# COMMUNICATION
## AND THE
## LAW

# *Communication and the Law*
## 2007 Edition
### Communication Law Writers Group
### W. Wat Hopkins, Editor

ISBN 1-885219-30-X

Vision Press
4195 Waldort Drive
P.O. Box 1106
Northport, Alabama 35476

On the cover: *Scene at the Signing of the Constitution of the United States*, by Howard Chandler Christy (1940), depicts the signing of the U.S. Constitution at Independence Hall in Philadelphia. The painting hangs in the House wing of the Capitol building in Washington.

Printed in the United States of America

**Communication Law Writers Group**

# COMMUNICATION

## AND THE

# LAW

2007 Edition

## W. Wat Hopkins, Editor

VISION PRESS

# Preface

The law is ever-changing.

While the guarantees of the First Amendment are provided in clear, succinct language, jurists, attorneys and free-speech advocates have come to learn that interpreting that language is often complicated. Communication law draws upon virtually every type and source of the law — from regulations to statutes, from contract law to constitutional law, from administrative law to the common law. In addition, each year Congress, regulatory agencies and the U.S. Supreme Court provide a wealth of information that those who follow communication law must locate, digest and come to understand.

So the law — and the interpretation of the law — continues to change.

The publication of the first edition of *Communication and the Law* in 1998 marked the beginning of an effort to keep up with that change in a concise, readable way. Sixteen authors — among them some of the leading communication law scholars in the country — agreed to update the text annually and to work for its continued improvement.

While authorship has changed — indeed, the number of authors has increased from sixteen to nineteen — the commitment to the comprehensive review of the law and to the continuing improvement of the textbook has not changed, as this, the tenth edition of *Communication and the Law,* reflects.

In addition to its comprehensive overview of communication law, this edition of the text contains discussion of some significant events that have had an impact on communication law over the past year. And it continues to follow the evolution of changes that occurred in recent years.

Specifically, this edition contains discussion of a number of cases that had not been decided a year ago. Indeed, this edition of *Communication and the Law* has references to more than 100 cases not mentioned in earlier editions. Some of those cases are discussed substantively, some marginally, but all demonstrate that the law must be continually updated.

The continually evolving law related to broadcasting and cable regulation — specifically related to cross-ownership, media mergers and government regulation of joint cable-Internet issues — is updated, as are sections of the text related to copyright, student expression, the flag-burning controversy and issues involving paparazzi. In addition, the chapter on regulating public relations has been updated to include more information on corporate speech.

The terrorist attacks of September 11, 2001, also continue to have considerable impact on how government agencies handle information and how the public responds to access, to criticism of the government and to other speech-related issues. Those issues are discussed at several places in the text.

This edition of the textbook is better than the first, but it can be better still. We continue to need the help of our readers. This edition was barely in the mail to the publisher before we began planning the 2008 edition. If you have comments or if there are changes you would like to see, don't wait — let us know now. Our goal is to provide a comprehensive, readable text that is concise but complete. The e-mail address of each author accompanies that author's biography at the end of the book. If you have comments, please let us know.

A number of people played a big part in making *Communication and the Law* possible. I would like to thank longtime friend and colleague David Sloan of the University of Alabama and Joanne Sloan of Vision Press for suggesting the project to me, for encouraging its completion and for their continued support. The eighteen people who, with me, make up the Communication Law Writers Group have been a pleasure to work with. I thank them for their willingness to engage in this venture and for their willingness to work hard to see it through.

As always, I am thankful for my colleagues in the Department of Communication at Virginia Tech, a wonderfully supportive group that makes it a pleasure to go to work each day. Finally, I owe special thanks to the members of my family, especially to my wife, Roselynn, for continued love and support. They make it a pleasure to go home each day.

**W. Wat Hopkins**
December 2006
Blacksburg, Virginia
whopkins@vt.edu

# Table of Contents

# Expanded Table of Contents

# CONTENTS

# 1

# The Law in Modern Society

## By Thomas A. Schwartz

---

 **Headnote Questions**

- *What is law?*
- *What are the sources of U.S. law?*
- *What is the difference between a trial court and an appellate court?*
- *What are the basic steps in a court case?*
- *How are judges chosen?*

---

"The language of the law," the erudite American jurist Learned Hand said in 1929, "must not be foreign to the ears of those who are to obey it."[1] He meant that the law ought to be clearly written and that, in a democracy, everyone should know the law. Law is too important to be left only to lawyers. Unfortunately, Americans today can hardly be expected to "know" the law, given its amount and density. Also of concern, they tend to know little about the nature and process of law and the officials and institutions that create, administer, interpret and enforce it.

To understand communication law – or any other area of the law – students need an introduction to the law generally. That is the purpose of this chapter. Although the law is a complex subject, its basics will be presented here so readers will have a framework within which to put any particular aspect of communication law.

Like the society it serves, law is dynamic. It is important to come to terms with the fundamentals of communication law, but it is also important to understand the forces that create and sustain the law, forces that inevitably will change the law, and how legal change comes about.

This chapter first offers some definitions and probes some of the assumptions of the legal system. The chapter then discusses how law is organized and the institutions that make, apply and interpret the law.

---

[1] Learned Hand, *Is There a Common Will?*, in THE SPIRIT OF LIBERTY: PAPERS AND ADDRESSES OF LEARNED HAND 56, 56 (1952).

## THE NATURE OF LAW

"Law" seems to have an unusual number of meanings. The law is usually defined as the rules of conduct established and enforced by authority in a society. The law of a society is one of its most fundamental characteristics; the kind and amount of behavior a society prescribes and proscribes for its members reveal much about the nature of that society. Also telling is how and why the law is applied and obeyed. Attitudes toward legal systems range from anarchism to authoritarianism.

The term "law" is also frequently used to refer to a particular law, usually an act or statute passed by a legislative body. When people say, "It's the law," however, they may be referring to any sort of official policy, whether it more technically should be called a court decision, administration regulation or municipal ordinance. When they use the word "law," people may also mean jurisprudence — the study of the law. Law in this sense refers to what law schools train lawyers to do: It is the profession of lawyers and judges.

## THE SOURCES OF LAW

All American law can be organized according to its sources. Any particular policy affecting communication may be categorized, roughly in the order in which the categories evolved, as common law, equity law, statutory law, constitutional law, administrative law or international law.

### Common Law

"Case law" refers to a body of law in which courts have applied the principles established in precedents. "Common law" refers specifically to a body of law in which courts create precedential principles. The term "common law," however, has come to embrace both meanings.

In the Twelfth Century, England began creating a system of local courts and law for resolving disputes between common people. Judges assigned to these courts were charged to determine and apply local customs and values to resolve the conflicts. Consistency became a prized feature of the common law. In the name of fairness, a kind of conflict resolved one day naturally should be resolved the same way the next day, the next year and, perhaps, indefinitely. For a community to be stable, law should be stable, too.

Thus developed the powerful common law principle known as *stare decisis*, part of a Latin phrase meaning that once established, a legal decision should not easily be changed. When a common law court makes a decision, a precedent is necessarily set. Courts within the same jurisdiction are required to reckon with that precedent in deciding similar cases. Today, one of the main functions of courts is to decide which precedents are applicable and how they apply to particular cases. Lawyers find precedent and argue that it should be construed in favor of their clients; judges determine the correct interpretation of precedent. Judges working in the common law tradition do not impose their own sense of right, good or wisdom but rather attempt objectively to find the correct law and apply it to the facts of a particular case. Common law judges are reluctant to reverse precedents.

Colonial America was subject to English common law, and a reformed system continues in modern American courts. Thoroughly researched opinions that American jurists write may still use British common law precedent as authority. Many areas of modern law are controlled principally by common law, sometimes called "judge-made" law. The development of this law, obviously very important in society, is generally left to the courts by the other branches of government. Other sources of law usually are not specific enough to handle each aspect of every dispute that arises in courts. Thus, judges have to make law to fill in the gaps.

The decisions and accompanying opinions — written rationales for the decisions — of courts are recorded and maintained chronologically. The reports of many trial courts and almost all appellate courts are continuously published according to jurisdiction in consecutive volumes of books called "reports" or "reporters." These bound reports constitute the seemingly endless rows of books on shelves in law libraries, law offices and courtrooms. Because these reports are organized by jurisdiction and chronologically, they would be impractical for use without the work of researchers who organize the law according to subject matter.

A number of these important analyses of English common law were performed near the turn of the Eighteenth Century. For instance, Sir William Blackstone, the first professor of law at Oxford University, collated English common law. The resulting set of volumes, which became known as *Blackstone's Commentaries*, organized the law according to subject matter, including the law of freedom of speech and the press. These scholarly collections and analyses of the law for use by lawyers and judges are referred to as legal "treatises." Almost as authoritative as the law itself are the treatises, called "restatements," that the American Law Institute publishes.

As readers will discover, the common law plays a central role in the law of communication, probably most prominently in the areas of libel and invasion of privacy.

### Equity Law

The United States also inherited the law of equity from England, where equity courts were established as early as the Fourteenth Century. Judges in equity courts, unlike common law judges, were empowered to use general principles of fairness, rather than custom or precedent, in resolving problems. Equity solutions to problems brought to these courts, however, were to be supplemental to the common law, not to supersede it. Issues in equity normally are too difficult to address with other kinds of law.

Equity actions by courts are usually in the form of what are called "extraordinary writs." The best known is the writ of *habeus corpus*, provided for in Article I of the U.S. Constitution. It is an order from a court to determine the status of a person detained by authorities. Extraordinary writs, most commonly in the forms of temporary or permanent injunctions or restraining orders, are judicial orders requiring people to do something that they do not want to do or stopping them from doing something that they want to do. Violation of such a court order would be a serious matter that can result in severe punishment.

Readers will see the law of equity at work in a number of cases in this book. For example, the famous Pentagon Papers case was instigated by an injunction a U.S. District Court judge issued requiring the *New York Times* to discontinue publishing a classified government history of American involvement in the Vietnam War. The case climaxed when the U.S. Supreme Court ordered that the injunction be lifted.[2]

### Statutory Law

America is a republican democracy. A succinct definition of a democracy is a political system in which citizens vote in regular elections. A republic is a democracy in which the majority rules through the representatives who are elected by the voters to represent them in political institutions. Representatives at the municipal, county, state and national levels meet regularly to enact legislation that reflects the will of the electorate. This legislation is statutory law.

---

[2] New York Times Co. v. United States, 403 U.S. 713 (1971).

Legislative bodies – city councils, county commissions, state assemblies and Congress, for example – tend to follow strict procedures to create statutory law. Students of politics have a good sense of how ideas typically become laws. In Congress, a representative or senator may propose a law in the form of a bill, which may be referred by congressional leadership to an appropriate committee for consideration. The committee may refer the bill to a subcommittee. The subcommittee examines the bill, perhaps by holding hearings or undertaking other studies. After this review, the subcommittee may vote on whether to recommend to the full committee that the bill – amended or not – be enacted as a statute. If the majority of the subcommittee members vote in favor of the bill, the committee may conduct additional deliberations before voting on whether to recommend the bill to the full chamber of Congress.

The full chamber may have additional discussion of the bill before voting on whether to enact it as law. In a bicameral legislature, such as Congress, a similar bill has usually followed a similar process in the other chamber. If the legislation is approved in the other chamber but in a different form, representatives of each chamber meet to work out the differences. Any compromises in Congress must be approved by both the House of Representatives and the Senate. Upon adoption, a bill is referred to the president, who has the power to veto it. Congress can override the veto by a two-thirds vote of each chamber.[3] Rescinding laws requires the same process. All states except Nebraska have bicameral legislatures, while local governments tend to have unicameral councils or commissions.

Other sources of law are apt to be deferential to statutory law because it is seen as the will of the people in a democracy. Statutory law, however, must be consistent with the Constitution and applied, enforced and interpreted by the executive and judicial branches of government. A state statute applies only to people in the state wherein it was adopted and must be consistent with both the federal and the state's constitutions; a federal statute applies to all people in the United States and must be consistent with the federal Constitution.

Statutory law plays an important role in communication law. State and federal legislation is key to understanding the law of obscenity, electronic media, intellectual property, marketing and journalistic privilege.

### Constitutional Law

America's most important contribution to thought about law in society is the written constitution. After the American Revolution, each of the thirteen states wrote and ratified a document that was intended to be a kind of powerful contract between the people and government. Carrying the idea of democracy to a new and original extreme, the state constitutions vested sovereignty in the people through the constitutions and designated public officials and government bodies as public servants.

Based on the model of the early state constitutions, the U.S. Constitution, written in 1787 and ratified in 1789, became a model for constitutions of other nations and for states that subsequently joined the union. The U.S. Constitution is made up of the Preamble, seven articles and twenty-seven amendments. The most important parts are the first three articles and the Bill of Rights, the first ten amendments.

Important to understanding American constitutional law is the concept of "limited government." The experience that led to the American Revolution taught the constitutional framers not to trust centralized power. They intended to create governments that would be explicitly excluded from almost all aspects of an individual citizen's life. Governments would be assigned only those functions in society that citizens could not perform for themselves. The Constitution was the device for the assignment of specific powers to government. The assumption was that government was powerless to do anything that it was not entitled to do in the Constitution.

Article I of the U.S. Constitution establishes Congress and enumerates its powers, including the powers to tax and mint money, declare war and regulate interstate commerce. Article II establishes the presidency and enumerates its powers, including leading the military, establishing foreign policy and appointing government officers. Article III establishes the federal judiciary and enumerates its powers, including hearing cases involving federal and international matters and disputes between states and between citizens of different states. According to the theory of limited government, all other powers are retained by the states, or no government can exercise those powers.

Since the framers believed that the federal government literally could not exercise any powers not enumerated in the Constitution, they rejected efforts to include a listing of individual rights and liberties, including freedom of speech or the press, that the government should be forbidden to abridge. Including such provisions in the Constitution, however, proved to be politically popular. In its first session, Congress approved twelve constitutional amendments, ten of which were ratified as the Bill of Rights, including the famous First Amendment provisions for freedom of religion and expression.

The Constitution, according to Article VI, is "the supreme Law of the Land," which has come to mean that any conflicting source of law must yield to constitutional law. Because the Constitution is brief and often ambiguous, however, its provisions are subject to multiple interpretations. What one person considers an exercise of First Amendment-protected "freedom of speech" may not be to another person.

Through their assertion of the power to declare statutory law inconsistent with constitutional law,[4] the courts, especially the

---

3 *See* U.S. CONST. art I, § 7, cl. 3.

4 Perhaps the most famous decision in U.S. constitutional history is *Marbury*

# FEDERAL JUDICIAL POWER

Article III, Section 2 of the U.S. Constitution provides that "the judicial Power shall extend to all Cases ... and Controversies":

1. "arising under this Constitution, the Laws of the United States, and Treaties made, ..."

2. "affecting Ambassadors, other public Ministers and Consuls, ..."

3. "of admiralty and maritime jurisdiction, ..."

4. "to which the United States shall be a Party, ..."

5. "between two or more States, ..."

6. "between a State and Citizens of another State, ..."

7. "between Citizens of different States" [also known as "diversity-of-citizenship" cases], ...

8. "between Citizens of the same State claiming Lands under the Grants of different States, ..."

9. "between a State, or Citizens thereof, and foreign States, Citizens or Subjects, ..."

All other matters are reserved for state courts.

Most cases in federal courts involve items 1, 4 and 7.

---

U.S. Supreme Court, are decisive in explaining and applying the Constitution. When reviewing a challenge to the constitutionality of a government action, the Court explains what the Constitution means, thus producing constitutional law. As Chief Justice Charles Evans Hughes once observed, the "Constitution is what the judges say it is."[5]

The Constitution can be amended either by calling a new constitutional convention, which has never happened, or by a vote of two-thirds of each of the houses of Congress and three-fourths of the state legislatures.[6]

Constitutional law, of course, provides the theoretical umbrella for all law, including communication law. Virtually every law affecting communication is ultimately answerable in some form to con-

stitutional law. Most important are the Supreme Court's constitutional theories based on the First Amendment clauses protecting the rights of free speech, free press, assembly and petition. This terse constitutional language has generated countless court decisions and opinions explaining what those words mean.

### Administrative Law

The nature of American life changed dramatically during the Industrial Revolution. In the decades following the Civil War, the national economy became dependent less on agriculture and more on manufacturing. Farmers went to work in factories. Immigration increased, with diverse populations streaming into the expanding cities and generating new political issues. Public services and mass communication and transportation took prominent places in commercial and social life.

As the economy became more centralized, industrialists and financiers came to dominate society, including politics and government. Farmers, small business owners and others in middle income groups became increasingly agitated over the behavior of monopolies that dictated wages and prices. Markets and governments seemed controlled by a wealthy few. Political groups calling themselves "populists" and "progressives" emerged to seek political change. Frustrated in its appeals to corrupt, reactionary and incompetent legislatures, executives and courts, the progressive movement pushed the concept of administrative law for reforming government.

The progressives reasoned that if unregulated capitalism resulted in reduced competition in the marketplace of goods and services, then the economy should be regulated by the government to ensure free enterprise. Some midwestern states first experimented with the idea of administrative law by regulating aspects of intrastate commerce. Then, in 1887, Congress created the first federal administrative agency, the Interstate Commerce Commission, to regulate commerce between states. Beginning in the 1910s, Congress created dozens of so-called "independent" agencies to regulate specific aspects of commerce; among these agencies are the Federal Communications Commission, the Federal Trade Commission and the Securities and Exchange Commission.

Framers of federal administrative law meant for commissioners to be apolitical experts in the fields they regulate. Instead of being elected in a political process that might be captured by the industries being regulated, a commissioner is appointed by the president to a fixed term, although the Senate can veto appointments. Congressional legislation attempts to restrict politics in the appointment process by limiting the number of members of one political party on a commission. On the five-member FCC, for example, a maximum of three can be from the same political party. Administrative law was to be created by people trained and experienced in the often complex issues of finance and technology that the appointees would address.

Administrative law is a creature of administrative agencies, most

---

v. *Madison*, 1 Cranch 137 (1803). In his opinion for the Court, Chief Justice John Marshall asserted the power of the U.S. Supreme Court to deem congressional enactments unconstitutional. At best, Article III of the Constitution is ambiguous as to whether the framers meant that the Court should have such power.

[5] Speech at Elmira, N.Y., May 3, 1907.

[6] *See* U.S. CONST. art V.

of which, unlike other political institutions, have quasi-legislative, quasi-executive and quasi-judicial powers. In short, an administrative agency can pass its own laws, execute those laws and adjudicate disputes over enforcement, unrestricted by considerations of the separation of powers that limit Congress, the president and the courts. The FCC can enact regulations affecting broadcasting licensees, punish an offending licensee and hear and resolve a challenge by the licensee to the regulations or enforcement. The sum total of the rules, regulations, decisions and other policy-making of these agencies make up the body of administrative law.

Also important to understanding federal administrative law is how it is affected by Congress, the president and the courts. Congress empowers the agencies through statutes. An agency can exercise only the power granted by the agency's enabling legislation. Federal agencies also are governed by the Administrative Procedures Act of 1946, which requires that agencies be fair and reasonable.[7] In addition, congressional legislation funds the agencies, and Congress sometimes threatens what it considers agency misbehavior with budget cuts. The agencies are accountable to the president most directly through the appointment of agency members. Decisions of the agencies can be appealed to federal courts which try to be deferential to the expertise of the agencies but also can rule agency actions to be unconstitutional or otherwise invalid.

Administrative law has a prominent place in the study of communication law. As examples, the FCC broadly regulates electronic media, the FTC regulates advertising and other marketing practices, and the SEC regulates communication by publicly held companies. Virtually every communication business must attend to at least some administrative law.

### International Law

Formal relationships between independent nations are governed by treaties, agreements that establish policies for how societies can interact politically and economically. Designated the commander in chief and head of state by Article II of the U.S. Constitution, the president has much unilateral authority to conduct American relations with other nations, but Article I empowers Congress to fund transnational initiatives, declare war and approve treaties. Article III grants federal courts exclusive jurisdiction to hear cases involving U.S. foreign affairs.

The United States has entered into numerous world and regional covenants subjecting the nation and its citizens to policies of various multinational organizations, the most important of which is the United Nations. The U.N. Charter commits member nations to participate in efforts to foster peace and prosperity throughout the world. The Universal Declaration of Human Rights, International Covenant on Civil and Political Rights, European Convention for the Protection of Human Rights and Ameri-

can Convention on Human Rights are examples of international and regional agreements that assert that human rights such as freedom of expression ought to be protected by governments.

Treaties such as the North American Free Trade Agreement between Canada, Mexico and the United States have important implications for both the amount and kind of communication between nations and the protection of freedom of expression in each nation. More specifically, agreements such as the Berne Convention for the Protection of Literary and Artistic Works and the Agreement on Trade-Related Aspects of Intellectual Property Rights attempt to establish harmonious policies for the international treatment of intellectual and creative property. (Intellectual property is discussed in Chapter 7.)

The development of new communication technology breaks down political and other barriers between nations, raising questions about international communication far faster than policy-making bodies can provide satisfactory answers. There is no doubt that international law will become increasingly influential as a source of communication law. (The regulation of new communication technologies is discussed in Chapter 12.)

Virtually every law examined in this book can be categorized into one of these six sources of law. When thinking about any particular law, a student should consider where it fits in the larger scheme of the law.

### COURTS

The focus of most interest in the law is the courtroom. Law schools train lawyers principally for careers in courts, not legislatures or administrative agencies whose members are not required to have law degrees. To practice law in most American courts, a person must have graduated from a law school, be licensed and be a member of the local bar.

Courts are at the center of the study of U.S. law for many reasons. Unlike judges of almost every other nation, American judges are vested with wide political authority. Through the power of judicial review – the ability to deem laws unconstitutional (and to have their decisions taken seriously) – courts are the ultimate forums for the resolution of disputes, whether between private or public parties. In theory at least, even the most powerful must answer to the least powerful in courts. Congress, the president and the states have largely acceded to the courts the ability to square other laws with the Constitution. "In truth, few laws can escape the searching analysis of judicial power for any length of time," asserted Alexis de Tocqueville, the prescient French observer of early America, "for there are few which are not prejudicial to some private interest or other, and none which may not be brought before a court of justice by the choice of parties, or by the necessity of the case."[8]

---

[7] 5 U.S.C. § 551 (1994).

[8] ALEXIS DE TOCQUEVILLE, DEMOCRACY IN AMERICA 75 (New American Library 1956) (1835, 1840).

As primary guardians of the Bill of Rights, the courts are protectors of individual rights and liberties, perforce an anti-majoritarian responsibility. The courts, however, tend to be cautious in exercising the power of judicial review. In its history, the U.S. Supreme Court has declared unconstitutional only about 100 acts of Congress and 1,000 acts of state and local governments.[9] The courts seem sensitive to the undemocratic image of an un-elected government body ruling invalid a law passed by elected representatives. Judges may also be aware, at least subconsciously, that their existence and funding depend on the legislatures. The power of the courts is sometimes called "the judicial myth" because courts actually have few resources to require obedience of their decisions. Courts generally have only public esteem as political capital.

A court hearing a case is supposed to resolve a carefully framed question in a genuine dispute between two or more parties, finding for one of them. The court should be apolitical, fair and principled in making a decision. The court is expected to follow strict legal procedure to ensure impartiality for all parties and fully to explain the rationale for the decision in a public document called the court's opinion. These decisions and opinions of American courts are not only important sources of law guiding everyday life but also of authoritative American political philosophy.

### Jurisdiction

Perhaps the most important way to distinguish between courts is by their jurisdiction, that is, their power to hear and rule in a case. "Jurisdiction" usually refers to the subject matter (the kinds of legal issues) on which a court is entitled to rule, or to geography, places or types of parties over whom a court has authority. One fundamental distinction to be made in considering court jurisdiction is between trial courts and appellate courts; almost all American courts are either courts of original jurisdiction or appellate jurisdiction.

There are two ingredients in a court case: the facts and the law. Trial courts find facts and apply the law. An appellate court reviews only the trial court's application of the law; the appeals court is generally powerless to seek new evidence or directly apply the law to the case under review. Appeals courts affirm or reverse trial court verdicts; they do not issue new verdicts. Most American court systems consist of trial courts ("law-applying and fact-finding" courts), intermediate appellate courts ("law-reviewing" courts) and courts of last resort. As courts of last resort, the federal and state supreme courts usually have limited, if any, original jurisdiction. They mainly deal with petitions to review reviews of law by other appellate courts.

Courts will have either general or limited subject-matter jurisdiction. A general jurisdiction court handles a wide array of criminal and civil matters. A limited-jurisdiction court may be created to handle only, for example, tax issues, bankruptcy issues or juvenile issues.

### Federal Courts

Article III of the Constitution says little about the number and sorts of federal courts, mentioning "one supreme Court" and "such inferior courts as the Congress may from time to time ordain and establish." With the Judiciary Act of 1789, as amended, and other legislation, however, Congress has developed an elaborate federal judiciary.

When Congress creates courts under Article III, a resulting court is called an "Article III court." When a federal court is created by way of other constitutional provisions, it is called a "non-Article III court." Article III provides that judges assigned to Article III courts have lifetime tenure, meaning they hold office until they die, are impeached and convicted or choose to retire (at age sixty-five with at least fifteen years of service or age seventy after at least ten years of service). A non-Article III judge may serve a term specified in the law that established the judge's court.

Examples of non-Article III courts are the Court of Federal Claims, the Court of Appeals for the Armed Forces and the Tax Court. These courts have specific jurisdiction suggested by their names. Article III courts include the district courts, courts of appeals and U.S. Supreme Court.

### U.S. District Courts

The ninety-four district courts are the federal courts of original jurisdiction. At least one is located in each state, Puerto Rico and the District of Columbia. As many as four are located in each of the most populous states. The number of judges assigned to each court ranges from two to twenty-eight, depending on the amount of work in the court. Normally, one judge presides in a case, with or without a jury, but a three-judge panel may be assigned to decide a case in special circumstances.

There are 610 judgeships in the fifty states and territories and fifteen in the District of Columbia. Each district also is assigned at least one magistrate, bankruptcy judge, marshal, clerk, U.S. attorney (federal prosecutor), probation officer and reporter. One of the judges in each district is appointed the chief judge to handle administrative matters.

In recent years, the district courts have heard an annual average of about 275,000 civil cases and 45,000 criminal cases. It takes about three and one-half years to dispose of a criminal felony case and seven years for a civil case. About half the civil cases involve contract and liability law. Half of the criminal cases involve narcotics, fraud and drunk driving and other traffic offenses.

### U.S. Courts of Appeals

The current system of the federal courts of appeals was estab-

9 See LAWRENCE BAUM, THE SUPREME COURT 167 (6th ed. 1998).

## THE AMERICAN JUDICIAL SYSTEM

| FEDERAL COURTS | | STATE COURTS |
|---|---|---|
| | **Courts of Last Resort** | |
| Supreme Court | | Supreme Court[*] |
| | **Intermediate Appellate Courts** | |
| Courts of Appeals | | Courts of Appeal[**] |
| | **Trial Courts of General Jurisdiction** | |
| District Courts | | Circuit Courts[***] |
| | **Trial Courts of Limited Jurisdiction** | |
| Court of Federal Claims | | *Examples:* |
| Court of International Trade | | Family Court |
| Court of Appeals for Veterans Claims | | Juvenile Court |
| Rail Reorganization Court | | Small Claims Court |
| Tax Court | | Traffic Court |

* In Maryland and New York, this court is called the Court of Appeals, and in Maine and Massachusetts, the Supreme Judicial Court. Texas and Oklahoma have both supreme courts and courts of criminal appeals as courts of last resort.
** Eleven states do not have intermediate courts of appeals. Twelve states call these courts by variations on this name, e.g., the Maryland Court of Special Appeals, the Florida District Court of Appeals and the Pennsylvania Superior Court.
*** Names of state trial courts include Circuit Court (18 states), District Court (16 states), Superior Court (13 states), Court of Common Pleas (Ohio and Pennsylvania), Supreme Court (New York) and Trial Court (Massachusetts). Vermont has both a District Court and a Superior Court.

---

lished by Congress in 1891.[10] These courts take appeals of decisions of the district courts and federal agencies. Except when the Supreme Court agrees to review decisions of appeals courts, the lower decisions are final. Since the Supreme Court in recent years has been granting full review to fewer than 100 of about 7,000 petitions it receives each term, clearly the courts of appeals are, as a practical matter, the courts of last resort in the federal judiciary.

There are 179 judgeships in eleven numbered multi-state circuits and the District of Columbia Circuit. Each circuit has one appeals court with six to twenty-eight permanent judgeships, depending on the docket size. Rather than involve all of the judges in every decision, an appeals court normally assigns a case to a three-judge subcommittee, called a "panel." When the entire court assembles to decide a case, it is said to act *en banc*.

About 62 percent of the 45,000 appeals court petitions each year involve civil matters. About 25 percent are criminal cases, and 10 percent are administrative cases. Only about 15 percent of the petitions result in formal hearings before the appeals courts.

A chief judge is assigned in each appeals court to handle administrative work for the circuit. In addition, a Supreme Court justice is chosen to be the supervising "circuit justice" for each circuit.

### U.S. Supreme Court

The Supreme Court of the United States, the federal court of last resort, is the only court specifically mentioned in Article III of the Constitution, but little else is said in the Constitution about how the Court was to be structured or how it was to conduct its work. Through legislation, Congress established the office of the Chief Justice of the United States and determined the number of justices, which was set at nine in 1869. A Supreme Court term opens on the first Monday in October, according to statute, and usually concludes at the end of June.

In the past thirty years, the annual number of petitions reaching the Court has grown from about 1,000 to about 7,000. The Court gave full-dress treatment to a peak of 174 cases in each of the 1982 and 1983 terms, but in recent terms, the Court has decided fewer than 100 cases per term this way.

Notice that the title of the federal judiciary's chief administrative officer is the "Chief Justice of the United States," not the "Chief Justice of the U.S. Supreme Court." The associate justices do not regard the chief justice as their boss. Rather, the chief justice is the head of the federal judiciary, chair of the Federal Judicial Conference (the policy-making body for the federal courts) and in charge of administrative matters for the Supreme Court, including its building. Also, the justices have agreed, the chief justice is the chair of the conferences of the justices in deciding cases and presides at public hearings for the Court. The chief justice is in a better position than anyone to set the Court's agenda, but the justices are not answerable to the chief justice, who, like each of them, has only one of the nine votes.

---

10 Everts Act of 1891, 28 U.S.C. ch. 3 (1994).

# THE U.S. COURT CIRCUITS AND DISTRICTS

**FIRST CIRCUIT**—The districts of Maine, Massachusetts, New Hampshire, Rhode Island and Puerto Rico.

**SECOND CIRCUIT**—The districts of Connecticut, Northern New York, Southern New York, Western New York and Vermont.

**THIRD CIRCUIT**—The districts of Delaware, New Jersey, Eastern Pennsylvania, Middle Pennsylvania, Western Pennsylvania and Virgin Islands.

**FOURTH CIRCUIT**—The districts of Maryland, Eastern North Carolina, Middle North Carolina, Western North Carolina, South Carolina, Eastern Virginia, Western Virginia, Northern West Virginia and Southern West Virginia.

**FIFTH CIRCUIT**—The districts of Eastern Louisiana, Middle Louisiana, Western Louisiana, Northern Mississippi, Southern Mississippi, Eastern Texas, Northern Texas, Southern Texas and Western Texas.

**SIXTH CIRCUIT**—The districts of Eastern Kentucky, Western Kentucky, Eastern Michigan, Western Michigan, Northern Ohio, Southern Ohio, Eastern Tennessee, Middle Tennessee and Western Tennessee.

**SEVENTH CIRCUIT**—The districts of Central Illinois, Northern Illinois, Southern Illinois, Northern Indiana, Southern Indiana, Eastern Wisconsin and Western Wisconsin.

**EIGHTH CIRCUIT**—The districts of Eastern Arkansas, Western Arkansas, Northern Iowa, Southern Iowa, Minnesota, Eastern Missouri, Western Missouri, Nebraska, North Dakota and South Dakota.

**NINTH CIRCUIT**—The districts of Alaska, Arizona, Central California, Eastern California, Northern California, Southern California, Hawaii, Idaho, Montana, Nevada, Oregon, Eastern Washington, Western Washington, Guam and Northern Mariana Islands.

**TENTH CIRCUIT**—The districts of Colorado, Kansas, New Mexico, Eastern Oklahoma, Northern Oklahoma, Western Oklahoma, Utah and Wyoming.

**ELEVENTH CIRCUIT**—The districts of Middle Alabama, Northern Alabama, Southern Alabama, Middle Florida, Northern Florida, Southern Florida, Middle Georgia, Northern Georgia and Southern Georgia.

**DISTRICT OF COLUMBIA CIRCUIT**—District of Columbia.

## State Courts

Article III seems to give broad authority to the federal courts to handle legal issues, but the vast majority of American judicial work is done in the state courts. Federal jurisdiction is actually limited, leaving most matters of civil and criminal law to states. Although the most important constitutional issues seem eventually to reach the federal courts, the state courts actually produce the law most directly affecting citizens on a day-to-day basis.

State court systems are generally organized like the federal court system, with trial and intermediate appellate courts and courts of last resort. Names of these courts vary in the states. Sixteen states call their general jurisdiction trial court the "district court," but New York calls it the "supreme court." Most intermediate appellate courts are called "appeals courts," but in Pennsylvania, this court is called the "superior court." Most courts of last resort are "supreme courts," but in Maryland it is called the "court of appeals."

Each state court system is independent of other state court systems and the federal system. A state supreme court is the ultimate authority on that state's law. Just as a state court cannot correct the U.S. Supreme Court in its interpretation of federal law, federal courts cannot correct a state supreme court in its interpretation of state law. The U.S. Supreme Court can overrule a state supreme court on a state law question only when the two courts disagree over whether state law violates federal law. The U.S. Constitution, as the supreme law of the land, prevails whenever it is violated by other law, even a state constitution. On the other hand, a state constitution can provide more and different rights than the federal constitution. "State constitutions, too, are a font of individual liberties," U.S. Supreme Court Justice William J. Brennan Jr. noted, "their protections often extending beyond those required by the Supreme Court's interpretation of federal law."[11]

State court systems have created a large number of courts in

---

11 William J. Brennan Jr., *State Constitutions and the Protection of Individual Rights,* 90 HARV. L. REV. 489, 491 (1977).

special subject-matter jurisdiction. Probate, traffic, domestic relations and juvenile courts are common. So are courts dealing in only minor crimes, such as justice of the peace courts, and in minor civil matters, such as small claims courts.

## LEGAL PROCEDURE

Law is either substantive or procedural. Most of what this book describes is the substance of communication law, for instance, whether a particular communication is defamatory or obscene.

Procedural law, on the other hand, includes the rules for how substantive law is created, administered and adjudicated. To protect against governmental abuse, the federal and state constitutions require that authorities treat individuals fairly, equally and decisively. Mandating that a criminal suspect be represented by legal counsel and be given an impartial trial by peers are examples of procedural law. In federal courts, the *Rules of Civil Procedure* and *Rules of Criminal Procedure* establish details as specific as the cost of filing records and the dimensions of the paper permitted to be submitted as court documents. States have similar procedural law. A case that is likely to be won on the merits may be lost for failure to follow procedure. If a plaintiff's lawyer does not file an action by the deadline established by procedural law, the court in that case will probably dismiss the action. That may be cause for the client to sue the lawyer for malpractice.

The procedure for a legal action depends on many factors, the most fundamental of which are whether the action is civil, criminal or administrative and where the action is brought. A civil action generally involves a dispute between private parties. Civil due process applies; the standard of proof is a "preponderance of the evidence" and remedies in equity, such as an injunction, or in law, such as monetary damages, are available.

A criminal action is brought by a prosecutor against an individual for committing a crime designated in legislation. Criminal due process applies; the standard of proof is "beyond a reasonable doubt," and remedies include fines and imprisonment. An administrative action may be brought by the subject of a regulation made by a government agency that has been authorized by legislation to regulate an individual or organization. The application of a regulation to a party can be appealed by the party for a hearing by the agency. Rules of administrative procedure are applied. Decisions by an agency's bureaucracy on fines and orders may be upheld, adjusted or dismissed by an agency's judges or by the agency's policy-making commissioners, acting as a kind of internal court of appeals. The administrative process is also subject to external judicial review.

Legal procedure also depends on where an action is brought. Although procedural rules in different systems resemble each other, each state has its own specific procedures for its courts and agencies. Federal courts and agencies have separate sets of procedures. Procedures will also differ depending on whether the action is in a trial court or appellate court.

### Trial Court Procedure

Courts are in the business of remedying or punishing social wrongs. Civil law was established to correct civil wrongs, such as torts or breaches of contracts, but has also become a way to achieve constitutional rights. Civil courts are intended to be places where civilized people will resolve their disputes rather than through violence or other inappropriate behavior. Criminal law was established to punish criminal wrongs, such as arson or larceny, although a major part of criminal law is devoted to protecting the constitutional rights of suspects.

### Civil Procedure

The victim of a civil wrong will first consult an attorney who may specialize in civil procedure. The attorney tries to determine whether the client has a cause for legal action based on the facts and the law and, if so, whether the law provides a remedy in equity or damages. The two major branches of civil law are torts and contracts. A tort is a non-criminal wrong committed by one party against another party. Libel and invasion of privacy are torts. A contract is an agreement between two parties. If one party violates the agreement, the other party may seek a remedy for breach of contract.

A typical civil case seeks monetary damages to help the plaintiff recover from various kinds of losses, for example, harm to reputation, shame and ridicule resulting from defamation. Generally, a plaintiff has to present evidence that the defendant was at fault for causing the harm to the plaintiff and that the plaintiff suffered as a result. The defendant can prevail by contradicting the plaintiff's evidence or introducing other evidence. The judge and jury decide on whether the plaintiff succeeds in the action by a "preponderance of the evidence."

The plaintiff's attorney, once satisfied that a client has a case, may begin to collect evidence to support the claim. An example of evidence would be affidavits — sworn statements by potential witnesses. The attorney will also conduct legal research. One initial decision will be in which court to bring the case. If the case involves state law and both parties are in the state, then the case should be filed in a court in that state. If the case involves federal law, then the case should be filed in the federal district of the legal wrong. If the parties are in different states, the case may be brought in a court in either state or in a federal district court. If the case involves state law, the law of the state in which the case is brought prevails, including in a federal court. The law in one state might be more favorable to the plaintiff than the law in another state. These variables figure into "forum shopping," the process of picking a court for an action. The parties must have at least some connection to the court district where the case is brought.

Other initial legal issues for the plaintiff's attorney are the statute of limitations and standing to sue. The statute of limitations, usually a year in a tort action, is the deadline for initiating a suit. A plaintiff must also establish "standing," the right to bring the action; that is, does the plaintiff have a legally established interest in the litigation? For example, survivors of a libel plaintiff who dies generally do not have standing to sue on behalf of the deceased.

The legal system tries to encourage litigants to settle the case out of court. After the initial investigation, the plaintiff's attorney may ask the defendants for an amount of money to settle the case before legal action is filed. A defendant may also volunteer to settle at any stage of the process. Settlements account for a much larger proportion of the dispositions of civil actions than do trials.

The pre-trial process consists of two stages: pleadings and discovery. The basic pleadings are the complaint and answer. The first formal document filed in a case is the complaint, in which the plaintiff states the grounds for the action and jurisdiction of the court and demands judgment. Upon receipt of the complaint and a filing fee, the clerk of court puts the case on the docket. The clerk issues a summons to be served on the defendant, notifying the defendant of the action. This step is called "service of process." The defendant is given a deadline within which to respond to the summons.

The defense attorney analyzes the complaint and researches other facts and law that may be relevant. If the defense does not challenge the complaint on the grounds of lack of jurisdiction or specificity, a document called an "answer" is prepared. The answer should admit as true the facts in the complaint that are not disputed and specify facts that are disputed. The answer may deny the allegations in the complaint and establish the defense, even if the defendant denies the plaintiff has a cause of action. The answer is delivered to the clerk of courts and sent to the plaintiff. At this stage and in subsequent pre-trial stages, the defendant can ask the court summarily to dismiss the case on the grounds that the plaintiff's case is insufficient as a matter of law.

The next stage of the civil process is discovery, during which each side of a case obtains information from the other side. In civil discovery, the parties have wide latitude in seeking this information. Refusal to cooperate can result in a citation for contempt of court. Discovery includes interrogatories, depositions and requests for documents or other evidence. An interrogatory is a list of written questions by one party of the other party. The answers are admissible as evidence in court.

A deposition is a transcript of a formal interview by an attorney of a witness who answers questions under oath. The transcript is prepared by a court reporter, and the deponent is allowed to read it before signing it as an accurate account of the interview. A deponent, as a potential witness in a case, is served a subpoena, a court order that the person appear at a time and place to give evidence. A subpoena *duces tecum* requires that the person also produce any documents or other evidence relevant to the issues in the case. All of this evidence, filed at court, is available to both parties.

After completion of the discovery stage, the attorneys for both sides meet to discuss where the case stands and whether a settlement is possible. If not, the attorneys will try to produce a stipulation, an agreement on which facts both sides consider settled and which facts are still at issue. After requesting a trial, the attorneys meet with the judge in the case. The judge may review the record of the case, encourage settlement and request that the attorneys file briefs on legal issues. A trial date is scheduled.

The first step in the trial stage of civil procedure is *voir dire*, the selection of the jury, assuming a jury is used. In certain kinds of cases, a jury may not be used, perhaps at the request of the parties to the case. A case without a jury is called a "bench trial." When used, a civil jury often has fewer than twelve jurors. Its job is to determine the facts, that is, to determine from the competing versions of the truth exactly what happened. If a jury is not used, the judge determines the facts as well as applies the law. Otherwise, the function of the judge is solely to apply the law.

Potential jurors are usually selected by the court clerk from drivers' registration lists. Failure to report for a call for jury duty can result in a citation for contempt of court. In *voir dire*, the judge and attorneys may question the members of the preliminary *venire*, seeking information that might prevent them from being fair and effective. After this questioning, the attorneys can ask the judge to remove some of the jurors "for cause," that is, for a reason that the judge finds acceptable. In addition, the attorneys are given an opportunity to remove a set number of jurors through "peremptory challenges," or without justifying the removals.

After the jury is impaneled, the trial begins. The judge normally gives preliminary instructions to the jury about the conduct of the trial. This is followed by the plaintiff's opening statement and then the defendant's opening statement. These are presentations by the attorneys of what they intend to show.

Next is the presentation of the evidence, first by the plaintiff, then by the defendant. Direct examination of a witness is conducted by the lawyer who calls the witness. Cross-examination is conducted by the opposing lawyer. Throughout the presentation of evidence, the attorneys may invoke various rules of evidence. Arguments over these rules are directed at the judge, not the jury, because these are questions of law, not facts. One side may object that the other side is violating some rule of evidence. For example, lawyers are not allowed to ask leading questions, that is to frame questions in such a way as to encourage specific answers. A lawyer also may not use "hearsay" evidence – evidence of a statement made out of court and, therefore, of questionable validity. In determining the proper application of the rule, the judge may sustain or overrule the objection. The side that loses these arguments may use them as bases for an appeal that the trial court judge misapplied the law.

At the conclusion of the plaintiff's presentation of the evidence, the defense may move that the judge dismiss the case on the grounds that the plaintiff failed to show with sufficient evidence a *prima facie* case, that is, a case that unless contradicted would likely prevail before a reasonable jury. Assuming the plaintiff has not failed, the defense presents its evidence and witnesses, subject to cross-examination by the plaintiff. Since the burden of proof is on the plaintiff, the defendant is not required to produce evidence but generally will do so. When the defense rests, the plaintiff's attorney presents closing arguments, followed by the defense attorney's closing arguments. Like the opening statements, closing arguments do not include presentation of evidence but are summaries of the evidence and arguments as to how the evidence should be interpreted.

After the closing arguments, the judge orally instructs the jury on the law as it applies to the case. These instructions to the jury are carefully written, sometimes in consultation with the attorneys in the case. The judge explains how a jury is supposed to use evidence, the plaintiff's burden of proof, the requirements necessary for the defense and any other law applicable to the jury's deliberations.

The jury retires to the jury room, selects a chairperson (often called a "foreman" or "forewoman") and deliberates until reaching a verdict in favor of one of the parties. In civil actions, depending on the jurisdiction, a party to the case may request that the jurors be unanimous in their decision. Often, only a majority vote is necessary for one side to prevail. The jury is usually asked not only to rule for one side of a civil action but also to determine how much in damages should be given to the plaintiff if the plaintiff wins. A jury is not expected to explain its decision.

After the jury decision is announced, the losing side is normally given a deadline within which to file a petition arguing that the jury's verdict should be set aside as a matter of law. In most jurisdictions, a judge has the power to order a judgment as a matter of law. The judge is expected to explain any decision that contradicts a jury's determination.

### Criminal Procedure

The legal system sees crimes as wrongs committed against society, not just against the victims of those crimes. As a result, an elaborate criminal justice system, including police, prosecutors, defense attorneys, judges and jailers, has been constructed with tax money to deal with crime. Crimes are usually categorized as felonies or misdemeanors. Felonies are serious crimes — such as treason, murder and rape — with penalties of capital punishment, lengthy prison terms and large fines. Misdemeanors are less serious crimes — such as reckless driving, marijuana possession and disorderly conduct — that carry penalties of lower fines and shorter jail terms.

Some assumptions of criminal law procedure resemble those in civil law procedure, but because the liberty and perhaps life of the criminal defendant may be at stake, criminal law procedure tends to be much more strict and specific than its civil law counterpart. Criminal rights in the Fourth, Fifth, Sixth and Eighth amendments of the U.S. Constitution have been the subject of great interest to the Supreme Court and other courts whose decisions on criminal

## TYPICAL STAGES OF LEGAL PROCEDURE

### CRIMINAL CASE
Investigation • Arrest • Arraignment • Complaint • Preliminary hearing • Grand jury indictment • Hearings and motions • Trial • Sentencing • Appeal

### CIVIL CASE
Complaint filed • Answer • Discovery • Hearings and motions • Settlement conference • Trial • Appeal

procedure have had a great impact on the work of police, prosecutors, courts and prisons.

Criminal law procedure includes the police investigation, arrest, complaint, initial appearance, preliminary hearing, prosecutorial investigation, indictment, arraignment, plea, defense investigation, discovery, trial, verdict, sentencing and punishment.

Police must follow certain procedures when investigating a crime. They must find and preserve physical evidence and question witnesses and others with information relevant to the crime. They are restricted by the Fourth Amendment prohibition against unreasonable search and seizure. They can obtain a search warrant by satisfying a judge that they have probable cause to believe that evidence related to a specific crime can be obtained at a location specified in the warrant. They must be careful to "Mirandize" suspects, that is, to advise them of their rights to have attorneys and not to speak to the police.[12] Police must know when to discontinue custodial interrogation and arrest a suspect.

An arrest occurs when a person related to a crime is taken into custody. An arrest is usually made with an arrest warrant, which is based on reasonable evidence that the suspect committed a crime. The suspect is taken before a magistrate for an initial appearance and further advised of his or her rights. The suspect, who is innocent until proven guilty, may ask to be released from custody until required to appear at subsequent proceedings. The magistrate considers whether to grant bail and, if so, how much the bail should be, based on the seriousness of the charge and the likelihood the suspect will appear at future court proceedings.

A suspect is entitled to a lawyer. If the suspect is indigent, one — probably a public defender — will be assigned by the court. The defense attorney represents the defendant at the preliminary hearing before a judge to determine whether there is probable cause to believe the suspect committed a crime. Depending on evidence presented, a judge can dismiss the case or "bind it over" for further proceedings.

Next, the prosecution is expected to file a bill of information or seek a grand jury indictment. A bill of information, normally used

---

[12] *See* Miranda v. Arizona, 384 U.S. 436 (1966).

in a less serious case, is a document read at a public hearing out-lining the charges and evidence. Witnesses may be examined and cross-examined. A presiding judge decides on whether the prose-cution can proceed. More commonly, especially in serious cases, an indictment is issued by a grand jury, a panel of citizens assem-bled in secret to determine whether there is sufficient evidence to support further prosecution.

The arraignment is another court hearing at which the defen-dant is expected to enter a plea to the charges filed by the prose-cutor, generally guilty or not guilty. A suspect may also plead *nolo contendere,* which essentially means that the defendant will not contest the charges. If the defendant pleads guilty, the judge will set a date for sentencing. If the defendant pleads not guilty, the judge will set a date for trial.

The criminal discovery process differs from that of a civil case. Depositions are abnormal in criminal discovery; they are used only when a witness is unable to appear at a trial. Defendants have the Fifth Amendment right not to make any statements to the prose-cution, but if they do, they probably will be required to respond under oath at the trial to a cross-examination by the prosecutor. In addition, the criminal record of a defendant may be suppressed as evidence against the defendant if it would unnecessarily preju-dice the jury against the defendant. The police and prosecutor are required to share evidence they obtain that may help the defen-dant. Each side is free to ask the other for evidence, but not all ev-idence is required to be presented before trial. Each side is re-quired to reveal to the other a list of witnesses expected to be called and exhibits to be presented.

The prosecutor will develop a theory about the motive and op-portunity of the defendant to commit the crime and how the crime itself was committed. In response, the defendant develops a de-fense strategy. To have enough time to gather evidence and oth-erwise develop a sound strategy, the defense may ask for addi-tional time through a motion for a continuance. Other pretrial mo-tions might include a motion to suppress evidence illegally ob-tained, a motion to change the place of the trial because of adverse publicity and a motion to remove the judge because of prejudice.

Prosecution and defense strategies are often dependent on what are called "aggravating" and "mitigating" circumstances. Ag-gravating circumstances are often named and defined in legislation as factors that must be shown in order to convict a defendant of a certain crime. In a death penalty case, for example, the prosecutor might be required by state law to show that the defendant killed a police officer or a minor, had previously been convicted of a vio-lent crime or was unusually cruel in committing the murder. Miti-gating circumstances may be argued by the defense attorney to convince the jury to convict a guilty defendant of a lesser crime or to decide on less punishment than the prosecutor seeks. For ex-ample, evidence may show that the defendant played a small role as an accomplice to the principal perpetrator of the crime, that the victim consented to the conduct leading to the murder or that the defendant felt the murder was morally justified.

*Voir dire* in criminal cases is usually taken more seriously than in civil cases. In trials involving felonies, twelve jurors are normal. In an attempt to avoid mistrials, additional jurors may be chosen as alternates in the event regular jurors, once seated, become sick or are disqualified. Lawyers usually get more peremptory chal-lenges than in civil cases. Jury selection in criminal cases can be lengthy and complicated. Behavioral experts may be hired as con-sultants to the lawyers in choosing jurors.

At the trial, the prosecutor makes an opening statement, fol-lowed by one by the defense attorney. The prosecutor presents the evidence with cross-examination by the defense. When the prosecution rests, the defense may ask the judge to dismiss the case on the grounds that as a matter of law, the prosecution failed to present evidence that the defendant was guilty "beyond a rea-sonable doubt." If the motion fails, the defense may present evi-dence, attempting to raise serious doubts about the defendant's guilt. The prosecutor's closing statement is followed by the de-fense attorney's. The judge's instructions to the jury are usually more detailed in a criminal case than in a civil case.

The twelve jurors retire to the jury room and, in almost all juris-dictions, must reach a unanimous vote on a verdict of guilty or not guilty. If a unanimous vote cannot be achieved, the judge gen-erally declares a mistrial. The jury forewoman or foreman an-nounces the verdict in court. The defendant is free of custody from the moment of a verdict of not guilty. If found guilty, the de-fendant will be held for sentencing, which is normally a separate proceeding, sometimes involving the jury. The judge may request a report from a probation officer on the defendant's background and seek recommendations on sentencing from witnesses, the prosecution and the defense. Ranges of possible sentences for convictions of crimes are established in legislation. Once sen-tenced, a convict is turned over to penal authorities.

Plea bargaining in criminal procedure should be noted because the vast majority of the dispositions of prosecutions end when deals are reached between the defense and prosecutor. In ex-change for pleading guilty to a crime, the defendant may be charged with a lesser offense or be offered a lesser punishment than if the defendant pleads not guilty and is found guilty at a trial. A plea bargain must be approved by a judge. Plea bargaining is used in about 95 percent of cases in pretrial stages in American courts.

### Appellate Court Procedure

New Hampshire, West Virginia and Virginia are the only states in which appellate courts have virtually complete discretion over the kinds of cases they accept. In most states, appellate courts are re-quired to consider appeals in some kinds of cases and have dis-cretion in accepting appeals in other kinds of cases.

In most jurisdictions, a notice of appeal must be filed within thirty days of a trial court's decision. The appellant, the party bringing the appeal, must take responsibility for providing the appeals court with the entire record of the lower court case. The appellant must also satisfy the appeals court that the case contains an appealable legal issue. The appellant can raise only questions of law, not fact, and must show not only that the trial court erred in applying the law but also that the error was prejudicial, that is, an error that actually harmed the appellant's ability to win the trial.

An appeals court will require that the appellant file its argument, called a brief, within thirty to sixty days after the appellant delivers the trial court record. The brief of the appellee is due thirty to sixty days after the appellant's brief is filed. Since an appeals court cannot overturn a jury's determination of the facts, the goal of the appellant is often to convince the appeals court that the record on which the jury based its decision was inadequate or unfair.

Appeals courts do not re-try cases but sometimes conduct oral hearings, allowing the parties to the case to supplement their briefs with public presentations before the judges. The judges usually ask questions of the attorneys during the hearings.

The appeals court can affirm or reverse the lower court decision. If ruling in favor of the appellant, an appeals court may nevertheless find that the error was not serious enough to have altered the outcome of the case. Further, an appeals court ruling in favor of an appellant is less likely to reverse the lower court than to remand the case to the lower court with directions on how to handle the legal issue that was appealed. This may require a new trial.

In most state systems and in the federal system, losers of court decisions get a second opportunity to appeal to a court of last resort, usually called a supreme court. Cases may arrive in the form of what are called appeals, but often they are technically petitions to the court to have the court review the lower court decision. As a result, many parties bringing the cases are called petitioners rather than appellants and those responding to the petitions are called respondents rather than appellees.

Appellate jurisdiction is sometimes subdivided into categories of mandatory and discretionary jurisdiction. Mandatory jurisdiction means the court is required by the constitution or legislation to take cases, either all cases brought to the court or cases addressing certain matters. Discretionary jurisdiction means the court can make the decision itself about whether to take a case.

### U.S. Supreme Court Procedure

A brief overview of procedure at the U.S. Supreme Court can foster understanding of the law for three reasons: (1) the Court is an example of a court of last resort, (2) the Court's procedures are models for other courts of last resort and (3) the Court is the most important of all courts in shaping law in the United States. Although the Court does not enact or carry out laws, it is an important national policy maker through its interpretation of law. The Supreme Court has been the most influential source of constitutional law.

The Court is highly secretive about its work. The justices rarely agree to interviews with journalists and rarely comment on cases.

Being politically unaccountable to the public, the justices apparently believe that the Court is best served by low visibility. When they do appear in public, the justices are highly courteous toward each other.

The Court receives about 7,000 petitions a year. There are a number of different kinds of ways of obtaining permission to have the Court review a lower court decision. One famous way, though it is rarely accepted by the Court, is through an *in forma pauperis* affidavit, a "pauper's petition." Even when an individual may not be able to afford a lawyer or use a formal process to get the Court's attention, the petitioner might be able to bring the case forward with a simple letter to the Court and no filing fee.

The Court is also required by Article III of the Constitution and by congressional legislation to hear certain cases. For example, when state or federal laws are declared by lower courts to be unconstitutional, the Court has mandatory jurisdiction. Over time, however, the justices have successfully sought more and more discretion over what cases are put on the docket. Almost every case the Court decides is accepted by grant of a petition for a writ of *certiorari*, an order to a lower court requiring that the records of the case be brought to the Supreme Court.

The clerk, using guidelines established by the Court, sorts the petitions into groups called "frivolous" and "nonfrivolous." Both groups are transmitted to the office of the chief justice, whose law clerks also screen the petitions, agreeing or disagreeing with the clerk. Petitions deemed frivolous by the chief justice are "deadlisted." Nonfrivolous petitions are put on the agenda for discussion by the justices and a vote on acceptance. Clerks for all of the justices review all the petitions, even those deadlisted.

Members of the Court have established criteria for granting or denying *certiorari*. For example, the Court will reject a petition unless the petitioner has exhausted all other legal remedies. In short, if it is possible to take the case to another court, the petitioner must do so before the Supreme Court will consider hearing the case. Unlike some state supreme courts, the U.S. Supreme Court will not give advisory opinions to anyone, including other branches of government. The Court deals in only *bona fide* disputes between real parties, not hypothetical situations or moot cases. The Court, however, has an exception to its mootness doctrine: When an important issue repeatedly arrives before the Court but cannot be decided because of mootness, the Court may agree to hear the case. The Court also rejects what it calls political questions, that is, issues presented in the form of cases when they should be resolved in the political branches of government. Some issues are not resolvable in the courts. Many disputes between branches of government and between the federal and state governments, according to the Court, should be solved in the political process, not the legal process.

Also influential in shaping the Court's docket is the Office of the Solicitor General in the U.S. Department of Justice. The solicitor general, representing the federal government when it is a litigant before the Supreme Court, is given considerable independence by the president and attorney general in deciding which cases the government should ask the Court to review. Since the federal government — the most frequent and important litigant in the federal courts — loses dozens of cases in U.S. appeals courts each year, the solicitor general has recently asked the Court to hear only about thirty cases. The Court, respecting this advice and the restraint shown by the solicitor general, usually grants review to most of these cases.

Only about 10 percent of all of the petitions survive to be formally presented by the chief justice at regular meetings of the nine justices in the conference room of the Supreme Court building. At this conference, the justices may agree that some cases can be decided summarily, for example, simply affirming or reversing a lower court decision with a brief explanation or with no explanation. Most of the cases are dismissed without explanation. The justices may agree to decide a case without an oral hearing. This is usually done when the justices are unanimous or nearly so on what they see as a fairly straightforward question. Normally, a short unsigned opinion – called a *per curiam* – accompanies such a decision.

If at the conference four of the nine justices agree that a case should be heard, then the case is accepted for review. This happens in only about 100 cases a year. Written briefs by each side addressing the merits of the case are submitted to the Court within forty-five days. The Court may also accept briefs from other parties interested in the case – *amici curiae*, or "friends of the court." Political scientists call these parties "judicial lobbies." State governments, corporations and political organizations frequently file *amici* briefs.

The Court also holds a public oral argument for each case. Before the justices hear a case, they meet in the cloak room adjacent to the hearing room. In a ceremonial tradition, they help each other don their robes, shake hands with each other, line up in order of seniority and walk into the courtroom. At the raised bench in the courtroom, the chief justice – who is always considered the senior-most justice, no matter how long his or her tenure – sits in the middle. The senior-most justice sits to the chief justice's right, the next most senior justice sits to the chief justice's left and so forth, so that the junior-most justices are sitting at the outer wings of the bench.

The chief justice presides at the hearing, calling the cases for argument and controlling a red light that, when lit, means a lawyer representing one side can speak. When the light is shut off, the lawyer's time has ended. Each side of a case is normally allocated thirty minutes to present arguments. Soon after a lawyer's presentation begins, however, the justices start asking the lawyer questions, which are often pointed and difficult. Most of the hearing is an exchange between the lawyer and the justices. After one side finishes, the other side presents. After one case is argued, the next case is called. When the scheduled cases have been heard, the chief justice adjourns the hearing, the justices rise and leave the courtroom, again in order of seniority. The justices "de-cloak" and return to their respective chambers.

The private conferences of the justices are held not only to decide on which cases the Court ought to accept for review but also to discuss and vote on the cases that have been heard. The chief justice brings up each case, beginning the discussion and indicating his vote. In order of seniority, the justices offer their perspectives on the case and vote, although any justice can change her or his mind anytime between the conference and the time the decision is announced to the public. The chief justice keeps track of the votes. After the conference vote on a case, one member of the prevailing side is assigned to write the Court's opinion, explaining the decision. The authorship of the Court opinion is assigned by the senior-most member of the majority. Since the chief justice tends to vote with the majority in most cases, the chief justice makes the assignments much more often than do associate justices. This is considered the most significant power of the chief justice because writing the Court's opinion – and explaining the law, especially in important cases – is a prized assignment among the justices.

Once assigned, a justice will draft an opinion and circulate it among the justices who react with comments. The author is under pressure to be responsive to these comments because, if not, the author risks losing the support of the other justices. Besides having a vote in each case, a justice has the option of writing a separate opinion and/or joining other opinions.

Members of the prevailing side in a case resulting in a split vote among the justices realize that the strength of the Court's decision and opinion depends on the size of the majority. If a justice, however, agrees with the outcome of the case but disagrees with the rationale in the opinion of the Court, the justice can choose not to join the opinion and write what is called an opinion concurring in judgment or result, explaining why the justice disagrees. The ethic of the justices is to strive for unanimous opinions, but the cases often produce split votes and separate opinions. A majority opinion of the Court is one with which at least five justices concur. A plurality opinion is an opinion of the Court that attracts more agreement than any other opinion written by the justices in the majority. Obviously a majority opinion is stronger than a plurality opinion.

Concurring and dissenting justices have a number of options regarding the writing and joining of opinions. If in agreement with the opinion of the Court, a concurring justice can simply join that opinion. The justice may join the opinion of the Court and write a concurring opinion to clarify certain points the justice thinks necessary. Or, as indicated, the justice can write an opinion concurring in the judgment. These separate writings may or may not be joined by other justices.

Dissenting justices are less systematic than majority justices in the opinion process. Dissenters do not normally try to produce a single opinion that they then "sign." To make matters more complicated, justices sometimes write opinions concurring in part and dissenting in part. This variety of writings can cause confusion over the strength and endurance of an opinion of the Court.

Once the justices have settled their votes and opinions, the record of the case is given to the branch of the Government Printing Office located in the basement of the Supreme Court building. Because Court decisions might have undue influence for some people if the decisions are leaked, the decisions and opinions are kept under tight security until the Court is ready to announce them to the public. At separate public proceedings, the justices again parade into the hearing room, and, with the chief justice presiding, announce the outcome of each case and summarize its opinions. At the same time, the printed versions of the judgments and opinions are distributed to the parties to the cases and journalists covering the court.

## JUDGES

Judges, through their decisions and opinions, are important in the creation of law affecting communication. The interpretations of the free speech and press clauses by the U.S. Supreme Court are especially crucial to understanding the system of freedom of expression in America. A sense of who these decision-makers are and how their decisions are affected by less formal influences is important to a complete understanding of communication law.

Throughout American history, the judiciary has been dominated by white, Anglo-Saxon, male Protestants. These men tend to come from families with high incomes and tend to attend elite universities and law schools. They and their families have often been politically active. Critics of the judiciary complain that this system has not represented the interests of all Americans.

States commonly require that a judge have a law degree and legal experience, but neither Article III of the Constitution nor federal statute requires that federal judges have either. There never has been a federal judge, however, who has not been trained in the law, although some federal judges have had sparse, if any, legal experience.

State systems for choosing judges vary considerably. A plurality of states use what is called the "Missouri Plan." When a judicial seat becomes vacant in one of these states, a judicial commission – usually made up of representatives of the legislature, the judiciary, the bar association and other constituencies – meets to create a short slate of candidates to fill the seat. The governor fills the seat with one of the candidates on the slate. After a substantial period in office, perhaps ten years, the judge runs not against another candidate, but in a retention election in which the voters are asked whether the judge should return to office for ten years. Given the low visibility of judicial elections, it is highly likely that, unless the judge's performance has been extraordinarily poor, the judge will remain in office indefinitely. Proponents of the Missouri Plan argue that it protects honest judges from partisan politics and other electoral influences but provides voters with some opportunity to make judges accountable.

Next most common among state judicial selection systems are elections. Eight states hold partisan elections; judges, like candidates for non-judicial offices, campaign for election for terms with endorsements of political parties. Fourteen states hold nonpartisan elections, forbidding party labels of judicial candidates on voter ballots. Four states provide for gubernatorial appointments of judges, usually requiring legislative approval of those appointments.

The framers of the Constitution intended to insulate federal judges from political influences by providing for nominations of judges by the president "with the Advice and Consent of the Senate,"[13] which has come to mean essentially that the president appoints them, but the Senate can veto the appointments. Article III further distances federal judges from political considerations by giving them lifetime tenure and protecting their salaries from being reduced.[14] Federal judges can be removed from office only by impeachment in the House of Representatives and conviction in the Senate.[15]

The countervailing forces that create judicial selection systems that range from partisan elections to executive appointments are the concerns for judicial accountability to the public, on the one hand, and judicial independence from undue influences, on the other hand. The results of comparisons of the quality of the judiciary resulting from these different selection systems are mixed.

How divorced federal judges are from politics may depend at least in part on how federal judges are chosen for nomination by the president for approval by the Senate. When a district court judge retires or dies, the president normally consults with the highest ranking members of Congress in the president's party from the state that contains the district court. The members of Congress consult with party leaders in the state on the person who should be recommended to the president. If the president nominates this candidate, the nomination is unlikely to meet resistance from other members because they will want similar support when they make recommendations to the president. In the Senate, this norm is called "senatorial courtesy." The Senate Judiciary Committee makes recommendations to the Senate concerning judicial appointments. This process is frustrated, however, when the Senate is controlled by the party opposite of the president's party, as was the case throughout the Clinton administration. President Bill Clinton had difficulty in the Republican-controlled Senate obtaining consideration, much less confirmation, of his nominations to fill judgeships. President George W. Bush has had some difficulty because of Democratic maneuvering despite the fact that Republicans have held a majority in the Senate.

A similar kind of politics plays a role in the filling of U.S. appeals court seats. Members of Congress from states in a federal circuit expect to be able to place an equitable share of judges from each of those states on the appeals court.

Since it is a national court and the most politically important

[13] U.S. CONST. art II, § 2, cl. 2.
[14] U.S. CONST. art III, § 1.
[15] U.S. CONST. art II, § 4.

# SYSTEMS FOR THE SELECTION OF JURISTS IN STATE COURTS OF LAST RESORT

## NOMINATING COMMISSION
### (USUALLY WITH GUBERNATORIAL APPOINTMENT)

Alaska, Arizona, Colorado, Delaware, District of Columbia, Florida, Hawaii, Indiana, Iowa, Kansas, Maryland, Massachusetts, Missouri, Nebraska, New Mexico, New York, Oklahoma, Rhode Island, South Carolina, South Dakota, Tennessee, Utah, Vermont, Wyoming

## NONPARTISAN ELECTIONS

Georgia, Idaho, Kentucky, Michigan, Minnesota, Mississippi, Montana, Nevada, North Dakota, Ohio (but with a partisan primary), Oregon, Washington, Wisconsin

## PARTISAN ELECTIONS

Alabama, Arkansas, Illinois, Louisiana, North Carolina, Pennsylvania, Texas, West Virginia

## APPOINTED BY CHIEF EXECUTIVE

California, Maine, New Hampshire, New Jersey, United States

## ELECTED BY LEGISLATURE

Virginia

## JUDICIAL SELECTION COMMISSION
### (THE COMMISSION SUBMITS A LIST OF CANDIDATES TO THE GOVERNOR, WHO APPOINTS ONE, WITH APPROVAL BY THE LEGISLATURE)

Connecticut

Set terms for these jurists range from six to fifteen years. The term in Massachusetts and New Hampshire is until the age of 70. In South Carolina and federal courts, a justice has lifetime tenure. The number of jurists on each of these courts is five (nineteen courts), seven (twenty-five courts), eight (only Louisiana) or nine (eight courts).

---

court, the U.S. Supreme Court is subject to different levels of politics. There are examples in Court history of presidents appointing senators, cabinet members and other politicians not experienced as judges to Supreme Court seats, presumably as pay-offs for political favors. Chief Justice William Rehnquist, formerly an assistant attorney general, had no judicial experience when President Richard Nixon nominated him to be an associate justice in 1972. Nor had some of those who have been considered great justices: Louis Brandeis, Felix Frankfurter, Charles Evans Hughes, Harlan Fiske Stone and Earl Warren. The story is frequently told that Warren, then governor of California and a presidential candidate, was named chief justice by President Dwight D. Eisenhower in return for helping him get elected.

Presidents tend overwhelmingly to appoint judges from their own political parties. Since most judges are ultimately chosen by state party leaders, this is not surprising. Both Bill Clinton and Jimmy Carter made attempts to increase the number of minorities and women on the federal bench. A nominee is subject to an official FBI background check and lobbying by a variety of special interest groups. In addition, a president is not likely to recommend a candidate whose credentials are poor. Although political litmus tests of federal nominees are seen as an overt politicization of the federal bench, presidential candidates often campaign for their election by promising that through judicial appointments, the

candidate will remake federal courts that produce unpopular decisions.

There are stories of how disappointed presidents have been in the nominations they have made to the Supreme Court. Eisenhower, a conservative Republican, said his biggest mistake as president was naming Earl Warren the chief justice. Warren, also a Republican, led what historians consider to be a constitutional revolution at the Supreme Court by aggressively taking cases and pronouncing decisions to advance civil rights and liberties and other liberal causes. Nevertheless, most judges, because of their political histories and perhaps interests in advancing to higher courts, perform predictably once on the bench.[16]

Discussion of judicial ideology tends to dwell not only on whether judges develop voting patterns consistent with conservative or liberal perspectives on the issues but also on judges' attitudes toward the role the courts should play in the political system. Judges called "activists" believe the courts have an active role to play in the political system. Judicial restraintists believe the courts have a modest role to play. Paragons of these opposing views were William O. Douglas and Felix Frankfurter, both named to the Supreme Court in 1939 by President Franklin Roosevelt.

---

[16] *See* JEFFREY A. SEGAL & HAROLD J. SPAETH, THE SUPREME COURT AND THE ATTITUDINAL MODEL (1993).

# THE JUSTICES OF THE SUPREME COURT OF THE UNITED STATES

| NAME | BORN | APPOINTED | IDEOLOGY |
|------|------|-----------|----------|
| **John Paul Stevens** | **1920** | **1975 by Ford** | **Independent** |

Born in Chicago and appointed from Illinois, Associate Justice Stevens is a former private practitioner, law professor and judge on the U.S. Court of Appeals for the Seventh Circuit. Northwestern University School of Law, 1947.

| **Antonin Scalia** | **1936** | **1986 by Reagan** | **Conservative** |
|------|------|-----------|----------|

Born in Trenton, N.J., but appointed from Virginia, Associate Justice Scalia is a former private practitioner, law professor, assistant U.S. attorney general and judge on the U.S. Court of Appeals for the District of Columbia Circuit. Harvard Law School, 1960.

| **Anthony M. Kennedy** | **1936** | **1988 by Reagan** | **Conservative** |
|------|------|-----------|----------|

Born in Sacramento and appointed from California, Associate Justice Kennedy is a former private practitioner, law professor and judge on the U.S. Court of Appeals for the Ninth Circuit. Harvard Law School, 1961.

| **David H. Souter** | **1939** | **1990 by Bush I** | **Moderate** |
|------|------|-----------|----------|

Born in Melrose, Mass., but appointed from New Hampshire, Associate Justice Souter is a former state attorney general, state trial court judge and associate justice of the New Hampshire Supreme Court. Harvard Law School, 1966.

| **Clarence Thomas** | **1946** | **1991 by Bush I** | **Conservative** |
|------|------|-----------|----------|

Born in Pinpoint, Ga., and appointed from Georgia, Associate Justice Thomas is a former chairman of the U.S. Equal Employment Opportunity Commission and judge on the U.S. Court of Appeals for the District of Columbia Circuit. Yale Law School, 1974.

| **Ruth Bader Ginsburg** | **1933** | **1993 by Clinton** | **Moderate** |
|------|------|-----------|----------|

Born in Brooklyn and appointed from New York, Associate Justice Ginsburg is a former law professor and judge on the U.S. Court of Appeals for the District of Columbia Circuit. Columbia Law School, 1959.

| **Stephen G. Breyer** | **1938** | **1994 by Clinton** | **Moderate** |
|------|------|-----------|----------|

Born in San Francisco and appointed from California, Associate Justice Breyer is a former law professor and chief judge of the U.S. Court of Appeals for the First Circuit. Harvard Law School, 1964.

| **John G. Roberts, Jr.** | **1955** | **2005 by Bush II** | **Conservative** |
|------|------|-----------|----------|

Born in Buffalo, N.Y., and appointed from Maryland, Chief Justice Roberts is a former private practitioner, lawyer in the Reagan and Bush I administrations, and judge on the U.S. Court of Appeals for the District of Columbia Circuit. Harvard Law School, 1979.

| **Samuel A. Alito, Jr.** | **1950** | **2006 by Bush II** | **Conservative** |
|------|------|-----------|----------|

Born in Trenton, N.J., and appointed from New Jersey, Associate Justice Alito is a former lawyer in the Justice Department of the Reagan and Bush I administrations, U.S. attorney for New Jersey and associate judge for the U.S. Courts of Appeals for the Third Circuit. Yale Law School, 1975.

*Roberts was nominated in 2005 by President Bush to be the 17th Chief Justice. Alito is the 110th justice to serve on the Court. The Judiciary Act of 1789 provided for a Chief Justice and five associate justices. Additional seats were added by Congress in 1807, 1837, 1863 and 1869, bringing Court membership to nine beginning after the Civil War.*

Douglas, a former chair of the Securities and Exchange Commission, and Frankfurter, a former Harvard law professor, had impeccable credentials as liberals in support of Roosevelt's New Deal program. But once on the Court, these two justices frequently disagreed, not only on how broad a Supreme Court decision should be, but even on whether the Court should be hearing a case. Douglas championed the courts as constitutional crusaders, equal partners with Congress and the president in running the country. He was unafraid to assume power for the Supreme Court to advance a sweeping political vision he saw in the Constitution.

Frankfurter, on the other hand, felt that no constitutional history or theory supported Douglas' activism. He urged the Court to be deferential to the political branches of government and to treat each case as narrowly as possible.

Most of the 110 justices in Supreme Court history would be properly categorized as conservative restraintists. Only during the Warren Court era of the 1950s and 1960s did liberal activists become a majority. In recent years, liberals accused the Rehnquist Court majority of being conservative activists,[17] although some say that is an oxymoron. The conservatives favor limited government, including a modest role for the Court in the political system.

In short, the idea of judicial politics should be kept in mind when trying to understand the law, including communication law.

## ALTERNATIVE DISPUTE RESOLUTION

Between 90 and 95 percent of all civil law disputes are settled out of court before trial but often not until years after the disputes arose. In the meantime, parties to the cases suffer prolonged delays and mounting legal costs that perhaps force unsatisfactory resolutions of the disputes. Isn't there a better way? As dissatisfaction with the clogged courts has risen, some legislatures, courts, attorneys' groups, business leaders and other reformers have been encouraging, with considerable success, alternatives to courts for the resolution of disputes.

Alternative dispute resolution (ADR, as lawyers call it) is a broad term encompassing a number of ways that litigants can avoid courts: negotiation, mediation, arbitration, private judging, expert fact-finding, mini-trials and summary jury trials.

Negotiation encourages the parties to communicate with each other about their dispute. Once one party gets a lawyer and especially after a lawsuit is filed, too often both parties see the case as inevitably headed toward litigation, preventing negotiation. Disputants, however, should be encouraged to come together calmly to argue their positions and to offer compromises. Some neighborhood organizations offer neutral settings where feuding residents can meet in an attempt to de-escalate a dispute. If this fails, both parties, of course, have rights to proceed with legal action, but negotiation may save them the trouble.

Mediation is a formal version of negotiation. A third party is engaged by the disputants to facilitate communication and reach a solution. The mediator need not be legally trained but should be knowledgeable in the area of dispute and effective at helping identify the problem and creating a resolution for the conflict. Mediation has been used in labor disputes for many years and has also become popular in the commercial world. A mediator may meet with the parties separately before bringing them together. The parties may stipulate that the proceedings are secret, not to be used as evidence in litigation should that follow the attempt to mediate.

Mediators may charge hourly fees, but sometimes communities offer trained mediators at neighborhood dispute centers for free or at low cost. Mediation is strictly voluntary and does not foreclose the possibility of litigation if one or both parties are unhappy with the outcome.

Arbitration is more formal than mediation. A neutral third party, called the arbitrator, is chosen by the parties, called disputants. The arbitrator acts with the authority of a judge, issuing a decision that is legally binding on the disputants. Arbitrators often are lawyers, sometimes retired judges, who charge fees. Arbitration is common in resolving contractual disputes between businesses, even at the international level. Contracts increasingly include provisions for arbitration should contractual disputes arise.

Although state law may prescribe procedures for arbitration, often the procedures of the American Arbitration Association are used. The disputants, likely to be represented by lawyers, may also agree to their own procedures. In any case, the procedures normally are more relaxed than those used in courts.

Generally, an arbitration case proceeds like a court case, and the arbitrator issues a decision, called an award, within thirty days after the proceeding ends. Arbitration has many advantages over courts. The cases can be conducted in secret, avoiding exposure of information that the parties would rather keep out of public court documents. Arbitration is speedier than court procedure. Finally, arbitration is less expensive than a court case.

Variations on arbitration include issue arbitration, non-binding arbitration and court-annexed arbitration. Issue arbitration means the disputants agree that only a part of their dispute will be handled by an arbitrator, who makes a decision on only that part of the dispute. Non-binding arbitration, as its name suggests, is used when the disputants want the formality of arbitration but also want to reserve the right to take their dispute to court. Court-annexed arbitration is when a part of a court proceeding is referred to an arbitrator, either with the consent of the parties or as a state law requirement that certain kinds of civil actions go to arbitration before they are permitted to enter the courts. Courts have the power to enforce arbitration awards. Losers in arbitration can appeal the awards in courts, but judges tend to be deferential to the arbitration decisions.

Private judging, also known as "rent-a-judge," is another ADR trend. Parties to a dispute, invoking state law, can hire a retired judge whose decision in what amounts to a private court is as final as that of a judge in a public court. Some states have provisions for rent-a-juries as well. Decisions in some states can be appealed to state appellate courts. Unlike other ADR choices, private judging is likely to be more expensive than regular court proceedings.

Expert fact-finding may be used when the parties to a case want to hire an expert to resolve only factual conflicts in a dispute. The expert investigates and produces a report attempting to establish the truth. This determination is not binding on the parties, but can obviously influence their decisions about litigation.

Short of going to court, other ways for potential litigants to try

---

[17] *See* David M. O'Brien, Storm Center: The Supreme Court in American Politics 61 (4th ed. 1996).

to sort out their arguments over who is right about the nature of their dispute is to conduct a "mini-trial" or a "summary jury trial." Sometimes businesses will conduct an informal mini-trial with corporate officers from both companies acting as the jury. Parties in a summary jury trial, unlike in a mini-trial, will hire private citizens as potentially "typical" jurors to act as mock petit jurors. Lawyers can present as much of a case as they wish and allow the mock jury to reach a verdict. The lawyers may interview the mock jury to anticipate how an actual jury might react to their arguments. Whether mini-trials or summary jury trials are binding on the parties depends on whether they agree to it.

ADR has little to offer the criminal justice system, but there is no doubt that ADR has helped ease the straining civil justice system. Still, the dockets of most courts continue to grow.

## LEGAL RESEARCH

Law is highly codified and organized in surprisingly sophisticated ways. Law libraries at major universities require considerable physical space for the vast published collections of all the sources of laws at the international, federal and state levels. On-line access to the law is helping to ease the strain of the ever increasing size of legal collections.

Most law libraries are organized consistent with the structure of government. The national collection will include the primary legal materials generated by the federal legislative, executive and judicial branches of government. Using similar systems of organization, parallel materials from each of the states, in alphabetical order, are stacked behind the national materials. Separate from these primary materials of research are the secondary materials — for example, legal dictionaries, encyclopedias, treatises and law journals.

Legislation is maintained in multi-volume sets of books, called "codes" or "revised statutes," according to topics, usually named "titles" or "chapters." Congressional legislation is officially published in the *United States Code*, organized in alphabetical order of fifty titles. Each enactment of Congress is assigned a title, and each part of the legislation is given a section number. When Congress enacts new legislation, it is assigned to the appropriate title and given new section numbers. If Congress amends statutes, it can specify exactly which sections are affected. If Congress rescinds legislation, the sections numbers and text are removed.

In legal research, a citation to the *United States Code* looks like this: Federal Freedom of Information Act of 1976, 5 U.S.C. 552 (1994). The name of the act, which usually includes the year in which the act was passed, is followed by a series of numbers and abbreviations. This act is located in Title 5 of the *United States Code* beginning at section 552. The year "1994" was when the Code book was published. Private publishers issue annotated versions of the *United States Code*, including not only all that is in the *Code* but also citations to court decisions that have interpreted provisions in the *Code*. Sets of codes and revised statutes usually have elaborate indexes to help users find laws.

Court decisions are maintained in continually published volumes of books called "reports" or "reporters." Official reports of court decisions are organized by jurisdiction, and the decisions and opinions of the court are reported in chronological order. For example, the U.S. Government Printing Office prints and publishes the official reports of the U.S. Supreme Court as *United States Reports*. The citation to a Supreme Court case looks like this: *Chaplinsky v. New Hampshire*, 315 U.S. 568 (1942). The case name includes the names of the parties to the case. In almost all jurisdictions, the first-named party is the party initiating the action, and the second-named party is the party against whom the first-named party initiated the action. At the trial court level, the action initiator is called the "plaintiff," and the reactor is called the "defendant." In an appellate case, they are, respectively, the "appellant" and the "appellee." When the case is taken by an appellate court, usually a court of last resort, in the form of a petition, the parties are called the "petitioner" and "respondent." The "v." is an abbreviation common in law for the word "versus." The abbreviation "U.S." has been assigned by the legal community to *United States Reports*. The first number refers to the number of the volume of *U.S.* in which the case appears. The second number is the first page of the report of the case in that volume. The parenthetical is the year in which the court made this decision. Thus, the case of *Chaplinsky v. New Hampshire*, decided in 1942, begins on page 568 in volume 315 of *United States Reports*. All reports of other courts also have been assigned unique abbreviations.

Administrative law is organized in several ways. Rules, decisions and other documents may be published officially or by private publishers in reports resembling court reports. For example, the Federal Communications Commission officially publishes its materials in *Federal Communications Commission Reports*. Citations to an agency's reports follow the format of a citation to a court case. To promulgate formal rules affecting the public or subjects of regulation however, an agency must publish notice of its intention to do so and invite the public to participate in the process in the *Federal Register*, an official daily public accounting of the activities of the agencies. If a rule is approved, it must be published in the *Federal Register* and then in the *Code of Federal Regulations*. Each agency is assigned a title like a title in the *United States Code*. Each part of a regulation is assigned a section number. Citations to the *C.F.R.* resemble citations to the *U.S.C.* Like the *U.S.C.*, the *C.F.R.* has detailed indexes to facilitate finding regulations.

Although legal research emphasizes using original primary sources of law, comprehensive banks of legal materials are becoming increasingly accessible on-line. Highly useful organizations of the law on-line are those provided by LEXIS-NEXIS and WESTLAW. These services are extremely expensive, designed for researchers in law offices and government. See the list of law-related Web sites at the end of the chapter for other services.

## SUMMARY

Law is a system of rules established and enforced by authority in a society. Law can be organized according to its sources: (1) common law, which is law made by judges in deciding cases; (2) equity law, which consists of orders by courts to resolve legal problems expeditiously; (3) statutory law, which is law enacted by legislative bodies; (4) constitutional law, which is documents containing the supreme rules for a society and the interpretation of the documents by courts; (5) administrative law, which is the rules and decisions of administrative agencies; and (6) international law, which is mainly treaties between nations.

Trial courts find facts and apply the law. Appellate courts review the application of the law by trial courts. Civil and criminal legal procedure differs at both the trial and appellate court levels. A civil case usually consists of the complaint, the answer, discovery, hearings and motions, the settlement conference, the trial and appeals. A criminal case usually consists of an investigation, the arrest, an arraignment, the complaint, a preliminary hearing, a grand jury indictment, hearings and motions, the trial, sentencing and appeals.

Federal judges are nominated by the president with the "advice and consent" of the Senate in order to protect them from politics, but the process of choosing a federal judge is political. States use variations on the appointive and electoral systems to choose state judges.

## FOR ADDITIONAL READING

Baum, Lawrence. *The Supreme Court,* 8th ed. Washington, D.C.: Congressional Quarterly Press, 2004.

Berch, Michael A., Rebecca White Birch & Ralph S. Spritzer. *Introduction to Legal Method and Process: Cases and Materials,* 3rd ed. St. Paul, Minn.: West Group, 2002.

Bonsignore, John J., et al. *Before the Law: An Introduction to the Legal Process,* 7th ed. Boston: Houghton Mifflin, 2002.

Burns, James MacGregor, J.W. Peltason, Thomas E. Cronin & David B. Magleby. *Government by the People,* 17th ed. Upper Saddle River, N.J.: Prentice Hall, 1998.

Flango, Carol & David B. Rottman, *Appellate Court Procedures,* Williamsburg, Va.: National Center for State Courts, 1998.

Harr, J. Scott. *Constitutional Law and the Criminal Justice System,* 2d ed. Belmont, Calif.: Wadsworth/Thompson Learning, 2002.

Jacobstein, J. Myron, Roy M. Mersky & Donald J. Dunn. *Fundamentals of Legal Research,* 8th ed. New York: Foundation Press, 2002.

Kerwin, C.M. *Rulemaking: How Government Agencies Write Law and Make Policy,* 3rd ed. Washington, D.C.: CQ Press, 2003.

Rehnquist, William H. *The Supreme Court.* New York: Knopf, 2001.

Scheb, John M., & John M. Sheb II. *An Introduction to the American Legal System.* Albany, N.Y.: West/Thompson Learning, 2002.

Siegal, Larry J. & Joseph J. Senna. *Introduction to Criminal Justice,* 10th ed. Belmont, Calif.: Thompson/Wadsworth, 2005.

## SELECTED LAW-RELATED INTERNET SOURCES

American Law Resources on-Line, http://www.lawsource. com, has links to legal materials in all states, Canada and Mexico.

Constitution of the United States of America, http://gpoaccess. gov/constitution/browse.html/, includes text, analysis and annotations of court interpretations.

CourtTV, http://www.courttv.com, provides background materials on high visibility trials, including news and features.

CSPAN America and the Courts, http://www.cspan.org, includes thoughtful television reports and documents on issues concerning courts and law.

Federal Courts Finder, http://www.law.emory.edu/FEDCTS, provides information about and links to federal courts.

FedWorld, http://www.fedworld.gov, offers access to thirty million government Web pages, including the *Statistical Abstract.*

FindLaw, http://www.findlaw.com, is probably the most comprehensive and searchable online resource for legal materials, including fascinating message boards for lawyers, clerks and associates and U.S. and world government links.

GPO Access, http://www.gpo.access.gov, is the searchable home site for the Government Printing Office, offering dozens of federal resources, including presidential materials, public and private laws, *Congressional Record, Code of Federal Regulations, Federal Register* and *U.S. Code.*

Hieros Gamos, http://www.hg.org, is a multi-purpose legal resource containing legal news and hundreds of links to other law-related sites.

Human Rights Library, http://www1.umn.edu/humanrts, includes a collection of about 21,000 documents and other materials in English and other languages concerning international human rights.

Internet Legal Resource Guide, http://www.ilrg.com, has comprehensive world resources, including newsgroups, on law and the legal process, with emphasis on the United States.

Jurist, http://www.jurist.law.pitt.edu, has many helpful features, including legal news, research and commentary from the United States, and elsewhere.

Law Lists, http://www.lib.uchigao.edu/~llou/lawlists/info.html, is an index to law-related discussion groups.

Legal Information Institute, http://www.law.cornell.edu, contains many law-related resources, including court decisions and previews of U.S. Supreme Court oral arguments.

National Center for State Courts, http://www.ncsc.dni.us/ ncsconline.org, is a source for information about state courts.

Thomas, http://thomas.loc.gov, is the Library of Congress server for legislative information, including bills, the *Congressional Register* and legislative histories.

U.S. Federal Judiciary, http://www.uscourts.gov, is the site of the Administrative Office of the U.S. Courts.

U.S. House of Representatives, http://www.house.gov, is a site especially useful for following current activity in the House of Representatives.

U.S. Senate, http://www.senate.gov, contains useful information about Senate actions and committees.

U.S. Supreme Court, http://www.supremecourtus.gov, includes the dockets, journal, calendar, oral argument transcripts, rules, *U.S. Reports,* maps and photographs of the Supreme Court building and related links.

World Wide Web Virtual Library: Law, http://www.law.indiana.edu/law/lawindex.html, is a site for finding miscellaneous legal information on the Internet.

# 2

## The First Amendment in Theory and Practice

*By Paul E. Kostyu*

---

 **Headnote Questions**

- *What are the guarantees of the First Amendment?*
- *How did freedom of the press and speech develop in the United States?*
- *Who helped develop the modern understanding of free speech and free press?*
- *What is the value of free speech?*
- *Why are the protections offered by the First Amendment not absolute?*
- *Why do individual First Amendment protections vary from person to person?*
- *How do the courts balance the right of expression against other personal rights or social interests?*
- *What is incorporation? Strict scrutiny? First Amendment due process?*

---

When Attorney General Alberto Gonzales said the government has the authority to prosecute journalists for publishing classified material, it represented still another, but certainly not the last, challenge for the First Amendment. Gonzales told ABC's "This Week" that journalists' obligation to national security is greater than the First Amendment right of a free press.[1]

Gonzales was even criticized by Mark Corallo, the spokesperson for former-Attorney General John Ashcroft, after Gonzales issued subpoenas to force two *San Francisco Chronicle* reporters to reveal the source of leaked grand jury testimony. Corallo called the subpoenas "the most reckless abuse of power I have seen in years."[2]

At few times in recent history has there been so much pressure on the freedoms the First Amendment guarantees. The terrorist attacks in New York, Pennsylvania and Washington, D.C., on Sept. 11, 2001, and the war in Iraq contributed to official, public and private debate and fallout about just what freedoms need to be protected and which ones need to be restricted.

"We're in a new world where we have to rebalance freedom and security," said former Rep. Richard Gephardt, a Democrat from Missouri. "We're not going to have all the openness and freedom we have had." Senator Trent Lott, a Mississippi Republican, added, "When you're in this type of conflict, when you're at war, civil liberties are treated differently."[3]

Among the immediate responses to the terrorist attacks were FBI agents monitoring private citizens' e-mail, high schools and museums curtailing expressive activity, and police and National Guard troops confiscating film from journalists and tourists. "Government officials and policymakers immediately called for measures that would chill public discourse, disrupt reporting by the press and interrupt the flow of information to the public," wrote Paul McMasters, First Amendment ombudsman for the Freedom Forum.[4]

In late 2005, the *New York Times* revealed in what would become a Pulitzer Prize-winning story that the National Security Administration has engaged in wiretapping the conversations of

---

[1] See Jaime Jansen, *Gonzales Says Reporters Can be Prosecuted for Publishing Classified Information*, May 22, 2006, *at* http://jurist.law.pitt.edu/.

[2] Joshua Pantesco, *Former Ashcroft Spokesman Blasts Gonzales for Journalist Subpoenas*, June 1, 2006, *at* http://jurist.law.pitt.edu/.

[3] Paul McMasters, *Freedom Flees in Terror From Sept. 11 Disaster*, July 16, 2002, *at* http://www.freedomforum.org.

[4] *Id.*

U.S. citizens for several years without court approval as required by the 1978 Foreign Surveillance Act. Several legal challenges are pending in federal courts.[5]

In June 2006, the federal government was in a Detroit courtroom defending its warrantless domestic-surveillance program. The ACLU, journalists, lawyers and schools want the program halted, saying it violates the rights to free speech and privacy. The government wants the case dismissed, saying the program is well within the president's authority to protect the country from terrorism.[6]

The war in Iraq has had its own First Amendment fallout. Those who protest the war are criticized as un-American and told they are misusing, if not abusing, their free speech rights. A protester at the Columbia, S.C., airport during a visit by President George W. Bush was arrested for holding a sign that said "No war for oil" even though he was on public property. He was charged with trespassing for being outside the zone established for demonstrators that day.[7]

At both the Democratic and Republican national conventions in 2004 protesters were arrested or otherwise detained for exercising their First Amendment rights. In Boston, the Democrats designated a "free speech" zone a block from the convention center which a federal judge described as an "internment camp" because it was surrounded by an eight-foot high chain link fence topped with razor wire and guarded by law enforcement officers.[8]

And an appearance at the Baseball Hall of Fame by actors Tim Robbins and Susan Sarandon was canceled after they both expressed opposition to the war. "A chill wind is blowing in this nation," Robbins said. "Every day the airwaves are filled with warnings, veiled and unveiled threats, spewed invective and hatred directed at any voice of dissent."[9]

The U.S. Supreme Court refused to hear a case involving journalists from *Time* magazine and *The New York Times* who refused to testify before a grand jury about the leak of an undercover CIA officer's identity.[10] One of them, Matthew Cooper of *Time*, was released from his confidentiality agreement by his source and testified. The other, Judith Miller, served 85 days in jail for contempt of court for refusing to identify her source.[11] And a federal appeals court upheld a contempt finding against four reporters who refused to reveal their sources for stories about former nuclear scientist Wen Ho Lee.[12]

William Rehnquist, the former Chief Justice of the United States, wrote that when America is at war, its citizens should get used to having fewer freedoms. There are, he wrote, limits on what courts will do to protect rights because there is reluctance to rule "against the government on an issue of national security during wartime."[13]

Free expression is essential to a free government and to U.S. society. "The First Amendment is not just another phrase, another document in American history," said Ken Paulson, executive director of the Freedom Forum's First Amendment Center. "It is a binding contract with the American people. It is the heart of what we are as a nation."[14]

McMasters agreed: "As much as we wish to be safe forever from the horrors [of the attacks], we simply cannot protect freedom by forsaking freedom. As much as we want relief from this time of national duress, we simply cannot make ourselves more secure by making fundamental freedoms less secure."[15]

The First Amendment gives us the right to express ourselves without fear of punishment. It also gives us access to information and protection from prior restraint. But only 11 percent of the respondents to a 1997 survey by the Freedom Forum could name freedom of the press as one of the five rights guaranteed by the First Amendment.[16] In 2005, just 16 percent could do so.[17]

In a similar survey in 2001 before the events of Sept. 11, less than half (46 percent) of all Americans said they believe the press has too much freedom.[18] That number improved in 2005, when 39 percent said the press had too much freedom. In 1999, more than half (53 percent) held that view. The number of people who believe the First Amendment goes too far in the rights it guarantees was 23 percent in 2005, down from 49 percent in 2003.[19]

Some other findings from the annual survey by the First Amendment Center suggest that Americans continue to embrace freedom of speech, even while they maintain some misgivings:

- Nearly 80 percent of the respondents agreed that broadcasters should be allowed to televise the proceedings of the Supreme

---

[5] *See The 2006 Jefferson Muzzles Go To,* June 12, 2006, *at* http://www.tjcenter.org/muzzles.html.

[6] *See* Associated Press, *Domestic Spying Defended in Court,* COLUMBUS (OHIO) DISPATCH, June 13, 2006, at A8.

[7] *See* John Leo, *Speech is Still Free, Sort Of,* THE REPOSITORY, May 6, 2003, at A5.

[8] The Jefferson Muzzles, *at* http://www.tjcenter.org, June 13, 2005.

[9] Associated Press, *Robbins: 'Chill Wind' is Blowing in America,* (NEW PHILADELPHIA, OHIO) TIMES-REPORTER, Apr. 17, 2003, at A6.

[10] *See* Associated Press, *High Court Won't Hear Reporters' Appeal Over Subpoena,* June 28, 2005, *at* http://www.firstamendmentcenter.org.

[11] *See* Associated Press, *Miller Ordered to Jail, Cooper Agrees to Testify in Plame Case,* July 6, 2005, *at* http://www.firstamendmentcenter.org.

[12] Associated Press, *Contempt Finding Upheld Against Reporters,* June 28, 2005 *at* http://news.findlaw.com. The case was eventually resolved when five major news organizations agreed to pay $750,000 to Wen Ho Lee to settle the case. *See* Josh Gerstein, N.Y. Sun, June 5, 2006, *available at* http://www.nysun.com/article/33833.

[13] Adam Cohen, *Justice Rehnquist's Ominous History of Wartime Freedom,* N.Y. TIMES, Sept. 22, 2002, at D12.

[14] Kenneth A. Paulson, 1999 Speech (Mar. 17, 1999), *available at* http://www.freedomforum.org.

[15] McMasters, *supra* note 3.

[16] The five rights are freedom of speech, freedom of the press, freedom of religion, the right of assembly and the right to petition the government.

[17] *First Amendment 2005 Survey Touches Headline Issues,* June 28, 2005, *at* http://www.firstamendmentcenter.org.

[18] Kenneth A. Paulson, *Good News, Bad News in Latest First Amendment Survey,* July 16, 2002, *available at* http://www.freedomforum.org.

[19] *First Amendment 2005 Survey, supra* note 17.

Court;

- Seventy-five percent said that as part of a classroom discussion, public school students should be allowed to express views that others might find offensive, but just 27 percent agreed that students should be allowed to wear T-shirts with messages or pictures that might offend others;

- Sixty percent opposed extending government authority to regulate content on broadcast television to programs on cable or satellite television systems, but 64 percent endorsed increased fines for over-the-air broadcasters who violate government rules regarding content;

- Sixty-three percent said the government should not be allowed access to records of materials borrowed by public library patrons, and 77 percent said those patrons should be told when the government asks for records of what they borrowed.

"The year 2001 was a pivotal time at every level of government for free speech, from national security concerns in the wake of Sept. 11 to the actions of city councils and state governments," wrote Richard T. Kaplar, vice president of The Media Institute. "But the First Amendment survived, which is a tribute to journalists, government officials and the American people."[20]

"Most Americans celebrate the freedoms guaranteed by the First Amendment," wrote McMasters of the Freedom Forum. "Yet they are not entirely comfortable with those freedoms. They are constantly reevaluating their commitment to First Amendment rights and values and rearranging their priorities, asking themselves whether life would be more civil, more orderly, less threatening if the excesses of expression were somehow subdued."[21]

"Free speech in the land of the free is not as free as you might think," Associated Press writer Nancy Benac wrote. "In a debate as old as the republic, Americans are weighing once again when it is proper to place limits on the First Amendment's protections of unbridled speech." Benac quoted free speech lawyer and scholar Floyd Abrams as saying, "First Amendment issues are always unpopular. That's why we need a First Amendment."[22]

Abrams is right.

## THE HERITAGE OF FREE EXPRESSION

Freedom of expression is not exclusive to the United States, and it has no identifiable "father" or "mother." It dates probably to the ancient Greeks, notably Plato and Socrates and their philosophical writings during the establishment of western civilization. But there is a more recent history.

In the mid-Fifteenth Century Johann Gutenberg developed movable type, and, shortly thereafter, William Caxton introduced the printing press to England. The concept of printing was new, so Caxton faced few, if any, restrictions. But that quickly changed. The British government recognized the power of the printed word and sought to control it.

The Sixteenth and Seventeenth centuries in England also saw battles that mixed politics and religion. Dissent was a capital offense. The monarchy and the Church of England wanted opposition silenced. Religious and political fighting were linked to economic differences between the aristocracy, a rising middle class and the poor. All sides in these battles came to understand the importance of the printing press.

Government became involved early, implementing a system of licensing in 1520. The licensing allowed officials to preview material, thus controlling both content and distribution. A license became a coveted commodity, so much so that licensed printers often protected their own self-interests by uncovering those who published without government approval. Often the government engaged in heavy-handed means to censor ideas it considered dangerous. People were jailed, tortured and executed for expressing ideas contrary to those espoused by government officials. Presses were wrecked, publications destroyed and buildings burned.

But the period was not without support for free expression. One of the most notable arguments came from poet John Milton, whose now-famous *Areopagitica* criticized government censorship in 1644. In the essay, subtitled *For the Liberty of Unlicensed Printing*, Milton protested a 1643 order by Parliament requiring the registration of all publications by the Stationer's Company, which was founded in 1557. Milton viewed the order as a means of establishing a system of censorship and wrote:

> Though all the winds of doctrine were let loose to play upon the earth, so Truth be in the field, we do injuriously by licensing and prohibiting to misdoubt her strength. Let her and Falsehood grapple; who ever knew Truth put to the worse in a free and open encounter?[23]

Milton's argument is that censorship, whatever the form, is unnecessary because truth will always win in a battle with falsity. Open debate, the argument goes, is the only way for people to discern the truth and reject falsehood. Milton was advocating what has come to be known as the "marketplace of ideas" theory, even though the metaphor, in its purest form, refers to an exchange or competition of ideas rather than a battle of ideas.

Milton made a lasting contribution to freedom of expression, but freedom had its limits, even to Milton. He opposed freedom of expression for Catholics and others who advocated ideas Milton considered dangerous, subversive, impious or evil. Seven years after writing *Areopagitica*, Milton joined Oliver Cromwell's govern-

---

[20] The Media Institute, *Unprecedented Events Created New First Amendment Challenges in 2001*, July 16, 2002, *available at* http://www.mediainst.org.

[21] Paul McMasters, *State of the First Amendment: A Survey of Public Attitudes*, May 15, 2000, *available at* http://www.freedomforum.org/first/sofa/1999/analysis.asp.

[22] Nancy Benac, *Free Speech Not Always as Free as You Think*, THE DELAWARE GAZETTE, June 23, 1997, at 4.

[23] JOHN MILTON, AREOPAGITICA AND OF EDUCATION 50 (George H. Sabine ed., 1951) (1644).

ment as a censor, helping impose a strict Puritanical doctrine on England. The beliefs of other religious groups were granted little tolerance by the government, despite Milton's earlier argument.

Though the most famous advocate of freedom of expression in the mid-Seventeenth Century, Milton was not alone. Roger Williams, a Baptist minister who had visited the North American colonies, wrote in the same year as Milton's *Areopagitica* that freedom of expression should be allowed even for Catholics, Jews and Muslims. The Levelers, a Puritan group of the same period who believed strongly in egalitarianism, also had consistently condemned censorship and licensing in their tracts. Suppressing the truth kept people ignorant, they argued, allowing tyrants to use that ignorance for unjust ends.

In the late Seventeenth Century, other philosophers advocating freedom of expression emerged. A notable among them was John Locke, who argued that government should answer to the people, instead of the people to the government.[24] People have natural rights, Locke wrote, including life, liberty and property ownership; government, through its grant by the people, should safeguard those rights, to which freedom of expression is central.

Free expression, of course, is linked to a free press. The ability to write one's thoughts and then pass them on to others is a foundation of free speech theory. The development of the theory continued into the Eighteenth Century. Perhaps the most quoted representative of that period is English jurist William Blackstone, who, in 1769, wrote:

> The liberty of the press is indeed essential to the nature of a free state: but this consists in laying no previous restraints upon publications, and not in freedom from censure for criminal matter when published. Every freeman has an undoubted right to lay what sentiments he pleases before the public; to forbid this, is to destroy the freedom of the press: but if he publishes what is improper, mischievous, or illegal, he must take the consequence of his own temerity. To subject the press to the restrictive power of a licenser ... is to subject all freedom of sentiment to the prejudices of one man, and make him the arbitrary and infallible judge of all controverted points in learning, religion, and government.[25]

Blackstone's point was that there must be a means for distributing ideas, that is, that there must be publication, but that writers must be held accountable for their words. Protection does not extend to false or other "mischievous" material.

Blackstone's view is important, not only because it advances the concept of a free press, but also because Blackstone was a ju-

rist rather than a philosopher; he had the power to do more than theorize — he could interpret the law. Blackstone's impact resonated long after his death. As late as 1907, Supreme Court Justice Oliver Wendell Holmes consulted his work when looking for guidance on expression issues.[26]

Other forces advancing freedom of expression were at work:
- Parliament gained a major victory over the monarchy in 1688, leading to strictly limited powers of the throne.
- A two-party system, which encouraged spirited debate, emerged. Both parties — the Whigs and Tories — relied on the printing press to espouse and circulate their views.

While licensing pressures lessened, punishment for seditious libel — criticism of the government — grew as the prevailing form of censorship. A prosecution for seditious libel did not allow truth as a defense. In fact, truth exacerbated the crime. Because true criticism would make people more suspicious of government, it provided the impetus for disorder or revolt. A key theory in a prosecution for sedition was the greater the truth, the greater the libel. Despite reforms, criticism of government was viewed as criminal throughout the Eighteenth Century. It wasn't until passage of the Fox Libel Act in 1792, which allowed juries instead of judges to decide what was libelous, that prosecutions began to diminish.

These same influences had significant impact on the current view of prior restraint, which is discussed in detail in Chapter 4.

## THE CONSTITUTION AND THE BILL OF RIGHTS

While the Mother Country was dealing with freedom of expression, parallel issues faced the American colonists. They had a strong desire to ensure that the censorship experiences of England didn't find a home in the new country. Censorship was part of the colonial way of life before the break with England, because colonial governors loyal to the crown exerted the same kinds of control in the New World. The assumption was, if restrictions could be imposed in England, they could be imposed in the colonies.

The First Amendment grew from those experiences. Colonists came to the new country to escape religious and political oppression, but found similar restrictions. Licensing became commonplace, and papers carried on their nameplates the words "published by authority," even after English papers had been freed from the requirement.

A variety of laws — from those prohibiting seditious libel to those, like the Stamp Act of 1765, requiring governmental stamps on published material — were used to control publishing. Colonists saw the laws as unfair, and their strict enforcement was one of the causes of the American Revolution.

One of the most famous seditious libel cases of the period was that of John Peter Zenger, a German immigrant who printed the

---

[24] John Locke, *Concerning the True Original Extent and End of Civil Government*, 35 GREAT BOOKS OF THE WESTERN WORLD 25-81. (Robert Maynard Hutchings ed., 1952).

[25] *See* WILLIAM BLACKSTONE, COMMENTARIES OF THE LAWS OF ENGLAND, 1765-1769 152 (William Carey Jones ed. 1916) (1769).

[26] *See* Patterson v. Colorado, 205 U.S. 454, 462 (1907). *See also* WILLIAM W. VAN ALSTRYNE, FIRST AMENDMENT CASES AND MATERIALS 6-21 (1991) (discussing Blackstone).

*New York Weekly Journal.* Lewis Morris and James Alexander, who backed the paper, were political opponents of New York's colonial governor, William Cosby. Zenger published harsh attacks on the governor — attacks probably written by Morris, Alexander and others — and was jailed for seditious libel in 1734. There was little doubt that Zenger was guilty of publishing the libel. Indeed, his attorney, Andrew Hamilton, admitted as much at trial. Hamilton, however, convinced the jury that no one should be jailed for publishing truthful information, even if it was critical of government or officials. Jurors ignored the law that obligated them to find Zenger guilty and acquitted the printer.

Some scholars interpret the Zenger case as a historic blow for freedom of the press, while others see it as a victory for free speech rights. The difference lies in the interpretation of Hamilton's action. Legal historians argue that Hamilton appealed to the wisdom of local juries and the right of a free people, rather than a free press, to criticize their government.

As the country moved toward independence, revolutionary leaders realized that they did not want to repeat the mistakes of the past. Before the end of the Revolutionary War, the Articles of Confederation, the nation's first constitution, provided the guidelines for the formation of a loose-knit federation of thirteen states with a weak federal government. The document contained no bill of rights, because the drafters thought the government didn't have the power to infringe upon the rights that would be enumerated in such a bill. Many of the rights, including freedom of expression, were found in most state constitutions. Freedom of the press, for example, was guaranteed by the Virginia constitution five years before the adoption of the Articles of Confederation.

But the government formed under the Articles began to falter, requiring fundamental changes in governmental structure. In 1787, the states — all but Rhode Island, that is — sent delegates to Philadelphia to rewrite the Articles. Instead, the delegates created a new charter — the Constitution — giving increased powers to a central government while keeping state law supreme in some matters.

Historians have little to go on regarding the discussions that took place at that constitutional convention, because no official record was kept, and the public was not admitted. But it seems clear that a bill of rights was not a high priority.

At least partly because of the absence of provisions protecting fundamental, individual rights, supporters of the Constitution had a difficult time winning ratification by three-quarters of the states. Some delegates wanted the protections listed first; others wanted them included somewhere in the document, and still others didn't want them included at all. Thomas Jefferson, writing to James Madison in 1787, found the absence of protection for fundamental rights one of the shortcomings of the Constitution: "I will now tell you what I do not like. First, the omission of a bill of rights, providing clearly ... for freedom of religion, freedom of the press...."[27]

The Constitution was ratified without a bill of rights, but legislators in some states supported the document only upon promises that attempts would be made in the first Congress to approve such a bill. James Madison, who made some of those promises in Virginia, introduced a bill of rights during the first session of the First Congress. His original amendment dealing with free expression read: "The people shall not be deprived or abridged of their right to speak, to write or to publish their sentiments and freedom of the press, as one of the great bulwarks of liberty, shall be inviolable."[28]

That wording did not survive congressional committees, however. Though it is impossible to tell how the courts over time would have interpreted Madison's original amendment, its wording seems to provide more broad-based protection for both speech and the press than the version eventually adopted:

Congress shall make no law respecting an establishment of religion, or prohibiting the free exercise thereof; or abridging the freedom of speech, or of the press; or the right of the people peaceably to assemble, and to petition the Government for a redress of grievances.

It's tempting to assign more importance to the protections of speech and press because they come first in the Bill of Rights, but, in fact, the First Amendment wasn't always first. When Madison's proposed bill of rights came out of a joint conference committee, there were twelve amendments. What would eventually become the First Amendment was third, behind an amendment providing for a fixed schedule for apportioning seats in the House of Representatives, and one restricting the way representatives and senators could give themselves raises. Those two amendments were not ratified, so the third amendment came to be first. Even had the amendment been listed first originally, however, there is no indication that courts would or should consider it more important than other rights. As Justice Harry A. Blackmun once wrote, "The First Amendment, after all, is only one part of an entire Constitution."[29]

It took two years for the required ten states — three-fourths of the thirteen original states — to ratify the Bill of Rights. Connecticut, Georgia and Massachusetts did not ratify the first ten amendments to the Constitution until 1941.

The First Amendment, unlike Madison's original proposal, applies only to Congress. The wording clearly represents the founders' fear that the new federal government might overpower the states. They wanted to ensure that states' rights came first by preventing Congress from interfering with the protection of speech or press found in state constitutions. Consequently, if newspaper publishers wanted to seek recourse from attempts to muzzle them by state governments, they would have to do so through

---

[27] Letter from Thomas Jefferson to James Madison (1787), *in* THOMAS JEFFERSON ON DEMOCRACY 47 (Saul K. Padover ed., 1939).

[28] 1 ANNALS OF CONGRESS 452 (1834).

[29] New York Times Co. v. United States, 403 U.S. 713, 761 (1971) (Blackmun, J., dissenting).

state constitutions; there was no help in the federal Constitution. It would take nearly 140 years for that interpretation to change.

## THE FIRST AMENDMENT APPLIED TO THE STATES

In 1925, the Supreme Court extended the prohibition on Congress' interference with free speech and press rights to the states. The ruling came in a case involving a Communist named Benjamin Gitlow, who had been convicted of criminal anarchy in New York. Gitlow's crime was advocating the violent overthrow of the government through his publications, *The Left Wing Manifesto* and *The Revolutionary Age*. The First Amendment does not explicitly prohibit the states from infringing upon speech and press rights, but Gitlow's attorney contended that Gitlow's conviction under state law still violated his First Amendment free press rights.

In 1868, some fifty-seven years prior to Gitlow's case arriving at the Supreme Court, the Fourteenth Amendment to the Constitution was adopted to endow newly emancipated slaves with the same constitutional rights as everyone else in the country. The amendment has several provisions, including the Constitution's only statement of citizenship. Its best known language, however, is that no state shall "deprive any person of life, liberty, or property, without due process of law; nor deny to any person within its jurisdiction the equal protection of the laws."

The language is almost identical to that of the Fifth Amendment. The Fifth Amendment is directed toward Congress, however, while the Fourteenth is directed at the states. Justice Edward Sanford, writing for the majority in *Gitlow v. New York*, applied the First Amendment to the states through the Fourteenth, though he did so in an almost backhand way: "We may and do assume that freedom of speech and of the press — which are protected by the First Amendment from abridgment by Congress — are among the fundamental personal rights and 'liberties' protected by the due process clause of the Fourteenth Amendment from impairment by the States."[30]

Sanford's *dicta* were a precursor to changes in the way of thinking about the Constitution that would have an enormous impact on expressive rights. In effect, Sanford said state governments, just like the federal government, are bound by the Constitution. While judges and scholars recognized that state constitutions could provide more expansive rights than those provided in the federal Constitution — indeed, some do — the concept that state laws and constitutions could not grant fewer rights was relatively new. This is called the "concept of incorporation." It didn't help Gitlow — the Court affirmed his conviction — but it provided a touchstone that has protected expressive rights ever since.

While the Court in *Gitlow* assumed the Fourteenth Amendment protected fundamental rights, it wasn't until 1931 that the Court actually struck down a state statute that it said violated the press clause of the First Amendment, doing so in *Near v. Min-*

*nesota*,[31] a prior restraint case.

Incorporation also gives federal courts authority to review the constitutionality of state laws, allowing them to be the final interpreters of freedom of expression. The Court would prefer not to rule on issues from states involving fundamental rights. If legislation does not affect these fundamental rights, the Court assumes the legislation is constitutional. It tries to avoid political battles and counteracting majority rule, though it is often accused of doing just that. But if legislation — state or federal — is seen to infringe First Amendment rights, the Court will not defer to the legislature. In First Amendment cases, the Court examines the whole record of a lower court decision to determine whether the decision handicaps freedom of expression.

The government usually cannot regulate expression based on its content. "If there is a bedrock principle underlying the First Amendment," wrote Justice William Brennan in 1989, "it is that the government may not prohibit the expression of an idea simply because society finds the idea offensive itself or disagreeable."[32] That is, a regulation must be content neutral — the regulation must be based on factors not related to the content of the message that will be hampered by the regulation. This is true unless the regulated speech falls into one of the categories of expression that is not protected by the First Amendment — obscenity, fighting words or information that would harm national security, for example.

In addition, the time, place and manner in which messages are expressed *can* be regulated. Time, place and manner regulations allow a local, state or federal government, for example, to require permits for parades, specifying the route the parade will follow and the time of day the parade can take place. The government can ban the parade because it would go down Main Street during rush hour, but cannot ban the parade because of the message being espoused by the marchers. Time, place and manner restrictions are constitutional as long as they are not arbitrary — for example, it might be unconstitutional to ban all messages without a valid reason — and as long as they are neutral — that is, they treat all messages the same way. A Cincinnati ordinance, for example, was ruled unconstitutional when city officials tried to ban both a Jewish menorah and a Ku Klux Klan cross from display on public property. The city said allowing the menorah was a violation of the separation of church and state, while permitting the cross constituted fighting words. A federal judge said the First Amendment protected a Jewish organization's right to display the menorah, and an appellate court said the city also had to allow the cross, even though the KKK offends many people.[33]

---

[30] 268 U.S. 652, 666 (1925).

[31] 283 U.S. 697 (1931). After *Near*, the Court, on a case-by-case basis, brought other clauses of the Bill of Rights under Fourteenth Amendment protection.

[32] Texas v. Johnson, 491 U.S. 397, 414 (1989).

[33] Knight Riders of the Ku Klux Klan v. Cincinnati, 72 F.3d 43 (6th Cir. 1995). *See also*, Chabad of Southern Ohio v. Cincinnati, 537 U.S. 1085 (2002); Associated Press, *Cincinnati Must Allow Jewish Display in Public*

The Supreme Court requires that there be what it calls "strict scrutiny" of any action that directly infringes on First Amendment freedoms. When a court uses strict scrutiny to determine whether a regulation is constitutional, it must find (1) that there is a compelling government interest for the regulation and (2) that the regulation is necessary and narrowly tailored to meet that government interest. That is, the government must take the least drastic measures to accomplish a necessary goal.

Regulations that are not specific enough or are not sufficiently narrow are generally ruled to be vague, overbroad or both. An unconstitutionally vague law is so unclear that persons of common intelligence must guess at its meaning and will differ in their methods of application. A vague law makes speakers unnecessarily cautious. An example of such a law was one preventing the desecration of the U.S. flag. The law prohibited contemptuous treatment of the flag in public. "Contemptuous" was not defined. Burning the flag may be "contemptuous," but so may be wearing a scarf or tie that appears to be a flag. Wearing a small flag on the seat of the pants or using a flag as a rug in an art gallery also might be contemptuous. A statute that leaves authorities broad discretion to curb expression and does not define the line between protected and unprotected expression is unconstitutionally vague.

An overbroad law, on the other hand, can be very clear about what it prohibits, but it prohibits too much. That is, it prohibits protected as well as unprotected speech. The Georgia Supreme Court struck down as overbroad a state statute regulating lewdness, because under the statute a bumper sticker reading "shit happens" would have been illegal.[34] A federal appeals court struck down a Cleveland ordinance that banned most billboard advertisements for alcoholic drinks, saying it was "unduly broad."[35]

Suppressing speech is not an easy task. The courts require that a specific legal procedure be followed that allows them to decide what expression is protected. The procedure, called "First Amendment due process," requires certain safeguards so that individual rights are protected. Those safeguards include requiring the government to notify an individual when action is being taken against the individual and providing an opportunity to be heard in court.

The process is left to the courts, which are seen as unbiased interpreters of government legislation and individual rights. This is part of the system of checks and balances of power. By following due process, the courts require the government to bear the burden of proving that legislation does not violate individual rights. That is, the courts assume that expression is protected unless the government proves otherwise.

First Amendment due process is intended to prevent self-censorship, which occurs when individuals are unable to distinguish between protected and unprotected expression. In order to pro-

tect themselves, store owners may not stock certain books, magazines or videos, for example, to avoid being prosecuted, even though that material may be protected expression. Another way to interpret due process is to view expression as innocent (protected by the First Amendment) until proven guilty (not protected).

The courts in their examination of First Amendment cases apply rules and principles that have been developed over time, primarily from legal precedent established in earlier cases. When First Amendment due process is involved, courts usually expedite the decision-making process, because the impact is much broader than in other types of cases.

## THE DISTINCTION BETWEEN "SPEECH" AND "PRESS"

The First Amendment requires that both speech and the press be protected. Almost from the time it was drafted, however, there has been debate over what the terms "speech" and "press" mean. Though the First Amendment says nothing about either "expression" or "conduct," for example, the Supreme Court has held that some expressive conduct is protected as "speech." Chapter 3 covers conduct and speech in greater detail.

In a 1989 case, Justice Brennan, an ardent supporter of the First Amendment who retired a year later, wrote that "the First Amendment literally forbids the abridgment only of 'speech,' but we have long recognized that its protection does not end at the spoken or written word."[36] Government restriction, he wrote, "is not dependent on the particular mode in which one chooses to express an idea."[37]

In the colonial period, speech manifested itself in meetings, on street corners, from pulpits and through traveling balladeers. The press produced bills of sale, advertisements, poetry, promotions, books, essays and newspapers. Colonists found value in their freedom to listen to the speechmakers and to read the output of the printers.

When the First Amendment was drafted, was there a clear sense of what "speech" and "press" meant? Scholars disagree. It may seem clear that "speech" is the spoken word and "press" is the written word, but as technology developed, the distinctions between these two have increasingly blurred. The blurring continues to challenge the courts to develop new interpretations of "speech" and "press." Computer technology has made it cheaper to provide information to a broad audience. We can publish *and* speak *via* the Internet. We can use computers to produce small special-interest publications cheaply and quickly. There has been an explosion of specialty magazines and newsletters addressing a variety of interests and needs. Internet weblogs ("blogs") blur the line between speech and press even more.

The word "press" no longer applies to only traditional newspapers and magazines. The term also must be applied to shows such

---

*Square, Supreme Court Says*, COLUMBUS DISPATCH, Dec. 17, 2002, at C9.

[34] Cunningham v. State, 400 S.E.2d 916 (Ga. 1991).

[35] Eller Media Co. v. Cleveland, 326 F.3d 720 (6th Cir. 2003).

[36] Texas v. Johnson, 491 U.S. at 404.

[37] *Id.* at 414.

as *Hard Copy*, *Inside Edition* and *Extra*; tabloids such as the *National Enquirer*, the *Star* and the *Globe*; documentaries and docudramas; and every special interest group or individual with a computer, printer and wireless card. Some officials throughout history have reacted to each new technology — books, photographs, movies, radio, television, the Internet — with an urge to regulate.[38]

The courts have found themselves wrestling with how to apply the freedoms the First Amendment provides. Are the speech rights less for some categories of people than others? Do freelance writers have the same rights as journalists who work for mainstream publications? What are the other expressive activities that may fall under the broad categories of oral and printed words? Do they include pictures, gestures, dances, the Internet?

The Supreme Court has had to interpret the words "speech" and "press" in a variety of ways. The Court has been required to go beyond the verbal and written communication of ideas based on what the framers were thinking — or what we think they were thinking — to issues involving the development of modern technology. Jefferson said as much in 1816 when he wrote, "I know also that laws and institutions must go hand in hand with the progress of the human mind.... As new discoveries are made, new truths disclosed, and manners and opinions change with the change of circumstances, institutions must advance also, and keep pace with the times."[39] The founders had no concept of film, videotape or computers when they wrote the First Amendment.

In a broad sense, the courts have provided First Amendment protection to expression, a term that incorporates speech, press and some conduct. Expression also incorporates many forms of entertainment like theater performances, movies and dancing.

Still not fully answered is the question of whether the protection of expression includes the right to gather information. The Court has said that newsgathering deserves some protection but has never backed up that *dicta* by providing protection.[40] The Court also has limited access to some public places and information. Chapters 16, 17 and 18 cover access to information and places in greater detail.

## THE THEORIES OF PROTECTING EXPRESSION

In its 2005-06 term, the Supreme Court reviewed or decided ten cases and refused to hear forty-three others that dealt with free press or speech issues. Among other things, the Court upheld restrictions on materials prisoners could receive; said universities receiving government money must give equal access to military recruiters; held federal extortion and racketeering laws cannot be used to ban demonstrations; ruled that statements made by gov-

ernment employees in the course of their official duties are outside protection of the First Amendment; said a lower court needs to look again at a challenge to federal restrictions on political advertisements.[41]

First Amendment issues, some of which never make it to the Supreme Court, manifest themselves in a variety of ways. The Court, for example, refused to hear a case involving a New York kindergarten student who had been prevented from using a poster of Jesus as part of a class assignment on ways to save the environment.[42] Here are some other recent episodes:

- Vandals tried to destroy 676 white, wooden crosses that Michael Astley put in a field as a memorial to fallen U.S. troops in Iraq.[43]

- A Maryland judge said mooning may be disgusting and demeaning, but it is protected communication. In a feud involving a homeowners association, Raymond McNealy of Germantown, Md., mooned a member of the association's board. The judge said his decision might have been different had McNealy been on trial for "being a jerk."[44]

- An Ohio court of appeals ruled a city law restricting the size of political signs is unconstitutional. The wife of a county Republican chairman was fined $75 per day for placing a 32 square-foot Bush-Cheney sign in her yard in Cuyahoga Falls. A city ordinance limited temporary yard signs to eight square feet.[45]

- Attorneys for Roger D. Blackwell asked a federal judge to rescind part of sentence he imposed that prevents the former Ohio State University professor from profiting from his crimes by writing a book about them. Blackwell was sent to prison for insider trading. His attorneys said the book ban would restrict Blackwell's First Amendment rights.[46]

- Three members of the Pickerington, Ohio, city council accused their colleagues of using e-mail messages to cut them out of policy discussions with the city's administration. The e-mails

---

[38] *See* David Hudson, *Government Regulation of New Technology is an Old Tale,* Mar. 16, 1999, *available at* http://www.freedomforum.org/speech/1999/3/16electronic.asp.

[39] Letter from Thomas Jefferson to Dr. Priestly (1802), *supra* note 27, at 67.

[40] *See* Branzburg v. Hayes, 408 U.S. 665 (1972).

[41] *See* Beard v. Banks, S.Ct. 126 S.Ct. 2572 (2006); Garcetti v. Ceballos, 126 S.Ct. 1951 (2006); Randall v. Sorrell, 126 S.Ct. 2479 (2006); Rumsfeld v. Forum for Academic & Institutional Rights, 126 S.Ct. 1297 (2006); Scheidler, et. al. v. National Organizations for Women, et. al., 126 S.Ct. 1264 (2005); Wisconsin Right to Life Inc. v Federal Election Commission, 126 S.Ct. 1016 (2006).

[42] Baldwinsville Central Sch. Dist. v. Peck, 126 S.Ct. 1880 (2006) (denying cert.). *See also* Associated Press, *High Court Stays Out of Dispute Over Kindergartner's Jesus Poster,* SAN DIEGO UNION-TRIBUNE, Apr. 25, 2006, at A5. *See also* http://www.firstamendmentcenter.org for list of cases denied review by the Supreme Court.

[43] *See* Ann Fisher, *An American's Dissent,* COLUMBUS (OHIO) DISPATCH, Jan. 2, 2006, at D1.

[44] *See* David Montgomery, *Judge Finds 'Mooning' Disgusting, Not Indecent,* COLUMBUS (OHIO) DISPATCH, Jan. 6, 2006, at A7.

[45] Hudson v. Arshinkoff, 2005-Ohio-6976 (2005). *See* April McClellan-Copeland, *Political Sign Limits Dismissed,* (CLEVELAND) PLAIN DEALER, Dec. 16, 2005, at B4.

[46] *See* Barnett D. Wolf, *Book-Deal Ban Draws Attorneys' Objection,* COLUMBUS (OHIO) DISPATCH, Dec. 24, 2005, at B1.

came to light after a councilman submitted a public information request and received more than 200 exchanges involving city officials.[47]

- Two editors of the student newspaper at the University of Illinois at Urbana-Champaign were suspended for printing cartoons depicting the prophet Muhammad. The same cartoons enraged Muslims and led to violent protests when they were published in Europe.[48]
- At the University of North Carolina at Chapel Hill and the University of Florida a columnist and political cartoonist, respectively, came under fire when they inflamed minority groups – Muslims and blacks – and caused protests and debate about what they published. The columnist was fired and the cartoonist condemned and threatened.[49]
- The Zanesville-Muskingum County Port Authority in Central Ohio disregarded Ohio's open government laws and met in secret to hire an executive director.[50]
- The Ohio Supreme Court ruled unanimously that the home addresses of state employees are not public records and can be shielded from disclosure.[51]
- Secrecy in the federal government accelerated, as departments classified documents at a rate of 125 per minute with vague labels such as "sensitive security information." In 2004, 15.6 million documents were classified, doubling the number from 2001. On the other hand, declassification of historical documents slowed to a crawl. In 2004, 28 million pages were declassified, down from 204 million pages in 1997.[52]
- The City of Toledo explored limiting a demonstration of neo-Nazis in a neighborhood where rioters looted businesses and threw bricks at police when the white supremacist organization marched the last time. The city wanted to move the demonstration to another part of the city.[53]
- A minister claimed his free-speech rights were violated when Madison, Wis., police told him to remove anti-homosexuality banners from highway overpasses. A federal appellate court agreed, saying the city's claim that the banner created a hazard by slowing traffic infringed on the rights of the Rev. Ralph

Ovadal. The city has since adopted an ordinance banning any display of banners or signs, except traffic signs, on overpasses.[54]

- Members of white supremacist groups, including the Ku Klux Klan, held a rally at the Antietam National Battlefield in Maryland in what is believed to be the first time a group was given permission to demonstrate at the site of the bloodiest day of the Civil War. Park Superintendent John Howard said, "The Supreme Court has ruled consistently that national parks in particular are places of freedom of expression."[55]
- Anti-abortion activists want a federal court to declare a Cleveland, Ohio, noise ordinance unconstitutional because their free-speech rights were violated when they were prevented from blaring a 911 recording outside a clinic.[56]

The list goes on and on. Can indecency be banned from the Internet? How do we balance free speech and sexual or racial harassment? When can a college administration tell a professor what not to say in the classroom? Can a college prevent political campaigning on its computer network? Can a private company fire an employee because of a shirt the employee wears to work? Can a school suspend a student for the message he wears on a T-shirt? Are state statutes preventing disparaging comments about agricultural products — called "veggie libel laws" — constitutional?

The First Amendment says "Congress shall make no law...." The words seem clear enough. They don't say Congress can make some laws, or it can make a few, reasonable laws. It says Congress can make *no law* that abridges the freedom of speech or the press. Yet, courts have often decided that, in some circumstances, speech and press rights must yield to other rights.

Columnist George F. Will wrote:

For several decades in America, the aim of much of the jurisprudential thought about the First Amendment's free speech provision has been to justify contracting its protections. Freedom of speech is increasingly "balanced" against "competing values." As a result, it is whittled down, often by seemingly innocuous increments, to a minor constitutional after-thought.[57]

Some First Amendment scholars and jurists, because of the clear language of the First Amendment, argue for absolute protection for all speech — regardless of content, motive of the speaker or consequences of the speech. Others argue that speech contributing to a self-governing society should receive absolute pro-

[47] *See* Kirk D. Richards, *Pickerington Council at Odds Over E-mail*, COLUMBUS (OHIO) DISPATCH, Sept. 26, 2005, at B3.

[48] *See* David Mendell, *2 Campus Editors Suspended Over Muhammad Cartoons, Judge Lets Union Dues go to Political Causes*, TIMES-REPORTER, Feb. 16, 2006, at A7.

[49] *See* Kathleen Parker, *College Columnist, Cartoonist Axed for Expressing Opinions*, TIMES-REPORTER, Oct. 15, 2005, at A4.

[50] *See Operating in the Dark*, COLUMBUS (OHIO) DISPATCH, Oct. 5, 2005, at A12.

[51] State ex rel. Dispatch Printing Co. v. Johnson, 106 Ohio St.3d 160 (2005). *See also* Randy Ludlow, *High Court Hides State Workers' Addresses*, COLUMBUS (OHIO) DISPATCH, Sept. 8, 2005, at D1.

[52] *See* Scott Shane, *Classifying of Federal Documents Skyrockets*, COLUMBUS (OHIO) DISPATCH, July 3, 2005, at A9.

[53] *See* Associated Press, *Legal Expert Doubts City Can Ban Neo-Nazi March*, COLUMBUS (OHIO) DISPATCH, Oct. 20, 2005, at C13.

[54] Ovadal v. City of Madison, No. 04-4030 (7th Cir. 2005). *See also* Associated Press, *Ruling: Removal of Anti-Gay Banners Didn't Violate Free Speech*, Dec. 14, 2005, *at* http://www.firstamendmentcenter.org.

[55] *See* Stephen Manning, Associated Press, *KKK Stages Rally at Site of Bloody Civil War Battle*, THE REPOSITORY, June 11, 2006, at A7.

[56] *See* Associated Press, *Abortion Foes Say Cleveland Law Violates Free Speech*, THE REPOSITORY, Jan. 25, 2006, at B10.

[57] George F. Will, Washington Post Writers Group, *Open Societies Tolerate Free Speech*, THE REPOSITORY, Feb. 27, 2006, at A5.

tection. Philosopher Alexander Meiklejohn, who promoted this theory, based it upon an analysis of the Constitution and Bill of Rights. He concluded that the document was intended only to protect speech of self-governing importance: "No one who reads with care the text of the First Amendment can fail to be startled by its absoluteness. The phrase 'Congress shall make no law ... abridging the freedom of speech,' is unqualified. It admits of no exceptions."[58]

Former Supreme Court Justice Hugo Black also had what some might call an "absolutist" view of the First Amendment. He argued that, because freedom of speech and press are explicitly mentioned, those forms of expression are protected. He believed that no expressive conduct was protected, however, because speech, not conduct, is explicitly mentioned in the First Amendment. In Justice Black's view, freedom of speech and press are contained within a circle of freedom; conduct lies outside that circle.

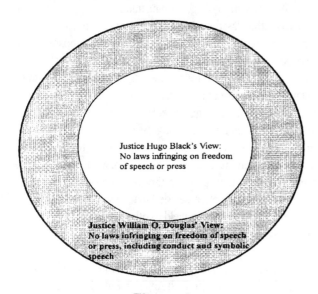

Justice Hugo Black's View:
No laws infringing on freedom of speech or press

Justice William O. Douglas' View:
No laws infringing on freedom of speech or press, including conduct and symbolic speech

**Figure 1**

Absolutist View of the First Amendment

William O. Douglas, also very nearly absolutist, took a broader view than his colleague. He believed symbolic speech — wearing armbands, burning draft cards — fell within the circle of protection. He was opposed to weighing the First Amendment against other values because, he said, doing so ran counter to the intent of the framers and the express language of the First Amendment. Given the events of Sept. 11, 2001, and their aftermath, Douglas' words could be used both by those who want First Amendment rights restricted and those who do not:

The First Amendment provides that "Congress shall make no law ... abridging the freedom of speech." The Constitution pro-

vides no exception. This does not mean, however, that the Nation need hold its hand until it is in such weakened condition that there is not time to protect itself from incitement to revolution. Seditious conduct can always be punished. But the command of the First Amendment is so clear that we should not allow Congress to call a halt to free speech.... The First Amendment makes confidence in the common sense of our people and in their maturity of judgment the great postulate of our democracy.... Unless and until extreme and necessitous circumstances are shown, our aim should be to keep speech unfettered and to allow the processes of law to be invoked only when the provocateurs among us move from speech to action.[59]

Despite the views of Justices Douglas and Black, nothing close to an absolute interpretation of the First Amendment has ever commanded a majority of the Supreme Court. As a result, a number of exceptions and limitations have been whittled into First Amendment law. Government in the United States, then, can be seen as falling on a spectrum. At one end is totalitarian government that controls all expression; at the other end is a pure libertarian government, which allows complete freedom — anarchy. The United States lies between those two poles.

One of the most notable conditions under which the government can bar expression occurs when speech threatens national security or public safety. But there are other reasons for barring expression. Exceptions to freedom of expression depend on what is said, who is speaking and the harm that may be caused by the expression. As you read this book, you will discover some of the exceptions. Pornography, for example, is protected while obscenity is not; some forms of commercial speech are protected, while others are not. Libel and reporting on trials push First Amendment protections to the edges of the circle. In the end, the only absolute — found dead center in the circle — is that political speech is protected all the time. The trouble, as with any issue, is in the definition. What constitutes political speech?

## THE VALUE OF FREE SPEECH

We value free speech because it advances some important social goals:

- *The discovery of truth*. If people have no access to the truth or to information, then they have no way of judging error and, thus, cannot make reasonable decisions.
- *The continuance of self-government*. People cannot govern themselves without understanding the issues.
- *A check on government power*. The media become a means through which the public can keep track of the three branches of government. It is through this role that the media came to

---

[58] ALEXANDER MEIKLEJOHN, FREE SPEECH AND ITS RELATION TO GOVERNMENT 17 (1948).

[59] Dennis v. United States, 341 U.S. 494, 590 (1951) (Douglas, J., dissenting).

be referred to as "the fourth estate," that is, as a fourth branch in the system of self-government.[60]
- *A promotion of stable change.* Free speech allows those who disagree with policy to work for change without seeking a violent overthrow of government.
- *Individual fulfillment.* Free speech encourages us to express ourselves and, thereby, enriches and enhances our lives.

Each of these benefits of free speech deserves some explication.

## Discovery of the Truth

Freedom of expression is widely believed to be an effective method of searching for truth. The model for this search is called "the marketplace of ideas." The theory is that, just as consumers search for the best products in a market, individuals are able, because free expression ensures a wide variety of ideas in circulation, to determine the most useful or original information, that is, the truth. The theory is that good ideas, like good products, will prevail in a free market. Under this theory, censorship is not only obnoxious, it is impractical.

John Stuart Mill espoused a different, but similar, philosophy in the Nineteenth Century. Mill valued free speech because, he argued, without it truth would have no chance to prevail in the marketplace. If people have no access to the truth, then they have no way of judging error and no way of substituting truth for error. Mill's classic work *On Liberty*, published in 1859, established the boundaries for authority and freedom in the modern state. Mill said the press plays a valuable role by providing security against "a corrupt or tyrannical government."

Mill argued that even one voice against a majority should not be silenced because "if the opinion is right, [the people] are deprived of the opportunity of exchanging error for truth: if wrong, they lose, what is almost as great a benefit, the clearer perception and livelier impression of truth, produced by its collision with error." In one of his most-quoted phrases, Mill wrote, "If all mankind minus one were of one opinion, and only one person were of the contrary opinion mankind would be no more justified in silencing that one person, than he, if he had the power, would be justified in silencing mankind."[61]

Mill offered four defenses for the diversity of opinion that is at the heart of freedom of expression:[62]

1. Some opinion may be false; thus other opinion may be true.
2. Conflict between opinion leads to a clearer comprehension of truth.
3. Conflicting opinions share truth between them.
4. Non-conforming opinion is needed to supply truth.

In order to maintain viability and vitality, truth needs to be challenged. If there are fewer avenues of challenge, Mill would argue,

then truth is injured. Thus, the marketplace suffers when more media outlets are concentrated under fewer owners. Such concentration could be as restrictive as government censorship. In addition, the marketplace means little to minorities, dissidents and fringe groups who do not have access to the media. First Amendment scholar Jerome Barron discounts the marketplace concept, saying that if it ever existed, it has long ceased to do so because "there is an inequality in the power to communicate ideas just as there is inequality in economic bargaining power."[63]

The marketplace of ideas may still be viable, but it is changing as media conglomerates grow, as new media are offered to consumers and as computers become cheaper and more versatile. The marketplace theory also suffers because of technology overload: 500 cable television channels, an untold number of home pages on the Internet, literally thousands of sources of information. With countless messages, how can truth rise to the top? Instead, the truth could become more obscured by the overwhelming number of false messages. While the discovery of truth is an ongoing process, in the short term a false message can cause harm. Thus, the government could argue, there is a need for intervention to protect the public.

## Governance

Thomas Jefferson, himself often maliciously criticized in the press, wrote in 1787 that people should have full information about public affairs through the press:

> The basis of our government being the opinion of the people, the very first object should be to keep that right; and were it left to me to decide whether we should have a government without newspapers, or newspapers without government, I should not hesitate a moment to prefer the latter.[64]

Alexander Meiklejohn is the best known modern proponent of freedom of expression as a value for the governance of a people. Discovery of the truth, he said in the 1940s, is needed for a democratic society to exist because citizens need to understand the issues before they can be expected to act. Free speech "is not, primarily, a device for the winning of new truth, though that is very important," Meiklejohn wrote. "It is a device for the sharing of whatever truth has been won. Its purpose is to give to every voting member of the body politic the fullest possible participation in the understanding of those problems with which the citizens of a self-governing society must deal."[65] Voting is the key act of self-governance, and Meiklejohn argued that the free flow of informa-

---

[60] *See, e.g.*, Potter Stewart, *Or of the Press*, 26 HASTINGS L.J. 633 (1975).

[61] JOHN STUART MILL, ON LIBERTY 18 (David Spitz ed., 1975) (1859).

[62] *Id.* at 44.

[63] Jerome Barron, *Access to the Press – A New First Amendment Right*, 80 HARV. L. REV. 1641, 1647 (1967).

[64] Letter from Thomas Jefferson to Edward Carrington (1787), *supra* note 27, at 93.

[65] MEIKLEJOHN, *supra* note 58, at 88-89.

tion, by protecting discussion, beliefs and associations, was part of the voting process. The theory is applied to education, philosophy, science, literature, the arts and public issues; it applies to any speech relating to public affairs. The First Amendment guarantee is "assured only to speech which bears, directly or indirectly, upon the issues with which voters have to deal — only, therefore, to the consideration of matters of public interest."[66]

As with any theory, Meiklejohn's has definitional problems. How does one define "matters of public interest," "political speech" or similar terms? Meiklejohn argued that political speech should be defined broadly, including the sciences, the arts and issues involving morality because they can all be related to self-government. Consequently, they become matters of public interest. In order to have robust and uninhibited debate on public matters, Meiklejohn advocated immunizing political speech unconditionally from government interference.

Clearly influenced by Meiklejohn, former Justice William Brennan developed his own theory about the First Amendment and its value. As one scholar wrote, Brennan adhered to the theory that "the First Amendment's primary purpose is to guarantee protection when speech touches on areas of self-government ... no individual or institution has greater or lesser free-speech protection than any other individual or institution. Therefore, when First Amendment rights come into conflict, those rights must be balanced."[67] Brennan's balancing scale was vested in the First Amendment's role in society, which the justice found paramount. For Brennan, free expression was guaranteed for its societal benefit, not its benefit to individuals. Justice Brennan argued that public debate must not only be "uninhibited, robust and wide open" but also informed.[68] In a democratic society, Brennan argued, "[T]he government, the press, and the people all have roles to play in the operation of society. Self-government of a society requires a communications process, and it is that process the First Amendment is designed to protect."[69]

Some critics argue that the promotion of democracy will only be realized if the media do a thorough and responsible job of covering public affairs. They say the media are a long way from that kind of coverage and won't do it without governmental encouragement. A movement called "public journalism" or "civic journalism" was an attempt by some media outlets to respond to this criticism.

Professor Zechariah Chafee Jr. was one of the earliest of these critics. He argued that it would prove difficult to separate political and private speech. He also questioned the role of the courts in defying legislatures. When the nation faces a crisis or an emer-

gency, particularly one involving a threat from outside its borders, then the mood of society will reflect less toleration for certain types of expression. If speech is viewed as putting the country at risk, then society, in general, won't have a problem with legislation controlling speech, because protection of society becomes more important than individual rights.[70] Professor Chafee's analysis rings true in light of the terrorist attacks on New York, Pennsylvania and Washington, D.C., and the war in Iraq. The government acted to suspend some rights in the interest of protecting society from future attacks. Congress passed and President George W. Bush signed the USA PATRIOT Act of 2001,[71] and states followed suit with their own anti-terrorism statutes.[72]

Many legislators, organizations and members of the public — conservative and liberal — oppose provisions of the PATRIOT Act saying it goes too far by infringing on protected civil rights. Two long-time members of the Senate Judiciary Committee, a Republican and a Democrat, introduced legislation that would restrict government powers granted under the PATRIOT Act. But a bill approved by the Senate intelligence committee would expand the government's powers in terrorism investigations allowing the FBI to more easily conduct secret searches and read suspects' mail.[73]

The ACLU and other organizations said sixteen provisions of the law should have been allowed to lapse on Dec. 31, 2005, "to bring the PATRIOT Act back in line with the Constitution."[74] But President Bush urged keeping the act in place. A spokeswoman for the Department of Justice said, "We have consistently said that full reauthorization of the PATRIOT Act is critical to ensuring that law enforcement has the tools they need to protect our country from future attacks."[75] In June 2005, the House of Representatives voted 238-187 to block part of the most controversial aspect of the act, Section 215, which allows federal investigators to access library, bookstore and other records secretly. The majority in the House supported eliminating library and bookstore records from the PATRIOT Act, but kept FBI access to records covering Internet usage at a library.[76] In March 2006, President Bush signed into law the renewal of the act. Law enforcement kept its anti-terror tools, but with some restrictions. Opponents of the renewal

---

[66] *Id.* at 79.

[67] W. Wat Hopkins, Mr. Justice Brennan and Freedom of Expression 83 (1991).

[68] Karen Green, "Uninhibited, Robust and Wide-Open" — But Informed: Justice Brennan's Structural Model of the First Amendment 2 (March 1998) (unpublished paper presented at the AEJMC Southeast Colloquium, New Orleans, La.).

[69] *Id.*

[70] *See* Zechariah Chafee Jr., The Blessings of Liberty (1956); Zechariah Chafee Jr., Free Speech in the United States (1941).

[71] Uniting and Strengthening America by Providing Appropriate Tools Required to Intercept and Obstruct Terrorism Act, Pub. L. No. 107-56, 115 Stat. 272 (2001).

[72] Every state has taken steps, through legislation, resolutions, appropriations or establishing offices and task forces to guard against possible dangers after Sept. 11, 2001. More than half have passed some form of anti-terrorism legislation. *See* John Nagy & Jason White, *State by State Security Update*, July 17, 2002, *available at* http://www.stateline.org.

[73] *See* Dan Eggen & Charles Babington, Washington Post, *More Restriction Planned Under Patriot Act*, The Repository, July 14, 2005, at A8.

[74] *Id.*

[75] *Id.*

[76] *See* Charles C. Haynes, *Debating the Patriot Act: Is the Sun Setting on Section 215?*, June 26, 2005, *at* http://www.firstamendmentcenter.org.

said the civil rights protections added to the bill were "almost meaningless."[77]

The controversy over the act's provisions spilled beyond Washington, D.C. At least 400 cities and counties and seven states passed resolutions opposing parts of the PATRIOT Act.

The PATRIOT Act's restriction of civil rights in an effort to help the government cope with terrorism follows the underlying philosophy of the clear and present danger test, which was first espoused by Justice Oliver Wendell Holmes in 1919:

We admit that in many places and in ordinary times the defendants in saying all that was said in the circular would have been within their constitutional rights. But the character of every act depends upon the circumstances in which it is done. The most stringent protection of free speech would not protect a man in falsely shouting fire in a theatre and causing a panic. It does not even protect a man from an injunction against uttering words that may have all the effect of force. The question in every case is whether the words used are used in such circumstances and are of such a nature as to create a clear and present danger that they will bring about the substantive evils that Congress has a right to prevent.[78]

Holmes developed his test as a way to prevent, or at least limit, legislatures from getting too repressive in times of crisis. In Holmes' view, determining what is a clear and present danger still falls to the courts, not the legislatures. Holmes' effort to protect speech backfired. The test did not provide a broad spectrum of protection for expression. Six months after enunciating the test, Holmes repudiated it as unworkable. However, the damage was already done. For more than fifty years the courts used the test, in one form or another, to limit expression.[79]

And while Meiklejohn's alternative to the clear and present danger test is absolute protection for all public or political expression, Chafee argued that such a view is unrealistic. Not all speech deserves protection, Chafee wrote. A form of the clear and present danger test can be applied to language that has no social interest — profanity, indecency or defamatory speech — because in those cases the speech is not essential to the development of ideas. Using language similar to Chafee's, the Court ruled that fighting words are not constitutionally protected speech.[80]

Justice Brennan's apparent acceptance of Meiklejohn's philosophy was manifested in the landmark case *New York Times Co. v. Sullivan*. In his unanimous opinion, Brennan wrote that a libel suit against a newspaper must be considered "against the background of a profound national commitment to the principle that debate on public issues should be uninhibited, robust, and wide-open."[81] Five years later, Justice Byron R. White, also for a unanimous Court, wrote in *Red Lion Broadcasting Co. v. FCC*: "It is the right of the public to receive suitable access to social, political, esthetic, moral, and other ideas and experiences which is crucial here." This right of the public, he wrote, is paramount: "It is the purpose of the First Amendment to preserve an uninhibited marketplace of ideas in which truth will ultimately prevail, rather than to countenance monopolization of the market whether it be by the Government itself or a private licensee."[82]

### Check on Government Power

The ability to express ideas freely and, with them, to critique government is an important check against abuse of power. The Constitution provided three branches of government, with a division of power, so the judiciary, legislature and executive could be checks on each other. Implicit in the Constitution, however, was the concept that government was of the people. Therefore, social critics argue, for people to be their own governors, they must know what the government is doing. In such a model, citizen critics are vital to the process, and the primary way most of us know what is transpiring is through the media.

A free press, therefore, is essential in bringing to light abuses of power. From Tammany Hall to Watergate, the media have been bringing down unscrupulous governments. Watergate is an outstanding example. The *Washington Post* was instrumental in uncovering political dirty tricks, wire tapping, money laundering and obstruction of justice by the Nixon Administration in the 1970s. When a Congressional committee made it clear that it would recommend that President Richard Nixon be impeached, he resigned.

Without the freedom to aggressively become a watchdog of government at all levels, the press would not be able to uncover these governmental abuses.

### Stable Change

Freedom of expression allows those who disagree with governmental or social policy to work for change within the system and without violence. Those in power often see public criticism as obstructionist, but the structure of government and protection for government criticism demonstrate the framers believed that flexibility and stability work together; tradition and change coexist. Stable change occurs because problems can be dealt with incrementally, reducing the need for drastic change, which could be disruptive.

Without freedom of the press and freedom of speech, real prob-

---

[77] Associated Press, *Patriot Act Awaits Bush's Signature*, Mar. 8, 2006, *at* http://www.firstamendmentcenter.org.

[78] Schenck v. United States, 249 U.S. 47, 52 (1919).

[79] *See, e.g.,* W. Wat Hopkins, *Reconsidering the 'Clear and Present Danger Test': Whence the 'Marketplace of Ideas'?, in* 33 FREE SPEECH YEARBOOK 707-08 (1995).

[80] *See* Chaplinsky v. New Hampshire, 315 U.S. 568 (1942).

[81] 376 U.S. 254, 270 (1964).
[82] 395 U.S. 367, 390 (1969).

lems of society may remain hidden and will fester; fear, hatred and resentment breed; no safety valve exists to allow the ventilation of problems. Compromise becomes more difficult under such circumstances and makes problem solving nearly impossible. Consequently, what erupts from this mix is social unrest and the potential for violent action against authority.

### Individual Fulfillment

Many of the arguments for free speech presented thus far are tied to the practical or functional aspects of expression, that is, free expression promotes self-government. In late seventeenth-century England, however, philosopher John Locke argued that free speech is a good unto itself, even if it does not add to the functioning of government. It is good, Locke argued, because it is self-fulfilling.

Locke's argument is based on the belief that expressing opinion is part of human nature. We want to express ourselves; indeed, we need to express ourselves. This helps each of us discover what it means to be human. If we feel good about ourselves, we can help society feel good.

In the early United States, Thomas Jefferson and James Madison were believers of the self-fulfilling role of free expression. "A right of free correspondence between citizen and citizen, on their joint interest, whether public or private, ... is a natural right," Jefferson wrote to James Monroe in 1797. "It is not a gift of any municipal law."[83]

### FIRST AMENDMENT TESTS

Despite the apparently absolute language of the Constitution, there is no absolute protection for speech or the press. The right of expression is often balanced against other personal rights or social interests. In addition, as will be demonstrated later in this book, some types of speech receive more protection than others. Under this hierarchy, speech critical of the government and speech broadcast over the airwaves that fulfills equal opportunity requirements mandated by federal communications law receive almost absolute protection.

Because most speech is not absolutely protected, courts have used a variety of tests to balance freedom of expression against other rights to determine which must give way. When a test is applied in a case, the outcome depends on the competing interests and the application of the test. Some of the most common tests — past and present — are discussed below.

### Bad Tendency Test

The bad tendency test was espoused in the early 1900s and pro-

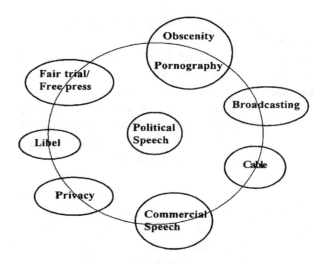

**Figure 2**

The First Amendment
through Supreme Court Interpretation

vided virtually no protection for speech. Thomas Tedford described the test as the "nip-it-in-the-bud," the "killing the serpent in its egg" or the "putting out the spark before the conflagration" approach.[84] Under the test, if expression was expected to cause the slightest tendency toward harm, the speech could be prevented.

The classic use of the test came in 1925 when Justice Edward T. Sanford, in upholding the conviction of Benjamin Gitlow, wrote:

> A single revolutionary spark may kindle a fire that, smouldering [sic] for a time, may burst into a sweeping and destructive conflagration. It cannot be said that the State is acting arbitrarily or unreasonably when in the exercise of its judgment as to the measures necessary to protect the public peace and safety, it seeks to extinguish the spark without waiting until it has enkindled the flame or blazed into the conflagration.[85]

Fortunately, the test was discontinued because speakers and writers had no way of knowing if they could be punished for their expression. There was no warning because the test was so vague that it could be applied multiple ways. Gitlow's actions, the Court said, were "inimical to the public welfare" and could "corrupt public morals," which was enough to stop him.[86]

### Clear and Present Danger Test

As previously indicated, the clear and present danger test was first enunciated by Justice Oliver Wendell Holmes in 1919. It allows expression to be controlled when there is a clear and present danger

---

[83] Letter from Thomas Jefferson to James Monroe (1787), *supra* note 27, at 15.

[84] THOMAS L. TEDFORD, FREEDOM OF SPEECH IN THE UNITED STATES 450 (1985).

[85] Gitlow v. New York, 268 U.S. 652, 669 (1925).

[86] *Id.* at 667.

that the expression will bring about substantive evils. The test was a significant improvement over the bad tendency test because it provided a judge with a narrower window for restricting expression. In theory, speech would have to pose a serious and immediate danger in order for the government to restrict it. The test was not rigorously applied, however, and Holmes later backed off its use. The Court held that the government need not wait until the very moment damage was imminent to restrict speech. If all the ingredients for trouble are present, the Court reasoned, the government has a right to halt the offensive speech. That interpretation gave the government flexibility Holmes had not intended.

The clear and present danger test was intended to punish threatening speech rather than the mere advocacy of illegal acts at some future time. If the advocacy is directed to incite or produce imminent lawlessness, however, it may be halted or, if the action is carried out, it may be punished. Holmes would allow speech to be regulated only if the danger was both clear and imminent, like a person falsely shouting "fire" in a theater and causing a panic.

In the 1969 case of *Brandenburg v. Ohio,* the Court held that the mere advocacy of illegal activity is protected by the First Amendment.[87] In what some scholars interpret as a variation of the clear and present danger test, the Court said only when there is an imminent danger of incitement of illegal activity can authorities step in to stop speech. In a *per curiam* decision, the Court found unconstitutional the 1919 Ohio Criminal Syndicalism Statute, which was used to convict a Ku Klux Klan leader. In doing so, the Court established a two-part test to evaluate the likelihood that speech will lead to illegal activity:

- Who is the speaker? Does the person have a history of illegal activity or affiliation with an organization that does so? Do people take the speaker seriously?
- Is there a likelihood that the espoused actions will be carried out?

A 1973 case involving an anti-Vietnam War street protester upheld the standard.[88] *Brandenburg,* which is still the precedent for such issues, essentially put an end to the use of sedition as a threat against anti-government speech, though the government has filed sedition charges against white supremacists, neo-Nazis and others involved in bombings, racketeering and robberies.

The clear and present danger test continues to survive, despite judicial urgings that it be abandoned.[89] The test, however, is used almost exclusively in areas related to the administration of government or the judiciary. In *Nebraska Press Association v. Stuart,* for example, the Court invalidated a gag order that was intended to restrict the reporting of a murder trial. Quoting appellate Judge Learned Hand, Chief Justice Warren Burger wrote that the Court had to determine whether "the gravity of the 'evil,' discounted by its improbability, justifies such invasion of free speech as is neces-

sary to avoid the danger."[90]

In addition, Virginia tried to protect the reputations of members of its judiciary by using the clear and present danger test to prevent the publication of confidential information about the proceedings of the state's judicial disciplinary commission. The state argued that publication of the information represented a clear and present danger to the administration of justice. The Court did not accept the argument, but the case illustrates how broadly the test may be stretched and how it can put expression — even political speech — at risk.[91]

### Balancing Test

A balancing test is implicit in all the methods used by courts to gauge the interests of speech in society. But when courts deliberately weigh the values of speech against conflicting values or interests, they are balancing those interests. Courts decide which value in a particular instance deserves greater protection. Balancing provides more flexibility than the clear and present danger test because the judge can assign weights to different facts as they appear in the case. The outcome, however, is often unpredictable.

### Strict Scrutiny

Courts employ strict scrutiny when confronted with governmental actions specifically aimed at restricting the content of expression. Under the strict scrutiny test, the government must show a compelling reason for instituting a regulation that abridges speech. The reason, in fact, must be so compelling that it requires free expression to take a subordinate role. In addition, the government must demonstrate that the regulation is narrowly tailored to meet the specific goal without restricting speech that is not related to the goal. The courts often will examine the circumstances of a case to see if the government could have taken action that was less destructive of First Amendment rights. If such a method exists, the courts will rule in favor of the First Amendment and strike down the regulation. In many cases, the burden is so great the government cannot meet it.

Strict scrutiny also is discussed in Chapter 3.

### THE LEVELS OF PROTECTED SPEECH AND SPEAKERS

A constant theme throughout this chapter — indeed, throughout this book — has been that the First Amendment is not absolute. There are instances in which speech — and speakers — can be restricted, and restrictions vary based on the type of speech employed, the speaker and the location of the speech. For example, the Minnesota Supreme Court ruled that neither the First Amendment nor the free-speech provision of the state constitu-

---

[87] 395 U.S. 444 (1969).

[88] Hess v. Indiana, 414 U.S. 105 (1973).

[89] *See, e.g., Brandenburg,* 395 U.S. at 452 (Douglas, J. concurring).

---

[90] 427 U.S. 539, 562 (1976).

[91] Landmark Communications, Inc. v. Virginia, 435 U.S. 829 (1978).

tion protects speech in shopping malls.[92] State courts in California, Massachusetts, Oregon and New Jersey, on the other hand, have interpreted their constitutions as providing some protection for speech in shopping malls.[93]

### The Hierarchy of Protected Expression

The Supreme Court has indicated that there are three levels of protection for speech:

- Political expression receives the highest level of protection. Speech that is of governing importance is strictly protected. The definition of "governing importance" can be broad. Indeed, some First Amendment advocates expand the definition beyond speech about government and politics to include topics as varied as education, health, agriculture and culture.
- Commercial speech receives less protection. The Court has recognized that advertising and other forms of commercial speech are protected. Commercial speech, however, is a particularly sturdy form of speech, that is, it has a tendency to survive despite restrictions. And, because the speaker has a vested interest, the Court has recognized that the government can impose stricter regulations on commercial speech.
- Obscene material, false advertising and fighting words are not protected.

Commercial speech and false advertising are discussed in Chapter 8; obscenity is discussed in Chapter 5; and fighting words are discussed in Chapter 3.

### Who Is Protected?

The rights of all people to speak and publish are basic. So are the rights to engage in symbolic speech and to associate with others. And, the Court has said, because of the right to speak and disseminate ideas, there may be an implied right to receive some kinds of information.

The First Amendment also guarantees the right to contribute money and to solicit funds, though with limits. In *Nixon v. Shrink Missouri Government PAC*, the Court upheld limits on campaign contributions as a way to prevent government corruption.[94] In a concurring opinion, Justice John Paul Stevens wrote, "Money is property; it is not speech.... The right to use one's money to hire gladiators, or to fund 'speech by proxy,' certainly merits significant constitutional protection. These property rights, however, are not entitled to the same protection as the right to say what one

pleases."[95] Yet, in a 5-4 decision, the Court upheld the constitutionality of the Party Expenditure Provision of the Federal Election Campaign Act of 1971, saying its limits on the coordinated expenditures of political parties did not violate the First Amendment.[96]

A court challenge to the Bipartisan Campaign Reform Act of 2002,[97] which bars issue advertising, was filed almost immediately by the Republican National Committee. Taking effect after the November 2002 election, the law prohibits broadcast ads paid for by non-profit groups and others when the ads refer to a specific candidate and run within sixty days of a general election or thirty days of a primary. The RNC said the law infringed on protected political speech. The Supreme Court combined eleven cases and upheld limitations on campaign funding.[98]

Freedom of expression also guarantees some right to remain silent. A person cannot be compelled to salute the flag, to affirm a belief in God or to associate with a political party or particular ideology.[99] New Hampshire, for example, lost its bid to require all car owners in the state to bear license plates with the slogan "Live Free or Die." The Court upheld the right of a Jehovah's Witness to block out the slogan because the Witness said it violated his religious beliefs. In its 2001-02 term, the Court invalidated a Missouri constitutional amendment that compelled its federal delegation and candidates for Congress to work and vote for a federal constitutional amendment setting term limits.[100]

In 1769 Justice Abraham Yates wrote, "It is certain every man has a right to keep his own sentiments, if he pleases. He has certainly a right to judge whether he will make them public or commit them only to the sight of his friends."[101] Yet there is a debate among legal scholars about whether there is indeed broad constitutional protection to not speak as suggested by Yates' opinion. Clearly, a person can be held in contempt of court for not answering questions during a trial. But is there a constitutional right to silence? Some think the Court's opinions have not gone that far; they view silence as a penumbra right attached to freedom of thought.

Levels of protection attach to classes of people, just as they do

---

[92] State v. Wicklund, 589 N.W.2d 793 (Minn. 1999).

[93] PruneYard Shopping Ctr. v. Robins, 592 P.2d 341 (Cal. 1979), *aff'd* 447 U.S. 74 (1980); Batchelder v. Allied Stores Int'l, Inc., 445 N.E.2d 590 (Mass. 1983); New Jersey Coalition Against War in the Middle East v. J.M.B. Realty Corp., 650 A.2d 757 (N.J. 1994); Lloyd Corp., Ltd. v. Whiffen, 849 P.2d 446 (Or. 1993).

[94] 528 U.S. 377 (2000).

[95] *Id.* at 398-99 (Stevens, J., concurring).

[96] Fed. Election Comm'n v. Colorado Republican Fed. Campaign Comm., 532 U.S. 923 (2001). *See also* Randall v. Sorrell, 126 S.Ct. 2479 (2006).

[97] 2 U.S.C. 431 (2002).

[98] McConnell v. FEC, 540 U.S. 93 (2003), included: National Rifle Association v. FEC, No. 02-1675; McCain v. McConnell, No. 02-1702; Republican National Comm. v. FEC, No. 02-1727; National Right to Life v. FEC, No. 02-1733; American Civil Liberties Union v. FEC, No. 02-1734; Adams v. FEC, No. 02-1740; Paul v. FEC, No. 02-1747; California Democratic Party v. FEC, No. 02-1753; American Federation of Labor and Congress of Industrial Organizations v. FEC, No. 02-1755; and Chamber of Commerce of the United States v. FEC, No. 02-1756.

[99] *See, e.g.,* Wooley v. Maynard, 430 U.S. 705 (1977); Elrod v. Burns, 427 U.S. 347 (1966); Torcasso v. Watkins, 367 U.S. 488 (1961); West Virginia Bd. of Ed. v. Barnett, 319 U.S. 624 (1943).

[100] Cook v. Gralike, 531 U.S. 510 (2001).

[101] Miller v. Taylor, 4 Burr. 2301, 2302 (1769).

to classes of speech. No person or class of people has absolute protection, and all classes of people have some free speech rights.

**Adults.** There is no language in the Bill of Rights that distinguishes categories of people and their levels of protection. Yet, over the years the courts have realized that there are distinctions, often based on age. The courts also have classified people by their employment — in the public versus the private sector — as well as whether they are in prison. Adult, private citizens enjoy the most rights. And, while many of those same rights apply to students, children and government employees, the level of protection is not the same. The ambiguity of protection is demonstrated in a ruling by the Washington Supreme Court. The court weighed the First Amendment rights of a newspaper to maintain its editorial integrity against the free speech rights of one of its reporters who was involved in political activism outside the workplace. The court ruled in favor of the paper.[102] And in 1999, the Supreme Court of California ruled that racial or ethnic epithets directed at Hispanic/Latino employees of Avis must be forbidden in the workplace regardless of their context.[103] The U.S. Supreme Court denied review in both cases.

**University Students.** For the most part, the Court has said the First Amendment has the same force on public college campuses as in the community at large: "Mere dissemination of ideas — no matter how offensive to good taste — on a state university campus may not be shut off in the name alone of 'conventions of decency.'"[104] College students cannot be held to a higher standard of expressive conduct just because they're on state university campuses. There is no "dual standard in the academic community with respect to the content of speech," the Court has said.[105] But that hasn't stopped the lower courts from threatening campus expression rights. For example, the Sixth U.S. Circuit Court of Appeals overturned a holding that the same restrictions applied to high school could be applied to the college and university press.[106] And the Seventh U.S. Circuit Court of Appeals ruled that a college student newspaper could be subject to administration control if it was created as a certain type of public forum and was funded by the school.[107]

Students at private colleges and universities may have even fewer expressive rights because the First Amendment is aimed at the government — it has no bearing on private entities. At public colleges and universities, the administration is tantamount to the government. Private colleges and universities, however, are not supported by state funds, so their administrations are not considered "governments" under the law, and the First Amendment does not apply. State laws, specifically state constitutions, may provide greater protection on both public and private campuses. Most states have affirmative speech provisions in their constitutions. Students on a private college campus also may find support for free expression in the institution's own mission statement.

**High School Students.** High school students, like adults, have some fundamental expressive rights. But while students are at school, administrators and teachers may more easily restrict those rights. A school district cannot prevent students from symbolically protesting a war — by wearing black armbands, for example — so long as the symbolic expression does not disrupt school activities.[108] The Supreme Court has recognized, however, that schools have specific functions that may be protected. Speech can be curbed if it disrupts class work or involves substantial disorder or invades the rights of others. And school-sponsored publications may be restricted if they don't support the pedagogical mission of the school.[109]

Student expressive rights are discussed in greater detail in Chapter 13.

**Government Employees.** Government employees have the right to speak and publish, but with limitations. They may speak as private persons on public issues, just as they may vote for whomever they want. They cannot be fired, for example, for remarks hostile to the government or even to their own governmental agency, unless those remarks are likely to impede the agency's operations. In addition, in 1991 the Court said employees of federally financed family planning clinics can be barred from providing information about abortions.[110] More recently, the Court said restrictions Congress imposed on the speech of federally funded lawyers who aid the poor were unconstitutional.[111]

For more than fifty years, federal government employees could not participate in political campaigns. That changed, however, when Congress passed, and President Clinton signed, the Hatch Act Reform Amendments of 1993.[112] Most government employees still cannot solicit campaign funds from the public and may not run for partisan office, but they can, if they choose, take active roles in campaigns.[113] The same law also states that employees

---

[102] Nelson v. McClatchy Newspapers, 936 P.2d 1123 (Wash. 1997).

[103] Avis Rent a Car System v. Aguilar, 980 P.2d 846 (Cal. 2000).

[104] Papish v. Board of Curators, 410 U.S. 667, 670 (1973).

[105] Id. at 671.

[106] Kincaid v. Gibson, 236 F.3d 342 (6th Cir. 2001), rev'g 191 F.3d 719 (6th Cir. 1999). See the discussion of this case in Chapter 13.

[107] Hosty v. Carter, 412 F.3d 731 (7th Cir. 2005), rev'g 325 F.3d 945 (7th Cir. 2005).

[108] See Tinker v. Des Moines Indep. Sch. Dist., 393 U.S. 503 (1969).

[109] See Hazelwood v. Kuhlmeier, 484 U.S. 260 (1988).

[110] Rust v. Sullivan, 500 U.S. 173 (1991).

[111] See Legal Services Corp. v. Velazquez, 531 U.S. 533 (2001).

[112] Pub. L. 103-94, Sec. 2(a), Oct. 6, 1993, 107 Stat. 1001 (1993).

[113] Employees of the following federal agencies may not participate in political campaigns: Federal Election Commission; FBI; Secret Service; CIA; National Security Council; National Security Agency; Defense Intelligence Agency; Merit Systems Protection Board; Office of Special Counsel; Office of Criminal Investigations of the Internal Revenue Service; Office of Investigative

cannot be forced to participate in a campaign, and allows conditions to be set involving participation in municipal elections in Maryland, Virginia and the immediate vicinity of the District of Columbia.

In its most recent case in this area of the law, the Court said in a 5-4 decision that statements made by government employees in the course of their official duties is outside protection of the First Amendment.[114] As Court-watcher Tony Mauro wrote: "But by also stating that government employees retain free-speech rights as citizens, and by giving a favorable nod to whistleblower-protection laws, the Court seemed to raise new questions and guarantee that this nettlesome area of law is far from settled."[115]

**Prisoners.** Prisoners have fewer rights to speak, publish and receive information than free adults. Prison officials can enact reasonable restrictions to control their access to people and information. Officials can regulate, for example, a prison newspaper. But prisoners in a federal penitentiary challenged a 1996 federal law that banned NC-17, R and X-rated movies, saying their First Amendment rights were violated.[116]

## SUMMARY

The First Amendment is essential to a free government and to U.S. society. Without it, there is no protection from frivolous libel or invasion of privacy suits; there is no right of access to government proceedings; there is no protection from prior restraint; there is no right to investigate or criticize government. Without the First Amendment, newspapers, magazines, broadcast stations and other media would not exist as we know them.

The Thomas Jefferson Center for the Protection of Free Expression at the University of Virginia annually awards Muzzles to those it thinks are guilty of censorship. Its most recent awards went to, among others:[117]

- President George W. Bush for a disregard of Constitutional principles when he bypassed Congress and the judiciary in using the National Security Administration to wiretap conversations involving U.S. citizens without authorization.
- The U.S. Department of Justice for seeking extensive access to Google search data not to protect national security but to "understand the behavior of current Web users, [and] estimate how Web users encounter harmful-to-minors material in the

course of their searches."

- Kevin Martin, chairman of the Federal Communications Commission, for telling cable and satellite TV providers to do more to shield children from adult-oriented content or be subject to FCC fines even though Congress and the Supreme Court have not given the FCC the authority to regulate cable in the same way that it regulates over-the-air broadcasts.
- The administration of William Patterson University in New Jersey for trying to issue a letter of reprimand to employee and part-time student Jihard Daniel for an e-mail he sent to a professor asking that he not be sent notices about the screening and discussion of a movie about lesbians. The professor filed a complaint saying she felt threatened by Daniel's response. The university found Daniel violated the state's anti-harassment policy because he used the word "perversion." He later was cleared by an impartial university hearing officer.
- U.S. Rep. Joe Barton, a Republican from Texas, who used his position as chairman of the House Energy and Commerce Committee to challenge scientific positions on global warming for political, not scientific, purposes. His actions had the effect of chilling scientists from presenting their findings for fear of a political backlash.
- The Supreme Court of Florida for ruling that two attorneys had to stop airing a TV commercial featuring a pit bull in a spiked collar and the firm's phone number, 1-800-PIT-BULL, as a way to seek legitimate business. Chief Justice Barbara Pariente said the ad implied the attorneys would get results "through combative and vicious tactics that will maim, scar or harm the opposing party." She said if such ads were allowed "images of sharks, wolves, crocodiles and piranhas could follow."
- The school administrations of Tennessee's Oak Ridge High School, Florida's Wellington High School and California's Troy High School for censoring the student press. In Tennessee, Principal Becky Ervin recalled 1,800 copies of the school's monthly newspaper because it had articles discussing birth control, tattoos and body piercing. In Florida, Principal Cheryl Alligood pulled copies of the school paper because it contained an article presenting student views on sex and virginity. In California, the student newspaper editor was removed by school officials for profiling three gay students even through all three willingly participated in the article.
- Hecklers in a University of Connecticut audience for preventing conservative columnist Ann Coulter from finishing her speech because of persistent boos, jeers, name-calling and songs. Even though the First Amendment gives the right to individuals to disagree with a speaker, it is contrary to the spirit of the amendment to do so in a way that prevents the audience from hearing a speaker's ideas.

The First Amendment's guarantees of free speech and press are not absolute. Courts throughout the country continue to interpret its language as new issues arise. Arguments and justifications for free expression are found in our English

---

Programs of the U.S. Customs Service; Office of Law Enforcement of the Bureau of Alcohol, Tobacco and Firearms; the Central Imagery Office, and the Criminal Division of the Department of Justice. In addition, FEC employees cannot contribute financially to political campaigns.

[114] 126 S.Ct. 1951 (2006)

[115] Tony Mauro, *Head-Scratching Follows Garcetti Ruling*, May 31, 2006, *at* http://www.firstamendmentcenter.org.

[116] Adam Liptak, *Appeals Court Reinstates Suit by Inmates Over Films Rated R*, N.Y. TIMES, July 28, 2002, at 1-23.

[117] Http://www.tjcenter.org/muzzles.html.

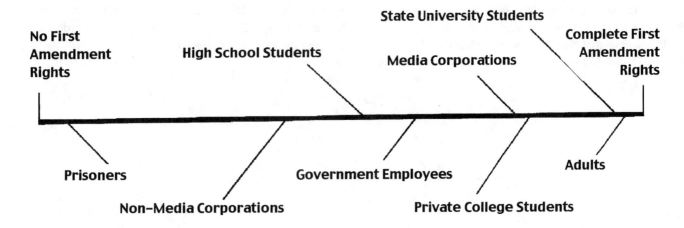

**Figure 3**

First Amendment Protection Spectrum

heritage in the words of John Milton, William Blackstone and others, who challenged the authority of government under threat of sometimes brutal punishment.

The First Amendment was the result of debate and political maneuvering among colonists. It was not always first. Thus, an argument can be made that it has no more weight than any of the other nine amendments that make up the Bill of Rights. Though it was initially interpreted to apply only to the federal government, the First Amendment became applicable to the states in 1925.

The rights found in the First Amendment manifest themselves in a variety of ways. People often claim a right of expression — a right to speak or publish — without understanding the limits on those rights. The Supreme Court has placed those limits as it balances conflicting rights. However, the Court has made it clear that any regulation of expression must be content neutral. The Court also has said that any government regulation that affects First Amendment rights must pass strict scrutiny. The government — whether it be federal, state or local — must be able to justify its action to control expression by demonstrating that it used the means least damaging to the First Amendment.

There is value in the First Amendment because it allows us to discover the truth, continue to govern ourselves, provide a check on government power, promote stable change and enrich ourselves. While not everyone enjoys the same protection offered by the First Amendment, everyone has some protection.

**FOR ADDITIONAL READING**

Demac, Donna A. *Liberty Denied, The Current Rise of Censorship in America*. New Brunswick, N.J.: Rutgers University Press, 1990.

Frohnmayer, John. *Out of Tune, Listening to the First Amendment*. Nashville: The Freedom Forum First Amendment Center, 1994.

Hentoff, Nat. *Free Speech for Me — But Not for Thee*. New York: Harper Collins Publishers, 1992.

Hopkins, W. Wat. *Mr. Justice Brennan and Freedom of Expression*. New York: Praeger, 1991.

*Quill*. September 1976. Special issue on the First Amendment.

Siebert, Fred. *Freedom of the Press in England 1476-1776*. Urbana, Ill.: University of Illinois Press, 1952.

Terry, Carolyn. "First Under Fire, Are Americans Having Second Thoughts About the First Amendment?" *Presstime*, September 1995, pp. 36-42.

Wriston, Walter B. *Mistress of the World, The Marketplace and Public Opinion in the Information Age*. New York: The Freedom Forum Media Studies Center, 1993.

**SELECTED INTERNET SOURCES**

American Booksellers Foundation for Free Expression, http://www.abffe.org.

American Civil Liberties Union, http://www.aclu.org.

American Library Association Office for Intellectual Freedom, http://www.ala.org/alaorg/oif.

Beacon for Freedom of Expression, http://www.beaconforfreedom.org.

Chilling Effects Clearinghouse, http://www.chillingeffects.org.

Electronic Frontier Foundation, http://www.eff.org.

Ellen K. Solender Institute in Free Speech and Mass Media Law, http://library.law.smu.edu.

Feminists for Free Expression, http://www.ffeusa.org.

The File Room, http://www.thefileroom.org.

First Amendment Law Review, http://falr.unc.edu.

First Amendment Project, http://www.thefirstamendment.org.

Freedom to Read Foundation, http://www.ftrf.org.

Free Expression Network Clearinghouse, http://www.freeexpression.org.

Free Expression Policy Project, http://www.fepproject.org.
Media Institute, http://www.mediainstitute.org.
Media Law Resource Center, http://www.medialaw.org.
National Coalition Against Censorship, http://www.ncac.org.

National Freedom of Information Coalition, http://www.nfoic.org.
Thomas Jefferson Center for the Protection of Freedom of Expression, http://www.tjcenter.or.

# 3

## Conduct and Speech

### By W. Wat Hopkins

---

 **Headnote Questions**

- *How does the Supreme Court determine whether conduct is expressive?*
- *How does the Supreme Court determine whether expressive conduct is constitutionally protected?*
- *What are the intermediate and strict scrutiny tests?*
- *What is the constitutional status of threatening speech, fighting words and intimidating speech?*

---

As readers of this book will no doubt learn — if they haven't already — much First Amendment jurisprudence depends upon interpretation and, beyond that, degrees of interpretation. One man's art is another's obscenity; one woman's opinion is another's libel; one author's fair use is another's copyright infringement.

One of the best examples of the divergence of attitudes toward free speech might be the battle waged in the 1960s and '70s between Justice Hugo Black and some of his brethren on the U.S. Supreme Court. Justice Black took the position that the government cannot restrict the distribution of material because that material is obscene, defamatory, indecent, or even because it might harm the national security. "I read 'no law ... abridging'" freedom of speech and press, Justice Black wrote, "to mean *no law* abridging."[1] Speech, he maintained, was absolutely protected.

The great free-speech advocate, however, had a very narrow definition of "speech." Just as "no law" meant "no law," in Justice Black's view, "speech" meant "speech" and nothing more. He disagreed, therefore, when the Court ruled that students could not be punished for wearing black arm bands to school, or that a protester could not be punished for wearing a jacket with an offensive slogan on the back. These cases, Justice Black contended, involved conduct and did not implicate the First Amendment; no "speech" was involved.

Fortunately for picketers, flag-burners and dozens of others who have chosen over the years to express their views by doing

rather than saying, a majority of the Supreme Court has never agreed with Justice Black's definition of "speech." Indeed, a majority of the Court has always recognized that "speech" is more than talking. Justice Abe Fortas, for example, wrote that those students who wore armbands to school to protest the Vietnam War were participating in activity that was "closely akin to 'pure speech.'"[2] Justice Fortas' was a momentous characterization. If something that was so clearly an action could be considered "pure speech," many other types of conduct could be recognized as speech as well and, therefore, eligible for First Amendment protection. Under such a construction, expression, which is not mentioned in the First Amendment, is protected alongside "speech" and "press."

That has long been the case in First Amendment jurisprudence. Indeed, the Court has recognized a variety of activities as being speech: carrying or displaying a flag; marching or picketing; burning a flag, cross or draft card.[3] The Court has also said that a sit-in is a form of expression, as is the "silent, reproachful presence" of a group of African Americans who refused to leave an all-white library.[4] In fact, in some circumstances, even sleeping could be described as "speech."[5]

This is not to say, however, that the First Amendment protects all expressive or symbolic conduct. Conduct, after all, may intrude

---

[1] Smith v. California, 361 U.S. 147, 157 (1959) (Black, J., concurring).

[2] Tinker v. Des Moines Indep. Sch. Dist., 393 U.S. 503, 505-06 (1969).

[3] *See* cases cited at *infra* footnote 10.

[4] Brown v. Louisiana, 383 U.S. 131, 141-42 (1966).

[5] *See* Clark v. Cmty. for Creative Non-Violence, 468 U.S. 288 (1984).

on individual rights more than other forms of speech. It may literally do what an old advertisement for a long-distance telephone company once suggested consumers figuratively do: Reach out and touch someone. The Court has said, therefore, that there must be some balance between the rights of the actor and the rights of others present when conduct is used as a means of expression. This tension between rights has been at the heart of expressive conduct cases since the 1960s, when the Court's first substantive analysis in this area of the law began.

## CONDUCT AS SPEECH

For First Amendment purposes, there are three kinds of conduct: (1) conduct that has no communicative value, (2) conduct that is purely communicative and (3) conduct that has a mix of communicative and non-communicative elements.

Sometimes it's easy to tell the difference. One spring, for example, a home owner noticed that his U.S. flag had become frayed and moth-eaten. The home owner decided to replace the flag and learned from the U.S. Code that one proper way of disposing of a damaged flag is by burning.[6] The home owner took the flag into the back yard, dropped it into the grill, doused it with lighter fluid and set it ablaze. No one saw the action, and the flag burner later disposed of the cold ashes by spreading them in the flower bed. The act had no communicative value; its purpose was solely to dispose of a damaged U.S. flag as suggested by the U.S. Code.[7]

Come summer, the home owner replaced the damaged flag and, on July 4, put it on a flag-pole attached to the garage. The act is purely communicative; the home owner displayed the flag to demonstrate patriotism on Independence Day.

But when fall arrived, the home owner became dismayed. An incumbent president had taken actions with which the home owner violently disagreed. The home owner had a series of arguments with a neighbor, who happened to be the local chairman of the president's political party. The home owner's irritation was inflamed even more because the president was using hundreds of flags in his re-election campaign, even using the flag as a background on campaign posters, bumper stickers and other paraphernalia. To demonstrate his distaste, the home owner doused his recently purchased flag with lighter fluid, set it ablaze and tossed it on the neighbor's front porch. The burning flag destroyed a "Welcome" mat and left a large, sooty spot, requiring the porch to be repainted.

This action by the home owner contains both communicative and non-communicative elements. The home owner communi-

cated displeasure with presidential politics, but also caused property damage.

Under Supreme Court rulings, purely communicative conduct may be regulated by the government only in extremely rare circumstances. Conduct that has both speech and non-speech elements, however, may be regulated more readily. Courts must balance the rights of an individual to express viewpoints through action against the rights of individuals who may be impacted by the action. The balancing is complex and often controversial.

Over the years, the Court has developed a series of tests it applies in adjudicating cases in which individuals or groups claim constitutional protection for symbolic speech. First, the Court asks, is the conduct expressive? If not, the First Amendment is not implicated, the inquiry ends, and the government may regulate the conduct. If the conduct *is* expressive, however, the Court then asks the more difficult question: Is the expressive conduct protected by the First Amendment?

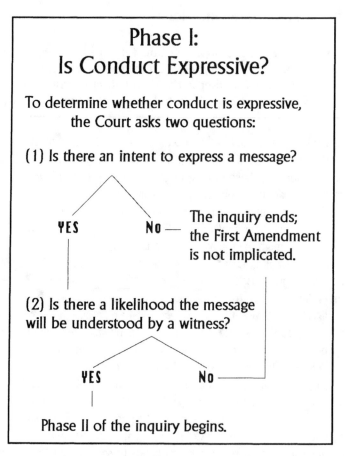

**Figure 1**

### Is the Conduct Expressive?

If conduct is expressive, that conduct is "speech." The expressive nature of the conduct is the element that moves action from simply doing to communicating. The home owner is no longer burning a damaged flag in his grill; the home owner is burning it in pub-

---

[6] Respect for the U.S. flag is covered in the U.S. Code, Title 4, Chapter 1, ß 8. Paragraph k of that section reads: "The flag, when it is in such condition that it is no longer a fitting emblem for display, should be destroyed in a dignified way, preferably by burning."

[7] Sometimes, however, ritualistic burnings of damaged flags are held as part of patriotic celebrations. *See, e.g.,* Keisha Stewart, *An Extra-Special Fourth of July*, ROANOKE TIMES, July 5, 2002, at B1, B6.

lic for the express purpose of communicating a message.

To determine whether conduct is purely utilitarian or has some communicative elements, the Court asks two questions: (1) Is there an intent to express a message? (2) Is there a likelihood the message will be understood by a witness? If there is no intent to express a message, or if it is not likely that a witness will understand the intended message, the conduct is not expressive, and the First Amendment does not apply.[8] Figure 1 demonstrates the flow of this inquiry.

The Court does not require that a viewer of expressive conduct understand the exact message the actor intends. Only a general understanding of the message is necessary. For example, when spectators watched in 1984 as Gregory Lee Johnson burned an American flag outside the meeting place of the Republican National Convention in Dallas, it was unnecessary that they knew Johnson was demonstrating his distaste for President Ronald Reagan, who was seeking re-nomination. It was sufficient that the spectators understood that Johnson was dissatisfied with some aspect of the United States or of the U.S. government — those entities symbolized by the flag.

Even though Johnson's action could be interpreted as a demonstration of disgust with Reagan, the Republican Party, the U.S. government *or* the United States itself, Justice William Brennan, upholding Johnson's right to burn the flag, wrote in *Texas v. Johnson*, "The expressive, overtly political nature of this conduct was both intentional and overwhelmingly apparent."[9]

Members of the Court have recognized a wide array of conduct to be expressive: burning a cross, nude dancing, displaying a license plate, burning a draft card, saluting a flag, displaying a flag.[10]

Not all these activities, however, are constitutionally protected. Once an action has been determined to be expressive, the Court must determine whether the expressive conduct is protected by the First Amendment. Cases involving expressive conduct date to the early Twentieth Century, but the Court's first substantive treatment of expressive conduct was in 1968. In *United States v. O'Brien*, the Court recognized that burning a draft card as a means of protesting the Selective Service system and U.S. involvement in Vietnam was expressive conduct, but ruled that other concerns outweighed David Paul O'Brien's right to burn the

card.[11] In *O'Brien*, the Court, for the first time, delineated the test for determining whether expressive conduct is protected by the First Amendment.

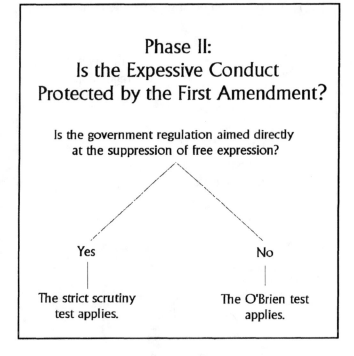

**Figure 2**

### Is the Expressive Conduct Protected?

At first glance, O'Brien's burning of his draft card is remarkably similar to Johnson's burning of a U.S. flag. Both men had audiences, both were expressing distaste with political agendas, and both were using an age-old method of destruction to demonstrate that distaste. In both cases, there was an intent to express a message, and there was a likelihood that the message would be understood by witnesses.

But the Court found significant differences in the two acts. Ironically, the differences were based primarily upon the intent of the government rather than upon the intent of the actors.

After the Court finds conduct to be expressive, it determines whether the conduct may be regulated by examining the rationale behind the government regulation being applied. The Court must determine whether the regulation is directed at the suppression of speech or at some other goal. If the purpose of the regulation is to restrict speech, the Court applies what it calls a "strict scrutiny test" to determine whether the regulation is constitutional; if the regulation is not directed at the suppression of speech, but at some other goal, the Court applies a test of intermediate scrutiny. Figure 2 demonstrates the flow of this inquiry.

---

[8] This test was first enunciated in *Spence v. Washington*, 418 U.S. 405, 410-11 (1974), but was refined significantly in *Texas v. Johnson*, 419 U.S. 397, 404-06 (1989).

[9] 491 U.S. at 406.

[10] *See* Virginia v. Black, 538 U.S. 343 (2003) (cross burning, in many instances, is intimidating speech); Barnes v. Glen Theatre, 501 U.S. 560 (1991) (nude dancing, though expressive, may be regulated); Wooley v. Maynard, 430 U.S. 705 (1977) (a person cannot be forced to display a license plate that contains an ideological message with which the person disagrees); United States v. O'Brien, 391 U.S. 367 (1968) (burning of draft card is not constitutionally protected); Stromberg v. California, 283 U.S. 359 (1931) (a regulation prohibiting the display of a red flag is not constitutional); West Virginia Bd. of Educ. v. Barnette, 319 U.S. 624 (1943) (students cannot be forced to salute the flag).

[11] 391 U.S. 367 (1968).

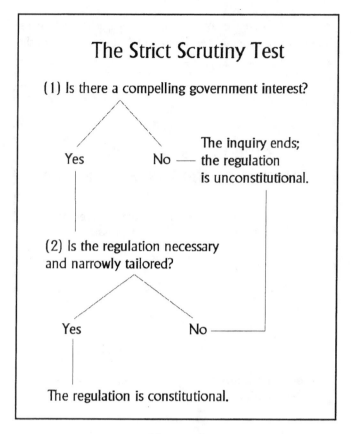

## The Strict Scrutiny Test

(1) Is there a compelling government interest?

Yes          No ——— The inquiry ends;
                     the regulation
                     is unconstitutional.

(2) Is the regulation necessary
and narrowly tailored?

Yes                    No ———

The regulation is constitutional.

**Figure 3**

**Strict Scrutiny.** Attorneys for Texas argued to the Texas and U.S. supreme courts that the state's purpose in adopting its flag desecration act was to protect the U.S. flag as a symbol of patriotism and unity. And, the attorneys argued, the state had the right to do so. The Court agreed that protecting the flag is a noble cause. The method used to protect the flag, however, was directed at the suppression of free speech; the statute would allow expression supporting the state's goals, but would not allow expression contrary to those goals. Because the statute was directly related to the suppression of speech, therefore, strict scrutiny was required to determine whether the statute was constitutional. Figure 3 demonstrates the flow of the strict scrutiny test, which requires the resolution of two questions:

- *Is there a compelling government interest for the regulation?* The government interest advocated by the regulation must be more than a passing interest; it must be vitally important to governmental operations. In *Texas v. Johnson,* Justice Brennan recognized that there may be a compelling government interest in protecting the flag as a symbol of national unity. National unity is important, Justice Brennan wrote, and the flag may be the single best symbol of the United States and that unity.

- *Is the regulation necessary and narrowly tailored to advance the government interest?* A necessary regulation is one that is essential, rather than optional, for the advancement of the government's interest. To survive strict scrutiny, a regula-

tion must be necessary, but it must also be narrowly tailored. Being narrowly tailored means that the regulation goes as far as necessary to advance the government interest, but does not overstep its bounds. In the area of speech, a narrowly tailored regulation is one that does not encompass protected speech in its prohibitions. Justice Brennan said the Texas act was not narrowly tailored. Even though protecting the flag is a compelling government interest, an individual's right to criticize the government is powerful. The government may promote the flag, Justice Brennan wrote, but may not control messages critical of the government simply because the flag is the medium of that criticism. "If there is a bedrock principle underlying the First Amendment," Justice Brennan wrote, "it is that the government may not prohibit the expression of an idea simply because society finds the idea itself offensive or disagreeable."[12]

**Intermediate Scrutiny: The O'Brien Test.** The Court came to a different conclusion in *United States v. O'Brien.*

When David Paul O'Brien burned his draft card, he was, like Johnson, voicing his discontent with government policy, specifically, with Selective Service. At the time, federal law required all men in the United States who were eighteen or older to carry draft cards until they surrendered them to Selective Service officials upon induction into the armed forces or until they were no longer eligible for the draft.

O'Brien did not deny burning his draft card but contended that the law prohibiting the destruction or mutilation of the card was unconstitutional because it inhibited free speech and served no legitimate legislative purpose. He was found guilty in federal district court in Massachusetts of violating the law. The First U.S. Circuit Court of Appeals found the statute unconstitutional but affirmed the conviction on grounds that O'Brien should have been convicted of the less serious offense of not having possession of the draft card.[13] Both the government and O'Brien appealed to the Supreme Court.

Chief Justice Earl Warren, writing for a seven-member majority, did not dispute O'Brien's contention that the burning of a draft card was expressive conduct. Instead, based upon the assumption that the conduct was sufficient to implicate the First Amendment, he took issue with O'Brien's argument that freedom of expression includes all modes of "communication of ideas by conduct." Wrote Warren: "We cannot accept the view that an apparently limitless variety of conduct can be labeled 'speech' whenever the person engaging in the conduct intends thereby to express an idea." When speech and non-speech elements combine in some form of expression, Warren wrote, a sufficiently important governmental interest in regulating the non-speech element of the communication can justify incidental limitations of First Amendment

---

12 Texas v. Johnson, 491 U.S. at 414.

13 O'Brien v. United States, 376 F.2d 538 (1st Cir. 1967).

freedoms.[14] Warren delineated a four-part test for determining when the government regulation is justified:[15]

- *Is the regulation within the constitutional power of the government?* The government has a right to raise and support armies, the Court noted, and to make all necessary and proper laws to that end; therefore, the Selective Service Act was within the power of the government.
- *Does the regulation further an important or substantial government interest?* Because the draft card and other Selective Service documents further the smooth and proper functioning of the system, Congress has a legitimate and substantial interest in preventing their wanton and unrestrained destruction and assuring their continuing availability by punishing people who knowingly and willfully destroy them.
- *Is the governmental interest unrelated to the suppression of free expression?* The non-destruction requirements of the law were aimed at the continued smooth operation of the Selective Service System, the Court held. That is, they were aimed at the non-communicative aspects of O'Brien's conduct and nothing else.
- *Is the incidental restriction of free expression no greater than is essential to the furtherance of the stated governmental interest?* The Court noted that the restriction O'Brien violated was narrowly drawn.

O'Brien's conviction was upheld, therefore. More importantly, however, the Court established a test to be applied in cases involving expressive conduct. The flow of the O'Brien Test is demonstrated in Figure 4.

### Flag Burning Revisited

Members of Congress — and of a number of state legislatures — were not happy with the Court's ruling in *Texas v. Johnson* and a follow-up case a year later.[16] Legislators began seeking ways to circumvent the Court's ruling, and those efforts continue.

Indeed, in June 2006, Congress came as close as it has ever come of clearing the first hurdle in amending the Constitution to prevent flag desecration. The Senate came one vote short of approving a constitutional amendment that had already been approved by the House of Representatives.[17] The House, for the sixth time since *Texas v. Johnson,* approved a proposed constitutional amendment by a vote of 286-130, well beyond the two-thirds vote required before an amendment can be submitted to the states for consideration.[18] An amendment must be ap-

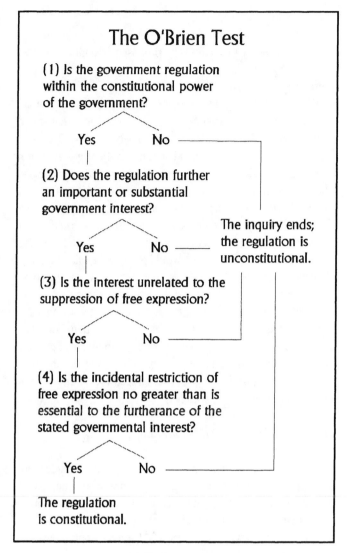

**Figure 4**

proved by a two-thirds vote in each house of Congress, however, and a Senate vote had never surpassed that margin.

In 1990, fifty-eight senators voted in favor of the amendment, and in May 2001 sixty-three did so.[19] Some observers of Congress believed that the Senate would approve the measure last year, and were nearly correct. In June the Senate vote favoring the amendment was 66-34, one vote shy of the 67 votes needed to achieve a two-thirds majority.

Senate approval would not have ended the debate, however. To become part of the Constitution, an amendment also must be approved by three-fourths of the states, a requirement that would apparently cause little problem: All fifty state legislatures have passed non-binding resolutions urging Congress to send them

---

[14] 391 U.S. at 376-77.

[15] *Id.* at 377-82.

[16] United States v. Eichman, 496 U.S. 310 (1990).

[17] *See* Carl Hulse, *Flag Amendment Narrowly Fails in Senate Vote*, N.Y. TIMES, June 28, 2006, at 1A.

[18] H.J. Res. 10, 109th Cong. (2005). The earlier votes came in 1995, 1997, 1999, 2001 and 2003.

---

[19] *See* Phillip Taylor, *House Approves Flag Amendment for Fourth Time in 6 Years*, FREEDOM FORUM ONLINE (July 18, 2002), *at* http://www.freedomforum.org.

the amendment for ratification.[20]

But the issue would not be resolved even if the amendment had been approved by the states. The proposed amendment stated: "The Congress shall have power to prohibit the physical desecration of the flag of the United States."

Congress, then, would have been required to draft a law that, among other things, described the kinds of activities that would constitute "physical desecration" and defined the word "flag" – no small tasks. For example, would spitting on the flag – an action that might require cleaning, but would not permanently damage the flag – constitute "physical desecration"? And could a person be arrested for burning a picture or some other representation of a flag? Much debate would be likely before Congress would pass a law punishing the physical desecration of the flag – and then the Supreme Court, at some point, would probably be called upon to determine whether that law was constitutional under the new amendment and balanced against the First Amendment.

All this activity is apparently taking place absent a strong mandate from the citizenry. A poll released by the Freedom Forum in June 2005 indicated that 63 percent of the respondents opposed such a constitutional amendment, up from 53 percent in 2004. Only 35 percent of the respondents favored the amendment – down from 45 percent a year earlier.[21]

### The Strange Case of Nude Dancing

Dancing, most people will agree, is a form of expression, at least in those contexts in which professionals perform for audiences. And it would seem just as obvious that when a professional dances nude, that dancer is attempting to express a message, and the message is apparent to an observer. The Supreme Court, however, has reached such conclusions begrudgingly and remains unwilling to grant constitutional protection to nude dancing.

The Court faced the issue most recently in *Erie v. Pap's A.M.*[22] The case began when the operator of a nightclub featuring nude dancing challenged an Erie, Pennsylvania, ordinance that prohibited public nudity. The nightclub owner claimed that the ordinance infringed his First Amendment free expression rights by prohibiting expressive conduct in the form of nude dancing. The Pennsylvania Supreme Court agreed,[23] but the U.S. Supreme Court overturned that opinion, ruling that the ordinance was constitutional. The Court was splintered in its rationale, however.

Writing for four justices, Sandra Day O'Connor found that, since the ordinance prohibited all nudity, not just nude dancing, it was not a content-based restriction and was constitutional under the

four-part O'Brien Test.[24] Justice O'Connor admitted that nude dancing is expressive conduct — though "it falls only within the outer ambit of the First Amendment's protection."[25] The two justices who concurred in the judgment, thereby allowing the ordinance to stand, were not willing to go that far. Antonin Scalia, joined by Clarence Thomas, wrote that nude dancing could be regulated as conduct, unless there was evidence that an ordinance aimed at the dancing was aimed specifically at the "communicative character" of the dancing rather than the nudity itself.[26]

Only Justices John Paul Stevens and Ruth Bader Ginsburg recognized that nude dancing is, indeed, expressive conduct, and regulations such as those enacted in Erie must face strict scrutiny. Discounting the Court's argument that the ban was aimed at the secondary effects of nude dancing — increased sex crimes, for example — Justice Stevens wrote that the Court held, for the first time, that such effects "may justify the total suppression of protected speech."[27]

What seems clear from the Court's opinion in *Erie* — as well as earlier nude dancing cases[28] — is that members of the Court are willing to allow certain types of expressive conduct to be regulated, not because the conduct is not expressive, but because they don't like the message the conduct is communicating.

## SPEECH AS CONDUCT

Before the discussion of conduct and speech is complete, two special cases must be addressed: threatening speech and picketing.

### Threatening Speech

Thus far, this discussion has centered on conduct that takes on the role of speech, that is, conduct that is expressive. Another area of law with which the Court has wrestled is the regulation of speech when that speech takes on additional characteristics, that is, when the speech takes on the role of conduct. This occurs with fighting words, threatening speech and intimidating speech.

Fighting words are words that are so vile or obnoxious that they are likely to prompt a physical reaction. For example, what might the result be if, during a hotly contested football game between two bitter rivals — say the University of Virginia and Virginia Tech — a Virginia Tech fan wandered into the U.Va. student section wearing a sweatshirt that read "Fuck the Cavaliers"?

The result might seem obvious, and the example is not as far-

---

[20] *See id.*

[21] Press Release, First Amendment Center, 63% Oppose Flag-Burning Amendment, New Survey Shows (June 10, 2005), *available at* http://www.firstamendmentcenter.org.

[22] 529 U.S. 277 (2000).

[23] Pap's A.M. v. Erie, 719 A.2d 273 (Pa. 1998).

[24] 529 U.S. at 296-97 (plurality opinion).

[25] *Id.* at 289 (citing Barnes v. Glen Theatre, 501 U.S. 560, 565-66 (1991)) (plurality opinion).

[26] *Id.* at 310 (Scalia, J., concurring in judgment).

[27] *Id.* at 317-18 (Stevens, J., dissenting).

[28] *See, e.g.,* Barnes v. Glen Theatre, 501 U.S. 560 (1991); Renton v. Playtime Theatres, 475 U.S. 41 (1986).

fetched as it might first appear. On April 26, 1968, Paul Robert Cohen walked into the Los Angeles County Courthouse wearing a jacket bearing the slogan "Fuck the draft." Cohen was arrested and convicted of violating that portion of the California Penal Code that prohibited maliciously and willfully disturbing the peace or quiet of any neighborhood or person by offensive conduct.

The Supreme Court, however, found that the conduct was speech and was protected.[29] Three justices disagreed. Harry Blackmun, Warren Burger and Hugo Black argued, in a dissent drafted by Blackmun, that "Cohen's absurd and immature antic ... was mainly conduct and little speech."[30] They said Cohen should have found another way of expressing his opinion on the draft.

In the majority opinion, however, Justice John Marshall Harlan pointed out the importance of the emotive as well as the cognitive force of speech:

We cannot overlook the fact, because it is well illustrated by the episode involved here, that much linguistic expression serves a dual communicative function: it conveys not only ideas capable of relatively precise, detached explication, but otherwise inexpressible emotions as well. In fact, words are often chosen as much for their emotive as their cognitive force. We cannot sanction the view that the Constitution, while solicitous of the cognitive content of individual speech, has little or no regard for the emotive function which, practically speaking, may often be the more important element of the overall message sought to be communicated.[31]

Even though the Court found Cohen's "absurd and immature antic" to be protected speech, the antic demonstrates the type of speech that can take on the role of conduct: The words become like actions. Either Cohen or the reckless Virginia Tech football fan could have been confronted by a person willing to respond to the words with physical violence.

The Court first recognized the so-called "fighting words" doctrine in 1942 in the case of *Chaplinsky v. New Hampshire*.[32] A Jehovah's Witness was arrested for calling a police officer a "damned fascist" and a "God damned racketeer." The Court upheld the conviction, calling the verbal assault an attack of fighting words, that is, words "which by their very utterance inflict injury or tend to incite an immediate breach of the peace." Such utterances, the Court said, "are no essential part of any expression of ideas, and are of such slight social value as a step to truth that any benefit that may be deprived from them is clearly out-weighed by the social interests in order and morality."[33]

Not only must the words be particularly violent or obnoxious,

they must be aimed directly at an individual for the fighting-words doctrine to apply, as the Court demonstrated seven years later in *Terminiello v. Chicago*.[34] A well-publicized speech by a right-wing anti-Semite was met by a crowd of protesters, some of whom were able to break into the meeting hall where the speech was held. The speaker, Arthur Terminiello, repeatedly referred to the protesters as "scum" or "slimy scum." The speech so stirred members of the crowd that police indicated they feared unrest. Like Chaplinsky, Terminiello was convicted of breaching the peace by using language that would stir the public to anger. In Terminiello's case, however, the Court reversed. Justice William O. Douglas, in one of his few free-speech majority opinions, wrote that free speech is designed to invoke dispute:

It may indeed best serve its high purpose when it induces a condition of unrest, creates dissatisfaction with conditions as they are, or even stirs people to anger. Speech is often provocative and challenging. It may strike at prejudices and preconceptions and have profound unsettling effects as it presses for acceptance of an idea. That is why freedom of speech, though not absolute ... is nevertheless protected against censorship or punishment, unless shown likely to produce a clear and present danger of a serious substantive evil that rises far above public inconvenience, annoyance, or unrest. There is no room under our Constitution for a more restrictive view.[35]

What's the difference in the two cases? *Terminiello* did not involve a face-to-face confrontation. In an important lower court case, the Illinois Supreme Court upheld the rights of neo-Nazis to march in Skokie, Illinois, displaying the swastika, which an appellate court ordered removed because of the fighting-words doctrine.[36] The state supreme court recognized, however, that the march removed the speech from that one-on-one dialogue to a more abstract insult. Ironically, after winning the right to march in Skokie, the neo-Nazis never did.

The confrontational nature of language has been important to the Supreme Court as well. The Court has consistently struck down as vague and overbroad state laws prohibiting the use of abusive, menacing, insulting or profane language, if those statutes had not been narrowed by state courts to focus on fighting words.[37] Though the Court has upheld convictions for the use of abusive language when there was a threat of a riot, the threat must be relatively direct. A speaker's shout that "We'll take the fucking streets," for example, was found not to be fighting words, nor did it tend to incite a riot, because the speaker was obviously not re-

[29] Cohen v. California, 403 U.S. 15 (1971).

[30] *Id.* at 27 (Blackmun, J., dissenting).

[31] *Id.* at 25.

[32] 315 U.S. 568 (1942).

[33] *Id.* at 571.

[34] 337 U.S. 1 (1949).

[35] *Id.* at 4.

[36] Vill. of Skokie v. Nat'l Socialist Party of Am., 373 N.E.2d 21 (Ill. 1978).

[37] *See, e.g.,* Lewis v. New Orleans, 415 U.S. 130 (1974); Plummer v. City of Columbus, Ohio, 414 U.S. 2 (1973); Gooding v. Wilson, 405 U.S. 518 (1972).

ferring to an imminent action, but, rather, to some possible future action.[38]

The Court has faced few fighting words cases, but did so in 1992. In *R.A.V. v. St. Paul,*[39] it held that a conviction for burning a cross in the yard of a black couple who had moved into a predominantly white neighborhood could not stand under the fighting-words doctrine. The cross that the juvenile burned didn't cause much of a fire — it was made from broken chair legs — but the Minnesota Supreme Court said the act amounted to fighting words. It upheld the conviction for violating a city ordinance prohibiting the burning of a cross, the placing of a Nazi swastika, or other similar action for the purpose of arousing anger, alarm or resentment "on the basis of race, color, creed, religion or gender."

The Supreme Court reversed. It said St. Paul could prohibit fighting words but that the ordinance allowed fighting words unless they were aimed at a member of one of the classes specified. It would be acceptable under the ordinance, the Court said, to use fighting words against someone based on political affiliation, union or non-union membership or sexual preference: "The First Amendment does not permit St. Paul to impose special prohibitions on those speakers who express views on disfavored subjects."[40] The Court recognized that the conduct was reprehensible but ruled that the subject was being unconstitutionally punished under an ordinance that advanced what amounted to viewpoint discrimination.

Revisiting the issue of cross burning during its 2002-03 term, the Supreme Court carved out a new category of speech that is not protected by the First Amendment — intimidation. In *Virginia v. Black,*[41] the Court held that when cross burning achieves the status of intimidating speech, it can be proscribed and punished, but the Court also held that not all instances of cross burning are intimidating. The Court found a Virginia state law to be unconstitutional because, in addition to banning cross burning that is designed to intimidate "any person or group," the law stated that the act of burning a cross was *prima facie* evidence of an intent to intimidate. The clause making cross burning automatically intimidating, the Court held, also made the law unconstitutional. While cross burning can be "a particularly virulent form of intimidation,"[42] Justice Sandra Day O'Connor wrote for the majority, and it always can be considered "a symbol of hate," it has also been used to communicate "messages of shared ideology."[43] Therefore, to be proscribed, cross burning must cross the line from being a symbol representing some ideology, celebration or ritual, and must become intimidating.

The Court had previously indicated that, in addition to fighting words, speech that constituted what it called a "true threat" could be proscribed.[44] And, indeed, some scholars and advocates argued that cross burning constituted threatening speech. The Court in *Virginia v. Black* held that cross burning constituted intimidating speech, and that intimidating speech as a type of threat could be proscribed and punished. Wrote Justice O'Connor: "Intimidation in the constitutionally proscribable sense of the word is a type of true threat, where a speaker directs a threat to a person or group of persons with the intent of placing the victim in fear of bodily harm or death."[45]

The Court did not elaborate on what kinds of speech might be intimidating, what the distinctions are between intimidating speech and true threats or how lower courts can make such determinations. But that is the way of the Court. Because the Court only answers questions put to it, the process of establishing tests can be long and arduous. The Court, for example, held that obscenity is not protected by the First Amendment in 1957, but it was 1973 before a majority of the Court agreed upon a test for obscenity.[46] The Court has taken similar paths in the area of expressive conduct[47] and commercial speech.[48] It may be years, therefore, before the Court develops a test for determining when speech in general and cross burning in particular become intimidating.

## *Picketing*

The Court has recognized that picketing is a time-honored method of expressing a message. It is often used by people who cannot afford to publish their complaints, and it is generally aimed at a narrow problem. Therefore, the Court has granted picketers broad protection, still balancing their rights against those of other individuals and against public peace and safety. It has held that peaceful picketing cannot be licensed, that restrictions on picketing must be content-neutral and that picketing cannot be banned from public property.

One of the Court's most important rulings on picketing came near the middle of the century. In striking down Alabama's statute prohibiting picketing a place of business, the Court noted that freedom of speech and press "are among the fundamental person-

---

[38] Hess v. Indiana, 414 U.S. 105, 107 (1973). *See also,* Feiner v. New York, 340 U.S. 315 (1951).

[39] 505 U.S. 377 (1992).

[40] *Id.* at 391.

[41] 538 U.S. 343 (2003).

[42] *Id.* at 363.

[43] *Id.* at 356-57.

[44] *See* Watts v. United States, 394 U.S. 705, 707 (1969).

[45] 538 U.S. at 360.

[46] The Court held that obscene material lies outside the protection of the First Amendment in *Roth v. United States,* 354 U.S. 476 (1957) and established the test of obscenity in *Miller v. California,* 413 U.S. 15 (1973). *See* the discussion of obscenity in Chapter 5.

[47] *See* the cases cited in footnote 10.

[48] The Court held that commercial speech is protected by the First Amendment in *Bigelow v. Virginia,* 421 U.S. 809 (1975) and *Virginia State Board of Pharmacy v. Virginia Citizens Consumer Council,* 425 U.S. 748 (1976), and established a test to determine when commercial speech may be regulated in *Central Hudson Gas & Electric Co. v. Public Service Commission of New York,* 447 U.S. 557 (1980). *See* the discussion of commercial speech in Chapter 8.

al rights and liberties which are secured to all persons" by the Constitution, and that picketing was one of the activities that "may enlighten the public on the nature and causes" of public debate.[49]

The rights of individuals to picket or distribute information often depend upon where the picketing occurs and the rationale behind government regulations restricting the picketing. Picketing in an area designated a public forum — like a park or sidewalk — is almost always protected, if the picketing is peaceful and if it does not interfere with other valid uses of the public forum.[50] Even in the absence of a public forum, the Court has held that absolute bans on First Amendment activity — including picketing — may be unconstitutional because the government cannot justify such bans.[51]

Picketing on private property is more problematic. Often, however, even the private property rights of individuals and corporations must give way when individuals choose to express themselves by picketing. While the Court has recognized that owners have certain rights over their property, when the property is used for a public purpose and when it's obvious that the picketers are expressing their own viewpoints and are not speaking for the property owners, the Court has allowed picketing on private property.[52]

The Court has also held that towns cannot restrict access to private homes to disseminate information. The Village of Stratton prohibited persons from distributing information door-to-door without first receiving a "Solicitation Permit." Apparently the issuance of the permit was *pro forma*, but the Jehovah's Witnesses of New York complained that the process of applying for the permit infringed their First Amendment rights. The Court agreed, ruling in June 2002 that persons engaging in door-to-door advocacy could not be required to identify themselves through an application and permit procedure.[53]

The Court, however, has also allowed some picketing to be restricted, including in shopping malls and at private residences. It also allowed the military to restrict picketing and the distribution of literature on military bases — even those portions of the bases open to the public.[54]

Finally, the Court has allowed restrictions on persons who picket abortion clinics and attempt to prevent women from obtaining abortions. It held that restrictions on picketing were not aimed at the anti-abortion message of the activists, but were aimed at conduct, that is, at efforts by the activists to interfere with people entering or leaving the clinics. The Court also upheld the use of zones in which picketing could be banned but held that 300-foot buffer zones were unreasonable and burdened more speech than necessary to serve the government's interest in guaranteeing the free flow of traffic.[55] It also held that a so-called "floating buffer zone" requiring picketers to stay at least fifteen feet from people or vehicles entering or leaving the clinics violated the First Amendment because it overburdened speech.[56]

In a related matter, the Court held in 2003 that a First Amendment challenge to a law prohibiting trespassing could not stand absent a showing that freedom of speech was being inhibited.[57] The case began when the city of Richmond and the Richmond Redevelopment and Housing Authority devised a plan to help reduce unwanted traffic in Whitcomb Court, a low-income housing project. The town gave to the housing authority the streets within and adjacent to the project, thereby closing those streets to public use. The housing authority then developed a set of rules governing foot traffic on those streets and authorized the Richmond Police Department to enforce the new trespass laws.[58]

Kevin Lamont Hicks was convicted of violating the trespassing law and appealed his conviction on grounds that his First Amendment rights had been violated.[59] He won before the Virginia Court of Appeals and the Virginia Supreme Court,[60] but the U.S. Supreme Court disagreed. The Virginia Supreme Court held that the law gave too much discretion to the manager of the housing project who, the court said, had "the unfettered discretion to determine not only who has a right to speak on the Housing Authority's property," but may also prohibit speech "she finds personally distasteful or offensive even though such speech may be protected by the First Amendment."[61]

The Supreme Court, however, held that the manager's discretion in allowing or prohibiting speech within Whitcomb Court was irrelevant, because there was no evidence that Hicks was attempting to speak. He had been barred from returning to the housing project, the Court noted, and, therefore, his challenge related solely to the rule that those barred could not reenter. He did not show and did not attempt to show that his banishment was related to speech.[62]

---

[49] Thornhill v. Alabama, 310 U.S. 88, 95 & 104 (1940).

[50] *See, e.g.,* Bachellor v. Maryland, 397 U.S. 564 (1970); Gregory v. Chicago, 394 U.S. 111 (1969); Cox v. Louisiana, 379 U.S. 536 & 559 (1965); Henry v. Rock Hill, 376 U.S. 776 (1964).

[51] *See* Bd. of Airport Comm'rs v. Jews for Jesus, 482 U.S. 569 (1987).

[52] *See, e.g.,* Pruneyard Shopping Ctr. v. Robins, 447 U.S. 74 (1974); Lloyd Corp., Ltd. v. Tanner, 407 U.S. 551 (1972); Amalgamated Food Employees Union v. Logan Valley Plaza, Inc., 391 U.S. 308 (1968).

[53] Watchtower Bible and Tract Soc'y of New York v. Vill. of Stratton, 536 U.S. 150 (2002).

[54] *See, e.g.,* Greer v. Spock, 424 U.S. 828 (1976). *But see also,* United States v. Albertini, 472 U.S. 675 (1985); Flower v. United States, 407 U.S. 197 (1972).

---

[55] *See* Madsen v. Women's Health Clinic, Inc., 512 U.S. 753 (1994).

[56] Schenck v. Pro-Choice Network of Western New York, 519 U.S. 357 (1997).

[57] Virginia v. Hicks, 539 U.S. 113 (2003).

[58] Hicks v. Commonwealth, 548 S.E.2d 249, 251-52 (Va. App. 2001).

[59] *Id.* at 252.

[60] Commonwealth v. Hicks, 563 S.E.2d 674 (Va. 2002).

[61] *Id.* at 681.

[62] 539 U.S. at 118-19.

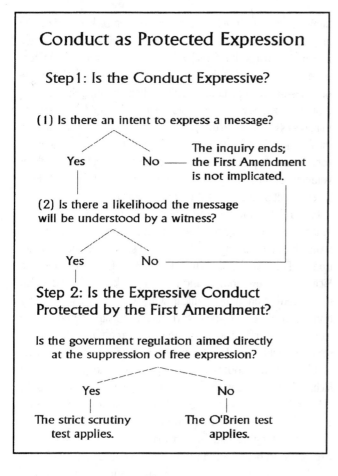

**Figure 5**

## SUMMARY

The speech/conduct conundrum consists of parallel issues: conduct that takes on the role of speech and speech that takes on the role of conduct.

Based on *United States v. O'Brien, Texas v. Johnson* and other Supreme Court cases, the Court has established a carefully delineated course in dealing with expressive conduct. That course is described in Figure 5.

In traveling that course, the Court must answer some specific questions.

*Is the conduct expressive?* The conduct is expressive if there is an intent to express a message and if there is a likelihood the message will be understood. If there is either no intent or no likelihood of understanding, the conduct is not expressive, the First Amendment is not implicated, and the inquiry is over. If the conduct is expressive, however, the inquiry continues.

*Is the expressive conduct protected?* The path to determining whether conduct is protected begins with the rationale behind the government regulation. The Court first determines whether the regulation is aimed directly at speech. If it is, the Court applies a strict scrutiny test by asking two questions: (1) Does the regulation advance a compelling government interest? and (2) is

the regulation necessary and narrowly tailored? If the answer to either question is no, the regulation is unconstitutional. If the answer to both questions is yes, the regulation is constitutional.

If the Court finds that the regulation is not aimed specifically at speech, it applies a test of intermediate scrutiny, called the "O'Brien Test," to determine whether the regulation is constitutional. Under the test, a regulation is required to meet four points: (1) The activity regulated must be within the constitutional power of the government; (2) the regulation must advance an important government interest; (3) the government interest must be unrelated to the suppression of free expression; and (4) the incidental restriction on speech must be no greater than necessary to advance the government interest.

Just as conduct can take on the role of speech, speech can sometimes become like conduct. Words can be so vile or obnoxious that they prompt a physical response. Courts allow such words to be regulated but take care to ensure that governments don't trammel free expression in their efforts to protect other individual rights. Statutes prohibiting offensive or abusive language, for example, have routinely been held to be unconstitutional unless they have been narrowed so they only prohibit fighting words. In addition, the Supreme Court has ruled that intimidation is a category of what it calls "true threats" and may be banned.

Finally, courts have recognized the value of picketing and have allowed individuals to picket on both private and public property. Picketing in areas traditionally held to be public fora is almost always allowed. Picketing on private property is more problematic, but the Supreme Court has often allowed such picketing.

## FOR ADDITIONAL READING

Baker, C. Edwin. *Human Liberty and Freedom of Speech.* New York: Oxford University Press, 1989.

Emerson, Thomas I. *The System of Freedom of Expression.* New York: Vintage, 1970.

Goldstein, R.J. *Saving "Old Glory": The History of the American Flag Desecration Controversy.* Boulder, Colo.: Westview Press, 1996.

Haiman, Franklyn S. *Speech and Law in a Free Society.* Chicago: University of Chicago Press, 1981.

Hopkins, W. Wat. "Cross Burning Revisited: What the Supreme Court Should Have Done in Virginia v. Black and Why it Didn't," 26 *Hastings Communication and Entertainment Law Journal (COMM/ENT)* 269 (2004).

Hopkins, W. Wat. *Mr. Justice Brennan and Freedom of Expression.* New York: Praeger, 1991.

Katsh, M. Ethan, ed. *Taking Sides — Clashing Views of Controversial Legal Issues.* Guilford, Conn.: Dushkin, 1995.

Russomanno, Joseph. *Defending the First.* Mahwah, N.J.: Lawrence Erlbaum Associates, 2005.

Smolla, Rodney A. *Free Speech in an Open Society.* New York: Vintage, 1993.

# 4

# Prior Restraint

*By Steven Helle*

---

 **Headnote Questions**

- *What is the origin of the doctrine against prior restraint?*
- *Did the framers of the First Amendment intend for the amendment to ban only prior restraint, or did they intend something more?*
- *What are the characteristics of prior restraint, historically and currently?*
- *Why is a doctrine against prior restraint important?*
- *What are the critical principles that courts consider in applying the doctrine?*

---

"Censorship" is a word casually used in editorials or angry speeches to denounce everything from postal rate increases, to obscenity prosecutions, to theft of campus newspapers. But the term meant something specific in historical usage, and it is rarely what writers or speakers mean today. Those who denounce contemporary attempts to control speech, however, are taking advantage of the considerable distaste that became associated with the historical form of censorship.

Therein lies the dilemma that runs throughout this chapter. The battles against the historical form of censorship have been won, and an extensive body of law seems to have extinguished the prospect of future censorship as long as the First Amendment retains any vitality. But is it advisable to expand the notion of censorship and the extent of protection available under the First Amendment in order to combat innovative forms of regulation that accomplish much the same thing as historical censorship? Or would stretching the First Amendment to offer the same degree of protection against more types of control ultimately dilute and weaken the protection, just as a balloon that expands becomes thinner — and more susceptible to breaking?

## HISTORICAL BACKGROUND

Much of U.S. law has its roots in English law. England, of course, imposed its law on its American colonies. But even after the Amer-

ican Revolution, twelve of the thirteen newly established states expressly adopted the common law of England as their own. Lawyers on this side of the Atlantic educated themselves primarily by reading Sir William Blackstone's *Commentaries on the Law of England.* "In the first century of American independence, the *Commentaries* were not merely an approach to the study of law; for most lawyers they constituted all there was of the law," wrote Daniel J. Boorstin, Librarian of Congress emeritus.[1] Because English law influenced not only U.S. law, but the framers of the U.S. Constitution as well, it is important to trace the English experience with censorship to better understand how and why U.S. law on the subject evolved the way it did.

Printing on a press was introduced to England in 1476, and not long afterward the Crown attempted to impose controls. The Roman Catholic Church was interested in suppressing what it considered heretical opinions. In 1501, Pope Alexander VI attempted to require printing to be licensed. In 1517, Martin Luther posted his *95 Theses* on the door of the Castle Church in Wittenberg, Germany, questioning the practice of contributing to the church as a means of buying forgiveness for sins. The Church burned the writings of Luther and others who questioned its authority or practices, dismissed them from the Church, prohibited the faithful from reading the works and issued rebuttals. But the demand —

---

[1] DANIEL J. BOORSTIN, THE MYSTERIOUS SCIENCE OF THE LAW 3 (1941).

and profit — for publishing the works only grew.

### King Henry VIII

King Henry VIII of England, at the request of the Church, used this religious debate as the impetus for asserting the Crown's control over printing. Henry, in fact, secretly encouraged the reformers while publicly condemning them, even publishing his own response to Luther. By appearing to lead the effort to denounce and control the heretics, he hoped to win the favor of Rome and the Pope's blessing for his divorce from Queen Catherine.

When the clergy was unable to control the speech of the heretics, Henry issued his first list of prohibited books in 1529, and several booksellers and others who possessed the banned books were executed. In 1530, Henry issued a proclamation establishing a licensing system, the first such system outside the church. He decreed that no person could print any religious book until it was examined and approved by the clergy, and every printer would obey or "answere to the kinges highnes, at his uttermost peryll." Executions, fines and imprisonment followed. When Henry did not get the dispensation he desired from Rome, he switched sides and began executing the Catholic faithful.

As historian Fredrick Siebert noted, Henry was fully aware of the influence of the printing press in easing his break with Rome. He was an early and excellent master of manipulating public opinion by controlling the press, and he certainly had the tools and will to exercise that control to its fullest. "His policy henceforth was not only to eliminate undesirable reading matter but to stimulate the circulation of that which would strengthen his cause," Siebert wrote.[2]

Thus, the Proclamation of 1538 extended the king's censorship to all printing, not just religious writings, including "errors and seditious opinions." Sedition, or criticism of government, had no ecclesiastical foundation. The matter is muddled because Henry had made himself the head of the Church of England. Therefore, an attack on the Church could be considered an attack on the state, or vice versa. But for the first time, speech that was expressly political was subject to censorship through a licensing system; and Henry's political appointees, not the Church, would decide what violated the regulations and deserved the King's displeasure. As Siebert noted: "The shift in the administration of the licensing regulations from the clergy to state officers was one of Henry's contributions to the regulation of the press. The method was subsequently adopted on the continent, even in Catholic countries."[3]

Henry also instituted the practice of requiring printers to post bonds, which would be forfeited if their publications offended him. He offered printers "privileges" – or copyrights – in certain works, which protected them from piracy. And the Tudor sovereigns who followed him engaged in a brilliant maneuver by recognizing a Sta-

tioner's Company, or organization of officially sanctioned printers. Just as broadcasters in this country did in the 1920s, these early printers actually sought government regulation. In the same way that the broadcasters favored by the U.S. government gained monopolies on the use of certain radio frequencies, the favored English printers obtained monopolies on the printing of certain works, such as the Bible, which were very profitable.

But the monopolies served the interests of the government, as well, because the economic interests of the printers ensured that they would do nothing to alienate the government and risk losing their monopolies. Furthermore, the government gained an ally in controlling unlicensed printing. The members of the Stationer's Company were given broad powers of search and seizure to protect their monopolies from renegade printers. Their zealousness in exercising these powers led directly to the enactment of the Fourth Amendment to the U.S. Constitution, prohibiting unreasonable searches and seizures and requiring warrants based on probable cause.

Henry's licensing system endured until the close of the Seventeenth Century; and it was more or less successful, depending on how aggressively it was enforced or evaded at any given time. It took a brave printer to risk forfeiture of property, fines, imprisonment, torture, amputation and execution for flouting the system. The Stationer's Company sniffed out the trail of a press that had been secretly moved all over England to avoid capture in 1589. John Hodgkins was finally arrested and charged with printing unlicensed Puritan tracts critical of the Church of England. He refused to confess, was tortured, jailed for a year and then put on the rack. There is no record of his fate after that.

Ingenious printers and authors attempted to circumvent the regulations, forging censors' signatures, changing manuscripts after they had been approved or writing ostensibly fictional dramas whose characters everybody understood to represent real-life figures. But the stakes, depending on the political temper of the times and one's choice of political patrons, could be high.

Parliament took control of the licensing system from the Crown in 1643, but the structure of censorship remained essentially what it had been in 1538. Publication came to be subject to other forms of governmental regulation, primarily prosecutions for seditious libel and taxation, and the penalties associated with those forms of regulation could be just as severe. But the licensing system was distinctive not only because it was first; but, because it applied to every publication, it gave the government complete discretion regarding the content of each publication, and it occurred in advance of publication. This latter feature indicates why this censorship was called "prior restraint."

Understandably, members of the Stationer's Company did not object to licensing (unless, as sometimes happened, some members obtained licenses that others did not). Objections came from those without licenses — and the philosophy and value of freedom of the press began to take shape. Two Puritans who wrote an unlicensed religious pamphlet in 1572 argued that they had pre-

---

[2] FREDRICK S. SIEBERT, FREEDOM OF THE PRESS IN ENGLAND, 1476-1776 47 (1965).
[3] Id. at 49.

sented the tract to Parliament and, in doing so, they should have the privilege of "writing and speaking freely." This, according to Siebert, was the first time that the ancient right of Englishmen to petition Parliament was translated into an argument for a free press.[4] The pair, however, was sentenced to a year in prison.

### Milton and Areopagitica

In 1644 John Milton presented in *Areopagitica,* which was itself unlicensed, what law professor Vincent Blasi has labeled the classic attack on prior restraint. Ironically, the impetus for this great treatise arose from Milton's having been cited for an earlier unlicensed tract on divorce, which was no easier for him to obtain than it had been for King Henry VIII. Milton framed his argument broadly:

> And though all the windes of doctrin were let loose to play upon the earth, so Truth be in the field, we do injuriously by licencing and prohibiting to misdoubt her strenth. Let her and Falshood grapple; who ever knew Truth put to the wors, in a free and open encounter.... [I]t is not possible for man to sever the wheat from the tares, the good fish from the other frie; that must be the Angels Ministery at the end of all mortall things. Yet if all cannot be of one mind, as who looks they should be? This doubtles is more wholsome, more prudent, and more Christian that many be tolerated, rather than all compell'd.[5]

Although it is an eloquent tribute to diverse expression without government suppression or endorsement of any one opinion, there is the view that Milton really was more interested in his divorce than in freedom of expression because he became a government censor just seven years after *Areopagitica.* In his defense, however, Professor Jeffery Smith noted that Milton's role as censor primarily involved overseeing publication of the government's own newsletter — and, as censor, he had to recall his arguments from *Areopagitica* when he was questioned for approving a catechism that Parliament afterward condemned. Smith noted that, although Milton's arguments showed up in a few other tracts in his time, he probably had more impact in later centuries as philosophers, statesmen and jurists crafted libertarian theory.[6]

An abridged version of *Areopagitica* was published in 1693, but when the Licensing Act came up for renewal in 1694, the treatise apparently had no influence on the decision by the House of Commons to let the act lapse. A list of eighteen reasons for not renewing the Act was presented in the House of Commons. The reasons, thought to be written by John Locke, had to do with the vagueness of the licensing standards, the impediments to free

trade, the ineffectiveness of the system, and other objections unrelated to the philosophy of freedom of the press.

Under the two-party political system that had evolved, censors risked offending somebody important whether they licensed a publication or not. Important people did not want to undertake the task of censoring, and they did not trust unimportant people to do it. As Thomas Macaulay wrote in his *History of England* nearly two centuries later, "On the great question of principle, on the question whether the liberty of unlicensed printing be, on the whole, a blessing or a curse to society, not a word is said."[7] After more than a century and a half, licensing was dead in England.

### The American Experience

Licensing continued in the American colonies until the 1720s. In 1723, the Massachusetts legislature, stung by constant criticism from James Franklin, publisher of the *New England Courant,* ordered Franklin never to publish the *Courant* or any other publication, "Except it be first Supervised, by the Secretary of this Province." Franklin published a new, unlicensed edition and went into hiding, making his brother Benjamin publisher. The legislature had not prohibited his soon-to-be-famous brother from publishing without a license.

James was eventually arrested, and the legislature sought an indictment from the grand jury, which historian Leonard Levy described as a mistake. The grand jury refused to indict, "probably motivated by a detestation of the licensing system which had ended a generation earlier in England.... Thus, Franklin went luckily free, and prior restraint of the press was at an end in Massachusetts," Levy wrote.[8]

Blackstone accurately summarized the law on both sides of the Atlantic when, in the late 1760s, he wrote in his *Commentaries* perhaps the most famous lines regarding the prior restraint doctrine:

> The *liberty of the press* is indeed essential to the nature of a free state; but this consists in laying no *previous* restraints upon publications, and not in freedom from censure for criminal matter when published. Every freeman has an undoubted right to lay what sentiments he pleases before the public: to forbid this is to destroy the freedom of the press; but if he publishes what is improper, mischievous, or illegal, he must take the conse-

---

[4] *Id.* at 96.

[5] JOHN MILTON, AREOPAGITICA 74-76 (Eng. Rep. 1972) (1st ed. n.p. 1644).

[6] JEFFREY A. SMITH, PRINTERS AND PRESS FREEDOM — THE IDEOLOGY OF EARLY AMERICAN JOURNALISM 33-35, 40 (1988).

[7] 5 THOMAS B. MACAULAY, THE HISTORY OF ENGLAND FROM THE ACCESSION OF JAMES II 16-17 (1889). Macaulay observed that the event produced no excitement and was little noted, probably because Parliament was preoccupied with the funeral for Queen Mary. But the vote by the House of Commons not to renew the Licensing Act did "more for liberty and for civilisation than the Great Charter or the Bill of Rights." *Id.* at 15-16. The House of Lords did not object, probably because it assumed a different bill for regulating the press would be introduced — and, indeed, one was, but it did not clear committee before the session ended. Macaulay noted that "petty grievances did what Milton's *Areopagitica* failed to do."

[8] LEONARD W. LEVY, EMERGENCE OF A FREE PRESS 32 (1985).

quences of his own temerity.[9]

Freedom from prior restraint seemed a lot when measured against the lack of any freedom whatsoever just a few generations before. If subsequent punishment remained an option, that may only seem to be meager progress when viewed from the vantage point of today. But there were voices, even as Blackstone wrote, who argued that freedom *did* mean more, that subsequent punishments such as seditious libel prosecutions were also inconsistent with the notion of freedom of the press.

### The Framers' Intent

What did the framers intend in 1791 — a little more than two decades after Blackstone's pronouncement — with the drafting of the First Amendment? Did they intend just to prohibit prior restraint, or did they mean to ban subsequent punishment as well? Professors Smith and Levy lead the opposing camps on this question. The arguments of Levy and the narrow constructionists — those who think the framers were only thinking of banning prior restraint — can be summarized this way:

- Blackstone's definition of the law was the notion of free speech and press commonly accepted at the time; so it must be what the framers were contemplating.

- If the framers thought they were banning subsequent punishment such as seditious libel prosecutions, then how could many of those same members of Congress, just seven years later, enact the Alien and Sedition Acts of 1798 with the express intent of punishing people who criticized government?

- Prosecutions for seditious libel may have ended with the John Peter Zenger trial in 1735, but state legislatures brought citizens up on contempt charges for criticizing government at least twenty times after that date and before passage of the First Amendment, thus indicating endorsement of subsequent punishment as an alternative to prior restraint.

The broad constructionists, who think the First Amendment went beyond banning prior restraint, counter:

- Blackstone may have summarized the English common law that had been practiced up to his time, but he was not summarizing U.S. law, and, indeed, why have a First Amendment at all if it was only intended to commemorate the common law supposedly already in place?

- The American experience with free press far exceeded the English common law. Not only were there no judicial prosecutions for seditious libel since 1735 and no examples of legislative contempt charges after independence in 1776, but politicians, printers and others exercised considerable freedom and espoused a distinctly libertarian theory of a free press in the century before the First Amendment. In short, how could there be so much freedom in practice if the law was so repressive?

---

[9] 4 WILLIAM BLACKSTONE, COMMENTARIES ON THE LAWS OF ENGLAND 151-52 (1769).

- James Madison, author of the First Amendment, passionately proclaimed that the Sedition Act violated the First Amendment and criticized the Federalist party members of Congress for returning America to "ancient ignorance and barbarism." The act expired by its own terms three years later, which was also the time that Republican Thomas Jefferson became president and pardoned the twenty-five or so Republican printers and journalists convicted under the act. Thus, it can be argued that Congress, as it has demonstrated many times since, was not invoking Constitutional principles in enacting the Sedition Act, but petty party politics.

- Why was a Sedition Act necessary if the common law already contemplated prosecution for seditious libel?

- Finally, the theme of the entire Constitution, not just the Bill of Rights, is the limiting of the power of government — in the words of Madison, "fortify[ing] the rights of the people against the encroachments of the government." A broad conception of freedom of speech and press is fundamental to limiting government and placing power in the people, and a narrow conception of the First Amendment would be inconsistent with the rest of the document. A freedom to criticize government without fear of prosecution is implicit in self-governing; so the First Amendment must have encompassed more than mere freedom from prior restraint.

It is impossible to provide a definitive answer to the question of whether the framers intended the First Amendment to go beyond freedom from prior restraint. Not only was there little debate on the question at the time, but the very issue of "framers' intent" is chimerical because there is no single way to gauge that intent. Whose intent? Do you look to Madison because he wrote the First Amendment, or to a poll of the legislators who voted on the measure, or to the sentiment in the states that ratified it? At what moment is the intent assessed? When proposed, when voted on, or when the framers first spoke on the meaning, which may be many years later? Does it matter if their understanding may be a bit different, more refined, or even contrary a few years later?

It may even be that there actually was no "intent" in the minds of the legislators at the time of passage. They may have deliberately left the First Amendment — and the rest of the Bill of Rights — vague to reduce controversy and facilitate passage. Who can be opposed to freedom of speech and press at that level of abstraction? The legislators may even have been forward-thinking enough to want to leave the interpretation to later generations, which would face problems the framers could not anticipate.

The answer is relevant because current interpretation of the Constitution often begins with an inquiry into the intent of the framers, and several Supreme Court justices seemingly would also end the inquiry there as well. But most jurists and scholars believe that the framers' intent is only one factor and that the Constitution is an evolving document that must take into account changing circumstances. So, even if we could determine what the framers intended regarding the First Amendment, and even if they only meant it to prohibit prior restraint, that would not necessarily bind current interpretation. Of course, once you break free from the historical intent, current interpretation could yield less as well as more freedom than the framers had in mind.

The strength of the doctrine against prior restraint, dating as it does to well before the First Amendment, is that it carries a certain cachet, a reminder of the baseline of individual freedom. The historical record of suppression and manipulation of the press by governments eager to promote their self-interest serves as evidence of what can happen in the absence of a prior restraint doctrine. The doctrine was created to serve two needs: individual freedom and limited government. At a minimum, the First Amendment was created to serve the same needs, with the same doctrine.

### Historical Prior Restraint Defined

A number of other conclusions can be drawn regarding the historical record. The nature of prior restraint that Blackstone, Milton and King Henry VIII had in mind involved a licensing system. Prior restraint, historically understood, involved (1) submitting *all* proposed publications (2) to government censors (3) who exercised considerable discretion regarding the content to be approved for publication, and it was (4) imposed specifically on publication (5) in advance of the publication.

Prior restraint did not refer to isolated efforts by government officials to suppress speech — a judge's order not to print a libelous tract, for example. Historically, the all-inclusiveness of the regulatory system, the fact that *every* proposed publication must be reviewed and approved, defined prior restraint. Therefore, even the works ultimately approved would still have been subject to prior restraint. "Prior review" is a phrase synonymous with "prior restraint."

Prior restraint meant suppression only by the government, although employers, parents and others obviously suppress speech regularly. Indeed, the historical system of prior restraint did not apply to speech at all, because licensing was a reaction to the introduction of the printing press, although speech in the form of parades or plays, for example, could conceivably be subjected to licensing or a permit system. But any interference with publication, even if it entirely precluded publication, did not constitute prior restraint if undertaken by individuals or institutions not associated with government.

If the standards for what could be published could ever be delineated clearly enough, then a censor's discretion would have been unnecessary, because the violations could be handled easily through subsequent punishment of individual violators. The considerable discretion exercised by censors is a critical objection to a system of prior restraint.

Of course, the aspects of prior restraint most commonly associated with it had to do with its narrow focus on controlling the actual publication, in advance of publication. Other government restrictions that might have the effect of inhibiting or entirely fore-closing publication would still not be included within the scope of prior restraint, even if they occurred in advance of publication. Restrictions on news gathering, for example, or punishment for not revealing a journalist's confidential source would not qualify as prior restraint because they were not directed specifically at stopping publication.

Consider the 1664 case of printer John Twyn. He was caught with proofs for a book claiming the government was accountable to the people and the people were entitled to revolt. Setting the standard for current journalists, Twyn refused to name the author. For his temerity he was hanged, drawn and quartered — a vicious and ultimate penalty that certainly precluded his publication. Technically, however, it was not prior restraint because the government did not specifically target publication.

A recent U.S. Supreme Court case is less brutal in its outcome but just as illustrative in its narrow conception of what constitutes prior restraint. In *Alexander v. United States*,[10] the government had prosecuted the owner of more than a dozen stores and theaters dealing in sexually explicit magazines and videotapes. Four magazines and three videotapes in the inventory were found to be obscene. Under a statute that allows the state to seize any property connected to a pattern of criminal behavior, the court ordered Ferris Alexander to forfeit his adult entertainment businesses and their inventories. The government then burned all of the magazines and videotapes.

Alexander maintained that the seizure and destruction of all his magazines and videotapes — which had *not* been found to be obscene and were therefore protected speech — constituted prior restraint. How could a ban on speech be more total than by destroying the speech, he argued? But the Court noted that the term "prior restraint" applied only to orders that forbid certain communications in advance of the communications; this, on the other hand, was only punishment for his obscenity convictions. Prior restraints, by their nature, stop the speech completely and perpetually, Chief Justice William Rehnquist wrote for the Court. Alexander could theoretically open another adult entertainment store the next day, restock with new inventory, and sell videotapes and magazines, all without obtaining prior approval from any court, Rehnquist wrote. The statute that allowed the government to seize property connected with criminal activity did not differentiate between expressive and non-expressive property, he noted, and to do so would encourage criminals to invest their ill-gotten gains in expressive property to protect them from forfeiture. He added:

By lumping the forfeiture imposed in this case after a full criminal trial with an injunction enjoining future speech, petitioner stretches the term "prior restraint" well beyond the limits established by our cases. To accept [Alexander's] argument would virtually obliterate the distinction, solidly grounded in our

---

[10] 509 U.S. 544 (1993).

cases, between prior restraints and subsequent punishments.[11]

## RATIONALES FOR PRIOR RESTRAINT

The doctrine against prior restraint can be considered merely a stepping-stone in the evolution of free speech and press; having served its purpose, it arguably can now be relegated to the dustbin of history. But there are reasons why distinguishing prior restraint from subsequent punishment still makes sense. The extent to which subsequent punishment is prohibited by the First Amendment is a different question, however, than whether prior restraint should be prohibited. The doctrine against prior restraint accords so wholly with the premises of limited government that disregarding the doctrine can be considered antithetical to the very form of government prescribed by the Constitution.

### Why Distinguish Subsequent Punishment?

Distinguishing prior restraint from subsequent punishment is a matter of some significance. The Supreme Court has said the First Amendment offers some protection from subsequent punishment. But the Court has also maintained that prior restraint is the most odious and least tolerable infringement of free speech. It would help to have some justification for the differential treatment beyond the venerable age of the prior restraint doctrine. After all, the point of subsequent punishment is to restrain speech in advance, too. Legislatures enact laws not to fill some prison quota, but to deter conduct; and laws punishing speech are no different. So how does the fact that the governmental force is applied prior to publication make it worse?

Professor Thomas Emerson attempted to answer that question more than forty years ago in an important essay.[12] First, he noted the *breadth* of prior restraint. Because all publications are subject to prior restraint, necessarily more communication is affected than when individual publications are targeted for subsequent punishment.

Second, Emerson emphasized the temporal aspect implicit in the two forms of regulation. With prior restraint, *timing and delay* are in the hands of government. At least with subsequent punishment, the publication reaches the marketplace of ideas, and the timing is at the discretion of the publisher. But the requirement of prior review imposes an obvious hitch in the editorial process, and sometimes mere delay can undermine the impact of a story, a factor of which the government is quite aware.

Third, a system of prior restraint has a *propensity toward an adverse decision.* To obtain a judgment after publication, no matter how stacked the trial may be, is still more bother than a system

of censorship, which entails, as Emerson wrote, "a simple stroke of the pen." The publisher has practical advantages after publication that are missing beforehand, when the advantages favor government. Thus, Emerson concluded, a system of prior restraint by its very nature makes it easier and more likely that the result will be adverse to the expression.

Similarly, matters of *procedure* favor the government in prior restraint. Prior restraint is an administrative procedure rather than a criminal procedure. In the latter, there are presumptions of innocence, burdens of proof, stricter rules of evidence — all of the trappings that are intended to make courts more deliberative and fairer forums than administrative agencies. Juries are available in criminal proceedings, but in an administrative proceeding the case is heard only by a minor bureaucrat.

Fifth, subsequent punishment provides an opportunity for *public appraisal and criticism.* Administrative proceedings can avoid the glare of publicity, but court hearings have a rich history of openness, which can be said to be more consistent with democracy and the goal of informing public opinion.

Sixth, the *dynamics of prior restraint* are such that absurd and unintelligent administration is foreordained. Emerson noted that the personality of a person willing to be a censor tends toward over zealousness. Not only that, but quite bluntly, "The function of the censor is to censor," Emerson wrote. The job title does not include promotion of expression: When in doubt, excise. The risk is far greater if the censor approves something that later meets with disapproval than if the censor censors. "The long history of prior restraint reveals over and over again that the personal and institutional forces inherent in the system nearly always end in a stupid, unnecessary, and extreme suppression," Emerson wrote.

Seventh, a system of prior restraint favors *certainty over risk.* Scholars and publishers sometimes note that the advantage of a licensing system is that there is a seal of approval if the work passes review, and the work is presumably immune from further sanction. But in a system of subsequent punishment, a publisher could be punished even if the publisher intended to remain within the law; the publisher may have made an error in interpretation and faced punishment for that error. Prior restraint reduces risk, Emerson agreed, but he added that favoring such a system implies a "philosophy of willingness to conform to official opinion and a ... timidity in asserting rights that bodes ill for a spirited and healthy expression of unorthodox and unaccepted opinion."

Finally, prior restraint systems have greater *effectiveness* going for them. When it comes to enforcement, the question is only whether the publication received prior approval. Everybody understands the rules of prior restraint. Indeed, the virtue of the system is its simplicity, at least from government's perspective. Cases are open and shut. Publishers either obey or they don't, and most do. Thus, prior restraint can be distinguished from subsequent punishment, not only definitionally, but rationally. "These ... considerations which underlie the doctrine of prior restraint ... are the reasons why the doctrine is not simply an arbitrary historical acci-

---

[11] *Id.* at 549-50.

[12] Thomas I. Emerson, *The Doctrine of Prior Restraint*, 20 LAW & CONTEMP. PROBS. 648 (1955).

dent, but a rational principle of fundamental weight in the application of the First Amendment," Emerson concluded.

### Premises of Prior Restraint

Apart from the definition, differentiation or appropriate treatment of subsequent punishment, prior restraint would be contrary to the First Amendment simply because it is inconsistent with a constitutional system of limited government. Professor Vincent Blasi, with a nod to Milton's *Areopagitica,* identified three premises underlying any system that endorses prior restraint, all of which are inconsistent with limited government and the libertarian theory that spawned the First Amendment:[13]

1. Prior restraint implies trust in the state rather than in the individual and public.
2. Speech is too risky in a democracy.
3. Individuals should have no autonomy from the state.

Blasi believes censorship to be an indignity to both writers and readers because the inherent paternalism of the state associated with censorship implies a general distrust of speakers and audiences. The state is a "suspicious, omnipresent tutor" if it must oversee and approve everything that is disseminated. "No system of political authority premised on the consent of the governed can admit the state to that role, whatever the behavioral consequences," Blasi wrote.

Preoccupation with government power is a trademark of the prior restraint doctrine and libertarian theory generally. Some contemporary free speech theorists are less skeptical of government and more concerned with what they see as the exercise of power by speakers, particularly the media and other corporations engaging in expression. They also are suspicious of the rational capacities of the public and propose a need for a "particularly active and absolute form of intervention by the state" that Blasi noted would be consistent with prior restraint.

Blasi responded that we may distrust the rationality of citizens, but the lesson of the First Amendment is that we distrust the state more. "To trust the censor more than the audience is to alter the relationship between the state and citizen that is central to the philosophy of limited government," Blasi wrote.

The second "troublesome premise" implicit in prior restraint is that speech is no different than other hazardous activities that are licensed or enjoinable. But licensing, Blasi explained, is a method of enforcing social norms. Free speech, by its nature, does not observe such norms; social conformity distorts public discourse. Speech — like democracy — is risky, but that is its virtue. "Only when the public views controversial speakers as normal people, with a legitimate role to play in the social system, can the fragile state-individual balance be maintained," Blasi noted.

The third and perhaps most obvious premise of prior restraint

is its subordination of individual autonomy. Blasi contended that prior restraints such as

licensing systems and injunctions coerce or induce speakers to relinquish full control over the details and timing of their communications. These regulatory systems must be premised, therefore, on the notion that either such control is not an essential attribute of the autonomy of speakers, or that such autonomy need not be respected. Either premise is objectionable.[14]

Thus, prior restraints cannot be consistent with the implementation of limited government. Those cases in which the Court has condemned the regulation as a prior restraint aptly illustrate the libertarian principles providing the intellectual foundation for the doctrine against prior restraint: distrust of government, acceptance of the risk inherent in speech, and individual autonomy from government.

## CASE LAW AND PREMISES

A review of the major cases embracing the prior restraint doctrine yields a treasure trove of commentary and rulings adopting the premises of the doctrine.

### Distrust of Government

In 1931, the Supreme Court in *Near v. Minnesota*[15] for the first time explicitly adopted the doctrine against prior restraint as constitutional law. In *Near,* the Court referred time and again to the danger of government regulation as a means of deterring criticism of government. The Court expressed concern about governmental abuse of its authority, with regard to both official misconduct and the exercise of the discretion necessary to implement the statute, which was intended to quell seditious libel. In striking the statute, the Court served notice that the prior restraint doctrine had broken free from its historical moorings.

The case involved a governmental ban on speech in advance of publication, based on content, but it was in the form of a nuisance statute enforced by judicial injunction. Jay M. Near had published in his *Saturday Press* malicious and scandalous libels adjudged to be nuisances. As partial punishment, he was ordered not to publish any more under threat of contempt of court.

Some Supreme Court justices argued that this was not a licensing system within the historical meaning of previous restraint but a remedy for past transgressions. The majority disagreed, however, arguing on three separate occasions in the opinion that the scheme "must be tested by its operation and effect." Thus understood, the Minnesota law was the "essence of censorship." Writing

[13] Vincent Blasi, *Toward a Theory of Prior Restraint: The Central Linkage,* 66 MINN. L. REV. 11, 69-82, 85 (1981).

[14] *Id.* at 85.
[15] 383 U.S. 697 (1931).

for the Court, Chief Justice Charles E. Hughes interpreted the statute as directed, not just at libels of private citizens, but "at the continued publication by newspapers and periodicals of charges against public officers of corruption, malfeasance in office, or serious neglect of duty."

This was a somewhat remarkable conclusion, given that the Court cited no specific language in the statute or in Minnesota Supreme Court opinions to support its conclusion that the statute concerned primarily libels of public officers. The Minneapolis mayor, a chief of police and a county attorney had been libeled by the defendant, but so had grand jurors, two newspapers and the "Jewish race." The Court, however, emphasized the "operation and effect" of the law when it noted that the newspaper had been targeted because its principal content was criticism of government. Seventeen times in the opinion, the Court expressed concern for protecting expression about official misconduct. Skepticism of government's capacity to oversee publications critical of government was hardly ameliorated by allowing a judge to determine if future issues of the *Saturday Press* were consistent with the "public welfare," the Court noted. If the statute operated to suppress expression critical of official misconduct, the doctrine against prior restraint was designed to thwart its operation as well as its effect.

The majority's expansion of the notion of prior restraint to include judicial injunctions, as well as administrative licensing systems, initiated an academic debate that continues to this day. It is significant, however, that in the Court's first pronouncement on prior restraint, it signaled its intention not to be bound by classical conceptions. Not coincidentally, it is also significant that this first opinion stands as tribute to the checking function, which the framers held dear and which presupposes governmental abuse of its authority.

The Court continued its concern for governmental exercise of discretion in matters relating to speech in a line of prior restraint cases, many of which were closer in kind to the licensing system contemplated by Blackstone. But a prior restraint case five years after *Near* illustrated that the Court considered taxation of the press as well as systems to suppress seditious libel as within the scope of prior restraint. The characteristic that was constant was a concern for government's abuse of its authority.

*Grosjean v. American Press Co., Inc.*[16] involved a Louisiana tax on selected newspapers that on its face did not even seem to qualify as a subsequent punishment. The tax was imposed, not on content, but on the basis of circulation, with all newspapers that circulated more than 20,000 copies weekly to pay a tax of 2 percent on gross receipts. The tax was imposed by statute, and the

penalty for failure to pay the tax was a possible fine of up to $500 as well as imprisonment not exceeding six months.

The Court traced the history of "taxes on knowledge" to the English experience, taking judicial notice of the framers' familiarity with that legacy. Writing for the unanimous Court, Justice George Sutherland observed that stamp taxes and taxes on advertising historically had not been intended to gain revenue, but to control the flow of information regarding government. They shared that characteristic with prior restraint, but of course, the same might have been said of seditious libel laws, which constituted subsequent punishments and which operated concurrently with the English system of taxes on the press. Justice Sutherland concluded his survey of English repression of the press with a quote from Eighteenth Century scholar and attorney Thomas Erskine: "The liberty of opinion keeps governments themselves in due subjection to their duties." The quote, although it is not clear from Sutherland's opinion, dates from the year after the First Amendment was enacted — and was made in defense of freedom from seditious libel.

The *Grosjean* case articulates quite nicely the checking function of the press and the threat that governmental abuse of its authority poses to that essential value of freedom of the press. Using the British government as its example, the Court assailed the "persistent effort" to curtail any criticism, true or false. The "predominant purpose" of the First Amendment was "to preserve an untrammeled press as a vital source of public information." The Court described public opinion as "the most potent of all restraints upon misgovernment." The key to informed public opinion is a free press performing the vital function of the Fourth Estate. "To allow it to be fettered is to fetter ourselves," the Court wrote.

From this emphasis on government's sensitivity to criticism and the importance of insulation for critics, the Court concluded that the First Amendment was meant to preclude "any form of previous restraint upon printed publications, or their circulation, including that which had theretofore been effected by these two well-known and odious methods," referring to a stamp tax and a tax on advertising.

A virtue of the prior restraint doctrine as it has come to be construed is that it puts a heavy burden, indeed an insurmountable burden if case outcomes are any indication, on government. While tests and even balancing have been advocated in the same breath as the doctrine against prior restraint, a great strength of the doctrine is that it brings historical weight to bear in asserting outright skepticism of government. Prior restraints are presumed unconstitutional, and it is up to government to bear the heavy burden of attempting to overcome that presumption. The doctrine has a pedigree that no test of compelling or overriding interests can match. The lessons embodied in the doctrine against prior restraint should not be forgotten, but they can easily be lost through mere balancing.

---

[16] 297 U.S. 233 (1936). Professor Emerson was particularly critical of the Court's application of the prior restraint doctrine in the tax cases. The doctrine could only be relevant to tax cases, he wrote, if it applied to any regulation that inhibited First Amendment freedom. "When employed in this way the concept becomes so broad as to be worthless as a legal rule," Emerson wrote. THOMAS I. EMERSON, THE SYSTEM OF FREEDOM OF EXPRESSION 511 (1970).

### Acceptance of Risk

Worst-case scenarios are integral to the second premise implicit in a system of prior restraint identified by Blasi: risk aversion. In imposing prior restraint, government is attempting to avert the consequences of speech that has yet to be uttered. This necessarily involves the government — including the courts that are passing on the constitutionality of the prior restraint — in gazing into crystal balls. Rationalizing the need for prior restraint thus lends itself to posing the worst possible consequence of the speech if it were to occur.

The only antidote to threats of worst-case scenarios is straightforward acknowledgment that speech does involve risk and that freedom includes freedom for the potent as well as the impotent. "That at any rate is the theory of our Constitution," Justice Oliver Wendell Holmes wrote. We "wager our salvation," he added, "upon imperfect knowledge." He addressed the penchant for concocting worst-case scenarios head-on when he then observed that we must be "eternally vigilant against attempts to check the expression of opinions that we loathe and believe to be fraught with death."[17] Freedom is not for the faint of heart.

Holmes' caveat against caution was tested in the Pentagon Papers case. There, if documents the government had classified as secret were published in the newspapers, then the alleged resultant danger would be "the death of soldiers, the destruction of alliances, the greatly increased difficulty of negotiation with our enemies, the inability of our diplomats to negotiate," as well as prolonging the Vietnam War and extended delay in freeing U.S. prisoners.[18] Dangers do not get any worse.

One might have wondered at this characterization of the danger, however, given that the Pentagon Papers were historical documents relating to U.S. involvement in the Vietnam War. They not only did not give away any planned troop movements or strategic objectives, but they contained nothing the North Vietnamese did not already know about. Indeed, the people most ignorant of their content was the constituency of the government that was attempting to conceal them.

The papers, for example, revealed that the U.S. government had deliberately engaged in a manipulative public relations campaign aimed at U.S. citizens and foreign allies with little relation to the actual war effort or negotiations, of which the North Vietnamese were, of course, intimately aware. Justice Hugo Black, voting with the majority to allow the *New York Times* and other newspapers to continue publication of a series based on the documents, identified what might have been the real danger that the U.S. government perceived: its own embarrassment.

In the last opinion he was to write before he died, Justice Black

zeroed in on the government's use of "national security" as its cover for censorship in the case. The phrase demonstrates a felicitous choice of words by the government. Advocating "security" is meant to be comforting, an appeal to our natural tendency to avoid risk. It also put the newspapers that would disclose these papers in the unappealing role of exposing us to hazards. But Justice Black cautioned that the word was "a broad, vague generality." He seemed to be suggesting that a government whose capacity for deception in conducting war was revealed in the papers would not hesitate to deceive in promising security to its citizens. Free speech does involve risks, but the framers of the First Amendment, who fully appreciated what it took to defend a nation, nevertheless understood that free speech provided the only real security, Black wrote.[19]

This paradox of security through risk is only one of many associated with the First Amendment: a freedom to espouse no freedom, freedom for the speech we hate, a right to be wrong. All, however, share an implicit acknowledgment of the risk of free speech. Such paradoxes perhaps explain why Professor Emerson wrote that the theory of freedom of expression "does not come naturally to the ordinary citizen, but needs to be learned."[20] One does not ordinarily choose the more hazardous course, much less associate risk with security. Prior restraint appeals to that impulse favoring the safer path. But the doctrine against prior restraint teaches not only that the government's worst-case scenarios seem not to come true when information is ultimately published, but that attempts to achieve security through suppression pose the greater risk. The risk is not in speech being published, but in it *not* being published. That, as Holmes said, at any rate is the theory of our Constitution.

### Regard for Individual Autonomy

The final premise of prior restraint that also conflicts with a constitutional system of limited government is a depreciation of individual autonomy. The Court in *Schneider v. State*,[21] for example, took note more than once of the police power to promote the public interest in regulating the public streets. But when municipal ordinances sought to license the dissemination of leaflets on those thoroughfares, the Court found that they infringed not only on individual speech, but a system of government:

This court has characterized the freedom of speech and that of the press as fundamental personal rights and liberties. The phrase is not an empty one and was not lightly used. It reflects the belief of the framers of the Constitution that exercise of the rights lies at the foundation of free government by free men. It stresses, as do many opinions of this court, the importance of

---

[17] Abrams v. United States, 250 U.S. 616, 630 (1919) (Holmes, J., dissenting).

[18] New York Times Co. v. United States, 403 U.S. 713, 763 (1971) (Blackmun, J., dissenting).

[19] *Id.* at 719 (Black, J., concurring).

[20] EMERSON, *supra* note 16, at 12.

[21] 308 U.S. 147 (1939).

preventing the restriction of enjoyment of these liberties.... Mere legislative preferences or beliefs respecting matters of public convenience may well support regulation directed at other personal activities, but be insufficient to justify such as diminishes the exercise of rights so vital to the maintenance of democratic institutions.[22]

If speaking in a public forum imposes burdens or inefficiencies on the state, such is the price of maintaining individual autonomy. The ordinance in *Schneider* was particularly odious to the Court in that it allowed a police officer, acting "as a censor," to determine what literature could be distributed and who would distribute it, and required pamphleteers to submit to an inquisition, photographing and fingerprinting. Such censorship struck at the heart of free expression because it placed discretion in the officer rather than the speaker. Moreover, the Court made clear that individual autonomy extended not only to the message but to the site of the speech: "[O]ne is not to have the exercise of his liberty of expression in appropriate places abridged on the plea that it may be exercised in some other place."[23]

The concept of individual autonomy answers the fundamental question in each prior restraint case: "Who is to decide?" The choice of what, when and where to speak is either left to the discretion of the speaker or overruled by the state. Autonomous speech is the condition precedent to the autonomous citizenship contemplated in the democratic model.

First Amendment doctrine, with its focus on individual autonomy, may be quaint in the eyes of those who advocate that individuals must yield to the public interest, whether the issue involves mandatory motorcycle helmets, zoning or bans on racist speech. But the First Amendment, as exemplified by the prior restraint doctrine in particular, is one of the last areas of constitutional law to uphold the democratic tradition as it was historically understood. If autonomy in speech is rejected, Robert Post observed, the implications go to the core of our belief in self-government, and "beguiling visions of progressive reform" should not obscure that democratic legitimacy, and not just autonomous speech, is at issue.[24]

## RECENT CASES

The doctrine against prior restraint shows amazing vitality despite having roots stretching back more than three centuries. Perhaps even more amazing is that cases involving prior restraint persist and questions still emerge. Drawing on those three centuries of history seems to facilitate answering the questions, however.

## *Origin of a Test*

The case in which the Supreme Court most recently employed the prior restraint doctrine shows evidence of distrusting government, embracing risk and prizing individual autonomy; and it contains the Court's most thorough analysis, which ironically was borrowed from some of its earliest First Amendment cases. Those early cases did not even involve prior restraint, and the analysis was taken not from the majority opinions, but from a dissent and a concurring opinion.

The first early case, *Abrams v. United States*,[25] involved a prosecution for publishing two leaflets in 1918 containing objections to U.S. military intervention against the Bolsheviks, who would ultimately form what came to be known as the Soviet Union. Justice Holmes had written an earlier opinion for the Court, in which he had framed the issue as "whether the words used are used in such circumstances and are of such a nature as to create a clear and present danger that they will bring about the substantive evils that Congress has a right to prevent."[26] He had endorsed the conviction of speakers in that case, but Harvard Law Professor Zechariah Chafee Jr. prevailed upon Holmes to impart more meaning to the clear and present danger test,[27] which he did in *Abrams*.

When he circulated his dissent to the majority opinion in *Abrams* and defended it at the justices' Saturday conference, Chief Justice Edward White, his long-standing friend and daily companion on the long walk home, asked him not to issue it. When he persisted, three justices took the highly unusual step of calling on him at his home, where his wife joined them in attempting to persuade him not to publish the dissent. Holmes did not relent, and the effect was electric. "A great noise of vilification and praise went up all over the country," wrote biographer Sheldon M. Novick.[28]

In his famous dissent, which has eclipsed the majority opinion and become the law of the land, Holmes stiffened the meaning of a "present danger." He wrote that "nobody can suppose that the surreptitious publishing of a silly leaflet by an unknown man, without more, would present any immediate danger." Opinions should be allowed "unless they so imminently threaten immediate interference with the lawful and pressing purposes of the law that an immediate check is required to save the country," he wrote. Holmes' stress on the immediacy of the danger before speech would be unprotected presents a nearly impossible hurdle to regulation, but, curiously, it also seems to protect only speech that is unimportant or ineffective or both. Still, it was a major milestone in the evolution of the First Amendment.

---

[22] *Id.* at 161.

[23] *Id.*

[24] Robert Post, *Meiklejohn's Mistake: Individual Autonomy and the Reform of Public Discourse*, 64 U. COLO. L. REV. 1109, 1137 (1993).

---

[25] 250 U.S. 616 (1919).

[26] Schenck v. United States, 249 U.S. 47, 52 (1919).

[27] *See* DONALD L. SMITH, ZECHARIAH CHAFEE JR., DEFENDER OF LIBERTY AND LAW 30 (1986); Fred D. Ragan, *Justice Oliver Wendell Holmes Jr., Zechariah Chafee Jr., and the Clear and Present Danger Test for Free Speech: The First Year, 1919*, 58 J. AM. HIST. 42-43 (1971).

[28] SHELDON M. NOVICK, HONORABLE JUSTICE — THE LIFE OF OLIVER WENDELL HOLMES 332 (1989).

Justice Holmes and Justice Louis Brandeis had a forty-year-old friendship before Brandeis was appointed to the Court, and they collaborated on some of the great opinions of their era. Brandeis joined in Holmes' dissent in *Abrams*, and Holmes joined Brandeis' concurrence in *Whitney v. California*,[29] a case in which a woman was convicted of criminal syndicalism for joining the Communist Labor Party. Brandeis' opinion concurring in the majority decision seemed to favor her acquittal, but because she did not raise at trial the argument that Brandeis presented, she could not do so on appeal, Brandeis wrote.[30]

This judicial restraint probably left Ms. Whitney unimpressed, but the plain fact is that Brandeis did not have the votes on the Court to overturn her conviction. So whether Brandeis labeled his lesson on First Amendment law a concurrence or a dissent seems less important than the fact that it fleshed out the clear and present danger test in a way that lower courts could apply it.

Brandeis pointed out that the Court had not yet determined "when a danger shall be deemed clear; how remote the danger may be and yet be deemed present; and what degree of evil shall be deemed sufficiently substantial to justify resort to abridgement of free speech." First, he turned the question around and suggested that the real danger lay in repression of speech and "that the path of safety lies in the opportunity to discuss freely supposed grievances and proposed remedies."

Brandeis believed that mere fear of serious injury did not justify suppression of speech. "Those who won our independence were not cowards.... They did not exalt order at the cost of liberty," he wrote. In the same libertarian vein, Brandeis indicated that the limited role of the state was to make individuals free to develop their faculties and to avoid "silence coerced by law — the argument of force in its worst form." He continued:

> To justify suppression of free speech there must be reasonable ground to fear that serious evil will result *if free speech is practiced*. There must be reasonable ground to believe that the danger apprehended is *imminent*. There must be reasonable ground to believe that the evil to be prevented is a *serious* one.[31]

To summarize, the speech must cause the alleged danger, the danger must be immediate, and it must be grave.

### Nebraska Press Association

Nearly a half century later, the Court expanded on these themes in its most recent press prior restraint case, *Nebraska Press Association v. Stuart*.[32] Erwin Simants had been arrested for the murder

of six people in a small Nebraska town. Three days later, Judge Hugh Stuart issued an order prohibiting the public dissemination of any testimony or evidence. The Nebraska Press Association appealed the prior restraint.

The Supreme Court granted *certiorari* and used the case to review its decisions involving the "heavy presumption" against the constitutional validity of prior restraint, including *Near v. Minnesota* and the Pentagon Papers case. That heavy presumption translated into a nearly impossible burden on government to justify the exercise of such authority and implicit trust in the state rather than speakers. "The thread running through all these cases is that prior restraints on speech and publication are the most serious and the least tolerable infringement on First Amendment rights," wrote Chief Justice Warren Burger for a unanimous Court.

He distinguished prior restraints from subsequent punishments, noting that penalties for violating a criminal statute or libel judgments do not become effective until after trial and all appeals are ended. "A prior restraint, by contrast and by definition, has an immediate and irreversible sanction," Burger wrote. "If it can be said that a threat of criminal or civil sanctions after publication 'chills' speech, prior restraint 'freezes' it at least for the time."

Burger noted the possible risk that pre-trial publicity posed for a defendant's Sixth Amendment right to a fair trial by unbiased jurors. But he also quoted from an earlier case praising the press as the "handmaiden" of justice, because it "guards against the miscarriage of justice."[33] As Brandeis might have put it, the risk of free speech is real, but the risk of enforced silence is greater. In particular, an effective check on governmental abuse would be missing.

In the Pentagon Papers case, Burger had voted with the three dissenters in favor of prior restraint. He seemed particularly bothered by the fact that the *New York Times* had three to four months to review and edit the classified documents, but the Court had very few days to digest the case. Why, he asked, after months of deferral, must the right to publish be vindicated so precipitously? He answered his own question five years later in *Nebraska Press Association*, noting it was a matter of the speaker's autonomy:

> Of course, the order at issue ... does not prohibit but only postpones publication. Some news can be delayed and most commentary can even more readily be delayed without serious injury, and there often is a self-imposed delay when responsible editors call for verification of information. But such delays are normally slight and they are self-imposed. Delays imposed by governmental authority are a different matter.[34]

As Brandeis had observed — and Milton before him — thinking and speaking are private, individual matters sensitive to governmental interference. If speakers are to maintain their autonomy,

---

[29] 274 U.S. 357 (1927).

[30] *Id.* at 379-80 (Brandeis, J., concurring).

[31] *Id.* at 375-76 (Brandeis, J., concurring) (emphasis added).

[32] 427 U.S. 539 (1976).

[33] *Id.* at 560 (quoting Sheppard v. Maxwell, 384 U.S. 333, 350 (1966)).

[34] *Id.* at 559.

the choice not only of what to say, but when to say it, must be left to individual discretion.

To uphold the prior restraint, Burger wrote,

[W]e must examine the evidence before the trial judge when the order was entered to determine (a) the nature and extent of pre-trial news coverage; (b) whether other measures would be likely to mitigate the effects of unrestrained pre-trial publicity; and (c) how effectively a restraining order would operate to prevent the threatened danger. The precise terms of the restraining order are also important. We must then consider whether the record supports the entry of a prior restraint on publication, one of the most extraordinary remedies known to our jurisprudence.[35]

First, Burger wrote, the trial judge had reasonably concluded that there would be intensive local and national press coverage. Judge Stuart had found "a clear and present danger that pre-trial publicity *could* impinge upon the defendant's right to a fair trial," the Court observed (emphasis added by the Court). But he was wrong. As Holmes and Brandeis had postulated, a clear and present danger requires immediacy; mere conjecture is insufficient.

Burger wrote that the trial judge's "conclusion as to the impact of such publicity on prospective jurors was of necessity speculative, dealing as he was with factors unknown and unknowable." Nobody could tell what would be disseminated, who would read or view it, what impact it would have, who would be picked as jurors, or whether they would be able to decide the case based solely on the evidence introduced in court. One cannot even be certain there will be a trial. Simants could plead guilty — or have a heart attack. When the Court referred to factors unknown and unknowable, the case was over. Once the burden of proof is assigned, that party loses, because it is impossible to prove factors unknown and unknowable. Because the government has a heavy burden to overcome the presumption of unconstitutionality, it loses.

Likewise, in the second step of the analysis, Burger noted that the government has the burden of proving no other measures would mitigate the effects of publicity. That, too, is unknown and unknowable, without actually implementing the measures. Multiple options exist: change of venue to a jurisdiction with less publicity, postponement of the trial to allow the effects of publicity to subside, intensive questioning of prospective jurors to determine possible bias, instructions to jurors on avoiding publicity and considering only evidence presented in court, sequestration of jurors, restraints on leaks by trial participants, and, of course, a new trial. The obligation to provide a fair trial is on the state, not the press, and if the state holds an unfair trial, it must hold another, fair trial or not try the defendant. The press cannot deny defendants their Sixth Amendment rights.

Third, the Court questioned the effectiveness of the prior restraint. That is, as Brandeis put it, would the danger result if the free speech in question were allowed? If the speech were stopped, would the danger stop, too? In *Nebraska Press Association,* the Court said the danger remained. The trial court might have had difficulty implementing its order regarding media outside the court's jurisdiction.

More telling, though, was the impossibility of stopping a whole community of 850 people from discussing the case and quite likely generating rumors that would be more damaging to the defendant than publicity. Although everybody was restrained from disseminating information about the case, only the media would leave behind evidence of disobeying the order. The townspeople — who constituted the pool of prospective jurors — would gossip no matter what the court decreed. If the restraint would be ineffective, that by itself is a reason for invalidating it.

Finally, the Court noted that the order was defective because it was vague and overbroad. Vague speech regulations inhibit speakers who cannot be sure if they will violate the regulation. An overbroad regulation might be constitutional if more narrowly crafted, but a regulation that proscribes protected speech as well as unprotected speech is constitutionally suspect. This court order, as modified by the Nebraska appellate court, banned "information strongly implicative of the accused." Would saying Simants had been arrested for six murders be "strongly implicative"? Too vague. If the order would cover such an allegation, then it would cover speech that would not prejudice the outcome because the jury would learn that as soon as the trial began anyway. Therefore, the order was overbroad as well.

### Applying the Test

So the case left a blueprint for how the Court would likely approach prior restraint cases in the future, whether the restraint involves fair trials or not. The Court is not willing, apparently, to merely determine if the government regulation qualifies as a prior restraint and declare it unconstitutional on those grounds alone, as it did in *Near v. Minnesota.*

First, the regulation must fit the definition of prior restraint, which has relaxed since the days of King Henry VIII, but is not so elastic to include every restraint on publishing, as the Court illustrated in *Alexander v. United States.*[36] Today, a licensing system would still qualify as prior restraint, unless the government imposed it on its own employees (as with CIA agents), a condition of accepting a government subsidy (although this area is still developing and the case law is somewhat inconsistent), or involved broadcasting or the high school or elementary press. As well, though, (1) a government prohibition (2) of a specific publication (3) based on its content (4) after the exercise of discretion and (5) in advance of publication would constitute prior restraint today.

---

[35] *Id.* at 562.

[36] *See* text accompanying *supra* note 10.

When a regulation is defined as prior restraint, it is presumed unconstitutional, and the government bears a heavy burden to overcome that presumption. This aspect cannot be emphasized too strongly, because the tendency is to give the government the benefit of the doubt and avoid the risk of speech. It is easy to concoct worst-case scenarios and hard to favor an abstract concept such as free speech, but the presumption weighs the balance solidly in favor of free speech at the outset.

To overcome the presumption of unconstitutionality, the government must prove that the danger is serious; that it is imminent; that the speech is the cause of the danger and that stopping the speech will stop the danger; that no alternatives to prior restraint will work; and that the terms of the prior restraint are neither vague nor overbroad. The prior restraint can fail at any of these steps and need fail only one to remain unconstitutional.

A danger can be serious without being imminent, as in the *Nebraska Press Association* case. Likewise, as Brandeis noted, a danger can be imminent without being serious. Advocacy of trespassing could be so persuasive that the speaker's audience immediately sought out backyards to traverse, but even so, it would not rise to the level of a serious danger justifying prior restraint. Seriousness is usually the easiest element of the test to meet, because the government's asserted danger is taken at face value, and the government is always able to posit a danger of some magnitude.

Imminence, on the other hand, is generally the element least likely to be demonstrated. Proving something will immediately and inevitably occur is almost impossible. Nobody can know what will happen in the future. The *Nebraska Press Association* Court echoed Brandeis' observation that fear of serious injury alone will not justify suppression when it wrote that the trial judge's conclusions regarding the impact of publicity were necessarily speculative. Conjecture is *always* possible; evidence of imminence rarely so.

But even if the danger is imminent, it need not be caused by the speech. If the danger occurs regardless of whether the speech is practiced, then the rationale for the restraint fails. This element of the test often comes into play when the proscribed speech is already in the public domain, as it was in the Pentagon Papers case where historical data was being suppressed. If the content of the speech is already available elsewhere, even if it poses an imminent danger, then there is no reason to stop the speech in a given case. The question is whether *the speech at issue in the case* causes the danger.

Alternatives to the prior restraint are almost always available to deal with the danger. The question here is not whether an alternative, narrower form of prior restraint would be preferable. That is an overbreadth question. Alternatives to regulating speech altogether are at issue in this context. Even if alternatives would impose substantial costs on government, as in moving the entire trial, regulating speech must be the last resort, not the first.

In any event, to preserve individual autonomy from government, the burden is on government to prove no means other than infringing on the speaker would adequately address the problem. Publishing something different or at a later time is not an alternative because it shifts the burden to the speaker, when government must do everything possible to defer to the speaker's discretion. The question is not why the speaker wishes to speak, but why the government wants to censor, and the burden is heavy.

### Legacy of Nebraska Press Association: CNN

Although the Supreme Court has not considered a prior restraint against the press in recent years, it did have the opportunity in 1990 and declined to do so. The case began when prison officials made tape recordings of conversations between Manuel Noriega and his attorney. Cable News Network obtained copies, but Noriega asked a judge to impose a prior restraint on the dissemination of the tapes to preserve his right to a fair trial.

The judge asked CNN to turn over the tapes so he could listen to them and decide whether they imperiled Noriega's fair trial right, but CNN refused. The judge imposed the ban, and CNN appealed. The case is muddied because the refusal to turn over the tapes became the issue that seemed to become more important in the court's mind than the constitutionality of the prior restraint. The case illustrates the legacy of *Nebraska Press Association* in the sense that the judge believed he had to have access to the tapes before he could apply the test. If the *Near v. Minnesota* approach had been in place, it would only have been necessary to define the regulation as a prior restraint and find it unconstitutional, without applying any test. Even though the burden seems impossible to meet after *Nebraska Press Association,* the fact that there is a test suggests that some prior restraints will pass the test; otherwise, why have a test?

As Professors Sigman Splichal and Matthew Bunker have noted, however, even if the trial judge had assumed the dissemination of the conversations on the tape posed a threat to Noriega's fair trial, without actually obtaining the tapes or hearing them, he could still have applied the test and the prior restraint would have been unconstitutional. Indeed, the prior restraint would have failed at every step of the test because of the questionable imminence, ineffectiveness of the restraint and availability of alternatives.[37]

In any event, the Supreme Court met and discussed the case on a Sunday morning, which it had not done in forty years, before deciding not to hear it. The denial of *certiorari* provoked a passionate dissent from Justice Thurgood Marshall, joined by Justice Sandra Day O'Connor. He considered the case to be "of extraordinary consequence for freedom of the press." Marshall noted the presumed unconstitutionality of prior restraint and that the proponent of "this drastic remedy" carries a heavy burden to justify it. He continued:

---

[37] Sigman L. Splichal & Matthew D. Bunker, *The Supreme Court and Prior Restraint Doctrine: An Ominous Shift?,* 3 MEDIA L. & POL'Y 11 (1994).

I do not see how the prior restraint imposed in this case can be reconciled with these teachings. Even more fundamentally, if the lower courts in this case are correct in their remarkable conclusion that publication can be automatically restrained pending application of the demanding test established by *Nebraska Press,* then I think it is imperative that we re-examine the premises and operation of *Nebraska Press* itself. I would grant the stay application and the petition for certiorari.[38]

The late Justice Marshall is no longer on the Court, and the fact that the Supreme Court declined to hear the case means it still has never actually decided in favor of a prior restraint against the press. Perhaps the best that can be said about this case is that it has not served as precedent for any other cases. Yet.

## Tory v. Cochran

The Supreme Court in 2005 decided a non-press prior restraint case, but it introduced no new law. Indeed, the Court took great pains to limit the scope of its ruling.

In the case, Ulysses Tory had been a client of well-known attorney Johnnie L. Cochran Jr., but Tory was dissatisfied with Cochran's services. Tory then engaged in several high-profile criticisms of Cochran, including writing letters to the bar association, picketing Cochran's office, and pursuing him in public while chanting threats and insults. As an example of Tory's criticisms, one of the signs used in the picketing read "Hey Johnnie, How Much Did They Pay $$ You to Fuck Me?"[39]

Cochran sued for libel in the California courts, and the court ruled that not only were the libels false and intended to extort money from Cochran, but that damages were an inadequate remedy because Tory said he would continue the campaign of defamation. So the court enjoined Tory and his agents or representatives from uttering, in the form of picketing or otherwise, any statements about Cochran in any public forum.[40] This, the U.S. Supreme Court ruled, was a prior restraint.

The Court unanimously found the restraint unconstitutional. It couched its nine-paragraph ruling in terms of causation and overbreadth. Tory's speech no longer represented any threat to Cochran because Cochran had died before the ruling came down. If the speech was not the cause of any danger, then it could not be restrained. Additionally, the terms of the restraint were so broad that the Justices noted in oral argument that it prohibited Tory's lawyer from criticizing Cochran — and even prevented Tory and his representatives from saying anything, including praise, regarding Cochran. Thus, the restraint was fatally overbroad.

If the Court had said no more, one might have been satisfied.

Indeed, one might even wonder why the Court had taken the case, because it added nothing to the law and the opinions of the California appeals court upholding the ruling had not even been published. Unfortunately, the Court said it left several questions unanswered, almost inviting further litigation.

Because Cochran had died, the Court said it did not resolve whether a permanent injunction could ever be issued in a defamation case against a public figure (a question First Amendment scholars had assumed had been resolved — in the negative — long ago). Furthermore, the Court said it did not resolve whether this injunction would have been valid before Cochran's death, which was the essential issue in the case.

Unless the Court was interested in rewriting many decades of prior restraint law, there could only be one outcome to this case. For the Court to say these remained unsettled questions is, well, unsettling.

## Business Week

In 1996, the U.S. Court of Appeals for the Sixth Circuit offered a ringing endorsement of the prior restraint doctrine.[41] Procter & Gamble had sued Bankers Trust, alleging fraud in a business deal. The trial judge authorized the parties before trial to interview each other and collect evidence that would be kept secret, although on file with the court. The secrecy order was intended to protect trade secrets and other confidential information.

The parties later notified the judge that *Business Week* magazine had obtained a copy of documents that the parties wanted to keep secret and asked the judge to order *Business Week* not to publish them. He sent a facsimile to McGraw-Hill, publisher of *Business Week,* imposing a prior restraint three hours before the presses would have rolled and without any chance for McGraw-Hill to contest the order.

The next day, McGraw-Hill's lawyers asked the judge to withdraw his order and also filed a request for an expedited appeal with the Sixth Circuit. The Sixth Circuit turned McGraw-Hill down on procedural grounds, as did Supreme Court Justice John Paul Stevens when McGraw-Hill asked him for an emergency stay of the order. McGraw-Hill was effectively at the mercy of the trial court.

The trial judge conducted hearings off and on for three weeks, during which he was most interested in learning how *Business Week* had obtained the documents in violation of the secrecy order. It turned out that someone in the Procter & Gamble public relations office had notified a *Business Week* reporter that some fascinating documents had been filed in the case, and another *Business Week* reporter had obtained them from an acquaintance at a New York law firm representing Bankers Trust. Apparently neither the reporter who obtained the documents nor the New York lawyer who provided them knew anything about the secrecy order.

---

[38] Cable News Network, Inc. v. Noriega, 498 U.S. 976 (1990) (Marshall, J., dissenting from *denial of certiorari*).

[39] Tory v. Cochran, 544 U.S. 734 (2005).

[40] *Id.* at 735-36.

---

[41] Procter & Gamble Co. v. Bankers Trust Co., BT Securities Corp., 78 F.3d 219 (6th Cir. 1996).

Upset that his order had been violated, the trial judge issued a permanent prior restraint ordering *Business Week* not to publish any of the documents it had obtained. But, at the same time, he held that the parties to the case had not given any good reason why the documents should be secret, and he made copies of them public — enabling *Business Week* and everybody else to obtain copies from the courthouse that could be published.

The Sixth Circuit panel concluded that the trial judge was trying to keep his prior restraint order from being appealed when he put the documents on the public record and allowed everybody, including *Business Week,* to publish them. But the Sixth Circuit was not fooled. Chief Judge Gilbert S. Merritt wrote that "appellate courts cannot allow themselves to be done out of their jurisdiction so cleverly.... So long as the permanent injunction remains technically in effect, we will review it as an injunction just as technically."

Merritt then turned to the First Amendment analysis, observing that the order was a "classic prior restraint" and therefore presumed unconstitutional. He applied textbook post-*Nebraska Press Association* analysis, beginning with a heavy burden on the proponent of prior restraint. The interests of Procter & Gamble and Bankers Trust fell vastly short of the "exceptional circumstances" required to justify prior restraint. According to the Sixth Circuit:

> Far from falling into that "single, extremely narrow class of cases" where publication would be so dangerous to fundamental government interests as to justify a prior restraint,... the documents in question are standard litigation filings that have now been widely publicized. The private litigants' interest in protecting their vanity or their commercial self-interest simply does not qualify as grounds for imposing a prior restraint. It is not even grounds for keeping the information under seal, as the District Court ultimately and correctly decided.... The permanent injunction, therefore, was patently invalid and should never have been entered.[42]

The court addressed three other bothersome aspects of the case. First, it criticized the trial judge for his extensive investigation into how *Business Week* obtained the documents. Not only did the trial court fail to conduct any First Amendment inquiry before sending the facsimile to *Business Week,* "but it compounded the harm by holding hearings on issues that bore no relation to the right of *Business Week* to disseminate the information in its possession," wrote the appeals court.

Preoccupation with the motive or knowledge of the speaker seems to cast the speaker in the role of suspect, when it is government whose motives are presumed suspect in prior restraint. Inquiring into how *Business Week* obtained the documents shifts the burden from the government to the magazine. In the Pentagon Papers case, the newspaper stories were based on documents that were not only classified, but stolen! Yet the origin of the stories was irrelevant to the outcome.

Second, the appeals court chided the trial court for relying on the Supreme Court opinion in *Seattle Times Co. v. Rhinehart*[43] as authority for its prior restraint. In that case, the Court ruled that if one litigant could be required to disclose confidential information to the opposing litigant, the opposing litigant could be required not to disseminate the information, at least until it was revealed in open court. The Sixth Circuit said *Rhinehart* only applied to the actual parties to a case. *Business Week* was not involved in this case and was not using a court to obtain information from another party; quite the opposite.

Third, the Sixth Circuit disapproved of the temporary prior restraint that stopped the *Business Week* presses and continued while the judge held hearings until the permanent prior restraint was issued. Temporary restraining orders, known in the legal trade as TROs, are common as a means of maintaining the status quo while a court gathers evidence and reaches a decision. Chief Judge Merritt quoted from a First Circuit case involving the *Providence Journal:* "This approach is proper in most instances, and indeed to follow any other course of action would often be irresponsible. But, absent the most compelling circumstances, when that approach results in a prior restraint on pure speech by the press it is not allowed."[44]

A temporary prior restraint is still a prior restraint. As the Sixth Circuit noted in considering if the situation was capable of recurring, there is no three-week exception to the prior restraint rule. Indeed, the court quoted from an opinion by Supreme Court Justice Harry Blackmun that "each passing day may constitute a separate and cognizable infringement of the First Amendment."[45]

The *Providence Journal* case should not be taken too far as authority, however. The First Circuit held that the newspaper could disobey a prior restraint order that was "transparently invalid" as long as it made a "good faith" effort to appeal it. That was contrary to earlier authority holding that the press should ordinarily abide by an order and work within the judicial system to overturn it, which is what McGraw-Hill did. The Supreme Court soon granted certiorari to hear the *Providence Journal* case.

"I have read the oral argument before Supreme Court and there is no doubt in my mind that the Supreme Court granted cert to reverse *Providence Journal,*" noted Ken Vittor, Senior Vice President and General Counsel for McGraw-Hill.[46] Perhaps fortunately for the press, media lawyer Floyd Abrams (who also argued the *Ne-*

---

[42] *Id.* at 225.

[43] 467 U.S. 20 (1984).

[44] In re Providence Journal, 820 F.2d 1342, 1351 (1st Cir. 1986), *modified on rehearing*, 820 F.2d 1354 (1st Cir. 1987).

[45] Nebraska Press Ass'n v. Stuart, 423 U.S. 1327, 1329 (1975) (Blackmun, J., in chambers).

[46] Speech during panel discussion at Practising Law Institute Seminar on Communication Law in New York City (Nov. 8, 1996).

*braska Press Association* case before the Supreme Court) was able to convince the Supreme Court to dismiss the *Providence Journal* case because of a procedural problem with the prosecutor who had been assigned to the case.

### Prior Restraint — of Terrorism?

Cryptography, or coding messages so that only the intended receiver can decipher them, dates to at least Julius Caesar. Decrypting, or attempts by unintended receivers to uncover the right "key" to break the code, probably dates back just as far. With the advent of computers, the science has taken a huge leap. The number of possible keys to recent encryption codes is 1 followed by 77 zeroes, or the total number of atoms in the universe, making the codes virtually unbreakable.[47]

Purchases made over the Internet are encrypted so that credit card data will be secure. Individual or corporate users can have other legitimate uses for encryption. Encryption can even be understood as the digital-age equivalent of the First Amendment right to be anonymous.[48] However, governments are greatly concerned about the use of encryption by terrorists, criminals and spies.

For example, Ramzi Yousef, who masterminded the bombing of the World Trade Center in 1993, apparently encrypted files that contained plans to crash eleven airliners, but the National Security Administration was able to crack his password and foil the plot. Al-Qaida operatives have used encryption in their communications, although it is not clear that any encrypted messages were used when they planned the September 11, 2001, attack on the World Trade Center.[49]

In the 1990s, in an effort to keep encryption techniques out of foreign hands, the U.S. government ruled that encryption technology was a "munition." Export of such technology had to be reviewed and licensed — and export included use of the Internet if foreign nationals might access the technology. Under Department of Commerce regulations, license applications could be held indefinitely, appeals of denials were to be decided "within a reasonable time," and there was no judicial review.[50]

Daniel Bernstein, a computer science professor at the University of Illinois in Chicago, developed a method of encryption, which he called "Snuffle." When informed he would need a license to distribute his source code within the general academic and scientific communities, he sued, claiming prior restraint.

The Court of Appeals for the Ninth Circuit determined that source code for encryption software was "speech." Computer programmers can read source code, and it expresses ideas little different from equations or graphs used in other fields. This was a controversial finding, to which the dissent objected because source code was "functional" rather than expressive. Source code is translated by computers into machine language (object code) – one's and zeroes – that then causes computers to work. Because source code controlled a computer without conveying information to humans during this translation, the dissent contended it could not be speech.[51]

But once the majority concluded that source code was, in fact, protected by the First Amendment, the court then found the regulations to be unconstitutional prior restraint. The regulations placed too much discretion in government officials and did not take into account the need for judicial oversight. "To the extent the government's efforts are aimed at interdicting the flow of scientific ideas — these efforts would appear to strike deep into the heartland of the First Amendment," the court wrote.

But what might have happened if this case had occurred after September 11, 2001? In a case the year after the Bernstein case, a professor at Case Western Reserve University wanted to post source code to his Web site, which would constitute exporting the code under the regulations. The Court of Appeals for the Sixth Circuit overturned the lower court finding that the code was not speech. Although the expressive elements were protected, the court indicated that the government's interest in regulating the functional elements must also be considered. In language that was prescient of 9/11, the court wrote that the exercise of presidential power on behalf of national security interests could sometimes outweigh free speech interests.[52]

The court returned the case to the lower court because changes in the encryption export regulations had just made it much easier to export source code, but the court's sensitivity to the balance of interests is mindful of a conclusion Professor Fredrick Siebert drew after surveying 300 years of English press law:

The area of freedom contracts and the enforcement of restraints increases as the stresses on the stability of the government and of the structure of society increase.[53]

Prior restraint doctrine does not exist in a vacuum. Judges interpret it, and they are subject to the same anxieties and pressures as anybody else. It follows that judicial opinions are a product of

---

[47] *See* Barak Jolish, *The Encrypted Jihad,* http://archive.salon.com/tech/feature/2002/02/04/terror_encryption (Feb. 4, 2002).

[48] *See* McIntyre v. Ohio Elections Comm'n, 514 U.S. 334 (1995); Talley v. California, 362 U.S. 60 (1960)(anonymous leafleting protected).

[49] *See* Lisa M. Krieger, *How Technology Is Used to Mask Communications,* SAN JOSE MERCURY-NEWS, Oct. 2, 2001, at 1F; Jolish, *supra* note 47; Jake Tapper, *Don't Blame it on Reno,* http://archive.salon.com/politics/feature/2002/01/02/reno/index_np.html (Jan. 2, 2002).

[50] Bernstein v. United States, 176 F.3d 1132, 1138 (9th Cir. 1999), *reh'g en banc granted and opinion withdrawn,* 192 F.3d 1308 (9th Cir. 1999).

[51] *Id.* at 1142. *See also* Junger v. Daley, 209 F.3d 481 (6th Cir. 2000)(also finding source code to be speech). Apparently, no rehearing was ever held in the *Bernstein* case because the government in 2000 changed its regulations to allow most exports of encryption products and software.

[52] Junger v. Daley, 209 F.3d 481 (6th Cir. 2000).

[53] SIEBERT, *supra* note 2, at 10.

their times. Sensitivity to First Amendment interests might well be waning in this period post-9/11 as people seem willing, even enthusiastic about trading freedom for what they hope to be security. Even the doctrine against prior restraint might not be adequate to protect speech in such a climate.

## SUMMARY

Questions remain in this age-old area of the law. If even temporary restraints are so disdained and obviously unconstitutional, should the speaker be able to maintain autonomy and speak at will? Can the judiciary effectively censor the press through TROs in a way that it would not allow the executive branch to do? Are speakers better off to sacrifice principles for pragmatism and obey the prior restraint so they can appear before the appellate court with "clean hands"? It probably helped *Business Week* that it could point out that the only party who had violated the court order was one of the litigants, and it obviously hurt CNN when it refused to turn over the tapes so the judge could review them.

The prior restraint doctrine will not survive simply because it has a venerable pedigree. The government will continue to attempt to control and manipulate expression, and the doctrine may have to adapt to remain viable. That's what happened in *Near v. Minnesota* when the Court expanded the doctrine to include judicial orders as well as administrative licensing. But the test that the Court used in *Nebraska Press Association* to test the constitutionality of a judicial prior restraint might be considered a step back, because the *Near* Court, and even Blackstone, contemplated a clear rule rather than a balancing test, albeit one heavily weighted in favor of speech. A test seems to open the door to temporary prior restraints at a minimum, and it may significantly diminish the strength of the doctrine in the long run.

Ultimately, the future of the doctrine depends on those who understand its roots and its rationale and can explain both, whether in editorials, court papers or coffee shops.

## FOR ADDITIONAL READING

Abrams, Floyd. "Prior Restraints," in 2 *Communications Law 2003,* New York: Practising Law Institute, 2003.

Anderson, David A. "The Origins of the Press Clause," 30 *UCLA Law Review* 455 (1983).

Barnett, Stephen R. "The Puzzle of Prior Restraint," 29 *Stanford Law Review* 539 (1977).

Bezanson, Randall P. *How Free Can the Press Be?* Urbana: University of Illinois Press, 2003.

Bickel, Alexander. *The Morality of Consent.* New Haven: Yale University Press, 1975.

Blanchard, Margaret A. "Filling in the Void: Speech and Press in State Courts Prior to Gitlow," in *The First Amendment Reconsidered — New Perspectives on the Meaning of Speech and Press,* Bill Chamberlin & Charlene Brown, eds. New York: Longman, 1982.

Friendly, Fred W. *Minnesota Rag: The Dramatic Story of the Landmark Supreme Court Case That Gave New Meaning to Freedom of the Press.* New York: Vintage Books, 1981.

Helle, Steven. "Prior Restraint by the Backdoor," 39 *Villanova Law Review* 817 (1994).

Helle, Steven. "Publicity Does Not Equal Prejudice," 85 *Illinois Bar Journal* 16 (January 1997).

Jeffries, John C. "Rethinking Prior Restraint," 92 *Yale Law Journal* 409 (1983).

Kalven, Jr., Harry. "The Supreme Court, 1970 Term — Forward: Even When a Nation is at War," 85 *Harvard Law Review* 3 (1971).

Knoll, Erwin. "National Security: The Ultimate Threat to the First Amendment," 66 *Minnesota Law Review* 161 (1981).

Litwack, Thomas R. "The Doctrine of Prior Restraint," 12 *Harvard Civil Rights-Civil Liberties Law Review* 519 (1977).

Mayton, William T. "Toward a Theory of First Amendment Process: Injunctions of Speech, Subsequent Punishment, and the Costs of the Prior Restraint Doctrine," 67 *Cornell Law Review* 245 (1982).

Meiklejohn, Alexander. *Free Speech and its Relation to Self-Government.* New York: Harper & Brothers, 1948.

Morland, Howard. "The H-Bomb Secret — How We Got It, Why We're Telling It," *The Progressive,* November 1979, p. 14.

Redish, Martin H. "The Proper Role of the Prior Restraint Doctrine," 70 *Virginia Law Review* 53 (1984).

Rudenstine, David. *The Day the Presses Stopped: A History of the Pentagon Papers Case.* Berkeley: University of California Press, 1996.

Scordato, Martin. "Distinction Without a Difference: A Reappraisal of the Doctrine of Prior Restraint," 68 *North Carolina Law Review* 1 (1989).

Strong, Frank R. "Fifty Years of 'Clear and Present Danger': From Schenck to Brandenburg — and Beyond," *The Supreme Court Review* 41 (1969).

Ungar, Sanford J. *The Papers & the Papers: An Account of the Legal and Political Battle Over the Pentagon Papers.* New York: Dutton, 1972.

# 5

# Regulating Pornography

*By F. Dennis Hale & W. Wat Hopkins*

☞ **Headnote Questions**

- *How are federal, state and local governments involved in the legal issue of obscenity?*
- *What is the difference between obscenity and indecency?*
- *How has the Supreme Court defined speech that is obscene and, therefore, not protected by the First Amendment?*
- *How does the law shield children from obscene or erotic messages?*
- *How are zoning laws used to regulate obscene material?*
- *How have ratings systems evolved?*

Cases involving Paul Cohen and Robert Mapplethorpe illustrate how judges, artists and jurors can disagree about what is obscene or indecent.

In 1968, Cohen was sentenced to thirty days in jail for disturbing the peace by wearing a jacket in the Los Angeles County Courthouse bearing the inscription, "Fuck the Draft." When the U.S. Supreme Court reversed the conviction, Justice John Marshall Harlan conceded that the message was distasteful to many people but noted that "it is nevertheless often true that one man's vulgarity is another's lyric."[1]

Two decades later, residents of Cincinnati debated issues of decency and taste when a grand jury indicted an art museum director for exhibiting photographs by Robert Mapplethorpe, some of which portrayed homoerotic subject matter. The photographer, accustomed to defending his controversial photographs, once said there is little difference between a photograph "of a fist up someone's ass" and a photograph of carnations in a bowl. At the conclusion of the criminal trial for obscenity, a Cincinnati jury sided with Mapplethorpe and exonerated the museum director.

Despite the outcomes of the two cases, many believe that both Cohen's jacket and Mapplethorpe's photographs are, if not obscene, indecent. The cases, then, demonstrate the subjectivity and disagreement that surround pornography and obscenity. A discussion of these controversial issues must necessarily begin with an understanding of terms, particularly "obscenity," "pornography," "erotica" and "indecency."

Indecency, the broadest of the four terms, refers to material — both sexual and non-sexual — that is offensive to manners or morals. Indecency is as much a question of taste and ethics as it is an issue of legality. Broadcast stations, newspapers and magazines generally avoid disseminating messages that would be judged indecent by most of their consumers — the repeated use of harsh profanities, for example.

Obscenity, as that term is commonly used, is similar to indecency because it is defined as including both sexual and non-sexual meanings. It is material that is disgusting to the senses or abhorrent to morality or virtue. On a ladder of offensiveness, obscenity is up a few rungs from indecency. The adjective "obscene" has been used to deride a variety of non-sexual targets including petroleum company profits, movie violence and television toy ads targeted at children. Most often, however, "obscenity" has a sexual connotation and refers to graphic portrayals of sex acts intended to arouse lustful thoughts.

The terms "pornography" and "erotica" also refer to graphic portrayals of sex for a lustful purpose. Some such portrayals, such as classic photographs or paintings of nude models, are less graphic

---

[1] Cohen v. California, 403 U.S. 15, 25 (1971).

and explicit. But even the milder portrayals of sexuality may be illegal if children are likely to be watching on television or if sold directly to children. "Erotica" is generally a more neutral term, while "pornography" is material that is demeaning.

In this chapter, the terms "pornography" and "obscenity" are used in the legal sense. "Pornography" refers to material that explicitly portrays sex acts for the purpose of sexual arousal. Such material is protected unless it is determined to be obscene. The term "indecency" is used in this chapter to refer to media portrayals of sexual behavior that are milder and less explicit than obscenity and that are protected by the First Amendment for adults. The terms "hard-core" and "soft-core" have similarly been used to distinguish between more explicit and less explicit sexual content.

Erotic expression and obscenity are important because they exist at the outer limits of protected speech. Obscenity, fighting words and threats are narrow categories of speech that are unprotected by the First Amendment. The expansion and contraction of these categories mirror the vigor of free speech and thought in the United States.

Obscenity is a legal issue that never dies. A constant tension exists between free speech liberals and conservatives over the control of sexually explicit speech. The controversy predates the Greek philosopher Aristotle, who advocated that legislators should banish from the state, as they would any other evil, all unseemly talk and indecent remarks. The Supreme Court, state appellate courts, Congress, state legislatures, city councils and local police and prosecutors are often involved in indecency issues — which seem to surface periodically.

## OBSCENITY AND THE LAW

The pornography issue is entertaining, controversial, stimulating, informative and even humorous. Many a cartoon in the 1960s made light of robed appellate court justices, representing the nation's keenest minds on constitutional law, watching hours of porn movies to determine whether they were obscene.

But there is a serious side as well. Obscenity laws make it a crime to sell some erotic materials, even to willing adults. A felony conviction for disseminating obscenity may result in years of imprisonment, hefty fines or attorneys' fees and the forfeiture of property. Such a conviction amounts to a socially sanctioned punishment for the dissemination of ideas. Some may find the ideas offensive, crude and without merit, but they are ideas nonetheless.

In addition, a person convicted more than once for disseminating obscene material may be classified a racketeer and punished even more severely under RICO laws — the abbreviation stands for *racketeer influenced and corrupt organizations.* An obscenity RICO conviction in Indiana means a maximum of ten years in prison, $20,000 in fines and forfeiture of business property.[2] When Ferris Alexander was convicted by federal authorities of disseminating obscenity, he was sentenced to six years in federal prison, fined $100,000 and ordered to forfeit $9 million in business assets.[3]

Supreme Court rulings in obscenity law fall into two basic areas. First, the Court interprets federal statutes and regulations that control or prohibit the creation and distribution of erotic material. This body of law includes the Federal Communications Act, rules and regulations of the Federal Communications Commission and U.S. Postal Service, laws controlling imports and exports, and regulations governing interstate commerce. Obscenity laws, like statutes on almost any subject, contain vague provisions that courts must interpret. For example, if U.S. Customs agents in New York City intercept pornographic films shipped from Germany to New Hampshire, what laws and standards apply — those of New York, Germany or New Hampshire? If federal statutes are silent on such issues, federal appellate courts must divine rules of law by relying on other legal precedents.

More importantly, the Supreme Court decides how far federal and state governments may go in restricting erotic speech. More than sixty years ago, in *Near v. Minnesota,* the Court said that obscenity was one of a few, narrow classes of speech that is unprotected by the First Amendment.[4] *Near* provided no guidelines, however, and it would be another twenty-six years before the Court began the difficult task of drawing the line between speech that was obscene (and therefore illegal), and speech that was nonobscene (and protected by the Constitution).

State legislatures and supreme courts are also sources of obscenity regulation. And local police and prosecutors are the major source of enforcement, or lack of enforcement, of state obscenity law. Neither the First Amendment nor federal statutes mandate that states enact and implement obscenity laws. State judges in Oregon and Hawaii, for example, have exercised their option to decriminalize the sale of obscenity to adults. And in some metropolitan areas, political liberalism and a profit motive discourage the enforcement of obscenity laws. By contrast, a few cities — like Cincinnati — vigorously prosecute obscenity.

When state and local governments control obscenity, they rely on a general principle called "police power." The term is not what it sounds like — it has little to do with the official duties of police officers. This broad legal power allows states to prohibit all things inimical to the comfort, safety, health and welfare of society. The police power authorizes the legislative branch of state governments to enact laws to protect the peace, good order, morals and health of communities. Of course, state and federal constitutions limit how far states may go in exercising their police powers.

## OBSCENITY AND SOCIETY

But is pornography clearly a threat to public safety, health and

---

[2] *See* Fort Wayne Books, Inc. v. Indiana, 489 U.S. 46 (1989).

[3] Alexander v. United States, 509 U.S. 544 (1993). *See also* United States v. X-Citement Video, Inc., 513 U.S. 64 (1994).
[4] 283 U.S. 697 (1931).

morality? The creation and sale of pornography traditionally have been entangled with other fringe and illicit services such as gambling, prostitution and drugs. But times change. Video rental stores located in malls and suburban neighborhoods isolated from illegal drugs and prostitution derive substantial revenue from sexually explicit videos that may or may not be legally obscene.

Sociologists and political activists are divided on whether adult pornography is harmful. Theoretically, private behavior should not be criminalized unless it is harmful to specific individuals. But researchers and political groups disagree about the effects of pornography. Two presidential commissions have studied the issue. President Lyndon Johnson created the Commission on Obscenity and Pornography in 1968. Two years and thousands of dollars later, during the Nixon Administration, the commission concluded that neither hard-core nor soft-core pornography leads to antisocial behavior and thus should not be prohibited. Eighteen years later, however, the U.S. Attorney General's Commission on Pornography, called the "Meese Commission" for then Attorney General Edwin Meese, concluded that pornography is pervasive in society and recommended vigorous enforcement of obscenity laws.

Many people, including a number of social scientists who have researched obscenity, oppose obscenity laws. They see erotica as a private, moral issue that exists beyond the reach of government. They argue that, in fact, moderate consumption of erotica — like wine, ice cream or even marijuana — is compatible with physical and mental health. Sallie Tisdale defended pornography for women in a 1992 *Harper's* magazine article and in a 1994 book.[5] She wrote: "I want never to forget the bell curve of human desire, or that few of us have much say about where on the curve we land." And Canadian philosopher F. M. Christensen provided a reasoned defense of pornography in his 1990 book, *Pornography: The Other Side*, in which he argued, "We constantly hear about sex criminals found to own pornography — ignoring all those who do not, and all the non-criminals who do. Similar stories of rapists and murderers who were Bible readers can equally well be found."[6]

Proponents of strict enforcement of obscenity laws cite history and research findings to defend their position. They point out that many cultures traditionally have controlled erotic expression. The *Bible* may include bawdy tales of prostitutes and adulterers, but it tells them discreetly without close-ups of genitals. They point to studies showing that men exposed to explicit videos become more callous in their attitudes toward women and to a study that shows a strong correlation between the consumption of men's girlie magazines and the incidence of sex crimes against women. Two feminists, Catherine MacKinnon and Andrea Dworkin, have

been particularly active in fighting pornography, which they define as the graphic, sexually explicit subordination of women. They argue that it presents women "as sexual objects for domination, conquest, violation, exploitation, possession, or use, or through postures or positions of servility or submission or display."[7] A 1984 ordinance in Indianapolis adopted this argument, but a U.S. Circuit Court of Appeals found it to be unconstitutional.[8]

Some federal judges, however, support attempts by states to control pornography and public nudity. Supreme Court Justice Antonin Scalia observed in 1991 that Indiana's nudity law would be violated "if 60,000 fully consenting adults crowded into the Hoosier Dome to display their genitals to one another, even if there were not an offended innocent in the crowd."[9] In March 2000, a more unified Supreme Court voted to uphold an Erie, Pennsylvania, ordinance that banned public nudity and thus prohibited erotic dancers in bars from performing totally nude.[10] The majority gave state and local governments broad latitude for creating and implementing such laws. Two justices said that local governments needed no justifications other than public morality to ban totally nude dancing in public. And four justices insisted on only the slimmest of justifications, stating that local government could justify such regulations by citing studies from other states and cities that documented secondary effects of nude, barroom dancing. Such secondary effects include sex crimes, prostitution and harm to property values.

## OBSCENITY AND THE SUPREME COURT

Justice Scalia's colorful observation — part of a lively history of Supreme Court jurisprudence in the area of erotic speech — is from a concurring opinion in a case involving nude dancing. Darlene Miller, a dancer at the Kitty Kat Lounge in South Bend, Indiana, argued that nude dancing was a form of protected expression. Indiana, however, said the state had a right to require all public performers to at least wear pasties and G-strings, and the Supreme Court agreed in a decision that is representative of the Court's history in pornography law.

In his majority opinion, Chief Justice William Rehnquist insisted that Indiana had a right to combat public nudity, conceding that nude dancing was "expressive conduct within the outer perimeters of the First Amendment." But, Rehnquist observed, "It is possible to find a kernel of expression in almost every activity a person undertakes."[11] Byron White, joined by three other justices, dissented, arguing that non-obscene, nude dancing performed before consenting adults was protected expression. Justice David

---

[5] SALLIE TISDALE, TALK DIRTY TO ME: AN INTIMATE PHILOSOPHY OF SEX (1994); Sallie Tisdale, *Talk Dirty to Me: A Woman's Taste in Pornography*, HARPER'S, Feb. 1992, at 37.

[6] F.M. CHRISTENSEN, PORNOGRAPHY: THE OTHER SIDE 126 (1990). *See also*, DENNIS HOWITT, CRIME, THE MEDIA AND THE LAW (1988) (reviewing the statistical studies of social scientists in America and Britain on the relationship between pornography and crime).

[7] ANDREA DWORKIN & CATHERINE MACKINNON, PORNOGRAPHY AND CIVIL RIGHTS: A NEW DAY FOR WOMEN'S EQUALITY 113-14 (1988).

[8] American Booksellers Ass'n v. Hudnut, 771 F.2d 323 (7th Cir. 1984).

[9] Barnes v. Glen Theatre, 501 U.S. 560, 575 (1991) (Scalia, J., concurring).

[10] Erie v. Pap's A.M., 529 U.S. 277 (2000).

[11] *Barnes*, 501 U.S. at 570.

Souter joined Scalia in his attack on the concept that consent should affect the outcome of the case.

This kind of fragmentation — and worse — dominated Supreme Court jurisprudence in obscenity law for more than thirty years. Typical was the 1966 case, *Memoirs v. Massachusetts*, in which Justice William Brennan presented a three-part test to determine whether a work was obscene.[12] Two other justices signed Brennan's plurality opinion holding that the 1749 novel, *Memoirs of a Woman of Pleasure*, was not obscene; two justices concurred and voted to overturn the conviction for reasons articulated in other Court opinions; another judge wrote his own concurrence; and three justices filed separate, dissenting opinions.

William Douglas, a staunch First Amendment supporter, concurred in the judgment, he wrote, because the First Amendment absolutely protected obscene speech: "Publications and utterances were made immune from majoritarian control by the First Amendment, applicable to the States by reason of the Fourteenth. No exceptions were made, not even for obscenity."[13]

Justice Tom Clark disagreed with both Douglas and Brennan. The new test, he wrote, "gives the smut artist free rein to carry on his dirty business" and "preying upon prurient and carnal proclivities for its own pecuniary advantage."[14]

The *Memoirs* definition of obscenity, which was an expansion of a definition in the 1957 case of *Roth v. United States*,[15] made it difficult to prosecute erotic works primarily because they were required to be "utterly without redeeming social value." Most films or books contain a kernel of a story line or smidgen of non-sexual plotting that amount to some social value.

The social value test was suggested in *Roth* and formally adopted in *Memoirs*. Under the combined *Roth/Memoirs* test, other appellate courts found most erotic materials to be non-obscene and thus protected by the Constitution. Adult bookstores and theaters proliferated; two presidential commissions studied pornography; and the Supreme Court generally ruled in favor of free speech on obscenity matters. Justices on the Supreme Court, however, were divided on how to define obscenity and whether they should be spending so much time perusing erotic materials. For example:

- In 1964, the Court invalidated the $2,500 fine of a Cleveland Heights theater manager for showing *Les Amants*. Justice Potter Stewart conceded that he could not intelligibly improve on the legal definition of obscenity: "But I know it when I see it, and the motion picture involved in this case is not that."[16]

- In 1966, Justice Hugo Black objected to "saddling this Court with the irksome and inevitably unpopular and unwholesome task of finally deciding by a case-by-case, sight-by-sight personal judgment of the members of this Court what pornography (whatever that means) is too hard core for people to see or read."[17]

- In 1967, the Court reversed obscenity convictions from New York, Kentucky and Arkansas for distribution of the publications *High Heels, Gent, Swank, Lust Pool* and *Shame Agent.* The justices disagreed on what rule of law to apply but deemed the material protected "whichever of these constitutional views is brought to bear."[18]

- In 1968, a justice noted that the Court had published fifty-five separate opinions for 130 obscenity cases since *Roth*, that this was a "chaotic state of affairs" that was "unmatched in any other course of constitutional adjudication."[19]

- And in 1970, Chief Justice Warren Burger complained about assuming the role of a "supreme and unreviewable board of censorship for the 50 states."[20]

The struggles the Court had in defining and regulating obscenity were mirrored throughout the judicial system. Some scholars, attorneys and judges joined Justices Black and Douglas in their opposition to all obscenity laws, but most jurists and observers agreed that the task was unavoidable. Indeed, many so-called absolutists who believe that consenting adults have a right to view whatever they desire, agree that lines must be drawn for material aimed at children, for required reading materials for juveniles in public high schools, or for material that is obtrusive and unavoidable, such as billboards.

If limits must be imposed for materials that are available to children, the central question becomes, "Where are those lines drawn?" Federal District Court Judge Bruce Jenkins emphasized the difficulty in drafting such definitions in a 1982 decision, in which he declared the Utah cable obscenity statute to be unconstitutional:

I'm an old legislator. I am appreciative of the legislative process. I was President of the State Senate some years ago. I respect those who participate in the legislative process very, very much. Nevertheless the extremely difficult drafting problems that exist in any effort to deal with the areas of expression requires exquisite care by the legislature and conscientious conformity to exacting constitutional standards. Free expression is so important to the well being of our whole social structure that any limitations must be viewed by the most critical of legislative eyes.[21]

[12] 383 U.S. 413 (1966). Under the test, a work was obscene if (1) the dominant theme of the material taken as a whole appealed to a prurient interest in sex; (2) the material was patently offensive because it affronted contemporary community standards relating to the representation of sexual matters; and (3) the material was utterly without redeeming social value.

[13] *Id.* at 427 (Douglas, J., concurring).

[14] *Id.* at 441-42 (Clark, J., dissenting).

[15] 354 U.S. 476 (1957).

[16] Jacobellis v. Ohio, 378 U.S. 184, 197 (1964).

[17] Mishkin v. New York, 383 U.S. 502, 516-17 (1966).

[18] Redrup v. New York, 386 U.S. 767, 771 (1967).

[19] Interstate Circuit v. Dallas, 390 U.S. 676, 704-05 (1968) (Harlan, J., concurring and dissenting).

[20] Walker v. Ohio, 398 U.S. 434, 443 (1970) (Burger, C.J., dissenting).

[21] Home Box Office v. Wilkinson, 531 F. Supp. 986, 995 (D. Utah 1982).

In 1973, the fragmentation on the Supreme Court abated when five judges, for the first time since *Roth,* agreed on where some of those lines should be drawn. The definition of obscenity established in *Miller v. California*[22] continues to be the law today.

### Miller v. California

Marvin Miller sent a mass mailing to California residents, promoting four illustrated books — *Intercourse, Sex Orgies Illustrated, Man-Woman* and *An Illustrated History of Pornography* — and a film — *Marital Intercourse.* A restaurant owner and his mother in Newport Beach who received copies of the brochure complained to police. Miller was eventually charged with violating California's obscenity statute.

The Supreme Court described the brochure as consisting primarily of "pictures and drawings very explicitly depicting men and women in groups of two or more engaged in a variety of sexual activities, with genitals often prominently displayed."[23] Five justices, in an opinion written by Chief Justice Warren Burger, found the brochure obscene under the Court's new definition:[24]

(1) whether the average person, applying contemporary community standards, would find that the work, taken as a whole, appeals to the prurient interest;
(2) whether the work depicts or describes, in a patently offensive way, sexual conduct specifically defined by applicable state law;
(3) whether the work, taken as a whole, lacks serious literary, artistic, political, or scientific value.

The first two parts of the *Miller* obscenity test were quite similar to the first two parts of the *Memoirs* test. In part three of the *Miller* test, however, the Court rejected the requirement that a work be utterly without redeeming social value and replaced it with the more restrictive requirement that the work lack serious value. In addition, the *Memoirs* definition used the broad adjective "social" to qualify value; the *Miller* test specified that the value be literary, artistic, political or scientific, omitting, for example, entertainment value. Thus, the *Miller* test appeared to make obscenity prosecutions easier by changing the third part of the *Memoirs* test.

On the same day that the Court decided *Miller,* it decided four other obscenity cases, all by 5-4 votes, clarifying a variety of constitutional provisions in obscenity law. Justice Douglas dissented in all cases, reiterating his position that the First Amendment protects even obscene material; Justice Brennan, joined by Thurgood Marshall and Potter Stewart, dissented, arguing that "obscenity" could not be defined sufficiently to give notice to producers of ex-

plicitly sexual material and, therefore, should be decriminalized.

In *Kaplan v. California,* the Court decided that photographs and drawings were not necessary for a work to be obscene; words alone are sufficient.[25] *Kaplan* involved *Suite 69,* a book sold by the Peek-A-Boo Bookstore, one of 250 adult bookstores in Los Angeles. The Court described the book as consisting "entirely of repetitive descriptions of physical, sexual conduct, 'clinically' explicit and offensive to the point of being nauseous."[26] The Court said the book contained almost every conceivable variety of sexual contact, homosexual and heterosexual, regardless of whether a reader sampled every fifth, tenth or twentieth page, and regardless of the page upon which the reader started.

In *Paris Adult Theatre I v. Slaton,*[27] the Court confirmed that adult movies were obscene, even when they were marketed discreetly. The Court described the Atlanta adult movie house as having a "conventional, inoffensive theatre entrance, without pictures." And the entrance door had the sign, "Adult theatre — you must be 21 and able to prove it. If viewing the nude body offends you, please do not enter." The fact that the theater had a tasteful, non-exploitative exterior and that it restricted its clients to interested adults did not exempt it from obscenity prosecution.

Finally, the Court upheld two federal prosecutions for importing obscene material into the United States for private, personal use and for the transportation of obscene material in common carriers in interstate commerce.[28]

### Miller Part 1: The Prurient Interest Test

The first prong of the *Miller* test — "Whether the average person, applying contemporary community standards, would find that the work, taken as a whole, appeals to prurient interest" — is the easiest to satisfy. It requires that an erotic work be judged according to average persons — not particularly susceptible and sensitive persons or totally insensitive persons. And the work is judged according to local, contemporary standards, which may vary from community to community. Wrote the *Miller* majority:

It is neither realistic nor constitutionally sound to read the First Amendment as requiring the people of Maine or Mississippi to accept public depiction of conduct found tolerable in Las Vegas or New York City.... People in different states vary in their tastes and attitudes, and this diversity is not to be strangled by the absolutism of imposed uniformity.[29]

The first part of the *Miller* test requires that the overall work

22 413 U.S. 15 (1973).
23 *Id.* at 18.
24 *Id.* at 24.

25 413 U.S. 115 (1973).
26 *Id.* at 116-17.
27 413 U.S. 49 (1973).
28 United States v. 12 200-Ft. Reels of Super 8mm Film, 413 U.S. 123 (1973); United States v. Orito, 413 U.S. 139 (1973).
29 413 U.S. at 32-33.

## The Transition of the Obscenity Test

### The rationale:

" ... implicit in the history of the First Amendment is the rejection of obscenity as utterly without redeeming social importance."

**Roth (1957)**
**Roth-Memoirs (1966)**
**Miller (1973)**

### Prurient Interest:

The average person, applying contemporary community standards must find that the dominant theme of the material, taken as a whole, appeals to the prurient interest.

The dominant theme of the material, taken as a whole, must appeal to the prurient interest in sex.

An average person, applying contemporary, local community standards, must find that the work, taken as a whole, appeals to the prurient interest.

### Patent Offensiveness:

The material is patently offensive because it affronts contemporary community standards.

The work depicts in a patently offensive way sexual conduct specifically defined by applicable state law.

### Value of the Work:

The material is utterly without redeeming social value.

The work lacks serious literary, artistic, political or scientific value.

---

judge noted: "The magazine's overwhelming effect, obviously planned, is to create sexual excitement and stimulation, to scratch the itch — or to create the itch itself — of prurient interest."[31]

### Miller Part 2: The Patently Offensiveness Test

The second prong of the *Miller* test is "Whether the work depicts or describes, in a patently offensive way, sexual conduct specifically defined by the applicable state law."

The same federal judge who found that *Penthouse* appealed to a prurient interest in sex also found that it satisfied the second part of the *Miller* test: The sexual portrayal was sufficiently graphic to be considered patently offensive. Ordinary photographs or drawings of nudes would not satisfy such a requirement, but the 108 photographs in the five photo features went beyond nudity. The judge noted that eighty-seven photos included exposed breasts, buttocks or genitals; nine included actual or simulated lesbian, oral sex; seven alluded to masturbation through the location of fingers in or near genitals; and sixteen photos showed legs spread to expose genitals, with six of those "close-up photographs showing nothing but women's groins."[32]

The patent offensiveness requirement separates hard-core sexual portrayals from other erotic expression. In order for a sexual portrayal to be obscene, it must be specifically enumerated in a state obscenity statute. In *Miller,* the Court said that such portrayals were of ultimate sexual acts, normal or perverted, actual or simulated, including masturbation, excretory functions and the lewd exhibition of genitals. State statutes that define the human behaviors whose portrayals may be obscene read like a catalog of sexual practices for heterosexual and homosexual couples and individuals.

Thus, communities are restricted in obscenity prosecutions to works containing explicit portrayals of hard-core sex acts. One year after *Miller,* the city of Albany, Georgia, fined theater manager Billy Jenkins $750 and sentenced him to twelve months of probation for showing the movie *Carnal Knowledge.* Some critics listed the film as among the ten best movies of 1971, and Ann-Margret received an Academy Award nomination for her performance. The Supreme Court reversed the obscenity conviction and pointed out that juries do not have "unbridled discretion in determining what is 'patently offensive.'" Sexuality may have been the major theme of the movie, the Court said, but it was not obscene: "There is no exhibition whatever of the actors' genitals, lewd or otherwise, during these scenes. There are occasional scenes of nudity, but nudity alone is not enough to make material legally obscene under the *Miller* standard."[33] The case, *Jenkins v. Georgia,* is a strong reminder to those individuals who mistakenly believe that *Miller* gave communities unlimited power to regulate erotic material.

---

have a prurient appeal, that is, the work arouses an immoderate or unwholesome interest in sex. The work, however, is judged on its entirety, not on isolated or fleeting passages or scenes that contain sexual descriptions or images. When a Cincinnati art museum was prosecuted for exhibiting photographs by Robert Mapplethorpe, the judge required the 175-photo exhibit to be judged on the basis of seven controversial photos that had been isolated from the others in the exhibit, violating the intent of the *Miller* test.[30]

Judges have conducted crude content analyses to determine the appeal of the overall work. One federal district court judge in Georgia concluded that an issue of *Penthouse* magazine satisfied the first part of the *Miller* test because most of the pages were devoted to photos emphasizing the genitals of nude women. The

---

[30] Cincinnati v. Contemporary Arts Ctr., 566 N.E.2d 214 (Ohio Mun. 1990).

[31] Penthouse v. Webb, 594 F. Supp. 1186, 1198 (N.D. Ga. 1984).
[32] *Id.*
[33] Jenkins v. Georgia, 418 U.S. 153, 161 (1974).

Subjectivity, imprecision and unpredictability occur in all three parts of the *Miller* test. Complicating this subjectivity, tolerance for erotic materials varies from community to community. The concepts of patently offensive and prurient interest vary according to community norms, which are reflected in the attitudes of court jurors.

### *Miller* Part 3: The Serious Value Test

The third and final determinant of obscenity is "Whether the work, taken as a whole, lacks serious literary, artistic, political or scientific value."

Even if a work appeals to the prurient interest and is patently offensive under state law, it must satisfy the third part of the *Miller* test to be obscene and to lie outside the protection of the First Amendment. In effect, the third part forces judges to play the role of artistic or social critics and evaluate the aesthetic merit of works containing sexual content. Prosecuting and defense attorneys may call expert witnesses to characterize the social value of the work for the jury. The Court ruled in 1987 that the third part of *Miller* involves national rather than community standards.[34]

The presence of a substantial amount of serious, non-sexual material may salvage a work that contains graphic sex, but the amount of non-sexual material must be substantial. One judge has cautioned: "A quotation from Voltaire in the flyleaf of a book will not constitutionally redeem an otherwise obscene publication."[35] Although some judges have classified *Penthouse* as obscene because of the quantity of explicit, erotic photographs, others have judged it non-obscene because of its serious articles. The Louisiana Supreme Court in 1980 found that the 228-page, June 1980 issue of *Penthouse* satisfied the first two parts of *Miller*, and that ninety-six pages of photo essays of women satisfied the third part because they constituted hard-core sexual conduct. However, the magazine as a whole was redeemed by sixty-seven pages of articles that clearly had serious value: "These articles convey ideas, and purport to convey serious information. They do not lack serious political and scientific value, nor even serious literary value."[36]

Similarly, in 1979 a Boston Municipal Court judge upheld First Amendment protection for the film *Caligula* by a legal thread. He found that the film lacked social value because it "does not lift the spirit, does not improve the mind, nor does it enrich the human personality or develop character." But a political scientist had testified that the film had a serious political theme about absolute power corrupting absolutely, and no rebuttal witness was presented on the issue. The judge ruled that the movie was protected because the government had failed to prove beyond a reasonable doubt that the film lacked serious political value.[37]

Judges are not free to serve as their own fact finders on the issue of social value. A federal district court judge found the lyrics of the 2 Live Crew album "As Nasty As They Wanna Be" to be obscene, but he ignored the testimony of critics who said that the music had political significance and literary conventions, and the government presented no evidence on the issue of artistic value. The U.S. Court of Appeals reversed the ruling, rejecting the argument that "simply by listening to this musical work, the judge could determine that it had no serious artistic value."[38]

A federal district judge demonstrated in 1991 that a modicum of political or literary value can salvage a work. The judge ruled that a truck driver's bumper sticker, "How's my driving? Call 1-800-EAT-SHIT," had serious literary value because it parodied bumper stickers that encouraged drivers to call truck companies with comments about the driving habits of truck drivers. The judge also said the bumper sticker had serious political value because it protested the "Big Brother" mentality that is promoted by serious versions of the sticker, and it did not satisfy the first two parts of *Miller* because it was not erotic.[39]

Other judges are not so quick to find serious value in sexually explicit material. In 1977, the Kentucky Supreme Court upheld an obscenity conviction and accompanying $4,000 fine against the Paducah Fourth Street Cinema for showing *Deep Throat*. After viewing the movie, the court held that it lacked serious value: "The story line consists entirely of the sexual activities of Miss Linda Lovelace. We failed to find any serious literary, artistic, political or scientific value in this motion picture."[40] A federal district court, four years later, similarly failed to find serious value in the film *Cinderella-96*, which was described as a translation of the fictional character, Cinderella, into a bawdy, lusty tale of recurring homosexual and heterosexual encounters. The judge said the "sum and substance of the movie is the almost unbroken string of sexual acts depicted." He concluded that the movie was obscene even though it contained no sexual penetration or ejaculation. And he said it lacked serious literary and artistic value even though it may be entertaining and enjoyable to some viewers.[41]

## OBSCENITY AND PUBLIC OPINION

*Miller v. California* should have increased obscenity convictions and diminished the availability of erotica. It didn't. Indeed, obscenity convictions decreased, and more erotica became available after 1973. Why?

The answer may be that the public doesn't want obscenity laws

[34] Pope v. Illinois, 481 U.S. 497 (1987).

[35] Kois v. Wisconsin, 408 U.S. 229, 231 (1972), *quoted in Miller*, 413 U.S. 15, 25 n.7 (1973).

[36] Louisiana v. Walden Book Co., 386 So. 2d 342, 346 (La. 1980).

[37] Massachusetts v. Saxon Theatre Corp., 6 Media L. Rep. (BNA) 1979 (Boston Mun. Ct. 1980).

[38] Luke Records, Inc. v. Navarro, 960 F.2d 134, 138 (11th Cir. 1992).

[39] Baker v. Glover, 776 F. Supp. 1511 (N.D. Ga. 1991).

[40] Western Corp. v. Kentucky, 558 S.W.2d 605, 607 (Ky. 1977).

[41] Septum, Inc. v. Keller, 7 Media L. Rep. (BNA) 1664 (N.D. Ga. 1981).

to be strictly enforced. Most prosecutors and judges — those people responsible for enforcing obscenity law — are elected, and members of the public serve on the juries that decide criminal obscenity cases. Studies show that many people use erotica or tolerate its use by others. A 1994 study, for example, reported that 41 percent of men and 16 percent of women questioned said they had purchased auto-erotic materials during the previous twelve months. Twenty-three percent of the men had watched sexually explicit movies, 22 percent had visited clubs with erotic dancers and 16 percent had purchased sexually explicit books or magazines. Only 34 percent of all subjects said they believed there should be laws prohibiting the sale of pornography to adults.[42]

Other studies report similar results. An Indiana survey found that 54 percent of all adults questioned had watched adult videos or movies at least once.[43] And a 1991 Gallup Poll found that 53 percent of adults either opposed tightening standards in their communities for the sale of sexually explicit material or wanted the standards to be less restrictive. In addition, more than 50 percent of adults said magazines with nudity, magazines that show adults having sexual relations, theaters showing adult movies and sexually explicit video rentals should be available to adults without restrictions or without public displays.[44]

Tolerance has no doubt increased in the years since the study.

These attitudes translate into high demand for erotic material. The Kinsey Institute estimated in 1990 that thirty-five million copies of "girlie" magazines are distributed each month.[45] The 2004 Standard Rate and Data Services *Consumer Magazine Advertising Source* reports that *Playboy* has a monthly circulation of three million with an advertising rate of $141,620 per colored page, and *Penthouse's* monthly circulation is 478,000 with an advertising rate of $26,000 per colored page.[46] *Writer's Market* does not list *Playboy* or *Penthouse* as welcoming submissions from freelance writers but does list eighteen magazines under its "men's magazine" category, including *Climax* (83,000 circulation), *Screw* (125,000), *Gallery* (500,000) and *Thigh High* (89,000). *Playboy* is rated the most tasteful of the top three girlie magazines (*Playboy, Penthouse* and *Hustler*), but a content analysis of *Playboy* centerfolds from 1953 to 1990 found that the portrayals became more explicit from 1971 to 1985. Explicitness was defined as the showing of pubic hair and opened legs.[47]

Reliable statistics on the sale of X-rated movie tickets or the rental of adult videos are unavailable, but the proliferation of home

videos and DVDs has played a major role in making erotic films more available to interested adults. The number of households with VCRs increased from less than 1 percent in 1978 to 73 percent in 1992. In 2002, more than 40 million American homes had DVD players, and the availability of erotic videos has skyrocketed. In 2001, a producer of pornographic videos estimated the size of the U.S. porn industry at $10 billion. This included 25,000 video outlets, 10,000 new adult video titles a year and 711 million rentals of hard-core sex films.[48]

The proliferation of girlie magazines, increased explicitness of the major men's magazines, growing availability of DVDs and erotic videos are developments that reflect a public that consumes more erotic material and is increasingly tolerant of erotica. This is a public that balks at obscenity prosecutions. Law professor Robert Riggs counted the number of obscenity cases appealed to higher courts before and after *Miller* and found a sharp upward trend from 1969 to 1974, the year after the decision, and an "almost equally sharp down turn" after 1974.[49] Political scientist Harold Leventhal detected similar trends when he surveyed local prosecuting attorneys about obscenity enforcement before and after *Miller*. Although prosecutors reported an increase in the quantity of obscenity in their communities after 1973, they reported a lower priority for prosecuting obscenity and a drop in the number of obscenity cases. Leventhal concluded that *Miller* failed to spur more obscenity prosecutions.[50] Similarly, University of Chicago law professor Cass Sunstein observed in 1993 that "realistically speaking, most people involved in the production of sexually explicit work have little to fear from the *Miller* test."[51]

So, while the three-part *Miller* test and the wording of some local obscenity statutes theoretically have made it easier to prosecute obscenity, the public has grown increasingly tolerant of erotic material and has reduced political pressures on elected officials to enforce obscenity laws. And members of that public have difficulty when they serve as jurors and are asked to restrict magazines or films that are similar to materials that the jurors may have rented or purchased recently.

## THE LIMITED TRADITION OF PROTECTING OBSCENITY

*Miller* and its companion cases were aimed at restricting the transportation and sale of explicit erotica, but what of the possession of sexually explicit material? Coexisting with the doctrine that obscenity may be regulated is a second doctrine at the core of which is the concept that when persons are in the privacy of their

---

[42] Robert Michael et al., Sex in America: A Definitive Survey (1994).

[43] June Reinisch & Ruth Beasley, The Kinsey Institute New Report on Sex (1990).

[44] The Gallup Poll Monthly, October 1991.

[45] Samuel Janus & Cynthia Janus, The Janus Report on Sexual Behavior (1993).

[46] Standard Rate and Data Services, 87 Consumer Magazine Advertising Source 478-80 (2004).

[47] Anthony Bogaert & Deborah Turkovich, *A Content Analysis of Playboy Centerfolds From 1953 Through 1990: Changes in Explicitness, Objectification, and Model's Age,* J. of Sex Research 30, 135 (1993).

[48] *See* Mark Cromer, *Porn's Compassionate Conservatism,* The Nation, Feb. 26, 2001, at 25.

[49] Robert Riggs, Miller v. California: *An Empirical Note,* 1981 BYU L. Rev. 247.

[50] Harold Leventhal, *An Empirical Inquiry into the Effects of* Miller v. California *on the Control of Obscenity,* 52 N.Y.U. L. Rev. 810 (1977).

[51] Cass Sunstein, Democracy and the Problem of Free Speech 211 (1993).

homes, the government may not interfere with their personal thought process or their perusal of words or pictures. Under this doctrine, the private possession of objectionable material is legal.

This concept that the mere possession of obscenity for private use is beyond the reach of government was articulated best, probably, by Justice Thurgood Marshall in *Stanley v. Georgia*, a 1969 case.[52] When police searched the home of Robert Eli Stanley for bookmaking equipment, they found no gambling devices but discovered three reels of sexually explicit 8mm film.

In his majority opinion overturning Stanley's conviction, Justice Marshall found that the mere private possession of obscene matter could not be a crime under the Constitution. The state has no right "to control the moral content of a person's thoughts," Marshall wrote, and the right to receive information and ideas is critical. Wrote Marshall:

If the First Amendment means anything, it means that a state has no business telling a man, sitting alone in his own home, what books he may read or what films he may watch. Our whole constitutional heritage rebels at the thought of giving government the power to control men's minds.[53]

*Stanley* was as much a victory for home sanctity as for free expression. A year later the Supreme Court upheld homeowners' prerogatives in another case involving erotica. In *Rowan v. U.S. Post Office*, the Court gave homeowners "complete and unfettered discretion" to prohibit a pornography distributor from mailing erotic material to a homeowner's address. "[W]e are often 'captives' outside the sanctity of the home and subject to objectionable speech," the Court noted. But that does not mean "we must be captives everywhere." The homeowner has sole discretion in deciding whether mailed material is erotically arousing or sexually provocative and can require the postal service to notify the mailer to stop sending the material to the homeowner.[54] Theoretically, a homeowner could judge a gun catalog or jewelry brochure, even one lacking human models, as erotic and order the distributor to cease further mailings.

State legislatures and supreme courts have minimized obscenity prosecutions. A state high court can do so by finding an obscenity statute unconstitutional as the Wisconsin Supreme Court did in 1980.[55] As long as the legislature remains inactive in redrafting a statute, obscenity prosecution is stymied. Similarly, in 1979 the Arkansas Supreme Court reversed a $1,000 fine and one-month jail term for the possession of one obscene film in a home.[56] And, as the result of decisions by the Iowa Supreme Court, the dissemination and ownership of obscene material was legal for adults in

Iowa from 1973 to 1977. In 1973, the court ruled that the state's obscenity statute was inconsistent with *Miller v. California*.[57] And, in 1977, the court ruled that state obscenity law restricted obscenity for minors but not for adults.[58] For twelve years, 1973 to 1985, there were no obscenity prosecutions in North Carolina because of the complexity of that state's law. A specific work could not be the target of a criminal obscenity prosecution until it first had been declared obscene in an advisory hearing.[59]

It is difficult for state legislators to get elected on a platform of decriminalizing obscenity. In 1990, a federal district court judge in Florida told opponents of obscenity laws: "In sum, if persons subscribe to the view that obscenity should be legalized, they should take their petitions to Tallahassee, the Florida capital, not to the steps of the U.S. courthouse."[60] But most state legislatures have been unsympathetic.

Most actions to abolish obscenity laws come from state supreme courts, which are more independent of voters than legislatures are. The most dramatic example is Oregon. In 1987, the Oregon Supreme Court voted unanimously to decriminalize the sale or ownership of obscenity for adults, though sale of sexually explicit material to minors continued to be prohibited.[61] The court reversed the conviction of Earl Henry, the operator of an adult bookstore in Redmond, ruling that the free expression clause of the state constitution was broader than the First Amendment and protected obscenity. The court reasoned that territorial law existing in 1857, when the state constitution was adopted, only prohibited the distribution of obscenity to minors. The court concluded: "In this state any person can write, print, read, say, or sell anything to a consenting adult even though the expression may be generally or universally considered 'obscene.'"[62]

Obscenity protection made other inroads in the Western United States. The Hawaii Supreme Court ruled that the right of privacy, which had been incorporated in its state constitution nine years earlier, protected adult possession of obscenity. "Since a person has the right to view pornographic items at home," the court said in a unanimous opinion, "there necessarily follows a correlative right to purchase such materials for this personal use, or the underlying privacy right becomes meaningless."[63] The court indicated in a footnote that it was not deciding the issue of child pornography, the sale to minors, the obtrusive public display of pornography, the showing of obscenity to a captive audience, or

---

[52] 394 U.S. 557 (1969).

[53] *Id.* at 565.

[54] 397 U.S. 728, 737 (1970).

[55] Wisconsin v. Princess Cinema, 292 N.W.2d 807 (Wis. 1980).

[56] Buck v. Arkansas, 578 S.W.2d 579 (Ark. 1979).

[57] State v. Wedelstedt, 213 N.W.2d 562 (Iowa 1973).

[58] Chelsea Theater Corp. v. Burlington, 258 N.W.2d 372 (Iowa 1977).

[59] *See* Samuel Currin & Robert Howers, *Regulation of Pornography — The North Carolina Approach*, 21 WAKE FOREST L. REV. 263 (1986).

[60] Skywalker Records, Inc. v. Navarro, 739 F. Supp. 578, 587 (S.D. Fla. 1990).

[61] State v. Henry, 732 P.2d 9 (Or. 1987).

[62] *Id.* at 18.

[63] State v. Kam, 748 P.2d 372, 380 (Haw. 1988).

films that depicted actual killings.

The Oregon obscenity doctrine almost crossed the Columbia River into Washington. There, the state's supreme court voted 5-4 that the Washington constitution did not afford obscenity greater protection than the federal constitution. The four-judge minority favored Oregon's approach.[64] One vote made the difference in public policy between the two Pacific Northwest states.

The most recent effort to use a state constitution to expand protection for erotica occurred in Wisconsin in 1999. The Crossroads News Agency, an adult bookstore located along Interstate 94, was fined $4,000 and court costs for the sale of the obscene videotape, *Anal Vision No. 5*. The Wisconsin Supreme Court unanimously rejected the argument that the Wisconsin constitution provided greater protection for obscenity than the U.S. Constitution. The court observed that Oregon was the only state that had created this kind of protection of the roughly one-third of the state jurisdictions that had interpreted their state constitutional speech clauses to protect obscenity.[65]

## PROTECTING CHILDREN AND JUVENILES

Even when obscenity is decriminalized for consenting adults, courts recognize the need to restrict sexually explicit material from view by juveniles and children. The exception has two manifestations. First, federal and state law strictly prohibits the distribution of materials portraying children or juveniles in sexually explicit situations. Second, federal and state laws prohibit the sale of sexual materials to minors.

These laws don't merely ban the sale of legally obscene materials to minors; they ban the sale of sexual materials that clearly would be legal if sold to adults. This concept has been called "variable obscenity." The government may be stricter in prohibiting the sale of sexual materials to juveniles than to adults.

In 1968, the Supreme Court upheld a New York statute that made it a crime to sell materials containing nudity to anyone under the age of sixteen. Sam Ginsberg, the owner of a Bellmore, Long Island, luncheonette, sold two girlie magazines to a sixteen-year-old on two different occasions. The magazines contained pictures of nude women that were clearly not obscene.[66] The Court upheld the conviction and denied that the statute lacked a rational justification, even though studies neither proved nor disproved a causal link between erotic material and the ethical and moral development of youths.

Events three decades later demonstrate that the doctrine of variable obscenity remains very much alive. In 1996, a panel of the U.S. Court of Appeals unanimously upheld a California statute that banned the selling of sexually oriented publications from un-

supervised news racks. The court held that the California legislature had a compelling interest in shielding juveniles from sexual materials that were not obscene for adults.[67] And the next year Phoenix police used a similar statute in Arizona to justify the seizure of fifteen coin-operated news racks for the local, sexually oriented weekly, the *Beat*, which had been published for thirty-three years and had a circulation of 8,500. The publisher, Jerry Evenson, commented: "We're not pornographic. We have no full nudity, there is no profanity. The only thing we have is bare nipples." Simply reporting on the Phoenix event caused a controversy for the trade magazine, *Editor & Publisher*. The magazine's Richmond, Virginia, printer refused to publish a two-inch reproduction of an ad from the *Beat* showing bare-breasted dancers.[68]

The Federal Communications Commission has applied the same logic in prohibiting the use of indecent language on commercial radio. The Supreme Court has said radio may be restricted more than print media because of its intrusiveness and its accessibility to children.[69] The case began when WBAI broadcast a twelve-minute monologue by George Carlin, "Filthy Words," at 2 p.m. His satire is an analysis of the seven words that originally were banned from broadcasting: shit, piss, fuck, cunt, cocksucker, motherfucker and tits. Though the station preceded the monologue with an advisory that it contained offensive language, a man who was driving with his young son missed the advisory and tuned in to the middle of the monologue. He was offended and complained to the FCC.

The Supreme Court voted 5-4 to uphold possible civil sanctions against the station, but the decision was based on the fact that radio is uniquely available to children. The majority said the decision balanced the significant interests of listeners in their homes against the broadcasters' interests. A concurring opinion indicated that the ruling did not apply to the isolated use of an offensive word in a broadcast. Eleven years later, in 1989, the Supreme Court underscored the importance of the intrusiveness factor and invalidated a ban on telephone indecency. The FCC was attempting to control the dial-a-porn business that made sexually oriented messages available to people who called 900 numbers. The Court indicated that the telephone was not nearly as intrusive as the radio: "Placing a telephone call is not the same as tuning in a radio and being taken by surprise by an indecent message."[70]

From 1989 to 1993, while Alfred Sikes was FCC chairman, the commission actively enforced radio's prohibition against indecency and levied fines of from $2,000 to $600,000. Most notorious was shock-jock Howard Stern, who paid a total of $1.7 million in fines for his off-color morning commentaries on the radio. He was cited for his numerous and explicit references to masturbation,

---

[64] State v. Reece, 757 P.2d 947 (Wash. 1988).

[65] County of Kenosha v. C & S Management, Inc., 588 N.W.2d 236 (Wis. 1999).

[66] Ginsberg v. New York, 390 U.S. 629 (1968).

[67] Crawford v. Lungren, 96 F.3d 380 (9th Cir. 1996).

[68] *See* Mark Fitzgerald, *News Racks Seized*, EDITOR & PUBLISHER, Oct. 11, 1997, at 8.

[69] FCC v. Pacifica Found., 438 U.S. 726 (1978).

[70] Sable Communications v. FCC, 492 U.S. 115, 128 (1989).

fornication, excretory functions and sexual organs. A study of broadcast indecency fines for 1987-1997 found that thirty-six fines were issued by the Federal Communications Commission. The study concluded that the FCC tended to fine stations "when humor is combined with patently offensive descriptions of sexual or excretory activities or organs, expletives, or sexual innuendo."[71]

In April 2001, the Federal Communications Commission attempted to clarify its indecency regulation that applies from 6 a.m. to 10 p.m. on AM and FM radio and commercial television. The FCC said that it applies three criteria to determine indecency: (1) explicitness or graphic nature of the depiction of sexual or excretory organs or activities; (2) whether the materials dwell on or repeat at length such sexual depictions; (3) the context and whether the depiction appears to pander or titillate, or is presented for shock value. The heart of the FCC statement was thirty-two explicit examples from FCC indecency cases, twenty-three of which were ruled indecent. The indecent examples included the *Howard Stern Show* and songs with titles like "Uterus Guy," "You Suck," "Sit on My Face" and "Penis Envy." The nine segments that were found to be not indecent were from the *Oprah Winfrey Show,* the *Geraldo Rivera Show,* the film *Schindler's List* and the National Public Radio show *All Things Considered.*[72]

In addition, in 2005 Congress passed and a year later President George W. Bush signed a bill providing for a ten-fold increase in fines the FCC could levy on broadcast stations for airing indecent material. Apparently fed up with sexual references and incidents like the exposure of Janet Jackson's breast in the 2004 Super Bowl, Congress set the maximum possible fine for each incident at $325,000. The Broadcast Decency Enforcement Act of 2005 was signed by the president in June 2006.[73]

The Supreme Court indicated in 1975 that there were limits to how far it would go to shelter children and disinterested adults from offensive speech that was not legally obscene. The Court ruled that a city ordinance prohibiting the showing of films with nudity in drive-in theaters with screens visible from streets or public places was unconstitutional.[74] The theater was prosecuted for the R-rated film, *Class of '74.* The outdoor screen was visible from two city streets and a church parking lot. The majority said that the censorship was not justified by the limited privacy interests of persons on public streets who could simply look away when confronted by offensive material. The Court said that "clearly all nudity cannot be deemed obscene even as to minors."[75] Such a rule

would bar films with pictures of baby's buttocks, nude bodies of war victims, cultures in which nudity is indigenous, the opening of art exhibits and bathers on a nude beach.

The Supreme Court applied similar logic when it invalidated the Communications Decency Act of 1996. The act made it a crime to communicate indecent material on the Internet to persons seventeen or younger. The act defined "indecency" as patently offensive descriptions of sexual or excretory activities or organs. The Supreme Court said in *Reno v. American Civil Liberties Union* that the act would allow Internet users to be punished for disseminating such things as the seven "dirty words" of the George Carlin monologue, discussions of prison rape or safe sexual practices, artistic images that include nudity or, arguably, the card catalog of the Carnegie Library.[76] The Court concluded that the Internet was not as available to children as radio and television and that it was unconstitutional to deprive adults of sexual matter that was indecent but not obscene. The court said that banning such material "threatens to torch a large segment of the Internet community" and was like "burning the house to roast the pig."[77]

In May 2000, the Supreme Court again invalidated a provision of the Telecommunications Act of 1996 that had restricted the dissemination of indecent and erotic material.[78] Two sections of the act had restricted the broadcasting by cable television of sexually oriented programming such as Playboy Television and Spice. The act required cable systems to fully scramble such erotic programs so that the occasional and accidental bleeding of sexual images would not be available to children, or to delay the broadcasts to the safe harbor time period of 10 p.m. to 6 a.m., when children were less likely to be watching. Most cable systems opted for the delayed broadcasting because the technology for effective scrambling of signals was too expensive. Five justices agreed that the regulation unconstitutionally burdened the disseminators of programs that were indecent and erotic but not obscene. The majority favored the less restrictive and less intrusive alternative of requiring cable systems to inform their subscribers of a blocking option that would entirely block such sexual channels from their home televisions.

Some observers have incorrectly interpreted *Reno v. ACLU* as legalizing obscenity on the Internet. The decision legalized indecency but not obscenity. Distributors of obscenity on the Internet have been successfully prosecuted. Robert and Carleen Thomas were sentenced to more than two years in federal prison and forfeited their computer system for operating a sex Internet site that they called "The Nastiest Place on Earth," from their Milpitas, California, home.[79] A U.S. postal inspector in Memphis, Tennessee, paid $55 to copy their files. The two defendants were prosecuted on the basis of community standards in the recipient community

[71] Milagros Rivera-Sanchez & Michelle Ballard, *A Decade of Indecency Enforcement: A Study of How the Federal Communications Commission Assesses Indecency Fines (1987-1997),* 75 JOURNALISM AND MASS COMM. Q. 143, 147 (1998).

[72] In the Matter of Indecency: Guidance on the Commission's Case Law Interpreting, 18 U.S.C. 1464 (2000); Enforcement Policies Regarding Broadcast Indecency, *available at* http://www.fcc.gov.

[73] Pub. Law 109-235 (2006).

[74] Erznoznik v. Jacksonville, 422 U.S. 205 (1975).

[75] *Id.* at 212.

[76] 521 U.S. 844 (1977).

[77] *Id.* at 882.

[78] United States v. Playboy Entertainment Group, Inc., 529 U.S. 803 (2000).

[79] United States v. Thomas, 74 F.3d 701 (6th Cir. 1996).

of Memphis. A panel of the U.S. Court of Appeals agreed that there was no need to adopt a new definition of community for obscenity prosecutions involving electronic bulletin boards.

In addition, in March 2006, the Supreme Court let stand a ruling by a federal three-judge panel from New York holding the obscenity provision of the Communications Decency Act was not overbroad.[80] The federal court for the Southern District of New York held that the plaintiff failed to meet its burden proving that the community standards prong of the Miller Test was not applicable to the widespread scope of the Internet.[81]

Congress has not given up in its attempt to protect children from Internet erotica. In 1998, following the *Reno* decision, Congress approved a statute that was narrower than the former Communications Decency Act. The new act, the Child Online Protection Act (COPA), prohibited easily accessible, commercial erotica on the World Wide Web that was harmful to minors. The statute provided a three-part test, similar to the *Miller v. California* test, to determine what content was harmful. Two of the three prongs were based on the application of community standards, which could mean local standards.

The U.S. Court of Appeals ruled that this use of community standards rendered the law substantially overbroad. The Supreme Court reversed the holding and ruled that it was just as valid to apply local standards to the Internet as to films, magazines and dial-a-porn telephone conversations, as the Court had in previous cases.[82] A dissenting Justice John Paul Stevens wrote that in the context of the Internet that "community standards become a sword, rather than a shield." He argued, "If a prurient appeal is offensive in a Puritan village, it may be a crime to put it on the World Wide Web."[83]

In 2004, the Supreme Court filed its second decision in the case — *Ashcroft v. ACLU* — and ruled on the constitutionality of the central provision of the Child Online Protection Act. A five-judge majority ruled that a COPA provision was unconstitutional that required Internet providers of erotica to verify the age of customers. The majority ruled that age verification was not the least restrictive means of shielding minors from Internet pornography. The majority concluded that filters and blocking software on home computers was a more effective method.[84]

Congress' third attempt to shield children from Internet erotica met with success before the Supreme Court. In 2000, Congress passed the Children's Internet Protection Act (CIPA), which required libraries that received federal subsidies to connect filters on all of their computers that were connected to the Internet. The purpose of the filters was to block child pornography and erotic material that was inappropriate for children.

In a plurality opinion by Chief Justice Rehnquist, the Court upheld CIPA. Rehnquist wrote: "Because public libraries have traditionally excluded pornographic material from their other collections, Congress could reasonably impose a parallel limitation on its Internet assistance program."[85] He noted that the statute allowed libraries to disconnect the filters for adults: "When a patron encounters a blocked site, he need only ask a librarian to unblock it or disable the filter."[86] Two other justices wrote concurring opinions that supported the four-judge plurality. Justice Anthony Kennedy wrote that the protection of minors was both compelling and legitimate.[87] And a concurring Justice Stephen Breyer wrote that the law posed a comparatively small burden that was similar to the traditional library practice of isolating some materials in closed stacks where access required a wait and a signature for a patron.[88] There were two dissenting opinions. Justice John Paul Stevens called the act a blunt nationwide restraint on adult access.[89] And Justice David Souter, joined by Ruth Bader Ginsburg, said that Congress could have protected children without restricting adults.[90]

The availability of erotica on the Internet continues to trouble many citizens, especially parents and lawmakers. One solution to the problem that does not involve government or the courts is for parents to install software on home computers that filters out most sexual images and messages. Cyber Patrol, Net Nanny and X-Stop Librarian are examples of such software. Lycos, a popular search engine, makes available at no charge a program called "Safety Net" that screens out most adult material.

The Constitution protects many portrayals of adults in sexual situations. But material that portrays minors in erotic or suggestive poses is another matter. The Supreme Court, Congress, state supreme courts and legislatures have been unequivocal in supporting the criminalization of what is known as "child pornography." In 1982 the Supreme Court upheld a state statute that prohibited the dissemination of material with sexual performances by children under the age of 16. *New York v. Ferber*[91] involved a Manhattan store that sold films of young boys masturbating. The Court conceded that material depicting children in sexual situations could be prosecuted even if the material would not be obscene had it depicted adults in the same situations. But, in reversing the highest appellate court in the state, the Court said that the paramount concern in such cases was protecting children who were portrayed in such materials from psychological, emotional and mental harm. This was clearly a compelling state interest that

[80] Nitke v. Gonzales, 126 S.Ct. 1566 (2006).

[81] Nitke v. Gonzales, 413 F.Supp. 2d 262, 268-69 (S.D.N.Y. 2005).

[82] Ashcroft v. American Civil Liberties Union, 535 U.S. 564 (2002).

[83] *Id.* at 603 (Stevens, J., dissenting).

[84] Ashcroft v. American Civil Liberties Union, 524 U.S. 656 (2004).

[85] United States v. American Library Association, 539 U.S. 194, 212 (2003) (plurality).

[86] *Id.* at 209 (plurality).

[87] *Id.* at 214 (Kennedy, J., concurring).

[88] *Id.* at 215 (Breyer, J., concurring).

[89] *Id.* at 220 (Stevens, J., dissenting).

[90] *Id.* at 231 (Souter, J., dissenting).

[91] 458 U.S. 747 (1982).

justified some limits on expression.

Eight years later, the Supreme Court upheld an Ohio child pornography law that prohibited the possession of materials depicting nude children unless they served a *bona fide* artistic, scientific or educational purpose.[92] Clyde Osborne was sentenced to six months in prison for the possession of four photographs of juvenile, nude males in sexually explicit positions. The Court said that the gravity of the state interest in protecting victims of child pornography justified the limits on free expression. The Ohio Supreme Court specified that it was limiting its ruling to the lewd exhibition or graphic focus on genitals to prevent punishment for possession of innocuous photographs of naked children.

During its 2001-02 term the Supreme Court decided a case concerning "virtual" or fabricated child pornography. In 1996 Congress amended the Child Pornography Prevention Act to criminalize child pornography images that do not involve real children but are computer images of fictitious children engaged in imaginary sexual conduct. The statute made illegal a visual depiction that appears to be or "conveys the impression" of a minor engaged in explicit sex. The Supreme Court ruled 6-3 that the statute was unconstitutional, concluding: "The Government has shown no more than a remote connection between speech that might encourage thoughts or impulses and any resulting child abuse." The Court held that the Constitution required a stronger, more direct connection to prohibit speech "on the ground that it may encourage pedophiles to engage in illegal conduct."[93] Child pornography, then, is one of the few categories of legally taboo speech in American society.

## PANDERING AND ZONING

Most of this chapter has analyzed the definitional approach for controlling obscenity. Zoning laws and the concept of pandering are other approaches for controlling sexually explicit material. The more obscure of the two is pandering.

**Pandering.** The classic pandering case is *Ginzburg v. United States*. Ralph Ginzburg was sentenced to five years in federal prison and fined $42,000 because of the method he used to promote his erotic but non-obscene books and periodicals. What was thought to be a liberal Supreme Court upheld the conviction by a 5-4 vote. Earl Warren and William Brennan voted to uphold the conviction because of Ginzburg's blatant pandering: "The business of purveying textual or graphic matter openly advertised to appeal to the erotic interest of their customers."[94]

Ginzburg — a former articles editor for *Esquire* and staff writer for NBC and *Reader's Digest* — mailed nine million copies of a brochure to promote the book, *The Housewife's Handbook on Selective Promiscuity;* the newsletter, *Liaison;* and the hardcover quarterly devoted to love and sex, *Eros.* The mailings generated 150,000, $25 subscriptions to *Eros.*

The Supreme Court said Ginzburg's method of promotion could be used to judge the content of the works: "Where the purveyor's sole emphasis is on the sexually provocative aspects of his publications, that fact may be decisive in the determination of obscenity."[95] Ginzburg had highlighted the erotic nature of his publications by mailing the promotions from cities whose names had sexual connotations: Intercourse and Blue Ball, Pennsylvania, and Middlesex, New Jersey.

The Court's decision was denounced by civil libertarians who pointed out that none of Ginzburg's publications were even close to satisfying the court's own definition of obscenity. *Eros* had received a number of national graphics awards, including one from the National Society of Art Directors. In order to secure a conviction, federal prosecutors had moved the trial from New York City to the more conservative Philadelphia, where the mayor had narrowly won election on a promise to rid the city of smut, and the police department's obscenity control squad recently had arrested twenty-two magazine dealers and confiscated seventeen vanloads of magazines. Ginzburg's appeal to the Supreme Court was supported by briefs of the American Civil Liberties Union, the Authors League of America and a group of writers that included Joseph Heller, James Jones, Norman Mailer and Arthur Miller.

**Zoning.** A decade after *Ginzburg,* the Supreme Court approved another non-content approach for the control of obscenity. In *Young v. American Mini Theatres, Inc.,* the Court allowed cities to use zoning laws to limit the location and concentration of businesses that specialize in erotic media.[96] The Pussy Cat, an adult theater in what had been a corner gas station, challenged a Detroit ordinance. The law said that an adult business could not be located within 1,000 feet of two other adult businesses, or within 500 feet of a residential neighborhood. Adult businesses included pool halls, pawnshops and adult bookstores and theaters. The intent of the ordinance was to prevent the concentration of such businesses on one street.

In an opinion by Justice John Paul Stevens, the Court upheld the Detroit ordinance. Stevens said the ordinance did not impose content limitations on the creators of adult movies or significantly restrict the viewing of such movies. Stevens concluded that the impact of the ordinance on free expression was at most incidental and minimal. He attempted to create a doctrine granting erotic speech less protection than political speech, noting that "it is manifest that society's interest in protecting this type of expression is of a wholly different, and lesser, magnitude, than the interest in untrammeled political debate."[97] But only a minority of jus-

---

[92] Osborne v. Ohio, 495 U.S. 103 (1990).

[93] Ashcroft v. Free Speech Coalition, 535 U.S. 234, 254 (2002).

[94] 383 U.S. 463, 467 (1966).

[95] *Id.* at 470.

[96] 427 U.S. 50 (1976).

[97] *Id.* at 70.

tices joined him on that point.

In 2002 the Supreme Court again supported the right of cities to limit the geographic concentration of adult businesses. The Court upheld a Los Angeles ordinance that prohibited the presence of more than one adult business in a building. The Court said that such uses of zoning laws must be backed up by studies that document a relationship between a concentration of adult business and undesirable secondary effects such as increases in crimes such as prostitution, robbery and assault.[98]

New York City Mayor Rudolph Giuliani used a Detroit-type ordinance to banish topless bars and X-rated peep shows from the Times Square area to an industrial district. And the highest court in the state, the New York Court of Appeals, upheld the law. The unanimous decision noted that the number of adult establishments in New York City had grown from nine in 1965 to 177 in 1993, with 107 being located in Manhattan.[99]

The advent of the DVD and the proliferation of video rental stores with adult movie sections, along with the growth of cable television with adult networks, has diminished the significance of the *Young* decision. In many cities adult theaters are a dying business.

## RATINGS AND LABELING

*Young* helped to shield disinterested adults from unwanted, erotic media. It empowered cities to isolate adult businesses from homes, schools and churches and made it easier for disinterested adults to avoid such businesses. Offensive businesses that are unobtrusive and easily avoided are easier to tolerate. The voluntary labeling of movies, recordings and video games has had the same effect. It gives adults fair warning about the explicit content of media and assists them in avoiding material they find offensive for themselves or their children.

The most successful of the rating systems was initiated by the Motion Picture Association of America after Jack Valenti took over as president in 1966. That year a new kind of frankness emerged in movies. *Who's Afraid of Virginia Woolf* included the word "screw" and the phrase "hump the hostess." More movies contained nudity. Because of the fear of government censorship, the movie industry decided to create its own system for rating films. The system has changed over the years. As it exists today, the system has five categories:

- *G — General Audiences.* All ages are admitted. The film contains nothing in language, nudity and sex, or violence that would offend parents whose children view the film. Snippets of language may go beyond polite conversation, but they are common, everyday expressions.
- *PG — Parental Guidance Suggested.* Some material may not be

suitable for children. There may be some profanity, violence or brief nudity, but these elements are not intense. There is no drug use content.

- *PG-13 — Parents Strongly Cautioned.* Some material may be inappropriate for children under 13. The rating is required for drug use content or use of harsher, sexually derived words.
- *R — Restricted.* The admission of people under age 17 requires accompanying parent or adult guardian. The movie contains some adult material: hard language, tough violence, nudity within sensual scenes or drug abuse.
- *NC-17 — No Children Under 17 Admitted.* The content of the movie is patently inappropriate for youngsters. The rating does not necessarily mean the content is obscene or pornographic. It can mean the presence of violence or sex or aberrational behavior or drug use that is too strong and therefore off-limits for viewing by children.

Leaders in the motion picture industry consider the movie rating system a success. The system has been embraced by the National Association of Theater Owners and by the Video Software Dealers Association. Polls conducted by the Opinion Research Corporation of Princeton, New Jersey, show that three-quarters of parents with children find the system very useful or fairly useful in selecting movies for their children.

The recording and video games industries have also adopted ratings, but in a more limited way. In 1985 the Recording Industry Association of America agreed to encourage its members to place the warning "Explicit Lyrics — Parental Advisory" on recordings containing references to explicit sex, violence or substance abuse. Instead of the warning, song lyrics may be printed on the back of the album cover. In 1994 the Software Publishers Association, following threats from Congress, agreed to encourage its members to label computer and video games. Games are labeled for age appropriateness and for the explicitness of violence, nudity or sex, and language.

The major advantage of such ratings is that, because they alert consumers to content, they tend to discourage the involvement of government in controlling that content. Congress has not been fully satisfied with the actions of the software industry, however, and several bills aimed at the industry were introduced but did not pass the 107th Congress.[100]

And in 1996, with pressure from Congress, most of the TV networks agreed to a voluntary rating system. The six classifications were:

- *TV-Y.* Children's programs acceptable for kids of all ages.
- *TV-Y7.* Children's programs for ages seven and older that might have material upsetting to younger kids.
- *TV-G.* Appropriate for audiences of all ages.

---

[98] City of Los Angeles v. Alameda Books, Inc., 535 U.S. 425 (2002).

[99] Stringfellows of New York, Ltd. v. City of New York, 694 N.E.2d 407 (N.Y. 1998).

[100] *See* Kyonzte Hughes, *Rating & Labeling Entertainment,* First Amendment Center, June 13, 2006, http://www.firstamendmentcenter.org. *See also,* Associated Press, *"Grand Theft Auto" Makers Settle With FTC Over Sex Content, available at* http://www.firstamendmentcenter.org.

- *TV-PG.* Parental guidance suggested, may contain violence, sexual material or offensive language.
- *TV-14.* Inappropriate for kids under fourteen because of more intense violence and sexual content.
- *TV-MA.* Not for children under seventeen, may contain sex, profane language or graphic violence.

Additional rating subcategories were: V — violence, S — sexual situations, L — coarse language, D — suggestive dialogue and FV — fantasy violence. New television sets with something called a "V-chip" may be programmed to censor different categories of programs.[101]

## SUMMARY

The centrist decision in *Miller v. California* displeased liberals, conservatives, civil libertarians and religious fundamentalists. The decision did not achieve the hoped-for effect of reducing the availability of erotica. In fact, explicit erotica has grown in popularity since *Miller,* thanks in part to changes in media technology and the developments with VCRs and DVDs, cable and the Internet. The increase in erotica has occurred despite the actions of virtually every state legislature to draft restrictive statutes to comply with *Miller.* Erotica also has become quite commonplace in Canada, which has an eighty-five-store chain called "Adults Only Video." Under Canadian Supreme Court rules, portrayals of explicit sex are legal if they do not include degradation or violence.

Why has erotica prospered while laws have become more restrictive? The answer is public opinion, which has grown quite tolerant of unobtrusive erotica. Liberal public opinion translates into less pressure on prosecutors and police to enforce obscenity laws. The concept of jury nullification also limits obscenity convictions: Jurors make their decisions based on conscience and overall justice and not on the law.

A constant tension exists in this country between liberals and conservatives about the availability of erotica. It is part of what some have termed a cultural war. This war has even influenced the U.S. military, as demonstrated by the Military Honor and Decency Act of 1996. The federal statute prohibits military exchanges, or PX's, from selling or renting sexual films, books or magazines in which a dominant theme portrays nudity, including sexual or excretory activities or organs, in a lascivious way. To implement the law, the Pentagon created an eight-member Resale Activities Board of Review to determine which of 153 erotic magazines carried in PX's violated the statute. *Playboy,* which sold 25,000 copies a month on military bases, was deemed acceptable; but *Penthouse,* which sold 19,000 copies, was unacceptable. This resulted in a legal challenge by *Penthouse.* A panel of the U.S. Court of Appeals upheld the statute on a split vote, concluding that the regulation constituted content discrimination that was legal and not viewpoint discrimination that was unconstitutional.[102] This kind of hair splitting, distinguishing between content and viewpoint discrimination, is typical of obscenity jurisprudence.

## FOR ADDITIONAL READING

Christensen, F. M. *Pornography: The Other Side.* New York: Praeger, 1990.

Dworkin, Andrea & Catharine A. MacKinnon. *Pornography & Civil Rights: A New Day for Women's Equality.* Minneapolis: Organizing Against Pornography, 1988.

Howitt, Dennis. *Crime, Media and the Law.* New York: John Wiley & Sons, 1998.

Lasky, Melvin J. *Profanity, Obscenity and the Media.* Somerset, N.J.: Transaction, 2004.

Lewis, Felice Flanery. *Literature, Obscenity, & Law.* Carbondale, Ill.: Southern Illinois University Press, 1976.

Linz, Daniel. "Estimating Community Standards: The Use of Social Science Evidence in an Obscenity Prosecution," 55 *Public Opinion Quarterly* 80-112 (Spring 1991).

MacKinnon, Catharine A. *Only Words.* Cambridge: Harvard University Press, 1993.

Michael, Robert T., et al. *Sex in America: A Definitive Survey.* New York: Little, Brown and Company, 1994.

Strossen, Nadine. *Defending Pornography: Free Speech, Sex, and the Fight for Women's Rights.* New York: Scribner, 1995.

[101] *See* Kelvin Childs, *No Rush to New TV Ratings,* EDITOR & PUBLISHER, Nov. 1, 1997, at 14.

[102] General Media Communications, Inc. v. Cohen, 131 F.3d 273 (2nd Cir. 1997).

# 6

# Defamation

*By Kyu Ho Youm*

---

  **Headnote Questions**

- *Why is libel considered an occupational hazard for media professionals?*
- *What are the key functions of libel law?*
- *What is the principal distinction between libel and slander? How are the causes of action related to what has been called a "defamacast"?*
- *What must a plaintiff prove to win a libel case?*
- *Why is "publication" called a term of art in libel law?*
- *What is the definition of "actual malice" in libel law?*
- *Why are state constitutions and common law important to libel law?*
- *What kind of damages are recognized in a libel action?*
- *What kinds of defenses are available to libel defendants?*
- *Why is it a crucial libel defense issue to determine whether a plaintiff is a public official, public figure or private person?*
- *What comes closest to being an ironclad libel defense?*
- *When can "opinion" be used as a libel defense?*
- *When can repeating a defamatory statement be defensible?*
- *Where does the law stand with regard to libel on the Internet?*
- *When do U.S. media face transborder libel litigation, and what are the implications of foreign libel judgments?*

---

Freedom of speech is not absolute. It must be balanced against other competing social interests. One area in which such balancing must occur is that of defamation. As the U.S. Supreme Court has noted: "[A]bsolute protection for the communications media requires a total sacrifice of the competing value served by the law of defamation."[1]

The libel law of a society indicates to a large extent how the society balances the importance of reputational interests with freedom of speech. Harm to reputation has been a criminal offense or a civil wrong since civilization's earliest days, but the social and cultural approach to reputation as a value varies from society to society. Professor Robert C. Post elaborates:

Defamation law would operate differently in a deference society than in a market society. In the latter, reputation is a quintessentially private possession; it is created by individual effort and is of importance primarily to those who have created it. Reputation's claim to legal protection is neither greater nor less than the claim to public protection of similar private goods. The preservation of honor in a deference society, on the other hand, entails more than the protection of merely individual interests. Since honor is not created by individual labor, but instead by shared social perceptions that transcend the behavior of particular persons, honor is "public good, not merely a private possession."[2]

---

[1] Gertz v. Robert Welch, Inc., 418 U.S. 341, 341 (1974)

[2] Robert C. Post, *The Social Foundations of Defamation Law: Reputation and*

In the United States, defamation was one of the earliest legal actions available against the press, and it is still the most common legal danger to the media. Libel is clearly an occupational hazard for professional communicators: Seventy percent of all libel actions are filed against the mass media; at least two-thirds of those are brought against newspapers.[3]

Libel, then, has the very real possibility of chilling speech, particularly when one considers the ramifications of a libel suit. As attorney Barbara Dill writes:

Libel law in the United States is at a critical juncture. The old broken formula of sue-and-be-sued is not working well for anyone but lawyers. It costs too much, takes too long, and clogs the courts with fencing matches that end most often in technical decisions that bypass the fundamental issues and satisfy neither side.[4]

The chill caused by libel law is clearly an irony in the United States, where press freedom is protected as a constitutional right, but reputation is not. In many ways, First Amendment scholar Frederick Schauer writes, "[T]he American approach ... reflects a society in which the press is considered to occupy a much more important role in the resolution of public issues. The press occupies a special position in the American system, a position that accounts for its strong protection against inhibiting defamation laws."[5]

Libel suits are common, and there are no guarantees, but professional communicators can be proactive in an attempt to stay out of trouble and to provide themselves with more protection should they be sued.

This chapter first reviews defamation law from the plaintiff's perspective and then provides an overview of libel defense strategies. It focuses on the elements of a cause of action for libel and related areas, including the technological impact of cyberspace and the emerging legal issues confronting news media and individuals around the world. It also explores various libel defenses the media use in accomplishing a great social good by publishing allegedly defamatory material.

## DEFAMATION DEFINED

Defamation — the publication of material that would tend to hold one up to hatred, ridicule, contempt or spite — consists of twin torts: libel and slander. In general, libel is the publication of defamatory matter by written or printed words or by some other physical form. Slander is defamatory communication by spoken words, gestures or other transitory means.[6]

The distinction between libel and slander originated when relatively few people could read, and the spoken word was more credible. Since then, the written word has gained more credibility, and defamation by writing is perceived to cause greater harm. More recently, however, new modes of communication have developed that often make the distinction between libel and slander obsolete. Defamation by means of television or radio, for example, might have more impact and greater reach than that by a small newspaper. Modern legal guides suggest that, instead of the form of communication medium, courts should consider the area of dissemination, the deliberate and premeditated character of a publication and the persistence of the defamation when classifying a defamatory statement as libel or slander.[7]

Jurisdictions often disagree on whether defamation by electronic means should be defined as libel or slander. Most states do not distinguish libel from slander with regard to broadcasting, but four, including California, treat defamatory radio and television broadcasts as slander, and thirteen states, including New York, treat it as libel. A New York court explained its rationale:

When account is taken of the vast and far-flung audience reached by radio today, often far greater in number than the readers of the largest metropolitan newspaper, it is evident that the broadcast of scandalous utterances is in general as potentially harmful to the defamed person's reputation as a publication by writing. That defamation by radio, in the absence of a script or transcription, lacks the measure of durability possessed by written libel, in nowise lessens its capacity for harm.[8]

Some states — Connecticut and Tennessee are two — make a distinction between a statement broadcast from a script — libel — and that which is ad-libbed — slander. An appellate court in Georgia, noting that television broadcasting contains both libel and slander, coined the word "defamacast" to describe broadcast defamation. The court said, "Perhaps the most perplexing problem is whether defamatory material shown on television should be classified as a libel, a slander or in some third category." The court decided to classify this type of material: "Believing as we do that the common law must adapt, and classically has adapted, to meet new situations, we now make that 'frank recognition...' that defamation by radio and television falls into a new category, thus completing the triptych. In this category, defamation by broadcast or 'defamacast' is actionable *per se.*"[9]

While debate on the issue continues, an increasing number of

---

*the Constitution,* 74 CAL. L. REV. 691, 702 (1986).

[3] DONALD M. GILLMOR, POWER, PUBLICITY AND THE ABUSE OF LIBEL LAW 133 (1992).

[4] Barbara Dill, *Libel Law Doesn't Work, But Can It Be Fixed?, in* MARTIN LONDON & BARBARA DILL, AT WHAT PRICE? LIBEL LAW AND FREEDOM OF THE PRESS 35 (1993).

[5] Frederick Schauer, *Social Foundations of the Law of Defamation: A Comparative Analysis,* 1 J. MEDIA L. & PRAC. 1, 18 (1980).

[6] *See* RESTATEMENT (SECOND) OF TORTS §§ 568(1), 568(2) (1977).

[7] *Id.* at § 568(3) (1977).

[8] Shor v. Billingsley, 158 N.Y.S.2d 476, 484 (N.Y. Sup. Ct. 1956).

[9] Am. Broad.-Paramount Theatres, Inc. v. Simpson, 126 S.E.2d 873, 876, 879 (Ga. Ct. App. 1962).

jurisdictions are accepting the position that, because of the wide dissemination and the increased power of the broadcast media, defamation by electronic means is closer to libel than slander.

## THE RATIONALE AND REACH OF LIBEL LAW

Libel law protects the reputational interests of individuals because it involves statements about them made by others. Legal scholar David Anderson has identified four types of reputational harm in the context of relational interest. The defamation may (1) interfere with the plaintiff's existing relationships with other people; (2) interfere with future relationships; (3) destroy a favorable public image; or (4) create a negative public image for a person who previously had no public image at all.[10]

Libel law also serves other important societal interests. It attempts to compensate for economic and emotional injury and promotes human dignity by providing a civilized forum in which a dispute is settled.

More importantly, however, libel law acts as a deterrent on the publication of false and injurious speech through the award of damages. The Supreme Court has noted, for example, that a state "may rightly employ its libel laws to discourage the deception of its citizens."[11] In addition, libel law serves a vital social interest by providing a check on media power. It opens the newsgathering and decision-making process of the media to public scrutiny and accountability. A federal judge in a libel action against *Time* magazine explained:

> *Time* has refused to issue any correction or to print plaintiff's denial. Only through the litigation process has plaintiff been able to uncover and publish the evidence from which *Time* claimed to have learned the contents of [a secret document relating to the Beirut massacre in 1982]. And only through this avenue has he been able to bring to light the process by which the allegedly offending statement came to be written, including evidence of the possible motivations and truthfulness of its author. That this process has proved enormously expensive, and painfully contentious, is as much the product of *Time's* all-out litigation strategy as of any plan by plaintiff to intimidate the press.[12]

### Constitutional and State Law

Although the Constitution does not explicitly recognize reputational rights, American courts have often noted the value of a good name. In an oft-quoted opinion, Justice Potter Stewart characterized an individual's right to protection of reputation as "a concept at the root of any decent system of ordered liberty." Justice Stewart continued: "The protection of private personality, like the protection of life itself, is left primarily to the individual States under the Ninth and Tenth Amendments. But this does not mean that the right is entitled to any less recognition by this Court as a basic of our constitutional system."[13] Therefore, the Supreme Court has recognized that "society has a pervasive and strong interest in preventing and redressing attacks upon reputation."[14]

The Constitution, of course, is not the only source of law to be used in balancing free speech and reputational rights. State constitutions and common law play a significant role in protecting press rights and in allowing individuals to protect their reputations. State statutes can also affect libel conflicts. Statutes of limitations — laws that prevent stale lawsuits from being adjudicated — and retraction statutes — which can mitigate or eliminate some damages — are examples of state laws that directly affect libel.

In addition, the First Amendment principle that prior restraint is presumptively unconstitutional applies to attempts to restrain material because it may be defamatory. State courts have rejected attempts to halt the publication of such material. However, one state supreme court did not rule out a possibility of defamatory statements being subject to prior restraint in limited circumstances. The Nebraska Supreme Court held in 1997: "[A]bsent a prior adversarial determination that the complained of publication is false or a misleading representation of fact, equity will not ... enjoin a libel or slander, unless such libel or slander is published (1) in violation of a trust or contract, or (2) in aid of another tort or unlawful act, or (3) injunctive relief is essential for the preservation of a property right."[15] In 2005, the U.S. Supreme Court refused to rule on the question of whether the First Amendment may ever allow a permanent injunction against defamation relating to a public figure. In *Tory v. Cochran*,[16] the Supreme Court sidestepped the substantive First Amendment issues over the injunction attorney Johnnie L. Cochran Jr. had obtained to prevent his former client Ulysses Tory from his continuing defamation. When Cochran died while the Supreme Court reviewed the California court's injunction, the Court ruled that the injunction was an overbroad prior restraint upon speech because it lacked "plausible justification."

### Criminal Libel

As the Media Law Resource Center noted in 2003, "[I]t is hard to square modern First Amendment principles with laws that pur-

---

[10] David A. Anderson, *Reputation, Compensation, and Proof,* 25 WM. & MARY L. REV. 747, 765-66 (1984).

[11] Keeton v. Hustler, 465 U.S. 770, 776 (1984).

[12] Sharon v. Time, 599 F. Supp. 538, 556 (S.D.N.Y. 1985).

[13] Rosenblatt v. Baer, 383 U.S. 75, 92 (1966).

[14] Milkovich v. Lorain Journal Co., 497 U.S. 1, 22 (1990) (quoting *Rosenblatt,* 383 U.S. at 86).

[15] Sid Dillon Chevrolet-Oldsmobile-Pontiac, Inc. v. Sullivan, 559 N.W.2d 740, 747 (Neb. 1997).

[16] 544 U.S. 734 (2005). For a detailed discussion of *Tory v. Cochran,* see Chapter 4.

port to criminalize statements that allegedly harm reputation."[17] Seventeen states and two U.S. territories have statutes that allow the government to prosecute people for defaming public officials, libeling the dead and using racial or ethnic epithets. These statutes are rarely used today, but they have been applied to Internet publishers recently. A Utah high school student, for example, was prosecuted under Utah's criminal libel law for his publication on a Web site of allegedly defamatory statements about his principal and classmates. In November 2002, however, the Utah Supreme Court invalidated the criminal libel law because it failed to recognize the actual malice standard.[18]

The U.S. Supreme Court has not repudiated criminal libel. Indeed, the Court, in *Garrison v. Louisiana*,[19] extended the actual malice rule — knowledge of falsity or reckless disregard of the truth — to criminal libel.

Criminal libel had its genesis in *De Libellis Famosis,* an English case in which Lord Coke delineated the principal points of the action:

> Every libel is made either against a private man, or against a magistrate or public person. If it be against a private man it deserves a severe punishment, for although the libel be made against one, yet it incites all those of the same family, kindred or society to revenge, and so tends *per consequens* to quarrels and breach of the peace, and may be the cause of the shedding of blood and greater inconvenience; if it be against a magistrate, or other public person, it is a greater offense; for it concerns not only the breach of the peace, but also the scandal of Government; for what greater scandal of Government can there be than to have corrupt and wicked magistrates to be appointed by the King to govern his subject under him.[20]

Courts have approached criminal libel in various ways, usually based upon the actual malice requirement. In 1991, for example, a U.S. district court struck down South Carolina's criminal libel statute, finding it unconstitutional because it allowed liability upon a showing of common law malice — ill will, spite or hatred — rather than actual malice.[21] Four years later, however, the Tenth U.S. Circuit Court of Appeals upheld the Kansas criminal libel statute. The court held that the law is not unconstitutional on its face because it requires actual malice to be proved in libel cases involving matters of public concern.[22] Then, in July 2001, the Alabama Supreme Court invalidated the state's criminal libel statute

because it did not require a showing of actual malice. The Alabama statute required proof that a defamatory statement about a public official or public figure be made "falsely and maliciously."[23] Most recently, the First U.S. Circuit Court of Appeals struck down Puerto Rico's criminal libel law on the ground that it lacked the actual malice requirement and truth as a defense.[24]

## THE PLAINTIFF'S CASE

Before the Supreme Court constitutionalized libel law in 1964 with *New York Times Co. v. Sullivan,*[25] the basic requirement for a plaintiff in making a case for defamation was proof that the defendant published a statement about the plaintiff that had a tendency to harm the plaintiff's reputation in the community or to discourage other people from associating or dealing with the plaintiff. The burden was on the plaintiff to prove three essential elements: identification of the plaintiff in the allegedly defamatory material, publication of the material by the defendant and the defamatory nature of the material.

But the requirements in a modern libel action are not that simple. To win damages, especially in libel actions against the media, a plaintiff must establish that: (1) a false *and* defamatory statement of fact concerning the plaintiff was published to a third party, (2) the publication was not privileged and was made with fault on the part of the publisher, and (3) the publication caused actual injury.

### Falsity

Under the common law, when a libel action was filed, statements upon which the action was based were presumed to be false. As a matter of constitutional law, however, that presumption of falsity has been rejected. Libel plaintiffs today must prove the statements are false, even if the statements were made with ill will.

Judge Robert Sack of the Second U.S. Circuit Court of Appeals, in the highly acclaimed *Sack on Defamation,* wrote that under the constitutional rule, "Truth is usually now not a *defense*. Proof of falsity is instead part of the plaintiff's case, at least in defamation suits brought by public officials, or involving communications about public issues, or both."[26]

### Defamation

In addition to being false, offending material must be defamatory. Identifying defamatory language is the first order of business in libel law. As one scholar wrote, however, "[W]ords are not single faced. They have many facets and may have many interpretations.

---

[17] Preface, *Criminalizing Speech About Reputation: The Legacy of Criminal Libel in the U.S. After Sullivan & Garrison,* MLRC BULLETIN (Mar. 2003).

[18] I.M.L. v. State, 61 P.3d 1038 (Utah 2002).

[19] 379 U.S. 64 (1964).

[20] 77 Eng. Rep. 250, 251 (1609).

[21] Fitts v. Kolb., 779 F. Supp. 1502 (D.S.C. 1991).

[22] Phelps v. Hamilton, 59 F.3d 1058 (10th Cir. 1995). *See also* State v. Carson, 95 P.2d 1042 (Kan. Ct. App. 2004).

[23] Ivey v. Alabama, 821 So.2d 937, 941 (Ala. 2001).

[24] Mangual v. Rotger-Sabat, 317 F.3d 45 (1st Cir. 2003).

[25] 376 U.S. 254 (1964).

[26] ROBERT D. SACK, SACK ON DEFAMATION 3-2 (3d ed. 2006).

Their values change with time, with place, and with association. Whether or not a word has a libelous connotation will therefore require analysis and perception in terms of its milieu and period."[27] Supreme Court Justice Oliver Wendell Holmes also observed: "A word is not a crystal, transparent and unchanged; it is the skin of a living thought and may vary greatly in color and content according to the circumstances and the time in which it is used."[28] Thus, the same words may communicate different meanings in different contexts.

## "Red-Flag Words"

Attorney and libel expert Bruce Sanford has listed a number of so-called "red flags," that is, words that courts often consider defamatory. They are:

addict, adultery, AIDS, alcoholic, atheist, bankrupt, bigamist, blacklisted, blackmail, bribery, cheater, child abuse, con artist, coward, crook, deadbeat, drug abuser, drunkard, ex-convict, fraud, gangster, gay, Herpes, hypocrite, incompetent, infidelity, Jekyll-Hyde personality, kept woman, Ku Klux Klan, Mafia, mentally ill, Nazi, neo-Nazi, peeping Tom, perjurer, plagiarist, prostitute, rapist, scam, scoundrel, seducer, shyster, slacker, stool pigeon, suicide, swindle, thief, unethical, unmarried mother, unprofessional, unsound mind, villain.

From Bruce W. Sanford, *Libel and Privacy* ß 4.13 (2d ed. 2006).

Socialism, love, democracy, communism and other words are capable of as many connotations and interpretations as there are situations in which they can be used. Consequently, words can be ambiguous. One cannot say with assurance that a word is or is not defamatory unless it has been placed in time, in location and in association so that its meaning can be determined. As the Hawaii Supreme Court said, whether a statement is defamatory "depends, among other factors, upon the temper of times, the current of contemporary public opinion, with the result that a word, harmless in one age, in one community, may be highly damaging to reputation at another time or in a different place."[29]

Compendiums of words cannot be considered a foolproof formula to divining how courts will rule on similar language, but they can often be warning signs for possible trouble. In addition, there are categories of words that are especially sensitive. For example, words that:

• impute to another a loathsome disease;

• accuse another of serious sexual misconduct;

• impugn another's honesty or integrity;

• accuse another of committing a crime or of being arrested or indicted;

• allege racial, ethnic or religious bigotry;

• impugn another's financial health or credit-worthiness;

• accuse another of associating with criminals or others of unsavory character;

• assert incompetence or lack of ability in one's trade, business, profession or office.[30]

**Interpreting Defamation.** Defamation is recipient-oriented. That is, it hinges on how the language is interpreted by its recipients. Thus, the first step in analyzing the defamatory nature of a statement is determining whether the readers could interpret the words to be defamatory and whether they did so. The value judgments, knowledge and background of recipients will affect their interpretations of statements. For example, people who support abortion as a constitutional right of privacy would not consider it defamatory for a person to be depicted as being "pro-choice," while those who view abortion as morally reprehensible might lose their reputations among a certain group by being depicted as "pro-choice." So, whose understanding of a defamatory statement is used in establishing the defamatory nature of the statement?

The *Restatement (Second) of Torts,* a legal tract designed to explain the law, states that "[i]t is enough that the communication would tend to prejudice [the plaintiff] in the eyes of *a substantial and respectable minority*" of the community, and "it is not enough that the communication would be derogatory in the view of a single individual or a very small group of persons, if the group is not large enough to constitute a substantial minority."[31]

As an example, a prison inmate was unsuccessful in maintaining a libel action when he was identified as an FBI informant because, the court said, he was not accused of unlawful or improper conduct. Noting that the defamatory statement must expose the plaintiff to public ridicule "in the minds of 'right thinking persons' or among 'a considerable and respectable class of people,'" the court stated: "It is true that a charge of informing may bring opprobrium from one's fellow inmates in the prison community. However, it is not one's reputation in a limited community in which attitudes and social values may depart substantially from those prevailing generally which an action for defamation is designed to protect."[32]

**Rules of Construction.** Most states use the reasonable construction rule to determine the defamatory nature of a statement. Under the rule, the meaning of a communication, according to the

---

27 Philip Wittenberg, Dangerous Words: A Guide to the Law of Libel 11 (1947).

28 Towne v. Eisner, 245 U.S. 418, 425 (1918).

29 Beamer v. Nishiki, 670 P.2d 1264, 1271 (Haw. 1983).

30 Neil J. Rosini, The Practical Guide to Libel Law 9 (1991).

31 Restatement, *supra* note 6, at § 559 comm. e (emphasis added).

32 Saunders v. WHYY, 382 A.2d 257, 259 (Del. Super. Ct. 1978).

*Restatement,* "is that which the recipient correctly, or mistakenly but reasonably, understands it was intended to express."[33] The rule does not allow a strained interpretation. The Alabama Supreme Court provided a good explication of the rule:

[T]he printed words are to be taken in their natural meaning, and according to the sense in which they appear to have been used and the idea they are adapted to convey to those who read them. A forced construction is not to be put upon them in order to relieve the defendant from liability, nor are they to be subjected to the critical analysis of a trained legal mind, but must be construed and determined by the natural and probable effect on the mind of the average lay reader.[34]

By contrast, the innocent construction rule, which is applied in Illinois and Ohio, requires a statement "to be considered in context, with the words and the implications there from given their natural and obvious meaning; if, as so construed, the statement may reasonably be innocently interpreted or reasonably be interpreted as referring to someone other than the plaintiff it cannot be actionable per se."[35]

The *Restatement* indicates that a report of a single act of misconduct by a person in the course of the person's business, trade, profession or office may be sufficient to support a libel action, even though the charge does not imply a habitual course or conduct. A number of states, however, have adopted the single instance rule, which provides that a charge of ignorance or a mistake on a single occasion is not actionable unless special damages can be shown. The rule is based on the common-sense premise that people make mistakes, and to state that a professional has made a mistake in a specific instance should not cause damage because the statement only implies that the person is human.

**Implication.** Defamation by implication occurs when false impressions arise from truthful statements. It demonstrates the larger problem of determining the meaning of an allegedly defamatory communication by examining the words in context. The Texas Supreme Court, for example, held: "A publication can convey a false and defamatory meaning by omitting or juxtaposing facts, even though all the story's individual statements considered in isolation were literally true or non-defamatory."[36] One example of defamation by implication is a story published by the *Memphis Press-Scimitar.* It reported that Mrs. Ruth A. Nichols was treated for a bullet wound she received when another woman found her with the woman's husband in the Nichols home. According to witnesses, the woman fired at her husband, then at Mrs. Nichols.

The story was true. The Tennessee Supreme Court held, however, that the story was defamatory because it omitted crucial facts.[37] What the newspaper did not report was that Mrs. Nichols and the suspect's husband were not alone in the Nichols home; Mrs. Nichols' husband and two neighbors were also there, and Mr. Nichols had attempted to prevent the shooting.

Defamation through implication often arises in one of three contexts: (1) when a writer tries to guide a reader to a conclusion without stating the conclusion; (2) when a writer is ambiguous, offering multiple meanings, at least one of which is defamatory; (3) when a writer juxtaposes one message with another, creating an implication that is not necessarily intended.

An important tract on the law of torts has explained that proof of defamation by implication requires a combination of elements, defined by the terms "inducement," "innuendo" and "colloquium," explained here:

If the plaintiffs themselves are not directly named they must show by "colloquium" that the statements were "of and concerning" them. If it is still not clear how the plaintiffs have been defamed, they must plead extrinsic facts that would permit a defamatory meaning to be applied to defendants' words. This allegation of extrinsic facts is called the "inducement...." Where a statement is not clearly defamatory on its face it is the function of the innuendo to assert the meaning that plaintiff attaches to the passage and any additions by colloquium and inducement. The innuendo is not a fact but is the plaintiff's assertion of how the passage would be understood by those who heard the defendant's words and knew the additional unstated facts.[38]

To state, for example, that John Doe ran his car into a utility pole is not defamatory since he has every right to do so. But when it is specifically pleaded as "inducement" that Doe insured the car and, as "innuendo," that the statement is construed to mean that he was defrauding the insurance company, a charge of property damage is clearly implied, which is defamatory.

The Supreme Court has not addressed the issue of whether those who defame through implication are liable for damages. Several lower courts, however — including courts in Connecticut, the District of Columbia, Louisiana and Michigan — have declined to recognize liability for defamatory implications. The basis for the rulings appears to be this premise:

If unrestrained ... the theory of libel by implication would allow a jury to draw whatever inferences it wished, truthful or otherwise, from statements of fact. It would thereby permit liability for the mere tone of a publication, for statements that are in

---

[33] Restatement, *supra* note 6, at § 563 (1977).

[34] Kelly v. Arrington, 624 So. 2d 546, 548-49 (Ala. 1993).

[35] Chapski v. Copley Press, 8 Media L. Rep. (BNA) 2403, 2406 (Ill. 1982).

[36] Turner v. KTRK Television, Inc., 38 S.W.3d 103, 114 (Tex. 2000).

[37] Memphis Publ'g Co. v. Nichols, 569 S.W.2d 412 (Tenn. 1978).

[38] T. Barton Carter et. al., The First Amendment and the Fourth Estate 91 (8th ed. 2001).

substance opinion or true, or for statements about public persons that do not pass the "actual malice" test because they do not constitute knowing falsity or "reckless disregard" for the truth.[39]

The California Supreme Court, for example, has noted that a false and defamatory meaning cannot be based on "the fact that some person might, with extra sensitive perception, understand such a meaning.... Rather, the test ... is whether by reasonable implication a defamatory meaning may be found in the communication."[40]

**Libel per se and libel per quod.** A statement that is libelous *per se* is defamatory on its face. That is, the defamation is apparent in the statement. If additional information is required before a statement is defamatory, the statement is libelous *per quod,* and a plaintiff must prove special damages — that there was, in fact, a loss of money — before the plaintiff can recover.

The distinction between libel *per se* and libel *per quod* was weakened in 1974 when, in *Gertz v. Robert Welch, Inc.,*[41] the Supreme Court required plaintiffs to prove damages before recovering, but in many jurisdictions the distinction remains as a rule of law. The Missouri Supreme Court no longer recognizes a distinction between libel *per se* and libel *per quod.* That court stated that the rule created unjustifiable inequities by requiring a higher standard of proof for certain defamations:

> [I]n defamation cases the old rules of *per se* and *per quod* do not apply and plaintiff need only to plead and prove the unified defamation elements. In short, plaintiffs need not concern themselves with whether the defamation was *per se* or *per quod,* or with whether special damages exist, but must prove actual damages in all cases.[42]

By contrast, Illinois is one of the jurisdictions where the *per se/per quod* distinction is still recognized. In *Bryson v. News America Publications, Inc.,* for example, the Illinois Supreme Court held that a statement is defamatory *per se* if it falls into one of five statutorily defined categories: (1) commission of a crime; (2) infection with a type of communicable disease that could cause the infected person to be avoided; (3) malfeasance in the performance of a job; (4) unfitness for one's profession or trade; and (5) if the statement falsely accuses plaintiff of "fornication or adultery."[43]

The plaintiff in *Bryson* sued the publisher of *Seventeen Maga-*

*zine* for an article in which she was described as a "slut." She claimed that the article was libelous *per se.* The Illinois Supreme Court agreed, stating that the article's reference to the plaintiff as a "slut" fell within the Illinois libel statute's classification of words that "amount to charge any person with having been guilty of fornication or adultery."[44]

### Statements of Fact

For an allegedly defamatory statement to be actionable — that is, for a lawsuit to be based upon the statement — the statement must be one of fact rather than of opinion. In *Gertz,* the Supreme Court said: "Under the First Amendment there is no such thing as a false idea. However pernicious an opinion may seem, we depend for its correction not on the conscience of judges and juries but on the competition of other ideas. But there is no constitutional value in false statements of fact."[45] And in *Milkovich v. Lorain Journal*[46] the Court held that for a statement to be actionable, it must be provably false.

The threshold question facing the opinion defense is how to distinguish fact from opinion. Whether a statement is a statement of fact or opinion is decided by the judge. If the judge cannot determine whether a particular statement constitutes fact or opinion, the determination is made by the jury. (Opinion as a defense is discussed later in this chapter.)

### Identification

In order to win a libel action, a plaintiff must prove that he or she was identified, that is, that the defamation was "of and concerning" the plaintiff. Identification has nothing to do with the intent of the publisher of the defamation. As one writer put it, "The test is not whom the story intends to name but who a part of the audience may reasonably think is named — 'not who is meant but who is hit.'"[47]

Identification does not always mean that the plaintiff must be named. The plaintiff can be identified by other information within the published material or by extrinsic facts not included in the published material. And the plaintiff need not show every viewer or reader of the material identified the plaintiff, but that some significant number did.

A landmark Illinois case, *John v. Tribune Co.,*[48] provides a good example of how identification can cause unique problems. The case began when the *Chicago Tribune* reported about a police raid on a prostitution operation in an apartment house. Two

[39] Sack, *supra* note 27, at 2-29.

[40] Forsher v. Bugliosi, 608 P.2d 716, 723 (Cal. 1980).

[41] 418 U.S. 323 (1974).

[42] Nazeri v. Missouri Valley College, 860 S.W.2d 303, 313 (Mo. 1993) (en banc).

[43] 672 N.E.2d 1207, 1215 (Ill. 1996).

[44] *Id.* at 1221.

[45] 418 U.S. at 339-40.

[46] 497 U.S. 1 (1990).

[47] Paul P. Ashley, Say It Safely 30 (4th ed. 1969).

[48] 181 N.E.2d 105 (Ill. 1962).

articles about the raid identified the arrested owner as Dorothy Clark, also known as "Dolores Reising, 57, alias Eve Spiro and Eve John." By sheer coincidence, a woman whose maiden name was Eve Spiro and whose name at the time of the raid was Eve John was living in the basement of the raided building. She was a practicing psychologist and was not involved with the prostitution operation. She sued for libel. The Illinois Supreme Court held that the alias names could not be read as identifying Eve Spiro John as the "target" of the publication.[49] Thus, there was no identification of the plaintiff in the *Tribune* story.

Pictures of persons identified with fictitious names can also create headaches for the media. In April 1982, *TV Guide* published an ad for an upcoming television documentary series on teenage pregnancy. The heading of the advertisement asked in large, bold letters: "GUESS WHAT LORI FOUND OUT TODAY." In the middle of the advertisement was a photograph of a diary that contained the handwritten entry: "Dear Diary: I found out today that I'm pregnant. What will I do now?" Directly below the diary was a photograph of a teenager embracing a young man.

Libby Sue Chumley sued the publisher of *TV Guide* for a false implication that she was pregnant. She claimed she was the girl in the picture and that she was not and had never been pregnant. She further asserted that she never engaged in sexual relations with the young man in the photograph or with anyone else.

In 1984, the Georgia Supreme Court ruled that the ad was "of and concerning" Chumley. The court rejected the argument that the advertisement did not identify Chumley because "Lori" was the name used in the ad even though the photograph of the advertisement was Chumley. The court reasoned that the bold print of the advertisement and the strategic placement of the photo made it possible for people to interpret Chumley to be "Lori," a pregnant teenager.[50]

In addition, the Supreme Court has said that races or other large groups of people cannot win libel actions because individual members of the large groups have not been identified. The *Restatement* delineates the "group libel doctrine" this way:

One who publishes defamatory matter concerning a group or class of persons is subject to liability to an individual member of it if, but only if: (a) the group or class is so small that the matter can reasonably be understood to refer to the member; or (b) the circumstances of publication reasonably give rise to the conclusion that there is a particular reference to the member.[51]

The rationale for the rule is that, "First, defamatory statements do little damage to the reputation of any member of a group larger than twenty-five if the defamation refers to all members of the

group.... Second, the price to be paid by making such statements actionable is simply too high" for freedom of expression.[52]

The cut-off point for identification probably ranges from about twenty-five to about one hundred. Indeed, a class of 637 commercial net fishermen was certainly too large for any individual net fisherman to sustain a libel action against two television stations. The Florida Circuit Court that ruled in the case noted that the group libel doctrine is "deeply entrenched" in the common law and "almost never operates to create liability when the allegedly defamed group is greater than twenty-five individuals.... No case has been reported that has ever applied the principle to a group larger than 60 individuals."[53]

While members of groups can be defamed if the groups are small enough, it is almost impossible for family members to be defamed based on the activities of other members of the family. A father cannot be defamed, for example, because of a report that his son was charged with some crime.[54]

## Publication

Publication is essential to a libel plaintiff's case. It is probably the easiest element to prove when the lawsuit involves the media, but legally, "publication" is a term of art. It occurs when defamatory material is intentionally or negligently disseminated to someone other than the person defamed. As one court put it, "A defamatory writing is not published if it is read by no one but the one defamed. Published it is, however, as soon as read by anyone else."[55]

The form of publication is irrelevant. Defamatory material can be published in written or spoken form or on computer bulletin boards. Especially noteworthy, however, is the congressional attempt to immunize online publication of defamatory statements from liability. In 1996, Congress enacted the Communications Decency Act, which provides, in part, that, "No provider or user of an interactive computer service shall be treated as the publisher or speaker of any information provided by another information content provider."[56] Thus, the federal law protects online service providers from state law causes of action for defamation. And, while repetition of a defamation generally consists of a new and separate libel, repetition by the defamed person generally does not constitute publication. Similarly, while each person involved in the publication of defamatory material may be sued, unless the involvement is direct, there is not likely to be liability. News vendors,

[49] *Id.* at 108.

[50] Triangle Publ'ns v. Chumley, 317 S.E.2d 534, 537 (Ga. 1984).

[51] RESTATEMENT, *supra* note 6, at § 5645a.

[52] REX S. HEINKE, MEDIA LAW 101 (1994).

[53] Adams v. WFTY, Inc., 24 Media L. Rep. (BNA) 1350, 1351 (Fla. Cir. Ct. 1995).

[54] Apparently only one Puerto Rico case violated this tenet of libel law. *Compare* Torre-Silva v. El Mundo, Inc., 3 Media L. Rep. (BNA) 1508 (P.R. 1977) *with* Rodriguez v. El Vocero De Puerto Rico, Inc., 22 Media L. Rep. (BNA) 1495 (P.R. 1994).

[55] Ostrowe v. Lee, 175 N.E. 505, 505 (N.Y. 1931).

[56] 47 U.S.C. 230(c) (Supp. 1996).

book sellers and libraries, for example, are not subject to liability for "publishing" defamatory material, if they had no reason to suspect that the material was defamatory.

The accurate republication of defamatory statements within quotation marks is automatically a republication. And, since accuracy is not necessarily the equivalent of truth, simply reporting what another person has said is no defense except where the neutral-reportage doctrine is recognized. (The defenses of truth and neutral reportage are discussed later in this chapter.)

At one time, each separate publication of a defamatory statement could prompt a cause of action. For example, if a newspaper sold 500,000 copies of an edition containing a libelous statement, a plaintiff could bring 500,000 different lawsuits. But courts have recognized the inherent unfairness of such a rule, and many have adopted the single-publication rule. The rule requires a plaintiff to recover all damages suffered from a libel published in any one edition of a magazine or newspaper in one action. This, of course, does not necessarily foreclose multiple causes of action against several defendants for a defamatory statement. Each person who is responsible for publication of the defamatory statement may be held liable for the publication.

The date of publication of an alleged libel is important because courts do not like to hear old lawsuits. Therefore, each jurisdiction in the United States has a statute of limitations, which bars legal actions after certain periods of time. The statute of limitations for libel actions in most states is one or two years. The key, therefore, is determining the actual date of publication of the libel. If each republication constitutes a new publication, therefore, a new statute of limitations applies to each republication.

Courts that have applied the single-publication rule, however, have held that the statute of limitations begins to run with the first publication. This single-publication rule applies to Internet postings. That is, "[D]espite the continued public availability," Judge Sack wrote, "[T]here is a single publication at the time the posting is made, and the statute of limitations begins to run then."[57] In addition, courts have distinguished between a "republication" and a "repetition" of the libel, the latter not being a publication for purposes of a lawsuit. An example of a repetition would be the distribution of a syndicated column. The publication occurred, one court held, with the distribution of the column, and each printing of the column thereafter was a repetition, not a republication. The statute of limitations of the state where the column first appeared should apply, the court held.[58]

### Fault

U.S. libel law is exceedingly complex, and one of the best examples

of that complexity might be the various degrees of fault that are applied. Public figures and public officials are required to prove actual malice — knowledge of falsity or reckless disregard for the truth — before they can win libel actions. Private persons, on the other hand, must only prove negligence in most states in order to win, but must prove actual malice if they want to win punitive damages or presumed damages.

The actual malice rule, which originated for constitutional purposes in *New York Times Co. v. Sullivan,*[59] is derived from the constitutional right of American people to express themselves about matters of public concern. Against the background of "a profound national commitment to the principle that debate on public issues should be uninhibited, robust, and wide-open," the Supreme Court declared, "erroneous statement is inevitable in free debate, and ... it must be protected if the freedoms of expression are to have the 'breathing space' that they 'need to survive.'"[60]

*Times v. Sullivan* arose from an advertisement published in the March 29, 1960, issue of the *New York Times.* The full-page ad, "Heed Their Rising Voices," was placed by the Committee to Defend Martin Luther King and the Struggle for Freedom in the South and, among other things, solicited funds for the legal defense of Dr. King. It started thus:

As the whole world knows by now, thousands of Southern Negro students are engaged in widespread non-violent demonstrations in positive affirmation of the right to live in human dignity as guaranteed by the U.S. Constitution. In their efforts to uphold these guarantees, they are being met by an unprecedented wave of terror by those who would deny and negate that document which the whole world looks upon as setting the pattern for modern freedom.

The advertisement alleged repressive actions taken by local authorities against civil rights demonstrations in the South:

In Montgomery, Alabama, after students sang "My Country, 'Tis of Thee" on the State Capitol steps, their leaders were expelled from school, and truckloads of police armed with shotguns and tear-gas ringed the Alabama State College Campus. When the entire student body protested to state authorities by refusing to re-register, their dining hall was padlocked in an attempt to starve them into submission.

The advertisement, without naming any individuals or organizations, asserted that "the Southern violators of the Constitution" were "determined to destroy the one man who, more than any other, symbolizes the new spirit now sweeping the South — the Rev. Dr. Martin Luther King, Jr., world-famous leader of the Mont-

---

[57] Sack, *supra* 26, at 7-6. *See also* McCandliss v. Cox Enters., Inc., 593 S.E.2d 856 (Ga. 2004) (holding that the single-publication rule applies to archived stories on the newspaper's Web site).

[58] Givens v. Quinn, 877 F. Supp. 485, 490 (W.D. Mo. 1994).

[59] 376 U.S. 254 (1964).

[60] *Id.* at 270-72.

gomery Bus Protest." It continued:

> Again and again the Southern violators have answered Dr. King's peaceful protests with intimidation and violence. They have bombed his home almost killing his wife and child. They have assaulted his person. They have arrested him seven times — for "speeding," "loitering" and similar "offenses." And now they have charged him with "perjury" — a felony under which they could imprison him for ten years.

L.B. Sullivan, a commissioner of public affairs for Montgomery, sued the New York Times Co. for libel. He claimed that because he was the commissioner responsible for supervision of the Montgomery police, the advertisement's allegations of police wrongdoing libeled him. He sought damages of $500,000, and a jury awarded him the entire amount. The Alabama Supreme Court affirmed the judgment, holding that the *Times* was irresponsible in publishing the false advertisement because the paper could have verified the allegations in the advertisement by checking its own files prior to publication. The Alabama court curtly rejected the *New York Times'* argument that the advertisement was protected by the U.S. Constitution. It reasoned in a single sentence that "The First Amendment of the U.S. Constitution does not protect libelous publications."[61]

The New York Times Co. appealed the decision to the U.S. Supreme Court. On March 9, 1964, the Court reversed the Alabama court decision unanimously. It was a stunning victory for free press and free speech in America. Alexander Meiklejohn, who had argued for years that political expression relating to the government should be immune from punishment, characterized the *Times* decision as "an occasion for dancing in the streets."[62]

Justice William Brennan, who wrote the opinion for the Court, began with the "general proposition that freedom of expression upon public questions is secured by the First Amendment." Noting the First Amendment's guarantee of freedom of expression as a right of American citizens, Justice Brennan wrote that the *Times* case should be examined "against the background of a profound national commitment to the principle that debate on public issues should be uninhibited, robust, and wide-open, and that it may well include vehement, caustic, and sometimes unpleasantly sharp attacks on government and public officials." Justice Brennan wrote that the advertisement in question was "an expression of grievance and protest on one of the major public issues of our time" and thus entitled to the constitutional protection. However, "The question is whether it forfeits that protection by the falsity of some of its factual statements and by its alleged defamation of re-

spondent."[63]

Justice Brennan answered by stating that "the First Amendment guarantees have consistently refused to recognize an exception for any test of truth." He recognized the flexibility of the concept of truth and warned against the chilling effect of penalizing honest mistakes: "A rule compelling the critic of official conduct to guarantee the truth of all his factual assertions — and to do so on pain of libel judgment virtually unlimited in amount — leads to a comparable 'self-censorship.'"[64]

Therefore, the Court established that a public official could win a libel action based upon criticism of official conduct only if the official could prove actual malice, defined as knowledge of falsity or reckless disregard for truth or falsity. "Actual malice" does not mean hatred, ill-will or spite, which is the definition of common law malice.

The Supreme Court has specifically said that actual malice is a subjective rather than objective standard. That means that the standard reflects an attempt by a publisher to, as Justice Brennan said in *New York Times*, injure through knowing or reckless falsehood. Thus, the conduct of a libel defendant is often examined to determine whether there is objective evidence of the subjective standard. One way a plaintiff can prevail in a libel action, therefore, is to demonstrate that there was knowledge of falsity or reckless disregard for the truth.

**Knowledge of Falsity.** Actual malice is proved much more often by showing reckless disregard on the part of the defendant than by showing knowing falsity. One reason — perhaps the foremost reason — is that professional communicators rarely publish anything knowing it is false. But there are exceptions. One was when Ralph Ginzburg published in *Fact* magazine that some psychiatrists he surveyed found Republican presidential candidate Barry Goldwater to be mentally unstable. Goldwater sued for libel, and his attorneys were able to show that the survey results were actually very favorable toward Goldwater, but Ginzburg ignored the positive comments and focused only on the negative. In addition, there was evidence that the publisher of the article knew before the survey was distributed what the tenor of the article would be. Goldwater was able to meet the actual malice standard by showing that, although the statements Ginzburg made were true individually, collectively they misrepresented the truth; that is, they were false and that the author knew this but published them anyway.[65]

While knowledge of falsity can be easily applied, it's not easily proved. Because "[t]he knowledge of falsity prong of Times Rule Actual Malice is based on a determination of what the publisher knew or did not know at the time of publication," one scholar wrote, the defendant's state of mind at the time of publication is

---

[61] *Id.* at 264 (quoting New York Times Co. v. Sullivan, 144 So. 2d 25, 40 (Ala. 1962)).

[62] Harry Kalven Jr., *The New York Times Case: A Note on "The Central Meaning of the First Amendment,"* 1964 SUP. CT. REV. 199, 221 n.125.

[63] 376 U.S. at 271.

[64] *Id.* at 279.

[65] Goldwater v. Ginzburg, 414 F.2d 324 (2d Cir. 1969).

key.[66] Proving state of mind with convincing clarity can be challenging at the least. Rarely will a libel defendant admit knowledge of falsity, so, most often, plaintiffs must use objective evidence. That's difficult, but it can be done. When editorial writers at a newspaper asserted that a public official was a liar, for example, but articles in the same newspaper demonstrated that the official had not lied, the editorial writers were found to have acted with actual malice — they *knew* their statements were false.[67]

A plaintiff's claim that a publication is false, while signaling that a publisher should investigate further, is not sufficient, standing alone, to show knowledge of falsity, particularly in the face of evidence from reliable, objective sources. If the evidence from those reliable sources raised questions about the truth of the material to be published, it's a different story. As one scholar wrote, "To publish in the face of such evidence would be to publish with knowledge of falsity. Similarly, to publish charges with little or no support for those charges has also been determined to be publishing with knowledge of falsity, as has the selective use of information to the detriment of the plaintiff."[68]

Thus, the determination of knowledge of falsity rests on what the libel defendant knew at the time of publication. And what the publisher knew often rests on the extent of the investigation before publication, along with the interpretation, editing and presentation of the material. In *Herbert v. Lando,*[69] for example, the Supreme Court concluded that a plaintiff could inquire as to a defendant's state of mind while preparing a report. Questions about why the defendant believed and disbelieved certain sources, why the defendant used some material over other material and like issues were permissible, Justice Byron White wrote for the majority.

Former Army Col. Anthony Herbert contended that he was defamed in a *60 Minutes* segment. Producer Barry Lando and correspondent Mike Wallace argued that the First Amendment protected them from testifying as to their thought processes or state of mind at the time the segment was being edited and produced. The Supreme Court disagreed, finding that state of mind was central to actual malice. In a previous case, the Court had held, "There must be sufficient evidence to permit the conclusion that the defendant in fact entertained serious doubts as to the truth of his publication."[70] The assertion by a defendant that he or she believed the publication to be true is inadequate standing alone, but may be sufficient when not refuted by the plaintiff.

What a libel defendant knew at the time of publication was also central to the 1984 case *Bose Corporation v. Consumers Union of United States.*[71] Bose filed suit against the publisher of *Consumer Reports* magazine for statements critical of stereo speakers developed by the company. Bose convinced a jury that the magazine had published false statements with actual malice. The U.S. Court of Appeals for the First Circuit reversed, however, and the Supreme Court upheld the reversal. Bose had succeeded in showing that the author of the critical report might not have expressed himself well and might have attempted, at trial, to cover up for that poor expression. That proof, the Court said, however, was irrelevant. What was important was the author's "state of mind when he wrote his initial report, or when he checked the article against that report."[72]

In short, it becomes essential to explore the libel defendant's state of mind at the time of the preparation and publication of the defamation in order to learn whether actual malice existed. The libel defendant should recognize that these are likely to be probed and should be prepared to justify both the actions and the state of mind that led to the choices made.

The publisher's state of mind toward the investigation and the material that is eventually published is also key to the question of knowledge of falsity. Indeed, the publisher's state of mind toward the *subject* of the report may be irrelevant because ill will toward the plaintiff is not sufficient to demonstrate actual malice. Ill will, however, may be introduced to demonstrate a defendant's motive for lying or publishing with reckless disregard for the truth. As one court noted, while "the concepts underlying malice and actual malice are not the same ... this does not preclude a relationship between them."[73] When courts permit evidence of ill will, hatred or spite to be introduced for their bearing on the actual malice question, they usually admonish juries that those elements, standing alone, can never establish actual malice.

Courts have also indicated that knowledge of falsity can be demonstrated by the way material is written, edited or presented. This may be particularly true with headlines. Wrote First Amendment scholar W. Wat Hopkins:

> When large headlines are not literally defamatory, for example, but raise the implication of wrongdoing not supported by the texts of the articles over which they appear, a libel verdict for a public official can stand because of sufficient evidence that the headlines were published with actual malice. When the headlines are merely ambiguous, however, there is no knowledge of falsity. Similarly, ambiguous language or internal inconsistencies in news stories, standing alone, are insufficient evidence of actual malice.[74]

[66] W. Wat Hopkins, Actual Malice Twenty-Five Years After Times v. Sullivan 144 (1989).

[67] *See* Costello v. Capital Cities Comm'ns, 505 N.E.2d 701 (Ill. Ct. App. 1987).

[68] Hopkins, *supra* note 66, at 138.

[69] 441 U.S. 153 (1979).

[70] St. Amant v. Thompson, 390 U.S. 727, 731 (1968).

[71] 446 U.S. 485 (1984).

[72] *Id.* at 495.

[73] DiLorenzo v. New York News, 432 N.Y.S. 2d 483, 486 (N.Y. App. Div. 1981).

[74] Hopkins, *supra* note 66, at 141-42.

In addition to a media defendant's state of mind, the editorial policies that govern or guide actions can play a role in the determination of predisposition. The idea that a media defendant preconceived a story line, then proceeded to skew reporting to fit that preconception, is evidence of knowledge of falsity. In *Burnett v. National Enquirer,* for example, the trial court suggested that the *Enquirer's* editorial predisposition may have contributed to its judgment. Entertainer Carol Burnett argued that she had been falsely portrayed by the *National Enquirer* as being "drunk, rude, uncaring, and abusive" in a Washington restaurant.[75] At trial, a reporter for the *Enquirer* testified that the article about Burnett was published even though he was unable to verify its accuracy.

Similarly, *Tavoulares v. Washington Post Co.*[76] resulted in some troubling law that courts may believe they need to follow. A *Washington Post* article implied that William Tavoulares, the president of Mobil Oil Co., misused his corporate position by setting up his son to head an international tanker fleet. A federal jury awarded Tavoulares $2 million in damages. Before the verdict was overturned by the full Court of Appeals for the District of Columbia,[77] a panel of that court had held that the *Post's* predisposition toward "hard-hitting investigative journalism" could be considered as evidence relevant to actual malice.[78] The suggestion that a practice generally revered in journalism could be used against a libel defendant sent shock waves throughout the field. Those feelings were eased, however, when a full-panel rehearing by the District of Columbia Circuit reversed, throwing out the $2 million verdict, ruling that actual malice had not been proven. Adding to the relief was the court's assertion that a media organization's reputation for aggressive reporting was not to be taken as evidence of actual malice.

Pressure exerted by newsroom supervisors to produce high-impact stories may also be construed as a predisposition toward certain kinds of stories with specific plot lines. Such pressure may contribute to reporters skewing facts to fit such predilections. First Amendment scholar and libel expert Rodney Smolla places this phenomenon within the context of freedom of expression:

At the very core of our first amendment jurisprudence lies the elemental wisdom that government has no business prescribing what is orthodox, genteel, or polite in politics and culture. A publication or broadcast outlet is not to be penalized because of its unique boldness, style, or flair. Indeed, in an era in which one of the great *economic* tendencies in the media is toward consolidation and centralization, often resulting in "play it safe" editorial styles that make all news sound the same, the first amendment's protection for those media outlets with special courage or uniqueness is more vital than ever. To actually preconceive a story is one thing — such an act is quite properly probative of actual malice — but merely to have an editorial image or slant is quite another.[79]

Thus, when circumstances permit, proving falsity can be easier than exploring a defendant's state of mind. It simply stands to reason that it is much more difficult to prove a particular state of mind compared to presenting evidence that suggests reckless oversights. But what happens when a defendant admits to altering an interviewee's quotations? Arguably, that is an example of knowing falsity. That is, if quotations were knowingly altered to the extent that their meaning was materially transformed, then the journalist must have been aware of the fact that they were false. Traditionally, journalistic practice suggests that words bracketed by quotation marks are the exact words of the person to whom they are attributed. When a journalist knowingly changes this material, the quoted information arguably has been knowingly falsified.

While that might be the case, publishing knowing falsehoods is only one element of a public figure's burden of proof. In *Masson v. New Yorker Magazine, Inc.,* the Supreme Court ruled that even the deliberate misquotation of a public figure cannot be libelous unless the wording materially changes the meaning of what was really said.[80] The Court said that in *Masson* the meaning had not been transformed. On remand, a federal district court jury ruled in favor of the journalist, even though she had admitted to condensing certain statements by the plaintiff.[81]

In his dissenting opinion, Justice Byron White addressed the issue of knowing falsehoods: "[T]he reporter ... wrote that Masson said certain things that she knew Masson did not say. By any definition of the term, this was 'knowing falsehood.'"[82] He was right, but the final word on this issue was in favor of the defendant, based on the statements at issue being substantially true.

**Reckless Disregard.** Reckless disregard for whether material is true or false, like knowledge of falsity, is a subjective test. But it can often be determined by the conduct of the publisher rather than by examining thought processes, state of mind, or predisposition at the time of publication.[83] Knowledge of falsity focuses on what the publisher knew; reckless disregard focuses on what the publisher reasonably *should have known*. The focus of the actual malice inquiry, as one scholar has written, "is on a defendant's attitude toward the truth or falsity of the publication," on "subjective awareness of its probable falsity" and on "actual doubts as to

---

[75] 193 Cal. Rptr. 206 (Cal. Ct. App. 1983).
[76] 759 F.2d 90 (D.C. Cir. 1985).
[77] Tavoulares v. Wash. Post Co., 817 F.2d 762 (D.C. Cir. 1987) (en banc).
[78] Tavoulares v. Wash. Post Co., 759 F.2d 90, 121 (D.C. Cir. 1985).

[79] Rodney A. Smolla, Law of Defamation § 3:73 (2005).
[80] 501 U.S. 496, 516 (1991).
[81] Masson v. New Yorker, 832 F. Supp. 1350 (N.D. Cal. 1993).
[82] *Masson,* 501 U.S. at 526 (White, J., dissenting).
[83] *See, e.g.,* W. Wat Hopkins, *Good News or Bad for the Press? Actual Malice as Purposeful Avoidance of the Truth,* 14 Newspaper Res. J. 99 (Summer/Fall 1993).

its accuracy." The "inquiry in 'actual malice' focuses largely on the defendant's belief regarding truthfulness."[84]

For recklessness to rise to the level of actual malice, it must be significant — it must be tantamount to lying; it must be obvious that the publisher did not care about the truth of the published information. When publishers have demonstrated adequate investigation of potentially libelous charges, courts have typically ruled that there was no reckless disregard. Therefore, a plaintiff cannot prove reckless disregard if the defendant can show the statements were adequately investigated prior to publication.

The seriousness of the charges being made is also weighed. The more serious the material in question, the more detailed an investigation into its truth should be. In addition, reckless disregard is more likely to be found when sources for published material are anonymous, biased or of questionable reputation. Courts look to the number of reputable sources when determining whether a sufficient investigation was conducted.

The Supreme Court has provided some guidance as to the meaning of reckless disregard. It has, for example, called reckless disregard publishing with a "high degree of awareness of their probable falsity."[85] And, the Court has said, for reckless disregard to exist, "[T]here must be sufficient evidence to permit the conclusion that the defendant in fact entertained serious doubts as to the truth of his publication."[86] Whether a defendant had such serious doubts can be established by circumstantial evidence including determining what the defendant's thoughts were leading up to publication of the challenged statements.

The mere failure to investigate charges is not sufficient, standing alone, to prove reckless disregard. Publishers often rely on the work of reputable writers. If there is no reason to doubt the truth of material submitted by those writers, it is not necessary for publishers to have conducted independent investigations. If plaintiffs can show that publishers had doubts about the truth of such material or reasonably should have had doubts, however, that's a different story. In such cases, the question of reckless disregard may be open. In short, a publisher must be able to demonstrate a reasonable belief in the truth of the published material. That may sometimes require an investigation into the facts, but the belief may also be based on the reputation of the original author. To establish actual malice, plaintiffs must go beyond proving that "a reporter failed to show significant initiative in corroborating, verifying, or further investigating the defamatory story at issue." Rodney Smolla wrote:

[T]he mere failure to investigate, even when that failure to investigate is less than reasonable or responsible journalism, does not in and of itself meet the actual malice test. There must be

some evidence of subjective suspicion that further investigation is needed. That evidence, of course, can be met by circumstantial data, including such things as the reliability or unreliability of the source or the inherent implausibility of the allegation, but something other than the stark failure to pursue investigation must be established.[87]

**Negligence.** At a minimum, the Supreme Court said in *Gertz v. Welch,* private persons seeking damages for the publication of false defamations related to matters of public interest must prove negligence. As a result, most states have ruled that negligence is the standard of fault for private-person libel plaintiffs.

Negligence has been defined in a variety of ways, but it is generally defined as failure to act as a reasonably or ordinarily careful person would under similar circumstances. A second definition — known as "journalistic malpractice" — is failure to adhere to standards of reporting and writing that are common to the news industry.

The reasonable care standard requires a libel plaintiff to establish that a libel defendant did not operate in a reasonable way, that is, that a reasonable person would have operated in a way significantly different from that of the defendant. The Arizona Supreme Court, for example, defined negligence this way:

conduct which creates an unreasonable risk of harm. It is the failure to use that amount of care which a reasonably prudent person would use under like circumstances. The question which the jury must determine from the preponderance of the evidence ... is whether the defendants acted reasonably in attempting to discover the truth or falsity or the defamatory character of the publication.[88]

Most states have adopted the reasonable person definition of negligence, but some — including Iowa, Kansas and Oklahoma — define negligence as journalistic malpractice. The *Restatement* defines journalistic malpractice this way:

The defendant, if a professional disseminator of news, such as a newspaper, a magazine or a broadcasting station, or an employee, such as a reporter, is held to the skill and experience normally possessed by members of that profession.... Customs and practices within the profession are relevant in applying the negligence standard, which is, to a substantial degree, set by the profession itself, though a custom is not controlling.... If the defendant is an ordinary citizen, customs of the community as a whole may be relevant.[89]

---

[84] SMOLLA, *supra* note 79, at § 3:43.
[85] Garrison v. Louisiana, 379 U.S. 64, 74 (1964).
[86] St. Amant v. Thompson, 390 U.S. 727, 731 (1968).

[87] SMOLLA, *supra* note 79, at § 3:49.
[88] Peagler v. Phoenix Newspapers, Inc., 560 P.2d 1216, 1222 (Ariz. 1977).
[89] RESTATEMENT, *supra* note 6, at § 580B cmt. g.

Regardless of the definition of negligence, some factors seem common when courts have ruled that defendants published material negligently. In his in-depth study of negligence as an actionable standard in post-*Gertz* cases, media law scholar W. Wat Hopkins identified three general negligence rules:

(1) [I]f there is a discrepancy between what a reporter says he was told by a source and what the source said he told the reporter, the court is more likely to believe the source and find that negligence is likely; (2) courts are likely to rule that negligence could be established if media representatives make little or no effort to contact a person against whom accusations are made or if a medium bases a story later found to be false upon a single source; (3) courts are likely to rule that negligence could be established if media fail to get all the information they should.[90]

### Actual Injury

Even if libel plaintiffs can prove they were identified in false, defamatory publications, and even if they can prove the requisite degree of fault, they must still prove actual injury in order to recover damages.

Warning against the "danger of media self-censorship" resulting from jury discretion in assessing punitive damages, the Supreme Court said that "punitive damages are wholly irrelevant to the state interest that justifies a negligence standard for private defamation actions. They are not compensation for injury. Instead, they are private fines levied by civil juries to punish reprehensible conduct and to deter its future occurrence." The Court noted, however, that the private libel plaintiff who establishes liability under a less demanding standard than actual malice may be limited to recovery of "only such damages as are sufficient to compensate him for actual injury."[91]

In a libel action, four types of damages are recognized.

*Nominal damages* are awarded to plaintiffs who have not suffered from provable injury to their reputations. They are granted in very small amounts, usually $1, and are awarded where a plaintiff does not seek compensation for loss, but a vindication of reputation in the form of a declaration that a published statement is false.

*Compensatory damages* are awarded for actual injury. They compensate, not for out-of-pocket loss, but for harm to reputation, humiliation, suffering and mental anguish. Awards of compensatory damages must be based upon the evidence, but if the damages are not outrageous, a jury can award damages in its own discretion. Compensatory damages are sometimes called "general damages."

*Special damages* are designed to compensate for actual pecuniary loss. Evidence of special damages will demonstrate an actual amount of money the plaintiff lost as a result of the defamation.

*Punitive or exemplary damages* are designed to punish the defendant for outrageous and willful defamation. They are designed to deter the defendant and others from repeating similar actions. Actual malice must be proved for recovery of punitive damages. Four states — Massachusetts, Michigan, Oregon and Washington — do not recognize punitive damages in libel cases, and other states have capped the amount of punitive damages a plaintiff can win. Some states require that both actual malice and common law malice be established in seeking punitive damages for libel.

## PUBLIC PERSONS

The Supreme Court has established that two categories of libel plaintiffs — public officials and public figures — must prove actual malice in order to win libel actions.

### Public Officials

Public officials for purposes of the actual malice rule are persons in government who are in or appear to be in policy-making roles. The Supreme Court has indicated that "the 'public official' designation applies at the very least to those among the hierarchy of government employees who have or appear to the public to have, substantial responsibility for or control over the conduct of governmental affairs."[92] The trial judge determines whether a plaintiff is a public official.

Determining just who qualifies as a public official is reasonably, but not entirely, clear-cut. In a 1979 case, the Supreme Court made it clear that "public official" is not synonymous with "public employee."[93] Whether a public employee is in or appears to be in a position to make policy and whether the employee has ready access to the media are key factors.

A public official must establish that a defamatory statement was directed at the official, rather than at the official's government unit. This is at the heart of First Amendment philosophy — that under the Constitution there is no such thing as libel against the government; there is no seditious libel.

A person remains a public official for the purposes of the actual malice rule even after leaving office, at least with regard to stories that refer to conduct while in office. The passing of time, however, eventually may erode public interest in the office-holder's conduct so that the *New York Times* rule would no longer apply. There may be cases "where a person is so far removed from a former position of authority that comment on the manner in which he per-

[90] W. Wat Hopkins, *Negligence Ten Years After Gertz v. Welch*, 93 JOURNALISM MONOGRAPHS 19 (Aug. 1985).
[91] Gertz v. Robert Welch, Inc., 418 U.S. 341, 350 (1974).

[92] Rosenblatt v. Baer, 383 U.S. 75, 85 (1966).
[93] Hutchinson v. Proxmire, 443 U.S. 111, 119 n.8 (1979).

formed his responsibilities no longer has the interest necessary to justify the *New York Times* rule."[94] But this exception is rare.

Any statement that touches on an official's fitness for office — even if the statement is about the official's private life — is considered protected. Said the Supreme Court:

> The *New York Times* rule is not rendered inapplicable merely because an official's private reputation, as well as his public reputation, is harmed. The public-official rule protects the paramount public interest in a free flow of information to the people concerning public officials, their servants. To this end, anything which might touch on an official's fitness for office is relevant.[95]

### Public Figures

In 1967, the actual malice rule was expanded to include public figures. In *Curtis Publishing Co. v. Butts*,[96] the Supreme Court ruled that there was little legal difference between persons who have widespread fame and notoriety — public figures — and public officials. "Many who do not hold public office at the moment," wrote Chief Justice Earl Warren, "are nevertheless intimately involved in the resolution of important public questions or, by reason of their fame, shape events in areas of concern to society at large."[97]

The rule was established in a roundabout way. Justice John Marshall Harlan had written a plurality opinion differentiating between public officials and public figures, but he also differentiated between the rules that should apply to the two categories. Chief Justice Warren wrote that the actual malice rule should apply to both categories of libel plaintiffs, and a sufficient number of justices joined his opinion so as to establish that rule.

The actual malice rule was extended in 1971 to any defamatory story involving matters of public or general interest, but the expansion was short-lived. In *Rosenbloom v. Metromedia, Inc.*,[98] a plurality of the Court had favored a rule that required private people involved in matters of public interest to prove actual malice when suing for libel based upon discussion of those matters. But the "Rosenbloom Rule" lasted only three years. In 1974, a 5-4 Court majority definitively rejected the rule by overruling *Rosenbloom* in *Gertz v. Robert Welch, Inc.*[99]

The *Gertz* case started in 1969 when *American Opinion*, a monthly periodical published by the John Birch Society, a far-right organization founded by Robert Welch, published an article critical of a Chicago civil liberties lawyer, Elmer Gertz. Gertz had been retained by the family of an African-American man who had been shot and killed by Chicago policeman Richard Nuccio. The article

claimed that Gertz, who was hired to initiate a wrongful death suit against Chicago and Nuccio, was the architect of the "frame-up" in the earlier prosecution of Nuccio for second-degree murder. It further maintained that the prosecution was part of a Communist effort to discredit the Chicago police. The article reported, in part:

> The file on Elmer Gertz in Chicago Police Intelligence takes a big Irish cop to lift.... He has been an official of the Marxist League for Industrial Democracy, originally known as the Intercollegiate Socialist Society, which has advocated the violent seizure of our government.... In fact, the only thing Chicagoans need to know about Gertz is that he is one of the original officers, and has been Vice President, of the Communist National Lawyers Guild ... which probably did more than any other outfit to plan the Communist attack on the Chicago police during the 1968 Democratic Convention.

Gertz sued Robert Welch, Inc., publisher of *American Opinion*, for libel. He said the statements about him were false. He had no criminal record, contrary to the implications of the article. He was not a member of the Marxist League for Industrial Democracy. Further, although he had been a member of the National Lawyers Guild fifteen years earlier, the Guild was not a Communist organization. Neither had he anything to do with the prosecution of Nuccio for murder.

In his complaint, Gertz claimed he was injured both as an individual and as an attorney. He sought $100,000 in actual damages and $500,000 in punitive damages.[100] In 1970, a jury awarded him $50,000 in damages, but the trial judge set aside the verdict because, he said, since the article discussed Gertz's public activity, the actual malice rule should apply. Gertz appealed, but the U.S. Court of Appeals for the Seventh Circuit applied *Rosenbloom* and affirmed the trial judge's ruling, stating that there was no clear and convincing evidence of actual malice.[101]

In his appeal to the Supreme Court, Gertz argued in part:

> Is every attorney, representing a client, to be exposed to the most scurrilous attacks, with absolutely no recourse? May a defamer concoct wholly fictitious stories about such an attorney which have no legitimate connections with the matter at hand? Are the members of the legal profession such public figures that they imperil their very livelihood to all unfounded attacks with absolutely no recourse? These issues must be considered very carefully and fully, not in an offhand manner.[102]

The Supreme Court agreed, holding that the actual malice rule applies to private-person libel plaintiffs only when they seek pre-

---

[94] *Rosenblatt*, 383 U.S. at 87 n.14.
[95] Garrison v. Louisiana, 379 U.S. 64, 77 (1964).
[96] 388 U.S. 130 (1967).
[97] *Id.* at 163 (Warren, C.J., concurring).
[98] 403 U.S. 29 (1971).
[99] 418 U.S. 323 (1974).

[100] ELMER GERTZ, GERTZ V. ROBERT WELCH, INC.: THE STORY OF A LANDMARK LIBEL CASE 40 (1992).
[101] 471 F.2d 801 (7th Cir. 1972).
[102] GERTZ, *supra* note 100, at 85-86.

sumed or punitive damages. Other than that, the Court said, states could determine the fault standard for private-person libel plaintiffs, so long as states did not allow liability without some degree of fault. The Court explained the distinction between public and private persons:

> Public officials and public figures usually enjoy significantly greater access to the channels of effective communication and hence have a more realistic opportunity to counteract false statements than private individuals normally enjoy. Private individuals are therefore more vulnerable to injury, and the state interest in protecting them is correspondingly greater. More important than the likelihood that private individuals will lack effective opportunities for rebuttal, there is a compelling normative consideration underlying the distinction between public and private defamation plaintiffs. An individual who decides to seek governmental office must accept certain necessary consequences of that involvement in public affairs. He runs the risk of closer public scrutiny than might otherwise be the case.[103]

In *Gertz*, the Court also differentiated between three types of public figures. General or all-purpose public figures are persons who have achieved pervasive fame or notoriety in their communities or are pervasively involved in the affairs of society. It is not easy to become an all-purpose public figure. The category is generally reserved for those people who have become so-called "household names" — that is, celebrities.

Far more common than the all-purpose public figure is the limited-purpose public figure. Limited-purpose public figures have "thrust themselves to the forefront of particular controversies in order to influence the resolution of issues involved."[104] This means, first, a public controversy must exist and, second, the nature and extent of the plaintiff's participation in that controversy must be determined. While it is clear that newsworthiness and public figure status are not synonymous, some courts have held that a person who creates a public controversy in order to affect the outcome of some public issue has met the limited-purposes criteria.

The Court also acknowledged that involuntary public figures may exist — at least in theory — but that such cases would be rare. Yet, an individual could be thrust into a matter of public controversy not merely through voluntary actions but also through bad luck. It is possible to become a public figure through no purposeful action. Meanwhile, as one media law scholar has noted:

> While the Supreme Court has provided at least some guidance for lower courts attempting to identify public officials, all-purpose public figures, and limited-purpose public figures, the

Court has provided little guidance in defining involuntary public figures. Indeed, some lower appellate courts have held that the Supreme Court has only established two categories of public figures status — all purpose and limited purpose — ignoring the language of *Gertz* to the contrary.[105]

The *Gertz* Court saw a relationship between public figures and public officials, in part, because individuals in both groups tend to have access to the media and, therefore, have the ability to set the record straight when inaccuracies occur. Private figures, on the other hand, usually have limited access to the media and are, therefore, more vulnerable to irreparable injury. In addition, there is a certain degree of risk that accompanies those in the public eye. While public officials "must accept certain necessary consequences [regarding their] involvement in public affairs," they also "run the risk of closer public scrutiny than might otherwise be the case.... Those classified as public figures stand in a similar position.... [T]he communications media are entitled to act on the assumption that public officials and public figures have voluntarily exposed themselves to increased risk of injury from defamatory falsehoods concerning them."[106] The Court noted that society's stake in news about private figures is not as great as when public people are involved. Society places a high value in protecting private figures against libel, so the level of fault they are required to meet is less demanding than it is for public people.

Distinguishing between public and private figures, however, is not an easy task. As one court reported, it "is much like trying to nail a jelly fish to the wall."[107] Being in the public eye and being a public figure are not the same. The case of Mary Alice Firestone is one example. She was married to the heir to the Firestone Rubber Co. fortune, was a prominent member of Palm Beach society and even subscribed to a clipping service so she could keep track of all the news published about her. In addition, when she and her husband became involved in a notorious divorce proceeding, Mrs. Firestone held daily press conferences. When she sued *Time* for incorrectly reporting that her husband was granted a divorce because of her adultery and extreme cruelty — rather than because "neither party is domesticated" — it seemed certain that she would be categorized as a public figure for libel purposes. But the Supreme Court said no. The Court said that a large number of people might be interested in the problems of the extremely wealthy, but those were not the kinds of matters the Court had in mind when it referred to a public controversy.[108]

A plaintiff cannot be made public merely by the actions of the media. This "bootstrapping" occurs when media defendants attach themselves to the protection of the actual malice standard by

[103] 418 U.S. at 344-45.
[104] *Id.* at 345.

[105] W. Wat Hopkins, *The Involuntary Public Figure: Not So Dead After All*, 21 CARDOZO ARTS & ENT. L.J. 1, 44 (2003).
[106] 418 U.S. at 345.
[107] Rosanova v. Playboy Enterprises, 411 F. Supp. 440, 443 (S.D. Ga. 1976).
[108] Time, Inc. v. Firestone, 424 U.S. 488 (1976).

# THE LIBEL PLAINTIFF'S BURDEN OF PROOF

1. **Publication**
2. **Identification**
3. **Defamation**

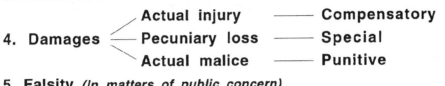

4. **Damages** — **Actual injury** —— **Compensatory**
   — **Pecuniary loss** —— **Special**
   — **Actual malice** —— **Punitive**

5. **Falsity** *(In matters of public concern)*

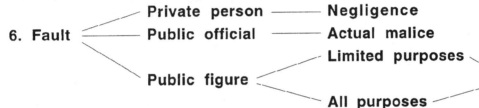

6. **Fault** — **Private person** —— **Negligence**
   — **Public official** —— **Actual malice**
   — **Public figure** — **Limited purposes** — **Actual malice**
   — **All purposes**

pointing to their own allegedly libelous media coverage of the plaintiff as evidence that the plaintiff is a public figure. The Supreme Court has said, "Clearly, those charged with defamation cannot, by their own conduct, create their own defense by making the claimant a public figure."[109] As a result, courts have noted that the public controversy at issue must have existed prior to the publication upon which the defamation claim is based. However, a court that rigidly applies the pre-existing controversy requirement may punish legitimate reporting that uncovers specific acts of wrongdoing. Courts, therefore, attempt to strike a delicate balance between which came first — the controversy or the story about the controversy.

Just as a media organization is not permitted to bootstrap itself into creating its own defense, a plaintiff may not avoid the actual malice standard by claiming that the attention was unwanted. The proper question is not whether the plaintiff volunteered for the publicity but whether the plaintiff volunteered for an activity from which publicity would foreseeably arise.

Even if an individual is not active within a particular sphere, mere presence within the sphere may satisfy a court's public-figure requirements. Where a person has

chosen to engage in a profession which draws him regularly into regional and national view and leads to fame and notoriety in the community, even if he has no ideological thesis to promulgate, he invites general public discussion.... If society chooses to direct massive public attention to a particular sphere of activity, those who enter that sphere inviting such attention overcome the *Times* standard.[110]

Thus, voluntary entry into a sphere of activity, the court reasoned, is sufficient to satisfy this element of the public figure inquiry.

Because the Supreme Court has said that someone with widespread fame or notoriety is a public figure, the individual's prominence is important in determining public-figure status. Moreover, that prominence may apply to a narrowly drawn context. Merely being an executive within a prominent and influential company does not by itself make a person a public figure. Professionals are typically not public figures, but under certain circumstances they can be. For example, voluntary use of controversial or unorthodox techniques may be enough to confer public-figure status. Publicly defending such methods or adopting other controversial stands also tends to bring about public status. Thus, a doctor who had written extensively on health issues as a newspaper columnist, who was also the author of various journal articles, and who had appeared on at least one nationally broadcast television program discussing health and nutrition issues was held to

---

[109] Hutchinson v. Proxmire, 443 U.S. 111, 135 (1979).

[110] Chuy v. Philadelphia Eagles Football Club, 431 F. Supp. 254, 276 (E.D. Pa. 1977).

be a public figure for a limited range of issues — those pertaining to health and nutrition.[111]

An individual may assume public-figure status within small publics but may revert to being a private figure in larger spheres. For example, a university professor may be a public figure on campus and in the adjacent academic community, but a private person beyond those boundaries. The professor, therefore, may be a public figure for purposes of an article in the university newspaper, but not for purposes of a regional newspaper or a national magazine. Thus, the professor's public-figure status is restricted. Similarly, an individual can attain the status of an all-purpose public figure within a particular geographical area.[112]

The passage of time may theoretically permit some people who were once public figures to regain private-figure status. To revert to private-figure status, it is likely that a plaintiff would need to demonstrate that the original status as a public figure was not connected to events or controversies that have become part of the permanent historical consciousness of the country.

*Gertz,* the most important libel case since *New York Times Co. v. Sullivan,* established a new set of guidelines for balancing the constitutional right of free speech against concerns for reputational interests.

First, the Court reaffirmed that public figures, along with public officials, must prove actual malice in libel cases involving matters of public concern.

Second, the Court held that "so long as they do not impose liability without fault, the states may define for themselves the appropriate standard of liability for a publisher or broadcaster of a defamatory falsehood injurious to a private individual," at least where the content of the defamatory statement "makes substantial danger to reputation apparent."[113]

Third, the Court stated that presumed or punitive damages may not be awarded absent a showing of actual malice. Those who cannot prove actual malice, the Court said, may be compensated only for actual injury.[114] In a later case, the Court held that the actual malice requirement for punitive damages does not apply to material "of purely private concern."[115]

As a result of *Gertz,* forty-one jurisdictions, including the District of Columbia, Puerto Rico and Virgin Islands, have established negligence as the private-person fault standard; five states — Alaska, Colorado, Indiana, Kansas and New Jersey — have adopted a variation of the Rosenbloom Rule; and one state, New York, requires "gross irresponsibility" when matters of public concern are involved. The New York Court of Appeals held in *Chapadeau v. Utica Observer-Dispatch* that where the content of

the article is arguably within the sphere of legitimate public concern, which is reasonably related to matters warranting public exposition, the party defamed may recover if he or she can establish "by a preponderance of the evidence, that the publisher acted in a grossly irresponsible manner without due consideration for the standards of information gathering and dissemination ordinarily followed by responsible parties."[116]

The "gross irresponsibility" standard in New York for private-figure libel plaintiffs is considered closer to "actual malice" than to negligence when it comes to difficulty of proof. Indeed, Judge Sack of the Second Circuit noted: "It is almost as difficult as 'actual malice' for plaintiffs to meet in most cases and more difficult in some."[117]

## DEFENSE STRATEGIES

The libel defendant is by no means defenseless. Any of a number of defenses or defense strategies is available to help prevent liability, depending on the circumstances of a case.

In libel law, the rights of individuals to be secure in their reputations are weighed against the rights of publishers to be heard on issues important to self-government. Broadly speaking, libel defenses assert that important issues of public concern should be debated in a free, open and uninhibited manner. A libel suit today, thanks to the precedent that *New York Times Co. v. Sullivan*[118] established, can be defended on constitutional grounds as well as through the common law.

Libel defenses begin by attempting to defeat the plaintiff's case — that is, by refuting any of the plaintiff's claims, a defense may be successful. In late 2004, for example, the Tenth U.S. Circuit Court of Appeals upheld a federal district court's dismissal of a libel suit because the plaintiff had suffered no reputational harm from two news stories.[119] The federal appeals court reasoned that he had too tarnished a reputation as a convicted murderer to be further damaged when the stories were published.

If defeating an element of the plaintiff's case doesn't work, defendants then have the opportunity to assert affirmative defenses.

## THE CONSTITUTIONAL DEFENSE

The First Amendment protects the freedoms of speech and press. Therein lies the heart of the so-called "constitutional defense" in libel law. The Supreme Court has recognized that free speech is vital because it ensures individual self-fulfillment and that it is a social good because it contributes to the search for truth. The First Amendment "rests on the assumption that the widest possible dissemination of information from diverse and antagonistic

---

[111] Renner v. Donsbach, 749 F. Supp. 987 (W.D. Mo. 1990).

[112] *See, e.g.,* Williams v. Pasma, 656 P.2d 212 (Mont. 1982).

[113] *Id.* at 347-48.

[114] *Id.* at 349-50.

[115] Dun & Bradstreet, Inc. v. Greenmoss Builders, Inc., 472 U.S. 749, 759 (1985).

[116] 341 N.E.2d 569, 571 (N.Y. 1975).

[117] SACK, *supra* note 26, at 6-14.

[118] 376 U.S. 254 (1964).

[119] Lamb v. Rizzo, 391 F.3d 1133 (10th Cir. 2004).

sources is essential to the welfare of the public."[120] Moreover, as Justice Louis Brandeis wrote during the era in which the Court truly began to interpret the meaning and scope of the First Amendment, "[F]reedom to think as you will and speak as you think are means indispensable to the discovery and spread of political truth."[121]

Thus, a libel defense, of sorts, has developed out of the notion that contributing significantly to public knowledge and information is important, and freedom of expression is a key element in that process.

The question becomes, does the speech contribute to the "profound national commitment to the principle that debate on public issues should be uninhibited, robust, and wide-open?"[122] At a base level, a media organization's defense on constitutional grounds is a claim that limiting its ability to convey information is an abridgment of the First Amendment guarantees of free speech and press. Carrying this argument to its logical conclusion, then, finding a media defendant responsible for libel is unconstitutional because doing so limits constitutionally protected freedoms. Moreover, knowing that such a verdict is possible in the wake of critical or less-than-positive statements about an individual may also limit freedom by producing a chilling effect. That is, the media may be less inclined to publish information containing critical statements knowing the dangers that may lie ahead in a libel trial.

The ability to criticize the government and government officials was central to *Times v. Sullivan*. At the root of Justice Brennan's opinion was the notion that statements about public officials — people who hold government positions — are most deserving of constitutional protection. The freedom to be critical of government and government officials, after all, was the basis and justification for the First Amendment's protection of speech and the press from interference by the state. Some scholars, in fact, have taken an unconditional approach to the issue. Alexander Meiklejohn, for example, has written that speech relevant to self-government is absolutely protected under the First Amendment.[123] Harry Kalven Jr. wrote that the central meaning of the First Amendment is uninhibited discussion of governmental affairs: "Political freedom ends when government can use its powers and its courts to silence its critics."[124]

It was the critical nature of the ability of citizens to criticize government and government officials that prompted Justice Brennan to appropriate the actual malice standard from state libel law and establish it as a constitutional rule. Unless a defendant's statement about a public plaintiff was made knowing it was false, or with reckless disregard for its truth, the defense will be successful.

The scope of the standard was soon thereafter expanded to apply to more than public official plaintiffs.

As previously indicated, the Supreme Court, in the 1967 case *Curtis Publishing Co. v. Butts*, applied the actual malice standard to public figures, that is, individuals who either possess widespread fame or notoriety or who have thrust themselves into a public controversy in order to influence its outcome.

Chief Justice Warren justified the extension, writing that the "differentiation between public figures and public officials and adoption of separate standards of proof for each have no basis in law, logic, or First Amendment policy."[125] The case established the principle that many people who do not hold governmental office are nevertheless intimately enough involved in the resolution of public issues that, like public officials, they are public figures and should be required to prove the defendant acted with actual malice.

Because of the dramatic difference in the level of fault required of public and private libel plaintiffs, defendants often exert great effort to demonstrate that a plaintiff is a public person. This effort, of course, while not purely a defense, is considered part of the so-called "constitutional defense" given that it stems from the actual malice concept. It is certainly an issue that libel defendants should consider as they formulate their defense strategies. How a libel suit unfolds hinges on this determination.

### The Nature of the Statement

Not only is the categorization of the plaintiff meaningful to the libel defendant, the nature of the statement at issue can also be important. In *Dun & Bradstreet v. Greenmoss Builders*[126] a private-person plaintiff contended that he was defamed by material the Supreme Court said was a matter of private concern. A Dun & Bradstreet credit report sent to five subscribers inaccurately reported that Greenmoss Builders had declared bankruptcy. Justice Lewis Powell, for the majority, wrote that the purpose of the speaker and the nature and size of the audience are among the criteria for determining when speech involves matters of public concern.[127] Thus, the Court sought to establish minimal standards of fault not only depending on the status of the plaintiff but also according to the nature of the subject matter.

### Opinion

The opinion defense has both constitutional and common law elements, causing discussion of this complex area of the law to become somewhat muddled. Traditionally, opinion as a libel defense stemmed from the common law. But the ability to voice opinions, particularly about issues of public concern, is now recognized as

---

[120] Citizen Publ'g. Co. v. United States, 394 U.S. 131, 139-40 (1969).

[121] Whitney v. California, 274 U.S. 354, 375 (1927) (Brandeis, J., concurring).

[122] *Times v. Sullivan*, 376 U.S. 254, 270 (1964).

[123] *See* ALEXANDER MEIKLEJOHN, POLITICAL FREEDOM 20-27 (1960).

[124] Kalven, *supra* note 62, at 205.

[125] 388 U.S. 130, 163 (1967) (Warren, C.J., concurring in the result).

[126] 472 U.S. 749 (1985).

[127] *Id.* at 783.

also being at the heart of the First Amendment's protection of expression. Constitutional derivations of the opinion defense are analyzed here; the common law components of opinion follow.

To attempt to separate statements of fact from statements of opinion is to venture onto one of the law's most slippery of slopes, yet to do so is vital in establishing the boundaries of the protection. In addition, state-to-state variations make the distinction all the more difficult.

In *Gertz*, the Supreme Court stated: "Under the First Amendment there is no such thing as a false idea. However pernicious an opinion may seem, we depend for its correction not on the conscience of judges and juries but on the competition of other ideas."[128] The question remained, however, just what is an opinion, and how is it different from a statement of fact?

The defining case in this area is *Ollman v. Evans*.[129] The 1984 ruling was by the D.C. Circuit Court of Appeals, whose judges later acquired greater notoriety in other venues. A college professor sued newspaper columnists Rowland Evans and Robert Novak, who wrote that he had no status within the profession, and that he used his classroom as an instrument to prepare for a Marxist revolution. The court was split in its decision. Judge Antonin Scalia decided that the columnists wrote a "classic and coolly crafted libel,"[130] but the court's majority, led by Judge Kenneth Starr, found the column to be opinion protected by the First Amendment and the principles enunciated in *Gertz*. Judge Robert Bork concurred. Moreover, Judge Starr noted the difficulty in distinguishing opinion from fact, and attempted to simplify the task by establishing a four-part test, now known as the *Ollman* test:[131]

1. The inquiry must analyze the common usage or meaning of the words.

2. Is the statement verifiable — "objectively capable of proof or disproof"? In other words, can the statement be proven either true or false?

3. What is the linguistic or journalistic context in which the statement occurs? The article or column must be considered as a whole: "The language of the entire column may signal that a specific statement that, standing alone, would appear to be factual, is in fact a statement of opinion."

4. What is the "broader social context into which the statement fits?"

Opinion was initially granted a wide berth of protection. But then came *Milkovich v. Lorain Journal*,[132] a case that reframed the interpretation of the opinion defense. It also forced recognition of the notion that where pure opinion may not exist, mixed opinion may. In *Milkovich*, a high school wrestling coach sued when a local newspaper columnist indicated that the coach lied

under oath about his role in a brawl during a wrestling match. For the first time, the Supreme Court addressed the "false idea" statement from *Gertz*. "[W]e do not think this passage from *Gertz* was intended to create a wholesale defamation exemption for anything that might be labeled 'opinion,'" Chief Justice William Rehnquist wrote for the Court. "Not only would such an interpretation be contrary to the tenor and context of the passage, but it would also ignore the fact that expressions of 'opinion' may often imply an assertion of objective fact."[133] Rehnquist wrote that facts can disguise themselves as opinions, and, when they do, they imply a knowledge of hidden facts that led to the opinion. While *Milkovich* holds that opinion is not protected as a category of speech, it provides a framework in which opinion *is* protected. That is, since an opinion cannot be proved to be false, it cannot be the basis for a successful libel action.

As noted above, opinion defenses are not limited to the constitutional category. Defenses such as "fair comment and criticism" and "letters to the editor" are common law libel defenses.

### Neutral Reportage

Neutral reportage is another defense with a constitutional foundation. It was first enunciated in 1977 in *Edwards v. National Audubon Society, Inc.*[134] Neutral reportage protects accurate, unbiased news reporting of accusations that prominent, responsible persons make against public figures. It recognizes that the actual malice rule does not protect a media defendant from reporting false, defamatory statements that are newsworthy even if the defendant knows those statements are false. The Second U.S. Circuit Court of Appeals — and other courts that have adopted the neutral reporting rule — believed that such statements, when made by public figures, are newsworthy and should be protected provided that they are reported accurately and objectively. The *Edwards* court overturned a jury verdict against the *New York Times*, saying it was constitutionally impermissible to hold the newspaper liable for publishing such statements:

> [W]hen a responsible, prominent organization ... makes serious charges against a public figure, the First Amendment protects the accurate and disinterested reporting of those charges, regardless of the reporter's private views of their validity.... We do not believe that the press may be required under the First Amendment to suppress newsworthy statements merely because it has serious doubts regarding their truth.[135]

Since the Supreme Court had said that serious doubts about a statement's truth constitutes actual malice, *Edwards* seemed to carve out an exception within the definition of actual malice. Neu-

[128] *Gertz*, 418 U.S. 323, 339-40 (1974).

[129] 750 F.2d 970 (D.C. Cir. 1984).

[130] *Id*. at 1038 (Scalia, J., dissenting in part).

[131] *Id*. at 979-83.

[132] 497 U.S. 1 (1990).

[133] *Id*. at 18.

[134] 556 F.2d 113 (2d Cir. 1977).

[135] *Id*. at 120.

tral reportage, it seemed, would create even greater breathing space for a media industry already provided latitude *via* the actual malice standard.

In the nearly three decades since its inception, several states — Alabama, Florida, Georgia, Illinois, Louisiana, New York, Oklahoma, Vermont and Washington — and the District of Columbia have accepted neutral reportage in some form. In addition, on the federal appeals level, the Fourth, Seventh and Tenth Circuit Courts have joined the Second in recognizing the privilege. Yet the judiciary has hardly embraced it. Indeed, a significant number of courts have rejected the libel defense, reasoning that it is neither First-Amendment-mandated nor justifiable on policy grounds. The recent rejection by the Pennsylvania Supreme Court of neutral reportage is illustrative. In *Norton v. Glenn,* the court held that the First Amendment creates no special rights for the news media in libel law over and above those enjoyed by ordinary citizens.[136] The court also stated that unless the Supreme Court changes the actual malice standard further in favor of the media, there is no public policy justification for adoption of the neutral reportage privilege.[137]

The Supreme Court has had virtually nothing to say about neutral reportage. While it remains an option in the libel defendant's strategy, the inconsistent manner in which courts have accepted neutral reportage makes it an unreliable defense.

## COMMON LAW DEFENSES

Libel defendants may also utilize defenses that originate with the common law. Traditional state rules governing libel law largely stem from laws and principles handed down through generations of legal precedent, mainly from English law. Early in the Sixteenth Century, the common law courts began to recognize a claim for defamation and, with it, various defenses. These grew out of the recognition that there is sometimes an interest in the free flow of information that is so important that some allowance for error must be made.

### Fair Comment and Criticism

Imagine a situation in which a newspaper writes a highly critical review of a local theater production. Should the subjects of the review be able to file a libel claim? At the turn of the century, the *Des Moines Leader* republished a review of an act by "The Cherry Sisters." Among other statements, the reviewer described one sister as "an old jade," a second as "a capering monstrosity," and the three of them as "strange creatures." When the sisters sued for libel, the Iowa Supreme Court accepted the *Leader's* defense:

One who goes upon the stage to exhibit himself to the public,

or who gives any kind of a performance to which the public is invited, may be freely criticised [sic].... [E]ntire freedom of expression is guaranteed [sic] to dramatic critics, provided they are not actuated by malice or evil purpose in what they write.[138]

Thus began the development of the fair comment and criticism doctrine. Originally the privilege provided only modest coverage, protecting commentary only when it was based on true facts, but over time it has expanded. Still, to qualify for the privilege, commentary must be fair, it must be made without common law malice (that is, ill will), and it must accurately reflect the opinion of the commentator.

Fair comment and criticism is a common law privilege that protects critics from lawsuits brought by individuals in the public eye. A "critic" can be anyone who comments on these individuals. A person in the public eye is anyone who enters a public sphere: artists, entertainers, dramatists, writers, members of the clergy, teachers — anyone who moves in and out of the public eye, either professionally or as an amateur. The privilege also protects commentary on institutions whose activities are of interest to the public or where matters of public interest are concerned.

Fair comment and criticism protects criticism based on facts that are stated, privileged or otherwise known to be available to the public. If the challenged statement conveys or implies a defamatory message, this defense may be lost and the implication may be the basis of a libel suit.

### Truth

Truth is a complete defense in a libel case. If it can be proved, there can be no liability. If a statement must be false for liability to attach, it cannot be the basis of a successful libel suit if, in fact, it is true. But there are a number of misconceptions about the truth defense, and the defense is not easy to prove.

For years, truth was considered a noble defense. After all, the media are supposed to be in the business of rooting out and publishing the truth. A turnabout in the law, however, has turned the truth-falsity distinction on its ear. In modern libel law, the burden of proof in this area lies with the plaintiff, not the defendant.

Just because the burden of proof lies with the plaintiff, however, a libel defendant does not stand idly by. The defendant's attorneys will attempt to demonstrate that the disputed material is true. The attorneys will do this by cross-examining the plaintiff's witnesses and, possibly, by producing evidence of truth. In such circumstances — and even when a defendant advances a defense of truth — the defendant need not demonstrate that a defamatory statement is completely true in order to maintain the defense. Substantial truth is all that is required. As one court said, "Slight inaccuracies of expression are immaterial provided that the defam-

---

[136] 860 A.2d 48, 53 (Pa. 2004).

[137] *Id.* at 57.

[138] Cherry v. Des Moines Leader, 86 N.W. 323, 325 (Iowa 1901).

atory charge is true in substance."[139] The Supreme Court has agreed, saying that substantial truth

> would absolve a defendant even if she cannot justify every word of the alleged defamatory matter; it is sufficient if the substance of the charge be proved true, irrespective of the slight inaccuracy in the details.... Minor inaccuracies do not amount to falsity so long as the substance, the gist, the sting of the libelous charge can be justified.[140]

Substantial truth means, for example, that if a newspaper reported that an individual was in police custody when, in fact, the individual had been released on bail, the story would be substantially true, because the individual had been in custody and it was only a quirk in time that had caused the mistake. If, however, a newspaper published that an individual had been charged with a crime when the individual had only been questioned and released, the story would not be substantially true. In short, the substantial truth defense can protect a libel defendant when *minor* inaccuracies appear in a report.

A phenomenon unique to the broadcast media may play a role in libel cases and, in turn, may have a bearing on the truth defense. Broadcasters have the ability to alter a message — and its believability, that is, its perceived "truth" — with voice inflections. A libel suit was filed against a Chicago television station claiming that one of its reporters gave a false impression of what had actually occurred, and thereby defamed the plaintiffs, with his skeptical tone of voice. That is, while his words themselves were innocent enough, the tone with which they were delivered was at the root of the libel claim. The judge, however, agreed with the defendant's position that the tone alone could not support the defamation suit, and he dismissed it.[141]

It is worthwhile to note a growing trend in lawsuits against media defendants. Plaintiffs are circumventing the issue of truth in the defendant's stories by filing suit for transgressions other than libel. A good example is *Food Lion v. Cap Cities/ABC*,[142] in which a supermarket chain that was unhappy with a television news magazine segment on its food preparation practices sued, not for libel, but because of the techniques used in gathering the information. This strategy enabled Food Lion to entirely bypass any obligation of proving that the broadcast was false.[143] Thus, whereas libel may have been the preferred sword for plaintiffs in cases like this, lawyers are more frequently advising their clients to avoid the realm in which media defendants have the shield of both constitu-

tional and common law protection at their disposal. (The *Food Lion* case is discussed in Chapter 18.)

## Qualified Privilege

Within some spheres of society, it is so vitally important that people be allowed to speak without fear of being sued for libel that they are granted immunity from liability. This privilege — called "absolute privilege" — typically occurs within the context of carrying out the business of government. Nothing a government official says that is relevant to the official's duties can be the subject of a successful libel suit. Moreover, an open society demands that members of the public have access to information relating to government proceedings. It logically follows, then, that people reporting on these proceedings or other absolutely privileged information also have the protection of privilege. This privilege, however, is conditioned or qualified on the fair and accurate reporting of the proceeding and is generally known as "qualified privilege."

The privilege may be lost if the allegedly defamatory material is published with common law malice, if it is not accurate, if it is not fair, if the gist of the article is not substantially correct or if the author draws conclusions or adds comments to the official report. According to the Supreme Court of Illinois, however, it is not defeated by either common law malice or *New York Times* actual malice.[144] Sometimes also referred to as the "fair report" or "official report" privilege, it proves to be an exception to the rule of republication, discussed later in this chapter. The fair report privilege protects media reports of official government actions, regardless of possible defamatory elements in those reports. The rationale is that citizens in a participatory democracy are entitled to such information. But that entitlement does not extend to official reports issued by governments other than those in the United States.[145]

The privilege covers officials and proceedings in the executive, judicial and legislative branches of local, state and federal governments and, often, private individuals communicating with the government.

**Executive Branch.** Reports on the official statements and proceedings of people in the administrative — or executive — branch of government are typically privileged. The reports and hearings administrators are required by law to prepare and conduct are covered, particularly when the information contained therein has been made available to the public.

Law enforcement agencies are included as part of the executive branch of government, so reports of police activity are conditionally privileged. Official reports and statements by police officials and officers qualify. A 2001 Illinois case illustrates how the privilege can work. A former Belleville, Illinois, police chief sued the *News-*

---

[139] Liberty Lobby, v. Dow Jones, 838 F.2d 1287, 1296 (D.C. Cir. 1988).

[140] Masson v. New Yorker Magazine, 501 U.S. 496, 516-17 (1991).

[141] Hanash and Yousef v. WFLD, 1998 U.S. Dist. Lexis 17738 (N.D. Ill. 1998).

[142] 964 F. Supp. 956 (M.D.N.C. 1997).

[143] A divided federal appeals court ultimately ruled that the newsgathering techniques used were not unlawful. *See* Food Lion, Inc. v. Capital Cities/ABC, 194 F. 3d 505 (4th Cir. 1999).

[144] *See, e.g.,* Solaia Technology LLC v. Specialty Publ'g Co., N.E.2d 2006 WL 1703487 (Ill. Jun 22, 2006).

[145] *See, e.g.,* Lee v. Dong-A Ilbo, 849 F.2d 876 (4th Cir. 1988).

*Democrat* there for libel (as well as invasion of privacy) after the newspaper reported he had been the subject of a rape investigation. A three-judge panel of the Appellate Court of Illinois unanimously dismissed the case, ruling that the fair report privilege protected the newspaper because its article was a fair and accurate report based on a local prosecutor's comments.[146]

Not every statement by a police officer is privileged, however. The Idaho Supreme Court, for example, refused to apply the privilege to statements a police officer made to a reporter during an interview.[147] These were not considered to be part of the officer's official duties, which is a key determinant in deciding whether the privilege applies.

**Legislative Branch.** Reports about the proceedings of Congress, state legislatures and local governing bodies are privileged. In addition, reports on documents — petitions and complaints, for example — that are filed with or submitted to these bodies are also privileged. It is important to remember, however, that documents coming from legislative meetings are not privileged until officials take possession of them.

**Judicial Branch.** Reports about judicial activities — the courts — are conditionally privileged. So media accounts of testimony, depositions, arguments, trials, verdicts, opinions and orders — those aspects that are typically open or available to the public — are among the proceedings covered. Also, documents that relate to the judicial branch are also typically privileged. Conversely, those parts of the judicial process that are closed are not privileged.

As a Massachusetts judge, Oliver Wendell Holmes Jr. was among those who reasoned that the public should be provided with information about judicial proceedings because "those who administer justice should act under a sense of public responsibility."[148] Nearly a century later, another Massachusetts court echoed Holmes and held that the value of granting privilege to media reports about the courts is "the security which publicity gives for the proper administration of justice."[149]

### Non-Publication and Republication

Since a plaintiff in a libel case must prove that a defamatory statement was published, a defendant may prevail by showing he or she did not publish the statement, that the statement was not understood by a third party, or that it was published so long ago (one year or more, depending on the state) that the statute of limitations expired.

Since republication is generally considered tantamount to pub-

lication, there is virtually no defense in arguing that the defendant merely repeated a defamatory statement. As one court ruled, "[O]ne who republishes a defamatory statement 'adopts' it as his own and is liable in equal measure to the original defamer."[150] Moreover, media organizations are especially prone to libel suits for repeating defamatory statements, because plaintiffs tend to sue defendants who are best able to pay damages. Neither the original publisher nor a reporter is as likely to be as financially capable as a media organization.

### Letters to the Editor

While the publication of letters to the editor represents a form of republication, letters are typically viewed as expressions of opinions rather than statements of fact. For that reason, newspapers and magazines have won most cases based on the publication of letters. Courts have sought to provide protection for their publication, often viewing them as part of an open forum for the general public.

The placement of a letter can have a bearing in determining whether it qualifies as opinion. That is, by appearing within a section of a newspaper or magazine that is clearly set aside for letters expressing opinions, a letter is much more likely to be viewed by a court as an expression of opinion.

Courts have held that some letters to the editor have been expressions that combined opinion and facts. Often cases based on such expressions are resolved in favor of libel plaintiffs. For example, a Florida appellate court ruled that a letter questioning a child psychologist's qualifications was defamatory because it was this sort of mixed expression and, therefore, not privileged.[151] On the other hand, the Ohio Supreme Court in 2001 supported the notion that writers of letters to the editor enjoy the same constitutional protection for opinions as journalists do: "The robust exchange of ideas that occurs each day on the editorial pages of our state's newspapers could indeed suffer if the nonmedia authors of letters to the editor published in these forums were denied the same constitutional protections enjoyed by the editors themselves."[152] Thus, the authors of letters that the news media publish are as shielded as the media themselves.

### The Wire Service Defense

Another exception to the republication rule is the publication of information from a business that expressly provides information to news organizations. This "wire service defense" is available to libel defendants if four factors are met:

(1) the defendant received the copy in which the defamatory

---

146 Hurst v. Capital Cities Media, 754 N.E.2d 429 (Ill. App. 2001).

147 Weimer v. Rankin, 790 P.2d 347 (Idaho 1990).

148 Cowley v. Pulsifer, 137 Mass. 392, 394 (1884).

149 Liquori v. Republican Co., 396 N.E.2d 726, 728 (Mass. App. 1979).

150 Liberty Lobby v. Dow Jones & Co., 838 F.2d 1287, 1298 (D.C. Cir. 1988).

151 Madsen v. Buie, 454 So. 2d 727, 729 (Fla. Dist. Ct. App. 1984).

152 Wampler v. Higgins, 752 N.E.2d 962, 975 (Ohio 2001).

statements are contained from a reputable news gathering agency;

(2) the defendant did not know the story was false;

(3) nothing on the face of the story could have reasonably alerted the defendant that it may have been incorrect; and

(4) the original wire service story was republished without substantial change.

In short, the wire service defense holds that the accurate republication of a story that a reputable news agency provided does not constitute fault as a matter of law.

The wire service defense originated with a 1933 case, *Layne v. Tribune Co.*[153] The Florida Supreme Court held that republication of wire service reports could not be libelous unless the publisher acted in a negligent, reckless or careless manner. "No newspaper could ... assume in advance the burden of specially verifying every item of news reported to it by established news gathering agencies," the court held.[154]

The wire service defense has succeeded even when a newspaper published a story that relied on past wire-service articles[155] and when a CBS affiliate broadcast network news reports.[156] Though by no means universally accepted, at least thirteen jurisdictions have adopted the wire service defense: Alaska, the District of Columbia, Florida, Georgia, Hawaii, Kentucky, Louisiana, Massachusetts, Missouri, New York, North Carolina, Wisconsin and Puerto Rico.

But what happens if the Associated Press republishes defamatory articles from reputable newspapers? The "reverse wire service defense" protects the AP from liability. The Massachusetts Court of Appeals, calling the relationship between the AP and its member newspapers and other media outlet members "symbiotic," noted that the AP employs its own staff to report original news stories but also often relies upon member newspapers as additional wire sources.[157]

### On-Line Republication

The publication of on-line computer material by Internet service providers is related to publication and republication. The issue in libel law is whether an on-line service can be held liable for defamatory statements that are published through that service.

The defining case in this area is *Zeran v. America Online*.[158] This case dealt with the issue of an ISP as publisher, but did so in light of the passage of the Communications Decency Act in 1996. One section of the act provides that "no provider or user of an interactive computer service shall be treated as the publisher or speaker of any information provided by another information con-

tent provider."

Kenneth Zeran sued America Online when the company included his name and telephone number in a series of bulletin board notices that advertised t-shirts and other items glorifying the 1995 bombing of a federal building in Oklahoma City. The inclusion of Zeran's name was part of a hoax by an unknown individual. A relevant section of the CDA stipulates that no provider of an interactive computer service can be treated as the publisher of any information provided by some entity other than the provider. A U.S. District Court ruled that while the CDA does not preempt all state law actions of this nature, it did preempt Zeran's claim of negligence on the part of AOL because it conflicts with both the language and purposes of the CDA.[159] On appeal, the Fourth U.S. Circuit Court of Appeals ruled that this section of the CDA "plainly immunizes computer service providers like AOL for liability for information that originates with third parties."[160] Thus, an on-line libel defendant may be able to utilize the CDA when similar circumstances present themselves.

### The Libel-Proof Plaintiff

A libel defendant may be able to invoke the concept of the "libel-proof plaintiff." When an individual's reputation in the community is so bad that even a false accusation could not further harm it, the individual is considered to be libel-proof and cannot win a defamation suit. The libel-proof doctrine was first articulated as a libel defense in *Cardillo v. Doubleday Co., Inc.*, a 1975 case.[161] Since then, two separate prongs of the libel-proof doctrine have developed — incremental harm and issue-specific publication.

**Incremental Harm.** If an individual is identified in an article as a thief, child molester and tax evader, and if all of those charges are true, does it make any difference if the individual is also identified falsely as a kidnapper? The doctrine of incremental harm says no. In such a case, the publisher could probably win, arguing that the single false statement causes harm that is merely incremental beyond what already exists and, therefore, is not grounds for a libel suit. In short, under these kinds of circumstances the false statement causes no harm to the reputation beyond the harm caused by the true statements, which are protected.

One of the leading incremental harm cases is *Herbert v. Lando*.[162] Anthony Herbert, a retired Army officer, sued over state-

---

[153] 146 So. 234 (Fla. 1933) (en banc).

[154] *Id.* at 239.

[155] McKinney v. Avery Journal, 393 S.E.2d 295 (N.C. App. 1990).

[156] Auvril v. CBS, 140 F.R.D. 450 (E.D. Wash. 1991).

[157] Reilly v. Associated Press, 797 N.E.2d 1204 (Mass. Ct. App. 2003).

[158] 129 F.3d 327 (4th Cir. 1997).

[159] Zeran v. America Online, 958 F. Supp. 1124, 1135 (E.D. Va. 1997).

[160] Zeran v. America Online, 129 F.3d 327, 328 (4th Cir. 1997).

[161] 518 F.2d 638 (2d Cir. 1975) (ruling that the passages of a book whose authors wrote that a habitual criminal was involved in various other criminal activities were not published with actual malice).

[162] 781 F.2d 298 (2d Cir. 1986), *aff'g, in part, rev'g, in part,* and *remanding,* 596 F. Supp. 1178 (S.D.N.Y. 1984). The case and its facts had been thoroughly explored by the courts on several previous occasions. *See* Herbert v. Lando, 73 F.R.D. 387 (S.D.N.Y.), *rev'd,* 568 F.2d 974 (2d Cir. 1977), *rev'd,* 441 U.S. 153 (1979).

ments made about him during a segment of *60 Minutes*. The segment questioned the validity of his claim that the U.S. Army had punished him for trying to disclose information about massacres by American forces in South Vietnam. The Second U.S. Circuit Court of Appeals ruled that if the charge that Herbert lied about reporting war crimes was not actionable, "[O]ther statements, even those that might be found to have been published with actual malice should not be actionable if they merely imply the same view, and are simply an outgrowth of and subsidiary to those claims upon which it has been held there can be no recovery."[163]

In several cases, however, the incremental harm doctrine has failed as a libel defense. A particularly noteworthy example was the outright rejection of the doctrine in *Liberty Lobby, Inc. v. Anderson*.[164] Journalist Jack Anderson described the founder of Liberty Lobby as a racist, fascist, anti-Semitic and neo-Nazi, and wrote that Liberty Lobby was founded to pursue his goals. Anderson argued that previous publications had already so irreparably tarnished the plaintiff's reputation that the libel-proof doctrine should apply. In an opinion written by Judge Antonin Scalia, the court rejected the claim, ruling that "we cannot envision how a court would go about determining that someone's reputation had already been 'irreparably' damaged — i.e., that no new reader could be reached by the freshest libel."[165]

Nevertheless, the doctrine remains a valuable defense weapon, particularly against frivolous libel suits, and especially given the Supreme Court's opinion that states are free to adopt the doctrine as they see fit.[166]

**Issue-Specific Publication.** Courts recognizing the issue-specific doctrine have found that libel plaintiffs with tarnished reputations with regard to a particular issue are libel-proof *only with respect to that topic area*. Libel claims pursued in the issue-specific context present the question of whether previous publicity or criminal convictions have so tarnished the plaintiff's reputation that the plaintiff should be barred from receiving a damage award.

In one case, for example, the media defendant had published an article stating that the plaintiff had used his relationship with actress Elizabeth Taylor for financial gain.[167] The court held that the plaintiff had a "reputation for taking advantage of women generally, and of Miss Taylor specifically." And it ruled that "[a]n individual who engages in certain anti-social or criminal behavior and suffers a diminished reputation may be 'libel-proof' as a matter of law, as it *relates to that specific behavior*."[168]

Thus, the doctrine of the libel-proof plaintiff may serve a defen-

dant who has published otherwise defamatory statements about an individual whose reputation is already so sullied as to render additional accusations moot, regardless of their falsity. The doctrine may apply to accusations of any nature or to those that relate only to a specific issue.

## OTHER DEFENSE ISSUES

While not defenses *per se*, several other issues can have a bearing on — and even strengthen — a libel defense.

### *Responsible Reporting*

As part of a defense strategy, a libel defendant may attempt to demonstrate to a court that it conducted itself in a responsible way. Within the context of a media organization, responsible reporting may be demonstrated through attempts to show that journalists acted without negligence or reckless disregard of the truth.

In attempting to prove that a libel defendant acted with reckless disregard, a plaintiff is likely to attempt to build a case bit by bit, demonstrating irresponsibility or carelessness in publishing. Courts have said that no single element is sufficient to prove clearly and convincingly that a defendant acted with actual malice, but each can be used as evidence. A libel defendant who is aware of certain claims of irresponsibility or carelessness, therefore, can be prepared to refute them. Some of the claims might be the following:

- failure to investigate sufficiently;
- failure to interview parties who have knowledge of facts related to the story, including the subject of the report;
- reliance on previously published material;
- reliance on biased stories;
- inaccurate reporting;
- reporting from a specific point of view in an investigative story;
- refusal to retract or correct if facts warrant;
- absence of a fixed deadline;
- ill-will or hatred toward the plaintiff.

Even if media defendants are unable to escape liability altogether, by refuting these points, and demonstrating responsible reporting, they are likely to mitigate damages.

A case in Ohio illustrates how a court may consider one or more of these elements of responsible reporting. Within the context of a libel suit, a state appellate court concluded that a reporter's failure to interview one of the police officers accused of brutality in a series of reports could be regarded as negligent behavior. The court ruled, however, that that irresponsibility alone did not support the officer's claim that the reporter had acted with actual malice.[169] Conversely, a television journalist argued that his

---

163 *Id.* at 312.

164 746 F.2d 1563 (D.C. Cir. 1984), *rev'd on other grounds*, 477 U.S. 242 (1986).

165 *Id.* at 1568.

166 *See* Masson v. New Yorker Magazine, 501 U.S. 496, 523 (1991).

167 Wynberg v. National Enquirer, 564 F. Supp. 924 (C.D. Cal. 1982).

168 *Id.* at 928 (emphasis added).

169 Early v. Toledo Blade, 720 N.E.2d 107 (Ohio App. 1998).

# THE DEFENDANT'S CASE

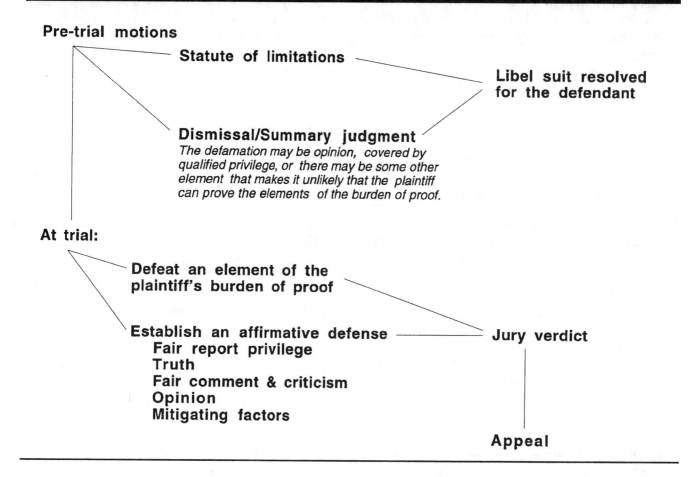

**Pre-trial motions**

**Statute of limitations**

**Libel suit resolved for the defendant**

**Dismissal/Summary judgment**
*The defamation may be opinion, covered by qualified privilege, or there may be some other element that makes it unlikely that the plaintiff can prove the elements of the burden of proof.*

**At trial:**

**Defeat an element of the plaintiff's burden of proof**

**Establish an affirmative defense**
    **Fair report privilege**
    **Truth**
    **Fair comment & criticism**
    **Opinion**
    **Mitigating factors**

**Jury verdict**

**Appeal**

---

reporting methods were responsible by maintaining that he spent four days interviewing thirty people and reviewing 500 pages of court records in preparing the story. That contributed to an appellate court overturning a libel judgment against him.[170]

Retractions, apologies and corrections for reputation-damaging reports can also be considered examples of "responsible reporting." In the eyes of the law, their impact varies greatly from state to state. In some states, a prompt and complete apology, correction and retraction will protect a defendant from punitive damages. In other states, jurors merely consider retractions in determining the amount of damages awarded.

While a retraction or apology is not a libel defense, a potential libel defendant is often advised to correct possibly libelous errors due to the correction's ability to alleviate the statement's defamatory sting in the eyes of a court. Admitting errors in such circumstances may be regarded as an aspect of responsible reporting.[171]

Moreover, many states have retraction laws that provide varying degrees of protection. Typically, they require a plaintiff to give a publisher an opportunity to retract a libelous statement prior to initiating a libel suit. If the publisher honors the request in a timely manner, the retraction may reduce the damages that the plaintiff may later seek should a lawsuit be filed. It should be noted, however, that the plaintiff may use a retraction, apology or correction as a defendant's admission of liability.

### Summary Judgment

A judge may summarily decide certain points of a case and issue a judgment dismissing the case. It can occur at any of several points in litigation.

A judge may issue a summary judgment on grounds that there is no genuine issue as to any material fact. Generally, this is a result of a plaintiff clearly being unable to meet at least one element in the plaintiff's burden of proof. On numerous occasions, the

---

[170] Dolcefino and KTRK Television, Inc. v. Turner, 987 S.W. 2d 100 (Tex. 1998).

[171] It should be acknowledged that retractions and/or apologies are sometimes discouraged by those who advise potential media defendants. To retract

or apologize, they say, is tantamount to an admission of guilt, thus increasing the challenge of mounting a successful defense.

Supreme Court said that when considering motions for summary judgment, courts "must view the facts and inferences to be drawn from them in the light most favorable to the opposing party."[172] The rationale behind this view is, if the summary judgment is granted, the plaintiff's opportunity to prove a case is ended, but if the defendant's motion for summary judgment is denied, the defendant still has an opportunity to prove its case.

Summary judgments are seen as important tools for protecting free expression, particularly in an environment in which plaintiffs have harassed the media by filing frivolous lawsuits. Allowing judges to dismiss claims without merit tackles the chilling effect on media coverage that these lawsuits can have. As one federal judge explained:

In the First Amendment area, summary procedures are even more essential. For the stake here, if harassment succeeds, is free debate. One of the purposes of the [New York] Times [actual malice] principle, in addition to protecting persons from being cast in damages in libel suits filed by public officials, is to prevent persons from being discouraged in the full and free exercise of First Amendment rights with respect to the conduct of their government. The threat of being put to the defense of a lawsuit brought by a popular public official may be as chilling to the exercise of First Amendment freedoms as fear of the outcome of the lawsuit itself, especially to advocates of unpopular causes.[173]

Until 1979, summary judgment was a preferred method of dealing with libel cases involving actual malice. When the defense submitted a motion for summary judgment — based on the contention that the plaintiff could not prove actual malice — the judge would either grant or deny it. If granted, the case was over; if denied, the case went to trial.

In 1979, Chief Justice Warren Burger cast doubt on the appropriateness of summary judgment in libel cases because, he argued, any examination of actual malice "calls a defendant's state of mind into question." Such a circumstance, Burger argued, "does not readily lend itself to summary disposition."[174] While some lower courts took Burger's admonition to heart — using it as a basis for denying summary judgment — motions for summary judgment are granted more often than not. Then, in 1986, Justice Byron White wrote that in deciding whether to grant motions for summary judgment, trial judges should decide whether public plaintiffs can meet the actual malice standard by "clear and convincing evidence." If not, summary judgment should be granted.[175] In short,

this tempered Burger's words, suggesting that summary judgment remains a viable option.

Today, judges may be somewhat more apt to grant motions for summary judgment in an effort to curtail the increasing cost of defending libel suits. About 80 percent of libel insurance costs are incurred, not through the compensation of injured plaintiffs, but merely in defense costs. Estimates regarding the average libel defense cost vary but typically range from $100,000 to $200,000. In major cases, defendants have spent millions of dollars. Moreover, libel defendants have discovered that juries are increasingly unsympathetic toward them. The median jury award increased from $200,000 in the early 1980s to an average of $1.5 million over that decade. According to the Media Law Resource Center, libel judgments against the media averaged $1.8 million in 2001.[176] In fact, juries seem to be punishing some libel defendants — those whose content or newsgathering techniques they find distasteful — particularly hard with punitive damages. Jury verdicts can reach into the millions, making it appear that juries base their decisions at least in part on a perceived unsavory nature of the defendant. In the wake of these awards, one scholar wrote, "The ability of juries to punish unpopular speakers by awarding punitive damages in ruinous amounts flies in the face of the First Amendment which protects unorthodox as well as mainstream speech."[177]

While approximately two-thirds of jury verdicts in media libel cases are rendered against media defendants, about 75 percent are reversed or reduced on appeal. The bottom line — and not necessarily a reassuring one — for those facing a libel suit may be that media defendants tend to win on the law rather than having to rely on the often emotion-based conclusions of jurors.

## GLOBALIZATION OF U.S. LIBEL LAW: JURISDICTION AND CHOICE OF LAW ISSUES

Increasingly, broadcasts and publications transcend the boundaries of one state, or even one country, causing complicated problems for potential libel plaintiffs. The site where a lawsuit is generally adjudicated is — in legal parlance — the "place of wrong," that is, the place where the alleged injury occurred. In past years, the place of wrong for libel actions was the jurisdiction where the defamatory publication was made, regardless of where it originated. More recently, however, libel actions have been adjudicated in the place with the most significant relationship to the case. Generally, the place with the most significant relationship to the case is the jurisdiction in which the plaintiff lives or works.[178]

The determination of which law should govern in multi-state or

---

[172] Mourning v. Family Publ'ns Serv., 411 U.S. 356, 382 (1973). See also United States v. Diebold, 369 U.S. 654, 655 (1979); Adickes v. Kress & Co., 389 U.S. 144, 157 (1970).

[173] Washington Post Co. v. Keogh, 365 F.2d 965, 968 (D.C. Cir. 1966).

[174] Hutchinson v. Proxmire, 443 U.S. 111, 120 n.9 (1979).

[175] Anderson v. Liberty Lobby, 477 U.S. 242, 244, 256 (1986).

[176] Press Release, Libel Defense Resource Center, Media Defendants' Win Rate Higher ... But So Are Damage Awards, available at http://www.ldrc.com/Press_Releases/bull2002-1.html.

[177] Nicole B. Casarez, Punitive Damages in Defamation Actions: An Area of Libel Law Worth Reforming, 32 Duq. L. Rev. 667, 687 (1994).

[178] See Restatement (Second) of Conflict of Laws § 150 (1971).

multi-nation lawsuits is called the "choice of law" issue. Transnational media litigation, which often involves libel cases in foreign countries against media defendants in the United States, is growing. This is especially the case in libel involving the Internet. A good illustration is the High Court of Australia's 2002 decision in *Dow Jones & Co. v Gutnick.*[179] Australian businessman Joseph Gutnick sued the U.S. company Dow Jones & Co. in the Supreme Court of Victoria for defamation in connection with online material published in *Barron's Online* magazine. Noting that the material at issue was downloaded by Victoria residents, the Australian court held that when defamatory statement is accessible to and read by ISP subscribers in an Australian state, a court of that state has jurisdiction to hear an action for defamation relating to the statements.

In a 2005 Internet libel case, however, a Canadian appellate court refused to exercise jurisdiction over an American newspaper. In *Bangoura v. Washington Post,*[180] the Ontario Court of Appeal held that there was "simply no real and substantial connection" between the libel action and Ontario. Cheikh Bangoura, a native of Guinea, who moved to Ontario in 2000, sued the *Washington Post* and its three reporters in a Canadian court for defamation. In 1997, the *Washington Post* published two articles claiming that Bangoura, then a U.N. official in Kenya, engaged in sexual harassment, financial improprieties and nepotism.

Generally, American courts hold that U.S. libel defendants are protected by the First Amendment from such foreign judgments if they are brought to the United States for enforcement.

In *Bachchan v. India Abroad Publications, Inc.,*[181] for example, an Indian national living in London asked a New York state court to enforce a libel verdict the plaintiff won in England against the publisher of a newspaper and news service for Asian Indians in the United States. Judge Shirley Fingerhood found that England's lack of an equivalent to the First Amendment to be significant and ruled that enforcing a foreign libel judgment would seriously jeopardize the First Amendment protections of speech and the press.

The Maryland Court of Appeals reached a similar conclusion five years later. A U.S. citizen was successfully sued in England for a letter he had written to the editor of the London *Daily Telegraph.* When the letter writer returned to the United States, specifically Maryland, the plaintiff in the case asked American courts to enforce the libel judgment.[182]

The Maryland Court of Appeals, however, noting England's adherence to strict liability in libel actions, the presumptive falsity of alleged defamations, the lack of distinction between private and public figures and differences in defenses, concluded that defamation law was totally different in England "in virtually every significant respect." The principles of libel law applied to the suit in Eng-

land, the court held, were "so contrary to Maryland defamation law, and to the policy of freedom of the press" that the judgment should not be recognized.[183]

More recently, a federal district judge in California held the French court's order against Yahoo! unenforceable in the United States. U.S. District Judge Jeremy Fogel stated in *Yahoo! Inc. v. La Ligue Contre le Racisme et l'Antisemitisme,* "Although France has the sovereign right to regulate what speech is permissible in France, this Court may not enforce a foreign order that violates the protections of the U.S. Constitution by chilling protected speech that occurs simultaneously within our borders."[184] The 2006 Internet hate speech case involved civil lawsuits filed by two French human rights groups against Yahoo! in a French court. The French court ordered Yahoo! to prevent France-based access to Yahoo!'s Internet auction service that displays Nazi artifacts and to any other site or service defending Nazism or contesting Nazi crimes.

## SUMMARY

Defamation law is designed to protect reputations so that individual relational interests are not harmed, while the guarantees of free expression are designed to promote the gathering and dissemination of information. Reputational rights are recognized in every society as a significant interest, but the degree of protection by law or custom varies greatly from country to country.

In the United States, though free expression is vigorously protected, libel law is one of the most visible legal restraints on expression. In recent years, the chill on expression caused by libel law has been a growing concern for the media. On the other hand, those critical of the excesses of the press welcome some degree of press chill. Notwithstanding the debate, there is no denying that libel law serves as a necessary mechanism for the balance between reputational rights and press freedom.

There are two types of defamation: libel, or written defamation, and slander, or spoken defamation. The traditional distinction between libel and slander is not as clear-cut as it once was because of new modes of communication. Broadcast defamation, for example, is more often than not treated as libel.

Nearly all libel cases are civil actions, in which plaintiffs claim monetary damages for reputational harm from the publication of defamatory statements. Libel is still recognized as a crime in some jurisdictions, but criminal libel statutes are rarely invoked.

To establish a cause of action against a non-media libel defendant, a plaintiff must prove that he or she was identified in a statement that was published to a third person, and that the statement was defamatory. When a media organization is the defendant, the plaintiff must establish two additional elements: (1)

179 194 A.L.R. 433 (2003).
180 258 D.L.R.4th 341 (Ont. Ct. App. 2005).
181 585 N.Y.S.2d 266 (1992).
182 Telnikoff v. Matusevitch, 702 A.2d 230 (Md. 1997).

183 *Id.* at 247-48.
184 145 F. Supp. 2d 1168, 1192 (N.D. Cal. 2001), *rev'd en banc,* 433 F.3d 1199 (9th Cir.), *cert. denied,* 126 S. Ct. 2332 (2006).

that the publication resulted from fault on the part of the defendant and (2) that the plaintiff suffered actual injury from publication of the defamatory statement.

Libel as a tort — a civil wrong — is premised on the requirement that a statement be false and defamatory. Thus, falsity is essential to a libel claim. Therefore, a libel claim for a statement of opinion — which cannot be proved to be true or false — cannot stand.

"Truth" in libel law is not synonymous with "accuracy." Verbatim quotations in a news story may be accurate but may not necessarily be true. "Truth" means that the substance of the quoted statement is factually verifiable.

It is difficult to determine when some language is defamatory; other language is clearly defamatory. The meanings of words change with the time, place and manner in which they are used. In some jurisdictions, the libel *per se* and libel *per quod* rules are still followed. Libel *per se* refers to words and phrases that are defamatory on their face and need no additional information. Libel *per quod* refers to a statement that is not defamatory in and of itself but that can be made defamatory if additional facts are known.

Family members or relatives of libel plaintiffs can rarely claim damages for libels unless they can individually establish that they suffered from damage to their reputations because of the publication of defamatory statements about them. Identification is not necessarily the specific reference to a plaintiff by name. If a plaintiff is identifiable to those who were exposed to the publication, the identification requirement is met. Individuals who are members of groups have increasing difficulty proving they were identified as the size of the group grows.

Publication has little to do with the ordinary meaning of printing or broadcasting a defamatory statement. Instead, it means that material is disseminated to someone other than the defamed person. Publication is rarely an issue in media libel actions because defamatory statements are usually disseminated to a wide audience when media publish them. Republication of a libelous statement can constitute a cause of action separate from the original publication. Whoever is substantially and directly involved in publishing a defamatory statement is liable and thus can be sued.

Libel plaintiffs must prove fault, but the degree of fault depends upon the status of the plaintiff. In most jurisdictions, private persons are required to prove negligence in order to win compensatory damages. Public figures and public officials must prove actual malice in order to win compensatory damages. In addition, every libel plaintiff must prove actual malice in order to win punitive or presumed damages.

Libel defendants have at their disposal a variety of tools they can use to defend themselves. Typically, their first option is to seek summary judgment. If there is reason to believe that the plaintiff is unable to prove all the elements of the burden of proof — whether on constitutional or common law grounds — a defense attorney may be able to prevail with a summary judgment.

When a case goes to trial, libel defendants can use both constitutional and common law defenses. Among the defenses in the latter category, "truth" is regarded as the most definitive, given that it refutes any claim that a statement is false. Other common law defenses for media defendants include the privilege of reporting the proceedings of all government branches. The privilege is qualified on the reporting being fair and accurate.

At the heart of the constitutional defense is the notion that there is a First Amendment value embedded in the media's freedom to express themselves. The creation of actual malice was designed to provide an additional layer of protection for media defendants in reporting about public officials. The doctrine was later extended to public figures. Thus, establishing the nature of the plaintiff is key. Libel defendants seek to have plaintiffs categorized as public because they then have to prove the defendant acted with actual malice — knowledge of falsity or reckless disregard for the truth.

Media organizations and their employees have the right to express opinions, and that right has its roots in the First Amendment freedom of the press. However, defining what qualifies as opinion has been a challenge, and largely rests with the four-part *Ollman* test. The protection of opinion is also derived from the common law. Those who are in the public eye subject themselves to fair comment and criticism by the media.

To some extent, defending a libel accusation involves refuting the elements of the plaintiff's case — that is, contesting the plaintiff's attempts to prove that the definition of libel was met. Given that one of those elements is that the statement at issue is false, if the defendant can prove that it is true, the defense is successful. Similarly, because publication is an element of the plaintiff's case, a defendant may attempt to prove that its publication qualifies as one of the exceptions to the republication rule — neutral reportage, the wire service defense, or on-line republication. With regard to the latter, the Communication Decency Act of 1996 offer protection to computer service providers.

Finally, media defendants want to portray themselves as reliable and trustworthy organizations that conduct themselves responsibly. While not a defense, per se, this representation can only help the defendant's image in the eyes of the court and jury. Moreover, journalistic integrity is simply the proper way to conduct business, and often tends to be the best way to avoid libel suits in the first place — and that is often the best defense.

Libel actions resulting from multi-state publications of defamatory statements create various choices of law questions for plaintiffs. The law of the state with "the most significant relationship" to the libel action is generally applied. Foreign libel judgments against transnational U.S. media cannot be enforced in the United States when they are found to violate First Amendment standards on freedom of speech and the press.

**FOR ADDITIONAL READING**

Braithwaite, Nick, ed. *The International Libel Handbook*. Oxford: Butterworth-Heinemann, 1995.

Carter-Ruck, Peter F., & Harvey Starte. *Carter-Ruck on Libel and Slander*, 5th ed. London: Butterworths, 1997.

Collins, Matthew. *The Law of Defamation and the Internet Law*, 2d ed. Oxford: Oxford University Press, 2005.

Elder, David A. *Defamation: A Lawyer's Guide.* Deerfield, Ill.: Clark Boardman Callaghan, 2004.

Gillmor, Donald M. *Power, Publicity, and the Abuse of Libel Law.* New York: Oxford University Press, 1992.

Hopkins, W. Wat. *Actual Malice.* Westport, Conn.: Praeger, 1989.

Hopkins, W. Wat. "The Involuntary Public Figure: Not So Dead After All," 21 *Cardozo Arts & Entertainment Law Journal* 1 (2003).

Jones, William K. *Insult to Injury: Libel, Slander, and Invasions of Privacy.* Boulder, Colo.: University Press of Colorado, 2003.

Lewis, Anthony. *Make No Law: The Sullivan Case and the First Amendment.* New York: Random House, 1991.

Lisby, Gregory C. "No Place in the Law: The Ignominy of Criminal Libel in American Jurisprudence," 9 *Communication Law and Policy* 433 (2004).

London, Martin & Barbara Dill. *At What Price?: Libel Law and Freedom of the Press.* New York: Twentieth Century Fund Press, 1993.

Metcalf, Slade R. *Rights and Liabilities of Publishers, Broadcasters and Reporters.* 2 vols. St Paul, Minn.: West Group, 2006.

O'Neil, Robert M. "*New York Times Co. v. Sullivan:* A First Amendment Lawyer's Retrospective," 9 *Communication Law and Policy* 423 (2004).

Rosini, Neil J. *The Practical Guide to Libel Law.* New York: Praeger Publishers, 1991.

Sack, Robert D. *Sack on Defamation: Libel, Slander, and Related Problems,* 3rd ed. New York: Practising Law Institute, 2006.

Sanford, Bruce W. *Libel and Privacy,* 2d ed. Englewood Cliffs, N.J.: Aspen Law & Business, 2006.

Smolla, Rodney A. *Law of Defamation,* 3d ed. St. Paul, Minn.: West Group, 2006.

Wimmer, Kurt A. "International Law and the Enforcement of Foreign Judgments Based on Internet Content," http://www.ldrc.com/Cyberspace/cyber12.html#_ftn1.

Youm, Kyu Ho. "The Interface Between American and Foreign Libel Law: U.S. Courts Refuse to Enforce Libel Judgments," 49 *International and Comparative Law Quarterly* 131 (2000).

# 7

## Intellectual Property

*By Dorothy Bowles*

---

☞ **Headnote Questions**

- *What is intellectual property?*
- *Do intellectual property laws help or hinder the mass media?*
- *Is a work copyrighted in the United States also protected in other countries?*
- *What does "fixed in tangible form" mean?*
- *What is copyright infringement?*
- *To what extent may copyrighted works be used for nonprofit or educational purposes?*
- *What is the fair use doctrine?*
- *What factors do courts consider when determining whether fair use applies?*
- *How does each of the fair use factors apply to downloading music from the Internet without paying for it?*
- *What is the difference between a copyright and a trademark?*
- *What is compulsory licensing? To which media does it apply?*
- *What challenges does the Internet pose for copyright law?*
- *How have entertainment industries attempted to protect their copyrights from illegal file sharing?*
- *What do "contributory infringement" and "vicarious infringement" mean?*

---

Most college students would not go into a store and steal a book or CD, even if they knew they wouldn't get caught. Yet, many of the same students exhibit few qualms about illegally downloading music or movies from the Internet although this is stealing from copyright owners. A 2005 national survey reported that two-thirds of a sample of college and university students said they had no ethical reservations about illegally downloading copyrighted digital files from the Internet for free or swapping them electronically with other people. Slightly more than half of the college-age respondents said they thought it was permissible at school or in the workplace to download software, music and movies.[1]

Patent, trademark and copyright laws protect the right of people who own "intellectual property" — original literary, musical or graphic works or unique devices, identifying words, phrases or symbols — to receive compensation from those who use their creative work.

Congress' authority to enact patent and copyright laws derives from the interstate commerce clause of Article I, Section 8 of the Constitution. The pertinent sentence is:

> The Congress shall have power... To promote the progress of science and useful arts, by securing for limited times to authors and inventors the exclusive right to their respective writings and discoveries.

The U.S. Supreme Court has interpreted the phrase "to promote" as being synonymous with the phrases "to stimulate," "to encourage" and "to induce."[2]

Intellectual property laws both hinder and help the mass media. On the one hand, copyright and trademark laws give news and entertainment companies an economic incentive to create material,

---

[1] Complete results of this survey, conducted for the Business Software Alliance, can be found at http://www.definetheline.com/research.html.

[2] *See* Goldstein v. California, 412 U.S. 546, 555 (1973).

knowing they can reap financial rewards from works their employees create and that others cannot steal the fruits of their labors. On the other hand, the media must take care not to publish material that infringes the intellectual property ownership rights of others. The limited monopoly bestowed by copyright serves the ultimate goal of stimulating activity and progress in the arts and sciences and thus enriching the public. As the Supreme Court has noted, the Copyright Act is intended to increase rather than impede the harvest of knowledge.[3] The act protects only the manner of expression, not ideas; thus, many people may create their own individual creative works about the same idea. The limited copyright monopoly rewards the individual author in order to benefit the public. By this reasoning, copyright and trademark law can coexist with the First Amendment.

## ELEMENTS OF COPYRIGHT LAW

The first federal copyright law in the United States was enacted in 1790, within two years of ratification of the Constitution. Congress passed major revisions about every forty years until 1909. Then roughly seventy years passed before Congress overhauled copyright law with passage of the Copyright Act of 1976,[4] which went into effect January 1, 1978. It, too, has been amended several times.

No "international copyright" exists to automatically protect an author's work worldwide. Until 1955, U.S. authors had little protection from international pirates because the United States had not signed the major international copyright treaties. Today, works copyrighted in the United States are generally protected from infringement in some eighty nations that agree to two multilateral treaties: the Universal Copyright Convention and the Berne Convention for the Protection of Literary and Artistic Property. The United States joined the Berne Union in 1989. Members of the union agree to a certain minimum level of copyright protection and agree to treat nationals of other member countries like their own for purposes of copyright. A work first published in the United States or another Berne Union country (or first published in a non-Berne country, followed by publication within thirty days in a Berne Union country) is eligible for protection in all Berne member countries.

International piracy in 2005 was estimated at $512 billion, with China blamed for nearly two-thirds of the counterfeit goods.[5] China adopted its first intellectual property laws in 2001 as a requirement to joining the World Trade Organization,[6] but enforcement has been lax.

The Digital Millennium Copyright Act (DMCA) of 1998[7] implemented two international treaties that supplement and update the Berne Convention as the source of the basic framework for international copyright. These treaties, combined with the enforcement obligations of the World Trade Organization, provide the legal framework to protect and enforce the rights of copyrighted works globally. They boost efforts to raise the minimum standards of copyright protection around the world, particularly with respect to network-based delivery of copyrighted materials. Each signatory country must specify that creators have the basic property right to control distribution of copies of their creations. The treaties also require each signatory country to provide in its law for a copyright owner's exclusive right of "making available" its works (or phonograms) to the public for on-demand access.

### Protected Works

The Copyright Act protects original works of authorship fixed in any tangible medium of expression, from which they can be perceived, re-produced or otherwise communicated, either directly or with the aid of some device. The medium of expression may already exist or may be developed in the future. Works of authorship include:

(1) literary works;

(2) musical works, including any accompanying words;

(3) dramatic works, including any accompanying music;

(4) pantomimes and choreographic works;

(5) pictorial, graphic and sculptural works;

(6) motion pictures and other audiovisual works;

(7) sound recordings; and

(8) architectural works.

These categories are illustrative, not limiting, and they are interpreted broadly. For example, the act defines literary works as "works, other than audiovisual works, expressed in words, numbers, or other verbal or numerical symbols or indicia, regardless of the nature of the material objects, such as books, periodicals, manuscripts, phonorecords, film, tapes, disks, or cards, in which they are embodied." Therefore, telephone directories and expressions used by computer programmers are copyrightable as "literary works," although processes used in developing computer programs are not within the scope of copyright protection.[8] Coin-operated electronic video games are copyrightable under the category "audiovisual works."[9] Maps may be registered as "pictorial, graphic, and sculptural works," as may advertisements, floral ar-

---

[3] See Harper & Row Publishers v. Nation Enter., 471 U.S. 539 (1985); Sony Corp. v. Universal City Studios, Inc., 464 U.S. 417 (1984).

[4] 17 U.S.C. §§ 101-118 (1976).

[5] See Eric A. Priest, The Future of Music and Film Piracy in China (Jan. 6, 2006), available at Social Science Research Network: http://ssrn.com/abstract =761064.

[6] See Ruth Taplin, Managing Intellectual Property in the Far East – the Case of China, TOMPSON SCIENTIFIC KNOWLEDGELINK NEWSLETTER (April 2005), available at scientific.thomson.com/ts/media/newsletterpdfs/2005-04/chinese-ip.pdf.

[7] Pub. L. No. 105-304, 112 Stat. 2863 (1998) (codified at 17 U.S.C.S. § 101 (LEXIS 2002)).

[8] See Gates Rubber Co. v. Bando Chemical Indus., Ltd., 9 F.3d 823 (10th Cir. 1993); Atari Games Corp. v. Nintendo, Inc., 975 F.2d 832 (9th Cir. 1992); Southern Bell Tel. and Tel. Co. v. Associated Tel. Directory Publishers, 756 F.2d 801 (11th Cir. 1985).

[9] See Midway Mfg. Co. v. Dirkschneider, 543 F. Supp. 466 (D. Neb. 1981).

rangements, bumper stickers, fabric, wall covering designs, patterns for sewing and stained glass designs.

Courts have distinguished among three separate concepts: originality, creativity and novelty. A work is "original" if it is the independent creation of its author. It is "creative" if it embodies a modest amount of intellectual labor. It is "novel" if it differs from existing works in some relevant respect. For a work to be copyrightable, it must be original and creative but need not be novel. This contrasts with patent law where novelty is a requirement.

In a case involving telephone directories published by rival telephone companies, the Supreme Court said the level of creativity required to meet the originality requirement is extremely low.[10] The Court said the time-honored tradition of compiling facts in alphabetical order did not possess the minimal creative spark required for protection under the Copyright Act. As a result, the Copyright Office no longer registers claims to the white pages of telephone books. However, a telephone directory or other compilation satisfies the "original work of authorship" requirement if the authors independently made subjective decisions regarding layout and design of pre-existing information.[11] These requirements are likely met in the yellow pages of a telephone directory.

As early as 1884, courts recognized that photographing a person or filming an event involves creative labor.[12] Abraham Zapruder's film of the assassination of President John F. Kennedy in 1963 was held copyrightable because it embodied elements of creativity. Among other things, Zapruder selected the kind of camera (movie, not still), the kind of film (color), the kind of lens (telephoto), the area in which the pictures were to be taken, the time they were to be taken and (after testing several sites) the spot on which the camera would be operated.[13] Similarly, a court said the many decisions made during the broadcast of a baseball game — camera angles, types of shots, the use of instant replays and split screens, and shot selection — supply the creativity required to copyright the telecasts.[14]

In the 1976 Copyright Act, Congress expressly afforded copyright protection to simultaneously recorded broadcasts of live performances such as sports events,[15] but such protection does not extend to the underlying events. The National Basketball Association sought to stop Motorola and its sports reporting partner from selling pagers and SportsTrax, a service that provides subscribers with almost up-to-the-minute information about NBA games in progress.[16] Among the NBA's six claims for relief was federal copyright infringement on grounds that it owned the basketball games and could control real-time transmission of information about those games. The professional baseball, football and hockey leagues filed friend of the court briefs in the case.

Both a New York district court and the Second U.S. Circuit Court of Appeals held that the sports events do not constitute "original works of authorship." The appeals court noted that despite considerable preparation for games, they are not "authored" in any common sense of the word; they have no script like movies, plays and many other forms of entertainment. Developments like the T-formation in football or new movements and techniques in figure skating, gymnastics or wrestling cannot be copyrighted so that other athletes are not allowed to duplicate the feats, the court wrote.[17] Some legal scholars promote the idea that routine-based athletic performances, such as figure skating and gymnastics, comply with the requirements of the Copyright Act because they are original and creative and may be fixed in a tangible medium of expression.[18]

In other cases, courts have said:

• The video display for Breakout, a game in which a "rectangular paddle" directed a "circular ball" into colored rectangular "bricks" while accompanied by audio signals, was lacking in the minimal artistic expression necessary for a copyright.[19]

• Acrylic panels used in a decorative supermarket display were sufficiently original and expressive.[20]

• The phrase "alpine Goldilocks" in a travel guide description of the average skier was an analogy constituting expression of original insight and thus protectable under the Copyright Act.[21]

• ZZ Top's guitar riff in *La Grange,* although similar to riffs other artists used in earlier songs, was sufficiently original to warrant protection from Chrysler Corporation's unauthorized use.[22]

Although the creativity threshold is low for copyright, independent authorship, rather than copying, is essential. This does not mean, however, that variations on existing works may never be copyrighted. So long as the variation goes beyond merely trivial, the added elements to the original may be copyrighted.[23]

[10] Feist Publ'ns v. Rural Tel. Serv. Co., 499 U.S. 340 (1991).

[11] *See* Southern Bell Tel. and Tel. Co. v. Associated Tel. Directory Publishers, 756 F.2d 801 (11th Cir. 1985).

[12] *See* Burrow-Giles Lithographic Co. v. Sarony, 111 U.S. 53, 60 (1884).

[13] Time, Inc. v. Bernard Geis Assocs., 293 F. Supp. 130 (S.D.N.Y. 1968). Although the Zapruder family owns the copyright on the film, the government confiscated it for use in its investigation of the assassination. In 1999, almost four decades after the 26-second film was made, a special arbitration panel ruled that the U. S. government must pay the family $16 million for the seized property.

[14] Baltimore Orioles, Inc. v. Major League Baseball Players Ass'n, 805 F.2d 663 (7th Cir. 1986).

[15] 17 U.S.C. § 101 (1976).

[16] Nat'l Basketball Ass'n and NBA Props., Inc. v. Motorola, Inc. and Sports Team Analysis and Tracking Sys., Inc., 105 F.3d 841 (2d Cir. 1997).

[17] *NBA v. Motorola,* 105 F.3d at 846.

[18] *See, e.g.,* William Tucker Griffith, Note and Comment: *Beyond the Perfect Score: Protecting Routine-Oriented Athletic Performance with Copyright Law*, 30 CONN. L. REV. 675 (1998).

[19] Atari Games Corp. v. Oman, 693 F. Supp. 1204 (D.D.C. 1988), *rev'd* 888 F.2d 878 (D.C. Cir. 1988).

[20] Designer's View, Inc. v. Publix Super Mkts., Inc., 764 F. Supp 1473 (S.D. Fla. 1991).

[21] Feder v. Videotrip Corp., 697 F. Supp. 1165 (D. Colo. 1988).

[22] ZZ Top v. Chrysler Corp., 54 F. Supp. 2d 983 (W.D. Wash. 1999).

[23] *See* Merritt Forbes & Co. v. Newman Inv. Sec., Inc., 604 F. Supp. 21 (D.N.Y. 1985).

## Unprotected works

Items not eligible for copyright protection include:

* an idea, procedure, process, system, method of operation, concept, principle or discovery, regardless of the form in which it is described, explained, illustrated or embodied;
* facts or works consisting entirely of information that is common property and containing no original authorship;
* works that have not been fixed in a tangible form of expression;
* names, short phrases and slogans; familiar symbols or designs; mere variations of typographic ornamentation, lettering or coloring (although these items may be protected under trademark law or law relating to unfair competition);
* mere listings of ingredients or contents;
* works produced by the U.S. government; and
* works that are in the public domain.

Some of these items require further explanation.

**Ideas and Facts.** A key copyright principle is that no person can own an idea or a fact. Our hypothetical Skool of Hard Nocks band, for example, may compose as many songs about the topic of love as it wishes, so long as it expresses its own sentiments about love, rather than copying or altering those of someone else. (See boxed sidebar, p. 121.) Other authors are likewise free to write about love.

One way to illustrate the difference between a fact or idea and protected expression — not always a clear-cut distinction — is to consider a court case involving two books and a movie about the tragic explosion of the Hindenburg. The colossal dirigible, built in Germany during Hitler's reign, burst into flames over a New Jersey landing site in 1937 before scores of onlookers. Thirty-six people perished in the fire, and the incident received widespread news coverage. A news event cannot be copyrighted, but the way the event is described in stories can be.

The official blame for the disaster was placed on static electricity igniting the hydrogen-filled airship. A different theory — that the Hindenburg was sabotaged — emerged from years of investigation by author A.A. Hoehling. In 1962, he published a book arguing that a crew member, seeking to impress his anti-Hitler girlfriend in Germany, planted a bomb aboard the dirigible, intending for it to explode after everyone had disembarked. Bad weather had delayed the flight, causing the premature detonation of the bomb, according to Hoehling's theory.

Would Hoehling's research and his new theory about the cause of the explosion be copyrightable? Hoehling thought so and brought a copyright infringement suit when Universal City Studios released a motion picture based on the theory. The acknowledged source for the movie was a 1972 novel by Michael Mooney, who used Hoehling's theory as the basis for his fictionalized account of the Hindenburg tragedy. Mooney was also named as a defendant in the infringement suit. A district court judge ruled for the defen-

dants and an appeals court affirmed, because neither research nor ideas are copyrightable.[24]

Another suit, brought by the widow of author Richard Wright, best known for *Native Son* and *Black Boy,* also turned, in part, on the fact-expression distinction. After Wright's death, a biography was written by one of his acquaintances, Dr. Margaret Walker, and published in 1988 by Warner Books. Wright's widow refused to give the biographer permission to use material from Wright's journals and letters and sued for copyright infringement.

A three-judge panel for the Second U.S. Circuit Court of Appeals examined ten journal entries and six letters, considering as a threshold matter whether material quoted or paraphrased in Walker's book bore "the stamp of the author's originality," making it copyrightable, or whether the material communicated facts or ideas.[25] First the judges distinguished between those parts of the journal entries that bore Wright's stamp of creativity (copyrightable) and those that conveyed mundane details of Wright's life or served only to illustrate Dr. Walker's friendship with Wright (not copyrightable).[26] Then the copyrightable portions became the basis for the court's determination of whether the fair use defense against copyright infringement applied. Fair use will be discussed later in this chapter.

The letters at issue in the Wright case were written by Richard Wright to Margaret Walker. Although she was the recipient of the letters and owned the paper on which they were written, Walker did not own the manner of expression contained within them. Richard Wright, and later his widow, retained ownership of the original expression contained in the letters.

**Useful Articles.** A procedure, process, system, method of operation, concept, principle or discovery, regardless of the form in which it is described, explained, illustrated or embodied in such a work, may be eligible for a patent, but not a copyright. While pictorial, graphic and sculptural works may be copyrighted, the mechanical or utilitarian aspects of such works are not copyrightable. The Copyright Act defines a "useful article" as an article having an intrinsic utilitarian function that is not merely to portray the appearance of the article or to convey information. Examples are clothing, furniture, machinery, dinnerware and lighting fixtures. An item that is normally part of a useful article may itself be classified as a useful article, such as an ornamental wheel cover on a vehicle. Yet, a useful article may have both copyrightable and noncopyrightable features. For example, the design of a piece of furniture may qualify for protection under patent law while unique ornate carvings on the furniture may be copyrightable.

The copyrightable work must be capable of existing independently of its utilitarian aspects. In a case where the form of a bicy-

---

[24] Hoehling v. Universal City Studios, 618 F.2d 972 (2d Cir. 1980).

[25] Wright v. Warner Books, Inc. and Margaret Walker, 953 F.2d 731, 735 (2d Cir. 1991).

[26] *Id.* at 736.

## Copyrights, Patents, Trademarks and the Skool of Hard Nocks

*To distinguish among copyrights, patents and trademarks, consider the following hypothetical situation:*

Several young musicians, calling themselves "Skool of Hard Nocks," begin practicing in hopes of hitting the big time. The group plays original songs as well as songs by popular artists. During a practice session in a garage one night, the musicians notice that a particular series of sounds on a synthesizer causes mice to rush from their hiding places and congregate in one corner. After experimenting a bit, the musicians invent the "Hard Nocks Mouse Trap," a contraption consisting of two boxes placed in opposite corners of a room. One tiny box emits the synthesizer sounds, and, shortly thereafter, the second, much larger box springs shut to capture the mice that huddle within it.

Do the songs or the mousetrap qualify for protection under intellectual property laws? Yes to both counts.

If the group has gone beyond merely playing its original songs and has taken the step of fixing the music and lyrics in tangible form, such as writing them on paper or making an audio tape, the works are **copyrighted**, even if they are not published. Copyright protection begins as soon as the songs are fixed in tangible form.

If a review of existing patents shows that the Skool of Hard Nocks has indeed invented a better mousetrap, the group can **patent** the invention to protect its right to potential profits.

The names "Skool of Hard Nocks" and "Hard Nocks Mouse Trap" might eventually become **trademarks**, but, unlike copyright protection, trademark protection is not automatic upon creation. To become recognized as trademarks, the names must be unique and widely used so that the public comes to identify them with the band or the mousetrap.

Skool of Hard Nocks might be guilty of **copyright infringement** if the band copies or publicly performs someone else's copyrighted songs without paying royalty fees. So long as that playing is confined to private practice sessions, no problems exist.

---

cle rack was inspired by a sculpture, the sculpture was eligible for copyright, but the bicycle rack was not because it was influenced in significant measure by utilitarian concerns. Therefore, its aesthetic elements could not be said to be conceptually separable from utilitarian elements.[27] However, a copyrighted work of art does not lose its protected status merely because it subsequently is put to functional use.

Clothing, even that based on elaborate designs of high fashion industry, is utilitarian and not copyrightable. When a designer claimed Halloween costumes were "soft sculptures," equally adaptable as wall hangings or decorations, courts disagreed. One said the artistic elements of the costumes advanced the utilitarian purpose of enabling wearers to masquerade, and the designer's artistic judgment was not exercised independently of functional influences.[28] On the other hand, decorative belt buckles used principally for ornamentation have been considered jewelry sufficiently original for copyright.[29] Not all jewelry meets such originality standards. A particular ring design, for example, was ruled ineligible for copyright protection because it was not exceptional, original or unique.[30] Copyright protection does not encompass games because they consist of abstract rules and play ideas.

**Works Produced by the U.S. Government.** Works created by the federal government are in the public domain, with the exception of standard reference data produced by the U.S. Secretary of Commerce under the Standard Reference Data Act.[31] When the federal government contracts with non-employees — a postage stamp designer perhaps — the copyright for the resulting work may or may not be assigned back to the government. In addition, the arrangement and pagination of government documents — if they reflect skill, discretion and effort — are copyrightable. Someone else could use the government material, but they could not use the particular layout.[32]

Works created by state governments are subject to copyright. Each state decides whether to retain the copyright or place the works in the public domain. No statute, case or regulation indicates that a state cannot copyright its laws. However, the U.S. Copyright Office takes the position that a state's laws may not be copyrighted. The Compendium of Copyright Office Practices (Compendium II) states, "Edicts of government, such as judicial opinions, administrative rulings, legislative enactments, public ordinances, and similar official legal documents are not copyrightable for reasons of public policy. This applies to such works whether they are federal, state, or local as well as to those of foreign governments." Although the Compendium II does not have force of law, apparently the Copyright Office would refuse registration to any state trying to register its laws.

---

[27] *See* Brandir Intern, Inc. v. Cascade Pac. Lumber Co., 834 F.2d 1142 (2d Cir. 1987).

[28] Whimsicality, Inc. v. Rubie's Costumes Co., 721 F. Supp. 1566, *aff'd in part, vacated in part*, 891 F.2d 452 (2d Cir. 1989).

[29] *See* Kieselstein-Cord v. Accessories By Pearl, Inc., 632 F.2d 989 (2d Cir. 1980).

[30] DBC of New York, Inc. v. Merit Diamond Corp., 768 F. Supp 414 (S.D. N.Y. 1991).

[31] 15 U.S.C. § 290(e) (2004).

[32] *See* West Publ'g Co. v. Mead Data Cent., Inc., 616 F. Supp 1571 (D.C. Minn. 1985).

Works containing material produced by the federal government published before March 1, 1989, when the United States became a party to the Berne Convention, were required to carry a notice. The notice is no longer required, but the Copyright Office strongly recommends it in order to defeat a claim of "innocent infringement," meaning that defendants in an infringement suit claim they did not know the material they used was protected by copyrighted. The Copyright Office suggests this copyright notice for works containing government material:[33]

---

*Copyright 2007 Jane Doe. Copyright claimed in Chapters 7-10, exclusive of U.S. Government maps.*

---

**Works in the Public Domain.** If a work is in the public domain, it is not copyrighted and can be used without securing permission and without attribution.[34] In addition to works produced by the federal government, works for which the copyright period has expired are in the public domain. The duration of copyright protection will be discussed later in this chapter.

### Exclusive Rights of Copyright Holders

If our hypothetical Skool of Hard Nocks heavy metal group has copyrighted its original musical compositions, it has exclusive rights:

(1) to reproduce the copyrighted work;

(2) to prepare derivative works based upon the copyrighted work;

(3) to distribute copies or phonorecords of the copyrighted work to the public by sale or other transfer of ownership, or by rental, lease or lending;

(4) to perform the copyrighted work publicly; and

(5) to display the copyrighted work publicly.

These rights are separate and distinct from each other, so Skool of Hard Nocks can authorize one company to reproduce its music and a different company to distribute the copies. Yet, if either of those companies prepared derivative works or sponsored public performances of the music without authorization, that company would be guilty of the crime of copyright infringement.

**Derivative Works.** The copyright owner of a work has the right to make or to authorize new works based on the original, such as translations, dramatizations, fictionalizations, motion picture versions, sound recordings, art reproductions, abridgments, condensations or any other forms of the work. A work consisting of editorial revisions, annotations, elaborations or other modifications that, as a whole, represent an original work of authorship is

a derivative work.

A work will not be considered derivative unless it substantially copies from the original, copyrighted work. Copyright infringement charges against makers of the popular play and screenplay *Driving Miss Daisy* were not justified, a court held, even though an earlier play titled *Horowitz and Mrs. Washington* was also about an elderly, white, Jewish woman who eventually became close friends with a black assistant. The court said that despite similarities, the works differed in their themes, settings and tone, plot and character development, so *Driving Miss Daisy* was not a derivative work.[35]

**Public Performance or Display.** Only a copyright owner can authorize the public performance or display of the work. After purchasing one or more copies of a work, a video store, for example, may rent those copies. It would be a copyright violation, however, for the store owner to set up a projector and screen a film for the public or make additional copies of it. It is not considered a public performance for a hotel to provide audiovisual materials for use in guest rooms. Similarly, one could play Skool of Hard Nocks music for family and acquaintances, for religious services or for face-to-face, non-profit teaching activities. However, to play it without authorization in a business to entertain customers would infringe copyright.

Case law establishes that restaurants or other businesses are allowed to play radio music over a single receiver and speakers of a kind commonly used in private homes[36] but that the use of multiple speakers constitutes a public performance and a copyright violation.[37] After lobbying by the National Restaurant Association, Congress changed the law in 1998 to exempt small businesses (restaurants and bars under 3,750 square feet or retail establishments under 2,000 square feet) from paying performance license fees for playing radio or television broadcasts.[38] Larger businesses can avoid fees if they use no more than six external speakers (but not more than four per room) or four televisions measuring fifty-five inches or less (but not more than one per room). These rules only apply to businesses that use radio or television. Firms that play pre-recorded tapes or CDs must pay royalties.

What about broadcast stations that play recorded music; isn't that a public performance? Yes, and those stations pay music licensing organizations — the two best-known are the American Society of Composers, Authors and Publishers (ASCAP) and Broadcast Music Inc. (BMI) — for the right to broadcast music. But the music industry is mired in other performance and copyright questions. Who actually controls performance rights among the many

---

[33] U.S. COPYRIGHT OFFICE, COPYRIGHT BASICS (1994).

[34] *See* Dastar Corp. v. Twentieth Cent. Fox, 539 U.S. 23 (2003).

[35] Denker v. Uhry, 820 F. Supp 722 (S.D.N.Y. 1992).

[36] *See* Cass Country Music Co. v. Vasfi Muedini, 821 F. Supp. 1278 (E.D. Wis. 1993).

[37] *See* Sailor Music v. Gap Stores, Inc., 668 F.2d 84 (2d Cir. 1981).

[38] Fairness In Music Licensing Act of 1998, Pub. L. No. 105-298, 112 Stat. 2830 (1998) (codified at 17 U.S.C.S. § 110 (LEXIS 2002)).

people involved in the creative process of developing a piece of music from a mere idea to the physical medium upon which it is fixed? Who — the composer, the record producer, the performer — shares licensing fees? Do musicians and others participating in the production of sound recordings have the right to prevent particular people or companies from performing their works? The answers to these and other copyright questions in the complex music industry are discussed in the "compulsory licensing for music and broadcasting" section of this chapter.

The use of a copyrighted visual work within another visual work may require permission to avoid unlawful infringement, but case law on this question is rather unclear. One court held that the use of an architectural drawing in a film was an infringement;[39] whereas another court denied an injunction to bar the showing of a film that included copyrighted film clips.[40] In a 1997 case, the Second Circuit said a jury or other fact-finder, rather than summary judgment, was necessary to determine whether the use of a copyrighted poster as set decoration in a television show constituted infringement.[41] The poster in question was visible in the background from 1.86 seconds to 4.16 seconds during several scenes in the show. A federal regulation provides that public broadcasting entities will pay royalty fees for the use of published pictorial and other visual works.[42] The regulation distinguishes between a "featured" display, a "full-screen or substantially full screen display for more than three seconds," and a "background" display, one that is less than full-screen or one that is full-screen but visible for less than three seconds.

**Moral Rights.** In addition to the five exclusive rights belonging to all copyright owners, a limited category of visual artists received more protection in a 1990 amendment to the Copyright Act.[43] Creators of visual art — paintings, drawings, prints, sculptures or photographic images, existing in up to 200 copies — received what are referred to as "authors' rights" or "moral rights." These rights prevent the use of an author's name on works that he or she did not create. The act also prevents the use of an author's name on a work that has been distorted, mutilated or otherwise modified so the use may harm the author's honor or reputation.

### Copyright Ownership

Initial copyright ownership is vested in the author or authors of a work as soon as the work is created in a tangible form.

**Joint Works.** The authors of a joint work are co-owners of the copyright. A joint work is one prepared by two or more authors with the intention that their contributions will be merged into inseparable or interdependent parts of a whole. Ownership of a copyright may be transferred in whole or in part or bequeathed by will to someone else.

**Works Made for Hire.** Journalists and other media employees generally do not own the copyrights to articles, photographs or other works they produce as part of their jobs. Unless an agreement between the employee and employer specifies otherwise, employees usually produce what are known as "works made for hire," with the employer owning the copyrights.

Copyright disputes between employers and employees sometimes turn on whether a work was produced within the scope of employment or whether a work was produced separate from the normal duties on the job. Major league baseball players argued that telecasts of games amounted to a misappropriation of their names, pictures and performances. A court rejected that argument, however, ruling that the players were employees whose performances before broadcast audiences were within the scope of their employment; hence, the performances were works made for hire.[44]

The 1976 Copyright Act also defines as a work made for hire one "specially ordered or commissioned for use as a contribution to a collective work, as a part of a motion picture or other audiovisual work, as a translation, as a supplementary work, as a compilation, as an instructional text, as a test, as answer material for a test, or as an atlas, if the parties expressly agree in a written instrument signed by them that the work shall be considered a work made for hire."[45] Freelancers typically work under these conditions, so unless both parties specify by contract that a commissioned work is a work-made-for-hire, then the freelancer maintains copyright ownership.

As might be expected, these issues have prompted a considerable number of lawsuits. In a 1989 opinion, the Supreme Court said that factors to consider in making this distinction include, but are not limited to
- skill required;
- amount of supervision;
- whether the hired worker set his or her own hours, owned equipment or tools needed for the job, or received employee fringe benefits;
- how payment was made;
- how taxes were paid; and
- whether the hired party independently hired and fired assistants.[46]

---

[39] Woods v. Universal City Studios, 920 F. Supp. 62 (S.D.N.Y. 1996).

[40] Monster Comm., Inc. v. Turner Broad. Sys., 935 F. Supp. 490 (S.D.N.Y. 1996).

[41] Ringgold v. Black Entn't Television, Inc., 126 F.3d 70 (2d Cir. 1997).

[42] 37 C.F.R. § 253.8 (1996).

[43] Visual Artists Rights Act, 17 U.S.C.A. § 106a (1990).

[44] Baltimore Orioles, Inc. v. Major League Baseball Players Ass'n, 805 F.2d 663 (7th Cir. 1986).

[45] 17 U.S.C.S. § 101 (2002).

[46] Cmty. for Creative Non-Violence v. Reid, 490 U.S. 730 at 751-53 (1989). See also, Marco v. Accenty Publ'g Co., 969 F.2d 1547 (3d Cir. 1992).

The Supreme Court said these factors should be considered as a whole with no single one being determinative.

**Collective Works.** Magazines, newspapers, anthologies and encyclopedias are examples of collective works in which a number of separate and independent articles are assembled into a whole. The 1976 Copyright Act says that each separate contribution to a collective work is distinct from the whole, and copyright belongs to the author of the contribution.

Unless the parties make other arrangements, the owner of the copyright of the collective work is presumed to have acquired only the privilege of reproducing and distributing the contribution as part of the whole, any revision of the collective work, and any later collective work in the same series. The Supreme Court has made clear that the party paying a fee is buying first-time rights.[47] The freelance author or artist retains other rights as well as the right to future uses of the material.

Newspaper and magazine publishers now commonly transfer their paper products to electronic databases that they control and to those operated by other companies, such as LexisNexis. Customers can locate individual articles or abstracts and buy copies of articles. This practice raises important questions about ownership of individual articles in the electronic versions of printed periodicals.

Freelance writers maintained that they had sold their articles for use in a collective work and that they should receive additional payment if those individual articles were sold separately from the collection. Publishers argued that the electronic database versions of their periodicals were simply revisions of a collective work, requiring no further payment to authors.

Two federal district courts considering the collective works question arrived at different conclusions, one in California agreeing with freelancers that they should be paid if their articles were photocopied from collected works and another in New York siding with publishers.

The defendants in the 1998 California case were the owners of UnCover, a citation database and document delivery company, that functions like a private interlibrary loan service.[48] UnCover sent copyright payments to publishers but did not seek permission from or send a royalty to the authors of the individual articles. The district court, refusing to accept the argument that reproduction of a single article was simply a revision of a collected work, held that the authors, not the publishers, owned the rights to the articles once they were separated from the collective work.

A New York district court, on the other hand, held for the *New York Times* and other electronic database publishers in a similar lawsuit. The court reasoned that the substantially similar electronic version amounted to a revision of a collective work for which publishers exercise creativity.[49] The Second U.S. Circuit Court of Appeals reversed, holding that publishers need permission from freelance authors before reproducing their material.[50] The appeals court rejected the publishers' argument that electronic databases were merely revisions of the collective work in which each author's individual contribution first appeared.

Eight years after the lawsuit began, the Supreme Court announced its decision, ruling that newspapers and magazines may not display printed freelance work on Web sites or electronic archives without first obtaining specific permission from freelancers.[51] The 7-2 majority rejected the publishers' analogy between electronic databases and microfilm and microfiche, noting that articles in databases appear disconnected from their original context, rather than as part of the collected work.

Finally, in 2005, after almost four years of court-mandated mediation talks, parties reached an $18 million settlement agreement plus attorneys' fees and court costs to cover freelance authors whose work on or after August 15, 1997, "has been reproduced, displayed, adapted, licensed, sold and/or distributed in any electronic or digital format, without the person's express authorization."[52] Some publishers, including the *New York Times*, chose to remove the freelance writers' works, as many as 115,000 articles, from Lexis/Nexis and other full-text databases if the writers did not waive their claims for compensation. The *Times* and others now require permission for electronic republication of works by freelance authors as part of their standard contract.[53]

The question of whether a complete copy of a printed publication can be transferred to a new medium, such as a CD-ROM, without compensating freelance authors has received conflicting answers from appellate courts. The National Geographic Society was ruled to have infringed copyrights of freelance authors and photographers by including their materials in a CD-ROM that compiled contents from more than 100 years of National Geographic Society magazines. The U.S. Court of Appeals for the Eleventh Circuit held that the CD-ROM was a new product, in a new medium, for a new market and did not qualify as a revision of a collective work.[54] The Supreme Court declined to review the case, and a federal jury in Florida awarded the plaintiff $400,000 in 2003 for willful infringement of copyright law.

When other freelancers sued National Geographic for royalty

[47] New York Times Co. v. Tasini, 533 U.S. 483, 497 (1990) (citing Stewart v. Abend, 495 U.S. 207, 229 (1990)).

[48] Ryan v. CARL Corp., 23 F. Supp. 2d 1146 (N.D. Cal. 1998).

[49] Tasini v. New York Times Co., 972 F. Supp 804 (S.D.N.Y. 1997). Other defendants were *Newsday*, Mead Data Central, Time Inc., University Microfilms International and the Atlantic Monthly Co.

[50] Tasini v. New York Times Co., 206 F.3d 161(2d Cir. 1999).

[51] New York Times Co. v. Tasini, 533 U.S. 483 (2001).

[52] In re Literary Works in Electronic Databases Copyright Litigation, MDL No. 1379 (U.S.D.C., S.D.N.Y., Mar. 31, 2005). The full text of the settlement agreement is available at http://www.copyrightclassaction.com/notice.pdf.

[53] *Timeline: A History of Copyright in the United States,* Association of Research Libraries (Nov. 22, 2002), *available at* http://www.arl.org/info/frn/copy/timeline.html.

[54] Greenberg v. Nat'l Geographic Soc'y, 244 F.3d 1267 (11th Cir. 2001), *cert denied,* 534 U.S. 951 (2001).

payments based on the use of their work in the same CD-ROM, a federal district court judge[55] issued a summary judgment for the magazine, and in 2005 the Second Circuit Court of Appeals upheld the ruling.[56] The three-judge panel considered the digital archive as akin to bound volumes or microfilm and not a new work. The Second Circuit distinguished the earlier *New York Times* case where each article had to be retrieved individually from a database, separate from the rest of the periodical in which it first appeared.

**Duration of Ownership.** Recall that the purpose of intellectual property law is to promote the progress of science and useful arts by securing for limited times to authors and inventors the exclusive right to their respective writings and discoveries. The framers of the Constitution recognized that eternal protection would not best serve public policy. After a term of protection expires, copyrighted works become part of the public domain, freely available for anyone.

In revising copyright law in the 1970s, Congress specified that protection begin immediately after a work is fixed in tangible form rather than at the time it is first published or registered as an unpublished work. In addition, Congress extended the number of years that copyright protected a work. Thus, to decide whether a particular work is still protected, it is important to consider whether the Copyright Act that went into effect on January 1, 1978, or previous copyright law protects the work.

Under heavy lobbying from major publishing groups and despite the objections of other interest groups, Congress amended copyright law in 1998 with the Sonny Bono Copyright Term Extension Act (CTEA),[57] granting protection for the lifetime of the author plus seventy years. (See the box on page 126 for the terms and lengths of copyright.) Without the passage of CTEA, many valuable properties controlled by book publishing houses, record and movie studios would have fallen into the public domain. Novels such as *The Great Gatsby,* movies such as *The Jazz Singer* and cartoon characters Mickey Mouse and Pluto could have been freely circulated.

The Supreme Court upheld the constitutionality of CTEA, with a seven-justice majority rejecting arguments that Congress had exceeded its power by extending the term for published works with existing copyrights.[58] Parties challenging CTEA maintained that the "limited time" language of the Constitution was a clear line beyond the power of Congress to extend for works whose original copyrights would expire earlier. The Court held that the act did not violate the copyright clause's "limited time" restriction because the "life plus seventy years" term was not perpetual, and, therefore, fit within Congress' discretion. The Supreme Court also noted that CTEA brought the United States in line with copyright duration in the European Union.

The Court rejected the argument that CTEA violated the First Amendment, reasoning that the proximity of adoption of both the First Amendment and the copyright clause indicates that the framers thought the two were compatible. The Court said the copyright law – by protecting expression but not ideas and by permitting fair use – contained built-in First Amendment accommodations. The Court also rejected the need to apply strict scrutiny (discussed in Chapter 3) to CTEA provisions.

Under the pre-1978 statute, the copyright term was for twenty-eight years from the date that the work was published or registered in unpublished form. During the twenty-eighth year of the term, the copyright owner could apply for a twenty-eight-year extension, making the total length of protection fifty-six years. If the copyright owner failed to apply for renewal, the work fell into the public domain. The act that went into effect at the start of the calendar year in 1978 extended the renewal term, and subsequent amendments further extended the renewal for works published between 1964 and 1977 to a total of ninety-five years and made renewal automatic. Knowing whether a particular work is in the public domain has become a rather complex matter as indicated by the chart above. The Copyright Office, in its Circular No. 22, offers suggestions for approaching a copyright investigation.

### Infringement

Anyone who violates the rights of a copyright owner may be found guilty of copyright infringement. "Piracy," "bootleg" and "plagiarism" are informal, nonlegal synonyms for "copyright infringement." To prove infringement, the copyright owner must be able to prove that

(1) the defendant had access to the copyrighted work, and

(2) the two works are substantially similar.

The statute of limitations for initiating an infringement action is three years. One who successfully establishes infringement may recover monetary damages, obtain an injunction against further infringing and, if the court so directs, collect attorneys' fees.

Monetary awards may be in the form of actual or statutory damages. Actual damages are out-of-pocket losses the copyright owner can prove resulted from the infringement. Often it is difficult to pinpoint actual damages; so the copyright owner can ask for statutory damages, which range from $750 to $30,000, as determined by the judge. If the plaintiff proves that the defendant's infringement was "committed willfully," the judge may award as much as $150,000 per infringement.[59] A copyright infringer might also face criminal charges if a judge determines that the infringement was willful and for purposes of commercial advantage or pri-

[55] Faulkner v. Nat'l Geographic Soc'y, 296 F. Supp. 2d 488 (S.D.N.Y. 2003).

[56] Faulkner et al. v. Nat'l Geographic Soc'y et al, 409 F.3d 26 (2d Cir. 2005).

[57] Pub. L. No. 105-298, 112 Stat. 2827 (amending 17 U.S.C. § 3) (1998).

[58] Eldred v. Ashcroft, 517 U.S. 186 (2003).

[59] Digital Theft Deterrence and Copyright Damages Improvement Act of 1999, Pub. L. No. 106-160, § 1, 113 Stat. 1774 (amending 17 U.S.C.S. § 504) (1999).

## TERMS OF COPYRIGHT PROTECTION
## UNDER 1999 TERM EXTENSION ACT

| DATE OF WORK | PROTECTION BEGINS | TERM OF PROTECTION |
|---|---|---|
| Created on or since Jan. 1, 1978. | When fixed in tangible medium of expression. | Life of the author plus 70 years; 95 years from publication or 120 years from creation, whichever is shorter, for works made for hire, anonymous, pseudonymous works or corporate author. |
| Published earlier than 1923. | Already in the public domain. | Has expired. |
| Published between 1923 and 1963. | When first published with notice. | 28 years with option for 67-year renewal, for total of 95 years; if not renewed, already in public domain. |
| Published between 1964 and 1977. | When first published with notice. | 28 years plus automatic renewal for 67 years (for a total of 95 years). |
| Created but not published before Jan. 1, 1978. | Jan. 1, 1978 | Life of the author plus 70 years or until Dec. 31, 2002, whichever is longer. |
| Created before Jan. 1, 1978, and published before Dec. 31, 2002. | Jan. 1, 1978 | Life of the author plus 70 years or Dec. 31, 2047, whichever is longer. |

vate financial gain. In addition to stiff fines, criminal conviction for copyright infringement carries a prison term.

### Registering a Work

Although a work fixed in tangible form, whether published or not, is automatically protected, registering a work with the Copyright Office carries advantages. Registering before infringement allows the copyright owner potentially to collect statutory damages and attorneys' fees, remedies that are unavailable if registration takes place after an infringement.

To register a copyright, a person must send three items — application form, fee and deposit material — in the same package to the Copyright Office, Library of Congress, Washington, D.C., 20559, within three months of the date of first publication. Effective July 2006, the basic registration fee increased from $30 to $45, with fees varying according to the type of work. Fee rates are included with the instructions for completing each application form. Generally, two copies of a published work or one copy of an unpublished work must be deposited with the Copyright Office. Some works are exempt from the deposit requirement.

As of March 1, 1989, the effective date of the Berne Convention implementation, no notice is required to retain copyright, but a notice prevents a defendant in an infringement suit from pleading "innocent infringement" to mitigate actual or statutory damages. The copyright notice should be affixed to copies or phonorecords in such a way as to "give reasonable notice of the claim of copyright." A proper copyright notice consists of three things:

- © (the letter "C" in a circle) or the word "Copyright" or the abbreviation "Copr." (The letter "P" in a circle for a sound recording);
- the year of first publication;
- the name of the copyright owner.

For example:

---

© 2007 Jane Doe

---

An inadvertent mistake on a copyright registration certificate will not invalidate a copyright and thus bar an infringement action unless the alleged infringer has relied to its detriment on the mistake, or unless the claimant intended to defraud the Copyright Office by making the misstatements.[60] The author or copyright owner may wish to place a copyright notice on any unpublished copies or phonorecords that leave his or her control. For example:

---

*Unpublished work* © 2007 *Jane Doe*

---

## COPYRIGHT AND FAIR USE

A copyright holder's bundle of rights is referred to in the Copyright Act of 1976 as "exclusive rights," but the act also places some

---

[60] *See* Urantia Found. v. Maaherra, 114 F.3d 955, 963 (9th Cir. 1997) (quoting Nimmer, § 7.20 at 7-201 and n.6).

# HOW TO OBTAIN FORMS
# FOR REGISTERING ORIGINAL WORKS

(1) Write the
U. S. Copyright Office
Library of Congress
101 Independence Avenue S.E.
Washington, D.C. 20559-6000

(2) Call the 24-hours-a-day forms hotline at (202) 707-9100, or

(3) Download from the Copyright Office Web site at http://www.copyright.gov/forms/.

---

limitations on those rights. The most controversial of these limitations is the fair use doctrine, created by the courts, but codified in the 1976 statute.

The fair use doctrine is designed to balance the rights of the copyright holder with the public's interest in dissemination of information affecting areas of universal concern, such as art, science and industry. It allows the use of copyrighted material in a reasonable manner without the consent of the copyright owner. Fair use has been justified this way:

Notwithstanding the need for monopoly protection of intellectual creators to stimulate creativity and authorship, excessively broad protection would stifle, rather than advance, the objective. First, all intellectual creative activity is in part derivative. There is no such thing as a wholly original thought or invention. Each advance stands on building blocks fashioned by prior thinkers. Second, important areas of intellectual activity are explicitly referential. Philosophy, criticism, history and even the natural sciences require continuous re-examination of yesterday's theses.[61]

For these reasons, the Copyright Act of 1976 provides that the fair use of a copyrighted work for purposes such as criticism, comment, news reporting, teaching (including multiple copies for classroom use), scholarship or research is not an infringement of copyright. As in many areas of law, a definitional problem exists.

The legislative history of the 1976 Act makes clear that because the doctrine is an equitable rule of reason, no generally applicable definition is possible. Each case raising the question of fair use must be decided on its own facts. Drawing on analyses used in court cases before the statute was enacted, Congress listed four factors for determining whether the use of a work was a fair use:

(1) the purpose and character of the secondary use;
(2) the nature of the copyrighted work;

(3) the amount and substantiality of the portion used in the secondary work; and

(4) the effect of the use upon the potential market for or value of the copyrighted work.

Courts have made it clear that the four factors must be explored together, rather than in isolation, that no one factor is determinative, and that the line between fair use and infringement must be drawn on a case-by-case basis.

A 1992 amendment to the Copyright Act makes fair use applicable for both published and unpublished works. The Digital Millennium Copyright Act also squelches the mistaken notion of some freewheeling Web site operators that the fair use doctrine permits wholesale copying of documents or images on the Internet.

## Purpose and Character of the Secondary Use

Although a key consideration is whether the secondary use is of a commercial nature or is for nonprofit educational purposes, the analysis is more complex than that. In weighing this factor, courts will consider whether the secondary use of the copyrighted material serves the public interest by stimulating creativity as copyright law intended. Courts will also ask other questions: Does the secondary use do more than paraphrase or repackage the original? Does it have what judges have referred to as "transformative" value; that is, does the secondary use add value to the original?

Examples of transformative uses are critical reviews of quoted material or summarizing parts of the original in order to comment on it. In an infringement case involving a parody, the Supreme Court held that the more transformative the new work is, the less significant are other factors, such as commercialism, that might weigh against the finding of fair use. The Court said transformative works lie at the heart of the fair use doctrine's guarantee of breathing space within the confines of copyright, but transformative use is not absolutely necessary for a finding of fair use.[62]

---

[61] Pierre N. Leval, *Commentary: Toward a Fair Use Standard*, 103 HARV. L. REV. 1105, 1109 (1990).

[62] *See* Campbell v. Acuff-Rose Music, 510 U.S. 569 (1994).

## Nature of the Copyrighted Work

That courts explore the nature of the copyrighted work implies that certain kinds of works are more amenable to fair use than others. Fair use is more likely to protect copying from an out-of-print work, for example, than from one available for purchase. For a work designed to be used only once — a workbook, for example — the commercial impact will be great if a teacher makes multiple copies of workbook exercises.

Whether the original work is fictional or factual influences judgments of fair use. A federal district court noted that public interest in dissemination becomes progressively stronger as we move along the spectrum from fancy to fact.[63] Another consideration is whether the original work was published or unpublished.

Courts have held that copying from unpublished work tends to negate the defense of fair use[64] although 1992 amendments to the Copyright Act make fair use applicable for both published and unpublished works.[65]

## Amount and Substantiality of Portion Used

This factor calls for both a quantitative and qualitative assessment of material used. If a large amount of the original copyrighted work or the most significant part of it is taken, the fair use defense may not protect the secondary use. No specific formula exists regarding the amount of an original work that can be used without defeating the fair use defense.

Courts consider the interaction between this factor and the first and fourth factors. In some instances, the transformative nature of the secondary use justifies taking only a small part of the original, whereas in other situations, a larger amount of copying might be essential to accomplish the transformative purpose of the secondary work. A court ruled, for example, that a teacher's "learning activity package" about cake decorating, consisting of about 50 percent of a copyrighted booklet on the subject, contained virtually no additional information and amounted to substantial quantitative and qualitative copying and, thus, was not fair use.[66]

On occasion, depending on the transformative purpose, the fair use doctrine might permit use of an entire work. In a lengthy critical study analyzing the structure, symbolism and meaning, literary antecedents and influences of a single poem, for example, fragments of the poem dispersed throughout the work of criticism could encompass the entire original work without compromising its market value. The impact on the market value of the original in such an example is likely nil, assuming that potential buyers would prefer to purchase the poem alone or as part of a collection of poems rather than buying a lengthy critical study.

## Effect on Potential Market or Value

Although judges weigh all four factors in determining whether a use is fair, they give special attention to the effect of the secondary use upon the potential market for or value of the copyrighted work. Several court opinions, including that of the Supreme Court in *Harper & Row Publishers, Inc. v. Nation Enterprises*, indicate that this is the single most important factor in analyzing the fair use defense.[67] In a more recent case, however, the Supreme Court noted a relationship between factors 1 and 4, saying, "[T]he more transformative the new work, the less will be the significance of other factors, like commercialism, that may weigh against a finding of fair use."[68]

## News Reporting and Fair Use

The 1985 *Harper & Row* case, which involved copying from former President Gerald Ford's unreleased memoirs, illustrates how the Court applies the four fair use factors and how slippery the interpretation of the fair use concept can be, even for judges. The Court was split 6-3, with the majority analyzing each of the four factors and holding that *The Nation*, a political commentary magazine, exceeded the limits of fair use. Meanwhile, three dissenting justices reasoned that the magazine's 2,250-word article, appropriating some 300 words of the total 200,000 words in the manuscript, did not constitute an unfair taking of a copyrighted work.

President Ford left the White House in January 1977 and a month later contracted with Harper & Row and *Reader's Digest* to publish his memoirs. Ford's book, to be titled *A Time to Heal: The Autobiography of Gerald R. Ford*, was to contain previously unpublished information about the Watergate scandal, White House discussions in the days before President Richard Nixon's resignation, Ford's subsequent pardon of Nixon, Ford's reflections on this period in U.S. history and the morality and personalities involved. In addition to the right to publish the Ford memoirs in book form, Harper & Row owned the exclusive right to license prepublication excerpts, known in the publishing industry as "first serial rights."

When the memoirs were nearly completed, Harper & Row negotiated a prepublication licensing agreement with *Time* magazine, which would pay $25,000 — half in advance and the other half at publication — for the right to excerpt 7,500 words from Ford's ac-

[63] Nat'l Bus. Lists, Inc. v. Dun & Bradstreet, Inc., 552 F. Supp. 89 (D. Ill. 1982). *See also* New Era Publ'ns Int'l v. Carol Publ'g Group, 729 F. Supp. 992 (S.D.N.Y. 1990), *aff'd in part, rev'd in part on other grounds*, 904 F.2d 152 (2d Cir. 1990).

[64] *See* Harper & Row Publishers v. Nation Enters., 471 U.S. 539 (1985); Salinger v. Random House, Inc., 811 F.2d 90 (2d Cir. 1987); New Era Publ'ns Int'l v. Carol Publ'n Group, 729 F. Supp. 992 (S.D.N.Y. 1990), *aff'd in part, rev'd in part on other grounds*, 904 F.2d 152 (2d Cir. 1990).

[65] Pub. L. No. 102-492 (1992) (amending 17 U.S.C. 107).

[66] Marcus v. Rowley, 695 F.2d 1171 (9th Cir. 1983).

[67] 471 U.S. 539 (1985). *See also* Ass'n of Am. Med. Coll. v. Cuomo, 928 F.2d 519 (2d Cir. 1991).

[68] Campbell v. Acuff-Rose Music, Inc., 510 U.S. 569, 579 (1994).

count of his Nixon pardon. The magazine excerpts were to appear approximately one week before shipment of the book version to bookstores. Exclusivity was an important consideration, and Harper & Row instituted procedures designed to maintain the confidentiality of the manuscript. In addition, *Time* retained the right to renegotiate the second payment if the material appeared in print before the *Time* excerpts.

Two to three weeks before the scheduled *Time* article, an unidentified person secretly delivered a copy of the Ford manuscript to Victor Navasky, editor of *The Nation*. According to the district court trial transcript, Navasky, knowing that he was unauthorized to possess the manuscript and that he needed to work quickly to return it to his source, hastily put together a story composed of quotes, paraphrases and facts drawn from the manuscript. He included no independent commentary, research or criticism in the 2,250-word article.

Immediately after *The Nation* article appeared, *Time* canceled plans to publish its own excerpts and refused to pay the second half of the $25,000 fee. Harper & Row brought suit against *The Nation's* parent company, alleging, among other things, a violation of the Copyright Act. At trial, *The Nation* argued that the information it published was of great public interest, that much of it was news or facts ineligible for copyright and that the article made fair use of the original manuscript. The district court rejected the arguments and awarded Harper & Row $12,500 in actual damages.[69]

A divided U.S. Court of Appeals for the Second Circuit reversed the district court decision. The majority said the lower court erred in assuming that the coupling of Ford's verbatim reflections with noncopyrightable facts transformed that information into a copyrighted totality. The majority held that when the noncopyrighted material was stripped away, *The Nation* article contained, at most, about 300 words that were copyrightable. The court of appeals focused on those words in its analysis of the four fair use factors, concluding that:

- the purpose of *The Nation* article was news reporting;
- the Ford book was essentially factual in nature;
- the 300 words appropriated were insubstantial in relation to the whole 2,250-word article; and
- the impact on the market was minimal because the court was not convinced that *Time's* decision not to publish the excerpts resulted from *The Nation's* scoop.

The court of appeals was especially influenced by the politically significant nature of the subject matter and its conviction that it is not "the purpose of the Copyright Act to impede that harvest of knowledge so necessary to a democratic state" or "chill the activities of the press by forbidding a circumscribed use of copyrighted works."[70]

The Supreme Court disagreed and reversed the appeals court decision. Justice Sandra Day O'Connor, writing for six members of the Court, acknowledged the factual nature of Ford's book but said, "Creation of a nonfiction work, even a compilation of pure fact, entails originality."[71] Further, she noted that the copyright principle of rewarding the individual author in order to benefit the public applies equally to works of fiction and nonfiction. Without the incentive guaranteed by copyright protection, Ford and other public figures might never document their reflections and unique perspective on historical facts. Justice O'Connor wrote that *The Nation's* use of excerpts from Ford's unpublished manuscript effectively usurped the right of first publication, an important marketable subsidiary right.

Then the opinion turned to a lengthy discussion of the fair use defense, applying each of the four fair use factors to the facts of the case. The purpose of *The Nation* article, the majority said, agreeing with the court of appeals, was news reporting, and *The Nation* had every right to seek to be the first to publish information. But, wrote Justice O'Connor, "*The Nation* went beyond simply reporting uncopyrightable information and actively sought to exploit the headline value of its infringement, making a 'news event' out of its unauthorized first publication of a noted figure's copyrighted expression."[72] *The Nation's* stated purpose was to scoop the forthcoming hardcover and *Time* abstracts. Thus, "*The Nation's* use had not merely the incidental effect but the *intended purpose* of supplanting the copyright holder's commercially valuable right of first publication."[73] The defendant's conduct is also relevant in analyzing the character and purpose of the use, the majority said, noting that the trial court had found that *The Nation* knowingly exploited a purloined manuscript.

The nature of the copyrighted work, the majority held, was an unpublished historical narrative or autobiography; copyright law generally recognizes a greater need to disseminate factual works than works of fiction or fantasy. The Court said the fact that a work is unpublished is a critical element of its nature and that the right of first publication encompasses not only the choice of whether to publish at all but also the choices of when, where and in what form first to publish a particular work. Noting that Harper & Row's contract with *Time* magazine required the abstract to be submitted to the copyright holder for prepublication review, the Court said, "*The Nation's* clandestine publication afforded no such opportunity for creative or quality control," a situation "difficult to characterize as 'fair.'"[74]

The amount and substantiality of the portion of *A Time to Heal* used by *The Nation* might appear to be insubstantial, Justice O'Connor wrote. Qualitatively, however, the taking was essentially the heart of the book. The portion of the book about the pardon

[69] Harper & Row Publishers v. Nation Enters., 557 F. Supp. 1067 (S.D.N.Y. 1983).

[70] Harper & Row Publishers v. Nation Enters., 723 F.2d 195, 208-09 (2d Cir. 1983).

[71] *Harper & Row*, 471 U.S. at 547.

[72] *Id.* at 540.

[73] *Id.* at 562 (emphasis in original).

[74] *Id.* at 564.

of former President Nixon was "the most interesting and moving part of the entire manuscript." *The Nation* editor had testified that he selected the most powerful passages in those chapters and quoted them verbatim to best convey Ford's distinctive expression.

Finally, the majority opinion focused on the effect *The Nation's* article had on the market, rejecting the circuit court's finding of no causal relationship between *The Nation* article and *Time's* refusal to pay. For the majority at the Supreme Court, there was "clear-cut evidence of actual damage." In addition to money lost from *Time* magazine, the Court considered harm to the *potential* market to the original copyrighted work as well as derivative works.[75]

Three justices dissented, arguing that the majority opinion applied a constricted reading of the fair use doctrine. After considering the threshold question of copyrightability, Justice William J. Brennan, joined by Justices Byron White and Thurgood Marshall, discussed each of the four fair use factors and concluded that the magazine's quotation of 300 words was fair use. Brennan accused the majority of jeopardizing the robust public debate essential to self-government by giving former public officials too much control on information about their terms of office.[76]

Another case concerning news reporting and fair use revolved around the widely circulated videotape of the beating of Reginald Denny during the April 29, 1992, riots in Los Angeles. The civil disturbance came in the aftermath of a jury verdict in favor of police officers accused of using excess force to subdue Rodney King, a criminal suspect. The Los Angeles News Service (LANS) shot the dramatic tape from a helicopter, broadcasting the scene live over a LANS licensee station. The news service then licensed the tape to the media, and other stations broadcast it later that evening. KCAL-TV aired the tape multiple times without a license and without credit. The district court granted summary judgment in KCAL's favor, holding that the doctrine of fair use exempted the station because:

• the Denny videotape was unique and newsworthy and had significant public interest and concern;

• KCAL used portions for the purposes of news reporting; and

• LANS failed to identify a commercial loss because of KCAL's conduct.

The Ninth U.S. Circuit Court of Appeal's analysis of the four factors of the fair use doctrine led it to reverse the district court and remand the case for further proceedings.[77] Concerning the purpose and character of use, the court said that although KCAL had not scooped LANS, as had *The Nation* in the Ford memoirs case, this did not mean that "KCAL's use of the Denny tape had neither the effect nor purpose of depriving LANS of its also valuable right of licensing its original videotape which creatively captured the

Denny beating in a way that no one else did."[78] The second factor — nature of the copyrighted work — weighed in favor of KCAL because of the informational and factual nature of the tape. The third factor — amount and substantiality of what was used — weighed against KCAL because although the station used only thirty seconds of the four-minute, forty-second videotape, it was the "heart" or most valuable segment of the original. Regarding the fourth factor — effect on the market — the appeals court wrote, "This case doesn't fit neatly into a traditional niche because 'news' isn't normally thought of as having a secondary market."[79] The court noted, however, evidence existed that KCAL's use of LANS's product without a license would destroy the news service's primary market. In considering impact on the market, courts must consider "whether unrestricted and widespread conduct of the sort engaged in by the defendant ... would result in a substantially adverse impact on the potential market for the original."[80]

In weighing the fourth factor, courts also consider whether disputing parties compete with each other. A district court in California said, for example, that actress Pamela Anderson Lee and the tabloid news program *Hard Copy* were not competing for the same market.[81] Further, *Hard Copy's* use of several short, blurry excerpts from a videotape of Lee and her boyfriend engaging in sexual activity would likely enhance the marketability of the tape.

The First U. S. Circuit of Appeals also considered differing markets in evaluating the fourth fair use factor in a copyright infringement case against a newspaper that used nude and semi-nude photographs of the reigning Miss Puerto Rico Universe.[82] Upholding the district court's grant of summary judgment to the newspaper, the court noted that the photographs were taken for a modeling portfolio and that the relatively poor newspaper reproduction would not change the demand for the portfolio and, in fact, might increase demand. Further, the appeals court held that by using the pictures in a newsworthy sense the newspaper had added transformative value to the photographs.

### Classroom Copying and Fair Use

The fact that a copyrighted work is copied for educational use rather than for profit does not insulate the user from a finding of infringement. The fair use section of the Copyright Act, however, specifically lists teaching (including multiple copies for classroom use) as one example where certain uses of copyrighted works may qualify as fair use. But Congress did not intend for classroom copying to substitute for the purchase of materials. Copying from works intended to be consumable — workbooks, exercises, stan-

---

[75] *Id.* at 567.

[76] *Id.* at 579 (Brennan, J., dissenting).

[77] Los Angeles News Serv. v. KCAL-TV Channel 9, 108 F.3d 1119 (9th Cir. 1997).

[78] *Id.* at 1121.

[79] *Id.* at 1122.

[80] *Id.*

[81] Michaels v. Internet Entm't Group, Inc., 5 F. Supp. 2d 823 (C.D. Calif. 1998).

[82] Nunez v. Caribbean Int'l News Corp., 235 F.3d 18 (1st Cir. 2000).

dardized tests, test booklets and answer sheets, for example — is specifically prohibited.

The Association of American Publishers and the Author's League of America agreed to guidelines to permit some copying for scholarly research and instructional use. According to these guidelines, teachers may make a single copy of a chapter from a book, an article from a periodical or newspaper, a short story, short essay, short poem, chart, graph, diagram, drawing, cartoon or picture from a book, periodical or newspaper. Multiple copies for classroom use (not to exceed more than one copy per student in a course) may be made, provided that the copying meets specific tests of brevity and spontaneity and each copy includes a copyright notice. The brevity guidelines are:

• Poetry: (a) A complete poem if less than 250 words and if printed on not more than two pages or, (b) from a longer poem, an excerpt of not more than 250 words.

• Prose: (a) Either a complete article, story or essay of less than 2,500 words, or (b) an excerpt from any prose work of not more than 1,000 words or 10 percent of the work, whichever is less, but in any event a maximum of 500 words.

• Illustration: One chart, graph, diagram, drawing, cartoon or picture per book or per periodical issue.

The use of multiple copies must be spontaneous, meaning that the decision to use the work and the moment of its use for maximum teaching effectiveness are so close in time that it would be unreasonable to expect a timely reply to a request for permission. In addition, no more than nine instances of such multiple copying for one course may be made during one class term except for current news periodicals and newspapers and current news sections of other periodicals. The legislative history of the Copyright Act indicates that Congress intended for similar guidelines to apply for the use of music for instructional purposes.

Courts have held that course-packs compiled by university instructors for reproduction and distribution by commercial copy centers exceed the brevity and spontaneity tests and do not qualify as fair use.[83] To avoid illegally infringing copyrights on photocopied compilations, copy shops must obtain permissions from the various copyright holders and pay them license fees. These costs are passed along to students, of course, but the alternative for students is to buy multiple published works.

The Copyright Act was amended in 2002 to allow increased flexibility for accredited nonprofit educational institutions to use the Internet to provide copyrighted materials to students enrolled in distance education courses.[84] The Technology, Education and Copyright Harmonization Act of 2002 (TEACH) improved the situation for distance education, but it imposed many requirements for the use of copyrighted materials beyond the limits for traditional classrooms. For example, TEACH does not allow scanning or uploading of full or lengthy works or storage on a Web site for access during an entire semester, and the law places limits on converting material from analog into digital formats.

## Parody and Fair Use

Material that mimics or makes fun of a copyrighted work may be protected by the fair use defense. The decision often turns on the third factor — the amount and substantiality of the portion. To be effective, a parody must copy enough to conjure up the original. Even more extensive use might be ruled fair, provided that the parody builds on the original, using it as a known element of modern culture and contributing something new for humorous effect or commentary.

Several court cases have involved advertising parodies. "McDonaldland" television commercials were ruled an infringement on a children's television show, "H.R. Pufnstuf."[85] On the other hand, Screw magazine's spoof of "Poppin' Fresh," a copyrighted trade character owned by Pillsbury Company, was considered a fair use. The magazine said its character, "Poppie Fresh," was meant to poke fun at Pillsbury's advertising campaign and corporate image in general. The court concluded that the magazine's use was more like an editorial or social commentary than an attempt to capitalize financially on the original, despite the commercial nature of the magazine.[86]

In another case, the Dr Pepper Company, which spent approximately $100 million over three years on its "Be A Pepper" campaign, was not amused when Sambo's Restaurants mimicked the campaign with its "Dancing Seniors" television commercials. "Wouldn't you like to be a Pepper too?" the soft drink commercials asked the viewing audience. The invitation from the restaurant chain was "Don't you want to be a Senior, too?" Applying the four fair use factors, a federal district court in Texas noted several similarities between the commercials and concluded that Sambo's copied the essence of the Dr Pepper commercial and jingle. The copying distracted from the uniqueness and originality of the "Be A Pepper" commercials and thus shortened the life of the campaign and the business goodwill it had brought the company.[87]

A parody case involving the rap music group 2 Live Crew and one of the music industry's leading publishers, Acuff-Rose, Inc., reached the Supreme Court. Luther Campbell, a 2 Live Crew member, wrote a satirical version of "Oh, Pretty Woman," a hit song from the 1960s by Roy Orbison and William Dees. Both the rap and the rock versions of the song opened with the line "Pretty Woman,

[83] See Princeton Univ. Press v. Michigan Document Serv., Inc., 99 F.3d 1381 (6th Cir. 1996); Basic Books, Inc. v. Kinko's Graphics Corp., 758 F. Supp. 1522 (S.D.N.Y. 1991).

[84] Technology, Education, and Copyright Harmonization Act of 2002, 107 Pub. L. No. 273, § 13301, 116 Stat. 1758 (amending 17 U.S.C. §110) (2002).

[85] Sid & Mary Krofft Television Prods. v. McDonald's Corp., 562 F.2d 1157 (9th Cir. 1977).

[86] Pillsbury Co. v. Milky Way Prods., No. C78-679A, 1981 U.S. Dist. LEXIS 1772, 8 Media L. Rep. (BNA) 1016 (N.D. Ga. 1981).

[87] Dr Pepper Co. v. Sambo's Rests., 517 F. Supp. 1202 (N.D. Tex. 1981).

walking down the street." Beyond that line, the two songs bear little resemblance. Whereas in the Orbison and Dees version the singer seeks the attention of a woman described as looking "lovely as can be," the sexually suggestive 2 Live Crew song is about a "bald headed, two timin' woman."

One appellate court judge characterized the rap song as "clearly intended to ridicule the white-bread original" and said it "reminds us that sexual congress with nameless street-walkers is not necessarily the stuff of romance and is not necessarily without its consequences. The [rap] singers have the same thing on their minds as did the lonely man with the nasal voice [Orbison], but here there is no hint of wine and roses."[88]

The manager for 2 Live Crew contacted Acuff-Rose Music, the copyright owner, offering to pay a fee for use of the song and enclosing a copy of the lyrics and a recording of the rap parody, but Acuff-Rose refused permission. Nonetheless, 2 Live Crew released records, cassette tapes and compact discs of "Pretty Woman" in a collection of songs titled "As Clean As They Wanna Be." The albums and compact discs identified the authors of the original "Pretty Woman" as Orbison and Dees and its publisher as Acuff-Rose. Almost a year later, after nearly a quarter of a million copies of the recording had been sold, Acuff-Rose sued 2 Live Crew and its record company, Luke Skyywalker Records, for copyright infringement.

The district court granted summary judgment for 2 Live Crew, reasoning that the commercial purpose of 2 Live Crew's song was no bar to fair use. The court added that 2 Live Crew's version was a parody, which "quickly degenerates into a play on words, substituting predictable lyrics with shocking ones" to show "how bland and banal" the rap group thinks the Orbison song is; that 2 Live Crew had taken no more than was necessary to "conjure up" the original in order to parody it; and that it was "extremely unlikely that 2 Live Crew's song could adversely affect the market for the original."[89]

The U.S. Court of Appeals for the Sixth Circuit reversed and remanded. Although it assumed for the purpose of its opinion that 2 Live Crew's song was a parody of the original, the court of appeals held that "the admittedly commercial nature" of the parody weighed against a finding of fair use. The court of appeals also said that, by "taking the heart of the original and making it the heart of a new work," 2 Live Crew had, qualitatively, taken too much. Finally, after noting the effect on the potential market for the original, as well as the market for derivative works, the appeals court faulted the district court for "refus[ing] to indulge the presumption" that "harm for purposes of the fair use analysis has been established by the presumption attaching to commercial uses."[90]

The Supreme Court reversed, with Justice David Souter writing for a unanimous Court and noting that this was the Court's first opinion on the question of whether fair use could protect a parody from a copyright infringement claim. Justice Souter wrote:

Suffice it to say now that parody has an obvious claim to transformative value, as Acuff-Rose itself does not deny. Like less ostensibly humorous forms of criticism, it can provide social benefit, by shedding light on an earlier work, and, in the process, creating a new one. We thus line up with the courts that have held that parody, like other comment or criticism, may claim fair use....[91]

The Court cited lower court cases holding that a song titled "When Sonny Sniffs Glue" parodying "When Sunny Gets Blue" was a fair use,[92] as was the *Saturday Night Live* television show skit featuring "I Love Sodom," a takeoff on the New York City tourism campaign song "I Love New York."[93] The Court also said that parody, like any other use, has to be judged on a case-by-case basis according to the four factors of fair use.

The Court applied the four factors to "Pretty Woman." Regarding the purpose of the use, the Court said, "While we might not assign a high rank to the parodic element here, we think it fair to say that 2 Live Crew's song reasonably could be perceived as commenting on the original or criticizing it, to some degree."[94]

The second factor — the nature of the copyrighted work — is not much help, the Court said, "in separating the fair use sheep from the infringing goats in a parody case, since parodies almost invariably copy publicly known, expressive works."[95]

For its analysis of the third factor — the amount and substantiality of the portion used in relation to the copyrighted work as a whole — the Court turned its attention "to the persuasiveness of a parodist's justification for the particular copying done," recognizing "that the extent of permissible copying varies with the purpose and character of the use." Souter wrote:

Parody presents a difficult case. Parody's humor, or in any event its comment, necessarily springs from recognizable allusion to its object through distorted imitation. Its art lies in the tension between a known original and its parodic twin. When parody takes aim at a particular original work, the parody must be able to "conjure up" at least enough of that original to make the object of its critical wit recognizable [citations omitted]. What makes for this recognition is quotation of the original's most distinctive or memorable features, which the parodist can

[88] Acuff-Rose Music, Inc. v. Campbell, 972 F.2d 1429, 1442 (6th Cir. 1992), *rev'd*, 510 U.S. 569 (1994).

[89] Acuff-Rose Music, Inc. v. Campbell, 754 F.Supp. 1150, 1158 (M.D. Tenn. 1991).

[90] *Acuff-Rose Music*, 972 F.2d at 1439.

[91] Campbell v. Acuff-Rose Music, Inc., 510 U.S. 569, 579 (1994).

[92] Fisher v. Dees, 794 F.2d 432 (9th Cir. 1986).

[93] Elsmere Music, Inc. v. Nat'l Broad. Co., 482 F. Supp. 741 (S.D.N.Y. 1980), *aff'd*, 623 F.2d 252 (2d Cir. 1980).

[94] *Campbell*, 510 U.S. at 583-84.

[95] *Id.* at 586.

be sure the audience will know. Once enough has been taken to assure identification, how much more is reasonable will depend, say, on the extent to which the song's overriding purpose and character is to parody the original or, in contrast, the likelihood that the parody may serve as a market substitute for the original. But using some characteristic features cannot be avoided.[96]

Souter wrote that while 2 Live Crew's copying the characteristic opening bass riff and first line of the Orbison lyrics may have gone to the "heart" of the original, thereafter the rap group's lyrics and music departed markedly from the original.[97]

Considering the fourth fair use factor — the effect of the use upon the potential market for or value of the copyrighted work — the Supreme Court noted that a parody is unlikely to act as a substitute for the original because the parody and the original usually serve different market functions. Here a rap version likely appealed to a different audience than the Orbison song.

In another lawsuit involving parody and the fair use doctrine, the publishers of an illustrated book about the infamous O.J. Simpson murder trial unsuccessfully argued that the book was a parody of Dr. Seuss' *The Cat in the Hat* and a fair use of Theodor S. Geisel's book for children.[98] The defendant's book was titled *The Cat NOT in the Hat! A Parody by Dr. Juice* and was described in promotional literature as telling "... the whole story in rhyming verse and sketches as witty of Theodore [sic] Geisel's best. This is one parody that really packs a punch!" The district court and the Ninth Circuit Court agreed that ordinary reasonable people would perceive that a substantial similarity existed between the two works.

Further, in applying the four-part fair use test, the appeals court drew from Justice Anthony Kennedy's concurring opinion in the 2 Live Crew parody of "Oh, Pretty Woman," noting that "The parody must target the original, and not just its general style, the genre of art to which it belongs, or society as a whole."[99] Despite its claim in the title and its broadly mimicking of Dr. Seuss' characteristic style, *The Cat NOT in the Hat!* was not a parody, the appeals court said, because it did not hold Seuss' style up to ridicule.

The court concluded that the author and illustrator of the infringing work merely used the cat's stove-pipe hat, the narrator ("Dr. Juice") and the title "to get attention" or maybe even "to avoid the drudgery in working up something fresh."[100] While Simpson was depicted thirteen times in the cat's distinctively scrunched and somewhat shabby red and white hat, the substance and content of *The Cat in the Hat* was not conjured up by the focus on the Brown-Goldman murders or the O.J. Simpson trial, the appeals court wrote, concluding that the infringing work did not create a transformative work with new expression, meaning or message.

In May 2002, a copyright infringement lawsuit pitting the owner of rights to Margaret Mitchell's *Gone With the Wind* against a book titled *The Wind Done Gone* was settled out of court. Publisher Houghton Mifflin Co. agreed to continue to sell the book, labeling it an "unauthorized parody," and to make a financial contribution to Morehouse College in Atlanta at the request of the Mitchell estate. Both parties reserved rights concerning future adaptations of their respective books.[101]

Although the copyright argument was never submitted to a jury, the Eleventh U.S. Circuit Court of Appeals determined that an injunction against the book's distribution was an unlawful prior restraint.[102] The circuit court applied the four fair-use factors and decided that, if the matter were submitted to a jury, it was likely that *The Wind Done Gone* would be entitled to the fair-use defense. Thus, the injunction should not stand. The Eleventh Circuit remanded the case for a trial on the merits of the copyright claim, but the parties settled before the case went to trial.

Mattel Inc., manufacturer of the Barbie doll, was denied a preliminary injunction against a photographer who used pictures of Barbie in a variety of poses, some with sexual overtones. Mattel argued that photographer Tom Forsythe violated both its copyright and its trademark rights. The company tried to convince a court that consumers could mistake the photos as advertisements. Furthermore, Mattel argued that "crudely sexual and violently misogynistic"[103] photographs tarnished its trademark.

Forsythe countered that his photographs were a fair use, displaying the theme of "Barbie's power as a beauty myth," and were intended as a parody or commentary.

For a preliminary injunction to be approved, Mattel would have to show there would be irreparable harm if the injunction were not granted, and that the company would likely succeed at an eventual trial. A three-judge panel at the Ninth Circuit Court of Appeals, after considering the four fair use factors and conditions for trademark infringement and trademark dilution, upheld a lower court's conclusion that Mattel failed to show the possibility of injury or its probable success in the case. The same court later upheld an order that Mattel pay Forsythe's legal fees totaling more than $1.8 million.[104]

[96] *Id.* at 588.

[97] *Id.*

[98] Dr. Seuss Enters. L.P. v. Penguin Books USA, Inc., 109 F.3d 1394 (9th Cir. 1997).

[99] *Id.* at 1400 (quoting *Acuff-Rose*, 510 U.S. at 597 (Kennedy, J., concurring)).

[100] *Id.* (quoting from *Acuff-Rose*, 510 U.S. at 580).

[101] The Reporters Committee for Freedom of the Press, *"Wind Done Gone" Copyright Case Settled* (May 29, 2002), *at* http://www.rcfp.org/news/2002/0529suntru.html.

[102] SunTrust Bank v. Houghton Mifflin Co., 268 F.3d 1257 (11th Cir. 2001).

[103] Mattel v. Mattel, Inc. v. Walking Mt. Prods., 4 Fed. Appx. 400, 2001 U.S. App. LEXIS 2610 (9th Cir. Feb. 15, 2001) (unpublished).

[104] Mattel v. Mattel, Inc. v. Walking Mt. Prods., 53 F.3d 792 (9th Cir. 2003).

## COMPULSORY LICENSING
## FOR MUSIC AND BROADCASTING

Just as copyright law authorizes fair use as a limitation on the five exclusive rights of a copyright owner, compulsory licensing limits those rights for five types of uses:

- phonorecords of musical works,
- musical works on jukeboxes,
- cable television,
- certain works on public broadcasting, and
- satellite retransmissions to the public for private viewing.

Generally, compulsory licensing is a system that compels the owner of certain types of intellectual property to allow others to use that property for a reasonable fee. For years the Library of Congress and the Copyright Office administered a series of Copyright Arbitration Royalty Panels that periodically reviewed and set rates for licensing fees, collected fees annually and distributed them to copyright owner representatives. Beginning in June 2005, three permanent Copyright Royalty Judges replaced the Royalty Panels.[105]

Recall that a copyright bestows five exclusive and divisible rights — to reproduce, to prepare derivative works, to distribute copies, to perform and to display the work. These rights have been compared to owning a stick of salami, which can be sold in its entirety or cut into several pieces, each sold or given away separately. Compulsory licensing means that owners of copyrighted musical works do not have the exclusive right to decide who may perform or display their works, because the law allows anyone who pays a royalty fee to use them.

It is also important to understand that the law recognizes protection for three different aspects of music: compositions, sound recordings and phonorecords. A musical composition consists of music, including any accompanying words. Sound recordings are defined in the law as "works that result from the fixation of a series of musical, spoken, or other sounds, but not including the sounds accompanying a motion picture or other audiovisual work." Generally, copyright protection extends to the contribution of the performers whose performances are captured on the recording and to the contribution of the person or persons responsible for capturing and processing the sounds to make the final recording. The right to make a recording of a musical work is referred to in copyright law as a mechanical right. A sound recording is not the same as a phonorecord, which is simply the physical object, such as a cassette tape, CD, LP or 45 r.p.m. disk, containing the recording and its underlying musical composition. This means that three entities — the composer, the producer/performer and the manufacturer of the phonorecord — may own separate copyrights for various aspects of a single phonorecord.

A new legal question concerning compulsory licensing is whether companies that sell ringtones for cell phone should qualify for such licenses instead of dealing individually with music publishers for mechanical licenses and the performing rights societies for public performance licenses.[106]

### Sound Recordings and Phonorecords

Musical compositions have always been eligible for copyright protection, but sound recordings and phonorecords did not receive federal protection until 1972, although common law and some state laws provided limited protection. The rationale for this lack of protection, predating the 1909 Copyright Act, was that piano rolls used to activate pianos were not copies of the underlying musical composition because they could not be read or deciphered by the naked eye.[107]

How much will our hypothetical band Skool of Hard Nocks make from royalty fees paid to publicly perform its copyrighted sound recordings, and how does it go about collecting those fees? The hundreds of broadcast stations and other entities that perform or display Skool of Hard Nocks music will not deal individually with the band. Instead, the band will join one of the performance rights organizations — ASCAP or BMI, for example — and grant it the right to license the band's songs. The Copyright Arbitration Royalty Panels will collect licensing fees for distribution to performance rights organizations, which will in turn pay royalties to members. The amount of royalty fees members receive is based on the frequency their music is performed.

It would be impractical for broadcast stations, nightclubs and other businesses to keep track of each time a recording is used. So these firms buy a blanket license, paying an annual fee to the performance rights organization that controls the right to the recording. Fees vary according to the gross receipts of the station or business. Broadcasters do not like these blanket licenses, arguing in numerous lawsuits over the years that they are monopolistic and violate the Sherman Antitrust Act. Eventually, ASCAP and BMI agreed to permit members to negotiate directly with broadcasters and others seeking licenses, but generally performers and composers prefer to leave the matter to ASCAP and BMI.

Broadcasters also object to the practice by which producers of syndicated programming sell the programs to stations without synchronization rights — the right to reproduce music in conjunction with video. This means that in addition to buying the programming, broadcasters must pay ASCAP or BMI for "performance" rights. Broadcasters say their costs would be reduced if producers negotiated with copyright owners for both synchronization and performance rights. Under the present system, however, copyright owners, ASCAP and BMI know that broadcasters cannot air the programming without performance rights. So they

---

[105] Copyright Royalty and Distribution Reform Act of 2004, Pub. L. No. 108-419, 118 Stat. 2341 (2004).

[106] *See* Mario F. Gonzalez, *Are Musical Compositions Subject to Compulsory Licensing for Ringtones?*, 12 UCLA ENT. L. REV. 11 (Fall 2004)

[107] *See* White-Smith Music Publ'g Co. v. Apollo Co., 209 U.S. 1 (1908).

have little incentive to bargain. In a 1984 lawsuit, hundreds of independent television stations presented this "lack of incentive to bargain" argument in court, but the Second U.S. Circuit Court of Appeals did not think it was sufficient to rule the blanket licensing procedure an illegal restraint of trade.[108]

### Jukeboxes

Another historically controversial copyright issue involves coin-operated phonorecord players or jukeboxes. The 1909 Copyright Act exempted jukebox operators, so, until the present law went into effect in 1978, they had free use of phonorecords. Apparently, music publishers did not oppose the exemption in 1909 because jukeboxes produced relatively little income, and they increased the popularity of particular songs, which in turn boosted sales. As jukebox revenues became increasingly significant, however, music publishers and other copyright holders took a very different position. During copyright law revision discussions in the 1970s, they denounced the jukebox exemption as an anachronistic historical accident that was unconscionable, indefensible, totally unjustified and grossly discriminatory.

After much controversy and many proposals in Congress, the 1976 Copyright Act established a compulsory license requirement with the fee set at $8 per year per jukebox, subject to periodic review and adjustment by the Copyright Arbitration Royalty Panels. One legal scholar called the requirement "one of the greatest failures of the 1976 Act, entirely due to deliberate lawlessness by the majority of jukebox operators."[109] Barely one-fourth of the jukeboxes in operation were licensed in 1978, and the number steadily declined between then and 1989, despite thousands of infringement suits brought by ASCAP, BMI and other performing rights organizations. Civil suits did not succeed in requiring licenses, and despite requests from the Copyright Office, the Justice Department did not take criminal action against the worst offenders.

In order for the United States to join the Berne Convention and have a measure of international copyright protection, the jukebox-licensing situation demanded change. After some four years of deliberations, the compulsory license provision for jukeboxes in the 1976 Copyright Act was suspended to allow the trade association representing jukebox operators, the Amusement and Music Operators Association, to negotiate licensing agreements with ASCAP, BMI and the Society of European Stage Actors and Composers. Failure to execute a license agreement and display a certificate on the jukebox is grounds for infringement.

### Cable Television Systems

Like jukebox operators, cable television system owners paid no fees for using copyrighted material until 1978. Broadcasters paid royalties for the programming they aired, but cable owners retransmitted that programming at no cost. Copyright infringement suits against cable operators were unsuccessful; the Supreme Court twice held that retransmission did not constitute a "performance."[110]

The revised copyright act changed this so that cable system operators now participate in a compulsory licensing plan that requires them to pay royalties in exchange for using copyrighted material without securing permission. Those fees are based on a complex formula that considers the gross revenues subscribers pay for the basic retransmissions, plus the number of distant television station signals retransmitted and whether they are network affiliates. The fee structure influences programming choices that cable companies make available to viewers because transmitting more non-local stations translates to larger royalty fees.

### Satellite Retransmissions

Home satellite dishes were new and expensive items when the Copyright Act was passed in 1976. Eventually thousands of U.S. homes were receiving broadcasts *via* satellites, but copyright owners received no royalties on these retransmissions. Congress responded with a provision in the 1984 revision of the Communications Act that encouraged the scrambling of broadcast signals so that home satellite dish owners could not receive signals without paying annual fees. Then, in a series of laws during the 1990s, Congress applied compulsory licensing to satellite carriers that retransmitted

• unaltered superstations and network stations to home satellite dishes for private home viewing;[111] and

• television station signals into a station's local market.[112]

Compulsory licensing also applies to cable and satellite digital audio services, webcasting and future forms of digital transmission.

### COPYRIGHT AND DEVELOPING TECHNOLOGY

In a sense, all copyright law has been in response to developing technology. After all, unauthorized copying was hardly a problem when each copy required laborious hand lettering. Infringement concerns began with the invention of movable type and multiplied with succeeding generations of faster, more efficient printing presses. The development of each new medium for fixing works in tangible form — photography, moving pictures, sound recordings, digital imaging — as well as each new means of reproducing or

---

[108] Buffalo Broad. Co. v. ASCAP, 744 F.2d 917 (2d Cir. 1984).

[109] 1 WILLIAM F. PATRY, COPYRIGHT LAW AND PRACTICE 982 (1994).

[110] Teleprompter Corp. v. Columbia Broad. Sys., 415 U.S. 394 (1974); Fortnightly Corp. v. United Artists Television, Inc., 392 U.S. 390 (1968).

[111] Satellite Home Viewer Act of 1994, Pub. L. No. 103-369, § 1, 108 Stat. 3477, (amending 17 U.S.C. §§ 111 and 119 (2003)).

[112] Intellectual Property and Communications Omnibus Reform Act, Pub. L. No. 106 § 113, 113 Stat. 1501 § 1 (1999). This act expressly allowed satellite delivery of local signals for the first time.

transmitting works — radio, television, photocopying machines, video tape recorders, satellites, fax machines, pagers, computers, the Internet, CDs and DVDs — challenged lawmakers and judges.

### Video Cassette Recorders

One such challenge was movie studios' claim that people who videotaped movies from television broadcasts were infringing on copyrights. The stations, of course, paid royalties for the right to broadcast the movies, but home viewers paid no fees for copying over-the-air broadcasts. Under the doctrine of "first sale," movie studios receive no royalties after the initial sale of a film, although a video store may recoup its purchase price many times over through repeated rentals of a single film. Home recording of movies broadcast over television further decreased the opportunity for studios to make that first sale.

Recognizing the futility of collecting fees from individuals who taped in their homes, Universal Studios and Walt Disney Productions attempted to hold the manufacturers of taping equipment responsible for what they considered to be the illegal use of the video recorders. The studios sued Sony and other manufacturers of videotape and recorders, arguing that the manufacturer and sales of taping equipment contributed to copyright infringement. The studios pointed out that the fair use doctrine had not been interpreted as protecting the copying of an entire copyrighted work where no transformational value was added. During a lengthy trial, both parties introduced survey results showing that the primary use of tape recorders was for taping television programs for later viewing, referred to as "time shifting." The surveys also showed that most viewers erased tapes and reused them.

The district court ruled in favor of the manufacturers, concluding that noncommercial home recording of off-the-air broadcasts was a fair use. Considering the four factors of the fair use doctrine, the court emphasized that the material was broadcast free to the public at large and that home taping was a private, noncommercial activity conducted entirely within the home. Further, the court reasoned that the purpose of this use served the public interest in increasing access to television programming. The district court said that even if time shifting were considered an infringement, the manufacturers could not be held liable as contributory infringers for merely selling a "product capable of a variety of uses, some of them allegedly infringing."[113]

The movie studios appealed, and the Ninth U.S. Circuit Court of Appeals reversed, reasoning that home taping of entire broadcasts was not a "productive use" and that it was therefore unnecessary for the studios to prove any harm to the potential market for their copyrighted works.[114]

In *Sony Corporation v. Universal City Studios,*[115] a sharply divided Supreme Court held that Sony and other defendants were not guilty of contributory infringement. The majority noted a significant likelihood that substantial numbers of copyright holders would not object to "time shifting" by private viewers. The Court said no showing existed that time shifting would cause significant harm to the potential market for the movies and other taped material. Four justices dissented, expressing the view that time shifting was not a fair use and that the recorder manufacturers were guilty of inducing and materially contributing to the infringement.

*Sony* applies to home taping intended for private use. It does not extend to commercial uses of a home-taped movie, such as selling it or charging admission for a public performance. Likewise, the decision does not protect a commercial service that tape records newscasts for sale to subjects of the broadcasts.[116]

Before *Sony,* some industry representatives suggested that consumers pay surcharges on video cassette recorders and blank tapes to compensate copyright owners for over-the-air broadcasts. Congress never acted on the suggestion, which was opposed because recorders and tapes have legitimate purposes other than copying protected movies. Perhaps because they acted while digital audio recording equipment was relatively unknown and the digital industry was without lobbying power, proponents of this method of generating royalty revenue successfully lobbied Congress to enact the Audio Home Recording Act of 1992.[117] It requires manufacturers of digital audio recorders for home use to make the equipment incapable of "serial copying," making a copy from a copy. In addition, manufacturers must pay royalty fees on both the taping devices and the blank tapes, costs that typically are passed along to consumers. This law applies to digital audio equipment and tapes alone, not video taping devices or blank videotapes.

### Digital Versatile Disks (DVDs)

In the early 1990s, movie studios began to experiment with distributing movies in digital as well as analog format. In addition to larger data capacity and greater durability, DVDs offered improved visual and audio quality over videotapes. The studios, however, were reluctant to release digital movies and risk losing sales unless they could prevent DVDs from being copied and distributed free over the Internet.

In 1996, computer experts, working on behalf of the studios, devised the Content Scramble System (CSS), an encryption method to protect movies on DVDs. The studios then licensed the encryption technology to DVD player manufacturers, who

---

[113] Universal City Studios, Inc. v. Sony Corp. of Am., 480 F. Supp. 429, 460 (D. Calif. 1979).

[114] Universal City Studios, Inc. v. Sony Corp. of Am., 659 F.2d 963 (9th Cir. 1981).

[115] 464 U.S. 417 (1984).

[116] *See* Georgia Television Co. v. TV News Clips of Atlanta, Inc., 718 F. Supp. 939 (N.D. Ga. 1989).

[117] Pub. L. No. 102-563, 106 Stat. 4237 (1992) (codified at 17 U.S.C.S. § 1001 (LEXIS 2002)).

contracted to keep the technology confidential. Thus, DVD players were equipped to unscramble CSS code so that movies in DVDs format could be displayed on a television or computer screen, but they could not be copied. In 1997, studios began distributing DVD movies, which quickly gained popularity and provided significant studio revenue.

Within two years, a computer programmer had reverse-engineered a licensed DVD player and devised a program (called DeCSS) to decipher CSS encryption. Soon afterward, the publisher of a magazine for computer hackers posted both the object and source code for DeCSS on the magazine's Web site. Eight movie studios obtained a court injunction that ordered publisher Eric Corley to remove DeCSS from his Web site and from linking to other sites containing the decryption program.[118] The basis for the injunction was the anti-circumvention and anti-trafficking provisions of the Digital Millennium Copyright Act.[119]

On appeal, Corley argued that these DMCA provisions violated the First Amendment. The Second Circuit found in favor of the movie studios.[120] The court held that although computer code is entitled to First Amendment protection, the DMCA's anti-circumvention and anti-trafficking provisions are content neutral because they concern only the nonspeech element of computer code. Further, the regulation serves a substantial governmental interest unrelated to the suppression of free expression and does not burden more speech than necessary to further that interest. The Second Circuit also rejected Corley's challenge to the DMCA on the basis that it unconstitutionally eliminated fair use of copyrighted materials, a claim the court termed "extravagant."[121]

In early 2004, federal district courts in California and New York both enjoined the sale of software used to copy CSS-encrypted DVDs, holding that the software violates the anti-circumvention provisions of the DMCA.[122]

Digital rights management software now exists to prevent unauthorized copying. It breaks a movie file into many pieces and saves them in various locations on a user's hard drive. The software then puts the pieces together to allow the movie to be played smoothly. In addition, the DRM software imbeds code into movie files that causes them to self-destruct after a specified period of time. Even if a user were able to assemble the pieces of the movie to make a copy, the file automatically would stop working.[123]

Each year since 2002, a bill titled the Digital Media Consumer's Rights Act has been introduced in the House of Representatives, but as of June 2006, the most recent version was stalled in various House committees and sub-committees.[124] The bill would amend the DMCA to allow usersto circumvent digital copy-protection measures if the purpose falls within the scope of traditional fair use. The bill would also allow companies to develop and market tools that bypass digital copy protections if those tools are capable of significant non-infringing use. Proponents of the measure, including the American Library Association, say it would permit a number of fair uses, including allowing consumers to backup movies they have bought.[125] Opponents argue that the bill would lead to increased piracy and more lost sales.[126]

### Computers and the Internet

Copyright questions raised by video and audio tape recorders pale in comparison to the avalanche of legal problems prompted by digital technology. Personal computers and software combine to enable users to infringe copyright with relative ease when the copyrighted material is in digital format. Further, uploading the digital copy to the Internet exposes it to literally millions of people around the globe. Each of those recipients has the capabilities to further manipulate, copy and display the copyright work along even more avenues on the information superhighway.

Google, the search engine giant, currently is scanning all the books housed in several large university libraries and converting the printed copies into digital format for loading to the Google Web site. Instead of securing copyright permission at the outset, Google has shifted the permission burden to copyright owners, who must notify Google and "opt out" to prevent their works from being used. Not surprisingly, book publishers, authors and other copyright owners oppose the Google endeavor.[127]

Publishers share Google's goal of making books more widely available and easier to search electronically, which they say is the purpose of the Open Content Alliance, a cooperative effort among publishers, libraries, and Yahoo!. The Alliance project will share its work with all search engines and will protect the rights of copyright holders, according to the Association of American Publishers. Talks between the publishers and Google failed to deter Google executives from their original plan.[128]

While Google claims that fair use protects this copying because

[118] Universal City Studios, Inc. v. Reimerdes, 111 F. Supp. 2d 346 (S.D.N.Y. 2000).

[119] 17 U.S.C. 1201 (1998).

[120] Universal City Studios, Inc. v. Corley, 273 F.3d 429 (2d Cir. 2001).

[121] Id. at 458.

[122] 321 Studios v. MGM Studios, 2004 U.S. Dist. LEXIS 2771 (N.D.Cal. 2004); Paramount Pictures Corp. v. 321 Studios, 2004 U.S. Dist. LEXIS 3306 (S.D.N.Y. 2004).

[123] See ZDNET, May 30, 2003, at http://zdnet.com.com/2100-1103_21011581.html.

[124] Digital Media Consumers' Rights Act of 2005, H.R. 1201, 109th Cong., 1st Sess., 151 Cong. Rec. H1263 (Mar. 9, 2005).

[125] Digital Media Consumers' Rights Act: Hearings Before the Subcomm. on Trade and Consumer Protection, H. Energy and Commerce Comm., 109th Cong. (May 12, 2004), available at http://www.ala.org/ala/washoff/Woissues/copyrightb?HR107testimonywritten051204.pdf.

[126] Revision to DMCA Gains Support, INTERNET NEWS, June 22, 2004, at http://www.internetnews.com/bus-news/article.php/3372091.

[127] See Jim Astrachan, Commentary: Great gobs of Google, KANSAS CITY DAILY RECORD, Dec.4, 2005 (Lexis/Nexis).

[128] See Publishers Sue Google over Digital Book Copies, 23 COMPUTER & INTERNET LAW. 22 (2006).

## Illegal Forms of Copying and Distributing Sound Recordings

- **Pirate:**

  Unauthorized duplication of only the sound of legitimate recordings, as opposed to all the packaging, i.e., the original art, label, title, sequencing, combination of titles.

- **Counterfeit:**

  Unauthorized recordings of the prerecorded sound as well as the unauthorized duplication of original artwork, label, trademark and packaging.

- **Bootleg** (or underground):

  Unauthorized recordings of a live concert or a musical broadcast on radio or television.

- **Online piracy:**

  Unauthorized uploading of a copyrighted sound recording and making it available to the public, or downloading a sound recording from an Internet site, even if the recording isn't resold. Online piracy may now also include certain uses of "streaming" technologies from the Internet.

---

it serves the public interest, publishers disagree, asserting that Google wishes to draw users to its site and gain commercially through increased advertising rates. Publishers express skepticism at Google's claims to allow viewers to see only portions of books unless the book is in the public domain or the copyright owner has consented. Once a work is in digital form, its escape onto the Internet is easy, publishers point out. Consequently, in late 2005, a group of major publishing companies claimed copyright infringement and asked a federal court for declaratory and injunctive relief.[129] Regardless of that court's eventual decision, the case is likely to be appealed and will be closely monitored by various segments of the public.

Should the transmission of a work in digital form be governed as a public performance, a reproduction or as distribution? Can it be all three at the same time? How do rules concerning the right of importation of copyrighted works from foreign nations apply in a digital environment? It is beyond the scope of this book to consider all existing law to address new technology and copyright issues, but many issues affecting mass media are addressed here.

**Computer Software.** Anyone who wrestles with shrink-wrapping on a computer software program receives notice that, by virtue of opening the package, he or she agrees to abide by copyright statutes protecting the enclosed disks. Owners of a lawful copy of a computer program are authorized to load the program into a computer and modify it as necessary.

The current Copyright Act also made it legal for the owner to create a backup copy, but only for archival purposes. Unless the copyright owner has authorized public distribution as "shareware," it is illegal to make multiple copies of computer software for friends or co-workers. Companies and educational institutions often purchase site licenses for a specified number of copies for office or classroom use.

Two university students, operating without the university's knowledge or authorization, eliminated copying safeguards on hundreds of software packages and made them available for free downloading. Both district and appeals courts rejected their fair use argument, and they were held liable for damages amounting to almost $1.5 million. Further, one student was sentenced to two years in prison and the other to eight months plus six months of community custody with supervised release.[130]

A computerized database is eligible for copyright protection as a "literary work" to the extent that it incorporates style rather than merely ideas or facts. Although the labor involved in typing factual information into a compilation does not constitute original, copyrightable expression, the Supreme Court has held that the specific selection and arrangement of facts, such as the layout and design of a database, may entail a minimal degree of creativity sufficiently original for copyright protection.[131]

Two U.S. District Court decisions in New York held that copyright protection extends to the user interfaces or "look and feel" of visual screen displays for computer software even when the underlying source code has not been copied.[132] This is important protection because newer graphical software relieves developers from much of the coding, permitting them instead to concentrate their creative efforts on designing user-friendly screen displays.

**Bulletin Board Systems and the World Wide Web.** Posting

---

[129] McGraw Hill Co. et al. v. Google, Inc., No. 05 CV 8881 (filed 10/19/2005 S.D.N.Y.) (Lexis/Nexis).

[130] *Copyright Law - Software Piracy*, CHI. DAILY LAW BULL., Nov. 12, 2003, *available at* LEXIS, Legal News Library.

[131] Feist Publ'ns v. Rural Tel. Serv. Co., 499 U.S. 340 (1991).

[132] O.P. Solutions, Inc. v. Intellectual Prop. Network Ltd., 1999 U.S. Dist. LEXIS 979, 50 U.S.P.Q.2d (BNA) 1399 (S.D.N.Y. 1999) ("OPS I"); 1999 U.S. Dist LEXIS 16639 (S.D.N.Y. 1999) ("OPS II").

digital reproductions of copyrighted photographs on computer bulletin board systems without authorization is an infringement. A company operating such a system made digital reproductions of 170 photographs from *Playboy* magazine and distributed the images to subscribers. A court rejected a fair use defense, noting that the use was clearly commercial; that the originals were for entertainment, not factual, purposes; and that, if widespread, such conduct would adversely affect the magazine's market.[133] In addition, the use of the magazine's trademarks "Playboy" and "Playmates" as file descriptors on the bulletin board system was held a violation of the federal law protecting trademarks.

**ISP Liability.** On the question of whether an Internet service provider shares in the liability for copyright infringement by its subscribers, one federal district court answered in the negative so long as the ISP had not undertaken any affirmative action that directly resulted in copying.[134] In that particular case, involving the Church of Scientology as plaintiff, the decision held that "although copyright is a strict liability statute, there should still be some element of volition or causation which is lacking where a defendant's system is merely used to create a copy by a third party."[135] This lack of involvement by the ISP differs from the bulletin board service operators in the *Playboy* cases, and another BBS operator who encouraged customers to download Sega video games into their computers after an unidentified subscriber made the games available on the bulletin board. Further, the BBS offered to sell subscribers an alternative to Sega's video cartridges. The court in the Sega case found the BBS operator guilty of contributing to copyright infringement although a subscriber rather than the operator originally uploaded the video games.[136]

The Digital Millennium Copyright Act[137] exempts Internet service providers from liability for customers' copyright infringement so long as the ISP promptly removes the material upon either becoming aware that it is infringing or receiving notice from the copyright owner claiming infringement. So long as the ISP acts in the good faith belief that the material is infringing and follows a specified notification procedure, the act also protects the ISP from liability for removing the material.

**Digital Manipulation.** Other computer-related copyright debates and ethical dilemmas spring from digital manipulation of images. Is a black and white movie that has been colorized or is a photograph that has been altered a derivative work that is eligible for copyright protection? Does such doctoring of images infringe the copyright owner's right to control derivative works?

Turner Network Television set off a firestorm of protest in some quarters when it used computer technology to colorize classic Hollywood films, including *Casablanca* and *It's a Wonderful Life*. Turner was not infringing copyright because the company had purchased rights to the movies, but protesters decried what they viewed as mutilation of cultural heritage. Prominent Hollywood figures urged Congress to protect the integrity of movies, painting the specter of digital imaging run amok, altering films to replace actors with "fresher faces" or to change the movement of speakers' lips to conform to new dialogue.

The upshot was the National Film Preservation Act of 1988, termed by copyright expert William Patry "one of the silliest pieces of legislation ever to pass Congress."[138] The act establishes a board authorized to designate as many as twenty-five films each year for registration as "classical films," a label denoting that the films are materially unaltered. Meanwhile, the Copyright Office passed a regulation requiring the deposit of the black-and-white version as well as the colorized version when copyright registration is sought for the newer version.

Digital manipulation technology also creates problems for the music industry. The technology allows sounds to be converted to digital bits and manipulated by a recording engineer. Sounds from copyrighted songs, perhaps just a single note or distinctive few notes, can be remixed and combined with other sounds, to create a new song. Courts have held that this musical "sampling" infringes copyright if the copying is sufficiently significant to result in a substantially similar work. The two musical works do not have to be substantially similar; there is infringement if there is similarity between qualitatively important portions of the two works.[139]

Noting that technological advances coupled with the popularity of hip hop or rap music have made instances of digital sampling extremely common and have spawned a plethora of copyright disputes and litigation, the Sixth Circuit Court of Appeals in 2005 said that the "substantially similar" test applies to the copyrighted musical compositions but not to sound recordings.[140] The case challenged the use of a George Clinton and Funkadelic's three-note guitar riff that ran two seconds. The rap group NWA lowered the guitar pitch, looped the sample, extended it to sixteen beats, and used the sample five times in its song *100 Miles and Runnin'*. The court said that such sampling requires a license. The Sixth Circuit includes Nashville, Tenn., where more than 800 lawsuits had been filed by early 2005 over unlicensed sampling of copyrighted works.

The ease and convenience of digital scanning technology brings with it increasing legal concerns for photographers, particularly freelancers. While direct copying of photographs and other visual

[133] Playboy Enters. v. Frena, 839 F. Supp. 1552 (M.D. Fla. 1993).

[134] Religious Tech. Ctr. v. Netcom On-Line Comm. Serv., Inc., 907 F. Supp. 1361 (N.D. Calif. 1995).

[135] *Id.* at 1370.

[136] Sega Enters. v. MAPHIA, 857 F. Supp. 679 (N.D. Calif. 1994).

[137] Pub. L. No. 105-304, 112 Stat. 2863 (1998) (codified at 17 U.S.C.S. § 101 (2002)).

[138] PATRY, *supra* note 109, at 101.

[139] *See* Jarvis v. A&M Records, 827 F. Supp. 282 (D.N.J. 1993); Grand Upright Music Ltd. v. Warner Bros. Records, 780 F. Supp. 182 (S.D.N.Y. 1991).

[140] Bridgeport Music, Inc. et al. v. Dimension Films, 410 F.3d 792 (6th Cir. 2005).

images without authorization — such as downloading an image from the Internet and displaying it on a Web page — is illegal, does infringement occur when portions of one or more photographs are digitally reproduced and combined to create a new photograph? Should fair use principles apply to such derivative works so long as the new work is sufficiently transformative?

Scholars differ in their analyses of these questions. Some argue that the mere act of scanning a copyrighted photograph without permission is copyright infringement, while others maintain that new images created from bits and pieces of scanned images should be eligible for copyright protection. Other writers call upon Congress or the courts to clarify the legal ambiguities.[141]

A 1999 case offers guidance. A company hired a photographer to take aerial photographs of the Las Vegas Strip and a graphic artist to combine and digitally alter the photographs to create an artistic depiction of the Strip. The company then sold postcards and posters bearing the computer-enhanced image. Another company scanned and digitally altered the image further and produced other novelty items for sale. The court determined that the copying did not qualify as a fair use and was copyright infringement.[142]

**Web Linking.** Yet, another potential legal situation involving copyright and the Internet is the widespread practice of directly linking one Web site to another.[143] While most Web enthusiasts probably view hyperlinking as analogous to recommending a book or citing a source, at least one legal scholar asserts that expanding e-commerce will promote "linking rights" governed by laws of unfair competition and intellectual property, rather than a free and uninhibited 'right' to link.[144] He predicts that "contrary to the original ethos of Internet use, which celebrated hyperlink technology and encouraged everyone to use it to the greatest extent possible, in the era of business use of the Internet, linkages will often be scrutinized and controlled — and sometimes discouraged, litigated, or penalized."[145]

The practice of "deep linking" — bypassing a site's home page and taking users directly to a specific page within the targeted site — particularly troubles some Web site owners, both from business and copyright standpoints.[146] Another legal scholar analyzed five years of cases worldwide and concluded that it was relatively rare for a Web publisher to face liability from linking to other Internet sites.[147]

The Washington Post Company and several other news organizations reached an out-of-court settlement with Total News, Inc., a company whose advertising-filled Web site included "framed" pages of news from other sites.[148] The publishers claimed that their own advertising banners were displaced by the Total News ads, actionable as common law misappropriation, federal and state trademark dilution, unfair competition, trademark infringement, copyright infringement and tortuous interference. The news organizations did not object to the hyperlinks *per se* but to the way they were viewed within a Total News frame, which blocked the original advertising and substituted other ads. The case was settled with Total News agreeing to a licensing arrangement with specified conditions for displaying pages from the publishers' Web sites.[149] The *Los Angeles Times* and *Washington Post* won a permanent injunction and $1 million in statutory damages from operators of an Internet bulletin board that posted articles without permission.[150]

In another case, a court granted a preliminary injunction against a Web site operator found to have contributed to copyright infringement.[151] The Web site operator, as ordered, removed the copyrighted *Church Handbook of Instructions* from his own site. Then he posted Web addresses directing users to other online sources for the *Handbook* and sent e-mail encouraging people to browse those sites, print copies of the *Handbook* and send them to others.

In yet another linking case, a defendant won summary judgment when a federal district court determined that his linking was fair use.[152] The defendant operated a "visual search engine." Unlike typical Internet search engines, this one retrieved images instead of descriptive text and produced a list of reduced, thumb-

---

[141] For discussions of legal issues involving digital photography, *see* Jonathan A. Franklin, *Digital Image Reproduction, Distribution and Protection: Legal Remedies and Industrywide Alternatives*, 10 COMPUTER & HIGH TECH. L. J. 347 (1994); Michael S. Oberman & Trebor Lloyd, *Copyright Protection for Photographs in the Age of New Technologies*, 2 B.U. J. SCI. & TECH. L. 10 (1996).

[142] Tiffany Design, Inc. v. Reno-Tahoe Specialty, Inc., 55 F. Supp. 2d 1113 (D. Nevada 1999).

[143] For a discussion of potential legal problems involving Internet material, *see generally*, Stephen Fraser, *The Conflict Between the First Amendment and Copyright Law and Its Impact on the Internet*, 16 CARDOZO ARTS & ENT. L. J. 1 (1998); David J. Loundy, *Revising the Copyright Law for Electronic Publishing*, 14 J. MARSHALL J. COMPUTER & INFO. L. 1 (1995); April M. Major, *Copyright Law Tackles Yet Another Challenge: The Electronic Frontier of the World Wide Web*, 24 RUTGERS COMPUTER & TECH. L. J. 24 (1998); Michael D. McCoy & Needham J. Boddie, II, *Cybertheft: Will Copyright Law Prevent Digital Tyranny on the Superhighway?*, 30 WAKE FOREST L. REV. 173 (1995).

[144] Mark Sableman, Link Law: The Evolving Law of Internet Hyperlinks (1998) (unpublished paper presented to the Law Division, Association for Education in Journalism and Mass Communication annual convention, Baltimore, Md.).

[145] *Id.* at 2.

[146] For a discussion of the need for specific Internet property rights to battle deep linking and software robots, *see* John D. Saba Jr., Comment, *Internet Property Rights: E-Trespass*, 33 ST. MARY'S L. J. 367 (2002).

[147] Mark Sableman, *Link Law Revisited: Internet Linking Law at Five Years*, 16 BERKELEY TECH. LJ. 1273 (2001).

[148] Wash. Post Co. v. Total News, Inc., 97 Civ. 1190 (PKL) (S.D.N.Y. filed Feb. 20, 1997).

[149] Stipulation Order of Settlement and Dismissal, Wash. Post Co. v. Total News, Inc., No. 97 Civ. 1190 (PKL) (S.D.N.Y. filed June 5, 1997).

[150] Los Angeles Times v. Free Republic, No. 98-7840, 2000 U.S. Dist. LEXIS 20484, 29 Media L. Rep (BNA) 1028 (C.D. Calif. 2000).

[151] Intellectual Reserve, Inc. v. Utah Lighthouse Ministry, Inc., 75 F. Supp. 2d 1290 (C.D. Utah 1999).

[152] Kelly v. Arriba Soft Corp., 77 F. Supp. 2d 1116 (C.D. Calif. 1999).

nail pictures related to the user's query. By selecting the desired thumbnail, a user could view the full-size version of the image and the address for the originating Web site. By clicking on the address, the user could link to that site.

After analyzing the fair use factors, the Court found two of the four factors weighed in favor of fair use, and two weighed against it. The first and fourth factors — character of use and lack of market harm — weighed in favor of fair use, the court said, because of the established importance of search engines and the transformative nature of using reduced versions of images to organize and provide access to them. The second and third factors — creative nature of the work and amount or substantiality of copying — weighed against fair use, but the court placed the most importance on the transformative use.

### Online Music and Movie Piracy

During the past decade, peer-to-peer file sharing initially shrunk music industry revenues, and, as bandwidth grew, so did P2P piracy of movies. The advent of MP3, a digital song-compression format, and increasingly faster Internet connections combined to change music distribution, thus pitting major record labels against electronics developers, independent recording artists, who sought to discover audiences for their music, P2P server operators, and, eventually, music fans.

Since 1998, the Recording Industry Association of America (RIAA) has sought to stem the flow of unauthorized copying by taking informal and legal actions against four groups of people:

- those who manufacturer MP3 players,
- those who operate Web sites containing pirated music,
- operators of search engines that help users locate online music files, and
- people who download music from the Internet without paying for it.

Some Internet pirates thought they could escape prosecution if they gave away rather than sold their stolen wares. The No Electronic Theft Act,[153] passed in 1997, plugged that loophole, and the Department of Justice won its first MP3 pirating conviction against a University of Oregon student. The student pleaded guilty to illegally distributing copyrighted music and other materials and could have been sentenced to three years in prison and a $250,000 fine.

**Actions Against Player Manufacturers.** The RIAA unsuccessfully sought an injunction to prevent Diamond Multimedia Systems from selling the Rio, an early MP3 player, claiming that it violated the Audio Home Recording Act of 1992.[154] That act requires specifically defined categories of digital audio copying devices to (1) register with the Copyright Office; (2) pay a statutory royalty on each device and piece of media sold; and (3) incorporate a serial copyright management system to prevent consumers from making multiple copies of recordings. The manufacturer won that first round after a 1999 ruling that neither computers nor the Rio qualified as digital audio recording devices as defined by the Audio Home Recording Act.[155] This meant that multipurpose devices like computers or MP3 players did not have to pay royalties or incorporate serial copyright management systems, but it did not exempt the manufacturers or consumers from copyright suits.

As copyright lawsuits continued, major factions in the controversy eventually forged several agreements to accommodate their individual interests. Diamond Multimedia announced that it would equip the Rio player with anti-piracy software, permitting customers to hear one or two tracks before the recording locked up. Individual recording labels or other copyright holders would determine terms for unlocking and downloading the music, ensuring royalty collections. MP3.com, a Web site that allows musicians to distribute their work online, entered into a licensing agreement with ASCAP and Universal Music Group and agreed to make its music available in digital formats compatible with players being made by other manufacturers. Large international music firms announced similar arrangements.

Competing interests decided compromise would eventually trigger the greatest business opportunities for each of them. The Secure Digital Music Initiative (SDMI), a consortium representing companies from the recording, home electronics and technology industries worldwide, forged a standard that eventually would prevent illegally duplicated music from being played on digital devices. Even after copyright protection – in the form of digital watermarks imbedded in CDs – was in place, portable digital players would still play the millions of CDs already in existence. The *New York Times* quoted the RIAA general counsel as saying, "For some companies we're talking about giving away a musical heritage. Think about Elvis, think about the Beatles – we're talking about giving away the catalog."[156]

Major record companies, unconvinced that security devices would be effective,[157] sued MP3.com, and, in 2000, a federal district judge sided with the recording industry.[158] Judge Jed S.

---

[153] Pub. L. No. 105-147, 111 Stat. 2678 (1997) (amending 17 U.S.C. § 506 (a)(1) and 18 U.S.C. § 2319 (2000)).

[154] Pub. L. No. 102-563, 106 Stat. 4237 (1992) (codified at 17, U.S.C.S. § 1001 (2002)).

[155] Recording Indus. Ass'n of Am. v. Diamond Multimedia Sys., 180 F.3d 1072 (9th Cir. 1999).

[156] Neil Strauss & Matt Richtel, *Pact Reached on Downloading of Digital Music*, N.Y. TIMES ONLINE (June 19, 1999), http://www.nytimes.com.

[157] The Digital Millennium Copyright Act (Pub. L. No. 105-304, 112 Stat. 2860 (1998) (codified at 17 U.S.C. § 101 (LEXIS 2002)) makes it a crime to circumvent technological protection measures that control access to protected works or to manufacture or traffic in such technology. Exceptions are made for law enforcement and intelligence agencies, as well as for nonprofit libraries, archives or educational institutions engaged in a good faith determination of whether to acquire a protected work. The act also makes it illegal to provide or distribute false copyright management information with the intent to induce or conceal infringement.

[158] UMG Recordings, Inc. v. MP3.com, Inc., 92 F. Supp. 2d 349 (S.D.N.Y.

Rakoff began his opinion with this statement: "The complex marvels of cyberspatial communication may create difficult legal issues; but not in this case. [MP3.com's] infringement of plaintiff's copyrights is clear."[159] The judge determined MP3.com's attempt to use the fair use defense was "indefensible" and labeled as "essentially frivolous" all other legal arguments MP3.com advanced to avoid an infringement finding. Ultimately, MP3.com was ordered to pay millions of dollars in penalties and to pay royalties to use music on its online services.[160]

Advances in digital technology continued to plague the music and movie industries, however, and by mid-2006 RIAA had launched new copyright challenges against makers of tiny devices capable of receiving and recording XM satellite radio transmissions. The time-shifting rationale from *Sony* may apply to these devices because they do not permit burning to CDs or transferring recordings to other media.[161] Similarly, major movie studios, along with ABC, CBS and NBC broadcast networks, filed suit to block an announced plan by Cablevision Systems Corp. to allow viewers to store and pause TV programs on the cable system rather than on set-top boxes. The plaintiffs viewed this new development as potential for copyright infringement, while Cablevision regarded it as another time-shifting method.[162]

**Suits Against File-sharing Services.** Another copyright infringement target was the original Napster, which began operation in 1999. With its P2P file sharing, Napster operated much like an Internet jukebox. Users downloaded the free software and used Napster's central data registry to locate other Napster users who had desired songs stored on their personal computers. Then Napster software transferred the file from computer to computer *via* a temporary connection. The RIAA referred to Napster as "a giant online pirate bazaar," and many universities, viewing it as a bandwidth bottleneck that caused delays and disruptions of Internet service to the academic community, blocked Napster on their campus networks.[163]

In 2000 and 2001 Napster lost before a federal judge in California[164] and at the Ninth Circuit Court of Appeals[165] when both courts found Napster guilty of contributory federal copyright in-

fringement and related state law violations. Napster unsuccessfully sought refuge in the Digital Millennium Copyright Act[166] "safe harbor" provision by arguing that it was an Internet service provider or a mere conduit. Further, Napster claimed that its posted statement notifying users that accounts of copyright infringers would be terminated also insulated it from liability.

After more legal wrangling, the Ninth Circuit affirmed a district court's preliminary injunction that, in effect, ordered Napster to shut down unless it could guarantee that it would block 100 percent of unauthorized songs from being downloaded *via* the Internet.[167] In 2002, Napster filed for bankruptcy protection, claiming $7.9 million in assets and $101 million in debts.[168] Today, new owners of the Napster name operate a paid music service.

By the time of original Napster's demise, new peer-to-peer file-sharing services were already in operation, and infringement suits from movie studios and record labels quickly followed. The Napster copycats, like Kazaa, Grokster and Morpheus, operated differently from the original. Instead of maintaining a centralized index on a server, they distributed file-sharing software that allowed users to connect and share files directly with one another.

Although a federal district court[169] and the Ninth Circuit Court[170] held that this difference sufficiently insulated the defendants from contributory infringement, the Supreme Court, in *MGM Studios v. Grokster*,[171] declared that those courts misapplied its Sony Betamax opinion.[172] The lower courts interpreted *Sony* as holding that the distribution of a commercial product capable of substantial non-infringing uses could not give rise to contributory liability for infringement unless the distributor had actual knowledge of specific instances of infringement and failed to act on that knowledge.

In June 2005, the Supreme Court reversed the lower courts and remanded the case for reconsideration of MGM's summary judgment motion. Justice Souter, for a unanimous Supreme Court, wrote:

> The question is under what circumstances the distributor of a product capable of both lawful and unlawful use is liable for acts of copyright infringement by third parties using the product. We hold that one who distributes a device with the object of promoting its use to infringe copyright, as shown by clear ex-

---

2000).

[159] *Id.* at 349.

[160] UMG Recordings, Inc. v. MP3.com, Inc., No. 00-C0472, 2000 U.S. Dist. LEXIS 17907 (S.D.N.Y. Nov. 14, 2000).

[161] *See* David Pogue, *XM Radio Fans Can Record It If They Hear It,* N.Y. TIMES, May 25, 2006, at C1.

[162] *See* James Bernstein & Richard J. Dalton Jr., *Newest Digital Dispute; Cablevision's Plan to Offer Remote Recording of Programs Spurs Suit on Copyright Charges From Hollywood Execs,* NEWSDAY, May 26, 2006, at A60.

[163] *See* Mary Deibel, *Singing the Blues Over Napster,* SCRIPPS HOWARD NEWS SERVICE, May 18, 2000 (quoting figures from Students Against University Censorship at Indiana University-Bloomington).

[164] A&M Records, Inc. v. Napster, Inc., 114 F. Supp. 2d 896 (N.D. Calif. 2000).

[165] A&M Records, Inc., v. Napster, Inc., 239 F.3d 1004 (9th Cir. 2001).

[166] 17 U.S.C. § 512 (2003).

[167] A&M Records, Inc. v. Napster Inc., Nos. 01-15998, 01-16003, 01-16011, 01-16308 (9th Cir., Mar. 25, 2002).

[168] *See* B. Garrity, *Copyright-Infringement Suits Frozen As File-Swapping Service Files For Bankruptcy Protection,* BILLBOARD, June 15, 2002, at 3.

[169] Metro-Goldwyn-Mayer Studios v. Grokster, Ltd., 259 F.Supp. 2d 1029 (D.C. Cal. 2003).

[170] Metro-Goldwyn-Mayer Studios Inc. v. Grokster Ltd., 380 F.3d 1154 (9th Cir. 2004).

[171] 545 U.S. 913 (2005).

[172] Sony Corp. of America v. Universal City Studios, Inc., 464 U.S. 417 (1984).

pression or other affirmative steps taken to foster infringement, is liable for the resulting acts of infringement by third parties.[173]

Whereas, there was no evidence that Sony had desired to bring about VCR taping in violation of copyright or had taken active steps to increase its profits from unlawful taping, the same could not be said of Grokster and StreamCast, the Supreme Court concluded, after studying the two companies' business models, their advertising, and their failure to develop filtering tools or other mechanisms to diminish the infringing activity. The Court acknowledged the tension between the competing values of supporting creativity through copyright protection and promoting technological innovation by limiting infringement liability. Despite offsetting considerations, the Court said the argument for imposing indirect liability in this particular case was powerful, given that the respondents' software accounted for billions of infringing downloads each month.

The Court noted that when a widely shared product is used to commit infringement, it may be impossible to enforce rights in the protected work effectively against all direct infringers, so the only practical alternative that remains is to act against the device's distributor for secondary liability on a theory of contributory or vicarious infringement. One infringes contributorily, the Court said, by intentionally inducing or encouraging direct infringement. Vicarious infringement occurs when one profits from direct infringement while declining to stop or limit it. Although "the Copyright Act does not expressly render anyone liable for [another's] infringement,"[174] these secondary liability doctrines emerged from common law principles and are well established in the law.[175]

In scores of newspaper and magazine articles immediately after the Supreme Court's *Grokster* ruling, representatives from the music and movie industries declared a great victory, while spokesmen for the file-sharing services urged caution and noted that the case still had to return to the district court. File-sharing interests voiced the possibility that they might be able to restructure their businesses to adhere to the Supreme Court guidelines for contributory and vicarious infringement.

The music and movie industries followed up the decision by filing thousands of lawsuits against individual consumers, while states began criminally prosecuting alleged copyright violators, from downloaders to game-store owners who sold modified Xboxes.

A government effort at limiting illegal file sharing is the Family Entertainment and Copyright Act,[176] which became law in 2005. It imposes criminal penalties of fines and up to three years in prison on anyone found guilty of possessing or distributing on the Internet any movie, music or software files that have not yet been released to the public. The law also makes it a crime to record movies from theater screens.

On a single day in June 2005, the FBI and law enforcement from ten other countries conducted more than ninety searches worldwide and made multiple arrests designed to disrupt and dismantle many organizations that illegally distribute and trade in copyrighted software, movies, music, and games on the Internet. The operation targeted top-level release groups that are primary suppliers to the for-profit criminal distribution networks that cost the copyright industry billions of dollars each year.[177]

**Attempts to Stop Individuals from File sharing.** For several years, record labels and individual bands like Metallica have applied pressure on individual users by employing the services of firms that work as an Internet police force, crawling the Web looking for copyrighted files being downloaded by consumers. When suspected infringers are detected, notification is sent to either the user's ISP or employer that the content must be removed and that copyright laws have been violated.[178] A major problem, however, is identifying the culprit, as most do not use their real names.

One tactic is to subpoena Internet service providers for the names of subscribers who commit copyright infringement. A federal district court ruled that under terms of the Digital Millennium Copyright Act, Verizon must comply with a RIAA subpoena seeking the identity of a particular subscriber,[179] but an appeals court reversed.[180] The court seemed sympathetic to the music industry plight but noted that P2P networks were nonexistent when the DMCA was written.

Another appeals court issued a similar ruling in 2005.[181] British courts, on the other hand, have ordered ISPs to identify subscribers targeted by the music industry in England as illegally sharing files.[182] The U.S. decisions do not prevent RIAA from filing suits, but industry representatives can no longer provide advance notice to individuals sued. RIAA files suits naming individual defendants as "John Doe" to compel ISPs to reveal subscriber names. Some defendants in these suits choose to settle out of court. Four college students, for example, each agreed to pay between $12,000 and $17,500 in May 2003 to avoid going to court.[183]

---

[173] Metro Goldwyn-Mayer Studios Inc., et al. v. Grokster, Lts., et al., 2005 U.S. LEXIS 5212 at 10 (June 27, 2005).

[174] *Sony,* 464 U.S. at 434.

[175] *Id.* at 486.

[176] 109 Pub. L. 9; 119 Stat. 218 (2005).

[177] *See Justice Department Conducts International Internet Piracy Sweep,* 22 COMPUTER & INTERNET LAW 34 (2005).

[178] *See* Mark Sweney, *MP3 Is Establishing Itself As a Music Format and Firms are Flocking to Setup Download Sites,* REVOLUTION, May 29, 2002, at 24.

[179] Recording Indus. Ass'n of Am. v. Verizon Internet Servs., No. 03-MS-0040 (D.D.C. Apr. 24, 2003).

[180] Recording Industry Ass'n of Am. v. Verizon Internet Servs., 351 F.3d 1229 (D.C. Cir. 2003).

[181] Charter Commc'ns., Inc., Subpoena Enforcement Matter v. Charter Communs., Inc., 393 F.3d 771 (8th Cir. 2005).

[182] *British Courts Order File Sharers to be Identified,* THE REGISTER, Apr. 20, 2005, *at* http://www.theregister.com/2005/04/19/bpi_p2p_lawsuits/.

[183] Associated Press, *Students and RIAA Settle Copyright Suits,* May 1, 2003, *at* http://www.nandotimes.com/technology/story/875081p610c.html.

In another suit, a University of Arizona student who had unauthorized possession of movies and music was fined $5,400 and was sentenced to three months in prison, three years' probation, and 200 hours of community service. In addition, he was ordered to take a course on copyright law and not to use file-sharing programs in the future.[184]

Having already filed approximately 6,000 individual lawsuits,[185] the RIAA, immediately after *Grokster* was decided in June 2005, filed a new wave of John Doe infringement suits[186] and also began to target students using university Internet2 facilities.[187] Recording industry associations in Denmark, Germany, Italy and Canada took similar actions in their countries.[188] The Motion Picture Association of America (MPAA), which represents the seven largest movie studios, had also begun to file lawsuits against individuals it accused of illegally trading movie files. Executives from the movie industry hoped that legal action would curtail illegal movie downloads before they rival illegal music downloads.[189]

RIAA also continued to report alleged copyright violations to college and university officials, urging officials to disallow peer-to-peer file sharing on school networks.[190] Many higher-education institutions have taken such steps, either to head off potential litigation or because student files-sharing activity is diverting valuable computer resources from research and other academic uses. The U.S. Naval Academy, for example, seized computers from approximately one hundred students suspected of improperly downloading copyrighted material. Those students face a variety of punishments, including court martial, if found guilty of copyright violations.[191]

Freshman orientation materials at many institutions of higher education now include copyright lessons and warnings about potential repercussions for infringement. Some universities are entering into deals with music providers to provide legal downloads of songs and movies as part of the effort to discourage illegal file trading. Universities also are installing various technological devices and restricting network access to deter the use of campus networks for illegal file sharing.[192]

In addition to its legal battles, the music industry has taken steps to attract customers to legal online music services. The "big five" companies – Bertelsmann Music Group (BMG), EMI, Sony, Universal and Warner Music – as well as some independent labels now sell licenses to file sharing services — FullAudio, MusicMatch, Pressplay, Peer Impact, Rhapsody and StreamCast Network, for example — which distribute Morpheus software. Shawn Fanning, the creator of the original Napster, worked with Universal Music Group to put that company's music collection online. AOL and Apple Computer also offer pay-for-music subscription services. Industry observers speculate, however, that the industry faces a huge challenge to persuade users to pay – at rates less than a dollar per song – for music that they have gotten for free, even at the risk of copyright infringement prosecution.[193]

The movie industry appeared to be making similar arrangements. Warner Brothers, for example, announced in 2006 that it planned to make hundreds of movies and television shows available for purchase over the Internet, using BitTorrent software, the same program widely used to download copyrighted material illegally.[194]

**Webcasting.** Another growth area for music online is webcasting or streaming audio. As user bandwidth increases, more entertainment Web sites stream audio and create genre-based, commercial-free programming. Statutes now establish a royalty system to compensate copyright owners for music played on the Web.[195] The U.S. Copyright Office designated the RIAA as administrative entity for digital performance rights for webcasting, similar to the roles of ASCAP and BMI for collecting and distributing royalties for music played on radio, television and other venues. Broadcasters unsuccessfully argued that they should be allowed to webcast without paying royalties.[196] Webcasters must meet certain criteria to qualify for a compulsory license rather than dealing with copyright owners individually.[197]

[184] *See* Cassie Tomlin, *RIAA Proscutes UA Student,* ARIZONA DAILY WILDCAT, Mar. 7, 2005, http://wwwwildcat.Arizona,edu/papers/98/112/01_4.html.

[185] *See MPAA to Begin File-Trading Lawsuits,* N.Y. TIMES ONLINE ARCHIVES, Nov. 5, 2004, *at* http://www.nytimes.com/2004/11/05/business/media/05film. html.

[186] *See RIAA Continues Enforcement Of Rights With New Lawsuits Against 784 Illegal File Sharers,* RIAA NEWSLETTER, June 29, 2005, *at* http://www.riaa.com/ news/newsletter/062905.asp.

[187] *See RIAA Expands Scope Of Illegal File-Sharing Lawsuits Against Student Abusers Of Internet2,* RIAA NEWSLETTER, May 26, 2005, *at* http://www.riaa.com /news/newsletter/052605.asp.

[188] *See* Mark Landler, *Fight Against Illegal File Sharing Is Moving Overseas,* N.Y. TIMES ONLINE ARCHIVES, Mar. 31, 2004, *at* http://nytimes.com.

[189] *See MPAA to Begin File-Trading Lawsuits, supra* note 185.

[190] *See* Wired News, May 2, 2003, *at* http://www.wired.com/news/digiwood /0,1412,58698,00.html.

[191] *See* CNET, Nov. 25, 2002, *at* http://news.com.com/2100-1023-971130 .html.

[192] *See UCLA Implements Antipiracy Software,* CHRON. OF HIGHER EDUC., Apr. 27, 2004, *at* http://chronicle.com/free/2004/04/2004042706n.htm.

[193] *See* Mike Langberg, *Bigger Selection Helps AOL's MusicNet, Other Pay Services,* MERCURY NEWS, Feb. 27, 2003, *at* http://www.siliconvalley.com/mld/ siliconvalley/business/technology/personal_technology.html.

[194] *See* Julie Bosman & Tom Zeller Jr., *Warner Bros. To Sell Movies Using the Software of Pirates,* N.Y. TIMES, May 9, 2006, at C3 (May 9, 2006).

[195] The Digital Performance Right in Sound Recordings Act, as amended by the Digital Millennium Copyright Act in 1998, now covers cable and satellite digital audio services, webcasters and future forms of digital transmission. Miscellaneous Provisions, Title IV of the Millennium Copyright Act, H.R. 2281, 105th Cong., 2d Sess. (1998).

[196] Bonneville Int'l Corp. v. Peters, 347 F.3d 485 (3d Cir. 2003).

[197] These criteria and other information about webcasting licenses are available at the Recording Industry Association of America Web site *at* http:// www.riaa.com.

## TRADEMARKS

Trademarks, service marks and trade names, like copyrighted works, are types of intellectual property protected by law. A federal statute defines a trademark as "any word, name, symbol or device or any combination thereof, adopted and used by a manufacturer or merchant to identify its goods and distinguish them from those manufactured or sold by others."[198] The term "service mark" is used for distinctive identifiers for a service rather than a product. A "trade name" is defined by statute as "any name used by a person to identify his or her business or vocation."[199]

"Proctor & Gamble" is the trade name of a business that identifies its products with many different trademarks, including Ivory soap, Tide detergent and Crest toothpaste. A single word — "Sears," for example — may be used for all three purposes: to identify products, to identify services and to identify the company that produces those products and services. The term "trademark" is used here to refer to all three forms of protected property. Examples of trademark symbols are the peacock feathers identifying the National Broadcasting Company and the golden arches of McDonald's. Even a color can be a trademark, the Supreme Court held, if that color has attained a secondary meaning and therefore identifies and distinguishes a particular brand and thus indicates a source.[200]

---

## TERMS

**Trademark:** a word, name, symbol or device, or any combination thereof, to identify products of a manufacturer or merchant and to distinguish them from goods manufactured or sold by others.

**Service mark:** distinctive identifiers for a service rather than a product.

**Trade name:** name used to identify a person's business or vocation.

---

In addition to identifying sources of goods and services, trademarks also function to warrant that goods coming from a particular source — even though consumers may not know the identity of that source — will be of consistent and desirable quality. The instant recognition value of trademarks permits companies to use shortcuts in advertising. Companies recognize the tremendous value of their trademarks and work zealously to protect them from infringement and from falling into generic use.

In addition to the "right of publicity" tort (covered in Chapter 14), celebrities sometimes use trademark law to prevent the use of their name or likeness without permission. For instance, attorneys for the Princess Diana's estate filed a suit against an American firm, the Franklin Mint, for selling an assortment of dolls, plates, jewelry and other items in memory of the former Princess of Wales. The estate was not deterred from its suit by the defendant's pledge that a portion of the proceeds would benefit the late Princess' charities. Golfer Tiger Woods had earlier won a financial payment and a permanent injunction against the Franklin Mint.[201] The National Basketball Association alleged trademark infringement and trademark dilution in obtaining a court order to stop use of an altered NBA logo in advertising for an album by rapper "Cam'ron." The magazine ad including the logo showed a silhouetted basketball player holding a handgun alongside the words "sports, drugs, entertainment." NBA Properties, Inc. objected to the implication that the NBA endorsed violence and drugs.[202]

### Trademark Registration

Registration is not essential for protection from the tort of trademark infringement, but it is recommended in order to give notice that the owner has the right of exclusive right to use the mark. Registration also establishes the date of inception of the use. Federal registration is possible if sales have occurred between at least two states or between the United States and a foreign country. In the Internet environment, trademark owners today seek international protection almost immediately to ensure that they can use their marks in e-commerce without risk.

Although a section of the Lanham Act provides a basis for bringing a federal action for infringement of an unregistered trademark,[203] the owner of an unregistered mark has the burden of showing that the mark is distinctive in order to win the suit. This means convincing a court that the mark is "inherently distinctive" or has become distinctive through extensive advertising and use resulting in "secondary meaning" or "acquired distinctiveness." The plaintiff in a federal lawsuit involving a registered trademark will have already met this burden by virtue of having been granted a federal registration.

A trademark registered with the U.S. Patent and Trademark Office should be accompanied by ® (an R in a circle) as notice. An unregistered trademark may use ™ as a notice. The Patent and Trademark Office provides free public access on its Web site to a trademark database of applications and registrations to conduct searches or obtain other information regarding marks.[204] The fee

---

[198] 15 U.S.C. 1121 (2003).

[199] 15 U.S.C. 1127 (2003).

[200] Qualitex Co. v. Jacobson Prods. Co., 514 U.S. 159 (1995).

[201] *Di's Estate Sues Franklin Mint Over Items; Company Accused of Ignoring Trademarks*, NEWSDAY, May 19, 1998, at A41.

[202] NBA Props. v. Entm't Records LLC., 99 Civ. 2933, 1999 U.S. Dist. LEXIS 7780 (S.D.N.Y. 1999).

[203] Trademark Act of 1946, 15 U.S.C. 1501 et seq. (1946) (popularly known as the Lanham Act).

[204] The URL for the U.S. Patent and Trademark Office is http://www.uspto. gov.

for registering a trademark is $375.

Under the Trademark Revision Act of 1989, a trademark no longer has to be in use before an application for registration is filed. An "intent to use" application gives the applicant six months (or up to three years under some circumstances) to begin using the mark. The mark is not actually registered until it is placed into use, but the "intent to use" provision protects it from infringement by someone else who has neither used the mark previously nor applied for it. Unlike copyright law, which protects a work from the moment it is fixed in tangible form even if it is never published, a trademark isn't protected until it is used in commerce. Further, for protection to continue, commercial use of the mark must continue. If a company ceases to use its trademark, it loses legal protection. Registration is renewable every ten years for as long as the mark remains in use.

State governments, usually through the secretary of state's office, also register trademarks to give notice of valid ownership. State registration is particularly important for companies doing businesses within a single state. Companies marketing goods or services with national or international distribution often forego the state registration process because the marks have federal protection. In today's global economy, all major corporations, especially those with products targeted by counterfeiters, now file their most relevant trademark and copyright registrations with U.S. Customs.

### Protection of Rights

Trademark disputes are frequent. Groups involved in such disputes in recent years include the U.S. Olympic Committee, Nike, Ford Motor Company, Marvel Comics Ltd., Levi Strauss & Co., American Angus Association, Playboy Enterprises, Twin Peaks Productions Inc., Stern's Miracle-Gro Products, Kohler Co., Wachovia Bank & Trust Co. and Walt Disney Co. Legal action generally comes after a trademark is threatened by the likelihood of confusion with another mark or by dilution.

**Likelihood of Confusion.** To determine whether consumers are likely to be confused as to the source, sponsorship or approval of a product, courts consider these factors:
• strength or weakness of the plaintiff's trademark, based on its distinctiveness;
• similarity of the plaintiff's and defendant's trademarks;
• the differences in the products or services being marketed under the same trademark;
• whether the original owner is likely to bridge the gap between the competing products or services;
• presence of actual confusion among consumers;
• whether the defendant acted in good faith in adopting the mark;
• the quality of the defendant's products or services;
• the sophistication of potential consumers;

• the trade channels for the products or services; and
• the similarity of the advertising media.

Like the four factors in the fair use defense in copyright, each of these factors must be examined individually, and no single factor is determinative. And the factors must be applied on a case-by-case basis.

Mead Data Central, for example, sought to prevent Toyota Motor Sales from naming its luxury automobile "Lexus," arguing likelihood of confusion with LEXIS, a computerized legal research service. The court denied the claim on the basis that the general public was unfamiliar with the LEXIS trademark and that LEXIS' primary customers were attorneys and law students who were unlikely to be confused because of their "recognized sophistication."[205] The New York Stock Exchange was unsuccessful in its attempt to stop a gambling casino from using "New York $lot Exchange" as its trademark. The court said the stock exchange mark was not "distinctive" within the meaning of the statute and the public was not likely to be confused.[206]

McDonald's Corporation went to court in Canada trying to prevent Coffee Hut Stores Ltd. from registering "McBeans" as a trademark for coffee, coffee beans, coffee makers and accessories. McDonald's had more than thirty registered trademarks with the prefix "Mc" combined with a food or food-type item. In U.S. courts the company had successfully prevented a variety of firms from using the prefix, ranging from "McSleep" for a motel chain to "McDental" for a dental practice.[207] The Canadian court, however, ruled in favor of Coffee Hut, determining that McDonald's and McBeans were different kinds of businesses and there was no likelihood of confusion.[208]

A federal district court permitted the Network Network, a technology consulting and training firm, to continue using the domain name "www.tnn.com," ruling that it neither infringed on CBS' trademark TNN nor diluted the mark. The court noted that Internet users seeking The Nashville Network program listings were not likely to be confused when they encountered listings of computer network maintenance seminars instead.[209]

Disney's use of Caterpillar equipment in the movie *George of the Jungle 2* sparked a lawsuit. Caterpillar claimed the villains' use of the equipment infringed, tarnished or diluted its trademark. A court disagreed, reasoning that viewers would recognize that men operating the machinery were the villains rather than the

---

[205] Mead Data Cent. v. Toyota Motor Sales, 875 F.2d 1026 (2d Cir. 1989).

[206] New York Stock Exch. v. New York, New York Hotel LLC, 69 F. Supp. 2d 479 (S.D.N.Y. 1999).

[207] Quality Inns Int'l v. McDonald's Corp., 695 F. Supp. 198 (D. Md. 1988); McDonald's Corp. v. Druck and Gerner, D.D.S., P.C., d/b/a McDental, 814 F. Supp. 1127 (N.D.N.Y. 1993).

[208] McDonalds' Corp. v. Coffee Hut Stores, Ltd., No. T-1205-92 (Fed. Ct. of Canada, Trial Div. 1994).

[209] Network Network v. CBS, 2000 U.S. Dist. LEXIS 4751 (C.D. Calif. 2000).

Caterpillar machinery.[210]

Where one company's parody of another's trademark leads to an infringement lawsuit, the likelihood of confusion rationale applies. As one authoritative source puts it: "Some parodies will constitute an infringement, some will not.... [T]here are confusing parodies and non-confusing parodies. All they have in common is an attempt at humor through the use of someone else's trademark. A noninfringing parody is merely amusing, not confusing."[211]

Trademark infringement was charged in the Dr. Seuss' *The Cat in the Hat* case discussed earlier in this chapter, and the parody argument did not protect the defendant publishers. The district court's preliminary injunction, upheld by the appeals court, was based in part on a finding that the good will and reputation associated with *The Cat in the Hat* character and title, the name "Dr. Seuss," and the cat's hat outweighed the expenses incurred by the defendants in publishing their book about the O. J. Simpson trial.[212]

The appeals court in that case cited examples from several cases in which courts have issued injunctions and held, in effect, that poking fun at a trademark is no joke. Examples include a diaper bag with green and red bands and the wording "Gucchi Goo," allegedly poking fun at the well-known Gucci name and design mark[213] and the use of a competing meat sauce of the trademark "A.2" as a pun on the famous "A.1" trademark.[214] The Hard Rock Cafe won a trademark infringement suit against a company using a "Hard Rain" logo. The claim of parody is no defense, the court said, "where the purpose of the similarity is to capitalize on a famous mark's popularity for the defendant's own commercial use."[215]

**Dilution.** Even where there is no likelihood of consumer confusion or no competition or relationship between the goods or services involved, at least half of the states have laws allowing a trademark owner to get an injunction to stop another party from diluting the distinctive quality of a trademark. Generally, this protection is available only to those marks that have acquired strength through long and substantial use or that were particularly distinctive to begin with, at least with a certain group of people, product line or territory.

Trademarks are categorized according to distinctiveness, ranging from coined or fanciful marks at the high end of the spectrum to marks that are merely descriptive at the low end of the continuum. Coined or fanciful marks are those created solely to serve as trademarks. Examples are EXXON and Kodak, which, as created, had no relationships to the products they represent.

At the other end of the trademark distinctiveness continuum are those that are merely descriptive of the quality or characteristic of the goods or service they represent, such as "Handyman" for a carpenter service or "Shine" for a floor polish. Geographic names and surnames used as trademarks are also considered merely descriptive; thus, companies operating within the same location or with the same surname would be free to use them.

A classic example of the potential of a trademark being diluted by having its image tarnished was the sale of a poster reading "Enjoy Cocaine" in flowing red and white script identical to that used in labels and posters for Coca-Cola. A court granted the soft drink company an injunction against sale of the poster.[216] Ringling Brothers' slogan "The Greatest Show on Earth" was found illegally diluted by a car dealer using the slogan "The Greatest Used Car Show on Earth."[217]

The doctrine of trademark dilution became part of federal law with the Federal Trademark Dilution Act (FTDA) of 1995, which protects famous trademarks from subsequent uses that blur the distinctiveness of the mark or tarnish or disparage it, even in the absence of a likelihood of confusion.[218] Before then, such protection was based on state law, which was inconsistent from state to state and not recognized in some states. Contrary to the patent and copyright arena, where federal law controls, the legislative history behind the Dilution Act specifically indicates that the Dilution Act was not meant to preempt existing state dilution statutes.[219] The act also made U.S. law consistent with the international obligations of the United States in the trademark area.

The Trademark Dilution Act provided for these three exemptions from liability:

(1) fair use by competitors in comparative advertising or promotion,

(2) noncommercial use of a mark and

(3) all forms of news reporting and news commentary.

In a case involving Victoria's Secrets stores, the Supreme Court addressed the legal question of whether the act required proof of actual harm to a famous trademark or whether the act was violated if consumers mentally associated a junior user's mark with a famous mark.[220] Circuit courts of appeals had expressed differing views about the "actual harm" issue.[221] The case before the

---

[210] Caterpillar, Inc. v. Walt Disney Co., 68 U.S. P.Q. 2d (BNA) 1461 (C.D. Ill 2003).

[211] McCarthy on Trademarks § 31.38[1], at 31-216 (rev. ed. 1995).

[212] Dr. Seuss Enters. L.P. v. Penguin Books USA, 109 F.3d 1394 (9th Cir. 1997).

[213] Gucci Shops, Inc. v. R.H. Macy & Co., 446 F. Supp. 838 (S.D.N.Y. 1977).

[214] Nabisco Brands v. Kaye, 760 F. Supp. 25 (D. Conn. 1991).

[215] Hard Rock Cafe Licensing Corp. v. Pacific Graphics, 776 F. Supp. 1454, 1462 (W.D. Wash. 1991).

[216] Coca-Cola Co. v. Gemini Rising, Inc., 346 F. Supp. 1183 (E.D.N.Y. 1972).

[217] Ringling Bros. — Barnum & Bailey Combined Shows v. Celozzi-Ettelson Chevrolet, 855 F.2d 480 (7th Cir. 1988).

[218] 15 U.S.C. § 1125 (1995).

[219] See S.L. Serad, Comment: *One Year after Dilution's Entry Into Federal Trademark Law*, 32 Wake Forest L. Rev. 215 (1997).

[220] Moseley v. V Secret Catalogue, 537 U.S. 418 (2003).

[221] See Kellogg Co. v. Exxon Corp., 209 F.3d 562 (6th Cir. 2000); Ringling Bros. — Barnum & Bailey Combined Shows, Inc. v. Utah Div. of Travel Dev., 170 F.3d 449 (4th Cir. 1999).

Supreme Court arose after Victor Moseley and his wife opened a small retail shop in Elizabethtown, Kentucky. Moseley's shop, named "Victor's Secrets," sold adult toys, gag gifts and lingerie. Upon receipt of a letter from the legal staff of the corporation that operated 750 Victoria's Secret stores with 1998 sales exceeding $1.5 billion, the Moseleys changed the name of their store to Victor's Little Secret. At that point Victoria's Secret filed a trademark dilution lawsuit.

The Supreme Court reversed the lower court decisions and remanded the case for further proceedings on the grounds that a mental association between the Moseley store and the famous brand did not automatically cause customers to form a different impression of Victoria's Secret. The Court noted the difficulty of establishing proof of actual dilution of a trademark but refused to accept such difficulty as a reason not to require proof.

**Generic Terms.** A generic term — one that designates the substance or "genus" of the product — cannot be used as a trademark. Anyone is free to use words like "automobile," "car," "soft drink" and "computer." Even if there were only one manufacturer of a particular product and the public associated only that manufacturer with that particular product, the name of that product would still be generic. An airline company's application to register "E-Ticket" was denied because it has become a generic term for computerized travel reservations and tickets. "Log cabin homes" was held generic when used in connection with building designs or kits for log homes. America Online, Inc. was not permitted exclusive use of "You Have Mail" or "Buddy List" as service marks because these are generic terms.

Some trademarks have become generic because of their use — or misuse — by the public. The King-Seeley Thermos Company, for example, originated the term "thermos" for vacuum-insulated containers during the 1920s, but the word fell into general use so that King-Seeley was unsuccessful in its attempts to prevent Aladdin Industries from referring to its vacuum-insulated products as "thermos" bottles.[222] Other examples of former trademarks that are now generic are "aspirin," "cellophane" and "yo yo."

To protect their marks from falling into generic use, trademark owners take steps — like advertisements — to educate the public that the mark should not be used in a generic sense. Companies also write warning letters to journalists and others who used trademarks incorrectly, such as using them as nouns or verbs, as in "Xerox this document" or "make a Xerox." Correct usage for a trademark is as an adjective followed by a noun: Xerox® copier, a Xerox® copy, Kleenex® tissue, Teflon® coating, Jeep® vehicle, Weed Eater® trimmer. Trademarks should be differentiated typographically from words around them by capitalization, italics, boldface, quotation marks or some other special type. As noted earlier in this chapter, registered marks should be indicated with ® (an R

in a circle), and the ™ symbol should follow unregistered trademarks. Plural forms should not be used. "She uses Kleenexes" is incorrect; the correct form is "She uses Kleenex tissues." Trademarks should not take the possessive form, as in "the Jeep's windshield." Instead, "the windshield on a Jeep® sport utility vehicle" is correct usage.

**Cybersquatting and Trademark Protection.** A get-rich-quick scheme of the early Internet era was "cybersquatting" also referred to as "cyberpiracy" — registering a famous trademark as a domain name and then selling the name to the rightful owner at exorbitant prices. Some trademark owners successfully used the Federal Trademark Dilution Act of 1995 to stop others from using their trademarks as Internet domain names.[223] A defendant in several such cases had registered multiple domain names based on trademarks and trade names, including aircanada.com, anaheimstadium.com, australiaopen.com, camdenyards.com, deltaairlines.com, eddiebauer.com, flydelta.com, frenchopen.com, lufthansa.com, neiman-marcus.com, panavision.com, northwestairlines.com and yankeestadium.com.[224]

Trademark owners now have two legal weapons against cyberpiracy: the Anticybersquatting Consumer Protection Act (ACPA)[225] and the Uniform Domain-Name Dispute Resolution Policy (UDRP).[226] The anticybersquatting legislation affords remedies, including injunction, actual damages and profits or statutory damages, to trademark owners who can show: (1) the mark was "distinctive" or "famous" at the time the accused cybersquatter registered the domain name, and (2) the accused acted with "a bad faith" intent to profit from the mark. The act lists nine factors to help courts determine "bad faith intent." The UDRP is a policy adopted by the Internet Corporation for Assigned Names and Numbers. The World Intellectual Property Organization (WIPO) established a panel that uses this policy for mediating domain name disputes.

During the first six months of operation, the new forum for domain name disputes received 727 cases involving 1,067 domain names.[227] Among many trademark owners who immediately launched suits when ACPA became law were Harvard University, the National Football League, *Teen* Magazine, New Zealand's America's Cup team and celebrities Courtney Love and John Tesh. The

---

222 King-Seeley Thermos Co. v. Aladdin Indus., 321 F.2d 577 (2d Cir. 1963).

223 For a discussion of these cases and others arising out of the act during the first year after its passage, *see* Serad, *supra* note 212. For information about various methods a company can utilize to curb Internet name poaching, *see* Stacy B. Sterling, Comment: *New Age Bandits in Cyberspace: Domain Names Held Hostage on the Internet*, 17 Loy. L. A. Ent. L. Rev. 733 (1997).

224 *See* Panavision Int'l, L.P. v. Toeppen, 141 F.3d 1316 (9th Cir. 1998); Intermatic, Inc. v. Toeppen, 947 F. Supp. 1227 (N.D. Ill. 1996).

225 15 U.S.C. 1125(d) (2002).

226 As approved by the Internet Corporation for Assigned Names and Numbers (ICANN), Oct. 24, 1999.

227 *See* Jeri Clausing, *In New Forum for Domain Name Disputes, Trademark Holders Dominate*, N.Y. Times on the Web Cyber L. J. (May 19, 2000), *available at* http://www.nytimes.com/library/tech/00/05/cyber/cyberlaw/.

World Wrestling Federation was the first complainant to use ICANN's dispute resolution policy, successfully showing bad faith on the part of a man who registered "worldwrestling-federation.com" and then offered to sell it to the WWF for $1,000.[228] The Uniform Domain-Name Dispute Resolution Policy specifies no remedies beyond transfer of the domain name to the trademark holder, but it is a less expensive and faster process than federal litigation under ACPA.

An early WIPO complaint that received extensive media coverage involved the Rev. Jerry Falwell, who sought to have a Web site stripped of its domain names jerryfalwell.com and jerryfallwell.com. The noncommercial site parodied the widely known minister, particularly his post-September 11, 2001, comments blaming the terrorists attacks on some segments of the population whose religious views differed from his own. The WIPO mediation panel ruled against Falwell because he failed to demonstrate that his name had ever been used as a trademark to label particular goods or services. Therefore, the panel considered the use of his name in a noncommercial Web site to be legitimate fair use commentary.[229] The WIPO panel noted that Falwell might have remedy under a tort claim or under the Anticybersquatting Consumer Protection Act, which expressly provides for protection of personal names.[230]

## SUMMARY

Intellectual property laws both hinder and help the mass media by providing companies an economic incentive to create material, but at the same time preventing the media from publishing material owned by others. The Copyright Act protects original works of authorship fixed in any tangible medium of expression, now known or later developed, from which they can be perceived, reproduced or otherwise communicated, either directly or with the aid of a machine or device. A key copyright principle is that expression or style, not ideas or facts, is protected.

Copyright owners have an exclusive bundle of rights that may be exercised separately or as a package: (1) to reproduce the work in copies or phonorecords, (2) to prepare derivative works, (3) to distribute copies or phonorecords, (4) to perform the work publicly and (5) to display the work publicly. The fair use doctrine and compulsory licensing limit these rights somewhat.

In determining whether copying constitutes fair use or infringement, courts apply four factors on a case-by-case basis. Even if the commercial value of the original is unharmed, secondary works that draw heavily from originals aren't likely to qualify as fair use unless they add significant transformative value to the original.

Publication is no longer essential to copyright protection. Works fixed in tangible form are "born protected." The duration of a copyright varies according to when a work was created or published, but current law protects works during the lifetime of the owner plus seventy years. Material not protected by copyright falls into the public domain, available for all to use without authorization.

Each new medium for fixing works in tangible form — photography, moving pictures, sound recordings, digital imaging — and each new reproduction and transmission method — radio, television, photocopying machines, VCRs, satellites, fax machines, computers, CDs, DVDs, the Internet — challenge lawmakers and judges to amend or interpret copyright law. Introduction of new technology generally outpaces law and policy adaptations. Internet-based software that allows users to bypass copyright owners and duplicate music, movies or other digital files currently pose multimillion dollar copyright concerns and legal questions. In addition to continued legal action against alleged infringers, the movie and music industries' latest tactic is to sue individuals who download online material without paying for it.

In addition to copyrighted works, other legally protected intellectual property includes trademarks, service marks and trade names. Trademarks identify sources of goods and services and warrant that goods coming from a particular source will be of consistent and desirable quality. Service marks are distinctive identifiers for a service, and a trade name is any name used by a person to identify his or her business or vocation.

## FOR ADDITIONAL READING

Albert, G. Peter, Jr. *Intellectual Property Law in Cyberspace.* Washington, D.C.: The Bureau of National Affairs, Inc., 1999.

Branscomb, Anne Wells. *Who Owns Information?* New York: Basic Books, 1994.

*Copyright Law Symposium.* New York: Columbia University Press. Published annually. (Award-winning research papers in a program sponsored by the American Society of Composers, Authors and Publishers (ASCAP)).

Lee, Lewis C. & J. Scott Davidson, eds. *Intellectual Property for the Internet.* New York: Wiley Law Publications, 1997 (updated with pocket parts).

Lessig, Lawrence. *Free Culture: How Big Media Uses Technology and the Law to Lock Down Culture and Control Creativity.* New York: Penguin, 2004.

Nimmer, Melville B. & David Nimmer. *Nimmer on Copyright: A Treatise on the Law of Literary, Musical and Artistic Property, and the Protection of Ideas.* New York: M. Bender, 1978. (Looseleaf for updating.)

Patent and Trademark Office. *Basic Facts about Registering a Trademark.* Washington, D.C.: U.S. Department of Commerce.

Patry, William F. *Copyright Law and Practice,* 3 Vols. Washington, D.C.: The Bureau of National Affairs, Inc., 1994 (1997, 1998 sup-

---

[228] World Wrestling Fed'n Entm't, Inc. v. Michael Bosman, Case No. D99-0001 (WIPO 2000).

[229] Falwell v. Cohn, WIPO Case No. D2002-0184 (June 3, 2002), *available at* http://www.citizen.org/documents/FalwellDecision.pdf.

[230] *Id.* at 5.

plements).

Patry, William F. *The Fair Use Privilege in Copyright Law.* Washington, D.C.: The Bureau of National Affairs, Inc., 1995.

Thorne, Robert & John David Vlera, eds. *Entertainment, Publishing and the Arts Handbook.* New York: Clark Boardman Callaghan (annual).

U.S. Copyright Office, *Copyright Law of the United States of America,* http://www.copyright.gov/title17/.

# 8

# Regulating Advertising

*By Karla K. Gower*

---

 **Headnote Questions**

- *What is commercial speech?*
- *How has constitutional protection for commercial speech changed over the years?*
- *Why doesn't commercial speech get the same First Amendment protection as other forms of speech?*
- *What is the four-part test courts use to determine the constitutionality of government restrictions on commercial speech?*
- *What is the Federal Trade Commission's role in regulating advertising?*
- *How does the Federal Trade Commission define deceptive advertising?*
- *What remedies can the Federal Trade Commission use to stop deceptive ads from being disseminated?*
- *What other remedies are available to prevent the dissemination of deceptive ads?*
- *What constitutes a lottery or contest?*
- *How does the advertising industry regulate itself?*

---

Advertising is everywhere in today's society: on television, the Internet, billboards, t-shirts and even fast-food wrappers. And it is used to sell everything, from the latest movie to the next president. Despite its apparent ubiquity, advertising is a highly regulated field. It is regulated at the federal level most directly by the Federal Trade Commission, but also by agencies such as the Food and Drug Administration and the Securities and Exchange Commission. Similar agencies at the state level also regulate advertising. Although advertising now receives some protection from government restrictions *via* the First Amendment, it was not always the case.

The U.S. Supreme Court first considered whether advertising was speech and therefore protected by the First Amendment in 1942.[1] At that time, the Court declared that advertising did not warrant First Amendment protection, finding that the "Constitution imposes no ... restraint on government as respects purely commercial advertising."[2]

But over the years, the Court has whittled away at the commercial speech doctrine until today advertising enjoys some protection under the First Amendment on the basis that "the free flow of commercial information is indispensable" to people's lives and their ability to be informed consumers.[3]

But the extent of protection remains a controversial issue. The Supreme Court has defined commercial speech as either speech that does "no more than propose a commercial transaction" or as expression "solely motivated by the desire for profit."[4] Scholars debate the value of such speech, with some taking a paternalistic stance, arguing that consumers need protection from unscrupulous advertisers and therefore commercial speech ought not to receive the protection it does. Others argue that consumers are capable of making their own decisions based on information provided to them and, therefore, commercial speech ought to receive even greater First Amendment protection. The Court itself vacillates between expanding and contracting the protection although

---

[1] Valentine v. Chrestensen, 316 U.S. 52 (1942).

[2] *Id.* at 54.

[3] Virginia State Bd. of Pharmacy v. Virginia Citizens Consumer Council, 425 U.S. 748, 765 (1976).

[4] Pittsburgh Press Co. v. Pittsburgh Comm'n on Human Relation et al., 413 U.S. 376, 385 (1973); Dun & Bradstreet v. Greenmoss Builders, Inc., 472 U.S. 749, 762 (1985).

overall expansion has ruled the day most recently.

## CONSTITUTIONAL PROTECTION
## FOR COMMERCIAL SPEECH

As indicated, one of the Supreme Court's earliest forays into the area of commercial speech came in 1942 with *Valentine v. Chrestensen.*[5] Chrestensen owned an old Navy submarine, which he moored at a state pier in the East River in New York City. He distributed handbills to pedestrians advertising tours of the submarine. City police told him to stop giving out the fliers because he was violating the city's sanitary code, which prohibited the distribution of handbills for commercial advertising. The ordinance only allowed handbills providing information or public protest to be distributed on city streets. Being resourceful, Chrestensen decided to print a new batch of handbills. On one side, the flier contained a message criticizing the City Dock Department for refusing him wharfage facilities at a city pier; the other side contained the original information promoting tours of his submarine, but without mention of the fee for the tour. Police officials said he was still in violation of the ordinance. He sued the police commissioner, seeking to enjoin the police from interfering with his distribution of advertising and claiming that the Constitution protected him.

The Supreme Court upheld the city's ordinance, saying it did not violate Chrestensen's freedom of speech or press. The Court said previous decisions made it clear that the streets are proper places for expressing opinion and spreading information, but that governments could regulate purely commercial advertising. The Court dismissed Chrestensen's political protest as an obvious attempt to dodge the restriction.[6]

The Court didn't soften its position on constitutional protection for advertising until 1964 with *New York Times Co. v. Sullivan.*[7] That case, known mainly for its contribution to libel law, involved a full-page, paid, political advertisement for a civil rights organization published in the *New York Times.* The ad criticized government officials in Montgomery, Alabama, for their handling of civil rights protests in the city and sought financial support for a civil rights organization. Lawyers for plaintiff L.B. Sullivan, the Montgomery police commissioner criticized in the ad, had urged the Court to dismiss the case on the grounds that advertising was not protected by the First Amendment. The Court refused to do so, indicating that because this was an editorial ad with a political message, it warranted protection. The Court left open the question whether purely commercial advertising would be protected.

Nine years later, in *Pittsburgh Press Co. v. Pittsburgh Commission on Human Relations,* the Court suggested that it might be willing to give constitutional protection to "an ordinary commer-

cial proposal," although the case in question did not involve one.[8] The case centered on the *Pittsburgh Press'* help-wanted ads. The newspaper organized job listings into sex-designated columns such as "Male Help Wanted," "Female Help Wanted." The Pittsburgh Commission on Human Relations, a governmental body, ordered the newspaper to stop segregating the ads this way. The practice, the commission said, violated a city ordinance prohibiting employment discrimination — and the aiding of such discrimination — on the basis of race, religion, ancestry or sex. The newspaper challenged the government's interference in its editorial practices on First Amendment grounds.

In rejecting the newspaper's argument, the Supreme Court said the help-wanted ads resembled the ad in *Valentine* rather than the ad in *Sullivan* because a help-wanted ad "is no more than a proposal of possible employment. The advertisements are thus classic examples of commercial speech."[9] That was not, however, the reason the First Amendment did not protect the ads in this case. The Court held that the commission was correct in ordering the newspaper to stop segregating the ads because segregation aided in illegal hiring practices. "We have no doubt that a newspaper constitutionally could be forbidden to publish a want ad proposing the sale of narcotics or soliciting prostitutes" because of the illegal nature of the activities being advertised, the Court wrote.[10] The Court noted, however, that there might be some First Amendment protection for an advertisement for an ordinary commercial proposal not tainted by illegality.[11]

Two years later, the question of the legality of the activity advertised arose again. In *Bigelow v. Virginia,* the managing editor of the *Virginia Weekly* had been convicted of violating a state law prohibiting the advertising or soliciting of abortions.[12] Bigelow had published an ad for an abortion referral service in New York. The ad pointed out that, although abortions were illegal in Virginia, they were legal in New York. The ad promoted the services of the Women's Pavilion in helping women gain access to accredited hospitals and clinics at low costs.[13]

The Supreme Court struck down the Virginia statute. The activities advertised were legal in New York, and Virginia could not keep from its residents information about legal activities in other states, the Court held. It pointed to the *Pittsburgh Press* case as standing for "the principle that commercial advertising enjoys a degree of First Amendment protection."[14]

Of course, the ad at issue in *Bigelow* was not purely commercial speech, as in *Valentine.* It told readers about legal abortion services in New York, which was information of clear public interest.

---

[5] 316 U.S. 52 (1942).
[6] *Id.* at 55.
[7] 376 U.S. 254 (1964).

---

[8] 413 U.S. 376, 389 (1973).
[9] *Id.*
[10] *Id.* at 388.
[11] *Id.* at 389.
[12] 421 U.S. 809 (1975).
[13] *Id.* at 811-14.
[14] *Id.* at 821.

*Bigelow* came just two years after the Court's 1973 ruling in *Roe v. Wade* that abortion was part of the constitutionally protected right of privacy.[15] The Court said Bigelow's First Amendment interests "coincided with the constitutional interests of the general public's."[16] Thus the Court was willing to protect political ads and ads with information promoting legal activities that were in the public interest.

### Expanding Protection for Purely Commercial Speech

The Court addressed the issue of First Amendment protection for purely commercial advertisements a year after *Bigelow* in *Virginia State Board of Pharmacy v. Virginia Citizens Consumer Council*.[17] A Virginia statute prohibited licensed pharmacists from advertising the price of prescription drugs. The state pharmacy board, which regulates pharmacists, said the restriction was necessary for several reasons. Without the ban on ads, pharmacists would have to participate in aggressive price competition, which would distract them from their important jobs as dispensers of drugs, possibly endangering consumers' health and harming the pharmacists' status as professionals. The pharmacy board also said the pressure of competition created by advertising might push some conscientious pharmacists out of business, and that pharmacists would pass advertising costs on to consumers. In addition, advertising would encourage consumers to shop around for the best prices rather than develop a trusting relationship with one pharmacist.

Among those challenging the advertising regulation was the non-profit Virginia Citizens Consumer Council, a group that represented many elderly and chronically ill people. The group argued that permitting the advertising would help consumers of prescription drugs. The group further contended that the First Amendment secures for prescription drug consumers the right to *receive* information from pharmacists, which would allow them to find the drugs they need at the best prices.

The Supreme Court agreed and recognized for the first time that the First Amendment protects purely commercial advertising. The Court said a consumer's interest in commercial information "may be as keen, if not keener by far, than his interest in the day's most urgent political debate."[18] The restriction hurt the sick, poor and elderly the hardest because much of their income went to purchasing drugs, and drug prices in Virginia varied widely from store to store, even within the same town or city.[19]

In addition, the Court reasoned, purely commercial speech contributes to public decision-making in a democracy. In a free-enterprise system, individuals allocate much of their overall resources by making many private economic decisions. "It is a matter of public interest that those decisions ... be intelligent and well informed," the Court held. "To this end, the free flow of commercial information is indispensable." The information was also crucial to the development of intelligent opinions about how to reform or regulate the economic system.[20]

The Court noted, however, that the government was still free to regulate ads that are false, misleading, deceptive or that promote illegal products or services.[21] In a footnote, the Court explained why "commonsense differences" between commercial speech and other, protected types of speech made government regulation of untruthful commercial speech more tolerable. First, advertisers may easily verify their commercial speech because they disseminate information about their own product or service and, therefore, know more about it than anyone else. In contrast, reporters and political commentators must rely on other sources as the basis for the information they distribute. Second, commercial speech is hardier than other types of speech because it is so necessary for generating profits that regulation would not chill an advertiser's speech.[22]

A year later, the Court used its decision in *Virginia State Board of Pharmacy* to invalidate an advertising regulation imposed upon another category of professionals: attorneys. *Bates v. State Bar of Arizona* began when two lawyers violated an Arizona state bar regulation that prohibited lawyers from advertising prices for legal services in the mass media.[23] The attorneys had advertised their prices for routine legal services, such as uncontested divorces and name changes, in a local newspaper.

The state bar argued, among other things, that advertising would make lawyers less dignified and professional, that it would stir up unnecessary lawsuits, and that it would result in higher costs for legal services. The Supreme Court rejected all of those arguments. People who have a legitimate need for legal services often do not know where to turn for advice or are afraid that legal services will cost too much, the Court held. Advertising could help these people.[24] The Court also noted that there is nothing inherently misleading about lawyers advertising the cost of routine legal services.[25]

In a second case involving advertising by attorneys, *Ohralik v. Ohio State Bar Association*, the Court clearly indicated the lower level of constitutional protection commercial speech receives.[26] Upholding the punishment of a lawyer who had personally solicited business from two victims of a car accident, the Court

[15] 410 U.S. 113 (1973).

[16] 421 U.S. at 822.

[17] 425 U.S. 748 (1976).

[18] *Id.* at 763.

[19] *Id.* at 754.

[20] *Id.* at 765.

[21] *Id.* at 771.

[22] *Id.* at 772 n.24.

[23] 433 U.S. 350 (1977).

[24] *Id.* at 370.

[25] *Id.* at 372.

[26] 436 U.S. 447 (1978).

noted that its decisions have "afforded commercial speech a limited measure of protection, commensurate with its subordinate position in the scale of First Amendment values, while allowing modes of regulation that might be impermissible in the realm of noncommercial expression."[27]

### The Central Hudson Test

A test for determining the extent of the protection for commercial speech came in 1980 with *Central Hudson Gas & Electric Co. v. Public Service Commission of New York.*[28] Central Hudson, and other electric utilities, had been promoting the use of electricity, a practice New York's public service commission said was contrary to the then national policy of conserving energy. The commission, which regulates utilities in the state, ordered electric utilities to stop the advertising. Central Hudson challenged the order as a violation of its First Amendment rights.

The Court enunciated a four-part test for determining when government restrictions of commercial speech are permissible, and applying the test to the case at hand, struck down the New York restriction.[29] Under the test, courts must consider each of the following:

(1) Is the ad true and not misleading, and does it advertise a legal product or service? The New York Public Service Commission did not claim that the advertising at issue was misleading, deceptive or for any illegal activity, so the analysis continued to the second question.

(2) Is the asserted governmental interest substantial? If the ad satisfies the first prong of the test, the burden of proof shifts to the government to show that it has a substantial interest in protecting the health, safety, morals and aesthetics of the public. Here the government's interest in energy conservation was certainly substantial, the Court said.

(3) Does the regulation directly advance the governmental interest? The Court found that there must be an immediate connection between advertising and electrical consumption, otherwise the company would not have been advertising. Therefore, a restriction on advertising would reduce electrical consumption, advancing the government's interest.

(4) Is the regulation no more extensive than necessary to serve the governmental interest? The Court found the regulation to be more extensive than necessary because it banned ads even for electric services or devices that were energy efficient.

The *Central Hudson* test was seen as a positive step toward protecting commercial speech from unreasonable government regulation. But six years later, the Court's application of the test in *Posadas de Puerto Rico Associates v. Tourism Company of*

*Puerto Rico* revealed the test's potential to be used to validate government restrictions on advertising rather than to protect such speech.[30] The case involved a ban on casino ads in Puerto Rico. The island had legalized gambling to promote tourism but banned casino ads because it did not want to encourage Puerto Ricans to gamble. A casino operator who was fined for violating the advertising ban sued, challenging its constitutionality.

Applying the *Central Hudson* test to the regulation, the Court found that the ads concerned a lawful activity and were not in any way misleading. The justices then moved to the second prong of the test. Reducing the demand for casino gambling by local residents, they held, was a substantial government interest because gambling was associated with increased crime and disruption of moral and cultural patterns.[31] The regulation also passed the third prong of the test. The Court said it was reasonable to assume that ads aimed at residents would increase the demand among those residents for casino gambling. And finally, because the Puerto Rican government could have legally banned casino gambling entirely but took the less drastic step of only banning ads for casino gambling, the regulation was no more extensive than necessary, the fourth prong.[32]

Justices William Brennan and John Paul Stevens wrote vigorous dissents. Brennan argued that government should not be allowed to suppress truthful commercial speech about a legal activity.[33] He questioned whether the Puerto Rican government truly believed that casino gambling would result in serious harms, because the government had legalized casino gambling and residents were allowed to patronize casinos. He also wrote that it was unclear whether banning casino advertisements would reduce crime and that there were much better ways to address the governmental interest, such as vigorously enforcing criminal laws.[34] Stevens wrote that the First Amendment does not permit the discriminatory nature of the ad ban, which singled out Puerto Rican residents for disfavored treatment.[35]

*Posadas* appeared to erode protection for commercial speech, and three years later that erosion continued in *Board of Trustees, State University of New York v. Fox.*[36] At issue was a regulation by the State University of New York prohibiting private commercial activities in university facilities. The university said the regulation sought to prevent commercial exploitation of students, maintain an educational atmosphere on campus, promote student safety and protect residential tranquillity. A representative of a housewares company who demonstrated the company's products in a dorm room was arrested for violating the regulation.

---

[27] *Id.* at 456.

[28] 447 U.S. 557 (1980).

[29] *Id.* at 566-70.

[30] 478 U.S. 328 (1986).

[31] *Id.* at 341.

[32] *Id.* at 345-46.

[33] *Id.* at 349 (Brennan, J., dissenting).

[34] *Id.* at 353-56 (Brennan, J., dissenting).

[35] *Id.* at 360 (Stevens, J., dissenting).

[36] 492 U.S. 469 (1989).

After working through the *Central Hudson* test, the Court clarified the meaning of the fourth part of the test, which asks whether a regulation is no more extensive than necessary to serve the governmental interest. This part seemed to inquire whether the regulation is "absolutely the least severe that will achieve the desired effect."[37] But, the Court said, it really asks whether there is a reasonable fit between the interest and the regulation, which the Court explained as "a fit that is not necessarily perfect, but reasonable" or "narrowly tailored to achieve the desired objective."[38] Thus, the "not more than necessary" requirement was changed to "a reasonable fit," making it easier for a government regulation to survive constitutional challenge.

### Recent Cases and Trends

Since those cases, however, the Court has strengthened the *Central Hudson* test, especially the third and fourth prongs. In a series of cases decided in the 1990s, the Supreme Court boosted constitutional protection for commercial speech by requiring solid proof to support government claims that regulations satisfied the *Central Hudson* test.

In 1993, the Court struck down a Cincinnati ordinance that banned free-standing commercial news racks, while permitting newspaper news racks. The Court held in *Cincinnati v. Discovery Network* that although commercial speech does not warrant the same level of protection as noncommercial speech does, the ordinance placed too much emphasis on the distinction between the two kinds of speech.[39] The justices found a lack of reasonable fit between the city's purpose of promoting the safety and aesthetics of its public streets and the banning of commercial, but not noncommercial, news racks.[40]

In the same year, the Court addressed the issue of commercial speech by professionals. *Edenfield v. Fane* concerned Florida's ban on in-person, uninvited solicitation of clients by certified public accountants.[41] According to the Florida Board of Accountancy, the ban helped protect consumers from fraud by CPAs and helped maintain CPA independence in auditing businesses and attesting to the financial statements of businesses. A Florida-based CPA, who had practiced in New Jersey where solicitation was allowed, claimed the ban violated his free speech rights.

The Court, in striking down the ban, noted that the board had presented "no studies that suggest personal solicitation of prospective business clients by CPAs creates the dangers of fraud, overreaching, or compromised independence that the Board claims to fear."[42] In fact, research indicated that the dangers of compromised independence were not associated with uninvited solicitation of new business, but with long-term service of clients.[43]

But two years later, the Court upheld a rule prohibiting lawyers from direct-mail solicitations to personal injury victims and their families for thirty days after the victims' accidents or disasters. In *Florida Bar v. Went For It Inc.*, a lawyer, who said he routinely sent such solicitations within thirty days and wanted to continue doing so, challenged the rule as an abridgment of his free speech rights.[44] The bar association argued in support of the rule that it served a substantial interest in protecting the privacy and peace of mind of personal injury victims and their relatives.

The Court noted that attorney advertising is commercial speech that deserves some First Amendment protection, but a public opinion study revealed that adult Floridians generally "'have negative feelings about those attorneys who use direct mail advertising.'"[45] Therefore, the Court held, the Florida Bar rule targeted a substantial state interest.

Although the Court has a tendency to uphold restrictions on lawyers' commercial speech, it is more expansive when it comes to what is known as vice advertising — advertising for alcohol, tobacco and gambling. In the same year that the Court upheld the Florida Bar rule on commercial speech, it struck down a federal provision that prohibited brewers from indicating alcohol content on beer labels. In *Rubin v. Coors Brewing Co.*, the Court found that the regulation failed the third and fourth prongs of the *Central Hudson* test.[46] The government asserted that allowing alcohol content on beer labels would lead to strength wars among brewers, which would in turn lead to an increase in alcoholism. The Court held that although the government had a substantial interest in preventing strength wars, the regulation did not advance that interest in a "direct and material way."[47] The federal government allowed the labels of distilled spirits to disclose alcohol content, required the labels of some wine bottles to do so and did not prohibit brewers from indicating alcohol content in advertisements.[48] In none of those cases did a strength war ensue. In addition, the regulation failed the fourth prong of the *Central Hudson* test because less intrusive alternatives, such as limiting the alcohol content of beer, existed.[49]

The Court continued its protection for vice advertising in *44 Liquormart v. Rhode Island*.[50] Rhode Island had a law that for-

---

[37] *Id.* at 480.

[38] *Id.*

[39] 507 U.S. 410 (1993).

[40] *Id.* at 417.

[41] 507 U.S. 761 (1993).

[42] *Id.* at 771.

[43] *Id.* at 772.

[44] 515 U.S. 618 (1995).

[45] *Id.* at 626-27 (quoting Magid Associates, Attitudes & Opinions Toward Direct Mail Advertising by Attorneys (Dec. 1987), Summary of Record, App. C(4), at 6).

[46] 514 U.S. 476 (1995) (striking down 27 U.S.C. § 205(e)(2)(1995)).

[47] *Id.* at 490.

[48] *Id.* at 488.

[49] *Id.* at 490.

[50] 517 U.S. 484 (1996).

bade the advertisement of prices of alcoholic beverages. The state claimed that the ban served the substantial government interest of reducing alcohol consumption among its residents. If alcohol retailers could advertise their prices, prices would fall and consumption would rise, the state reasoned.

The Court unanimously rejected Rhode Island's ban on the price advertising of alcohol. Because the state presented no evidentiary support, the Court said it could not agree that the ban would significantly advance the state's interest in promoting temperance.[51] Plus, the ban was more extensive than necessary because alternative methods, such as educational campaigns or increased sales taxes, would be more likely to meet the goal of promoting temperance.[52]

In making the ruling, the Court indicated that its earlier decision in *Posadas* was incorrect. "*Posadas* erroneously performed the First Amendment analysis," the Court wrote. The government "does not have the broad discretion to suppress truthful, non-misleading information for paternalistic purposes that the *Posadas* majority was willing to tolerate."[53] Thus, the Court said it would apply a "more stringent constitutional review" when the government completely suppresses truthful expression.[54]

The Court's pronouncement, however, did not mean a change in the *Central Hudson* test. The majority continues to apply the test, seeing no reason to change it. In *Greater New Orleans Broadcasting v. United States*, a 1999 case, the Court found that the federal regulatory regime governing the broadcasting of advertising by privately operated casinos was "so pierced by exemptions and inconsistencies that the Government cannot hope to exonerate it."[55] A group of broadcasters from New Orleans challenged a federal law banning broadcast advertising for casinos.[56] The broadcasters wanted to be able to air ads for private commercial casinos that are legal in Louisiana and Mississippi.

The Court had earlier, in the case of *United States v. Edge Broadcasting*, upheld a similar federal provision prohibiting the broadcasting of lottery advertising in non-lottery states on the basis that the stations were located in a state in which gambling was not legal and that states had a right to discourage gambling by choosing to not have a lottery.[57] But this time, the Court was unanimous in its decision to strike the law. The Court first noted that no one contested that the ads were truthful and for a legal activity.[58] The two interests the federal government identified as justifying the federal law were reducing the social costs of gambling and assisting states that restrict or prohibit gambling.[59] While the Court was willing to accept that these two interests were substantial, it pointed out that the federal government had shown that those interests were in some cases outweighed by the economic benefits of gambling because the government approved of casinos operated by Indian tribes and exempted state-run lotteries and casinos from federal gambling laws.[60]

The Court rejected the argument that the law directly advanced the governmental interest in reducing the social costs of gambling by reducing the demand for it. "While it is no doubt fair to assume that more advertising would have some impact on overall demand for gambling, it is also reasonable to assume that much of that advertising would merely channel gamblers to one casino rather than another," the Court wrote.[61] It said the government had failed to connect broadcast advertising for casinos to the ill effects of gambling. In conclusion, the Court said that speakers and audiences, rather than government, should be allowed to evaluate accurate and non-misleading information about legal conduct.[62]

In *Lorillard Tobacco Co. v. Reilly*, the majority held that the broad sweep of Massachusetts regulations on outdoor and point-of-sale tobacco advertisements indicated the Attorney General had not "'carefully calculate[d] the costs and benefits associated with the burden on speech imposed' by the regulations," as required by the fourth prong of *Central Hudson*.[63] Among its regulations, Massachusetts banned all tobacco advertising that could be seen within 1,000 feet of schools and playgrounds.

The Court found that although the intent of the restrictions was to protect children from the influence of tobacco advertising, the regulations also limited the tobacco industry's First Amendment right to communicate with adults about legal products. They banned outdoor advertising but also advertising inside a store if visible from outside and restricted advertisements of all sizes. Thus, the regulations were unconstitutional because they covered too much communication.

The Court has also struck down provisions of the federal Food and Drug Administration Modernization Act of 1997 that precluded pharmacists from advertising compounded drugs.[64] Under the FDAMA, compounded drugs – those custom-made for patients by pharmacists – did not have to comply with the FDA's drug approval process if providers refrained from advertising or promoting them. This restriction sought to balance the government's interests in protecting public health through the FDA approval process for manufactured drugs and continuing to permit pharmacists to compound drugs that had not been tested for

---

[51] *Id.* at 505.

[52] *Id.* at 507.

[53] *Id.* at 509-10.

[54] *Id.* at 508.

[55] 527 U.S. 173, 190 (1999).

[56] 18 U.S.C. § 1304 (1996).

[57] 509 U.S. 418 (1993).

[58] 527 U.S. at 184.

[59] *Id.* at 185.

[60] *Id.* at 186-87.

[61] *Id.* at 189.

[62] *Id.* at 195.

[63] 533 U.S. 525, 561 (2001) (quoting Cincinnati v. Discovery Network, 507 U.S. 410, 417 (1993)).

[64] Thompson v. Western States Medical Ctr., 535 U.S. 357 (2002).

safety or efficacy. After a group of licensed pharmacies challenged the limitation as a violation of their free-speech rights, the Supreme Court ruled in a 5-4 decision that the restriction was too broad. While acknowledging that protecting the integrity of the FDA's drug approval process was a substantial interest, the Court held that the interest could have been advanced by other means that did not include restrictions on speech. "We have made clear that if the Government could achieve its interests in a manner that does not restrict speech, or that restricts less speech, the Government must do so," the Court wrote.[65]

Over the years since it first enunciated a test for commercial speech cases, the Court has expanded protection for such speech but faced so far with regulations that do not pass the *Central Hudson* analysis, it has seen no need to depart from the test. However, the Court is deeply divided over the test, with some justices calling for equal protection for noncommercial speech and truthful, non-misleading commercial speech.

## REGULATION OF DECEPTIVE ADVERTISING

Commercial speech can be regulated at both the federal and state levels, but the primary regulatory body is the Federal Trade Commission.

### *The Federal Trade Commission*

The Federal Trade Commission was established by Congress in 1914.[66] The five commissioners are nominated by the president and confirmed by the Senate for terms of seven years. No more than three commissioners may be of the same political party. The FTC is responsible for administering a variety of federal statutes that "promote competition and protect the public from unfair and deceptive acts and practices in the advertising and marketing of goods and services."[67] Ten regional offices are responsible for enforcing regulations, investigating complaints and educating the public.[68] The FTC focuses on national advertising, referring purely local concerns to state and local government agencies. While the FTC staff itself monitors national ad campaigns for potentially deceptive claims, letters from consumers or businesses, Congressional inquiries, or news stories on consumer or economic topics may also trigger FTC investigations.

The FTC is responsible for protecting consumers from both unfair and deceptive advertising.

Unfairness is defined by the Commission as an act or practice that "causes or is likely to cause substantial injury to consumers, which is not reasonably avoidable by consumers themselves and

not outweighed by countervailing benefits to consumers or to competition."[69] Unfairness arises more often in a business' relationship with a consumer than in advertising; for example, a company may be found to have acted unfairly if it coerces a customer to buy expensive unnecessary parts or services.

The FTC is more concerned with deception than with unfairness. The Commission defines a deceptive ad as one that contains a material representation, omission or practice that is likely to mislead a consumer acting reasonably under the circumstances. The definition, then, has three key parts:

• *The representation, omission or practice must be material.* "Material" means the representation, omission or practice "is likely to affect the consumer's conduct or decision with regard to a product or service." Types of material statements include those about the health, safety, cost, quality, durability, performance or efficacy of a product or service.[70] A claim such as "You will save 50 percent with our long distance service" would be material because it is a statement about price that is likely to influence a consumer's purchasing decision. Express claims as to the attributes of a product are always considered material. Ads involving health and safety are usually presumed to be material, as are those containing information that pertains to the central characteristic of the product. A Colgate-Palmolive claim that its Rapid Shave shaving cream was so good it could be used to shave sandpaper is an example of a material representation. In the TV commercial, Rapid Shave was apparently spread on sandpaper and then a few seconds later shaved off. The FTC complained that the ad was deceptive and a material misrepresentation because it was not sandpaper, but rather sand sprinkled on glass. Colgate-Palmolive argued that the product really could shave sandpaper if left on long enough, but that on TV, sand and paper were the same color. Glass had to be used to get the proper visual impression. The Supreme Court agreed with the FTC that this was a material misrepresentation.[71]

Not all fake demonstrations will result in an allegation of material misrepresentation. Only those that are used to suggest a product attribute will be. For example, a fake television could be used in an ad for satellite TV service because no claim about the quality of the television is being made. A fake television could not be used to advertise the television itself, especially if the ad were extolling the virtues of the sharp, clear quality of the screen image.

• *The representation, omission or practice must be likely to mislead.* The advertisement does not have to actually mislead or cause deception so long as it appears likely to do so. A deceptive statement may mislead expressly (e.g., "Using Listerine prevents colds") or by implication, in which the ad suggests that the prod-

---

[65] *Id.* at 371-72.

[66] 15 U.S.C. § § 41-48 (1999).

[67] 16 C.F.R. § 0.1 (1999).

[68] The offices are in Atlanta, Boston, Chicago, Cleveland, Dallas, Denver, Los Angeles, New York, San Francisco and Seattle.

[69] FTC Act Amendments of 1994, 15 U.S.C.A. § 45(n) (West Supp. 1995).

[70] Federal Trade Commission, *FTC Policy on Deception*, Oct. 14, 1983, http://www.ftc.gov/bcp/policystmt/ad-decept.htm.

[71] FTC v. Colgate-Palmolive Co., 380 U.S. 374 (1963).

uct contains certain elements or does certain things.[72] Omission of important or material information can make an ad deceptive. For example, if a company advertised that people could save 50 percent with its long distance service but failed to say that it required customers to spend at least $100 to get the savings, the omission would make the claim misleading.

• *The representation, omission or practice must be likely to mislead a reasonable consumer.* The FTC has said that the key question is "whether the consumer's interpretation or reaction is reasonable."[73] The FTC does not seek to protect people who are "foolish or feeble-minded."[74] In addition, the FTC will consider the intended audience for the ad in deciding whether an ad is deceptive. For example, for a claim in an advertisement targeting children, the agency would evaluate the ad from the perspective of how reasonable children of the age group targeted would be likely to respond. Similarly, the agency would evaluate a claim in a prescription drug ad directed to doctors taking into account the knowledge and sophistication of the highly educated target audience. Also, the FTC will evaluate the impact of the advertisement *as a whole* on reasonable consumers, rather than focusing on isolated, out-of-context words or imagery.

In addition to the standards for deceptive ads described above, since 1971 the FTC has required prior substantiation of claims from advertisers. Advertisers must be able to substantiate the explicit and implied statements in ads that make objective claims about their products and services before the claims are made. That is, they must have "a reasonable basis" for their claims before they make them. Without such a basis, companies are deemed to have violated Section 5 of the FTC Act.[75] An advertiser must have at least the level of evidence the ad says exists.

In June 2005, the FTC settled a lawsuit against Tropicana in which it alleged Tropicana made false and unsubstantiated claims about the beneficial health effects of orange juice. Tropicana claimed in its ads that daily consumption of its "Healthy Heart" orange juice would lead to dramatic benefits for blood pressure, cholesterol and homocysteine levels, citing three clinical studies as proof. The FTC alleged that the studies did not in fact substantiate Tropicana's claims. As part of the settlement, Tropicana was prohibited from promoting any food as affecting cholesterol and blood pressure levels or the risks of developing heart disease, stroke or cancer without "competent and reliable scientific evidence."[76]

Exaggerations or hyperbole in ads are considered *puffery* and not generally deceptive. Puffery claims are ones that reasonable people do not believe are true qualities and are incapable of being proved true or false. They usually involve subjective matters such as taste or appearance. Examples of puffery would be describing a soft drink as the "World's Best" or "the perfect summer drink."

Testimonials and endorsements by experts or celebrities, on the other hand, are regulated because they are considered to carry special weight with consumers. An expert must be an expert in the product category. For example, a NASCAR driver could be considered an expert on the handling of an automobile, but not necessarily on the quality of adjustable wrenches. Celebrities and ordinary citizens must actually use the products they endorse because the ads imply that consumers will experience the same satisfaction with the product as the endorser.

The FTC engages in a number of activities to help prevent deceptive ads from appearing in the marketplace including:

• *Advisory opinions.* An advertiser may seek an advisory opinion from FTC commissioners or FTC staff on a proposed advertisement or specific issue of concern. An advisory opinion is a statement giving an informed judgment about a legal question or issue. The Commission may provide an advisory opinion if the request "involves a substantial or novel question of fact or law and there is no clear Commission or court precedent" and the request is a matter of significant public interest.[77] Because advisory opinions are only opinions and are not legally binding, the Commission may later reconsider the question and rescind or revoke its opinion.[78] Advisory opinions become part of the public record after they are issued.[79]

• *Industry guides.* The FTC publishes detailed guides that tell advertisers how to avoid creating advertising that is deceptive. Some of the guides, for example, describe how advertisers may avoid deception in testimonials and endorsements in ads and in the use of the word "free." The Commission has also created industry guides specific to advertising for particular types of products — jewelry, dietary supplements and foods, for example. The FTC may take action against an advertiser who fails to comply with industry guides.[80]

• *Policy statements.* The FTC may publicly state its regulatory philosophy in a policy statement. For example, the FTC issued a policy statement about comparative advertising after examining the advertising industry's codes and standards on the subject.[81] Finding that its codes and standards seemed to discourage the

---

[72] Warner-Lambert Co. v. FTC, 562 F.2d 749 (D.C. Cir. 1977).

[73] Federal Trade Commission, *FTC Policy on Deception*, Oct. 14, 1983, http://www.ftc.gov/bcp/policystmt/ad-decept.htm.

[74] Heinz W. Kirchner, 63 F.T.C. 1282, 1290 (1963).

[75] Federal Trade Commission, *FTC Policy Statement Regarding Advertising Substantiation*, http://www.ftc.gov/bcp/guides/ad3subst.htm (last visited June 16, 2003).

[76] *Tropicana Settles FTC Lawsuit*, June 28, 2005, http://www.advertisinglaw.com/blogs/blog/52 (last visited June 30, 2005).

---

[77] 16 C.F.R. § 1.1 (1999).

[78] 16 C.F.R. § 1.3 (1999).

[79] 16 C.F.R. § 1.1 (1999), 16 C.F.R. § 1.3 (1999), 16 C.F.R. § 1.4 (1999).

[80] 16 C.F.R. § 1.5 (1999).

[81] The FTC defines comparative advertising as "advertising that compares alternative brands on objectively measurable attributes or price, and identifies the alternative brand by name, illustration or other distinctive information." 16 C.F.R. § 14.15 (1999).

use of comparative advertising, the FTC wanted to clearly state its position that "industry self-regulation should not restrain the use by advertisers of truthful comparative advertising." The FTC's policy on comparative advertising "encourages the naming of, or reference to, competitors, but requires clarity, and, if necessary, disclosure to avoid deception of the consumer.... Comparative advertising, when truthful and non-deceptive, is a source of important information to consumers and assists them in making rational purchase decisions."[82]

- *Rulemaking*. The FTC may establish Trade Regulation Rules, which have the force of law, to address widespread deceptive practices. The commission holds informal hearings at which interested parties and the public may participate and give their opinions about the proposed rule.[83]

If the FTC decides that an ad is deceptive, it has a number of remedies at its disposal. One problem the FTC has is that ad campaigns can be over long before the FTC catches up with the company and brings a complaint. On the other hand, the FTC does have publicity working in its favor. Companies do not like the negative publicity that comes with a charge of false advertising; so publicity can be a powerful sanction.

- *Consent agreements*. If the FTC believes that an advertisement is deceptive, it may issue a complaint to the advertiser detailing its charges. The advertiser may then choose to settle the charges with the FTC by signing a consent agreement. Generally, the advertiser does not admit liability but agrees to start or stop doing something. The advertiser, for example, may stop running a particular ad or may stop making specific claims in an ad. The agreement also provides that the advertiser waives the right to judicial review. The FTC places proposed consent agreements on the record for sixty days to allow public comment before they become final.

- *Cease-and-desist orders*. If a consent agreement cannot be reached and the advertiser chooses to fight the charges, the FTC's complaint will be adjudicated before an FTC administrative law judge in a proceeding similar to a trial. At the end of this quasi-judicial proceeding, the judge will issue a decision stating findings of fact and conclusions of law and recommending either a cease-and-desist order or dismissal of the complaint. A cease-and-desist order is an order for the advertiser to start or stop doing something. The decision of the administrative law judge may be appealed to the full commission. The advertiser may appeal the commission's decision to a federal court of appeals, and either party may appeal that decision to the U.S. Supreme Court.

- *Corrective advertising*. In some cases the FTC will require a company to correct its advertising message in future ads to clear up any misleading impressions that were left from the deceptive ads. This remedy is usually reserved for long-running and success-ful ad campaigns where the FTC fears the public will be left with false information. For example, Warner-Lambert was ordered in the late 1970s to state in its future advertising for Listerine that "contrary to prior advertising, Listerine will not help prevent colds or sore throats or lessen their severity."[84]

- *Court injunctions*. Rather than taking an administrative route first, the FTC may go directly to federal court to seek a preliminary or permanent injunction.[85] The FTC is likely to take this step in cases of ongoing consumer fraud to attempt to stop it before too many consumers are harmed.

- *Civil and criminal penalties*. The FTC can ask a federal district court to impose civil penalties for a number of reasons, including to reimburse all consumers who bought an advertiser's product, because an advertiser violated a federal statute that imposes fines on violators, or because an advertiser has violated an FTC order. To get consumer redress, the FTC must show that an advertiser demonstrated conduct that a "reasonable man would have known under the circumstances was dishonest or fraudulent."[86] The FTC can also refer cases to the Justice Department for criminal prosecution.

The FTC is active in regulating advertising and marketing practices on the Internet. Advertising on the Internet must conform to the same rules as advertising in other media. The FTC has been working with the Food and Drug Administration and other governmental agencies to fight deceptive advertising and marketing of health-related products online. In a six-month period ending July 2003, for example, the FTC filed or settled actions with companies promising rapid and permanent weight loss, a cure for cancer, and the elimination of snoring.[87] The FTC estimated that the products targeted totaled more than $1 billion in consumer sales.[88]

### Legal Liability

The basic defense against any false advertising complaint is truth, that is, providing evidence proving that the product does what the ad says it does, or has the attributes the ad claims it does. Advertising agencies may be held legally liable, along with their clients, for deceptive claims, because they have a responsibility to independently check claims made in ads.

---

[82] 16 C.F.R. § 14.15 (1999).

[83] 15 U.S.C. § 57 (a)(b)(3) (1999).

[84] Warner-Lambert Co. v. FTC, 562 F. 2d 749, 752 (D.C. Cir. 1977).

[85] 15 U.S.C. § 53 (b) (1999).

[86] 15 U.S.C. § 57 (b) (1999).

[87] Federal Trade Commission, *FTC Enforcement Activities: Dietary Supplement and Health Fraud Actions*, July 2003, http://www.ftc.gov/opa/2003/07/diethealth.htm.

[88] Federal Trade Commission, *Federal Trade Commission Attacks $1 Billion in Deceptive Health Marketing Since December*, July 10, 2003, http://www.ftc.gov/opa/2003/07/diethealth.htm (last visited June 16, 2004).

### Lanham Act

At the federal level, the Lanham Act also provides redress for people and businesses harmed by false or deceptive advertising. The Lanham Act is the federal trademark protection law, but it contains a section dealing with advertising. Section 43(a) reads, in part, as follows: "Any person who ... in commercial advertising or promotion, misrepresents the nature, characteristics, qualities, or geographic origin of his or her or another person's goods, services, or commercial activities, shall be liable in a civil action by any person who believes that he or she is or is likely to be damaged by such act."[89] The section creates a "distinct federal statutory tort designed to afford broad protection against various forms of unfair competition and false advertising."[90]

Because of the Lanham Act's focus on protection of commercial interests, as opposed to consumers, courts have not generally given consumers standing to bring an action under Section 43(a). The act allows businesses or people to sue others for competitive harm arising from false advertising. For a claim, the plaintiff must establish that the advertiser made a false representation about a product or service; that the representation deceives, or has a tendency to deceive, a substantial segment of the target audience; that the representation is material; and that it resulted or is likely to result in injury to the plaintiff. Although the elements are similar to the FTC's standards for deceptive advertising, the biggest difference is the requirement of injury. In Lanham Act cases, the plaintiff must show that it has or is likely to have suffered commercial harm by the defendant's deceptive advertising claims. The plaintiff also must show that the claim was in fact false and not just that the advertiser lacked prior substantiation.

### State Laws

All fifty states have enacted their own legislation similar to the Federal Trade Commission Act, prohibiting deceptive advertising. Unlike the federal law, however, most of the state statutes permit private lawsuits to be brought by consumers and competitors against advertisers and allow plaintiffs to sue for damages in addition to an injunction stopping the ads. Some national advertisers, such as tobacco companies and airlines, have sought to avoid state penalties by claiming the state law is pre-empted by federal law. Commercial speech is an area of law that is shared by the state and federal governments. When a conflict between the two arises, the federal law takes precedence.

### Lotteries and Contests

A lottery has three elements: a prize, chance and consideration.

The *prize* is what the winner receives, such as money, a trip or merchandise. *Chance* means that the prize is awarded based on luck and not skill. *Consideration* refers to what the participant must give in exchange for the potential prize. That is, the participant must buy a product, pay for a ticket, or expend some effort for the prize. All three elements must be present to constitute a lottery. Under the Charity Games Advertising Clarification Act of 1988,[91] the media may advertise lotteries provided the lotteries are legal in their state, but for the most part lotteries are highly regulated and controlled by states.

Contests, on the other hand, face less regulation. To be a contest, only two of the three elements of a lottery can be present. Thus, contests can involve a prize and chance or a prize and consideration, but not all three. Most contests avoid the lottery regulations by asking the winner a skill-testing question, which makes winning based on knowledge or skill rather than chance. Or they say there is no purchase necessary, which removes the consideration element. The FTC has rules regulating contests, as does the Federal Communication Commission.

### Industry Self-regulation

The advertising industry has developed a variety of schemes and units for self-regulation. Among them are the National Advertising Division, the National Advertising Review Board and the Children's Advertising Review Unit.

**The National Advertising Division.** The main advertising industry group that regulates ads is the National Advertising Division, which is a program of the Council of Better Business Bureaus. The advertising community created the NAD in 1971 "to provide a system of voluntary self-regulation, minimize government intervention and foster public confidence in the credibility of advertising."[92] Self-regulation allows advertisers to resolve disputes quickly and inexpensively, without government involvement and assessment of penalties.

The NAD reviews national advertising and investigates complaints about the truth or accuracy of claims. It focuses on product performance, superiority, and scientific and technical claims, but "is not the appropriate forum to address concerns about the 'good taste' of ads, moral questions about products that are offered for sale or political or issue advertising," the Better Business Bureau reports.[93]

While the NAD cannot force an advertiser to comply with a recommendation or accept its findings, it exerts pressure on advertisers by publishing its conclusions in the *NAD Case Reports* and

---

[89] Lanham Act, 15 U.S.C. § 1125(a), § 43(a) (1999).

[90] Estate of Presley v. Russen, 513 F. Supp. 1339, 1376 (D.N.J. 1981).

[91] 18 U.S.C.A. § 1307 (West Supp. 1995).

[92] Better Business Bureau, *The National Advertising Division,* http://www.bbb.org/advertising/advertiserAssist.asp.

[93] National Advertising Bureau, *About NAD,* http://www.nadreview.org/AboutNAD.asp.

by issuing press releases announcing decisions.

**The National Advertising Review Board.** Either an advertiser whose claim is in question or a challenger of an advertising claim may appeal a finding of the NAD to the National Advertising Review Board. The NARB is a group of about eighty-five advertising professionals who work in ad agencies, companies that advertise, academia and government. It sits in panels of five members to decide NAD appeals. If an advertiser does not accept the NARB panel's decisions and recommendations, which the Better Business Bureau says is rare, the NARB refers the case to an appropriate law-enforcement agency, such as the Federal Trade Commission.[94]

**The Children's Advertising Review Unit.** To combat misleading and socially irresponsible advertising aimed at children, the advertising industry created the Children's Advertising Review Unit in 1974, which, like the NAD, operates as part of the Council of Better Business Bureaus. The CARU reviews and analyzes advertising targeting children under the age of twelve by monitoring advertising on television, radio, children's magazines, comic books and online services.

In addition to monitoring ads, the organization will also take complaints from consumers, including children. If the CARU finds that an ad is misleading or inaccurate or that it violates a set of industry rules known as the "Self-Regulatory Guidelines for Children's Advertising," the CARU will try to work with the advertiser to change or discontinue the ad.

## SUMMARY

Commercial speech is defined as expression that proposes a commercial transaction or expression related solely to the economic interests of the speaker and its audience. The saga of the development of constitutional protection for commercial speech began in 1942 with a Supreme Court pronouncement that commercial advertising received no First Amendment protection. The Court modified that initial view, later saying that the First Amendment protected even purely commercial expression, though government was free to restrict advertising that was false, misleading or deceptive, or promoted illegal products or services. The Court said commercial speech receives a lower level of protection than other types of expression because the truth of its content is more easily verified and because it is an economic necessity for companies; thus, commercial advertising could better tolerate government regulation.

In 1980, the Court articulated a four-part test, commonly referred to as the "*Central Hudson* Test," to determine whether a regulation on commercial speech is constitutional:

(1) Is the commercial speech true and not misleading, and does it advertise a legal product or service?

(2) Is the asserted governmental interest substantial?

(3) Does the regulation directly advance the governmental interest?

(4) Is the regulation no more extensive than necessary to serve the governmental interest?

The Court later clarified the fourth part of that test, explaining that there need only be a reasonable fit between the regulation and the governmental interest. Because of that less rigorous interpretation and because of a decision that upheld government restriction of truthful commercial speech for a legal activity, the Court's decisions by the end of the 1980s seemed to have reduced protection for commercial speech.

But in the 1990s the pendulum appeared to have reversed, with the Court applying the *Central Hudson* Test more stringently if truthful commercial speech for legal products and services was involved. In the latest cases, the Court has been requiring proof to support government assertions that regulations pass the *Central Hudson* Test.

The Federal Trade Commission is the federal governmental agency that regulates deceptive advertising in the United States. The FTC's definition of a deceptive ad is an ad that contains a representation, omission or practice that is material and likely to mislead a consumer acting reasonably in the circumstances.

The Commission uses various tools — offering advisory opinions to advertisers, issuing policy statements, publishing industry guides, making rules and requiring substantiation — to try to prevent deceptive advertising from appearing in the marketplace. Once advertisers disseminate deceptive claims to consumers, the FTC seeks remedies — through a consent agreement, cease-and-desist order, injunction, or civil or criminal penalties — to stop such claims from continuing to deceive consumers and to seek redress for harms advertisers have inflicted on consumers.

Competitors and others harmed by false and deceptive advertising can seek redress through the Lanham Act. In Lanham Act cases, the plaintiff must show that it has suffered or is likely to suffer commercial harm by the defendant's false and deceptive claims. State laws also regulate advertising, and many allow consumers and competitors to sue for damages in addition to an injunctive relief.

Advertisers should be aware of the rules and regulations regarding the promotion of lotteries and contests.

Self-regulation by the advertising industry can be an effective and quick way of addressing concerns about deceptive or unsupported claims in national advertising and about various issues relating to children's exposure to advertising. The National Advertising Division, Children's Advertising Review Unit, and National Advertising Review Board, which all operate as part of the Better Business Bureau, are the main industry groups involved in the self-regulatory process.

---

[94] National Advertising Division, *NAD/NARB/CARU Procedures*, (visited June 23, 2003), http://www.nadreview.org/Procedures.asp.

## FOR ADDITIONAL READING

An, Soontae. "From a Business Pursuit to a Means of Expression: The Supreme Court's Disputes Over Commercial Speech," 8 *Communication Law and Policy* 201 (2003).

Baker, C. Edwin. "Commercial Speech: A Problem in the Theory of Freedom," 62 *Iowa Law Review* 1 (1976).

Better Business Bureau Advertising Review Programs Web site, http://www.bbb.org/advertising.

Federal Trade Commission Web site, http://www.ftc.gov.

Hoefges, Michael. "Protecting Tobacco Advertising Under the Commercial Speech Doctrine: The Constitutional Impact of Lorillard Tobacco Co.," 8 *Communication Law and Policy* 267 (2003).

Kozinski, Alex, and Stuart Banner. "Who's Afraid of Commercial Speech?" 76 *Virginia Law Review* 627 (1990).

Post, Robert. "The Constitutional Status of Commercial Speech," 48 *UCLA Law Review* 1 (2000).

Redish, Martin H. "The First Amendment in the Marketplace: Commercial Speech and the Values of Free Expression," 39 *George Washington Law Review* 429 (1971).

Schmidt, Richard M. Jr., and Robert Clifton Burns. "Proof or Consequences: False Advertising and the Doctrine of Commercial Speech," 56 *University of Cincinnati Law Review* 1273 (1988).

Stern, Nat. "In Defense of the Imprecise Definition of Commercial Speech," 52 *Maryland Law Review* 55 (1999).

# 9

# Regulating Public Relations

*By Greg Lisby*

---

 **Headnote Questions**

- *When might a public relations practitioner be considered an "insider" under the SEC's misappropriation test?*
- *When would a public relations practitioner have an actionable claim for unfair competition?*
- *What is required for a "no-compete" clause in a public relations practitioner's employment contract to be enforceable?*
- *How is the ownership of public relations practitioners' works-made-for-hire determined?*
- *What is the difference between corporate speech which is protected by the First Amendment and corporate action which is not?*
- *Under what circumstances is corporate speech deemed political speech and when is it commercial speech?*
- *What are the dangers of standard form contracts in the practice of public relations?*
- *When may a public relations practitioner sue a journalist based on a claim of promissory estoppel?*

---

The economy — the foundation and fiber of the United States — is based upon the exchange of goods and services and upon the marketing and promotion of those exchanges. In no other country does capitalism exist as such a crucial part of society. As a result, corporate entities have many of the same rights and privileges as natural persons under the Constitution, especially in the area of free expression, even though they might be considered artificial persons at best.[1] Corporations as well as people, for example, have the right to publicize their positions about issues they believe to be important — especially political positions — and the corporations may use corporate monies to fund the process.[2] In addition, both have the right of self-promotion and the right to

make money off their likenesses and activities.[3] That is, they have the right of publicity. They are also protected by the Fifth Amendment's protections against double jeopardy.[4] But no person — natural or artificial — can be forced to disseminate a view with which that person disagrees.[5] Yet corporations enjoy no constitutional right of privacy.[6] They can be required to testify against themselves, and their corporate records may be used to incriminate them in court proceedings.[7]

Historically, there were few restrictions on these marketplace rights. *Caveat emptor* — let the buyer beware — was the rule. That

---

[1] *See* First Nat'l Bank of Boston v. Bellotti, 435 U.S. 765 (1978). They were first deemed "persons" entitled to the Constitution's equal protection guarantees in *Santa Clara County v. Southern Pac. R.R.*, 118 U.S. 394, 396 (1886), and to its due process guarantees in *Smyth v. Ames*, 169 U.S. 466, 522 (1898).

[2] *See* Cort v. Ash, 422 U.S. 66 (1975).

[3] *See* Zacchini v. Scripps-Howard Broad. Co., 433 U.S. 562 (1977).

[4] *See* United States v. Martin Linen Supply Co., 430 U.S. 564 (1977).

[5] *See* Hurley v. Irish-American Gay, Lesbian, and Bisexual Group of Boston, 515 U.S. 557 (1995) (unanimously holding that an organization cannot be forced to adopt or incorporate an unwanted message).

[6] *See* California Bankers Ass'n v. Schyultz, 416 U.S. 21 (1974); United States v. Morton Salt Co., 338 U.S. 632 (1950).

[7] *See* Anderson v. Maryland, 427 U.S. 463 (1976); Wilson v. United States, 221 U.S. 361 (1911); Hale v. Henkel, 201 U.S. 43 (1906).

is not the case today; corporations and the public relations practitioners who communicate their views also have legal responsibilities to the public.

No one has ever successfully contended that the Constitution protects one's right to say anything, at any time, at any place. Consequently, time, place and manner restrictions — as long as they are content neutral — may be used to balance opposing rights. The restrictions may not single out a particular type of expression, though they may incidentally restrict or inhibit expression, and they must serve some significant governmental interest. These restrictions traditionally involve the maintenance of peace and quiet in a neighborhood or park, litter-free public areas, uninterrupted traffic flow and the like. The test is: Does the importance of free expression outweigh the social interests furthered by the regulation being proposed?

Public safety, aesthetics and other community concerns may take precedence when courts consider the right to communicate through economic speech. Thus, public relations practitioners need to know the regulations governing a variety of activities, including where lobbyists must register, what lobbying activities are legally permissible, where to obtain proper permits for collecting signatures, how to stage rallies and protests and how to determine the exact noise level at which an ordinance regulating the use of loud speakers at public events denies a speaker freedom of expression.

An employer, for example, has a free speech right to communicate his views to his employees but may not disseminate an expression containing material misrepresentations of fact or prejudicial racial appeals.[8] On the other hand, many union organizing and election restrictions — permissible in a labor relations context — would be inappropriate in a political context. And in many cases permits are required prior to some expressive activities. Clearly, these and similar situations pose complex questions whose solutions may not be subject to uniformity or consistency. Answers may depend upon individual situations.[9]

## PUBLIC RELATIONS LAW DEFINED

Public relations law has been described as plain, old business law polished with a veneer of First Amendment protections. In fact, it is not really an area of law — such as defamation or copyright — but a study of the application of other areas of law to particular practices — the practices of public relations, which may be defined as the explanation of business or institutional concerns to the public. The importance of a broad knowledge of public relations law was highlighted by the results of a 1996 survey of public relations practitioners who admitted a general lack of familiarity with

the main categories of law that appear on the accrediting examination of the Public Relations Society of America.[10]

What might be termed economic expression was historically unprotected by the First Amendment. The assumption was that economic expression, which includes commercial expression, was not vital to the nation's well-being. Only expression contributing to informed self-government (that is, political expression) was thought to fit that description, even though a consumer's "interest in the free flow of commercial information ... may be as keen, if not keener by far, than his interest in the day's most urgent political debate."[11]

In *Virginia State Board of Pharmacy v. Virginia Citizens Consumer Council*, the U.S. Supreme Court provided for First Amendment protection for truthful marketing of legal products and services. The fact that a businessman's interests are "purely economic," the Court said, "hardly disqualifies him from protection under the First Amendment."[12] In addition, the Court concluded, the First Amendment protected the consumer's right to receive economic information. It wrote:

So long as we preserve a predominantly free enterprise economy, the allocation of our resources in large measure will be made through numerous private economic decisions. It is a matter of public interest that those decisions, in the aggregate, be intelligent and well informed. To this end, the free flow of economic information is indispensable. And if it is indispensable to the proper allocation of resources in a free enterprise system, it is also indispensable to the formation of intelligent opinions as to how that system ought to be regulated or altered. Therefore, even if the First Amendment were thought to be primarily an instrument to enlighten public decision-making in a democracy, we could not say that the free flow of information does not serve that goal.[13]

By the late 1970s, the Court appeared to be applying a kind of "public interest" test to determine what economic expression was constitutionally protected and what was not. This seemed especially apparent in its ruling in *First National Bank of Boston v. Bellotti*.[14] There, agreeing that corporate speech was constitutionally protected, a sharply divided Court took pains to point out that the promotion — which stated the bank's position on a proposed amendment to the Massachusetts consti-

---

[8] *See* Nat'l Labor Relations Bd. v. Gissel Packing Co., 395 U.S. 575 (1969).

[9] For example, should a shopping center owner be able to stop people from passing out anti-war pamphlets in a part of the mall otherwise open to and regularly used by all? *See* Lloyd v. Tanner, 407 U.S. 551 (1972).

[10] *See* Kathy Fitzpatrick, *Public Relations and the Law: A Survey of Practitioners*, PUBLIC RELATIONS REV., Mar. 22, 1996, at 1. The categories are libel, copyright, privacy, access to information, contracts, commercial speech, financial public relations, Securities & Exchange Commission regulations and professional malpractice.

[11] Virginia Bd. of Pharmacy v. Virginia Citizens Consumer Council, 425 U.S. 748, 763 (1976).

[12] *Id.* at 762.

[13] *Id.* at 765 (citations and references omitted).

[14] 435 U.S. 765 (1978).

tution — was the type of speech indispensable to decision-making in a democracy, and this is no less true because the speech comes from a corporation rather than an individual. The inherent worth of the speech in terms of its capacity for informing the public does not depend upon the identity of its source, whether corporation ... or individual.[15]

In an attempt to provide more predictability in this area of the law, the Court, in *Central Hudson Gas & Electric Corp. v. Public Service Commission*, differentiated between commercial and political advertising, and established a four-part test for determining when a commercial claim may be regulated.[16] As a result, economic expression, as long as it promotes lawful products and services, is protected by the First Amendment but may be regulated in certain narrow circumstances.

However, twenty-five years later, the Court's jurisprudence in this area appears to be more ad hoc than reasoned and stable. In *Glickman v. Wileman Brothers & Elliott*,[17] for example, members of the Court disagreed over whether First Amendment publicity rights — and incidentally the freedom from compelled speech — were implicated at all. They determined instead that the 1937 federal requirement that agricultural commodity producers fund generic marketing campaigns promoting their fruits was only one of ordinary business regulations affecting economic policy. Then, in *United States v. United Foods*,[18] the Court ruled that requiring mushroom growers to run ads promoting mushroom sales violated the First Amendment. It distinguished its *Glickman* ruling on the grounds that the compelled speech there was merely ancillary to – or supplemented – a more comprehensive agricultural marketing program. And in *Johanns v. Livestock Marketing Association*,[19] the Court concluded that a federal beef promotion program was not compelled speech violating the First Amendment, as the program only funded government speech which is not susceptible to being challenged as compelled speech.

## CONSTITUTIONAL LAW

In addition to federal copyright law and the First Amendment's protection of privacy and commercial expression — as well as its seismic effects on the common law tort of defamation — public relations practitioners must have a basic understanding of their responsibilities to clients under corporate speech case law and federal trademark law.

### *Corporate Expression*

Since the 1970s, corporate expression has been constitutionally protected, though the degree of this protection varies, depending upon the type of expression. Campaign expenditures and corporate political expression, both broadly protected by the First Amendment, require a compelling governmental interest before either may be regulated.[20] Campaign contributions and commercial expression — advertising — are moderately protected by the First Amendment and require only a substantial governmental interest before either may be restricted.[21] A corporation also has a constitutional right not to be associated with expression it opposes.[22]

Though philosophical questions still exist as to the full extent of the comparative constitutional rights of natural persons and corporations, it is clear that corporations are artificial persons under the Constitution, entitled to the protections of the First Amendment. Without regard to the communicative power of corporate speech, the only questions now remaining are the extent to which corporate actions are communicative in nature and the type of evidence needed to meet the relatively high standard required to justify limiting corporate expression.

On the grounds that large political campaign contributions create fears of improper influence on the political process, which in turn undermines citizens' faith in government honesty and integrity, the Supreme Court in *Buckley v. Valeo* upheld limits on contributions, which the Court did not believe were a form of direct expression, as long as the regulation was "closely drawn" and matched a "sufficiently important [governmental] interest."[23] The elements of this test, of course, are basically the same as the requirements of *Central Hudson Gas & Electric v. Public Service Commission*[24] and *S.U.N.Y. v. Fox*,[25] which mandate a reasonable

---

[15] *Id.* at 777.

[16] 477 U.S. 557, 566 (1980): "At the outset, we must determine whether the expression is protected by the First Amendment. For commercial speech to come within that provision, it at least must concern lawful activity and not be misleading. Next, we ask whether the asserted governmental interest is substantial. If both inquiries yield positive answers, we must determine whether the regulation directly advances the governmental interest asserted, and whether it is not more extensive than is necessary to serve that interest." The Court modified the final part of the test to require only a reasonable fit between state interests and the regulatory methods used to protect them in *Board of Trustees of the State University of New York v. Fox*, 492 U.S. 469 (1989).

[17] 521 U.S. 457 (1997).

[18] 533 U.S. 405 (2001).

[19] 544 U.S. 550 (2005). *See* Linda Greenhouse, *In Free-Speech Ruling, Justices Say All Ranchers Must Help Pay for Federal Ads*, N.Y. TIMES, May 24, 2005, at A15.

[20] *See* Buckley v. Valeo, 424 U.S. 1 (1976) (campaign expenditures); First Nat'l Bank v. Bellotti, 435 U.S. 765 (1978) (corporate political expression). This *Bellotti* decision was expanded to include ideological groups and entities — those formed to disseminate political ideas, rather than amass economic capital — in *Fed. Election Comm'n v. Massachusetts Citizens for Life*, 479 U.S. 238 (1986).

[21] *See* Buckley, 424 U.S. 1 (1976); Virginia Bd. of Pharmacy v. Virginia Citizens Consumer Council, 425 U.S. 748 (1976).

[22] *See* Pac. Gas & Elec. v. Pub. Util. Comm'n, 475 U.S. 1 (1986).

[23] 424 U.S. at 25.

[24] 447 U.S. 557 (1980).

[25] 492 U.S. 469 (1989).

fit between the "substantial" governmental interest in the regulation of advertising and the regulatory method used.

Thus, case law in the years since has focused on (1) whether a corporate disbursement was an expenditure or a contribution, and (2) whether a particular expression was or was not political. For example:

- In *Consolidated Edison of New York v. Public Service Commission*,[26] the Supreme Court concluded that the discussion of public policy controversies in the form of monthly inserts in utility bills was political expression.

- In *Federal Election Commission v. National Right To Work Committee*,[27] the Court upheld a legislative restriction on the solicitation of contributors to corporate political funds, concluding that this was not political expression.

- In *Federal Election Commission v. National Conservative Political Action Committee*,[28] the Court concluded that campaign expenditure limits on political action committees were unconstitutional infringements on protected corporate political expression.

- In *Austin v. Michigan Chamber of Commerce*,[29] the Court upheld a state statute prohibiting corporate expenditures on behalf of a candidate for election, concluding that this was a campaign contribution.

- In *Nixon v. Shrink Missouri Government P.A.C.*,[30] the Court upheld a state statute setting limits on contributions to political candidates, but concluded that its 1976 *Buckley* decision did not require a specific dollar limit on political contributions that would still be appropriate and applicable twenty-four years later. Rather, the Court ruled, the test was whether the limitation was so low as to prohibit candidates from being able to advocate effectively for their election.

Though *First National Bank v. Bellotti* is considered the "Magna Carta" of corporate speech doctrine,[31] the decision by no means settled all questions regarding the role of corporations in public life, their influence on the democratic process, and their involvement in the political sphere through "soft money" assistance to political parties. In 2002, Congress again tackled the issue and enacted the Bipartisan Campaign Reform Act,[32] called "the most ambitious effort since Watergate to reduce the influence of big donations on the political process."[33] The statute was immediately challenged in eleven separate lawsuits, which were consolidated

into a single action: *McConnell v. Federal Election Commission*.[34] A special three-judge panel upheld most of the statute but found that its two most important provisions were an unconstitutional infringement of free expression, including its restrictions on large political donations from corporations and labor unions to political parties and its prohibitions against issue advertisements paid for by those same entities. Concluding that "soft money" contributions are not corporate speech, the Supreme Court reversed the lower court's ruling while upholding its decision regarding "electioneering communications" by corporate political action committees.[35] The Court in 2006 again declined to revise its definitional distinctions between campaign expenditures and contributions and did not overturn the constitutional protection for spending in *Randall v. Sorrell*,[36] though "the patchwork of six separate opinions" also showed that the Court continues "to grapple with how far it is permissible to go in limiting" corporate and individual campaign contributions.[37]

The line separating corporate action from corporate expression and commercial expression from corporate speech, however, is still dim and uncertain. As corporations can only "express" themselves by spending money, they would prefer that all expressive activity be deemed corporate speech, as it is protected by the First Amendment, while action may be regulated. And, too, they would prefer that all corporate speech be deemed political speech, which requires a higher level of judicial scrutiny to justify regulation than does commercial speech. Yet, to cite *First National Bank v. Bellotti* as an example of the essential nature of both corporate expression and its constitutional protection ignores the plain fact that *Bellotti* also involved the advertising of corporate views on a political referendum. Clearly, the question of what is and is not corporate political or corporate commercial speech is not easily answered,[38] though there is no doubt that materially false or misleading corporate expression, affirmatively and knowingly de-

---

[26] 447 U.S. 530 (1980).

[27] 459 U.S. 197 (1982).

[28] 470 U.S. 480 (1985).

[29] 494 U.S. 652 (1990).

[30] 528 U.S. 377 (2000).

[31] Norman Dorson & Joel Gora, *Free Speech, Property, and the Burger Court: Old Values, New Balances*, 1982 SUP. CT. REV. 195, 212.

[32] 2 U.S.C. 441a *et seq.* (2000).

[33] Neil A. Lewis & Richard A. Oppel Jr., *U.S. Court Issues Discordant Ruling on Campaign Law*, N.Y. TIMES, May 3, 2003, at A14.

[34] 251 F. Supp. 2d 176 (D. D.C. 2002).

[35] McConnell v. Fed. Elections Comm'n, 540 U.S. 93 (2003). *See* Linda Greenhouse, *Justices, in a 5-to-4 Decision, Back Campaign Finance Law That Curbs Contributions*, N.Y. TIMES, Dec. 11, 2003, at A1. *See also* Glen Justice, *Even with Campaign Finance Law, Money Talks Louder Than Ever*, N.Y. TIMES, Nov. 8, 2004, at A16.

[36] 126 S.Ct. 2479 (2006).

[37] Linda Greenhouse, *Justices Reject Campaign Limits in Vermont Case*, N.Y. TIMES, June 27, 2006, at A1.

[38] In *Nike v. Kasky*, 45 P.3d 243 (Cal. 2002), the California Supreme Court concluded that Nike's non-advertising defense of its corporate reputation and its controversial business and labor practices in Southeast Asia constituted commercial expression, because the expression was motivated primarily by pecuniary interests, and not political speech through which Nike was participating in a public debate. Because commercial expression must be truthful to be protected by the First Amendment and because the California court concluded that Nike's speech was both false and misleading, it determined that the expression could be regulated and Nike penalized for its falsity. The Supreme Court refused to hear the case, and it was settled out of court, leaving the important question of whether Nike's speech was political speech or commercial speech unanswered. 539 U.S. 654 (2003).

## CONTINUUM OF TRADEMARK PROTECTION

| **Most** | | | | **Least** |
| --- | --- | --- | --- | --- |
| Fanciful | Arbitrary | Suggestive | Descriptive | Generic |

**Figure 1**

signed to misinform consumers, is not protected by the First Amendment.[39]

### Trademarks/Service Marks

Words or designs, or a combination of the two, that denote a specific product, service or company may be protected by the Lanham Act of 1946.[40] The basic federal requirement for a trademark or service mark is that it be distinctive, though it also must not be scandalous or deceptive, consist of a flag or emblem of any country, resemble a person's signature or likeness without consent, resemble any other trade or service mark, be merely descriptive of the product, be geographically descriptive of origin, and must not be a surname. Once registered with the U.S. Patent and Trademark Office, a mark is good for ten years and may be renewed for unlimited ten-year periods, as long as it is regularly used in commerce.

The degree of protection varies along a continuum, with fanciful marks receiving the most protection and generic marks no protection whatsoever, as Figure 1 demonstrates.

Fanciful marks are generally coined words or designs with no dictionary meaning, such as "Exxon." Arbitrary marks are commonplace words or symbols that do not describe the product or company with which they are associated, such as "Apple" computers. Suggestive marks, on the other hand, are familiar words or phrases that are used to suggest what the product or service really is, such as the Nickelodeon children's television network. As might be surmised, descriptive marks actually describe the thing or company, such as *Personal Finance*, a financial investment magazine. Generic marks are the names of the product or service itself and cannot function as trademarks, such as aspirin, an over-the-counter pain reliever, also sometimes known as acetyl salicylic acid. (At one time, "aspirin" was a protected trademark of the Bayer Company, but it fell into common usage, no longer distinguishing the product of a particular manufacturer and was invali-

dated.[41] Corporations thus are constantly on the look-out for public misuse of their trade and service marks to prevent what has been called "generecide" — the killing of trademarks by common or generic use.)

Corporations and public relations practitioners should therefore be extremely careful when adapting ideas, slogans, images or logos that might be protected by trademark or copyright law.[42] However, in a case involving Victoria's Secret and Victor's Little Secret, retailers with similar names and little else, similarity alone is insufficient to support a claim for trademark dilution. Actual economic harm must be proven, though not the consequences of dilution, such as, actual loss of sales or profits.[43]

Minimally, the corporate attorney should conduct a trademark search to determine if a similar logo or company name is already in use by a company in a similar line of business. Failure to do so could expose the corporation or public relations practitioner to a lawsuit seeking to prevent the use of the logo or mark, even though it is already in use and developing business and goodwill for the company, in addition to a tort claim for unfair competition.[44] For example, an embarrassing public relations situation developed when Ty, Inc., introduced a white tiger Beanie Baby, named "Blizzard," forgetting that Dairy Queen owned the name as a trademark for one of its ice cream desserts. The Beanie Baby was quickly retired, and when McDonald's introduced its Teenie Beanie Baby version of the tiger in 2000, its name had been changed to "Blizz." In another instance, Burger King found itself facing a lawsuit filed by Chick-fil-A when its promotional materials for the movie *Chicken Run* were a little too similar (though with the opposite message) to Chick-fil-A's popular advertisements featuring cows urging customers to "Eat Mor Chikin."

---

[39] *See* Illinois v. Telemarketing Associates, 538 U.S. 600 (2003). *See also* Linda Greenhouse, *Justices Rule Charity May Be Charged with Fraud*, N.Y. Times, May 6, 2003, at A1. Fraud in advertising was determined by the Court to be without First Amendment protection in *FTC v. Colgate-Palmolive*, 380 U.S. 374 (1965).

[40] 15 U.S.C. 1051 (2000). Even without federal trademark protection, a mark may also be protected under the common law or state statute.

[41] Bayer Co. v. United Drug Co., 272 F. 505 (S.D. N.Y. 1921).

[42] *See* MGM-Pathe Communications v. Pink Panther Patrol, 774 F. Supp. 869 (S.D. N.Y. 1991) (where a gay rights organization was held to have infringed on a trademark because ordinary individuals could mistakenly assume that the trademark owners sponsored or otherwise supported activities of the organization).

[43] Moseley v. V Secret Catalogue, 537 U.S. 418 (2003). *Also* Linda Greenhouse, *Ruling on Victor vs. Victoria Offers Split Victory of Sorts*, N.Y. Times, Mar. 5, 2003, at A16.

[44] *See* Matt Haig, Brand Failures: The Truth About the 100 Biggest Branding Mistakes of All Time (2003).

## ADMINISTRATIVE LAW AND REGULATIONS

The turn of the last century ushered in a new type of American law, specifically designed to deal with the growing complexities and technical intricacies of the modern business marketplace. Administrative law is different from other types of law because it is not based on the separation of powers, in which the legislative branch of government makes the law, the executive branch enforces the law, and the judicial branch interprets the law. In establishing administrative agencies that promulgate rules, regulations and guidelines, Congress and the states, in essence, called upon experts to administer a new type of law. Administrative regulations are used to correct what economists refer to as a "market failure," which means – in the case of the Food and Drug Administration, for example – that free market forces would lead to the consumption of many drugs with high risks in relation to their benefits. Thus, in the drug industry example (though the justification for regulation may also be applied to the securities industry and others, too), "the hypothesized source of this market failure is a lack of information on the part of drug consumers – in other words, patients and doctors – and a lack of incentives for pharmaceutical firms to provide sufficient information,"[45] which justifies the regulation of such communication.

Each of the so-called "alphabet agencies" — the IRS, FCC, FAA and others — makes its own regulations, enforces them and provides initial judicial review — acting as all three branches of government rolled into one. The result is that it is almost impossible to beat administrative agencies at their own game. Generally, courts defer to the expertise of these appointed specialists, except when they overstep the boundaries of their authority or violate their own internal procedures. Agencies that directly affect the practice of public relations include the Securities and Exchange Commission, the Food and Drug Administration,[46] the Federal Trade Commission,[47] the Consumer Product Safety Commission and the Federal Communications Commission.[48]

While, arguably, it is impossible for a public relations practitioner to have a complete knowledge of every federal and state agency with a regulatory interest in a particular corporate or public communication, the practitioner should be aware of certain important concepts and definitions regularly used by each administrative agency with which his or her client deals.

### *Securities and Exchange Commission*

The SEC is particularly concerned with the regulation of the buying and selling of stocks and bonds and with the corporate communication surrounding that buying and selling.[49] Its guiding principle was stated by the late President Franklin Roosevelt, following the stock market crash of 1929: "No essentially important element [may] be concealed from the buying public."[50] The purpose of the agency and the myriad of securities laws enacted in the early 1930s, the Court said, is "to substitute a philosophy of full disclosure for the philosophy of caveat emptor and thus to achieve a high standard of business ethics in the ... industry."[51]

The question today is still: How much corporate openness is enough? Though the stock exchanges have decided against requiring stock analysts not to speak with journalists who did not report the analysts' disclosed conflicts of interest in news articles, in the wake of the Enron scandal and corporate collapse, the SEC is expanding its list of conditions requiring disclosure of corporate information, as well as accelerating the time frame within which information must be disclosed to the agency and to the public.

The rule is this: Companies must disclose in a timely manner material information which would affect or have a connection with stock sales or purchase decisions. Such information must not be knowingly false or misleading. Inaccurate information must be corrected.

A duty to disclose material information exists where there is a fiduciary relationship, knowledge of insider information or knowing participation in a fraudulent scheme.[52] Recently, this duty has been extended to include the long established practice of giving important corporate news first to stock analysts and mutual fund managers before announcing it publicly, as well as to the disclosure of cancellations of stock purchases by corporate execu-

[45] Henry G. Grabowski, Drug Regulation and Innovation: Empirical Evidence and Policy Options 11 (1976). *See also* John Milton, Areopagitica – A Speech for the Liberty of Unlicensed Printing 51-52 (John W. Hales ed., Oxford University Press 1961) (1644) (in which the concept of a free, unregulated marketplace of ideas which would lead to the discovery of truth was first articulated). The concept was incorporated into American law in *Abrams v. United States*, 250 U.S. 616, 630 (1919) (Holmes, J., dissenting).

[46] Promotional claims and press releases by pharmaceutical companies, for example, must be submitted to the FDA for its approval prior to their public release. Another example of how FDA rules impact the practice of public relations is the FDA's recent announcement that it would consider regulating the nicotine in cigarettes as it does other drugs.

[47] The FTC has recently been concerned with the extent to which companies' claims of environmentally friendly products are fact-based and meet the FTC's so-called green guidelines. *See* Michale C. Lasky, *PR and Legal Issues: Earth-Friendly PR Claims Must Meet FTC's 'Green' Guidelines*, O'Dwyer's PR Services Report, Feb. 1995, at 51.

[48] The FCC has recently been concerned with the extent to which ownership restrictions actually promote diversity in the broadcast industry. *See*

Stephen Labaton, *Ideologically Broad Coalition Assails F.C.C. Media Plans*, N.Y. Times, May 28, 2003, at C6.

[49] Annual reports and other SEC filings from 1994 to date are available at http://www.sec.gov/.

[50] Message of the President to Congress, House of Representatives Report No. 85, 73rd Congress, 1st Sess. 2 (Mar. 29, 1933).

[51] SEC v. Capital Gaines Research Bureau, 375 U.S. 180, 186 (1963). These laws include the Securities Act of 1933, 15 U.S.C. 78 (2000); the Securities Exchange Act of 1934, 15 U.S.C. 78 (2000); the Public Utility Holding Company Act of 1935, 15 U.S.C. 79 (2000); the Trust Indenture Act of 1939, 15 U.S.C. 77 (2000); the Investment Company Act of 1940, 15 U.S.C. 80 (2000).

[52] For an example of a case where there was no knowing participation, *see* Strong v. France and the Nat'l Ass'n for Stock Car Auto Racing, 474 F.2d 747 (9th Cir. 1973).

tives.[53] This duty requires that there be a fact-based, supported basis for all business reports and projections issued by a corporation. As a rule of thumb, anything other than objectively verifiable statements of fact are presumptively misleading. The corporation, however, has no legal responsibility for independent reports and projections. Disbelief or undisclosed belief or motivation as to the reality of a situation does not require the corporate officer or public relations practitioner to disclose the information unless the disbelief is accompanied or supported by factual evidence.

Companies must also disclose in a timely manner important financial information that reveals a full and complete understanding of their fiscal conditions — every "essentially important element," in Roosevelt's words. Failure or delay in doing so can be evidence of deceptive or misleading actions on the part of a company or even proof of an intent to defraud. On the other hand, the information must be "available and ripe for publication" before there commences a duty to disclose. To be ripe under this requirement, the content must be verified sufficiently to permit the officers and directors to have

> full confidence in [its] accuracy. It also means ... that there is no valid corporate purpose which dictates the information not be disclosed. As to the verification of the data aspect, the hazards which arise from an erroneous statement are apparent, especially when it has not been carefully prepared and tested. It is equally obvious that an undue delay not in good faith in revealing facts can be deceptive, misleading, or a device to defraud....[54]

Corporate communication may not hide any material or significant fact or claim from the buying public, defined as reasonable and objective persons and investors making purchasing decisions. The claim need not actually influence an investor's decision to buy, nor must the investor actually lose money for the claim to be considered deceptive. The material fact must only have the capacity to affect an investor's choices. Such an omission — however inadvertent — makes the information false and misleading, according to the Securities and Exchange Commission. According to the Supreme Court:

> An omitted fact is material if there is a substantial likelihood that a reasonable shareholder would consider it important in deciding how to vote.... Put another way, there must be a substantial likelihood that the disclosure of the omitted fact would have been viewed by the reasonable investor as having signifi-

cantly altered the "total mix" of information available.[55]

Corporations traditionally considered material facts requiring disclosure as those that would affect a company's earnings by 5 percent or more. In 1999, however, the SEC broadened its definition of items companies must report as material, stating that it is as important to consider whether a reasonable investor would consider the information to be important or immaterial in the context of the company's overall financial situation. Such extensive disclosure requirements reinforce Congress' belief that "there cannot be honest markets without honest publicity. Manipulation and dishonest practices of the marketplace thrive on mystery and secrecy."[56]

Everything used in connection with the sale or purchase of securities in a manner "reasonably calculated to influence the investing public" is inappropriate and subject to SEC sanction.[57] This would include false financial statements, deceptive corporate press releases or incomplete public communication by the corporation.

As in the area of advertising, corporate release of knowingly false and misleading information may be equated with fraudulent misrepresentation and may even give rise to private enforcement actions, as long as the misrepresentation actually caused a loss.[58] In such instances, "[T]he seller is made to assume the burden of proving lack of scienter," defined as guilty knowledge that the information is false and misleading.[59] Information may be fraudulently misrepresentative when a corporation uses "indefinite and unverifiable" terms — such as "high value" or "fair" — in its public communication. In fact, "[S]uch conclusory terms in a economic context are reasonably understood to rest on a factual basis that justifies them as accurate, the absence of which renders them misleading." Corporate expression "should be to inform, not to challenge, the reader's critical wits."[60] Disclosure that is made with honesty of purpose and freedom from fraudulent intent, without the knowledge of any circumstances that would cause a reasonable individual to inquire further, is good faith disclosure.

A company may have a legal responsibility – a duty to correct – to remove material errors from non-corporate reports. It must do so if it has become so involved in the preparation of the reports projections by others outside the company that there is "an im-

---

[53] *See* Danny Hakim, *S.E.C. Approves Regulation Against Selective Disclosure,* N.Y. TIMES, Aug. 11, 2000, at C7; Floyd Norris, *S.E.C. Tells Concerns to Disclose Cancellations of Stock Purchases,* N.Y. TIMES, Feb. 1, 2001, at C1.

[54] Financial Industrial Fund v. McDonnell Douglas Corp., 474 F.2d 514, 519 (10th Cir. 1973).

[55] TSC Indus. v. Northway, 426 U.S. 438, 449 (1976). The falsehood's materiality is its "natural tendency to influence, or [capacity for] influencing, the decision of the ... body to which it was addressed." Kungys v. United States, 485 U.S. 759, 770 (1988).

[56] House of Representatives Report No. 1383, 73rd Congress, 2d Sess. 11 (1934).

[57] 17 C.F.R. 240.10b-5 (2000).

[58] *See* J.I. Case Co. v. Borak, 377 U.S. 426 (1964). *See also* Dura Pharmaceuticals v. Broudo, 544 U.S. 336, (2005); Linda Greenhouse, *Securities Fraud Standards Upheld by Supreme Court,* N.Y. TIMES, Apr. 20, 2005, at C3.

[59] Wilko v. Swan, 346 U.S. 427, 430 (1953).

[60] Virginia Bankshares v. Sandberg, 501 U.S. 1083, 1097 (1991).

plied representation that the information ... is true or at least in accordance with the company's views." Such involvement "is a risky activity, fraught with danger; management must navigate carefully between ... misleading stockholders and the public by implied approval of reviewed analyses and ... tipping material inside information by correcting statements which it knows to be erroneous."[61] However, there is no duty to correct erroneous reports if the company has a policy of refraining from commenting on earnings forecasts.

The time-worn attitude that public relations is simply a conduit for corporate expression is no longer workable. Public relations practitioners are not considered by the Securities and Exchange Commission and the courts to be mere publicists with no responsibility for the accuracy of corporate financial statements, although neither are they necessarily guarantors of such information. The courts require them to make fair, proper and appropriate investigations as to the accuracy of such statements.

In modern corporate law, the term "insider" is generally defined as one who has company information that is not available to the general public, that is, one who normally is involved in confidential relationships in the conduct of business. Corporate officers and directors obviously fall into this category.[62] Public relations practitioners, at times, also may be so classified. An insider, however, must act for personal gain in order to be in violation of the law. In addition, one has a duty to disclose information in one's possession to the public if the information in question could change the mind of an average individual making an investment decision. This tendency to change an investor's mind meets the standard of materiality discussed earlier. In a seminal case from the late 1930s, the federal courts held that the SEC could release sales, cost and gross profit data filed with the agency by the American Sumatra Tobacco Company, because the data were in the public interest, even though the release could put the company at a competitive disadvantage in the marketplace.[63] Only if disclosure would so seriously affect the company as to wreck its business would release of the information not be required.

But the mere possession of non-public market information does not necessarily require its disclosure. For example, one who has no connection with a company has no concomitant duty to disclose information in his or her possession. However, under the SEC's "misappropriation theory," even someone who is not a true company insider may still be restricted as an insider would be from taking advantage of market information obtained from sources outside the company itself. The theory has been the core of some of the most highly visible insider-trading cases of the 1980s, including the prosecution of takeover specialist Ivan Boesky and junk-bond king Michael Milken. In 1997, the Supreme

Court refused to restrict the SEC's regulatory direction, reviving a federal lawsuit against a Minneapolis attorney who had been convicted of making more than $4.3 million by trading on confidential information about a planned takeover bid for Pillsbury Company, even though he had no formal connection with or legal obligation to the company or its shareholders.[64] The attorney was a partner in the firm that had been retained to represent Pillsbury's interests in the takeover offer, but did no work on the representation himself. Yet the Court concluded that he knew or should have known that the information he used had been obtained from an insider or someone working on that person's behalf. The SEC may thus prohibit actions that are not in and of themselves fraudulent if its prohibition is "reasonably designed" to prevent actions that are fraudulent, such as insider trading based on non-public information.

More recently, the SEC has begun going even further in revising its rules restricting insider trading to include regulations governing "selective disclosure" — in which publicly traded companies provide information to analysts through the use of conference calls and other non-public events — and the "fiduciary" responsibility spouses and family members owe each other when one gives another inside information.[65]

### Food and Drug Administration

Congress initially enacted the Pure Food and Drugs Act of 1906, as an exercise of its power under the Commerce Clause, to protect the wholesomeness of products being sold across state lines and to protect the public from fraud.[66] The best known test of that use of the Commerce Clause is *Hippolite Egg Co. v. United States*.[67] The case began when an interstate shipment of preserved eggs was confiscated because the label failed to disclose that the product contained traces of boric acid. The government termed the acid a "deleterious" ingredient, making the eggs "adulterated" under the statute and subject to confiscation and destruction. A unanimous Supreme Court rejected the attack on Congress' power. The FDA was subsequently established to change this remedial power into a proactive regulatory one.[68] Today, the FDA has to approve all press releases, advertising, package inserts or other promotional copy about medical devices (including condoms) and prescription and non-prescription drugs.[69]

---

[61] Elkind v. Liggett & Myers, 635 F.2d 156, 163 (2d Cir. 1980).

[62] *See* SEC v. Texas Gulf Sulfur Co., 401 F.2d 833 (2d Cir. 1968).

[63] American Sumatra Tobacco Corp. v. SEC, 110 F.2d 117 (D.C. App. 1940).

[64] United States v. O'Hagan, 521 U.S. 642 (1997).

[65] *See* Neal Lipschutz, *New Rules Force Companies To Be More Forthcoming,* ATLANTA J.-CONSTITUTION, Aug. 15, 2004, at Q2.

[66] 21 U.S.C. 301 (2000).

[67] 220 U.S. 45 (1911).

[68] *See* Mark E. Boulding, *The Statutory Basis for FDA Regulation of Scientific and Educational Information,* 4 J. PHARMACY & LAW 123 (1995).

[69] 21 U.S.C. 343(a) (2000). The "definitions of labeling and advertising taken together cover — at least in the FDA's opinion — virtually all information-

The Federal Trade Commission, not the FDA, controls the contents of book, magazine or non-label advertising of food and non-prescription drug products, and evaluates them under a "truthful and not misleading" standard.[70] The FDA only regulates the claims that appear on the product's packaging, which includes "all labels and other written, printed, or graphic matter upon any article or any of its containers or wrappers, or accompanying such article,"[71] though it does regulate the advertising of all prescription drug products.[72] A product is deemed to be misbranded "unless its labeling bears adequate directions for use."[73] This includes the regulation of pharmaceutical trade or generic names, pesticides and similar products, and promotional materials.[74]

In general, the FDA bars all health claims from labels without its prior approval. The Food and Drug Administration Modernization Act of 1994 allowed health claims to be made on food labels if supported by authoritative statements from certain health research and protection agencies, such as the National Academy of Sciences, provided that the FDA was given a pre-marketing notice.[75] Out of "concern over excessive regulation of dietary supplements and the suppression of truthful information,"[76] Congress enacted the Dietary Supplement Health and Education Act of 1994, which allowed certain health claims to be made on the labels of dietary supplements without petitioning the FDA for its approval.[77] These claims include statements that dietary supplements restore nutrient deficiency, claims regarding how the human body uses the nutrient and proclamations that dietary supplements contribute to one's general well-being.[78] Yet these may only be made if the manufacturer has substantiation that the claim is "truthful and not misleading," if the label expressly states that the FDA has not evaluated the claim, and if the FDA is notified thirty days before the marketing claim is made.

In response to congressional passage of the Nutrition Labeling and Education Act of 1990,[79] the FDA enacted regulations allowing health claims to be made only when it

determines, based on the totality of publicly available scientific evidence (including evidence from well-designed studies conducted in a manner which is consistent with generally recognized scientific procedures and principles), that there is significant scientific agreement, among experts qualified by scientific training and experience to evaluate such claims, that the claim is supported by such evidence.[80]

A lawsuit claiming that the requirements were an unlawful prior restraint of truthful commercial speech by the FDA was determined to be without merit in 1998.[81]

In 2002, the FDA began a wide ranging review of its rules that regulate what corporations can say about their products (specifically, food, drugs, cosmetics or supplements) — what is "scientific truth"? The review came after the Supreme Court overturned a ban prohibiting pharmacies from advertising the availability of "compounded" pharmaceuticals, drugs pharmacists mix themselves for the specific needs of certain types of patients.[82] Scolding the government for its failure to consider alternatives to a complete advertising ban, the Court offered a ringing defense of free expression: "If the First Amendment means anything, it means that regulating speech must be a last — not first — resort."[83] Recognizing the challenge, the FDA stated:

False or misleading claims concerning foods, drugs, biologics, medical devices, cosmetics, or veterinary medicines may harm individuals who rely on these claims. Truthful claims, by contrast, may improve public health. If advertising of prescription drugs, for instance, leads to better informed consumers or to more physician visits to treat under-diagnosed illnesses, more people will be better off. On the other hand, if advertising of prescription drugs results in the inappropriate prescription of pharmaceuticals, the effect on public health will be negative.... The FDA must continue to pursue regulation of products for purposes of protecting the public health with a full recognition of the evolving judicial landscape in areas that directly affect its ability to regulate words. To be sure, the FDA will continue to

---

disseminating activities by or on behalf of a ... drug manufacturer." David A. Kessler & Wayne L. Pines, *The Federal Regulation of Prescription Drug Advertising and Promotion*, 264 J. AM. MED. ASS'N 2409, 2410 (1990). *See also* Greg Winter, *F.D.A. Survey Finds Faulty Listings of Possible Food Allergens*, N.Y. TIMES, Apr. 3, 2001, at C1.

[70] 21 U.S.C. 343(a) (2000).

[71] 21 U.S.C. 321(m) (2000). *See also* Marian Burros, *U.S.D.A. Enters Debate on Organic Label Law*, N.Y. TIMES, Feb. 26, 2003, at D1; Joyce Cohen, *Amid a Lawsuit, Keeping Track of a Candy Wrapper's Fine Print*, N.Y. TIMES, Nov. 9, 2005, at D18.

[72] FDA rules concerning the content of prescription drug ads may be found beginning at 21 C.F.R. 202.1.a (2000). *See, e.g.*, Stuart Elliott, *FDA Criticizes Viagra Ads, Prompting Pfizer To Halt Them*, N.Y. TIMES, Nov. 16, 2004, at C6.

[73] 21 U.S.C. 352(f) (2000). *See also* Heckler v. Chaney, 470 U.S. 821 (1985).

[74] *See* Ruckelshaus v. Monsanto, 467 U.S. 986 (1984) (applying the Federal Insecticide, Fungicide and Rodenticide Act of 1972, 7 U.S.C. 135FF (2000)); Abbott Labs v. Gardner, 387 U.S. 136 (1967); United States v. Exachol, 716 F. Supp. 787 (S.D.N.Y. 1989).

[75] 21 U.S.C. 343(r) (2000).

[76] Nutritional Health Alliance v. Shalala, 953 F. Supp. 526, 528 (S.D. N.Y. 1997).

[77] 21 U.S.C. 343(r) (2000).

[78] *See* Donald G. McNeil Jr. & Sherri Day, *F.D.A. to Put New Rules on Dietary Supplements*, N.Y. TIMES, Mar. 8, 2003, at A13. *See also* Donald G. McNeil Jr., *Sometimes, the Labels Lie*, N.Y. TIMES, Sept. 9, 2003, at D7.

[79] 21 U.S.C. 301 (2000).

[80] 21 C.F.R. 101.14(c) (2000).

[81] Nutritional Health Alliance v. Shalala, 144 F.3d 220 (2d Cir. 1998).

[82] Thompson v. Western States Medical Ctr., 535 U.S. 357 (2002). *See also* Gina Kolata, *Stung by Courts, F.D.A. Rethinks Its Rules*, N.Y. TIMES, Oct. 15, 2002, at D1.

[83] *Id.* at 373. *See also* Linda Greenhouse, *Citing Free Speech, Justices Lift a Ban on Advertising Mixed-to-Order Drugs*, N.Y. TIMES, Apr. 30, 2002, at A20.

regulate commercial speech as part of its mandate. In particular, the FDA intends to defend [its regulations] against constitutional challenges [while seeking] to ensure ... that its regulations, guidances, policies, and practices comply with the First Amendment.[84]

## Federal Trade Commission

While a number of federal statutes also govern marketing do's and don'ts, the Federal Trade Commission Act of 1914 gives the FTC the authority to define and control unfair practices in the marketplace, though primarily after the fact.[85] While its effectiveness has varied greatly over the years as a result of differing political attitudes, the agency has the power to ban types of promotional claims and to order that certain claims be altered so they are no longer improper. Required alterations may include warnings, disclosures and corrections of earlier deceptive claims. The FTC's rulings and reports not only determine the scope of federal regulation but also set standards for industry regulatory bodies.

This authority has evolved slowly. While early judicial decisions raised questions about the extent of the FTC's power, the Supreme Court in 1922 backed a broad interpretation of its ability to define unfair means of competition.[86] The Court subsequently brought marketing excesses within the FTC's power to regulate unfairness in 1937,[87] and Congress responded the following year with an amendment to the FTC Act, which allowed the agency to act to protect consumers as well as competing businesses from unfair claims. In the 1970s, Congress authorized the FTC to seek injunctive relief against publicity that violates federal law and later to regulate publicity affecting all commerce, not just interstate commerce.

Publicity is considered deceptive if (1) it is likely to deceive (2) a reasonable consumer (3) with an omission or material representation of fact so significant that it has the capacity to affect a decision to purchase or to act on its recommendation. Material claims have included omissions or claims about health, safety, durability, performance, warranties, efficiency, cost and quality. Deception may take place through express falsehoods or false implications. It might even take place through an omission, if the consumer needs the omitted information to form an impression.

Puffery, on the other hand — statements about subjective matters, such as taste, smell, appearance and feel — are not improper.

The FTC assumes that consumers do not take puffery seriously, until marketing claims falsely imply material assumptions of superiority. For example, the promotional claim that a sports car is the "sexiest" car on the road or that Bayer aspirin "works wonders" is acceptable. A claim that a television antenna was an "electronic miracle," however, was held by the FTC to go beyond acceptable puffery because the statement, taken with a series of other claims, could lead consumers to believe falsely that the antenna was generally superior to others. Puffery becomes deceptive when exaggerated claims falsely imply material assumptions of superiority.

A claim does not actually have to deceive someone to be improper. Taken as a whole, it only has to be likely to or have a tendency or capacity to mislead, regardless of the businessperson's intent, a substantial number of reasonable consumers — those in the target group at whom the advertisement is directed, acting reasonably in the circumstances.[88] Where the deception is not fully clear, the FTC relies on expert testimony and the results of consumer surveys to assess the likelihood of deception. In addition, publicity acceptable in certain circumstances may not be proper in others. For example, an announcement exaggerating the medicinal powers of a product might not deceive average, healthy adults but could be deemed deceptive if directed to the terminally ill who are desperately seeking solutions. Also, misleading promises of easy weight loss might not deceive the consumer of average weight but could deceive a chronically obese consumer.

Deceptive practices, of course, are not limited to advertising and marketing. A June 1998 FTC study revealed that 92 percent of 600 World Wide Web sites surveyed collected personal information on visitors and subscribers, while only 2 percent provided privacy statements that disclosed how the information would be used. Recently, Geocities, a popular Web site, reached an agreement with the FTC, the first Internet privacy enforcement action, to settle charges that it had deceived customers by promising them that the company would not provide subscriber information — including age, education, occupation, income and personal interests — without permission to third parties. The FTC made it plain at the time that Geocities was not required to keep such information private and not to sell it, and the company admitted no wrong-doing. The company was only required to be truthful in its Web privacy statement and to disclose to consumers what it does with the information it collects. Even more recently, the FTC has focused its regulatory sights on deceptive, junk e-mail, also known as "spam," encouraging consumers to send any deceptive spam they receive to: uce@ftc.gov.

In addition to deceptive advertising, the FTC also regulates unfair business practices. Section 5 of the FTC Act defines "unfairness" very broadly: It is the extent to which a practice offends public policy, is immoral or unethical, or causes substantial injury to

---

[84] 67 Fed. Reg. at 34943 (May 16, 2002). *See also* Gardiner Harris, *FDA Moves Toward More Openness with the Public*, N.Y. TIMES, Feb. 20, 2005, at A19.

[85] 15 U.S.C. 45 (2000). These laws include the Sherman Anti-Trust Act of 1890, 15 U.S.C. 1 (2000); the Clayton Act of 1914, 15 U.S.C. 12 (2000); the Wheeler-Lea Amendment of 1938, 15 U.S.C. 53 (2000); and the Consumer Product warranties and Federal Trade Commission Improvements Act of 1975 (also known as the Moss-Magnuson Act), 15 U.S.C. 57 (2000).

[86] *See* FTC v. Winstead Hosiery Co., 258 U.S. 483 (1922).

[87] *See* FTC v. Standard Educ. Soc'y, 302 U.S. 112 (1937).

[88] *See* FTC v. Colgate-Palmolive, 380 U.S. 374 (1965).

consumers or businesses.[89] The FTC has generally narrowed the focus of its unfairness inquiries to examine whether marketing practices cause substantial injury that is not outweighed by offsetting benefits to consumers or competitors who cannot reasonably avoid the injury. Thus, the concept of unfairness may most easily be seen in a company's treatment of its customers.[90] The harm must be substantial and, more often than not, monetary, as when sellers coerce consumers into purchasing unwanted goods or services or acting against their own best interests. However, the unfair treatment may not be unsubstantiated or trivial. But the commission has also found unfairness in certain promotional practices that bring unwarranted safety or health risks, such as the inclusion of free sample razor blades in copies of a newspaper.

A false or misleading claim may also have an unfair or anti-competitive effect on trade, sufficient to constitute an antitrust violation, a rule the Supreme Court established in 1934.[91] The Court revisited this issue during its 1998-99 term in *California Dental Association v. FTC*,[92] a case that challenged the association's enforcement of its mandatory code of ethics prohibiting a member dentist from false and misleading promotional statements, in this instance the promotion of discounted services. The FTC in 1993 had alleged that the association violated the Sherman Antitrust Act of 1890 because it applied its code in a way that also restricted truthful, non-deceptive claims. The Court upheld the ban, concluding that the restrictions were not anti-competitive on their face — they were, after all, designed to avoid deceptive claims and "might plausibly be thought to have a net pro-competitive effect, or possibly no effect at all on competition." Because the association's reasoning was not implausible, the FTC could not conclude that the restrictions were "presumptively wrong."

All fifty states have also enacted legislation that prohibits unfair competition, unfair acts and practices, and allows citizens and companies to sue over deceptive claims. Under many state laws, consumers (as well as competitors) can also sue to recover damages and attorney's fees.

## TORT LAW

Tort law has three purposes: compensation, justice and deterrence. It deals with fairly compensating individuals for losses that have been caused by the actions of others. The harms, among others, may be physical (such as battery, trespass to land or intrusion upon physical solitude), mental (such as assault or infliction of emotional distress), reputational (such as defamation or misappropriation). Thus, a tort is

- a result of conduct — by an act of either commission or omission,
- that has a detrimental affect on one's legal interest in either person or property,
- usually committed with a certain state of mind (such as recklessness or carelessness),
- that causes damage, assuming that the consequences were at least "reasonably foreseeable."

Without an adequate defense, a defendant must pay at least nominal damages, usually compensatory damages and sometimes punitive damages to the injured individual.

### *Interference with Contract or Prospective Advantage*

When a claim for breach of contract might not be actionable, a tort claim for interference with contract or prospective advantage — which does not require an enforceable contract — might be. A claim for interference with contract requires that there be some sort of a contractual relationship in existence, that the defendant must have been aware of that contractual relationship, and that the defendant acted to cause a breach in that relationship. A claim for interference with prospective advantage requires a prospective or future relationship advantageous to the parties involved (and not an existing contract), the intentional or negligent interference with that relationship, resulting in damage caused by that interference.

The tort's most controversial application as it relates to public relations has stemmed from its use as a weapon by corporations to keep employees from joining labor unions during the early part of the last century.[93] A more recent example was the 1980s takeover battle between Texaco and Pennzoil for Getty Oil, which created a public relations fiasco for Texaco. A tortuous interference claim filed by Pennzoil when Texaco topped the Pennzoil offer for Getty Oil — interfering with the two companies' agreement — resulted in a verdict of $7.53 billion in actual damages and $2.5 billion in punitive damages for Pennzoil, a final appeal to the Supreme Court, and an ultimate settlement of $3 billion.[94]

Interference with prospective advantage may most frequently be found in unlawful efforts to prohibit attempts — through public relations or other acts — to hinder or deter potential customers from dealing with a particular business. The basic rule is that one owes a duty to take reasonable measures to avoid the risk of caus-

---

[89] 15 U.S.C. 45(a)(1) (2000).

[90] *See* Cinderella Career & Finishing Sch. v. FTC, 425 F.2d 583 (D.C. Cir. 1970).

[91] FTC v. Algoma Lumber Co., 291 U.S. 67 (1934).

[92] 526 U.S. 756 (1999).

[93] *See* Hitchman Coal & Coke Co. v. Mitchell, 245 U.S. 229 (1917). The miners' decision to join a labor union was ruled to have violated their "yellow dog" contracts in which they agreed not to join a union while employed by the mining company. The outcome was first changed by enactment of the Norris-Laguardia Act of 1932, 29 U.S.C. 101 (2000), which prohibited the enforcement of "yellow dog" contracts in federal courts. These type of contracts were finally outlawed by the National Labor Relations Act of 1935, 29 U.S.C. 151 (2000), which made it an "unfair labor practice" to discriminate against employees because of their union membership.

[94] *See* Texaco v. Pennzoil, 485 U.S. 994 (1988); Texaco v. Pennzoil, 729 S.W.2d 768 (Texas App. 1987).

ing economic damages to identifiable persons or businesses who will suffer or are reasonably likely to suffer damages from such conduct.

## Unfair Competition

The tort of unfair competition may take several forms, but the two most important to the practice of public relations are cases involving what might be termed "passing off" and "malice in trade."

*Passing off* is similar to misrepresentation in that it involves a business selling or presenting its goods and services in such a way that they appear to be the goods and services of another business, allowing the first to benefit from the good reputation of the second. The name, image or representation of the product or service may be protected by trademark law. However, the unfairness lies in the manner — either expression or act — in which the first company conducted its business.

*Malice in trade* cases involve companies overstepping the proper bounds of competition, seeking to drive others out of business through malicious public relations or actions.[95]

The seminal case illustrating unfair competition is *International News Service v. Associated Press*.[96] On the grounds that the Associated Press' news stories were "quasi-property," the Supreme Court held that actions by International News Service redistributing the news as its own, without authorization, denied the AP full value for its news-gathering efforts, leading customers to believe that the news stories in question, which had been copied and rewritten, originated with the INS. The Court concluded that the AP thus had a legal right to protect its publication of news from improper interference by the INS:

> Not only do the acquisition and transmission of news require elaborate organization and a large expenditure of money, skill, and effort; not only has it an exchange value to the gatherer, dependent chiefly upon its novelty and freshness, the regularity of the service, its reputed reliability and thoroughness, and its adaptability to the public needs; but also, as is evident, the news has an exchange value to one who can misappropriate it.[97]

From a public relations perspective, then, presentation of a campaign or program to the public does not lessen the monetary value to public relations practitioners of their hard work, especially when those efforts are viewed in comparison or competition with the efforts of another company "endeavoring to reap where it has not sown and ... appropriating to itself the harvest of those

who have sown."[98]

## Duty To Warn/Failure To Disclose

A public relations practitioner's duty to warn arises most commonly in product liability situations, in which the manufacturer of a product could be held liable for failing to warn consumers of dangerous conditions associated with the product.[99] The general rule is that for a duty to warn to exist, a product must be dangerous beyond the extent to which a reasonable consumer, with knowledge common to the community as to the product's characteristics, would use it. To mitigate a product's inherent danger, a seller could be required to provide directions as to the use of the product. In the situation where a product contains a dangerous ingredient — or one whose danger is not widely known or which an average consumer would not reasonably expect to find contained in the product — a seller could be required to provide a warning with each sale of the product. For example, warnings as to appropriate use are generally required for poisonous drugs. Where a warning is given, the seller may assume that it has been read and heeded. However, sellers are not generally required to warn consumers about products or ingredients that are only dangerous or potentially dangerous when consumed in excessive amounts, over an extended period of time, or when the danger is generally known and recognized. This is known as the "common sense" defense. Thus, the threshold question is, first, whether the circumstances of a case demand a duty to warn at all and, second, whether the warning is adequate.

To determine the adequacy of directions or warnings, judges must balance "the likelihood that the product would cause the harm complained of, and the seriousness of that harm, against the burden on the manufacturer of providing an adequate warning."[100] Adequacy may be

> measured not only by what is stated, but also by the manner in which it is stated. A reasonable warning not only conveys a fair indication of the nature of the dangers involved, but also warns with the degree of intensity demanded by the nature of the risk. A warning may be found to be unreasonable in that it was unduly delayed, reluctant in tone, or lacking in a sense of urgency.[101]

Adequacy also requires resolving other questions: How explicit must the warning be?[102] In whose language must the warning be

---

[95] The leading American authority is *Tuttle v. Buck*, 119 N.W. 946 (Minn. 1909).

[96] 248 U.S. 215 (1918).

[97] *Id.* at 238.

[98] *Id.* at 239-40.

[99] *See* Albright v. Upjohn Co., 788 F.2d 1217 (6th Cir. 1986).

[100] Ayers v. Johnson & Johnson Baby Products Co., 818 P.2d 1337, 1346 (Wash. 1991).

[101] Seley v. G.D. Searle Co., 423 N.E.2d 831, 837 (Ohio 1981).

[102] In *Ayers*, the Court concluded that because Johnson & Johnson's Baby Oil was marketed as "pure and gentle," consumers could reasonably have con-

made?[103] At what point is a warning sufficient?[104] On the other hand, when a federal statute dictates the specific wording of a product's labeling requirements, federal law preempts state tort law claims.[105] More broadly, public relations practitioners must always be sensitive to situations in which state regulation of corporate business practices are preempted by federal law.[106]

The same rule also applies to product warranties and marketing promises by manufacturers. For example, a company that promoted its "Golfing Gizmo" as "completely safe" was held liable when a 13-year-old boy hit the ball in an unusual manner and was hit in the head when the ball bounced back. The device consisted of a golf ball attached to an elastic cord. It was supposed to allow users to improve their golf swings without having to retrieve golf balls. The company's promotional literature urged users to "drive the ball with full power" since the "ball will not hit player." The court upheld an award based on claims of breach of warranty and misrepresentation.[107]

### Misrepresentation

The core of the tort of misrepresentation is a person's reliance on a false statement. Thus, if a false statement is material — substantially central to a person's decision to rely on the statement — if the public relations practitioner knows that it is false, if his or her intent is to induce others to make economic decisions based upon the statement, if justifiable reliance results and causes damages, the practitioner may be liable for fraudulent misrepresentation. "Puffing" — subjective statements about quality — may be fraudulent if the parties to the exchange do not enjoy equal bar-

gaining power to determine their truthfulness.[108]

Negligent misrepresentation occurs when a public relations practitioner makes a false representation of a material fact in his or her professional capacity, when he or she fails to use reasonable care to determine the statement's truth, and when the practitioner owes a duty to the person who justifiably relied on it, causing damages. However, the general rule is that nondisclosure, when two parties are dealing independently and knowingly, "at arm's length," is not grounds for a misrepresentation claim.[109] Third parties, such as public relations practitioners, are not generally liable for negligent misrepresentation unless: (1) they know their statements will be used for a particular purpose; (2) they know another specific party will rely on their statements; and (3) they are somehow linked to that party and understand the consequences of that party's reliance on their statements.[110]

## BUSINESS LAW REGULATION OF PUBLIC RELATIONS

Because public relations involves the marketing of corporate ideas and ideals, as well as the defense of economic actions and transactions (such as contracts), a close, symbiotic relationship exists between business law and public relations law. Public relations practitioners must understand the extent to which the general laws of business also govern their field; both they and the media are subject to the normal laws of business, such as antitrust regulations, even though their expression may be protected by the First Amendment.

### Ownership of Work and Proposals

The Supreme Court ruled in 1989 that, unless an express contractual agreement exists to the contrary, independent contractors, also sometimes known as "free-lancers," own the copyright to works they create.[111] Historically, corporate clients assumed they owned such works-made-for-hire because they had contracted with PR practitioners to create a particular campaign, program,

---

cluded that it was safe even if accidentally inhaled and, therefore, a more explicit warning was required. 818 P.2d at 1346-1347.

[103] *See* Ramierz v. Plough, 863 P.2d 167 (Cal. 1993) (holding that warnings in English only regarding the dangers of non-prescription drugs were adequate).

[104] *See* MacDonald v. Ortho Pharmaceutical Corp., 475 N.E.2d 65 (Mass. 1985) (holding that warnings included with oral contraceptives must be given to all "who it is foreseeable will come in contact with, and consequently be endangered by" the product, except in certain, narrow circumstances when the manufacturer only has a duty to warn a "responsible, ... learned intermediary," such as a physician).

[105] *See* King v. E.I. Dupont De Nemours & Co., 996 F.2d 1346 (1st Cir., 1993) (holding that a manufacturer's labeling was adequate based on the duties the Federal Insecticide, Fungicide and Rodenticide Act of 1972, 7 U.S.C. 136 (2000), required of manufacturers). *See also* Cipollone v. Liggett Group, 505 U.S. 504 (1992) (holding that federal regulation of cigarette warning labels in the Federal Cigarette Labeling and Advertising Act of 1965, 15 U.S.C. 1331 (2000), and its successor, the Public Health Cigarette Smoking Act of 1969, 15 U.S.C. 1331-1340 (2000), preempted state labeling requirements); however, *see also* Bates v. Dow Agrosciences, 544 U.S. 431, (2005) (holding that farmers whose crops are damaged by federally approved pesticides may sue in state court); Linda Greenhouse, *Supreme Court Says Farmers May Sue In State Courts*, N.Y. TIMES, Apr. 28, 2005, at C11.

[106] *See* Crosby v. Nat'l Foreign Trade Council, 530 U.S. 363 (2000).

[107] Hauter v. Zogarts, 534 P.2d 377 (Cal. 1975).

[108] *See* Vulcan Metals Co. v. Simmons Mfg. Co., 248 F. 853 (2d Cir. 1918) (holding that a company's ability to test a product placed it on equal footing from a bargaining standpoint with the company which made unverified marketing claims as to the product's performance).

[109] *See* Swinton v. Whitinsville Sav. Bank, 42 N.E.2d 808 (Mass. 1942) (holding that a vendor who failed to disclose as a latent defect that the house was infested with termites did not commit misrepresentation). It is important to note that many jurisdictions by state statute require termite inspections by licensed inspectors before a house may be sold. For another type of transaction *see Osborn v. Gene Teague Chevrolet*, 459 P.2d 988 (Or. 1969) (upholding a fraud verdict when a used car dealer had reset a vehicle's odometer from 100,000 miles to 62,000 miles, even in the absence of any verbal statement misrepresenting the vehicle's condition).

[110] *See* Credit Alliance Corp. v. Andersen & Co., 483 N.E.2d 110 (N.Y. 1985) (where the detrimental reliance on a report by certified public accountants was at issue).

[111] Cmty. for Creative Non-Violence v. Reid, 490 U.S. 730 (1989).

project or plan. A close look at the works-made-for-hire provisions of the Copyright Act of 1976, however, reveals that the corporation owns the finished work only if the creator is an employee acting "within the scope of his or her employment."[112] Other works, "specifically ordered or commissioned," require an express agreement "that the work is to be considered a work-made-for-hire."[113] Even then, the corporation may not own all rights to the work, because the Copyright Act defines "works-made-for-hire" in a limited way, as "a contribution to a collective work, as a part of a motion picture or other audio-visual work, as a translation, as a supplementary work, as a compilation, as an instructional text, as a test, as answer material for a test, or as an atlas."[114]

Generally, PR campaigns, projects, programs or plans created by independent practitioners do not fit into one of these categories and, thus, continue to be owned by their creators even if the copyright is assigned to the corporation. So corporations and public relations practitioners should carefully agree to the origin and ownership of public relations plans in very specific contractual terms. Because prospective clients can easily use part or all of a proposal after having seen it during a presentation, a statement of ownership should be included on the proposal's title page.

### Letters of Agreement/Employment Contracts

A contract is simply a promise that the law will enforce.[115] To be legally binding, a contract must include: an offer to do something, consideration — defined by law as a bargained-for exchange, something given in exchange for a promise to act in some way — and a legal detriment in that the person making the promise agrees to do something he or she does not have to do — and acceptance by both parties or mutual assent. Agreements and contracts spell out the responsibilities and mutual obligations in a relationship:

• To the public relations practitioner: the terms of work to be produced, timeliness, deadlines, billing routines, the use of freelancers through sub-contracting and other pertinent data;
• Of the employer or client: the terms of supplying information, timetables for review of work and payment schedules.

These points should be thoroughly understood before either side agrees. The final version of the contract should be read before it is signed. With only slight exaggeration, it has been said: "The whole panoply of contract law rests on the principle that one is bound by the contract which he knowingly and voluntarily signs."[116]

The law assumes that a contractual agreement has been fully negotiated between its parties, even though standard form contracts are commonplace in business life, reflecting the impersonality of the mass market. Though such contracts take advantage of the lessons of experience, save time and effort, and provide for the simplified interpretation of other, similar contracts, they are also inherently dangerous legally, for one party can use a contract to impose its will on another unwilling or unwitting party. First, standard form contracts generally provide no opportunity for one party to bargain over terms. Second, a party to such contracts with no real opportunity to study the terms may thus be unfamiliar with the provisions of the agreement. Third, because the bargaining is not between equals, usually the party in the weaker bargaining position may not understand what he or she is signing. Such agreements are known as "contracts of adhesion" and are legally unenforceable if they include "an absence of meaningful choice on the part of one of the parties together with contract terms which are unreasonably favorable to the other party."[117]

### Hold-Harmless Clauses

Letters of agreement and employment contracts should also include "hold-harmless/duty to read" or indemnification clauses. Such a clause should clearly state that the public relations practitioner shall not be held responsible for any material approved by the client or corporate officers for public dissemination that results in negative or unwanted publicity or legal action. Such a clause would generally be unenforceable if it (1) is unconscionable, (2) is a violation of public policy or (3) lacks true mutual and informed assent. A successful challenge to such a clause could arise if one party to the agreement unfairly shifts the burden of responsibility for any act of wrongdoing to the weaker party, wrongly taking advantage of that party.

In some instances, provisions might also include payment of legal costs and damages if the covered individual is sued.

### No-Compete Clauses

Letters of agreement and employment contracts may also include no-compete clauses, which restrict the employment of the public relations practitioner by a company's competitors.[118] The common law prohibition against contracts in restraint of trade is one of the oldest and most firmly established in the law.[119] Public policy concerns still generally disfavor such restraints and favor an individual's freedom of contract and right to work.[120] Thus, no-

---

[112] 17 U.S.C. 101 (2000); 17 U.S.C. 201 (2000).

[113] Id.

[114] 17 U.S.C. 101(A)(2) (2000).

[115] For an example of a lawsuit over the terms of an employment contract in the entertainment industry involving the actress Shirley Maclaine, see Parker v. Twentieth Century-Fox Film Corp., 474 P.2d 689 (Cal. 1970).

[116] Nat'l Bank of Washington v. Equity Investors, 506 P.2d 20, 36 (Wash. 1973).

[117] Williams v. Walker-Thomas Furniture Co., 350 F.2d 445, 449 (D.C. Cir. 1965).

[118] See David Koeppel, Lose the Employee, Keep the Business, N.Y. TIMES, May 5, 2005, at C5.

[119] See Dutch Maid Bakeries v. Schleicher, 131 P.2d 630, 634 (Wyo. 1942).

[120] For example, chapter 237 of the Acts of 1998 of the Commonwealth of

compete clauses in employment agreements are generally unenforceable, unless the following four requirements are met:

1. The clauses are in writing.

2. The clauses are part of the contract at the initial time of employment or change in the employee's status and involve consideration or payment.

3. The clauses are reasonable in both duration (time) and space (geography).

4. The clauses are reasonably necessary to protect the business interests or activities of the employer.

"Reasonableness" is a determination to be made by the court as a matter of law, not a factual determination for the jury.

Despite the obvious importance of the fourth element — especially when one realizes that the employee is usually at a disadvantage both procedurally (that is, the potential for unfairness in the process of making the bargain) and substantively (that is, the potential for unfairness in the terms or outcome of the agreement) when contracting for employment — most debate focuses on the third element. The test is whether the restraint of trade is unreasonable. Is the time or geographic limitation greater than required to protect the employer's interests? Do the limitations impose an undue hardship on the employee's ability to profit from his or her skills? Is either limitation injurious to the public's interest, which favors free competition in the market? Essentially, no-compete clauses must not deny the practitioner the right to earn a living.

The traditional disfavor in which such agreements are usually held means that courts construe them against the party — the employer — seeking to enforce them. Thus, the initial burden is on the employer to prove that the no-compete clause is reasonable, is fairly related to and is necessary to protect the employer's business interests or activities. The employer is not entitled to protection against ordinary competition in the market. For example, even if a business were national in scope, an agreement not to compete anywhere in the nation would be unreasonable.

When examining covenants "not-to-compete," courts tend to apply one of three strategies:

1. Under the "all-or-nothing" approach, if any part of the employment contract is objectionable, then it is completely unenforceable. The legal trend has been steadily away from this tactic toward one of the two other forms of judicial modification.

2. Under the "blue line" method, courts mark out what is objectionable in the contract. The remaining provisions are enforceable.

3. The "rule of reasonableness" method requires courts to assume that the parties to the agreement intended some type of restriction, absent any evidence of "bad faith" on the part of either party, and then modify the problematic parts of the contract as best they can to match that intent.

*Massachusetts (amending chapter 149 of the General Laws of the Commonwealth of Massachusetts) prohibits the use of such clauses in employment contracts in the broadcasting industry.*

### Confidentiality Agreements

Because public relations professionals — unlike doctors, attorneys, ministers and, in some cases, journalists — cannot claim that a legally privileged relationship exists between themselves and their clients, some corporations require contractual agreements forbidding any sharing of information outside the organization.

If there is a difficulty with the legality of these agreements, some public relations practitioners recommend involving the company's attorney, when necessary, in public relations discussions and creating a privileged, confidential relationship in that manner.

### Consent Agreements/Release Forms

Many types of consent agreements may be necessary to effective public relations. Although releases may not be necessary in every situation, the basic rule of thumb is that if the use is economic — if it is for purposes of trade — releases are necessary. An ideal consent release should be in writing and contain these elements:

1. Consideration or exchange of value,

2. Identification of parties' names and ages,

3. A statement as to the agreement's scope and duration,

4. Words binding one's legal successors and representatives,

5. A statement that the agreement is the full agreement, that no promises were made not plainly stated in the release.

It might also be wise to tie the agreement to one that has a purpose much broader than consent, but minimally open-ended consent/release agreements should be obtained to protect future uses of the material. Of course, the parents or guardians of minors must enter into such agreements on the behalf of those minors.

*The bottom line is this: Whenever there is any doubt as to the origin of any material to be used in an economic campaign, copies of all consent agreements or releases should be obtained to protect against corporate liability from improper use of the material.*

## INTERACTING WITH THE MEDIA

A few simple and practical actions can help corporations, public relations practitioners and other business communicators successfully to interact with the media and avoid misunderstandings and lawsuits.

### Recording Interviews

Corporate clients should be advised to tape-record all interviews with journalists. Deliberate misquoting that materially changes the meaning of what was said can be the legal equivalent of actual malice, which is an essential element in some libel suits, and a tape recording can demonstrate the changes.[121] Tape recording is also a good policy in any antagonistic situation, although care must be taken not to violate state privacy laws governing consensual monitoring. Some states allow recording with the consent of one party; others require the consent of both parties.

### Careful Public Actions

Public relations practitioners and their corporate clients should never do or say anything they do not want disseminated by the media, especially if they are engaged in some newsworthy activity. They should remember that courts generally allow the media broad leeway in defining "newsworthiness."[122]

### Off-the-Record Remarks

The rules for off-the-record remarks are difficult to understand simply because they are almost always unwritten. Indeed, each individual journalist or media organization may have its own understanding of what the so-called "rules" are. It is always best to clarify rules or expectations at the beginning of a conversation with any member of the media. Conversations are generally considered to fall into one of several categories:

*On the record.* Every comment made by a corporate employee may be attributed to the employee through either direct quotations or paraphrases.

*For background.* The corporate employee may be quoted directly, but his or her name may not be used.

*For deep background.* The information may be used but may not be attributed to the individual.

*Off the record.* The journalist may not use the information.

### Promises of Confidentiality

A journalist's verbal promise of confidentiality is enforceable under the principle of *promissory estoppel*, if justifiably relied upon by the person to whom the promise is made.[123] It is wise in such situations to have the journalist repeat the confidentiality agreement and to use the word "promise." For this reason, corporate officers and public relations practitioners should tape-record all conversations with journalists in case the promise of confidentiality is broken.

### SUMMARY

Public relations, which generally may be defined as the explanation of business or institutional concerns to the public, involves the management and marketing of corporate ideas and ideals, and the defense of economic actions and transactions. Public relations law has been described as plain, old business law polished with a veneer of First Amendment protections. In fact, it is not really an area of law — such as defamation and copyright — but a study of the application of other areas of law to the practice of public relations. Because of this, a close, symbiotic relationship exists between public relations law and the general laws of business.

In modern corporate law, for example, the term "insider" is generally defined as one who has company information that is not available to the general public. However, under the Securities and Exchange Commission's misappropriation test, public relations practitioners who are not true company insiders may still be restricted from taking advantage of market information obtained from sources outside the company itself and, therefore, must be careful what they do with such information. Similarly, they must be careful not to misrepresent a company's products or services to the public in such a way as to overstep the proper bounds of competition, or the company they represent could be sued for the tort of unfair competition.

In the area of employment law, public relations practitioners must understand who owns the public relations plans they create. Independent contractors generally own the copyright to the works they create. And because such plans generally do not fall into the "works-made-for-hire" definition included in the Copyright Act of 1976, they continue to be owned by their creator even if the copyright is assigned to a corporate employer. In addition, "no-compete" clauses in employment contracts are enforceable only if such clauses are in writing, if such clauses are a part of the employee's contract at the beginning of the particular work or employment, if such clauses are reasonable in both duration and space, and if such clauses are reasonably necessary to protect the business interests of the employer. Finally, just as a journalist's verbal promise of confidentiality may be enforceable under the principle of *promissory estoppel* — if justifiably relied upon by the person to whom the promise is made — public relations practitioners should be aware of the potential legal consequences of their promises and agreements, whether written or oral.

Written agreements are generally more easily enforced than oral ones, but even written agreements — whether they be employment contracts or confidentiality agreements — if presented for signature without opportunity for negotiation may not be enforceable. The law assumes that all contractual agreements have been fully negotiated between the parties to them. Standard "form" agreements are inherently dangerous legally as they may be the means by which one party to a contract imposes its will on another unwilling or unwitting party in that they generally provide no opportunity for parties to bargain over terms, they provide parties with no real opportunity to even study the terms, and they are not agreements reached as the result of bargaining between equals.

---

[121] *See* Masson v. New Yorker, 501 U.S. 496 (1991).

[122] *See* Sidis v. F-R Publishing Co., 113 F.2d 806 (2d Cir. 1940).

[123] *See* Cohen v. Cowles Media, 501 U.S. 663 (1991).

## FOR ADDITIONAL READING

Gower, Karla. *Legal and Ethical Restraints on Public Relations*. Prospect Heights, Ill.: Waveland Press, 2003.

Lamb, Robert, William Armstrong & Karolyn Morigi. *Business, Media, and the Law: The Troubled Confluence*. New York: New York University Press, 1980.

Lisby, Greg, et al. "Integrating the Public Relations Perspective into the Mass Communications Law Course," 48 *Journalism Educator* 67-73 (Summer 1993).

Moore, Roy, Ronald Farrar & Erik Collins. *Advertising & Public Relations Law*. Hillsdale, N.J.: Lawrence Erlbaum, 1998.

Parkinson, Michael & Marie Parkinson. *Law for Advertising, Broadcasting, Journalism & Public Relations*. Mahweh, N.J.: Lawrence-Erlbaum, 2006.

Simon, Morton. *Public Relations Law*. New York: Appleton-Century-Crofts, 1969.

Stevenson, Russell. *Corporations and Information: Secrecy, Access and Disclosure*. Baltimore: Johns Hopkins University Press, 1980.

Walsh, Frank. *Public Relations and the Law*. Sarasota, Fla.: Institute for Public Relations Research and Education, 1992.

Wolfson, Nicholas. *Corporate First Amendment Rights and the SEC*. New York: Quorum Books, 1990.

# 10

# Broadcast Regulation

*By Michael A. McGregor*

---

 **Headnote Questions**

- *Why are broadcasting media regulated differently than print media?*
- *What are the powers of the Federal Communications Commission?*
- *What are the main structural regulations of the broadcast media?*
- *What are the main content regulations of the broadcast media?*
- *What role do the courts play in the regulation of broadcasting?*
- *How will the transition to digital transmission affect broadcasters and consumers?*

---

Broadcast regulation is one of the most complex and dynamic areas of communication law. To better understand how broadcasting came to be regulated as it is today, it is necessary to review some of its history. That history will be followed by a discussion of regulation as it affects broadcasting today.

## THE DEVELOPMENT OF BROADCAST REGULATION

Few people involved in radio's development, which began more than one hundred years ago, foresaw its becoming a form of mass communication. "Wireless," as it was originally called, initially was considered an extension of the telegraph and the telephone. Only much later did it become a mass medium.

### Broadcasting's Early History

Guglielmo Marconi, generally considered the first person to send radio signals without wires, believed his "wireless radio," used for ship-to-shore and ship-to-ship radio transmissions, would be commercially successful. He competed fiercely with rival companies to retain rights to his invention. Employees of Marconi Wireless Company of America, for example, refused to recognize signals sent to shore from ships using equipment that other firms manufactured. Concern that distress signals might be ignored led Congress to adopt the Wireless Ship Act of 1910, which required

large ships to have wireless equipment and radio operators on board. The law also made it illegal not to retransmit or answer wireless transmissions from ships. The 1910 law was the first American regulation of devices using the electromagnetic spectrum, a natural resource through which radio signals are transmitted.

When ships began using wireless equipment, many radio signals filled the spectrum. Signals would interfere with each other, so only static was heard, causing problems not only for U.S. vessels but also for ships throughout the world. In an effort to deal with the problem, representatives from a number of countries met to establish certain standards for radio use. They also insisted that individual nations adopt laws requiring that the standards be followed. This agreement and one tragic event led to the United States replacing the 1910 law with the Radio Act of 1912.

### The Radio Act of 1912

The tragedy was the sinking of the *Titanic*. The supposedly unsinkable ship hit an iceberg in the Atlantic Ocean, and more than 1,500 people died. The irony that tied the *Titanic* tragedy to broadcast regulation was the fact that a ship only a few miles away could have saved many lives. No one on the nearby ship knew of the *Titanic's* desperate radio transmissions, however, because, even though the ship met the provisions of the 1910 Act and possessed the required radio equipment, the radio operator had gone off duty. While the 1910 Act required radio equipment, it did not require a radio operator to be on duty twenty-four hours a day.

The *Titanic* tragedy focused public and congressional attention on radio legislation. Congress adopted the 1912 Act, which, in addition to closing some of the loopholes of the earlier act, became the first law directly affecting commercial radio. Among other provisions, it allowed the U.S. Secretary of Commerce to award licenses for radio stations and to assign the spectrum frequencies those stations would use. In an era when wireless was considered a point-to-point medium, the 1912 Act worked well enough. Dramatic changes in the use of wireless, however, soon demonstrated the act's limitations.

Following World War I, rather than simply communicate with each other, wireless "hobbyists" began using their stations to deliver information and entertainment to a broader audience of listeners. This form of mass communication, which became known as "broadcasting," quickly became very popular with listeners and caught the attention of major electronics manufacturers. General Electric, Westinghouse, the Radio Corporation of America (RCA) and other companies, anticipating the revenue potential of broadcasting, began acquiring radio licenses around the country. The problems with the 1912 Act became apparent. Although the act gave the secretary of commerce the power to grant licenses, it did not allow the secretary to reject license applications. All the secretary could do was award a license to anyone who applied. The secretary of commerce faced other limitations as well. Station operators would unhesitatingly change frequencies and the height of transmission towers. An operator might even move a station from city to city. Under the 1912 statute, federal courts ruled, Secretary of Commerce Herbert Hoover had no power to control these actions.[1] The U.S. Attorney General agreed.[2]

So, as commercial radio began to develop, the government granted and registered licenses, but could neither refuse a license to an applicant nor limit the purposes for which radio stations were used. This inability to control the use of the spectrum led to serious interference problems. By 1920, many commercial broadcasters and hobbyists believed radio was doomed as a public medium unless the government could control both the number of radio stations on the air and the broadcast frequencies. In an attempt to deal with the chaos on the airwaves, Hoover convened several radio conferences between 1922 and 1926 but could not convince radio station owners to cooperate with one another. At first, Congress ignored calls to adopt legislation controlling radio broadcasting. In most major cities, interference constantly interrupted radio stations' signals. Eventually, the problem became so serious that Congress cooperated.

### Radio Act of 1927

Recognizing radio's importance to the public and the country's commerce, and realizing the need to control spectrum use, Congress adopted the Radio Act of 1927. The act established a five-member Federal Radio Commission, each commissioner representing a different region of the country. The FRC was given the power to grant and deny radio station licenses, assign frequencies and prevent spectrum interference, but it did not have the power to censor content.

The 1927 Act was important because it was the first law giving the U.S. government, through the FRC and Congress, control over radio broadcasting to the public. The act established definitively that the electromagnetic spectrum belonged to the public – it was not to be privately owned. In addition, the act required the FRC to act in the "public interest, convenience or necessity," the standard the Federal Communications Commission still uses. The act also established that broadcast stations were not to be regulated as common carriers, that is, the licensee was responsible for the content of the station's transmissions. The 1927 law did not explicitly give the federal government exclusive jurisdiction over broadcast regulation, but the Supreme Court later interpreted it as doing so and as forbidding the states from interfering.[3] Each of these points continues to be an important element in broadcast regulation.

### Communications Act of 1934

In adopting the 1927 Act, Congress expected that the FRC could be disbanded after completing its task of allocating licenses to radio stations, but it soon became apparent that the federal government would need to oversee broadcasting on a continuing basis. Another problem was that the 1927 Act had added yet another federal agency, the FRC, to the list of bureaucracies — including the Interstate Commerce Commission, the Department of Commerce and the Postmaster General's Office — with control over spectrum use and telephony. To continue jurisdiction over broadcasting, but also to simplify the regulatory process, Congress adopted the Federal Communications Act of 1934, establishing the Federal Communications Commission. The Commission had jurisdiction over "radio and wire communication service," that is, broadcasting and various aspects of telephone service. The 1934 Act replaced the 1927 law, and the FCC superseded the FRC.

In the seventy years since the adoption of the act, the FCC has had to decide how to deal with satellites, cellular telephones and other new technologies that use the spectrum but which, of course, were not mentioned in the act and were not imagined by any member of Congress in 1934. To address these new technologies, Congress has amended the act many times. The most recent major amendment occurred in 1996, when Congress adopted and President Bill Clinton signed the Telecommunications Act of 1996.

---

[1] *See* Hoover v. Intercity Radio Co., 286 F. 1002 (D.C. Cir. 1923); United States v. Zenith Radio Corp., 12 F.2d 614 (N.D. Ill. 1926).

[2] *See* 126 Op. Atty. Gen. (1)-(c) (1926).

[3] *See* Fed. Radio Comm'n v. Nelson Bros., 289 U.S. 266 (1933).

This act significantly altered many rules regarding broadcasting, as well as cable, telephone service, satellite television transmission and other communications media. (Cable regulation is discussed in Chapter 11, and the Telecommunications Act is discussed in Chapters 11 and 12.)

## RATIONALES FOR BROADCAST REGULATION

The First Amendment states that the government "shall make no law ... abridging the freedom of speech, or of the press...." Does that mean broadcasters are fully protected, having the same First Amendment rights as publishers of the print media? The Supreme Court has said "No," holding that various mass media may be treated differently under the First Amendment, and that broadcasters' rights are not equal to those of the print media.[4]

### Print v. Broadcast

When the Supreme Court began making rulings involving broadcasting, it had precedent for not treating the industry the same as the print media. From 1915 until 1952, the Court held that motion pictures were entertainment and, therefore, not entitled to First Amendment protection.[5] As radio developed into a major mass medium, it primarily offered entertainment. By the mid-1930s, First Amendment rights essentially had been applied only to the print media, and courts found no reason to extend the same type of protection to broadcasting. For example, just one year after the Supreme Court ruled in *Near v. Minnesota*[6] that a state could not stop a newspaper from printing "malicious, scandalous, and defamatory" attacks on public officials, a federal appellate court upheld the FRC in denying a radio license renewal to a church whose minister, Dr. Robert Shuler, used the station to attack government officials, labor unions and religions other than his own.[7]

Three decades later, the Supreme Court took a similar approach. In 1964, a small Pennsylvania radio station carried a fifteen-minute program in which the Rev. Billy James Hargis attacked Fred J. Cook, the author of *Goldwater — Extremist on the Right.* Hargis said Cook was fired as a newspaper reporter because he made false charges against city officials, that Cook had worked for a Communist publication, had denounced then FBI chief J. Edgar Hoover and the Central Intelligence Agency, and set out to "destroy Barry Goldwater," Republican presidential candidate in 1964. When Cook learned of the broadcast, he asked the station for free time to reply under the FCC's personal attack rule. The

station refused. Cook complained to the FCC, which ordered the station to offer Cook time. The station appealed to the courts.

In 1969, the Supreme Court found in *Red Lion Broadcasting Co. v. FCC* that "those who are licensed stand no better than those to whom licenses are refused. A license permits broadcasting, but the licensee has no constitutional right ... to monopolize a radio frequency to the exclusion of his fellow citizens." Therefore, the Court held, the First Amendment does not prohibit "requir[ing] a broadcaster to permit answers to personal attacks occurring in the course of discussing controversial issues...."[8]

Five years later, the Supreme Court heard a case in which a newspaper refused to abide by a state statute that required the newspaper to provide free space for a candidate it had criticized. The *Miami Herald* had published an editorial highly critical of a candidate for the Florida House of Representatives. When the candidate demanded space for a response under Florida law and the newspaper refused, he sued. The Supreme Court, in *Miami Herald Publishing Co. v. Tornillo,* held that it is unconstitutional for the government to force a newspaper to publish anything it chooses not to. The Court said that a "responsible press is an undoubtedly desirable goal, but press responsibility is not mandated by the Constitution and like many other virtues it cannot be legislated."[9]

The Court apparently thought of "press" as "print media," not broadcasting. *Red Lion* required a radio station to provide a right of reply, while the Court held in *Tornillo* that the same requirement could not be applied to newspapers. This does not mean broadcasters have no First Amendment rights. The Supreme Court has found that they do. But it has said that "of all forms of communication, it is broadcasting that has received the most limited First Amendment protection."[10] Courts have used several rationales for the proposition that print media have greater First Amendment rights than broadcasters. The rationales are spectrum scarcity, the concept of public trusteeship, pervasiveness and the special impact broadcast media can have, especially on children.

### Spectrum Scarcity

The electromagnetic spectrum is the array of energy that includes radio waves.[11] Radio and television stations use transmitters to send radio waves to receiving antennas. Transmitters radiate several thousands or millions of radio waves per second. This is the "frequency" at which the station is broadcasting. The FCC assigns frequencies to stations and requires them to transmit only on

---

[4] *See, e.g.,* Red Lion Broad. Co. v. FCC, 395 U.S. 367 (1969) (upholding limits on broadcasters' First Amendment rights).

[5] *See* Joseph Burstyn, Inc. v. Wilson, 343 U.S. 495 (1952); Mutual Film Corp. v. Indus. Comm'n of Ohio, 236 U.S. 230 (1915).

[6] 283 U.S. 697 (1931). *Near v. Minnesota* and prior restraint are discussed in Chapter 4.

[7] Trinity Methodist Church, South v. Fed. Radio Comm'n, 62 F.2d 850 (D.C. Cir. 1932).

[8] 395 U.S. at 389, 392.

[9] 418 U.S. 241, 256 (1974).

[10] FCC v. Pacifica Found., 438 U.S. 726, 748 (1978).

[11] Other portions of the spectrum are identified as "infrared," "X-rays," "gamma rays" and "ultraviolet." For a discussion of broadcast technology, *see* F. LESLIE SMITH, DAVID OSTROFF & JOHN WRIGHT, PERSPECTIVES OF RADIO AND TELEVISION (1998).

those frequencies.

Groups of frequencies can be used only for certain types of broadcasting. FM radio stations are assigned frequencies within a certain portion of the spectrum, as are AM radio stations and UHF television stations. VHF television stations are found in three sections of the spectrum — channels 2, 3 and 4 are located in one portion, channels 5 and 6 in a second portion, and channels 7 to 13 in a third. Because of the way the federal government has allocated the spectrum for broadcasters' use, only a limited number of radio and television stations can be on the air. Adding more would cause harmful interference. Therefore, only a relatively few people or companies may use the spectrum for broadcasting. So there is a spectrum scarcity; there are not enough frequencies to allow all who want to broadcast to do so. Courts have decided that Congress may impose certain obligations to serve the public on those fortunate enough to have broadcast licenses.

However, most cities have more radio and television stations than newspapers. Where, then, is the scarcity? As the courts see it, this is not simply a matter of numbers. There are so few newspapers because a newspaper is very costly to begin and operate, and advertisers and subscribers for competing newspapers are limited. This is an economic limitation, the courts say, while spectrum scarcity is a physical and technical limitation, that is, a limitation of nature. No matter how much money might be available to begin a new broadcast station, if there is no room on the spectrum — if a station cannot be added without causing signal interference with other stations — the new station may not go on the air.

Therefore, the award of a broadcast license is considered to be a grant of a privilege. Another person or company who wants to communicate with the community by owning a broadcast station simply may not do so if no frequencies are available in the area.

The Supreme Court adopted the spectrum scarcity rationale in 1943. The Court was straightforward, stating that radio's "facilities are limited; they are not available to all who may wish to use them; the radio spectrum simply is not large enough to accommodate everybody. There is a fixed natural limitation upon the number of stations that can operate without interfering with one another."[12] The Court echoed the point twenty-six years later in *Red Lion*: "[I]t is idle to posit an unabridgeable First Amendment right to broadcast comparable to the right of every individual to speak, write, or publish."[13]

### *The Concept of Public Trusteeship*

Unlike some countries where the government owns and controls all broadcasting outlets, in the United States nearly all commercial stations are privately owned. But because the spectrum remains in the government's hands, those who are given licenses hold portions of the spectrum in trust for the public, that is, they are pub-

lic trustees. The courts have said that Congress and the FCC may require broadcasters to operate in the public interest if they are to be granted the privilege of holding broadcast licenses. The Supreme Court has accepted this approach, stating in *Red Lion*:

> There is nothing in the First Amendment which prevents the Government from ... requiring a licensee to ... conduct himself as a proxy or fiduciary with obligations to present those views and voices which are representative of his community.... [T]he people as a whole retain their interest in free speech by radio and their collective right to have the medium function consistently with the ends and purposes of the First Amendment. It is the right of the viewers and listeners, not the right of the broadcasters, which is paramount.... Licenses to broadcast do not confer ownership of designated frequencies, but only the temporary privilege of using them.[14]

In 1973, just four years after deciding *Red Lion*, the Court wavered on this point. The CBS television network refused to accept advertisements from the Business Executives' Move for a Vietnam Peace, which, together with the Democratic National Committee, asked the FCC to rule that broadcasters could not "refuse to sell time to responsible entities ... for comment on public issues."[15] The Commission rejected the request. The Supreme Court ruled that broadcasters did not have to take any and all advertisements.

*Red Lion*, which held that a radio station must give time for an individual to reply to a personal attack, and the CBS case, which held that broadcasters need not sell time for commercials about public issues, may not be as contradictory as they appear. The two decisions suggest that there is no general right for the public to have access to broadcast stations. But Congress may require access under certain circumstances, such as when a political candidate running for federal office wants to purchase airtime to reach the public. This still leaves broadcasters less protected than the print media under the First Amendment.

The spectrum scarcity and public trustee rationales have been attacked often as being unsupportable. By the mid-1980s, even the Supreme Court suggested that it would consider a "signal from Congress or the FCC that technological developments have advanced so far that some revision of the system of broadcast regulation may be required."[16] That is, the Court recognized that, since audiences may receive video signals from cable television, satellites, microwave transmissions and other new technologies, the scarcity of spectrum space for broadcast stations may not limit communication with the public through the electronic media. Also, technologies exist to put more stations on the AM and FM bands without causing interference. In 1983, for example, the FCC

---

[12] Nat'l Broad. Co. v. FCC, 319 U.S. 190, 213 (1943).
[13] 395 U.S. at 388.

[14] *Id.* at 394.
[15] Columbia Broad. Sys. v. Democratic Nat'l Comm., 412 U.S. 94, 98 (1973).
[16] FCC v. League of Women Voters, 468 U.S. 364, 376 n.11 (1984).

adopted a spectrum allocation for FM radio which added more than 1,000 stations nationwide.[17]

A former chair of the FCC has argued that even if there is a spectrum scarcity, all goods are scarce to some degree.[18] Newsprint is scarce and increasingly expensive, for example. Does that justify government ownership of all newspapers or limits on the First Amendment rights of newspaper publishers?

### Pervasiveness

Another rationale courts use to justify differential First Amendment treatment of broadcasters is that radio and television are ubiquitous — they are heard and seen in homes, stores and in many other places, and are constantly intrusive, especially on the lives of children. Further, a listener or viewer has no idea what is being broadcast until a receiver is turned on.

Exactly that kind of confrontation was at the center of a case in which the Supreme Court noted that broadcasting is different from other media. In *FCC v. Pacifica*,[19] a child inadvertently was exposed to indecent language when his father turned on the car radio. The Court said that with many forms of speech — like movies or words on jackets[20] — people have a responsibility to avoid the communication; they can turn their heads or avert their eyes, for example. But, the Court said, radio and television are omnipresent; they are intruders rather than forms of communication people invite into their lives. The Court was particularly concerned that when radio or television comes into the home, children may be exposed to material their parents do not want them to see or hear. Broadcasting's intrusiveness and omnipresence make it unique among mass media, the Court said. These characteristics justify treating radio and television differently than print media under the First Amendment.

### Special Impact

A few courts have articulated an additional rationale for broadcast regulation. They suggest that radio and television have a greater impact on audiences than do print media.[21] Considering a law forbidding cigarette and small cigar advertising on television, a federal appellate court in the 1960s, without clearly explaining the grounds for its assertion, stated that

an ordinary habitual television watcher can avoid these com-

mercials only by frequently leaving the room, changing the channel, or doing some other such affirmative act. It is difficult to calculate the subliminal impact of this pervasive propaganda, which may be heard even if not listened to, but it may reasonably be thought greater than the impact of the written word.[22]

In 1996, Congress decided that televised violence presented enough of a threat to the well-being of children that it passed a law calling for a voluntary system that rated television violence, profanity and sexual content. The law — known as the "v-chip law" — will be discussed later in this chapter.

In addition, the Supreme Court has said that the broadcast media can have a powerful impact on children when it comes to indecent programming. In *Pacifica*, the Court said that while parents may be able to shield their children from offensive books or motion pictures, broadcasting is "uniquely accessible to children, even those too young to read."[23] As a result, an indecent broadcast could instantly enlarge the vocabulary of very young children. The Court found that in order to protect children, the FCC could constitutionally channel indecent broadcasts to times when children were less likely to be in the audience.

## THE FEDERAL COMMUNICATIONS COMMISSION

The FCC is the government agency responsible for regulating broadcasting, other spectrum uses such as satellite communications and amateur radio, and various aspects of telephone service.

### Structure of the FCC

The FCC is one of the federal government's independent agencies, similar in that respect to the Securities and Exchange Commission or the Federal Trade Commission. But the FCC cannot be considered truly independent. Congress allocates the FCC's budget in a bill that the president must approve. The Commission's five members are selected by the president and confirmed by the Senate. They serve five-year terms and can be reappointed.[24] The president decides which of the five commissioners will be chair. While the FCC is not intended to be political — only three of the five commissioners can be from the same political party — political considerations do play a part in the appointment process and in many Commission decisions. In many ways, the FCC is imbued with politics, as evidenced by straight party-line votes on important policy issues. The Commission's 2003 action on ownership rules provides an excellent example: All three Republicans voted to ease ownership restrictions, and both Democrats vigorously op-

---

[17] Modification of FM Broadcast Station Rules to Increase the Availability of Commercial FM Broadcast Assignments, 94 F.C.C.2d 152 (1983).

[18] Mark Fowler & Daniel Brenner, *A Marketplace Approach to Broadcast Regulation*, 60 TEXAS L. REV. 207 (1982).

[19] 438 U.S. 726 (1978).

[20] *See* Erznoznik v. Jacksonville, 422 U.S. 205 (1975); Cohen v. California, 403 U.S. 15 (1971).

[21] *See, e.g.,* Robinson v. American Broad. Co., 441 F.2d 1396 (6th Cir. 1971); Banzhaf v. FCC, 405 F.2d 1082 (D.C. Cir. 1968).

[22] *Banzhaf,* 405 F.2d at 1101.

[23] 438 U.S. at 749.

[24] The FCC initially had seven commissioners instead of the FRC's five, since the FCC had more responsibilities. Congress reduced the number of commissioners to five in 1982.

posed further deregulation. (A discussion of the decision appears later in this chapter.)

The FCC employs more than 2,000 staff members across six bureaus. Of these six bureaus, three are of particular relevance to broadcasters:

- The Media Bureau (formerly the Mass Media Bureau) administers the policy and licensing programs related to electronic media, including radio, television and cable television. It also handles post-licensing matters related to direct broadcast satellite.
- The Consumer and Governmental Affairs Bureau, among other things, tries to encourage more public participation in the works of the Commission.
- The Enforcement Bureau resolves complaints involving radio frequency interference, indecent communications, and false distress signals, among others.

As an independent regulatory agency, the FCC has judicial, legislative and executive powers.

## *Judicial Power*

When the FCC makes decisions that affect individual licensees — taking action to revoke a license, for example — it acts much as a court does. Such cases that deal with individual parties are decided initially by administrative law judges (ALJ) within the Commission. An ALJ will hold a hearing that might look much like a trial. The parties to the hearing are represented by counsel. They present evidence and witnesses, and witnesses may be cross-examined. After all the evidence is presented, the ALJ weighs the evidence and writes an opinion, referred to as the "Initial Decision." A losing party may appeal the decision to the five commissioners.

## *Legislative Power*

The FCC also acts much as a legislative body, adopting policies affecting an entire industry. The Commission or an interested outside party may initiate the legislative process. When a decision is made to begin the process, FCC staff members prepare a Notice of Proposed Rule Making (NPRM), stating what regulations the FCC is considering adopting, changing or rescinding, and explaining the reasons behind the new regulations. When the commissioners agree on the NPRM's language, they make it public. Members of the public — although that usually means corporations and lobbying groups representing companies that may be affected by the rules — submit comments to the FCC. The Commission makes them public and then accepts reply comments — written arguments supporting or rebutting the initial comments. The staff and commissioners review the comments and replies, discuss the proposed rules and finally adopt a Report and Order. The regulations in the order may be the same as those originally proposed in the NPRM, or they may be different, based on the public comment or changes made by commissioners for other reasons. After an order

is released, members of the public may ask the FCC to reconsider the decision, which the Commission may or may not do.

## *Executive Power*

The FCC may impose an array of penalties to enforce its decisions, rules, regulations and policies — from a letter of reprimand inserted into a licensee's file, to a fine, to renewing a license for less than a full term, to revocation or non-renewal of a license. Short-term license renewals and non-renewals are harsh penalties, and the Commission normally prefers to impose no more than a fine, called a "forfeiture," when it finds a licensee has violated FCC rules. But the threat of losing a license generally keeps broadcasters in line.

Final Commission decisions, whether reports and orders, license awards or other determinations, may be appealed to a federal appellate court. Most appeals from FCC decisions are taken to the U.S. Court of Appeals for the District of Columbia Circuit. The case may then be appealed to the Supreme Court, which may grant or deny *certiorari*. An appellate court is to give deference to the FCC's interpretation of the Communications Act.[25] And when the FCC rules on a factual matter — whether a licensee lied to the Commission, for example — a court can overturn the FCC's decision only if it was "arbitrary, capricious [or] an abuse of discretion."[26]

## *The Public Interest Standard*

In both the 1927 and the 1934 acts, Congress required the FCC to regulate broadcast licensees so that they function in the "public interest, convenience and necessity."[27] The public interest standard, adopted from the 1890 Interstate Commerce Act, is the standard that is supposed to govern Commission decisions. The Communications Act does not define the term, leaving it to the FCC and the courts to give it substance. This allows the Commission much flexibility in establishing policies and deciding cases. There are several problems with this scenario. The FCC may give the words different meanings at different times, for example, depending upon its make-up. It has used the standard both to adopt and later reject the same regulation, and the Commission and the courts cannot always agree on what the term means.

In 1928, the FRC issued a statement providing certain technical and content guidelines for radio that it believed were required to meet the public interest.[28] Later it used a 1929 case involving a dispute among three Chicago area stations to further amplify its un-

---

25 *See* Chevron U.S.A., Inc. v. Natural Resources Defense Council, 467 U.S. 837 (1984).

26 5 U.S.C. § 706 (2)(A) (2000).

27 47 U.S.C. §§ 302(a), 307(d), 309(a) & 316(a) (2000).

28 Public Interest, Convenience, or Necessity, 2 F.R.C. Ann. Rep. 166 (1928).

derstanding of the public interest.[29] These suggestions included ways to limit spectrum interference, provide radio signals to much of the country, limit the private use of commercial radio frequencies and provide well-rounded programming. The FRC also recommended that it would be in the public interest for stations to limit the "use of phonograph records" as program material.

In addition, the FRC applied the public interest standard when evaluating broadcast content. For example, in the 1920s Dr. John R. Brinkley aired a program called the

"Medical question box," devoted to diagnosing and prescribing treatment of cases from symptoms given in letters.... Patients are not known to the doctor except by means of their letters.... The doctor usually advises that the writer of the letter is suffering from a certain ailment, and recommends the procurement from one of the members of the Brinkley Pharmaceutical Association, of one or more of Dr. Brinkley's prescriptions.... [For instance,] "Sunflower State, from Dresden Kans[as]. Probably he has gall stones. No, I don't mean that, I mean kidney stones. My advice to you is to put him on Prescription No. 80 and 50 for men, also 64. I think that he will be a whole lot better. Also drink a lot of water."[30]

The FRC refused to renew the station's license, stating that Dr. Brinkley's programs did not serve the public interest. On appeal, the court agreed that Brinkley operated the station only to earn revenue for himself and that public health was being endangered. Brinkley argued that his First Amendment rights were being abridged, but the court found that the Commission "has merely exercised its undoubted right to take note of appellant's past conduct, which is not censorship."[31]

Similarly, the FRC refused to renew a radio station licensed to a church. When evaluating the station's renewal application, the FRC found that the Rev. Robert Shuler used his access to the airwaves to issue attacks against public officials and various religious groups. On appeal, the court upheld the FRC's decision finding that "the evidence abundantly sustains the conclusion of the Commission that the continuance of the broadcasting programs is not in the public interest.... [I]t is manifest, we think, that it is not narrowing the ordinary conception of 'public interest' in declaring his broadcasts — without facts to sustain or to justify them — not within that term."[32]

The FCC often has discussed its understanding of the public interest in its policymaking rulings affecting the entire broadcast industry, but also has done so in its licensing decisions. And the interplay between the FCC and the courts also has helped define the public interest. For example, the Supreme Court agreed with the FCC that the Commission could not take into consideration any possible impact on an existing radio station's revenues when it granted a license for a new station in the same city.[33] The public interest meant being concerned with the public, not the licensee, the Court said. Three years later, the Court reinforced this interpretation in *National Broadcasting Co. v. FCC*: "The 'public interest' to be served under the Communications Act is ... the interest of the listening public...."[34] The Court has held that judges have limited powers to overturn a Commission public interest determination. If the FCC balances the various interests at stake, it is up to the Commission to define the public interest.[35]

In 1946, the FCC attempted to give station licensees better guidance about how to operate in the public interest. A set of informal programming guidelines, known as the "Blue Book" after the color of its cover, suggested that stations broadcast non-sponsored programs, live programs originated locally, and programs "devoted to public discussions."[36] The Blue Book also urged stations to limit the number of commercials and to be careful of their content. Although broadcasters feared the Blue Book was an attempt by the FCC to scrutinize programming practices, the fact is that the Commission never denied the renewal of a station's license for violation of the Blue Book guidelines.[37]

In 1960, the FCC replaced the Blue Book with a formal programming statement that specified fourteen program categories as "the major elements usually necessary to meet the public interest."[38] The categories included children's, religious, educational, public affairs, agricultural, news, sports, entertainment and weather programs, and "opportunit[ies] for self-expression, ... the development and use of local talent" and "service to minority groups."

After decades of protecting the public interest by imposing regulations on broadcast stations and networks, the FCC, in the 1980s, moved toward a marketplace approach. The Commission said that competition among stations and from other forms of electronic media would be sufficient to ensure that licensees operate in the public interest and that extensive regulation would be unnecessary.

The FCC took significant steps to deregulate radio in 1981[39]

---

[29] *See* Great Lakes Broad. Co., 3 F.R.C. Ann. Rep. 32 (1929), *rev'd on other grounds,* 37 F.2d 993 (D.C. Cir. 1930).

[30] KFKB Broad. Ass'n v. Fed. Radio Comm'n, 47 F.2d 670, 671 (D.C. Cir. 1931).

[31] *Id.* at 672.

[32] Trinity Methodist Church, South v. Fed. Radio Comm'n, 62 F.2d 850, 852 (D.C. Cir. 1932).

[33] *See* Sanders Brothers v. FCC, 309 U.S. 470 (1940).

[34] 319 U.S. 190, 216 (1943).

[35] *See, e.g.,* FCC v. WNCN Listener's Guild, 450 U.S. 582 (1981).

[36] FCC, Public Service Responsibility of Broadcast Licensees (Mar. 7, 1946), *reprinted in* F. Kahn, Documents of American Broadcasting 132 (3d ed. 1978).

[37] *See, e.g.,* Hearst Radio, Inc. (WBAL), 15 F.C.C. 1149 (1951).

[38] En Banc Programming Inquiry, 44 F.C.C. 2303, 2314 (1960), *aff'd sub nom.,* Henry v. FCC, 302 F.2d 191 (D.C. Cir. 1962).

[39] Deregulation of Radio, 84 F.C.C. 2d 968 (1981), *aff'd in part, remanded in part sub nom.,* Office of Communication of the United Church of Christ v. FCC, 707 F.2d 1413 (D.C. Cir. 1983).

and television in 1984.[40] In these and other actions, the Commission eliminated a number of programming guidelines; requirements for surveying community leaders, interest groups and individuals to ascertain programming needs and preferences; most limits on how much time could be used for commercials; complex license renewal processes; certain technical rules; and a number of other minor regulations. But the Commission left many other broadcasting rules in place.

Despite its deregulatory stance during the 1980s and 1990s, the FCC is still trying to grapple with how to interpret the concept of public interest. For instance, in December 1999 the FCC issued a Notice of Inquiry asking how broadcasters can serve the public interest during the transition to digital technology.[41] In attempting to understand the meaning of the public interest, it may be safe to say that the public interest means what the FCC says it means at any given time, subject to congressional oversight and judicial review.

## STATION LICENSING

In large part, the Federal Radio Commission was created to ensure that stations broadcast without interfering with other stations' signals. That responsibility continues, but today the FCC's duties extend much farther. The Communications Act of 1934 gave the FCC the authority to allocate frequencies, that is, to assign frequencies to companies that the Commission has decided may operate radio and television stations. The act requires that the FCC do this in a "fair, efficient and equitable" manner.[42]

The Commission first must decide which portions of the spectrum will be used for what purposes — satellite transmissions, AM or FM radio, cellular communications or for police and fire department use. For example, in 1948, the FCC decided to use the portion of the spectrum it had designated "channel 1" for purposes other than VHF (very high frequency) television. Therefore, today the VHF channels in use are 2-13; there is no frequency called "channel 1." Once it has decided which portion of the spectrum is assigned to a particular use, the FCC selects who will be given the right to use a particular frequency. The Federal Radio Commission had assigned four experimental television frequencies in 1928. The FCC established standards for television and allocated experimental television channels in the 1930s. But the Commission waited until 1941 to adopt the first nationwide television allocation plan.[43] The plan allowed interested individuals and companies to apply for permission to operate television stations

in the cities to which the Commission allocated frequencies. However, U.S. involvement in World War II stopped station licensing and construction.

In 1945, the FCC assigned VHF channels to individual cities, being certain that broadcasting on a frequency — say, channel 2 — in one city did not interfere with a channel — for example, channel 3 — in the same city or in a neighboring community. But the Commission soon recognized that basing the country's television allocations on twelve VHF frequencies — channels 2 to 13 — limited the number of stations that could be on the air. In 1948, the FCC stopped awarding television licenses and did not resume until 1952. During that time the Commission considered the role UHF (ultra high frequency) stations should play as well as other issues, such as how to provide television service to as many communities as possible.

When the license freeze ended, the Commission established new television allocations, added seventy UHF channels and set aside certain frequencies for noncommercial television stations.[44] Congress later helped to foster UHF stations by adopting the All-Channel Receiver Act, requiring that all television sets sold in the United States have UHF capacity.[45]

As technology evolves and demand for the spectrum continues to grow, the FCC's job of allocating this valuable resource becomes more complex and demanding. In November 1999, the FCC issued a policy statement outlining guiding principles for the management of the spectrum.[46] These principles pave the way for the Commission to reclaim portions of the spectrum that are not being used efficiently and relocate some technologies to under-used parts of the spectrum. These actions will benefit the public by providing additional spectrum for technologies such as high-speed wireless Internet connections.

### Awarding Station Licenses

Obtaining a broadcast license begins with submitting an application to the FCC. The applicant must give notice to the public that the application was submitted. The FCC staff processes the application, and, barring objections or challenges by the staff or the public, and assuming there are no other applications for the same frequency, will approve it if the applicant is qualified. According to the Communications Act, all applicants for broadcast licenses must be technically, financially and legally qualified.[47]

---

[40] Commercial Television Stations, 98 F.C.C. 2d 1076 (1984).

[41] In the Matter of Public Interest Obligations of TV Broadcast Licensees, 14 F.C.C.R. 21633 (1999). As of mid-2006 the Commission had not yet answered this question.

[42] 47 U.S.C. § 303 and § 307(b) (2000).

[43] Rules and Regulations Governing Commercial Television Broadcast Stations, 6 Fed. Reg. 2284 (1941).

---

[44] Amendment of Section 3.606 of the Commission's Rules and Regulations, Amendment of the Commission's Rules, Regulations and Engineering Standards Concerning the Television Broadcast Service, Utilization of Frequencies in the Band 470 to 890 Mcs for Television Broadcasting, 41 F.C.C. 148 (1952). This decision is commonly known as the "Sixth Report and Order."

[45] Pub. L. No. 87-529 (1962), codified at 47 U.S.C. § 303(s) (2000).

[46] In the Matter of Principles for Reallocation of Spectrum to Encourage the Development of Telecommunications Technologies for the New Millennium, 14 F.C.C.R. 19868 (1999).

[47] 47 U.S.C § 308(b) (2000).

To be technically qualified, an applicant must have access to technical expertise sufficient to operate the station. That means having sufficiently planned for the equipment and engineering personnel needed. To be financially qualified, an applicant must demonstrate sufficient financial backing, through funds on hand or loan commitments, to run the station for the first three months without advertising or other income.

There are several aspects to being legally qualified. The first criterion is U.S. citizenship. The Communications Act forbids granting a broadcast station license to foreign governments or alien individuals, or their representatives, or to foreign corporations.[48] In addition, foreign interests may own no more than 20 percent of the stock of a corporation holding a broadcast license. For a corporation that is controlled by another corporation, the controlling entity may not have more than 25 percent of its stock owned or voted by foreign interests. In 1995, the FCC waived this last rule to allow Rupert Murdoch and his companies to continue owning Fox television stations and the Fox television network. Murdoch had changed his citizenship from Australian to American in order to own television stations in the United States. But, in fact, his Australian company, News Corporation, was the owner of the Fox properties. Because Murdoch controls News Corporation, however, and because changing Fox's ownership structure might have caused economic harm sufficient to damage the network's attempt to compete with ABC, CBS and NBC, the FCC granted the waiver, finding it was in the public interest.[49]

A second criterion for licensure is that the applicant be of good character. Specifically, the Commission will not award licenses to companies run or controlled by individuals who have engaged in fraudulent conduct or who have been convicted of felonies or of violating antitrust laws involving the mass media.[50] The FCC is particularly concerned with applicants who have lied or made misrepresentations to the Commission. For example, the FCC revoked the licenses of Contemporary Media because its sole shareholder, Michael Rice, was convicted of sexually abusing children.[51] Contemporary Media informed the FCC of Rice's arrest and told the Commission that Rice was removed from his managerial role of the company as a result of the arrest. However, the FCC later learned that Rice was actually involved in the affairs of his company after his conviction and revoked the company's licenses and construction permits. Contemporary Media appealed the FCC's decision, but the D.C. Circuit upheld the Commission's decision as reasonable.[52] While the fact that Contemporary Media lied to the FCC probably tipped the balance against the licensee, this case ratified the Commission's authority to base its licensing decisions on the issue of character.

The final aspect of being legally qualified to be a licensee relates to the Commission's media ownership rules. In certain instances, FCC regulations forbid one company from owning more than a specified number of stations in a market.[53] If an applicant for a license is not eligible to own the station for which it is applying due to the Commission's ownership rules, it may not be awarded the license. These specific ownership regulations will be discussed below under the heading "Structural Regulation of Broadcasting."

### Mutually Exclusive Applications

If two or more applicants for the same broadcast license meet the basic qualifications set by the FCC, the agency must choose among them. Prior to 1993, the Commission held full-blown evidentiary hearings to determine which one of the applicants would best serve the public interest. To make such a determination, the Commission applied a set of comparative standards that it developed in 1965.[54] In a 1993 case, *Bechtel v. FCC*, a federal appellate court rejected one of the comparative factors the FCC had been using.[55]

The factor to which the District of Columbia Circuit objected is called "integration." For nearly thirty years, the Commission had said the public interest was best served if station owners were involved in the station's day-to-day management. For several years before the court invalidated this factor, many comparative hearing decisions had turned on integration. But the court held that the FCC had offered no proof that the integration of ownership and management had led to better broadcast service than absentee ownership. So, the court held that there was no evidence that using the integration factor was in the public interest.

Other criteria used in comparative hearings included prior broadcast experience and the likely reach of a station's signal. The FCC also considered whether a minority applicant was involved in the management of the station. The Commission has acknowledged that minorities are underrepresented as station licensees and granted the minority preferences in order to further diversify media ownership. The Supreme Court upheld this approach in 1990.[56] In 1995, however, the Court issued a decision that limited the FCC's ability to grant preferences on the basis of race.[57]

The Commission also has argued that women are underrepresented as station owners and, for a time, awarded a preference to female applicants who were integrated into the management of the station. But the District of Columbia Circuit found that the FCC had not presented sufficient evidence that giving female applicants a preference helped to increase the level of programming across

[48] 47 U.S.C. § 310 (2000).

[49] Fox Television Stations, Inc., 11 F.C.C.R. 5714 (1995).

[50] Character Qualifications in Broad. Licensing, 5 F.C.C.R. 3252 (1990); Character Qualifications in Broad. Licensing, 102 F.C.C.2d 1179 (1986).

[51] In re Contemporary Media, Inc., 13 F.C.C.R. 14437 (1998).

[52] Contemporary Media, Inc. v. FCC, 214 F.3d 187 (2000).

[53] 47 C.F.R. § 73.3555 (2005).

[54] Policy Statement on Comparative Hearings, 1 F.C.C.2d 393 (1965).

[55] 10 F.3d 875 (D.C. Cir. 1993).

[56] Metro Broad., Inc. v. FCC, 497 U.S. 547, 563 (1990).

[57] Adarand Constructors, Inc. v. Pena, 515 U.S. 200 (1995).

the country devoted, or of interest, to women and ordered the FCC to stop giving preferences to women.[58]

For many years the FCC's comparative hearing process for awarding broadcast licenses when there was more than one qualified applicant was heavily criticized. Even the Commission criticized its own method as one that "can be described most charitably as laborious, exceedingly time consuming, expensive and often resulting in choices based on, at most, marginal differences."[59] Others suggested that the hearing process was highly discretionary, inconsistent, unpredictable and an inadequate way to award radio and television licenses that may earn millions of dollars for those who receive them.

Due to these criticisms and the *Bechtel* decision, in 1993 the agency stopped using comparative hearings in these kinds of licensing cases. As early as 1982 the FCC experimented with lotteries to grant certain kinds of licenses, including low-power television. But it moved away from using lotteries shortly thereafter. It continued to search for ways to deal with mutually exclusive applications[60] but took no final action. Congress finally resolved the matter in the Balanced Budget Act of 1997, which required the FCC to use auctions to award commercial broadcast licenses when there are mutually exclusive applications.[61] In order to assure that licenses do not always go to the applicant with the deepest pockets, and to help diversify the ownership of broadcast media, the FCC provides what it calls "bidding credits" to qualified small businesses. These credits allow the small business applicants to bid more money for the license than they actually have. Since the auction process took effect in 1998, more than 650 broadcast frequencies have been licensed to the applicant who can bid the most, adding nearly $315 million to the U.S. treasury.[62]

### License Renewals

Both radio and television station licenses are awarded for eight-year periods, after which the licenses must be renewed. The renewal application is much smaller and simpler than the application for the original license. Licensees who have engaged in serious misconduct during the license term may not have their licenses renewed, but the vast majority of license renewal applications are routinely granted.

The Telecommunications Act of 1996 requires the FCC to take a two-step approach to broadcast license renewal. First, the Com-

mission must decide whether to renew the current license holder, without considering whether the public interest would be better served by a different licensee. The Commission must renew the license unless it finds that the incumbent broadcaster has not operated in the public interest, has committed serious violations of the Communications Act or FCC rules, or in any other way has shown a pattern of abusing the law or Commission regulations. The Commission also is to consider any comments submitted by the public to the station or the FCC about a licensee's performance. If the FCC decides under these standards that a broadcast license should not be renewed, the Commission then will move to the second step and put the license up for auction. While the Telecommunications Act of 1996 seems to ensure that most broadcast licenses will be renewed, the FCC still may refuse to renew a license on grounds that the station owner has not operated in the public interest.

### Transferring Broadcast Licenses

A broadcast station's facilities — its transmitter, compact disk players, desks and trucks — belong to the station owner and can be sold to anyone at any time. But the facilities are useless without a license to broadcast. The license belongs to the federal government and is given to a licensee for a specified period of time. If the licensee — the station owner — wants to sell the station, it is unlikely anyone would purchase it without also being able to use the station's license, and that requires asking the FCC to transfer the license. Generally, the FCC will transfer a license upon request if the new licensee meets the basic criteria. Currently, more than three-quarters of broadcast licenses are held by companies other than the ones to which the licenses first were granted.

### Public Involvement in Licensing

It may seem obvious that since the FCC's standard is the public interest, the public should have a voice in the Commission's decision-making process. It took a court decision, however, to require the FCC to allow public involvement. The FCC assumed it had the authority and responsibility to determine how the public interest standard applied. In essence, it presumed that it represented the public and, therefore, that the public need not be involved.

In 1964, a public interest group accused television station WLBT in Jackson, Mississippi, of selecting its programming based on racial bias. The FCC would not allow the group to participate in the license renewal proceeding for WLBT, but a federal appellate court held that members of the public had a right to be part of the process.[63] Then, after the FCC renewed WLBT's license, a court overturned the Commission's decision. The court said that when the public participates in FCC proceedings, it only has to draw the

---

[58] Lamprecht v FCC, 958 F.2d 382 (D.C. Cir. 1992).

[59] Amendment to the Commission's Rules to Allow the Selection from Among Competing Applications for New AM, FM and Television Stations by Random Selection (Lottery), 4 F.C.C.R. 2256, 2256 (1989).

[60] *See* Reexamination of the Policy Statement on Comparative Broadcast Hearings, 9 F.C.C.R. 2821 (1994) (seeking comment on the effect of the *Bechtel* decision on comparative hearings).

[61] Pub. L. No. 105-33, § 302(a)(1), codified at 47 U.S.C. § 309(j)(2000).

[62] *See generally* the FCC Auctions home page *at* http://wireless.fcc.gov/auctions/.

[63] Office of Communication of the United Church of Christ v. FCC, 359 F.2d 994 (D.C. Cir. 1966).

Commission's attention to pertinent issues; the public is not required to prove the charges are true.[64] The Commission must investigate the claims, if it decides they have credence.

Since 1966, then, members of the public have been able to participate in licensing proceedings. The FCC may set certain limits, such as allowing participation only by groups representing listeners or viewers who actually will be affected by the Commission's action. The usual method of public participation is the filing of what is called a "petition to deny" the granting of a construction permit, broadcast license or license renewal. The Commission may reject the petition or attempt to gather additional information needed to make a decision on the petition's complaint.

Another broadcast station may intervene in the licensing process also, either because it believes its signal will be degraded if the FCC grants or renews a license, or because it claims it will suffer financially. But a claim that it will lose revenues only allows a station to be involved in the license proceeding; it is not sufficient grounds for denying or not renewing a license.[65] The FCC is not required to protect other broadcasters' economic interests from competition by a new or renewed station.

### Regulatory Fees

For seven decades, broadcasters paid essentially nothing to the federal government for licenses. The costs of obtaining a license were substantial, but they were for engineering studies and attorneys' fees to assist with the application process; the government did not charge fees for licenses. Beginning in 1989, Congress authorized the FCC to impose and collect application processing fees.[66] These fees, which range from $3,720 for a new television station construction permit to $150 for a renewal application, go directly to the U.S. Treasury and are not available to the Commission. Beginning in 1993, in an effort to recover the FCC's costs, Congress required the Commission to collect additional regulatory fees.[67] These fees range from several hundred dollars to more than $60 thousand per year, depending on the type of service — AM, FM, VHF, UHF — and the size of the market in which the station operates. These regulatory fees cover approximately 99 percent of the agency's total costs.[68]

### The Birth of a New Service – Low Power FM Radio

The Communications Act of 1934 makes it illegal to operate a radio or television station in the United States without a license from the FCC. Stations operating without licenses — known as pirate stations — can be subject to civil fines, court injunctions, seizures of their radio equipment, and even criminal penalties including jail time.[69] Although there have always been pirate stations, in recent years the Commission has cracked down on numerous illegal stations across the country, citing concerns that they can interfere with licensed broadcast stations and even with aircraft, police and fire communications, creating a potential for harm to public safety.[70] Pirate station operators claim that the mergers in the broadcast industry have eliminated programming diversity and the illegal stations are trying to fill the void. Former FCC Chairman William Kennard, sympathetic to the claims of pirate station operators, led the way for the creation of a low power radio service.

In 2000, the Commission voted to authorize the creation of a new, low power FM service.[71] With time, the action will create two types of stations: LP 100 stations, with power ranging from fifty to 100 watts, which would serve areas of about 3.5 miles, and LP 10 stations, with power ranging from one to ten watts, which would serve an area of about one to two miles. The new LPFM stations will be non-commercial.

As could be expected, full-power broadcasters, led by the National Association of Broadcasters, vigorously opposed the low-power stations, citing the possibility of interference. Congress, primarily responding to the lobbying efforts of the NAB, reacted to the FCC's action by passing a law that significantly restricted the number of LPFM stations the FCC could license.[72] At the same time, Congress required the Commission to conduct a study of LPFM interference to determine whether more channels could be added. The FCC submitted its report to Congress in February 2004, concluding that additional channels would not significantly interfere with existing full-power stations.[73] The Commission recommended that its original interference standards, as adopted in 2000, be re-instituted, thus permitting additional LPFM stations.[74] To date no action has been taken on the Commission's recommendation. As of mid-2006, approximately 700 LPFM stations were on the air, mostly in midsized and small markets.

### Broadcast Networks

Most programs that broadcast television stations carry are, or

---

[64] Office of Communication of the United Church of Christ v. FCC, 425 F.2d 543 (D.C. Cir. 1969).

[65] See FCC v. Sanders Bros., 309 U.S. 470 (1940).

[66] 47 U.S.C. § 158 (2000).

[67] 47 U.S.C. § 159 (2000).

[68] FCC, Regulatory Fees (2006), at http://www.fcc.gov/fees/regfees.html.

[69] See Press Release, FCC, Rayon Sherwin "Junior" Payne Sentenced to Prison for Unlicensed Radio Operation (May 12, 2003).

[70] See, e.g., Press Release, FCC, Shlomo Malka Found in Contempt of Court-Ordered Injunction, Fined $35,000.00 for Unlicensed Radio Operation (Mar. 6, 2003).

[71] In the Matter of Creation of Low Power Radio Service, 15 F.C.C.R. 2205 (2000).

[72] Making Appropriations for the Government of the District of Columbia for FY 2001 and for other Purposes, Pub. L. No. 106-553 § 632(a), 114 Stat. 2762, 2762A-111 (2000). This legislation primarily concerned budget provisions for various agencies and programs of the federal government.

[73] Report to the Congress on the Low Power FM Interference Testing Program (Feb. 19, 2004), available at http://www.fcc.gov/mb/audio/lpfm/.

[74] Id. at 4.

once were, network shows. The same was true of radio from 1930 to 1952. A "network" distributes programs to stations, and the stations broadcast the programs. For example, NBC will send *The Tonight Show* to more than two hundred stations throughout the country, all of which receive the program the same evening, although networks send programs at several different times to accommodate the country's different time zones. That makes NBC a network, as are ABC, CBS, Fox, and the newly established CW. Most of the stations receiving the programs from the networks are known as affiliates because they have contractual obligations to carry the programming the networks distribute. Some stations, however, are licensed to the networks and are known as "O & O's" — owned and operated by the networks.

The FCC licenses only broadcast stations. "Broadcasting" means sending a signal intended for general reception. The signals a network sends — *via* satellite today, formerly by telephone wires — are meant only for the stations affiliated with the network, not for the general public. Therefore, networks do not broadcast and are not licensed by the FCC. Each of the major networks has licenses for several television stations it owns and operates. So the FCC, which licenses those stations, has indirect control over the networks. Also, courts have allowed the FCC to set certain rules for the networks because of the networks' contractual relations with the broadcast stations over which the Commission does have jurisdiction.[75]

## STRUCTURAL REGULATION OF BROADCASTING

In order to fulfill its public interest goals without intruding on a licensee's programming discretion, the Commission often adopts rules that regulate the structure of the broadcast industry. These rules, for example, set limits on the number of stations a company can own in a single market or restrict the kinds of businesses in which a licensee can engage.

The FCC long has acted on the assumption that the public interest is best served when many different licensees operate stations. Diverse ownership, the Commission asserted, would lead to diverse viewpoints in programming and increased economic competition. For decades the FCC has limited the number of stations, as well as other media outlets, a single owner can control.[76]

The ownership restrictions were designed to prevent undue concentration of ownership at both the national and the local levels. The national rules first limited the number of stations that a company could own to seven AM, seven FM and seven TV (no more than five of which could be VHF stations).[77] During the

1980s and 1990s, the Commission modified the national ownership limits several times, finally setting the limits at twenty AM, twenty FM and twelve TV stations.[78] The Commission also added an additional requirement for television group ownership: the stations could cover no more than 25 percent of the nation's television households.[79] Another FCC rule prohibited one company from controlling two television broadcast networks. Broadcast networks were also not allowed to own cable television systems.

At the local level, the anti-duopoly rule limited a licensee to only one station of the same service in a market. (AM radio, FM radio and television each is a "service.") The one-to-a-market rule barred an entity from owning both a commercial television station and any radio station in the same market (although this rule was often waived to permit such combinations). There were also cross-ownership restrictions: A company could not own a cable system and a broadcast station in the same local market, for example. Over the years, the FCC significantly amended its local ownership rules. Moreover, Congress sharply modified some ownership limits in passing the Telecommunications Act of 1996.[80] The act further directed the Commission to review every two years whether the remaining ownership restrictions continued to serve the public interest.[81]

Due in part to court opinions requiring the Commission to reconsider some of its ownership rules, plus the Congressional requirement that the agency review its ownership rules every two years, the FCC in September 2002 issued a Notice of Proposed Rule Making that addressed all ownership regulations.[82] This proceeding was very controversial, with most industry groups and a majority of the commissioners favoring further deregulation, and consumer groups plus the two Democrat commissioners very much opposed to any action that would permit increased media concentration. Over the course of the proceeding, interested parties submitted more than 520,000 comments, the vast majority opposing further deregulation.[83]

On June 2, 2003, the FCC, citing significant changes in the media marketplace, adverse court decisions and operating efficiencies of consolidated ownership, substantially amended the remaining ownership requirements to permit increased consolidation.[84] In

---

[75] *See, e.g.,* Nat'l Broad. Co. v. FCC, 319 U.S. 190 (1943) (upholding the FCC Chain Broadcasting Rules which regulated the contractual relationships between broadcast networks and their affiliates).

[76] *See, e.g.,* Broadcast Services Other than Standard Broadcast, 6 Fed. Reg. 2282 (1941) (imposing national ownership restrictions on television broadcast stations).

[77] Rules and Regulations Relating to Multiple Ownership, 18 F.C.C. 288

(1953), *aff'd sub nom.* United States v. Storer Broad. Co., 351 U.S. 192 (1956).

[78] Radio Multiple Ownership Rules, 7 F.C.C.R. 2755 (1992).

[79] Multiple Ownership, 100 F.C.C.2d 74 (1985).

[80] Telecommunication Act of 1996, Pub. L. 104-104, 110 Stat. 136 § 202 (1996).

[81] *Id.* at § 202(h).

[82] 2002 Biennial Regulatory Review—Review of the Commission's Broadcast Ownership Rules and Other Rules Adopted Pursuant to Section 202 of the Telecommunications Act of 1996, 17 F.C.C.R. 18503 (2002).

[83] Press Release, FCC, FCC Sets Limits on Media Concentration (June 2, 2003), *available at* http://www.fcc.gov/ownership/documents.html#brdcastownrlmt.

[84] 2002 Biennial Regulatory Review — Review of the Commission's Broadcast Ownership Rules and Other Rules Adopted Pursuant to Section 202 of the

June 2004, however, a federal court vacated most of the new rules and remanded the case back to the Commission for further analysis.[85] As of mid-2006 the Commission had taken no final action on the remand. Thus, it is unclear whether or the extent to which the new rules will be implemented. Because of this uncertainty, both versions of the rules are discussed here.

### Radio

Congress, in the 1996 Act, rescinded the national ownership limits for radio stations.[86] Thus, one company may own as many stations throughout the country as it wants. Rules continue to restrict ownership within each local market. The limit depends on the number of stations in the market:

- In communities with up to fourteen radio stations, a licensee can have no more than five radio operations, no more than three of which may be AM or FM stations, and no single licensee may control more than half of the total radio stations in a market.
- In markets with fifteen to twenty-nine radio stations, one owner may control up to six radio stations, but no more than four AM or four FM stations.
- In communities with thirty to forty-four radio stations, one owner may control up to seven radio stations, but no more than four AM or four FM stations.
- In markets with forty-five or more radio stations, one owner may control up to eight radio stations, but no more than five AM or five FM stations.[87]

The Commission's 2003 Order did not change these numerical limitations on radio ownership, but the Commission amended its definition of local radio markets in an effort to make the rules more predictable and understandable.[88]

### Television

The 1996 Act removed all limits on the number of television stations one company may own, but owners could not control stations capable of reaching more than 35 percent of the country's households with television sets.[89] The FCC was forced to review the 35 percent rule after the D.C. Circuit Court ordered it to justify whether keeping the rule continued to serve the public interest.[90] In its 2003 Order, the Commission raised the coverage cap to 45 percent, finding that there was a need to retain some ownership limits but that increasing the limits would benefit the public by allowing large group owners, such as the broadcast networks, to expand their holdings and channel increased revenues into expensive, high-quality programming.[91] In the only Congressional action to formally overrule part of the 2003 Order, Congress amended this provision to state that group-owned stations could cover no more than 39 percent of all U.S. television households.[92]

Prior to 2003, rules allowed common ownership of two television stations within the same Designated Market Area (as defined by Nielsen Media Research) if eight full-power independent television stations (commercial and non-commercial) remained in operation after the merger — the "eight-voices exception." The rule only allows common ownership if one of the stations is not among the top four-ranked stations in the market based on audience share. The rule was also challenged in court. In April 2002, the D.C. Circuit ordered the FCC to review its TV duopoly rule and its eight voices exception. According to the court, the FCC had failed adequately to explain its rationale.[93]

In its 2003 Order, the Commission amended the local television ownership limits to allow "triopolies" in larger television markets. According to the new rules:

- In markets with five or more TV stations, a company may own two stations, but only one of them may be among the top four in ratings.
- In markets with eighteen or more TV stations, a company may own three TV stations, but only one of them may be among the top four in ratings.
- In deciding how many stations are in the market, both commercial and non-commercial TV stations are counted.
- The FCC will use a waiver process for markets with eleven or fewer TV stations in which two top-four stations seek to merge. The FCC will evaluate on a case-by-case basis whether

---

Telecommunications Act of 1996 (MB Docket No. 02-277); Cross-Ownership of Broadcast Stations and Newspapers (MM Docket No. 01-235); Rules and Policies Concerning Multiple Ownership of Radio Broadcast Stations in Local Markets (MM Docket No. 01-317); Definition of Radio Markets (MM Docket No. 00-244), FCC 03-127, 18 F.C.C.R. 13,620 (2003).

[85] *Prometheus Radio Project v. F.C.C.*, 373 F.3d 372 (3d Cir. 2004), *cert. denied*, 125 S.Ct. 2904 (2005). In June 2006, the Commission issued a Further Notice of Proposed Rule Making to address the issues raised by the court. *See* FCC Public Notice, FCC Opens Media Ownership Proceeding for Public Comment (June 26, 2006), *at* http://hraunfoss.fcc.gov/edocs_public/attachmatch/DOC-266033A1.pdf.

[86] Telecommunications Act of 1996, Pub. L. 104-104, 110 Stat. 136, § 202(a) (1996).

[87] 47 C.F.R. § 73.3555(a) (2004).

[88] Press Release, *supra*, note 83, at 6. The FCC replaced its signal contour method of defining markets (i.e., the extent to which various stations' signals overlapped with other signals), with Arbitron's market method, in which every radio station is assigned to a single specific geographic market.

[89] Telecommunications Act, *supra* note 80, at § 202(b).

[90] Fox TV v. FCC, 280 F.3d. 1027 (D.C. Cir. 2002). The court also struck down an FCC rule that prohibited the common ownership of a broadcast television station and a cable television system in the same community. The court found that the FCC had failed to justify the retention of the rule as necessary to safeguard competition or the public interest. *Id.* at 1051.

[91] Press Release, *supra*, note 83, at 5.

[92] Consolidated Appropriations Act of 2004, Pub. L. No. 108-199, Div. B, § 629, 118 Stat. 3, 99-100 (2004). Congress chose the 39 percent figure because two group owners, Viacom and News Corp., had already reached the 39 percent mark by virtue of the Commission's waiving the rules. Setting the cap at 39 percent thus foreclosed the possibility that these two companies would have to divest any of their television properties.

[93] Sinclair Broad. Group v. FCC, 284 F. 3d 148 (D.C. Cir. 2002).

such stations would better serve their local communities together rather than separately.[94]

## Media Cross Ownership

Before the 2003 Order, the FCC maintained two separate cross-ownership restrictions — one regulating the common ownership of radio and television stations in the same market and the other regulating the common ownership of broadcast stations and newspapers in the same market. The pre-2003 regulations allow one owner to control up to two television stations and six radio stations in markets with twenty additional independent media voices. For purposes of this rule, independent media voices include full-power television stations, radio stations, daily newspapers and cable television systems. A company may own up to two television stations and four radio stations in markets with ten additional voices. There are no restrictions on owning one TV and one radio station in a market.[95] The second cross-ownership restriction generally forbids the common ownership of a daily newspaper and any commercial broadcast station — radio or television — in the same community,[96] although over the years, the FCC has granted a handful of waivers.

In its 2003 Order, the Commission eliminated both the radio-television cross-ownership ban and the broadcast-newspaper cross-ownership ban in markets that contain nine or more television stations. The Commission asserted that neither rule could be justified for larger markets in light of the abundance of media in those areas. The Commission placed some cross-media limits on ownership in smaller markets. According to the new rules:

- In markets with three or fewer TV stations, no cross-ownership is permitted among TV, radio and newspapers. A company may obtain a waiver of that ban if it can show that the television station does not serve the area served by the cross-owned property (the radio station or the newspaper, for example).
- In markets with between four and eight TV stations, combinations are limited to one of the following:
  (A) A daily newspaper; one TV station; and up to half of the radio station limit for that market (if the radio limit in the market is six, for example, the company may only own three) or
  (B) A daily newspaper; and up to the radio station limit for that market; (for example, no TV stations) or
  (C) Two TV stations (if permissible under local TV ownership rule); and up to the radio station limit for that market (no daily newspapers, for example).[97]

## Broadcast Networks

At one time, broadcast networks could not own cable systems, but Congress ordered the rescission of the rule in 1996.[98] The dual network rule, which prohibits a company from owning two national television broadcast networks, still exists,[99] but the Commission has interpreted the rule to prohibit only the merger of the four major broadcast networks, ABC, CBS, NBC and Fox.[100] The agency made no changes in this regulation in its 2003 Order.

## REGULATION OF BROADCAST PROGRAMMING

The Communications Act forbids the FCC from censoring broadcast programming, but that has not prevented the FCC and Congress from adopting a number of regulations and laws affecting broadcast content. Some broadcasters argue that these limitations amount to censorship, but courts generally have allowed content requirements and restrictions.

## Formats

While most television stations offer a broad selection of programming, radio stations adopt formats that provide a relatively limited range of content. A radio station's format may be country and western music, adult-oriented albums, oldies or another sub-genre of rock, sports or news and talk. Listeners tune to a radio station because of its particular programming and may be upset if the station changes formats. This is particularly true if the format is unusual — jazz, classical music or children's programming, for example. Indeed, at one time courts told the FCC that the public interest requires the Commission to give approval, and to allow citizens' groups to have an opportunity to express their views, before a station could change a unique format.[101]

Several years later, however, the Commission decided that stations should be able to choose their formats without FCC approval, based upon the rationale that market forces should determine the formats of the large number of stations on the air. The Supreme Court upheld that decision.[102] Stations now may change formats at will, no longer needing FCC permission, the rationale being that if a sufficient number of listeners will support a station offering a particular format, a station in the market will respond to that consumer demand.

---

[94] Press Release, *supra,* note 83, at 4.

[95] 47 C.F.R. § 73.3555(c) (2004).

[96] 47 C.F.R. § 73.3555(e) (2004).

[97] Press Release, *supra* note 83, at 7.

[98] Telecommunications Act of 1996, Pub. L. 104-104, 110 Stat. 136 § 202(f)(1) (1996).

[99] 47 C.F.R. § 73.3613(a)(1) (2005).

[100] Dual Network Order, 16 F.C.C.R. 11115 (2001).

[101] *See* Citizens Comm. to Save WEFM v. FCC, 506 F.2d 246 (D.C. Cir. 1973); Citizens Comm. to Preserve the Voice of the Arts in Atlanta v. FCC, 436 F.2d 263 (D.C. Cir. 1970).

[102] FCC v WNCN Listeners Guild, 450 U.S. 582 (1981).

## Fairness Doctrine

Broadcasters have argued that many rules and laws affecting programming conflict with their First Amendment rights, but the fairness doctrine particularly nettled them. The FCC developed the fairness doctrine in a number of decisions beginning in 1949. The doctrine required broadcasters to inform audiences about controversial issues of public importance in the stations' license areas and to present contrasting viewpoints about the issues. This was to be done in overall programming, not necessarily through any individual program.[103] The Supreme Court, in *Red Lion Broadcasting v. FCC*, effectively upheld the FCC's right to impose fairness requirements.[104]

By the mid-1980s, however, the Commission began to question whether it needed the doctrine, since the number of broadcast and other outlets available to most people for dissemination of news and opinions about controversial issues had grown significantly. The Commission also concluded that the doctrine in fact had a chilling effect on speech because broadcasters would often avoid controversial issues altogether rather than open themselves to complaints about presenting contrasting viewpoints. For these reasons, in 1987 the FCC rescinded the doctrine, a decision the courts upheld.[105] Some public interest groups, however, continue to press Congress to codify the doctrine, and bills that would do so were introduced (but not passed) in both the 108th and 109th Congresses.[106]

## Indecent Programming

No electronic media may carry obscene material. The First Amendment protects obscenity on radio or television no more than in any other mass medium. (Obscenity is covered in Chapter 5.) In addition to possibly violating criminal laws, broadcasters who air obscene material are subject to stiff fines for not complying with FCC rules. Broadcasters, however, are also forbidden from airing "indecent or profane" programs,[107] a restriction not placed on other mass media. Over the years, the FCC has focused primarily on regulating indecent programming and has not attempted to regulate profanity. As we shall see, that policy changed in 2004.

During broadcasting's first fifty years, no station was punished solely on grounds that it aired indecent material.[108] But in the 1970s, the face of radio was changing, and some stations allowed — indeed, encouraged — on-air personalities to discuss sexual topics in a joking way, often at times when children could be listening.[109] Reacting to complaints from the public, the FCC fined some stations and stated that it expected such programming to stop.[110]

Then, in 1973, the FCC was faced with what it considered an egregious example of indecent material. During a weekday mid-afternoon, a father and son driving through New York City turned on the car radio and heard on WBAI, an FM station licensed to the Pacifica Foundation, a portion of an album by comedian George Carlin. Recorded live, the twelve-minute routine was based on Carlin's list of seven words "you can't say on the public ... airwaves."[111] The father complained to the FCC, and, after a hearing, the Commission warned Pacifica that if it broadcast indecent programming again, the FCC could impose sanctions. Pacifica appealed, and the Supreme Court upheld the FCC.[112]

The Court adopted the FCC's definition of indecent communication as words that "describe, in terms patently offensive as measured by contemporary community standards for the broadcast medium, sexual or excretory activities and organs, at times of the day where there is reasonable risk that children may be in the audience."[113] The Court recognized that the restriction on indecent programming limited broadcasters' First Amendment rights but found the restriction acceptable because (1) broadcasting is pervasive, and (2) the Carlin monologue was aired at a time children likely could be listening. Both points were important.

First, the Court assumed that people could be exposed to radio or television at any time, in any place, with little control over what they would hear or see. Because broadcasting differs in this regard from print media, which normally require a decision to purchase and a conscious effort to read, broadcasters' First Amendment rights could be narrowed. Second, since the primary concern was preventing children from being exposed to indecent programming, the FCC and Supreme Court did not hold that stations never could carry such material. Rather, they could not air indecent material when children were likely to hear or see it. Accordingly, the Commission has chosen 10 p.m. to 6 a.m. as a "safe harbor" during which broadcasters are permitted to carry indecent programming.[114]

---

[103] *See* Editorializing by Broad. Licensees, 13 F.C.C. 1246 (1949).

[104] 395 U.S. 367 (1969).

[105] Syracuse Peace Council v. FCC, 867 F.2d 654 (D.C. Cir. 1989). *See also* Arkansas AFL-CIO v. FCC, 11 F.3d 1430 (8th Cir. 1993).

[106] Media Ownership Reform Act of 2004, 108th Cong. § 3 (2004); Fairness and Accountability in Broadcasting Act of 2005, 109th Cong. (2005).

[107] 18 U.S.C. § 1464 (a provision of the United States Criminal Code); 47 U.S.C. §§ 312(a)(6), 503 (b)(1)(D) (2000).

[108] *But see,* Robinson v. FCC, 334 F.2d 534 (D.C. Cir. 1964) (in which the FCC found that a disk jockey told offensive jokes, capable of indecent meaning, on the air, but based its non-renewal of the station's license on grounds that the station management had lied to the FCC).

[109] *See* Sonderling Broad. Corp., 41 F.C.C.2d 777 (1973) (for example, a caller saying, "... I used to spread [peanut butter] on my husband's privates.... [W]omen should try their favorite...," and the announcer replying, "Whipped cream, marshmallow....").

[110] *See* Illinois Citizens Comm. for Broad. v. FCC, 515 F.2d 397 (D.C. Cir. 1974).

[111] The words were shit, piss, fuck, cunt, cocksucker, motherfucker and tits.

[112] FCC v. Pacifica Found., 438 U.S. 726 (1978).

[113] *Id.* at 732.

[114] New Indecency Enforcement Standards, 2 F.C.C.R. 2726 (1987).

Until a few years ago, most indecency fines were levied against radio stations, usually for broadcasts involving live shows that feature sexually graphic or suggestive discussions, expletives or lewd songs. For example, from 1987 through mid-1995, the FCC fined Infinity Broadcasting a total of $1.7 million for carrying the Howard Stern program, which included material the FCC found indecent. In an effort to help the broadcast industry avoid violating the indecency rules, the FCC issued a Policy Statement in 2001 which listed the various factors the Commission uses to determine whether material is indecent.[115]

Several notable events in 2003 and 2004 led both the FCC and Congress to reconsider the ways indecent and profane broadcasts are regulated. First came a string of high-profile violations involving radio shock jocks. One instance involved the "Opie and Anthony Show," during which descriptions of couples having sex in St. Patrick's Cathedral were aired live.[116] Another involved a call-in show in which callers described in detail explicit sexual and excretory experiences.[117] A third involved Clear Channel's "Bubba the Love Sponge," who consistently spoke of sexual organs and explicit activities.[118] The incident most credited with provoking Congress, however, was the famous "costume malfunction" during the Super Bowl halftime show in which Janet Jackson's breast briefly was revealed. In response to these and other violations and the resulting complaints from thousands of citizens, in 2006 Congress amended the Communications Act to raise the permissible penalty for airing indecent language from $32,500 to $325,000 per incident.[119]

In another development, the FCC, in a departure from long-established practice, announced that it will begin to act against stations airing profanity. This issue arose when Bono, while accepting a Golden Globe award on live television, said the award was "fucking brilliant." After review, the FCC's Enforcement Bureau, citing past precedent, declared that the one-time, fleeting use of the word — even though it was broadcast outside the safe harbor — was not indecent.[120] The word was used as an adjective, not as a reference to sexual activity. Congress responded with resolutions condemning the decision.[121] Several months later the full Commission reversed the bureau's decision, finding the use of the word to be profane, and indicating that future use of such profanity outside the safe harbor will result in forfeitures.[122] The Commission defines profanity as "language so grossly offensive to members of the public who actually hear it as to amount to a nuisance."[123]

Based on this decision, many television licensees declined to carry the annual Veteran's Day airing of the award-winning World War II movie *Saving Private Ryan* due to the profanity in the film. Several stations did carry the program, and many complaints about the language were filed at the Commission. The FCC ruled that the program was not profane or indecent, arguing that the language was integral to the film's objective of presenting the horror of war.[124] However, when the same language was spoken by musicians in a critically acclaimed documentary on the blues, the FCC ruled the language was profane.[125] In 2006, the FCC declared that use of the word "shit" outside the safe harbor also was profane and could lead to sanctions.[126] As a result of all these actions, the four major broadcast networks have indicated they will challenge the FCC's decisions in court.[127]

## Children's Programming

For decades Congress and the FCC have fought with broadcast television networks over children's programming. Early on, the battle involved excessive violence in shows children watched. Later, advocates for better children's television programming convinced Congress that there simply were not enough shows that helped children learn about themselves and their world. Congress held a number of hearings about children's television and tried to convince broadcast network executives to pay more attention to the quality of children's programs.

Finally, in 1990, Congress adopted a law requiring broadcast stations to provide certain types of children's programs, which essentially meant that networks and syndicators would need to supply the shows.[128] The statute also limited the amount of commercial time that could be inserted before, during and after children's programming on broadcast stations and cable networks.

The Children's Television Act requires all broadcast television

---

[115] In the Matter of Industry Guidance on the Commission's Case Law Interpreting 18 U.S.C. § 1464 and Enforcement Policies Regarding Broadcast Indecency, 16 F.C.C.R. 7999 (2001). The factors are (1) the explicitness or graphic nature of the description or depiction of sexual or excretory organs or activities; (2) whether the material dwells on, or repeats at length, descriptions of sexual or excretory activities or organs; and (3) whether the material appears to pander, is used to titillate, or appears to have been presented for shock value.

[116] Infinity Broadcasting Operations, Inc. et al., 18 F.C.C.R. 19954 (2004).

[117] Infinity Broadcasting Operations, Inc., 18 F.C.C.R. 6915 (2003).

[118] Clear Channel Broadcasting Licenses, Inc. et al., 19 F.C.C.R. 4975 (2004).

[119] Broadcast Decency Enforcement Act of 2005, Pub. Law 109-235 (2006).

[120] Complaints Against Various Broadcast Licensees Regarding Their Airing of the "Golden Globe Awards," 18 F.C.C.R. 19859 (Enforcement Bur. 2003).

[121] H. Res. 500, S. Res. 283, 108th Cong. (2003).

[122] Complaints Against Various Broadcast Licensees Regarding Their Airing of the "Golden Globe Awards," 19 F.C.C.R. 4975 (2004).

[123] *Id.* at 4977.

[124] Complaints Against Various Television Licensees Regarding Their Broadcast on November 11, 2004, of the ABC Television Network's Presentation of the Film "Saving Private Ryan," 20 F.C.C.R. 4507 (2005).

[125] Complaints Regarding Various Television Broadcasts Between February 2, 2002, and March 8, 2005, 21 F.C.C.R. 1664, paras. 72-86 (2006).

[126] *Id.* at paras. 100-145.

[127] *See* Frank Ahrens, *Networks Sue Over Indecency Rulings; Lawsuits Say FCC Exceeded Authority*, WASH. POST, Apr. 15, 2006, at D1.

[128] Children's Television Act, Pub. L. No. 101-437, 104 Stat. 996 (1990) (codified at 47 U.S.C. § 303(a-b) (2000).

stations to provide programming intended for children sixteen years old or younger that will serve their "educational and information needs."[129] The law also encourages stations to offer educational and information programming that is meant for families — adults, as well as children. Nature programming is an example. Additionally, the act suggested that stations could show their concern about children's programming in other ways. They could air announcements for children's shows on public television, for example, or they could help pay for study guides for educational and information programs.[130] The law did not specify how much programming aimed at children would be required for a station to be in compliance, but the voluntary activities could help convince the FCC that a station has met the requirements.

By the mid-1990s, several FCC commissioners and some members of Congress had said that television broadcasters were not fulfilling their responsibilities under the Children's Television Act. To give the law more teeth, in 1996 the Commission adopted rules making it clear what stations would have to do.[131] Specifically, stations were to broadcast three hours per week of programs designed to serve children's intellectual/cognitive and social/emotional needs. The programs are required to be at least thirty minutes long, regularly scheduled on a weekly basis and broadcast between 7 a.m. and 10 p.m. These rules establish what is termed "core programming," and stations' compliance with the rules is considered at license renewal.

A station that does not broadcast quite three hours of core programming can still have its license renewed by airing public service announcements, programs fewer than thirty minutes in length and programs not scheduled weekly — all of which are designed to meet children's intellectual and emotional needs and which the station persuades the FCC are equivalent to meeting the three-hour requirement. Stations not coming within either of these categories will have to convince the FCC commissioners that they deserve to have their licenses renewed.

Moreover, recent studies indicate that the networks are preempting children's shows for sports programs during the weekend, especially in the western time zone. However, the FCC rules require that preempted children's shows be rescheduled.

While the programming requirements apply to broadcast stations and not to cable systems, the Children's Television Act has commercial limits that apply to both. It restricts advertising time before, during and after programming specifically directed at children twelve years old and younger. Commercials are limited to twelve minutes per hour during the week and ten and one-half minutes per hour on Saturdays and Sundays. These limits are prorated; a half-hour program could carry only six minutes of commercials on Thursday afternoon, for example. The FCC has fined several stations thousands of dollars for exceeding these limits. After reviewing recent license renewal applications, the FCC found that about 26 percent of all stations have exceeded the limits. In response, it announced its intention to conduct unannounced audits to identify violators. The Commission also has ruled that characters in children's programs cannot appear in commercials before, during or after those programs.[132]

### V-Chip and Television Program Ratings

In the mid-1990s, rumblings from the public and politicians about the perceived amount of violence and sex on television rose to a roar. Congress addressed the complaints in the Telecommunications Act of 1996, which required that, beginning in 1998, all television sets sold in the United States include a means for viewers to prevent certain programs from being seen on the sets. A microprocessor chip — called a "v-chip" — within the set picks up an electronic signal embedded within certain television programs. The signal indicates the program's rating. The v-chip in a set may be instructed to prevent programs rated for mature audiences, for example, from being seen on that set.

Congress encouraged the television industry to develop a voluntary rating system for television programs and required the FCC to establish a committee to do so if the networks refused, or if they failed to meet the Commission's standards for rating programs. The four major broadcast networks chose Jack Valenti, head of the Motion Picture Association of America, to chair a group devising a ratings system.

There are two sets of parental guidelines, as the ratings are known. One category applies to programs designed solely for children. A TV-Y rating means a program is appropriate for all children; TV-Y7 means a program is designed for children age seven and above. The second rating category applies to programs designed for the entire audience. TV-G means that most parents would find the program suitable for all ages. TV-PG means the program contains material that parents may find unsuitable for younger children. TV-14 means the program contains some material that many parents may find unsuitable for children under 14. Finally, TV-MA means that a program is specifically designed for an adult audience and is, therefore, unsuitable for children under 17. Additionally, the ratings include letters that identify various types of content. For example, "V" stands for violence, "FV" for fantasy violence, "S" for sexual material, "L" for strong language, and "D" for suggestive dialogue. Sports and news programs are not rated.

While the law does not require a rating to be applied to any individual program, once a program is rated the rating must be imbedded on the signal carrying the show. In January 2000, the FCC released a survey that indicated that all the broadcast networks and most of the basic cable networks were encoding their

---

129 47 U.S.C. § 303(b) (2000).

130 Children's Television Programming, 6 F.C.C.R. 2111 (1991); Children's Television Programming, 6 F.C.C.R. 5093 (1991).

131 Policies and Rules Concerning Children's Television Programming, 11 F.C.C.R. 10660 (1996).

132 Children's Television Programming, 6 F.C.C.R. 7199 (1990).

programming.[133]

As another way of protecting children from violent content on television, some groups and the chairman of the FCC, Kevin Martin, have called for reinstituting a family viewing hour, once suggested to television stations by the National Association of Broadcasters, an industry group. Programs shown in the hour prior to prime time and in the first hour of prime time — 6-8 p.m. — were to have a reduced level of sex and violence. The standard was challenged in federal court,[134] but the NAB already had dropped its suggestion. Nevertheless, the networks voluntarily continued the family viewing hour for several more years before abandoning it in 1983. Responding to public concern about the coarsening of television content, in 2004 both Houses of Congress introduced bills in the 108th Congress that would have either reinstituted the family viewing hour or channeled violent programming to late-night time periods.[135] Neither House acted on the proposals.

### Political Broadcasting

Under Section 315 of the Communications Act, once a legally qualified candidate for an elective office has used a station — has been given or sold time — all other legally qualified candidates for the same office must be given an equal opportunity. That is, candidates for the same office have the right to approximately the same amount of time during a period of the day when they are likely to be seen or heard by the same size and type of audience. Section 315 applies to legally qualified candidates running for all types of elective office — local, state or federal.

While the FCC has held, essentially, that the public interest requires candidates to be given access to broadcast stations, Congress made certain of that for those running for federal offices. Section 312(a)(7) of the Communications Act requires broadcast stations to give federal candidates "reasonable access" to radio and television audiences. The term "reasonable access" is interpreted liberally. In 1980, the Carter-Mondale Committee asked ABC, NBC and CBS to sell it thirty minutes of time. The networks refused, and the Supreme Court upheld the FCC's decision that the refusal violated section 312(a)(7).[136] The Commission also has stated that "reasonable access" does not mean free time for federal candidates; stations may charge candidates for air time, a ruling also upheld in court.[137]

Section 312(a)(7) guarantees that a candidate for federal office

cannot be denied time on broadcast stations. Otherwise, federal candidates are subject to the provisions of Section 315, just as are candidates for non-federal offices.

A point of contention between broadcasters and candidates for federal office has been the length of political ads. Broadcasters usually sell time to commercial advertisers in thirty- and sixty-second slots. But some candidates have sought to buy five-minute time slots in order to present a more detailed message to voters. Consequently, the FCC issued an order stating that candidates cannot be barred from purchasing advertising time in lengths most useful for their purposes simply because broadcasters traditionally sell commercial time in thirty- and sixty-second slots.[138]

**Legally Qualified Candidate.** A legally qualified candidate is one who has announced publicly that she or he is running for an office. This means more than telling a few friends. The person must have made a widely disseminated statement. Second, the person must meet qualifications for the office — age or residency, for example. Third, the person must either (a) have qualified for a place on the ballot, usually by having a sufficient number of registered voters sign a nominating petition or being nominated by a political party, or (b) be a publicly committed write-in candidate. Independent candidates can be legally qualified, and even candidates with no reasonable chance of winning the election can insist upon equal opportunity.

A candidate claiming equal opportunity in reaction to another candidate's appearance must be running for the same office. Clearly, two candidates seeking the mayor's seat or two seeking a Senate seat are running for the same office. But other scenarios are not so clear. Assume two Republicans are running in a primary election for mayor, as are two Democrats. A Republican buys a minute of time on a radio station, and one of the Democrats insists on a similar purchase. Under Section 315, the station need not sell time to the Democrat. The FCC has ruled that the Democrat and Republican are not running for the same "office": The Democrat is running for the Democratic nomination, and the Republican is running for the Republican nomination. If both candidates were to win their primary races and face each other in the general election, they would be running for the same office, and so would any third-party or independent candidates for mayor.

A station could avoid all these problems by not selling advertising time to any candidates for state and local offices under Section 315, although the FCC has indicated it would frown on such action. But the requirement under Section 312(a)(7) that broadcast stations offer reasonable access for federal candidates essentially means that a station must sell time to even the first candidate for a federal office asking to run an advertisement.

---

[133] News Release, FCC, FCC V-Chip Task Force Releases Updated Survey on the Encoding of Video Programming (Jan. 11, 2000), *at* http://www.fcc.gov/Bureaus/Miscellaneous/News_Releases/2000/nrmc0004.html.

[134] *See* Writers Guild of America, West, Inc. v. FCC, 609 F.2d 355 (9th Cir. 1979).

[135] Children's Protection from Violent Programming Act, H.R. 3914, 108th Cong. (2004); Broadcast Decency Enforcement Act of 2004, S. 2056, 108th Cong. (2004).

[136] CBS, Inc. v. FCC, 453 U.S. 367 (1981).

[137] Kennedy for President Comm. v. FCC, 636 F.2d 417 (D.C. Cir. 1980).

[138] People for the American Way and Media Access Project, FCC 99-231 (Sept. 7, 1999), *at* http://ftp.fcc.gov/Bureaus/Mass_Media/Orders/1999/fcc99231.pdf.

**Use.** "Using" a station, which triggers Section 315 for competing candidates, happens when a candidate, the candidate's picture or the candidate's identifiable voice appears on the air. This can be a campaign commercial, or it can be an appearance on a station's cooking show with no mention of the election. There is no use if the appearance is disparaging, which would occur, for example, if an opponent used the candidate's picture in a belittling way.

In 1959, Congress amended Section 315 by specifying four news exemptions to the use rule. In these instances, even if a candidate's voice or picture is used on the air, Section 315 does not apply because there has been no use under the law. Congress' intent was to be certain that Section 315 did not artificially limit news coverage of political campaigns and candidates.

First, on-the-spot coverage of a news event will not trigger Section 315. The FCC and courts have ruled that press conferences, speeches and debates among candidates generally will be considered news events, and coverage of them will not constitute a use. For example, President Jimmy Carter, running for re-election in 1980, used a press conference to attack Edward Kennedy, his opponent for the Democratic nomination. Kennedy demanded time to reply, but the FCC and the courts found that a press conference is a bona fide news event and, therefore, is an exception to Section 315.[139]

Similarly, debates among candidates are news events and, therefore, exempted from Section 315 regardless of who sponsors them — the candidates, broadcasters or a nonpartisan group.[140] The FCC and the courts have said that it is not required that all candidates for an office be included in a debate, and those who are excluded cannot claim time under Section 315.[141] In 1998, the Supreme Court said that even state-owned public television stations may exclude minor political candidates from on-air debates. The 6-3 opinion held that public stations could exercise their journalistic discretion as long as the exclusion of minority candidates was not based on the candidate's views.[142]

In 1996, the FCC allowed ABC, Fox and the Public Broadcasting Service to provide free time for the major party presidential candidates.[143] The Commission said that the candidates' appearances would be exempt from the equal opportunities requirement of Section 315 as coverage of a bona fide news event.

Second, a candidate's appearance on a regularly scheduled newscast is not considered a use. The appearance could be an interview with a candidate, coverage of a candidate's campaign activities or other such activities. Courts have interpreted this exception broadly. Candidates appearing on *The McLaughlin Group*,

for example, a television program featuring discussions among panelists as well as presentations of news events, are considered to be involved in news coverage, even though the appearance was not in a typical newscast.[144]

The FCC does not interpret the broadcast exemption broadly in relation to on-air personalities who are running for office. While it may seem, for example, that a news program anchor who is a political candidate would come under the newscast exemption, the Commission has held otherwise.[145] Congress recognized that the broadcasting of news about candidates for public office is important to viewers; so it amended Section 315 to exclude appearances by candidates in newscasts. Appearing in a news story, however, and appearing on a news program as a reporter or anchor are not the same. A person presenting the news does not help the public learn more about the campaign; it simply gives the candidate an unfair opportunity to become known by voters. Therefore, an anchor on a Sacramento station who was a candidate for town council in a nearby community had to choose between being on the air or being a candidate during the campaign period. Had he been both, the station would have been required to offer more than thirty hours of free time to other candidates for the same office to comply with the requirements of Section 315.

Third, a candidate's appearance on a regularly scheduled news interview program is not a use and does not trigger Section 315. Interview programs like *Meet the Press* and *Issues and Answers* are exempt. The FCC has extended the definition of a "news interview program" to include *The Today Show*, *Entertainment Tonight* and similar programs.[146] Even interview segments of call-in talk shows can be exempt.[147] To fall under the exemption, the program must have been regularly scheduled beginning well before the election period, and the station must control the content, format and guests.

Fourth, a candidate's appearance on a news documentary program is not a use if the appearance is incidental to the campaign. For example, a water engineer who is running for governor could be in a documentary about water conservation in the state. But a documentary about the political views of a mayoral candidate would not qualify under the exemption.

**Application Time of Section 315.** Section 315 applies whenever there are two or more legally qualified candidates for the same elective office. That may be only a short time before an election, or months prior to an election.

[139] Kennedy for President Comm. v. FCC, 636 F.2d 417 (D.C. Cir. 1980).

[140] *See* League of Women Voters Educ. Fund v. FCC, 731 F.2d 995 (D.C. Cir. 1984) (without opinion).

[141] *See* Johnson v. FCC, 829 F.2d 157 (D.C. Cir. 1987).

[142] Arkansas Educ. Television Comm'n v. Forbes, 523 U.S. 666 (1998).

[143] Fox Broad. Co., Public Broad. Serv. and Capital Cities/ABC, 11 F.C.C.R. 11101 (1996).

[144] Telecommunications Research and Action Center, 7 F.C.C.R. 6039 (1996).

[145] *See* Branch v. FCC, 824 F.2d 37 (D.C. Cir. 1987).

[146] *See, e.g.,* Paramount Pictures Corp., 3 F.C.C.R. 245 (1988) (*Entertainment Tonight*); Multimedia Entertainment, 56 Rad. Reg. 2d (P & F) 143 (1984) (*Donahue*).

[147] Request of Infinity Broadcasting Operations Inc. for Declaratory Ruling, DA 03-2865, 18 F.C.C.R. 18603 (2003).

**Requesting Time.** Under Section 315, a candidate whose opponent has used a broadcast station must ask for equal opportunity. The station has no obligation to notify candidates. Information about candidates who have requested time and who have appeared must be kept in public files available at broadcast stations. Requests for time must be made within seven days of the appearance that triggered Section 315.

**Lowest Unit Rate.** Section 315 provides that candidates purchasing time for political commercials must be charged no more than the station's most-favored advertiser would pay. That is, whatever the rate would be for the advertiser who purchases the most minutes during the year on a station is the rate a candidate would be charged. This is true even if that minute is the only time the candidate will purchase during the entire campaign.[148] But if the appearance triggering Section 315 was free to the first candidate — a candidate appears on a local children's program only to read a story aloud — opponents may demand equivalent free time.

The lowest-unit-rate provision takes effect forty-five days before a primary election and sixty days before a general or special election. Outside those periods, stations and cable systems may charge political candidates what any other advertiser would be charged (not just their best advertiser) for a comparable purchase of advertising time.

Many members of Congress, upset with the high cost of political campaigns, have sought revisions in the lowest unit rate provisions that would make political advertising even less expensive. As part of the campaign finance reform efforts in the 107th Congress, bills were introduced that would have forced broadcasters to provide free time to politicians or even fund political air time through a voucher system that broadcasters would have paid for.[149] Broadcast lobbyists successfully argued against these measures, and they were not included in the legislation that ultimately became law.[150]

**Content of Political Commercials.** Broadcast stations cannot edit political advertisements, nor can they refuse to run a candidate's commercial because they believe the message will offend their audience. At the same time, stations are not liable for anything said or shown in political commercials. Broadcasters cannot be sued for libel, invasion of privacy or any other tort based on material in a candidate's presentation under Section 315.[151]

The general rule that political advertisements cannot be censored was severely tested in the 1990s when some candidates chose to show aborted fetuses as part of their commercials. A Georgia candidate for the U.S. House of Representatives included in a commercial depictions of "the actual surgical procedure for abortion ... [including] graphic depictions and descriptions of female genitalia, the uterus, excreted uterine fluid, dismembered fetal body parts, and aborted fetuses."[152] The FCC held that while such commercials are not indecent, stations and cable systems may decide to carry such advertisements only in the safe harbor hours used for indecent programming if they find that the commercials could be harmful to children.[153] But a federal appellate court found that this would permit "broadcasters to take the content of a political advertisement into account" in determining whether to confine the commercial to the safe harbor period, allowing broadcasters "standardless discretion."[154] The court said that, on balance, candidates' rights as specified in sections 315 and 312(a)(7) of the Communications Act took precedence over concerns about children being exposed to possibly offensive material.

**Zapple Rule.** While not a part of Section 315, an FCC doctrine known as the "Zapple rule" applies to political appearances and works as a quasi-equal opportunity rule.[155] Originally a part of the fairness doctrine, the Zapple rule takes effect when a candidate's supporters — but not the candidate or the candidate's picture or voice — use a station. For example, a candidate's campaign manager might appear in a commercial supporting the candidate's election. Under the Zapple rule, the station must offer comparable time to supporters of the candidate's opponent. This offer does not extend to the opponent. The doctrine applies only to supporters of major candidates and is subject to the same "use" exemptions as Congress adopted for Section 315.

The Zapple rule, named for a congressional staff member who first brought the issue to the FCC's attention, does not require broadcast stations to sell time to a candidate's supporters in the first place. If they do sell them time, they need not do so at the lowest unit rate.

**Ballot Issues.** Section 315 and the Zapple rule apply only to candidates for public offices and their supporters; they do not apply to ballot issues. Supporters and opponents of such issues may purchase broadcast time if they wish, but there is no requirement

---

[148] *See* Political Programming Policies, 7 F.C.C.R. 678 (1991).

[149] *See, e.g.,* A Bill to Amend the Communications Act of 1934 to Revise and Expand the Lowest Unit Cost Provision Applicable to Political Campaign Broadcasts, to Establish Commercial Broadcasting Station Minimum Airtime Requirements for Candidate-Centered and Issue-Centered Programming Before Primary and General Elections, to Establish a Voucher System for the Purchase of Commercial Broadcast Airtime for Political Advertisements, and for Other Purposes, S. 3124, 107th Cong. (2002).

[150] *See* Bipartisan Campaign Reform Act of 2002, Pub. L. 107-155 (2002).

[151] Farmers Educ. & Coop. Union of America v. WDAY, 360 U.S. 525

(1959).

[152] Gillette Communications of Atlanta v. Becker, 807 F. Supp. 757, 763 (N.D. Ga. 1992) (finding the commercial to be indecent), *dismissed without opinion and remanded,* 5 F.3d 1500 (11th Cir. 1993).

[153] Petition for Declaratory Ruling Concerning Section 312(a)(7) of the Communications Act, 9 F.C.C.R. 7638 (1994) (disagreeing with the *Gillett* decision that such commercials are indecent).

[154] Becker v. FCC, 95 F.3d 75, 81 (D.C. Cir. 1996).

[155] Letter to Nicholas Zapple, 23 F.C.C.2d 707 (1970).

that such time be sold or that equal opportunities be provided.

## *Other Programming Requirements*

The FCC has imposed on broadcasters several other rules affecting program content. When those rules have been challenged as violating broadcasters' First Amendment rights, courts have generally upheld them.

**Lotteries.** A lottery is a contest that has a prize of more than token value, uses chance rather than skill to determine winners and requires some form of consideration — like the purchase of a ticket — to enter. FCC rules and federal criminal laws have long restricted the information broadcasters may carry about lotteries. The exception has been state-run lotteries in states where the stations are located. Congress changed all that in 1988.

Broadcasters may carry information about certain lotteries. As before, they can provide facts about state lotteries if the station is located in a state that has a lottery. They may also carry news or advertisements for gaming conducted by Native American tribes.[156] And they may provide information about a lottery legal in the state where it is conducted and that a governmental or nonprofit organization offers or is sponsored by a person or company not primarily in the business of sponsoring lotteries.[157] Thus, reports or advertisements for bingo games at churches or a cereal company giving away an automobile are acceptable if state law permits. But until recently, stations could not carry information or advertisements for private (non-Native American) gambling casinos or sports betting. In 1999, the Supreme Court unanimously struck down the ban on television and radio advertising of private casino gambling in states where such gambling is legal, finding that the ban was "so pierced by exemptions and inconsistencies that the government cannot hope to exonerate it."[158]

**Sponsorship Identification.** Broadcasters must identify clearly any individual or group providing money, or anything else of value, in return for the dissemination of a message.[159] The purpose of the rule is to ensure that viewers and listeners will not confuse paid advertisements with entertainment or news programs. If the sponsor is obvious — a cereal, a laundry detergent, a fast food restaurant — the requirement is met. Other messages are not so clearly identifiable. If, for example, a local company provides funds for a "Clean Up The Parks" advertising campaign, those ads must carry the company's name as a sponsor. Concerns over "product placement" advertising (advertisers paying television producers to place their products as props in television shows) and the recent controversy over the Bush Administration's practice of producing video "news" segments supporting its policies for placement in local newscasts has prompted the FCC to issue a consumer alert regarding its sponsorship identification policies.[160]

**Hoaxes and News Distortion.** The FCC prohibits the broadcasting of hoaxes. Under the regulation, a hoax occurs when a station knowingly broadcasts false reports of crimes or catastrophes that "directly cause foreseeable — immediate, substantial and actual public harm."[161]

WALE-AM radio in Providence, Rhode Island, perpetuated a hoax in 1991 when the news director announced over the air that a WALE talk show host had been shot in the head while outside the station's studio. About ten minutes later, the station stated that the shooting had been a dramatization. Before the second announcement, several police officers rushed to the scene, as did several members of the media. WALE apologized to the public and offered to repay the Providence Police Department for any costs resulting from the hoax. The FCC admonished the station's owner, citing the Commission's policy "requiring licensees to program their stations in the public interest."[162]

The Commission also has a policy against news distortion. One example of distortion occurred when a Chicago television station had a group of people stage a gathering at which marijuana was smoked in order to film a "pot party." The FCC expressed its concern about manufacturing news but did not threaten action against the station.[163] In another instance, the CBS documentary *Hunger in America* showed a child said to be suffering from malnutrition but who was afflicted with a different illness.[164] The Commission took no action against CBS but used the case to establish a policy forbidding intentional news distortion. The Commission, however, distinguishes deliberate distortion from a mistake or negligent reporting.

**Cigarette Advertising.** Concerned with the costs to public health that cigarette smoking causes, Congress made it "unlawful to advertise cigarettes on any medium of electronic communication" after January 1, 1971.[165] The law was upheld despite a challenge based on broadcasters' First Amendment rights.[166]

---

[156] Indian Gaming Regulatory Act, Pub. L. No. 100-497, § 21, codified at 25 U.S.C. § 2720 (2000).

[157] *See* Charity Games Advertising Clarification Act of 1988, Pub. L. No. 100-625, § 2(b), codified at 18 U.S.C § 1307 (2000).

[158] Greater New Orleans Broad. Ass'n v. United States, 527 U.S. 173, 190 (1999).

[159] 47 U.S.C. § 317 (2000).

[160] *See* The FCC's Payola Rules, *at* http://www.fcc.gov/cgb/consumerfacts/PayolaRules.html.

[161] Broadcast Hoaxes, 7 F.C.C.R. 4106, 4106 (1992).

[162] Letter to WALE-AM, 7 F.C.C.R. 2345, 2346 (1992).

[163] WBBM-TV, 18 F.C.C.2d 124 (1969).

[164] Hunger in America, 20 F.C.C.2d 151 (1969).

[165] 15 U.S.C. § 1335 (2000).

[166] Capital Broad. Co. v. Mitchell, 333 F. Supp. 582 (D.C. 1971), *aff'd without opinion*, 405 U.S. 1000 (1972).

**Distilled Spirits Advertising.** A more recent controversy arose when, in 1997, a television station aired an advertisement for Seagrams. The ad represented a departure from a four-decade long, self-imposed ban of hard liquor advertising on television. Congress and the FCC became concerned that the distilled spirits industry was going to begin advertising on television on a regular basis. The FCC, along with some members of Congress, began to discuss whether there should be a statutory ban on such ads. While the ban on cigarette advertising provides a precedent for a ban on distilled spirits, the current issue is complicated by the fact that beer and wine ads appear regularly on television. Thus, the issue becomes whether the government can constitutionally ban the advertising of some types of alcohol products on television — such as distilled spirits — while allowing others — such as beer and wine. As yet, Congress has not acted on this issue.

## NONCOMMERCIAL BROADCASTING

Certain parts of the broadcast spectrum are set aside for use by noncommercial stations. Radio broadcasting was using the AM band before any government agency could consider whether to reserve frequency assignments for noncommercial uses. The FCC, however, was able to set aside portions of the FM band and reserve certain television frequencies for nonprofit organizations, usually educational institutions and state governments, but also religious groups. The Commission recognized that some educational institutions might be tempted to sell their stations to commercial broadcasters, in part because of the high costs of keeping a station on the air, unless certain frequencies were reserved only for nonprofit, educational use.

In 1967, Congress aided noncommercial broadcasting by adopting the Public Broadcasting Act, which established the Corporation for Public Broadcasting, an agency through which federal government and other funding is used to produce programming for noncommercial stations. The FCC has no jurisdiction to enforce any provisions of the Public Broadcasting Act,[167] such as that requiring "strict adherence to objectivity and balance in all programs or series of programs of a controversial nature."[168]

One section of the act insisting on objectivity and another forbidding noncommercial stations from supporting political candidates raise questions of First Amendment protection for public stations. The Supreme Court rejected the provision forbidding public stations from supporting political candidates and the Public Broadcasting Act's ban on noncommercial stations editorializing. The Court said that First Amendment protection of journalistic freedom should also apply to public stations.[169]

Most public stations receive federal and possibly state funds, and government agencies own many of them. The tension be-

tween the public nature of noncommercial stations and First Amendment freedoms was reflected in the *Death of a Princess* case. The docudrama, intended for showing on public television, portrayed the execution in Saudi Arabia of a woman and her lover accused of adultery. The government of Saudi Arabia had strong objections to the program, and several public television stations decided not to carry it.[170] Viewers took government-owned stations in Alabama and Houston, Texas, to court, hoping to force them to broadcast the program.[171] In part, the suits claimed that the public stations were arms of the government and were engaging in censorship, as well as violating viewers' First Amendment rights. A federal appellate court found that, as licensees under the Communications Act, the stations were permitted to use their editorial judgment in selecting what programs to carry.[172]

Most of the regulations that apply to commercial stations also apply to non-commercial stations, but there are several differences. In comparative licensing situations, for example, Congress has forbidden the use of auctions in awarding noncommercial licenses. Accordingly, the FCC has developed a point system that compares objective criteria such as local diversity and technical superiority.[173] Another regulatory difference relates to the multiple- and cross-ownership limitations, which do not apply to noncommercial licensees.[174] Finally, as the name implies, noncommercial stations are not permitted to carry advertisements.[175] However, they are permitted to acknowledge entities that contribute money to the station or underwrite programming. These underwriting announcements differ from commercial advertising in that they contain no qualitative statements about the underwriter's products or services, they cannot make comparisons among products, they cannot provide price information, and there can be no calls to action or inducements to purchase.[176]

## THE MOVE TO DIGITAL

Following almost ten years of study and testing, the FCC, in consultation with various industry groups, adopted a new digital television (DTV) transmission standard in 1996.[177] The new standard,

---

[167] *See* Accuracy in Media, Inc. v. FCC, 521 F.2d 288 (D.C. Cir. 1975).

[168] 47 U.S.C. § 396(g)(1)(A) (2000).

[169] FCC v. League of Women Voters, 468 U.S. 364, 402 (1984).

[170] *See, e.g.,* Barnstone v. Univ. of Houston, KUHT-TV, 487 F. Supp. 1347, 1348 (S.D. Tex. 1980).

[171] In Alabama, all public stations operate under a statewide agency; in Texas, the public television stations operate independently of one another.

[172] *See* Muir v. Alabama Educ. Television Comm'n, 688 F.2d 1033 (5th Cir. 1982) (en banc).

[173] In the Matter of Reexamination of the Comparative Standards for Noncommercial Educational Applicants, 15 F.C.C.R. 7386 (2000), *aff'd sub nom.* American Family Ass'n v. FCC, 365 F.3d 1156 (D.C. Cir. 2004).

[174] 47 C.F.R. § 73.3555(f) (2004).

[175] 47 U.S.C. § 399B (2000).

[176] Commission Policy Concerning the Noncommercial Nature of Educational Broadcast Stations, 7 F.C.C.R. 827 (1992).

[177] Advanced Television Systems and Their Impact Upon the Existing Television Broadcast Service, 11 F.C.C.R. 17771 (*Fourth Report and Order*, 1996).

which allows for transmission of multiple program streams as well as high definition television (HDTV) will replace the analog transmission standard that broadcasters have used since the 1940s. The Commission proposed a ten-year transition period during which broadcasters and consumers would replace their incompatible analog transmission and receiving equipment with new digital equipment. Every full-power television broadcaster was given a second six-megahertz channel on which to broadcast its digital signal. During the transition, all broadcasters would send out two signals, the old analog signal and the new digital signal. At the end of the transition period as originally established (December 31, 2006), all television broadcasters were to end their analog transmissions and broadcast solely using their digital signals. The spectrum no longer being used for analog broadcasting was to be auctioned for other uses.[178]

Fearing that not enough television consumers would have digital equipment by the end of the transition period, Congress amended the end-of-analog deadline by requiring that analog signals be turned off only when 85 percent of television households in a market could receive the digital signals. Subsequently, the transition slowed based on a number of factors including the expense of digital broadcasting and receiving equipment. Although most television stations are now broadcasting a digital signal, few consumers have the equipment necessary to receive the digital transmissions.[179]

Irked by the lack of progress and anxious to reallocate valuable spectrum for other uses (not to mention collecting the billions of dollars that would be realized from auctioning the spectrum currently used for the second broadcast channel), Congress changed course again and set a firm transition deadline for February 17, 2009.[180] After that date all analog television transmissions will cease. Congress also allocated $1.5 billion to fund a program that will provide $40 vouchers to consumers to help pay for analog-to-digital converter boxes.[181] This program will be administered by the National Telecommunications and Information Administration.[182]

The transition to digital broadcasting for terrestrial radio will be much simpler than the television transition. For radio, the FCC has approved a digital transmission system that allows stations to provide both analog and digital signals on the same frequency si-

multaneously.[183] Accordingly, this system, known as In-Band On-Channel (IBOC), does not require the allocation of additional frequencies. Digital radio provides much higher quality signals plus the ability to broadcast more than one program stream at the same time.[184]

## EQUAL EMPLOYMENT OPPORTUNITIES

The FCC, in conjunction with the Equal Employment Opportunity Commission, a federal agency established in 1964, requires that broadcasters not discriminate in hiring, promoting or firing on the basis of race, gender, religion, color or national origin. While the EEOC is expected to notify the FCC of any discrimination complaints filed against broadcast licensees, the FCC also enforces its own equal employment rules.

These regulations require licensees to widely disseminate information concerning full-time job vacancies, provide notice of full-time job vacancies to recruitment organizations, and complete a series of longer-term recruitment initiatives – such as job fairs, internships and mentoring programs – over a two-year period.[185]

## SUMMARY

The broadcast media play an integral role in the dissemination of news and information, but the Supreme Court has said that of all forms of mass media, broadcasting has the least protection under the First Amendment. In other words, as long as the FCC issues licenses, broadcasters are required to serve the public interest, which subjects them to more regulation than other mass media. That is, of course, unless the Supreme Court reverses itself and rules that all media are entitled to the same rights under the First Amendment.

It will be interesting to see how the government deals with stations that purchased the right to use the spectrum — those that bid for a radio or a television license. Will they have more protection under the First Amendment? And, as new technologies emerge, will the FCC or the courts eventually change the definition of "scarcity"? After all, spectrum scarcity will always exist because it takes time to develop technologies that open new portions of the spectrum to public use. Forecasting the answers to these questions is not easy, but at some point — as new technologies give the public more information and entertainment choices — the regulatory scheme under which broadcasting operates is likely to change.

While the FCC's role may change, for now it will continue issuing licenses, reviewing the transfer of licenses, making spectrum al-

[178] Advanced Television Systems and Their Impact Upon the Existing Television Broadcast Service, 12 F.C.C.R. 12809 (*Fifth Report and Order*, 1997).

[179] Second Periodic Review of the Commission's Rules and Policies Affecting the Conversion to Digital Television, 19 F.C.C.R. 18279 (2004).

[180] Deficit Reduction Act of 2005, Pub. L. No. 109-171, § 3002 (2006).

[181] *Id.* at § 3005.

[182] For more information on the act and the voucher program, *see* NTIA's digital transition web page *at* http://www.ntia.doc.gov/otiahome/dtv/index.html. Additional information about the transition can be found at the FCC's digital television web page *at* http://www.fcc.gov/cgb/consumerfacts/digitaltv.html.

[183] Digital Audio Broadcasting Systems and Their Impact on the Terrestrial Radio Broadcast Service, 17 F.C.C.R. 19990 (2002).

[184] For more information on digital radio, *see* the FCC's digital radio page *at* http://www.fcc.gov/cgb/consumerfacts/digitalradio.html.

[185] 47 C.F.R. § 73.2080 (2005).

locations, settling controversies among competing parties, issuing fines, and developing policy that will affect the broadcast media as well as other new technologies. But the FCC will not be doing all of this on its own. Regardless of whether its powers are changed or limited in any way, the FCC will always operate under the watchful eye of the courts and the Congress.

## FOR ADDITIONAL READING

Aufderheide, Patricia. *Communications Policy and the Public Interest.* New York: Guilford Press, 1999.

Botein, Michael & Douglas H. Ginsburg. *Regulation of the Electronic Mass Media: Law and Policy for Radio, Television, Cable and the New Video Technologies,* 3d ed. St. Paul: West, 1998.

Carter, T. Barton, Marc A. Franklin & Jay B. Wright. *The First Amendment and the Fifth Estate: Regulation of Electronic Mass Media,* 5th ed. Westbury, N.Y.: Foundation Press, 1999.

Creech, Kenneth C. *Electronic Media Law and Regulation,* 3rd ed. Boston: Focal Press, 1999.

Einstein, Mara. *Media Diversity: Economics, Ownership, and the FCC,* Mahwah, N.J.: Lawrence Erlbaum Associates, 2004.

Krattenmaker, Thomas G. *Telecommunications Law and Policy.* Durham, N.C.: Carolina Academic Press, 1998.

Lipschultz, Jeremy H. *Broadcast Indecency: F.C.C., Regulation and the First Amendment.* Boston: Focal Press, 1996.

McChesney, Robert W. *The Problem of the Media: U.S. Communication Politics in the 21st Century.* New York: Monthly Review Press, 2004.

Minow, Newton N. & Craig L. LaMay. *Abandoned in the Wasteland: Children, Television, and the First Amendment.* New York: Hill and Wang, 1995.

Powe, Lucas A., Jr. *American Broadcasting and the First Amendment.* Berkeley, Calif.: University of California Press, 1987.

Smith, F. Leslie, David Ostroff & John Wright. *Perspectives of Radio and Television: Telecommunication in the United States,* 4th ed. Mahwah, N.J.: Lawrence Erlbaum Associates, 1998.

Tillinghast, Charles H. *American Broadcast Regulation and the First Amendment: Another Look.* Ames, Iowa: Iowa University Press, 2000.

"The Vast Wasteland Revisited," 55 *Federal Communications Law Journal* 395-614, May 2003.

# 11

# Regulating Cable Communication

*By Matt Jackson*

---

 **Headnote Questions**

- *What is the legal history of cable television?*
- *What are the rationales for the government's regulation of cable television?*
- *What level of First Amendment protection does cable enjoy?*
- *Why do courts allow more stringent governmental structural regulations on cable than on the print media?*
- *What kinds of regulations are designed to protect each of the various cable-related interest groups – broadcasters, programmers, competitors, consumers?*

---

Cable television is the primary source of news and entertainment for most television viewers. Indeed, 60 percent of the television households in the United States subscribe to cable, and another 26 percent subscribe to direct broadcast satellite (DBS) or some other type of subscription television service. Cable industry revenues are approximately $6 billion per year.[1] So it is no surprise that cable has drawn the attention of regulators and politicians. Cable originally was regulated because of the threat it posed to broadcasting. Over time, cable regulations evolved in response to concerns about monopoly power. Today, regulators are trying to foster competition between the cable, satellite, telephone and broadcast industries.

Government regulators try to protect consumers and preserve competition in all large industries. However, cable, broadcasting and other forms of telecommunications receive special attention because of their role in transmitting speech. Policymakers are aware that these media are important to the proper functioning of democracy. A handful of large companies like Time-Warner control the communications infrastructure that citizens rely on for information and political participation. So, in addition to normal concerns regarding competition, cable regulation also is based on free speech principles and a desire to foster a marketplace of ideas. But regulators must avoid violating the First Amendment rights of cable operators in their attempt to promote the First Amendment rights of others.

The Constitution was written long before the development of the electronic communication technologies that dominate our world today, so it is not clear how the First Amendment should be applied to each new technology. The U.S. Supreme Court has recognized that the unique traits of each mass medium permit different constitutional standards.[2] Yet the unique characteristics of a new communication technology often are not apparent until long after the technology is introduced and adopted by the public. Often it is unclear whether the technology used should affect the legal protection of the message conveyed.

Convergence of the media industries also creates problems for policymakers. Originally, cable merely provided video programming. Today, cable operators are rapidly expanding to offer Internet access, telephone service, interactive television and other new services. As the distinctions between cable companies, telephone companies and broadcasters blur, their different regulatory schemes come into conflict. For example, telephone companies

---

[1] Twelfth Annual Report: In re Annual Assessment of the Status of Competition in the Market for the Delivery of Video Programming (FCC 06-11), 20 F.C.C.R. 2755 at paras. 8, 11 (Mar. 3, 2006) (hereinafter *Twelfth Annual Report*).

[2] *See, e.g.,* Times Film Corp. v. Chicago, 365 U.S. 43 (1961).

have to share their wires with competing telephone companies. Now that cable companies offer telephone and Internet service, should they have to share their cable wires as well?

Cable regulations can be classified broadly as either structural or content-based. Most cable content regulation is similar to content-based regulation of broadcasting and print. The same standards for defamation and invasion of privacy apply to cable as well. As with broadcasting, courts evaluate the content regulations in light of the unique characteristics of the technology. Structural regulation is grounded in modern economic theory. As a general rule, economists believe that companies behave best when faced with competition. Competition leads to efficient use of society's resources, a wide range of choices for consumers and continual product innovation. When there is little or no competition, powerful companies can take advantage of consumers, suppliers and would-be competitors. Antitrust law, which is applied to all industries, is designed to preserve competition in the marketplace.

But some industries have unique characteristics that make competition more difficult to achieve or sustain. The large infrastructure costs and economies of scale involved in operating a cable system led many regulators to believe that cable, like the telephone industry, was a natural monopoly. In other words, it is more efficient for one company to run a single cable down the street and serve every house than for two companies to run two separate cables down the street with each company serving half the houses. Theoretically, one company could offer the service more cheaply than two competing companies. Yet without a competitor, that company might raise its prices since consumers would have no alternative. Similarly, a monopoly cable provider can take advantage of program suppliers because the program supplier has few other potential customers.

In most areas of the country, each home is served by only one cable operator, typically a huge company that owns hundreds or thousands of cable systems across the nation. This has led regulators to impose special structural regulations on operators so that they cannot abuse their monopoly positions. Today regulators are trying to promote competition in the hope that it will reduce the need for regulation of the industry. Often the regulations created to encourage competition, however, are just as complex as the regulations that are utilized when there is no competition.

Sometimes the law contains elements of both content and structural regulations – the access and must-carry requirements, for example. This creates special problems for First Amendment analysis. On the one hand, the purpose of these laws is to assure citizens have access to a robust marketplace of ideas. Lawmakers are concerned when one company has the ability to control much of what consumers see or hear. At the same time, the Supreme Court has said that those companies have First Amendment rights.

To make matters even more complex, cable operators must negotiate franchise agreements with local communities for the right to run their cables over (or under) city streets. Broadcasters, who don't need to use wires to distribute their signals, don't need permission to use the public rights-of-way. Thus, cable companies must deal with both federal and local regulations. As we shall see, many times this results in conflicting rules.

## HISTORY OF CABLE TELEVISION REGULATION

When cable television was introduced in the late 1940s, broadcasters welcomed the new technology because it expanded the audience for local stations by physically extending the reach of broadcast signals. Cable providers erected tall antennas to pick up television signals and strung coaxial cables to transmit the signals to homes unable to receive the broadcast signal clearly. Television stations saw cable as an ally that increased the number of homes that could receive their signals.

Beginning in the mid-1950s, these community antenna television – CATV – systems, as they were then known, began using microwave technology to import signals from distant television stations located in other markets. The systems' wires carried the distant signals alongside local broadcast signals to cable subscribers who enjoyed an increased variety of programming. Local broadcasters quickly realized that these new channels would siphon away parts of their audiences and ultimately reduce advertising revenues. So broadcasters asked the Federal Communications Commission to control the cable industry.

The FCC was caught in a bind. On the one hand, increased viewing choices clearly promoted the FCC's mandate to serve the public interest and foster diversity. But broadcasters argued that if enough cable viewers stopped watching local TV stations, the stations would go bankrupt, leaving those homes that did not subscribe to cable without any television at all. Broadcasters reminded the FCC that part of its mandate was to promote broadcasting.

At first, the FCC was unsure if it had the authority to regulate cable operators. A broadcast station transmits its signal from its transmitting tower over the public airwaves to receiving antennas attached to television sets or homes. The courts have relied upon this use of the scarce electromagnetic spectrum by broadcasters, as discussed in Chapter 10, as a rationale to support regulation of broadcasting. But spectrum scarcity does not apply to cable television. Cable systems are not permitted to use the spectrum or to allow their signals to leak from their cables and cause interference with broadcasters. The technological differences between broadcasting and cable made it difficult for the FCC to decide upon a framework for cable regulation.

### Early Federal Regulation of Cable Television

When Congress adopted the Communications Act of 1934, it created a framework for regulating broadcasting and wire communications like telegraph and telephone. One portion of the act gave the FCC power over common carriers – companies that allow anyone to use their facilities and do not limit or control the content that can be transmitted. Another portion of the act gave the FCC jurisdiction over broadcasting. At that time, Congress could not have envisioned cable television. Consequently, the Federal Communication Commission initially said the Communications Act did not grant the Commission power to regulate cable; the Commission's legal jurisdiction was limited to radio, broadcast television, other technologies using the electromagnetic spectrum and common carriers. Through the 1950s, the FCC refused to assume control over cable, even at the request of broadcasters.[3]

As cable grew, broadcasters continued to call for its regulation. In the end, the FCC said it could regulate cable because of the effect cable had on broadcast television. It said the general language of the Communications Act gave the Commission power over "interstate ... communication by wire" and the responsibility to adopt rules and regulations needed to "make available ... [an] efficient ... radio communication service..." in the "public interest, convenience and necessity." In 1962, the FCC decided it was required to regulate cable in the public interest because cable involves interstate communication by wire and because cable may harm efficient television service.[4] The Commission suggested that television stations, particularly UHF stations (which had weaker signals than VHF stations) and stations in smaller markets, could be harmed financially, even driven off the air, if viewers switched from local stations to stations imported by cable from other cities.

In 1968, the Supreme Court supported the FCC's interpretation, ruling that because the Communications Act of 1934 gave the FCC responsibility to foster the growth of broadcast television, the FCC could regulate cable as long as the regulation was "reasonably ancillary" to the Commission's jurisdiction over broadcast television.[5] The Court's opinion did not mention the First Amendment.

Based on its new-found authority, the FCC adopted rules requiring cable systems to carry all local broadcast signals and severely limiting the number of distant broadcast signals a system could import.[6] The FCC also issued an expansive order in 1972 covering many facets of cable regulation.[7] The Commission required larger cable systems to produce local programming. Although the Supreme Court upheld that program origination rule, the Commission removed the requirement shortly thereafter.[8]

Later, the FCC required systems to make channels available to the public, government officials and school administrators, and to provide cameras and other equipment for those who wanted to use these access channels. This time the Supreme Court said the FCC had gone too far; the Communications Act did not allow the Commission to force cable systems to open their channels to everyone and to provide the equipment needed for such use.[9] The Court said it was one thing to require cable operators to create their own programming, but quite another to force the cable operator to act as a common carrier and provide an outlet for everyone else.[10] The FCC could not assert that much power without direct authorization from Congress. Congress later gave local franchise authorities the power to require these public, educational and government access (PEG) channels.

As technology improved, cable networks emerged, providing programming that was not available on either local or distant broadcast stations. Programmers' signals were sent from a transmitter on the ground to a satellite, which retransmitted the signals to ground receiving dishes owned by cable systems, which then distributed the signals to cable customers. At first, the FCC tried to restrict the growth of cable by creating complex rules that prevented cable companies from taking advantage of the new satellite technology. The rules prevented premium channels – channels for which a subscription is required, such as HBO – from carrying movies between three and ten years old or most major sporting events. The rules were designed to prevent premium channels from siphoning away popular programming from free, over-the-air broadcast stations. After the Court of Appeals for the District of Columbia struck down the Commission's pay cable rules, subscription-based premium channels like HBO began to prosper.[11]

### Early Local Regulation of Cable Television

The number of cable subscribers skyrocketed between 1975 and 1985, and cable operators, local authorities, broadcasters and program producers disagreed about who should regulate cable and how it should be regulated. Each group lobbied the FCC and Congress for rules that favored its own interests. During this period, the FCC prevented city and state authorities from regulating pay television. Yet states, counties and local governments imposed extensive requirements on cable systems through an elaborate franchising process. Local governments had authority over cable systems because cable systems must run their wires from the headend to subscribers' homes over streets and other public land. Local authorities control this use of public rights-of-way and, therefore, can impose conditions, in the form of franchise agreements, on cable operators.

---

[3] *See* Frontier Broad. Co. v. Collier, 24 F.C.C. 251 (1958).

[4] *See* Carter Mountain Transmission Corp., 32 F.C.C. 459 (1962), *aff'd*, Carter Mountain Transmission Corp. v. FCC, 321 F.2d 359 (D.C. Cir. 1963).

[5] *See* United States v. Southwestern Cable Co., 392 U.S. 157, 178 (1968).

[6] First Report and Order in Dockets 14895 and 15233, 38 F.C.C. 683 (1965); Second Report and Order, 2 F.C.C.2d 725 (1966).

[7] Cable Television Report and Order, 36 F.C.C.2d 143, *recon.*, 36 F.C.C. 2d 326 (1972), *aff'd sub nom.*, ACLU v. FCC, 523 F.2d 1344 (9th Cir. 1975).

[8] *See* United States v. Midwest Video Corp., 406 U.S. 649 (1972) (*Midwest*

*Video I*).

[9] *See* FCC v. Midwest Video Corp., 440 U.S. 689 (1979) (*Midwest Video II*).

[10] *Id.* at 700-01.

[11] *See* Home Box Office v. FCC, 567 F.2d 9 (D.C. Cir. 1977).

A franchise is essentially a contract between the two parties. Many franchising authorities wanted to control the programming carried by cable, the rates cable systems charged, the customer services provided by cable systems and other aspects of cable business. Franchising authorities also required cable systems to pay a portion of their revenues in return for permission to use public rights-of-way. Many of the early franchising agreements imposed such a heavy burden on new cable operators that the systems failed. In 1984, the Supreme Court helped reduce this problem when it held that the FCC, not local authorities, had broad power regarding cable and that certain regulatory powers belonged to the commission alone.[12]

### The Cable Acts and the Telecommunications Act

In 1984, thirty-five years after the introduction of CATV and fifty years after the adoption of the Communications Act, Congress decided the Communications Act needed to be amended to include cable regulation. After lengthy debate, Congress adopted the Cable Communications Policy Act of 1984[13] to distinguish the areas of responsibility of local and federal authorities. The 1984 Cable Act freed cable operators to determine the prices they would charge subscribers and forced cable systems to provide service to their entire franchise areas. The law also limited the fees local franchising authorities could charge cable operators and prevented franchisers from arbitrarily refusing to renew a cable operator's franchise. By deregulating cable television, the act permitted increased growth of cable.

But soon complaints arose that the larger, powerful cable television business was concerned more with profits than with customer service. Customers complained about rapidly rising prices. Localities complained about unfulfilled franchise obligations. So Congress, believing the 1984 Cable Act had eliminated too much regulation, again amended the 1934 Communications Act with the Cable Television Consumer Protection and Competition Act of 1992.[14] Among other provisions, the 1992 Cable Act gave television broadcast stations the choice of requiring cable systems to carry their signals (must-carry) or to insist on payment or other compensation for being carried (retransmission consent). It also regulated rates for many cable services and required the FCC to adopt rules to allow cable television's competitors to have access to much of the programming cable television carries. Federal courts have upheld several of the act's provisions.[15] While the 1984 Act was designed to *deregulate* the cable industry, the 1992 Act was passed to *re-regulate* the industry.

Four years later, again changing its mind, Congress passed the Telecommunications Act of 1996, which reduced some regulations and eliminated others affecting cable television.[16] The Act focused on increased competition – rather than federal regulation – to assure communications services in the public interest. It reflected a belief among lawmakers and many economists that regulations were stifling, rather than protecting, competition. At the same time, rapid changes in technology (particularly wireless technology) made policymakers question the earlier assumption that the cable and telephone industries were natural monopolies. Policymakers now believed that terrestrial and satellite wireless companies, telephone companies and possibly even electric companies (who also have wires into every home) could offer the same services as cable companies.

The Telecommunications Act sought to encourage competition by allowing local telephone companies, long distance telephone companies and cable companies to enter each others' businesses. Instead of competition, however, the law has prompted mergers and buyouts within and between cable and telephone companies.[17] The Telecommunications Act also maintained existing cable system content requirements but prohibited the FCC from imposing new content obligations on cable operators. The 1996 Act also requires the FCC to review its ownership rules every two years with a mandate to repeal or modify any ownership rule that is no longer in the public interest.[18]

## CABLE AND THE FIRST AMENDMENT

In 1986, the Supreme Court held for the first time that cable operators clearly had First Amendment interests and enjoyed some level of constitutional protection. In *Los Angeles v. Preferred Communications, Inc.*, the Court said cable television operators engage in "some of the aspects of speech and the communication of ideas as do the traditional enterprises of newspapers and book publishers...."[19] The Court said a franchising authority could not use the franchising process to grant a cable monopoly. Instead, the Court held that Los Angeles was required to show that its interests in refusing to issue a competing franchise outweighed the First Amendment interests of the cable applicant.

In 1991, the Court said in *Leathers v. Medlock* that cable is "engaged in 'speech' under the First Amendment."[20] Nevertheless, it held that a state could tax cable system revenues, even if other

---

[12] *See* Capital Cities Cable, Inc. v. Crisp, 467 U.S. 691 (1984).

[13] Pub. L. No. 98-549, 98 Stat. 2779 (1984) (codified at 47 U.S.C. §§ 601-639).

[14] Pub. L. No. 102-385, 106 Stat. 1460 (1992).

[15] *See* Time Warner Ent. Co. v. FCC, 93 F.3d 957 (D.C. Cir. 1996); Time Warner Ent. Co. v. FCC, 56 F.3d 151 (D.C. Cir. 1995).

[16] Pub. L. No. 104-104, 110 Stat. 56 (1996).

[17] *See* Jeffrey P. Cunard, *Cable Remains Dominant and Strong*, CABLE TV & NEW MEDIA L. & FINANCE, Jan. 1999, at 1; Andrea Foster, *Panels Will Study AT&T Cable TV*, NAT'L L.J., June 14, 1999, at B1; Tom McGhee, *Cable Industry Due for Mergers*, DENVER POST, Apr. 26, 2004, at C1; *Telecom Act in Action; Vision of Competition Blurred by Consolidation*, N.Y. L.J., Sept. 10, 1998, at 5.

[18] Pub. L. No. 104-104, § 202(h), 110 Stat. 56 (1996).

[19] 476 U.S. 488, 494 (1986).

[20] 499 U.S. 439, 444 (1991).

mass media aren't taxed, so long as the tax is unrelated to speech and is a non-discriminatory, property and service tax applied to a large number of other businesses. In neither of these two cases did the Court specify what standards courts should use to determine whether a cable operator's First Amendment rights had been abridged.

The Court finally did so in *Turner Broadcasting System, Inc. v. FCC*.[21] In response to a First Amendment challenge to the must-carry provisions of the 1992 Cable Act, the Court drew a distinction between content-based and content-neutral regulations of cable and upheld the constitutionality of the must-carry rules, which require cable systems to carry local broadcast programming. The Court held that the First Amendment is to be applied to cable television in two ways. First, governmental regulations directed toward the content of cable television programming must pass the strict scrutiny test to be constitutional. That is, the government must show that the law directly advances the least restrictive means to protect a compelling governmental interest of the highest order. This is the same standard applied to content regulations of newspapers.[22]

If a cable regulation is not directed at content, however, and imposes only an incidental burden on a cable operator's speech, the Court held that the regulation need be tested only under the intermediate First Amendment standard established in *United States v. O'Brien* and *Ward v. Rock Against Racism*.[23] Intermediate scrutiny of content-neutral regulations requires the government to show that the regulation is a reasonable way to achieve an important or substantial government interest. Here again, the Court applied the same level of protection it would afford to core First Amendment speakers. In general, structural regulations of cable are treated as content-neutral and thus face only intermediate scrutiny.

## CABLE STRUCTURAL REGULATIONS

Cable operators face many structural regulations. This stems in part from the government's early view of cable as a video delivery business that was not engaged in speech in the same way as a newspaper or broadcast station. Instead, cable was viewed as a threat to free speech since it threatened the viability of free, over-the-air broadcast stations, especially marginal TV stations. In addition, cable was assumed to be a natural monopoly. Congress and the FCC have imposed ownership and rate regulations to protect consumers and program producers from unfair business practices on the part of large cable operators. However, many of the regulations are being rescinded as cable operators face more competition from DBS providers and other multi-channel competitors.

### Rate Regulation

For decades, cable television operators, the FCC and franchising authorities have received complaints about rates charged for cable services. Attempts to limit rates have competed with concerns that cable's growth as a business would be stunted if government interfered by setting prices. In 1971, the FCC prohibited franchising authorities from regulating rates for pay-per-channel services but did not address rate regulation for other cable services.[24]

The 1984 Cable Act restricted the ability of local franchising authorities to regulate cable rates. It stated that rates could not be regulated if the cable operator faced what it called "effective competition." The FCC defined effective competition as the ability of subscribers to receive three or more over-the-air broadcast signals, effectively freeing most cable operators from price controls. Cable prices rose rapidly, and Congress reimposed rate regulation in the 1992 Cable Act. Under the 1992 Act, the basic tier of local broadcast and public access channels would be regulated by the local franchising authority, and the cable tier (including the common package of cable networks such as CNN, MTV, ESPN and TBS), would be regulated by the FCC. Premium channels such as HBO, Showtime and Cinemax, digital cable services and pay-per-view channels remained unregulated. The FCC's regulation of the cable tier expired in 1999.

Currently, only the basic tier faces rate regulation by the franchise authority and only if the cable company faces no effective competition. Cable rates rose an average of 5.4 percent in 2003, lower than the preceding five years when prices rose an average of 7.5 percent each year. However, since most cable systems have added more channels, the average cost per channel has remained roughly the same.[25] Cable systems that face competition charge an average of 7.3 percent less than systems that have no competition.[26] However, only 3.7 percent of the more than 33,000 cable systems in the United States are classified as facing effective competition.[27]

### Ownership Restrictions

In addition to rate regulation, cable operators face various ownership and conduct restrictions. This is because the government historically has been concerned with cable's position as a monopoly bottleneck that controls consumers' access to video programming. At one time, federal law and FCC rules designed to pre-

---

[21] 512 U.S. 622 (1994).

[22] *See, e.g.,* Miami Herald Publ'g Co. v. Tornillo, 418 U.S. 241 (1974) (applying strict scrutiny to content-based regulation of newspapers).

[23] 391 U.S. 367 (1968); 491 U.S. 781 (1989).

[24] *See* Time-Life Broad., Inc., 31 F.C.C. 2d 747 (1971).

[25] In re Implementation of Section 3 of the Cable Television Consumer Protection and Competition Act of 1992 (FCC 05-12), 20 F.C.C.R. 2718, para. 7 (Feb. 4, 2005).

[26] *Id.* at para 12.

[27] Eleventh Annual Report: In re Annual Assessment of the Status of Competition in the Market for the Delivery of Video Programming (FCC 05-13), 20 F.C.C.R. 2755 at para. 136 (Feb. 4, 2005).

vent concentration of media ownership prohibited the owner of a broadcast television station from owning a cable system in the same area. The purpose of the so-called "cross-ownership rule," first adopted by the FCC in 1970 and later made part of the 1984 Cable Act, was to protect diversity of ownership and content. The ban on broadcast-cable cross-ownership was intended to prevent a broadcast owner from favoring the owner's station and refusing to carry competing broadcasters on the cable system. In 1992, the FCC recommended that Congress repeal the cross-ownership ban, in part because the must-carry rules (discussed later in this chapter) would prevent discrimination against other local stations. Congress took that action in the Telecommunications Act of 1996, but the FCC never repealed its own version of the rule. The FCC cross-ownership ban was struck down in February 2002 by the U.S. Court of Appeals for the D.C. Circuit.[28] The court said the FCC had failed to justify why the rule should be kept, but the court did not evaluate whether the rule violated the First Amendment. Cable systems now can own local television stations.

Another cross-ownership rule imposed by the 1992 Cable Act generally prohibited a cable operator from owning a wireless cable or a satellite master antenna television system, both discussed in the next chapter, in the same area served by the cable system. The 1996 Act removed that joint ownership ban if the cable system faces competition from another company providing multi-channel video service. There are no legal restrictions on ownership of cable systems by citizens of other countries or owners of newspapers or other print media in the areas the cable system serves.

### Horizontal and Vertical Ownership Limits

Some of the most contested ownership rules deal with horizontal and vertical integration. The 1992 Cable Act directed the FCC to impose horizontal and vertical ownership limits to make sure cable operators won't have so much power as gatekeepers that they are able to prevent unpopular views from being heard.[29] The largest cable operators (AOL Time Warner, Comcast and Cox, for example) own hundreds of cable systems and are referred to as "multiple system operators." The horizontal ownership limits were imposed to prevent one MSO from becoming so large that it could take advantage of program suppliers. For example, assume that a new cable network is being launched. If one MSO controlled 60 percent of the nation's cable subscribers and refused to carry that network, the network would likely fail because it cannot reach 60 percent of the population.

The FCC imposed a 30 percent limit on the number of subscribers one MSO can control. The FCC assumed that a new cable network would need the opportunity to reach at least 40 percent of the nation's homes in order to be viable. If each MSO was lim-

ited to a 30-percent reach, a new cable programmer would have a chance to succeed even if the two largest MSOs refused to carry the new network. The FCC believed this would encourage diversity of programming and prevent the largest MSOs from refusing to pay a fair price for programming.

In the 1990s, Congress also raised concerns about increased ownership of cable programming networks by cable system operators (vertical integration). Two of the country's largest cable system owners at the time, TCI and Time Warner, Inc., invested in the company that owns TNT, CNN and other cable networks. Then Time Warner purchased the networks outright in 1996. During debate of the 1992 Cable Act, Congress expressed concern that cable companies that own their own networks might exclude competing networks from reaching viewers. In response, a provision of the 1992 Cable Act ordered the FCC to adopt rules to limit the number of cable networks in which a cable owner had invested that the owner could carry on its cable system.

The FCC ruled that no more than 40 percent of a system's first seventy-five channels could be used for programming affiliated with the system's owner. The remaining 60 percent of the first seventy-five channels had to be available for carriage of broadcast television stations and cable programming in which the system's owner had no more than a 5 percent interest.[30] Slightly more of a system's channels could be used for cable programming in which the system owner had an interest if the services were controlled by minority individuals or businesses. Local and regional cable networks were exempt from this rule. If a system had more than seventy-five channels, those additional channels would not be affected by the regulation.

For example, AOL Time Warner owns all of the Turner and CNN cable networks (TBS, TNT, Cartoon Network, Headline News, CNNSI and others). In communities where AOL Time Warner owns the local cable franchise, only 40 percent of the first seventy-five channels could be affiliated networks. The purpose of this rule was to make sure unaffiliated programmers had a chance to reach local viewers. Regulators feared that the MSO would refuse to carry cable networks that competed with its own cable networks. The FCC rule was designed to promote competition among program suppliers and diversity of programming.

Time Warner and AT&T, the two largest MSOs at the time, challenged the FCC's horizontal and vertical ownership rules in court. The D.C. Circuit Court of Appeals said that both the horizontal and vertical ownership regulations were content-neutral and should be reviewed under intermediate scrutiny. The court said Congress and the FCC could impose some horizontal and vertical ownership limits without infringing on the First Amendment rights of cable operators.[31] However, in 2001 the same court ruled that

---

[28] Fox Television Stations, Inc. v. FCC, 280 F.3d 1027 (D.C. Cir. 2002).

[29] 47 U.S.C. § 533 (2000).

[30] Development of Competition and Diversity in Video Programming Distribution and Carriage, 8 F.C.C.R. 8565 (1993); 47 U.S.C. § 536 (2000).

[31] Time Warner Ent. Co. v. United States, 211 F.3d 1313 (D.C. Cir. 2000).

the FCC had not provided adequate justification for the specific 30 percent horizontal limit or the 40 percent vertical limit that it had chosen.[32] The FCC must now create a better justification or develop new limits before they can be enforced. It has been five years since the appeals court told the FCC to reevaluate its ownership limits, and the agency appears no closer to making a decision. Indeed, the FCC is asking for additional information before making its decision.[33]

### Media Mergers

Media mergers and acquisitions have filled the headlines since the passage of the Telecommunications Act of 1996, and the cable industry is no exception. Since the passage of the act, AT&T purchased TCI and MediaOne to create AT&T Broadband, Viacom purchased CBS, and AOL purchased Time Warner. In the latest large merger, Comcast purchased AT&T Broadband in November 2002 to become the largest MSO with more than 21 million subscribers.[34] At the end of 2004, the four largest MSOs (Comcast, AOL Time Warner, Charter and Cox) controlled 68 percent of all U.S. cable subscribers.[35]

Cable faces increasing competition from DBS, which now serves more than 26 million homes (27 percent of total subscribers). However, even including DBS and all other forms of subscription television, the top four cable companies still control about 48 percent of all subscribers.[36] Since the appeals court remanded the FCC's vertical and horizontal cable ownership rules and the current FCC commission has attempted to ease other ownership rules, it is very likely the FCC will raise the cable ownership limits, leading to a new wave of mergers in the cable industry. In 2005, Comcast and AOL Time Warner proposed purchasing the assets of the bankrupt Adelphia cable company, currently the fifth largest cable MSO. If the sale is approved, Comcast will add 700,000 subscribers, giving the largest MSO a total reach of 29 percent of all subscription TV households. AOL Time Warner would acquire more than 3.5 million cable households, giving the company 18 percent of all subscribers.[37]

### Access to Cable Networks

The 1992 Cable Act requires companies that supply affiliated cable systems with programming *via* satellite to offer such programming to cable's competitors as well.[38] The act prevents cable systems and programmers from entering into exclusive agreements or in other ways limiting access to programming by such multi-channel video distributors as direct broadcast satellite systems. In other words, AOL Time Warner, which owns CNN, must allow DBS provider DirecTV to offer CNN to its customers. The purpose of this rule is to make sure cable's competitors can offer popular programming services to potential customers to create more competition and reduce the power of large MSOs. If one company had the exclusive right to distribute the most popular cable networks like MTV and ESPN, few consumers would be willing to switch to a competing distributor. Notice that like the vertical and horizontal ownership rules discussed previously, the concern is potential anticompetitive behavior by large, vertically integrated cable operators. Whereas the vertical and horizontal ownership rules are primarily aimed at protecting content producers (cable networks) to ensure content diversity, the access rules are primarily aimed at protecting competing distributors. The ban on exclusive agreements between cable programmers and cable operators was set to expire in October 2002. In 2002, the FCC issued a Report and Order extending the ban for five years.[39] The ban does not cover networks that rely on terrestrial distribution. Many MSOs have regional sports or news channels that are not distributed *via* satellite. The MSOs do not have to share these networks with their competitors.

### Interactive Television

Digital technology has created countless new opportunities for interactive television. These services include interactive program guides, personal video recorders like TiVo and Replay, video on demand and other enhanced services like immediate product purchases while viewing TV. Many of these new interactive services will be made available through the Internet or sophisticated set top boxes. The FCC has opened an inquiry to determine if large, vertically integrated cable operators might discriminate in favor of affiliated ITV providers.[40] This is similar to the concern that cable operators would favor affiliated networks that eventually led to the vertical ownership limits. In 2006, Congress was considering an overhaul of the Telecommunication Act of 1996. One focus of debate was the issue of "net neutrality" which would prohibit the companies that control the physical infrastructure of the Internet

---

[32] Time Warner Ent. Co. v. United States, 240 F.3d 1126 (D.C. Cir. 2001).

[33] In re the Commission's Cable Horizontal and Vertical Ownership Limits, Second Further Notice of Proposed Rulemaking (FCC 05-96), 20 F.C.C.R. 9374 (May 17, 2005).

[34] *See* Barnaby J. Feder, *U.S. Clears Cable Merger of AT&T Unit With Comcast,* N.Y. TIMES, Nov. 14, 2002, at C7.

[35] This percentage is based on only counting cable subscribers, not households that subscribe to DBS or some other form of multichannel subscription service. Looking at MVPDs as a whole, DirecTV and Echostar are the second and fourth largest MVPDs respectively. *See Twelfth Annual Report, supra* note 1, at Table B-3.

[36] *Id.*

[37] FCC Public Notice (DA 05-1591), June 2, 2005.

[38] 47 U.S.C. § 548 (1992). *See* Time Warner Ent. Co. v. FCC, 93 F.3d 957 (D.C. Cir. 1996), *reh'ng denied*, 105 F.3d 723 (D.C. Cir. 1997).

[39] 47 C.F.R. § 76.1002 (2002).

[40] In re Nondiscrimination in the Distribution of Interactive Television Services Over Cable (FCC 01-15), 66 Fed. Reg. 7913 (Jan. 26, 2001).

(mostly large cable and telephone companies) from discriminating against competitors in the delivery of content, or charging more to transmit video over the Internet than e-mail or other types of data. By the summer of 2006, both the House and Senate had rejected the requirement for net neutrality in the bills under consideration.[41]

## CABLE ACCESS REGULATIONS

As mentioned earlier in this chapter, cable was initially regulated because local broadcasters felt threatened by its ability to import distant signals and add original, cable-only programming. Another aspect of this concern was that attaching a coaxial cable to the back of a television set effectively meant unplugging the antenna. So, if viewers wanted to watch a local TV station that was not carried on the cable system, they would have to switch back and forth between cable reception and antenna reception. Broadcasters and the FCC believed that most viewers would not be willing to make this extra effort, meaning that local stations not carried by the cable system would lose that portion of their audience who subscribed to cable. These broadcasters wanted to make sure they had access to cable viewers. The FCC and Congress were concerned that if a local station was not carried by the cable system, it would lose so many viewers that it might go out of business, leaving the viewers who *don't* subscribe to cable with fewer stations to choose from. This led to a long evolution of must-carry rules. The basic premise is that the local cable operator is a gate-keeper with the ability to determine which channels viewers can receive. Many observers believe this power threatens the marketplace of ideas. Regulators also feared that cable operators would have an incentive to not carry local broadcast stations because they compete with those stations for advertising revenues.

### Must-Carry Rules

Although the FCC began in 1965 to adopt various rules forcing cable to carry broadcast stations, federal appellate courts twice ruled that the so-called "must-carry rules" unconstitutionally infringed cable operators' First Amendment rights.[42] The courts did not say the rules could never be applied to cable operators, but both said the FCC had not adequately demonstrated why it favored broadcasters' concerns over cable operators' rights. In the 1992 Cable Act, Congress attempted to resolve the problem by allowing a television station either to choose must-carry status with the local cable system or to negotiate with the cable operator on the terms for retransmitting the broadcaster's signal. The latter option is called "retransmission consent." In adopting these provisions,

Congress presented more than a dozen rationales to justify imposing must-carry rules.

In 1994, in *Turner Broadcasting System, Inc. v. FCC (Turner I)*, the Supreme Court found the must-carry rules content-neutral and asked the lower court to determine their constitutionality.[43] The lower court found the rules constitutional in 1995,[44] and the Supreme Court agreed in 1997. By a 5-4 vote, it said the must-carry rules were a narrowly tailored, content-neutral means to protect the broadcast industry from extinction (Turner II).[45] It said the rules were an appropriate means by which the government could assure that cable operators would not force broadcasters out of business and deprive consumers of broadcast programming.

Four members of the majority said Congress had justified the rules for three reasons: (1) they protect the strength of local television broadcasting that enhances the diversity of content available to viewers; (2) they ensure that viewers who are not cable subscribers have access to local news, information and opinions; and (3) they promote competition for the delivery of video programming. They found the rules did not impermissibly favor broadcast programming but were a content-neutral means to protect the broadcast industry and enhance competition. In essence, the majority said the rules were content-neutral because they merely favored one mode of delivery (free, over the air broadcasting) over another mode of delivery (pay cable) without regard to the specific content being delivered. As the Court said in Turner II:

> It is true that the must-carry provisions distinguish between speakers in the television programming market. But they do so based only upon the manner in which speakers transmit their messages to viewers, and not upon the messages they carry: Broadcasters, which transmit over the airwaves, are favored, while cable programmers, which do not, are disfavored. Cable operators, too, are burdened by the carriage obligations, but only because they control access to the cable conduit. So long as they are not a subtle means of exercising a content preference, speaker distinctions of this nature are not presumed invalid under the First Amendment.

> Our review of the Act and its various findings persuades us that Congress' overriding objective in enacting must-carry was not to favor programming of a particular subject matter, viewpoint, or format, but rather to preserve access to free television programming for the 40 percent of Americans without cable.[46]

In contrasting the case to *Miami Herald v. Tornillo*,[47] in which the Supreme Court struck down a state right-of-reply law applying

---

[41] Bloomberg News, *Senate Panel Rejects Rule on Access Fee*, N.Y. Times, Jun. 29, 2006, at C4.

[42] *See* Century Communications Corp. v. FCC, 835 F.2d 292 (D.C. Cir. 1987); Quincy Cable TV, Inc. v. FCC, 768 F.2d 1434 (D.C. Cir. 1985).

[43] 512 U.S. 622 (1994) (Turner I).

[44] Turner Broad. Sys., Inc. v. FCC, 910 F. Supp. 734 (D.D.C. 1995).

[45] Turner Broad. Sys., Inc. v. FCC, 520 U.S. 180 (1997) (Turner II).

[46] 512 U.S. at 645-46.

[47] 418 U.S. 241 (1974).

to newspapers, the majority noted that the Florida right-of-reply law punished newspapers based on the content of their editorial columns, while the must-carry law was not based on the programming decisions of the cable operator. Cable systems had to adhere to the must-carry requirements regardless of which cable networks they picked, whereas the right-of-reply law was only enforced when a newspaper criticized a candidate for office. Unlike the Florida newspapers, cable operators were not being punished for choosing specific programming to include on their systems. The justices said the must-carry rules were a reasonable way to achieve important government interests, and the rules had no greater impact on cable operators' and programmers' free speech rights than was necessary to achieve their goals.

Justice Stephen Breyer provided the fifth vote affirming the constitutionality of the must-carry rules but based his opinion on the need to protect local and educational broadcast programming.[48] He did not endorse the reasoning that the rules promote competition in the video delivery market.

In a sharp dissent, Justice Sandra Day O'Connor said Justice Breyer's opinion actually supported the argument that the must-carry rules were an unconstitutional content-based means to promote the speech of broadcasters over cable operators. O'-Connor noted that Congress stated that it specifically wanted to protect local and educational programming.[49] Therefore, the law was based at least in part on the content of the broadcasters' speech. The dissenting justices would have applied strict scrutiny to the must-carry rules and struck them down as favoring local (broadcast) speech over national (cable) speech.[50]

The case was remanded for the district court to determine if, in fact, local television stations would be in danger of going out of business in the absence of must-carry rules. After eighteen months of additional fact finding, a three-judge federal district court, in a 2-1 decision, found that the rules do not violate the First Amendment, and the Supreme Court agreed.[51]

Generally, the must-carry rules apply to all except the smallest cable operations. Systems with twelve or fewer channels must carry at least three eligible television stations, and systems with more than twelve channels must devote up to one-third of their channels to carrying eligible stations. All full-power commercial stations located in the community served by a cable system may demand to be carried. Rules also require non-commercial stations to be carried, but they cannot choose to negotiate for carriage under the retransmission consent rules.[52]

Under the law, every three years commercial television stations must decide whether to negotiate terms for carriage or to demand carriage under the must-carry standards. When the law was passed, stations hoped cable operators would pay for the signal, just as the operators pay cable networks. However, most cable operators have refused to pay cash to carry broadcast stations, believing that the local stations need cable carriage more than the cable company needs the local station. Operators that own multiple cable systems have instead negotiated non-monetary deals with companies that own a number of television stations. For example, some cable operators agreed to carry the new FX cable network if Fox would permit the operators to retransmit the television stations Fox owned. Similarly, Capital Cities/ABC (now a part of Disney) agreed to allow carriage of television stations it owned in exchange for cable systems carrying ESPN2, the sports cable network owned in part by ABC. Retransmission consent agreements continue to foster controversy as companies that own broadcast stations demand cash or prime channel space for their cable networks in return for giving the cable operator permission to carry their local broadcast stations.[53]

### Digital Must-Carry

The 1996 Act gave broadcasters a second channel to help ease the transition to digital broadcasting. Once most consumers have switched to digital tuners, the broadcasters will give back their original analog channels to the government. In the meantime, a contentious issue is whether cable operators should have to carry a local broadcaster's digital signal in addition to its analog signal. Broadcasters point out that 65 percent of households subscribe to cable. If cable doesn't carry the new digital signal, consumers won't have any incentive to purchase new digital televisions and the transition to digital will take much longer, or possibly not happen at all. Cable operators argue that broadcasters are offering little digital programming and that few consumers own the new digital sets. The cable companies don't want to give up valuable space on their systems that can be used for new cable channels or other digital services just so that broadcasters can transmit the same programming over two separate channels.

In January 2001, the FCC adopted new rules for carriage of digital broadcast signals.[54] Under the new rules, stations with both an analog and digital signal can demand must-carry for the analog signal but not the digital signal. A station that only has a digital signal can demand must-carry for that signal. With digital signals, it is possible for a broadcast station to transmit more than one program at a time (multicasting) and to transmit other information as well (electronic program guides and Internet services, for example). When a digital-only TV station demands must-carry, the cable

---

[48] 520 U.S. at 225-26 (Breyer, J., concurring in part).

[49] *Id.* at 232-35 (O'Connor, J., dissenting).

[50] *Id.* at 234 (O'Connor, J., dissenting).

[51] *Turner Broad. Sys.,* 910 F. Supp. 734 (D.D.C. 1995), *aff'd,* 520 U.S. 180 (1997).

[52] 47 U.S.C. § 535 (2000).

[53] *See* John M. Higgins & Dan Trigaboff, *Stations Mean Business on Retrans,* BROADCASTING & CABLE, Jan. 6, 2003, at 6.

[54] In re Carriage of Digital Television Broadcast Signals; Amendments to Part 76 of the Commission's Rules (FCC 01-22), 66 Fed. Reg. 16, 523 (Mar. 26, 2001), 16 F.C.C.R. 2598, codified at 47 C.F.R. § 76.56, 76.62 (2001).

operator only has to carry the primary video and program-related content such as closed captioning or v-chip data. The FCC considered modifying these rules if the transition to digital broadcasting stalled but reaffirmed its 2001 decision in February 2005.[55]

### Leased-Access Channels

The must-carry rules grew out of concerns that the local cable system is usually a monopoly provider that controls the programming options for subscribers. As discussed earlier, this concern is alleviated in part by the vertical ownership restrictions that force cable operators to carry cable networks in which they don't have a financial interest. To foster competition and a marketplace of ideas, additional access requirements have been imposed as well.

The 1984 Cable Act requires large cable systems to provide channels for purchase by commercial users and allows franchising authorities to negotiate with cable systems to offer channel capacity for use by the public and by educational and governmental organizations (PEG channels). Requirements for commercial leased-access channels and public, educational and governmental access channels do not violate cable operators' First Amendment rights, according to a federal appellate court.[56]

Under the 1984 Act, cable systems with thirty-six to fifty-four channels must designate 10 percent of their channels for this purpose. Systems with fifty-five or more channels must set aside 15 percent of their channels for leased access. These channels may be leased for a fee by anyone who wants to put programming on the cable system. The FCC has jurisdiction over the rates, terms and conditions of commercial leased-access contracts. Cable systems often use access channels for purposes other than leased access, such as carrying cable network programming, until they are requested for leased-access purposes. Under the 1992 Cable Act, a cable system may use up to one-third of its leased-access channels for certain educational or minority cable programming services and still count the channels as being used for leased access. While the purpose of the leased-access provisions was to make sure alternative viewpoints could be heard on cable systems, as a practical matter few programmers can afford to lease a channel full-time. This severely limits the potential audience for any program transmitted on a leased-access channel.

### Leased-Access Content Restrictions

Cable operators generally act as common carriers of commercial, leased-access channels; they do not control the content they deliver. But the 1992 Cable Act gave cable systems the right to reject leased-access programming that the operator "reasonably believes describes or depicts sexual or excretory activities or organs in a patently offensive manner as measured by contemporary community standards."[57] The 1996 Act permits a cable system operator to refuse to carry a program or portion of a program "which contains obscenity, indecency or nudity" on a commercial, leased-access channel.

Congress also developed a complex method of segregating indecent leased-access material that operators carried. The Communications Decency Act of 1996 required cable operators to put all such programming on separate channels scrambled or blocked in some way. A subscriber was required to ask in writing for such a channel to be unblocked and, later, could also ask for it to be re-blocked. The cable operator has thirty days to comply with a written request for unblocking or re-blocking.

In 1996, a divided Supreme Court reviewed a First Amendment challenge to the law's indecency and obscenity restrictions and upheld the provision permitting cable operators to reject obscene programming.[58] But the Court rejected the parts of the law that required operators to segregate indecent material and force subscribers to request it. Several justices noted that, unlike obscenity, indecency is protected by the First Amendment. They said alternative means that would interfere less with viewers' First Amendment rights could still protect children and sensitive viewers from the material. In addition, the justices expressed concern that cable customers who wanted access to some or all of the segregated programming might hesitate to request access in writing for fear their names would be released.

The U.S. Court of Appeals for the Second Circuit in 1999 dismissed a First Amendment challenge against Time Warner Communications for its refusal to transmit sexually explicit and violent sexual programming over its leased-access channels.[59] But the court said Time Warner had infringed the free expression rights of programmers through its blanket refusal to consider future programming submissions from any programmer who had submitted programs Time Warner deemed indecent. The court enjoined Time Warner from applying its blanket refusal policy.

### PEG Access Channels

The 1984 Cable Act permits, but does not require, franchising authorities to negotiate with cable operators to provide access channels for members of the public, educational institutions and governmental bodies (PEG channels). The agreements need not require all three types of programming, and a system may devote one channel to multiple purposes. For example, a system could use one channel for educational access during daytime hours and

---

[55] In re Carriage of Digital Television Broadcast Signals: Amendments to Part 76 of the Commission's Rules (FCC 05-27), 20 F.C.C.R. 4516 (Feb. 23, 2005).

[56] *See* Time Warner Ent. Co. v. FCC, 93 F.3d 957 (D.C. Cir. 1996).

[57] 47 U.S.C. § 532(h) (2000).

[58] Denver Area Educ. Telecomm. Consortium, Inc. v. FCC, 518 U.S. 727 (1996).

[59] Life Without Shame v. Time Warner Ent. Co., 191 F.3d 256 (2nd Cir. 1999).

for governmental access during the evening.

Access channels grew out of competitive offerings from cable operators attempting to land franchises in large cities. Beginning more than thirty years ago, cable operators promised PEG access and other features as a means to win franchises. Then, in 1969, the FCC encouraged cable operators to offer PEG channels[60] and in 1972 required systems to do so.[61] In 1979, the Supreme Court ruled that the Commission did not have the authority to require PEG channels,[62] but the ruling did not prevent cable systems and franchising authorities from voluntarily agreeing to have them. Finally, the 1984 Cable Act gave franchising authorities the right to negotiate with cable operators to have PEG channels.

### PEG Channel Content Restrictions

Cable operators have very limited control over the content of PEG channels and are not liable for material they cannot prohibit. This means a cable system cannot eliminate specific programming or public-access provisions to exclude ideas it dislikes or disfavors. For example, when the Ku Klux Klan attempted to offer a program on the Kansas City, Missouri, cable system's public-access channel, the city council removed the public-access channel requirement from the city's cable franchise. With the requirement gone, the operator stopped providing the channel, and the Klan had no way to offer its program. The Klan sued the cable system. A federal district court ruled in favor of the Klan because the city could not show that it had not eliminated the channel requirement as a way to limit the Klan's First Amendment rights to free speech.[63] The city re-established the public-access provision, and the Klan presented its program.

The 1984 Cable Act says franchising authorities and cable systems can agree that cable services — including PEG channels — will not present material that is "obscene or otherwise unprotected by the United States Constitution."[64] The 1992 Cable Act went further. It allowed cable operators to prohibit "obscene material or sexually explicit content or material soliciting or promoting unlawful conduct" on PEG channels and withdrew operators' protection against lawsuits based on their presentation of such material. The Supreme Court found this provision violated the First Amendment.[65] The Court said both public and private groups provided sufficient oversight of public-access channels to exclude the type of material to which Congress objected. Moreover, the government had not provided sufficient evidence to demonstrate that further control by the cable operator was required to protect children from indecent material. The Court also said cable operators permitted to exclude programming from public-access channels might restrict borderline material that otherwise might be protected under the First Amendment.

In 1998, the U.S. Court of Appeals for the Second Circuit upheld the right of an independent program producer to broadcast a sexually explicit show on public-access channels. The court said that although the 1984 Cable Act permits local authorities to enforce franchise agreements and control the operation of public-access channels, the law also prohibits cable operators from exercising editorial control over public-access programming and assures that cable systems provide the widest possible diversity of information services and sources to the public.[66]

In 1999, the U.S. Court of Appeals for the Fifth Circuit said a Houston city franchise rule giving preference to locally produced programming on PEG access channels permissibly advanced the government interest in programming diversity.[67] The court said the city's practice of charging a fee for all non-locally produced programming was a constitutional, content-neutral rule that did not distinguish between favored and disfavored speech. Instead, the court said, the rule advanced the city's substantial interest in promoting localism. The court of appeals remanded the case to the lower court to determine whether the general fee schedule was narrowly tailored to advance this interest.

### Access Rules and the First Amendment

Notwithstanding the restrictions on obscene and indecent content discussed previously, the motivation behind the various access rules is that for the 65 percent of homes that subscribe to cable, the cable operator is the gatekeeper that controls which programs and channels are available. Newspapers and other print publishers do not have the burden of must-carry, leased access or other access requirements. All of these structural access rules imposed on cable operators very likely would be struck down as unconstitutional if applied to newspapers. Why the different treatment? The Supreme Court provided some insight in its *Turner I* decision:

> Although a daily newspaper and a cable operator both may enjoy monopoly status in a given locale, the cable operator exercises far greater control over access to the relevant medium. A daily newspaper ... does not possess the power to obstruct readers' access to other competing publications.... The same is not true of cable. When an individual subscriber to cable, the physical connection between the television set and the cable

[60] Community Antenna Television System, 20 F.C.C. 2d 201 (1969).

[61] Cable Television Report and Order, 36 F.C.C. 2d 143 (1972).

[62] FCC v. Midwest Video Corp., 440 U.S. 689 (1979) *(Midwest Video II)*.

[63] Missouri Knights of the Ku Klux Klan v. Kansas City, 723 F. Supp. 1347 (W.D. Mo. 1989).

[64] 47 U.S.C. § 544(d) (2000).

[65] *See* Denver Area Educ. Telecomm. Consortium, Inc. v. FCC, 518 U.S. 727 (1996).

[66] McClellan v. Cablevision of Connecticut, Inc., 149 F.3d 161 (2nd Cir. 1998).

[67] Nationalist Television v. Access Houston Cable, 179 F.3d 188 (5th Cir. 1999).

network gives the cable operator bottleneck, or gatekeeper, control.... A cable operator, unlike speakers in other media, can thus silence the voice of competing speakers with a mere flick of the switch.[68]

In a certain sense, the Court is justifying cable regulation based on the scarcity of inputs on the back of a television set just as it justified broadcast regulation based on the scarcity of frequencies (broadcast regulation is discussed in Chapter 10). Newer digital television sets often have multiple inputs that viewers can easily select using a remote control device.

## LOCAL CABLE REGULATION

As previously indicated, cable operators must adhere to local as well as federal regulations because cables are placed on public property. Congress has periodically given and then taken away the power of local authorities to regulate cable franchises. In addition, local laws cannot violate the First Amendment or other constitutional restrictions.

### Cable System Franchises

The 1984 Cable Act made it clear that local authorities have a right to grant cable franchises and that a cable system is required to have a franchise in order to offer service. A few states grant franchises; in some other states, franchises are awarded by cities or counties and must be approved by the state; most frequently, however, franchises are granted by cities or counties.

The franchise award process will generally begin when a city asks interested companies to submit proposals outlining details about the system to be installed, the kinds of programming to be carried and information about customer service. The 1992 Cable Act forbids franchising authorities from awarding exclusive franchises. That is, they cannot agree to grant one, and only one, franchise. At first, communities liked awarding exclusive franchises because they could then ask for more in return from the cable operator. The prohibition on exclusive franchises is supposed to encourage competition.

Most communities have franchised only one company to offer cable service because other companies have not sought franchises; they do not want to invest the large amounts of money necessary to build competing cable systems (known as "overbuilds"). This is in large part because of the economies of scale that led observers to refer to cable as a natural monopoly. The Telecommunications Act of 1996 gave telephone companies the right to compete with cable, but most telephone companies have moved slowly to build competing systems.[69]

A city can also own a cable system, even in competition with a cable company offering service in the municipality. Courts have held that a franchising authority can build a system and compete with an existing cable operator in the city[70] and even grant a city agency a cable franchise with better terms than the company against which the city will compete.[71] The 1992 Act allows cities to operate their own cable systems without a franchise.

Courts have also ruled that technologies that compete with cable generally are not required to obtain franchises from local government. The U.S. Courts of Appeals for the Seventh and Fifth Circuits ruled in 1999 that neither satellite master antenna television systems nor telephone video systems are required to obtain franchises to offer video to consumers.[72]

Recently many states have passed or considered legislation that would allow for statewide franchises. The goal is to make it easier for telephone companies to compete with cable operators. Nine states have already passed legislation with Virginia and California the most recent examples.[73] The phone companies complain that having to negotiate local agreements with numerous municipalities creates a barrier to entry. In addition, bills being considered by the U.S. House and Senate in 2006 would allow companies to obtain national franchises, severely limiting the power of local communities to negotiate terms and conditions for individual franchise agreements.[74]

### Cable Franchise Provisions

Franchises can be short or hundreds of pages long, depending on the complexity of the agreement between the franchising authority and cable system. Certain provisions, however, will be found in most franchises.

*Franchise fees.* For decades, franchising authorities have required cable systems to pay franchise fees as part of the agreement to use public rights-of-way. At one time, franchise fees would be set as high as 36 percent of a cable system's revenues. In 1972, however, the FCC limited franchise fees, and the 1984 Cable Act set a franchise fee ceiling of 5 percent of gross annual revenues. The act does not define "gross annual revenues," allowing cable operators and franchising authorities to negotiate definitions. Some cable operators have argued that having to pay any franchise

---

[68] 512 U.S. 622, 656 (1994).

[69] *Twelfth Annual Report, supra* note 1, at para. 15.

[70] *See* Warner Cable Communications, Inc. v. City of Niceville, 911 F.2d 634 (11th Cir. 1990).

[71] *See* Paragould Cablevision, Inc. v. City of Paragould, 739 F. Supp. 1314 (E.D. Ark. 1990), *reb'g denied*, 930 F.2d 1310 (8th Cir. 1991).

[72] City of Chicago v. FCC, 199 F.3d 424 (7th Cir. 1999); City of Austin v. Southwestern Bell Video Services, 193 F.3d 309 (5th Cir. 1999).

[73] *See* Tom Chorneau, *Telecom Bill Opposition Fades,* S.F. CHRONICLE, Jun. 28, 2006, at C3; Cheryl Bolen, *New State Video Franchise Laws May Help Shape Federal Debate,* PIKE & FISCHER NEWS AND ANALYSIS (May 4, 2006).

[74] *See* Stephen Labaton, *House Backs Telecom Bill Favoring Phone Companies,* N.Y. Times, Jun. 9, 2006, at C3; Jim Puzzanghera, *Senate Panel OKs Troubled Telecom Bill,* L.A. Times, Jun. 29, 2006, at C3.

fees violates their First Amendment rights, but most courts hearing such cases have decided that cable's use of public rights-of-way justifies imposing franchise fees.[75] In 2005, a federal district court ruled that under federal law, the 5 percent franchise fee could only be applied to revenues from cable services. Minneapolis wanted to include revenues from cable modem service as well. The court noted that the FCC had already declared that cable modem Internet access did not constitute a cable service.[76]

*Programming.* The 1984 Cable Act allows franchising authorities to specify broad categories of video programming that the cable operator will be required to carry, such as movies, children's programming, sports and news and public affairs. Franchisers, however, are not permitted to specify which programming services a cable system must provide, such as CNN or ESPN, or to forbid a cable operator from offering specific services.

*Duration.* Franchises also specify the duration of the agreement, which typically is from eight to fifteen years. Most franchises specify that the cable operator must ask the franchising authority's permission to transfer or sell the franchise to a new owner. Most cable owners invest heavily in the equipment needed to operate their systems and hope to renew franchises and continue providing service beyond the initial franchise period. The 1984 Cable Act established a franchise renewal process that creates renewal expectancy so that cable operators would be willing to invest in upgrading their systems. As we shall see in the next section, local governments have attempted to use the franchising process as a means to regulate new services offered by cable companies.

## CABLE AND THE INTERNET

Perhaps no change within the cable industry has created more problems for regulators than the provision of broadband (high-speed) access to the Internet. As the Internet and the World Wide Web rapidly increased in popularity in the late 1990s, more and more consumers became interested in broadband access. Broadband access allows users to surf the Web and download Web pages, software, audio and video literally hundreds of times faster than a standard telephone modem.[77] For example, a ten-megabyte file that would take twenty-four minutes to download using a 56k modem can be downloaded *via* a cable modem in less than twenty seconds.

There are many different ways to achieve a broadband connection, including cable modems, digital subscriber line telephone service (DSL), wireless and satellite. The two most popular methods are cable modems offered by cable operators and DSL offered by telephone companies. Currently, cable modem service is 50 percent faster than DSL service on average.[78] While each method has its own drawbacks, most commentators agree that cable modems have a competitive advantage, primarily because of cable's head start in signing up broadband customers and the fact that DSL is limited to buildings located within three miles of the telephone company's central office equipment.[79] In 2003, twice as many subscribers used cable modems compared to DSL service.[80]

With a cable modem, users connect to the Internet using their coaxial cable connection rather than their telephone wire. If you use your telephone company to connect to the Internet, you can choose any Internet service provider that you would like. If you are using a dial-up modem and want to switch from one ISP to another, you simply dial a different telephone number. The telephone company is considered a common carrier and is not allowed to tell you who you can and cannot call. Even with telephone DSL service, different companies can lease the portion of the wire that is used to provide high-speed Internet access, so it is still possible to choose among competing DSL providers.

However, if you want to connect to the Internet through your cable company, your cable company gets to choose your ISP. You cannot demand that your cable company connect you to a different ISP because cable operators are not regulated like common carriers. For example, if your cable company chooses @Home as its ISP and you want to switch to AOL, you have to go through @Home to connect to AOL. You end up paying for @Home even though you don't use any of its content.

### *Open Access Requirements*

As more and more Internet users switch to cable modems, independent ISPs are concerned that they will lose their customers to ISPs that are owned by the cable companies. Competitors and consumer groups are afraid that cable-affiliated ISPs will favor cable-affiliated content providers. For example, if you get your broadband access through AOL Time Warner, maybe Time Warner-owned Web sites like CNN.com will download faster than competing Web sites. This is similar to the earlier concern that cable systems would favor affiliated cable networks. The horizontal and vertical ownership limits, leased access rules, and access to cable networks were all designed to prevent these types of anticompetitive practices in provision of cable service. Independent ISPs and consumer groups want laws that require cable operators to pro-

---

[75] *See, e.g.,* Group W Cable, Inc. v. City of Santa Cruz, 679 F. Supp. 977 (N.D. Cal. 1988).

[76] City of Minneapolis v. Time Warner Cable, Inc., 2005 U.S. Dist. Lexis 27743 (D. Minn. Nov. 10, 2005)(unpublished opinion).

[77] *See* DEBORAH A. LATHEN, FCC, BROADBAND TODAY, A STAFF REPORT TO WILLIAM E. KENNARD, CHAIRMAN (1999), *available at* http://www.fcc.gov/Bureaus/Cable/Reports/broadban.pdf.

[78] *See* Matt Stump, *ComScore Charts Cable, DSL Speeds,* MULTICHANNEL NEWS, May 5, 2003, at 34.

[79] *See* LATHEN *supra* note 77, at 27.

[80] *See* Matt Richtel, *Cable is Confident of Internet Lead Over Phone Rivals,* N.Y. TIMES, June 12, 2003, at C6.

vide open access for competing ISPs to use the cable system to reach customers for Internet service as well.

Cable operators refer to such demands as "forced access." They argue that they would have no incentive to spend the money to build broadband networks if they then have to share those networks with their competitors. In addition, they argue that the current lack of regulation encourages investment in competing broadband technologies such as DSL and wireless access.

In 1999, the FCC released a report stating that it did not intend to require open access at that time.[81] Meanwhile, AT&T was completing its mergers with TCI and MediaOne, two large MSOs, and the newly merged company was beginning to offer @Home broadband access through its cable lines. A number of ISPs, including AOL, lobbied the government to force AT&T to provide open access to its cable customers. While the FCC refused to require open access, consumer groups and competitors convinced some local franchise authorities to require open access as a condition of the franchise transfer or renewal. This resulted in court cases in three different cities where the local franchise had to be transferred to AT&T.

*AT&T v. City of Portland* began when AT&T sued the franchising authority for refusing to grant the franchise transfer.[82] The authority had included a requirement stating that the franchise could not be transferred unless AT&T agreed to provide open access for competing ISPs. The district court rejected AT&T's argument that Portland did not have the authority to impose such a requirement, but the Court of Appeals for the Ninth Circuit reversed the decision. The appeals court stated that cable Internet access is a telecommunications service, not a cable service, and that the Communications Act bars local franchising authorities from regulating telecommunications services.[83]

In a Virginia case, the Fourth U.S. Circuit Court of Appeals reached a similar conclusion.[84] In both cases, the courts distinguished between (1) the provision of Internet content and services (such as e-mail access and Web storage space on the ISPs server) and (2) the provision of transmission services between the ISP and the subscriber. Both courts concluded that the connection between the subscriber and the ISP, whether *via* a copper telephone line operated by the local telephone company or a coaxial cable operated by the cable company, should be classified as a telecommunications service. While such a classification precludes local franchise authorities from demanding open access as condition of franchise approval, it leaves the door open for the FCC to

begin regulating cable Internet access as a telecommunications service. This could result in the imposition of common carrier requirements and force cable companies to contribute to the universal service fund to support affordable telephone service unless the FCC chooses to forebear from imposing those requirements.

In the Florida case of *Comcast Cablevision of Broward County v. Broward County,* a district judge held that the franchise authority's attempt to impose open access requirements violated the First Amendment.[85] Without classifying broadband cable modems as a cable service or a telecommunications service, the court reasoned that the open access requirement was a content-based regulation similar to that in *Miami Herald v. Tornillo*[86] because the cable operator is essentially punished if it chooses to offer Internet access. The court also said that even if the regulation were content-neutral it would fail intermediate scrutiny because the county did not conduct adequate fact-finding to establish that a substantial governmental interest was at risk.

After initially lobbying for regulations requiring open access to cable modems, AOL abruptly changed its position upon acquiring Time Warner.[87] Time Warner's holdings included Time Warner Cable, the second largest MSO in the nation with 12.7 million subscribers. Now that AOL had purchased its own cable systems, it opposed government regulation in this area. Ironically, the Federal Trade Commission and the FCC required AOL Time Warner to provide open access for competing ISPs as a condition of allowing the merger between the two companies, even though there is no general requirement that other MSOs have to offer open access.[88] Thus, after AOL stopped lobbying for open access, it became the only company required to provide open access.

In March 2002, the FCC issued a ruling that cable modem service would be classified as an information service rather than as a telecommunications service or cable service.[89] This important decision would prevent local governments from requiring open access to cable modems or regulating cable Internet service in any way. The ruling also means that cable companies avoid any of the common carrier regulations that telephone companies face. The FCC recently eliminated most of the open access regulations imposed on telephone DSL lines as well.[90]

In declaring cable modem service to be an information service,

[81] In re Inquiry Concerning the Deployment of Advanced Telecommunications Capability to All Americans in a Reasonable and Timely Fashion, and Possible Steps To Accelerate Such Deployment Pursuant to Section 706 of the Telecommunications Act of 1996 (FCC 99-5), 14 F.C.C.R. 2398 (1999).

[82] 43 F. Supp. 2d 1146 (D. Or. 1999).

[83] AT&T v. City of Portland, 216 F.3d 871 (9th Cir. 2000).

[84] Media One Group, Inc. v. County of Henrico, 257 F.3d 356 (4th Cir. 2001).

[85] 124 F. Supp. 2d 685 (S.D. Fla. 2000).

[86] 418 U.S. 241 (1974).

[87] *See* Kathy Chen, *AOL Changes Tune in Debate on Cable Access,* WALL ST. J., Feb. 14, 2000, at B5.

[88] *See* Stephen Labaton, *FCC Approves AOL-Time Warner Deal, With Conditions,* N.Y. TIMES, Jan. 12, 2001, at C1.

[89] In re Inquiry Concerning High-Speed Access to the Internet Over Cable and Other Facilities, Internet Over Cable Declaratory Ruling: Appropriate Regulatory Treatment for Broadband Access to the Internet Over Cable Facilities (FCC 02-77), 17 F.C.C.R. 4798 (2002) [hereinafter Internet Over Cable Ruling].

[90] Press Release, FCC, FCC Adopts New Rules for Network Unbundling Obligations of Incumbent Local Phone Carriers (Feb. 20, 2003).

the commission ignored the *Portland* court analysis that said cable modem service has two components: an information service component (such as Web pages and e-mail) and a telecommunications component (the transmission of data between the cable headend and the home subscriber). Instead, the FCC said that cable modem service is a "single, integrated service."[91] The commission also ruled that cable modem service is interstate because most Internet data crosses state boundaries. This means that state regulators don't have jurisdiction to regulate cable modems either. The FCC also issued a Notice of Proposed Rulemaking to decide what regulations (if any) should be imposed on cable modem service. Independent ISPs and consumer groups appealed the FCC's ruling to the Court of Appeals for the Ninth Circuit, the same court that ruled cable Internet access is a telecommunications service in the *Portland* case. In 2003, the Ninth Circuit ruled that its decision in the *Portland* case was binding precedent that controlled its review of the FCC's declaratory ruling.[92] Therefore, the court stated that it was compelled to vacate the FCC's determination that cable modem service did not include a telecommunications service. In June 2005, the Supreme Court resolved this conflict between the Ninth Circuit's *Portland* decision and the FCC's declaratory ruling regarding the proper classification of cable modem Internet service. The Supreme Court held that the FCC's classification of cable modem service as an information service (rather than a telecommunications service) was reasonable.[93] Furthermore, when a court precedent conflicts with an agency's interpretation, the court must accept the agency's interpretation *unless* the statute is unambiguous and contrary to the agency's interpretation. Thus, the Court held that it was reasonable for the FCC to declare cable modem service to be an information service rather than a telecommunications service and the courts must defer to the agency interpretation.

### Pole Attachment Agreements

Cable operators need permission to attach their cables to poles or run them through underground conduits that are owned by telephone companies or electric companies. To prevent telephone and power companies from charging unreasonably high rental prices or refusing cable use entirely, Congress adopted the Pole Attachment Act in 1978. The act gives the FCC authority to regulate the rates, terms and conditions of agreements between most pole owners and cable systems. In addition, the Telecommunications Act of 1996 *requires* pole operators to allow cable companies to rent pole or conduit space. The act also extends the pole attachment provisions to cable operators' use of poles or conduits for non-video services – such as data or voice transmissions

– that compete with telephone offerings.[94] The law permits a state, rather than the FCC, to oversee pole rental contracts within the state. Nearly twenty states have decided to do so.

The FCC is struggling to determine the fees cable Internet service providers should be charged for pole use and the status of wireless carriers that attach their equipment to poles. Early in 1998, the FCC established a formula for fees for pole attachments by cable and wireless telephone services unable to negotiate terms in states that do not regulate pole attachments.[95] Internet services carried by cable will be charged at the rate applied to cable services, which currently is half the rate applied to telephone services. These rules were challenged by utility companies.

The Eleventh U.S. Circuit Court of Appeals ruled that the FCC did not have the authority to require pole attachments for wireless providers or to set the compensation rates for Internet service providers. The Supreme Court overturned the ruling and held that the FCC *does* have the authority to set rates for any pole attachment made by a cable company even if the attachment is used for purposes beyond providing cable services.[96]

## CONTENT AND PROGRAMMING REGULATIONS

Despite court decisions establishing that the First Amendment protects cable from content-based regulations, Congress has placed a variety of content-related and access regulations on cable television. Courts have allowed many of the laws to stand. In addition to the content restrictions imposed on leased access and PEG channels discussed earlier, Congress has also tried to regulate sexually explicit programming on commercial cable channels.

### Sexually Explicit Programming on Commercial Channels

The 1996 Telecommunications Act required the FCC to establish rules regarding sexually explicit programming on channels used primarily for such material (adult channels such as Playboy and Spice).[97] The commission issued a regulation that these channels would have to be fully scrambled or otherwise blocked, unless a subscriber chose to receive them. The purpose of the law was to address the problem of signal bleed whereby the audio or portions of the video are still viewable even though the channel has been scrambled. The rule said if cable operators do not completely

---

[91] Internet Over Cable Ruling, *supra* note 89, at 4823.

[92] Brand X Internet Serv. v. FCC, 345 F.3d 1120 (9th Cir. 2003).

[93] Nat'l Cable and Telecomm. Ass'n v. Brand X Internet Services, 125 S.CT. 2688 (2005).

[94] 47 U.S.C. § 224 (2000). *See also* Texas Utilities Elec. Co. v. FCC, 997 F.2d 925 (D.C. Cir. 1993); Heritage Cablevision v. Texas Utilities Elec. Co., 6 F.C.C. Rcd. 7099 (1991).

[95] In re Implementation of Section 703(e) of the Telecommunications Act of 1996, 13 F.C.C.R. 6777 (1998) (codified at 47 C.F.R. §§ 1.1401 - 1.1418 (1999)).

[96] Gulf Power Co. v. United States, 208 F.3d 1263 (11th Cir. 2000), *rev'd sub nom.* Nat'l Cable & Telecomms. Ass'n v. Gulf Power Co., 534 U.S. 327 (2002).

[97] 47 U.S.C. § 561 (2000).

scramble such channels, they must provide a safe harbor free of sexually oriented programming from 6 a.m. until 10 p.m. The Supreme Court applied strict scrutiny to strike down the requirement as a content-based restriction on speech that violated the First Amendment.[98] In a 5-4 decision, the Court said the law was an impermissible content-based restriction that singled out particular programmers. It noted that since blocking methods were either very expensive or not completely effective, most cable operators had to limit the transmission of sexually oriented cable channels to between 10 p.m. and 6 a.m. Thus, many adult viewers, including those who do not have children, were being denied access to protected content. Another provision of the law already required cable operators to block access to channels for individual households on request — clearly a less restrictive alternative solution. The Court held the government had not demonstrated the harm was real or that a less restrictive alternative was not available.

### Other Content Laws and Rules

Cable systems also must comply with certain federal laws and FCC rules that apply to broadcasters regarding political advertising, bans on carrying obscene material, limitations on information about lotteries and sponsorship identification rules (broadcast regulation is covered in Chapter 10). Cable systems must comply with the limits on commercial time during children's programs, but unlike broadcast stations, they do not have to provide three hours of children's educational programming per week.

## OTHER CABLE REGULATION ISSUES

Cable operators face numerous other regulations, some of which are briefly covered here.

### Exclusivity and Nonduplication Rules

The FCC has adopted two rules in addition to must-carry designed to protect broadcast stations from cable competition: syndicated exclusivity and network nonduplication. Syndicated programming is sold by exclusive contract to individual stations in different cities. When cable systems import distant broadcast stations' signals, those signals may include the same syndicated programming being shown by a local station under an exclusive contract. To address this duplication and protect local stations, the FCC adopted syndicated exclusivity rules in 1972.[99] These rules permitted a local station to require a cable system to black out any syndicated program on an imported signal that also was being carried by the station. The commission rescinded the rules in 1980

but reinstated them in 1988,[100] and they continue in force and have been upheld as content-neutral by the U.S. Court of Appeals for the D.C. Circuit.[101] Similar rules for network programs allow television stations affiliated with a broadcast network to demand that a cable system black out network programming being carried on an imported station affiliated with the same network.[102]

Another FCC blackout rule permits a professional sports team to require a cable operator to black out the local telecast of a local sports event involving that team if tickets to the event are not sold out.[103] A blackout cannot be required, however, if a local television station in the same area as the cable system and the sports event is broadcasting the event. The National Football League has agreed that its team owners will not ask for a blackout if a game is sold out seventy-two hours prior to game time.

### Cable and Copyright

Broadcast programming is protected under copyright law, which, as discussed in Chapter 7, requires that permission be granted for use of the material. Broadcast television stations, or the networks with which the stations are affiliated, pay the producers of television programming for the right to broadcast their shows. Similarly, when cable systems began to retransmit local broadcast signals, program producers argued that cable television was required to obtain permission as well. Producers said they had sold their shows to broadcast television, not to cable. Broadcast stations also argued that cable should be required to obtain permission to carry local programming – like evening news shows – for which local stations held the copyrights.

In 1968 and again in 1974, the Supreme Court said a cable system's retransmission of a broadcast station's signal did not violate the copyright law in effect at that time.[104] Instead, the Court said the cable was simply an extension of the viewer's antenna. Program producers and broadcasters reached a compromise with cable operators that Congress adopted as part of the Copyright Act of 1976.[105] The new copyright law's compulsory copyright license for broadcast television and radio programs permits cable operators to carry such programming for a fee without asking permission.[106] A complex formula determines the amount each cable system must pay, but the fee is less than the system would pay if it

---

[98] United States v. Playboy Ent. Group, 529 U.S. 803 (2000).

[99] Cable Television Report and Order, 36 F.C.C. 2d 143 (1972).

[100] Syndicated Exclusivity Rules, 79 F.C.C. 2d 663 (1980); In re Rules Relating to Program Exclusivity in the Cable and Broadcast Industries, 3 F.C.C.R. 5299 (1988).

[101] See United Video, Inc. v. FCC, 890 F.2d 1173 (D.C. Cir. 1989).

[102] First Report and Order in Dockets 14895 and 15233, 38 F.C.C. 683 (1965); In re Rules Relating to Program Exclusivity in the Cable and Broadcast Industries, 3 F.C.C.R. 5299 (1988).

[103] 47 C.F.R. § 76.111 (2002).

[104] Fortnightly Corp. v. United Artists Television, Inc., 392 U.S. 390 (1968); Teleprompter Corp. v. Columbia Broad. Sys., 415 U.S. 394 (1974).

[105] Pub. L. No. 94-553, 94 Stat. 2541, 17 U.S.C.S. §§ 101 et seq. (1976).

[106] 17 U.S.C. § 111 (1976).

negotiated separately with the copyright holder of each individual program. Cable payments are made to a fund administered through the Copyright Office, which distributes the money to the copyright holders. The broadcast stations and networks do not receive any of the money unless they are copyright owners.

Copyright issues continue to play a major role in cable television. As consumers and the various industries switch from analog to digital television, program producers are concerned that viewers will begin to trade movies and television programs on the Internet the same way they trade MP3 music files. HBO would find it difficult to rent or sell DVD copies of *The Sopranos* if consumers were trading the episodes for free. In addition, fewer viewers might subscribe to HBO if they could get the programs for free on the Internet. To prevent the illegal trading of copyrighted programs, cable companies, broadcast outlets, copyright owners and consumer electronics manufacturers are developing special encryption software and digital watermarks to prevent consumers from copying and/or distributing television programs.

In order to speed the transition from analog to digital broadcasting, the FCC passed a rule in 2003 that would require all digital television receivers manufactured after July 1, 2005, to recognize a "broadcast flag" — a digital code inserted in the broadcast to prevent redistribution of the content. Thus, the FCC was requiring copyright protection measures be built into TV sets.

In 2005, the Court of Appeals for the D.C. Circuit struck down the requirement and ruled that the FCC had exceeded its statutory authority. The court reasoned that the FCC can impose requirements related to the reception of television signals, but that it could not impose requirements controlling television sets *after* the transmission is complete.[107]

### Cable Companies as Telephone Providers

The Telecommunications Act of 1996 opened local telephone service to competition. For nearly 100 years, a residential telephone user could obtain service from only one local company. But the 1996 act permits any firm to offer local telephone service and requires telephone companies to make their facilities available, on a nondiscriminatory basis, to others who want to compete in the local telephone market. In return, local telephone companies will be allowed to offer long distance service.

Congress incorrectly expected cable to seize the opportunity provided by the 1996 Act to rush into and provide competition in the lucrative local telephone market. After all, local telephone service providers earned more than $66 billion a year, nearly three times the $23 billion in revenues earned from cable television service at the time. Moreover, cable lines — already in nearly two-thirds of American homes and passing more than 95 percent of homes — were permitted to carry a full range of communications

services: local telephone, Internet access, cable video and other services such as online banking. But such communications packages require fiber optic cable, and many cable operators hesitated to make the major investment necessary to upgrade their coaxial lines. Other cable operators entered the telephone market cautiously and selectively because they lacked experience or expertise in interactive services billed by usage.

In its most recent annual report on competition, the FCC noted that most cable companies are waiting for improved Internet protocol (IP) telephony technology before trying to offer telephone service on a large scale. Currently about 3.6 million customers get some form of telephone service through their cable company.[108]

### Cable Customer Privacy

In the 1984 Cable Act, Congress reacted to a concern that cable companies could collect private information about their customers and share that information with others without subscribers' permission. Congress particularly focused on cable company access to customer information through cable's two-way capabilities, such as banking-from-home. Most of these two-way services have not fully developed yet, but cable systems are limited in the information they can gather and release about their customers.

Private information includes the customer's name, address, telephone number, cable services taken and other information that identifies a particular subscriber. Cable systems annually must inform customers in writing what private information the system collects, what use the system makes of the information, to whom the information is disclosed and why, how long the information will be kept by the system, when and where the customer may see the information the system keeps, the limits placed by law on the system's right to collect and disclose private information, and what steps the customer may take if the cable system violates those limitations.

Without a customer's permission, a cable operator may collect only the private information needed to offer cable or other services ordered by the customer and to be certain customers are not stealing services. Similarly, a cable operator may not release private information to others without permission except as needed to provide services to the customer or for the system's legitimate business needs, such as giving information to a company that sends the cable system's monthly bills.

### Equal Employment Opportunity Requirements

The FCC has had equal employment opportunity rules for broadcasters and cable systems in place for twenty-five years, but the

---

107 American Library Ass'n v. FCC, 406 F.3d 689 (D.C. Cir. 2005).

108 *Twelfth Annual Report, supra* note 1, at para. 66.

1984 and 1992 cable acts codify these rules for cable systems and other multi-channel video programming providers. Generally, the law forbids cable systems and their corporate owners from discriminating on the basis of national origin, race, color, age, religion or gender in employment.

The rules also required that the employees in certain job categories, such as managers and technicians, reasonably reflect the makeup of the pool of possible employees in the cable system's area. Further, cable systems and their owners had to establish programs to ensure that no discrimination occurred in any phase of employment, including hiring, training, promotions and firing. However the validity of the rules were put into doubt when the D.C. Circuit Court of Appeals rejected similar rules which the FCC had put into place for broadcasters.[109]

The FCC created new rules in 2002 for broadcasters and cable companies that require them to conduct broad outreach when filling job vacancies and file an annual report concerning their EEO efforts. Under the new rules cable companies do not have to show that the racial makeup of their employees reflected that of the community.[110]

### Theft of Cable Service

Cable companies lose millions of dollars each year due to theft of cable services. Individuals tap into cable wires to obtain service without being subscribers, or they may use illegal set-top boxes to receive premium channels. The 1984 Cable Act forbids intercepting or receiving any cable service, or assisting anyone in doing so. Violators face up to two years in jail, $50,000 in fines or both. The law also forbids the manufacture and distribution of equipment intended to be used to steal cable service. Another section of the Communications Act makes it illegal to intercept signals not intended for the general public and to manufacture or sell equipment used to intercept such signals. Additionally, more than forty states have laws that may be used to prosecute theft of cable service.

### SUMMARY

Since cable television's commercial development in the 1950s, Congress, the FCC and the courts have vacillated about how it should be regulated. In general, Congress and the FCC have imposed regulation on cable operators when cable's growth and market dominance appeared to jeopardize over-the-air broadcasting or the public's interest in diverse content, quality service and fair pricing. Cable also has been regulated to protect the public, especially children, from indecent or obscene programming. Al-

though the courts view cable systems as part of the media protected by the First Amendment, some regulations treat cable more like a common carrier and require that the public, government and educational institutions, and even competitors, have access to a cable system's delivery network. Cable operators face such a complex array of regulations in part because of their size and economic power and in part because of their central role in disseminating news and other content.

In the early 1960s, the FCC asserted its authority to regulate cable television as "reasonably ancillary" to its obligation to protect an efficient broadcast system. The Supreme Court agreed and generally has deferred to the power of Congress to regulate cable. In fact, the Court has affirmed the authority of the FCC, rather than local or state governments, to regulate many aspects of cable systems. However, local governments maintain some power over cable systems through their franchising authority. Congress finally gave the FCC explicit authority to regulate cable in 1984.

In 1986, the Supreme Court said in *Los Angeles v. Preferred Communications* that cable operators enjoy some First Amendment protection. The Supreme Court has reviewed most structural regulation of the cable industry under intermediate scrutiny and generally has upheld content-neutral laws that advance the government's interest in providing broad access, encouraging a diversity of programming, or controlling excessive market power. In 2000, however, the Court, in *United States v. Playboy Entertainment*, afforded cable full First Amendment protection and applied strict scrutiny to strike down a federal law requiring cable operators to fully scramble indecent programming.

Many of the FCC's most important structural regulations are currently on hold. The FCC has not yet revised its cable vertical and horizontal ownership rules, which were remanded by an appeals court in 2001. In 2002, the FCC declared that cable modem Internet access constituted an information service rather than a cable or telecommunications service. This ruling was recently affirmed by the Supreme Court.

Policymakers continue to be driven by the belief that competition serves the public interest and protects competitors and consumers better than regulation. Most current regulatory efforts are designed to be short-term measures that protect small competitors until they are strong enough to compete with the large established incumbents. These regulatory efforts are complicated by the convergence of cable, telephone and Internet services; each with its own history of regulation. Ten years after the passage of the Telecommunications Act of 1996, increases in competition have been modest at best. Cable operators now control only 69 percent of the subscription television market, down from 95 percent just ten years ago.[111] In 2006, the Congress was considering replacing local franchise agreements with a national franchise as a way to encourage large telephone companies to compete more vigorously

---

[109] Md/DC/DE Broadcasters Ass'n v. FCC, 236 F.3d 13 (D.C. Cir. 2001).

[110] In re Review of the Commission's Broadcast and Cable Equal Employment Opportunity Rules and Policies (FCC 01-363), 67 Fed. Reg. 1704 (2002).

[111] *Twelfth Annual Report, supra* note 1, at para. 8.

with cable operators. However, as more and more video services migrate to the Internet, the regulatory focus may shift from cable service to Internet access. Time will tell if the changing regulatory landscape serves to enhance the marketplace of ideas.

## FOR ADDITIONAL READING

Aufderheide, Patricia. *Communications Policy and the Public Interest: The Telecommunications Act of 1996.* New York: Guilford Press, 1999.

Brock, Gerald W. *Telecommunication Policy for the Information Age: From Monopoly to Competition.* Cambridge: Harvard University Press, 1994.

Crandall, Robert W. *Cable Television: Regulation or Competition.* Washington, D.C.: Brookings Institution, 1996.

Ferris, Charles D., et al. *Cable Television Law.* New York: Mathew Bender, 1984-1998.

Hanson, Jarice. *Connections: Technologies of Communication.* New York: HarperCollins, 1994.

Huber, Peter W., et al. *The Telecommunications Act of 1996: Special Report.* Boston: Little, Brown, 1996.

Parsons, Patrick. R. *Cable Television and the First Amendment.* New York: Free Press, 1987.

Parsons, Patrick R. & Robert M. Frieden. *The Cable and Satellite Television Industries.* Boston: Allyn and Bacon, 1998.

Pool, Ithiel de Sola. *Technologies of Freedom.* Cambridge, Mass.: Belknap Press, 1983.

Rosston, Gregory L. & David Waterman, eds. *Interconnection and the Internet.* Mahwah, N.J.: Lawrence Erlbaum Associates, 1997.

# 12

## New Communication Technologies

*By Jeremy Harris Lipschultz*

---

☞ **Headnote Questions**

- *Why are convergence and diffusion useful concepts in technology law?*
- *How will new telephone and digital television services challenge existing law and regulation?*
- *How has the Internet redefined communication law and regulation?*
- *What role have the courts played in interpreting digital law?*
- *How have recent U.S. Supreme Court decisions set cyberlaw precedents?*

---

Communication law and regulation are experiencing an ongoing revolution because of social challenges unleashed by a wide array of new technologies. As new media allow individuals to take on the role of publishers (such as through the use of weblogs and podcasts), there are new freedoms and responsibilities.

Consider the case of a University of Louisiana at Monroe professor who, on his Web site, alleged that administrators had mismanaged funds. The professor first sought to remain anonymous and appealed a lower court decision that ordered a California Internet service provider (ISP) to name him so that a university vice president could sue for libel and slander.[1] The professor later identified himself, and the ISP removed the page.[2] Ultimately, the suit was dismissed when a court applied Louisiana anti-SLAPP law (strategic lawsuits against public participation), which grants First Amendment freedoms to Web publishers.[3] On a broader scale, Web sites such as RateMyProfessors.com offer students the ability to openly criticize instructors, and these postings may spawn liti-

gation. Internet Web site public access is one development among many in the history of new media technology law and regulation.

As noted in the last chapter, regulators have termed "new communication technologies" as those mass media developed after broadcast television; but it is fair to say that the printing press, the telegraph, the telephone, radio and television at one time were all considered revolutionary. While all new media seem to borrow or are said to be a form of remediation from "old" media,[4] an "antithetical" argument notes that "we are dealing with a unique form of communication" in the online world.[5] The diffusion of new technologies often involves the adoption of new ideas: "The newness means that some degree of uncertainty is involved in diffusion."[6]

The diffusion of the World Wide Web has been explosive since its introduction to the general public around 1994. By 2006, 172 million American (more than 77 percent) adults were using the Web – an increase of about 5 percent per year since 2002.[7] Nielsen/NetRatings estimated that there were more than 200 mil-

---

[1] *See* Dan Carnevale, *Professor Who Runs Web Site Can Remain Anonymous for at Least a While Longer,* Chron. of Higher Educ., Feb. 6, 2002, *at* http://chronicle.com/free/2002/02/2002020601t.htm.

[2] *See* Associated Press, *Anonymous University Web Critic Steps Forward,* The First Amendment Center, June 3, 2002, *at* http://www.firstamendmentcenter.org/news.aspx?id=3823&printer-friendly=y.

[3] *See Web Site Defamation Suit Against Professor Dismissed,* Reporters Committee for Freedom of the Press, May 29, 2003, *at* http://www.rcfp.org/news/2003/0529baxter.html.

[4] *See* Jay David Bolter & Richard Grusin, Remediation, Understanding New Media 5 (1999).

[5] Larry Pryor, *Online Journalism and the Threat of Two Cultures,* 57 Journalism & Mass Comm. Educator 302, 302 (2003).

[6] Everett M. Rogers, Diffusion of Innovations 6 (4th ed. 1995).

[7] The Harris Poll, May 24, 2006, *at http://www.harrisinteractive.com/harris_poll/printerfriend/index.asp?PID=668; cf.* The Media Audit, Apr. 25, 2002, *at* http://www.themediaaudit.com/growth.htm.

lion users in the United States.[8] About 135 million of those were said to be active users, and there may be as many as one billion online across the world.[9] As the number of users continues to rise, the convergence of printed text, photographs, audio and video presents challenges across the legal spectrum, from libel and privacy to obscenity and copyright issues.[10]

## CONVERGING VOICE, DATA AND VIDEO TECHNOLOGIES

Ongoing technological developments and market pressures are leading telephones, television and computers to converge into single services. The development of high-speed links *via* broadband services has opened doors to a variety of interactive programming and communication options.

The convergence of voice, video and data seemed to be driven by a desire for highly personalized media: "The computer's promise of immediacy comes through the combination of three-dimensional graphics, automatic (programmed) action, and an interactivity that television cannot match."[11] However, digital television has now begun to offer many personal computer-like features, and more are expected as the digital transition continues. Even traditional television viewing has been transformed through digitization. Digital recording devices, for example, allow for personalized media, time shifting and some control over live broadcasts. Such rapid technological change has produced an uncertain business environment.

Digital technology also unleashed stiff competition among potential providers of video services, and some of the regulatory battles were about which companies and media technologies would survive and prosper. Telecommunication deregulation allowed, for example, telephone companies to provide video services and cable companies to offer telephone services. This form of cross-media competition came at a time of mergers and corporate consolidation. Telecommunications cartels like Time Warner threatened to monopolize mass media, including the Internet: "Advertising and other corporate promotion on the Internet seem to grow exponentially, with 'the system' becoming more fully embedded in the cyber world each day."[12] As historian Randall Stross noted in 2005, marketers have gone from counting noses to counting Web eye-

balls and podcast eardrums.[13] Just one year later, vodcasts — video podcasts — were becoming popular. On Capitol Hill, lawmakers debated Net Neutrality legislation, which sought to limit Internet pricing tied to connection speeds and perhaps introduce further inequality among content providers on the Web.[14] Cable and telephone ISPs, for example, wish to charge Google and Yahoo! to send and receive data faster in a highly competitive environment. Against this backdrop, regulators and courts have been asked to decide what constitutes fair competition. One example is the persistent issue about whether the software giant Microsoft abused monopoly power. There is a larger question: What constitutes a monopoly in a global multimedia world?

Any study of new media technologies should begin with a reading of the writings in free expression and legal thinking, but it also must go beyond the law to view social change in an increasingly technological world.

### *The First Amendment and Cyberspace*

New communication technologies are not mentioned in the First Amendment, but lawmakers, regulators and the courts have attempted a variety of strategies to determine how it applies. For example, the U.S. Supreme Court has recognized that the unique traits of each mass medium permit different constitutional standards.[15] Yet, the unique characteristics of a new communication technology often are not apparent until long after it is introduced and adopted by the public.

Thus, Congress, the Federal Communications Commission (FCC), the Federal Trade Commission (FTC), other regulatory bodies applying administrative law, and the courts must choose either to: (1) regulate an emerging technology before it is well understood or widely used; (2) regulate during the uncertain developmental and evolutionary period; (3) attempt to formulate logical and consistent regulatory models after the new technology is in general use; or (4) avoid regulation altogether. Often, it is unclear whether, or how much, the technology of a medium should affect the legal protection of the message conveyed.

Constitutional standards of regulation are difficult to obtain, even after a new technology ages. Developmental history of a technology — such as telephone service — appears to affect the willingness of the courts to apply the First Amendment.[16] The result is a highly detailed, sometimes inconsistent and often confusing array of regulations and First Amendment rulings.[17]

---

[8] Neilsen/NetRatings, June 11, 2004, *at* http://http://www.netratings.com/news.jsp.

[9] *Population Explosion!*, CLICKZ, Mar. 16, 2005, *at* http://www.clickz.com/stats/sectors/geographics/article.php/5911_151151.

[10] *See, e.g.*, Leibovitz v. Paramount, 137 F. 3d 109 (2d Cir. 1998) (copyright); Zeran v. America Online, 129 F.3d 327 (4th Cir. 1997) (libel); Apollo-Media Corp. v. Reno, 19 F. Supp. 2d 1081 (N.D. Cal. 1998) (obscenity); Blumenthal v. Drudge and America Online, 992 F. Supp. 44 (D.D.C. 1998) (libel); Jessup-Morgan v. America Online, Inc., 20 F. Supp. 2d 1105 (E.D. Mich. 1998) (privacy); Cubby v. CompuServe, 776 F. Supp. 135 (S.D.N.Y. 1991) (libel).

[11] BOLTER & GRUSIN, *supra* note 4, at 224.

[12] BEN H. BAGDIKIAN, THE MEDIA MONOPOLY X (6th ed. 2000).

[13] Randall Stross, *The Battle for Eardrums Begins with Podcasts*, N.Y. TIMES, July 3, 2005, at 3.

[14] Kim Hart & Kara Kehaulani Goo, *Tech Faceoff: Net Neutrality, In the Eye of the Beholder*, WASH. POST, July 2, 2006, at F4.

[15] *See, e.g.*, Times Film Corp. v. Chicago, 365 U.S. 43, 50 (1961).

[16] *See, e.g.*, Susan D. Ross, *A Decade After Divestiture: Regional Bells, Video Programming and the First Amendment*, 21 RUTGERS COMPUTER & TECH. L. J. 143 (1995).

[17] *See, e.g.*, AT&T v. Iowa Utilities Bd., 525 U.S. 366, 397 (1999) (noting that

Consider, for example, the action by at least ten state legislatures to pass a patchwork of data privacy laws,[18] while state legislatures and the federal government also became concerned about unwanted e-mail, called "spam." A study by the FTC found deception in 66 percent of unsolicited commercial e-mail.[19] Many people view spam as a serious problem for businesses and individuals. While legislation may be designed to solve the nagging concern of e-mail spam, such a social problem goes beyond the full reach of law and regulation.

Legislation frequently is challenged in the courts on First Amendment and other grounds. State privacy law, for example, remains an unsystematic set of measures related to arrest, banking, medical and school records, computer crime and justice, government data, employment and other issues.[20]

Another example of confusing regulation is the FTC implementation of the Children's Online Privacy Protection Act,[21] known as "COPPA," originally part of congressional attempts to protect children in cyberspace.[22] Web sites were faced with a rule that required operators to post privacy policies, provide notice and obtain parental consent prior to collecting certain personal information from children.[23] The rule allowed Internet operators to submit their own self-regulatory plans for dealing with children under age thirteen, and many Web sites responded by restricting access.

The FTC rule was aimed at protecting identifiable information such as names, addresses, e-mail addresses and telephone numbers.[24] In response, about 147 individuals and corporations filed comments with the FTC. Retailer Amazon.com, for example, complained that the rule was "likely to interfere with the overall customer experience and inherent benefits of the Internet."[25] The Federal Trade Commission, however, voted to ask Congress to expand FTC regulatory authority over Internet consumer privacy, even as state legislatures considered more laws, because fewer than half of the Web sites studied had implemented adequate privacy protections.[26] In the end, Internet e-business and shopping

continued to grow under the new rules,[27] which may or may not have done much to protect personal privacy; Congress responded with hearings on the issue; and the political process failed to resolve the many ongoing privacy concerns. The blending of such Internet new technology issues with converging questions about telephone and video regulation raised the prospect that the legal landscape would continue to be complex.

## Video Services and Telephone Companies

There have been arguments for decades about whether companies providing local telephone service also should be allowed to own cable systems or offer video programming. Under the Communications Act of 1934, telephone companies were *common carriers* that must provide non-discriminatory services at similar rates to anyone wishing to send messages over their systems.

Different portions of the Communications Act govern telephone companies, broadcast stations and cable systems, which makes the law a cumbersome vehicle. More importantly, for a number of years many government regulators believed that telephone companies would use their large size, their universal penetration and their economic power to drive other multi-channel video providers out of business. Of course, cable and broadcast lobbyists helped fuel these fears within the political, policy-making system.[28] Concerns about telephone company behavior pre-date the break-up initiated in the 1970s and settled in the 1980s.

American Telephone & Telegraph's Bell System dominated local and long-distance telephone service in the United States during the first seven decades of the Twentieth Century. For consumers, it was a time when the telephone was a wired-only technology used primarily for voice communication between individuals. As early as the 1960s, there were video-phone demonstrations, but these were treated in the consumer market as experimental and futuristic. The focus remained on highly concentrated voice telephone service.

The problem of ownership concentration was known from the dawn of the telephone age. The dominance was so great that the federal government filed lawsuits against AT&T in 1914 and again in 1956. The government charged that AT&T violated antitrust laws by attempting to monopolize local and national telecommunications markets for service and equipment. Each time, AT&T signed

---

"it would be a gross understatement to say that the Telecommunications Act of 1996 is not a model of clarity").

[18] *See* Rachel Zimmerman & Glenn R. Si, *Lobbyists Swarm to Stop Tough Privacy Bills in State,* Apr. 21, 2000, *at* http://www.djreprints.com.

[19] *False Claims — Spam: A Report by the FTC's Division of Marketing Practices, at* http://www.ftc.gov/opa/2003/2004/spamrpt.htm.

[20] Electronic Privacy Information Center, *Privacy Laws by State,* June 13, 2001, *at* http://www.epic.org/privacy/consumer/states.html.

[21] 16 CFR 312.10(a) (2003). *See also* 65 F.R. 45 (Mar. 7, 2000), at 11947.

[22] Federal Trade Commission, Children's Online Privacy Protection Rule, 15 U.S.C. § 6501 (1999).

[23] 65 F.R. 45 (Mar. 7, 2000), at 11947.

[24] The Federal Trade Commission Web site is http://www.ftc.gov.

[25] *Children's Online Privacy Protection Rule, Public Comments Received, available at* http://www.ftc.gov/privacy/comments/amazoncom.htm (June 11, 1999).

[26] *See* Robert L. Jackson, *FTC Seeks Online Privacy Law From Congress,* L.A. TIMES, May 23, 2000, at C3.

[27] The Media Audit, May 14, 2003, *at* http://www.themediaaudit.com: "[T]he number of those making five or more purchases on the Internet during the past year increased by more than four million." Bob Jordan, co-chairman of International Demographics, Inc., said: "The dot com bust, corporate scandals and a sluggish economy seem to have had no impact on Internet shopping."

[28] Industry critics claim regulated industries exert too much influence through their frequent access to regulators. *See* ERWIN G. KRASNOW ET AL., THE POLITICS OF BROADCAST REGULATION (3d ed. 1982). *See also* Philip M. Napoli, *The Federal Communications Commission and Broadcast Policy-Making — 1965-1995: A Logistic Regression Analysis of Interest Group Influence,* 5 COMM. L. & POL'Y 203 (2000).

a consent decree, promising that it would no longer engage in the impermissible actions.

Similar concerns arose during the early years of the cable industry, when telephone companies could own cable systems. Cable systems often needed to string their lines above ground, but local government officials sometimes refused to allow cable operators to erect their own poles, which was also expensive and inefficient. Cable operators, then, often rented space on existing poles owned by telephone or power companies. However, from cable's earliest days through the 1960s, the FCC heard many complaints that affiliated cable operators were not being allowed to rent space on telephone poles.

In 1960, the FCC responded by adopting the telephone-cable cross-ownership ban to eliminate the incentive for telephone companies to discriminate against cable competitors. In 1974, the U.S. Department of Justice filed a third antitrust suit against AT&T, claiming that the 1956 consent decree had failed to prevent the telephone giant from monopolizing the business.

The new agreement, settled in 1982, became known as the "Modification of the Final Judgment," or the "MFJ."[29] It forced AT&T to sell off its local telephone service divisions. AT&T became only a long-distance provider. The newly formed regional and local telephone companies were limited to local phone services.

Two years later, Congress adopted the FCC's cross-ownership ban as part of the 1984 Cable Act. The law prevented all telephone companies in the United States – including the approximately 2,500 independent telephone companies not formerly affiliated with AT&T – from owning or operating cable systems.[30]

The companies that were divested from AT&T in 1982 – called "RBOCs" for "Regional Bell Operating Companies" – became the nation's largest providers of local telephone service. The RBOCs chafed at many restrictions in the MFJ, including the ban on information services. In 1991, Harold Greene, the federal district court judge overseeing the consent decree, essentially removed the information services ban.[31] However, that left in place the 1984 Cable Act ban on telephone-cable cross-ownership. Several RBOCs brought lawsuits and argued in court that their First Amendment rights to free speech were being abridged by the ban. Beginning in 1993, every court which heard such a case agreed and overturned the ban.[32]

While the RBOCs were in court challenging the Cable Act ban,

## THE REGIONAL BELL OPERATING COMPANIES (RBOCs) IN 2006

**at&t** (lower-case letters) (including **SBC** and **Bell-South**) - Covering the large states of California, Texas Illinois, Michigan and Ohio, SBC, formerly Southwestern Bell, acquired Ameritech (Michigan Bell, Ohio Bell and Wisconsin Bell) and Pacific Telesis (Pacific Bell and Nevada Bell). The Bell South (South Central Bell and Southern Bell) territory in the southeast was renamed.

**Qwest** - Qwest acquired all of the former USWest (Montana Bell, Northwestern Bell and Pacific Northwestern Bell) territory in the upper midwest, west and northwest.

**Verizon** - Bell Atlantic purchased Nynex (New England Telephone and New York telephone) and later became Verizon. This now also includes what was GTE and MCI.[33]

the FCC also gave telephone companies a way to be involved in video. In 1992, the Commission allowed the RBOCs to offer a common carrier video service called "video dialtone" or VDT.[34] With VDT, a telephone company would use its wires and support services to provide video similar to television signal quality.

Telephone companies were required to provide the service on a non-discriminatory, first-come-first-served basis. Telephone companies, historically viewed as common carriers, provided households access to shared long distance lines. In this environment, the telephone companies were not involved in content or editing. Nevertheless, video services seemed to redefine telephone companies: A telephone company also could offer its own video services over a VDT system on a limited basis. Unlike cable television, VDT systems did not require local franchises – neither the telephone company nor any of the programming services met the legal definition of a cable system.[35] Cable companies opposed VDT systems and argued that the absence of franchising requirements gave VDT systems an unfair advantage.

The Telecommunications Act of 1996 resolved some of the complex questions about telephone companies offering video services. The law eliminated the telephone-cable cross-ownership ban and allowed local telephone companies to provide video programming in one of four ways:

- A firm offering local telephone service could own a cable sys-

---

[29] See United States v. Western Elec. Co., 552 F. Supp. 131 (D.D.C. 1982).

[30] 47 U.S.C. § 613(b) (1984).

[31] See United States v. Western Elec. Co., 767 F. Supp. 308 (D.D.C. 1991). See also United States v. Western Elec. Co., 900 F.2d 283 (D.C. Cir. 1990).

[32] See Chesapeake & Potomac Tel. Co. v. United States, 830 F. Supp. 909 (E.D. Va. 1993), aff'd 42 F.3d 181 (4th Cir. 1994), vacated and remanded, 516 U.S. 415 (1996); Ameritech Corp. v. United States, 1994 U.S. Dist. LEXIS 4920 (Apr. 11, 1994). After adoption of the Telecommunications Act of 1996, 104 Pub. L. 104, the Supreme Court found this series of decisions moot, since Congress had answered the question of whether telephone companies could offer video services. See United States v. Chesapeake & Potomac Tel. Co. of Virginia, 516 U.S. 415 (1996).

[33] The Telecommunications Act of 1996 allowed the "Baby Bells" (RBOCs) to compete in the long-distance market. At the same time, long-distance providers, such as AT&T and Sprint, were allowed to compete in the local telephone market. By 2004, the largest U.S. long distance carrier, AT&T, considered moving some of its traffic onto the McLeodUSA network to avoid Baby Bell network charges. See Business In Brief, L.A. TIMES, JULY 8, 2004, at C3.

[34] See Telephone Company-Cable Television Cross-Ownership Rules, 7 F.C.C. Rcd. 5781 (1992).

[35] See Nat'l Cable Television Ass'n v. FCC, 33 F.3d 66 (D.C. Cir. 1994).

tem as a separate subsidiary company. Telephone-owned cable systems would need to comply with all of the laws and local and state cable franchise requirements.

• A telephone company could operate a common carrier video service similar to VDT (although that term is no longer used) on a first-come-first-served basis. Under this approach, the telephone company's video service would be regulated much as its common carrier telephone service.

• The Telecommunications Act created a new way for telephone companies to offer video – the "Open Video System." OVS providers served *both* as common carriers of others' programming and as program providers. If outside demand for video carriage exceeds system capacity, then the OVS provider could program no more than one-third of its channels, with the remainder offered to other video providers on a first-come-first-served basis. The systems were not required to obtain franchises, but local governments *could* require OVS fees equivalent to the franchise fees of a cable operator. By acting as video common carriers, OVS providers are absolved of some regulatory obligations.

• A telephone company could offer video services through what is called "wireless cable." Wireless technology is discussed later in this chapter and is perhaps the most important current development in the new media technology area.

In 1999, the Fifth U.S. Circuit Court of Appeals overturned the law's exemption of OVS systems from local franchising in Dallas.[36] However, the same court found that Southwestern Bell Video Services, a subsidiary of SBC Communications that provided video to apartment complexes, need not enter into a cable franchise agreement with Austin, Texas, because it did not own all of its equipment and was not a "cable operator" under federal and state law.[37] The FCC was left to reexamine its OVS rules. The 1996 act seemed to permit, but not require, franchising of OVS.

In general, telephone companies want to be free to compete with cable companies in the video business, but they would also like to be free from oversight and financial obligations imposed in franchising agreements. In a federal case out of Florida, a district court, citing the Dallas decision, held that Palm Beach was limited by a flurry of state and federal regulations to narrow right-of-way regulation of BellSouth's services.[38] BellSouth failed to get the court to strike down the entire local ordinance as an unconstitutional violation of due process and the Commerce Clause, and Palm Beach was allowed under federal law to charge reasonable compensation for use of the public rights-of-way.[39] The court lim-

ited Palm Beach under Florida law to collect no more than 1 percent of gross receipts on local telephone services. One must understand, however, that each state has been allowed to delegate state regulatory authority to its local governments, if it so chooses.[40] Thus, a state could also preempt all home-rule by cities, towns, counties and other local units. In general, state public service commissions tend to exert a lot of control over these instate telephone issues.

In another case, a federal appeals court rejected Cablevision of Boston's claim that the city did not do enough to level the playing field when Boston Edison entered a joint venture to wire underground fiber optic cable for video services.[41] At issue was whether the cable company had been given a chance to participate.[42] The court held that under federal law the city was only required to manage disruption caused by the work. It had no obligation to monitor the fiber optic business deal. State or federal regulators, however, might concern themselves with such issues. State regulators may be concerned with service quality and consumer rights.

A telephone company generally is not permitted to purchase an existing cable system located in the same service area. Nor is a cable system allowed to buy a telephone company where both provide service. A rule the FCC adopted before passage of the 1996 Act prohibited any cable system operator from passing its wires by more than 30 percent of all homes passed by cable in the United States (35 percent if the company is minority-controlled).[43] A federal appellate court ruled that a challenge to this regulation was not yet ready to be heard by the courts.[44]

The RBOCs also challenged provisions of the 1996 law. They argued that the law unfairly punishes them by requiring delays until competition exists before providing advanced services. In 1998, one federal circuit court upheld the FCC's effective competition standard before allowing a RBOC to offer long-distance services.[45] The same court later rejected another RBOC's constitutional challenge to the Telecommunications Act's mandate that Bell companies provide electronic publishing only through separate affiliates.[46] The court said the rule was a well-justified, content-neutral mechanism to prevent monopolies and unfair competition. The Supreme Court refused to review these and other lower court rulings that upheld special restrictions of the RBOCs.

Even before the 1996 Act was adopted, USWest (now a part of

---

[36] City of Dallas v. FCC, 165 F. 3d 341 (5th Cir. 1999).

[37] City of Austin v. Southwestern Bell Video Servs., 193 F. 3d 309 (5th Cir. 1999).

[38] Bellsouth Telecomm. v. Town of Palm Beach, 127 F. Supp 2d 1348 (S.D. Fla. 1999), *aff'd in part, rev'd in part,* 252 F.3d 1169 (11th Cir. 2001).

[39] *See* Federal Telecommunications Act of 1996, 47 U.S.C. § 253 (1999). The act preempted local control over telecommunications in general, but allowed for nondiscriminatory regulation of rights-of-way. *See* Bellsouth v. City of Coral Springs, 42 F. Supp. 2d 1304 (S.D. Fla. 1999).

[40] *See* AT&T Commc'ns v. City of Dallas, 8 F. Supp. 2d 582 (N.D. Texas 1998).

[41] Cablevision of Boston v. Public Improvement Comm'n., 184 F.3d 88 (1st Cir. 1999).

[42] *Id.* at 92-93.

[43] Horizontal and Vertical Ownership Limits, Second Report and Order, 8 F.C.C. Rcd. 8565 (1993).

[44] Time Warner Ent. Co. v. FCC, 93 F.3d 957 (D.C. Cir. 1996).

[45] SBC Commc'ns v. FCC, 138 F.3d 410 (D.C. Cir. 1998).

[46] BellSouth v. FCC, 144 F.3d 58 (D.C. Cir. 1998) (challenging that the special provisions violate the phone company's First and Fifth Amendment rights and constitute illegal punishment without a trial).

Qwest) had invested in Time Warner. Shortly after the act's passage, USWest agreed to acquire Continental Cablevision for $5.3 billion. Through these two transactions, USWest had a potential reach of more than sixteen million customers, approximately one in every four cable subscribers. In 1997, the FCC approved another major merger between British Telecom and MCI Communications. At the same time, concerns about unfair competition persisted. In 1997, the Supreme Court refused to review a circuit court of appeals ruling granting a small telephone provider $1.54 million and possible punitive damages as a result of AT&T's unfair and anti-competitive treatment of the company, but a year later the case was reversed.[47]

### Rates, Services and Access

Rates for service and competitor access to new marketplaces continue to be important issues. For example, the Supreme Court decided a limited case about the FCC methods for determining interconnection rates that new entrants pay to so-called "incumbent local telephone companies" (or "incumbent local exchange carriers," ILECs) to access a market and provide competitive services.[48] The D.C. Court of Appeals, however, after two previous interventions, refused to overturn the FCC method for determining fair charges for coinless pay telephone calls.[49] However, that same court vacated one FCC order that would have transferred licenses from Ameritech to SBC Communications as part of a merger and forced regulators to revisit the scope of services allowed to be included.[50] Companies and the Commission also have bickered over the release of required audit data the FCC uses to determine fairness of rates.[51]

Merger mania abounded in the past decade among the so-called "Baby Bells" and others: Pacific Telesis and SBC, Bell Atlantic and NYNEX, Ameritech and SBC, Bell Atlantic and GTE, AT&T and Tele-Communications, and AT&T and MediaOne, USWest and Qwest.[52] Three new giants emerged in 2006 — Verizon, Qwest and the new at&t. The buzzword of the day was "competition" for Internet and data services.[53] Expansion outside regions was allowed, as the new companies were active in the growing wireless telephone and data services business, spurred by development of new hand-held telephones that doubled as computers. The U.S.

marketplace appeared highly volatile. When the auction winner of high-speed wireless PCS spectrum licenses filed for bankruptcy and the FCC revoked for failure to pay, the Supreme Court, with an 8-1 vote, sided with creditors of NextWave, a company that had promised to pay more than $4 billion to serve ninety-five cities.[54] Later in the year, NextWave agreed to sell 20 percent of radio spectrum licenses to Cingular, an SBC/BellSouth joint venture, for about $1.3 billion.[55] The FCC previously reviewed a proposed merger between the nation's second and third largest long-distance telephone companies — MCI, WorldCom and Sprint:

> In a telecommunications world increasingly dominated by two poles — former Bell companies such as SBC Communications Inc. and Bell Atlantic Corp., and cable companies such as AT&T Corp. and Time Warner Inc. — their merger would create a third, providing greater choice and lower prices to consumers.[56]

However, that merger would have placed 80 percent of the residential long-distance market back in the hands of just two companies, AT&T and MCI (WorldCom). In July 2000, the two giants called off the $129 billion deal following regulatory challenges in the United States and Europe.[57] At the same time, the world's largest merger involved $342 billion Vodaphone Mannesmann and signaled a shift toward global telecommunications giants.[58] Further, convergence of technology meant that the AOL Time Warner deal produced what one writer called a sort of "unstoppable wave" of "juggernauts" battling over profitable new markets in the United States, Europe and Asia.[59]

By 2002, a national economic downturn and questionable business practices led to a dramatic shakeout of the more than 600 competing U.S. telecommunications companies. Global Crossing and McLeodUSA filed for bankruptcy protection.[60] WorldCom, which suffered a bankruptcy collapse, eventually admitted to $11 billion in fraud, agreed to pay shareholders $500 million, and signed on to a settlement that included a $1.5-billion Securities and Exchange Commission fine.[61] The deal allowed MCI to continue to operate the business.

From a regulatory perspective, the two questions involving the mergers and telecommunication companies (known as "telcos")

---

[47] Central Office Tel. v. American Tel. & Tel., 108 F.3d 981 (D.C. Cir. 1997). *Certiorari* in the case was granted Dec. 12, 1997, but then denied three days later. 522 U.S. 1036 (1997). The case, however, was later reversed in *Am. Tel. and Tel. Co. v. Central Office Tel., Inc.*, 524 U.S. 214 (1998), *reh'g denied*, 424 U.S. 972 (1998).

[48] Verizon Commc'ns v. FCC, 531 U.S. 1124 (2001).

[49] American Public Commc'n Council v. FCC, 215 F.3d 51 (D.C. Cir. 2000).

[50] Ass'n of Commc'ns Enterprises v. FCC, 235 F.3d 662 (D.C. Cir. 2001).

[51] *See* Qwest v. FCC, 229 F.3d 1172 (D.C. Cir. 2000).

[52] *See Merger Mania*, THE NAT'L J., June 26, 1999, at 1883.

[53] *See* Andrew Backover, *U S West Boldly Enters "Foreign" Realm*, DENVER POST, May 11, 2000, at C1.

[54] FCC v. NextWave Personal Commc'ns, Inc., 537 U.S. 293 (2003).

[55] *See* Simon Romero, *$1.3 Billion Deal. See for NextWave Radio Spectrum*, N.Y. TIMES, May 28, 2003, *at* http://www.nytimes.com.

[56] Peter S. Goldman, *WorldCom, Sprint Face Skeptics*, WASH. POST, Apr. 6, 2000, at E2.

[57] *See* Matt Moore, *Sprint, WorldCom Call Off Merger*, AP ONLINE, July 13, 2002, *at* http://wwwwire.ap.org.

[58] *See What Next?*, ECONOMIST, Feb. 12, 2000, at 1.

[59] *Unstoppable Wave*, J. OF COMMERCE, Feb. 17, 2000, at 5.

[60] *See* Kenneth Gilpin, *The Strong Will Survive the Fallout In Telecom*, N.Y. TIMES, Feb. 3, 2002, *at* http://www.nytimes.com.

[61] Associated Press, *WorldCom's Settlement Closely Watched*, N. Y. TIMES, May 27, 2003, *at* http://www.nytimes.com.

are: (1) Is there a settling point between free-wheeling marketplace economics and regulatory limits on monopolization of the market? (2) What role will the courts play in managing the telecommunication marketplace in such an environment?

The Supreme Court in 2002 began to address key issues raised by expanding telephone services and wireless delivery methods by ruling in two important cases. In *National Cable & Telecommunications Association v. Gulf Power,* the Court held that the Federal Communications Commission had authority under the Pole Attachments Act to set reasonable rates and conditions for high-speed Internet, traditional cable and wireless services.[62]

The court found that "the subject matter here is technical, complex, and dynamic; and as a general rule, agencies have authority to fill gaps where the statutes are silent."[63] Moreover, in *Verizon Communications v. FCC,* the Court upheld rules that require the large local telephone companies to lease to new competitors reasonably priced access to existing networks.[64] The decision was generally hailed as a victory for smaller competitors but was by no means the end of attempts by existing telephone powerhouses to retain a competitive advantage.[65]

In *AT&T v. FCC,* the D.C. Circuit Court of Appeals held that regulators might allow Bell operating companies expanded access to new long-distance customers, if competitors have access to local networks that meet the public interest.[66] In *SBC v. FCC,* circuit judges denied review of $6 million in FCC fines for merger agreement violations.[67]

The three proposed remaining "Baby Bell" RBOC telephone companies – the new at&t, Qwest and Verizon – earlier had faced millions of dollars in fines because they withheld or delayed providing access for competitors to lines and equipment, a small price to pay to gain a competitive edge in a business worth billions of dollars.[68] By 2004, the FCC was forced to draft new rules promoting competition after the Supreme Court left standing an appeals court decision that tossed out government rules. The inability to create legal regulation at first threatened AT&T and MCI, long-distance companies "struggling ... to launch their own brands of local service,"[69] however, the new mergers pushed MCI to Verizon, and the SBC deals assumed the AT&T brand. At stake were the huge profits to be made from providing wireless and high-speed Internet services. The U.S. House of Representatives had earlier voted to deregulate the business further and allow Baby Bells to

offer DSL high-speed Internet service without being required to provide competitors with access to equipment and networks, but the fate of that legislation remained in doubt. The proposed bill placed those promoting new technologies in opposition to lawmakers who viewed Baby Bells as too large.[70] Nevertheless, the business deals continued. Dell, a major computer manufacturer and seller, agreed to offer customers high-speed DSL Web access through BellSouth (FastAccess), SBC (Yahoo!) and Verizon (Online) in thirty-eight states.[71] One report suggested that SBC and Verizon "benefited immensely" as local telephone market incumbents: "In addition to their vast telephone networks, built over decades with ratepayer dollars, the companies have established relationships with loyal customers who are unlikely to jump ship to an unproven rival."[72]

DSL high-speed Internet competition was one issue. Consumers sometimes found their interests at odds with those of the large corporations. Two days after FCC rules designed to crack down on "slamming" – the illegal practice of switching long-distance service without permission – went into effect, for example, the U.S. Court of Appeals for the District of Columbia halted enforcement.[73] The one-page order did not address the validity of the rules, which would give consumers up to thirty days to avoid paying long-distance charges when their service is illegally switched. MCI sought suspension of the rules to allow the Commission to consider an industry plan to address the fast-growing problem.[74]

The FCC defined "slamming" as unauthorized changes in the preferred telephone carrier of a consumer. If a competing company switched a consumer without an explicit request, that would be considered slamming under anti-slamming rules, which took effect in 1999. The FCC's March 1999 strengthening of liability rules to allow consumers to avoid a month of slamming charges were stayed by the U.S. Court of Appeals for the District of Columbia Circuit in May 1999 following a request from telephone companies.

Similarly, there has been concern expressed about telemarketing. The public complained about the prevalence of unsolicited telephone sales calls. Again, the FTC this time responded with a national do-not-call list in 2003. In the first day alone, 735,000 numbers were registered.

[62] 534 U.S. 327 (2002).

[63] Id. at 339.

[64] 535 U.S. 467 (2002).

[65] *See* Stephen Labaton, *Leasing Rules for Phone Start-Ups Are Upheld,* N.Y. Times, May 14, 2002, *at* http://www.nytimes.com.

[66] 369 F.2d 554 (D.C. Cir. 2004).

[67] 373 F.3d 32 (D.C.Cir. 2004).

[68] *See* Peter J. Howe, *Rivals Question Impact of Financial Penalties on Baby Bells,* Boston Globe, May 20, 2002, at C1.

[69] *See* Christopher Sterling, *Local Phone Service Rules Left to Expire,* Wash. Post, June 10, 2004, at A01.

[70] *See* Susan Milligan, *House OKs Baby Bell-Backed Broadband Bill Plan,* Boston Globe, Feb. 28, 2002, at C2.

[71] *See* Colin C. Haley, *Dell Offers DSL Through Baby* Bells, InternetNews.Com, Jan. 8, 2003, *at* http://www.internetnews.com/bus-news/article.php/1566111.

[72] Joelle Tessler, *Baby Bells Emerging as Winners In Telecom Wars,* Mercury News, Jan. 27, 2002, *at* http://www.siliconvalley.com/mld/siliconvalley/3560255.htm.

[73] United States Telecom. Ass'n v. FCC, 295 F.3d 1326 (D.C. Cir. 2002).

[74] *See* Jeannine Aversa, *Appeals Court Halts Enforcement of FCC's New "Slamming" Rules,* Legal Intelligencer, May 19, 1999, at 4.

## THE FCC AND SLAMMING

The FCC rules were at the core of the agency's efforts to eliminate slamming by giving consumers meaningful recourse. There was a decline in slamming complaints the FCC received (with local telephone companies also reporting similar declines) after April 1999:

• In April 1999 the FCC received 1,355 slamming complaints, compared to only 840 complaints in May 1999.

• Records showed that in April 1999, SBC telephone company received 23,484 slamming complaints, compared to only 15,271 complaints in May 1999.

• Bell Atlantic's records revealed that in March 1999 it received 35,556 slamming complaints but that these numbers dropped to 19,263 in April 1999 and to 15,951 in May 1999.

A group of major long distance carriers – including MCI WorldCom, AT&T, Sprint, and Qwest – sought a waiver of the liability rules, and MCI WorldCom sought a stay while the D.C. Circuit was asked to review them. The rules required telemarketers to receive verification before switching a consumer's long-distance carrier.

Slamming has been the single largest source of complaints to the Commission in recent years. The number of complaints rose from 12,795 in 1966 to 21,868 in 1999, and there were about 3,000 written complaints during the first quarter of 2000. Since April 1994, the Commission has fined eight companies more than $10 million for slamming violations. Another twelve carriers accepted more than $2 million in fines, and there are more than $7 million in pending fines against five companies. The FCC claimed that its enforcement and fines have made a dent in the slamming problem.

### OTHER NEW ELECTRONIC MASS MEDIA

While cable systems provide service to nine of the country's ten multichannel video customers, other technologies also send video signals to viewers. Some federal regulators and members of Congress hope several of these will provide serious competition to cable. Through most of the 1990s, Congress held hearings, and the FCC devised research aimed at producing fair rates. The hope was that this competition would improve cable operators' customer service, reduce prices and increase programming diversity.

### *Direct-to-Home Services*

In 1934, when Congress passed the Communications Act, it did not envision satellites circling the earth and remaining in a fixed position relative to cities below. Science fiction writer Arthur C. Clarke first advanced this concept – known as "geosynchronous orbit" – in 1945.[75] It is not surprising, then, that the Communications Act did not mention direct broadcast satellites (DBS) that use modern technologies such as digital band compression to beam down hundreds of channels of video programming.

Provisions in the Communications Act do not precisely fit DBS, but the FCC clearly has jurisdiction over DBS because satellites use the electromagnetic spectrum to send signals to receiving dishes. The FCC licenses all DBS operations. In 1982, when the Commission faced the issue of how to regulate DBS, it realized that DBS could be seen as (1) a broadcasting service, distributing signals to terrestrial antennas, just as broadcast stations do, or (2) a service much like local telephone companies, renting space on the satellite to anyone who wants to send signals. The Commission chose not to clearly classify DBS and to adopt simplified, flexible regulations to allow it to develop.[76] Broadcasters challenged the fairness of this approach, and a federal appellate court disagreed, in part, with the Commission's strategy.[77]

The court found that DBS met many of the legal characteristics of a broadcast medium and could be regulated in a new way only to the extent that the FCC could justify such distinctions. The court said DBS could be regulated as a non-local broadcast service without the local programming obligations the Commission placed on broadcasters. A later court decision held that DBS was more like subscription services than broadcasting because DBS does not use the spectrum to transmit to the general public.[78] The confusion, which arose partly because of the different ways in which satellites may be used to provide services, caused the FCC to reconsider its terminology as well as its regulatory approach.

The Commission now uses the term "direct-to-home" to comprise services sending video signals to receivers in the United States. One type of DTH service is DBS, the service sending transmissions to receiving dishes eighteen to twenty-four inches in diameter. Operators such as DirecTV and U.S. Satellite Broadcasting offer this service using high-power signals. Another company, PrimeStar, offers DBS service using medium power. DBS is becoming increasingly popular.

The FCC informally refers to a second type of satellite service as "home satellite dish," but its proper name is "fixed satellite service." This service requires a receiving dish, about four to eight feet in diameter. The larger receiver is necessary because HSD uses a lower power signal than does DBS, requiring a larger surface to capture the signal. HSD was the first to develop commercially – particularly in rural and remote areas where stringing cable did not

---

[75] Arthur C. Clarke, *Extra-Terrestrial Relays – Can Rocket Stations Give World-Wide Radio Coverage?*, WIRELESS WORLD, Oct. 1945, at 305.

[76] Direct Broadcast Satellites, 90 F.C.C. 2d 676 (1982).

[77] Nat'l Ass'n of Broadcasters v. FCC, 740 F.2d 1190 (D.C. Cir. 1984).

[78] Nat'l Ass'n for Better Broad. v. FCC, 849 F.2d 665 (D.C. Cir. 1988).

make economic sense.

Under international agreements, the United States had eight positions for DTH satellites in the geosynchronous orbit. Each position used up to thirty-two transmission channels. But with digital signal compression, a technology allowing several signals to be transmitted in the portion of the spectrum previously needed for a single signal, hundreds of channels may fit on a single satellite. In the past, the FCC awarded the orbital positions through competitive hearings or by lottery. Now it auctions the slots; one DBS license auctioned in 1996 for $682.5 million.[79]

Seeking to promote competition among multi-channel video providers, to offer viewers with access to multiple choices for video programming and to strike a balance between the interests of tenants and landlords, the FCC, in 1999, prohibited property owners from unreasonably restricting tenants from installing satellite dishes.[80]

Satellite operators must comply with federal laws and FCC regulations, but they also must operate under standards adopted by the International Telecommunications Union, the worldwide body overseeing spectrum use. U.S. satellite operators need not strictly comply with ITU rules, but ultimately the ITU must approve the deviations from its standards, or the operators must come into compliance.

The 1992 Cable Act required the FCC to establish certain public interest obligations of satellite operators, such as rules regarding political communication, retransmission consent (but not the must-carry rules) and equal employment opportunities.[81] Broadcasters and cable operators argued that DBS had an unfair competitive edge and should have been subjected to government mandated must-carry rules. In 1998, the FCC adopted rules requiring DBS providers to set aside 4 percent of their channel capacity for noncommercial educational or informational programming, as required by the public interest section of the law.[82] The FCC has interpreted the 1992 Act to apply these requirements to DBS operators, but not to HSD services. A federal appellate court held that satellite operators, like cable operators, may use the compulsory copyright license.[83]

The FCC's 1998 ruling also limited programmers to the use of only one DBS channel, and it began the study of options for permitting DBS operators and other DTH services to retransmit local

television signals and provide data services to subscribers. The inability of DTH services to gain access to broadcast programming has limited their ability to compete with cable for viewers.[84] EchoStar, a leading DBS provider, brought a federal lawsuit against the television networks to obtain legal permission for retransmission of programming to residents where over-the-air reception of such signals is marginal.[85]

The broadcast regulation system was originally designed to promote the success of local broadcasters because it was believed they had an ability to serve the unique "public interest, convenience or necessity" of a particular community.[86] Under the 1992 Cable Act, the Commission was instructed to determine whether DBS operators also should be subject to such "localism" rules. Under the Communications Act of 1934, the FCC employed its licensing power to promote local ownership and programming. However, the FCC could not determine how a service that sends a signal nationally and offers a wide variety of programming options could be concerned with "localism" in the same way as a local broadcast station. Regardless, the general trend toward deregulation has led to little emphasis on the concept of localism in the licensing process.

The 1996 Act limited the ability of cities, homeowners' associations and others to place restrictions, such as zoning laws or appearance requirements, on satellite dishes. Congress' intent was to ensure that the growth of DBS would not be stymied. The FCC, in 1998, moved to consolidate and streamline regulation of DBS as a means to encourage and speed growth of the services and to promote competition with cable, whose rates continued to climb.[87]

### Satellite Master Antenna Television Systems

A satellite master antenna television system, also called "private cable," is essentially a cable system contained within an apartment building or several buildings. Similar to cable, a SMATV system collects local TV signals through an antenna and satellite signals through receiving dishes, all placed on top of the building. It sends these signals through wires that run through the building and into individual apartments. The SMATV system may serve other commonly owned buildings on the same plot of private land, and the system's wires will run to and through each building. If the wires go across public rights-of-way, such as a public street,

[79] *See* C. Thomas Veilleux, *EchoStar: Extra Channel Capacity,* 70 HFN, Feb. 12, 1996, at 53. For a broader history, *see* Time Warner Enter. v. FCC, 93 F.3d 957 (D.C. Cir. 1996).

[80] Restrictions on Over-the-Air Reception Devices, Second Report and Order, 63 FR 246, 47 CFR Part 1 (Jan. 22, 1999). *See also* David E. Bronston & Jeffrey A. Moerdler, *Tenants Right to Install Satellite Dish Antennas,* N.Y.L.J., Apr. 23, 1999, at 5.

[81] *See* Implementation of Section 25 of the Cable Television Consumer Protection and Competition Act of 1992, 8 F.C.C. Rcd. 1589 (1993).

[82] *See* Jeffrey P. Cunard, *DBS' Public Interest Duties Given Minimal Definition,* CABLE TV & NEW MEDIA L. & FIN., Dec. 1998, at 1.

[83] NBC v. Satellite Broad. Networks, 940 F.2d 1467 (11th Cir. 1991). *See also* Nat'l Ass'n for Better Broad. v. FCC, 849 F.2d 665 (D.C. Cir. 1988).

[84] *See* Jeffrey P. Cunard, *No Relief for DBS Subscribers Facing Loss of Network Signals,* CABLE TV & NEW MEDIA L. & FIN., Feb. 1999, at 1.

[85] *See* Michael L. Landsman, *EchoStar Takes on TV Networks,* CABLE TV & NEW MEDIA L. & FIN., Nov. 1998, at 8.

[86] *See* CHRISTOPHER H. STERLING & JOHN M. KITTROSS, STAY TUNED, A CONCISE HISTORY OF AMERICAN BROADCASTING 236-37, 557-80 (2d ed. 1990). *See also,* Nat'l Broad. Co. v. United States, 319 U.S. 190 (1943).

[87] Policies and Rules for the Direct Broadcast Satellite Services, Notice of Proposed Rulemaking, FCC 98-26, IB Docket No. 98-21 (Feb. 26, 1998).

the operation becomes a cable, not a SMATV, system.[88] However, the FCC and one court have ruled that a SMATV may use telephone lines to transmit signals across rights-of-way without shedding its status as a non-regulated private cable system.[89]

The FCC has chosen to impose few regulatory burdens on SMATV systems, thus allowing them to develop into competition for cable. Further, the Commission has held that there can be no local or state regulation of SMATV.[90] As a result, the systems must comply with the FCC's equal employment opportunity rules – unless they serve fewer than fifty subscribers – but do not face rate regulation, franchise fees, customer service standards or most of the other regulatory requirements imposed on cable systems.

### Wireless Cable

In 1970, the FCC dedicated part of the spectrum to a service for business communications. By 1974, the Commission realized that part of the spectrum could be used to send video signals to subscribers and established the "Multipoint Distribution Service." The FCC permitted two video channels to be provided in the country's fifty largest markets and one video channel in other markets. It increased the number of available channels in 1983, then again in 1991.[91] The business became known as "Multichannel Multipoint Distribution Service."

"Wireless cable" sent as many as thirty-three channels by microwave signals to small antennas on subscribers' homes. The signals then were sent by wire from the antenna to television sets. Wireless cable used microwaves, part of the electromagnetic spectrum, and, therefore, it was licensed and regulated by the FCC. Because wireless cable did not cross public rights-of-way, it was not considered a cable system and did not require a local franchise.

Wireless cable became a viable business when the FCC permitted its operators to combine their spectrum allocations with other portions of the spectrum dedicated to other types of wireless services. By combining spectrum allocations, wireless cable systems could compete with cable systems in some cities. Wireless cable was helped by the 1992 Cable Act requirement that cable networks offer their programming to wireless cable and other multi-channel multi-point video providers.

The FCC did not permit cities or states to regulate wireless cable operations, and, as with satellite operators, the Commission allowed wireless operators to act as conduits for other video programmers or to themselves provide programming.[92] In either case,

the Commission imposed very few regulatory requirements on wireless cable, but it must approve any non-subscription service supplied by MDS or MMDS.[93] As with DBS, wireless cable services had to comply with the retransmission consent rules requiring operators to obtain permission from any broadcast stations the wireless cable service carries.

In 1997, the FCC issued its first rulings preempting restrictions on the installation and use of satellite dishes imposed by local governments and homeowners associations in four states. That same year, the FCC began a proceeding to adopt more flexible regulation of wireless cable and to encourage use of the medium for interactive services. In a 1998 decision intended to strengthen the floundering wireless cable industry, the Commission adopted rules that allowed MDS operators to offer two-way digital services, such as Internet access and videoconferencing.[94]

The FCC used auctions to award hundreds of wireless cable licenses. As technological advances enabled wireless cable operators to offer a number of video signals on each of their thirty-three channels through digital signal compression, wireless cable licenses became more valuable. Several telephone companies have expressed an interest in purchasing wireless cable operations because the 1996 Telecommunications Act permits telephone companies to provide video services through wireless cable.

In 1998, the Commission auctioned portions of the spectrum to be used for local MDS, which uses transmitters to send voice, data or video within a six-mile radius. The FCC awarded more than 859 LMDS licenses and raised approximately $580 million. The FCC was not expected to permit local telephone companies or cable companies to bid for most LMDS licenses within their service areas, hoping that other small companies will develop LMDS to compete with local telephone and cable services.[95]

### Digital Television

"Digital television" is a term applied to a technological standard for a new form of television, affecting both the transmission and display of television signals. Other terms, such as "advanced television" and "high definition television," also are used to refer to these new standards. The conversion to digital from analog was slowed by the historic investment in traditional analog television systems. The transmission standard in use in the United States since 1941, called "NTSC" for the National Television System Committee, which suggested its adoption to the FCC, was rapidly being phased out in the new century.

An international DTV standard would improve significantly on

---

[88] *See* FCC v. Beach Commc'ns, Inc., 508 U.S. 307 (1993).

[89] *See* City of Austin v. Southwestern Bell Video Services, 1998 U.S. Dist. Lexis 16332 (Aug. 3, 1998). *See also* Frank W. Lloyd, *Litigation Update Court OKs Telco Video Service Without Cable Franchise*, CABLE TV & NEW MEDIA L. & FIN., Sept. 1998, at 8.

[90] *See* New York State Comm'n on Cable Television v. FCC, 669 F.2d 58 (2d Cir. 1982).

[91] Private Video Distribution Systems, 6 F.C.C. Rcd. 1270 (1991).

[92] Multipoint Distribution Service, 2 F.C.C. Rcd. 4251 (1987).

[93] Revisions to Part 21 of the Commission's Rules Regarding the Multipoint Distribution Service, Second Report and Order, FCC 98-70, CC Docket No. 86-179 (Apr. 14, 1998).

[94] *FCC Watch*, CABLE TV & NEW MEDIA L. & FIN., Sept. 1998, at 6.

[95] Rulemaking to Establish Rules and Policies for Local Multipoint Distribution Service and for Fixed Satellite Services, Fourth Report and Order, FCC 98-77, CC Docket No. 92-297 (May 6, 1998).

NTSC transmissions by providing better pictures, DVD-quality sound and a picture shaped more like a movie theater screen than traditional screens. Any of the electronic mass media — broadcasting, cable, SMATV, wireless cable, satellite — could transmit DTV programming, but existing television sets are not able to receive DTV signals and translate them into viewable pictures without a converter box.

DTV development, initially called HDTV, began in Japan in the mid-1960s. Later work was undertaken in Europe on a different HDTV standard incompatible with the Japanese technology. The United States began work on HDTV late, but the delay allowed American companies to use a digital rather than an analog transmission scheme. In 1987, the FCC established the Advisory Committee on Advanced Television Systems to coordinate American HDTV research. After years of work, the "Grand Alliance," comprised of several companies that had been competing to develop DTV, agreed upon a technical standard that is different from Japanese and European electronic engineering.

In 1996, the FCC approved a standard for signal transmission protocols, giving television set manufacturers the confidence to build and sell sets able to receive DTV signals. Televisions compatible with both the Grand Alliance and the FCC standards reached the market, and broadcasters and cable companies began to provide digital programming while simulcasting existing analog programs. Computer companies also sold what were being called PC-TVs or PC-Theater machines that display DTV programs as well as act as personal computers. Many desktop and laptop machines feature video cards and DVD drives capable of handling theater quality digital video.

In 1997, the Commission gave current full-power television broadcasters a second channel to use for DTV. DTV broadcasts have become a reality in most, but not all, markets. Stations are expected to offer programming on both NTSC/analog and digital channels so that existing television sets still may be used. In 1998, the FCC affirmed its commitment that conversion to DTV be completed by the year 2006, when analog channels were scheduled to go dark.[96] However, in early 2006 a provision of the Deficit Reduction Act delayed the death of analog television until February 17, 2009.[97] There has been some pressure on the FCC to impose certain public interest obligations on broadcasters in return for the new digital channels. During the 1990s, the government considered what those should be, with suggestions ranging from free air time for political candidates to not carrying hard liquor advertisements.

While it is expected the transition periods may take longer than the FCC foresees, eventually consumers who want to watch broadcast television will need sets capable of receiving digital signals, or set-top boxes that will convert digital signals to analog without HDTV-quality pictures or sound.

The digital channels allocated in 1997 could be used for high definition television, or for "multiplexing," that is, offering up to four television signals that would be an improvement on current quality but not up to the level of HDTV. Using digital compression, several television signals, plus data and other services, such as paging, could be provided on the spectrum space now devoted to one channel. The 1996 Act states that if broadcasters are given second channels, and they use them to provide services for which they charge a fee, they must compensate the federal government for using those channels.

The digital television revolution is likely to unleash a wide range of interactive, computer-like services that interface with television programming.[98] The digital television spectrum space is now viewed as a lucrative environment for datacasting, according to technology writer Glen Dickson: "Broadcasters are finally seeing DTV as a way to compete in the broadband space with cable MSOs and telcos that are rolling out fast pipes to the home."[99] Still, it is unclear how quickly broadcasters – particularly those in small markets or with small public broadcasting budgets – and their viewers will make the substantial investment to shift to digital. Further, technical issues present roadblocks to fully converting to DTV.[100] It appears that regulators promoting the transition might be overly optimistic about the consumer demand for such new technology. Consumer prices for digital sets have dropped dramatically, and this should help accelerate the pace of adoption. Also, the convergence of TV and computers and telephones offers more promise because consumers have already invested in expensive computer equipment capable of receiving digital TV signals. One RBOC, SBC, has an ambitious plan to offer television services to customers in its thirteen states, but this innovation is not happening very quickly. Verizon is also said to be interested in the digital television business. Nevertheless, the shift from analog VHS tape to DVD and digital video recording equipment promotes excitement about the new digital media age.

### Interactive Video and Data Services

Interactive Video and Data Services combine data transmission and interactivity to permit home shopping, banking and other

---

[96] Advanced Television Systems and Their Impact Upon Existing Television Broadcast Service, Memorandum Opinion and Order, FCC 98-24, MM Docket No. 87-268 (Feb. 23, 1998).

[97] *See* Amy Schatz, *Deadline in 2009 is Set for Digital-TV Switch,* WALL STREET JOURNAL, Dec. 20, 2005, at D1. *Also see* Jim Barnett & Michelle Cole, *Federal Cuts Sting Social Services,* OREGONIAN, February 3, 2005, at B01. The appropriated $7.5 billion from the sale of broadcast rights to assist consumers and public safety agencies make the costly switch from analog to digital signals.

[98] *See* Glen Dickson, *Calling All Digital Tiers,* BROADCASTING & CABLE, May 8, 2000, at 96-98.

[99] Glen Dickson, *Datacasting for Dollars,* BROADCASTING & CABLE, Apr. 24, 2000, at 56-57.

[100] *See* Michael Grotticelli, *A Two-In-One Fix for Digital TV,* BROADCASTING & CABLE, Oct. 1, 2001, at 42-43.

services. Some IVDS providers entered the business by buying available portions of the spectrum through FCC auctions that offered preferences for women and minorities. In 1997, a federal circuit court ruled that a constitutional challenge to these preferences must be reviewed on its merits by the FCC.[101] An IVDS provider argued that the preferences unconstitutionally favored select groups and inflated auction prices. Indeed, the FCC has been concerned by the number of auction and lottery winners who have defaulted.

These developments seemed less important than the broadening low-cost access made available *via* the World Wide Web. For a few hundred dollars, anyone may launch a multimedia site and attempt to compete with major media players without assistance or approval from government regulators. Still, the vast wealth of global media giants created an unfair playing field for true market competition. Digital broadcasters, for example, have begun to collaborate with computer people on interactive programming projects. Microsoft CEO Steve Ballmer predicted that television would seamlessly blend with Internet services."[102] This is likely to become increasingly interesting, as the online world becomes more accessible through portable devices.

## THE INTERNET

The Internet has become a means for people across the globe to be entertained, to exchange electronic mail and to access information through such services as the World Wide Web. The Web has grown from a handful of sites in 1994 to millions of sites today, and global online advertising had apparently surpassed $33 billion in 2004, although the estimates vary.[103] A 2006 estimate places the worldwide number of Internet users at more than 1.1 billion (with 229 million users in North America) and hosts at more than 500 million, with more sites in the United States than any other country. These numbers have grown dramatically each year. In fact, the most recent estimates suggested that more than three-fourths of adults in the United States used the Web, and the global trend was toward ubiquitous access.[104] The number of Web pages has been estimated to be around 55 billion,[105] but nobody knows for sure.

Everyone seems to agree, however, that the Internet will continue to expand and be a dominant force for years to come.

Anyone connected to this international grouping of computer networks can become a publisher, sending material to millions of people in many countries. Called the "national information infrastructure" or the "information superhighway" in the United States, the Internet is being connected to television sets through cable systems and telephone companies. Wireless access to Internet services is threatening to again change the online landscape before the dust settles from the technological revolution of recent years.

The Internet is a part of the convergence of telephone, television and computers, providing an extensive, international broadband network. Some analysts predict that a single broadband network could replace television, radio, telephones, mail, newspapers and other forms of communication. To assure the continued strength and growth of this communications network, some Internet service providers (ISPs) are lobbying Congress for laws that would require local cable television companies to provide access to their lines for Internet use. This policy is known as "unbundling" or "open access."

The Internet presents legal problems, some familiar and some new. For example, communication through the Internet can be undertaken anonymously, copyrighted material can be distributed without the copyright holder's permission, and information stored on computers can be obtained by people with no right to it. In 2000 this was noted when the world organization that registers trademarks and protects copyrights ruled that so-called "cybersquatters" may not buy and sell World Wide Web addresses using for-profit trade names such as the World Wrestling Federation.[106] And Canadian and American broadcasters filed suit against iCraveTV.com, a Toronto company that had been re-transmitting network programs on the Web. Broadcasters maintained their rights to license Web broadcasts of their programs.[107] As time passed, it became increasingly clear that the Web was less revolutionary than first predicted and more an extension of traditional media in terms of American communication law.

### The Internet and Indecency

A portion of the Telecommunications Act of 1996, called the Communications Decency Act (CDA), made it illegal to knowingly send or make available to minors any indecent or obscene material.[108] The CDA was one of four unsuccessful U.S. government attempts (under two presidents and three sessions of Congress) to restrict or filter access by children to pornography, particularly on the Internet. The CDA of 1996, the Child Pornography Prevention

---

[101] Graceba v. FCC, 115 F.3d 1038 (D.C. Cir. 1997).

[102] *See* Ken Kerschbaumer, *Ballmer: Place Your Bets, Microsoft's CEO Pushes Broadcasters to Take Risks in the Media Revolution*, BROADCASTING & CABLE, Apr. 12, 2000, at 13.

[103] *See* First Quarter 2005 Highest Internet Ad Revenue in Nine Consecutive Growth Quarters. Interactive Advertising Bureau. http://www.iab.net/news/pr_2005_6_6.asp.

[104] *See* Internet World Stats, *at* hhttp://www.internetworldstats.com/stats.htm. From 2000 to 2006, the number of users doubled. The top five nations in terms of Internet use are the United States, Japan, the United Kingdom, Germany and Canada. The five fastest growing countries for Internet use are Estonia, Poland, Belgium, Ukraine and Sweden.

[105] *See* Wayback Machine, *at* http://www..archive.org/web/web.php. The number of Internet users in Asia, which has more than half the world's pupulation, is estimated to be 400 million.

[106] *See* WWF *Wins Case Against Cyber-Squatter*, CBC ARCHIVES, Jan. 23, 2000, *at* http://cbc.ca.

[107] *See* CBC *Among Broadcasters Launching Lawsuit Against iCraveTV*, CBC ARCHIVES, Feb. 1, 2000, *at* http://cbc.ca.

[108] 104 Pub. L. 104, tit. 5, 110 Stat. 56 (1996).

Act of 1996 (CPPA), and the Child Online Protection Act of 1998 (COPA) all have failed various legal challenges. In 2003, however, the Supreme Court reversed a lower court and upheld the Children's Internet Protection Act of 2000 (CIPA).

In 1997, the Supreme Court found part of the CDA's indecency provisions unconstitutional. In *Reno v. ACLU,*[109] the Court acknowledged Congress' concern with preventing children from being the targets of, or having access to, sexually explicit communications. But the Court said the CDA's ban on indecency was both vague and overbroad. The law did not define indecency in a way that conformed to previous Court decisions.

In its ruling against the law that would have defined as criminal making such content accessible to children, the Court distinguished the Internet from broadcasting. The Internet does not use the limited public spectrum, and people are not as likely to be exposed inadvertently to sexually explicit material on the Internet as they might be on broadcast stations. Accordingly, adult Internet users should not suffer the reduced First Amendment protections that apply to radio and television station operators, the Court reasoned. However, the Court concluded that obscene material may be banned from the Internet because the First Amendment does not protect any obscene messages, regardless of medium. Most importantly, the Court treated Web site operators as publishers: "Publishers may either make their material available to the entire pool of Internet users, or confine access to a selected group, such as those willing to pay for the privilege."[110] The Court has consistently called for narrowly tailored restrictions on Internet speech and application of traditional obscenity law. From a legal perspective, the Internet was viewed as similar to print media with respect to the First Amendment.

The *Reno* decision reflected the Court's 1989 position in *Sable Communications v. FCC*, when it said Congress may prohibit obscene telephone communications but may not impose a complete ban on indecent "dial-a-porn" messages available *via* telephone for a fee.[111] Although the Court had ruled in 1978 in *FCC v. Pacifica Foundation* that the FCC could constitutionally restrict indecency on broadcast stations,[112] it found in *Sable Communications* that telephones are markedly different from broadcasting. Broadcasting is ubiquitous, uniquely powerful and easily available to children, the Court held. In contrast, a person must consciously and actively choose to access a dial-a-porn telephone service providing indecent material. Likewise, people pay to subscribe to gain access to the Internet, and filtering software is available to assist parents in protecting their children from offensive messages. And pornography sites often are supported by additional user subscription fees. Congress later adopted a law requiring dial-a-porn businesses to make their services available only through a

## FIVE KEY COURT CASES: NARROWLY TAILORING LAWS THAT RESTRICT INTERNET FREE SPEECH

Between 1997 and 2004 the United States Supreme Court addressed issues related to Internet pornography, obscenity and indecency in five important opinions:

• In *Reno v. ACLU* (1997) the Court by a vote of 7-2 found unconstitutional portions of the Communications Decency Act (CDA), which was part of the Telecommunications Act of 1996. The majority found CDA language too vague and rejected Justice Sandra Day O'Connor's call for zoning the Internet.

• In *Ashcroft v. ACLU* (2002) the Court voted 8-1 that the Child Online Protection Act of 1998 (COPA) should be remanded to lower courts to reconsider application of the obscenity test from *Miller v. California* (1973). The case appeared to apply the traditional obscenity test to Internet content. The case was remanded again in 2004 on a 5-4 decision to seek fresh evidence comparing site age verification blocking to user-based filtering software.

• In *Ashcroft v. Free Speech Coalition* (2002) the Court by a vote of 6-3 rejected a ban on "virtual" child pornography, as defined on the Child Pornography Prevention Act of 1996 (CPPA), as violating the First Amendment.

• In *United States v. American Library Assn.* (2003), a lower court decision was reversed in a 6-3 vote. The Children's Internet Protection Act of 2000 (CIPA), which requires libraries supported by federal funds to install filtering software on all computers, was found to be a constitutional and effective measure to block pornographic images deemed harmful to children. The Supreme Court rejected First Amendment arguments that public libraries are a public forum subject to the strict scrutiny standard. Instead, libraries make content-based decisions.

• In *Ashcroft v. ACLU* (2004) (*Ashcroft II*), the Supreme Court, by 5-4 vote blocked the latest iteration of COPA. The Court remanded the case to a lower court and sought fresh evidence on filtering software effectiveness.

pre-subscription arrangement, credit card payment or other method that would make it difficult for children to gain access to the indecent messages.[113] Attempts to enact similar restrictions for the Internet have been more problematic.

While courts use the *Miller v. California*[114] definition of obscenity for print and visual media, questions existed about applying it to the Internet. For example, the Sixth U.S. Circuit Court of Appeals upheld the conviction on federal obscenity charges of two people who operated a computer bulletin board from their California home.[115] The subscriber bulletin board service offered sex-

[109] 521 U.S. 844 (1997).
[110] *Id.* at 853.
[111] 492 U.S. 115 (1989).
[112] 438 U.S. 726 (1978).
[113] 47 U.S.C. 223(b) (1994).
[114] 413 U.S. 15 (1973).
[115] United States v. Thomas, 74 F.3d 701 (6th Cir. 1996). *See also* Pamela A. Huelster, *Cybersex and Community Standards,* 75 B.U. L. Rev. 865 (1995).

ually explicit materials. The couple was charged in Memphis with transmitting obscene material. A postal official had subscribed to the bulletin board, obtained computer files and ordered six video-tapes, all containing sexually explicit material. A jury found that the material violated the local community standards of Memphis and convicted the couple of transporting obscene images across state lines *via* the Internet. The lower court rejected the argument that the ruling effectively established a national standard for obscenity, contrary to the Supreme Court's *Miller* test, or that upholding the conviction would mandate that all material sent over the Internet be no more explicit than permitted by the most restrictive com-munity. The court said the defendants could, and should, have made certain when screening subscribers that their materials would not be received in restrictive communities.

Concerned by the high court's elimination of the CDA's online indecency ban, Congress enacted and President Bill Clinton signed the Child Online Protection Act (COPA) in October 1998 to prevent children from accessing material harmful to minors. Six months later, the U.S. Department of Justice was in the U.S. Court of Appeals for the Third Circuit to challenge a district court order that enjoined enforcement of the new law.[116] In February 1999, a federal judge in Pennsylvania stopped application of Congress' second attempt to shield children from Internet pornography.[117] COPA would have required commercial Web sites to collect credit card numbers or some other proof of age before they allow Inter-net users to access targeted materials. The law called for a fine of $50,000 and up to six months in prison for any commercial pro-vider who knowingly made harmful material available to minors under the age of 17.

In June 2000, an appeals court struck another blow to COPA by upholding the district court ruling.[118] The Third U.S. Circuit Court of Appeals held that the ACLU's attack on the constitution-ality of the act would likely succeed.

Then, in 2002, the Supreme Court held in *Ashcroft v. ACLU* that community standards may be used to identify material that is harmful to minors.[119] Ruling on COPA, the Court found use of *Miller v. California* language distinguishable because all three prongs of the test must be used. While the earlier *Reno* decision failed because only the patently offensive standard was utilized, the COPA statute also employed *Miller's* "prurient interest" and "serious value" tests. Justice Clarence Thomas, writing for the 8-1 majority, reiterated the point that, unlike the first two prongs, the third allows a court to set aside community standards in favor of "whether a reasonable person would find ... value in the material,

taken as a whole."[120] The decision remanded the case for further review by lower courts. Only Justice John Paul Stevens dissented, contending: "In the context of the Internet ... community stan-dards become a sword rather than a shield. If a prurient appeal is offensive in a puritan village, it may be a crime to post it on the World Wide Web."[121]

In 2004, the Supreme Court sided 5-4 with a lower court deci-sion to block COPA, but the case was remanded to update evi-dence on the effectiveness of Internet filters, as well as other exist-ing laws and technologies.[122] In an opinion written by Justice An-thony Kennedy, the Court held: "Content-based prohibitions, en-forced by severe criminal penalties, have the constant potential to be a repressive force in the lives and thoughts of free people."[123] The Court noted that Congress had since passed two other laws, one prohibiting misleading domain names, and another creating a "Dot Kids" domain. The decision to return the case to the district court relied upon the *Reno* decision and the idea that filtering software satisfies the least restrictive means test better than forc-ing commercial Web sites to verify user age. The Supreme Court, however, refused to accept the appellate court conclusion that use of community standards was overbroad. The Court distin-guished and clarified the differences between the district court opinion, which held that the statute must be narrowly tailored to serve a compelling government interest, and the appellate court's unconstitutional finding, which the Court's majority refused to accept without fresh evidence.

The Court's majority sought, by placing the burden on the gov-ernment, to seek less restrictive alternatives: "The purpose of the test is to ensure that speech is restricted no further than neces-sary to achieve the goal, for it is important to assure that legitimate speech is not chilled or punished."[124] The Court affirmed its belief that filters are less restrictive and more effective in blocking all porn sites, not just those in the United States. Minors may be able to obtain credit cards and access a pornographic Web site, and fil-ters also are not entirely effective. However, filters go beyond Web sites and may be used to block e-mail. The Court concluded that parents and libraries may be encouraged to use filters.

Justices Stevens and Ruth Bader Ginsburg would have gone fur-ther. Their concurrence supported the appellate court reasoning that use of community standards warranted striking the law down as unconstitutional.

However, Justice Antonin Scalia dissented, arguing that restrict-ing commercial pornography is consistent with existing law. Justice Stephen Breyer's dissent, meantime, found that COPA ad-vanced a compelling interest and followed the *Miller* test. The

116 *See Recent and Pending Cases,* MULTIMEDIA & WEB STRATEGIST, Apr. 1999, at 8. *See also* Michael Rubinkam, *DOJ to Appeal COPA Injunction,* LEGAL INTELLI-GENCER, Apr. 5, 1999, at 5.

117 American Civil Liberties Union v. Reno, 31 F. Supp. 2d 473 (E.D. Penn. 1999).

118 American Civil Liberties Union v. Reno, 217 F.3d 162 (3d Cir. 2000).

119 535 U.S. 564 (2002).

120 *Id.* at 579 (quoting Pope v. Illinois, 481 U.S. 497, 501 (1987)).

121 *Id.* at 603 (Stevens, J., dissenting).

122 Ashcroft v. ACLU, 542 U.S. 656 (2004).

123 *Id.* at 664. The government has the burden to prove that user-based fil-ters are not at least as effective as site-based age verification systems.

124 *Id.* at 667.

Court was severely divided on the question of whether filters solve the problem, as well as how best to fit restrictions within the requirements of the First Amendment .

In 1999, the Supreme Court had let stand a lower court ruling upholding another part of the Communications Decency Act.[125] The Court issued a one-sentence order that allowed the government to enforce a CDA ban on obscene and indecent e-mail that is intended to harass or annoy the recipient. In *ApolloMedia Corp. v. Reno*, a San Francisco company challenged a provision that made it a felony to initiate "the transmission of, any comment, request, suggestion, proposal, image, or other communication which is obscene, lewd, lascivious, filthy, or indecent, with intent to annoy, abuse, threaten, or harass another person."[126] Annoy.com had allowed people to send anonymous and lewd electronic mail to public officials. San Francisco Attorney William Bennett Turner argued that the provision unconstitutionally punishes indecent material under the *Miller* test:

> There is no conceivable government interest that could justify § 223's content prohibition of "indecent" speech.... The government cannot even advance the interest in protecting children from exposure to "indecent" material — the interest that it unsuccessfully urged to support the other provisions of the Act held unconstitutional.... The provisions at issue here apply regardless of the age of the recipient, govern communications among adults, and have no safe harbor defenses.[127]

Nevertheless, the Supreme Court refused to revisit its earlier decision.

In another case dealing with children's access to sexually explicit materials online, a federal judge enjoined enforcement of a Virginia library's policy to block public access to such Internet sites.[128] While recognizing a compelling government interest in reducing illegal access to pornography, the court suggested that the library had adopted an overbroad policy to address speculative concerns with no evidence of either illegal access or citizen complaints. At issue was whether a public library could use content categories to restrict Internet access. The lawsuit against the library board alleged such a policy violated the First Amendment and was an unconstitutional prior restraint. An earlier ruling declared: "The First Amendment applies to, and limits, the discretion of a public library to place content-based restrictions on access to constitutionally protected materials within its collection."[129] The

court held that receiving Internet information was consistent with the type of public forum routinely offered by the library.[130]

In another twist on the library issue, seven Minneapolis librarians claimed that the amount of pornography on Central Library computers created a "hostile, offensive, palpably unlawful working environment."[131] Library patrons downloading pornographic images prompted at least two bills in Minnesota to require blocking or filtering software on all school and library computers. Ultimately, the library director apologized to the public and announced plans to require sign-ins at workstations, as well as limiting computer use to thirty minutes.

A three-judge panel in the Third Circuit (Philadelphia) at first rejected the Children's Internet Protection Act (CIPA), which requires filtering software on computers at all libraries supported by federal funds. The court unanimously ruled the law unconstitutional.[132] It found filters tended to overblock educational content:

> While most libraries include in their physical collection copies of volumes such as *The Joy of Sex* and *The Joy of Gay Sex*, which contain quite explicit photographs and descriptions, filtering software blocks large quantities of other, comparable information about health and sexuality.... One teenager testified that the Internet access in a public library was the only venue in which she could obtain information important to her about her own sexuality. Another ... witness described using the Internet to research breast cancer and reconstructive surgery for his mother.... Even though some filtering programs contain exceptions for health and education, the exceptions do not solve the problem of overblocking constitutionally protected material ... not only information relating to health and sexuality that might be mistaken for pornography or erotica, but also vast numbers of Web pages and sites that could not even arguably be construed as harmful.[133]

The district court found that the four most popular filtering software programs blocked thousands of Web sites that were not pornographic, and this raised First Amendment issues. The court rejected the government's argument that current technology is

---

[125] ApolloMedia Corp. v. Reno, 526 U.S. 1061 (1999) (without opinion).

[126] Communications Decency Act, 47 U.S.C. § 223(a)(1)(A)(ii); 47 U.S.C. § 223(a)(2).

[127] Brief for Appellant, ApolloMedia Corp. v. Reno, 526 U.S. 1061 (1999), *available at* 1996 U.S. Briefs 511 (Feb. 27, 1997).

[128] Mainstream Loudon v. Bd. of Trustees of the Loudon County Library, 24 F. Supp. 2d 552 (E.D. Va. 1998).

[129] Mainstream Loudon v. Bd. of Trustees of the Loudon County Library, 2 F. Supp. 2d 783, 794-95 (E.D. Va. 1998).

[130] *See* Perry Educ. Ass'n v. Perry Local Educators' Ass'n, 460 U.S. 37 (1983). There are three categories of fora, according to the Supreme Court: (1) a traditional forum, such as a public park; (2) a limited forum, such as a public meeting; and (3) a non-public forum, such as a public employee's mailbox. A library may not be open to all forms of free expression, but it has been designated as a place where the public goes to find information. Under this reasoning, a court might be less sympathetic to someone using a library computer to send information.

[131] *See* Paul Levy, *Minneapolis Public Library Revises Internet Policy*, STAR TRIBUNE, May 18, 2000, at 3B; Paul Levy, *Complaints Filed Over Web Porn*, STAR TRIBUNE, May 4, 2000, at 1B.

[132] American Library Ass'n v. United States, 201 F. Supp. 2d 401 (E.D. Pa. 2002).

[133] *Id.* at 406.

imperfect but effective in blocking most hard-core porn sites. The court accepted the plaintiff's argument against the government that libraries constitute a public forum subject to a strict scrutiny First Amendment analysis:

> Because the filtering software mandated by CIPA will block access to substantial amounts of constitutionally protected speech whose suppression serves no legitimate government interest, we are persuaded that a public library's use of software filters is not narrowly tailored to further any of these interests. Moreover, less restrictive alternatives exist that further the government's legitimate interest in preventing the dissemination of obscenity, child pornography, and material harmful to minors, and in preventing patrons from being unwillingly exposed to patently offensive, sexually explicit content.[134]

The court noted that there are less restrictive options such as enforcement of library rules prohibiting access to pornography or making available unfiltered computers in restricted areas.[135] Instead, the measure would have restricted federal funds to any library that failed to keep minors from visual depictions of content found to be obscene, child pornography or generally harmful to minors. Citing *FCC v. League of Women Voters of California* and other cases, the district court concluded that the government has no right to restrict speech for content reasons: "By interfering with public libraries' discretion to make available to patrons as wide a range of constitutionally protected speech as possible, the federal government is arguably distorting the usual functioning of public libraries as places of freewheeling inquiry."[136] CIPA, which would have been enforced through actions of the FCC and provisions of the Library Services Technology Act, was enjoined from going into effect while the Supreme Court considered an appeal. The Court was faced with a series of arguments outlined by the American Civil Liberties Union about the CIPA law. The ACLU contended:

* It violates the First Amendment.
* Web site blocking is erratic and ineffective.
* It was passed against the advice of Congress' own experts.
* Web blocking is contrary to the mission of public libraries.
* It will widen the digital divide.[137]

Nevertheless, six justices agreed to reverse the lower court and uphold the new law. Chief Justice William Rehnquist, for a plurality, wrote that Internet pornography has been a serious problem for public libraries: "Some patrons also expose others to pornographic images by leaving them displayed on Internet terminals or printed at library printers."[138] The federal government provides two sources of funding to public libraries: (1) discounted rates for Internet access and (2) technology grants for equipment. The Court considered filtering "reasonably effective."[139] Further, the law allows libraries to disable filters "to enable access for bona fide research or other lawful purposes."[140] The plurality rejected the First Amendment issues that the lower court raised but noted library decision-making and the need for broad discretion.

The Chief Justice found instead that "the government has broad discretion to make content-based judgments in deciding what private speech to make available to the public."[141] Funding decisions typically use content-based criteria: "Public library staffs necessarily consider content in making collection decisions and enjoy broad discretion in making them."[142] In this view, a public library is not a public forum: "A public library does not acquire Internet terminals in order to create a public forum for Web publishers to express themselves, any more than it collects books in order to provide a public forum for the authors of books to speak."[143] Instead, the plurality said library resources exist "to facilitate research, learning, and recreational pursuits by furnishing materials of requisite and appropriate quality."[144] Because the Chief Justice found a library is not a public forum, he refused to apply a strict scrutiny standard:

> A library's need to exercise judgment in making collection decisions depends on its traditional role in identifying suitable and worthwhile material; it is no less entitled to play that role when it collects material from the Internet than when it collects material from any other source. Most libraries already exclude pornography from their print collections because they deem it inappropriate for inclusion. We do not subject these decisions to heightened scrutiny; it would make little sense to treat libraries' judgments to block online pornography any differently, when these judgments are made for the same reason.[145]

The decision held that adults may ask a librarian to unblock a site or disable a filter because "the Constitution does not guarantee the right to acquire information at a public library without any risk of embarrassment."[146]

In a separate concurring opinion, Justice Stephen Breyer also rejected the strict scrutiny approach: "The statutory restriction in

---

[134] *Id.* at 410.

[135] *Id. See also* Children's Internet Protection Act, 20 U.S.C.A. § 9134 (2003), at 342; 47 U.S.C.A. § 254, at 359.

[136] *Id.* at 490 n.36, *citing* FCC v. League of Women Voters, 468 U.S. 364 (1984).

[137] *American Civil Liberties Union, Blocking Programs On Trial: Why CIPA is Unconstitutional,* Mar. 30, 2002, *at* http://www.aclu.org/court/CIPA_Intro. html.

[138] United States v. American Library Ass'n, 539 U.S. 194, 200 (2003).

[139] *Id.*

[140] *Id.* at 201 (quoting 20 U.S.C. § 9134(f)(3); 47 U.S.C. § 254(h)(6)(D)).

[141] *Id.* at 204.

[142] *Id.* at 205.

[143] *Id.* at 206.

[144] *Id.* at 204 (holding: "To fulfill their traditional missions, public libraries must have discretion to decide what material to provide their patrons.").

[145] *Id.* at 208.

[146] *Id.* at 209.

question is, in essence, a kind of 'selection' restriction (a kind of editing)."[147] CIPA "seeks to restrict access to obscenity, child pornography, and, in respect to access to minors, material that is comparably harmful."[148] This is especially true when there is a need to be "shielding" children from exposure.[149]

But in a dissenting opinion, Justice Stevens wrote that CIPA "operates as a blunt nationwide restraint on adult access to 'an enormous amount of valuable information' that individual librarians cannot possibly review."[150] He argued that government "may not suppress lawful speech" and reduce adult access to "only what is fit for children."[151] He wrote:

Unless we assume that the statute is a mere symbolic gesture, we must conclude that it will create a significant prior restraint on adult access to protected speech. A law that prohibits reading without official consent, like a law that prohibits speaking without consent, "constitutes a dramatic departure from our national heritage and constitutional tradition."[152]

Justice Stevens saw local library discretion as similar to academic freedom at a university, and penalizing funding violates the First Amendment: "An abridgment of speech by means of a threatened denial of benefits can be just as pernicious as an abridgment by means of a threatened penalty."[153]

In a strident separate dissent, Justice David H. Souter, joined by Justice Ruth Bader Ginsburg, wrote that the CIPA statute "says only that a library 'may' unblock, not that it must."[154] Souter criticized the statute:

Children could be restricted to blocked terminals, leaving other unblocked terminals in areas restricted to adults and screened from casual glances. And of course the statute could simply have provided for unblocking at adult request, with no questions asked. The statute could, in other words, have protected children without blocking access for adults or subjecting adults to anything more than minimal inconvenience, just the way (the record shows) many librarians had been dealing with obscenity and indecency before the imposition of federal conditions.[155]

Justice Souter wrote that a local library could not, on its own, impose adult restrictions. He found CIPA to sanction censorship, not editing of materials. And he said the Court's opinion ignored that when a library does not have a book, a patron may use interlibrary loan to get it. He wrote:

[T]he Internet blocking here defies comparison to the process of acquisition. Whereas traditional scarcity of money and space require a library to make choices about what to acquire, and the choice to be made is whether or not to spend the money to acquire something, blocking is the subject of a choice made after the money for Internet access has been spent or committed... Thus, deciding against buying a book means there is no book (unless a loan can be obtained)... The proper analogy therefore is not passing up a book that might have been bought; it is either to buying a book and then keeping it from adults lacking an acceptable "purpose," or to buying an encyclopedia and then cutting out pages with anything thought to be unsuitable for all adults.[156]

Souter wrote that CIPA and the Supreme Court's support for it defied the history of American libraries. He reminded the Court that by the time of McCarthyism, the American Library Association had explicitly opposed censorship in its own Bill of Rights. The American library tradition has favored adult access to materials and adult inquiry:

Quite simply, we can smell a rat when a library blocks materials already in its control, just as we do when a library removes books from its shelves for reasons having nothing to do with wear and tear, obsolescence, or lack of demand. Content-based blocking and removal tell us something that mere absence from the shelves does not.[157]

Souter concluded: "There is no good reason, then, to treat blocking of adult enquiry as anything different from the censorship it presumptively is."[158]

The Court has become increasingly interested in visiting issues addressed in Internet law, especially when there is concern about children accessing obscene or pornographic content and when children are victimized by the pornography industry.

The question of whether computer animated "virtual child pornography" could be restricted came before the Supreme Court in 2001. An appeals court held that the Child Pornography Prevention Act of 1996 (CPPA) was unconstitutional in prohibiting the use of computer images that do not involve real children but simply appear to be minors.[159] At issue was whether there was a gov-

---

[147] *Id.* at 216 (Breyer, J., concurring) (citing Miami Herald Co. v. Tornillo, 418 U.S. 241, 256-58 (1974)).

[148] *Id.* at 218 (Breyer, J., concurring) (citing Miller v. California, 413 U.S. 15, 18 (1973)).

[149] *Id.* at 219 (Breyer, J., concurring) (citing New York v. Ferber, 458 U.S. 747, 756-57 (1982)).

[150] *Id.* at 220 (Stevens, J., dissenting).

[151] *Id.* at 222 (Stevens, J., dissenting) (quoting Ashcroft v. Free Speech Coalition, 535 U.S. 234, 252, 255 (2002)).

[152] *Id.* at 225 (Stevens, J., dissenting) (quoting Watchtower Bible & Tract Soc. of N.Y. v. Vill. of Stratton, 536 U.S. 150, 166 (2002)).

[153] *Id.* at 227 (Stevens, J., dissenting).

[154] *Id.* at 233 (Souter, J., dissenting).

[155] *Id.* at 234 (Souter, J., dissenting).

[156] *Id.* at 236-37 (Souter, J., dissenting).

[157] *Id.* at 241 (Souter, J., dissenting).

[158] *Id.* at 242 (Souter, J., dissenting).

[159] Free Speech Coalition v. Reno, 198 F.3d 1083, 1086 (9th Cir. 1999)

ernment interest beyond attempting to protect real victims of child pornography.[160] In a 6-3 decision, the Supreme Court ruled CPPA violated the First Amendment.[161]

The Court held that because the statute defined images as "any visual depiction, including any photograph, film, video, picture, or computer-generated image or picture" that "is, or appears to be, a minor engaging in sexually explicit conduct," the language was "overbroad and unconstitutional."[162] The Court explicitly cited *Sable* in rejecting government arguments that virtual child pornography could be used by pedophiles to seduce children.

Justice Anthony Kennedy's opinion found the law went beyond law the Court set forth in its child pornography case, *New York v. Ferber*: "As a general rule, pornography can be banned only if obscene, but under *Ferber*, pornography showing minors can be proscribed whether or not the images are obscene under the definition set forth in *Miller*."[163] However, the restriction on images that are the product of computer morphing were found to be too sweeping. By directly quoting the First Amendment, it was clear that Justice Kennedy and the Court's majority found CPPA to be a disturbing intrusion on First Amendment rights:

[A] law imposing criminal penalties on protected speech is a stark example of speech suppression. The CPPA's penalties are indeed severe. A first offender may be imprisoned for 15 years.... A repeat offender faces a prison sentence of not less than 5 years and not more than 30 years.... While minor punishments can chill speech,... this case provides a textbook example of why we permit facial challenges to statutes that burden expression. With these severe penalties in force, few legitimate movie producers or book publishers, or few speakers in any capacity, would risk distributing images in or near the uncertain reach of this law. The Constitution gives significant protection from overbroad laws that chill speech within the First Amendment's vast and privileged sphere. Under this principle, the CPPA is unconstitutional on its face if it prohibits a substantial amount of protected expression.[164]

The articulation of a "vast and privileged sphere" of First Amendment protection is expansive in terms of the type of speech under the umbrella of safety. Outside the safe zone are "defamation, incitement, obscenity, and pornography produced with real children."[165] By contrast, the Court was concerned that CPPA might render illegal Shakespeare's *Romeo and Juliet* or the popular movie *American Beauty*. CPPA, the Court found, failed to distinguish isolated sexual scenes from the *Miller* requirement to evaluate the "work as a whole." Interestingly, the Court rejected the argument that because virtual child pornography and real child pornography might soon be impossible to distinguish, prosecution would become difficult:

The hypothesis is somewhat implausible. If virtual images were identical to illegal child pornography, the illegal images would be driven from the market by the indistinguishable substitutes. Few pornographers would risk prosecution by abusing real children if fictional, computer images would suffice.[166]

In his concurrence, Justice Thomas wrote that the government failed to provide evidence of any case in which someone charged with production of illegal child pornography had raised reasonable doubt by contending the images were virtual and not of real children.[167]

Justice O'Connor, writing for Chief Justice Rehnquist and Justice Antonin Scalia, offered a partial dissent. They disagreed that CPPA's virtual-child pornography ban was overbroad: "Such images whet the appetites of child molesters, ... given the rapid pace of advances in computer-graphics technology, the Government's concern is reasonable."[168] Chief Justice Rehnquist added in a separate dissent that the CPPA statute had clearly defined explicit content as sex that was "genital-genital," "oral-genital," "anal-genital or oral-anal," "bestiality," "masturbation," "sadistic or masochistic abuse," or "lascivious exhibition of the genitals or pubic area."[169] Chief Justice Rehnquist and Justice Scalia argued unsuccessfully that the definition relates only to hard-core child pornography and not to classic plays or movies.

Attorney General John Ashcroft responded to the decision by suggesting that it provided "a dangerous window of opportunity for child abusers... left law enforcement at extreme disadvantage," and further opened a "thriving market for child pornography."[170]

---

(reviewing the CPPA, 18 U.S.C. § 2556(8) (1996), definition prohibiting depictions that "convey the impression" that they are "sexually-explicit portrayals of minors").

[160] *See New York v. Ferber*, 458 U.S. 747 (1982). Justice Stevens posed a hypothetical example: "If a child actor resided abroad, New York's interest in protecting its young from sexual exploitation would be far less compelling than in the case before us." *Id.* at 779. If a New York theater were offered a serious art film, which contained one lewd scene, a "federal interest in free expression" would be relevant. *Id.* Extended to virtual child pornography, there may be a weak state interest in stopping production and distribution of the content.

[161] Ashcroft v. Free Speech Coalition, 535 U.S. 234 (2002).

[162] *Id.* at 241 (quoting 18 U.S.C. § 2251, 2256(8)(B) and (D) (1996)).

[163] *Id.* at 240 (citing New York v. Ferber, 458 U.S. 747 (1982); Miller v. California, 413 U.S. 15 (1973)).

[164] *Id.* at 244.

[165] *Id.* at 246.

[166] *Id.* at 254.

[167] *Id.* at 259-60 (Thomas, J., concurring).

[168] *Id.* at 263-64 (O'Connor, J., concurring in judgment and dissenting in part). The government contended that advancing technology would allow a pornographer to hide behind the defense that there was no real victim to be found.

[169] *Id.* at 268 (Rehnquist, C.J., dissenting) (quoting 18 U.S.C. § 2256(2) (1996)).

[170] David Stout, *Ashcroft Pushes for Legislation to Ban Virtual Child Pornography*, N.Y. TIMES, May 1, 2002, *at* http://www.nytimes.com.

### Libel on the Internet

Portions of the Telecommunications Act of 1996 not struck down by the Supreme Court's ruling in *Reno v. ACLU* have been used to protect Internet service providers from liability for libel and civil torts.[171] A federal district court in 1998, for example, protected America Online from a libel suit brought by a Clinton administration official and his wife against the Drudge Report.[172] The couple sued after the report, republished on AOL's site, said the husband had a history of spousal abuse. The court relied on the act that protects providers of interactive services from liability for the content of third-party materials. The court said, even though AOL exercises some editorial control and is more than a passive carrier, the law dictates that online providers be protected from liability. Internet gossip columnist Matt Drudge was left to defend himself in the libel suit.

### Copyright on the Internet

The Internet presents questions about protection of intellectual property rights for computer originated and transmitted material. Original material is protected by copyright upon its creation, and the creator has exclusive rights to reproduce and distribute the work, as well as the right to create other works derived from the original. Therefore, uploading a document, copying an Internet posting and re-transmitting the posting without permission all could violate copyright law.[173] Even browsing through material on a computer, which causes a copy of the digital information to be held in temporary memory, could possibly constitute illegal copying. Alternately, this might be interpreted as the digital form of reading a book in a library or a magazine at a newsstand, and not a copyright infringement.[174]

The growth of Internet sites that link to or frame a small section of another site's content raised a new question of copyright infringement. In 1997, the *Washington Post* and five other news organizations charged a group of Internet news sites with copyright infringement for republishing and repackaging the media Web pages for profit.[175] Media organizations charged that the news sites copied their trademarks for use as links and republished their copyrighted material with advertising that generated revenue for the pirates rather than the copyright holders. The suit was settled out of court when the news sites agreed to provide links but not to frame any content from the news organization's sites. The *Los Angeles Times* won its case against FreeRepublic.com – a Web site that reprinted full-text online news stories and invited caustic reader reaction.[176]

Other questions surround the copyright protection of computer-generated materials. To qualify for copyright protection, material must be fixed in a tangible medium and must be original. Therefore, if an online document is a copy of material that already exists on paper, it is unclear whether the online document should be considered "original" and therefore protected. Additionally, it remains to be determined whether material created and transmitted electronically is "fixed in a tangible medium."

For example, a live television broadcast is not fixed in a tangible medium and, therefore, is not protected, unless, for example, it is simultaneously put on videotape. In contrast, a document put on a floppy or hard disk or a CD-ROM is fixed.[177] The question then is whether material created on a computer, sent over the Internet (as e-mail, for example) and then not saved on the computer is fixed in a tangible medium and thus subject to copyright protection. One court has held that material in a computer's random access memory is sufficiently fixed to be protected.[178]

In 1995 and again in 1998, Congress updated copyright laws in part to deal with these issues. Congress enacted the Digital Millennium Copyright Act (DMCA) of 1998 to eliminate an apparent loophole in the Digital Performance Rights in Sound Recordings Act that had permitted Webcasters to digitally transmit recordings without copyright licenses or fees. The new law grants Webcasters a statutory license to transmit, with certain limitations, recordings at fees established voluntarily or by a Copyright Arbitration Royalty Panel.[179] The established fees put an end to many Web casts as cost-prohibitive. For example, some college radio stations ended Web casts when forced to pay as much as $20,000 in additional music licensing fees.[180]

In the meantime, the Supreme Court upheld the Sonny Bono Copyright Term Extension Act of 1998 as a constitutional exercise of congressional powers.[181] The 7-2 decision dismissed concerns about free expression. However, Justices Stevens and Breyer wrote dissenting opinions, which raised concerns about the large proportion of unused content protected under the latest extension. Justice Breyer wrote: "The Copyright Clause and the First Amendment seek related objectives – the creation and dissemination of

---

[171] *See* Zeran v. America Online, 129 F.3d 327 (4th Cir. 1997).

[172] Blumenthal v. Drudge and America Online, 992 F. Supp. 44 (D.D.C. 1998).

[173] *See* Playboy Enters., Inc. v. Frena, 839 F. Supp. 1552 (M.D. Fla. 1993).

[174] *See* Religious Technology Ctr. v. Netcom On-Line Commc'ns Servs., 907 F. Supp. 1361, 1378 n.25 (N.D. Cal. 1995).

[175] Washington Post Co. v. Total News Inc., No. 97 Civ. 1190 (S.D.N.Y., complaint filed Feb. 20, 1997).

[176] Los Angeles Times v. Free Republic, 2000 U.S. Dist. LEXIS 5669, No. 98-7840 (C.D. Cal. 1999).

[177] *See* Mai Sys. Corp. v. Peak Computer, Inc., 991 F.2d 511, 518 (9th Cir. 1993).

[178] *Id. See also* Triad Sys. Corp. v. Southeastern Express Co., 64 F.3d 1330 (9th Cir. 1995).

[179] Miscellaneous Provisions, Title IV of the Digital Millennium Copyright Act, H.R. 2281 (105th Cong., 2d Sess. 1998).

[180] *See* Mark L. Shahinian, *Why College Radio Fears the DMCA*, Dec. 18, 2001, *at* http://www.salon.com.

[181] Eldred v. Ashcroft, 537 U.S. 186, 223 (2003), *reh'g denied*, 538 U.S. 916 (2003).

information."[182] In this view, the two should work together to promote free expression and dissemination of ideas. The law extended the existing copyrights on, for example, Disney's Mickey Mouse for another twenty years to 2023.[183] The extension kept many Twentieth Century icons, as well as lesser known media content, out of the public domain for general use.

On another front, the rock music band Metallica sued the Napster.com site in 2000 for copyright infringement and racketeering over its free software that allowed users to trade MP3 copies of music on an unrestricted basis. The digital music format allowed compact disc quality songs to be converted into a personal computer format, and this made possible the easy distribution of pirated copies over the Internet. The software made it so easy that thousands of music bootleggers clogged university campus network systems.

The international distribution *via* the Internet of illegal copies is a problem for Internet service providers and computer users. A German judge ruled that ISPs may be held liable for their roles in distributing illegal copies. However, the Supreme Court has let stand a New York Court of Appeals ruling that said ISPs are not liable for transmissions, but are akin to telephone and telegraph companies accorded common law qualified privilege against liability.[184] That ruling protected the Prodigy service from a defamation lawsuit. In the Metallica case, two of three universities – Yale and Indiana – blocked access to Napster.com in exchange for being dropped from the lawsuit. The band claimed large numbers of university students were using campus computer systems to access the site and trade pirated music. Metallica also identified 335,000 Napster screen names in 60,000 pages of documents.[185] The Napster.com site posted warnings about copyright, but it has looked away as its software users trade music files. However, Napster ultimately yielded to legal pressures by removing 317,377 users, a move that did not prevent the traders of bootleg music from returning.[186]

At the same time, the company MP3.com settled its lawsuit by halting access to major label songs after a federal district court ruled its database of more than 80,000 songs was copyright in-

fringement against Time Warner, Sony and others.[187] The Web site agreed to pay licensing fees to music companies. The Napster case, though, attracted much attention.

"Napster has built a business based on large-scale piracy," the complaint alleged.[188] The Recording Industry Association of America (RIAA) also sued over the distribution of MP3 music. A district court held that record companies and artists owned the music and issued an injunction prohibiting Napster from "engaging in, or facilitating ... copying, downloading, uploading, transmitting, or distributing ... copyrighted recordings."[189] The Ninth U.S. Circuit Court of Appeals agreed, holding that Napster infringed upon the music reproduction and distribution rights and that the sharing software went beyond a fair use.[190] The court distinguished Internet file sharing from the Supreme Court's ruling in *Sony Corp. v. Universal Studios, Inc.* that video cassette recorders constituted a fair use.[191] Following the decision, Napster was unable to reach an agreement with music companies to compensate them.[192] Subsequently, federal District Court Judge Marilyn Patel in San Francisco ordered Napster to curb trading of copyrighted music.[193] Napster went ahead with plans to develop a fee-based system, even though the company had no initial agreement with record companies.[194] At the same time, alternative services such as Gnutella, Aimster, Grokster and Kazaa prompted new legal challenges, as record companies struggled to develop their own pay sites.[195] Ultimately, the controversy appeared to be moving toward resolution *via* business deals: Vivendi Universal (teaming with Sony and Yahoo! to form Duet) purchased MP3.com for about $372 million; and Bertelsmann aligned with Napster, EMI, AOL Time Warner and RealNetworks to form MusicNet.[196] In 2002, four of five record companies suspended legal action against

[182] *Id.* at 244 (Breyer, J., dissenting).

[183] *See* Lawrence Lessig, *Protecting Mickey Mouse at Art's Expense*, N.Y. Times, Jan. 18, 2003, at A17. Seven justices found that: "[T]he Constitution grants Congress an essentially unreviewable discretion to set the lengths of copyright protections however long it wants, and even to extend them." Linda Greenhouse, *Supreme Court to Intervene in Internet Copyright Dispute*, N.Y. Times, Feb. 19, 2002, *available at* http://www.nytimes.com.

[184] *See* Lunney v. Prodigy Servs. Co., 529 U.S. 1098 (2000). *See also* Richard Carelli, *Supreme Court Lets Stand Decision Freeing Internet Providers from Liability for E-Mail Content*, AP Online, May 1, 2000, *at* http://wire.ap .org.

[185] *See Metallica Delivers List of Alleged Music Pirates to Online Firm*, AP Online, May 5, 2000, *at* http://wire.ap.org.

[186] *See Napster Removes Users*, Cnet News, May 9, 2000, *at* http://www.cnet. com.

[187] *MP3.com Settles Lawsuit*, Reuters, May 10, 2000, *at* http://www.reuters .com.

[188] John Borland, *Metallica Sues Napster, Colleges*, AP Online, Apr. 14, 2000, *at* http://wire.ap.org.

[189] A&M Records, Inc. v. Napster, Inc., 114 F. Supp. 2d 896, 927 (N.D. Cal. 2000).

[190] A&M Records, Inc. v. Napster, Inc., 239 F.3d 1004 (9th Cir. 2001).

[191] 464 U.S. 417 (1984).

[192] *See* Ron Harris, *Napster Offers Millions to Nix Case*, AP Online, Feb. 21, 2001, *at* http://wire.ap.org.

[193] *See* Matt Richtel, *Judge Orders Napster to Police Trading*, N.Y. Times, Mar. 7, 2001, at C1.

[194] *See* Matt Richtel, *Napster Planning Fees Starting in the Summer*, N.Y. Times, Feb. 21, 2001, at C6.

[195] *See* Hana C. Lee, *Aimster Gets the Napster Treatment*, The Standard, May 24, 2001, *at* http://www.thestandard.com.; Rob Tedeschi, *E-Commerce Report: Record Labels Struggle With Napster Alternatives*, N.Y. Times, Apr. 23, 2001, at 7. Aimster, later known as Madster, used instant-messaging to allow file sharing between people on a buddy list. The company said it could not police private Internet exchanges. They were faced with a lawsuit in New York. While it and Napster continued to operate, another firm called "Scour" declared bankruptcy.

[196] *See* Andrew Ross Sorkin, *Vivendi in Deal to Acquire MP3.com*, N.Y. Times, May 21, 2001, at C1.

Napster in order to avoid inquiries into their copyright actions; Napster continued to be threatened with bankruptcy; and Bertelsmann ultimately agreed to pay $8 million for Napster's assets.[197]

While the original Napster no longer exists, services such as Gnutella, Grokster, Madster, KaZaA and a host of others flourished and were faced with various legal challenges in the lower courts. In 2003, the recording industry filed lawsuits against hundreds of people, including parents of teens who illegally shared music online. However, it lost a case before the D.C. Circuit Court of Appeals that would have required Verizon and other ISPs to comply with court subpoenas to turn over the names of customers.[198]

In 2005, the Supreme Court overturned Ninth Circuit Court summary judgments that had insulated Grokster and Streamcast Networks from copyright infringement liability. In *MGM v. Grokster*, the Court held that "one who distributes a device with the object of promoting its use to infringe copyright, as shown by clear expression ... is liable."[199] The peer-to-peer networks featured the sharing of mostly copyrighted works, without any attempt to filter. Instead, the services sold advertising, which was delivered during downloads. The Court found that file sharing was not similar to VCR recording technology, which was protected from liability by the 1984 *Sony* decision. The number of downloads each day influenced the Court in its decision, but the opinion stopped short of revisiting the earlier law: "It is enough to note that the Ninth Circuit's judgment rested on an erroneous understanding of *Sony* and to leave further consideration of the *Sony* rule for a day when that may be required."[200] Digital video recording devices, such as TiVo, however, may hasten the day when the Court will need to reconsider whether the VCR recording protection afforded in the *Sony* case for the purpose of time-shifting program viewing will survive.

The copyright challenges raised the issue of whether Napster-like sites could survive economically by charging user fees to supplement advertising revenues. Napster was forced to show it was eliminating illegal file swapping and creating new software to monitor behavior of users around the world.[201] Thus, the once legal adversaries became partners.[202] One of the success stories is Apple's iTunes Music Store. It allows computer users to legally and swiftly download high quality music for ninety-nine cents per song.[203] The software enables users to listen to thirty-second clips and assemble custom compact discs for under $10.

The copyright liability of online service providers remains unclear. If a subscriber uses one of these services to send material that clearly is protected under copyright, is the service as well as the user guilty of copyright violation? For example, a company could print a hard copy of a magazine and then put the contents online. A user could copy a story from the online magazine and send it to millions of other Internet users. Who is liable?[204] Two courts have found Internet service providers – now called ISPs – liable for their subscribers' copyright infringements,[205] and one has found to the contrary.[206] A key factor affecting the rulings was whether the provider had, or should have had, prior knowledge of the infringement. Online providers who electronically screen or preview material may be held accountable for copyright infringements while providers who act as common carriers may not.

DVD copying is also a serious problem. A former engineering student faced a movie industry lawsuit for publishing on the Internet a code to unscramble encryption for copy protection.[207] Representatives of the Motion Picture Association of America (MPAA) have testified to Congress that an estimated 350,000 movies are being downloaded illegally each day at a cost of billions of dollars to the industry.[208]

The 1995 committee report of the U.S. Patent and Trademark Office to consider copyright questions on the Internet failed to resolve these issues.[209] While the committee suggested that computer transmissions should be considered "copies" similar to photocopies of a book page, it decided that existing copyright law was generally adequate to deal with the Internet.[210]

Conditions are changing so quickly on the Internet that one policy group suggested that Napster and similar file-sharing software should be outlawed. However, measures to protect intellectual property by gathering user data clash with those wishing to increase online privacy protection.

---

[197] *See* Matt Richtel, *Judge Grants a Suspension of Lawsuit on Napster*, N.Y. TIMES, Jan. 24, 2002, at C4; Matt Richtel, *Plaintiffs Sought Timeout After Turn in Napster Case*, N.Y. TIMES, Jan. 31, 2002, at C5; Matt Richtel, *Turmoil at Napster Moves the Service Closer to Bankruptcy*, N.Y. TIMES, May 15, 2002, at C1; John Schwartz, *Bertelsmann, In a Reversal, Agrees to Acquire Napster*, N.Y. TIMES, May 18, 2002; Neil Strauss, *Record Labels' Answer to Napster Still Has Artists Feeling Bypassed*, N.Y. TIMES, Feb. 18, 2002, at A1.

[198] RIAA v. Verizon, 351 F.3d 1229 (D.C. Cir. 2003).

[199] Metro-Goldwyn-Mayer v. Grokster, 545 U.S. 913, 125 S.Ct. 2764, 277 (2005), *remanded*, 419 F.3d 1005 (2005).

[200] 125 S.Ct. at 2779.

[201] *See* Christopher Stern, *Napster Signs Deal to Offer Music from Record Giants*, WASH. POST, June 6, 2001, at E1.

[202] *See* David D. Kirkpatrick & Matt Richtel, *Napster Near Accord on Music Sales*, N.Y. TIMES, June 5, 2001, at C1.

[203] *See* http://www.Apple.com/music/store.

[204] *See* Playboy Enters. v. Frena, 839 F. Supp. 1552 (M.D. Fla. 1993).

[205] *Id. See also* Sega v. MAPHIA, 857 F. Supp. 679 (N.D. Cal. 1994).

[206] Religious Technology Ctr. v. Netcom On-Line Commc'ns Servs., 907 F. Supp. 1361 (N.D. Cal. 1995).

[207] *See* Andrea L. Foster, *Free-Speech Group Backs Former Purdue U. Student Accused in DVD-Decoding Case*, N.Y. TIMES, May 2, 2002, *at* http://www.ny-times.com.

[208] *See* Press Release, Motion Picture Association of America, Valenti Testifies to Studios' Desire to Distribute Movies Online to Consumers (Apr. 23, 2002), *at* http://www.mpaa.or/MPAAPress/.

[209] Working Group on Intellectual Property Rights, Information Infrastructure Task Force, Intellectual Property and the National Information Infrastructure (1995) (White Paper).

[210] *See* Jeri Clausing, *Report Proposes Update of Copyright Act*, N.Y. TIMES, May 22, 2000, at C6.

# KYLLO v. UNITED STATES
## 533 U.S. 27 (2001)

In an unusual 5-4 decision authored by Justice Scalia and joined by Justices Souter, Thomas, Ginsburg and Breyer, the Supreme Court ruled that police had violated Fourth Amendment privacy protections by using thermal imaging technology to identify hot spots within a home produced by marijuana grow lights. In effect, the Court ruled that a warrant was required, and an illegal search had been conducted.

In 1992, Interior Department agents used an imager to investigate suspect Danny Kyllo's Florence, Oregon, home. Using informant tips, utility bills and the imaging, agents obtained a search warrant and found more than 100 marijuana plants. The Court's majority held there was a reasonable expectation of privacy that had been violated: "We think that obtaining by sense-enhancing technology any information regarding the interior of the home that could not otherwise have been obtained without physical 'intrusion into a constitutionally protected area,' ... constitutes a search — at least where (as here) the technology in question is not in general public use. This assures preservation of that degree of privacy against government that existed when the Fourth Amendment was adopted. On the basis of this criterion, the information obtained by the thermal imager in this case was the product of a search."

Justice Stevens dissented and was joined by Chief Justice Rehnquist and Justices O'Connor and Kennedy. They found the majority opinion confusing in that it appeared both to expand and to contract privacy protection by linking it to availability: "[T]his criterion is somewhat perverse because it seems likely that the threat to privacy will grow, rather than recede, as the use of intrusive equipment becomes more readily available." Stevens wrote that the imaging device simply enhanced one's senses: "Just as 'the police cannot reasonably be expected to avert their eyes from evidence of criminal activity that could have been observed by any member of the public,' ... so too public officials should not have to avert their senses or their equipment from detecting emissions in the public domain such as excessive heat, traces of smoke, suspicious odors, odorless gases, airborne particulates, or radioactive emissions, any of which could identify hazards to the community. In my judgment, monitoring such emissions with 'sense-enhancing technology,' ... and drawing useful conclusions from such monitoring, is an entirely reasonable public service." While the majority saw the enhancement as "through-the-wall" surveillance, the dissenters interpreted the majority view to be "off-the-wall" observations.

Florida, police arrested a 41-year-old who had hacked into a home network by parking his SUV nearby and using a laptop computer.[211] The case was considered one of the first instances in the nation in which charges were pressed and raised significant legal issues about what might constitute theft of online bandwidth. In the Florida case, the home owner had failed to encrypt the wireless signal. Further, in apartment complexes, a computer user might "see" more than one access point; and it is possible for there to be confusion over legal (with permission) and illegal access. Clearly, the convenience of wireless networking comes at a price – the availability of signals for potentially illegal activities and the possibility of invasion of privacy of legal and paying users.

### The Internet and Privacy Issues

Privacy protection is difficult on the Internet. At work, employees who occasionally use the Internet for personal reasons could find that their employers have access to everything sent and received online. People using the Internet from home for such services as banking or shopping and for sending e-mail messages could find they have less privacy protection than when engaging in such activities by mail or in person.

New technologies also have threatened to erode traditional common law views about the sanctity of privacy in one's home. Privacy becomes a question when law enforcement authorities want to tap into computer transmissions the way they do telephone calls. While a court order is required for either, it may be possible for computer users to encrypt transmissions. In 1993, the National Security Agency proposed a clipper chip, a technology to allow decoding of encrypted messages. The government's homeland security efforts since September 11, 2001, to fight terrorist threats also have caused new privacy concerns.

Web-based telephone services, such as Vonage, posed an interesting problem for regulators and the courts. The U.S. Court of Appeals, District of Columbia Circuit, upheld the Federal Communications Commission decision that law enforcement agencies required wiretap-compatibility. However, the court exempted university and private and networks, as well as instant messaging.[212] The clarification of the scope of the Communications Assistance for Law Enforcement Act, CALEA, meant that voice over Internet protocol (VoIP) was not exempt from telecommunication regulation under all circumstances.

Another privacy issue involves Web site content that is considered a threat. A federal jury in Portland, Oregon, ordered abortion protesters to pay $109 million in damages resulting from the Nuremberg Files site.[213] The site was ordered closed down for re-

A new problem has arisen from the theft of wireless network signals from homes and business. At times, people have been found to be breaking into private networks in order to facilitate their illegal file transfers. In 2005, for example, in St. Petersburg,

---

211 See Alex Leary, WiFi Cloaks a New Breed of Intruder, ST. PETERSBURG TIMES, July 4, 2005, at 1A.

212 American Council of Educ. v. FCC, 2006 U.S. App. LEXIS 14174.

213 See Planned Parenthood of Columbia/Willamette, Inc. v. Am. Coalition of Life Activists, 41 F. Supp. 2d 1130 (D.Or. 1999).

## JESSUP-MORGAN v. AMERICA ONLINE
### 20 F. Supp. 2d 1105 (S.D. Mich. 1998)

In 1996 a court granted Philip Morgan a divorce from Barbara Smith-Morgan in Michigan. Within weeks, Philip Morgan married Terry Jessup-Morgan, although the couple had a lengthy relationship prior to the divorce. Jessup, prior to the divorce and subsequent marriage, used her AOL screen name "Barbeeedol" to harass Barbara Smith-Morgan with the following posting:

Call me.... I'm single, lonely, horny and would love to have either phone sex or a [sic] in person sexual relationship....
My name is Barbara and I'm a single white female looking for just about any kind of sex I can have with someone other than myself....
If you can help, call me at (810) 977-9476

The telephone number was Barbara Smith's parents' home, where she and her two small children were staying during the messy divorce. The message had been posted on the newsgroup "alt.amazon-women.admirers." To the distress of Smith and her parents, a number of people called the phone number. Smith's brother, Kenton, used his AOL account to find the posting. He informed AOL of the problem *via* e-mail and asked for the identity of "Barbeeedol." In response, AOL terminated Jessup's account for "excessive USENET abuse" but informed Kenton that it only identified users "in response to a subpoena." Barbara Smith's divorce attorney served AOL with a civil subpoena in February 1996, and AOL responded by identifying "Barbeeedol" as Jessup.

Terry Jessup-Morgan later sued AOL, claiming release of her identity to Barbara Smith was "unlawful, tortuous, and a breach of contract." She alleged:
1. The release of stored electronic information violated the Electronic Communication Privacy Act;
2. AOL breached its contract;
3. AOL's release of information was negligent;
4. AOL engaged in fraud and misrepresentation in its contract;
5. AOL invaded her privacy and disclosed private facts about her;
6. AOL violated the Michigan Consumer Protection Act; and
7. AOL violated the Michigan Pricing and Advertising of Consumer Items Act.

Jessup admitted her fraudulent Internet posting, but she argued that the release of information by AOL adversely affected her child custody hearings and Philip Morgan's divorce case. Lawyers for AOL sought summary judgment and dismissal of the case in their favor.

The court found that Jessup, to become an AOL member, had agreed to Terms of Service that prohibited use of the online service to "harass, threaten, embarrass, or cause distress." The court found that the Electronic Communication Privacy Act was inapplicable in the case because identifying someone was "separate from the 'content' of electronic communication," and quoted the ECPA:

Except as provided ... a provider of electronic communication service or remote computing service *may* disclose a record or other information pertaining to a subscriber to or a customer of such service (not including the contents of communications covered by ... this section) to any person *other than a government entity.*

Jessup-Morgan's behavior was found to be a breach of the AOL contract, and the court issued summary judgment in favor of America Online on that claim. U.S. District Judge John Feikens ruled in favor of America Online on all seven claims, and the case was dismissed. The ruling made it clear that online users are subject to identification when an Internet service provider is subpoenaed for the information. The case might have implications for online journalists wishing to protect anonymous sources of information published, particularly if a source used e-mail to offer a reporter information. Faced with a subpoena, an ISP would likely disclose the identity of an e-mail screen name. Thus, it might be impossible for a reporter to guarantee anonymity to a source using e-mail if the screen name of the source became known.

---

sembling a hit list of abortion providers, some of whom were the victims of anti-abortion violence.[214] Names and towns of doctors providing abortions were listed on the site that featured dripping blood and fetus parts. The case was appealed on First Amendment grounds, and one legal scholar worried about the dangerous

precedent: "If [the case] is upheld on appeal the decision may be used in the future as a precedent to hold protesters liable for the violent acts of others."[215]

### Beyond the Internet and Future Regulatory Issues

The 106th Congress proposed at least fifty bills seeking to regulate

---

[214] *See* Ashley Packard, *Threats or Theater? Does* Planned Parenthood v. American Coalition of Life Activists *Signify That Tests for "True Threats" Need to Change?*, 5 COMM. L. & POL'Y 234 (2000).

[215] *Id.* at 266.

various aspects of the Internet – pharmacy consumer protection, online investor protection, spam advertising limitations, e-mail protection and e-commerce protection.[216] One bill sought to limit sales of prescription drugs by requiring Web sites to include a page that lists licensed pharmacists.[217] The mood to regulate was promoted by cases such as that of a Seattle doctor ordered to halt online prescribing of the sexual dysfunction drug Viagra after a sixteen-year-old boy and a woman posing as a man obtained prescriptions.[218] The Food and Drug Administration raised concerns about the rampant online sale of prescription drugs. State attorneys general, meanwhile, maintained that licensing and monitoring of health care professionals should continue to be a matter of state regulation. Nevertheless, former U.S. Senate Democratic Leader Tom Daschle of South Dakota concluded that Congress had not kept pace with technological change: "Internet users are often promised basic privacy protection, only to have their expectations disappointed and their personal information put up for sale or disseminated in ways to which they never consented."[219]

The global nature of telecommunications will pose new challenges. In the United Kingdom, for example, the government has plans for a spy center capable of tracking every e-mail and Web site hit, but civil libertarians were outraged by the multi-million dollar effort to crack down on cyber crime.[220] It was clear that as the integration of the Internet and television continued to advance the pressure to regulate at all levels of government would remain strong.[221] Author Ken Auletta has observed that we live in a confusing time with respect to mass media: "I think we have to look at the world as a great paradox.... On the one hand, you've got growing concentration.... On the other hand, you've got this democratic instrument, this technology, that basically challenges companies."[222] Daschle's Electronic Rights for the Twenty-First Century Act was not given serious consideration. There was, however, some support in 2001 for the Platform for Privacy Preferences standard that would allow online consumers to manage their personal data.

## SUMMARY

This chapter has focused on how technological and social

changes may create new legal and regulatory issues. The focus on telephones, digital television and the Internet led people to think about the predicted convergence of online and wireless media. It is predicted that the courts, as they have done with other so-called "new technologies," will continue to struggle to find legal and regulatory standards that pass constitutional muster years after the technological developments are no longer new.

Changing social and political conditions with the fallout from the September 11, 2001, terrorist attacks presented a new level of complexity. New communication technologies may be used for good or evil, and regulators struggle to allow for advancements without making it easier to harm people.

The Web continues to present new issues: fraudulent business practices, the sale of World Trade Center items on eBay auctions, and attempts by France to impose fines on Yahoo! for sale of Nazi memorabilia, in violation of French law.[223] The boundaries and limitations of communication and business in cyberspace remain unsettled. As one scholar of computer-mediated communication has noted, digital and Internet technologies present a paradox: "Utopian and dystopian views about the future of the Internet describe two very different future scenarios."[224] Faced with such uncertainty, we are likely to see much action within the courts, as parties dispute the virtual landscape.

In the business world, communication technologies remain very important. Competition between previously separate industries, such as is happening with cable and telephone companies, have created unfair situations that may force future government intervention.[225] At the same time, advances in technology will continue to present new legal challenges to the First Amendment freedom of speech and press.

In conclusion, the study of communication technology, cyberspace law and telecommunication issues on the Internet presents many challenges and opportunities. Within the broader context of communication and the law, regulation and court challenges are literally redefining the field.

## FOR ADDITIONAL READING

Bagdikian, Ben H. *The Media Monopoly*, 6th ed. Boston: Beacon Press, 2000.

Barnes, Susan B. *Computer-Mediated Communication, Human-*

---

[216] *See* Thomas, 106th Congress (1999-2000), Bill Text, *at* http://thomas. gov.

[217] Internet Pharmacy Consumer Protection Act, H.R. 2763, § 503B (Aug. 5, 1999).

[218] *See* Carol M. Ostrom, *Doctor Told to Halt Internet Prescriptions,* SEATTLE TIMES, Jan. 29, 2000, at A9.

[219] Tom Daschle, Report Card of the 106th Congress on Privacy, United States Senate, Dec. 14, 2000, *at* http://www.thomas.loc.gov.

[220] *See To Civil Libertarians, It Smacks of Big Brother.com,* AP ONLINE, May 11, 2000, *at* http://wire.ap.org.

[221] *See Couch Potatoes: Let Your Fingers Do the Talking,* NEWSWEEK, Jan. 17, 2000, at 57.

[222] Cable News Network, Millennium 2000: Media in the New Century (Jan. 1, 2000), Lexis-Nexis database, News/Transcripts/CNN.

---

[223] *See* Michael Cooper, *eBay is Asked to Remove Trade Center Items,* N.Y. TIMES, Feb. 22, 2002, *at* http://www.nytimes.com.; Carl S. Kaplan, *French Decision Prompts Questions About Free Speech and Cyberspace,* N.Y. TIMES, Feb. 11, 2002, *at* http://www.nytimes.com; Jennifer Lee, *3 Web Sites Closed In Spam Inquiry,* N.Y. TIMES, Mar. 12, 2002, at C6, *available at* http://www.nytimes.com.

[224] SUSAN B. BARNES, COMPUTER-MEDIATED COMMUNICATION 331 (2003).

[225] *See* Seth Schiesel, *Cable Giants Refuse to Sell Ads to Internet Competitors,* N.Y. TIMES, June 13, 2001, *at* http://www.nytimes.com. Time Warner Cable in New York refused to sell advertising to Verizon Communications promoting high-speed DSL Internet service that competes with cable modem service, and no laws or regulations appeared to prevent the block on competitors.

*to-Human Communication Across the Internet.* Boston: Allyn and Bacon, 2003.

Bucy, Erik P. *Living in the Information Age, A New Media Reader.* Belmont, Calif.: Wadsworth, 2002.

Hester, D. Micah, & Paul J. Ford, eds. *Computers and Ethics in Cyberage.* Upper Saddle River, N.J.: Prentice Hall, 2001.

Jashua, Gay, ed. *Free Software, Free Society: Selected Essays of Richard M. Stallman.* Boston: GNU Press, 2002.

Lievrouw, Leah A., & Sonia Livingstone, eds. *The Handbook of New Media, Updated Student Edition.* London: Sage, 2006.

Lipschultz, Jeremy H. *Free Expression in the Age of the Internet, Social and Legal Boundaries.* Boulder, Colo.: Westview Press, 2000.

Lister, Martin, Jon Dovey, Seth Giddings, Iain Grant & Kieren Kelly. *New Media: A Critical Introduction.* New York, NY: Routledge, 2003.

McChesney, Robert W. *Rich Media, Poor Democracy, Communication Politics in Dubious Times.* Urbana, Ill.: University of Illinois Press, 1999.

Rogers, Everett M. *Diffusion of Innovations,* 4th ed. New York: Free Press, 1995.

# 13

# Regulating Student Expression

*By Thomas Eveslage*

---

 **Headnote Questions**

- *How do the free expression rights of students differ from the rights of other citizens?*
- *Why are the free expression rights of high school and college students different?*
- *Why is it important that high school and college publications be identified as public forums?*
- *How and why do student press freedoms differ from freedom for the professional media?*
- *Under what circumstances can school or college officials restrict the free expression rights of students?*
- *What problems has computer technology posed for school officials trying to regulate student expression?*

---

Public high schools and colleges have changed in the thirty-eight years since the U.S. Supreme Court said that students do not "shed their constitutional rights to freedom of speech or expression at the schoolhouse gate."[1] Today we know that not all schoolhouse gates are the same. Some have narrow passages. Over-protective gatekeepers guard others.

Yet the Supreme Court's premise remains: Students are citizens even when they're on school property. The Court has said that no mental detector should prevent students from bringing their beliefs to school or to college and expressing them. Educational institutions, the Court implied, can be laboratories for young citizens trying to grasp the First Amendment's meaning and applications.[2]

High schools and universities are microcosms of society — with government-like figures of authority; with co-existing organizations, social classes and races; and with student media trying to interpret and help their audiences understand their learning communities. An examination of freedom of speech and press within the educational environment is a lesson in the scope and boundaries of individual liberties.

Just as all citizens discover that freedom of expression has strings attached, student journalists learn that they do not have the absolute freedom to say anything they want, anywhere they want. Courts have ruled that the First Amendment lets government officials regulate in a reasonable way where, when and how citizens speak, as long as those officials have valid reasons and are not suppressing ideas just because the government does not like them.

Student journalists, especially those on college publications, have many of the freedoms accorded their professional counterparts. Both groups face similar legal obligations and are subject to the same standards regarding libel, privacy, copyright and even the more peripheral student media concerns of broadcast regulation and confidentiality of sources.

Because the education of young people is of paramount concern in society, educators have some legal latitude when regulating speech on school property. But differences between high school and college experiences and educational objectives often lead judges to rule differently in the two settings. Because the learning environments are different, as are the age and maturity of their students and the responsibilities of those in charge, the freedom available and school officials' ability to restrict that freedom vary from high school to college.

Some free-speech concerns — especially prior restraint and access to information — pose special problems for the student

---

[1] Tinker v. Des Moines Indep. Sch. Dist., 393 U.S. 503, 506 (1969).

[2] *See* Nadine Strossen, *Keeping the Constitution Inside the Schoolhouse Gate — Students' Rights Thirty Years After* Tinker v. Des Moines Independent Community School District, 48 DRAKE L. REV. 45 (2000).

press. Denial of access to crime statistics and disciplinary proceedings has led to conflicts with college administrators. Censorship has been more of a problem for the high school press, primarily because courts give public officials more latitude when protecting children from potentially harmful material, and administrators interpret "harmful" broadly.

Fear and uncertainty regarding the Internet and the public's concerns with personal safety following the terrorist attacks of September 11, 2001, and the war in Iraq have chilled serious, sometimes intense, discussion of controversial topics on high school and university campuses. Compounding the problem, college students boldly proclaiming their actions to be personal, public "expression" have stolen newspapers carrying controversial content.

Since the 1999 shootings at Colorado's Columbine High School and 9/11 terrorist attacks, parents and the public seem more willing to give authorities latitude in controlling the school environment and student expression, and less-tolerant, more vigilant school officials have followed some students home to punish what they are saying on their personal Web sites.[3] To complicate matters, Supreme Court rulings of the past decade reveal both support for free-speech tolerance in the schools and reluctance to curb administrative authority. And although a federal appellate court in 2001 strongly rebuked arguments that college publications share the same free-speech constraints as the high school press, the appellate court in a neighboring circuit in 2005 suggested that a 1988 U.S. Supreme Court case limiting speech rights in the high school could be applied to colleges and universities.[4]

This chapter reviews principles of free expression as they extend to students. Court cases affecting the student media reveal legal arguments used to limit students' freedom of speech and how the physical environment, the age of young citizens, societal interests, computer technology and public-forum theory affect the expressive rights of students.

## A FRAMEWORK FOR STUDENT EXPRESSION

Most Americans understand that citizens are not free to speak or publish anything they wish, that there are limits and penalties, that circumstances affect constitutional liberties. To understand

that concept better, college students only have to look around or think back to their high school days. Whether individually or as student journalists, they have experienced some of the societal tensions that influence free expression.

### School as Society

At least in public colleges and high schools, a microcosm of American society exists that can help young citizens learn and appreciate what "free speech" and "free press" mean. This society has organizations and social classes, rules established to benefit all citizens, various outlets for free expression and government officials who make and enforce regulations.

When the abstract principle of free expression becomes real in the educational laboratory, high school and college journalists learn what professionals know — there is no special free-speech privilege for the press. By balancing legal rights and ethical responsibilities, journalists maintain credibility and earn public support.

The college campus more closely parallels society than does the high school, where students today often must express themselves responsibly or risk losing their freedom. Adults, including college students, have not faced that limitation. In fact, as will be demonstrated, courts historically have considered college campuses to be public forums where students' freedom to exchange ideas is central to the educational mission. Just as government officials have little power to stop or punish professional journalists who express unpopular or embarrassing ideas, college administrators historically have had little control over content of the student press.[5] There still are efforts to control expression — by citing campus speech codes, by creating "speech zones" on campus, by denying the student press access to information about crime on campus, by refusing to punish those who steal or destroy student newspapers and, most recently, by refusing to recognize student publications as public forums.

### The Legal Foundation

Students and educators have asked the courts to address two central questions: How does one balance the competing interests of individual freedom and institutional responsibility? And how much intellectual freedom do young citizens have while in high school and college? A review of court guidance reveals common ground for the First Amendment within high schools and colleges and beyond those institutions' boundaries. The legal foundation was laid more than sixty years ago.

In 1943 the Supreme Court told students that they bring the

---

[3] Public support for the rights of high school students remains low. The Freedom Forum's 1999 State of the First Amendment report revealed that 71 percent of adults surveyed believe students should not be allowed to wear t-shirts with messages or pictures "that others may find offensive." In 2004, 72 percent agreed with this statement; in 2005, 73% agreed. In 2001, the Freedom Forum's First Amendment Center released research results showing that 71 percent of high school teachers and administrators believe student journalists should not be allowed to report on controversial issues without school officials' approval. *See also Legal Requests to the SPLC Continue to Grow*, STUDENT PRESS LAW CENTER REP., Fall 2003, at 3; *Censorship on the Rise*, STUDENT PRESS LAW CENTER REP., Fall 2002, at 3.

[4] *See* discussion accompanying *infra* note 70.

[5] Less freedom exists for broadcast journalists than for print journalists on the university campus. *See First Amendment on the Air*, STUDENT PRESS LAW CENTER REP., Spring 2000, at 29. But editorial discretion survives. *See* Knights of the Ku Klux Klan v. Curator of the Univ. of Missouri, 203 F.3d 1085 (8th Cir. 2000).

right of free expression with them to school. In *West Virginia State Board of Education v. Barnette,*[6] it applied the long-standing free speech concept that government should neither require nor suppress expression. A high school policy requiring students to pledge allegiance to the flag, the Court ruled, unconstitutionally forced them to express beliefs they did not hold. When sitting in silent protest does not interfere with other students' rights, school officials may not punish such expression.

Despite the *Barnette* ruling, the prevailing judicial sentiment for the next quarter century would be that public school officials have a parent-like role that entitles them discretion in their control of high school students. First Amendment cases with a college setting did not reflect this attitude, however. Differences in the environment, maturity of students and educational function led courts to view public-college administrators as facilitators rather than parents.

### Strengthening the Foundation

High school and college students, including young journalists, received a boost when the high Court revisited the public school twenty-six years after *Barnette* and stated more emphatically that constitutional rights extend to students, even when they're on public-school property. *Tinker v. Des Moines Independent School District*[7] focused on the limits that public school officials have in the regulation of student expression. What the Court said about students, administrators and the educational environment had sweeping implications that touched all young citizens, including student journalists.

Mary Beth and John Tinker and their friend Christopher Eckhardt wore black armbands to school in December 1965 to express their opposition to the Vietnam War. Their form of silent protest clashed with a hastily prepared school policy. Officials thought that such expression was conduct and would disrupt the school. When the students refused to remove the armbands, they were suspended and sent home.

Legal action challenging the suspensions raised larger questions about whether fundamental First Amendment principles the Court applied outside of the school setting would pertain in school as well. Some questions were:

- Would any special circumstances justify different standards for regulating student expression?
- Is it protected symbolic speech or unprotected conduct to wear an armband to school?
- Will public school officials have to meet the same burden that courts have placed on other government regulators?
- What overriding interests would justify suppressing student expression?

Federal district and circuit court rulings in *Tinker* upheld the suspensions, reflecting the prevailing view that school officials should be given broad authority. The Supreme Court disagreed, ruling 7-2 that students, even when they're in school, share First Amendment protection with other citizens. The freedom has limits, but, the Court ruled, public school officials who wish to restrict expression must meet the burden of other government decision-makers and justify suppressing or punishing speech.

Officials obligated to maintain an orderly learning environment can control student behavior inside the high school. The *Tinker* Court, however, ruled that wearing an armband is not conduct but a symbolic form of speech that can be stopped or punished only when educators can show that such expression would cause a "substantial disruption of or material interference with school activities."[8]

*Tinker* tells us that, whether on or off school grounds, public officials are not to stop or punish speech solely because they find it offensive. In the words of Justice Abe Fortas, writing for the Court:

> Students in school as well as out of school are "persons" under our Constitution.... In our system, students may not be regarded as closed-circuit recipients of only that which the State chooses to communicate. They may not be confined to the expression of those sentiments that are officially approved. In the absence of a specific showing of constitutionally valid reasons to regulate their speech, students are entitled to freedom of expression of their views.[9]

The Supreme Court placed the burden on school officials, but offered several valid reasons that would justify regulation. The most common, and the one most often challenged in court, is the school's claim that expression would disrupt the educational process. A reasonable forecast of "material and substantial disruption" justifies suppression of speech, the Court said, but officials must show a factual basis for their prediction.

Another argument used to restrict student expression is that *Tinker* does not protect speech that is an invasion of the rights of others. High school officials have used this to justify censorship of defamatory material or, as in *Hazelwood School District v. Kuhlmeier,*[10] discussed later in this chapter, because of fear that content invades someone's privacy. Because libel and privacy are defined no differently inside the school than outside, the student press and professional media are equally vulnerable, but share the same legal defenses.

---

[6] 319 U.S. 624 (1943).
[7] 393 U.S. 503 (1969).
[8] *Id.* at 514.
[9] *Id.* at 510.
[10] 484 U.S. 260 (1988).

### The Tinker Philosophy

The Supreme Court brought the First Amendment onto school grounds with *Tinker* because educational institutions are appropriate laboratories for learning the marketplace of ideas philosophy. "Freedom of expression would not truly exist," the Court said, "if the right could be exercised only in an area that a benevolent government has provided as a safe haven for crackpots."[11]

The Court knew the risks of free speech, but was willing to take those risks with young people. As Justice Fortas wrote:

> Any word spoken in class, in the lunchroom, or on the campus, that deviates from the views of another person may start an argument or cause a disturbance. But our Constitution says we must take this risk.... Our history says that it is this sort of hazardous freedom — this kind of openness — that is the basis of our national strength and of the independence and vigor of Americans.[12]

The Student Press Law Center, an Arlington, Virginia-based source of legal advice and support for student journalists, considers *Tinker* "undoubtedly the most important student First Amendment case in the nation's history."[13] Little wonder. State and federal courts have cited *Tinker* in hundreds of high school and college cases. Free-speech advocates value the Court's emphasis on individual liberties and its assertion that speech — even on school property — is protected unless officials can demonstrate a reason to restrict it. With *Tinker*, a free-speech philosophy applied to all citizens clearly embraced high school students. And the case provided a solid foundation for a long line of higher-education cases that declare college students to be adults worthy of rights accorded citizens off campus.

*Tinker* was a *student rights* case, but not a *student press* case. During the 1970s and 1980s, however, many lower courts adopted the *Tinker* philosophy and applied it to cases involving student publications. Courts saw public high school and college students as citizens, and officials in all public institutions as arms of the government. More recently, the Supreme Court reminded school officials that they could not sponsor student-led prayer before football games, but also could not allow an outside group such as the Boy Scouts to use school facilities while denying access to another group simply because it was a religious organization.[14]

### Limitations in Private Schools

It's different in private institutions. The First Amendment does not tell citizens that they must speak or what they must say if they do; it tells government not to interfere with their expressive rights. The First Amendment applies, therefore, when there is government involvement or what is called "state action." When taxpayers are not heavily funding an educational institution or dictating its policies — and when those making decisions for it are not elected by, paid by or working for taxpayers — there is no state action. The assumption is that private-school officials are not obligated to abide by First Amendment constraints on government.

Students in private institutions, then, do not have First Amendment protection within those institutions.[15] But that does not mean that students cannot be given the "right" to express themselves. Where a private school's promotional material or written philosophy, policies and practices promise certain freedoms, students may argue that reneging on those promises constitutes breach of contract.[16]

A state's constitution and legislature may be additional vehicles for private-school students to obtain free-speech rights. In 1995, a California superior court upheld what then was the only state law in the country that extended First Amendment protection to students at private, post-secondary schools. In *Corry v. Stanford University*,[17] the court found the university's speech code unconstitutional and rejected Stanford's argument that as a private school it was not bound by the First Amendment. The state's content-neutral 1992 Leonard Law extended First Amendment protection to more California citizens (those on private-college campuses), the court said. It does not require a university to express ideas or to provide a platform for speech, the court added, nor would it lead the public to associate a college with ideas expressed on its campus.[18]

Despite this ruling, the reality is that beyond the walls of California educational institutions First Amendment protection extends to private-school students only when those who operate such schools and colleges allow it or a state constitution provides it.[19] If private-school practices and stated policies permit expression, students can benefit from them. If restrictions abound, students may stay at the school and abide by its rules or transfer to a public institution or a more permissive private school.

---

[11] 393 U.S. at 513.

[12] *Id.* at 508.

[13] LAW OF THE STUDENT PRESS 27 (2nd ed. 1994).

[14] *See* Good News Club v. Milford Central Sch., 533 U.S. 98 (2001); Santa Fe Ind. Sch. Dist. v. Doe, 530 U.S. 290 (2000).

[15] *See Legal Guide for the Private School Press*, STUDENT PRESS LAW CENTER REP., Winter 2002-03, at 33, *available at* http://www.splc.org/legalresearch.

[16] LAW OF THE STUDENT PRESS, *supra* note 13, at 65-73. *See also* Schaer v. Brandeis Univ., 735 N.E.2d 373 (Mass. 2000).

[17] No. 740309 (Cal. Super. Ct., Santa Clara Cty., Feb. 27, 1995).

[18] The Leonard Law is the basis of a lawsuit filed by Jason Antebi, who claims his firing as a host on KOXY, Occidental College's student radio station, violated his constitutional rights as a student at the California private college. *See Former Calif. University Shock Jock Sues School for First Amendment Violations*, STUDENT PRESS LAW CENTER NEWSFLASH, Apr. 5, 2005, at http://www.splc.org/newsflash.

[19] *See, e.g.*, Mercer Univ. v. Barrett, 610 S.E.2d 138 (Ga. Ct. App. 2005) for rationale precluding application of Georgia's Open Records Law to a private college.

## THE COLLEGE ENVIRONMENT

It may have surprised some people when a California judge in *Corry* upheld the state law that imposed First Amendment obligations on the managers of private institutions. But the court's unwillingness to distinguish between First Amendment protection on and off campus did not surprise those familiar with free-speech cases involving college students. With few exceptions, courts have equated the university campus with a public forum open to as far-reaching a collection of ideas as one might expect in a public park, and judges have given post-secondary students the adult-citizen status they would have if they were not in college.

Trying to meet their obligation to control disruptive student conduct, yet allow their students the right to express themselves on campus, officials at universities sprinkled throughout the country have, in greater number, established "free speech zones." In these designated places, individuals could distribute literature, give speeches or stage demonstrations without college interference. Schools came under fire, though, when they either imposed restrictions on speech elsewhere on campus or denied "speech zone" use to non-students. Courts have told university officials that they cannot narrowly define campus locations that operate as public forums. But officials have been given more leeway when they prevent non-students from having access to a limited public forum.[20] It is too early to know whether the 2005 ruling in *Hosty v. Carter* by the Seventh U.S. Circuit Court of Appeals will affect the prevailing legal view of the student press as a public forum.[21]

In *Kincaid v. Gibson,* a Kentucky district court and a three-judge panel of the Sixth U.S. Circuit Court of Appeals suggested an ominous exception to the public-forum status of college publications. But in January 2001, the full appeals court overturned the earlier rulings and declared the university yearbook a limited public forum.[22] The *Kincaid* and *Hosty* cases will be discussed later in this chapter.

### Distinguishing Student Expression

The concerns courts normally consider when they address student expression make it easier to distinguish high school and college cases than to differentiate between cases involving college students and those affecting citizens beyond campus boundaries.

Three factors have been central to the court's reasoning in cases concerning regulation of student expression.

**(1) The age of the speaker and audience.** When calls to

"protect the children" accompany efforts to regulate cyberspace and computer access to sexual material, the courts are asked to reconcile a legal dilemma that has distinguished high school and college students.[23] Courts for years have ruled that children are more vulnerable and deserve more protection than adults. This has led to different legal standards for sexual material and indecent, over-the-air broadcasts. Judges have said that high school students more comfortably qualify for the special protection of children than do college students, who are legally adults.

Both a three-judge federal court in Pennsylvania, when it enjoined enactment of the Communications Decency Act (CDA) in 1996, and the Supreme Court, when it held the act unconstitutional a year later, were careful not to refute the notion that children deserve to be shielded from indecency. Both courts held that regulation must not be so sweeping that it prohibits adults from obtaining or disseminating material that is legally protected for adults.[24] This is particularly true, the Court has said, when alternative means are available to shield children from objectionable material.[25] In 1999, a federal district court blocked enforcement of a new law meant to address constitutional defects in the CDA. The Third U.S. Circuit Court of Appeals affirmed the ruling,[26] in language similar to the Tenth U.S. Circuit Court of Appeals' rebuke of New Mexico's ban on Internet speech that the law termed "harmful to minors" but defined in sweeping terms.[27]

By an 8-1 vote in 2002, the Supreme Court remanded the case, asking for closer scrutiny of the "vague and overbroad" criteria. It agreed that a narrowly defined "community standards" criterion for identifying harmful online content could withstand a constitutional challenge but that the appellate court's ruling that the Child Online Protection Act (COPA) is overbroad requires review of more than the "community standards" criterion. After reconsideration, the Third Circuit reaffirmed its ruling.[28] In June 2004, the Supreme Court agreed 5-4 that COPA likely is overbroad because it denies adults access to material protected for adults. But the Court asked the lower court to see if the latest technology could allow enforcement of the law in a way that both protects children and allows adults access.[29]

The adult status accorded college students in a First Amendment context seemed to spare universities the task of monitoring cyberspace to the extent required of high school officials striving

[20] *See Zoning Free Speech,* STUDENT PRESS LAW CENTER REP., Winter 2004-05, at 32. *See also* Thomas J. Davis, *Assessing Constitutional Challenges to University Free Speech Zones Under Public Forum Doctrine,* 79 IND. L.J. 267 (2004).

[21] 412 F.3d 731 (7th Cir. 2005) (en banc), *cert. denied* 126 S.Ct. 1330 (2006). *See* discussion accompanying *infra* note 70-71.

[22] 236 F.3d 342 (6th Cir. 2001), *rev'g* 191 F.3d 719 (6th Cir. 1999).

[23] *See* Leora Harpaz, *Internet Speech and the First Amendment Rights of Public School Students,* 2000 BYU EDUC. & L.J. 123-162. *See also* D.F. v. Bd. of Ed. of Syosset Central Sch., WL 1236145 (2nd Cir. May 9, 2006).

[24] Reno v. ACLU, 521 U.S. 844 (1997), *aff'g* 929 F. Supp. 824 (E.D. Pa. 1996).

[25] *See* Sable Commc'ns v. FCC, 492 U.S. 115 (1989).

[26] ACLU v. Reno, 31 F. Supp. 2d 473 (E.D. Pa. 1999), *aff'd* 217 F.3d 162 (3d Cir. 2000).

[27] *See* ACLU v. Johnson, 194 F.3d 1149 (10th Cir. 1999).

[28] Ashcroft v. ACLU, 535 U.S. 564 (2002), *aff'd on remand,* 322 F.3d 240 (3d Cir. 2003).

[29] Ashcroft v. ACLU, 542 U.S. 656 (2004).

to shield minors. But the ease of access to a broad range of on-line information and unresolved questions about liability led to close monitoring and tighter regulation on some campuses. One example is administrative response to students' use of university computer facilities to access Napster and download music. Before the federal courts put the brakes on Napster,[30] the Student Press Law Center reported that more than 100 American colleges and universities banned access to Napster.com because so much server space was being used and because universities feared lawsuits for copyright infringement.[31] After a federal district court judge protected Grokster and other file-sharing services from liability when consumers illegally copy music or movies, the entertainment industry shifted its attention to individuals. Four college students file-sharing on their schools' networks were the first targets. From September 2003 through April 2005 the Recording Industry Association of America sued almost 4,000 individuals.[32]

**(2) Where the speech occurs.** The public high school is a different setting than either a college campus or a public street. High school students are closer to a captive audience, with less freedom to come and go. Because the university is more open and enrollment is voluntary, judges have been reluctant to give college officials more regulatory authority over their students than city officials have over a public demonstration or parade.

But judges have given broad regulatory latitude to public high school officials who argue that discipline and control of behavior are necessary to provide an effective learning environment. Complicating matters today for the courts and school officials is the temptation to regulate and punish online expression high school students generate off campus but about school-related issues and individuals. Although students are winning most legal challenges, school officials, in increasing numbers, continue to punish such expression.[33] One relevant case involves a junior high student expelled for one year for using violent and profane language in a personal letter he wrote at home, but never sent, to his ex-girlfriend. A three-judge panel of the U.S. Court of Appeals for the Eighth Circuit upheld a district court's ruling that the off-campus speech was protected, but the appeals court vacated the ruling and after

rehearing it upheld the expulsion by a 6-4 vote.[34] In Arkansas, however, a federal judge recently ruled that school officials unconstitutionally punished two honors students for what was posted on their personal Web sites. The judge called the Web site's content "crude, vulgar and juvenile," but said that because it posed no threat and in no way disrupted the educational process, the content was protected speech.[35]

**(3) The educators' responsibilities.** The Supreme Court, during the past twenty years, has given high school officials more discretion when regulating speech they believe is inconsistent with educational goals and moral values.[36] During this time, the gap continually widened between freedom of speech in high school and college because courts consistently held that universities should be forums for exchanging ideas and that college officials should encourage, not interfere with, that process. This view was strongly stated in the Sixth Circuit's *Kincaid v. Gibson* ruling, but the Seventh Circuit has retreated from this position.[37]

### The Legal Arguments

In general, five topics must be addressed in determining the status of speech in the college environment.

**(1) Lack of disruption.** *Tinker* has been cited to support college free-speech positions because it solidified the "substantial disruption" standard applied even earlier in a college press case. In that 1967 case, editor Gary Dickey was suspended from Troy State College for his published protest of student newspaper censorship. The Alabama federal district court judge who lifted the suspension said that only reasonable regulations needed to maintain order and to operate "in a manner conducive to learning" are appropriate.[38]

After the Supreme Court reinforced the disruption standard in *Tinker*, the Court applied it to the college setting with two decisions in the early 1970s. In *Healy v. James*[39] and *Papish v. Board of Curators of the University of Missouri,*[40] the Court said there is no less need for order in universities than elsewhere in society, but that there also is no less First Amendment protection. That

---

[30] *See A&M Records, Inc. v. Napster, Inc.,* 239 F.3d 1004 (9th Cir. 2001).

[31] *Universities Block Access to Popular Music Site,* STUDENT PRESS LAW CENTER REP., Spring 2000, at 37.

[32] *See MGM Studios v. Grokster, Ltd.,* 243 F. Supp. 1073 (C.D. Cal. 2003); 259 F. Supp. 2d 1029 (C.D. Cal. 2003). *See also Court Ruling and 4 Settlements Shift Debate over File-Sharing Programs,* CHRON. OF HIGHER ED., May 9, 2003, at A34; *Record Industry Sues 493 More U.S. Music Swappers,* Reuters, May 24, 2004, *available at* http://www.riaa.com/news.

[33] *See A Legal Manual for Online Publishers of Independent Student Web Sites,* http://www.splc.org/legalresearch, *reprinted in part, Guide to Internet Law,* STUDENT PRESS LAW CENTER REP., Spring 2004, at 40. *See also Students Increasingly Punished for Internet Postings,* STUDENT PRESS LAW CENTER REP., Winter 2005-06, at 21.

[34] Doe v. Pulaski County Special Sch. Dist., 263 F.3d 833 (8th Cir. 2001), *vacated & reh'g granted,* 306 F.3d 616 (8th Cir. 2002). *See also* J.S. v. Bethlehem Area Sch. Dist., 807 A.2d 847 (Pa. 2002).

[35] *See* Neal v. Efurd, Civ. No. 04-2195 (W.D. Ark. 2005), *available at* http://www.splc.org.

[36] *See* Bethel Sch. Dist. No. 403 v. Fraser, 478 U.S. 675 (1986).

[37] 236 F.3d 342 (6th Cir. 2001). *See also* Hosty v. Carter, No. 01-4155 (7th Cir. 2005) (en banc), after 325 F.3d 945 (7th Cir. 2003) was *vacated & reh'g granted, cert. denied* 126 S.Ct. 1330 (2006).

[38] Dickey v. Alabama State Bd. of Ed., 273 F. Supp. 613, 617 (M.D. Ala. 1967).

[39] 408 U.S. 169 (1972).

[40] 410 U.S. 667 (1973).

means, the Court said, that school officials may not silence a student organization just because it has a philosophy of disruption and violence (as in *Healy*) or suspend a graduate student just because the alternative newspaper she was distributing contained offensive language (as in *Papish*). In both instances, the Court ruled, such speech is consistent with the notion that universities are forums for exchanging ideas and expression may be restricted only if officials can show that the learning process is substantially disrupted.

**(2) Public forums.** Whether a student publication is a public forum, until recently seldom questioned on the college campus, is a recurring concern at the high school level. Sidewalks and parks traditionally have been public forums for sharing ideas, and the government has no authority to be selective about who speaks there. Not all public property is automatically a forum, but may become one, as when a city-owned building becomes a civic center open to community groups. The purpose of utility poles is not to carry signs, but if a city lets citizens post notices, the poles have been designated a public forum, and officials may not arbitrarily allow some messages and prohibit others.

The public-forum doctrine has been an important concept that has helped distinguish free-speech and free-press rights in high school and college. The Supreme Court underscored this point with three rulings — one involved a university,[41] and two concerned high schools.[42] A public high school is not traditionally a place for all citizens, or even all young people, to exchange ideas. Nor is all of a high school a public forum. And a student newspaper may not be a public forum because its function may not be to allow all students to express themselves; the newspaper must clearly be identified, by practice or policy, as a public forum.

There was no public forum in the Santa Fe School District of suburban Houston, the Supreme Court said. The Court rejected what school officials called private, voluntary, student-led prayer before football games. The district had not established a protected public forum for expression, the Court said, but instead had set guidelines that not only defined "appropriate" messages but also precluded minority viewpoints. Without "viewpoint neutrality," Justice John Paul Stevens wrote for the 6-3 majority, school officials not only sanctioned and sponsored prayer, they controlled its content.[43]

So as not to be accused of "sponsoring" religious worship, administrators denied a private community group access to the Milford Central School facilities. The Good News Club argued that this action was discriminatory because the school had created a limited public forum when it allowed community groups such as the 4-H Club and the Boy Scouts to use the school after hours. In a 6-3 ruling, the Supreme Court agreed that school officials were not deciding in a content-neutral way on the use of the established forum.[44]

The university press has not faced such rigid restrictions. Courts often have found the state university campus, by the nature of its mission and environment, to be a limited public forum. Remaining viewpoint-neutral is not only constitutionally required of administrators at public colleges and universities, it is central to the role of higher education. That message from the Supreme Court in *Board of Regents v. Southworth* upheld the University of Wisconsin's system of using student fees to support organizations representing a range of ideologies.[45]

Scott Southworth was one of five conservative, Christian students who objected to the university's activities fee that supported almost twenty organizations with political or ideological perspectives these students opposed. The federal district court and the Seventh U.S. Circuit Court of Appeals agreed with the students, who argued that the required fee forced them to express ideas they did not hold.[46] But the Supreme Court viewed the regulation as beneficial to all students rather than a burden to some and unanimously overturned the circuit court ruling.

Using some of the language heard from the Court in the Milford student prayer case, Justice Anthony Kennedy said that a fee-distribution system that is "viewpoint neutral" is constitutional. Wisconsin's program funded a range of controversial student organizations across the political spectrum, the Court ruled. Individual students may disagree with some of the funded organizations' ideas, the Court said, and a university could find a way to refund fee money to objecting students if it wished. But the system in place, operating as a public forum, was consistent with the mission of a university as a marketplace of ideas.[47] In the words of Justice Kennedy: "The university may determine that its mission is well served if students have the means to engage in dynamic discussion of philosophical, religious, scientific, social and political subjects in their extracurricular campus life outside the lecture hall."[48]

Notwithstanding pressure to quell anti-American sentiment expressed on campus after the terrorist attacks of September 11, 2001, most administrators acknowledge what the courts have long recognized — that a university is by nature closely aligned with the notion of a public forum. A federal district court in Utah said as

---

[41] Bd. of Regents of the Univ. of Wisconsin Sys. v. Southworth, 529 U.S. 217 (2000).

[42] Good News Club v. Milford Central Sch., 533 U.S. 98 (2001); Santa Fe Ind. Sch. Dist. v. Doe, 530 U.S. 290 (2000).

[43] 530 U.S. at 308-09. *See also* Adler v. Duval County Sch. Bd., 250 F.3d 1330 (11th Cir. 2001), *cert. denied,* 534 U.S. 1065 (2001). A school policy allowing the senior class to choose a classmate to deliver a graduation "message" was ruled constitutional because students made all decisions, even though each "message" for four years had been religious in nature.

[44] *Good News Club,* 533 U.S. 98 (2001).

[45] 529 U.S. at 234.

[46] 151 F.3d 717 (7th Cir. 1998).

[47] 529 U.S. at 232-33.

[48] *Id.* at 233.

much when it allowed a student group to construct shanties on the grounds of the University of Utah to protest apartheid and the university's South African investment policies.[49] And a federal appellate court in 1992 ruled that policy and practice at Southwest Texas State University clearly established all outdoor grounds "owned or controlled by the university" as a public forum.[50] Similarly, courts have said that once a university has established a newspaper, it has created a limited forum for the exchange of ideas[51] but a forum where student editors retain control over content.[52] Even a public radio station on a state university campus is free to reject an organization's request to sponsor programming.[53]

A Kentucky federal district court judge late in 1997 took a different position in a case of great concern to the collegiate press. The judge ruled that administrators at Kentucky State University could refuse to distribute about 2,000 copies of the student-produced yearbook and could remove the faculty adviser who would not force editors to print positive stories about the university. Students argued that university censorship based on dissatisfaction with negative newspaper stories and with the yearbook's content, grammatical errors, missing photo captions and the color of its cover abridged the students' First Amendment rights. In ruling for the university, Judge Joseph M. Hood became the first federal judge to apply to a college media case the Supreme Court's decision in the high school case of *Hazelwood v. Kuhlmeier*.[54]

Rejecting student arguments that the newspaper and yearbook were public forums, Judge Hood instead cited *Hazelwood* and deferred to the "intent of the publisher," in this case a university administration that the judge said did not intend to open the pages but retain them as "an educational tool."[55]

If collegiate journalists were upset that a federal judge ignored three decades of court rulings that equated press freedom on campus with that of the professional news media, they were stunned late in 1999 when a three-judge panel of the Sixth U.S. Circuit Court of Appeals upheld the lower court decision.[56] Adding to the injury was the appellate court's reliance on the high school case of *Hazelwood* when it rejected public-forum arguments and defined as "reasonable" broad administrative censor-

ship powers.

Writing for a 2-1 majority, Judge Alan Norris said that explicit administrative intent is necessary if a student publication is to function as a public forum. He concluded that school officials intended to manage their publications and thus could reasonably confiscate the yearbook or refuse to distribute any university publication "that might tarnish, rather than enhance" the school's image.[57]

Student Press Law Center Executive Director Mark Goodman struggled with the appellate court's reasoning. "If allowed to stand," Goodman wrote, "the decision ... will gut student journalism programs at some colleges and universities," just as *Hazelwood* has in many high schools.[58]

Sixth Circuit Judge R. Guy Cole Jr. shared these sentiments in a strong dissent. He argued that different students and settings at the high school and college levels make it inappropriate to apply the *Hazelwood* ruling, and he asserted that the yearbook was indeed a public forum.[59] After the Sixth Circuit vacated the 2-1 ruling and reheard the case, Judge Cole presented his arguments again, this time for a 10-3 majority that overturned the district court decision.[60]

Staff members of university newspaper and yearbook staffs breathed a sigh of relief. They had escaped a threat that limited their freedom to that of their high school counterparts. And the language of the Sixth Circuit's final ruling in *Kincaid v. Gibson* strongly reaffirmed the public-forum role of the student press, especially on a university campus.

University policy and publication board practices at Kentucky State clearly identified student publications as limited public forums, Judge Cole said. The court made no distinction between the roles or content of yearbooks and newspapers. Besides considering KSU's written policy and its "hands off" practice as indices of the yearbook and a public forum, the appellate court examined the publication's content.

In Judge Cole's words: "There can be no serious argument ... that in its most basic form, the yearbook serves as a forum in which student editors present pictures, captions, and other written material, and that these materials constitute expression for purposes of the First Amendment."[61]

The court also eloquently equated the college campus with a public forum. "The university environment is the quintessential 'marketplace of ideas,' which merits full, or indeed heightened, First Amendment protection," Judge Cole wrote. The court also found the age of the students relevant. Because readers likely are

---

[49] Univ. of Utah Students Against Apartheid v. Peterson, 649 F. Supp. 1200 (D. Utah 1986).

[50] Hays County Guardian v. Supple, 969 F.2d 111 (5th Cir. 1992).

[51] *See* Bazaar v. Fortune, 489 F.2d 225 (5th Cir. 1973).

[52] *See* Leeds v. Meltz, 85 F.3d 51 (2d Cir. 1996); Sinn v. Daily Nebraskan, 829 F.2d 662 (8th Cir. 1987); Mississippi Gay Alliance v. Goudelock, 536 F.2d 1073 (5th Cir. 1976); Lee v. Bd. of Regents of State Colleges, 441 F.2d 1257 (7th Cir. 1971).

[53] Knights of the Ku Klux Klan v. Curators of the Univ. of Missouri, 203 F.3d 1085 (8th Cir. 2000).

[54] Kincaid v. Gibson, Civ. No. 95-98 (E.D. Ky, Nov. 14, 1997), *applying* 484 U.S. 260 (1988).

[55] *Id.*

[56] Kincaid v. Gibson, 191 F.3d 719 (6th Cir. 1999).

[57] *Id.* at 729.

[58] Press Release, Student Press Law Center, U.S. Court of Appeals Upholds Confiscation of 2,000 Student Yearbooks at Kentucky State University (Sept. 8, 1999).

[59] 191 F.3d at 730-31 (Cole, J., dissenting).

[60] Kincaid v. Gibson, 236 F.3d 342 (6th Cir. 2001).

[61] *Id.* at 351.

young adults, the court said, the university has "no justification for suppressing the yearbook on the grounds that it might be 'unsuitable for immature audiences.'"[62]

Finally, the court said, even if a publication is not involved or expression occurs in a nonpublic forum, university officials "must not attempt to suppress expression based on the speaker's viewpoint." Confiscating a publication is among "the purest forms of content alteration," Judge Cole wrote, an unconstitutional way "to coerce speech that pleases the government" and an action that the court said it would not tolerate.[63] Regulation must be reasonable, not "a rash, arbitrary act" of censorship.[64]

The university chose not to appeal the ruling, so KSU students whose activity fees had paid for their yearbooks seven years earlier finally received their 1994 yearbooks. The court also ordered the university to pay editors Capri Coffer and Charles Kincaid $5,000 each, plus $60,000 in attorneys' fees and court costs.

But campus celebrations of the *Kincaid* ruling were short-lived. Despite the appellate court's strongly worded free-speech rationale and the court's refusal to apply the *Hazelwood* standard to the college press, the issue resurfaced almost immediately, this time before the U.S. Circuit Court of Appeals for the Seventh Circuit, consisting of Illinois, Indiana and Wisconsin. The Illinois Attorney General's Office, on behalf of Governors State University, argued that the restrictive, high-school-based *Hazelwood* decision justified administrative review and approval of the college student newspaper's contents prior to publication.[65]

The case followed telephone calls the university's Dean of Student Affairs and Services made to the printer of the student newspaper, *The Innovator*. Dean Patricia Carter told the printer not to print any issue until a university official reviewed the content. Editors filed suit, claiming that such action was unconstitutional prior restraint. University officials argued that university funding and the *Hazelwood* criteria should give administrators such discretionary authority.

In April 2003, a three-judge panel unanimously rejected the university's arguments. In *Hosty v. Carter,* the court cited twenty years of legal precedence in holding that administrators can censor only when student media content is "legally unprotected or if they can demonstrate that some significant and imminent physical disruption of the campus will result from the publication's content." The court added that the *Hazelwood* rationale is "not a good fit" for university students. Obvious differences in the missions of high schools and colleges — as well as differing needs, ages and maturity levels of the respective students — also reveal why *Hazelwood* reasoning is inappropriate, the court noted.[66]

What the Student Press Law Center called a "major victory," two years after an equally strong decision in *Kincaid v. Gibson*, left student press supporters euphoric — temporarily. Because the ruling was clear, direct and unanimous, there was some surprise when the state attorney general filed for a rehearing before the entire court. Few were prepared for the circuit court's decision on June 25, 2003, to vacate the three-judge ruling and rehear the case *en banc*. No one expected it would be two years before the full court would rule in the case.[67]

High school journalists have been told that the best legal protection from censorship is designation of the student publication as a public forum. The Supreme Court in *Hazelwood v. Kuhlmeier*[68] gave school officials more authority to regulate speech in school-sponsored venues than in public forums. Forum designation was important in the more controlled environment of a high school. At a university, however, where the exchange of ideas is encouraged throughout the campus, student publications presumably have been the public forums that the Sixth Circuit described in its *Kincaid* ruling. *Hosty v. Carter* suggests that may change.

Writing for the majority in a 7-4 ruling in June 2005, Judge Frank Easterbrook said that one cannot assume that a student publication is a public forum.[69] Judge Easterbrook applied what he called the "framework" of *Hazelwood*, which gives administrators the authority to regulate expression if there is a reasonable pedagogical justification. However, such control exists only in a non-public forum, the court said, making it essential in every college free-speech case to first determine whether the ideas were expressed in a limited or designated public forum.

The court said it was not clear whether the student newspaper at Governors State University was a public forum, either by practice or by policy. For that reason, Judge Easterbrook wrote, Dean Carter had qualified immunity from charges that she purposefully denied students their constitutional rights when she stopped the printing of the *Innovator*.

Mark Goodman, executive director of the Student Press Law Center, said that most college student publications would remain protected because they have functioned as public forums for years. He is more concerned that college officials will incorrectly interpret the court's references to *Hazelwood* as justifications to restrict objectionable content without considering whether a public forum exists to permit such content.[70] One thing is certain: all student publications — at the college or high school level — are better protected when clearly identified and officially recognized as

[62] *Id.* at 352.

[63] *Id.* at 355.

[64] *Id.* at 356.

[65] Hosty v. Governors State Univ., 174 F. Supp. 2d 782 (N.D. Ill., Nov. 13, 2001), *rev'd* 325 F.3d 945 (7th Cir. 2003).

[66] *See* Hosty v. Carter, 325 F.3d 945, 948 (7th Cir. 2003).

[67] *See Battle for College Free Press Continues,* STUDENT PRESS LAW CENTER REP., Fall 2003, at 29.

[68] 484 U.S. 260 (1988).

[69] 412 F.3d 731 (7th Cir. 2005).

[70] *See U.S. Court of Appeals Upholds Censorship by Governors State University Officials,* STUDENT PRESS LAW CENTER NEWSFLASH, June 20, 2005, *at* http://www.splc.org/newsflashes.

public forums. All student journalists are being encouraged to see that their publications are clearly identified as public forums.[71]

**(3) Requiring civil discourse.** The Student Press Law Center stated in 1994 that "First Amendment protections for college students ... appear as strong today as they were 25 years ago."[72] The *Kincaid v. Gibson* court struggle, the perplexing *Hosty v. Carter* case and renewed assaults by zealous college officials and dissatisfied students have tempered this optimistic assessment.[73] New threats have emerged, especially through the efforts of vocal advocates of politically correct speech and school officials who would rather mandate civility than risk unruly confrontation.[74] But many courts continue to strike down sweeping, well-intentioned restrictions. For evidence, one need look no further than cases involving speech codes created to curb hate speech on campus or the "free speech zones" discussed earlier in this chapter.

When college officials were faced with incidents of bigotry and racism on campus, they tried to curb verbal harassment rather than do nothing and appear to condone such incidents. Aware that courts had given broad protection to on-campus speech, officials attempted to equate verbal abuse with easier-to-control conduct and with unprotected fighting words. But the codes clearly focused on offensive expression, and when they were challenged, courts continued to hold that on-campus speech restrictions were no more permissible than off-campus restrictions.

A federal court, for example, found that a University of Michigan policy was so vague and sweeping that it punished constitutionally protected speech, even though the university's motive was to provide a comfortable learning environment for all students.[75] Even a more focused policy in the University of Wisconsin system was declared overbroad in 1991 and sent back to the board of regents for revision. Designed to punish only those who directed racial slurs or epithets at specific individuals, the code went beyond restricting fighting words and also forbade speech that created an undefined "intimidating, hostile or demeaning environment for education."[76]

When the Supreme Court unanimously rejected a city's hate-speech ordinance as unconstitutional, it seemed unlikely that a campus speech code could withstand a court challenge.[77] For a time, many campuses abandoned efforts to draft speech codes, chose to keep them but not enforce them or decided to punish hate speech only when it was tied to a criminal action.[78] But the mood seems to have changed, with tensions again rising over campus speech restrictions. During the 2002-03 academic year, the Student Press Law Center reported clashes over speech policies at nine universities in Texas, West Virginia, California, Illinois, Pennsylvania, Maryland and Wisconsin.

Courts, however, continue to find most policies unconstitutionally overbroad.[79] In 2003, a federal judge stopped a Pennsylvania university from enforcing what the court said was an unconstitutionally vague and overbroad code used to make students remove from dormitory-room doors anti-Osama Bin Laden posters the university said were offensive. Early in 2004, Shippensburg University announced it had rewritten the code. Threats of lawsuits challenging policies at the University of Texas-El Paso and Southwest Missouri State University led those schools to adopt less restrictive codes.[80]

Courts clearly have continued to equate college students with adults and hold public-university administrators, when trying to regulate student expression, to the same First Amendment strictures as off-campus government officials. The contrasting atmosphere for free expression at the high school and university levels will be clearer after discussion of the Supreme Court's *Hazelwood* ruling later in this chapter.

**(4) Access to crime reports.** College journalists share the First Amendment freedom that professional journalists enjoy, but face similar struggles to exercise those freedoms. One of the major battles continues to rage over access to campus crime information.

Professional journalists know that once they have information, the First Amendment makes it hard for government to stop publication. But it is just as clear that the First Amendment does not require that government agencies release information. State and federal legislation — FOI acts — can call for the release of such information. Journalists use these tools to joust with public officials over access to information some government employees would prefer to keep quiet.

Some university officials react with the same reservations when student journalists seek details about the types and extent of crimes on campus. Traci Bauer, while editor-in-chief of the South-

---

[71] *See Going Public*, STUDENT PRESS LAW CENTER REP., Spring 2006, at 6; *SPJ Drafts Statement to Designate Student Media as Public Forums*, May 30, 2006, http://www.spj.org/news.

[72] LAW OF THE STUDENT PRESS, *supra* note 13, at 51.

[73] *See* Gregory Lisby, *Resolving the Hazelwood Conundrum: The First Amendment Rights of College Students in Kincaid v. Gibson and Beyond*, 7 COMM. L. & POL'Y 129 (2002). *See also* Daniel Applegate, *Stop the Presses: The Impact of* Hosty v. Carter *and* Pitt News v. Pappert *on the Editorial Freedom of College Newspapers*, 56 CASE W. RES. L. REV. 247 (Fall 2005).

[74] *See Questionable Content*, STUDENT PRESS LAW CENTER REP., Spring 2002, at 10.

[75] Doe v. Univ. of Michigan, 721 F. Supp. 852 (E.D. Mich. 1989).

[76] UWM Post, Inc. v. Univ. of Wisconsin Bd. of Regents, 774 F. Supp. 1163, 1165 (E.D. Wis. 1991).

[77] *See* RAV v. St. Paul, 505 U.S. 377 (1992).

[78] *See* Scott Jaschik, *Campus "Hate Speech" Codes in Doubt After High Court Rejects a City Ordinance*, CHRON. OF HIGHER EDUC., July 1, 1992, at A19.

[79] *See, e.g.*, *Campus Speech Rules Scrutinized by Courts, Students, Advocates*, STUDENT PRESS LAW CENTER REP., Winter 2002-03, at 6; *Free-Speech Zones Frustrate Students*, STUDENT PRESS LAW CENTER REP., Fall 2002, at 8.

[80] *See* Bair v. Shippensburg Univ., 280 F. Supp. 2d 357 (M.D. Pa. 2003). *See also Colleges Adopt New Policies on Free Speech*, STUDENT PRESS LAW CENTER REP., Spring 2004, at 28; *Turning Off Political Speech*, STUDENT PRESS LAW CENTER REP., Winter 2003-04, at 29.

west Missouri State University newspaper, was the first to win a federal court decision granting access to incident reports from the campus police. A Missouri judge rejected the university's argument that police reports were education records that the Family Educational Rights and Privacy Act (also known as the Buckley Amendment) required be closed to protect student privacy. Judge Russell Clark, in *Bauer v. Kincaid*, cited the First Amendment and the Missouri Sunshine Law when he granted students access to the same type of information other police departments in Missouri must provide.[81]

The *Bauer* ruling did not stop colleges and universities from resisting the release of crime information, and the U.S. Department of Education fueled this tension by rejecting the judge's interpretation in that case. It wasn't until the Student Press Law Center took the DOE to court[82] and federal legislation was passed in the summer of 1992 that crime records were released from the bonds of Buckley Amendment secrecy. Or so it seemed.

This did not end legal struggles for campus crime information, however. The Federal Campus Security Act of 1990 requires that colleges and universities receiving federal aid publish annual figures for the number of crimes reported on campus. Instances of incomplete or misleading reports of campus crime prompted the U.S. House of Representatives to unanimously pass a resolution late in 1996 urging the U.S. Department of Education to monitor crime reports more closely.

Matters did not improve, and in 1997 the DOE reported to Congress that 60 percent of post-secondary institutions required to compile report crime statistics did not follow federal guidelines defining campus crimes. The report fueled additional congressional activity, and 1998 amendments to the Higher Education Act removed some loopholes and strengthened reporting requirements of the Campus Security Act, renamed the Jeanne Clery Disclosure of Campus Security Policy and Campus Crimes Statistics Act. The new federal legislation also complemented and reinforced state open-records laws.[83]

The 1998 legislation requires better disclosure of crime on campus — more access to campus police logs and to student disciplinary records and proceedings. The law also requires public and private colleges and universities to keep, and open to the public, records of all criminal incidents reported to campus police or security personnel. That information must be made public within two business days of authorities being notified.

This legislation was, in part, a response to an access battle college journalists have, with modest success, fought in court. At the University of Georgia, student journalists spent more than five years in court seeking entry to university disciplinary board hearings and records. In 1993, the state supreme court cited Georgia's open meeting and open-records laws and released the records from a hearing involving fraternity hazing[84] and from a different hearing about a gay-bashing incident.[85] In 1997, the Ohio Supreme Court ruled that Miami University of Ohio officials were wrong to consider disciplinary records from the campus court to be "education records" and thus deny student journalists access to them. Records of the proceedings are not protected by the Buckley Amendment's privacy provisions, the court said.[86] Department of Education regulations that went into effect in 2000 require not just campus police and security personnel to report offenses as part of annual campus crime statistics; now any administrator responsible for "student and campus activities," including coaches, housing officials and deans of students, must report incidents they're aware of, regardless of whether the campus police are involved.[87]

Despite these rulings and clearer federal regulations, student journalists often have to go to court to gain access.[88] Although the Supreme Court refused to hear the Miami University of Ohio case, the U.S. Department of Education continued to oppose disclosure. In 1995, the DOE said state open-meetings laws may provide access to campus judicial proceedings and colleges may open their disciplinary proceedings. But, taking a position that would put it on a collision course with the state courts, the DOE also said that all disciplinary records, even those related to criminal misconduct, remain "educational records" subject to the Buckley Amendment.[89]

Early in 1998, the DOE sought a court order to prevent Ohio State University and Miami University of Ohio from releasing unedited campus disciplinary records. In a surprise ruling inconsistent with previous court decisions, including those from the highest state courts in Ohio and Georgia, U.S. District Judge George Smith, in 2000, declared student disciplinary records to be "educational" and not akin to law-enforcement files subject to

---

[81] 759 F. Supp. 575 (W.D. Mo. 1991).

[82] *See* Student Press Law Ctr. v. Alexander, 778 F. Supp. 1227 (D.C.D.C. 1991).

[83] The Student Press Law Center reports that many schools try to use state laws to justify their refusal to disclose campus crime information. When Arkansas State University did, the state's attorney general, in February 2000, said that student disciplinary records are not "scholastic records" and that state law requires disclosure. *See Same Game, Different Rules*, STUDENT PRESS LAW CENTER REP., Spring 2004, at 16.

[84] Red & Black Publ'g Co. v. Bd. of Regents, Univ. of Georgia, 427 S.E.2d 257 (Ga. 1993).

[85] John Doe v. Red & Black Publ'g Co., 437 S.E.2d 474 (Ga. 1993) (without opinion).

[86] Miami Student v. Miami Univ. of Ohio, 680 N.E.2d 956 (Ohio 1997).

[87] The DOE has a database of college and university crime statistics at its Office of Postsecondary Education Web site: http://www.ope.ed.gov/security. *But see A Light in the Darkness*, STUDENT PRESS LAW CENTER REP., Winter 2003-04, at 15; *Crime Under Wraps*, STUDENT PRESS LAW CENTER REP., Fall 2003, at 16.

[88] *See* Cmty. College of Philadelphia v. Brown, 674 A.2d 670 (Pa. 1996). The Pennsylvania Supreme Court denied the student newspaper access to campus crime records. Pennsylvania's open records act does not apply to the state's educational institutions, the court said, because they are not agencies performing an "essential governmental function."

[89] *See* Mac McKerral, *Changes to Buckley Amendment Keep Campus Crime Reports Hidden*, QUILL, May 1995, at 17.

Ohio's Public Records Act.[90] The U.S. Court of Appeals for the Sixth Circuit upheld the decision, preventing the *Chronicle of Higher Education* from obtaining the same information that Miami University student journalists had acquired *via* Ohio's open-records law.[91]

This ruling from 2002 suggests the battle for access to campus crime information continues. It also raises questions about the U.S. Department of Education's willingness to enforce the stronger provisions on reporting campus crime and forestalls conclusions about the impact of recent access legislation. A 2002 Supreme Court decision offered some hope for easier access to campus crime information. In *Gonzaga University v. Doe*[92] the Court ruled 7-2 that individuals cannot sue colleges that release private student records protected by the Family Educational Rights and Privacy Act (FERPA). The Court said that schools not complying with federal law face sanctions from the Department of Education, adding that no FERPA provisions allow students or their parents to sue the institutions. The Vermont Supreme Court, however, even denied a commercial newspaper access to disciplinary records of state-college students, ruling such records to be "educational."[93]

Other incentives are opening campus crime records. The Tennessee legislature amended the state's open-records law to require public colleges and universities to reveal the names of students disciplined for sexual or violent offenses. It became law in July 2004.[94] Despite an increase in court battles for access to college records in 2003-04, students at private universities have found it much harder to gain access than their counterparts at public universities.[95] During the past three years, administrators at private universities in Massachusetts, Georgia, Missouri, New York and Indiana have stymied students' efforts to get campus crime information. When taken to court, officials have successfully argued that because they are private, not public, state open-records laws do not apply to them. While federal law may stipulate that all colleges and universities record and release crime-related incident reports, state laws that call for release of details such as those in arrest records apply to government agencies. Private colleges have escaped obligatory disclosure, although laws have recently opened police records at private universities in Virginia and Georgia and similar legislation is pending in Massachusetts.[96]

A Missouri judge early in 1999 cited amendments to the campus crime legislation when he told Southwest Missouri State University officials they were wrong to use the Buckley Amendment to deny the student newspaper access to results of a campus disciplinary proceeding.[97] Since then, colleges have faced fines as well as reprimands. Mount St. Clare College in Iowa paid $15,000 as the first school fined by the DOE for violating the Clery Act.[98] New Jersey's William Patterson University was threatened with a $55,000 fine for violating the Jeanne Clery Act in 2003, and Salem International University in West Virginia paid a $200,000 fine in 2005 for failing to maintain records and report campus crime from 1997 to 1999.[99]

There was early evidence that some universities were complying with the new regulations,[100] although Security on Campus, a national watchdog group, found 340 colleges had violated the Clery Act between 1991 and 2000.[101]

**(5) Special press problems.** College journalists face a few free-speech problems the professionals are spared. One that the Supreme Court has addressed concerns student fees, an essential revenue source for many campus publications. Student governments usually have a hand in dispersal of this money and occasionally try to place content requirements on the newspaper as a condition of funding.[102] So collegiate journalists closely watched the case involving University of Wisconsin students who challenged mandatory student fees as unconstitutional.

The Seventh U.S. Circuit Court of Appeals had said that the university should not force students to financially subsidize speech with which they disagree, ruling that students can refuse to pay activity fees that support organizations with ideologies students find objectionable.[103] Because student activity fees help to subsidize student publications on most campuses, and student newspapers carry editorials and opinion pieces that often are political or ideological, some collegiate journalists feared that an adverse

[90] United States v. Miami Univ., 91 F. Supp. 2d 1132 (S.D. Ohio 2000).

[91] *See* United States v. Miami Univ., 294 F.d 797 (6th Cir. 2002). *See also Federal Appeal Court Prohibits Release of Student Disciplinary Records Under FERPA,* STUDENT PRESS LAW CENTER NEWSFLASH, June 27, 2002, at http://www. splc.org/newsflash.

[92] 536 U.S. 273 (2002).

[93] *See* Caledonian-Record v. Vermont State Colleges, 833 A.2d 1273 (Vt. 2003).

[94] TENN. CODE ANN. § 10-7-504 (2004).

[95] *See Same Game, Different Rules,* STUDENT PRESS LAW CENTER REP., Spring 2004, at 16.

[96] *See, e.g.,* Mercer Univ. v. Barrett, 610 S.E.2d 138 (Ga. Ct. App., Feb. 3,

2005); Harvard Crimson, Inc. v. President & Fellows of Harvard College, 840 N.E.2d 518 (Mass. 2006). *See also Access Granted,* STUDENT PRESS LAW CENTER REP., Spring 2006, at 14.

[97] Bd. of Governors v. Nolan, No. 198CC4344 (Mo. Cir. Ct. Jan. 26, 1999).

[98] *See College Pays $15,000 to Education Dept.,* STUDENT PRESS LAW CENTER REP., Winter 2000-01, at 35.

[99] *See Record Fine Issued for Clery Act Violations,* STUDENT PRESS LAW CENTER REP., Fall 2004, at 20; *College Settles With DOE Over Clery Act Violations,* STUDENT PRESS LAW CENTER REP., Fall 2005, at 32.

[100] *See Smoother Sailing for Campus Crime Reporting,* STUDENT PRESS LAW CENTER REP., Spring 1999, at 19. *See also Two Schools Release Campus Court Records,* STUDENT PRESS LAW CENTER REP., Winter 1999-2000, at 28.

[101] *See Clery Act Violators Number More Than 300,* STUDENT PRESS LAW CENTER REP., Winter 2000-01, at 33. *See also* Dennis Gregory & Steven Janosik, *The Clery Act: How Effective is It? Perceptions From the Field on the Current State of the Research and Recommendations for Improvement,* 32 STETSON L. REV. 7 (2002).

[102] *See Who Controls the Purse Strings at Your Newspaper?,* STUDENT PRESS LAW CENTER REP., Winter 2001-2002, at 26.

[103] Southworth v. Bd. of Regents of Univ. of Wisconsin Sys., 151 F.3d 717, 732 (7th Cir. 1999).

Supreme Court ruling could mean that the content of their publication would determine their level of financial support.[104]

The Supreme Court emphatically reassured apprehensive students when it ruled unanimously that divergent views should be encouraged on a university campus. As long as its system of distributing student fees dealt with all student organizations in a viewpoint neutral way, the Court said, the university could require fees of all students and determine how to allocate those resources.[105] And when the university's plan for collecting mandatory activity fees still was not viewpoint-neutral less than a year later, a federal district court judge threatened to dissolve the fee system if it weren't appropriately revised within sixty days.[106] The university's fee policies continued to get court scrutiny.[107]

Other threats to the collegiate press remain, however, including:
• University officials inappropriately withholding funds from the student newspaper because of disagreement with its content.[108]
• Student newspaper advisers increasingly finding their jobs at risk because college administrators want fewer controversial stories and more positive news published.[109] Ron Johnson, nationally recognized adviser of the Kansas State *Collegian*, went to court when he lost his advising job based on a "content analysis" of the newspaper. Despite three decades of court rulings that call such action unconstitutional, a federal district court judge ruled that Johnson's First Amendment rights were not denied.[110]
• Students stealing and destroying campus newspapers as a means of expressing dissatisfaction with content or policies. The Student Press Law Center continues to report increases in the number of schools where campus newspapers are stolen. The SPLC reported more than 129 thefts of college newspapers from 2000 to 2005. Fifteen colleges and universities reported thefts in 1999-2000. In 2001-02 the SPLC reported thefts on twenty-nine campuses, including 30,000 newspapers stolen on six different campuses during one week. During the 2004-05 school year, the SPLC

reported newspaper thefts on eighteen campuses.[111] School officials have been reluctant to bring criminal charges, although the SPLC reported that more penalties were imposed on violators during the 2002-03 academic year, when thefts occurred on campuses in at least sixteen states.[112] Colorado has a new state law criminalizing the theft of free newspapers, San Francisco and Berkeley have ordinances punishing such theft, and students in Oregon, Indiana and Florida were among those fined or sentenced to community service as newspaper editors in increasing numbers put a price tag on the theft of their publications.[113]
• With reports of binge drinking and increased alcohol use on campus, college newspapers have become the targets of efforts to ban ads for alcoholic beverages.[114] Pennsylvania law allowed the Liquor Control Board to revoke the liquor license of any establishment advertising in a college newspaper. A federal district court and the Third U.S. Circuit Court of Appeals both initially rejected a request by the University of Pittsburgh's student newspaper to stop enforcement of the state law. The appellate court said the burden may be economic, but the law was not so onerous as to threaten the publication's constitutional rights.[115] But after the U.S. Supreme Court remanded the case, the Third Circuit in July 2004 ruled unconstitutional the state ban on paid ads in the student media.[116] Pennsylvania's attorney general chose not to appeal the ruling. In July 2006, Virginia's attorney general was preparing a defense in a lawsuit challenging a regulation prohibiting alcohol advertising in that state's student publications. The two college publications fighting the regulation are using arguments that the Third Circuit supported.[117]

Notwithstanding these special concerns and the *Hosty* ruling, most college publications remain closer to equal First Amendment footing with the professional press than the high school press does. The 2001 *Kincaid v. Gibson* ruling strengthened the legal foundation for student expression at colleges and universities. It did so with language that should echo far beyond campus bound-

---

[104] *See Paying for Free Speech*, STUDENT PRESS LAW CENTER REP., Spring 1999, at 30.

[105] Bd. of Regents of Univ. of Wisconsin Sys. v. Southworth, 529 U.S. 217 (2000). *See also* Rosenberger v. Rector & Visitors, Univ. of Virginia, 515 U.S. 819 (1995).

[106] *See* Fry v. Bd. of Regents of Univ. of Wisconsin Sys., No. 96-C-0292-S (W.D. Wisc. Dec. 8, 2000).

[107] *See* Southworth v. Bd of Regents of the Univ. of Wisconsin Sys., 307 F.3d 566 (7th Cir. 2002).

[108] *See, e.g.*, Stanley v. Magrath, 719 F.2d 279 (8th Cir. 1983). *See also Slashed Budgets Threaten Journalism Programs, Papers*, STUDENT PRESS LAW CENTER REP., Spring 2003, at 8.

[109] *See Court Revokes Order That Blocked Kansas State from Removing Newspaper Adviser*, STUDENT PRESS LAW CENTER NEWSFLASH, July 15, 2004, at www.splc.org/newsflashes; Leo Reisberg, *When Student Newspapers Offend, Advisers May Pay With Their Jobs*, CHRON. OF HIGHER EDUC., July 17, 1998, at A53. *But see Adviser Settles with Ga. University*, STUDENT PRESS LAW CENTER REP., Spring 2002, at 12 (A fired Georgia newspaper adviser won $192,000 settlement from Fort Valley State University.).

[110] *See* Lane v. Simon, No. 04-4079-JAR, 2005 WL 1366521, 2005 U.S.Dist.LEXIS 11330 (D.C. Kan., June 2, 2005) (slip opin.).

[111] *See Taking Out the Trash*, STUDENT PRESS LAW CENTER REP., Spring 2004, at 30; *Four Face Charges for Stealing Student Papers*, STUDENT PRESS LAW CENTER REP., WINTER 2005-06, at 38.

[112] *See Colleges Discipline Thieves*, STUDENT PRESS LAW CENTER REP., Fall 2002, at 10; Michael Koster, *The New Campus Censors*, COLUMBIA JOURNALISM REV., Sept./Oct. 1994, at 19; *Newspaper Thefts Rise Sharply*, STUDENT PRESS LAW CENTER REP., Spring 2002, at 14.

[113] COLO. REV. STAT. § 18-4-419. *See also Criminalizing Theft in Question*, STUDENT PRESS LAW CENTER REP., Fall 2003, at 30.

[114] *See Drinking in Victory*, STUDENT PRESS LAW CENTER REP., Winter 2004-05, at 16.

[115] Pitt News v. Fisher, 215 F.3d 354 (3d Cir. 2000). The newspaper was no more successful when arguing that the law is a content restriction. The case was dismissed on summary judgment. *See* CIV. NO. 99-529 (W.D. Pa., Feb. 14, 2003).

[116] *See* Pitt News v. Pappert, 379 F.3d 96 (3d Cir. 2004).

[117] *See Two College Newspapers Challenge State Regulation Prohibiting Alcohol Ads*, STUDENT PRESS LAW CENTER NEWSFLASH, June 2006, http://www.splc.org/newsflash.

aries in the Sixth Circuit (Kentucky, Tennessee, Ohio and Michigan). It is too early to know how much the 2005 *Hosty v. Carter* ruling affects college publications in and beyond the Seventh Circuit (Wisconsin, Illinois and Indiana), but collegiate journalists nationwide have become more assertive of press freedom and in establishing the public-forum status of their publications.[118]

## REGULATING HIGH SCHOOL EXPRESSION

During the 1970s and much of the 1980s, lower courts, with increasing regularity, stressed the *Tinker* testament to individual expression. They made it hard for school officials to censor the student press, telling them to write guidelines before regulating expression. And courts rejected vague and overbroad guidelines that allowed administrators to suppress material that, while embarrassing or disturbing to school officials, neither was substantially disruptive nor infringed on the rights of others.[119] In the mid-1980s, however, the Supreme Court began signaling a shift that would make it far harder for high school journalists to exercise the rights acknowledged in the *Tinker* decision.[120]

*Tinker*, with its inspirational free-speech rhetoric, remains good law for individual expression in the high school, although some courts have given school officials more discretion in controlling threats from students using personal, off-campus Web sites.[121] Meanwhile, the many students in supervised speech-related activities, such as student publications, now have less First Amendment protection. This can be traced to high school cases where the Supreme Court refocused its attention.

### A Shift in First Amendment Philosophy

Instead of concentrating on students and viewing constitutional freedom as an instrument to help those in high school learn societal values, the Supreme Court has turned its attention to school officials and what they must do to meet their responsibility to instill those values in the young. Administrators now have more latitude. When school-sponsored activities are involved, the burden shifts to students, who more easily can be silenced in public schools because of who they are, where they are and why they're there.

A 1986 Supreme Court case introduced this philosophy and foreshadowed a landmark high school newspaper case two years later. *Bethel School District v. Fraser*[122] began when a student gave a two-minute campaign speech during a school-sponsored assembly. Matthew Fraser used no four-letter words, but he did use sexual innuendo. He described the candidate as "firm — he's firm in his pants, he's firm in his shirt, his character is firm" and as one who "takes his point and pounds it in.... He doesn't attack things in spurts; he drives hard, pushing and pushing until finally — he succeeds."

Several students in the audience of 600 hooted during the speech, but when Fraser finished, the candidate spoke briefly, and the end-of-school assembly concluded. The next day, several teachers complained, and Fraser was suspended for three days. He filed suit and won when federal district and appellate courts agreed that because it was not substantially disruptive, his speech was protected.

But the Supreme Court disagreed. The disruption standard stemmed from *Tinker*, which dealt with students who wore armbands as individuals expressing political beliefs. Because circumstances were different in *Bethel*, the Court said, a different standard applies. First, school officials have more control over the content of a school-sponsored assembly than over what a student says in the corridors. Second, school officials should see that public education instills moral values and encourages civility. To do this, the Court said, school officials must be free to disassociate the school from "vulgar and lewd speech" that undermines the educational mission and is "inconsistent with the 'fundamental values' of public school education." The Court said it was more important that school officials have discretionary power to identify and inculcate "fundamental values" than that they establish and follow narrow regulations.[123]

Although the Court said that *Bethel* did not overturn *Tinker*, it was not clear until two years later whether the Court intended the *Tinker* standard to remain in place for serious idea speech (similar to that of a war protest) or whether *Tinker* was to apply only to speech not under the control of school officials. In 1988, the Court's *Hazelwood School District v. Kuhlmeier*[124] ruling clarified this: *Tinker* would apply when students spoke on their own in school, but a different set of rules applied to students using a school-sponsored vehicle such as the student newspaper.[125]

### The Hazelwood Standard

The *Spectrum* was very much a part of Hazelwood East High

[118] *See Life After Hosty*, STUDENT PRESS LAW CENTER REP., Spring 2006, at 24; *Hosty Q&A*, STUDENT PRESS LAW CENTER REP., Spring 2006, at 26; *Hosty v. Carter: An Analysis*, STUDENT PRESS LAW CENTER REP., Fall 2005, at 27.

[119] *See* Gambino v. Fairfax County Sch. Bd., 564 F.2d 157 (4th Cir. 1977); Nitzberg v. Parks, 525 F.2d 378 (4th Cir. 1975).

[120] *See Sacking News Coverage*, STUDENT PRESS LAW CENTER REP., Spring 2003, at 20.

[121] *See* J.S. v. Bethlehem Area Sch. Dist., 575 A.2d 412 (Pa. Comm. Ct. 2000), *aff'd* 807 A.2d 847 (Pa. 2002). *See also Schools Extend Reach to Punish Students for Off-Campus Speech Made on Internet*, STUDENT PRESS LAW CENTER REP., Fall 2001, at 35.

[122] 478 U.S. 675 (1986).

[123] *Id.* at 685-86.

[124] 484 U.S. 260 (1988).

[125] *See Rulings Emphasize Tinker Standard*, STUDENT PRESS LAW CENTER REP., Winter 2003-04, at 9. *See also*, Justin Peterson, *School Authority v. Students' First Amendment Rights: Is Subjectivity Strangling the Free Mind at Its Source?*, 2005 MICH. ST. L. REV. 931 (2005).

School. Its adviser taught most staff members, who were in their second journalism course at the suburban St. Louis, Missouri, school. The student newspaper had covered serious topics in earlier issues and put together a spring edition that included two pages featuring stories on teenage concerns, including pregnancy and divorce.

It was established practice to let Hazelwood East principal R.E. Reynolds review page proofs before publication. He objected to two stories. In one, three unnamed students described their pregnancies. In the other, students were quoted discussing the impact of their parents' divorces. Concerned that these stories might offend young readers and invade students' and parents' privacy, Reynolds pulled the two pages that included the offending articles. Three staff members, who learned of the censorship when the printed paper was delivered, filed suit.

A federal district court said that the principal's actions were reasonable and that he had authority because the newspaper was part of the school curriculum instead of a public forum.[126] The Eighth U.S. Circuit Court of Appeals said the *Spectrum* was part of the curriculum but also a public forum. The appellate court built its decision on a number of student-press cases grounded in *Tinker* and concluded that school officials had no reason to forecast substantial disruption and no liability for any libel or invasion of privacy suit.[127]

The same day the Eighth Circuit overturned the district court decision and supported the Hazelwood East students, the Supreme Court ruled in *Bethel v. Fraser*. Six months later, the Court agreed to review *Hazelwood*.

The Supreme Court almost effortlessly applied its *Bethel* rationale to *Hazelwood*. In reversing the Eighth Circuit ruling, the Court described a high school setting and citizenry in stark contrast to those of the university or society at large.[128] As it had done two years before, the Court stressed the obligation school officials have and the authority they need to educate youth. The content of the censored *Spectrum* stories was less important than whether the principal's actions were reasonable.

**The educator's role.** A public-school official doesn't quite have the autonomy of a true publisher, but does have more control over expression than do most government officials. The Court has come close to granting public school administrators the same un-

questioned authority of a private newspaper's owner.[129]

State or local government officials and public university administrators have strict limits on their censorship power and must justify restrictions. High school officials also have to defend any censorship, but today that is much easier. The tone and substance of the *Hazelwood* decision encourage close scrutiny of student expression. School officials may regulate "in any reasonable manner" the content of any "supervised learning experience," the Court said. In the words of Justice Byron White: "[E]ducators do not offend the First Amendment by exercising editorial control over the style and content of student speech in school-sponsored expressive activities so long as their actions are reasonably related to legitimate pedagogical concerns."[130] These concerns include "speech that is ... ungrammatical, poorly written, inadequately researched, biased or prejudiced, vulgar or profane, or unsuitable for immature audiences."[131] The school does not need specific written guidelines in order to control school-sponsored publications, the Court said, and violates the First Amendment only when censorship serves no valid educational purpose.

Several subsequent court rulings suggest that administrators' authoritative sphere is expanding. The U.S. Court of Appeals for the Ninth Circuit said in *LaVine v. Blaine School District* that school officials justifiably expelled a student who asked a teacher to comment on a poem he wrote about a fictitious shooting in a school.[132] The school district's safety concerns superseded the student's First Amendment rights, the court said.

In *Fleming v. Jefferson County School District*, the U.S. Court of Appeals for the Tenth Circuit let Columbine High School administrators prevent the display of decorative tiles with religious symbols.[133] Citing *Hazelwood*, the court said the school's decision was legitimately related to the need to create a safe environment for Columbine High's students.

Safety, security and substantial disruption remain the primary justifications school officials use to curtail the expression of individual students. A California student was told he could not wear in school a t-shirt that said "Homosexuality is Shameful," and a New Hampshire high school student was prevented from wearing a "no Nazis" patch with a line through a swastika. In both cases the courts sided with school officials who warned of disruptive consequences.[134]

But two recent federal district court cases in Ohio and Michigan

---

[126] Kuhlmeier v. Hazelwood Sch. Dist., 607 F.Supp. 1450 (D. Mo. 1985).

[127] Kuhlmeier v. Hazelwood Sch. Dist., 795 F.2d 1368 (8th Cir. 1986).

[128] In footnote 7 of the *Hazelwood* decision, the Supreme Court said only, "We need not now decide whether the same degree of deference is appropriate with respect to school-sponsored expressive activities at the college and university level." Although the Court did not foreclose that possibility, it was more than ten years before a federal judge applied the *Hazelwood* standard in a college press rights case. The Sixth Circuit refused to apply *Hazelwood* at the college level in *Kincaid v. Gibson*, 236 F.3d 342 (6th Cir. 2001), but the Seventh Circuit applied the *Hazelwood* "framework," if not the holding, to a college press case in *Hosty v. Carter*, 412 F.3d 731 (7th Cir. 2005).

[129] *See* Bd. of Educ. of Pottawatomie County v. Earls, 536 U.S. 822 (2002). This 5-4 Supreme Court decision allowing broad drug testing in public high schools is recent evidence that the rights of students must defer to administrative decisions and an overriding health and safety concern related to drug use.

[130] 484 U.S. 260, 273 (1988).

[131] *Id.* at 271.

[132] 257 F.3d 981 (9th Cir. 2001).

[133] 298 F.3d 918 (10th Cir. 2002), *cert. denied* 537 U.S. 1110 (2003).

[134] *See* Harper v. Poway Unified Sch. Dist., No. 04-57037 (9th Cir. Apr. 20, 2006); Governor Wentworth Reg'l Sch. Dist. v. Henderson, No. 05CV-133-SM, 2006 WL 658936 (D.N.H. Mar. 15, 2006).

remind administrators of limits to their authority.[135] *Draudt v. Wooster City School District* and *Dean v. Utica* will be discussed later in this chapter.

**The learning environment.** *Hazelwood* said that a more narrowly defined educational environment and a broader definition of curriculum give officials more regulatory control over student expression in high schools than in colleges.

Hazelwood East students argued successfully at the appellate court level that the *Spectrum* was a public forum that should be free of content-based regulation, but the Supreme Court disagreed. It ruled that because the newspaper had not been clearly designated as a public forum, school officials were free to oversee its content.

The Court did not assume what lower courts had come to accept — that the ideas exchanged in the student newspaper made it a public forum. Although it covered controversial issues and carried letters to the editor, *Spectrum* had not become a public forum because no school board policy clearly stated such intent, and the practice of submitting the newspaper for administrative review indicated the school wanted to retain control. While acknowledging that a student newspaper functioning as a public forum is harder to censor, the Court implied that stated school policy would be the only sure way to establish such a forum.[136] Federal judges have ruled in two recent cases that school policy can be revealed in a number of ways, and a publication allowed to function as a forum can gain legal standing as a limited public forum.[137]

**Age and maturity.** When it supported school officials, the Supreme Court in *Hazelwood* applied a legal philosophy built on the premise that, for legitimate reasons, government decision-makers can deny children constitutional rights that adults have. The age and maturity of high school students put their rights of free expression second to the rights of adults responsible for advancing the school's educational goals.

The Court held that school officials could use censorship to protect students from a newspaper story on coping with teenage pregnancy. Then the Court applied the legal rationale it had used in previous rulings to protect children from sexual material.

The Supreme Court earlier had defined and defended "variable obscenity" as a permissible way for the government to protect minors from the potential harm of sexual content. In *Ginsberg v.*

*New York,*[138] the Court held that when evaluating sexual material available to minors, the test for judging a work as obscene for adults can be modified and the material restricted if it meets a lesser standard. In 1982, the Court unanimously upheld a state child-pornography law directed at material not obscene for adults but illegal because it involved minors.[139] The rationale, once more, was a valid state interest in protecting vulnerable youth. In *Hazelwood,* the Court again decided that the First Amendment permits government — in this case, high school officials — to consider the "emotional maturity of the intended audience" when determining "whether to disseminate speech on potentially sensitive topics."[140]

As computers and Internet resources have entered the classroom and become tools for research and learning, school officials have had the added burden of protecting the young from adult material on the net. Even in decisions citing the unconstitutionality of the Communications Decency Act and the Child Online Protection Act, federal courts have acknowledged the valid government interest in protecting minors.[141] Today some overly protective school administrators are denying student journalists access to Internet resources useful in reporting, and publication staffs have to resolve privacy concerns before their newspapers are allowed to go online.[142] Schools' reliance on filters to deny students access to some online material poses problems, as a panel of federal judges determined in June 2002, declaring the Children's Internet Protection Act unconstitutional. The Supreme Court saw no problem here, ruling that the state interest in protecting children from pornographic material is more persuasive when adults can gain access to online library materials by removing the filtering blocks.[143] Infrequent, but highly publicized incidents of school violence and acute apprehension about national security and online predators also have made administrators quick to respond to insensitive student behavior and youthful impulse.[144]

[135] *See* discussion of *Draught v. Wooster City Sch. Dist.,* 246 F. Supp. 2d 820 (N.D. Ohio 2003), and *Dean v. Utica,* 345 F. Supp. 2d 799 (E.D. Mich. 2004), accompanying *supra* notes 133, 141, 151, 159, 163-65.

[136] *See* Andrew D.M. Miller, *Balancing School Authority and Student Expression,* 55 BAYLOR L. REV. 623 (Fall 2002).

[137] *See* Draudt v. Wooster City Sch. Dist. Bd. of Educ., 246 F. Supp. 2d 820 (N.D. Ohio 2003); Dean v. Utica Community Schs. 345 F. Supp. 2d 799 (E.D. Mich. 2004).

[138] 390 U.S. 629 (1968).

[139] New York v. Ferber, 458 U.S. 747 (1982).

[140] *See Hazelwood,* 484 U.S. 260, 272 (1982).

[141] *See* ACLU v. Reno, 31 F. Supp. 2d 473 (E.D. Pa. 1999.), *aff'd,* 217 F.3d 162 (3d Cir. 2000), *aff'd* Ashcroft v. ACLU, 535 U.S. 564 (2002), *aff'd on remand* 322 F.3d 240 (3d Cir. 2003), *aff'd* 542 U.S. 656 (2004).

[142] *See Off-Campus Web Sites Endure Censorship,* STUDENT PRESS LAW CENTER REP., Winter 2004-05, at 15. *See also,* Student Press Law Center's *CyberGuide: A Legal Manual for Online Publishers of Independent Student Web Sites,* http://www.splc.org/resources/cyberguide.html; *Paying the Price,* STUDENT PRESS LAW CENTER REP., Winter 2002-03, at 23.

[143] United States v. American Library Ass'n, 539 U.S. 194 (2003), *rev'g* 201 F. Supp. 2d 401 (E.D. Pa., May 31, 2002). *See also,* Candace Perkins Bowen & John Bowen, *First Amendment Also Protects Right to Hear,* ADVISER UPDATE, Spring 2005, at 18A.

[144] *See FERPA Fundamentalism,* STUDENT PRESS LAW CENTER REP., Spring 2001, at 35-39 (discussing how schools use this federal privacy law to require parental permission before student publications can publish the names or photographs of students).

### Arguing for Free Speech

The Supreme Court has not left students powerless to speak in the public schools. Valid legal arguments for free expression remain, as students learned in several recent student press-rights cases. Some questions relating to the most persuasive of those arguments are addressed here.

**Is there a legitimate reason to regulate?** In American society, the government must show that a legitimate public good will occur as a result of any regulation of an individual's speech. It's no different in public educational institutions. In high school, it is easier for officials to find valid reasons, especially when regulations are closely linked to educational objectives.

A seventh-grader in Derby, Kansas, learned this when a federal district court and the Tenth U.S. Circuit Court of Appeals upheld his suspension from school for drawing a Confederate flag while sitting in math class. T.J. West was suspended for violating a zero tolerance policy the school adopted after a racial disturbance. The appellate court said that the school needed latitude to prevent disruptive conduct and approved the policy that said students could not wear or possess material that is "racially divisive or creates ill will or hatred."[145]

*Hazelwood* gave school officials more authority over school-sponsored speech than over content students generate on their own. The proliferation of computers and the relative ease with which students can publish online and create Web sites have given the term "underground press" a new dimension. Off-campus use of the Internet qualifies as individual expression, subject to punishment by school officials only if it can meet the "substantial disruption" standard of *Tinker*.[146] But school administrators, in increasing numbers, are willing to punish potentially disruptive personal expression when a student's off-campus Web site touches the school.[147]

Despite court rulings that support students' off-campus expression, school officials persist in punishing this individual expression. Sometimes school officials can justify the punishment. When a Wisconsin high school student told readers of an underground newspaper how to crack the security of the school's computer system, he was expelled. A federal district court, applying *Tinker* to this off-campus expression, lifted the expulsion because the article did not cause substantial disruption. On appeal, the

Seventh U.S. Circuit Court of Appeals agreed that expulsion was excessive but said punishment was justified because the article was a substantial threat to the school.[148]

Despite the public's willingness to defer to school administrators and tight regulations when the health and safety of children are at stake, the courts have not been as willing to ignore infringements on the constitutional rights of students and teachers. Students who appeal their punishment by overzealous administrators continue to find support in the courtroom.[149] The Ninth Circuit Court of Appeals said so in a 2006 ruling that dealt with student speech outside of school, and an eighth-grader in New Jersey won a $117,500 cash settlement after school officials punished him for using his at-home Web site as a forum for students who found school boring.[150]

The refrain from the courts is consistent: School officials are not allowed to punish a student for posting on a personal Web site material that neither disrupts the educational process nor threatens the health or safety of students or school personnel. A Missouri federal judge in 1998 said as much in the country's first court ruling on this topic.[151] The same message came following the suspensions of students in Washington for posting mock obituaries of several friends[152] and in Pennsylvania for making fun of the athletic director.[153] Before awarding Karl Beidler $62,000 in damages and attorneys' fees, Judge Thomas McFee said that even the Web site posting of crude images of school officials by an "immature and foolishly defiant student" was protected speech because it did not disrupt the educational process.[154]

As discussed earlier, once a student publication is recognized as a limited public forum, school officials have limited control of the publication's content. If not a public forum, the publication is subject to what can be a broad interpretation of the school's "legitimate pedagogical concerns" justifying censorship.

Students have successfully challenged administrators to demonstrate in court that speech restrictions are reasonably related to educational goals. One early victory came from the New Jersey Supreme Court, which ruled unanimously that the principal of Clearview Junior High School had not met the *Hazelwood* standard when he censored two movie reviews by Brien Desilets. The principal had no problem with the content of the eighth-

---

[145] West v. Derby Unified Sch. Dist. No. 260, 206 F.3d 1358, 1361 (10th Cir. 2000), *cert. denied*, 531 U.S. 825 (2000). *See also Speech v. Safety*, STUDENT PRESS LAW CENTER REP., Winter 2005-06, at 8.

[146] *See* Mahaffey v. Aldrich, 236 F. Supp.2d 779 (E. Mich. 2002).

[147] *See* Jennifer Kathleen Swartz, *Beyond the Schoolhouse Gates: Do Students Shed Their Constitutional Rights When Communicating to a Cyber-Audience?*, 48 DRAKE L.R. 587 (2000). *See also* Pangle v. Bend-La Pine Sch. Dist., 10 P.3d 275 (Ore. 2000); *Off Campus, Not Off Limits*, STUDENT PRESS LAW CENTER REP., Winter 2003-2004, at 33; *The Domain Game*, STUDENT PRESS LAW CENTER REP., Spring 2006, at 20.

[148] Boucher v. Sch. Bd. of Greenfield, 134 F.3d 821 (7th Cir. 1998).

[149] *See Guide to Internet Law*, STUDENT PRESS LAW CENTER REP., Spring 2004, at 40. *See also* Flaherty v. Keystone Oaks Sch., 247 F. Supp.2d 698 (W.D. Pa. Feb. 26, 2003); *Students' Off-Campus Web Publications Out of Schools' Reach, Two Courts Affirm*, STUDENT PRESS LAW CENTER REP., Spring 2005, at 15.

[150] *See* Frederick v. Morse, 439 F.3d 1114 (9th Cir. 2006); Dwyer v. Oceanport Sch. Dist., No. 03-6005, slip. op. (D.N.J. Mar. 31, 2005).

[151] Beussink v. Woodlands Sch. Dist., 30 F. Supp.2d 1175 (E.D. Mo. 1998).

[152] Emmett v. Kent Sch. Dist., 92 F. Supp.2d 1088 (D.C. Wash. 2000).

[153] Killion v. Franklin Regional Sch. Dist., 136 F. Supp.2d 446 (W.D. Pa. 2001).

[154] Beidler v. North Thurston County Sch. Dist., No. 99-2-00236-6 (Thurston Cty. Super. Ct., July 18, 2000).

grader's reviews for the student newspaper but censored them because the films — *Rain Man* and *Mississippi Burning* — are R-rated, which school officials said meant the subject matter was inappropriate for junior-high students. The state supreme court disagreed and concluded that there were insufficient educational grounds to justify the censorship.[155]

The judge in a recent federal case noted that the quality of journalism that editor Katy Dean and the *Arrow* staff of Utica High School practiced overshadowed any censorship justifications that administrators offered. Officials tried to stop publication of an investigative story about a lawsuit that two community members filed against the school district, claiming that diesel fumes from idling buses constituted a nuisance, violated their privacy rights and harmed their health. Ruling for the students, Judge Arthur Tarnow noted the thoughtful and thorough investigation of a story that "was relevant to the school community." He reviewed each of the *Hazelwood* court's bases for reasonable censorship and concluded that there was no evidence that censorship of the student newspaper story in Utica High School was "reasonably related to any stated pedagogical concern."[156]

School officials also have used the *Hazelwood* ruling and a low-tolerance atmosphere in schools to exercise more control over what teachers say. Often school authorities link sanctions to a teacher's performance in the classroom and justify their actions as properly related to administrative oversight of the curriculum. The Fourth U.S. Circuit Court of Appeals upheld sanctions of a North Carolina drama teacher whose selection of a controversial play led school officials to remove the production from state competition and transfer the teacher to another school. The court said that although the teacher always selects the play, the drama is part of the curriculum that administrators can legitimately control as school-sponsored speech.[157] Publication advisers do much of their work with journalism students outside of the classroom, but these teachers also risk losing their jobs as advisers or being abruptly transferred to a different school if their performance dissatisfies administrators.[158]

**Is it school-sponsored speech that's being regulated?** The *Hazelwood* Court clearly gave high school officials more control than they had before over expression that is school-sponsored or supervised by faculty members. A 2002 Supreme Court decision that clarifies the parameters of school sponsorship should help student journalists. Students who speak on their own still have

constitutional safeguards in high schools. Before 1988, pre-publication review of school newspapers was permitted in most of the country, as long as constitutional procedural guidelines existed. The *Hazelwood* majority removed the requirement of guidelines for school-sponsored speech, but said it was not yet eliminating that safeguard for individual expression.

Speech that does not come through a faculty-supervised activity has more protection because it is subject to the *Tinker* standard and must be permitted unless school officials can show the speech is substantially disruptive or invades the rights of others. Post-*Hazelwood* cases that support this view deal with students wanting to distribute religious materials or publish alternative student newspapers.

The same year as *Hazelwood*, the Ninth U.S. Circuit Court of Appeals ruled that school officials were wrong to discipline five students who distributed their newspaper at a class picnic without getting prior approval. This court said the school's broad control over curriculum does not extend to a policy controlling content of non-school-sponsored speech.[159] A federal district court also rejected a prior-review policy applied to a religious pamphlet distributed in a Florida elementary school. The judge said school officials showed no evidence that distribution would be disruptive.[160] The *Tinker* disruption standard was applied in district court cases that supported students' right to distribute religious literature in Texas and Colorado,[161] and a school district was told it could not impose viewpoint based restrictions and prevent the display of a kindergarten student's artwork that included a depiction of Jesus.[162]

In *Owasso Independent School District v. Falvo*[163] the Supreme Court did not address a student press issue, but did address the federal privacy law that school officials have used to prevent publication or Web posting of student names and photos. FERPA, also known as the "Buckley Amendment," requires schools to get parental consent before releasing a high school student's "educational records." Administrators have applied FERPA to the student media, requiring parental approval before publishing identification of students or even conducting student surveys.

The parents of Kristja Falvo sued the Oklahoma school district, claiming that the classroom practice of having students exchange and grade quizzes and then read the results aloud violated FERPA. But the Supreme Court unanimously disagreed. Writing for the Court, Justice Kennedy said that students are not "acting for" the school when they grade quizzes at a teacher's request, nor does

---

[155] Desilets v. Clearview Regional Bd. of Ed., 647 A.2d 150 (N.J. 1994). *See also In re* George T, 93 P.3d 1007 (Cal. 2004).

[156] Dean v. Utica Cmty. Schs., 345 F. Supp. 2d 799, 809 (E.D. Mich. 2004).

[157] Boring v. Buncombe County Bd. of Ed., 136 F.3d 364 (4th Cir. 1998).

[158] *See* Amanda Lehmert, *Advisers Removed — But is it Censorship?*, QUILL, July-Aug. 2002, at 22. *See also Advisers in Limbo*, STUDENT PRESS LAW CENTER REP., Fall 2002, at 23; *Silencing the Rebellion*, STUDENT PRESS LAW CENTER REP., Fall 2002, at 20.

[159] Burch v. Barker, 861 F.2d 1149 (9th Cir. 1988).

[160] Johnston-Loehner v. O'Brien, 859 F. Supp. 575 (M.D. Fla. 1994).

[161] *See* Clark v. Dallas Ind. Sch. Dist., 806 F. Supp. 116 (N.D. Texas 1992); Rivera v. East Otero Sch. Dist., 721 F. Supp. 1189 (D. Colo. 1989).

[162] Peck v. Baldwinsville Cent. Sch. Dist., 426 F.3d 617 (2d Cir. 2006, *cert. denied*, 126 S.Ct. 1880 (2006).

[163] 534 U.S. 426 (2002).

reading grades aloud meet the FERPA requirement of a school-maintained educational record. This ruling should make it easier for student journalists to argue that they also are not "agents" of the school, and their published work will not open the district to a charge of violating FERPA.

**Is the publication a public forum?** A city is not required to create a public park or stock one with benches where people can share ideas. But if there is a park, public officials can't decide which political ideas may be expressed on a park bench and which may not. Students have used this public forum principle to defend their right to express ideas on school property. The *Hosty* ruling notwithstanding, courts consistently have found a public university's campus and student newspaper to be public forums, certainly for the university's students and faculty. The courts have not said that about high school corridors and publications. High school students and publication staffs will have more legal right to freedom of expression if school officials acknowledge that the newspaper and yearbook are public forums, but today neither high school nor college students can assume that their publications are forums.[164]

The Ninth U.S. Circuit Court of Appeals has clarified what it means for a school to designate a public forum. A Nevada school district gave principals the authority to set guidelines for acceptable advertising in student publications and reject ads that did not meet the guidelines. The school set a review procedure and refused to run Planned Parenthood ads considered unsuitable. Before deciding whether the broad administrative discretion of *Hazelwood* applied to this case, the court had to decide whether the publications were public forums, thus limiting administrative control. It said the newspaper was not a public forum just because it accepted advertising or reported on controversial issues. It was not a forum because school officials, with their policy and practice of prior review, clearly retained control and had not turned it over to the staff.[165]

Even when school officials allow students to make editorial decisions, it does not mean that the student publications are public forums open to anyone who wants access to the newspaper or yearbook. When the Supreme Court refused in June 1998 to hear his case, a Massachusetts businessman lost his argument that a high school newspaper had to accept his political advertisement encouraging sexual abstinence. Douglas Yeo wanted the ad in the newspaper and yearbook, but the student editors said no. Yeo rejected the students' offer to write a letter to the editor after they cited an unwritten policy not to accept political or advocacy ads. The First U.S. Circuit Court of Appeals initially ruled for Yeo, but a six-judge panel of the appellate court reheard the case and unanimously ruled for the students. The court said in *Yeo v. Lexington* that where high school officials (here under the mandate of a Massachusetts statute) grant editorial control to students, there is "no legal duty here on the part of school administrators to control the content of the editorial judgments of student editors of publications."[166]

In a recent New Hampshire case, a student sued his school district because a senior photo of him posing with a shotgun over his shoulder would not be published in the student yearbook. A district court judge ruled that the student's First Amendment rights were not denied because the yearbook staff, not school officials, made the editorial decision. Judge Steven McAuliffe implied that the student may have had a claim if the administration had banned the photo.[167]

An Ohio federal judge offered useful guidance on the public-forum issue when deciding a newspaper censorship case in 2003. Noting that a student newspaper is not always a public forum, Judge James Gwin discussed and weighed nine factors that he said should be used to determine whether a student publication is protected as a limited public forum. When he found that six of the nine criteria were met, he declared the Wooster High School newspaper a limited public forum. The school district then settled the case, agreeing to pay the students' legal fees of $30,000 and to donate $5,000 to charities of the students' choice.[168]

In *Dean v. Utica,*, a case that SPLC Executive Director Mark Goodman calls "[t]he most important student-newspaper censorship case since *Hazelwood*,"[169] the judge noted in detail how both practice and policy identified the publication as a limited public forum. Among other things, he cited the school's description of the journalism class, the course's curriculum guide and the newspaper's printed masthead as evidence that the publication was a forum.[170]

For more than a decade, free press advocates have encouraged high school journalists to clearly establish their publications as public forums. Where school authorities clearly have sanctioned the newspaper as a limited public forum, or where administrators have given students editorial control over content, it is likely that the standard from *Tinker*, not *Hazelwood*, will apply. The news-

---

164 *See* Draudt v. Wooster City Sch. Dist. Bd. of Ed., 246 F. Supp. 2d 820 (N.D. Ohio 2003); Hills v. Scottsdale Unified Sch. Dist., 329 F.3d 1044 (9th Cir. 2003). *See also Going Public,* STUDENT PRESS LAW CENTER REP., Spring 2006, at 6; *Hosty v. Carter: An Analysis,* STUDENT PRESS LAW CENTER REP., Fall 2005, at 27.

165 Planned Parenthood v. Clark County Sch. Dist., 887 F.2d 935 (9th Cir. 1989).

166 131 F.3d 241, 253 (1st Cir. 1997).

167 *See* Douglass v. Londonderry Sch. Bd., 413 F. Supp. 2d 1 (D.N.H. 2005). *See also N.H. Court Rejects Student's Claim That School Unfairly Banned Photos,* STUDENT PRESS LAW CENTER REP., Spring 2005, at 9.

168 *See* Draudt v. Wooster City Sch. Dist. Bd. of Educ., 246 F. Supp. 2d 820 (N.D. Ohio 2003). *See also School Board Pays $35,000 to Settle Wooster Blade Censorship Lawsuit,* STUDENT PRESS LAW CENTER REP., Winter 2003-04, at 8.

169 *See Court Releases Opinion on Utica High School Censorship Case,* STUDENT PRESS LAW CENTER NEWSFLASH, Nov. 18, 2004, *at* http://www.splc.org.

170 *See* Dean v. Utica Community Schs., 345 F. Supp. 2d 799, 807-08 (E.D. Mich. 2004).

paper or yearbook can become a forum through state law, school board policy, curriculum materials or an agreement with school officials, reinforced by practice and a staff policy that demonstrate the newspaper is used for an exchange of opinions.

### Do officials know that editorial control brings liability?
Whether a student newspaper is, by policy or practice, a public forum is important to students. But school officials also can benefit when they decide not to review copy before publication and give the staff responsibility for newspaper content.[171]

Officials at a high school or college who fear they will be held responsible for harmful expression should be reassured that they will be as liable as a private publisher if they routinely review and regulate publication content.[172]

Private publishers are legally responsible for defamatory content they print because they and their editors are free to decide what to publish. The Supreme Court, however, said that a television station carrying the defamatory comments of a political candidate was not responsible because the station had no editorial control. Broadcasters cannot be held accountable for content that Congress, through Section 315 of the Communications Act, denied station owners the power to edit, the Court said.[173]

School authorities may argue for the same immunity when the student newspaper at their school, by policy or by practice, has become a public forum and the administration does not review content. This was true when editors chose photos for the school yearbook[174] and may apply as well to a school-hosted Web site.[175] In public universities, where administrators have little control over student publication content, it is unlikely that a court would hold school officials legally liable for what is printed. In the high school, officials have more authority to oversee content but are not required by *Hazelwood* to do so. The more oversight and influence the administration exercises, the more likely it is that the school will be legally liable for what is published. By turning editorial decisions over to a staff and/or faculty adviser, school officials are in a better position to argue for the immunity that at least four courts have accorded state universities.[176] The most recent of these was a Minnesota appeals court in 2005 that

protected university officials from liability in a libel suit against the student newspaper. The court said that the university did not have the liability of a private publisher when college policy and First Amendment constraints prevented the university from controlling newspaper content.[177]

### Has law or policy given students more free-speech rights?
The Supreme Court has clearly indicated that lawmakers may give citizens more free speech protection than the Constitution provides. That's what students learned when the Court unanimously upheld their rights under the California Constitution to distribute literature at a privately owned shopping mall.[178]

California also passed a law in 1971 that codified the *Tinker* "substantial disruption" standard and protection for the speech and press rights of high school students. By the early 1980s, federal courts regularly cited and applied *Tinker*, and some free-speech observers thought the California law merely re-stated the Supreme Court precedent.

Then along came the *Hazelwood* decision, and within weeks a high school administrator tried to apply the new ruling and censor a California student newspaper. But the censorship was challenged, and a judge ruled that the state law granting students more free-speech rights takes precedence over the *Hazelwood*-based argument that educational goals justified censorship.[179]

Since then, the Student Press Law Center reports, twenty-nine other states have considered or debated legislation on student expression. Massachusetts followed California's lead and enacted legislation in July 1988. Then came Iowa, Colorado, Kansas and Arkansas. No similar state legislation has been passed since 1995. Bills to restrict student press censorship failed to gain approval during 1999 legislative sessions in Connecticut, Missouri and Illinois. In Nebraska, legislation carried over from 1999 to the 2000 session died when no compromise could be reached to advance the bill for a vote. Only two states — Alabama and Oregon — had legislative activity on free-speech laws in 2001. Both efforts hit snags. For the second consecutive year, amendments diluted and stalled legislation in Alabama.[180]

SPLC Director Goodman said in 2003 that legislation seemed to have a low priority among journalism educators, who were not committed to the planning and coalition-building needed to pass a law. During the twelve years since the last *Hazelwood* legislation

---

[171] *See Hold That Thought,* STUDENT PRESS LAW CENTER REP., Fall 2003, at 36.

[172] *See Gallo v. Princeton Univ.,* 656 A.2d 1267 (N.J. 1995); McEvaddy v. City Univ. of New York, 633 N.Y.S.2d 2 (N.Y. App. Div. 1995); LAW OF THE STUDENT PRESS, *supra* note 13, at 159. *See also* Ruth Walden, *The University's Tort Liability for Libel and Invasion of Privacy in the Student Press,* 65 JOURNALISM Q. 616 (Fall 1988).

[173] Farmers Educ. & Coop. Union of Am. v. WDAY, 360 U.S. 525 (1959).

[174] *See Douglass v. Londonderry Sch. Bd.,* 413 F. Supp. 2d 1 (D.N.H. 2005).

[175] *See Guide to Internet Law,* STUDENT PRESS LAW CENTER REP., Fall 2004, at 40, 42.

[176] *See Milliner v. Turner,* 436 So. 2d 1300 (La. Ct. App. 1983); Mazart v. State, 441 N.Y.S. 2d 600 (N.Y.Ct.Cl. 1981); Lewis v. St. Cloud State Univ., No. C2-04-2244 (Dist. Ct. Ramsey County, June 9, 2004), *affd.,* 693 N.W.2d 466 (Minn. Ct. App. Mar. 22, 2005); Doe v. New York University, No. 109457/04 (N.Y.Sup.Ct., New York County, Dec. 8, 2004).

[177] *See Lewis v. St. Cloud State Univ.,* 693 N.W.2d 466 (Minn. Ct. App., Mar. 22, 2005).

[178] *See Pruneyard Shopping Center v. Robins,* 447 U.S. 74 (1980).

[179] Leeb v. DeLong, 243 Cal. Rptr. 494 (Cal. Dist. Ct. App. 1988). *But see, Principals Censor Newspapers at Two Calif. Schools,* STUDENT PRESS LAW CENTER REP., Spring 2000, at 24 (describing censorship incidents where administrators ignored the state law).

[180] *See Student Press Supporters Pessimistic About Future of Free-Expression Bills,* STUDENT PRESS LAW CENTER REP., Spring 2001, at 41.

was passed, school personnel have struggled with the aftermath of Columbine, and budget deficits have preoccupied legislators.[181] What has been called anti-*Hazelwood* legislation was introduced during 2005 in Vermont and Michigan, although no bill was passed in either state. The court case involving Katy Dean and Utica High School journalism students got the legislature's attention in Michigan,[182] but that legislation stalled in 2006 after the Michigan Press Association refused to support it. Some encouragement came in California when two bills were introduced, one giving college journalists First Amendment protection that would negate the threat of *Hosty v. Carter*, the other addressing newspaper theft by making it a misdemeanor to take more than twenty-five copies of a free newspaper.[183]

But nationwide, other legislative obstacles have discouraged censorship:

- California's "Leonard Law," discussed earlier in connection with campus speech codes, extends First Amendment protection to high school and college students in both public and private schools.
- Students in Oregon and New Jersey have argued that their state constitutions protect student expression.
- The New York Commissioner of Education said that the publication policies of Long Island's Northport High School reveal the school's decision to set free-speech standards more permissive than *Hazelwood*'s.
- Two states – Pennsylvania and Washington – have added protection in "student rights" sections of their state education codes. In its code, Pennsylvania's Department of Education used *Tinker* to build a standard for freedom of expression that the state's scholastic press association uses to help police censorship efforts in the schools. Student press advocates have had to monitor efforts to weaken the protection of state codes. Pennsylvania successfully fought off such an assault in 2002, only to face and successfully thwart State Board of Education attempts in 2004 and 2005 to revise the code.

## SUMMARY

High school and college students today experience quite different First Amendment freedoms and tensions on their campuses. In public institutions, students have many rights other citizens have, and administrators are considered public officials subject to some of the same constitutional restrictions all government officials face. But freedoms of speech and press have limits in the schools, just

as they have parameters elsewhere in society, and some observers fear that the reach and power of cyberspace may blur some legal distinctions among educational institutions.

The legal springboard for student free-speech rights is the Supreme Court's 1969 ruling in *Tinker v. Des Moines Independent School District*, which stressed the value of free expression and said that school officials could stop student speech only by showing that the expression would substantially disrupt the school or infringe on the rights of others. Hundreds of high school and college cases during the next seventeen years were based on *Tinker* and its premise that free speech should be encouraged, even in school.

Some educators, especially in high schools, continued to argue for different regulatory standards based on school officials' responsibility to teach the young. That plus the relative immaturity of students and the need for an environment conducive to learning were reasons administrators gave for denying students freedom in school that they might have elsewhere.

The Supreme Court eventually agreed that free-speech distinctions and tighter restrictions are appropriate when dealing with high school students. Until recently, students in post-secondary schools have been considered adults, with the same First Amendment rights accorded adults elsewhere in society. A lower court in Kentucky tried to apply *Hazelwood* at the college level before an appellate court overturned the ruling. *Kincaid v. Gibson* removed some uncertainty about the context for free expression on college campuses, distancing student publications here from the restrictive free-speech rationale of *Hazelwood*. But the Seventh Circuit's 2005 ruling in *Hosty v. Carter* kept ties to *Hazelwood* alive and implied that college publications should clearly be identified as limited public forums to remain censorship-free.

In the past decade, college students have successfully challenged speech and conduct codes that the courts ruled too broad and restrictive, and college journalists have had some success in the Congress and the courts during frequent battles for access to campus crime information. High school officials have found it easier to restrict expression, but student journalists have tried to curb censorship by getting the school to recognize the student press as a public forum. And the Internet, with its ease of access, wealth of information and potential for abuse and harm, has imposed added responsibility on school officials. As they gauge public opinion while balancing the learning potential and their obligation to protect vulnerable youth, school authorities seem more willing to err on the side of close regulation.

## FOR ADDITIONAL READING

College Media Advisers, http://www.collegemedia.org.
*Death by Cheeseburger: High School Journalism in the 1990s and Beyond.* Arlington, Va.: The Freedom Forum, 1994.
*First Amendment Center*, http://www.firstamendmentcenter.org.

---

[181] *See Censorship on the Rise,* STUDENT PRESS LAW CENTER REP., Spring 2002, at 20; *Sad State of Affairs,* STUDENT PRESS LAW CENTER REP., Spring 2003, at 27.

[182] *See Legislatures Have Journalists in Mind,* STUDENT PRESS LAW CENTER REP., Spring 2005, at 4.

[183] *See California Legislation Protecting Student Newspapers Moves Forward,* STUDENT PRESS LAW CENTER NEWSFLASH, May 11, 2006, http://www.splc.org/newsflash.

Ingelhart, Louis E. *Student Publications: Legalities, Governance, and Operation.* Ames, Iowa: Iowa State University Press, 1993.

Journalism Education Association, http://www.jeapressrights/org.

*Law of the Student Press,* 2nd ed. Arlington, Va.: Student Press Law Center, 1994.

Student Press Law Center, http://www.splc.org.

*Student Press Law Center Report.* Thrice-yearly magazine of the SPLC, Arlington, Va.

# 14

# Privacy and the Professional Communicator

*By Sigman Splichal and Samuel A. Terilli, Jr.*

---

## ☞ Headnote Questions

- *What expectation of privacy do individuals have in American society?*
- *What kinds of information are private?*
- *What legal remedies are available for individuals who believe their privacy has been invaded?*
- *Are any legal remedies available to the news media when they report about private matters?*
- *Is a right of privacy recognized in the U.S. Constitution?*
- *Do students have any privacy rights?*
- *What special privacy issues or concerns do computers raise?*

---

*Privacy.*

The word resonates within American society, its citizens often making social and legal claims based on the belief they have a fundamental right, as U.S. Supreme Court Justice Louis Brandeis once put it, "to be let alone."[1] Privacy is a social concept as old as the nation, imbedded in its beginning, from the first settlers drawn to a new land in search of religious and political freedom in the Seventeenth Century to revolutionary patriots affronted by England's cavalier disregard for the autonomy of their businesses and the sanctity of their homes. The concept of privacy can be found in the liberal theories of Enlightenment philosophers, whose emphasis on individual liberties based on natural rights inspired the Founding Fathers' generation as it began to envision a new nation.[2] Indeed, essential elements of privacy are woven into the nation's most hallowed documents.

Yet, while privacy as a social value was apparent during the nation's formative years, privacy as the basis for *legal* claims remained elusive. Only in the last 100 years has privacy been propelled into the legal mainstream, mainly due to changes in the way Americans live and think.

Privacy is a dynamic value that continues to evolve, as do all social values, norms and customs. To be understood in an information-driven society — both in social and legal contexts — privacy must be viewed as a value that changes as society tries to balance rights of individuals with its needs and desires for information. The Ninth U.S. Circuit Court of Appeals put it aptly in a 1975 privacy case: To resolve privacy claims, courts must consider "the customs and conventions of the community; and in the last analysis what is proper becomes a matter of community mores."[3]

This chapter looks, first, at the evolution of the concept of privacy. It then focuses on the development of privacy as a distinct legal doctrine and its treatment in the common law of the states. It then discusses the four distinct privacy torts courts have identified: (1) publication of embarrassing private facts, (2) physical and technological intrusion, (3) false-light invasion of privacy and (4) commercialization. It also briefly addresses constitutional and statutory privacy, both of which place limits on government use of personal information — limits that have important implications for journalists, especially in the era of databases, the World Wide Web, the Internet and reporters' growing reliance on computer-assisted reporting. Finally, the chapter looks at ethical implications of privacy as the rights to gather and receive news are balanced with the rights of individuals to be let alone, and it examines the tort of intentional infliction of emotional distress.

---

[1] Olmstead v United States, 227 U.S. 438, 478 (1928). Actually, Judge Thomas M. Cooley had used the term forty years earlier in his A TREATISE ON THE LAW OF TORTS 29 (2d ed. 1888).

[2] *See, e.g.,* JOHN LOCKE, THE SECOND TREATISE ON GOVERNMENT (T. Peardon ed., 1952) (1690).

[3] Virgil v. Time, Inc., 527 F.2d 1122, 1129 (9th Cir. 1975).

## THE EVOLUTION OF A RIGHT TO PRIVACY

The concept of privacy, though never expressed as it is understood today, was not unknown in English common law, the legal system dominant in Colonial America and later adopted by the fledgling nation. Cases dating to the Norman Conquest recognized a value resembling privacy in the property rights of individuals. In 1741, the House of Lords, then England's highest court, invoked a property-rights doctrine to protect contents of personal letters from unauthorized publication.[4] This case, *Pope v. Curl,* is important in the development of privacy in American law because it acknowledged a property right in individuals' retention and control of personal ideas and information in letters sent to others, not only in the letters themselves.

In the development of American social and legal values, the basic characteristics of modern privacy predate the American Revolution. English philosopher John Locke, whose writings influenced Thomas Jefferson and other founders, argued that government had a duty to protect fundamental rights such as life, liberty and property.[5] These inalienable rights were described in the Declaration of Independence, the Constitution and the Bill of Rights. The Supreme Court, almost 200 years later, gleaned from the fundamental concept of liberty a constitutional right of privacy.[6]

In his book *Privacy in Colonial New England,* historian David H. Flaherty explored the precursors to modern privacy. He observed that although privacy as a legal doctrine evolved slowly, its underlying values were expressed in colonial customs and in the courts. Courts, he suggested, protected privacy values indirectly by enforcing laws against trespass, by limiting government searches and seizures, by hearing defamation cases and by recognizing privileged communications between wives and husbands. Ironically, as Flaherty pointed out, there was little physical privacy — in the modern sense — in most homes and public accommodations. Homes often lacked individual sleeping quarters, and families congregated in common beds. Communal sleeping arrangements were also common in public inns.[7] Traces of the practice remained as late as 150 years ago: During his early career as a struggling, small-town lawyer, Abraham Lincoln shared a room and bed above his office with a law partner.[8]

Flaherty noted that the concept of informational privacy was officially recognized during Benjamin Franklin's tenure as postmaster general before the American Revolution. Postmasters were required to swear an oath that they would not "wittingly, willingly, or knowingly open ... any letters which shall come into their hands."[9]

Values underlying privacy also were apparent as the Revolutionary War drew near and played a central role in the colo-

nists' growing hostility toward British rule. In 1761, Boston lawyer James Otis, speaking against the practice of general search warrants, noted: "Now one of the most essential branches of English liberty, is the freedom of one's own house. A man's house is his castle; and while he is quiet he is as well guarded as a prince in his castle."[10] On the eve of the Revolutionary War, each colony drew up a list of grievances against the British authorities. Atop each list was concern about general warrants, which authorized government agents to search premises at will without first presenting evidence of a specific violation of the law. After the colonies won independence, James Madison, the major proponent of a bill of rights spelling out individual liberties, introduced a proposal at the Constitutional Convention in 1789 to limit the scope of government searches. That proposal, which established "the right of the people to be secure ... against unreasonable search and seizures," was later adopted as the Fourth Amendment.

Values supporting privacy also found expression in the writings of nineteenth-century English philosopher John Stuart Mill, whose works were widely read in the United States. Mill argued in his influential *On Liberty* that the government should have no say in certain kinds of personal conduct, absent a compelling social interest. Expounding on this concept of personal liberty, he wrote: "The only part of conduct of anyone for which he is amenable to society is that which concerns others. In the part which merely concerns himself, his independence is, of right, absolute."[11]

## PRIVACY AS A LEGAL RIGHT

Legal concerns related to privacy developed slowly during the nation's first century, in large part because of the agrarian nature of society. Conflicts were as few and far between as the nation's early inhabitants. This physical distance reduced unwanted contacts and intrusions and the need for legal resolutions. Yet cases reflecting privacy concerns did surface. One nineteenth century case worth mentioning for its unusual facts is *Demay v. Roberts.* The case arose after a doctor took along an untrained assistant to help deliver a baby. The parents sued when they learned the assistant was not medically trained, arguing their privacy had been violated. The Michigan Supreme Court agreed, holding the mother had a "legal right to the privacy of her apartment at such a time."[12]

The demographics of American society shifted dramatically as the Industrial Revolution hit full force. Technological developments such as the steam engine led to manufacturing-based cities populated by factory workers. Physical distance between people shrank as populations converged in cities, and those in foreign lands began a new flow of immigration. In those crowded cities, the barriers of time and space common to rural settings no

---

[4] *See* Morris L. Ernst & Alan U. Schwartz, Privacy: The Right To Be Let Alone 5-6 (1962).

[5] Locke, *supra* note 2, at 55-81.

[6] *See* Griswold v. Connecticut, 381 U.S. 479, 486 (1965).

[7] David H. Flaherty, Privacy in Colonial New England (1972).

[8] David Herbert Donald, Lincoln 70 (1995).

[9] Flaherty, *supra* note 7, at 121.

[10] Richard F. Hixson, Privacy in a Public Society: Human Rights in Conflict 13 (1987).

[11] John Stuart Mill, On Liberty 13 (Currin V. Shields ed., 1956).

[12] 9 N.W. 146, 148 (Mich. 1881).

longer insulated individuals from unwanted contacts. Between 1870 and 1900, the population of the United States doubled, and the number of urban residents tripled.

Dramatic technological developments in the nineteenth century that threatened privacy were traced by Alan F. Westin in *Privacy and Freedom*, a comprehensive study of privacy issues. Westin noted that several technological developments in the late nineteenth century "altered the balance between personal expression and third-party surveillance that had prevailed since antiquity."[13] These innovations were the microphone and telephone in the late 1870s, the Kodak camera with its potential for "instantaneous photographs" in the 1880s and the dictograph recorder in the 1890s.

In 1877, the *New York Times* expressed concern about the effect of new technology on privacy. It called the telephone "a nefarious instrument" with "vast capabilities for mischief" that promised to rob individuals of their personal privacy. Responding to a decision by the city to allow telephone wires to be attached to city lamp posts, the *Times* cautioned:

> Every confidential remark made to a lamp-post by a belated Democratic statesman could be reproduced by a telephone connected with any other lamp-post.... Men who had trusted to friendly lamp-posts, and embraced them with the utmost confidence in their silence and discretion, would find themselves shamelessly betrayed, and their unsuspecting philosophies literally reported to their indignant families.[14]

While technology spurred the growth of industrial cities and development of such privacy-altering inventions as the telephone, other innovations — high-speed newspaper presses and advanced photography — spawned an aggressive kind of journalism, a distant cousin to that espoused by the colonial and revolutionary printers who catered to society's well-read and politically astute. New printing processes reproduced newspapers quickly and cheaply, and a new kind of journalism developed that often directed its content at the baser instincts of the swelling numbers of city dwellers. The "penny press" era of the mid-nineteenth century later yielded to "yellow journalism," sensationalistic news coverage to boost newspaper circulations that reached its peak toward century's end. Newspaper readers, not so interested in the complexities of politics and other public issues, sought information about misdeeds and travails. This new readership, coupled with journalists armed with cameras intruding into new, heretofore private areas, sometimes brought newspaper practices and privacy concerns into conflict. These conflicts created new social and legal issues to be sorted out.

In 1890, a pair of former law partners and Harvard Law School classmates took issue with the newspaper practices and technologies of the day. Louis Brandeis and Samuel Warren, uppercrust Boston lawyers, penned "The Right to Privacy" for the *Harvard Law Review*. The seminal article would steer the notion of a legal right of privacy toward the mainstream of American law. Attempting to document what they considered a climate of journalistic excess, the authors stated, somewhat hyperbolically: "Instantaneous photographs and newspaper enterprise have invaded the sacred precincts of private and domestic life; and numerous mechanical devices threaten to make good the prediction that 'what is whispered in the closet shall be proclaimed from the house-tops.'"[15] Brandeis and Warren argued that individuals possessed certain attributes, such as sentiments and intellect, over which they exercised rights akin to those governing personal property. The authors identified these rights in analogous laws on breach of trust, assault, copyright and defamation.

In 1895, six years after "The Right to Privacy" was published, the New York Court of Appeals addressed the issue of privacy in *Schuyler v. Curtis*.[16] The family of a prominent woman sued a private organization to halt plans to erect a life-size statue in her memory. The woman had never been a public personality, and the statue was an invasion of privacy, her family argued. The court acknowledged that it lacked clear guidance from previous cases and rejected the family's claim. It focused on the fact the woman was dead and concluded that any privacy interest followed her to the grave, thus stopping short of fully exploring the legal issues.

In some early privacy cases, before psychiatry and psychology had gained credence in legal circles, courts expressed fundamental concerns about awarding damages for mental harm. In 1902, for example, the New York Court of Appeals refused to recognize a right of privacy in *Roberson v. Rochester Folding Box Co.*, a case addressed more fully in the discussion of the tort of appropriation. In *Roberson*, the family of a young girl sued a flour company for using the girl's photograph in an advertisement. The family argued the advertisement caused the girl to be "greatly humiliated by the scoffs and jeers of persons who recognized her face and picture."[17] The court, while sympathetic, refused to recognize a legal remedy for an intangible mental harm, fearing such a precedent might trigger similar lawsuits that would clutter the courts. It also expressed concern that privacy liability would place unreasonable burdens on the press, which often used photographs of individuals without permission.

While New York's highest court was hesitant to embrace privacy, the Georgia Supreme Court was not, reaching the opposite result in a similar case, and becoming the first court to recognize unauthorized use of a person's identity as a violation of privacy.[18] The ruling prompted Louis Brandeis to write that he was encouraged to see privacy as a distinguishable legal right recognized by the courts.[19]

In addition to promoting privacy as a legal doctrine, the article by Brandeis and Warren may have helped elevate privacy in public discourse. In 1902, the *New York Times* took issue with new

---

[13] ALAN F. WESTIN, PRIVACY AND FREEDOM 338 (1967).

[14] Editorial, *The Telephone Unmasked*, N.Y. TIMES, Oct. 12, 1877, at 4.

[15] 4 HARVARD L. REV. 193, 195 (1890).

[16] 42 N.E. 22 (N.Y. 1891).

[17] 64 N.E. 442, 443 (N.Y. 1902).

[18] Pavesich v. New England Life, 50 S.E. 68 (Ga. 1905).

[19] 1 LETTERS OF LOUIS D. BRANDEIS 306 (M. Urofsky & D. Levy eds., 1971).

photographic technology, which no longer required willing subjects to sit motionless. Echoing the concerns of Brandeis and Warren, the newspaper complained in an editorial that "Kodakers lying in wait to photograph public figures had become a wanton invasion of privacy that demands legal control."[20]

While the Brandeis and Warren article nudged the issue of privacy onto the social and legal stage, the development of a unified legal theory remained elusive. In the ensuing decades, the legal contours of privacy developed piecemeal and with many variations. Seventy years after "The Right to Privacy" proposed a separate legal remedy for invasion of privacy, torts expert William Prosser summarized the extent of the common law development of privacy in an article in the *California Law Review*. Titled simply "Privacy," it dealt with tort law and not with constitutional or statutory questions of privacy. After reviewing some 200 privacy-related cases, Prosser identified four separate torts: (1) disclosure of embarrassing private facts about individuals; (2) intrusion, the physical or technological violation of an individual's privacy; (3) false light, the intentional dissemination of highly offensive false publicity about another; and (4) appropriation, or the use of another person's likeness without permission.[21]

## THE PRIVACY TORTS

American law assumes members of society have certain duties toward one another. These duties, derived from customs, mores and values, are often recognized in common law cases and in various statutes; they form the basis of tort law. Under the theory of tort law, when a member of society violates a duty toward another person that results in an identifiable harm, the injured person may recover damages. One class of duties deals with privacy and the harm — usually mental — that results when it is violated. When the news media are involved, courts have balanced individual privacy with other interests, such as the free flow of information to society about matters of public concern. Since the nature of the harm is usually mental, privacy torts apply only to individuals, not to businesses or corporations that exist merely as creatures of law.

Tort law varies from state to state. So any generalizations are based on trends in cases from the various states. Actual application of law in privacy cases may vary considerably, not only from state to state, but also among judicial jurisdictions within a state. Professional communicators need to be well versed in the laws and customs where they work.

### Embarrassing Private Facts

*Definition: The tort involving embarrassing facts is publication of private information that would be highly offensive to a reasonable person and is not a matter of legitimate public concern.*

The common law acknowledges that some information about

individuals should remain beyond the reach of neighbors — and the news media — and that disclosures normally would lead to unwarranted embarrassment or humiliation. The embarrassing private facts tort rests on several questions, each of which a plaintiff must answer effectively to advance a legal privacy claim.

*What is publication?* In libel law, "publication" has a specialized meaning. At a minimum, a libel plaintiff must prove a defamatory communication reached at least one person other than the plaintiff and defendant. Under the embarrassing private facts tort, however, "publication" means "publicity," that is, widespread communication. Publication in a newspaper, magazine or other print medium satisfies this requirement, as would dissemination by broadcast or cable. While laws governing libel and privacy in computer communications are still evolving, it is reasonable to assume that widespread communication of private information *via* a commercial database, user groups, bulk e-mail, Web page or similar means would meet this requirement.

*Is the information private?* As a threshold, an embarrassing private facts plaintiff must establish that the information in question is, in fact, private. What happens in public, or what appears in public records, normally is not considered private. In *Cox Broadcasting Co. v. Cohn*, the Supreme Court held that the news media are not to be held liable for publication of personal information, even if the media violate a state statute designed to protect rape victims, if they "merely give further publicity to information about a plaintiff which is already public."[22] In a California case, a privacy claim failed because the information was gleaned from public records.[23] A person involved in an automobile accident or the victim of a crime, therefore, cannot claim invasion of privacy based on photographs of or stories about the accident. As a Massachusetts court noted: "Many things which are distressing and lacking in propriety or good taste are not actionable."[24] Likewise, a participant in a public rally or parade cannot later claim privacy related to those actions.[25] At least one court, however, has said a crime victim's privacy might outweigh newsworthiness and the right to publish, even when the name is a matter of public record. In *Times Mirror Co. v. San Diego Superior Court*, a California appellate court reasoned that a crime witness' safety and the state's interest in prosecuting the crime might outweigh the media's right to publish and the public's right to know the name of the witness.[26]

Even intimate personal information cannot normally be the basis for a privacy claim if it is already widely known, as Oliver Sipple learned after he thwarted an assassination attempt on President Gerald Ford. Subsequent news accounts of Sipple's heroism disclosed that he was a homosexual, a fact already known within the San Francisco gay community.[27]

Consent is also a factor in determining whether personal information should be considered public or private. While the ques-

---

[20] WESTIN, *supra* note 13, at 338.
[21] William Prosser, *Privacy,* 48 CAL. L. REV. 383-84 (1960).

[22] 420 U.S. 469, 494 (1975).
[23] Briscoe v. Reader's Digest Ass'n, 483 P.2d 34 (Cal. 1972).
[24] Kelley v. Post Publ'g Co., 98 N.E.2d 286, 287 (Mass. 1951).
[25] Sipple v. Chronicle Publ'g Co., 201 Cal. Rptr. 665 (Cal. Ct. App. 1984).
[26] 244 Cal. Rptr. 556 (Cal. Ct. App. 1988).
[27] *Sipple,* 104 Cal. App. 3d at 1044.

tion of consent will be addressed more fully in a later discussion of private facts defenses, it should be noted that a person cannot normally provide information knowingly to the news media and subsequently claim an invasion of privacy, although in some instances consent might be effectively withdrawn.

*What kind of information might be considered highly offensive to a reasonable person?* A memorable case based on a "Where Are They Now?" story about child prodigy William Sidis offers a definition. Sidis sued for invasion of privacy based on a 1937 article in *The New Yorker*, published more than a quarter century after he made headlines as a preteen math whiz. He claimed the magazine's delving into his present life was offensive. On appeal, the Second U.S. Circuit Court of Appeals disagreed, holding that to be sufficiently offensive, a private disclosure must "outrage the community's notions of decency."[28] A more recent California case defined offensiveness differently, suggesting the public's legitimate interest in personal information ends when a publication forgoes legitimate news values and "becomes a morbid and sensational prying into private lives for its own sake."[29]

What kind of disclosure, then, would outrage a community's sense of decency or constitute sensational prying? Another oft-cited case is instructive and suggests that stories dealing with medical or other intimate health conditions are most problematic for journalists. Dorothy Barber was dubbed a "starving glutton" in a *Time* magazine article about a bizarre medical condition that caused her to lose weight despite eating large quantities of food. She sued *Time* for invasion of privacy after the magazine published a photograph showing her in a hospital room. The Missouri Supreme Court, citing the long-standing privacy protection accorded doctor-patient relationships, held that disclosure of the unusual eating disorder was embarrassing to Barber and invaded her privacy. The court acknowledged the public's interest in such medical maladies but reasoned that identifying Barber was not necessary to tell the story about the medical disorder.[30] As a rule, invasive stories or pictures that deal with physical or mental illness, or that expose the intimate parts of the body, require particular caution. The court's reliance on doctor-patient privilege in the Barber case also suggests disclosures that involve information normally protected under common law privileges could be considered highly offensive. *The Restatement of Torts* suggests several problem areas: sexual relations, humiliating illnesses, intimate personal letters, family disputes, details of home life, stolen photos or photos taken in private places, and information from individual tax returns.[31]

A plaintiff must prove the *widespread publicity* of intimately private material that a *reasonable person* would find *highly offensive*, and that the information was *not* related to a *matter of public concern*. At this juncture in most private facts cases involving the news media, plaintiffs fail, because most of what is printed or broadcast is chosen because it *is* newsworthy.

*What constitutes a matter of public concern?* Even if a plaintiff can establish that disclosure is highly offensive to a reasonable person, the likelihood of winning a privacy suit is slim if the plaintiff has become part of a public event or controversy. Information related to traditional news values is likely to deal with matters of public concern. Information about politics, law enforcement, crime, domestic violence, suicide, medical advances and social trends falls within the realm of traditional news.

The 1982 case of Hilda Bridges, who became an unintended actor on a very public stage, dramatically underscores the dearth of privacy protection for individuals caught up in news events. Bridges was dragged into a public matter when police officers — and members of the news media — surrounded her apartment after she was taken hostage by her estranged husband, who forced her to undress to prevent her from fleeing. During a standoff with police, the husband shot himself and police rushed the apartment. Bridges fled naked and distraught into the street, clutching only a hand towel. After *Today* newspaper in Cocoa Beach, Florida, published a revealing photograph, Bridges sued for invasion of privacy and infliction of emotional distress.

Satisfied that such publicity was unwarranted and highly offensive, a Florida jury awarded Bridges $10,000. A Florida appellate court, however, unanimously set aside the award, ruling that the law had not been properly followed. The jury had erred, the court reasoned, because events in question happened in public and because crime was a matter of public concern. Judge James Dauksch noted that privacy at some point must yield to the public interest. "Just because the story and photograph may be embarrassing or distressful does not mean the newspaper cannot publish what is otherwise newsworthy."[32] While publication of the photograph raised numerous ethical questions, Bridges' chances of eventual success were virtually nil because she had become caught up in a public drama. Years earlier in a privacy case, a Florida court had concluded: "Even though the plaintiff's role of 'actor' in an event having news value was not of his own volition ... the fact remains that he was in a public place and present at a scene where news was in the making."[33]

The result was essentially the same when a bystander at a public event thwarted an attempt to assassinate President Gerald Ford during his visit to San Francisco in 1975. As described earlier, Oliver Sipple's act of heroism drew him into the limelight, illuminating his Vietnam War record as well as his homosexuality. Sipple, well known in San Francisco's gay community before the Ford episode, sued the *San Francisco Chronicle* and other newspapers for invasion of privacy. He argued that while his public actions were newsworthy, his private life was not, and that disclosure of his sexual orientation caused him embarrassment because his homosexuality was not widely known. A California appellate court held that both Sipple's heroism and his homosexuality were newsworthy, noting that his heroic behavior cut

[28] Sidis v. F-R Publ'g Co., 113 F.2d 806, 809 (2d Cir. 1940).

[29] Virgil v. Time, Inc., 527 F.2d 1122, 1129 (9th Cir. 1975).

[30] Barber v. Time, Inc., 159 S.W.2d 291 (Mo. 1942).

[31] RESTATEMENT (SECOND) OF TORTS § 652D, comments b, g (1977).

[32] Cape Publ'ns, Inc. v. Bridges, 423 So.2d 426, 428 (Fla. Ct. App. 1982).

[33] Jacova v. Southern Radio and Television Co., 83 So.2d 34, 40 (Fla. 1955).

against stereotypes of gays.[34]

In Florida, a federal district court judge ruled that a suicidal sixteen-year-old girl filmed by a crew from the Fox Television docudrama *Cops* had no right of privacy because the filming resulted from her call to authorities seeking help. After the call was routed to 911, the film crew, riding with deputies that night, went to the girl's home, where she was videotaped in an open garage. When the footage was televised, the girl's face was intentionally blurred. The judge said a person who commits public acts that result in police intervention cannot expect such circumstances to remain private.[35]

While much of what is newsworthy deals with matters of social and political importance, any mass communication student knows newsworthiness also can be defined as anything out of the ordinary. Unusual occupations, hobbies, talents and other qualities that attract public attention are newsworthy. Two cases are prime examples. The first was based on a story in *Sports Illustrated* about a California body surfer well known for his derring-do. Michael Virgil sued *Sports Illustrated* for invasion of privacy after the magazine included accounts of his unusual personal behavior in a story about his surfing exploits. The information, discussed freely with a reporter, included his eating insects and burning himself with cigarettes, as well as diving headlong down a flight of stairs to impress women. *Sports Illustrated* included the material despite Virgil's request that personal information not be used. In rejecting Virgil's privacy claim, the Ninth U.S. Circuit Court of Appeals concluded that inclusion of the personal information in the story about the daring body surfer was a "legitimate journalistic attempt" to give a full portrait of the body surfer.[36]

*Sidis v. F-R Publishing Corp.* began with a *New Yorker* magazine story about a former child prodigy leading a recluse's life in Boston, never having realized his incredible promise. The court rejected Sidis' privacy claim, reasoning that his childhood acclaim gave rise to legitimate public interest about his present accomplishments.[37]

As *Sidis* suggests, newsworthiness normally stands the test of time in privacy actions. The Kansas Supreme Court reached that conclusion in 1975 after a newspaper republished a story about a police officer fired some ten years earlier. Noting that once "facts are in the public domain they remain there," the court held that republication of a newsworthy event was not an invasion of privacy. It said official government misconduct "is newsworthy when it occurs and remains so for as long as anyone thinks it worth retelling."[38]

In *Forsher v. Bugliosi*, the California Supreme Court stated it another way. Quoting tort expert William Prosser, it said, "[O]nce a man becomes a public figure, or news, he remains a matter of legitimate recall in the public's mind until the end of

his days."[39]

What about instances when the subjects of news accounts revealing private information are public officials or public figures? As a rule, most activities of public persons are newsworthy by virtue of their public status. When the *Miami Herald* disclosed that Democratic presidential contender Gary Hart spent the night with a woman who was not his wife, for example, questions were raised about proper bounds of reporting and the *Herald* was criticized, but the legal question of privacy was never raised. Robert Dole, a contender at the time for the Republican presidential nomination, put the privacy issue this way: "Once you stand up and say you're going to be a candidate for president, all bets are off."[40]

Similarly, had former football star and broadcaster Frank Gifford sued the *Globe* for publishing a story and photographs about his being videotaped with a woman not his wife, he would have little legal recourse unless the publication was false. The public's interest in his behavior was heightened by the fact that his wife, talk show host Kathie Lee Gifford, has been a vocal proponent of family values.

**Private Facts and Constitutional Protections.** The news media have some protection under the First Amendment when they publish truthful, lawfully obtained information about matters of public concern. Several cases help define the scope of this protection.

In *Cox Broadcasting Corp. v. Cohn*, parents of a teenage girl who was raped and murdered sued an Atlanta television station for broadcasting the girl's name. The suit was based on a Georgia statute that forbade publication of names of alleged rape victims. The station, WSB-TV, had obtained the victim's name from records provided at an open court hearing. The Georgia Supreme Court upheld the parents' right to pursue the lawsuit, but the U.S. Supreme Court reversed, focusing on the fact that the information was revealed in judicial records. It said the onus should be on government to ensure privacy by keeping certain information out of the public domain. Allegations of crime and the resulting proceedings, the Court said, "are without question events of legitimate concern to the public" that the press has a duty to report.[41]

Similarly, when the *Florida Star*, a small weekly newspaper, published the name of a rape victim as part of its routine police report, copied from a public bulletin board at the Duval County Sheriff's Department, the Court held that the report was protected. The rape victim sued the newspaper, claiming that violation of the state criminal statute barring publication of names of alleged rape victims constituted evidence of breach of duty and that she should be awarded civil damages for invasion of privacy. A jury agreed and awarded her $100,000. The Supreme Court overturned the verdict, holding that the Constitution prevents

---

[34] Sipple v. Chronicle Publ'g Co., 201 Cal. Rptr. 665 (Cal. Ct. App. 1984).

[35] *See* David Kidwell, *Woman Loses Privacy Suit Against TV Crime Show,* MIAMI HERALD, May 13, 1994, at 1B.

[36] Virgil v. Sports Illustrated, 424 F. Supp. 1286, 1289 (S.D. Cal. 1984).

[37] 113 F.2d 806 (2d Cir. 1940).

[38] Rawlins v. Hutchinson Publ'g Co., 543 P.2d 988, 996 (Kan. 1975).

[39] 608 P. 2d 716, 726 (Cal. 1980).

[40] Deborah Gersh, *Privacy and the Presidency,* EDITOR & PUBLISHER, Oct. 13, 1990, at 15.

[41] 420 U.S. 469, 492 (1975).

states from punishing the news media — even by allowing civil damages — for publishing truthful, lawfully obtained information. As in *Cox Broadcasting*, the Court reasoned that the government shoulders the burden in protecting such privacy interests and that news media could be punished for publishing truthful information only when the punishment advanced a "state interest of the highest order."[42] The Georgia Supreme Court, citing the *Florida Star* ruling, overturned a jury verdict awarding damages to a sexual assault victim who shot her assailant. The story identified the victim but never said specifically she had been sexually assaulted. The Georgia Supreme Court said both the state and federal constitutions protected the right of the newspaper to "accurately report the facts regarding the incident," including the name.[43]

**Consent as a Defense.** Normally, individuals cannot knowingly and willingly disclose their own personal information and then claim an invasion of privacy. As a rule, the more intimate the information, the more important for the reporter to be sure consent was clearly given, either explicitly or implicitly. Consent is explicit when professional communicators ask for and receive permission to use personal information for publication. There are few problems when people know they are speaking about themselves for publication. Consent must come from someone with authority to provide the information.. A friend could not give consent for the use of private information about a college roommate. A day-care operator cannot independently give consent for children under his or her care, nor can a hospital official give consent when the privacy of patients is involved. Minor children cannot give legal consent. Consent need not be in written form, but written consent is almost always easier to prove in court than oral consent.

Can explicit consent later be withdrawn? One court has said no — if the person providing information is newsworthy and the private information is used for legitimate journalistic purposes.[44] ABC News took no chance in June 2001 and decided not to air portions of a program titled *Tampering With Nature* after some parents of elementary school children interviewed for the program withdrew their consent. In a letter to ABC before the program was to air, parents complained that John Stossel asked the children leading questions.[45]

The Supreme Court has limited the freedom of reporters to change reporter/source agreements that rise to the level of rudimentary contracts. In *Cohen v. Cowles Media*, it said a reporter's promise to keep a source's name private could be treated by states as an oral contract without violating the First Amendment rights of the journalist. Journalists had argued that the source's name was newsworthy, and the ultimate decision to use or not use newsworthy information should reside with the

news media.[46] This suggests that journalists should be doubly careful about the terms under which they seek consent to publish private information.

**Implied Consent.** Reporters frequently talk to sources and use the information without specifically asking for permission to do so. Members of the public generally understand the function of reporters in American society. If journalists identify themselves, and sources talk willingly, there should be no problem. Implied consent is problematic if private information is obtained from someone who does not understand that the information is likely to be published.[47]

### *Intrusion*

*Definition: Intrusion is the highly offensive invasion of another person's solitude, either physically or by use of technological devices.*

The fundamental purpose of the tort of intrusion — to protect a person's solitude — can be traced to many of the nation's early values. But the notion of intrusion has gone beyond the traditional legal doctrine of trespass, or physical intrusion, to mechanical and electronic violations of private space. The means by which intrusion occurs have changed from the "instantaneous photography" that so riled Brandeis and Warren to the miniature video cameras that left ABC's *Prime Time Live* reeling from a $3.5 million fraud and trespass verdict in 1996. (That verdict was later reduced to $2 for breach of loyalty and trespass.) Whether physical or technological, the tort of intrusion deals with the *process of gathering information*, not the content of the information gathered.

**Privacy in Public and Quasi-Public Places.** Under common law, people in public places have little expectation of privacy. People engaging in public activities must assume they might be photographed, filmed or recorded.

While people in public places do not forgo all rights to privacy, journalists encounter few legal problems when they photograph or report information on such individuals, so long as they report what would reasonably be considered public. A New Jersey court, for example, granted a newspaper summary judgment in a privacy suit brought by the owner of a historic house when a photograph appeared in the newspaper. It reasoned that the photograph, taken from a public street, simply recorded what any passerby might see.[48] A Kentucky court held that a man photographed stepping fully clothed from a portable toilet on a college campus had no basis for a privacy claim, because he was stepping back into public view.[49] Similar reasoning has been applied to individuals on private property that is customarily open

[42] Florida Star v. B.J.F., 491 U.S. 524, 533 (1989).

[43] Macon Telegraph Publ'g Co. v. Tatum, 436 S.E.2d 655, 658 (Ga. 1993).

[44] *See* Virgil v. Sports Illustrated, 424 F. Supp. 1286 (D.C. Cal. 1976).

[45] *See* Associated Press, *Stossel Segment Scraped*, MIAMI HERALD, June 29, 2001, at 4A.

[46] 501 U.S. 663 (1991).

[47] *See* Prahl v. Brosamle, 295 N.W.2d 768 (Wis. 1980).

[48] Bisbee v. Conover, 452 A.2d 689 (N.J. 1982).

[49] Livingston v. Kentucky Post, 14 Media L. Rep. (BNA) 2076, 2077 (Ky. Cir. Ct. 1987).

to the public, such as malls, restaurants and businesses. One court has held that a dog trainer waiting backstage to perform his act was in a public place that afforded little expectation of privacy.[50] However, the Iowa Supreme Court reinstated a lawsuit filed by a woman filmed by a television crew in a pizza restaurant. The restaurant owner had given the crew permission to enter the restaurant. A lower court had dismissed the suit, reasoning that the woman was in public and not cast in a false light, and that the broadcast was for news rather than commercial purposes. The state supreme court disagreed, saying the woman should have an opportunity to present evidence that she was harmed by the telecast.[51]

Courts also have suggested that journalists may be persistent when encountering people in public without invading their privacy, so long as the behavior is not highly intrusive or overzealous. Journalistic behavior that is simply annoying is not necessarily an invasion of privacy.[52] Images come to mind of Mike Wallace doggedly pursuing a reluctant subject across a parking lot or down a public street to get a statement for *60 Minutes*. Persistence in pursuing a story or source is normally considered a virtue in journalistic circles, but behavior can become legally problematic when it is menacing or harassing. Such was the case with paparazzi Ron Galella and his pursuit of Jacqueline Kennedy Onassis, widow of President John F. Kennedy. A federal court, citing Onassis' right to be left alone, ordered Galella to stay at least twenty-five feet away from her in public. At issue was not Galella's right to photograph Onassis in public, but his overly intrusive efforts to obtain exclusive photographs.[53] The death of Princess Diana also spawned efforts to pass restrictive legislation. (See Chapter 18 for additional discussion of this legislation.)

**Trespass or Physical Intrusion.** According to *The Restatement of Torts*, anyone who enters private property without the consent of the owner or possessor commits a trespass.[54] Everyone has seen "No Trespassing" signs posted to warn away unwanted visitors. Private property is protected from intruders under both the common law and statutes, which spell out specific penalties. Entering private property without permission or staying on private or quasi-private property after being asked to leave poses legal dangers for journalists, whose rights are normally no different from those of any other citizen.

As a rule, a visitor on private property must obtain permission before entry. Permission must be obtained from the possessor of the property, be it the owner or someone with contractual control over the property, such as a renter or tenant. For example, a court held that journalists did not invade the privacy of a farmer when they obtained permission from a caretaker to enter the

property and photograph dead cattle.[55]

Consent may be either explicit or implied. Explicit consent occurs when a visitor asks for and is granted permission. A reporter might request an interview at a residence or at a business office, for example. When the purpose of the visit is obscured, however, or when journalists simply lie about their intentions, the question of trespass is much less clear.

Two court cases involving the same television news program show how troublesome the question of lawful access to private property can be.

In 1997, a North Carolina jury awarded the Food Lion food chain $3.5 million in damages after ABC's *Prime Time Live* carried a report, afforded by hidden video cameras, that Food Lion relabeled and restocked meat after its expiration date. The judge had allowed the jury to consider fraud and trespass charges against ABC without considering the veracity of the network's report on Food Lion's business practices. The jury based its award on the fact that *Prime Time Live* producers had committed a trespass by obtaining access to Food Lion facilities through fraudulent job applications.[56] Although the Food Lion judgment was reduced on appeal, it illustrates the dangers reporters face in a society that appears to be increasingly wary of certain reporting techniques.

The Food Lion decision stands in contrast to a ruling by the Seventh U.S. Circuit Court of Appeals in a case involving ABC's *Prime Time Live*. In *Desnick v. ABC*, the court rejected a trespass claim when reporters with hidden cameras posed as patients to obtain information based on claims that a Desnick Eye Center was performing cataract operations unnecessarily. The court drew an analogy between food critics appearing at a restaurant anonymously and unannounced and *Prime Time Live*'s undercover actions, even though *Prime Time Live* had gained the cooperation of the center by promising not to employ undercover tactics.[57]

ABC didn't fare as well in a subsequent case when it was successfully sued for intrusion after a network reporter went undercover as a telephone psychic and surreptitiously videotaped colleagues discussing their work. The California Supreme Court said that while employee conversations were not completely private, employees did have a reasonable expectation that they would not be videotaped.[58]

ABC prevailed in another more recent case when its undercover reporters and hidden cameras examined medical laboratories that evaluate women's pap smears and exhibit a high frequency of testing errors possibly caused by pressure on lab technologists to work too quickly.[59] ABC's *Prime Time Live* used hidden cameras and a fictitious health clinic to request tests and obtain interviews as well as a lab tour, but they did not obtain or

[50] People for Ethical Treatment of Animals v. Berosini, 867 P.2d 1121 (Nev. 1994).

[51] Stressman v. American Blackhawk Broad. Co., 416 N.W.2d 685 (Iowa 1987).

[52] *See* Dempsey v. Nat'l Enquirer, Inc., 702 F. Supp. 927 (D. Maine 1988).

[53] Galella v. Onassis, 353 F. Supp. 196 (S.D.N.Y. 1972).

[54] RESTATEMENT (SECOND) OF TORTS § 158, at 277 (1965).

[55] Wood v. Fort Dodge Messenger, 13 Media L. Rep. (BNA) 1614 (Iowa Dist. Ct. 1986). *See also* Lal v. CBS, 551 F. Supp. 356 (E.D. Pa. 1982).

[56] *See* Estes Thompson, *Jury: ABC Committed Fraud To Get Food Story*, MIAMI HERALD, Dec. 21, 1996, at 10A.

[57] 44 F.2d 1345 (7th Cir. 1995).

[58] Sanders v. American Broad. Cos., 978 P.2d 67 (Cal. 1999).

[59] Medical Lab. Mgmt. Consultants v. ABC, 3006 F.3d 806 (9th Cir. 2002).

reveal any personal or private information about the people interviewed or any patients. The court emphasized that the ABC crew did not intrude upon the reasonably expected seclusion of the lab's offices or the reasonable expectation of privacy of the owner who was secretly videotaped.

**Technological Intrusion.** Modern journalists are armed with an array of devices that enhance newsgathering, from telephoto lenses, to sensitive listening devices, to miniaturized video cameras. Technological intrusion is as old as the discussion of privacy. As noted, in 1890 Brandeis and Warren were concerned about a new kind of "instantaneous" photography that no longer required willing subjects to remain perfectly still. Today the culprit likely would be a miniaturized video camera. As a rule, the use of technology that enhances viewing or listening is legal as long as the device does not effectively let the journalist hear or see what normally could not be observed. If a device simply allows a journalist to see or hear what might be witnessed in public, there is no intrusion. People who go into public places — streets, parks and college campuses, for example — enjoy very little privacy, as long as they are not menaced or harassed. That is, the zone of privacy they enjoy is very small compared to the privacy they can expect in their homes or other strictly private places.

In *Dietmann v. Time, Inc.,*[60] the court awarded $1,000 damages to an unconventional healer. Reporters for *Life* magazine gained entry to Dietmann's home posing as prospective patients and secretly photographed and recorded their conversations as he performed his healing ritual. The Ninth U.S. Circuit Court of Appeals soundly rejected media arguments that subterfuge and secret photographing and recordings were essential to telling the story. "We strongly disagree," it said, "that the hidden mechanical contrivances are indispensable tools of newsgathering."[61]

In contrast to *Dietmann*, a Kentucky court rejected an intrusion claim after newspaper reporters persuaded a woman indicted on drug charges to secretly record a conversation with her lawyer, who she said had offered to bribe a judge. In *McCall v. Courier Journal & Louisville Times*, the court noted that the woman had not lied to gain access to her lawyer's office and that he had waived his privacy when he continued to talk to her though he suspected he was being taped.[62]

In a 1996 case, a federal court found grounds for technological intrusion when the television show *Inside Edition* used a shotgun microphone to eavesdrop on conversations inside a home. The court said use of a sensitive directional microphone, which could pick up conversations sixty yards away, was an invasion of privacy. Journalists for *Inside Edition* were sued by an official of a Pennsylvania health care business who had refused requests to be interviewed for a story on executive salaries. Using a van and a shotgun microphone, reporters waited outside the executive's

home to obtain information.[63]

A California court also drew a sharp distinction between photographing or videotaping an accident victim in public versus after the victim was placed inside a rescue helicopter and transported to a hospital. Producers for a reality program arranged to record and videotape inside the helicopter and were sued by the victim for intrusion and disclosure of embarrassing private facts. The California Supreme Court threw out the private facts claim but allowed the case to proceed on intrusion, resulting in an out-of-court settlement.[64]

Cellular telephones capable of taking and transmitting digital photographs have raised new privacy concerns, prompting businesses — particularly health clubs — to ban them. Florida, for example, went further and made it a crime to secretly record people dressing or undressing when they have a reasonable expectation of privacy. The statute, an extension of an existing law, covers both private and commercial distribution of such images and makes "video voyeurism" a felony.[65] Most states now have similar video voyeurism or cyber-peeping laws. In late 2004, President George Bush signed the federal Video Voyeurism Prevention Act of 2004, applicable to improper photographs, film, and videotape taken on federal property when an individual has a reasonable privacy expectation.[66]

Similar issues can arise in the context of the paparazzi. For example, in late 2005, actress Jennifer Anniston filed a lawsuit over topless photographs of her that, she argued, had to have been taken from a great distance and therefore with an intrusive telephoto lens and trespass or other unlawful means. Anniston and the photographer settled in 2006 — amicably, but confidentially.[67]

**Custom and Usage.** While explicit consent requires a request of the property owner or possessor, implied consent occurs in a number of ways under the "custom and usage" legal doctrine. As the name suggests, a degree of access is implied by custom or typical use of private and quasi-private property. It is customary to cross private property to ring someone's doorbell to solicit contributions or sell a product, absent a locked gate, a "No Trespassing" sign or other warning. It is also customary for shoppers and diners to enter stores and restaurants. This kind of access assumes the visitor does not engage in unwanted activities and leaves when asked.

The Florida Supreme Court accepted the argument that custom and usage justified a news photographer's entry onto private property with government officials. In *Fletcher v. Florida Publishing Co.*, the mother of a teenager killed in a house fire sued the *Florida Times-Union* for invasion of privacy when it published a photograph, over the caption "Silhouette of Death," showing the outline of where the body of the young victim had

---

[60] 449 F.2d 245 (9th Cir. 1971).

[61] *Id.* at 249.

[62] 623 S.W.2d 882 (Ky. 1981).

[63] Wolfson v. Lewis, 924 F. Supp. 1413 (E.D. Pa. 1996).

[64] Shulman v. Group W. Prod., 955 P.2d 469 (Cal. 1998).

[65] FLA. STAT., ch. 801.145 (2004).

[66] 18 U.S.C. § 1801 (West 2006).

[67] *See The Daily Dish*, BUFFALO NEWS, Dec. 7, 2005, at C3; *Names & Faces*, WASH. POST, Sept. 4, 2006, at C03.

lain.[68] The mother learned of her daughter's death from the newspaper account. Complicating the case was the fact that the photographer was asked to take photographs for fire officials, thus also acting in a quasi-official capacity. In court, the newspaper successfully argued that it was customary for journalists to accompany officials onto private property where crimes or disasters occurred, a position supported by statements from government officials.

The reasoning of *Fletcher*, however, has not been widely followed. To the contrary, in 1992 a federal court in New York emphatically rejected the *Fletcher* reasoning when journalists for CBS's *Street Stories* accompanied Secret Service agents during a search for documents in a credit card fraud investigation. During the raid, based on a search warrant, CBS employees videotaped a suspect's wife and child despite their repeated requests they not be photographed.[69] The Second U.S. Circuit Court of Appeals upheld a lower court ruling against the Secret Service, underscoring the position that law enforcement officials have no authority to allow journalists into private residences without the owners' permission, even when the property is under police control. Flatly rejecting any constitutional defense to justify the presence of CBS, the court found a clear Fourth Amendment violation by the Secret Service based on the presence of unauthorized journalists during the search. It concluded that the journalists served no legitimate law enforcement need and that their presence was "calculated to inflict injury on the very value that the Fourth Amendment seeks to protect — the right of privacy."[70] In apparent response to the ruling, the FBI in its *Law Enforcement Bulletin* cautioned local, state and federal law enforcement agencies that "media participation in enforcement activities that occur in private areas should be specifically prohibited, unless the media obtain consent from individuals occupying those areas."[71]

The Supreme Court, for the first time, in May 1999 indicated that individuals can win lawsuits on privacy grounds when law enforcement officers take journalists into private homes. *Wilson v. Layne*[72] began in 1992 before the Second Circuit ruling.

The *Wilson* case began when federal marshals and sheriff's deputies from Montgomery County, Maryland, raided the Rockville home of Charles and Geraldine Wilson. Officers were looking for the Wilsons' son, Dominic, on charges that he violated probation. The early-morning raid was part of "Operation Gunsmoke," a program started in 1992, with the blessing of the U.S. Attorney General, in which law enforcement agencies routinely invited journalists to accompany them in apprehending fugitives. A reporter and photographer from *The Washington Post* accompanied officers on the raid of the Wilson home. Dominic Wilson was not there at the time. The Wilsons sued the officers for violating their Fourth Amendment rights against unreasonable search and seizure by bringing into the home journalists who had no official role in the search.

Chief Justice William Rehnquist, writing for a unanimous court, conceded that reporter ride-alongs were common at the time of the raid and that the law governing the practice was uncertain. Nevertheless, he concluded that the presence of third parties with no legitimate law enforcement roles during the execution of a search warrant violated the Fourth Amendment's core interest in residential privacy.

Rehnquist rejected the officers' arguments that the presence of journalists during raids served a number of legitimate law enforcement purposes. First, he rejected the general proposition that officers should be able to exercise reasonable discretion about when the presence of journalists would advance law enforcement goals. "It may well be that ride-alongs further the law enforcement objectives of the police in a general sense, but that is not the same as furthering the purposes of the search," Rehnquist wrote. The Fourth Amendment "would be significantly watered down" by such a vague law enforcement objective.[73]

Rehnquist next rejected the argument that the publicity that resulted from ride-alongs significantly benefited the government by publicizing efforts to combat crime. The news media play an important role by informing the public about law enforcement activities, he wrote, but Fourth Amendment concerns were paramount in the *Wilson* case. "Surely the possibility of good public relations for the police is simply not enough, standing alone, to justify the ride-along intrusion into a private home," he wrote.[74]

Finally, Rehnquist rejected the argument that the presence of journalists could, in some instances, minimize abuse of suspects and protect the safety of officers. It may be reasonable for police to videotape their own actions, he wrote, but that is significantly different from allowing journalists to be present. "The *Washington Post* reporters in the Wilsons' home were working on a story for their own purposes," Rehnquist wrote. "They were not present for the purpose of protecting the officers, much less the Wilsons."[75] Rehnquist also noted that the officers might have a qualified immunity defense against liability on grounds that state law on ride-alongs was not clearly established at the time of the intrusion.

Clearly, consent from the owner is the best defense for journalists who enter private property.

**Recording Conversations With Sources.** Journalists often record conversations with their sources to create verbatim records of complicated information and lengthy direct quotes. In most states, this practice poses no legal problems because the law assumes that an exact account of a conversation can only benefit all parties involved. Parties to a conversation may legally recount

---

[68] 340 So. 2d 914 (Fla. 1976). *See also* Higbee v Times Advocate, 5 Media L. Rep. (BNA) 2372 (S.D. Cal. 1981).

[69] Ayeni v. CBS, 848 F. Supp. 362 (E.D.N.Y. 1994).

[70] Ayeni v. Mottola, 35 F.3d 680, 686 (2d Cir. 1994).

[71] *Media Participation in Police Raids May be History*, FLA. PRESS ASS'N BULL., Nov. 1994, at 3.

[72] 526 U.S. 603 (1999).

[73] *Id.* at 612.

[74] *Id.* at 613.

[75] *Id.*

a conversation to others, and the law simply extends this reasoning to allow taped conversations.[76] In some states, however, it is illegal to record a conversation without the consent of *all* parties. In these states, the reasoning assumes that if a person knows a conversation is being taped, the person might behave or respond differently. Perhaps the source would be more cautious or guarded in his or her comments or say nothing at all. Linda Tripp's recordings of her conversations with Monica Lewinsky are a stark illustration. Twelve states require that all parties to a conversation know when the conversation is being recorded. This knowledge can be conveyed in a number of ways. In cases involving personal contact, a journalist either may ask permission or may assume consent if a tape recorder is in full view and turned on. It is always a good idea to state before the conversation begins that it is being taped. This creates a record of consent. For telephone conversations, consent should be requested before taping begins and restated at the beginning of the conversation.

In Illinois, where state law requires all parties to agree to recordings, a court has added another legal twist, suggesting that where privacy is not expected, no such right exists. In *Russell v. American Broadcasting Co.*, a court held that ABC's *Prime Time Live* did not violate the privacy of a fish market manager when it secretly taped the manager coaching an undercover reporter about the finer points of selling fish.[77] Because the manager expressed no desire to keep the conversation private, the court reasoned, no privacy right was violated by the taping.

In 2005, a columnist in Miami stirred up significant controversy when he disclosed that he had reflexively, and without consent, recorded a telephone call with a county commissioner, who exhibited considerable stress during the call and moments later committed suicide in the newspaper's lobby. The newspaper fired the reporter for violating its policies and the state attorney initiated a criminal investigation, which was later dropped because the columnist had no intent to violate the law.[78]

The Supreme Court, in 2001, addressed the issue of news media liability for publication or broadcast of illegal recordings made independently by third parties and subsequently given to journalists. The case began in 1993 when the chief negotiator for a teachers union sued public affairs radio commentator Frederick Vopper, who broadcast parts of an illegally recorded cellular telephone conversation sent to him anonymously. The suit alleged Vopper violated Pennsylvania and U.S. wiretapping laws, which allow civil and criminal penalties for unlawful intercepts. The Third Circuit of the U.S. Court of Appeals, weighing Vopper's First Amendment claims, reversed the lower court, citing

the undue burden the laws placed on the news media.[79]

The Supreme Court agreed, refusing to apply the so-called "general laws doctrine" applied previously in cases involving reporter privilege, source confidentiality agreements and newsroom searches. The doctrine states that journalists are not immune from content-neutral laws that apply generally in society and do not unduly burden the news media. The Court concluded that privacy concerns were outweighed by the interest in publication of matters of public concern, noting that loss of privacy was often a cost of participation in public affairs. The Court held news media blameless so long as the journalists had no role in the illegal recording, obtained it lawfully, and the content involved a matter of public concern.[80]

### False Light

*Definition: False light invasion of privacy is the publication of highly offensive false information about an individual with actual malice, that is, knowing the information is false or with reckless disregard for its truth or falsity.*

*Newsweek*'s cover on March 28, 1988, showed a young man, hands clasped behind his head, being frisked by police against a backdrop of flashing patrol-car lights. The headlines stated: "The Drug Gangs/Waging War on America's Cities/Anti-Drug Sweep in Los Angeles." On April 25, the photo reappeared on an inside page over the small headline "Correction." A caption explained that the young man in the photo was released without being charged and that *Newsweek* did not mean to suggest that the man was being arrested. It is not known what transpired between *Newsweek* editors and the young man pictured on the cover, but one can suppose the discussion raised the specter of legal action against the news magazine because the man was cast in a false light.

Had the *Newsweek* case resulted in a lawsuit for false light invasion of privacy, the plaintiff would have had some of the same burdens of proof as a libel plaintiff. Consequently, false light cases are often filed in tandem with libel actions. Plaintiffs would have to prove the communication identified them (not always a given in a fictionalization), that it was false, and that the news medium was at fault — typically that it was published recklessly or with knowledge of falsity.

False light plaintiffs, however, would not allege loss of reputation; instead, they would argue that being cast in a highly offensive false light caused some other kind of harm. Also unlike libel, a false-light plaintiff must prove widespread publication — publicity — not just the legal publication.

**False Light and Actual Malice.** In most jurisdictions all false light plaintiffs — not just public officials and public figures, as in libel actions — must prove actual malice if involved in matters of public concern, a standard established by the Supreme Court in

---

[76] Federal law permits a party to a conversation to record it, so long as the recording is not for criminal purposes. However, the Federal Communication Commission, under penalty of lost phone service, requires all parties to consent. *See* 18 U.S.C.A. § 2511 (West Supp. 1996).

[77] 23 Media L. Rep. (BNA) 2428 (N.D. Ill. 1995).

[78] *See* Terry Aguayo, *Ex-columnist Will Not Be Tried for Taping Calls*, N.Y. TIMES, Sept. 10, 2005, at A8; Abby Goodnough, *Miami Paper Fires Columnist Adding Own Twist to Tale of Sex, Politics and Suicide*, N.Y. TIMES, July 28, 2005, at A14.

[79] Bartnicki v. Vopper, 200 F.3d 109 (3d Cir. 1999).

[80] Bartnicki v. Vopper, 532 U.S. 514 (2001).

the 1967 case of *Time, Inc. v. Hill*.[81] The case began in 1952 when three escaped convicts entered the home of James Hill near Philadelphia and held the Hill family hostage for a day. The ordeal received sensational play in Philadelphia newspapers and was the inspiration for Joseph Hayes' *The Desperate Hours*, a novel about the fictional Hilliard family. It was later the basis for a Broadway play and a film starring Humphrey Bogart. In 1955, *Life* magazine published a story titled "True Crime Inspires Tense Play" that purported to describe what actually happened to the Hill family. *Life* carried photos from the Philadelphia tryouts for the play, including one of the sons being mistreated by a "brutish convict." Another photo showed the daughter biting the hand of an abusive convict. Both photos were embellishments, since the real captors did not harass the family.[82] Arguing that *Life* used the family's name and experience for trade purposes, the Hill family sued for invasion of privacy. The Hills won at trial in 1963, but the Supreme Court set aside the damages in a 5-4 vote, applying the new legal rule that false light plaintiffs involved in matters of public concern must prove actual malice. (A point of interest: The Hills' lawyer was Richard M. Nixon.)

Courts are most likely to find disclosures highly offensive in two ways:

(1) Fictionalization is the embellishment or addition of information to an otherwise factual presentation, a device more common to television or stage dramatizations than to news coverage.

(2) Distortion occurs when elements of a story are deceptively juxtaposed, or when information is omitted, presented out of context or presented in an improper context.

**Fictionalizations.** As the *Time, Inc. v. Hill* case suggests, when a drama or novel is modeled on real events, false light problems can arise even when names and other facts have been changed. Fictionalization also can pose problems when the name of a real person is used, but use of a real name normally will not sustain privacy action unless the identity of the person is also appropriated; both a name and facts are usually necessary for there to be legal problems. The fact that the name used in the publication is coincidentally the same as the name of some real person not intended by the publisher or otherwise related or even similar to the character in the published material will not support a false light privacy claim.[83] For example, in *Geisler v. Petrocelli*, a federal judge refused to dismiss a false light claim because characteristics ascribed to the character and plaintiff significantly resembled her.[84] Novels, films and television programs often carry disclaimers, advising readers and viewers that their plots and characters are fictional and that any similarities to real people are coincidental. While disclaimers might prove helpful in marginal

cases, they are not a fail-safe way to prevent false-light claims.[85]

Fictionalization also can occur in simple news stories when facts and quotes are added or implied. While such distortions are deplorable as a matter of ethics, they also can result in legal problems. In *Cantrell v. Forest City Publishing*, for example, the widow of an accident victim successfully sued for invasion of privacy after a reporter for the *Cleveland Plain Dealer* wrote a story that implied he had spoken to the woman at her home.[86] She argued that the story held her and her family up for pity and ridicule, humiliating them and causing mental distress. The Supreme Court upheld the verdict, agreeing that the family was knowingly cast in a false light by substantial misrepresentations in the story.

To succeed, a false light plaintiff must prove misrepresentations were significant. Minor falsifications, as in libel cases, will not sustain a false light privacy claim.

A plainly unbelievable story — one with facts that defy reason and logic — still can be the basis of a successful false light claim. A 97-year-old Arkansas woman, Nellie Mitchell, won a $1.5 million false light judgment against *The Sun*, a tabloid published by Globe International, after it pulled a ten-year-old photo of her from company files and used it to illustrate an admittedly contrived story under the headline "World's Oldest Newspaper Carrier, 101, quits because she's pregnant." A federal court held the false publication could reasonably be deemed highly offensive and rejected Globe International's contention that it had a First Amendment right to publish an obviously fake story.[87]

**Distortions.** Until the recent upsurge in so-called television "docudramas" and "infotainment," news organizations were much more likely to find themselves defending false-light lawsuits over instances involving information out of context or inappropriately juxtaposed with other information. The *Newsweek* example is illustrative. The subject, photographed in a public place in the course of a newsworthy event, would have had little recourse if a photo caption simply had said he was being frisked by police during a drug sweep. However, the use of the photo with the various headlines and cutlines implied the subject of the photo was a suspect in a drug sweep that was part of the war on drugs.

Concern about the relationship of photos to text was also evident in a series by the *Miami Herald* titled "Collars for Dollars." The series documented excessive overtime by police officers who attached their names to drunken driving reports so they

---

[81] 385 U.S. 374 (1967).

[82] *Id.* at 377 (1967).

[83] *See* Botts v. New York Times Co., 2003 WL 23162315 (D.N.J.) (dismissing false light and intentional infliction of emotional distress claims based on an advertisement for the United Negro College Fund).

[84] 616 F.2d 636 (2d Cir. 1980).

[85] *See, e.g.,* Muzikowski v. Paramount Pictures Corp., 322 F.3d 918 (7th Cir. 2003) (A disclaimer stating that a motion picture, though in part inspired by actual events, was a "fictitious story and no actual persons. . . have been portrayed" was held to be insufficient to support dismissal of false light claim by well-known little league coach.).

[86] 419 U.S. 245, 253 (1973).

[87] Peoples Bank & Trust v. Globe Int'l, Inc., 786 F. Supp. 791 (W.D. Ark. 1992). A case that creates an interesting contrast is *Pring v. Penthouse*, 695 F.2d 438 (10th Cir. 1982), in which the court found no basis for the plaintiff's claim that a fictional story might be believed when it suggested a beauty queen was able to make sexual partners levitate during sex.

could earn overtime pay as witnesses. As part of a two-page spread of photos and text, the *Herald* carried this disclaimer: "About the photos. The police officers pictured here were photographed doing their jobs. Some were arresting drunk drivers at roadblocks. Others were at the courthouse, waiting for cases to be heard by a judge. Except where noted, there is no evidence that they are Collars for Dollars cops."[88] Courts will closely scrutinize the accuracy and context of any cut lines or descriptions of the photographs or other artwork appearing with text. In *Raveling v. HarperCollins Publishers,* for example, the court dismissed the plaintiff's claim that by including her picture holding her mobster brother-in-law's baby at a christening that the book in question portrayed her as involved with organized crime.[89] The court found persuasive not only the accuracy of the published description, but the absence of any suggestion in the book that she was somehow involved in organized crime.

Journalistic use of file photos and video street scenes is commonplace in most news organizations but can pose problems. Such practices should raise red flags when the subject matter is sensitive or individuals might be identified. Editors should take special care when selecting file photos or footage of auto accidents to illustrate stories on drunken driving or using street scenes for hard-to-illustrate stories. When a Washington, D.C., television station broadcast a story about a treatment for the sexually transmitted disease herpes, for example, it used a street scene to provide visuals. The snippet of tape included a clear view of passer-by Linda Duncan as the reporter was saying the following: "For the twenty million Americans who have herpes, it is not a cure." Duncan sued, and a court refused to dismiss the action.[90] A jury subsequently awarded her $750, an amount she unsuccessfully challenged in court as grossly inadequate.

In a few disturbing cases, jurors have found distortions and false light invasions of privacy in news stories in which every statement of fact was conceded to be true. The argument in these cases appears to have been that the order of the sentences or the selection of words might lead some readers to reach — at least momentarily — a false conclusion or impression regarding the plaintiff. One such case is the $18.28 million verdict in December 2003 against the *Pensacola News Journal* in a case filed by an influential local businessman, Joe Anderson. In 1998, the newspaper published an article about Anderson and his successful paving business and noted that he had shot and killed his wife in 1988.[91] The article also reported that the shooting had occurred two days before he had filed for divorce and that law enforcement officials determined the shooting to be a hunting accident. The article included seven paragraphs about the inci-

dent, including Anderson's explanation that a deer ran between him and his wife, leading to the accident. Anderson did not contest the accuracy of the report, but claimed the story portrayed him as a murderer through its juxtaposition of facts and use of particular words. The verdict has been appealed.

## Appropriation

*Definition: Appropriation is the use of another person's name, likeness or image, without permission, for commercial gain.*

Appropriation was one of the first privacy torts to develop, in part because it resembled property rights — an area of law familiar to Nineteenth Century courts. But it is also a tort with which courts initially had difficulty because it alleged a mental harm based on unwanted publicity. The field of psychology was not highly developed, and the notion that something as intangible as mental suffering could be quantified for the purpose of monetary damages troubled courts.

The turn-of-the century *Roberson v. Rochester Folding Box. Co.* case, discussed earlier, illustrates some early problems courts had with mental or psychic damages, as well as newspaper concerns about potential problems associated with the use of personal photos in their news pages. The case began when a New York company that processed baking flour used a picture of young Abigail Roberson in advertisements for its products. Her family sued for invasion of privacy, saying the unwanted attention the girl received in public caused severe embarrassment and humiliation. The court, by a 4-3 margin, rejected the argument that the mental anguish caused by unwanted publicity could give rise to measurable damages. The majority was concerned about the implications of recognizing damages for such an intangible harm. The court said its understanding of the law "leads us to the conclusion that the so-called right of privacy has not yet found an abiding place in our jurisprudence."[92]

This case of unwanted publicity generated much publicity of its own, with the public siding with the beleaguered Abigail Roberson. Public sentiment was not lost on the New York legislature, which passed a law prohibiting the commercial use of a person's name or likeness without permission.[93]

While the New York court was unwilling to recognize a legal right of privacy, the Georgia Supreme Court was more receptive. In *Pavesich v. New England Life Insurance Co.*, in 1905, it became the first state supreme court to recognize the unauthorized commercial use of one's identity as a violation of privacy.[94] Pavesich sued the insurance company after it used his photograph without permission in a testimonial advertisement that purported to express his sentiments about life insurance. In awarding Pavesich damages, the court focused on the commercial nature of the use. Though private people sometimes make claims of commercial appropriation, most claims deal with celebrities trying to protect the commercial value of their names and like-

[88] Lisa Getter, Gail Epstein & Jeff Leen, *Cops Cashing In*, Miami Herald, July 14, 1997, at 8A.

[89] 2004 WL 422538 (N.D. Ill. 2004).

[90] Duncan v. WJLA-TV, 10 Media L. Rep. (BNA) 1395 (D.C.D.C 1984).

[91] *See* Reporters Committee for Freedom of the Press News Media Update, *Jury Awards $18 Million in False Light Lawsuit*, Dec. 16, 2003, *available at* http://www.rcfp.org/news/2003/121anders.html; Stephen Nohlgren, *Case's Verdict Shows Truth No Certain Shield for Media*, St. Petersburg Times, Jan. 4, 2004, at 1B.

[92] 64 N.E. 442, 556 (N.Y. 1902).

[93] N.Y. Civ. Rights Law §§ 50-51 (McKinney 1992).

[94] 122 Ga. 190 (1905).

nesses — a more recent legal development.

**A Right to Publicity.** One issue the *Roberson* court found troubling was the distinction between public and private individuals. For politicians and celebrities, who seek out and depend on publicity, claims of damages based on mental anguish from unwanted attention would be inconsistent with their *intentional* forays onto the public stage. Courts consistently have balked at the notion that people who seek public attention could claim a mental harm based on public exposure.

While courts are not likely to award public persons damages for mental harm in appropriation cases, they have recognized a property-like right when the name or likeness of a celebrity or other public person is used for financial gain without authorization.

In some states, this right to publicity can be bartered and inherited. The Georgia Supreme Court blocked the unauthorized sale of plastic models of the Rev. Martin Luther King Jr., holding that the slain civil rights leader's publicity rights could be inherited even if they were not exercised during his lifetime.[95] Similarly, two circuits of the U.S. Court of Appeals have held that Elvis Presley's right of publicity could be exploited exclusively by his heirs.[96] In a 2003 cover story, *Parade* magazine estimated that the Presley estate earned $34 million the previous year.

Most commercial appropriation cases involve advertising or related enterprises, where the defendant has attempted to capitalize on a celebrity's name and identity. For example, an enterprising portable toilet business borrowed the phrase "Here's Johnny," Ed McMahon's nightly introduction of the star of *The Tonight Show With Johnny Carson,* to advertise its product. To underscore the link, the firm also advertised itself as "The World's Foremost Commodian." Even though neither his complete name nor likeness was used, Carson won his appropriation claim.[97]

The use of celebrity look-alikes and sound-alikes is common practice in advertising and sometimes results in appropriation lawsuits. A jury awarded singer Bette Midler $400,000 after Ford Motor Co. ran ads in which a singer imitated Midler's distinctive style and voice, an award upheld by the Ninth U.S. Circuit Court of Appeals in California, an influential authority on celebrity matters. It concluded that "to impersonate her voice is to pirate her identity."[98] A few years later, the Ninth Circuit upheld a $2.5 million judgment for singer Tom Waits, whose raspy voice was imitated in an advertisement for Frito-Lay corn chips. The court held that Waits had a property right "to control the use of his identity as embodied in his voice."[99] It also upheld a portion of the damage award based on mental distress.

*Wheel of Fortune* letter-turner Vanna White successfully sued an electronics firm for unauthorized use of her likeness. In an advertisement by Samsung Electronics, a well-dressed robot appeared wearing a white wig and turned letters on a giant video board. The Ninth Circuit agreed that Samsung had taken White's identity, observing that the identities of stars "are not only the most attractive for advertisers, but the easiest to evoke without resorting to obvious means such as name or likeness or voice."[100]

It is not a violation of publicity for a news publication to use an individual's name or likeness to promote the news content of the publication. In *Namath v. Sports Illustrated,* for example, the Supreme Court of New York County held that use of photos of former football star Joe Namath was permissible in promotional ads to establish the news content of *Sports Illustrated.*[101] The Ninth U.S. Circuit Court of Appeals reached a different result when the use of a celebrity's name and photo suggested she endorsed the publication. Actor-singer Cher sued for misappropriation after an interview she granted one publication was sold to another magazine, which used her name and photo for its own advertising. The court upheld a judgment, finding that the advertising implied that Cher endorsed the publication.[102]

In the only appropriation case it has decided, the Supreme Court held that the news exemption did not apply in the case of a performer who earned his living being shot from a cannon. Dubbed the "Human Cannonball," Hugo Zacchini's entire performance from cannon to net lasted fifteen seconds. When a television station broadcast his entire act on a news program, Zacchini sued for appropriation and won. The Supreme Court refused to block a jury trial on the $25,000 damage claim despite its newsworthiness because broadcast of the "entire act poses a substantial threat to the economic value of that performance."[103]

The use of names and likenesses also can pose problems in literary works, films, television and other forms of communication. Obtaining consent or permission is an important defense. In the popular 1997 film *Men in Black,* a spoof on the theory that space aliens reside among us, a television monitor tracks aliens who, disguised as humans, have become celebrities. To avoid legal problems, director Barry Sonnenfeld said, he obtained permission from Dionne Warwick, Danny DeVito, Sylvester Stallone, Newt Gingrich and other celebrities to use their likenesses.[104]

Actress Brooke Shields learned belatedly about the issue of consent when she tried to prevent publication of nude photographs taken of her when she was ten years old. She learned her mother had signed a standard photographic consent agreement that gave the photographer complete control to use or sell the images.[105] Baseball star Orlando Cepeda also learned the hard way that a person's identity can be contracted away. He sued Swift & Co. to stop its use of his name and picture, only to discover he had signed a licensing contract lending his name to

[95] Martin Luther King, Jr., Ctr. for Soci. Change v. American Heritage Prod., Inc., 296 S.E.2d 697 (Ga. 1982).

[96] *See* Factors, Inc., v. Pro Arts, Inc., 4 Media L. Rep. (BNA) 1144 (2d Cir. 1978); Elvis Presley Enter. v. Elvis Tours, 14 Media L. Rep. (BNA) 1053 (6th Cir. 1987).

[97] Carson v. Here's Johnny Portable Toilets, Inc., 698 F.2d 831 (6th Cir. 1983).

[98] Midler v. Ford Motor Co., 849 F.2d 460, 463 (9th Cir. 1988).

[99] Waits v. Frito-Lay, Inc., 978 F.2d 1093, 1100 (9th Cir. 1992).

[100] White v. Samsung Electronics of America, Inc., 971 F.2d 1395, 1399 (9th Cir. 1992).

[101] 363 N.Y.2d 276 (N.Y. Co. Sup. Ct. 1975).

[102] Cher v. Forum Int'l, 692 F.2d 634 (9th Cir. 1982).

[103] Zacchini v. Scripps Howard Broad., 433 U.S. 562, 575 (1977).

[104] *Invasion of the Body Snatchers,* MIAMI HERALD, July 12, 1997, at 2A.

[105] Shields v. Gross, 448 N.E.2d 108 (N.Y. 1983).

the meat company.[106] But former Chicago Bulls basketball star Dennis Rodman stopped an entrepreneur from marketing a long-sleeve T-shirt bearing images similar to Rodman's numerous upper body tattoos. U.S. District Judge Alfred Wolin granted Rodman's request for a restraining order, ruling that the t-shirt maker appeared to be profiting unfairly from Rodman's fame and tattoos without obtaining his permission.[107] Religion, too, can be a hot topic. In 2006, comic Jackie Mason sued Jews For Jesus, claiming their use of his image in their materials unfairly used his likeness to promote their beliefs and seek converts.[108]

**Definition of Commercial.** The potential breadth and definition of what is or is not a commercial use became a hotly contested issue in Florida following the release in 2000 of the film *The Perfect Storm.* Not only did the surviving family members of the fishermen killed during the storm claim a false light invasion of privacy as explained above, they also argued that Warner Brothers' dramatization of the events involving the storm and the crew of the Andrea Gail violated Florida's commercial misappropriation statute.[109] They argued the film amounted to a commercial use of their deceased family members' names and likenesses without consent. The court of appeals dismissed the false light privacy claim but certified to the Florida Supreme Court the question regarding the meaning of Florida's commercial misappropriation law. Arguments were heard in 2004.[110] In April 2005, the Florida Supreme Court answered that the commercial purpose contemplated by that state's misappropriation statute did not apply to the film because the film did not directly promote a product or service.[111] The case underscored the potential breadth and impact of some states' commercial misappropriation laws.

## INTENTIONAL INFLICTION OF EMOTIONAL DISTRESS

The wide berth the First Amendment affords professional communicators makes it difficult for many people who feel harmed by the media to succeed in court. Libel law, discussed in Chapter 6, requires plaintiffs to prove not only that information is false, but also that the publishers of alleged defamations were at fault — that publication resulted from either negligent or reckless practices or with outright knowledge of falsehood. False light invasion of privacy typically imposes similar burdens on plaintiffs, and plaintiffs under the embarrassing private facts tort have little chance of recovering damages when involved in matters of public concern. As a result, innovative lawyers sometimes file other

kinds of legal actions, often in tandem with libel or privacy suits, based on general legal doctrines that have largely developed outside the umbrella of the First Amendment protections.

One such end-run approach is the tort of intentional infliction of emotional distress, based on something akin to the common law doctrine of malice, or ill will.[112] The emotional-distress tort allows recovery of damages for severe emotional harm or deliberate or reckless conduct that is deemed outrageous and extreme,[113] a judgment normally determined by the sensibilities of a particular jury.

The leading media case on intentional infliction of emotional distress unfolded in the mid-1980s after a dispute between pornography mogul Larry Flynt, publisher of *Hustler* magazine, and the Rev. Jerry Falwell, a prominent Virginia-based television evangelist. The case was the subject of the critically acclaimed feature film *The People v. Larry Flynt.* Falwell sued Flynt and *Hustler* for libel, invasion of privacy and intentional infliction of emotional distress after the magazine ran a crude take-off of "The first time ..." advertising campaign of Campari Liqueur. The campaign focused on celebrities who recalled their first experiences imbibing the upscale liqueur. Double-entendre in the interviews gave readers the impression – until the ends of the ads – that the celebrities were discussing their first sexual experiences. *Hustler* cast Falwell in one of the "first-time" interviews, ostensibly reporting that his first time sexual encounter was with his mother in an outhouse.

The magazine published a disclaimer stating that the page was an advertising parody "not to be taken seriously." The Roanoke, Virginia, jury found in favor of *Hustler* on the libel claim, holding that no reasonable person would believe the parody to be true. The judge dismissed the privacy claim, because only appropriation is recognized as an invasion of privacy action in Virginia, and Falwell's identity had not been appropriated for commercial purposes. But the jury awarded Falwell $200,000 on the emotional distress claim. The U.S. Court of Appeals for the Fourth Circuit upheld the judgment, reasoning that the actual malice standard for public figures in libel cases did not apply to emotional distress.[114] Flynt and *Hustler* appealed to the Supreme Court.

After the lower court rulings, communication professionals had expressed grave concerns, in part because of the unsympathetic character of Flynt and his publication. They feared other public figures could routinely skirt protective libel and privacy laws and win judgments against the media on grounds unrelated to the truthfulness of what was published. Especially troubled were political and social satirists and editorial cartoonists whose purpose often is to hold public figures and institutions up to scorn and ridicule.

Much to their relief, the Supreme Court unanimously overturned the lower courts.

Citing journalism's long history of political caricature and car-

---

[106] Cepeda v. Swift & Co., 415 F.2d 1205 (8th Cir. 1969).

[107] Associated Press, *Tattoo T-Shirts Barred, for Now,* Chicago Tribune, May 29, 1996, at S5.

[108] Anthony Ramirez, *Jackie Mason In Court to Sue Jews for Jesus,* N.Y. Times, Aug. 26, 2006, at B.

[109] Tyne v. Time Warner Entm't Co., 336 F.3d 1286 (11th Cir. 2003); Fla. Stat., ch.540.08 (1998).

[110] *See* Mike Caputo, *Supreme Court: Films' Take on Captain Stirs a Tempest,* Miami Herald, Feb. 5, 2004, at 6B.

[111] Tyne v. Time Warner Entm't Co., 901 So. 2d 802 (Fla. 2005).

[112] *See* William Prosser, *Intentional Infliction of Mental Suffering: A New Tort,* 27 Mich. L. Rev. 874 (1939).

[113] Restatement (Second) of Torts § 46 comment d (1965).

[114] Hustler Magazine v. Falwell, 797 F.2d 1270 (4th Cir. 1986).

tooning and its place in the nation's political past and present, Chief Justice William Rehnquist reasoned that allowing public figures to collect damages without proving actual malice would unconstitutionally chill social and political discourse. He noted that the essence of political cartooning often focused on "unfortunate physical traits or politically embarrassing events — an exploration often calculated to injure the feelings of the subject of the portrayal. The art of the cartoonist is often not reasoned or evenhanded, but slashing and one-sided." The outrageousness requirement, he noted, was highly subjective and "would allow a jury to impose liability on the basis of the jurors' tastes or views, or perhaps on the basis of their dislike of a particular expression." To prevail, Rehnquist said, public officials or public figures must prove the communication was false and that it was published with knowledge or reckless disregard for whether it was true or false.[115]

Private individuals fare better in emotional distress cases. Consider again the case of the tabloid newspaper *Sun*, which lost an emotional distress suit in an Arkansas court after it published the fabricated story about the 101-year-old woman who became pregnant. To illustrate the story, the *Sun* used a photo of a 97-year-old Arkansas woman from its files, believing the woman had died. Among other things, the jury found the *Sun* guilty of intentional infliction of emotional distress and awarded hefty damages.[116] Courts typically will not allow plaintiffs to assert emotional distress claims to evade the defenses applicable to defamation claims, particularly if the emotional distress claim merely recasts a defamation claim.[117]

A variant of intentional infliction of emotional distress is the tort of outrage, which focuses exclusively on the behavior of the defendant. For example, in 1988, personnel from a Florida television station went to a local police department after officials disclosed that skeletal remains found a year earlier were those of a six-year-old boy reported missing three years before. A police officer removed the child's skull from a drawer in a laboratory. Images of the skull were broadcast as part of a report on crime. After the family of the boy watched a newscast showing a dramatic close-up of the skull, they filed an invasion of privacy and outrage lawsuit. Trial testimony centered on callous comments made during the television station's newsroom debate over whether to air the close-up footage. A Florida appellate court rejected the privacy claim but held that the newscast easily surpassed the outrageousness requirement. In a caustic rebuke of the decision to broadcast the close-up, the court said that if this case "did not constitute the tort of outrage, then there is no such tort."[118]

Plaintiffs also have been awarded damages in some jurisdictions for negligent infliction of emotional distress, which occurs when media behavior exposes individuals to dangers that

the media should have reasonably foreseen. For example, a California court held a radio station responsible after a young driver was killed trying to keep up with a disc jockey who traveled about awarding prizes. It reasoned that the accident was a foreseeable consequence of the station's promotion, which encouraged prize-seekers to rush from place to place.[119] Other courts, however, have been unwilling to hold the media accountable for the unforeseeable or speculative consequences, such as copy-cat behavior.[120]

## CONSTITUTIONAL AND STATUTORY PRIVACY

The privacy torts do not present the only reasons for special caution when gathering and disseminating information. Constitutional concerns and privacy statutes, which place limits *on government,* still have implications for journalists seeking information under government control. Limits on how government uses personal information indirectly place limits on journalists. And such limits on government use of private information — in this information-soaked era with its headlines about government and private enterprise abuses — are politically attractive to politicians and other policy-makers and record custodians.

Constitutional privacy is especially significant because it provides individuals a constitutional platform from which to challenge journalists in certain situations, potentially offsetting the presumption favoring publication of private facts about matters of public concern. Likewise, statutory privacy designed to protect individuals from government abuse also provides a rationale — sometimes unwarranted — for withholding information from the public and the news media.

### Constitutional Privacy

Over time, the Supreme Court has defined a range of constitutional privacy protections. Although the word "privacy" appears nowhere in the Constitution, the Court has nonetheless recognized a right to be free from government intrusion and eavesdropping. For example:

- Reasoning that freedom from intrusion is based on a "zone of privacy" surrounding a person, not a specific place, the Court ruled unconstitutional a government wiretap on a telephone booth.[121]
- In *NAACP v. Alabama,* the Court struck down an Alabama law that required certain organizations, including civil rights groups, to turn over membership rolls to the state.[122] The Court held the rule violated the associational rights of current and potential members of the NAACP, who might not exercise those rights out of fear of government retaliation.
- In *Griswold v. Connecticut,* a case challenging a state law

[115] Hustler Magazine v. Falwell, 485 U.S. 46, 55-56 (1988).

[116] Peoples Bank & Trust v. Globe Int'l Publ'g, Inc., 20 Media L. Rptr. (BNA) 2097 (1992).

[117] *See, e.g.,* Yohe v. Nugent, 321 F.3d 35 (1st Cir. 2003).

[118] Armstrong v. H&C Communications, Inc., 575 So. 2d 280, 282 (Fla. Ct. App. 1991).

[119] Weirum v. RKO General, Inc., 539 P.2d 36 (Cal. 1975). *See also* Robert E. Dreschel, *Negligent Infliction of Emotional Distress,* 12 PEPP. L. REV. 889 (1985).

[120] *See* Zamora v. CBS, 480 F. Supp. 199 (S.D. Fla. 1979); Olivia v. NBC, 178 Cal. 888 (Cal. App. 1981).

[121] Katz v. United States, 389 U.S. 347 (1967).

[122] 357 U.S. 449 (1958).

barring dissemination of birth control information, the Court fashioned a right of decisional privacy based on rights implied in the "penumbra" of various amendments to the Constitution.[123] The case laid the foundation for the controversial *Roe v. Wade* decision that recognized the right of a woman to have an abortion.[124]

Citing its decisions in *Griswold, Roe* and related cases, the Supreme Court, in June 2003, returned to constitutional privacy in *Lawrence v. Texas.*[125] By a 6-3 vote, it struck down a state statute that made criminal consensual sodomy between adults of the same sex. Writing for the majority, Justice Anthony Kennedy articulated a rationale based on respect for the private lives and intimate choices of the two Texas men who were arrested while in an apartment:

Liberty protects the person from unwarranted government intrusions into a dwelling or other private places. In our tradition the state is not omnipresent in the home. And there are other spheres of our lives and existence, outside the home, where the state should not be a dominant presence. Freedom extends beyond spatial bounds. Liberty presumes an autonomy of self that includes freedom of thought, belief, expression, and certain intimate conduct. The instant case involves liberty of the person both in its spatial and more transcendent dimensions.[126]

The decision overruled the Court's contrary 1986 holding in *Bowers v. Hardwick*[127] and prompted a stinging dissent from Justice Antonin Scalia, who, together with Chief Justice William Rehnquist and Justice Clarence Thomas, questioned the existence of any fundamental constitutional right to engage in homosexual conduct.[128] Justice Thomas added his own dissent in which he also questioned the existence of any general constitutional right of privacy.[129]

Most importantly to media professionals, however, has been the recent willingness of the Supreme Court to recognize a constitutional right of informational privacy — the right of individuals to control information about themselves. Concerns about privacy had been raised in several cases addressing government use of computers to gather, store and disseminate information about private individuals.

In 1976, concerns about the effects of new information technologies on privacy were first expressed on the Court by Justice William Brennan. In *United States v. Miller*, the majority held that individuals retained no privacy interest in information voluntarily given to a bank. Cautioned Brennan: "Development of

photocopying machines, electronic computers and other sophisticated instruments has accelerated the abilities of government to intrude into areas which a person normally chooses to exclude from prying eyes and inquisitive minds."[130]

A year later, the Court acknowledged a right of informational privacy in upholding a New York state practice of compiling and storing in a computer certain prescription drug records on individuals. Such a practice did not violate individuals' constitutional right of privacy, Justice John Paul Stevens wrote, so long as strict security was in place to ensure the privacy of the information. Wrote Stevens: "We are not unaware of the threat to privacy implicit in the accumulation of vast amounts of personal information in computerized data banks or other massive government files."[131] Justice Brennan, in a concurring opinion, echoed concerns about the threat of computers to privacy, noting prophetically: "The central storage and easy accessibility of computerized data vastly increases the potential for abuse of that information, and I am not prepared to say that future developments will not demonstrate the necessity for some curb on such technology."[132]

In *Department of Justice v. Reporters Committee for Freedom of the Press*, the Court reacted to a long-standing concern about the threat computers pose to personal privacy when it articulated the practical obscurity doctrine in response to a news media request for information contained in a government database.[133] In essence, the Court reasoned that computers have obliterated traditional barriers of time and space that once afforded individuals a measure of "practical obscurity" — or distance from their official past. Because of computers, the Court noted, individuals no longer can move to another place to escape past deeds or count on the passage of time to dim official memories. Following this reasoning, it suggested that information compiled in central government computers — even information gathered from various *public* records — regained a privacy interest when brought together in one place. In fact, the Court reasoned, if the information were indeed *public*, reporters should have no need to see a government database.[134] Under the reasoning of the *Reporters Committee* case, public-record information about individuals can be shielded from disclosure simply because it exists in a computer database.

### The Freedom of Information Act

Since the Great Depression, government's appetite for information has grown steadily, hitting full stride with the Great Society programs of the 1960s that coincided with the growth of systems analysis — a management technique that depended on vast amounts of data. To balance governmental need for information, much of it personal, statutes were passed to ensure that government gathered information only for specific purposes and that it

---

[123] 381 U.S. 479, 484 (1965).
[124] 410 U.S. 113 (1973).
[125] 539 U.S. 558 (2003).
[126] *Id.* at 562.
[127] 478 U.S. 186 (1986).
[128] 539 U.S. at 586 (Scalia, J., dissenting).
[129] *Id.* at 605 (Thomas, J., dissenting).

[130] 425 U.S. 435, 451 (1976).
[131] Whalen v. Roe, 429 U.S. 589, 605 (1977).
[132] *Id.* at 607 (Brennan, J., concurring).
[133] 489 U.S. 749 (1989).
[134] *Id.* at 780.

be used only for those purposes. One of the first such statutes was the federal Freedom of Information Act, passed in 1966 to ensure maximum access to records of federal executive agencies. While the act espouses openness, it also attempts to balance access with competing values. The result was nine exemptions, several of which raise privacy concerns as grounds for withholding information. (The federal Freedom of Information Act is discussed in Chapter 17.)

*Exemption 3* protects certain kinds of information, as defined by other federal statutes, from disclosure. For a statute to qualify under the exemption, it must specify exactly what information must be withheld and must allow no discretion on the part of agency personnel. Laws governing numerous agencies, including the Internal Revenue Act, which protects personal income tax records, fall into this category. The exemption also covers the Census Bureau, the Consumer Products Safety Commission and the Federal Trade Commission.

*Exemption 6,* which applies to personnel, medical and similar files, shields information that would "constitute a clearly unwarranted" invasion of privacy. Implicit in this language is the understanding that a balancing process must occur to determine whether withholding would be warranted. The "similar files" wording has been applied to a range of information. The State Department invoked the exemption to successfully withhold disclosure of the citizenship status of individuals. In *Department of State v. Washington Post Co.,* the Supreme Court supported use of the exemption and said information need not be highly personal to be covered.[135] Information could be withheld, it said, when disclosure could lead to injury or embarrassment. The Court also upheld the State Department when it argued that the privacy interests of Haitians whose asylum claims were rejected outweighed the public interest in disclosure.[136]

Privacy claims also were successfully raised by the National Aeronautics and Space Administration in a bid to prevent disclosure of an audio tape of the last communications from the space shuttle Challenger, which exploded after takeoff and killed its seven astronauts, including a high school teacher. In *New York Times Co. v. NASA,* the space agency argued that release of the audiotape, transcripts of which had already been made public, would only add to the anguish of the victims' families.[137] The *Times* countered that background noises and inflections of the astronauts' voices might yield significant information about the tragedy. A federal court rejected that reasoning and adopted the concept of relational privacy that extended protection to family members.

A state judge cited the Challenger ruling in the murder trial of Danny Rolling, convicted of killing five young people near the University of Florida in 1990. At the behest of prosecutors, Circuit Judge Stan Morris limited public access to graphic autopsy and crime scene photos — evidence jurors viewed before imposing Rolling's death sentence. The photos were public records

under Florida law. Faced with the prospect of the photos appearing in print and further traumatizing victims' families, the judge ordered that they be bound in folders and made accessible to the public only under court supervision. Under the ruling, copies of photos could not leave the courthouse.[138]

In 1998, concern about publication of autopsy photos led a Miami-Dade County circuit judge to seal autopsy photographs in the sensational murder of fashion designer Gianni Versace, who was gunned down on the steps of his Miami Beach mansion. Such photos, notwithstanding the ruling in the Gainesville murder case, were public records. During a brief hearing, with no lawyers for the news media present, a Versace family lawyer said his clients feared photos might appear on the Internet, as happened with the autopsy photos of Nicole Brown Simpson in the O.J. Simpson murder case. The judge sealed the records.[139]

In 2001, in the wake of the death of stock car driver Dale Earnhardt at the Daytona 500 NASCAR race, concerns about publication of autopsy photos prompted the Florida legislature to amend the state's record law to exempt autopsy photos unless a judge approved disclosure. Initial controversy focused on attempts by the *Orlando Sentinel* to have a medical expert view the photos to make an independent determination of the cause of Earnhardt's death. The newspaper, focusing on the issue of auto racing safety, expressed no interest in publishing the photos. The legislation restricts both viewing and copying. Violation of the law is a third-degree felony, allowing up to five years in prison and a $5,000 fine. Lawyers for *The Independent Florida Alligator* at the University of Florida and Websitecity.com, a Florida-based Web site, challenged the exemption as unconstitutional. Websitecity.com previously had published autopsy photos of auto racing fatalities. A circuit judge in Daytona Beach, however, upheld the legislation in June 2001.[140] In 2002, a state district court of appeals affirmed the trial court's ruling and held that the statute exempting photographs was not overbroad because it did not apply to the written autopsy report and because it allowed for release upon a showing of "good cause" — a term not defined by the statute.[141] In 2003, the Florida Supreme Court declined to hear the case.

*Exemption 7* covers disclosure of certain law enforcement records, including disclosures that would invade privacy. In the *Reporters Committee* case mentioned previously, the court recognized privacy interests in certain compilations of criminal records — even records that were public at their original source. For example, if a record is contained in a central government database, such as an FBI computer, that record might be considered private. The same record at a courthouse in the jurisdiction where the crime occurred would be a public record. The court said that since the privacy/access balance typically favors with-

[135] 456 U.S. 595 (1982).
[136] Dep't of State v. Ray, 502 U.S. 164 (1991).
[137] 782 F. Supp. 628 (D.D.C. 1991).
[138] Florida v. Rolling, 22 Media L. Rep. (BNA) 2264 (Fla. Cir. Ct. 1994).
[139] David Lions, *Judge Seals Versace Autopsy Pictures,* MIAMI HERALD, May 1, 1998, at 2B.
[140] *See* Mike Branom, Associated Press, *Judge Upholds Autopsy Photo Law, Denying Bid by Newspaper, Website,* MIAMI HERALD, June 12, 2001, at 5B.
[141] Campus Communication, Inc. v. Earnhardt, 821 So. 2d 388 (Fla. Dist. Ct. App. 2002).

holding records when they are contained in computer compilations, courts need not engage in case-by-case balancing with the public interest in disclosure. The simple determination that a record is in a computer compilation was sufficient to withhold such a record, the court reasoned.

In March 2004, the Supreme Court ruled in *Favish v. Office of Independent Counsel*,[142] a case that directly raised these privacy and FOIA issues, including the question of the privacy interests of family members of a deceased person. The *Favish* case grew out of requests for photographs taken during the investigation into the death of Vince Foster, a former deputy counsel in the Clinton White House.

In July 1993, Foster was found dead in a park in Washington, D.C. The National Park Service, the FBI, committees of the House and Senate, and the Office of Independent Counsel independently investigated the death. The conclusion of each was that it was a suicide, but rumors and doubts lingered. The District of Columbia Court of Appeals denied, in 1999, the records request of Accuracy in Media, a media watchdog organization, which had requested the photographs from the National Park Service. Favish, a lawyer who had participated in that litigation, renewed the request in California by serving it upon the Office of Independent Counsel, seeking 150 photographs.

The office released more than 100 photos but withheld several for reasons at first not clearly articulated. Favish later dropped twenty-one photos from his request. Eventually the office relied upon the privacy language of Exemption 7. The district court ruled for Favish on one photo and certain issues regarding the quality of the photos but withheld ten to protect the privacy interests of Foster's family. The Ninth Circuit Court of Appeals reversed the district court's ruling and held that, though the privacy interests of the family were a valid consideration, they had to be weighed against the public interest in the investigation. Because the Court of Appeals did not have the photos in question before it, the case was remanded to the district court for further analysis and the required balancing of the privacy and access interests. On remand, the district court ordered the release of five photos and withheld, on privacy grounds, the other five. The Ninth Circuit affirmed. In March 2004, the Supreme Court reversed the appellate court and held that under the FOIA surviving family members have a right to personal privacy regarding the photographic images of the scene of a close relative's death. The Court said such privacy interests outweighed, under the FOIA, the public's interest in disclosure.

### The Privacy Act of 1974

The Privacy Act was meant to create a "Code of Fair Information Practices" to regulate government agencies. The Senate report on the legislation noted that one purpose of the act was "to promote government respect for the privacy of citizens" by ensuring that executive branch agencies follow certain rules regarding the gathering and disclosing of information.[143] The Privacy Act is most likely to affect requests for information that is not clearly covered by the legislation. In such cases, custodians of records tend to be very cautious because the Privacy Act imposes penalties on custodians who release protected information. Withholding information that should be disclosed, on the other hand, may violate the federal Freedom of Information Act, but that legislation poses no penalties for wrongly withholding information.

### Other Privacy Concerns

A number of other federal and state statutes raising privacy concerns can erect barriers to information gathered and kept by government and, in some cases, private institutions.

**Driver's Privacy Protection Act.** Driver's license records have long been a source of useful information for journalists, more so in recent years with the growth of computer-assisted reporting. In 1991, for example, the *Miami Herald* used a computer analysis of state Division of Motor Vehicle records to show that many drunken drivers were being put back on the road. Beginning in September 1997, however, federal legislation began limiting access to such records. The legislation, passed in 1994, was partly in response to the slaying of California actress Rebecca Schaeffer by a fan who located her address through driver records obtained through a private investigator. The intent of the law is to inhibit stalkers and anyone else who might harm an individual after linking a name with an address.[144] The federal legislation contains a provision that allows states to disclose such information if they enact a provision notifying drivers that they have an option to withhold personal information.

Several states challenged the federal law, arguing that Congress had overstepped its authority in attempting to regulate a state practice. The Seventh and Tenth Circuits of the U.S. Court of Appeals upheld the federal law. The Fourth Circuit, however, sided with South Carolina, which had argued the law was unconstitutional because state driver's license information constituted internal state activity and, therefore, lay beyond the scope of congressional jurisdiction.[145] The U.S. Supreme Court, in *Condon v. Reno*, reversed the Fourth Circuit.[146] In a unanimous opinion by Chief Justice William Rehnquist, the Court held that the release or sale of drivers' license information constituted interstate commerce, thereby giving Congress regulatory authority.

**The Buckley Amendment.** Enacted as the Family Educational Rights and Privacy Act, the Buckley Amendment requires educational institutions receiving federal money to keep certain student records private. Directory information such as names, addresses and majors — which appear in most student directories

---

[142] 541 U.S. 157 (2004).

[143] 5 U.S.C. § 552a (1974).
[144] Driver's Privacy Protection Act of 1994, 18 U.S.C.S. § 2721 (1994).
[145] Condon v. Reno, 155 F.3d 453 (4th Cir. 1998).
[146] 528 U.S. 141 (2000).

— is not covered; academic records, including non-criminal disciplinary records, are. Before 1992, the Department of Education was advising institutions that campus crime records should be considered student disciplinary records under the Buckley Amendment — a position that was frustrating many news organizations, especially campus newspapers. A 1992 amendment, however, specifically states that crime reports are not educational records and cannot be withheld as disciplinary records.[147]

**Rape Shield Laws.** Whether to publish the name of a rape victim is a controversial topic, both legally and ethically. Rape shield laws were designed to encourage victims to come forward by preventing the additional trauma of publicity. Some courts have specifically upheld rape shield laws.[148] In Florida, however, the state supreme court in 1994 upheld a ruling that the state's law was unconstitutional in a case spawned by the William Kennedy Smith rape trial.[149] The court relied heavily on *Florida Star v. B.J.F.*, which held the news media should not be punished for publishing truthful, lawfully obtained information about matters of public concern absent a state interest of the highest order.[150] The Georgia Supreme Court, also citing *Florida Star*, overturned a verdict against a state newspaper in a civil case based on disclosure of the name of a sexual assault victim.[151]

**Juror Shield Laws.** Much has been said and written about protecting jurors' privacy, particularly since the Rodney King police brutality trial and O.J. Simpson murder trial. Since the Supreme Court's ruling in *Press-Enterprise v. Superior Court*,[152] jurors' selection and identity have been presumptively public matters. But after the King and Simpson cases, and the Timothy McVeigh trial in the Oklahoma City bombing, the tide appears to be changing. Citing privacy, judges appear to be routinely impaneling anonymous juries, a practice once reserved for the trials of organized crime kingpins when juror safety was a factor.[153] At least one state, Texas, has passed a law allowing anonymous juries. The law creates a presumption that juries will be anonymous in all criminal trials. Robert Dawson, a University of Texas criminal law professor, believes the 1993 statute was responsible for the growing number of private juries: "Before, a judge would have to go out on a limb to justify such a ruling. Now, he doesn't have to."[154] Jane Kirtley, former executive director of the Reporters Committee for Freedom of the Press, says the concept of juror privacy "has become almost epidemic." It is not a question of "media access or exploitation," she says. "It's the notion of public

oversight of the system."[155]

**Computer Privacy.** Journalists depend increasingly on information contained in computer databases and from other computer-based sources, such as the World Wide Web and Internet. Indeed, going online is allowing journalists greater speed and access to more information. Many significant news stories are based on analysis of government databases. Most laws dealing with computer privacy are designed to place limits on government. The Computer Matching and Privacy Act of 1988, for example, limits the ability of government to routinely cross-reference information in various government databases.[156] The Electronic Communications Privacy Act of 1986 made interception of computer communications a crime,[157] and the Computer Crime Act of 1986 made it unlawful to access or disclose certain records in computer form.[158] Many of the laws, reflecting some of the constitutional and statutory concerns discussed previously, treat computerized information as more threatening to privacy than similar information in paper files. Such laws can be vague or over-inclusive in ways that inhibit legitimate journalists.

The computer/privacy debate also has begun to focus on private-sector information practices. One survey of Internet users found that 55 percent favored privacy limitations.[159] In June 1997, the Federal Trade Commission held four days of hearings that suggested support for the self-regulation of privacy in computer communications. In May 2000, after conducting a series of Web site surveys, the FTC abandoned its long-standing policy supporting self-regulation. Instead, the agency announced support for federal legislation to protect online consumers, much to the dismay of the Online Privacy Alliance, an informal industry coalition that included some of the biggest online companies. In a report and in subsequent testimony before the Senate Commerce Committee, the FTC officials recommended that Congress establish "Basic standards of practice for the collection of information online."[160]

A related and growing privacy concerns involves the posting online of information, diary entries and other information by individuals on various social networking sites, such as MySpace.com and Facebook.[161] Many students and others have found that once information is posted and widely shared, the expectation of privacy may lessen. Employers, government agencies and others have used many of these sites to gather information about individuals.

**Health Insurance Privacy.** The privacy rules under the Health

---

[147] 20 U.S.C.S. § 1232g(a)(4)(B)(ii) (1995).

[148] *See, e.g.*, Nappier v. Jefferson Standard Life Ins. Co., 322 F.2d 502 (4th Cir. 1963).

[149] Florida v. Globe Communication Corp., 648 So. 2d 110 (Fla. 1994).

[150] 491 U.S. 524 (1989).

[151] Macon Tel. Publ'g Co. v. Tatum, 436 S.E.2d 655 (Ga. 1993).

[152] 464 U.S. 501 (1984).

[153] *See* Tony Mauro, *Trend to Press Restriction Escalates in Denver*, FIRST AMENDMENT NEWS, May 1997, at 1.

[154] Wendy Benjaminson, *Shroud of Secrecy Increasingly Veils Trials in Texas*, HOUSTON CHRONICLE, Mar. 13, 1994, at 1.

[155] Mauro, *supra* note 152, at 6.

[156] 5 U.S.C. § 552a (1988).

[157] 18 U.S.C. § 2510 (1986).

[158] 18 U.S.C. § 1030 (1986).

[159] *See* Dan Harrison, *Computer Users Back Net Privacy Law*, DM NEWS, June 16, 1997, at 3.

[160] Deborah Branscum, *Guarding Online Privacy*, NEWSWEEK, June 5, 2000, at 77.

[161] *See* Sam Terilli, *The Internet: Privacy Matters*, MIAMI HERALD, June 29, 2006, at 27A.

Insurance Portability and Accountability Act of 1996 (HIPAA)[162] took effect in April 2003. HIPAA is the law that governs, among other things, when a group health plan may impose pre-existing conditions on health insurance coverage. The HIPAA privacy rules will not directly apply to journalists, but will affect many businesses, including hospitals. Those hospitals will be more likely to refuse to release information about patients or even to confirm that an accident victim has been admitted. In addition, the law may set the tone and direction of future privacy legislation.

The HIPAA rules limit the use and disclosure of individuals' health information by the doctors, hospitals, health-care clearinghouses, insurance plans, their business associates and even many employers who provide health care or coverage. For example, employers may not use health care information to make personnel decisions and any covered entity may only disclose the information for purposes related to treatment, payment and health care operations, unless the individual has provided a clear, voluntary authorization permitting disclosure. The rules also require that each covered business adopt privacy procedures and train a designated privacy official to assure compliance.

The rules do not provide for private lawsuits seeking enforcement, but do provide for investigations by the Department of Health and Human Services, which can seek civil and criminal penalties for violations. Examples of exceptions allowing disclosure, even without authorization by individuals, include public health investigations, law enforcement, emergencies and national security, but there is no exception for any reports to journalists — even for the release of limited information concerning admission and discharge dates of patients.

### Privacy After September 11, 2001

The terrorist attacks that took place on September 11, 2001, have had a far-reaching impact on society, laws and notions of privacy. These matters are still evolving. Two extraordinary examples of the changes are the remarkably fast and debate-free passage of the USA PATRIOT Act in October 2001, and the draft of PATRIOT II, which was leaked to the media in early 2003 and which generated some public debate and criticism.[163]

The PATRIOT Act increased federal authority in a number of ways. For example, it relaxed restrictions on the sharing of information between domestic law enforcement agencies and intelligence agencies, enhanced the government's subpoena power to obtain and inspect e-mail records of suspected terrorists, expanded bank record-keeping requirements to track transactions and money laundering, and permitted roving wiretaps of sus-

pected terrorists. More than 300 pages long, the law received virtually no debate or congressional oversight before its passage, though it unquestionably broadened governmental power. The sense of urgency and fear following the attacks and the fact that the law included a provision for its sunset in five years facilitated its quick enactment.

The Domestic Security Enhancement Act — PATRIOT II — was not released to the public by the government, but was leaked in February 2003. If enacted, it would further the unprecedented expansion of governmental powers without any sunset provision. PATRIOT II would, for example, expand grand jury secrecy rules to cover witnesses, give the government greater control over grand jury investigations, broaden surveillance powers even beyond the PATRIOT Act, further erode the distinction between international terrorism and domestic terrorism, and further contract access under the Freedom of Information Act.

In the months following the release of the draft of PATRIOT II, criticism of the proposal mounted. Attorney General John Ashcroft and the Justice Department quietly dropped the matter before the 2004 elections.

Not long after his reelection in November 2004, President Bush began pushing for renewal of expiring PATRIOT Act provisions as well as expansion of certain powers of government to obtain records without judicial approval.[164] The president vowed to continue his support for the act and its expansion.[165] After months of negotiations with concerned members of Congress and amid media reports of secret government wiretapping of international telephone calls through the National Security Administration,[166] a compromise was reached in March 2006. The act was renewed with a few modifications limiting some government powers to obtain routine library records and providing people served with terrorism-related subpoenas the right to challenge the nondisclosure and gag order requirements of the subpoenas. The renewal, though, made permanent most of the PATRIOT Act's provisions.[167]

During the coming years, the pressure to vest government with new powers and to use computer technology and the Internet to track and prevent terrorism will continue to be strong. The results may include not only a contraction of the privacy rights of individual, but also a contraction of sources of information available to journalists.

---

[162] 42 U.S.C.A. § 1320d-4 (1996).

[163] Public Law 107-56 (2001). USA PATRIOT is an acronym for Uniting and Strengthening America by Providing Appropriate Tools Required to Intercept and Obstruct Terrorism. The proposed PATRIOT ACT II can be found at various Web sites, including http://www.publicintegrity.org (The Center for Public Integrity) and http://www.ire.org (Investigative Reporters and Editors).

[164] *See* Eric Lichtblau, *Plan Would Broaden FBI's Terror Role*, N.Y. TIMES, May 18, 2005, at A19; Editorial *Patriot Act Redux, and in the Dark*, N.Y. Times, June 1, 2005, at A20.

[165] *See* Carl Hulse, *House Rejects One Provision of Patriot Act*, N.Y. TIMES, June 16, 2005, at A1.

[166] *See* Charles Babington, *White House Working to Avoid Wiretap Probe; But Some Republicans Say Bush Must Be More Open About Eavesdropping Program*, WASH. POST, Feb. 20, 2006, at A08; Bob Deans, *White House Steps up Defense of Surveillance Bush's Wiretap Actions Called Legal Safeguard*, ATLANTA JOURNAL-CONSTITUTION, Jan. 20, 2006, at 3A.

[167] *See* Charles Babington, *Congress Votes to Renew Patriot Act, With Changes*, WASH. POST, Mar. 8, 2006, at A3; Steve Chapman, *The Surprising Lessons Offered By The Patriot Act*, BALTIMORE SUN, July 10, 2006, at 11A.

## SUMMARY

Despite assaults on their privacy from various quarters — and perhaps in part because of those assaults — Americans remain strong in their belief in the right to be let alone. Privacy concerns are manifested in constitutions, statutes and common law cases that attempt to balance individual rights with competing values, including the right of the news media to publish and the right of the public to be informed. It is to be expected, then, that the rights of individuals and the rights of a free and vigorous press often will clash. In many instances, the balance has traditionally tilted toward the press because of the bedrock principle that a democratic society works best when information flows freely.

Yet journalism in today's information-filled environment is practiced in widely varying ways, from the *National Enquirer* to the *Philadelphia Inquirer*, from *Hard Copy* to *The News Hour.* At times, reporters engage in journalistic behavior that, although technically within the bounds of the law, is ethically questionable. Journalistic excesses are not lost on the public, whose declining opinion of journalism is reflected in some polls. The results of declining confidence in the news media can be seen in the outcome of some court cases, such as the Food Lion case. Lack of public confidence in the press also can embolden politicians to pass laws limiting press freedoms in the name of privacy.

Privacy is an important value that the news media must respect — while never surrendering the responsibility to tell the hard truth whenever necessary.

## FOR ADDITIONAL READING

Coleman, A.D. "Private Lives, Public Places: Street Photography Ethics," 2 *Journal of Mass Media Ethics* 60 (Spring/Summer 1997).

Ernst, Morris L. and Alan U. Schwartz. *Privacy: The Right to be Let Alone.* New York: Macmillan, 1962.

Flaherty, David H. *Privacy in Colonial New England.* Charlottesville: University Press of Virginia, 1972.

Hixson, Richard F. *Privacy in a Public Society: Human Rights in Conflict.* New York: Oxford University Press, 1987.

Pember, Don. *Privacy and the Press.* Seattle: University of Washington Press, 1972.

Prosser, William. "Privacy," 48 *California Law Review* 383 (1960).

Sanford, Bruce W. *Libel and Privacy,* 2d ed. Englewood Cliffs, N.J.: Prentice-Hall, 1993.

Thomason, Tommy, ed. *Newspaper Coverage of Rape: Dilemmas on Deadline.* Fort Worth: Texas Christian University Press, 1994.

Warren, Samuel D. and Louis D. Brandeis. "The Right to Privacy," 4 *Harvard Law Review* 220 (1890).

Westin, Alan F. *Privacy and Freedom.* New York: Atheneum, 1967.

# 15

# Confidential Sources and Information

*By Cathy Packer*

---

 **Headnote Questions**

- *What are the recent developments in reporter's privilege law?*
- *What are the basic arguments for and against a reporter's privilege?*
- *What three elements must an attorney prove to compel testimony from a reporter who is protected by a qualified First Amendment privilege?*
- *What are the bases for the way the privilege varies from one jurisdiction to another?*
- *In what circumstances can law enforcement personnel legally search newsrooms?*
- *What can be the legal consequences of a journalist's revealing the identity of a source to whom he or she has promised confidentiality?*

---

Since early 2004 some thirty journalists and news organizations have dealt with subpoenas ordering them to appear in federal court proceedings to identify their confidential sources or hand over other information about stories they have covered. Almost a dozen journalists from major news organizations have been cited for contempt of court for refusing to testify.[1] In four "notorious losses,"[2] journalists who refused to identify their confidential sources suffered confinement and/or their employers paid costly fines or settlements. *New York Times* investigative reporter Judith Miller spent eighty-five days in federal prison, a television journalist spent four months under house arrest and paid an $85,000 fine, the *Boston Globe* was forced to pay $1.68 million to a libel plaintiff and five media organizations agreed to pay $750,000 to help settle a lawsuit so their reporters wouldn't have to testify and wouldn't be punished for refusing to do so.[3]

All of this litigation represents the most severe attack on the right – or privilege – of journalists to keep the identities of sources or other information confidential in at least thirty years. One legal scholar wrote, "We're seeing outright contempt for an independent press in a free society. The fact that courts have no appreciation for this is new, is troubling, and you cannot overestimate the import it will have over time."[4] An attorney for a plaintiff in a lawsuit seeking reporters' testimony countered, "We do not consider this to be any type of assault on the First Amendment but rather seeking justice.... We believe [the plaintiff] is entitled to this information under the law."[5]

There is some good news amidst all that bad news, however. In the spring of 2006 a compromise proposal for a federal shield law that would give reporters some protection against having to testify in court was introduced into the U.S. Senate, and its backers said

---

[1] *See* Lucy Dalglish, *Happy Birthday to the RCFP*, NEWS MEDIA & THE L., Spring 2005, at 1; Lucy Dalglish, *Back to Square One, 34 Years Later*, NEWS MEDIA & THE L., Fall 2004, at 1.

[2] James C. Goodale et al., *Reporter's Privilege: Recent Developments 2004-2005*, *in* 3 COMM. LAW 351, 351 (2005) (Goodale used this language to refer to the Miller, Wen and *Boston Globe* cases, but the Taricani case clearly belongs on this list, too.).

[3] *See* Adam Liptak, *Reporter Jailed After Refusing to Name Source*, N.Y. TIMES, July 7, 2005, at A1; Grant Penrod, *A Journalist's Home is His Prison*, NEWS

MEDIA & THE L., Winter 2005, at 10; Ayash v. Dana-Farber Cancer Inst., 13 Mass. L. Rep. 1 (Mass. Super. 2001), *aff'd*, 822 N.E.2d 667 (Mass. 2005), *cert. denied*, 126 S.Ct. 397 (2005); Reporters Committee for Freedom of the Press, *Settlement Reached in Lee Case Involving Reporter's Subpoena*, *available at* http://rcfp.org/news/2006/0602-con-settle.html (last visited July 11, 2006).

[4] Adam Liptak, *Courts Grow Increasingly Skeptical of Any Special Protections for the Press*, N.Y. TIMES, June 28, 2005, at A16 (quoting Jane Kirtley).

[5] Adam Liptak, *Judges Affirm Decision That Found 4 Reporters in Contempt*, N.Y. TIMES, June 29, 2005, at A14 (quoting Brian A. Sun).

it has a reasonable chance of becoming law.[6] Also, Connecticut adopted its first shield law.[7] All states but one, Montana, recognize that journalists have some rights not to testify in court.

The most highly publicized of the recent reporter's privilege cases, that of Judith Miller, began in 2003 when columnist Robert Novak published the identity of undercover CIA officer Valerie Plame, citing two unnamed administration officials as his sources. Several other journalists received the same information from confidential sources. The leaked information was considered newsworthy because it was widely believed to be a Bush Administration attack on Plame's husband, former Ambassador Joseph C. Wilson IV. Wilson had publicly criticized the administration's claim that Iraq attempted to buy uranium from the African nation of Niger to make nuclear weapons.

A special prosecutor then began investigating who in the federal government might have violated federal law by leaking Plame's identity to the media. The special prosecutor subpoenaed several reporters to testify before a federal grand jury. Some of the reporters gave limited testimony with their sources' permission. Miller, however, of the *New York Times,* and Matthew Cooper of *Time* magazine refused to testify. They were ordered to go to jail for eighteen months or until the end of the grand jury session, whichever came first. Time Inc. also was ordered to turn over documents concerning the case or pay a fine of $1,000 a day. The fines and jail sentences were postponed pending appeal.

The appeals ended in 2005 when the U.S. Supreme Court declined to review the contempt convictions of Miller, Cooper and *Time* magazine.[8] Miller then vowed not to testify, saying, "Journalists simply cannot do their jobs without being able to commit to sources that they won't be identified. Such protection is critical to the free flow of information in a democracy."[9] She was sent to federal prison and released after eighty-five days when she said her source was voluntarily releasing her from her promise of confidentiality and agreed to testify before the grand jury.[10] Shortly thereafter Miller's source, vice presidential aide I. Lewis "Scooter" Libby, was indicted for perjury and obstruction of justice.

The Supreme Court's refusal to hear the appeal in the case prompted *Time* to hand over its reporter Mathew Cooper's notes to the special prosecutor conducting the grand jury investigation. This was the first time in modern history that a major news organization complied with a government subpoena to reveal the identity of a confidential course.

Norman Pearlstine, Time Inc.'s editor-in-chief, explained his de-

cision this way: "I found myself coming to the conclusion that once the Supreme Court has spoken in a case involving national security and a grand jury, we are not above the law and we have to behave the way ordinary citizens do."[11] The magazine made its decision over Cooper's objections. Cooper eventually testified before the grand jury and avoided going to jail after his source, White House political adviser Karl Rove, released Cooper from his promise of confidentiality.[12] Thus far, four reporters have testified before this federal grand jury, and two others have given deposition testimony.[13]

The journalist held under house arrest was Jim Taricani, a Providence, Rhode Island, television reporter.[14] He was subpoenaed by a special prosecutor seeking to discover who had given Taricani a copy of an FBI surveillance tape in possible violation of a gag order. The tape showed a city official accepting a bribe. Taricani was sentenced to house arrest rather than jail because of his poor health.

The *Boston Globe* lost its libel case when a judge granted a default judgment against the newspaper because the newspaper refused to identify a confidential source used in story about Dr. Lois Ayash.[15] The *Globe* reported in 1995 that one of its columnists died due to an overdose of cancer drugs and that Ayash led the team of doctors who treated the columnist. When the *Globe* refused to identify its confidential hospital source during the discovery process, the court entered the default judgment. The judge reasoned that the newspaper had no testimonial privilege in the case because the plaintiff's need for the information outweighed the public's interest in the free flow of information. Ayash was awarded $1.68 million against the newspaper and $420,000 against the reporter who wrote the story. The judgment was upheld by the Supreme Judicial Court of Massachusetts, and in 2005 the U.S. Supreme Court refused to hear an appeal.[16]

The case in which five news organizations paid $750,000 so their reporters would not be compelled to testify centered around Wen Ho Lee, a former scientist at Los Alamos National Laboratory, who was suspected of espionage on behalf of China. After pleading guilty to a lesser charge, Lee sued the federal government for violating the federal Privacy Act by leaking information about him to the media. Lee's attorneys in his civil case subpoenaed six reporters as part of the discovery process in an attempt to uncover the source

[6] Reporters Committee for Freedom of the Press, *Shield Bill Introduced in Senate, available at* http://rcfp.org/news/2006/0518-con-shield.html (last visited July 14, 2006).

[7] An Act Concerning Freedom of the Press, 2006 Conn. Pub. Acts 140.

[8] Miller v. United States, 125 S.Ct. 2977 (2005).

[9] *See* Adam Liptak, *Court Declines to Rule on Case of Reporters' Refusal to Testify,* N.Y. TIMES, June 28, 2005, at A1.

[10] *See* David Johnston & Douglas Jehl, *Times Reporter Free From Jail; She Will Testify,* N.Y. TIMES, Sept. 30, 2005, at A1.

[11] *See* Adam Liptak, *Time Inc. to Yield Files on Sources, Relenting to U.S.,* N.Y. TIMES, July 1, 2005, at A1.

[12] *See* Adam Liptak, *Reporter Jailed After Refusing to Name Source,* N.Y. TIMES, July 7, 2005, at A1; Nancy Gibbs, *The Rove Problem,* TIME, July 25, 2005, at 23.

[13] *See* Casey Murray, *Under Oath: Journalists are Under Increasing Pressure to Testify in Court, Threatening Their Independence and Leading Many to Consider a Federal Shield Law,* NEWS MEDIA & THE L., Winter 2006, at 10.

[14] *In re* Special Proceedings, 373 F.3d 37 (1st Cir. 2004), *aff'g* 291 F. Supp. 2d 44 (D.R.I. 2003).

[15] Ayash v. Dana-Farber Cancer Inst., 13 Mass. L. Rep. 1 (Mass. Super. 2001).

[16] Ayash v. Dana-Farber Cancer Inst., 822 N.E.2d 667 (Mass. 2005), *cert. denied,* 126 S.Ct. 397 (2005).

of the government leak.

The reporters refused to answer questions about their sources. In 2004, a U.S. District Court judge found five of the six reporters in contempt and fined them $500 per day each until they revealed their sources.[17] On appeal, the U.S. Court of Appeals for the D.C. Circuit agreed that five of the reporters must identify their sources or be held in contempt. The court recognized that reporters have a First Amendment-based testimonial privilege, but held that the privilege is not absolute. The D.C. Circuit held the lower court had not abused its discretion in deciding that the reporters must testify because the reporters' information went to the heart of Lee's case and Lee had exhausted all reasonable alternative sources of information.[18] The court reversed the contempt order against the sixth reporter because he had not refused to answer questions but had repeatedly denied knowledge of the identity of sources who had spoken to reporters about Lee.[19]

The case, which involved ABC News, the Associated Press, the *Los Angeles Times*, the *New York Times* and the *Washington Post*, was settled before the Supreme Court decided whether to hear the reporters' appeals. The news organizations said in a joint statement that they paid Lee "to protect our confidential sources, to protect our journalists from further sanction and possible imprisonment, and to protect our news organizations from potential exposure. We were reluctant to contribute anything to this settlement, but we sought relief in the courts and found none."[20]

The causes of these problems include the failure of an increasing number of federal courts to recognize a First Amendment-based testimonial privilege for journalists, the fact that state shield laws generally do not apply in federal courts, the fact that the attorney general's guidelines governing media subpoenas do not apply in all cases and are only guidelines when they do apply, and the lack of a federal shield law. Disappointed by the Supreme Court's unwillingness to intervene, journalists and their supporters increasingly are pinning their hopes on proposals for a federal shield law.

Subpoenas have been a persistent problem for journalists for more than a century — but usually a less difficult and dramatic problem than today. In 2006, the Reporters Committee for Freedom of the Press listed on its Web site twenty journalists jailed since 1984 — about one a year in all of the nation's state and federal courts.[21] Every year a few other journalists who refused to comply with judicial orders to reveal the identities of confidential sources, to hand over work materials, or to testify in court were found guilty of contempt and were fined or ordered to perform community service. Other journalists avoided such penalties but paid a high price in legal fees and time. Representatives from about 320 newspapers and television stations surveyed by the Reporters Committee for Freedom of the Press reported that they received a total of 823 subpoenas in 2001.[22] The Reporters Committee said those numbers had remained fairly consistent for the previous thirteen years — the time period for which it had studied media subpoenas.

Even if the demands of the subpoenas are met, media outlets must expend significant time and resources to deal with them. This expense can be thousands of dollars in employee hours and legal costs. News outlets often must remove reporters from news stories because of subpoenas. This burden is especially onerous because in most cases the media aren't party to the underlying lawsuits; because the material is often available through other means, such as electronic databases; and because litigants can make broad demands for material.[23]

Problems typically arise when a reporter is served a subpoena to provide documents or answer questions at a judicial proceeding. Ignoring a subpoena may result in a citation for contempt of court; complying may result in the loss of important sources of information.

Newspapers and television stations responding to the Reporters Committee survey fully complied with about 70 percent of the subpoenas issued to them in 2001. In about 20 percent of cases, journalists reported, they were able to persuade the individuals who requested the subpoenas to withdraw them. In 8 percent of cases, the media challenged the subpoenas, and in 75 percent of those cases, they were successful in having the subpoenas quashed.[24]

Journalists who object to testifying or turning over work materials generally claim they are protected from doing so by a reporter's testimonial privilege. The privilege is actually a bundle of privileges including the privilege not to reveal the identity of a confidential source, the privilege to be free from turning over published information or unpublished work materials and the privilege to be free from testifying at judicial proceedings. It also includes protection from newsroom searches by law enforcement agencies. The reporter's privilege is related to the common law doctor-patient, lawyer-client and priest-penitent testimonial privileges that have long granted one party in a relationship the right to refuse to testify against the other. The reporter's privilege, however, appears to have diminishing support among federal jurists, and the Supreme Court has said it does not exist as a constitutional right.

The reporter's privilege varies dramatically from state to state

[17] Lee v. Dep't of Justice, 287 F. Supp. 2d 15, 16-17 (D.D.C. 2004).

[18] Lee v. Dep't of Justice, 413 F.3d 53, 60 (D.C. Cir. 2005).

[19] *Id.* at 63.

[20] Reporters Committee for Freedom of the Press, *Settlement Reached in Lee Case Involving Reporter's Subpoena, available at* http://rcfp.org/news/2006/0602-con-settle.html (last visited July 11, 2006).

[21] Reporters Committee for Freedom of the Press, *Paying the Price: Reporters Who Went to Jail, available at* http://www.rcfp.org/jail.html (last visited July 11, 2006).

[22] Reporters Committee for Freedom of the Press, *Agents of Discovery, available at* http://www.rcfp.org/agents/intro.html (last visited July 11, 2006).

[23] *Id.*

[24] *Id.*

and among federal jurisdictions. That's because the privilege is based on a patchwork of federal and state constitutional law, federal and state statutes, state common law, judicial rules and attorney general guidelines. The privilege also varies according to the type of proceeding to which a reporter is subpoenaed. For example, while the privilege has been recognized in both criminal and civil cases, a reporter is more likely to be compelled to testify in a criminal case where a defendant has a strong Sixth Amendment right to a fair trial. The privilege also varies according to the nature of what a reporter is being asked to reveal. Reporters are more likely to be compelled to testify about crimes they witnessed, for example, than about crimes of which they have second-hand knowledge.

## THE PROS AND CONS OF A REPORTER'S PRIVILEGE

A natural question arises in the debate over the benefit of allowing journalists to protect sources and information: Why would a journalist refuse to testify if the journalist had information that would help a court determine the truth in a case? Isn't it the business of journalists to uncover and publish the truth? Certainly it is, but journalists argue that they sometimes need to conceal certain information in order to protect the free flow of other information to the public. That's just one argument that is at the heart of the debate over a privilege of confidentiality. There are others:

• Criminal defense attorneys argue that a client's Sixth Amendment right to a fair trial outweighs the privilege of a journalist to refuse to testify. The criminal defendant's right is characterized as the right to "every man's evidence" to prove innocence. That right is closely tied to the right of the public to fair and effective law enforcement. Courts often emphasize that all citizens — including reporters — are obliged to testify when they have knowledge pertinent to the outcome of a criminal case.

• Journalists counter that they need to be exempt from some of the duties of other citizens. They argue that they should have greater First Amendment protection because they have the difficult task of serving as watchdogs over powerful governments. This raises the question, which will be discussed later in this chapter, of whether the First Amendment provides more protection for journalists than it provides for other citizens.

• If a reporter is forced to reveal the identity of a confidential source, the reporter's supply of confidential sources might dry up, journalists argue. They say sources often have information that the public needs for democratic self-governance — information that cannot be obtained by other means. Furthermore, revealing the identities of sources might subject the sources to harassment or retaliation from those about whom they provided the information. Much important news would go unreported without these sources, the argument goes, and without a guarantee of confidentiality, the sources would not provide information. Journalists point to Deep Throat and the media's investigation of the Watergate scandal as evidence of the importance of the informa-

tion that can be obtained only from confidential sources. The common counter argument is that there is no proof that subpoenas create a chilling effect on the gathering and dissemination of the news.

• The burden of having either to testify or to fight a subpoena keeps journalists in court and away from their important jobs, which raises First Amendment concerns. Subpoenas and search warrants also can prompt journalists to censor their writing to avoid being subpoenaed or deter them from recording and preserving their recollections for future use. Journalists say the burden on newsgathering outweighs the public interest in disclosure. Opponents of a reporter's testimonial privilege say the problem of subpoenas being served on journalists only arises when a source is implicated in a crime or possesses information about a crime or other matter being investigated, which does not describe the vast bulk of confidential sources.

• Journalists argue that reporting styles changed in the late 1960s and early 1970s and created greater need for confidential sources, particularly when the media sought news about minority cultural and political groups or dissident organizations suspicious of the law and public officials. Today journalists argue they need confidential sources to uncover what's happening in a government that has operated with increasing secrecy since the September 11, 2001, terrorist attacks.

• Journalists fear the government might use its subpoena power to harass the news media, to disrupt a reporter's relationships with sources or to retaliate when the news media are critical of the government. Judges and others counter that rules governing the use of subpoenas are designed to prevent such abuses.

• When police and prosecutors rely on journalists for information, they make the media an arm of law enforcement, which is not their proper role in a democracy and undermines their credibility with sources. Journalists are supposed to be watchdogs of law enforcement. In civil cases, a journalist might be forced into the position of preparing a litigant's case. Also, some journalists argue that if a journalist can find information, police or other investigators should be able to do the same — unless they're just too lazy.

• Journalists argue that law enforcement officials who search newsrooms armed with warrants threaten to interfere with their publication schedules. The government argues that the Fourth Amendment's protection against unreasonable searches and seizures provides ample protection for journalists — the same protection it provides for all citizens. It is the magistrate's job to ensure that a search warrant is not issued without probable cause or in a manner that unnecessarily interferes with publication.

These arguments appear in court opinion after court opinion as reporters resist orders to testify.

## THE HISTORY OF THE PRIVILEGE

Reporter's privilege cases are not new. For more than one hundred years, journalists have been resisting judicial — and sometimes Congressional — efforts to compel them to testify, and for most of those years journalists were without any testimonial privilege. In 1873, for example, an editor of the *New York Tribune* was subpoenaed to appear before a New York grand jury to identify the author of an allegedly libelous article that had been published in the newspaper.[25] The editor appeared but refused to identify the author. Newspaper policy prohibited him from disclosing the identities of any writers, he explained, because the newspaper, not the author, is responsible for the article's contents. The editor was found in contempt of court and sent to the county jail.

Some of the earliest reporter's privilege cases involved Congressional subpoenas. The Constitution gives Congress the power to investigate, which is accompanied by the power to subpoena.[26] In the mid-1850s, J.W. Simonton, Washington correspondent for the *New York Times*, reported that certain unnamed congressmen were soliciting bribes to influence their actions regarding the disposal of public lands. Simonton was called before the House to divulge the names. When he refused, the House cited him for contempt and imprisoned him for more than two weeks until he decided to testify. After he testified, several congressmen resigned. At the time, the only punishment for an individual who refused a congressional subpoena was imprisonment during the current session of Congress.[27] Harsher penalties were adopted later.[28]

While no reporter has been found in contempt of Congress for several decades, some have been threatened with contempt citations. In 1992, a special counsel appointed by the Senate wanted to compel Nina Totenberg of National Public Radio and Timothy Phelps of *Newsday* to disclose the sources of stories in which they reported that law professor Anita Hill told Senate investigators she had been sexually harassed by Supreme Court nominee Clarence Thomas. The leadership of the Senate Rules Committee decided not to order the two journalists to testify because of the chilling effect such an act would have on the media.

More recently, the reporter's privilege issue has arisen in the context of an international war crimes trial. In late 2002, the appeals court for the United Nations International Criminal Tribunal, which was investigating war crimes in the former Yugoslavia, recognized a qualified reporter's privilege for war correspondents. The tribunal, located in The Netherlands, had ordered a former *Washington Post* correspondent to comply with a subpoena to appear as a witness in the trial of a former Bosnian Serb accused of genocide and deportation of non-Serbs during the 1992-95 Bosnian War. The reporter and the *Post* argued that testifying would undermine their neutrality and endanger the lives of war correspondents. The first international war crimes court to address this is-

sue, the appeals court agreed. The court said a subpoena can be issued to a reporter only if the information sought is of direct and important value in determining the core issue in the case and cannot reasonably be obtained elsewhere.[29]

Year after year, journalists have argued that compelled testimony chills newsgathering, violates their employers' rules and violates professional codes of ethics. Not until 1959, however, did courts address the question of whether the First Amendment provided reporters a testimonial privilege. In *Garland v. Torre*, the U.S. Court of Appeals for the Second Circuit refused to exempt the reporter from her obligation to testify but, for the first time, recognized that "compulsory disclosure of a journalist's confidential sources of information may entail an abridgment of press freedom by imposing some limitation upon the availability of news."[30]

The case involved a breach of contract and libel suit filed against CBS by actress Judy Garland. She claimed that a network executive made false and defamatory statements about her to *New York Herald Tribune* columnist Marie Torre, who published them. During pre-trial discovery, Garland's legal counsel subpoenaed Torre, who testified that the statements in her column were the statements made to her by a CBS informant. But she refused to identify the source, arguing that doing so would violate her promise of confidentiality, even when ordered to do so by a federal judge. The judge held her in contempt of court, and Torre appealed.

Judge Potter Stewart wrote the opinion for the Second Circuit, and later, as a Supreme Court justice, he would use the reasoning from that opinion as the basis for what was arguably the most influential judicial opinion ever written regarding the reporter's testimonial privilege. The Second Circuit ruled that the First Amendment did not exempt the newspaper columnist from her obligation to testify and identify a confidential source. Stewart explained that the court's task was to balance the interest served by compelling the witness to testify against the resulting impairment of First Amendment freedoms. Noting that the balancing was not difficult in this case, Stewart explained that the First Amendment interest was the witness's right to decide whether to speak or remain silent, a privacy right. If freedom of the press also is involved, he wrote:

[W]e do not hesitate to conclude that it too must give place under the Constitution to a paramount public interest in the fair administration of justice. "The right to sue and defend in the courts is the alternative of force. In an organized society it is the right conservative of all other rights, and lies at the foundation of orderly government."[31]

The court suggested limits on the government's power to com-

[25] People ex rel. Phelps v. Fancher, 2 Hun. 226 (N.Y. Sup. Ct. 1874).

[26] U.S. CONST. art. I, §§ 1, 8. *See also* McGrain v. Daugherty, 273 U.S. 135, 174 (1927).

[27] *See* JAMES HAMILTON, THE POWER TO PROBE: A STUDY OF CONGRESSIONAL INVESTIGATIONS 91 (1976).

[28] *See* 2 U.S.C. 192, 194 (2000).

[29] Prosecutor v. Brdjanin, Decision on Interlocutory Appeal, No. IT-99-36-AR73.9 (Dec. 11, 2002).

[30] 259 F.2d 545, 548 (2d Cir. 1958).

[31] *Id.* at 549 (quoting Chambers v. Baltimore & Ohio R.R. Co., 207 U.S. 142, 148 (1907)).

pel reporters to testify, however. Judge Stewart pointed out that compelling Torre to testify did not involve curtailing unorthodox political, economic or religious views; the wholesale disclosure of a newspaper's confidential sources; or a case in which the identity of the news source was of doubtful relevance. Stewart also wrote that the district court had not abused its discretion in ordering Torre to testify because the court found the deposition was being taken in good faith, was a necessary step in the preparation for trial and was not being taken in a manner as to unreasonably annoy, embarrass or oppress the witness. While ruling against the media, Stewart was planting the seeds for a First Amendment-based qualified testimonial privilege for reporters.

The constitutional question did not come before the Supreme Court until *Branzburg v. Hayes*, fourteen years later. By then, subpoenas were being served on reporters in dramatic numbers. CBS and NBC, for example, received 121 subpoenas in a thirty-month period in the late 1960s and early 1970s; and a *Chicago Sun-Times* reporter was subpoenaed eleven times in eighteen months. This was the result of tumultuous social and political events that included the civil rights movement, the Vietnam War, the Watergate scandal, an increase in investigative reporting, the increased use of confidential sources as the basis for stories and the Nixon administration's desire to maintain law and order in an increasingly unstable society.

## BRANZBURG V. HAYES

In 1972, the Supreme Court decided by a 5-4 vote that the First Amendment does not provide journalists with the right to be free from having to appear before grand juries and testify about criminal behavior they had witnessed. The landmark opinion in *Branzburg v. Hayes*[32] was a stinging defeat for three reporters who had refused to testify before grand juries. Twenty years later, however, *Branzburg* was widely interpreted by lower courts as providing journalists with a qualified, or conditional, First Amendment-based testimonial privilege. Now the courts seem to have reversed direction again. What has caused these apparent shifts?

*Branzburg* was actually four separate cases consolidated in one opinion because the four cases raised the same First Amendment issue. Two of the cases involved Paul Branzburg, a reporter for the *Louisville Courier-Journal*. He was first subpoenaed to testify before a grand jury after he wrote a story in which he described watching two people synthesize hashish from marijuana. His second subpoena arrived after he wrote a story detailing the use of drugs in Frankfort, Kentucky, the state capital. In the second story, Branzburg reported that he spent two weeks interviewing dozens of drug users and seeing several of them smoke marijuana. In both stories, Branzburg concealed the identities of his drug-using and manufacturing sources, and, when subpoenaed, he appeared but refused to identify those sources, claiming a testimo-

nial privilege under the Kentucky shield law and the Kentucky and U.S. constitutions. The Kentucky Court of Appeals denied his claims, saying he had no legal right to refuse to testify about crimes he observed.[33]

The third case involved Paul Pappas, a newsman-photographer for a Massachusetts television station. As part of his coverage of civil disorders, he was invited into Black Panther headquarters on the condition that he not disclose anything he saw or heard except those events he might cover in an anticipated police raid. There was no raid, and Pappas reported no story. He was, however, subpoenaed to appear before a state grand jury investigating criminal acts allegedly committed by the Panthers during civil unrest. Pappas testified before the grand jury but refused to say what he saw and heard inside the Black Panther headquarters. The Massachusetts Supreme Judicial Court rejected his claim of a First Amendment privilege,[34] and Massachusetts had no shield law.

The fourth case in the *Branzburg* quartet involved Earl Caldwell, a *New York Times* reporter also covering the Black Panther Party and other black militant groups. He was subpoenaed and told to bring his notes and tape recordings about the aims and activities of the Black Panthers to a federal grand jury investigating crimes allegedly committed by the Black Panthers, including assassination threats against President Richard Nixon.

Caldwell objected to the broad scope of the subpoena, and the district court compromised. The court ordered him to divulge whatever information had been given to him for publication but said that he would not be required "to reveal confidential associations, sources or information received, developed or maintained by him as a professional journalist in the course of his efforts to gather news for dissemination to the public through the press or other news media."[35] The court held that the First Amendment afforded Caldwell a privilege to refuse to disclose such confidential information until the government showed a compelling and overriding national interest in the information that could not be served by any other means. Caldwell, however, objected to having to appear at all. He argued that having to appear before a grand jury, which meets behind closed doors, violated his First Amendment rights and, if enforced, would drive "a wedge of mistrust and silence between the news media and the militants."[36]

When Caldwell refused to appear, he was found in contempt. The U.S. Court of Appeals for the Ninth Circuit overturned that decision,[37] ruling that the First Amendment afforded reporters a qualified testimonial privilege and that requiring Caldwell to testify "would deter his informants from communicating with him in the

---

[32] 408 U.S. 665 (1972).

[33] Branzburg v. Pound, 461 S.W.2d 345 (Ky. Ct. App. 1970); Branzburg v. Meigs, 503 S.W.2d 748 (Ky. Ct. App. 1971). At the time these cases were decided, the appeals court was Kentucky's highest court.

[34] *In re* Pappas, 266 N.E.2d 297 (Mass. 1971).

[35] Application of Caldwell, 311 F. Supp. 358, 362 (N.D. Cal. 1970).

[36] *Branzburg*, 408 U.S. at 676.

[37] Caldwell v. United States, 434 F.2d 1081 (9th Cir. 1970).

future and would cause him to censor his writings in an effort to avoid being subpoenaed."[38] The government appealed to the Supreme Court.

Justice Byron White, for the Court, declared that the general obligation of each citizen to appear before a grand jury or at a trial and testify outweighs journalists' First Amendment interests. He explained that grand juries, which are mandated by the Fifth Amendment for defendants suspected of a capital or "otherwise infamous crime," are essential to fair and effective law enforcement because they protect a person from having to stand trial unless there is probable cause that the person committed a crime. The journalists' interests, on the other hand, were only slightly affected by this decision, White wrote. He held the decision would have no effect on what journalists can publish and would not affect a large number of their sources; the journalists' argument that having to testify would constrict the news flow from their sources was "to a great extent speculative."[39] History, he wrote, suggests the press can operate effectively without a testimonial privilege.

Justice White's opinion made it clear that the Court was not about to create a testimonial privilege for journalists that other citizens do not also enjoy. This point goes a long way toward explaining not only why the journalists lost the case, but why, six years later, student journalists would also lose *Zurcher v. Stanford Daily*.[40] In that case, the *Stanford Daily* asked the Court to establish a First Amendment protection against otherwise legal newsroom searches — a protection not afforded to other citizens.

In both *Branzburg* and *Zurcher*, the Supreme Court refused to interpret the First Amendment as giving journalists more protection than other citizens. In the view of the Court, the First Amendment applies equally to all citizens, and, furthermore, the Court did not want the task of deciding who is a journalist. This has consistently been the view of the majority of the Court.

Justice Stewart, for one, disagreed. He argued in a 1974 speech that the Press Clause was intended to extend rights to the press beyond those of other persons, who are protected by the speech clause. The press clause is needed to enable the media to act as watchdogs of government, he argued, and if the press and speech clauses do not have different meanings, they are no more than "a constitutional redundancy."[41]

When, in 1980, the media again came to the Supreme Court asking for an expanded interpretation of the First Amendment — this time for a right of access to criminal trials — the Court said "yes." The different result in *Richmond Newspapers v. Virginia*[42] undoubtedly was due in large part to the fact that the media requested the right of access for themselves and the public; the newspaper did not ask the Court to create a First Amendment

protection for journalists beyond that afforded to others.

Also, in *Branzburg* the Court stated that "news gathering is not without its First Amendment protection,"[43] a simple statement that has tremendous potential as a precedent for expanding the traditional scope of First Amendment freedoms. Traditionally the First Amendment has been interpreted as protecting the right to publish the news but not the right to gather it. That changed somewhat in 1980, when the *Branzburg* decision served as a precedent for guaranteeing the media and the public access to criminal trials, as established in *Richmond Newspapers*. But journalists have been unsuccessful in their attempts to have the reach of *Branzburg* extended to include a First Amendment right of access to prisons or jails — places that are not open to the general public and where security is very important.[44]

In *Branzburg*, White also noted that the grand juries in all four cases were conducted properly. Grand juries not conducted in good faith would raise different First Amendment issues, he said. White also warned law enforcement officials that they were not to use subpoenas to harass the media.

Finally, White pointed out that Congress and state legislatures had the power to create testimonial privileges for reporters by statute if they determined they were necessary and desirable. This illustrates the legal principle that while the government cannot take from citizens rights protected by the First Amendment, the government can create rights beyond those provided by the First Amendment. Shield laws do just that, as do state and federal statutes that grant the public and the media rights of access to government meetings and records.

In a three-paragraph concurring opinion, Justice Lewis Powell emphasized the limited nature of the majority opinion and opened the door for lower courts to reinterpret the *Branzburg* decision. "The Court does not hold that newsmen, subpoenaed to testify before a grand jury, are without constitutional rights with respect to the gathering of news or in safeguarding their sources," Powell wrote.[45] He noted that harassment of journalists would not be tolerated and explained that journalists can move to quash subpoenas if their information is only remotely related to grand jury investigations or if there is no legitimate law enforcement need for the information. He advocated balancing First Amendment and law enforcement interests on a case-by-case basis.

Justice Powell's concurrence opened the door to lower-court reinterpretation of the Court's decision because, although he voted with the majority to deny a First Amendment-based testimonial privilege in the four cases under review, he appeared to support a qualified journalistic privilege — a privilege that would be afforded to journalists if their information was only remotely re-

---

[38] *Branzburg*, 408 U.S. at 679.

[39] *Id*. at 694.

[40] 436 U.S. 547 (1978).

[41] Potter Stewart, *Or of the Press*, 26 HASTINGS L.J. 631, 633 (1975).

[42] 448 U.S. 555 (1980).

[43] 408 U.S. at 707.

[44] *See* Houchins v. KQED, 438 U.S. 1 (1978); Saxbe v. Washington Post Co., 417 U.S. 843 (1974); Procunier v. Pell, 417 U.S. 817 (1974). These cases are discussed in Chapter 18.

[45] *Branzburg*, 408 U.S. at 709 (Powell, J., concurring).

lated to a grand jury investigation or if there were no legitimate law enforcement need for the information. So, when the lower federal and state courts looked beyond who won or lost in *Branzburg* to which justices supported some degree of First Amendment-based privilege, they added Powell's position to those of the four dissenters. The result was a majority in favor of at least a qualified privilege for reporters.

In light of that reinterpretation, Justice Stewart's dissenting opinion became enormously important. Arguing that the Court had displayed a "crabbed view" of the First Amendment and "a disturbing insensitivity to the critical role of an independent press in our society,"[46] he proposed a three-part test to determine when a journalist must testify. In order to defeat a reporter's motion to quash a grand jury subpoena, he proposed, the government must prove:

- there is probable cause to believe the reporter has information that is clearly relevant to a probable crime;
- the information cannot be obtained by alternative means less destructive of First Amendment rights;
- there is a "compelling and overriding interest" in the information.[47]

These criteria are a version of the qualifications Stewart first suggested in *Garland v. Torre*. From those two media losses came a partial — if temporary — victory.

By the early 1990s, most appellate courts had interpreted *Branzburg* as a precedent for a qualified First Amendment-based privilege for reporters and had adopted Stewart's three-part test, or some variation thereof, as criteria for the privilege to stand. That is, the privilege is not absolute. A reporter can successfully claim a First Amendment right not to testify only if the government fails to prove all three parts of the test. If the government is able to prove what the court demands of it, the reporter must testify or chance being cited for contempt of court.

In the 1990s, however, some courts began withdrawing their support for a First Amendment-based privilege on the grounds that *Branzburg* was never intended to create a testimonial privilege for journalists, especially in grand jury cases, and had been misinterpreted by lower courts. In 1998, the U.S. Court of Appeals for the Fifth Circuit rejected a television station's claim of a First-Amendment based privilege, saying the media had no more First Amendment protection than anyone else.[48] The television station had been ordered to hand over outtakes of an interview with an arson suspect. In 2003, the Court of Appeals for the Seventh Circuit suggested a First Amendment-based privilege does not exist.[49] The court said the decisions of other federal courts that reinterpreted *Branzburg* to create a qualified privilege were "surpris-

ing" and "audacious."[50] So while the First Amendment-based privilege is still recognized in some jurisdictions, its judicial support seems shaky at best and journalists planning to claim the privilege should proceed with great caution.

## APPLYING THE FIRST AMENDMENT PRIVILEGE

It is not enough to know which circuits or states recognize the First Amendment-based privilege. Journalists should be aware that the qualified privilege is formulated differently in different jurisdictions. In most cases, the circuit courts have applied the three-part test from Stewart's dissent in *Branzburg* to decide whether a journalist must testify. Sometimes a fourth prong is added to the test: The underlying claim being litigated must clearly have merit. At other times neither a three- nor a four-part test is used. For example, the U.S. Court of Appeals for the First Circuit employs case-by-case balancing of "the potential harm to the free flow of information ... against the asserted need for the requested information."[51] Usually, however, the application of the three-part test decides a case. Here are examples of how each element of the three-part test has been applied by the circuit courts to protect journalists.

### (1) There is probable cause to believe the reporter has information that is clearly relevant to a probable crime.

In 1980, the U.S. Court of Appeals for the Fifth Circuit vacated a contempt decree against a reporter who had refused to obey a court order to reveal the identity of a confidential source at an *in camera* hearing.[52]

An *in camera* hearing takes place before a judge in chambers and provides an opportunity for the judge to review the reporter's information to decide if it should be revealed in open court. In this case, the subpoena had been sought by a discharged school official who sued the school district for allegedly publicizing false and stigmatizing charges against him and for failing to afford him a hearing in violation of his Fourteenth Amendment due process rights. The discharged school official claimed the defamatory charges had been leaked to the education reporter for the *Dallas Morning News*. He sought the identities of the reporter's confidential sources.

The Fifth Circuit found the reporter had a qualified First Amendment-based right to withhold the identities of confidential sources because their identities were not relevant to what the court determined to be the only possibly valid claim in the case — that the plaintiff had requested and been refused a hearing. Therefore the reporter could not be compelled to testify until the plaintiff first proved he had indeed been denied a hearing. Then, the court said,

---

[46] *Id.* at 725 (Stewart, J., dissenting).

[47] *Id.* at 743 (Stewart, J., dissenting).

[48] United States v. Smith, 135 F.3d 963 (5th Cir. 1998).

[49] *See* McKevitt v. Pallasch, 339 F.3d 530 (7th Cir. 2003).

[50] *Id.* at 532.

[51] Bruno & Stillman, Inc. v. Globe Newspaper Co., 633 F.2d 583, 596 (1st Cir. 1980).

[52] *In re* Selcraig, 705 F.2d 789 (5th Cir. 1983).

the reporter's testimony would be relevant to possible punitive damages.

### (2) The information cannot be obtained by alternative means less destructive of First Amendment rights.

In 2003, the U.S. District Court in Washington, D.C., ruled that Linda Tripp, the former White House secretary who taped telephone conversations with Monica Lewinsky about her affair with President Clinton, could not compel a reporter to testify because Tripp had not exhausted alternative sources.[53]

Tripp sued the U.S. Department of Defense under the federal Privacy Act, alleging that the department violated her privacy rights by telling a reporter for *Stars and Stripes*, the military newspaper, that she had applied for a job at a defense department facility in Germany. Tripp subsequently subpoenaed the reporter in an attempt to discover the identity of the reporter's confidential source in the defense department. The court ruled that the reporter had a qualified First Amendment-based testimonial privilege and that Tripp failed to overcome that privilege because she did not adequately seek alternate sources of information. The court said Tripp had "not even attempted to obtain the information requested from other sources, and therefore has not met the exhaustion requirement set forth by relevant case law." The D.C. Circuit has held that "'efforts made by the litigants to obtain the information from alternative sources is ... of central importance ...reporters should be compelled to disclose their sources only after the litigant has shown that he has exhausted every reasonable source of information.'"[54] The court said there were several defense department employees Tripp could have questioned.

### (3) There is a compelling and overriding interest in the information.

In 1983, the U.S. Court of Appeals for the Second Circuit allowed *Sports Illustrated* to refuse to comply with a subpoena for documents and tapes related to a story about a basketball point-shaving scandal at Boston College. The defense at the criminal trial resulting from the scandal sought the documents and tapes in order to impeach the credibility of one of the authors of the article, reputed underworld figure Henry Hill. The article was his first-person account of the point-shaving scheme. The court ruled that the magazine had a qualified privilege not to turn over its work materials to the court and that the defense failed to overcome that privilege because it failed to prove that the documents were "necessary and critical" to its case. The court explained that Hill had been thoroughly impeached already and that further evidence against him would serve "a solely cumulative purpose."[55] Hill had admitted under oath that he was a career criminal who had committed robbery, arson, hijacking, extortion and loan sharking and had trafficked in illegal drugs.

## THE WHO, WHAT AND WHERE OF THE FIRST AMENDMENT PRIVILEGE

Even when a court recognizes a First Amendment testimonial privilege, the protection afforded to journalists who refuse to testify varies based on three factors: (1) the type of proceeding in which the journalist is subpoenaed to testify; (2) the type of information or material the journalist is being asked to divulge, including whether the journalist is being asked to testify as an eyewitness, whether the journalist promised confidentiality to a source, and whether the information sought had been published; and (3) whether the person ordered to testify is, in fact, a journalist.

### The Type of Proceeding

Because the Supreme Court said in *Branzburg* that journalists do not have a First Amendment right to refuse to testify before a properly conducted grand jury, journalists today generally have the least protection when called to testify before grand juries. Courts usually interpret *Branzburg* as rejecting a First Amendment privilege unless the grand jury is harassing a witness or otherwise not acting in good faith.

This is a critical factor in the cases of some of the dozens of reporters recently subpoenaed. The reporters in the Valerie Plame case, for example, were subpoenaed to testify before a federal grand jury – the type of proceeding in which they have the weakest case for a testimonial privilege. There is no First Amendment privilege not to testify before a grand jury, and state shield laws generally do not apply in federal court.

This also was central to the ruling of the U.S. Court of Appeals for the Fifth Circuit in the case of Vanessa Leggett, an aspiring book author who spent 168 days in jail in 2001 and 2002 for refusing to comply with a federal grand jury subpoena. Leggett investigated the murder of a Houston socialite in order to write a book about the case, but then a grand jury subpoenaed all of her tape-recorded conversations with thirty-four people and any transcripts of those tapes. Leggett refused to comply, claiming a First Amendment privilege not to testify. The U.S. District Court held her in contempt and sent her to jail until the grand jury term expired. The U.S. Court of Appeals for the Fifth Circuit affirmed the lower court's decision, citing *Branzburg* and explaining it recognized no such privilege against a grand jury subpoena "absent evidence of governmental harassment or oppression," and it found no such evidence.[56] The Supreme Court refused to review the case.[57] No journalist had ever spent so much time in jail for refusing to testify.

---

[53] Tripp v. Dep't of Defense, 284 F. Supp. 2d 50 (D.D.C. 2003)

[54] *Id.* at 60 (quoting Zerilli v. Smith, 656 F.2d 705, 713 (D.C. Cir. 1981)).

[55] United States v. Burke, 700 F.2d 70, 77-78 (2d Cir. 1983).

[56] *In re* Grand Jury Subpoenas, 29 Media L. Rep. (BNA) 2301, 2304 (5th Cir. 2002).

[57] Leggett v. United States, 535 U.S. 1011 (2002) (denying cert.).

Some courts use *Branzburg* as a precedent for denying reporters a testimonial privilege in other types of criminal proceedings as well. In such cases, the courts generally conclude that the criminal defendant's Sixth Amendment right to "every man's evidence" outweighs First Amendment interests. For example, in 1988 the U.S. Court of Appeals for the First Circuit enforced a pre-trial subpoena issued to NBC requesting outtakes of an interview with a prospective key witness in the mail and wire fraud trial of Lyndon H. LaRouche and workers in his 1984 presidential campaign. Only a small portion of the interview had been aired. The court decided the case by balancing the journalists' First Amendment interests against the criminal defendants' interests. According to the court, the legitimate First Amendment interests in this case were (1) the threat of administrative and judicial intrusion into the newsgathering and editorial processes; (2) the disadvantage of a journalist appearing to be an investigative arm of the judicial system, the government or a private party; (3) the disincentive to compile and preserve non-broadcast material; and (4) the burden on journalists' time and resources in responding to subpoenas. The defendants' interests, as articulated by the court, were "their constitutional rights to a fair trial under the Fifth Amendment [the right to a grand jury and the guarantee of due process, for example] and to compulsory process and effective confrontation and cross-examination of adverse witnesses under the Sixth Amendment."[58] The weightier were the defendants' interests, the court ruled.

According to the survey conducted by the Reporters Committee in 2001, the largest number of subpoenas reported were issued in connection with criminal cases. The second largest category comprised subpoenas served in connection with civil cases. In civil cases, reporters generally have greater success in quashing subpoenas than in criminal cases because no party to the case has a Sixth Amendment fair trial interest.

When the management of a Florida television station received a subpoena in a civil case for its audio and videotapes of a county school board meeting, it claimed a qualified privilege under the First Amendment. A U.S. District Court judge granted the privilege because there were no Sixth Amendment interests in the case to outweigh the First Amendment interests. The judge explained: "This Court must only weigh the first amendment interest of the press — the independence in selection and choice of material for publication — against 'the interest served by the liberal discovery provisions embodied in the Federal Rules of Civil Procedure.'"[59]

A reporter who is a party to civil litigation, however, as in a libel or invasion of privacy suit, is more likely to be ordered to testify than a reporter who is not a party. In a 1974 case, for example, the U.S. Court of Appeals for the D.C. Circuit upheld a lower court's decision that a reporter who was being sued for libel had to disclose the identity of a confidential source. The libel plaintiff was attempting to prove the reporter had not used reliable sources. The plaintiff had to prove actual malice to prevail in the libel case, and there were no other means of proving it. The court explained that although it recognized a qualified privilege, the argument in favor of compelling disclosure was strong because the information sought went "to the heart of the matter."[60]

A reporter's right not to reveal a confidential source in a libel case is further weakened by the Supreme Court's 1979 decision in *Herbert v. Lando*.[61] The Court ruled in that libel case that there is no First Amendment privilege against discovery into the editorial process and, therefore, reporters could be compelled to testify about the details of the newsgathering and writing process. *Herbert* did not involve confidential sources.

### Type of Information Sought

Two potentially important considerations in determining if a reporter will be ordered to disclose information are whether the information is confidential and whether it has been published. Journalists traditionally have had greater success in protecting confidential information — especially the identities of confidential sources — than in protecting non-confidential information and sources. And journalists who object to handing over unpublished work products such as outtakes, notes, unpublished photographs and internal memos generally are more successful than those who object to handing over published work materials such as photographs, stories, audiotape and videotape. Published work products are the most common targets of subpoenas, according to the Reporters Committee study.

Publication and non-confidentiality were key factors when a U.S. District Court ordered reporters to testify in a 1990 case. The reporters were subpoenaed after reporting statements by several defendants in a case involving the arson of a bingo hall on a New York state Indian reservation.[62] The U.S. attorney sought to have the reporters testify that the defendants, who were identified in the story, made the statements attributed to them. The reporters moved to quash the subpoenas, claiming a First Amendment privilege. The court said the reporters enjoyed a qualified privilege but that the privilege was diminished by two factors: The information was not confidential, and it had been published. The reporters were required to testify. The court said there was a long list of such diminishing factors, including when a trial at which a reporter is called to testify is criminal, when the questions put to a reporter are narrowly limited and when the reporter is subpoenaed to testify about his or her observation of happenings in public places.

Reporters must almost always testify if they are eyewitnesses to

---

[58] United States v. LaRouche Campaign, 841 F.2d 1176, 1182 (1st Cir. 1988).

[59] Hatch v. Marsh, 18 Media L. Rep. (BNA) 1686, 1687 (M.D. Fla. 1990) (quoting Loadholtz v. Fields, 389 F. Supp. 1299, 1300 (M.D. Fla. 1975)).

[60] Carey v. Hume, 492 F.2d 631, 636 (D.C. Cir. 1974) (quoting Garland v. Torre, 259 F.2d 545 (2d Cir. 1958)).

[61] 441 U.S. 153 (1979).

[62] United States v. Markiewicz, 732 F. Supp. 316 (N.D.N.Y. 1990).

crimes. A U.S. District Court judge in California ruled, for example, that a television news cameraman's personal observations of force used by San Francisco police officers on a citizen were not privileged. The judge said the cameraman had not been asked to reveal any confidential sources or information, nor had he been requested to produce or discuss any resource materials. Rather, he was requested to disclose information that goes to the "very heart" of the plaintiff's claim that the police violated his rights, the court said, and there is no legal authority to support a testimonial privilege in such a case.[63]

Finally, if a journalist is accused of a crime, usually the only testimonial privilege available is the Fifth Amendment protection against self-incrimination.

### *Who Asserts the Privilege?*

Clearly a full-time professional journalist employed by a print, broadcast or cable outlet can successfully claim a First Amendment-based testimonial privilege if the privilege is recognized in a particular jurisdiction. The protection is not always granted to others who have information they do not want to disclose, however. The general rule is that the witness claiming the privilege must demonstrate that he or she sought, gathered or received the information in dispute with the intent — from the start of the newsgathering process — to distribute it to the public.

The person claiming the privilege need not work for a mainstream or commercial news organization. Medical newsletters, trade association magazines, investment analysts' reports and reports from Standard & Poor's credit rating agency also qualify, as do student and military publications. Freelance writers and book authors often qualify, as well, and pay is not a factor.[64] Scholars have had mixed success in claiming the privilege.[65] One individual who did not qualify was a personal friend of accused murderer Claus Von Bulow. The U.S. Court of Appeals for the Second Circuit said she could not obtain a privilege merely by claiming she planned to write a book about Von Bulow's trial because she had no contract and had previously published nothing.[66]

The U.S. Court of Appeals for the Fifth Circuit described Vanessa Leggett as an "English teacher and aspiring freelance writer."[67] It observed in a footnote that her published work consisted of a single article in an FBI publication and one fictional short story and that she had published nothing on the murder

she was investigating. However, the court did not decide whether she was a journalist for purposes of a journalist's testimonial privilege because it found there was no privilege in her case.

Recently there has been discussion in media circles about whether bloggers qualify as journalists under the First Amendment. There has been no court ruling on that issue.

## OTHER PROTECTIONS AGAINST SUBPOENAS

In addition to First Amendment protections, there is a body of state and federal law that provides reporters with protection from revealing sources and information.

### *State Shield Laws*

While the First Amendment-based reporter's privilege is failing to protect dozens of journalists in federal court proceedings, state shield laws continue to provide strong protection to journalists in state courts. Today thirty-two states and the District of Columbia have shield laws. Since the recent spate of journalist subpoenas, Connecticut has adopted its first shield law, and in 2006 Massachusetts and Utah were considering doing the same. Maryland adopted the first state shield law in 1896. However, shield laws do not always protect journalists completely; they vary significantly from state to state, and judges often interpret them very narrowly.

One way in which shield laws vary is in whom they protect. Arizona's shield law, for example, specifically applies to persons "engaged in newspaper, radio, television or reportorial work, or connected with or employed by a newspaper, radio or television station."[68] So, when the notes and other documents gathered by a freelance author for a book project were subpoenaed in a criminal case, an Arizona court ruled that the shield law did not apply to the freelance author. The court said the freelancer did not "gather and disseminate news on an ongoing basis as part of the organized, traditional, mass media."[69] Similarly, Ohio's shield law protects people "engaged in the work of, or connected with, or employed by" newspapers, press associations, or radio or television stations or networks.[70] A federal district court in Ohio refused to extend that law's protection to the publisher of bimonthly financial reports.[71] The Minnesota law provides broader protection. The law says the testimonial privilege is for any person "directly engaged in the gathering, procuring, compiling, editing, or publishing of information for the purpose of transmission, dissemination or publication to the public."[72]

---

[63] Dillon v. City and County of San Francisco, 748 F. Supp. 722, 726 (N.D. Cal. 1990).

[64] *See* James C. Goodale et al., *Reporter's Privilege*, 3 COMM. LAW 347, 398-402 (2005).

[65] *Compare* Cusumano v. Microsoft Corp., 162 F.3d 708 (1st Cir. 1998) (granting a testimonial privilege), *with* In re Grand Jury Subpoena, 750 F.2d 223 (2d Cir. 1984) (denying a testimonial privilege).

[66] Von Bulow v. Von Bulow, 811 F.2d 136 (2d Cir. 1987).

[67] *In re* Grand Jury Subpoenas, 29 Media L. Rep. (BNA) 2301, 2302 (5th Cir. 2002).

[68] ARIZ. REV. STAT. ANN. § 12-2237 (1994).

[69] Matera v. Superior Court, 825 P.2d 971, 973 (Ariz. Ct. App. 1992).

[70] OHIO REV. CODE ANN. §§ 2739.04 & 2739.12 (Page 1981).

[71] Deltec, Inc. v. Dun & Bradstreet, Inc., 187 F. Supp. 788 (N.D. Ohio 1960).

[72] MINN. STAT. ANN. §§ 595.021-595.025, 595.023 (West 1997) (as amended 1998).

| Jurisdictions With Shield Laws | | | |
|---|---|---|---|
| Alabama | Florida | Minnesota | North Dakota |
| Alaska | Georgia | Montana | Ohio |
| Arizona | Illinois | Nebraska | Oklahoma |
| Arkansas | Indiana | Nevada | Oregon |
| California | Kentucky | New Jersey | Pennsylvania |
| Colorado | Louisiana | New Mexico | Rhode Island |
| Delaware | Maryland | New York | South Carolina |
| District of Columbia | Michigan | North Carolina | Tennessee |

A proposal to amend the Maryland shield law to cover bloggers was unsuccessful in 2005. The proposal would have extended the current shield law's absolute privilege for sources and qualified privilege for unpublished news or information to people who gather or disseminate news or information through a blog.[73] However, it appeared that bloggers already were protected by the law, which defines the news media it protects as "any printed, photographic, mechanical, or electronic means of disseminating news and information to the public."[74]

In 2006, a California appeals court ruled that online reporters and bloggers are entitled to protection under the state's shield law. In a case that involved attempts by Apple Computer Inc. to identify the sources of leaked product information, the court interpreted the phrase "periodical publication" in the shield law to include the work of online reporters and bloggers. The court explained, "In no relevant respect do they appear to differ from a reporter or editor for a traditional business-oriented periodical who solicits or otherwise comes into possession of confidential internal information about a company."[75]

State shield laws also vary in the strength of the protection they provide. For example, New York's shield law provides absolute protection against having to reveal confidential information or the identity of a confidential source.[76] Other states — Michigan and Oklahoma are two — have shield laws that offer a qualified privilege. Michigan's law stipulates that in cases involving crimes punishable by life imprisonment, reporters may be compelled to reveal their sources if that information is essential to the proceeding and is not available from another source.[77] Oklahoma's law says a reporter may be compelled to reveal a source if the material sought is relevant to a significant issue in the legal action and not other-

wise available "with due diligence."[78] As these examples illustrate, qualified privileges often rely, at least in part, on the three-part test from Stewart's dissent in *Branzburg*.

Furthermore, some shield laws offer the same protection to journalists seeking to conceal the identity of a source and to journalists seeking to conceal other information; other laws distinguish between the two. For example, while the District of Columbia's shield law provides absolute protection for the identities of sources, it provides only qualified protection for news or information.[79]

Also, some states distinguish between situations in which a journalist has promised a source confidentiality and those in which the journalist has not. Rhode Island's shield law, for example, applies only to confidential sources and information,[80] while the District of Columbia law protects journalists who do not want to reveal the identities of sources "whether or not the source has been promised confidentiality."[81] State shield laws that do not clearly stipulate whether the identity of the source or information must have been received on a promise of confidentiality leave it to the courts to decide that question.

Some state shield laws include a libel exemption, that is, a provision that the testimonial privilege does not apply when the journalist asserting the privilege is a defendant in a libel case and asserts a defense based on the content or source of such information.[82] The logic is clear. A libel plaintiff often needs to know the source of the reporter's allegedly libelous story in order to meet the plaintiff's burden of proof. Keeping such information from the plaintiff denies the plaintiff the opportunity to prove the source was untrustworthy or ill-informed, which often is held to be evidence of actual malice or negligence, the two most common stan-

---

[73] *See* Grant Penrod, *The State of the Shield*, NEWS MEDIA & THE L., Spring 2005, at 23.

[74] MD. CODE, CTS. & JUD. PROC., § 9-112(a)(9) (2005).

[75] O'Grady v. Superior Court, 44 Cal.Rptr.3d 72 (Cal. Ct. App. 2006).

[76] N.Y. CIV. RIGHTS LAW § 79-h (McKinney 1992 & Supp. 1997).

[77] MICH. STAT. ANN. § 28.945(1) (Callaghan 1985 & Supp. 1996).

[78] OKLA. STAT. ANN. tit. 12, § 2506, 2506(B)(2) (West 1993 & Supp. 1997).

[79] D.C. CODE ANN. §§ 16-4702 & 16-4073 (Supp. 1996).

[80] R.I. GEN. LAWS §§ 9-19.1-1 to 9-19.1-3, 9-19.1-2 (1985 & Supp. 1996).

[81] D.C. CODE ANN. §§ 16-4702 & 16-4703, 16-4702(1) (Supp. 1996).

[82] *See, e.g.,* TENN. CODE ANN. § 24-1-208, 24-1-208(b) (1980 & Supp. 1996); OR. REV. STAT. §§ 44.510-44.540, 44.530(3) (1995).

dards of fault in libel cases. To deny the plaintiff the opportunity to learn the identity of the source of a story would doom the plaintiff's case to failure. Instead, some states with shield laws refuse to let reporters use those laws to conceal the identities of sources of allegedly libelous accusations.

### A Federal Shield Law?

Several bills to create a federal shield law were introduced in Congress in 2005 and 2006 in response to the recent wave of reporter subpoenas and at the time of this writing were still in committee. This effort comes thirty years after the last serious attempt by Congress to adopt a federal shield law and more than seventy-five years after its first attempt. Federal shield legislation first was introduced in Congress in 1929, and it has been reintroduced periodically since then, but it has never passed.

A flurry of activity was prompted by what appeared to be a major news media loss in *Branzburg v. Hayes* and by the Court's suggestion that Congress could create a statutory reporter's privilege. Journalistic organizations drafted model legislation, and bills were introduced. Exhaustive hearings were held in both the House and the Senate in the early 1970s. There were many points of dispute, however. How would the law define who was a member of the press? Should the testimonial privilege only protect the identities of confidential sources? Should it apply in criminal cases in which the constitutional right to a fair trial was at stake? Should a privilege be absolute or qualified? And if Congress could offer a privilege, could it take the privilege away — or something worse? Some journalists objected to encouraging Congress to legislate their rights lest it think it also could legislate controls over the media. Those journalists preferred to persist in the struggle for judicial recognition of a First Amendment-based privilege that would not be subject to political will or whim. Division among members of the media and Congressional opposition to the various proposals ultimately caused the media to abandon efforts to obtain a federal shield law.

In 2005, as federal prosecutors became more aggressive about seeking information from journalists, two bills were introduced into the U.S. Senate and one into the House or Representatives.[83] Those bills appeared to have broad support from the journalistic community, but congressional leaders said they were too strong. The 2005 bills would have provided an absolute privilege for reporters to refuse to reveal the identities of confidential sources.

In the spring of 2006, a compromise shield law bill was introduced in Congress that appeared to have a better chance of success than the 2005 bills.[84] The compromise bill proposes a qualified privilege for confidential sources and information – not an absolute privilege – for use in both criminal and civil cases. To compel reporters to testify, requesters would have to prove they had exhausted all alternate sources of information, they had reason to believe the information was relevant, the information was critical to the case and the public interest in revealing the confidential source outweighed the public interest in newsgathering and the free flow of information. The bill includes exceptions for journalists' eyewitness observations of crimes, preventing death or substantial bodily injury, and national security interests.

Journalists working for passage of a federal shield law said journalists are sorely in need of protection in federal courts where state shield laws generally do not apply. They added that this shield law would not be perfect, but it probably is the best they can do in the current political climate.[85] Meanwhile, the Justice Department has repeatedly objected that a federal shield law would hamper law enforcement and make it more difficult to fight terrorism.[86]

### Attorney General's Guidelines

In 1973 the U.S. Department of Justice adopted a policy that limits the authority of federal law enforcement officials to subpoena reporters or their telephone records in criminal or civil cases. The policy explains its purpose this way:

> Because the freedom of the press can be no broader than the freedom of reporters to investigate and report the news, the prosecutorial power of the government should not be used in such a way that it impairs a reporter's responsibility to cover as broadly as possible controversial public issues. This policy statement is thus intended to provide protection for the news media from forms of compulsory process ... which might impair the news gathering function.[87]

From 1993 to mid-1998, federal prosecutors sought permission to issue seventy-seven subpoenas to reporters. Of those, fifty-seven were approved, four were not approved, and sixteen were withdrawn. From 1991 through the summer of 2001, the Justice Department reported, it authorized eighty-eight subpoenas of the news media, including seventeen subpoenas that sought information that could identify a source or source material.[88] Since 2001,

---

[83] The Free Flow of Information Act, S. 1419, 109th Cong. (2005) and the Free Flow of Information Act, H.R. 3323, 109th Cong. (2005) are identical to each other. The other Senate bill was the Free Speech Protection Act, S. 369, 109th Cong. (2005).

[84] The Free Flow of Information Act of 2006, S. 2831, 109th Cong. (2006).

[85] *See* Reporters Committee for Freedom of the Press, *Shield Bill Introduced in Senate, available at* http://rcfp.org/news/2006/0518-con-shield.html (last visited July 14, 2006).

[86] *See* Lorne Manly, *Bill to Shield Journalists Gets Senate Panel Hearing*, N.Y. TIMES, July 21, 2005, at A11; Casey Murray, *Under Oath: Journalists are Under Increasing Pressure to Testify in Court, Threatening Their Independence and Leading Many to Consider a Federal Shield Law*, THE NEWS MEDIA & THE L., Winter 2005, at 11.

[87] 28 C.F.R. § 50.10 (1996).

[88] Reporters Committee for Freedom of the Press, *Justice Releases Statistics*

the Justice Department has approved subpoenas seeking confidential sources from at least seven reporters.[89]

The guidelines did not apply in many of the recent cases in which reporters are subpoenaed, however. The guidelines apply only to subpoenas sought by the U.S. Department of Justice. They do not apply to cases like the Wen Ho Lee case in which a civil litigant sought information from a reporter. The guidelines also do not apply to cases like the Valerie Plame case in which a special prosecutor sought information from a reporter.

The Justice Department policy says that in each case the decision on whether to issue a subpoena for a journalist's telephone records or to obtain information from a journalist should be made by balancing the public's interest in the free flow of information against the public's interest in effective law enforcement and the fair administration of justice. The policy lays out a set of rules federal law enforcement officials must follow in making such decisions. Those rules are similar to Justice Stewart's three-part test for a reporter's testimonial privilege in *Branzburg*:

• All reasonable attempts should be made to obtain information from alternate sources before issuing subpoenas to obtain information from journalists or to obtain their telephone records.

• Negotiations with the news media are to be pursued before seeking subpoenas to obtain information from journalists or to obtain their telephone records. Where the investigation permits, the policy says, "[T]he government should make clear what its needs are in a particular case as well as its willingness to respond to the particular problems of the media."

• No subpoena shall be issued to obtain information from journalists or to obtain their telephone records without authorization of the U.S. Attorney General. The only exception is when the journalist agrees to provide the information and the information has already been published or broadcast. In that case, authorization can be granted by a U.S. attorney or an assistant attorney general.

• When the attorney general is to decide whether to authorize a subpoena to obtain information from a journalist, six principles apply:

(1) In criminal cases, there must be reasonable grounds to believe — based on nonmedia sources — that a crime has occurred and that the information sought is essential to a successful investigation and will directly establish guilt or innocence.

(2) In civil cases, there should be reasonable grounds to believe — again based on nonmedia sources — that the information sought is essential to the successful completion of the litigation in a case of substantial importance.

(3) The government should first have attempted to obtain the information from alternative, nonmedia sources.

(4) The use of subpoenas to obtain information from journalists

should, except in emergencies, be limited to the verification of published information and surrounding circumstances that relate to the accuracy of the published information.

(5) Subpoena authorization requests should be treated with care to avoid harassment of the media.

(6) Subpoenas should, whenever possible, be directed at information on a limited subject, should cover a reasonably limited time period, should avoid requiring a large volume of unpublished material and should give reasonable and timely notice of the demand for documents.

• When the attorney general is to decide whether to authorize a subpoena to obtain a journalist's telephone records, essentially the same principles apply as when the attorney general is deciding whether to issue a subpoena to obtain information directly from a journalist. The notable differences have to do with the guidelines' requirements that the government notify journalists that their telephone records are going to be or already have been subpoenaed. Obviously, when a subpoena is served directly on a journalist, the journalist knows the subpoena has been served. A subpoena for telephone records is served on a telephone company, however, and a journalist might never know the records have been obtained by the government or another party in a case. Journalists argue that not knowing deprives them of the opportunity to challenge subpoenas or to warn sources that their identities have been disclosed. In fact, they took that argument to court but lost. In 1978, the U.S. Court of Appeals for the D.C. Circuit, relying on *Branzburg*, rejected reporters' arguments that the Constitution required the government to notify them when their phone records were subpoenaed from phone companies.[90]

The guidelines require that when the government has negotiated with a journalist about telephone records, the journalist shall be given reasonable and timely notice of the attorney general's decision to authorize the subpoena. When that notice is not given, the journalist should be notified as soon as notification will no longer present "a clear and substantial threat to the integrity of the investigation."[91] In any event, the journalist must be notified within forty-five days of the records being turned over to the government unless an assistant attorney general authorizes a forty-five-day delay. Also, the guidelines say that telephone records obtained by the government should be closely held to avoid disclosure to unauthorized persons or use for improper purposes.

It is important for reporters to remember that the Justice Department guidelines are just that – guidelines. They provide no legal recourse to journalists who object to the guidelines or the way they are applied.

A number of media organizations have joined in proposing revisions to the guidelines. The proposal was submitted to the FBI for review in June 2005.

on *Subpoenas of Reporters*, available at http://www.rcfp.org/news/2001/1206grassl.html (last visited July 13, 2006).

[89] *See* Casey Murray, *Sparring Over a Shield*, NEWS MEDIA & THE L., Fall 2005, at 14.

[90] Reporters Comm. for Freedom of the Press v. AT&T, 593 F.2d 1030 (D.C. Cir. 1978).

[91] 28 C.F.R. § 50.10 (1996).

### State Law and Rules of Evidence

Every state except Wyoming recognizes a reporter's privilege based on either a shield law, the First Amendment or common law. Courts in New York, New Hampshire and Wisconsin have recognized a reporter's qualified privilege based on the free press provisions of their state constitutions.[92] In 1980, California's constitution was amended to create an explicit reporter's privilege.[93] In addition, some states have recognized a common-law reporter's privilege.[94]

Finally, Section 403 of the Federal Rules of Evidence allows judges to quash subpoenas if the information sought would duplicate information already available, and New Mexico has a court rule that grants reporters a qualified privilege.[95]

### PRACTICAL ADVICE AND ETHICAL CONSIDERATIONS

What should you do if you are served a subpoena? Never ignore it, but never comply without first consulting your supervisor, who, in turn, should consult the news organization's legal counsel. Never destroy the requested notes or other work materials being subpoenaed; to do so could lead to a finding of contempt of court or obstruction of justice. Also, do not talk to the attorney who is responsible for the subpoena. If you do, you might accidentally waive your reporter's privilege.

Generally your choices will be to move to quash the subpoena, to appear and assert the privilege on a question-by-question basis as necessary or to appear and testify fully. Testifying might be appropriate when no confidential sources are involved or when a reporter is being asked only to confirm that the reporter wrote a particular article and that the information in it is accurate.

Some newsroom managers report that their aggressive opposition to all subpoenas served on their reporters eventually results in fewer subpoenas being issued, so fighting the subpoena should always be considered. Furthermore, media attorneys sometimes are successful in convincing the party behind the subpoena to withdraw it by explaining the relevant law and the news organization's intention to oppose the subpoena.

Even before you are confronted with this problem, however, you should be familiar with your news organization's policy regarding the retention of notes, tapes and other work materials. Some news organizations require the destruction of notes and related materials as soon as a story is published. Others wait specified periods of time before destroying these materials. Some routinely destroy photographs of traffic accidents to avoid having them subpoenaed in civil litigation.[96] One scholar has suggested that any reporter who writes a "controversial or unflattering" story should save the interview notes at least until the required statute of limitations for a libel suit has elapsed and that reporters whose employers resist adopting a document retention policy should develop their own routine for saving and destroying notes.[97] More recently some media leaders have recommended that reporters never store the identities of anonymous source electronically because those records might be subpoenaed from non-newsroom employees who do not understand the implications of complying with such subpoenas.[98]

You should also be aware of your media organization's policy governing the use of confidential sources. Some news organizations require management approval before a reporter can promise a source confidentiality. Some policies require reporters to reveal the source's identity to an editor. Others require reporters to tell sources that if a subpoena is served the source will have to come forward. If your organization does not have a policy, you should encourage your editors to consider one.

The code of ethics adopted by the Society of Professional Journalists in 1996 offers additional advice:

• Identify sources whenever feasible. The public is entitled to as much information as possible on sources' reliability.

• Always question sources' motives before promising anonymity.

• Clarify conditions attached to any promise made in exchange for information.

• Keep promises.[99]

If you fail in your attempt to have a subpoena quashed by a judge, you might be caught between the ethical mandate to keep your promise to a confidential source and a judge's determination to put you in jail if you do. Nobody can make that choice for you. At this point, however, you might want to ask your source to release you from your promise of confidentiality.

### NEWSROOM SEARCHES

Reporters also claim a privilege when law enforcement officials armed with search warrants arrive unannounced to search newsrooms for evidence. There are striking parallels between the law on newsroom search warrants and the law on subpoenas, including the Supreme Court's reasoning in denying a First Amendment privilege, the creation of statutory protection for reporters and the

---

[92] *See* New Hampshire v. Siel, 444 A.2d 499 (N.H. 1982); O'Neill v. Oakgrove Constr., Inc., 523 N.E.2d 277 (N.Y. 1988); Zelenka v. Wisconsin, 266 N.W. 2d 279 (Wis. 1978); State v. Knops, 183 N.W.2d 93 (Wis. 1971).

[93] CAL. CONST. art. I, § 2.

[94] *See, e.g.,* Senear v. Daily Journal-Am., 641 P.2d 1180 (Wash. 1982).

[95] N.M. SUP. CT. R. OF EVIDENCE 11-514.

[96] *See* Reporters Committee, *Agents of Discovery, supra* note 25.

[97] *See* Andi Stein, Taking Note of the Law: A Study of the Legal and Ethical Issues in Cases Involving Reporters' Interview Notes (1996) (paper presented to the Association for Education in Journalism and Mass Communication).

[98] *See* Grant Penrod, *Diverging Interests: The Saga of Matt Cooper and Judith Miller Raises Serious Questions About Notes, E-mail and Anonymous Sources,* NEWS MEDIA & THE L., Summer 2005, at 6-7.

[99] *Code of Ethics,* QUILL, Oct. 1996, at 1.

arguments for and against such privileges.

Over the years, journalists have had fewer problems with search warrants than with subpoenas, but search warrants are especially troublesome because they cannot be challenged in court before they are executed. As explained earlier in this chapter, a subpoena commands a reporter to appear at a certain time and place to give testimony and/or to produce certain materials. Thus, the reporter has time to go to court to challenge the subpoena before appearing. Search warrants provide no such option. A search warrant authorizes a law enforcement officer to search for and seize any property that constitutes evidence of a crime. The officer merely shows the warrant at the newsroom door and enters.

### Zurcher v. Stanford Daily

Just six years after the Supreme Court decided in *Branzburg v. Hayes* that the First Amendment does not protect reporters from giving testimony, the Court decided in *Zurcher v. Stanford Daily* that the First Amendment does not protect reporters from newsroom searches.[100] Justice White wrote the opinions for the Court in both cases and, in both, said there was no conclusive evidence that the outcomes of the cases would cause sources to dry up. Justice White suggested — again, in both cases — that Congress and state legislatures could create protection for the media where none exists under the First Amendment. Furthermore, both cases illustrate that the First Amendment protection is the same for all citizens and does not provide special protection for members of the media.

The *Zurcher* case began when nine police officers were injured during a clash between police and student demonstrators at the Stanford University Hospital in California. Two days later, the university's student newspaper, the *Stanford Daily*, published photographs and articles about the violent clash. Investigators obtained a search warrant from the local municipal court to search the *Stanford Daily*'s newsroom for information that would help to identify individuals who had assaulted the police. No newspaper employee was alleged to have committed any crime. Police searched the photo laboratories, filing cabinets, desks and wastepaper baskets. Locked drawers and cabinets were not opened, but police had the opportunity to read reporters' notes and correspondence.

The newspaper sued Zurcher, the local chief of police, claiming that the newsroom search violated its Fourth Amendment protection against unreasonable searches and seizures and its First Amendment free press rights. Reporters said they feared law enforcement officers searching newsrooms would uncover the identities of confidential sources or other sensitive information, causing sources to dry up and interrupting the free flow of information that is essential to a healthy democracy. The paper won in federal district court and the federal court of appeals, but the Supreme

Court reversed on a 5-3 vote.

First, the Court said, the lower courts erred when they ruled that the Fourth Amendment prohibited the issuance of search warrants to search the premises of any innocent third parties — parties not suspected of committing crimes. The Court said there was no precedent for such a "sweeping revision" of the Fourth Amendment, noting that search warrants are directed not at individuals but at places. Therefore, it makes no difference whether the person who owns or controls the premises to be searched is suspected of a crime.

The Supreme Court also rejected lower courts' holdings that the First Amendment allows newsroom searches only in the rare circumstances when there is a clear showing that important materials will be destroyed or removed and a restraining order would be futile. Subpoenas, the lower courts had said, were the preferred method of obtaining information from news organizations. The Supreme Court, however, said the First Amendment did not create a constitutional barrier against warranted searches of newsrooms. White wrote that the general rules protecting all citizens from improper searches are sufficient protection for the news media as well. "Properly administered," he wrote, "the preconditions for a warrant — probable cause, specificity with respect to the place to be searched and the things to be seized, and overall reasonableness — should afford sufficient protection against the harms that are assertedly threatened by warrants for searching newspaper offices." He noted, however, that the rules must be applied "with particular exactitude when First Amendment interests would be endangered by the search."[101] He wrote that magistrates can guard against searches that might interfere with a newspaper's publication schedule or that might allow police to "rummage at large" through newspaper files.[102]

### Privacy Protection Act of 1980

Congress responded to *Zurcher* by adopting the Privacy Protection Act of 1980, which severely limits the government's power to obtain search warrants for newsrooms. The federal statute, which applies to law enforcement agencies at all levels of government, does not mention newsrooms. Rather, the statute makes it illegal for police or other government officials investigating a crime to search for or seize work products or other documentary materials possessed by "a person reasonably believed to have a purpose to disseminate to the public a newspaper, book, broadcast, or other similar form of public communication" when the person is not suspected of a crime.[103]

Four exceptions are spelled out in the law, and they distinguish between work materials and documentary materials. Work materials are defined as materials that are created in anticipation of com-

---

100 436 U.S. 547 (1978).

101 *Id.* at 565.
102 *Id.* at 566.
103 42 U.S.C.A. § 2000aa(a) (1996).

munication to the public and include impressions, conclusions, opinions or theories of the journalist. Documentary materials are obtained in the course of investigating a story but do not contain a reporter's ideas. They include written or printed materials, photographs, motion picture films, negatives, videotapes, audio tapes and computerized records. Neither category includes material evidence — items used in the commission of a crime or possessed illegally.

The four exceptions to the prohibition against such searches are:

(1) Police may use search warrants when a person possessing work products or documentary materials is suspected of a crime related to those materials — that is, when the journalist is not an innocent third party — and when the alleged crime is not related specifically to the handling of the material in question. When the alleged crime is the receipt, possession, communication or withholding of materials, police may use search warrants only if the materials relate to national defense, classified information or restricted data.

(2) Police can use search warrants to obtain work product or documentary materials when there is reason to believe that the immediate seizure of such materials is necessary to prevent death or serious injury.

(3) Police can use search warrants to obtain documentary materials when there is reason to believe the advance notice inherent in the serving of a subpoena would result in the destruction, alteration or concealment of the materials.

(4) Police can use search warrants when documentary materials have not been produced in response to a subpoena and either all appellate remedies have been exhausted or there is reason to believe that the delay caused by further court proceedings relating to the subpoena would threaten the interests of justice. If the latter exception applies, the journalist must be given an opportunity to submit an affidavit opposing the search.

A journalist who believes he or she was the subject of a search in violation of the act can sue the government for damages. But the law stipulates that a law enforcement or other government official who can demonstrate a "reasonable good faith belief in the lawfulness of his conduct" is not liable for damages.

## WHICH LAW APPLIES?

The mix of legal protections described throughout this chapter raises the question of which protections apply in which courts. While the answer is not always clear, generally the extent to which a reporter can successfully claim a testimonial privilege hinges on whether the case in which the reporter is being asked to testify is being tried in federal or state court.

### In Federal Court

In cases involving questions of federal law, reporters can rely on the First Amendment-based privilege if it is recognized in the jurisdiction where the case is being heard. As previously noted, this means a journalist can anticipate a strong privilege in some instances and little or no protection in others. In some cases, a journalist will not know what to expect because the federal court has not decided a reporter's privilege case. Also, some federal courts have turned to state shield laws as guides to help them determine the appropriate scope of the reporter's privilege, but the state law is not binding on the courts.

Federal Rule of Evidence 501 provides that in civil cases in federal court in which the central issue is one of state law, the state law applies. The clearest example of when this rule applies is in a diversity action, in which the case turns on a question of state law but is brought in federal court because the parties reside in different states. In such a situation, the federal court applies the law of the state in which the federal court is situated.

### In State Court

In state cases, courts first look to a state shield law for guidance. If there is none, courts then look to the state common law, then to the state's constitution. Finally, state courts consider whether there is a First Amendment privilege.

## THE RIGHT TO REVEAL SOURCES

After decades of struggling for the right to honor their promises not to reveal the identities of confidential sources, in the 1980s and 1990s reporters found themselves in court arguing for the right to do just that — to publish the name of a confidential source because they deemed the name newsworthy. In a case that provoked significant disagreement among journalists over the ethics of breaking a promise of confidentiality, the *Minneapolis Star and Tribune* and the *St. Paul Pioneer Press Dispatch* argued unsuccessfully that the First Amendment afforded them the right to publish the name of a confidential source after promising confidentiality.

The case began in 1982 when Republican Party worker Dan Cohen offered four reporters, including one from the *Pioneer Press Dispatch* and one from the *Minneapolis Star and Tribune*, documents relating to a candidate for state lieutenant governor. Cohen sought and received promises that he would not be identified as the source of the documents, which showed that the candidate had been charged with three counts of unlawful assembly in 1969 and convicted of petit theft in 1970. Further investigation by the media revealed that the unlawful assembly charges, which were dismissed, stemmed from the candidate's participation in a protest against the city's failure to hire minority workers for its construction projects. The petit theft conviction, which was later vacated, was for stealing $6 worth of sewing materials from a store. That incident apparently occurred during a time when the candidate was emotionally distraught.

When the reporters returned to their newsrooms, their editors demanded to know the identity of the confidential source. The editors decided the source's identity was as newsworthy as the political candidate's brushes with the law and published stories identifying Cohen as the source of the information. "The fact that one party was using this tactic to malign the other was as important, if not more important, as the story itself," said the associate editor of the *Star and Tribune*.[104] He also said the newspaper had a clear policy that the decision to conceal the identity of a source was the editor's, not the reporter's.

The advertising agency for which Cohen worked fired him, and Cohen filed suit against both newspapers alleging breach of contract and fraudulent misrepresentation. A jury awarded Cohen $200,000 in compensatory damages and $500,000 in punitive damages. The Minnesota Court of Appeals affirmed the breach of contract finding, but reversed the punitive damage award after concluding that Cohen had failed to establish fraudulent misrepresentation, the only claim that could justify punitive damages.[105] The appeals court found that the reporters had not engaged in fraud because they had entered into their agreement with Cohen with every intention of keeping their promises of confidentiality, had no reason to anticipate their editors would do otherwise and strenuously objected to their editors' decision to publish Cohen's name.

The Minnesota Supreme Court reversed the compensatory damages award, holding that the reporters' promise to keep the source's identity confidential was not a legally enforceable contract. The court explained it was not persuaded that "in the special milieu of media newsgathering a source and a reporter ordinarily believe they are engaged in making a legally binding contract,"[106] but rather are making a moral commitment. The state supreme court also said the First Amendment interest of the newspapers in covering a story involving political sources in a political campaign — "the quintessential public debate in our democratic society" — outweighed the state's common law interest in protecting a promise of confidentiality.[107]

The Supreme Court reversed on a 5-4 vote, rejecting the newspapers' argument that deciding the case in favor of Cohen would violate their First Amendment right to publish lawfully obtained, truthful information, absent a need to further a state interest of the highest order. The Court ruled that generally applicable laws, such as those that require an individual to keep a promise, "do not offend the First Amendment simply because their enforcement against the press has incidental effects on its ability to gather and report the news."[108] In this case, the law of general applicability was Minnesota's doctrine of *promissory estoppel. Promissory*

estoppel is a legal doctrine similar to contract law that holds that when a clear promise is intended to and does induce a specific action, that promise is binding if injustice can be avoided only by enforcing it. The Court said the doctrine required those making promises to keep them. This was the first time the doctrine of *promissory estoppel* had been applied in a case involving the media.

The Court explained that the news media are subject to many generally applicable laws and that the Court has repeatedly refused to interpret the First Amendment as exempting the media from those laws. The Court compared the application of the doctrine of *promissory estoppel* to the media to the application of copyright law, antitrust law, nondiscriminatory taxes and the obligation to testify before a grand jury.

The case was remanded to the Minnesota Supreme Court for a decision under the theory of *promissory estoppel*. The court reinstated the $200,000 verdict in favor of Cohen.[109]

The principle established in *Cohen v. Cowles Media Co.* — that a journalist who breaks a promise to keep the identity of a source confidential is liable for damages that result from breaking the promise — has been applied in several subsequent cases. For example, in another Minnesota case a reporter for *Glamour* magazine was sued by a source who claimed she was identified in a story about therapist-patient sexual abuse after being promised her identity would be concealed.[110] The reporter did not use the source's name in the story but identified her as a Minneapolis attorney who served on a state task force that helped write a state law criminalizing therapist-patient sex. The source said she was identified because she was the only female attorney on the task force. In the story, the source told about incest committed by her father when she was a child and her sexual exploitation by her therapist. The case went up and down through the courts, with the U.S. Court of Appeals for the Eighth Circuit finally deciding the reporter's promise not to identify the source was an enforceable contract under the theory of *promissory estoppel.* ·

In other cases the courts have rejected such suits.[111]

## SUMMARY

Today more than ever, a reporter who receives a subpoena or whose newsroom is searched by law enforcement personnel needs to be familiar with the patchwork of reporter's privilege law and alert to the way it is now being interpreted by federal courts. Reporter's privilege law is based on the U.S. and state constitutions, federal and state statutes, common law, judicial rules and law enforcement guidelines. The legal protection afforded to re-

---

[104] Tony Mauro, *The Name of the Source: Editors Want to Know*, Wash. Journalism Rev., Sept. 1987, at 37.

[105] Cohen v. Cowles Media Co., 445 N.W.2d 248 (Minn. App. 1989).

[106] Cohen v. Cowles Media Co., 457 N.W.2d 199, 203 (Minn. 1990).

[107] *Id.* at 205.

[108] Cohen v. Cowles Media, 501 U.S. 663, 669 (1991).

[109] Cohen v. Cowles Media Co., 479 N.W.2d 387 (Minn. 1992).

[110] Ruzicka v. Conde Nast Publications, Inc., 939 F.2d 578 (8th Cir. 1991), *on remand*, 794 F. Supp. 303 (D. Minn. 1992), *vacated*, 999 F.2d 1319 (8th Cir. 1993).

[111] *See, e.g.*, Morgan v. Celender, 780 F. Supp. 307 (W.D. Pa. 1992).

porters who do not want to testify in judicial proceedings or to turn over work materials varies from jurisdiction to jurisdiction. Within a single jurisdiction, the privilege varies even further according to who is claiming the privilege, the type of proceeding in which a journalist is being asked to testify and the nature of the potential testimony.

One common theme of reporter's privilege law has been the qualified privilege suggested by Supreme Court Justice Potter Stewart in his landmark dissent in *Branzburg v. Hayes*. Stewart suggested that in order to defeat a reporter's motion to quash a subpoena, the government must prove each of the following:

• there is probable cause to believe the reporter has information that is clearly relevant to a probable crime;

• the information cannot be obtained by alternative means less destructive of First Amendment rights;

• there is a "compelling and overriding interest" in the information.

These three elements are at the core of the First Amendment-based reporter's privilege and many state shield laws.

Furthermore, the government's power to obtain search warrants for newsrooms is severely limited by the Privacy Protection Act of 1980. However, in recent cases some journalists have been found liable for breach of contract when they either intentionally or unintentionally revealed the identity of a source to whom they had promised confidentiality.

The extent of reporter's privilege is increasingly a subject of legal conflict and controversy, in part because of the important interests at stake. Journalists generally claim that they need to be allowed to refuse to testify in judicial proceedings in order to protect the free flow of information from their sources to the public. That free flow of information, they argue, is essential to a healthy democracy. Judicial and law enforcement personnel and the parties in civil and criminal court cases frequently counter that a reporter's information is crucial to the administration of justice and that a reporter is not exempt from every citizen's duty to testify in a judicial proceeding. These arguments are strongest in criminal cases where the defendant has a Sixth Amendment right to compel testimony that might prove he or she is not guilty. Considering the weighty arguments on each side of this debate, a single and simple solution seems highly improbable.

## FOR ADDITIONAL READING

Alexander, Laurence B. & Ellen M. Bush. "Shield Laws on Trial: State Court Interpretation of the Journalist's Statutory Privilege," 23 *Journal of Legislation* 215 (1997).

Baron, Jerome A. "Cohen v. Cowles Media and its Significance for First Amendment Law and Journalism," 3 *William & Mary Bill of Rights Journal* 419 (1994).

Boyd, J. Kirk. "Legislative Response to Zurcher v. Stanford Daily," 9 *Pepperdine Law Review* 131 (1981).

Ervin, Jr., Sam J. "In Pursuit of a Press Privilege," 11 *Harvard Journal on Legislation* 233 (1974).

Fargo, Anthony L. "Analyzing Federal Shield Law Proposals: What Congress Can Learn From the States," 11 *Communication Law and Policy* 35 (2006).

Fargo, Anthony L. "The Journalist's Privilege for Nonconfidential Information in States With Shield Laws," 4 *Communication Law and Policy* 325 (1999).

Fargo, Anthony L. "The Journalist's Privilege for Nonconfidential Information in States Without Shield Laws," 7 *Communication Law and Policy* 241 (2002).

Goodale, James C., et al. "Reporter's Privilege," *Communications Law*, vol. 3. New York: Practising Law Institute, 2005.

Reporters Committee for Freedom of the Press. "The Reporter's Privilege," http://www.rcfp.org/privilege/index.html.

Stone, Geoffrey R. "Why We Need a Federal Reporter's Privilege," 34 *Hofstra Law Review* 39 (2005).

Woodward, Bob. *The Secret Man: The History of Watergate's Deep Throat*, New York: Simon & Schuster, 2005.

# 16

## Access to Courts

*By Ruth Walden*

---

 **Headnote Questions**

- *How might media coverage of the criminal justice system interfere with a defendant's right to a fair trial?*
- *What remedies are available to judges to compensate for prejudicial publicity?*
- *Under what circumstances may a judge impose a gag order on the media?*
- *What might be the consequences of disobeying a judicial gag order?*
- *Under what circumstances may a judge impose a gag order on attorneys' or other trial participants' extrajudicial statements?*
- *What test is used to determine if a journalist can be held in contempt of court for commentary on or coverage of the judicial process?*
- *What test do courts apply to determine if the media may be punished for publishing information?*
- *When may a court proceeding be closed to the press and public?*
- *Do the press and public have a right of access to judicial records?*
- *What types of judicial records are considered confidential?*
- *Does the U.S. Constitution prohibit cameras in courtrooms? Does it require courts to admit cameras?*

---

From the 1935 trial of Bruno Hauptmann for the kidnapping of the Lindbergh baby to the 1995 murder trial of O.J. Simpson and the 2006 fraud trial of Enron executives Kenneth Lay and Jeffrey Skilling, sensational court cases have attracted massive media attention, resulting in concerns about the effects of press coverage on trial fairness and allegations of "trial by media." The free press-fair trial issue is generally viewed as a conflict between rights guaranteed by two amendments to the U.S. Constitution — the First Amendment right of freedom of the press and the Sixth Amendment right of a criminal defendant to a fair trial by an impartial jury. Some argue that allowing unrestrained media coverage of crimes, arrests, pretrial proceedings and trials seriously threatens defendants' Sixth Amendment rights and that restrictions must be placed on the media to ensure the proper operation of the criminal justice system. Others contend that the First Amendment cannot be subordinated to the Sixth Amendment, that a free press plays a critical role in ensuring the proper functioning of the judicial system and that it is the government's duty to find ways to accommodate both sets of rights.

As the cases discussed in this chapter will demonstrate, the U.S. Supreme Court has adopted a balancing approach in dealing with free press-fair trial conflicts, steadfastly refusing to declare one set of rights more important than the other. Instead, it has consistently instructed trial judges to take steps to vigorously protect the rights of defendants without limiting the rights of journalists to attend court proceedings and report on crime and the operation of the court system. In general, the Supreme Court has held that restrictions on the media may be imposed only as the last resort if all else fails to ensure the defendant's right to a fair trial.

### THE NATURE OF THE PROBLEM

Generally the conflict between freedom of the press and the right to a fair trial is manifested in three ways:

(1) *Pretrial publicity* may make it difficult to find impartial jurors who have not made up their minds as to the defendant's guilt

— or, in unusual cases, innocence — before the trial begins.

(2) *During-trial publicity* may taint a sitting jury, causing jurors to base a verdict on what they read, see or hear in the media, rather than solely on the evidence presented at trial.

(3) *The presence of journalists* and their equipment in the courtroom may cause physical and/or psychological disruption.

Let's consider each of those three potential problems by looking, primarily, at cases decided by the Supreme Court.

### Pretrial Publicity

Jurors are supposed to arrive at a verdict based solely on the evidence presented to them in the courtroom. The rules of evidence under which courts operate prevent certain types of information from being presented to the jury. Anyone who has watched a courtroom drama on TV — real or fictional — knows that such things as hearsay or the opinions of non-experts are usually ruled inadmissible. But, of course, the media don't follow court rules of evidence in deciding what to publish. Thus, considerable information that will never reach the jury in the courtroom could reach potential jurors as they watch TV or read newspapers.

The Supreme Court has made it clear that jurors need not be "totally ignorant of the facts and issues involved" in a case to be considered impartial. Exposure to "information about a ... defendant's prior convictions or to news accounts of the crime with which he is charged" is not, standing alone, enough to disqualify a potential juror.[1] The most frequently quoted definition of an impartial juror comes from Chief Justice John Marshall's opinion in *United States v. Burr*, the trial of Aaron Burr for treason in 1807:

> Were it possible to obtain a jury without any prepossessions whatever respecting the guilt or innocence of the accused, it would be extremely desirable to obtain such a jury; but this is perhaps impossible, and therefore will not be required. The opinion which has been avowed by the court is, that light impressions which may fairly be supposed to yield to the testimony that may be offered, which may leave the mind open to a fair consideration of that testimony, constitute no sufficient objection to a juror; but that those strong and deep impressions which will close the mind against the testimony that may be offered in opposition to them, which will combat that testimony, and resist its force, do constitute a sufficient objection to him.[2]

The trick, of course, is to determine what types of publicity can result in jurors possessing "strong and deep impressions" that may render them biased. Numerous court decisions, especially those in which criminal convictions have been overturned on appeal, have discussed the types of news stories that can cause

prejudice. In addition, the American Bar Association and voluntary bench-press-bar committees in several states have developed guidelines to help identify potentially prejudicial material. Most of these guidelines recognize that reporting the following types of information can create a danger of prejudice:

**Prior Criminal Records.** This is perhaps the most problematic category of potentially prejudicial information for journalists. In most cases, prior criminal charges and convictions are part of the public record, and journalists may believe it is important for the public to be informed that, say, a person accused of rape and murder had been previously charged with three sexual assaults and convicted once twelve years prior to the current charge. But normally a criminal record is not admitted as evidence at trial since the jury is supposed to base its verdict on evidence relating to the *current* charge only. Officially keeping information about a defendant's past record from jurors may be fruitless if the jurors have unofficially been informed of the defendant's past through the media. It's important to recall, however, that the Supreme Court has said knowledge of a defendant's prior criminal record *alone* is not enough to disqualify a potential juror.

**Confessions or Other Admissions by a Defendant.** Even today, with the requirement that police "Mirandize" anyone arrested ("You have the right to remain silent...."), criminal defendants sometimes make statements to the police that they — and their lawyers — later regret. If a judge can be convinced that a confession or other damaging statement was coerced or obtained before the defendant was informed of his or her rights to remain silent and have an attorney, the statement may be declared inadmissible at trial because of the Fifth Amendment's protection against forced self-incrimination. As with criminal records, jurors who have heard or seen media reports of a confession, or even references to the existence of a confession, may have a hard time forgetting those reports when they deliberate.

**The Results of Investigative Procedures or Tests.** Reporting the results of fingerprint, DNA, polygraph, blood and ballistics tests or the refusal of the accused to submit to such tests can cause problems. The admissibility of test results can often be the basis for a key battle in a criminal case, and such information is often kept from a jury. Reporting that the accused refused to submit to a lie detector test could well leave the impression that the defendant had something to hide.

**Opinions Regarding the Character, Personality, Guilt or Innocence of the Accused.** As some of the cases discussed later in this chapter will show, it is not unheard of for the media to attach derogatory nicknames to suspects, to report alleged character flaws or unusual lifestyles, or to conduct on-the-street interviews about a defendant's guilt or innocence. Furthermore, some-

---

[1] *Murphy v. Florida*, 421 U.S. 794, 799-800 (1975).
[2] 25 F. Cas. 49, 50-51 (D. Va. 1807) (No. 14,692g).

times officials themselves — police, prosecutors and even judges — make derogatory statements about defendants, which are then reported in the media. Such publicity not only may cause prejudice within a community but also may result in jurors feeling pressured to bring in the verdict the public wants.

**Speculation on Evidence or Witnesses.** Speculation about potential evidence and opinions as to the credibility or character of prospective witnesses are conjecture, often based on incomplete knowledge, guesswork or even malice. Prospective witnesses who tell journalists what they intend to say in court may change their minds or be prevented from making certain statements in front of the jury. Police officers and lawyers may often be the source of leaks about potential evidence or witnesses, thereby adding a ring of authority to the speculation or opinion.

In addition to those five categories of information, any sensational or inflammatory coverage of a crime and its aftermath is potentially prejudicial. Editorials demanding the arrest of a suspect or suggesting a suspect is getting special treatment because of wealth or position, lurid headlines or gory pictures of victims, and emotional outpourings by victims' friends and families all can stir up emotions in a community that may be inconsistent with the impartiality the Sixth Amendment demands. A look at some cases in which the Supreme Court considered claims that pretrial publicity robbed defendants of their rights to impartial juries provides specific examples of prejudicial coverage as well as an understanding of the types of publicity that may constitute grounds to overturn a conviction.

*Irvin v. Dowd*,[3] decided in 1961, marked the first time the Supreme Court overturned a state criminal conviction solely because prejudicial publicity interfered with a defendant's right to a fair trial. "Mad Dog" Irvin, as the media dubbed him, was charged with the murder of Whitney Wesley Kerr, who was one of six victims in a series of well publicized murders that occurred in the vicinity of Evansville, Indiana, beginning December 2, 1954. Although Irvin was being tried for only one murder, the police, the prosecutor and media made it clear they believed he was responsible for all six. The Supreme Court described the publicity surrounding the Irvin trial as "a barrage of newspaper headlines, articles, cartoons and pictures." News stories revealed Irvin's juvenile record, his prior convictions for arson and burglary, and his court-martial on AWOL charges during World War II. The media also reported that he had confessed to the six murders and offered to plead guilty if promised a ninety-nine-year sentence. One story characterized Irvin as "remorseless and without conscience."[4]

According to the Court, the effects of this publicity barrage were evident during *voir dire*, the questioning of potential jurors. The court excused 268 of 430 prospective jurors "as having fixed opin-

ions as to the guilt" of Irvin. Almost 90 percent of the potential jurors questioned "entertained some opinion as to guilt — ranging in intensity from mere suspicion to absolute certainty." Of the twelve jurors finally chosen, eight had admitted they thought Irvin was guilty. All twelve, however, told the judge they would be fair and impartial. In reversing Irvin's conviction and death sentence, the Supreme Court said, "With his life at stake, it is not requiring too much that [Irvin] be tried in an atmosphere undisturbed by so huge a wave of public passion and by a jury other than one in which two-thirds of the members admit, before hearing any testimony, to possessing a belief in his guilt."[5] Irvin was retried and again found guilty of murder. He was sentenced to life imprisonment.

Two years after *Irvin,* the Supreme Court again reversed a conviction, this time based on the pretrial broadcast of the defendant's confession. Wilbert Rideau was arrested and charged with bank robbery, kidnapping and murder. Without being informed of his right to remain silent and to have an attorney, Rideau confessed to the crimes — both off and on camera. A twenty-minute film of an interview with Rideau, during which he was "flanked by the sheriff and two state troopers," was broadcast for three consecutive days to estimated audiences of 24,000, 29,000 and 53,000 in Calcasieu Parish, Louisiana, with a population of about 150,000. Rideau's motion for a change of venue was denied, and the trial was held with a jury that included three persons who admitted to having seen the televised confession. Rideau was convicted and sentenced to death.

The Supreme Court ruled that the judge's refusal to move the trial to a community in which Rideau's confession had not been televised violated the defendant's due process rights:

> For anyone who has ever watched television the conclusion cannot be avoided that this spectacle [the televised interview], to the tens of thousands of people who saw and heard it, in a very real sense *was* Rideau's trial — at which he pleaded guilty to murder. Any subsequent court proceedings in a community so pervasively exposed to such a spectacle could be but a hollow formality.[6]

On retrial Rideau was once again convicted, and the Louisiana Supreme Court upheld that second conviction.

Among lawyers, judges and journalists, *Sheppard v. Maxwell*[7] has become synonymous with prejudicial publicity. The U.S. Supreme Court's reversal of Sheppard's conviction in 1966 was based on all three free press-fair trial problems listed earlier in this chapter — prejudicial pretrial publicity, during-trial publicity reaching an unsequestered jury and the activities of journalists in the

---

[3] 366 U.S. 717 (1961).
[4] *Id.* at 725-26.

[5] *Id.* at 727-28.
[6] Rideau v. Louisiana, 373 U.S. 723, 726 (1963).
[7] 384 U.S. 333 (1966).

courtroom. Here the focus will be on the nature and extent of the pretrial coverage.

In the early morning hours of July 4, 1954, Marilyn Sheppard was beaten to death as she lay in bed in her home in Bay Village, a suburb of Cleveland, Ohio. Her husband, Samuel, a surgeon and member of a wealthy, prominent, local family that ran an osteopathic hospital, said he had fallen asleep on the couch downstairs and was awakened by his wife's cries. According to his testimony at trial, Dr. Sheppard ran upstairs to the bedroom, where he saw a "form" by his wife's bed. He was struck on the back of the neck and knocked unconscious. When he came to, Sheppard said he checked his wife's pulse and "felt that she was gone." He next checked his son, who was asleep in another upstairs bedroom, and found him undisturbed. Sheppard said he then went downstairs, saw a "form" running out the door and pursued it to the lake behind his home. He struggled with the person he had chased and was again rendered unconscious. When he awoke, he returned to the house, again checked his wife and determined she was dead. Shortly before 6 a.m. he called a neighbor, who called the police and Sheppard's brother.

The pretrial publicity that followed was relentless and, according to the Supreme Court, virulent. Within days of the murder, the Cleveland newspapers began emphasizing Sheppard's alleged lack of cooperation with the police — which the Supreme Court later indicated was untrue — and refusal to take a lie detector test and be injected with "truth serum." Front-page editorials charged "Somebody's Getting Away with Murder" and demanded an inquest. The inquest, which was promptly called for the day after the editorial appeared, was held in a school gymnasium and broadcast live. During and after the inquest, news stories emphasized incriminating evidence, much of which was never presented at the trial. The media also focused on Sheppard's personal life, especially his admitted affair with one woman and alleged — but never admitted or proven — affairs with others. A few days after the inquest, a front-page editorial asked, "Why Isn't Sam Sheppard in Jail?" and demanded, "Quit Stalling — Bring Him In." At about 10 p.m. the day it appeared, Sam Sheppard was arrested for his wife's murder.

Alfred Friendly and John Goldfarb in their book, *Crime and Publicity*, reported that between July 5, when the murder was first reported in the media, and July 30, the day Sheppard was arrested, the *Cleveland Plain Dealer* ran a page-one story about the case twenty-five of the twenty-six days, with twelve of those stories under banner headlines. The *Cleveland Press* ran a page-one story each of the twenty-three days it published during the same period and printed three page-one editorials.[8]

According to the Supreme Court, after Sheppard's arrest, "The publicity ... grew in intensity until his indictment August 17." In its opinion overturning Sheppard's conviction — eleven and one-half years after the jury verdict — the Court listed numerous examples

of prejudicial and sensational coverage, concluding, "There are five volumes filled with similar clippings from each of the three Cleveland newspapers covering the period from the murder until Sheppard's conviction in December 1954." Before jury selection began, all three Cleveland papers published the names and addresses of the prospective jurors. "As a consequence, anonymous letters and telephone calls, as well as calls from friends, regarding the impending prosecution were received by all of the prospective jurors." The trial judge, Edward Blythin, who was running for reelection, refused to grant Sheppard's motion to move the location or delay the start of the trial, despite the fact that all but one of the twelve jurors selected admitted reading about the case in the newspapers.[9]

Despite the evidence of massive, prejudicial pretrial news coverage, the Supreme Court said that the pretrial publicity alone was not sufficient to prove Sheppard had been denied due process. Instead, the Court said its decision was based on the "totality of the circumstances," which included juror exposure to publicity during the trial and disruptions the media caused.[10]

### During-Trial Publicity

The same types of stories that could prejudice potential jurors if published before a trial could also taint a sitting jury. Reading in the newspaper that the person whose guilt or innocence they are supposed to decide has already confessed to the crime or has a record of arrests and convictions for similar crimes could affect jurors' decisions, even if such information is never presented in court. In fact, the Supreme Court has concluded that the effect of highly prejudicial information "may indeed be greater" when it reaches jurors through the media rather than through testimony in court "for it is then not tempered by protective procedures."[11]

Despite its potential for harm, during-trial publicity is usually not considered as serious a problem as pretrial publicity for a number of reasons. First, once a trial begins the media have the trial itself to cover and are less likely to resort to speculation and prediction. Second, in sensational, widely publicized cases, jurors are often sequestered and thereby protected from media stories about the case. Finally, even if jurors are not sequestered, judges routinely instruct them not to read, listen to or watch anything about the trial, and studies have found that jurors tend to take such admonitions seriously.[12]

Nonetheless, juror exposure to publicity during trial can and

---

[8] ALFRED FRIENDLY & RONALD L. GOLDFARB, CRIME AND PUBLICITY 14 (1967).

[9] 384 U.S. at 342, 354 n.9.

[10] *Id.* at 352.

[11] Marshall v. United States, 360 U.S. 310, 313 (1959).

[12] *See, e.g.,* Fred S. Siebert, *Trial Judges' Opinions on Prejudicial Publicity, in* FREE PRESS AND FAIR TRIAL 1, 12 (Chilton R. Bush ed., 1970); Rita J. Simon, *Does the Court's Decision in* Nebraska Press Association *Fit the Research Evidence on the Impact on Jurors of News Coverage?*, 29 STAN. L. REV. 515, 528 (1977).

has resulted in the reversal of convictions. It happened in 1959 in *Marshall v. United States*, the first case in which the Supreme Court reversed a federal criminal conviction solely on the basis of prejudicial publicity. (*Irvin v. Dowd* was the Court's first reversal of a *state* conviction due to prejudicial publicity.)

Howard R. Marshall was charged with illegally dispensing drugs to an undercover Food and Drug Administration inspector. During Marshall's trial in federal court, two potentially damaging newspaper articles appeared. One reported Marshall had two prior felony convictions, had written prescriptions for dangerous drugs, and, while serving a forgery sentence in Oklahoma, had told a legislative committee he practiced medicine with a $25 mail-order diploma. The article also stated that Marshall "acted as a physician and prescribed restricted drugs for Hank Williams before the country singer's death in December, 1953." The second article said Marshall had been arrested with his wife, who was convicted of drug charges and sentenced to jail.[13]

The judge had refused to admit as evidence much of the information published in the two articles, specifically because of its highly prejudicial nature. After learning of the articles, the judge questioned each juror individually and learned that seven had seen at least one of the stories. But the jurors assured him they could continue to be impartial, and the judge denied Marshall's motion for a mistrial. The jury brought in a conviction, which the Supreme Court overturned because of the jurors' exposure to prejudicial information without the safeguards that generally attend the introduction of evidence at trial.

As previously indicated, during-trial publicity played a major role in the reversal of Sam Sheppard's conviction in 1966. In *Sheppard v. Maxwell*, the Supreme Court gave this summary:

Much of the material printed or broadcast during the trial was never heard from the witness stand, such as the charges that Sheppard had purposely impeded the murder investigation and must be guilty since he had hired a prominent criminal lawyer; that Sheppard was a perjurer; that he had sexual relations with numerous women; that his slain wife had characterized him as a "Jekyll-Hyde"; that he was "a bare-faced liar" because of his testimony as to police treatment; and, finally, that a woman convict claimed Sheppard to be the father of her illegitimate child. As the trial progressed, the newspapers summarized and interpreted the evidence, devoting particular attention to the material that incriminated Sheppard, and often drew unwarranted inferences from testimony. At one point, a front-page picture of Mrs. Sheppard's blood-stained pillow was published after being "doctored" to show more clearly an alleged imprint of a surgical instrument.[14]

The Sheppard jury was not sequestered until it began deliberations, and the judge failed to give adequate instructions regarding juror exposure to the media. The judge suggested and requested that jurors avoid media coverage of the case, but he never ordered them to do so. Several times throughout the trial Sheppard's attorney requested that the judge question jurors about their exposure to specific, highly prejudicial coverage. The judge refused all but once. That one instance resulted from a television and radio broadcast in which Walter Winchell reported that a woman under arrest in New York for robbery said she was Sheppard's mistress and the mother of his child. Two jurors admitted hearing the broadcast — despite the judge's suggestions and requests. After the jurors assured him the broadcast would not affect their decisions in the case, the judge "merely asked the jury to 'pay no attention whatever to that type of scavenging.... Let's confine ourselves to this courtroom, if you please.'" The Supreme Court considered the admonitions insufficient to protect the jury from outside influence.[15]

## The Effects of Publicity

While there is widespread agreement about the types of publicity that are prejudicial, there is significantly less agreement about the actual *effects* of such publicity on jurors. The Sixth Amendment does not guarantee a defendant freedom from inflammatory publicity; it guarantees a trial by an "impartial jury." The key question, then, is whether news coverage of a case, whether pretrial or during trial, actually affects jurors' impartiality. Opinions and evidence are mixed. In all of the cases discussed previously, the jurors told the judges that, despite the publicity, they could be impartial. But Justice Tom Clark, who wrote the opinion of the Court in *Irvin v. Dowd*, voiced skepticism about such claims: "No doubt each juror was sincere when he said that he would be fair and impartial," but "[w]here so many, so many times, admitted prejudice, such a statement of impartiality can be given little weight."[16]

Numerous efforts to measure the effects of publicity on jurors during the past five decades have proved inconclusive. A key problem with empirical studies is that they generally involve mock trials and juries — experimental simulations — rather than real jurors deciding real cases. Real juror deliberations are conducted behind closed doors, and courts fear that allowing researchers to tape deliberations might improperly influence jurors.[17] "Jurors" in the ex-

---

13 360 U.S. at 311-12.

14 384 U.S. at 356-57.

15 *Id.* at 348-58.

16 366 U.S. 717, 728 (1961).

17 For example, in early 2003 a Texas appellate court refused to allow PBS to videotape jury deliberations in a Houston murder case for use in the documentary series *Frontline*. The trial judge had agreed to let PBS place an unmanned camera in the jury room, but, citing "the ancient and centuries-old rule that jury deliberations should be private and confidential," the appeals court reversed that order. Rosenthal v. Poe, 98 S.W.3d 194 (Tex. Crim. App. 2003). Periodically courts have allowed the taping of jury deliberations, however. For example, ABC was allowed to tape jury sessions in both Arizona and Colorado for its series titled *State v.*, which debuted in summer 2002. *See*

periments are often exposed to news stories after which the "trial" immediately begins. This ignores the fact that, in real life, exposure to prejudicial coverage may go on for months before the trial actually starts. Real jurors have had the time to either forget much of what they saw in the media or, perhaps because of repeated references, become convinced of its accuracy. Furthermore, in the experiments, all "jurors" are exposed to the same news stories, another unrealistic circumstance that may affect the studies' results.

Despite their drawbacks, though, experimental research and studies of public reaction to news stories are the main sources of data for lawyers, judges and scholars trying to determine the effects of prejudicial publicity. An article in the *Stanford Law Review* summarized the results of empirical studies:

> Experiments to date indicate that for the most part juries are able and willing to put aside extraneous information and base their decisions on the evidence. The results show that when ordinary citizens become jurors, they assume a special role in which they apply different standards of proof, more vigorous reasoning and greater detachment.[18]

This confirms what many judges and lawyers firmly believe: Individuals called to jury duty generally take their responsibility very seriously; they listen to and obey the judge's instructions; they recognize that a human being's liberty and perhaps life are in their hands; and they want to make the right decision based on the evidence and the law.

In the landmark 1966 study *The American Jury,* not one of 555 judges who had presided over 3,576 criminal cases during the 1950s mentioned prejudicial publicity as a factor affecting the jury's decision in a case.[19] That's largely due to the fact that most criminal cases receive little or no publicity. Trials like those of Sheppard, O.J. Simpson, Michael Jackson and the Enron executives can cause us to lose sight of the fact that "prejudicial publicity is a factor in the rare, sensational case; elsewhere it appears to be close to nonexistent."[20] A 1999 study reported that of 134 federal, first-degree murder cases, 65 percent received little or no newspaper coverage. The study also found no significant relationship between the amount of publicity a case received and the verdict. Conviction rates in cases that generated high levels of publicity were virtually identical to those in cases involving no publicity at all.[21]

### Disruption in the Courtroom

Publishing or broadcasting prejudicial material isn't the only way in which the media might interfere with a fair trial. The presence of journalists and their equipment in a courtroom could physically disrupt the proceedings, perhaps distracting jurors and trial participants or creating an atmosphere inconsistent with fairness and calm, reasoned deliberation. Some people, including Supreme Court justices, have argued that the presence of cameras in courtrooms causes psychological disruption sufficient to violate a defendant's Sixth Amendment rights.

The trial of Bruno Hauptmann in 1935 for the kidnapping of Charles and Anne Morrow Lindbergh's eighteen-month-old son is generally cited as one of the earliest examples of journalists disrupting the judicial process and as the reason the American Bar Association recommended in 1937 that cameras be banned in all courtrooms.

Because of the international popularity of Charles Lindbergh, the first person to fly across the Atlantic Ocean nonstop, journalists from around the world crowded into the small town of Flemington, New Jersey, where the trial was held. Estimates of the number of media people present have ranged from about 200 to nearly 1,000. While the Hauptmann trial may have been the impetus for the camera ban, the evidence indicates most journalists obeyed the judge's ban on photographing while court was in session. One photographer, however, "muffled his camera in a soundproof hood, installed in it a recording device with a remote control, and recorded some of the testimony."[22] Apparently more disruptive than the photographers and their cameras were the messengers who ran in and out of the courtroom carrying the reporters' copy to be transmitted back to their newsrooms.

The Hauptmann case has been repeatedly cited as evidence of press misbehavior, but various accounts of the proceedings seem to indicate that court officials and the general public contributed to the lack of decorum as much as, if not more than, the media:

> When the court was not in session sightseers were admitted. Placards were placed around the courtroom showing where principal participants in the trial sat. However, as a sign of decorum, "members of the Rotary Club kept sightseers from cutting their initials in the judge's bench." At the trial, the public applauded state witnesses. The whole proceeding was wild, raucous, and unrestrained. The court itself scarcely attempted to correct it.[23]

Regardless of who was actually to blame for what occurred in the courtroom, the Hauptmann trial became a frequently mentioned example of media interference with the judicial process.

---

Sara Thacker, *District Attorney Petitions Appeals Court to Vacate Judge's Order Permitting "Frontline" to Tape Jury,* NEWS MEDIA & L., Winter 2003, at 23.

[18] Simon, *supra* note 12, at 528.

[19] HARRY KALVEN JR. & HANS ZEISEL, THE AMERICAN JURY (1966).

[20] FRIENDLY & GOLDFARB, *supra* note 8, at 69.

[21] Jon Bruschke & William E. Loges, *Relationship Between Pretrial Publicity and Trial Outcomes,* J. COMM., Dec. 1999, at 104.

[22] FRIENDLY & GOLDFARB, *supra* note 8, at 12.

[23] *Id.*

By the 1960s, when Texas financier Billie Sol Estes went on trial for swindling, two states — Colorado and Texas — permitted televising trials under some conditions. From the outset, Estes' attorney objected to broadcasting the proceedings, but the judge allowed both radio and television to broadcast the pretrial hearing live. According to the Supreme Court, twelve cameramen moved around the courtroom; cables and wires were "snaked across" the floor; three microphones were set up on the judge's bench; and "others were beamed at the jury box and the counsel table."

During the trial itself, four cameras — one for each of the three major networks and one for a local station — and camera operators were confined to a booth specially constructed at the rear of the courtroom and painted to blend into the walls. Only the state's opening and closing arguments and the delivery of the jury's verdict were broadcast live with sound. Other portions of the trial, however, were filmed, without sound, and broadcast during regular newscasts.

In the light of the exhaustive, gavel-to-gavel coverage of recent trials, all of this seems relatively tame and nonthreatening. Nonetheless, the Supreme Court voted 5-4 to overturn Estes' conviction, saying he had been deprived of "that judicial serenity and calm to which [he] was entitled."[24] Justice Tom Clark, for the Court, contended that televising trials caused both physical and psychological disruptions and could negatively impact the jury, judge, witnesses and defendant.

The *Sheppard* case provides the classic example of disruptions resulting from media presence in the courtroom. Journalists were allowed to literally take over the courthouse. They filled most of the seats in the 26-by-48-foot courtroom. The judge allowed about twenty newspaper and wire service reporters to sit at a temporary table inside the bar directly behind the table where Sheppard and his attorney sat, making "confidential talk among Sheppard and his counsel almost impossible during the proceedings. They frequently had to leave the courtroom to obtain privacy." The journalists' frequent movement in and out "caused so much confusion that, despite the loud-speaker system installed in the courtroom, it was difficult for the witnesses and counsel to be heard."

The media were permitted to use and install private telephone lines and telegraphic equipment in all of the rooms on the floor where the courtroom was located. In addition, a radio station set up broadcasting facilities in a room on the third floor next to the jury room. Cameras were not permitted in the courtroom, but, "In the corridors outside the courtroom there was a host of photographers and television personnel with flash cameras, portable lights and motion picture cameras." Jurors, witnesses, attorneys and the defendant were repeatedly filmed as they entered and left the courtroom.[25]

The Supreme Court summarized the situation this way: "The fact is that bedlam reigned at the courthouse during the trial and newsmen took over practically the entire courtroom, hounding most of the participants in the trial, especially Sheppard."[26] The existence of this "carnival atmosphere," coupled with the prejudicial publicity that saturated the community before and during the trial, led the Court to reverse Sheppard's conviction. When he was retried a few months later, Sheppard was found not guilty.

## COMPENSATING FOR PREJUDICIAL PUBLICITY

If media coverage of the judicial process can cause problems, the inevitable question is: What can be done to remedy the situation? There are two broad categories of remedies:

(1) Measures designed to compensate for the existence of prejudicial publicity

(2) Measures designed to prevent, or at least diminish, prejudicial publicity and to control the presence and/or activities of journalists in the courtroom.

The key difference between the two types of remedies is that the former seeks to mitigate or lessen the *effects* of media coverage without restricting the coverage. Therefore, use of the first category of remedies does not raise First Amendment concerns because no interference with the operations of the press occurs. In contrast, the remedies in the second category are designed to impact journalists and their coverage of trial proceedings. Use of these measures raises serious First Amendment issues.

The Supreme Court has repeatedly declared that the trial judge has the responsibility to protect a defendant's right to a fair trial. In *Sheppard*, *Estes*, *Rideau* and *Irvin*, it indicated its disapproval of and disenchantment with the press' performance. But, more importantly, it focused on what the judges could have and should have done to safeguard the defendants' rights. Some of the remedies it suggested, such as regulating the behavior of journalists in the courtroom and controlling the dissemination of information by police, witnesses and attorneys, will be discussed later. Here we will focus on the traditional tools that judges can use to compensate for the effects of publicity without restricting publication.

### Change of Venue

When a trial is moved to a new location, that's a change of venue. The new location is one in which the publicity has not been as intense and, therefore, potential jurors are less likely to have been influenced by pretrial coverage. Change of venue requires, however, that a defendant give up another Sixth Amendment right — the right to be tried in the "district wherein the crime shall have been committed." Generally this presents no problem since the motion for a venue change comes from the defense attorney.

Whether a change of venue will be effective in mitigating the im-

---

[24] Estes v. Texas, 381 U.S. 532, 536-37 (1965).

[25] 384 U.S. 333, 333-44 (1966).

[26] *Id.* at 355.

pact of prejudicial publicity depends on several factors, one being how far the trial is moved. In *Irvin v. Dowd*, the judge agreed to move the trial from Vanderburgh County to neighboring Gibson County. Considering that 90 percent of the prospective jurors questioned said they believed Irvin was guilty, it would appear that moving the trial such a short distance did little to protect Irvin's right to an impartial jury.

If a case is subject to massive, nationwide publicity, like the Enron cases, it's unlikely that moving it anywhere in the country would make a difference in prospective jurors' exposure to media coverage. Defense lawyers tried to get the trial of Kenneth Lay and Jeffrey Skilling moved out of Houston, citing a pretrial survey showing more than 80 percent of potential jurors believed the two Enron executives were guilty, but U.S. District Court Judge Sim Lake refused, saying adequate safeguards existed to ensure the fairness of a Houston jury.[27]

Sometimes a defendant seeks to move the site of the trial not only because of the potential effects of publicity but also because of the perceived impact of the crime itself on the community in which it occurred. For example, Terry Nichols and Timothy McVeigh, the two men found guilty in the bombing of the federal building in Oklahoma City in 1995, successfully sought a change of venue to Denver. Their attorneys argued not only that prejudicial publicity was more intense and pervasive in Oklahoma than elsewhere in the country but also that the bombing had such significant emotional, psychological and economic effects on "every prospective juror in the state" that an impartial jury could not be found anywhere in Oklahoma.[28]

While a change of venue may make it easier to find unbiased jurors, it also increases the costs and inconveniences associated with a trial because attorneys, police officers and witnesses are forced to travel extra distances. One of the major objections to moving the Nichols and McVeigh trial to Denver was the hardship the move would create for survivors of the bombing and victims' families who wanted to attend the proceedings. In response, Congress passed a law requiring the closed-circuit televising of a federal trial when it is moved from its original location out of the state and more than 350 miles away so that victims and their relatives can view the televised proceedings.[29]

Change of venue can also result in unanticipated drawbacks for a defendant. For example, a judge in Durham, North Carolina, explained why he once was reluctant to grant a change of venue to a defendant accused of murdering her husband, a high school coach. The case had generated considerable publicity in the local media, but the judge was familiar with the pattern of jury verdicts in the state and believed that the defendant, if convicted, was less likely to be sentenced to death by a Durham jury than by juries in other communities in the state. He was right. The trial was moved to Fayetteville, where the defendant was convicted and sentenced to death. Her conviction was reversed on appeal, and the second trial was held in Durham, where the crime had occurred. She was again found guilty but was sentenced to life in prison.

### Change of Venire

"Venire" refers to the pool of potential jurors from which a jury will be selected to hear a trial. To change the venire, therefore, is to import jurors from another community. The tool is much less common than change of venue. As with change of venue, a change of venire only works if the publicity has been confined to the location in which the crime occurred. In addition, it can be an expensive option since it requires the state to pay for transporting, housing and feeding jurors for the duration of the trial.

### Continuance

To continue a trial is to delay it. Like change of venue, it requires a defendant to sacrifice a constitutional right — the right to a speedy trial — in the hope of enhancing juror fairness. Postponing a trial may be an effective remedy if publicity surrounding a trial and arrest can reasonably be expected to diminish over time. Studies have shown that people forget much of what they read in newspapers or hear on television and radio news, and, especially in large cities, a continuance often means another crime will have taken over the headlines by the time the trial begins. Of course, there's always the possibility that publicity will flare up again once a trial starts. In addition, for defendants who are not granted bail or are unable to pay it, delaying a trial means they must remain in jail longer awaiting trial.

### Voir Dire

"Voir dire" is the term for the process at the beginning of a trial when potential jurors are questioned to determine if they can be impartial. It is a crucial part of the trial and, in highly publicized, sensational trials, can take weeks, with hundreds of jurors questioned. In the *Irvin* case, 430 potential jurors were called, and in the trial in which O.J. Simpson was acquitted of murdering his ex-wife and her friend, 304 prospective jurors were questioned in a *voir dire* that took eleven weeks.

Jurors may be questioned not only about their familiarity with the case and opinions regarding the defendant's guilt but also about their occupations, religious beliefs, attitudes towards the death penalty, and racial, religious or lifestyle prejudices. They will

[27] Mary Flood, *Lay, Skilling Try Again to Get Trial Postponed, Moved*, HOUS. CHRON., Jan. 25, 2006, *available at* http://www.chron.com/disp/story.mpl/special,/enron/3611743.html.

[28] Motion for Change of Venue and Supporting Brief: Evidentiary Hearing Requested at 2, United States v. McVeigh and Nichols (CR 95-110-A) (W.D. Okla. 1995).

[29] Antiterrorism and Effective Death Penalty Act, 42 U.S.C. § 10608(a) (Supp. 1999).

be asked if they know the defendant, the victim or any of the lawyers in the case. Depending on the nature of the case, they might be asked if they or any members of their families have been victims of sexual abuse, domestic violence or other crimes. In the Simpson case, for example, a juror was dismissed part way through the trial for having lied about whether she had experienced domestic violence.

Both the prosecution and defense can challenge an unlimited number of jurors for cause. It is then up to the judge to determine if there is sufficient reason to believe the potential juror is biased or for some other reason, such as a relationship with the victim or defendant, unsuited to sit on the jury. In the Irvin trial, 268 jurors were dismissed as obviously prejudiced against the defendant.

The attorneys for both sides also can dismiss a limited number of jurors with peremptory challenges. An attorney does not need to provide a reason for using a peremptory challenge to dismiss a juror. While lawyers still base many peremptory challenges on instinct, jury selection has now become a form of social science. Law journal articles and books describe the ideal and the worst jurors for particular types of cases. Jury selection consultants can be hired to help lawyers devise the desired juror profile for a specific case. Thus, a lawyer may use peremptory challenges to eliminate from the jury pool people who, because of demographic or socioeconomic factors, are considered less likely to be sympathetic to his or her side.

The number of peremptory challenges available to each side differs depending on the type of case and jurisdiction. For example, in North Carolina each side is entitled to fourteen peremptory challenges in capital cases and six in non-capital cases.[30] In California, the number of peremptory challenges allowed ranges from twenty in cases involving the death penalty or life imprisonment to six in cases in which the maximum penalty is ninety days in jail.[31]

Judges, including the Supreme Court justices, place a great deal of faith in the *voir dire* process and believe that, if correctly used, it can be effective in weeding out potentially prejudiced jurors. Critics, however, note that potential jurors can and do hide the truth, either consciously or unconsciously. No doubt it can be difficult for people to openly admit that they have racial or religious prejudices or were so influenced by media coverage of a case that they can no longer be impartial. Sometimes people are not even aware of their own biases. And, as the Simpson case demonstrated, jurors might purposely withhold information, as did the juror who failed to disclose her own history of domestic abuse.

### Admonitions to the Jury

A judge may order jurors not to read, watch or listen to any media coverage of or commentary on the trial and not to discuss the trial with anyone except other jurors and then only when deliberations begin. These admonitions are intended to impress upon jurors their responsibility to decide the case solely on the basis of the law and evidence presented in court. Failure to follow the orders can result in removal from the jury, citation for contempt of court or both. Recall that in *Sheppard* the Supreme Court found the jury admonitions to be insufficient since the judge merely requested that the jurors avoid media coverage of the trial. Whether appropriate jury admonitions in the form of direct orders actually prevent juror exposure to media coverage of the trial is open to debate. However, as with *voir dire*, most judges indicate they believe that jury admonitions are effective in most cases.

### Sequestration

Sequestration is the most extreme, costly and seldom used of the remedies designed to shelter jurors from prejudicial publicity. Sequestration means isolating the jury for the duration of the trial. It entails housing the jurors in a hotel, screening their phone calls and monitoring their use of mass media to ensure that they do not see or hear any media coverage of the trial. While sequestration can be very effective in preventing jury exposure to prejudicial publicity, it is a remedy that also has many drawbacks. First, it adds significantly to the cost of the trial because the state must transport, house, feed and guard the jurors. Perhaps more importantly, though, sequestration causes significant disruptions to jurors' lives and effectively eliminates from juries people who cannot leave their families or jobs for weeks or even months. In addition, keeping jurors away from family, friends and normal routines for an extended period of time may have unintended psychological effects, causing jurors to resent the defendant and blame him or her for disrupting their lives.

### PREVENTING OR DIMINISHING PUBLICITY

Despite the existence of the traditional remedies discussed above, trial judges sometimes try to prevent or diminish the publicity itself. These judicial efforts to control what information journalists have access to and what the media publish or broadcast raise significant First Amendment implications, and during the past twenty years the Supreme Court has severely limited their use. Remedies aimed at eliminating or reducing prejudicial publicity and media interference with fair trial rights fall into six categories: (1) gag orders aimed at the media, (2) restrictions on trial participants, (3) post-publication sanctions, (4) court closures, (5) denials of access to court records and (6) bans or limits on cameras in the courtroom.

### Gag Orders on the Media

In *Sheppard v. Maxwell*, the Supreme Court provided a list of tools trial judges could use to protect defendants' fair trial rights.

---

[30] N.C. Gen. Stat. § 15A-1217 (2000).

[31] Cal. Code Civ. Proc. § 231 (Deering 2001).

## The Questions a Trial Judge Must Consider Before Issuing a Gag Order on the Press

1. Has there been intense and pervasive publicity that is likely to affect the fairness of the trial?
2. Are there no alternatives to a gag order that would protect the defendant's fair trial rights?
3. Is a gag order likely to be effective?

Only if the answers to all three questions are "yes" may a judge gag the media.

---

The Supreme Court, however, never suggested judges issue restrictive orders directly prohibiting the media from publishing information that might be prejudicial. Nonetheless, that's exactly what some judges did.

While comprehensive data are not available, a number of different sources reported an increase in gag orders on the press during the decade following *Sheppard*. A study by the Reporters Committee for Freedom of the Press identified thirty-nine gag orders directed at the media between 1967 and 1975. What is especially remarkable about the Reporters Committee data is the acceleration in such restraints over time. From 1967 through 1971, the committee identified a total of four gag orders on the press, averaging not even one per year. In the next four years, 1972 to 1975, the committee identified thirty gag orders on the press, reaching a peak of fourteen in 1975 alone.[32]

In 1975, Judge Howard Medina, who had headed the New York Bar Association's Special Committee on Radio, Television and the Administration of Justice, wrote in the *New York Times*: "It must be that trial judges like this show of authority. In any event, the number of these omnibus gag orders has vastly increased."[33] The Twentieth Century Fund's Task Force on Justice, Publicity and the First Amendment, in a report issued in 1976, criticized trial judges' "excessive use of restrictive orders."[34]

Journalists and attorneys were as concerned about the absurd nature of some of the gag orders as they were about the increased numbers. In one case a judge prohibited publication of a jury verdict entered in open court; in another, the court barred publication of the names of public witnesses for six months; in still another, a judge forbade publication of information about a recent jail break. The excessiveness of trial judges' responses to the "free press-fair trial problem" was illustrated by the results of a 1972 Reporters Committee survey, which showed that in every case in which the media challenged a gag order, an appellate court struck down the order.[35] But, as the post-1972 figures demonstrate, lack of success with appeals courts did not deter trial judges from imposing restrictions on the press.

Finally, in 1976, the Supreme Court put a halt to the indiscriminate use of gag orders on the press. The landmark case of *Nebraska Press Association v. Stuart*[36] began on Saturday evening, October 18, 1975, when police arrived at the Henry Kellie home in Sutherland, Nebraska, to find six members of the family with shotgun wounds to their heads. Five were already dead, and the sixth died later that night. Fear spread through the town of 850 as the local radio station reported that an armed murderer was in the area and advised residents to stay indoors and keep their doors locked.

The next day a neighbor of the Kellies, Erwin Charles Simants, 30, was arrested and charged with the six murders. Simants had apparently confessed to his thirteen-year-old nephew and his parents, who called the police. Simants admitted to police that he had killed the Kellies and was arraigned a few hours after his arrest. Reporters learned of Simants' confessions and publicized the information, along with speculation — later confirmed by autopsies — that Simants had sexually assaulted some of the victims after murdering them.

Both geography and Nebraska law complicated protecting Simants' right to a fair trial by an impartial jury. The court in which Simants was to be tried was in North Platte, population 19,000, the county seat of Lincoln County, just twenty miles east of Sutherland. Publicity about the crime had, of course, been as widespread in North Platte, the largest city in southwest Nebraska, as in Sutherland itself. Nebraska law severely restricted the use of two traditional techniques for mitigating the effects of prejudicial publicity — continuance and change of venue — by requiring that the accused be brought to trial within six months and allowing a change of venue only to an adjoining county, all of which were smaller than Lincoln County.

On Tuesday, October 21, the county attorney proposed a solution to County Judge Ronald Ruff — a gag order prohibiting publication of potentially prejudicial material. The next day Judge Ruff issued an order barring publication of testimony and evidence presented during the preliminary hearing. In addition, he ordered journalists to abide by the Nebraska Bar-Press Guidelines, a set of voluntary recommendations for minimizing prejudicial publicity.[37]

The media immediately appealed Judge Ruff's order to District

---

[32] Jack Landau, *Fair Press and Free Trial: A Due Process Proposal*, 62 A.B.A.J. 55, 57 (1976).

[33] Howard Medina, *Omnibus "Gag" Rulings*, N.Y. Times, Nov. 30, 1975, at 4-13.

[34] Twentieth Century Fund Task Force, Justice Publicity and the First Amendment, Rights in Conflict 4 (1976).

[35] Landau, *supra* note 32, at 56, 59.

[36] 427 U.S. 539 (1976).

[37] *Id.* at 542.

Court Judge Hugh Stuart, who found that there was a "clear and present danger that pre-trial publicity could impinge upon the defendant's right to a fair trial." Judge Stuart vacated Judge Ruff's order and entered his own, which also incorporated the bar-press guidelines and prohibited publication of specific information — including the existence and contents of Simants' confession and information relating to the sexual assaults — until after a jury had been impaneled. Stuart's order also prohibited the media from reporting on the exact nature of the gag order itself.[38]

The media made numerous attempts to have the gag order vacated or stayed. Finally, on December 1, after considerable prodding from Harry Blackmun, the Supreme Court justice who was overseeing the federal circuit that included Nebraska, the Nebraska Supreme Court modified Stuart's order to eliminate references to the bar-press guidelines but continued the ban on reporting confessions and "other facts 'strongly implicative' of the accused."[39] On December 12, 1975, the Supreme Court agreed to review the case; on January 5, 1976, Simants' trial began with jury selection; on January 8, the jury was sworn and sequestered, and Stuart's gag order was lifted; on January 16, Simants was found guilty on six counts of first degree murder and sentenced to death; on April 19, *Nebraska Press Association v. Stuart* was argued before the Supreme Court; and on June 30, a unanimous Court held that Stuart's gag order was a prior restraint on the press that violated the First Amendment. Incidentally, Simants' conviction was eventually overturned on the ground that a sheriff had tried to influence the sequestered jury. On retrial Simants was found not guilty by reason of insanity, which was his original plea.

In *Nebraska Press Association,* all nine justices agreed that the gag order was unconstitutional. They did not all agree, however, on the reasons for the conclusion. Chief Justice Warren Burger, writing for himself and four other justices, took a balancing approach, utilizing a variation of the clear and present danger test, which had been developed in the context of sedition cases. After acknowledging that prior restraints "are the most serious and the least tolerable infringement on First Amendment rights," Burger said the constitutionality of a gag order had to be determined by looking at the circumstances of a particular case and deciding whether "'the gravity of the "evil," discounted by its improbability,'" justified a gag order.[40] To determine this, Burger said three factors must be considered:

(1) the nature and extent of pretrial news coverage;

(2) whether other measures would be likely to mitigate the effects of unrestrained publicity; and

(3) how effectively a restraining order would operate to prevent the threatened danger.[41] Judges still use this three-part test to decide whether restrictive orders can be imposed on the media.

Burger said Judge Stuart was correct in concluding there would be intense and pervasive pretrial publicity. However, he failed to consider whether alternative measures might have protected Simants' right to a fair trial. Furthermore, the Chief Justice voiced doubts about the effectiveness of the gag order. Noting the crimes took place "in a community of 850 people," Burger wrote, "It is reasonable to assume that, without any news accounts being printed or broadcast, rumors would travel swiftly by word of mouth. One can only speculate on the accuracy of such reports, given the general propensities of rumors; they could well be more damaging than reasonably accurate news accounts."[42] Thus, Stuart's order failed Burger's balancing test and was declared unconstitutional.

Three justices — William Brennan, Thurgood Marshall and Potter Stewart — were willing to go even further. They concurred in the ruling but said gag orders on the press would always be unconstitutional. Two other justices — White and Stevens — indicated they might agree to an absolute ban on gag orders at a later date.

A year after *Nebraska Press Association,* the Supreme Court underscored the point that gag orders on the media would rarely be constitutional when it struck down an order prohibiting publication of the name and picture of an eleven-year-old charged with murder. The juvenile court judge had allowed journalists to attend the detention hearing for the accused boy but then banned publication of the child's name and the photo, which had been taken outside the courthouse. By the time the judge issued the gag order, the boy's name and picture had already been widely published and broadcast. In *Oklahoma Publishing Co. v. District Court,*[43] the Supreme Court said that once the judge permitted journalists to attend the hearing, he could not prohibit them from publishing the information they gathered while in attendance.

*Nebraska Press Association* and *Oklahoma Publishing Co.* have made it extremely difficult for a trial judge to justify gagging the press. Periodically judges still try, but such orders are almost always struck down on appeal. For example, appellate courts have struck down gag orders prohibiting publication of the names of jurors,[44] evidence presented in open court but outside the presence of the jury,[45] videotapes made during the government's investigation of alleged drug trafficking,[46] the identities of juvenile of-

---

[38] *Id.* at 543-44.

[39] *Id.* at 545.

[40] *Id.* at 559, 562 (quoting United States v. Dennis, 183 F.2d 201, 212 (2d Cir. 1950), *aff'd,* 341 U.S. 494 (1951)).

[41] *Id.* at 562.

[42] *Id.* at 567.

[43] 430 U.S. 308 (1977).

[44] *See* Capital Cities Media v. Toole, 463 U.S. 1303 (Brennan, Circuit Justice 1983); Times Publ'g Co. v. Florida, 632 So. 2d 1072 (Fla. Dist. Ct. App. 1994); Des Moines Register & Tribune Co. v. Osmundson, 248 N.W.2d 493 (Iowa 1976); State v. Neulander, 801 A.2d 255 (N.J. 2002); New Mexico *ex rel.* New Mexico Press Ass'n v. Kaufman, 648 P.2d 300 (N.M. 1982); Ohio *ex rel.* Chillicothe Gazette, Inc. v. Ross County Court of Common Pleas, 442 N.E.2d 747 (Ohio 1982); Pennsylvania v. Genovese, 487 A.2d 364 (Pa. 1985).

[45] *See* Florida *ex rel.* Miami Herald Publ'g Co. v. McIntosh, 340 So. 2d 904 (Fla. 1976).

[46] *See* CBS v. Dist. Court, 727 F.2d 1174 (9th Cir. 1984) (involving an FBI

fenders and victims[47] and defendants' prior criminal records and nicknames, such as "Quapaw Quarter rapist" and "Sugarhouse rapist."[48]

Television's fascination with "docudramas" based on sensational crimes has led a number of defendants to seek — unsuccessfully — to prevent such broadcasts. One of the best known of these cases involved an attempt by Lyle and Erik Menendez to prevent the broadcast in Los Angeles County of *Honor Thy Father and Mother: The True Story of the Menendez Murders* while the brothers awaited retrial on charges of murdering their parents. The Menendez brothers, who ultimately were convicted, claimed that airing the program in the county would make it impossible to find an unbiased jury. Applying the *Nebraska Press Association* test, a California federal district court disagreed, holding that the trial judge could adequately protect the defendants' fair trial rights through *voir dire* and jury instructions.[49]

In 1996, the Sixth U.S. Circuit Court of Appeals declared unconstitutional an unusual gag order issued in a civil case involving Procter & Gamble Co. and Bankers Trust Co. An attorney who worked for the firm representing Bankers Trust provided a *Business Week* reporter copies of documents relating to the lawsuit. Trial Judge John Feikens, however, had sealed the documents, a fact apparently unknown to both the attorney who provided the documents and the reporter who received them. Hours before the *Business Week* story based on the documents was to go to press, both Procter & Gamble and Bankers Trust asked Judge Feikens to issue a restraining order barring publication of the story. Without holding a hearing or giving McGraw-Hill, publisher of *Business Week*, a chance to protest, Judge Feikens issued the gag order. A few weeks later, Judge Feikens unsealed the documents on which the *Business Week* story was based, making them available to the public. Amazingly, however, the judge still refused to rescind his order barring the magazine from publishing its original article. In March 1996, the U.S. Court of Appeals for the Sixth Circuit ruled

that the case involved a "classic case of a prior restraint" in violation of the First Amendment. Judge Feikens had failed to demonstrate that irreparable harm to a substantial government interest would result from publication of the article, the appellate court wrote. Furthermore, he had not provided McGraw-Hill the opportunity to argue the merits of the gag order.[50]

Since *Nebraska Press Association*, only a few gag orders on the media have been upheld on appeal. In 2004, the Colorado Supreme Court affirmed in part a gag order in the Kobe Bryant rape case.[51] Eventually, the charge against the NBA star was dropped when the woman refused to continue participating in the case. Before that, though, the trial judge issued a gag order prohibiting seven media outlets from publishing information from transcripts of closed proceedings they had received erroneously. Because of the massive media interest in the case, the trial court had set up an e-mail list to disseminate public proceeding transcripts. Inadvertently, the court reporter e-mailed transcripts of closed hearings held to determine the admissibility of evidence relating to the accuser's prior and subsequent sexual conduct. The trial judge ordered anyone who had received the transcripts "to delete and destroy any copies and not reveal any contents thereof."[52] Holding that preventing public disclosure of irrelevant information about the accuser's sexual history was a compelling interest, the Colorado Supreme Court narrowed the order by striking the requirement that recipients delete and destroy all copies and limiting the ban on disclosure to just those portions deemed "not relevant and material" to the case under the state's rape shield law.[53]

In 1990, the Eleventh U.S. Circuit Court of Appeals refused to lift a temporary gag order prohibiting CNN from disseminating the contents of tape recordings of conversations between deposed Panamanian dictator Manuel Noriega, who was in jail in Miami awaiting trial on federal drug charges, and his lawyers. Jail officials had allegedly made the tapes, and CNN had obtained them legally. On a motion from Noriega's attorneys, a U.S. district judge issued a temporary restraining order prohibiting CNN from broadcasting the tapes and ordered the network to submit the tapes to him so he could decide whether their dissemination would present a "clear, immediate, and irreparable danger" to Noriega's fair trial rights and, therefore, should be permanently banned.[54] The next

---

sting operation targeting car manufacturer John DeLorean, who was ultimately acquitted).

[47] *See* Arkansas Democrat-Gazette v. Zimmerman, 20 S.W.3d 301 (Ark. 2000); KGTV Channel 10 v. Superior Court, 32 Cal. Rptr. 2d 181 (1994); Lesher Communications, Inc. v. Alameda County Superior Court, 22 Media L. Rep. (BNA) 1383 (Cal. Ct. App. 1994); San Bernardino County Dept. of Pub. Soc. Servs. v. Superior Court, 283 Cal. Rptr. 332 (1991); Sarasota Herald-Tribune v. J.T.L., 502 So. 2d 930 (Fla. Dist. Ct. App. 1987); *In re* a Minor, 537 N.E.2d 292 (Ill. 1989); Minneapolis Star & Tribune Co. v. Schmidt, 360 N.W.2d 433 (Minn. Ct. App. 1985); Minneapolis Star & Tribune Co. v. Lee, 353 N.W.2d 213 (Minn. Ct. App. 1984); New Jersey *ex rel.* H.N., 632 A.2d 537 (N.J. 1993).

[48] Arkansas Gazette v. Lofton, 598 S.W.2d 745 (Ark. 1980); KUTV v. Conder, 668 P.2d 513 (Utah 1983).

[49] Menendez v. Fox Broad. Co., 22 Media L. Rep. (BNA) 1702 (C.D. Cal. 1994). *See also* Hunt v. NBC, 872 F.2d 289 (9th Cir. 1989); Goldblum v. NBC, 584 F.2d 904 (9th Cir. 1978); Corbitt v. NBC, 20 Media L. Rep. (BNA) 2037 (N.D. Ill. 1992); Clear Channel Communications, Inc. v. Murray, 636 So. 2d 818 (Fla. Dist. Ct. App. 1994); Zamora v. Adams, 25 Media L. Rep. (BNA) 1638 (Tex. Dist. 1997).

[50] Proctor & Gamble Co. v. Bankers Trust Co., 78 F.3d 219, 225 (6th Cir. 1996).

[51] People v. Bryant, 94 P.3d 624 (Colo.), *stay denied sub nom.* AP v. District Court, 542 U.S. 1301 (Breyer, Circuit Justice 2004).

[52] *Id.* at 626.

[53] *Id.* at 637. *See also* KUTV v. Wilkinson, 686 P.2d 456 (Utah 1984) (upholding an order prohibiting the media from reporting a criminal defendant's alleged ties to organized crime).

[54] United States v. Noriega, 752 F. Supp. 1032, 1034-35 (S.D. Fla.), *aff'd sub nom. In re* Cable News Network, Inc., 917 F.2d 1543 (11th Cir.), *cert. denied*, 498 U.S. 976 (1990). *See also In re* State Record Co., 504 S.E.2d 592 (S.C. 1998), *cert. denied*, 526 U.S. 1050 (1999) (upholding a gag order prohibiting media coverage of a secretly recorded conversation between a de-

day the judge limited his order to material that was privileged. CNN appealed the judge's order but also disobeyed it by continuing to air the excerpts from the tapes it had broadcast prior to the issuance of the gag order.

The court of appeals refused to lift the district court's order, saying CNN's failure to allow the judge to inspect the tapes had made it impossible for the court to balance the network's First Amendment rights against Noriega's Sixth Amendment rights.[55] The Supreme Court denied *certiorari*, despite a vigorous dissent from Justices Thurgood Marshall and Sandra Day O'Connor, who said the trial judge's order could not be reconciled with *Nebraska Press Association* and the Pentagon Papers case.[56] CNN eventually turned the tapes over to the district judge, who, after reviewing them, concluded that broadcast of the remaining unaired portions would not violate Noriega's rights.[57]

Despite the fact that the gag order was ultimately lifted, CNN was found in contempt of court for airing portions of the tapes while the temporary restraining order was in force, fined $85,000 and ordered to broadcast a public apology.[58] This case illustrates an important point that journalists must keep in mind: Even if a court order is eventually declared unconstitutional, a person who violates the order while it is in effect can be found guilty of contempt of court and subject to fines and/or imprisonment. This is known as the "collateral bar rule," which states that a person who disobeys a court order may not collaterally challenge the constitutionality of the order as a defense to the contempt of court charge. The reasoning behind the rule is simple and generally sound: The effectiveness of the entire judicial system would be severely hampered if individuals were free to make their own decisions as to which court orders they would obey and which they would ignore. Under many circumstances, waiting for appellate review of a court order imposes little or no hardship on the individual subject to the order. But the situation changes when gag orders are imposed on the media since timeliness is the essence of news and waiting for an appellate court ruling could change news into history.

A 1972 case decided by the U.S. Court of Appeals for the Fifth Circuit illustrates the traditional strict application of the collateral bar rule. In *United States v. Dickinson*,[59] two Baton Rouge, Louisiana, reporters were held in contempt and fined $300 each for disobeying a federal judge's order not to report on anything that took place during a hearing that had been open to the public. The hearing was held to investigate the motives of the state in prosecuting a federal volunteer worker charged with conspiring to murder the Baton Rouge mayor. The volunteer contended the charges were brought to harass him because of his civil rights activities. Because the volunteer worker might later be tried on the criminal charges, the U.S. district judge ordered that there be no media coverage of what occurred at the hearing. On appeal, the Fifth Circuit struck down the trial court's gag order as unconstitutional but sustained the contempt convictions of the two reporters. The court wrote:

> We begin with the well-established principle in proceedings for criminal contempt that an injunction ... *must be obeyed*, irrespective of the ultimate validity of the order. Invalidity is no defense to criminal contempt.... "People simply cannot have the luxury of knowing that they have a right to contest the correctness of the judge's order in deciding whether to willfully disobey it.... Court orders have to be obeyed until they are reversed or set aside in an orderly fashion."[60]

While the court recognized that "[t]imeliness of publication is the hallmark of 'news,'" it went on to say: "But newsmen are citizens, too.... They too may sometimes have to wait."[61] It is somewhat ironic that having recognized the importance of timeliness in news reporting, the Fifth Circuit itself took five months to issue an opinion in the case.

More than a decade later, the First U.S. Circuit Court of Appeals adopted a somewhat more flexible approach, ruling that a "transparently invalid" gag order could be violated with impunity as long as the publisher first made "a good faith effort" to have an appellate court reverse the order. The case resulted from the *Providence Journal*'s violation of a judge's order prohibiting publication of information the paper had received from the FBI. The information, which the FBI had gathered through illegal wiretaps in the 1960s, related to reputed organized crime leader Raymond L.S. Patriarca, who had died in 1985. In 1976, the *Journal* had sought access to transcripts of the wiretaps under the federal Freedom of Information Act, but the FBI denied the request and a federal court upheld the denial, ruling that release of the transcripts would violate Patriarca's privacy. However, after Patriarca's death, the FBI released the transcripts to the *Providence Journal* as well as other news organizations. After a Providence radio station aired some of the information from the transcripts, Patriarca's son sued to prevent further publication, claiming dissemination of the information would violate his privacy.[62]

---

fendant in a murder trial and his attorney).

[55] 917 F.2d 1543, 1544 (11th Cir. 1990).

[56] New York Times Co. v. United States, 403 U.S. 713 (1971).

[57] United States v. Noriega, 752 F. Supp. 1045 (S.D. Fla. 1990).

[58] United States v. CNN, 865 F. Supp. 1549 (S.D. Fla. 1994). Beginning at 6 p.m. on Dec. 19, 1994, CNN broadcast an apology every hour for twenty-two hours. The statement said, in part: "CNN realizes that it was in error in defying the order of the court and publishing the Noriega tape while appealing the court's order. We do now and always have recognized that our justice system cannot long survive if litigants take it upon themselves to determine which judgments or orders of court they will or will not follow."

[59] 465 F.2d 496 (5th Cir. 1972).

[60] *Id.* at 509 (quoting Southern Railway Co. v. Lanham, 408 F.2d 348, 350 (5th Cir. 1969) (Brown, C.J., dissenting)).

[61] *Id.* at 512 (citation omitted).

[62] *In re* Providence Journal, 820 F.2d 1342, 1353 (1st Cir. 1986), *modified*, 820 F.2d 1354, 1355 (1st Cir. 1987) (en banc), *cert. dismissed*, 485 U.S. 693

## Violating Court Orders & Contempt of Court

**The *Dickinson* Rule**:

A journalist must obey a court order, even an obviously unconstitutional gag order, until an appellate court overturns it.

**The *Providence Journal* Rule**:

A journalist may violate a "patently invalid" gag order after making a "good faith effort" to get an appellate court to overturn it.

On November 13, 1985, Judge Francis Boyle issued an order barring publication of the wiretap information; on November 14, the *Journal* published an article in direct disobedience of that order; on November 19, Judge Boyle vacated his order, acknowledging that it was most likely unconstitutional; and on March 17, 1986, Judge Boyle held the *Journal* and its editor, Charles Hauser, in contempt of court, fining the newspaper $100,000 and giving Hauser an eighteen-month suspended sentence and ordering him to perform 200 hours of community service. The *Journal* appealed, and a three-judge panel of the First Circuit reversed the contempt convictions. While the court recognized that the collateral bar rule is the "general rule," it went on to emphasize that this case involved a prior restraint on speech, which, it said, represents "an unusual class of orders because they are presumptively unconstitutional." The court held the *Nebraska Press Association* test was the standard that applied to evaluating the constitutionality of Judge Boyle's gag order and that it was "patently clear" the order did not meet that test. In fact, the judge had failed to even consider two prongs of the test. Furthermore, the court noted that the purpose of a temporary restraining order, such as Judge Boyle issued, is to preserve the status quo while the court considers the case. However, for newspapers, the court said, the status quo "is to publish news promptly that editors decide to publish. A restraining order disturbs the status quo and impinges on the exercise of editorial discretion."[63]

A few months later, the First Circuit reheard the case *en banc*, affirmed the three-judge panel's ruling, but added a modification. The full court said that in the future a publisher had to "make a good faith effort to seek emergency relief from the appellate courts" before violating a patently invalid gag order. "If timely access to the appellate court is not available or if [a] timely decision is not forthcoming," the publisher may go ahead and publish in violation of the order, subsequently challenging the constitution-

ality of the order as a defense to a contempt citation. The requirement to seek appellate review before violating a court order was not applied to the *Providence Journal* case, the court said, because that would be unfair. Besides, the court indicated it was not clear whether timely appellate relief was available in this case.[64]

The Supreme Court failed to reconcile the apparent conflict between the Fifth Circuit and the First Circuit when it dismissed the appeal from the government in the *Providence Journal* case on procedural grounds.[65]

In attempting to understand these two cases, it's important to keep in mind that *Dickinson* is binding precedent only in the Fifth Circuit, and *Providence Journal* is binding precedent only in the First Circuit. In addition, both cases are federal cases, and individual states are free to devise their own rules regarding application of the collateral bar rule when state court judges issue gag orders on the press.[66] A few courts have chosen to follow the First Circuit's lead, ruling that journalists who disobey patently invalid court orders can escape contempt of court convictions. For example, in December 1998, the Mississippi Supreme Court unanimously overturned the contempt conviction of a *Delta Democrat Times* reporter who had disobeyed a trial judge's order not to report on a criminal defendant's juvenile record, which was discussed in open court. The state high court, noting that the trial judge did not consider the *Nebraska Press Association* test, said, "Without this determination, we are left with a presumption of invalidity."[67] Likewise, in 1994 the Kansas Supreme Court reversed the contempt conviction of the *Atchison Daily Globe* and its publisher, who had violated a trial court's order not to report a felony defendant's prior criminal record.[68]

However, in 2002 a New Jersey trial judge held four *Philadelphia Inquirer* reporters in contempt and fined them $1,000 each for printing the name of a juror in a high-profile murder trial even though two months earlier the New Jersey Supreme Court had ruled the order prohibiting publication of jurors' names was unconstitutional.[69] Thus, despite some successes in challenging

---

[63] *Id.* at 1346-53.

(1988).

[64] 820 F.2d 1354, 1355 (1st Cir. 1986).

[65] 485 U.S. 693 (1988). The special prosecutor who was handling the government's case had failed to obtain the U.S. Solicitor General's authorization to petition the Supreme Court for *certiorari*.

[66] For example, in 1984, two years before the First Circuit ruled in *Providence Journal*, the Washington Supreme Court, relying on both the state and U.S. constitutions, struck down a contempt citation against a television and radio station that had violated a "patently invalid" gag order. *Washington v. Coe*, 679 P.2d 353 (Wash. 1984).

[67] *Jeffries v. Mississippi*, 724 So. 2d 897, 900 (Miss. 1998). The judge who found the reporter in contempt and jailed her for seventy-two hours was found guilty of misconduct by the Mississippi Supreme Court in 2000, primarily because of her handling of the *Jeffries* case. The judge, who had already been defeated in her bid for reelection, was publicly reprimanded and fined. Mississippi Comm'n on Judicial Performance v. Byers, 757 So. 2d 961 (Miss. 2000).

[68] *Kansas v. Alston*, 887 P.2d 681 (Kan. 1994).

[69] *See* Phillip Taylor, *Colliding With Contempt*, NEWS MEDIA & L., Summer

contempt convictions resulting from disobeying gag orders, many attorneys still advise journalists to obey such orders until they are reversed on appeal or, at the very least, to make a sincere effort to obtain appellate court review of the order before disobeying it.

### Restrictions on Trial Participants

Judicial gag orders on trial participants became front-page news in 2005 when one such order temporarily barred *Tonight Show* host Jay Leno from telling jokes about Michael Jackson during the singer's child molestation trial. The judge in the Jackson case had issued a sweeping order prohibiting all trial participants, including witnesses, from speaking publicly about the case. Leno, who had received a phone call from Jackson's accuser a few years earlier during which the boy had asked for money to help with his cancer treatments, was subpoenaed by the defense and, thus, fell within the provisions of the gag order. After Leno called in surrogate comedians to deliver his Jackson jokes, the judge clarified his order, saying it did not prevent Leno from joking about the case but only from discussing his own part in it.[70]

While the *Nebraska Press Association* test has made it very difficult for judges to gag the media, it is easier for them to restrict the flow of information to the media by issuing gag orders aimed at trial participants, especially attorneys. In *Sheppard v. Maxwell*, the Court specifically said the judge "might well have proscribed extrajudicial statements by any lawyer, party, witness, or court official which divulged prejudicial matters."[71] Generally, courts view gag orders on trial participants as less distasteful under the First Amendment because they do not prevent the media from disseminating information but simply make it more difficult for journalists to obtain information. In addition, courts have greater power over trial participants, especially lawyers, than they do over non-participant journalists. Newsgathering, however, receives some First Amendment protection, and trial participants have their own First Amendment rights to speak. Thus, there are limits on judges' gag powers. Before considering how those limits apply to the typical gag orders aimed at attorneys, witnesses, defendants and jurors, a somewhat unusual situation — a gag order aimed at newspapers that were themselves participants in the case — will be addressed.

In *Seattle Times Co. v. Rhinehart*, the Supreme Court said that the strict *Nebraska Press Association* test did not apply when the media themselves were parties to the litigation and had obtained information through the pretrial discovery process.[72] The *Seattle Times* and *Walla Walla Union-Bulletin* were defendants in a libel and invasion of privacy lawsuit brought by Keith Rhinehart, head

of a religious group called the Aquarian Foundation. The newspapers wanted information about the foundation's members and donors, but the foundation refused, arguing that publication of such information would violate the members' and donors' First Amendment rights. A Washington state trial judge ordered the group to release the information but issued a protective order prohibiting the newspapers from publishing what they learned as parties to the lawsuit.

The Supreme Court unanimously upheld the trial judge's order, saying it was not a "classic prior restraint that requires exacting First Amendment scrutiny." Nonetheless, the Court said the state needed to demonstrate that a substantial government interest justified restricting the newspapers' right to publish the information. Preventing abuse of the discovery process constituted a substantial governmental interest, it concluded, and, therefore, the protective order was not a violation of the First Amendment. However, it noted that the papers could publish the same information if they obtained it through some other way.[73]

*Seattle Times v. Rhinehart* was an unusual case. Usually restrictive orders prohibit attorneys or witnesses from making extrajudicial, public statements that might prejudice the outcome of a trial. While such orders limit the flow of information to the media, they do not ban the media from disseminating information they possess; the orders are aimed at the parties, not the media.

The American Bar Association's Model Rules of Professional Conduct provide that an attorney should not make extrajudicial, public statements that "have a substantial likelihood of materially prejudicing" a pending case. While not expressly prohibiting any particular types of comments, the rules list certain subjects "more likely than not to have a material prejudicial effect on a proceeding." These include statements about the character, credibility, reputation or criminal record of a party, suspect or witness; the existence or contents of a confession or a suspect's refusal to make a statement; the results of examinations or tests or the refusal of a suspect to take a test; opinions as to a defendant's guilt or innocence; or even that "a defendant has been charged with a crime, unless there is included therein a statement explaining that the defendant is presumed innocent until and unless proven guilty."

In 1994, amidst the massive publicity surrounding the O.J. Simpson case, the ABA amended its rules to add a right-of-reply for defense lawyers. The provision says that an attorney "may make a statement that a reasonable lawyer would believe is required to protect a client from the substantial undue prejudicial effect of recent publicity not initiated by the lawyer or the lawyer's client." At the same time, the ABA added language directing prosecutors to "refrain from making extrajudicial comments that have a substantial likelihood of heightening public condemnation of the accused."[74]

2002, at 4.

[70] Lisa de Moraes, *For Jay Leno, Michael Jackson Jokes Are in Order*, Mar. 12, 2005, http://www.washingtonpost.com/wp-dyn/content/article/2005/03/25/AR2005032507531.html.

[71] 384 U.S. 333, 361 (1966).

[72] 467 U.S. 20 (1984).

[73] *Id.* at 33-35.

[74] MODEL RULES OF PROF'L CONDUCT R. 3.6 cmt., and R. 3.8(g) (1994).

About forty states have adopted rules, most following the ABA's model, allowing an attorney to be disciplined for public statements that could prejudice a trial even if the judge hasn't issued an order specifically limiting extrajudicial statements. Attorneys have challenged such rules, arguing that they are prior restraints on speech and, therefore, should be subject to the *Nebraska Press Association* test. In 1991, however, the Supreme Court ruled that the "substantial likelihood of material prejudice" standard, used in most states' attorney rules, does not violate the First Amendment. Chief Justice Rehnquist, noting that lawyers are "officers of the Court," justified applying a different standard to attorneys than to the media and general public. "Because lawyers have special access to information through discovery and client communications," he wrote, "their extrajudicial statements pose a threat to the fairness of a pending proceeding since lawyers' statements are likely to be received as especially authoritative."[75]

The case, *Gentile v. State Bar of Nevada*, involved a challenge to Nevada's disciplinary rules by a lawyer who had held a press conference in which he declared that his client, charged with felony theft, was innocent and questioned the integrity of the grand jury witnesses. The state bar subsequently disciplined the attorney for violating a Nevada Supreme Court rule, which was virtually identical to the ABA's model rule. While the Supreme Court sanctioned use of the substantial likelihood standard for lawyers, it declared Nevada's rule unconstitutionally vague because it did not provide clear notice of exactly what types of statements were permitted. A portion of the rule, which listed acceptable public statements by attorneys, the Court wrote, had misled Gentile "into thinking that he could give his press conference without fear of discipline."[76]

Whether a state has adopted specific rules limiting attorneys' extrajudicial statements, a trial judge has the inherent power to issue gag orders aimed at attorneys. One of the key criticisms of Judge Lance Ito's conduct of the O.J. Simpson trial was his failure to regulate the out-of-court comments of the attorneys. Ito justified his failure to gag the lawyers by noting that California had not adopted a rule limiting attorney speech, but most commentators agreed that Ito, as the trial judge, did not need a bar association or state supreme court rule to provide him with the power to prohibit prejudicial statements by the lawyers. In fact, during the subsequent civil lawsuit brought against Simpson by the families of the victims, Judge Hiroshi Fujisaki imposed a wide-ranging gag order on all trial participants, including the lawyers.

If an attorney violates a gag order, the result can be a contempt of court conviction, just as when a journalist violates a court order. For example, in 1995 the Second U.S. Circuit Court of Appeals upheld the criminal contempt conviction of Bruce Cutler, attorney for alleged organized crime boss John Gotti, because he had vio-

lated a trial court order prohibiting extrajudicial statements by attorneys if there was a "reasonable likelihood" that such statements would interfere with a fair trial. The trial court had found that Cutler knowingly and willfully violated its order by repeatedly speaking to journalists. Cutler was sentenced to ninety days of house arrest, three years of probation and 180 days suspension from the practice of law in the Eastern District of New York.[77]

Gag orders on lawyers, however, have been struck down when they were found to be overbroad or when the trial judge failed to consider alternative measures for protecting the defendant's right to a fair trial. In a case resulting from the trial of the people accused of the 1993 bombing of the World Trade Center, the Second U.S. Circuit Court of Appeals vacated a gag order prohibiting the attorneys from publicly discussing any aspect of the case. The trial judge had issued the blanket order without ever considering whether less restrictive means were available to protect the defendants' fair trial rights, the appeals court said.[78] In 1986, a sweeping order prohibiting attorneys from "any discussion of this case with the news media," including telling reporters what time court was to convene, was overturned as "vague and overbroad" by a New York appeals court.[79] The following year, a trial judge's order banning "any public statement" to the media during a sensational murder trial was declared unconstitutional because, first, it prohibited all statements, not just prejudicial ones, and second, the judge had failed to consider whether there were other measures that might have ensured the defendant's fair trial rights.[80]

As the Michael Jackson case illustrated, occasionally judges issue gag orders aimed at witnesses. Just as with restrictions on attorney speech, such orders will be upheld if they are necessary to protect the defendant's right to a fair trial and alternative measures are not available. In 1984, a U.S. district judge in North Carolina issued an order prohibiting all potential witnesses in a murder trial from making "any extrajudicial statement relating to the testimony in this case that such potential witnesses may give, or relating to any of the parties or issues such potential witnesses expect or should reasonably expect to be involved in this case, or relating to the events leading up to and culminating" in the crime. The order specifically forbade potential witnesses from giving interviews to the press relating to those same topics. The case involved the trial of Ku Klux Klan and Nazi party members for the shooting deaths of

---

[75] Gentile v. State Bar of Nevada, 501 U.S. 1030, 1074 (1991).

[76] *Id.* at 1048.

[77] United States v. Cutler, 58 F.3d 825, 828 (2d Cir. 1995). This case provides an excellent example of the collateral bar rule at work. The appeals court upheld Cutler's contempt conviction but refused to consider the constitutionality of the gag order since Cutler had violated it without first seeking appellate review.

[78] United States v. Salameh, 992 F.2d 445 (2d Cir. 1993).

[79] NBC v. Cooperman, 501 N.Y.S.2d 405 (App. Div. 1986).

[80] Connecticut Magazine v. Moraghan, 676 F. Supp. 38 (D. Conn. 1987). *See also In re* New York Times Co., 878 F.2d 67 (2d Cir. 1989); Levine v. United States Dist. Court, 764 F.2d 590 (9th Cir. 1985); United States v. Marcana Garcia, 456 F. Supp. 1354 (D.P.R. 1978); Breiner v. Takao, 835 P.2d 637 (Haw. 1992).

five people in Greensboro. In upholding the gag order, the U.S. Court of Appeals for the Fourth Circuit noted that there had already been "tremendous publicity" and that many of the potential witnesses were relatives of the victims. The appellate court also agreed with the trial judge that alternative remedies, such as change of venue, jury admonitions or sequestration, would be ineffective or impractical.[81]

In 1990, the Supreme Court upheld the right of a grand jury witness to publish his own testimony after the grand jury term had ended. A grand jury is an investigative body that does not decide a person's guilt or innocence but, instead, determines if there is sufficient evidence to indict, or formally charge, someone with a crime. Grand juries meet in secret, and the grand jurors themselves are prohibited from revealing what goes on during the proceedings. Florida law took the traditional grand jury secrecy even further, however, by prohibiting witnesses from disclosing their own testimony.

Because of articles he had written, Michael Smith, a reporter for the *Charlotte Herald-News*, was called to testify before a grand jury investigating alleged wrongdoing in the State Attorney's Office and Sheriff's Department in Charlotte County. The prosecutor warned Smith that Florida law prohibited him from revealing his own testimony. After the grand jury term ended, Smith wanted to use his testimony in his writing and claimed he had a First Amendment right to do so. Noting that the information Smith wanted to publish related to government misconduct and thus constituted "speech which has traditionally been recognized as lying at the core of the First Amendment," the Supreme Court unanimously held the Florida law unconstitutional.[82] Its opinion was narrow, however, restricted solely to a witness publishing his *own* testimony *after* the grand jury term ended.

Occasionally judges also try to gag defendants, with mixed results. Some appellate courts have struck down gag orders on defendants using the same test applied to the media in *Nebraska Press Association* while others have upheld restrictions on defendants' speech by applying the *Gentile* standard. For example, the Sixth Circuit used the *Nebraska Press* test to strike down a gag order that prohibited a congressman, on trial for mail and bank fraud, from commenting publicly on his own case outside of Congress. In *United States v. Ford* the court wrote:

We see no legitimate reasons for a lower threshold standard for individuals, including defendants, seeking to express themselves outside of court than for the press.... A criminal defendant awaiting trial in a controversial case has the full power of government arrayed against him and the full spotlight of media attention focused upon him. The defendant's interest in replying to the charges and to the associated adverse publicity, thus, is at a peak.... The "accused has a First Amendment right to reply publicly to the prosecutor's charges, and the public has a right to hear that reply...."[83]

In contrast, the Fifth Circuit upheld a sweeping gag order in a high-profile, federal corruption and racketeering case involving former Louisiana Gov. Edwin W. Edwards, state Insurance Commissioner James Harvey Brown and others. The trial court had prohibited parties, lawyers and witnesses from giving "any extrajudicial statement or interview" to "any public communications media" that "could interfere with a fair trial or prejudice any defendant, the government, or the administration of justice," including statements "intended to influence public opinion regarding the merits of the case."[84] Commissioner Brown appealed the gag order to the Fifth U.S. Circuit Court of Appeals, which, in July 2000, upheld it, saying that if a trial court "determines that there is a 'substantial likelihood' (or perhaps even merely a 'reasonable likelihood,' a matter we do not reach) that extrajudicial commentary by trial participants will undermine a fair trial, then it may impose a gag order on the participants, as long as the order is also narrowly tailored and the least restrictive means available."[85] The U.S. Supreme Court refused to review that decision.[86] A few weeks after the Fifth Circuit ruled, former Gov. Edwards was fined $1,700 — $100 per word — for violating a similar gag order in a related case by discussing allegedly exculpatory evidence with reporters outside the courtroom.[87]

In the wake of the O.J. Simpson trial, media attempts to interview jurors and post-trial statements by jurors generated considerable controversy. Jurors, of course, are always prohibited from discussing the trial in which they are involved while it is going on, just as they are prohibited from reading, viewing or listening to news reports about the trial. Such during-trial restrictions on ju-

---

[81] *In re* Russell, 726 F.2d 1007, 1008-10 (4th Cir. 1984). *See also* South Bend Tribune v. Elkhart Circuit Court, 691 N.E.2d 200 (Ind. Ct. App. 1998) (upholding a gag order on participants in a murder trial).

[82] Butterworth v. Smith, 494 U.S. 624, 632 (1990). In a similar case, the Third U.S. Circuit Court of Appeals ruled that reporters who testified about the alleged misconduct of a Pennsylvania Supreme Court justice before a state Judicial Review Board could not be prohibited from revealing their own testimony. They could, however, be barred from revealing the testimony of other witnesses or information they overheard during their appearances before the board. First Amendment Coalition v. Judicial Inquiry & Review Bd., 784 F.2d 467 (3d Cir. 1986).

[83] 830 F.2d 596, 598-99 (6th Cir. 1987) (quoting Monroe H. Freedman & Janet Starwood, *Prior Restraints on Freedom of Expression by Defendants and Defense Attorneys:* Ratio Decidendi v. Obiter Dictum, 29 STAN. L. REV. 607, 618 (1977)). *See also* United States v. Krzyske, 836 F.2d 1013 (6th Cir.) (striking down a judge's ruling that a defendant could go free on bail as long as he promised not to discuss his views on income taxes with anyone other than his attorney); Ohio *ex rel.* Dispatch Printing Co. v. Golden, 442 N.E.2d 121 (Ohio Ct. App. 1982) (striking down a municipal judge's gag order on the defendant, as well as members of the defendant's immediate family and counsel).

[84] United States v. Brown, 218 F.3d 415, 418-19 (5th Cir. 2000).

[85] *Id.* at 428.

[86] 531 U.S. 1111 (2001) (denying cert.).

[87] *See* S.L. Alexander, *A Reality Check on Court/Media Relations*, 84 JUDICATURE 146 (2000).

rors are considered essential to preserving the integrity of the jury process. Questions arise, however, when judges impose restrictions on post-verdict juror speech. The two most common reasons for post-verdict restrictions are to protect jurors' privacy and to ensure the secrecy of jury deliberations. Judges have expressed special concern about jurors being asked to reveal the votes and comments of their fellow jurors who may refuse to be interviewed by the press.

The Supreme Court has never ruled on the constitutionality of restrictions on post-verdict juror interviews, but a number of lower courts have upheld narrowly tailored restrictions. For example, in the case discussed above in which the New Jersey Supreme Court struck down an order prohibiting publication of jurors' names, it upheld a ban on contacting the jurors who had been dismissed after failing to reach a verdict until after a new trial was held in the case.[88]

If the ban on juror interviews is overly broad, however, it is not likely to survive constitutional scrutiny. In 1991, for example, the Ohio Supreme Court struck down an order prohibiting anyone, including journalists, from discussing a highly publicized murder case with jurors. It said the order was unconstitutionally overbroad.[89] More than a decade earlier, the U.S. Court of Appeals for the Ninth Circuit had struck down a similar order requiring everyone, including the media to "stay away from the jurors."[90]

In 1982, the Fifth U.S. Circuit Court of Appeals struck down a trial judge's restriction on post-verdict interviews with jurors who had convicted two men of transporting illegal aliens. The order prohibited interviews without the permission of the court, and permission would be granted only on a showing of "good cause." When a newspaper and its reporter were denied permission to conduct interviews, they appealed to the Fifth Circuit, which declared the order unconstitutional, saying, "The first amendment right to gather news is 'good cause' enough."[91] But a year later the same court upheld a more limited order prohibiting journalists from asking jurors about the votes of their colleagues and from repeatedly attempting to interview jurors who had said they did not want to be interviewed.[92]

Sometimes restrictions on juror interviews will be modified or upheld in part by appellate courts in an attempt to balance the interests at stake. For example, in 1994 the Third U.S. Circuit Court of Appeals upheld a trial judge's order informing jurors that they were under no obligation to speak to journalists and banning journalists from asking a juror about the votes or statements of other jurors. The appellate court, however, struck down two other limitations the trial court had tried to impose on journalists: a ban

on repeated requests for an interview from any one juror and a requirement that if a juror asks to end an interview the reporter must immediately stop asking questions.[93]

In 1995, two federal district courts in California declared unconstitutional state laws designed to prevent jurors and witnesses from selling their stories to the media. The California legislature enacted the laws in response to the publicity surrounding the O.J. Simpson trial. One law made it a misdemeanor for a juror or ex-juror to accept a benefit of more than $50 to talk or write about his or her jury service until ninety days after the conclusion of the trial. It also prohibited anyone from paying a juror or ex-juror more than $50 for the juror's story. The other law prohibited crime witnesses from accepting payment for their stories until one year after the crime had occurred or, if a criminal prosecution had begun, until a final verdict was reached.

Michael Knox, one of the original jurors in the Simpson case who was dismissed part way through the trial, challenged the juror gag law. He wanted to write a book about his experiences, and the Los Angeles district attorney informed him and his publisher they would be prosecuted if they entered into a publishing agreement in violation of the new California law. The federal court ruled that the law was a content-based prior restraint and was not narrowly tailored to serve a compelling government interest. Furthermore, it said the law was unconstitutionally overbroad and vague.[94] In the other case, a coalition of media organizations challenged the witness gag law as unconstitutional. The court agreed, holding that it violated both the U.S. and California constitutions.[95]

### Post-Publication Sanctions

Just as the Supreme Court has established constitutional limitations on judges' powers to gag the media, so too has the Court set up First Amendment barriers to post-publication punishment of the press for reporting about and commenting on the operation of the judicial system. Post-publication sanctions can be divided into two categories: contempt of court citations issued by judges and criminal penalties imposed by statutes for the publication of certain types of information.

**Contempt of Court.** Judges have the power to find people in contempt if they disobey court orders, show disrespect for the court or otherwise engage in conduct that interferes with the administration of justice. A contempt of court citation can result in a fine, imprisonment or both. Generally there are two types of contempt of court: civil and criminal.

A civil contempt citation is intended to be coercive, to force an

[88] State v. Neulander, 801 A.2d 255 (N.J. 2002).

[89] Ohio ex rel. Cincinnati Post v. Court of Common Pleas, 570 N.E.2d 1101 (Ohio 1991).

[90] United States v. Sherman, 581 F.2d 1358, 1360 (9th Cir. 1978).

[91] In re Express-News Corp., 695 F.2d 807, 810 (5th Cir. 1982).

[92] United States v. Harrelson, 713 F.2d 1114 (5th Cir. 1983).

[93] United States v. Antar, 38 F.3d 1348 (3d Cir. 1994).

[94] Dove Audio v. Lungren, No. CV 95-2570 RG (JRX), 1995 WL 432631 (C.D. Cal., June 14, 1995).

[95] California First Amendment Coalition v. Lungren, No. C 95-0440-FMS, 1995 U.S. Dist. LEXIS 11655 (N.D. Cal., Aug. 9, 1995).

individual to obey a court order. For example, if a judge orders a reporter to reveal a confidential source and the journalist refuses, the judge might cite the journalist for civil contempt and order the reporter jailed until the source is named. It is also possible that the judge might impose a fine, say $500 per day for as long as the refusal to testify continues. Civil contempt, since it is designed to be coercive not punitive, is not at issue here but is of concern in Chapter 15, which discusses confidential sources.

Criminal contempt, on the other hand, is intended to punish disobedience of a court order or disrespect for or obstruction of the judicial process. If a reporter tries to interview potential jurors during jury selection, for example, the reporter could be held in criminal contempt of court. Or, if a judge issues a gag order prohibiting the media from publishing certain information and a newspaper disobeys that order, the newspaper, the journalists involved or both could be held in criminal contempt and punished. Some judges have used their criminal contempt powers to punish criticism of and commentary about their own actions and the judicial process. In the 1940s, however, the Supreme Court imposed strict limitations on judges' ability to use contempt to punish critics. It ruled that out-of-court commentary could not be punished as contempt of court unless it presented a "clear and present danger" of interfering with the fair administration of justice.

The first such case to reach the Supreme Court was a joinder of two appeals, *Bridges v. California* and *Times Mirror Co. v. Superior Court*.[96] In the first case, labor leader Harry Bridges was held in contempt after he publicly called a judge's ruling in a labor dispute "outrageous" and threatened to tie up the docks on the Pacific coast if the judicial order against him and his union was enforced. In the second case, the *Los Angeles Times* was held in contempt for a series of anti-union editorials, which, the trial court contended, were aimed at influencing judicial decisions in pending labor disputes. Ironically, the Supreme Court used the same opinion to strike down the contempt convictions of both militant labor leader Bridges and the anti-union *Los Angeles Times*.

Writing for a five-member majority, Justice Hugo Black summarily dismissed the argument that judges' contempt powers were an appropriate tool for preserving public respect for the courts. "The assumption," he wrote, "that respect for the judiciary can be won by shielding judges from published criticism wrongly appraises the character of American public opinion.... [A]n enforced silence ... would probably engender resentment, suspicion, and contempt more than it would enhance respect."[97] Resurrecting the old "clear and present danger test," which the Court had first used in World War I sedition cases,[98] Black wrote that judges could punish commentary on pending cases only if such publications presented an imminent and extremely serious threat to justice.

Just what a formidable obstacle the clear and present danger test presented to judges attempting to punish their critics was demonstrated in 1946 and 1947 when the Supreme Court heard two more contempt cases. In the first, *Pennekamp v. Florida*, the *Miami Herald* and its editor, John D. Pennekamp, were held in contempt and fined for editorials that accused the courts of working harder to protect criminals than to protect law-abiding citizens. This time the Court unanimously struck down the contempt citations, declaring, "Free discussion of the problems of society is a cardinal principle of Americanism — a principle which all are zealous to preserve."[99]

The second case, *Craig v. Harney*, resulted from a contempt citation against the *Corpus Christi Caller-Times* for criticizing a judge who had issued a directed verdict in a civil case. Admitting that the offending articles were unfair and contained significant errors, the Supreme Court said: "But inaccuracies in reporting are commonplace. Certainly a reporter could not be laid by the heels for contempt because he missed the essential point in a trial or failed to summarize the issues to accord with the views of the judge who sat on the case."[100]

*Bridges*, *Pennekamp* and *Craig* have virtually eliminated the ability of judges to punish criticism of themselves or general commentary on the judicial system. It's important to remember, however, that none of those cases involved efforts to influence jury decisions, disobedience of court orders or in-courtroom disruptions of judicial proceedings. Judges can and do continue to use their contempt powers to punish such conduct, whether the perpetrator is a journalist or not.

**State Statutes.** It is not unusual for state laws to declare certain information relating to the justice system — such as juvenile offender, adoption and involuntary commitment records — confidential. Such laws generally prohibit government officials from releasing the information to unauthorized individuals, including journalists. Some states, however, have tried to go even further in protecting confidentiality by enacting laws that penalize the media for publishing certain information relating to the courts. In two cases in the 1970s, the Supreme Court ruled such state laws unconstitutional, holding that government could not punish the publication of truthful information that had been lawfully obtained unless there was a compelling need to do so.

In the first case, the *Virginian Pilot* was fined $500 for violating a state statute that made it a crime to publish information about the confidential proceedings of the Virginia Judicial Inquiry and Review Commission. The commission, established to hear complaints about judges' misconduct or disabilities, conducted its proceedings in secret to encourage the public to file complaints and to protect judges from the reputational harm that could result

---

96 314 U.S. 252 (1941).

97 *Id.* at 270-71.

98 *See* Schenck v. United States, 249 U.S. 47 (1919); Abrams v. United States, 250 U.S. 616 (1919).

99 328 U.S. 331, 346 (1946).

100 331 U.S. 367, 374-75 (1947).

from unwarranted complaints. The *Virginian Pilot* identified a judge who was being investigated and accurately reported that the commission had not filed a formal complaint against the judge. Acknowledging that the commission could meet in secret and keep its records confidential, a unanimous Supreme Court said in *Landmark Communications v. Virginia*, that imposing criminal sanctions on the publication of such information, which "lies near the core of the First Amendment," was unconstitutional.[101]

The following year, the Court struck down a West Virginia law that made it a crime for newspapers to publish the names of youths charged as juvenile offenders unless they first obtained written approval from the juvenile court. Two Charleston papers were indicted for identifying a fourteen-year-old who had shot and killed a classmate. The name of the youth was obtained through interviews with witnesses, the police and an assistant prosecuting attorney. Once again the Supreme Court unanimously ruled in favor of the press. The newspapers had argued that the statute imposed a prior restraint on publication since it required a judge's permission to publish a juvenile's name. In *Smith v. Daily Mail Publishing Co.*, the Supreme Court said it didn't matter whether the law was labeled prior restraint or not since "First Amendment protection reaches beyond prior restraints."[102]

Relying on its decision the previous year in *Landmark Communications*, the Court said that publication of lawfully obtained, truthful information could be punished only "to further a state interest of the highest order." While protecting the anonymity of juvenile offenders to enhance their chances of rehabilitation was an important interest, the Court held it was not sufficient to justify the infringement of First Amendment rights caused by imposing criminal sanctions for the publication of true information. It noted that while every state had a law providing for the confidentiality of juvenile proceedings, only five states "impose criminal penalties on nonparties for publication of the identity of the juvenile." Finally, the Court said the statute didn't even accomplish its goal since it only punished newspaper publication of juveniles' names. Radio stations in the area had broadcast the youth's name but were not indicted because the statute did not prohibit broadcasts.[103]

### Court Closures

As noted, the Supreme Court in *Sheppard v. Maxwell* did not suggest that gag orders on the press be used as a remedy for prejudicial publicity. Nor did it suggest closing the courtroom door to the press and public. In fact, in *Sheppard* it specifically reiterated its antipathy toward judicial secrecy:

The principle that justice cannot survive behind walls of silence has long been reflected in the "Anglo-American distrust for secret trials...." The press does not simply publish information about trials but guards against the miscarriage of justice by subjecting the police, prosecutors, and judicial processes to extensive public scrutiny and criticism. This Court has, therefore, been unwilling to place any direct limitations on the freedom traditionally exercised by the news media for "[w]hat transpires in the court room is public property."[104]

But, like gag orders, court closures became popular tools with judges seeking to avoid the problems they believed media coverage of trials caused. A study by the Reporters Committee for Freedom of the Press identified sixty-one instances of closures of court proceedings or records between 1967 and 1975. As with gag orders in that same period, the number of recorded closures steadily climbed, reaching a peak of twenty-five in 1975.[105] The 1976 report of the Twentieth Century Fund's Task Force on Justice, Publicity and the First Amendment lamented judges' "excessive reliance on secrecy" in the years following *Sheppard*.[106]

**Criminal Trials.** In 1980, however, the Supreme Court began limiting the ability of judges to shut off access to their courtrooms by ruling in *Richmond Newspapers v. Virginia*[107] that the press and public have a First Amendment right to attend criminal trials. It may seem odd that the Court used the First Amendment's guarantee of freedom of the press as a source of access rights, especially since the Sixth Amendment specifically provides for public trials. But it had earlier ruled that the Sixth Amendment's guarantee of a public trial, like its other guarantees of a speedy trial by an impartial jury in the district in which the crime was committed, was a right that was personal to the defendant.[108] If the defendant agreed to give up his constitutional right to a public trial, then the press or members of the public could not claim a Sixth Amendment violation.

In 1978, John Paul Stevenson, charged with murdering a hotel manager, *did* waive his right to a public trial. The prosecutor said he had no objections to closure; so Hanover County, Virginia, Circuit Court Judge Richard Taylor agreed to conduct Stevenson's trial behind closed doors.

It's easy to understand why Stevenson's attorney moved to close the trial and why Judge Taylor and the prosecution agreed. This was to be Stevenson's fourth trial on the same charge. The Virginia Supreme Court had overturned his 1976 conviction because of the use of inadmissible evidence. A second trial ended in

---

[101] 435 U.S. 829, 839 (1978).

[102] 443 U.S. 97, 101 (1979).

[103] *Id.* at 103-05. Since *Smith v. Daily Mail*, at least two other state laws prohibiting the publication of juvenile offenders' names have been declared unconstitutional. *See* Florida Publishing Co. v. Morgan, 322 S.E.2d 233 (Ga. 1984); *In re* Johnson, 5 Media L. Rep. (BNA) 2512 (S.C. Fam. Ct. 1980).

[104] 384 U.S. 333, 349-50 (1966) (citations omitted) (quoting *In re* Oliver, 333 U.S. 257, 268 (1948), and Craig v. Harney, 331 U.S. 367, 374 (1947)).

[105] Landau, *supra* note 32, at 57.

[106] TWENTIETH CENTURY FUND TASK FORCE, *supra* note 34, at 5.

[107] 448 U.S. 555 (1980).

[108] Gannett Co., Inc. v. DePasquale, 443 U.S. 368 (1979).

## When May a Judicial Proceeding Be Closed?

A judge must follow a specific path to determine whether a judicial proceeding may be closed:

**First**, the judge must determine whether a First Amendment right of access attaches to the particular type of proceeding. The Supreme Court has held that there is a right of access to criminal trials and preliminary hearings, but if a judge is evaluating a closure motion for a different type of proceeding, the judge must consider:
- whether this type of proceeding has historically been open to the public (the experience test); and
- whether public access plays a significant positive role in the functioning of the particular proceeding in question (the logic test).

**Second**, if the judge decides, as a result of the experience and logic tests, that a right of access exists, the judge must determine whether that right can be overcome by a compelling interest. To close the courtroom, the judge must issue specific, written findings that:
- closure is essential to preserve higher values, such as the defendant's fair trial rights or jurors' or victims' privacy rights; and
- the closure is narrowly tailored, that is, as brief as possible to serve the interest.

**Third**, if the overriding interest justifying closure is the defendant's right to a fair trial, the judge must find that:
- there is a substantial probability that an open proceeding will interfere with that right;
- closure will be effective in protecting the right; and
- there are no reasonable alternatives to closure.

---

a mistrial when one of the jurors had to be excused for illness and no alternate was available. A third trial, which Judge Taylor also agreed to close, ended in a mistrial when one prospective juror told others about Stevenson's previous trials.

After Judge Taylor ordered the fourth trial closed, Richmond Newspapers protested and asked for a hearing, which Judge Taylor conducted in secret. At the conclusion of the hearing, Taylor stuck by his decision that the extraordinary circumstances justified a closed trial. The next day Judge Taylor dismissed the jury, ruled the state had not presented sufficient evidence to justify a guilty verdict and declared Stevenson not guilty. The decision was reported in a two-sentence order, and, since the trial had been conducted behind closed doors, there was no way for the public to determine if Judge Taylor's conclusion was justified.

Richmond Newspapers appealed the trial closure to the Virginia Supreme Court, which refused to overturn Judge Taylor's decision. The U.S. Supreme Court, however, ruled 7-1 that the closure was unconstitutional. (Justice Lewis Powell, a Virginian, did not participate in the decision because he was acquainted with some of the people involved in the case.) As in *Nebraska Press Association*, the justices in *Richmond Newspapers* were divided over their reasoning. The majority of seven produced six different opinions, with no opinion garnering the endorsement of more than three justices.

Chief Justice Burger, joined by Justices White and Stevens, rested his opinion on the history and tradition of open trials in the Anglo-American justice system. Contending that trials had been open "to all who care to observe" since before the Norman

Conquest, Burger said open trials discouraged perjury and official misconduct, inspired public confidence in the justice system, and have "significant community therapeutic value," helping to defuse community outrage over crime. Although the First Amendment contains no express language regarding access to criminal proceedings, Burger wrote that the guarantees of freedom of speech and press and the rights to assemble and petition the government all "share a common core purpose of assuring freedom of communication on matters relating to the functioning of government. Plainly it would be difficult to single out any aspect of government of higher concern and importance to the people than the manner in which criminal trials are conducted." The public right of access to a criminal trial can be overcome only by "an overriding interest," Burger concluded, and only if the trial judge finds that "alternative solutions" are inadequate to ensure fairness. The Chief Justice expressly declined to provide examples of overriding interests that might justify closure, saying Judge Taylor had "made no findings to support closure [and] no inquiry ... as to whether alternative solutions would have met the need to ensure fairness."[109]

In a concurring opinion, which later became very influential in the development of a test for determining when courtrooms could be closed, Justice Brennan, joined by Justice Marshall, stressed the structural value of open courts, that is, the role openness plays in self-government. "[P]ublic access to trials acts as an important check, akin in purpose to the other checks and balances that infuse our system of government," Brennan wrote. Open tri-

---

[109] 448 U.S. at 564-81.

als, he said, "play a fundamental role" in ensuring defendants receive fair trials and in assuring the public that "procedural rights are respected, and that justice is afforded equally. Closed trials breed suspicion of prejudice and arbitrariness, which in turn spawns disrespect for law."[110]

Two years after *Richmond Newspapers*, the Supreme Court ruled 6-3 that a blanket rule requiring courtroom closure during the testimony of minor victims in sex crime cases violated the First Amendment.[111] The case began in 1979 when a trial judge in Norfolk County, Massachusetts, closed the trial of a man charged with raping three girls, two sixteen-year-olds and one seventeen-year-old. The judge relied on a state statute, which he interpreted as mandating closure of the entire trial. On appeal, the Supreme Judicial Court of Massachusetts interpreted the statute more narrowly than the trial judge, holding that it only required closure during the testimony of minor sex crime victims. The *Boston Globe* appealed to the Supreme Court.

In *Globe Newspaper Co. v. Superior Court*, Justice Brennan, for the majority, wrote that closure of criminal trials had to be determined case by case on the basis of a "compelling governmental interest" and had to be "narrowly tailored to serve that interest." While Brennan conceded that protecting "minor victims of sex crimes from further trauma and embarrassment" was a compelling interest, it did not justify a *mandatory* closure law since such a measure was not narrowly tailored. Case-by-case determinations were needed to consider such factors as "the minor victim's age, psychological maturity and understanding, the nature of the crime, the desires of the victim, and the interests of parents and relatives." Brennan questioned the state's second justification for the law — that closure encouraged minor victims to come forward and testify — because there was no empirical evidence to support the claim that mandatory closure accomplished that goal. Furthermore, since trial transcripts were open to the public, there was no way to guarantee a victim's testimony would remain secret.[112]

In a dissenting opinion, Chief Justice Burger focused again on history, contending, "There is clearly a long history of exclusion of the public from trials involving sexual assaults, particularly those against minors." Because a transcript of the trial was publicly available, Burger argued, the Massachusetts law did not deny the press or public access to information. Therefore, the Chief Justice contended that the only questions were "whether the restrictions imposed are reasonable and whether the interests of the Commonwealth override the very limited incidental effects of the law on First Amendment rights." Closing a trial during a child victim's testimony rationally served the state's interest, Burger concluded.[113]

Continuing the trend of opening the nation's courtrooms to the press and public, the Supreme Court ruled in 1984 that jury selection is an integral part of a criminal trial and, therefore, is subject to the First Amendment presumption of access. *Press-Enterprise Co. v. Riverside County Superior Court* (which is known as *Press-Enterprise I* to distinguish it from a later case of the same name) began when a California judge closed almost six weeks of the *voir dire* — jury selection proceedings — in a rape and murder trial involving a teenage victim. After the defendant was convicted and sentenced to death, the judge still refused to release the transcript of the *voir dire*, saying that "some of the jurors had some special experiences in sensitive areas that do not appear to be appropriate for public discussion."[114] After failing to obtain relief from the California appellate courts, the *Press-Enterprise* petitioned the Supreme Court to grant *certiorari*, which it did.

The Court unanimously ruled that closure of the *voir dire* violated the First Amendment. Chief Justice Burger, who wrote the opinion of the Court, used both the historical arguments he had articulated in *Richmond Newspapers* and the structural/functional arguments of Justice Brennan. The "historical evidence," he wrote, indicates that "since the development of trial by jury, the process of selection of jurors has presumptively been a public process with exceptions only for good cause shown." As for the functional argument, he said: "The open trial thus plays as important a role in the administration of justice today as it did for centuries before our separation from England.... Openness ... enhances both the basic fairness of the criminal trial and the appearance of fairness so essential to public confidence in the system."[115]

Just as Justice Brennan had held in *Globe Newspaper Co.*, the Chief Justice in *Press-Enterprise I* said that the presumption of open *voir dire* proceedings "may be overcome only by an overriding interest based on findings that closure is essential to preserve higher values and is narrowly tailored to serve that interest." Furthermore, the trial judge must present specific, written findings to justify closure and demonstrate that alternatives to closure are not available to protect the interests at stake, Burger wrote. In this case, the trial judge failed to present findings supporting his conclusion that closure was necessary to protect the defendant's fair trial rights and the jurors' privacy rights. Furthermore, the judge "failed to consider whether alternatives were available to protect the interests of the prospective jurors."[116]

**Other Criminal Proceedings.** In 1986, the Supreme Court extended the First Amendment presumption of openness to a criminal pretrial proceeding, specifically a preliminary hearing. In some states a preliminary hearing is known as a "show-cause" hearing; it is designed to determine if the government has sufficient evidence

---

110 *Id*. at 595-96 (Brennan, J., concurring).

111 Globe Newspaper Co. v. Superior Court, 457 U.S. 596 (1982).

112 *Id*. at 607-10.

113 *Id*. at 614-16 (Burger, C.J., dissenting).

114 464 U.S. 501, 504 (1984).

115 *Id*. at 505, 508.

116 *Id*. at 510-11.

to bind a defendant over for trial. *Press-Enterprise v. Riverside County Superior Court*, generally known as *Press-Enterprise II*, resulted from the closure of a forty-one-day preliminary hearing in the case of Robert Diaz, a nurse accused of murdering twelve patients by administering massive doses of a heart drug.[117] The case required the Court to determine whether the constitutional right of access extended to other types of judicial proceedings as well.

As he had in *Press-Enterprise I*, Chief Justice Burger, again writing for the majority, combined the historical justifications he relied upon in *Richmond Newspapers* with Justice Brennan's concern for the structural value of openness to establish a two-pronged test for deciding when a constitutional right of access attaches to a particular type of judicial proceeding.

The preliminary hearing at issue in *Press-Enterprise II* passed the so-called test "of experience and logic." First, the Court said, "there has been a tradition of accessibility to preliminary hearings of the type conducted in California," and second, "preliminary hearings are sufficiently like a trial" to justify the conclusion that openness was necessary for the proper functioning of the process. Burger noted that the preliminary hearing was often the "final and most important" criminal proceeding since so few cases proceed to trial and, therefore, often presented the only opportunity for the public to observe the criminal justice system. Furthermore, the absence of a jury at a preliminary hearing made public and press attendance even more important to protect "'against the corrupt or overzealous prosecutor and against the compliant, biased, or eccentric judge.'"[118]

Deciding that a First Amendment right of access attached to the preliminary hearing was only the first step in the analysis, however, since, as the Court had noted in all of its previous cases, that right was a qualified one and could be overcome by an overriding or compelling interest. A trial judge, therefore, before closing such a proceeding must provide "specific, on the record findings" that "'closure is essential to preserve higher values and is narrowly tailored to serve that interest.'" Furthermore, the Court said that, if the overriding interest to be served by closure was the defendant's right to a fair trial, a judge had to find that there was "a substantial probability" of prejudice resulting from an open proceeding, that closure would prevent the harm and that reasonable alternatives to closure would not protect the defendant's rights.[119]

The closure test articulated by the Court in *Press-Enterprise II* is similar to the gag order test it used in *Nebraska Press Association*, both emphasizing the judge's responsibility to evaluate the effectiveness of the order and to try all other alternatives before infringing on First Amendment rights. A few court closure cases demonstrate how the *Press-Enterprise II* test has been applied to

a variety of different types of proceedings.

In 1989, a federal magistrate in Charlotte, North Carolina, agreed to close a pretrial change of venue hearing in the well-publicized fraud case involving televangelist Jim Bakker and his partner in the PTL religious organization, Richard Dortch. Attorneys for Bakker and Dortch had sought the change of venue claiming adverse pretrial publicity in the Charlotte area. The magistrate closed the hearing, stating that "permitting the public and press to attend this hearing would pose the risk that the alleged prejudicial publicity of which the Defendants complain would be republished and re-aired in the print and electronic media."[120] Such republication would impair the defendants' right to a fair trial, the magistrate concluded. The chief judge for the Western District of North Carolina affirmed the magistrate's order.

A number of media organizations appealed to the Fourth Circuit, which declared the closure unconstitutional. As for the first part of the closure test — determining if a right of access attaches to the particular type of proceeding at issue — the court, citing *Press Enterprise II*, simply assumed that there was a presumptive right of access to all criminal trial and pretrial proceedings, including change of venue hearings. Since the compelling interest to be served by closure was the defendants' fair trial rights, the court jumped to the last portion of the *Press-Enterprise II* test and evaluated, first, whether there was a substantial probability that an open hearing would prejudice the defendants' rights and, second, whether closure would prevent the harm. The court said it was "highly dubious" that "republication of portions of publicity earlier put in the public domain" would cause the defendants' rights to be "decisively prejudiced" beyond the harm already done by the initial publications. More importantly, it said the magistrate "was simply wrong in thinking that, as a practical matter, closure would prevent that result.... [A]ny press barrage and frenzy occasioned by an open hearing would be as nothing to the firestorms of purely speculative 'republications' that would occur if press access to the hearing is denied." Finally, the court said the magistrate gave "too short shrift" to alternatives to closure, especially *voir dire*. Several highly publicized cases, such as the Watergate, ABSCAM and John DeLorean trials, had demonstrated that juries were "unaffected (indeed, in some instances, blissfully unaware of or untouched) by that publicity."[121]

In another highly publicized case, the Ninth U.S. Circuit Court of Appeals ruled in 1988 that closure of a pretrial detention hearing violated the First Amendment.[122] Stella Nickell was charged with murdering her husband and a woman whom she did not know by placing poison in Excedrin capsules on store shelves to make her husband's death look like a random product-tampering murder. The detention hearing was to determine whether she would be

---

[117] 478 U.S. 1 (1986).

[118] *Id*. at 10-13 (quoting Duncan v. Louisiana, 391 U.S. 145, 156 (1968)).

[119] *Id*. at 13-14 (quoting Press-Enterprise v. Riverside County Superior Court (I), 464 U.S. 501, 510 (1984)). *See also* El Vocero de Puerto Rico v. Puerto Rico, 508 U.S. 147 (1993) (per curiam).

[120] *In re* Charlotte Observer, 882 F.2d 850, 851 (4th Cir. 1989).

[121] *Id*. at 852-55.

[122] Seattle Times v. United States Dist. Court, 845 F.2d 1513 (9th Cir. 1988).

released pending her trial.

Applying the first portion of the *Press-Enterprise II* test, the Ninth Circuit acknowledged that pretrial detention hearings were relatively new proceedings, and thus, there was no history of public access. However, it said the structural arguments in favor of openness were sufficient to support a constitutional right of access to the proceeding. The court then concluded that there was inadequate evidence that an open detention hearing would prejudice Nickell's right to a fair trial and that the trial judge had not sufficiently considered alternatives to closure.

Based on both the First Amendment right of access and a state constitutional provision guaranteeing open courts, a North Carolina trial court in 1994 refused to close pretrial evidence suppression hearings in the case resulting from the murder of Michael Jordan's father, James Jordan.[123] Evidence suppression hearings present special problems since their sole purpose is to determine whether certain evidence will ever be presented to a jury. If evidence, say an allegedly coerced confession or the results of an allegedly illegal wiretap, is declared inadmissible during a public hearing, the media are free to report on its existence. The fear, then, is that potential jurors will learn about the evidence, remember it and perhaps be influenced by it even though it was never used in court.

On the other hand, evidentiary hearings are often crucial to the outcome of a criminal case because they can determine the strength of the prosecution's case. If, for example, a judge refuses to suppress a particularly damaging piece of evidence, such as a confession or the results of certain laboratory tests, the case against the defendant may be so strong that he or she decides to plead guilty and no trial is ever held. Furthermore, evidentiary hearings often deal with allegations of police and prosecutorial misconduct, which are important to bring to public attention.

In 1979, the Supreme Court held that the Sixth Amendment did not provide the press and public with a right to attend pretrial evidence suppression hearings.[124] That case, however, preceded *Richmond Newspapers* and was based not on the First Amendment but on the Sixth Amendment. Since the Supreme Court began articulating a broad First Amendment right of access to judicial proceedings, many lower courts have reached the same conclusion as did the North Carolina trial court in the James Jordan murder case and have recognized a constitutional right of access to pretrial evidentiary hearings.[125]

Courts have also held that a constitutional right of access attaches to numerous other types of criminal proceedings, including plea and sentencing hearings;[126] bail hearings;[127] a post-trial examination of jurors about potential misconduct;[128] a hearing on a motion to compel a defendant to give a blood sample for an HIV test;[129] and a hearing on a criminal defendant's recusal motion (asking the judge to remove himself from the case).[130] However, some types of criminal proceedings, most notably grand jury proceedings, have historically been conducted behind closed doors, and courts continue to rule that the First Amendment presumption of openness does not apply.[131] This point was underscored in 1998 when the D.C. Court of Appeals ruled that the media did not have a right of access to court proceedings and documents related to the grand jury investigation of the Monica Lewinsky-President Clinton affair.[132]

**Juvenile Proceedings.** Juvenile proceedings historically were closed to the public. The primary goal of the juvenile justice system was considered rehabilitation rather than punishment. State laws, therefore, often provided for closed hearings and confidential records to avoid stigmatizing minors by making their identities and crimes known to the public. Prompted by a rash of high profile, serious crimes by juveniles during the 1990s, however, many states have now opened up their juvenile proceedings and records to the public and press, especially when the crimes involved would be felonies if committed by adults.

The Supreme Court has not ruled on whether the First Amendment right of access applies to juvenile proceedings. However, because there is a history of secrecy associated with juvenile proceedings and because many people who work with juvenile offenders believe confidentiality plays an important role in rehabilitation, several courts have held that the First Amendment right of access does not apply to such proceedings. For example, in 1981 the Vermont Supreme Court flatly declared, "[A] juvenile proceeding is so unlike a criminal prosecution that the limited right of access described in *Richmond Newspapers* does not govern."[133]

---

[123] North Carolina v. Demery, 22 Media L. Rep. (BNA) 2383 (N.C. Super. Ct. 1994).

[124] Gannett Co. v. DePasquale, 443 U.S. 368 (1979).

[125] *See, e.g.,* United States v. Klepfer, 734 F.2d 93 (2d Cir. 1984); Gannett Westchester Rockland Newspapers v. Lacava, 551 N.Y.S.2d 261 (Ct. App. 1990); New York v. Franklin, 22 Media L. Rep. (BNA) 1255 (N.Y. Crim. Ct. 1993); Ohio v. Nobles, 21 Media L. Rep. (BNA) 1500 (Ohio Ct. Cm. Pls. 1993).

[126] *See* United States v. Eppinger, 49 F.3d 1244 (7th Cir. 1995); United States v. Soussoudis, 807 F.2d 383 (4th Cir. 1986); United States v. Byrd, 812 F. Supp. 76 (D.S.C. 1992); Baltimore Sun Co. v. Colbert, 593 A.2d 224 (Md. 1991); New York Times v. Demakos, 529 N.Y.S.2d 97 (App. Div. 1988); Washington v. Campbell, 21 Media L. Rep. (BNA) 1895 (Wash. Super. Ct. 1993).

[127] *See In re* Globe Newspaper Co., 729 F.2d 47 (1st Cir. 1984); United States v. Chagra, 701 F.2d 354 (5th Cir. 1983).

[128] *See* United States v. Simone, 14 F.3d 833 (3d Cir. 1994). *But see* United States v. Edwards, 823 F.2d 111 (5th Cir. 1987).

[129] *See* Florida v. Jenkins, 21 Media L. Rep. (BNA) 2159 (Fla. Cir. Ct. 1993).

[130] *See* Glen Falls Newspapers, Inc. v. Berke, 614 N.Y.S.2d 628 (App. Div. 1994).

[131] *See, e.g., In re* Subpoena to Testify Before Grand Jury, 864 F.2d 1559 (11th Cir. 1989); *In re* Multicounty Grand Jury Proceedings, 847 P.2d 812 (Okla. Crim. App. 1993).

[132] *In re* Dow Jones & Co., 142 F.3d 496 (D.C. Cir. 1998).

[133] *In re* J.S., 438 A.2d 1125, 1128 (Vt. 1981). *See also In re* T.R., 556

On the other hand, some courts have found a constitutional right of public and press access to juvenile proceedings — either based on the First Amendment or on state constitutional provisions. In 1995, for example, the Tennessee Supreme Court ruled that the public has a qualified First Amendment right to attend the hearings at which juvenile court judges determine whether youths charged with crimes will be transferred to adult court for trial.[134] And both the Oregon and South Carolina supreme courts have interpreted their state constitutions to provide a qualified right of access to juvenile proceedings.[135]

State statutes have become an increasingly important source of access rights as more state legislatures have enacted laws declaring that juvenile proceedings shall be open to the public.[136] Some states — Florida and Arizona are two — provide that a judge can close a proceeding only if closure "would best serve the public interest and the welfare of the child"[137] or "to protect the best interests of a victim, a witness, the state, or a clear public interest."[138] About one-third of the states now require public proceedings when minors are charged with crimes that would constitute felonies by adults or with certain enumerated serious, violent crimes, such as street gang activity, murder, rape, kidnapping and arson.[139] A few states base openness on the age of the juvenile.[140] Illinois has a unique provision declaring juvenile hearings closed "except for the news media and the victim." The law also says that the court may prohibit anyone in attendance at a hearing from disclosing the juvenile's identity.[141] Despite the trend toward openness, about one-third of the states still provide that juvenile proceedings be closed.[142] In some of those states, though, the judge has the discretion to permit some individuals to attend the proceedings if they have "a proper interest in the case"[143] or "if their attendance is compatible with the best interests of the child."[144]

**Civil Proceedings.** Although the Supreme Court has not expressly ruled that civil trials are subject to the same First Amendment right of access as criminal proceedings, numerous lower courts, both state and federal, have held that the press and public enjoy a right of access to civil judicial proceedings. Some courts have based this right of access on the First Amendment, following the reasoning articulated by the Supreme Court in *Richmond Newspapers* and its progeny; others have found a common law or state constitutional basis for access; and still others have used a combination of constitutional and common law.

One of the most frequently cited cases involving access to civil proceedings is *Publicker Industries v. Cohen*,[145] decided by the U.S. Court of Appeals for the Third Circuit in 1984. Reporters for the *Philadelphia Inquirer* and *Wall Street Journal* appealed when they were denied access to hearings in a lawsuit resulting from a corporate proxy fight. The Third Circuit recognized both a constitutional and a common law right of access to civil proceedings, saying that "the public's right of access to civil trials and records is as well established as that of criminal proceedings and records."[146] Other courts have followed the Third Circuit's lead, finding a right of access to an array of civil proceedings.[147]

Not every type of civil proceeding, however, is open to the press and public. Like grand jury and juvenile proceedings, some types of civil hearings traditionally have been closed and remain closed

N.E.2d 439 (Ohio); Sherman Publishing Co. v. Goldberg, 443 A.2d 1252 (R.I. 1982); *In re* N.H.B., 769 P.2d 844 (Utah Ct. App. 1989).

[134] Tennessee v. James, 902 S.W.2d 911 (Tenn. 1995). *See also* Florida Publishing Co. v. Morgan, 322 S.E.2d 233 (Ga. 1984).

[135] Oregonian Publishing v. Deiz, 613 P.2d 23 (Or. 1980); *Ex parte* Columbia Newspapers, Inc., 333 S.E.2d 337 (S.C. 1985).

[136] *See, e.g.,* COLO. REV. STAT. § 19-1-106(2) (2001); MD. CODE ANN., CTS. & JUD. PROC. § 3-818 (2001); MICH. COMP. LAWS § 712A.17(7) (2002); MONT. CODE ANN. § 41-5-1502(7) (2001); NEV. REV. STAT. § 62.193(1) (2001); N.C. GEN. STAT. § 7B-2402 (2001); N.M. STAT. ANN. § 32A-2-16(B) (2001); TEX. FAM. CODE ANN. § 54.08 (2002).

[137] FLA. STAT. ANN. § 985.04 (2001).

[138] ARIZ. JUV. CT. R. 7(c) (2001).

[139] *See, e.g.,* CAL. WELF. & INST. CODE § 676 (2001); DEL. CODE ANN. tit. 10, § 1063(a) (2001); GA. CODE ANN. § 15-11-28(c) (2001); IDAHO CODE § 20-525 (2000); IND. CODE § 31-32-6-3 (2000); LA. REV. STAT. ANN. § 879(B) (2002); ME. REV. STAT. ANN. tit. 15, § 3307(2) (2001); MD. CODE ANN., CTS. & JUD. PROC. § 3-818 (2001); MASS. GEN. LAWS ANN. ch. 119, § 65 (2002); MINN. STAT. § 260.155(1) (2001); MO. REV. STAT. § 211.171(6) (2001); N.J. STAT. ANN. § 2A:4A-60 (1999) & N.J. COURT RULES, 1969 R. 5:19-2 (2002); PA. CONS. STAT. ANN. tit 42, §6336 (2002); S.D. CODIFIED LAWS § 26-7A-36 (2001); TENN. CODE ANN. § 37-1-153 (2001); UTAH CODE ANN. §78-3a-115 (2000); VA. CODE ANN. § 16.1-302 (2000).

[140] *See, e.g.,* KAN. STAT. ANN. § 38-1652 (2001) (open if the juvenile was 16 at the time of the offense); S.D. CODIFIED LAWS § 26-7A-36 (2001) (open if juvenile was 16 and the crime was violent or a drug felony); TEX. FAM. CODE ANN. § 54.08 (2002) (closed if juvenile is under 14 at the time of the hearing); UTAH CODE ANN. §78-3a-115 (2000) (open if juvenile is 14 and charged with a felony or is a repeat offender).

[141] 705 ILL. COMP. STAT. 405/1-5 (1998).

[142] ALA. CODE § 12-15-65(A) (2001); ALASKA STAT. § 47.10.070 (2001); CONN. GEN. STAT. ANN. § 46B-122 (2001); D.C. CODE ANN. § 16-2316(E) (2001); KY. REV. STAT. ANN. § 610.070(3) (Michie 2001); MISS. CODE ANN. §43-21-203(6) (2001); N.H. REV. STAT. ANN. § 169-B:34 (2000); N.D. CENT. CODE § 27-20-24(5) (2002); OKLA. STAT. ANN. tit. 10, § 7003-4.1 (2002); OR. UNIF. TR. CT. R. 3.180 (1998); R.I. GEN. LAWS § 14-1-30 (2001); S.C. CODE ANN. § 20-7-755 (2001); VT. STAT. ANN. tit. 33. § 5523(c) (2001); WASH. REV. CODE § 13.34.110 (2001); W. VA. CODE 49-5-2(I) (2001); WIS. STAT. § 48.299 (2001); WYO. STAT. § 14-6-224(b) (2001).

[143] ALA. CODE § 12-15-65(a) (2001).

[144] ALASKA STAT. § 47.10.070 (2001).

[145] 733 F.2d 1059 (3d Cir. 1984).

[146] *Id.* at 1066.

[147] *See, e.g.,* Newman v. Graddick, 696 F.2d 796 (11th Cir. 1983) (pretrial and post-trial hearings in a class action suit charging overcrowding in a state prison); NBC Subsidiary (KNBC-TV), Inc. v. Superior Court, 980 P.2d 337 (Cal. 1999) (proceedings held outside the jury's presence in a civil lawsuit against actor Clint Eastwood by his former companion); Barron v. Florida Freedom Newspapers, Inc., 531 So. 2d 113 (Fla. 1988) (divorce proceeding); *In re* Brown, 18 Media L. Rep. (BNA)1460 (Fla. Cir. Ct. 1990) (child custody hearing); Bingham v. Struve, 591 N.Y.S.2d 156 (1992) (libel trial); Hutchinson v. Luddy, 18 Media L. Rep. (BNA) 1071 (Pa. Super. Ct. 1990) (pretrial proceedings in a civil suit against a Catholic priest charged with sexual misconduct).

## Challenging a Courtroom Closure

Journalists need to be familiar with their First Amendment rights of access and be prepared and willing to protest closure motions. If faced with a motion to close a judicial proceeding, you should do the following:

- Raise your hand, stand and identify yourself as a reporter.
- Formally object to the closure.
- Request the judge hold a hearing at which your news organization's attorney can appear.
- Immediately call your editor so he or she can contact your attorney.
- Be sure to remain respectful as you are registering your objection.

Here's the statement the North Carolina Press Association recommends journalists use in protesting a closure motion:

Your honor, I respectfully request the opportunity to register on the record an objection to the motion to close this proceeding to the public, including the press. Our legal counsel has advised us that standards set forth in recent U.S. Supreme Court decisions regarding the constitutional right of access to judicial proceedings recognize the right to a hearing before the courtroom is closed. Therefore, I respectfully request such a hearing and a brief continuance so I can call our counsel to come to explain our position.

---

under state statutes. Involuntary commitment and adoption proceedings are two of the most commonly closed types of civil proceedings. And, just as with criminal proceedings, judges sometimes find that even when a right of access exists for a particular type of civil proceeding, that right can be overcome by a compelling interest as long as the closure is narrowly tailored to serve that interest. Two of the most common interests used to justify closing civil proceedings are preventing the disclosure of trade secrets and protecting individual privacy, especially if the litigation involves a child.[148]

Civil discovery proceedings have generated a number of access lawsuits. Discovery is the pretrial phase of a lawsuit during which the litigants attempt to collect the information they need from one another and from third party witnesses. Traditionally, discovery in civil litigation has not been open to the press and public. In fact, it is usually conducted in attorneys' offices rather than in public courthouses. Because there is no history of public access and because so much of the information gathered during discovery never becomes part of the official court record, judges often rule that there is no right of access to discovery proceedings during which depositions are taken.[149] There have been exceptions, however. In one case a federal district court held that representatives of the media should be allowed to attend sessions when depositions

from the New York mayor and a former police commissioner were being taken in a lawsuit against the city. Because of the great public interest in the case, the court ruled that four journalists be admitted to serve as pool representatives for the rest of the press.[150] During the antitrust suit the federal government filed against Microsoft in 1998, the D.C. Court of Appeals ruled that journalists were entitled to attend the depositions from several Microsoft employees, including CEO Bill Gates. It based its decision on a little-known 1913 statute, which provided that depositions taken as part of Sherman Antitrust Act lawsuits "shall be open to the public as freely as are the trials in open court."[151]

**Immigration Hearings.** In the wake of the September 11, 2001, attacks on the World Trade Center and Pentagon, a new access controversy arose, this one involving closed deportation proceedings. Ten days after the terrorist attacks, Chief Immigration Judge Michael J. Creppy issued a directive mandating closure of all "special interest" immigration hearings. "Special interest" cases are those in which sensitive or national security information may be presented, including any information related to terrorist investigations.

In December 2001, a Michigan immigration judge held a closed hearing to decide if Rabih Haddad, who had overstayed his tourist visa and was suspected of having connections to al-Qaeda, could be deported. Several media organizations, along with members of

---

[148] *See, e.g.,* Woven Elec. Corp. v. Advance Group, Inc., 19 Media L. Rep. (BNA) 1019 (4th Cir. 1991); *In re* Iowa Freedom of Info. Council, 724 F.2d 658 (8th Cir. 1983); Doe v. Indep. Sch. Dist., 933 F. Supp. 647 (S.D. Tex. 1996); Morgan v. Foretich, 528 A.2d 425 (D.C. 1987); Milo v. Milo, 6 Media L. Rep. (BNA) 2524 (Ohio Ct. C.P. 1981).

[149] *See* Amato v. Richmond, 157 F.R.D. 26 (E.D. Va. 1994); Kimberlin v. Quinlan, 145 F.R.D. 1 (D.D.C. 1992); Fort Myers Broad. Co. v. Nelson, 460 So. 2d 420 (Fla. Dist. Ct. App. 1984).

[150] Estate of Rosenbaum v. New York City, 21 Media L. Rep. (BNA) 1987 (E.D.N.Y. 1993). *See also* United States v. Didrichsons, 15 Media L. Rep. (BNA) 1869 (W.D. Wash. 1988); Avirgan v. Hull, 14 Media L. Rep. (BNA) 2136 (D.D.C. 1987).

[151] United States v. Microsoft Corp., 165 F.3d 952, 953 (D.C. Cir. 1999).

Haddad's family and the public, sued, contending the closed proceeding was unconstitutional. Both a federal trial court and the U.S. Court of Appeals for the Sixth Circuit agreed that the First Amendment right of access established in *Richmond Newspapers* applied, even though the immigration hearings were not actually court proceedings but administrative, quasi-judicial proceedings. The courts held that the Creppy directive requiring blanket closure of all "special interest" hearings was unconstitutional.[152]

A few months later, in a case involving closed deportation hearings in Newark, New Jersey, the Third Circuit issued a contradictory decision, ruling 2-1 that there was no constitutional right of access to such proceedings.[153] In May 2003, the U.S. Supreme Court refused to hear an appeal in the New Jersey case, thereby failing to resolve the conflict between the two circuits.[154]

### Denials of Access to Court Records

In the wake of *Richmond Newspapers v. Virginia*, many lower courts have presumed that the First Amendment right of access to court proceedings extends to the documents filed in connection with those proceedings. Indeed, the Supreme Court in deciding *Press Enterprise I* and *II* didn't distinguish between access to a judicial proceeding itself and access to at least one type of court record — the transcript of the proceeding. In *Press Enterprise II*, Chief Justice Burger wrote, "Denying the transcript of a 41-day preliminary hearing would frustrate what we characterized as the 'community therapeutic value' of openness."[155]

The Constitution, however, is not the only source of a right of access to court records. Many states have statutes providing for public access to judicial documents.[156] In addition, both state and federal courts have long recognized a common law right of access to judicial records. Two years before it decided *Richmond Newspapers*, the Supreme Court, in *Nixon v. Warner Communications, Inc.*, acknowledged that the common law created a "presumption ... of access to judicial records."[157]

Courts have ruled that this general right of access applies to a wide array of both criminal and civil court records. For example, in 2002 the Ohio Supreme Court held that a newspaper had a right to access jury lists and questionnaires in a murder case.[158] In 1983,

the Ninth U.S. Circuit Court of Appeals ruled that the pretrial motions and documents filed in the John DeLorean drug prosecution had to be available to the press and public. "There is no reason to distinguish between pretrial proceedings and the documents filed in regard to them," the court declared in finding a constitutional right of access.[159] The same court also held that there is a right of access to post-conviction records, including pre-sentencing reports and post-sentencing documents filed in connection with a motion to reduce a sentence.[160] In civil cases, courts have found a right of access to pleadings, documents filed in connection with pretrial motions, summary judgment papers and settlement agreements.[161]

Some types of court records, however, are not generally available to the press and public. For example, grand jury proceedings are closed as are most grand jury records, including transcripts and evidence. However, when a grand jury hands down an indictment, that becomes a public record although sometimes a court is allowed to seal an indictment until an arrest has been made. Adoption and involuntary commitment records are documents that are also often declared confidential by state law and, therefore, not available to the press and public.

As more judicial records are becoming available electronically *via* Web sites, growing concerns about privacy and potential misuse of such records are fueling efforts to restrict electronic access. In October 2002, the National Conference of Chief Justices and the Conference of State Court Administrators released a set of guidelines aimed at helping states develop rules regarding electronic access to their court records. The stated goal of the guidelines "is to provide maximum public accessibility to court records, consistent with constitutional or other provisions of law and taking into account public policy interests that are not always compatible with unrestricted access."[162]

The guidelines suggest, however, that states consider restricting online access to some types of public court records, such as addresses, phone numbers and other contact information for victims and witnesses in criminal cases and photographs of "involuntary nudity," which would then "only be accessible at the court facility."[163] The guidelines suggest shutting off all access to some

---

[152] Detroit Free Press v. Ashcroft, 195 F. Supp. 2d 948 (E.D. Mich. 2002), *aff'd*, 303 F.3d 681 (6th Cir. 2002).

[153] North Jersey Media Group, Inc. v. Ashcroft, 308 F.3d 198 (3d Cir. 2002), *cert. denied*, 538 U.S. 1056 (2003).

[154] North Jersey Media Group, Inc. v. Ashcroft, 538 U.S. 1056 (2003).

[155] 478 U.S. 1, 13 (1986).

[156] *See Judicial Records: A Guide to Access in State & Federal Courts*, NEWS MEDIA & L., Summer 1995, at 1.

[157] 435 U.S. 589, 602 (1978).

[158] Beacon Journal Publ'g Co. v. Bond, 781 N.E.2d 180 (Ohio 2002). *See also* People v. Mitchell, 592 N.W.2d 798 (Mich. Ct. App. 1999) (holding the press has a qualified right of post-verdict access to jurors' names and addresses).

[159] Associated Press v. United States Dist. Court, 705 F.2d 1143, 1145 (9th Cir. 1983).

[160] United States v. Schlette, 842 F.2d 1574 (9th Cir. 1988); CBS v. United States Dist. Court, 765 F.2d 823 (9th Cir. 1985).

[161] *See* Leucadia, Inc. v. Applied Extrusion Techs, Inc., 998 F.2d 157 (3d Cir. 1993); Rushford v. New Yorker Magazine, Inc., 846 F.2d 249 (4th Cir. 1988); Bank of Am. Nat'l Trust & Sav. Ass'n v. Hotel Rittenhouse Assocs., 800 F.2d 339 (3d Cir. 1986); Resolution Trust Corp. v. Dean, 854 F. Supp. 626 (D. Ariz. 1994); Soc'y of Prof'l Journalists v. Briggs, 675 F. Supp. 1308 (D. Utah 1987); Willie Nelson Music Co. v. Comm'r, 85 T.C. 914 (1985); Shenandoah Publ'g House, Inc. v. Fanning, 368 S.E.2d 253 (Va. 1988); Goldberg v. Johnson, 485 So. 2d 1386 (Fla. Dist. Ct. App. 1986).

[162] CCJ/COSCA GUIDELINES 4 (Oct. 18, 2002), *available at* http://www.courtaccess.org/modelpolicy.

[163] *Id.* at 40.

types of court records that are now often public, including "[p]hotographs depicting violence, death or children subjected to abuse" and "[a]ddresses and phone numbers of litigants in cases." They even suggest prohibiting access to juror questionnaires, which, as mentioned above, the Ohio Supreme Court recently declared are subject to a First Amendment right of access.[164]

In a special report, the Reporters Committee for Freedom of the Press warned, "The model guidelines encourage states to consider further limits on access even to records at the courthouse by taking state statutes that *may* allow restrictions of particular information in certain circumstances and including them in a list of items that will be automatically excluded from public access."[165] Some states already have policies regarding online access to court records, and some are now considering the CCJ/COSCA Guidelines.[166]

**Secret Dockets.** As demonstrated above, the media are often successful in challenging courtroom closures, but such success requires knowledge that a proceeding is occurring. Courts dockets, which serve as indices of all judicial proceedings and documents filed in connection with those proceedings, are supposed to be public records. Sometimes, however, judges keep cases off the public dockets, preventing the press and public from even knowing the cases exist. In 2006, the Reporters Committee for Freedom of the Press reported that during the preceding five years, 469 cases in the U.S. District Court in Washington, D.C., had been "prosecuted and tried in complete secrecy, with no public knowledge even of the cases' existence and no way for the public to challenge the secrecy."[167] While the reasons for secret docketing might include protecting the safety of parties and witnesses or national security, such a system is ripe for abuse. In June 2006, the Florida attorney general announced an investigation into a secret Broward County docket that included more than 100 divorce and other civil cases involving TV personalities, judges, elected officials and other prominent individuals.[168]

Although the Supreme Court has not addressed the issue, two U.S. Courts of Appeals have ruled secret dockets violate the First Amendment. In 1993, the Eleventh Circuit held that dual dockets — one open, one secret — maintained by the U.S. District Court for the Middle District of Florida was "an unconstitutional infringement on the public and press' qualified right of access to

criminal proceedings."[169] In 2004, the Second Circuit struck down the Connecticut state court system's secret docketing system that had kept thousands of civil cases concealed from the public during the preceding forty years. The court said the presumption of open dockets could be overcome only by a showing that secrecy "'is essential to preserve higher values and is narrowly tailored to serve that interest.'"[170]

**Juvenile Records.** Just as access to juvenile proceedings has increased during the past few years so, too, has access to juvenile court records. While most states still consider most juvenile records confidential, some now permit access to records of cases involving felonies or specific serious, violent offenses.[171] In addition, several courts have recognized at least a qualified right of access to juvenile records.[172] Sometimes judges allow the press access to redacted versions of juvenile records in which the names have been omitted. For example, in one of the cases involving the Federal Juvenile Delinquency Act discussed above, the judge prohibited access to proceedings but did permit release of records that had been edited to hide the identities of the defendants.[173]

**Discovery Documents.** As previously indicated, access to civil discovery is sometimes an area of controversy. Journalists and members of the public not only have sought to be present during the actual taking of depositions but also have tried to obtain access to deposition transcripts and documents obtained as part of discovery. They have enjoyed the most success when seeking access to discovery documents that have been filed with a court but are less likely to be granted access to unfiled materials.

A 1988 D.C. Court of Appeals case, *Mokhiber v. Davis*,[174] illustrates the distinction well. Russell Mokhiber, an investigative reporter, sought access to a variety of discovery documents from a civil lawsuit that had been settled four years earlier. The court held that Mokhiber had no right to see discovery materials that had never been submitted to the court but did have a right of access to "papers submitted to the court for decision," including papers obtained *via* discovery.[175] Likewise, in an antitrust case, a federal

---

[164] *Id.* at 48-49.

[165] *Electronic Access To Court Records: Ensuring Access in the Public Interest*, NEWS MEDIA & L., Fall 2002, at 25, 27.

[166] *See* http://www.rcfp.org/courtaccess/viewstates.cgi for a state-by-state listing of electronic access policies.

[167] Kirsten B. Mitchell & Susan Burgess, *Disappearing dockets*, NEWS MEDIA & L., Winter 2006, at 4, *available at* http://www.rcfp.org/news/mag/30-1/cov-disappea.html.

[168] AP, *Fla. attorney general probes county's secret court docket*, June 16, 2006, *available at* http://www.firstamendmentcenter.org/news.aspx?id=17025.

[169] United States v. Valenti, 987 F.2d 708, 715 (11th Cir. 1993).

[170] Hartford Courant Co. v. Pellegrino, 380 F.3d 83, 96 (2d Cir. 2004) (quoting Press-Enterprise v. Riverside County Superior Court, 464 U.S. 501, 510 (1984)).

[171] *See, e.g.,* ARK. CODE ANN. § 9-27-309 (2001); CAL. WELF. & INST. CODE § 389 (2001); IND. CODE § 31-39-2-8 (2000); OKLA. STAT. tit. 10, § 7307-1.2 (2002); TENN. CODE ANN. § 37-1-153 (2001); UTAH CODE ANN. § 78-3a-206 (2000).

[172] *See, e.g., In re* K.F., 559 A.2d 663 (Vt. 1989); Orange County Publ'ns v. Sawyer, 14 Media L. Rep. (BNA) 1766 (N.Y. Sup. Ct. 1987); *In re* Richmond Newspapers, Inc., 16 Media L. Rep. (BNA) 1049 (Va. Cir. Ct. 1988).

[173] United States v. Three Juveniles, 862 F. Supp. 651 (D. Mass. 1994), *aff'd*, 61 F.3d 86 (1st Cir. 1995).

[174] 14 Media L. Rep. (BNA) 2313 (D.C. Cir. 1988).

[175] *Id.* at 2327.

district court in California held that a common law right of access attached to documents as soon as they were filed with the court in either civil or criminal cases.[176] In a few instances, courts have ruled that there is no right of access to discovery materials until the trial has begun or the documents have been introduced at the trial.[177]

While most courts have refused to recognize a right of access to unfiled discovery documents, a few judges have ruled in favor of openness and declined to seal discovery materials except upon a showing of "good cause."[178] For example, a Minnesota trial court in 1992 denied a motion from a St. Paul City Council member who was a defendant in a civil lawsuit to seal all discovery materials on the grounds that disclosure would cause her public humiliation and reputational harm. The court said there was a common law and statutory presumption of openness and, therefore, rejected the closure request as overbroad. However, it did agree to temporarily seal unfiled materials relating to medical, financial and psychological records.[179]

Other courts have also agreed to seal certain discovery documents to protect personal privacy. The Sixth U.S. Circuit Court of Appeals ruled in 1987 that protecting the associational privacy rights of non-parties was sufficient cause to justify sealing a list of Ku Klux Klan members that had been obtained as part of discovery in a civil lawsuit resulting from the fire-bombing of a black couple's home.[180] Other reasons frequently given for denying access to discovery materials are to protect trade secrets and to ensure the efficient functioning of the judicial process. A good example of the latter is a 1991 decision of the U.S. District Court for Arizona, which denied access to unfiled discovery materials in a class action suit resulting from savings and loan association failures. The court said that access would impede the progress of the case and create administrative burdens for both the court and parties.[181]

**Audio-visual Records.** As the use of audio-visual materials in the courtroom has increased, so too have efforts by journalists, especially broadcasters, to obtain copies of such materials. Sometimes the parties to litigation and judges are reluctant to allow broadcasters to copy audio-visual records because they fear the airing of such tapes will invade privacy, interfere with fair trial rights, implicate innocent third parties and/or sensationalize and distort the judicial process. Some judges have argued that the right of access to court records is met by simply allowing journalists to see or hear audio-visual evidence when it is used in the courtroom or by providing reporters written transcripts of tapes. Broadcasters who want to air portions of tapes are seldom satisfied with such limited access and claim a right to copy as well as to see and hear audio-visual records.

The Supreme Court addressed the issue in 1978 when it denied media requests to copy former President Richard M. Nixon's Watergate audio tapes. As noted previously, in *Nixon v. Warner Communications,* the Court recognized a common law presumption of access. However, Justice Powell, writing for the Court, noted that "the right to inspect and copy judicial records is not absolute."[182] In this case, the common law presumption of access was superseded by the Presidential Recordings and Materials Preservation Act, passed by Congress within weeks of President Ford's pardon of Nixon for his involvement in the Watergate scandal. That act gave the Administrator of General Services the responsibility for processing and arranging public access to the Nixon tapes.[183]

Since *Richmond Newspapers* in 1980, lower courts have generally recognized either a constitutional or common law right to inspect and copy audio-visual records. That right, however, like all of the other access rights discussed thus far, is not absolute and can be outweighed by other interests. Several good examples of how courts balance the interests for and against access came in the early 1980s, when two FBI sting operations, known as ABSCAM and BRILAB, resulted in four different access-to-tapes lawsuits. During ABSCAM, the FBI videotaped government officials allegedly accepting bribes from undercover agents. In BRILAB, the tapes were of Texas officials allegedly accepting bribes in the awarding of state employee insurance contracts. Understandably, broadcasters wanted to obtain copies of those tapes to show on the air.

In the first ABSCAM tape case, resulting from the trial of former Congressman Michael Myers, the Second U.S. Circuit Court of Appeals allowed the media to copy the tapes, saying that once such evidence was introduced in court, "[I]t would take the most extraordinary circumstances to justify restrictions on the opportunity of those not physically in attendance at the courtroom to see and hear the evidence, when it is in a form that readily permits sight and sound reproduction." The court considered the impact that broadcasting the tapes might have on the fair trial rights of Myers and future ABSCAM defendants but concluded that the risks were not sufficient to justify "curtailing the public's right of access to courtroom evidence." It added: "Defendants, as well as the news media, frequently overestimate the extent of the public's

---

[176] *In re* Coordinated Pretrial Proceedings in Petroleum Products Antitrust Litigation, 101 F.R.D. 34 (C.D. Cal. 1984).

[177] *See In re* Reporters Comm. for Freedom of the Press, 773 F.2d 1325 (D.C. Cir. 1985); Tavoulareas v. Washington Post, 724 F.2d 1010 (D.C. Cir. 1984); Booth Newspapers, Inc. v. Midland Circuit Judge, 377 N.W.2d 868 (Mich. Ct. App. 1985); *appeal denied*, 425 Mich. 854 (1986).

[178] The "good cause" standard is based on Rule 26(c) of the Federal Rules of Civil Procedure and similar provisions in state rules of civil procedure.

[179] Baloga v. Maccabee, 20 Media L. Rep. (BNA) 2201 (Minn. Dist. Ct. 1992). *See also* Glenmede Trust Co. v. Thompson, 56 F.3d 426 (3d Cir. 1995).

[180] Courier-Journal v. Marshall, 828 F.2d 361 (6th Cir. 1987).

[181] *In re* Am. Continental Corp./Lincoln Sav. & Loan Sec. Litig., 18 Media L. Rep. (BNA) 2303 (D. Ariz. 1991).

[182] 435 U.S. 589, 598 (1978).

[183] Pub. L. No. 93-526, 88 Stat. 1695 (1974).

awareness of news."[184]

In the other two ABSCAM cases, the federal appellate courts for the Third and D.C. circuits also granted broadcasters the right to copy the tapes despite claims that airing the tapes would interfere with the defendants' fair trial rights and invade the privacy of unindicted third parties.[185] The D.C. Circuit, however, told the trial judge that he could edit the tapes before releasing them to eliminate portions that might harm innocent third parties.

In the BRILAB case, *Belo Broadcasting Corp. v. Clark*, the Fifth Circuit upheld the trial court's refusal to allow copying of the FBI sting tapes.[186] First, it said that the media's First Amendment right of access was satisfied when journalists were allowed to view the tapes as they were played in open court and were provided transcripts of the contents. While the court acknowledged that there was a common law right of access to the tapes, it said the fair trial rights of a defendant who had not yet been tried outweighed the access right.

Since ABSCAM and BRILAB, media have continued to try to obtain copies of audio-visual materials used in the courtroom with mixed results. For example, in 1996, the Eighth U.S. Circuit Court of Appeals followed the approach taken by the Fifth Circuit in the BRILAB case and denied media access to the videotape of President Bill Clinton's testimony in the Whitewater-related fraud trial of James B. McDougal. The videotape had been played in an open courtroom, and transcripts of the tape were released to the public. The court said the press and public "were given access to the information contained in the videotape," and this met First Amendment requirements.[187] In contrast, in 1998 a federal court in Illinois followed the ABSCAM decisions and ruled the press and public had the right to inspect and copy the videotape of Illinois Gov. Jim Edgar's testimony during the trial of the trial of a state official for mail fraud and misapplication of government property.[188]

### Cameras in Courtrooms

In 1976, only two states — Texas and Colorado — allowed cameras in their courtrooms. In 2006, every state allowed at least some camera coverage of state courts. A key reason for this shift was the technological advances that eliminated the need for obtrusive flashes, bulky cameras and electrical cords snaking across courtroom floors. Also important, however, were changing public and judicial attitudes. At the same time courts were recognizing the importance of allowing public and press access to the judicial process, video cameras were becoming part of everyday life for most Americans. People became accustomed to being videotaped as

they did their shopping and banking, rode on elevators and attended weddings and parties.

The situation was significantly different earlier in the Twentieth Century when cameras were obvious and intrusive, and their presence in the courtroom was viewed as inconsistent with judicial dignity and decorum. The first official bans on cameras in the courtroom followed the 1935 trial of Bruno Hauptmann for the kidnapping of the Lindbergh baby. In 1937, the American Bar Association adopted Canon 35 as part of its Canons of Professional and Judicial Ethics. Canon 35, which declared that cameras "detract from the essential dignity of the proceedings, degrade the court and create misconceptions with respect thereto in the mind of the public," recommended that cameras be banned in all courtrooms. That recommendation, which was amended in 1952 to specifically include television cameras, was followed by most states for more than four decades.

When the Supreme Court heard its first cameras-in-the-courtroom case, *Estes v. Texas*, it agreed with the ABA that television cameras intruded upon "the solemn decorum of court procedure." Justice Tom Clark, writing for the Court, held that jurors could be distracted by the equipment and by the mere knowledge that the trial was being televised. "Not only will the juror's eyes be fixed on the camera," he wrote, "but also his mind will be preoccupied with the telecasting rather than with the testimony." The judge, Clark continued, had enough to do supervising the trial without also worrying about supervising television crews. Witnesses, he wrote, "may be demoralized and frightened, some cocky and given to overstatement; memories may falter, as with anyone speaking publicly, and accuracy of statement may be severely undermined. Embarrassment may impede the search for truth, as may a natural tendency toward over-dramatization." Finally, for the defendant, the presence of TV cameras "is a form of mental — if not physical — harassment, resembling a police line-up or the third degree," Clark wrote.[189]

Chief Justice Earl Warren, in a concurring opinion, referred to the noise and disorder of TV equipment but was most concerned about the psychological effects, concluding that the real evil was "the trial participants' awareness that they are being televised."[190] Justice John Marshall Harlan also wrote a concurring opinion. He shared his colleagues' fears about television's potential for disrupting the judicial process, or as he put it, causing "serious mischief," but also seemed to recognize that effect was the result of the novelty of the medium. Harlan speculated that someday television might become "so commonplace ... in the daily life of the average person" that its disruptive influence would disappear.[191]

By the 1980s, Justice Harlan's prediction had nearly come true. In its second cameras-in-the-courtroom case, *Chandler v. Florida*,

---

[184] United States v. Myers, 635 F.2d 945, 952-53 (2d Cir. 1981).

[185] *In re* Application of NBC (Criden), 648 F.2d 814 (3d Cir. 1981); *In re* Application of NBC (Jenrette), 653 F.2d 609 (D.C. Cir. 1981).

[186] 654 F.2d 423 (5th Cir. 1981).

[187] United States v. McDougal, 103 F.3d 651, 659 (8th Cir. 1996).

[188] United States v. Berger, 990 F. Supp. 1054 (C.D. Ill. 1998).

[189] 381 U.S. 532, 546-49 (1965).

[190] *Id.* at 570 (Warren, C.J., concurring).

[191] *Id.* at 597 (Harlan, J., concurring).

the Supreme Court in 1981 held that "no one has been able to present empirical data sufficient to establish that the mere presence of the broadcast media inherently has an adverse effect on that process."[192] Florida was one of several states that had begun experimenting with allowing cameras in its courtrooms in the 1970s. In *Chandler*, which involved two Miami Beach police officers charged with burglarizing a restaurant, the judge allowed a television camera in the court despite the defendants' objections. Although only about three minutes of the trial were ultimately broadcast, the officers appealed their conviction, claiming that the televising of trials was "inherently a denial of due process."

Writing for a unanimous Court, Warren Burger — who throughout his tenure as Chief Justice steadfastly opposed the introduction of cameras into federal courts — declared that the mere presence of cameras in the courtroom did not automatically deprive a defendant of a fair trial. Burger wrote that broadcast coverage might, in some cases, violate a defendant's constitutional rights, but the mere possibility of prejudice did not justify a ban on televising trials. Instead, an individual defendant would have to prove that "the presence of cameras impaired the ability of the jurors to decide" the specific case. "To demonstrate prejudice in a specific case a defendant must show something more than juror awareness that the trial is such as to attract the attention of broadcasters," Burger wrote.[193]

While *Chandler v. Florida* permits states to open their courtrooms to cameras, it does not require them to do so. The Supreme Court did *not* say that photographers have a First Amendment right to take their equipment into courtrooms. Instead it simply said that states were free to experiment with television coverage of trials. This point was underscored just two years later in another case out of Miami. U.S. District Judge Alcee Hastings, who was charged with accepting a bribe, asked to have his trial televised and was joined by news media organizations in challenging the ban on cameras in federal courts. After the trial court denied the motion, the media appealed to the Eleventh U.S. Circuit Court of Appeals, which upheld the lower court ruling, saying there was no constitutional right, under either the First or Sixth Amendment, to bring cameras into courtrooms.[194]

As of 2006, cameras were still banned in most federal courtrooms and in District of Columbia courts. The Federal Rules of Criminal Procedure have prohibited the televising of federal criminal trials for more than fifty years. In the early 1990s, limited television coverage of civil proceedings was tried under an experimental program authorized by the Judicial Conference of the United States, which sets policy for the federal courts. An evaluation of the program by the Federal Judicial Center found that judges became more favorable toward cameras in the courts after the experiment began; judges and court personnel believed the guidelines governing the program were workable and that journalists were generally cooperative; and judges and attorneys reported minimal or no effects of cameras in the courtrooms. Despite such favorable reactions, the Judicial Conference in September 1994 voted 19-6 to terminate the program.

In March 1996, the Judicial Conference revisited the camera question and voted to allow each of the thirteen U.S. Courts of Appeals to "decide for itself whether to permit the taking of photographs and radio and television coverage." The conference continued to voice its opposition to television coverage of federal trial court proceedings, however.[195] Despite that opposition, a few federal trial courts have allowed cameras. In addition, in November 2000, in *Bush v. Gore*, the U.S. Supreme Court for the first time released audiotapes of oral arguments immediately after the arguments were completed; and in February 2001, the U.S. Court of Appeals for the District of Columbia allowed live audio broadcasting of oral arguments in the Microsoft antitrust case.

During the past few years, Congress has repeatedly considered legislation to permit federal judges, both trial and appellate, to open their courtrooms to cameras. As of summer 2006, however, no camera access bill had managed to pass both houses.

While the federal courts have been loath to allow cameras, the same has not been true of state courts. The extent of coverage permitted, however, as well as the specific rules journalists must follow, differs greatly among the states, and journalists are well advised to study their individual state rules carefully before taking a camera or tape recorder into a courtroom. The best sources for information about cameras-in-the-courtroom rules in the fifty states is the Web site of the Radio-Television News Directors Association at http://www.rtnda.org/foi/scc.shtml.

At one end of the spectrum is Florida, where there is a presumption of camera access that can be overcome only by a finding that electronic coverage of a trial would have a "qualitatively different" effect than other types of media coverage.[196] At the other end of the spectrum are states like Alabama, where the consent of all parties and attorneys is needed; Utah, where only still cameras are allowed in trials; Nebraska, where only audio coverage of trials is permitted; and New York, Illinois, Delaware and Indiana, where only appellate courts coverage is permitted.

Most states require the consent of the presiding judge, and many place restrictions on the photographing of jurors and certain types of trial participants, such as juveniles, victims of sex crimes and undercover officers. Most states also limit the number of cameras allowed in the courtroom and specify where cameras

---

[192] 449 U.S. 560, 578-79 (1981).

[193] *Id.* at 581.

[194] United States v. Hastings, 695 F.2d 1278 (11th Cir.), *cert. denied sub nom.* Post-Newsweek Stations v. United States, 461 U.S. 931 (1983). *See also* Conway v. United States, 852 F.2d 187 (6th Cir.), *cert. denied*, 488 U.S. 943 (1988).

[195] *Judicial Conference Acts on Cameras in the Courts*, THE THIRD BRANCH, THE NEWSLETTER OF THE FEDERAL COURTS, Apr. 1996, *at* http://www.uscourts.gov/ttb /apr96/judconf.htm.

[196] Florida v. Green, 395 So. 2d 532, 536 (Fla. 1981).

may be placed. State rules often require pooling agreements among the various media.

Despite significant advances in the past twenty years, cameras in the courts continue to be a contentious issue, and judges often decide to ban coverage of highly publicized trials. For example, in late 2002 and early 2003, two Virginia judges in separate rulings refused to allow cameras into the criminal proceedings for Lee Boyd Malvo and John Allen Muhammad, who were subsequently convicted of murder in the Washington, D.C., area sniper shootings.[197] In 2004, a California trial judge prohibited camera coverage of the murder trial of Scott Peterson, accused of killing his wife, Laci, and their unborn child;[198] and in 2005, another California judge banned cameras during the child molestation trial of pop star Michael Jackson.[199] In contrast, on the other side of the country in North Carolina, another Peterson — this one Michael, a novelist and former newspaper columnist and mayoral candidate — was convicted of murdering his wife in a trial broadcast live on Court TV.[200]

Journalists who violate the rules governing electronic coverage can be found in contempt of court. For example, during a 1991 murder trial in North Carolina, Asheville station WLOS-TV inadvertently broadcast approximately three seconds of film showing some jurors. The trial judge, who had specifically warned station employees not to photograph jurors, found the station in contempt, imposed a $500 fine and prohibited WLOS from bringing cameras or recording equipment into the county courthouse for the next sixty days. In September 2000, an Ohio trial judge banned AP reporters from a murder trial after an AP photographer took pictures of jurors while they viewed the crime scene along a highway. The judge also threatened to ban any other reporters who gave photos or information to the Associated Press.[201]

## SUMMARY

While concern about press coverage of crimes and trials dates back at least two centuries, debate over the so-called free press-fair trial issue escalated during the 1960s when the Supreme Court overturned several murder convictions on the grounds that prejudicial publicity had deprived the defendants of their Sixth Amendment right to a fair trial. Televised and often sensationalized coverage of the O.J. Simpson trial in 1995 again brought the controversy to the forefront of public attention, and high-profile Twenty-First Century cases, such as the Michael Jackson child molestation trial, Kobe Bryant rape case and Enron trials, have kept the debate going. The perceived conflict between the First and Sixth Amendments can occur in three ways: pretrial publicity can make it difficult to find impartial jurors; during-trial publicity can influence a sitting jury; and the presence of journalists and/or their equipment in the courtroom can cause physical or psychological disruption.

Two broad categories of remedies are available to judges. First are the traditional remedies designed to compensate for — but not eliminate — publicity. The most commonly used of these compensatory remedies are change of venue, continuance, *voir dire* and jury admonitions. The second category of remedies consists of those aimed at reducing or eliminating publicity. These remedies are much more problematic since they directly impact on the media's ability to obtain and report information related to the judicial system, and, beginning in the mid-1970s, the Supreme Court began placing First Amendment restrictions on their use.

In 1976, in *Nebraska Press Association v. Stuart*, the Supreme Court said that gag orders on the press constituted prior restraints and could be used only if there was pervasive publicity likely to interfere with a fair trial, no other remedies were available and a gag order would be effective in preventing prejudicial publicity. This test made it extremely difficult for a trial judge to justify gagging the media and significantly reduced the number of gag orders issued and upheld on appeal. Journalists must keep in mind, however, that if a judge *does* issue a gag order, violating it can result in a contempt of court citation even if subsequently the order is struck down on appeal. While some appellate courts have ruled that journalists can violate a patently invalid gag order if timely relief is not available from an appeals court, others have enforced the so-called collateral bar rule, which says that a person cannot disobey a judicial order and then challenge its constitutionality as a defense to contempt of court.

Gag orders aimed at trial participants generally are not subject to the same rigorous test of constitutionality as gag orders aimed at the media. In *Gentile v. State Bar of Nevada*, the Supreme Court said it was permissible to punish an attorney who made extrajudicial statements that posed a "substantial likelihood" of interfering with a fair trial. While trial judges have greater leeway in restricting the speech of lawyers and other trial participants, there are First Amendment limits. A gag order cannot be overbroad and cannot be issued unless necessary to protect a defendant's right to a fair trial and no other alternative measures are available.

In addition to restricting the use of prior restraints on media coverage of the courts, the Supreme Court has also applied the First Amendment to limit the use of post-publication sanctions. In the 1940s, it ruled that judges could not use their contempt of

---

[197] *See Judge Rules Against Cameras in Sniper Suspect Trial,* Dec. 17, 2002, http://www.cnn.com/2002/LAW/12/12/sniper; *Judge Bars Cameras from Malvo Trial,* Mar. 3, 2003, http://www.cnn.com/2003/LAW/03/03/malvo.hearing/.

[198] *See Judge Bars Cameras from Peterson Courtroom,* Feb. 2, 2004, http://www.cnn.com/2004/LAW/02/02/peterson.case/.

[199] *See* Tina Susman, *Wheels of Justice Turn Secretly,* June 13, 2005, http://www.newsday.com/news/nationworld/world/ny-usjack134302689jun13,0,7754064.story.

[200] *See* http://www.courttv.com/trials/novelist/.

[201] *See* Reporters Committee for Freedom of the Press, *Judge Bans AP Photographer From Courtroom* (Sept. 22, 2000), *at* http://www.rcfp.org/news/w000/0922.

court powers to punish coverage of and commentary on the judicial process unless such publications presented a "clear and present danger" of interfering with the fair administration of justice. This stringent standard has virtually eliminated the practice of judges citing for contempt journalists and others who criticize the courts. Three decades later the Court strengthened the media's protection against post-publication punishments when it ruled that the media could not be punished for publishing lawfully obtained, truthful information unless necessary to serve a compelling governmental interest.

In a series of cases in the 1980s, the Supreme Court also put a halt to the widespread use of court closures as a means of controlling publicity when it ruled that the press and public enjoyed a First Amendment right of access to criminal proceedings. The Court established a multi-part test for determining when a judicial hearing could be closed, which requires a judge to issue written findings that, among other things, closure is essential to serve higher values and is as narrowly tailored as possible. While the Supreme Court has not ruled directly on whether a constitutional right of access exists to civil proceedings, most lower courts that have considered the issue have found a qualified First Amendment right of access and have used the same test the Court mandated for closing criminal proceedings.

Many lower courts have also presumed that the First Amendment right of access extends to judicial records. Whether they recognize a constitutional right of access, however, courts are unanimous that the common law provides both the press and public the right to inspect certain judicial records. However, increasing online access to judicial records is generating concerns about misuse of public information and privacy invasions, prompting some efforts to restrict electronic access. Media attempts to gain access to some types of judicial records, especially juvenile records, discovery materials and audio-visual records, have caused numerous conflicts in recent years, and courts have often disagreed about the extent of access rights.

One of the major free press-fair trial battles has involved cameras in the courtroom, especially the televising of trials. In 1965, the Supreme Court overturned a criminal conviction on the grounds that television cameras in the courtroom caused both physical and psychological disruptions inconsistent with the Sixth Amendment's guarantee of a fair trial. In the decades that followed, as cameras became less obtrusive and television became more ubiquitous, some states began to allow video coverage of judicial proceedings, ultimately leading the Court to revise its position. In *Chandler v. Florida* in 1981, it ruled that the mere presence of cameras did not automatically deny a defendant a fair trial. While there is no constitutional right to bring cameras into courts, states are free to experiment with camera coverage, and as of 2006, all fifty states allowed some form of camera coverage of courts. Most federal courts, however, continued to ban cameras despite generally favorable responses to a limited experiment with camera

coverage during the early 1990s.

Every day the news is filled with stories related to the judicial system. Whether it's a celebrity charged with murder, a movie star's messy divorce, charges of rape against a sports star, the trial or deportation hearing for a suspected terrorist or a challenge to a university's affirmative action policies, the courts generate news that affects the public and in which the public is interested. Conflicts between the press and the judiciary are inevitable since each is committed to advancing a different interest and those interests often appear to be at odds with one another. Judges and attorneys see their primary responsibility as ensuring fair trials and the proper functioning of the judicial process. Their key concern is protecting the rights of litigants, witnesses and jurors. Journalists, on the other hand, see their primary responsibility as informing the public and serving as a watchdog over government, including the judicial branch. Their key concern is protecting freedom of the press and the public's right to know.

Certainly sometimes less lofty goals motivate both sides, adding problems. During the last few decades, however, the Supreme Court has made it clear that the First and Sixth Amendments are of equal importance in our constitutional scheme. Neither takes precedence over the other, nor can one be used as the justification for infringement of the other. The press has broad First Amendment rights to observe and report on the judicial process, and the judiciary must find ways to respect those rights while at the same time ensuring that trials are fair, jurors unbiased and the judicial process operates smoothly, effectively and openly.

## FOR ADDITIONAL READING

Buddenbaum, Judith M., et al. *Pretrial Publicity and Juries: A Review of Research*, Research Report No. 11, School of Journalism, Indiana University (1981).

Bunker, Matthew D. *Justice and the Media: Reconciling Fair Trials and a Free Press*. Mahwah, N.J.: Lawrence Erlbaum Associates, 1997.

Connors, Mary M. "Prejudicial Publicity: An Assessment." *Journalism Monographs* 41 (1975).

Hengstler, Gary A. "Pressing Engagements: Courting Better Relationships Between Judges and Journalists," 56 *Syracuse Law Review* 419 (2006).

Levine, Raleigh Hannah. "Toward a New Public Access Doctrine," 27 *Cardozo Law Review* 1739 (2006).

Minow, Newton and Fred Cate. "Who Is an Impartial Juror in an Age of Mass Media?" 40 *American University Law Review* 631 (1991).

Sandys, Marla and Steven M. Chermak. "A Journey into the Unknown: Pretrial Publicity and Capital Cases," 1 *Communication Law & Policy* 533 (1996).

# 17

# Access to Public Documents and Meetings

*By Sandra F. Chance*

 **Headnote Questions**

- *Why is access to information important?*
- *Does the U.S. Constitution guarantee a right of access to government information?*
- *What laws provide for a right of access to government records and meetings?*
- *How is the need for access to information balanced with the need for security and government secrecy?*
- *What is FOIA? Does it apply to state and local records?*
- *What are the exemptions to FOIA?*
- *Why is there conflict between the right to privacy and the right of access to information?*
- *Are computer records covered by access laws?*
- *How have the September 11, 2001, terrorist attacks and threats of terrorism affected access to information?*

From the earliest days of the United States, citizens, elected officials, journalists, scholars, attorneys and judges have recognized that speech about government is more credible when it is based on information. That information must come, in large part, from the government's own meetings and records. James Madison observed, for example:

Nothing could be more irrational than to give people power, and to withhold from them information with which power is abused. A people who mean to be their own governors must arm themselves with power which knowledge gives. A popular government without popular information or the means of acquiring it is but a prologue to a farce or a tragedy, or perhaps both.[1]

Despite the logic of observations like that, governments at all levels — national, state and local — have a lengthy tradition of closing their records and meetings to public scrutiny. Madison himself

opted to exclude the press and public from the deliberations on the same First Amendment used today to argue for open meetings and records.

Tension between government secrecy and public access to government information runs through U.S. history. Scandals during the administrations of Presidents Ulysses S. Grant and Warren G. Harding, for example, brought demands for specific information about government. But only in comparatively recent times has access become an issue of continuing and widespread interest.

Before the Great Depression of the 1930s, people understood their government by watching the activities in the Oval Office, the legislative bodies — from Congress to town councils — and a few administrative agencies. With the New Deal that followed in the wake of the Depression, however, government surged in size and complexity. New agencies were established to perform specialized functions once handled, if at all, by elected representatives. Congress, for example, delegated much of its authority over advertising regulation to the Federal Trade Commission.

For all its Byzantine structure and process, Congress is a much easier organization to follow and evaluate than the FTC. Multiply

---

[1] Letter to W.T. Barry (Aug. 4, 1822), *in* 1 THE WRITINGS OF JAMES MADISON 103 (Gaillard Hunt ed. 1910).

this remote agency by the hundreds of others that were created on the local, state and federal levels and the sense of frustration felt by many citizens is understandable. Government couldn't be understood, and that loss of understanding was accompanied by a sense of loss of control.

The secrecy precipitated by World War II compounded the problem. Shortly after the armistice, a movement emerged to make government more accessible. At first spearheaded by journalists who demanded a legally enforceable "right to know," the movement gradually broadened to include public interest groups and business interests. Over time it was enormously successful in mobilizing the passage of federal and state access statutes. Today these freedom-of-information or right-to-know laws are the primary legal means by which citizens have access to government meetings and records. But they are not the only tools. Federal and state constitutions and the common law also play important roles.

A study of access law — or any law — requires an attempt to pinpoint the policy or objectives behind it. Frequently, the purpose of those behind it — whether judges, legislators or the Founding Fathers — is considerably different from those who use it.

Some laws, like many state right-to-know laws, often enunciate their rationales. But many others, including the federal Freedom of Information Act, don't. Courts are left to grope for clues in legislative histories and other sources to discover what to guide the interpretation of ambiguous language.

The importance of this search shouldn't be underestimated. If a statute's purpose is, for example, the discovery of truth or self-fulfillment, there just isn't much government information that wouldn't qualify for disclosure in order to foster that policy. If, on the other hand, the objective of a law is to prevent secret rules and regulations — if only final decisions need be made public — it is a narrow right-to-know policy, indeed. Most often, the policy is to permit citizens to participate effectively in government, a standard of openness that comes somewhere in the middle. The benefits of guaranteeing access to government information generally parallel those associated with protecting speech. That is, access to information promotes the discovery of truth, self-government, orderly change and self-fulfillment. Access also enables the press to perform its watchdog function.

In contrast, a government's instinctive preference for secrecy has several specific roots.

First, finding and copying public records requires time and labor, and providing facilities for public meetings is inconvenient and expensive. Limited resources can best be directed at whatever a particular government agency regards as its primary function, perhaps issuing drivers' licenses or collecting garbage.

Second, officials argue that opening meetings and records chills creativity and effectiveness in government. If the casual suggestions and give-and-take of frank, brainstorming discussions are open to public examination, and perhaps ridicule, innovators and risk-takers in government won't make bold or daring proposals.

The quality of decision-making will suffer.

Third, they point out, some interests such as national security and personal privacy are more important than the public interest in access to government information.

And, finally — though seldom, if ever, stated explicitly — secrecy prevents disclosure of government waste, incompetence, unfairness and criminal activity.

To these specific objections, advocates of public access respond that providing information is not just an annoying appendage to the duties of government and officials; rather, it is a primary function of government. The public has a need to know what its government is doing if democracy is to work. They also argue that members of the public have good ideas. By excluding them from the early stages of decision-making, government is deprived of a fertile source of imaginative suggestions. And by denying the public access during the formative stages of a proposal, it is being excluded at the very time its input can be most effective. Moreover, access to ideas that are rejected can sometimes be as telling about the governmental processes as those that are accepted.

While most right-to-know advocates concede that there are times when a specific interest, such as the movement of troops, will trump a generalized interest in disclosure, they argue that any exceptions must be specific. Officials may attempt to use a narrow, reasonable exception to a general policy of disclosure as a catchall to hide information that ought to be available.

Keep these policies and attitudes in mind as you go through the survey of constitutional, common law and statutory access issues.

## CONSTITUTIONAL ACCESS

In *New York Times Co. v. Sullivan,*[2] the U.S. Supreme Court declared that the "central meaning" of the First Amendment is that it protects discussion about government and officials. Without guarantees of free speech, self-governance is an unobtainable goal. But the Court has been reluctant to extend that guarantee to access to the government information necessary to give content to that speech.

Only in the context of criminal trials has the Court fully considered the access issue. First in *Richmond Newspapers v. Virginia,*[3] then in *Press-Enterprise Co. v. Superior Court (II),*[4] it held that the acquisition of newsworthy information was entitled to First Amendment protection. It took pains, however, to limit its holding to a particular kind of access — that of criminal trials. In-

---

[2] 376 U.S. 254 (1964).

[3] 448 U.S. 555 (1980).

[4] 478 U.S. 1 (1986). *Press-Enterprise II* involved the question of whether judicial proceedings, other than trials, are required by the First Amendment to be open; the Court held that they are. *Press-Enterprise Co. v. Riverside County Superior Court (I)*, 464 U.S. 501 (1984), involved the question of whether *voir dire* proceedings — the questioning of jurors to determine whether they are competent to sit in a particular trial — must be open to the public; the Court held that they must be. Both cases are discussed in Chapter 16.

deed, at least two justices emphasized this narrow focus in concurring opinions.

But the logic of the case can't be confined to criminal-justice proceedings. The Court based its decision, first, on the premise that access to criminal trials contributes to the self-governing function and promotes the democratic process. It added that criminal trials are historically open. Whether this latter observation is an independent test or merely evidence of the truth of the first part is unclear, but several lower federal courts have seized on the language to allow access based on the First Amendment.

A federal district court in Ohio, for example, found that the public had a qualified right to access to a city council meeting since such meetings were historically open to the public and the subject matter contributes to the functioning of government.[5] And a district court in Puerto Rico used the same First Amendment analysis to order the governor of Puerto Rico to disclose a record.[6] Both decisions were reversed on other grounds, and not without the appellate courts expressing skepticism that a broadly based constitutional right of access existed.

On the state level, the New York Court of Appeals adopted the Supreme Court's test but used it to deny access to a dentist's disciplinary hearing since there was no evidence that public access plays a significant role in the functioning of that proceeding.[7]

The Supreme Court's own reluctance to take the logical next step after the courtroom cases may be the "slippery slope" problem: Once a court requires some records and proceedings to be open, can a principled, constitutional line be drawn between matters that must be open and those where secrecy is appropriate? Even Justice William Brennan, one of the Court's staunchest free expression advocates, was wary of runaway access: "Analysis is not advanced by rhetorical statements that all information bears upon public issues [and therefore must be disclosed]; what is crucial in individual cases is whether access to a particular government process is important in terms of that very process."[8]

The Supreme Court decided an important First Amendment case in 1999. *Los Angeles Police Department v. United Reporting Publishing Corp.*[9] illuminates the growing conflict between open records and a citizen's right to privacy. The Court ruled that a California law limiting who could get access to police records listing names and addresses of arrested suspects did not, on its face, violate the First Amendment. The California law limits access to names and addresses of arrestees and crime victims to those who seek the information for "scholarly, journalistic, political or gov-

ernmental purposes." The law bars businesses from using the information "to sell a product or service."[10]

Writing for the majority, Chief Justice William Rehnquist said that this "is not a case in which the government is prohibiting the speaker from conveying information that the speaker already possesses." The law merely requires that if a company "wishes to obtain the addresses of arrestees, it must qualify under the statute to do so." According to the Court, the California law did not abridge anyone's right to engage in speech; it simply regulated access to information in the government's hand.[11]

State constitutions may also provide access rights to government information. Five states contain explicit provisions concerning the public's right to know. The constitutions of Florida, New Hampshire, North Dakota, Louisiana and Montana all guarantee access to government meetings and records.[12] The Montana Constitution, for example, provides that "No person shall be deprived of the right to examine documents or to observe the deliberations of all public bodies or agencies ... except in cases in which the demand of individual privacy clearly exceed the merits of public disclosure." Montana's is unusually explicit, but most state constitutions have provisions paralleling the First Amendment that can be employed in the right circumstances.

Claims based on either federal or state constitutions face uncertain prospects. The law continues to emerge, with issues related to electronic access helping to define the constitutional parameters. For example, in 1998, a federal district court in Tennessee ruled against a newspaper's claim that the First Amendment provided a right to the Web browser history and so-called "cookie" files of a government employee.[13] The newspaper wanted to know what Web sites the employee had visited online.

Courts of last resort often move with great caution. Edicts based on the constitution have no appeal short of the unwieldy task of amending the constitution itself. When courts err in interpreting statutes, on the other hand, Congress or state legislatures can easily make adjustments, at least in theory. Without finding a workable rule that can be applied to each of the millions of records and meetings whose openness they would otherwise have to resolve on a case-by-case basis, courts won't rush into this complex area.

Constitutional change may thus seem to move with the speed of glaciers. But the law will never be developed on that level if those seeking access don't make and pursue claims based on First Amendment theories. It was more than three decades after Justice William O. Douglas declared in 1947 that "a trial is a public

---

[5] WJW-TV v. Cleveland, 686 F. Supp. 177 (N.D. Ohio 1988), *rev'd on other grounds,* 878 F.2d 906 (6th Cir. 1989).

[6] El Dia, Inc. v. Colon, 783 F. Supp. 15 (D.P.R. 1992), *rev'd on other grounds,* 963 F.2d 488 (1st Cir. 1992).

[7] Johnson Newspaper Corp. v. Melino, 564 N.E.2d 1046 (N.Y. 1990).

[8] *Richmond Newspapers,* 448 U.S. at 589 (Brennan, J., concurring in judgment).

[9] 528 U.S. 32 (1999).

[10] Cal. Gov't Code § 6254(f)(3) (1995).

[11] 528 U.S. at 40.

[12] Fla. Const. art. I, § 24 (1992); N.H. Const. Part I, art. 8 (1976); N.D. Const. art. XI, § 5 (1974); La. Const. art. XII, § 3 (1974); Mont. Const. art II, § 9 (1972).

[13] Pitman Pit, Inc. v. City of Cookeville, 23 F. Supp. 2d 822 (M.D. Tenn. 1998).

event" before the Court declared that the Constitution requires courtrooms to be open.[14]

## COMMON LAW ACCESS

Under the common law of England — the traditional, judge-made law passed from generation to generation — access to public information was limited. The doors of legislative bodies were usually closed to the public, and citizens were allowed to inspect or copy public records only if they could show what was called a "proper interest." Just what formed a "proper interest" was uncertain for citizens then and historians now.

Virtually all reported judicial decisions describe controversies over records, not meetings. Evidently there was no right of access to meetings. After the American Revolution, meetings of legislative bodies on both sides of the Atlantic became more open, without judicial prodding. The outcomes in the great majority of these older common law cases turned on whether an interest — a need to see the record — was so important that the record would be available in a lawsuit. If a citizen, say, wanted to see all the town's utility bills out of personal curiosity, his interest wasn't proper. If, on the other hand, access to the record was essential to proving he had paid his own bill, then the interest was proper and access was granted.

These cases have long captured the attention of scholars and litigants. But largely forgotten are those cases in which citizens sought access, not to serve some personal or private interest, but to serve the general or public welfare. Given the common law's bad reputation, it may be surprising to learn that those who claimed to represent the public interest were often successful.

By the middle of the Nineteenth Century, for example, English courts were regularly opening the financial records of municipalities for taxpayer inspections. They often reasoned that citizens were like shareholders in a corporation; they had a right, limited though it was, to review the records of their enterprise, in these cases, their government. In the leading case, *Rex v. Guardians of Great Farrington,*[15] an English court held flatly that municipal financial records could no longer be withheld because a taxpayer failed to prove a special interest.

In the United States, as in England, most of the reported decisions concerned the demands of individuals seeking to serve private purposes. Sometimes the interest was merely curiosity; sometimes it was financial. A century ago, for example, title companies — companies that insured the ownership of land — found they could abstract information from deeds and other land records, repackage it and resell it at a profit. Officials, fearful of losing both income and control of what they perceived as their property, frequently resisted these incursions. Often requests for these purposes were unsuccessful. There are similar conflicts today between government and resellers of government information — on-line services, for example.

There were only a few reported cases where plaintiffs, usually newspapers, claimed their business was to represent the public interest. It's not clear why there weren't more. It may be that media seldom requested records or that they got them whenever they did. On the other hand, it is also possible that when access was denied, cases were not contested in court.

The media almost invariably won those cases that *were* contested, however. Courts typically recited the common law's narrow, historical "proper interest" restrictions and then declared that the "public interest" was a "proper interest." In a leading case, the Michigan Supreme Court concluded in 1928: "If there is any rule of English common law that denied the public the right of access to public records, it is repugnant to the spirit of our democratic institutions. Ours is a government of the people."[16]

A 1994 decision illustrates how the common law of access functions today. In *Washington Legal Foundation v. United Sentencing Commission,*[17] a public interest group sought access to records the commission used in formulating recommendations. The threshold question was whether the records were "public records" under the common law. Not every document contained in a government file qualifies. Common law records are generally only those that record official actions or are vital to the functioning of government. Even if a record is a "public record," it may still be withheld if, the court said, its "specific interests favoring secrecy outweigh the general and specific interests favoring disclosure."[18] This means the broad public interest in knowing about government may be insufficient to force disclosure; a particular public might also be necessary. It wasn't necessary to do the balancing in this case, however, for the threshold test wasn't met. The records sought were held to be "predecisional" and thus public records under the common law.

Despite its limitations, the common law can be a highly effective access tool. In one case, for example, a common law-based suit forced a government official to create a record that did not exist, something a statute never does. A sheriff had negotiated a settlement with a discharged deputy but kept no documents relating to the settlement. He said the law did not require any. A newspaper filed suit under the state freedom of information act and under the common law. The state supreme court ruled that no statute obligated the sheriff to create or maintain records of the settlement agreement. Thus, there was no record to be demanded under the state's right-to-know law.

But the common law claim fared better. The court held that the common law required a record to be made:

Whenever a written record of the transaction of a public officer,

---

[14] Craig v. Harney, 331 U.S. 367, 373 (1947).
[15] 109 Eng. Reprint 202 (1829).

[16] Nowack v. Fuller, 219 N.W. 749, 750 (Mich. 1928).
[17] 17 F.3d 1446 (D.C. Cir. 1994).
[18] *Id* at 1451.

in his office, is a convenient and appropriate mode of discharging the duties of his office, it is not only his right but his duty to keep that memorial, whether expressly required to do so or not; and when it is kept it becomes a public document.[19]

The common law required the sheriff first to create a record that he then was ordered to disclose.

In another case, a newspaper that had been excluded from a meeting of the Atlantic City Convention Center Authority demanded access to audiotapes recorded at the meeting. The newspaper's claim was based on the New Jersey right-to-know law and the common law. The statutory claim was dismissed since the meeting was taped only to make the drafting of minutes easier and more accurate, and, therefore, the tapes weren't public records under the state's narrow right-to-know law. On the common law claim, however, the New Jersey Supreme Court held that the records were indeed public records since recording was a "convenient, appropriate or customary method" of documenting official action.[20]

Access to records not available otherwise may be possible through requests based on a common-law theory. Legislative bodies, for example, typically exclude themselves from the reach of right-to-know statues. In *Schwartz v. Department of Justice*,[21] however, a federal district court noted that all three branches of government are subject to the common law right of access, and it ordered records of Peter A. Rodino Jr., then chairman of the House Judiciary Committee, released.

These decisions, of course, are binding only in jurisdictions where the rulings were made, but they represent some creative or last-resort uses to which the common law can be put.

The use of common law is limited, however. Its answer to the question of what is a public record is narrow — generally confined to documents that memorialize some official transaction such as a deed or minutes of a meeting. Even when a document is clearly a public record and the requester's purpose proper, a custodian may withhold it if disclosure is outweighed by some other interest, such as personal privacy.

The discretionary aspect of the common law can frustrate the usual judicial remedy: a writ of mandamus. A writ of mandamus is a court order for an official to comply with the law. Since the common law permits discretion, some courts are reluctant to overrule a custodian who has exercised that discretion in good faith, however wrong the custodian may have been on the primary issue.

In the everyday world, a demand based on the common law is so unusual it is likely to be met by an official with a puzzled or blank look. It will probably only be pursued to a conclusion when more conventional means, such as access statutes, are unavailing;

and it will almost certainly entail a time-consuming and expensive suit with an uncertain outcome. Still, given the right circumstances, the common law can be exploited to fill the cracks left by constitutions and statutes.

## THE FEDERAL FREEDOM OF INFORMATION ACT

The federal Freedom of Information Act[22] is, in several respects, the most important access tool today. It is certainly the most visible and most analyzed right-to-know law, governing access to the country's largest group of records. A study of the policies and issues of the federal act will also provide insights into comparable state laws, since it provides a framework for analyzing in detail each of the fifty state right-to-know laws, an individual analysis that is beyond the scope of this book.

The FOIA is the outgrowth of the Administrative Procedure Act of 1946. That act was, in turn, a response to the explosive growth of government that began during the 1930s. The emergence of highly specialized, independent regulatory agencies, like the Federal Trade Commission, and the activities of agencies of the executive branch, like the Department of Labor, triggered fears not just about secrecy but about incomprehensibility. Each of the agencies had its own rules and procedures, causing many to feel out of touch with government.

The Administrative Procedure Act attempted to restore a sense of order to government by standardizing the procedures used to adopt and enforce rules and by making sure those procedures were accessible to the public. Though this was a considerable improvement, particularly for those regularly doing business with an agency, in another sense it failed because of its focus on how things were done, rather than on what was being done and why. And agencies remained largely their own judges of how well they complied with the act.

In response to these problems and the swelling interest in the public's right to know, the Administrative Procedure Act was amended in 1966 by the Freedom of Information Act. For the first time, the public had a clear right of access to records of the executive and administrative agencies of government. In contrast to the common law, the legal burden was on the government to justify withholding, not on the requester to justify release. The law is now forty years old and has provided access to extraordinarily important information about governmental operations.

However, some agencies adopted tactics to undermine the law: The exemptions were given sweeping interpretations; fees for finding, copying and segregating exempt from non-exempt material were exorbitant; long delays became routine; and agencies claimed they couldn't find the requested information. As a result, the act was extensively amended in 1974. The changes sought to ensure compliance, for example, by limiting the fees agencies could charge

---

[19] *Daily Gazette Co. v. Withrow*, 350 S.E.2d 738, 747 (W.Va. 1986).

[20] *Atlantic City Convention Ctr. Auth. v. South Jersey Publ'g Co.*, 637 A.2d 1261, 1267 (N.J. 1993).

[21] 435 F. Supp. 1203 (D.C. 1977), *aff'd* 595 F.2d 889 (D.C. Cir. 1979).

[22] 5 U.S.C. § 552 (1966).

to actual costs, expediting the scheduling of FOIA cases and allowing a wrongly denied requester to recover attorney's fees from the agency. The act was again amended in 1976 and in 1986.

How well it works, of course, isn't measured strictly by what it says or how courts interpret it. The attitude of government leadership can be a powerful influence on the practical, day-to-day functioning of the FOIA. In contrast to its predecessors, the Clinton Administration did a lot, at least on paper, to encourage agencies to comply with the spirit, as well as the letter, of the FOIA.

In 1993, for example, the attorney general reversed the previous administration's policy and ordered agencies to presume that a requested document should be disclosed, rather than search for an exemption under which to hide it. The Office of Management and Budget now assists agencies in making their information available, particularly with electronic access. And, in 1995, President Bill Clinton issued a long-awaited executive order that sharply reduced the number of documents that may be classified for national security. He said his order would "lift the veil" on millions of documents and keep others from ever becoming classified. The *New York Times* characterized it as the least secretive policy on government records since the beginning of the Cold War.[23]

Despite this "presumption of openness" promised by Clinton's order on classification in 1995, the government, four years later, succeeded in its efforts to keep a document secret, taking the case all the way to the Supreme Court.[24] By granting *certiorari* and ruling on the substantive issues, the Supreme Court was poised to interpret the national security exemption to FOIA for the first time. In an unusual decision, it vacated the appellate court's ruling before the oral arguments were even heard. As a result, the Court deferred to the government's unsubstantiated claim that national security would be damaged and set the tone for increased governmental discretion over release of information.

The case began in 1994, when attorney Leslie Weatherhead filed FOIA requests with the Justice and State departments. He wanted copies of correspondence between the British Home Office and its American counterparts regarding his client's extradition to stand trial for conspiracy in an attempt to murder a U.S. attorney in Oregon. Initially, the agencies claimed they did not have any letters. Ultimately, the Justice Department found a letter but refused to give a copy to Weatherhead, claiming diplomatic concerns and a national security exemption to FOIA. Weatherhead filed suit in federal court. Initially, the trial judge relied on Clinton's 1995 executive order and ruled that this type of correspondence could be withheld only upon a showing that the British government expected the letter to remain secret when it was written. In addition, the judge said the government failed to prove that releasing the record would threaten national security. Following an appeal by the government, the judge reversed his position and said the letter

should not be released.[25] A federal appeals court reversed him and ruled that disclosure would not threaten national security.[26]

In a bizarre twist, the government released the originally unclassified letter two weeks before the Supreme Court was to hear oral arguments, with no apparent national security consequences. The government's attorney said the Ninth Circuit's ruling must be vacated in order to prevent it from "chilling future confidential communications between the United States and ... foreign governments."[27] *United States v. Weatherhead* was the second case in three years in which the Court set aside an appellate court ruling favorable to a requester without a hearing,[28] and it continued a line of cases narrowing what the act is meant to do and, thus, the kinds of records it makes available. In a key FOIA case, for example, Justice John Paul Stevens wrote for the majority:

[T]he basic purpose of the Freedom of Information Act [is] to open agency action to the light of public scrutiny.... Official information that sheds light on an agency's performance of its statutory duties fall squarely within that statutory purpose. That purpose, however, is not fostered by disclosure of information about private citizens that is accumulated in various government files but that reveals little or nothing about an agency's own conduct.[29]

For many, this view is unsupported by the language of the statute. Justice Ruth Bader Ginsburg observed in another leading case that the "'core purpose' limitation is not found in FOIA's language. A FOIA requester need not show that ... disclosure would serve any public purpose, let alone a 'core purpose' of 'opening agency action to the light of public scrutiny' or advancing 'public understanding of the operations of activities of the government.'"[30]

Advocates of an expansive interpretation of the FOIA argue that the law's purpose is the discovery of truth. The more restrictive view is often based on the argument that the purpose of the FOIA is only to disclose the final actions of government. The law itself contains no statement of purpose, leaving plenty of room for interpretation.

### Overview of the FOIA

In general, the FOIA requires federal government agencies to make

---

[23] Douglas Jehl, *Clinton Revamps Policy on Secrecy of U.S. Documents*, N.Y. TIMES, Apr. 18, 1995, at A1.

[24] *See* United States v. Weatherhead, 528 U.S. 1042 (1999).

[25] *See Without Hearing, High Court Overturns Decision on Openness of British Letter*, NEWS MEDIA & THE L., Winter 2000, at 4.

[26] Weatherhead v. United States, 157 F.3d 735, 741 (9th Cir. 1998).

[27] Joan Biskupic, *Case of Extradition Letter Dismissed*, WASH. POST, Dec. 4, 1999, at A2.

[28] The first was *Bibles v. Oregon Natural Desert Ass'n*, 519 U.S. 355 (1997).

[29] Dep't of Justice v. Reporters Comm. for Freedom of the Press, 489 U.S. 749, 772 (1989).

[30] Dep't of Defense v. Fed. Labor Relations Auth., 510 U.S. 487, 507 (1994).

their records available for inspection and copying unless the records fall into one of nine categories. The act does not apply to Congress, the courts or the president's staff.

Some information must be published by an agency — statements of its organization, functions, procedures and rules, for example, and steps one must take to obtain information, including copies of decisions. Many agencies, including all those of special interest to communications law, have public reading rooms where this and other information is available.

Other agency records must be specifically requested. The FOIA does not define "agency record," but judicial interpretations are so broad as to include almost anything containing information, so long as it was created by and is under control of the agency. Audio tapes and computer disks, as well as written materials, are agency records. Some records — appointment books, calendars and telephone logs, for example — may exist only for the convenience of individual employees. They aren't agency records. And the FOIA does not require an agency to create a document that does not exist.

The FOIA requires that a record be "reasonably described" by a requester so it can be located. An agency can charge reasonable search and copying fees. There are standard fee schedules, but individual requirements vary, so a requester should ask for an estimate of costs. The law authorizes waivers for educational and non-commercial scientific institutions and for the news media when the requested information will "contribute significantly to public understanding of the operation or activities of Government." To qualify for consideration, a requester will have to explain the purpose of the request, something not otherwise required.

Though the FOIA requires a quick response to a request, substantive compliance — the production of the record or specific grounds for denial — can take months or even years. Some federal agencies are overwhelmed by requests.

If a request is ultimately refused, the FOIA provides for an administrative appeal to the head of the agency and then to U.S. District Court. There are hundreds of judicial decisions resolving FOIA disputes. The legal burden of justifying secrecy is on the agency. A court can — but is not required to — order the government to pay attorneys' fees if a requester "substantially prevails."

### FOIA Exemptions

An agency may withhold a record under the FOIA only if it is covered by at least one of the act's nine exemptions. Even in those cases, the law doesn't require a record to be withheld. The exemptions are discretionary; although other laws may require secrecy, the FOIA never does. Moreover, if part of a document is legitimately exempt from required disclosure and the remainder is not, the custodian must release the non-exempt portion if, in the words of the law, it is "reasonably segregable."

**Exemption 1: National Security.** This exemption authorizes the president to make and enforce rules to keep information secret in the interest of national defense or foreign policy. The rules are established by executive order without congressional involvement. While the president has leeway to decide what documents should be protected, the order must make plain both the procedures for classifying and declassifying and the underlying criteria for determining whether a specific document should be classified.

The exemption has become one of the most important weapons in the war on terrorism, as the federal government institutes new rules and President George W. Bush issues new executive orders classifying large amounts of information in the name of national security. However, some argue that the new orders cover more than national security matters. For instance, many people do not associate national security with trade agreements, but under a new executive order, any document received from a foreign government "is presumed to cause damage to the national security" and will not be subject to release.[31] This is not unexpected; administrations since that of George Washington have withheld information because of national security concerns. Even the most outspoken advocates of public access concede that the release of certain information would be devastating for the country. But critics claim that national security has also been used to shield misconduct or incompetence from public view.

As originally enacted, the exemption gave the executive branch virtually blanket authority to classify information in the interest of national security or foreign policy. In 1973, for example, the Supreme Court held that the mere fact that the administration had classified a document was enough to justify withholding the document.[32] The FOIA, it ruled, just did not allow a national security classification to be challenged. Partly in response to that decision, Exemption 1 was amended in 1974 to permit a court to examine a document in private to determine whether it should be released. The amendment also allowed courts to order the release of non-classified portions of otherwise properly classified documents, that is, segregating portions of a document.

Courts today scrutinize agency actions closely to see whether the government follows its own procedures to classify documents. But they remain reluctant to overrule government experts as to whether the release of a particular document would threaten national security. Given the potential consequences of a mistake, the line between information that is safe and that which is harmful may be too fine for courts to draw with confidence. The Clinton Administration, for example, refused to disclose details of a $25 million telephone system at the White House. Would disclosure expose national secrets? Or extravagance? Or both.

**Exemption 2: Administrative Documents.** This exempts

---

[31] Exec. Order No. 13,292, 68 C.F.R. 15,315 (2003), *available at* http://www.whitehouse.gov/news/releases/2003/03/20030325-11.html.

[32] Environmental Protection Agency v. Mink, 410 U.S. 73 (1973).

from required disclosure routine and insignificant matters that are "related solely to the internal personnel rules and practices of an agency." And, though the decisions of lower courts are not uniform, the exemption also protects agency manuals and rules — such as law enforcement manuals — if their release would help people dodge the law. (Materials like these are often also exempt under Exemption 7, law enforcement records.)

The exemption protects routine administrative documents, such as rules about lunch hours or sick leave, because it would be burdensome for an agency to assemble and maintain the material for public inspection, and the public wouldn't reasonably be expected to have an interest. On the other hand, the mere fact that an FOIA request has been made is evidence that information is not of interest solely to an agency.

Some agencies attempt to use Exemption 2 to conceal significant information. The leading case is *Air Force v. Rose*,[33] in which the Supreme Court rejected the contention that summaries of hearings concerning violations of the Air Force Academy Honor and Ethics Code were merely internal personnel matters. The Court found there was enough legitimate public interest in the integrity of its military academies to remove the records from the shield of this exemption.

**Exemption 3: Other Laws.** This exempts from required disclosure records that are "specifically exempted from disclosure by statute ... provided that such statute (a) requires that matter be withheld from the public in such a manner as to leave no discretion on the issue, or (b) establishes particular criteria for withholding or refers to particular types of matters to be withheld." An example is 50 U.S.C. sec. 403(g), under which the Central Intelligence Agency is not required to disclose its organization, functions, names, official titles, salaries or number of personnel employed. There are probably hundreds of statutes that authorize withholding. A complete list isn't available.

This exemption applies only to statutes and not to agency rules and regulations. Thus, an agency can't exempt itself; only Congress can do that. Similarly, an agency cannot invoke the exemption because a state law may protect certain records. A federal appellate court has held that state juvenile records in possession of federal authorities could not be withheld under this exemption because the federal law protected only federal juvenile delinquency proceedings from disclosure.[34] A record exempt from disclosure under state law may be available under the FOIA. The opposite may also be true.

**Exemption 4: Trade Secrets.** This exemption protects "trade secrets and commercial or financial information" that individuals and businesses supply to government. For Exemption 4 to apply, the information must be commercially valuable, actually used in a

trade or business and maintained in secret.

The idea is to protect the competitive positions of those who submit confidential information to the government. If companies that voluntarily submit information cannot depend upon it being held in confidence, they may refuse to cooperate, and government's ability to get information will be impaired. When the government compels production of the information, the rationale becomes strained, and this exemption would seem not to apply.

This distinction was muddied, however, by a 1992 case in which the Court of Appeals for the District of Columbia held that when a company submits information voluntarily, even if the government could have compelled disclosure, the information enjoys exempt status.[35] This decision has been criticized, for it seems to invite collusion between an agency and a business when neither wants the information to be made public. An agency and a business simply agree to voluntary submission, undermining a line of cases that refused to recognize an agency's pledge of confidentiality as a substitute for meeting the standards of Exemption 4. Whether the other circuits will follow this court's lead is unknown. But because of the number of FOIA cases it decides due to its location in the District of Columbia, and the expertise it has developed in this area, the FOIA decisions of the D.C. Circuit merit special attention. They are highly influential.

Businesses themselves sometimes try to protect their interests in secrecy through "reverse FOIA" suits. In these, a business that has provided information to the government sues the government to stop it from making the information public. Reverse FOIA suits only involve information that falls into an exempt category, usually Exemption 4, and that the government has the discretion to release. These suits challenge the release as an abuse of discretion.

**Exemption 5: Inter- and Intra-Agency Memoranda.** The exemption protects agency memoranda or letters and reflects several common law privileges. Under the common law, some communications are privileged, that is, protected from forced disclosure by a court. These privileges seek to protect some larger purpose. The attorney-client privilege, for example, is said to make the criminal justice system function better, even though it may create injustices in a particular case by denying access to some evidence.

Because of the privileges, Exemption 5 is probably the most complex and most important exemption: More than 95 percent of all documents are inter- or intra-agency memoranda.

The exemption protects the deliberative process of government that leads to a decision — candid advice and recommendations or the open exchange of ideas — in what is called "executive privilege." The exemption doesn't apply to the final decisions and opinions themselves, and it doesn't apply to statements of policy and instructions to staff that affect the public.

In deciding whether the privilege is applicable, courts examine whether a particular "predecisional" document is "so candid and

---

[33] 425 U.S. 352 (1976).

[34] McDonnell v. United States, 4 F.3d 1227 (3rd Cir. 1994).

[35] Energy Project v. NRC, 975 F.2d 871 (D.C. Cir. 1992) (en banc).

personal in nature that public disclosure is likely in the future to stifle honest and frank communication within the agency," whether it is in the form of a recommendation or a draft and whether it considers the "pros and cons ... of one view-point or another."[36]

The privilege protects only opinions, not factual information. The distinction between fact and opinion, however, isn't always self-evident and can't be made mechanically. Sometimes the factual component of a document is so merged with the deliberative component that it cannot be segregated. The D.C. Court of Appeals, for example, held that factual material about former United Nations Secretary General Kurt Waldheim was not required to be disclosed under Exemption 5.[37] The department was considering whether to exclude Waldheim as an undesirable alien in light of his alleged activities in World War II. The discretionary selection of material from a large number of primary documents, the court said, revealed significant insights into the Department of Justice's deliberations. In contrast, a complete chronological account of Waldheim's military service was not exempt since it did not suggest the thinking of the decision-makers.

The Supreme Court decided an important FOIA case involving Exemption 5 in March 2001. In *Department of the Interior v. Klamath Water Users Protective Association*,[38] it unanimously ruled in favor of public disclosure of correspondence between American Indian tribes and the Department of the Interior. The case involved a dispute over water rights in the Klamath River Basin in Oregon and California.

Water users, competing with a handful of Native American tribes for water-use rights, filed FOIA requests for documents the tribes had turned over to the Bureau of Indian Affairs in the Interior Department. The government denied the request, saying the papers were inter-agency memoranda and should be withheld from the public under Exemption 5. The Court reiterated several of its earlier FOIA rulings, stating that the "limited exemptions do not obscure the basic policy that disclosure, not secrecy, is the dominant objective of the Act."[39] It also pointed out that FOIA mandates a "general philosophy of full agency disclosure," which would "help ensure an informed citizenry, vital to the functioning of a democratic society."[40]

In addition to executive privilege, Exemption 5 incorporates several other common law privileges, including attorney-client confidences and a lawyer's work product — documents prepared in anticipation of actual or foreseeable litigation. But courts also have cited lesser-known privileges, including, for example, one that protects commercial information created by government itself if its disclosure would put the government at a competitive disadvantage in, say, contract negotiations.

**Exemption 6: Personal Privacy.** This exemption protects "personnel and medical files and similar files the disclosure of which would constitute a clearly unwarranted invasion of personal privacy." Congress enacted the exemption to protect intimate and personal details in government files. No specific kinds of files are categorically exempt, though some are more likely to contain the sort of highly intimate, personal information the exemption is designed to protect. The term "similar files" has been interpreted broadly. One appellate court, for example, held that the voice recordings of the crew in the Challenger rocket was a "similar file" since the tape revealed personal information about particular individuals.[41] The tapes contained the final radio transmissions before the rocket exploded, killing everyone on board.

Some recent decisions, however, have hardly concerned the sort of records usually associated with medical and personnel records. In *Department of Defense v. FLRA*,[42] for example, two unions sought the home addresses of certain federal employees. The privacy interest at stake was that of individuals not wanting to be bothered at home with work-related matters.

The Supreme Court reversed a lower court that had ordered release of those addresses. It balanced the competing interests and found that if the privacy interest of the employees was slight, the weight on the public interest side of the judicial balance beam was even slighter. Disclosure of home addresses would not shed appreciable light on government operations or activities. With this case, the Court has instructed lower courts to consider only the broad purpose of the FOIA in striking a balance — to what extent does disclosure enlighten the public about the operations of government? The particular purpose of the requester is irrelevant. Compare this categorical kind of balancing with that of the common law, which may consider the particular use to which the information will be put.

**Exemption 7: Law Enforcement Records.** The purpose of this exemption is to protect law enforcement records and other information whose disclosure would jeopardize investigations. This could happen because the details of a specific investigation were released, or because of the release of general investigative techniques or policies. The exemption also protects the physical safety of officials, informants and others in the criminal justice system.

As originally enacted, the exemption applied to "investigatory files compiled for law enforcement purposes." Courts interpreted that to give a blanket exemption to any file that met the threshold

---

[36] Coastal States Gas Corp. v. Dep't of Energy, 644 F.2d 854, 866 (D.C. Cir. 1980).

[37] Mapother v. Dep't of Justice, 3 F.3d 1533 (D.C. Cir. 1993).

[38] 532 U.S. 1 (2001).

[39] *Id.* at 8 (quoting Dep't of the Air Force v. Rose, 425 U.S. 352, 361 (1976)).

[40] *Id.* at 16 (quoting NLRB v. Robbins Tire & Rubber Co., 437 U.S. 214 (1987)).

[41] New York Times Co. v. NASA, 920 F.2d 1002 (D.C. Cir. 1990) (*en banc*).

[42] 510 U.S. 487 (1994).

test of being "investigatory." In one case, a court ruled that, even though there was no on-going or contemplated law enforcement proceeding, an analysis of the bullet that killed President John F. Kennedy was exempt because it remained part of an "investigatory" file.[43]

Congress narrowed the exemption in 1976 to avoid results like that. First, it limited withholding only to situations where release would cause any of several specific kinds of harm, disclosure of the identity of a confidential source, for example. Second, it allowed only the withholding of records, not entire files. Authorities had often withheld an entire file even if only one record in the file contained exempt material. One result of this amendment was to give historians and others access to a wealth of important material — such as that related to executed spies Julius and Ethel Rosenberg — that had remained sealed for decades as an "investigatory file." Agencies complained that the amendment went too far in the other direction and no longer gave adequate protection to some sensitive law enforcement information, particularly training manuals and other non-investigatory materials. So the exemption was again amended in 1986.

For a record to be exempt from required disclosure, a two-part test must be met. First, it must be determined that the records or information were compiled for "law enforcement purposes." This includes more than investigatory records; training manuals, for example, are exempt.

The Supreme Court answered one crucial question in 1989: Could an agency invoke Exemption 7 to deny access to information that was originally compiled for a purpose other than law enforcement but was later assembled for a criminal investigation? A majority of the Court said it could; the language of the statute did not require the original purpose of the information to be considered.[44] Justice Antonin Scalia dissented, arguing that the majority focused too tightly on the words of the law. He complained that the decision allows the policy behind the exemption to be "readily evaded (or [made] illusory) if it requires nothing more than gathering up documents the government does not wish to disclose, with a plausible law-enforcement purpose in mind. This is a hole one can drive a truck through."[45]

Whether the information is compiled for law enforcement purposes is only the first part of the test. For the exemption to apply, it must also be shown that release of the information "could reasonably be expected to cause" one of six specific kinds of harm. Four are noncontroversial and have received little judicial attention. They are:

- the withholding of records when disclosure would deny a person a right to a fair trial or impartial adjudication;
- withholding of information that would "endanger the life or physical safety" of an individual;

- withholding of records that would disclose law enforcement techniques, guidelines and procedures "if such disclosure could reasonably be expected to risk circumvention" of the law; and
- withholding records that protect the identities of confidential sources so long as there is a mutual expectation of a confidential relationship.

The remaining categories produce much litigation and confusion. One allows withholding if disclosure could "interfere with enforcement proceedings." If enforcement proceedings are over, however, or if none are on the horizon, this exemption shouldn't apply. Nonetheless, some agencies claim the exemption on the basis that a case may arise or be reopened.

Records or information may also be withheld if their release could "reasonably be expected to constitute an unwarranted invasion of personal privacy." This exemption is similar to Exemption 6 in that a balancing of the privacy interest and the public interest is required. A comparison of the wording of the two exemptions suggests that privacy interests should receive greater weight here. Before the privacy interest prevails in Exemption 6, the intrusion must be "clearly unwarranted." Here it must only be "unwarranted." In *Department of Justice v. Reporters Committee for Freedom of the Press,* the Court held that a request for information about a person's criminal history was unwarranted since it shed little light on "public understanding of the operations or activities of government."[46]

The case is important, not just for an explanation of the substantive test to be used here, but for the insights it provides about the Court's attitude toward electronic data. Most of the records the Reporters Committee sought were available in one place or another in the form of accessible, traditional, paper records. Getting them would require a lot of leg work. The federal government had them all in one place — a computer. But the Court said the records, in electronic form, were qualitatively different; the power of the computer to assemble and manipulate the data held vastly greater potential to violate personal privacy.

In 2004, the Supreme Court decided another important FOIA case involving the conflict between access and privacy and ruled in favor of "survivor privacy" in *National Archives and Records Administration v. Favish.*[47] California attorney Allan Favish sued for access to photos taken at the death scene of former top aide to President Clinton, Vince Foster. The Court held exemption 7(C) allowed the government to withhold documents that "could reasonably be expected to constitute an unwarranted invasion of personal privacy."[48] The Court ruled that survivors of a deceased person could assert a privacy interest in "their own piece of mind and tranquillity."[49]

[43] Wiesberg v. Dep't of Justice, 489 F.2d 1195 (D.C. Cir. 1973).
[44] John Doe Agency v. John Doe Corp., 492 U.S. 146 (1989).
[45] Id. at 163 (Scalia, J., dissenting).

[46] 489 U.S. 749, 775 (1989).
[47] 541 U.S. 157 (2004).
[48] Id. at 171.
[49] Id. at 166.

The government has interpreted *Favish* broadly, advising federal agencies to "take heed of the Court's explicit recognition in *Favish* that unfortunately today's 'sensation-seeking culture' breeds the potential for 'unwarranted public exploitation' of FOIA-disclosed records."[50]

**Exemption 8: Records of Financial Institutions.** This applies to records related to government supervision of financial institutions such as banks and savings and loans. The purpose is to protect the security and integrity of financial institutions.

**Exemption 9:** The exemption applies to "geological and geophysical information and data, including maps, concerning wells." This exemption protects oil well data.

## THE ELECTRONIC FOIA

The access guaranteed by the FOIA, however, has not kept pace with this electronic revolution. Some government agencies used their conversion to computerized record-keeping as an excuse not to release information to the public and the press. These bureaucrats argued that the new formats make reproducing information too expensive or unwieldy, or that releasing electronic data was not required by the FOIA. In addition, agencies under pressure to raise revenues, began charging fees for data that would have been free in paper form.

To solve some of these problems, Congress passed the Electronic Freedom of Information Act Amendments in 1996, thirty years after the FOIA was passed.[51] The EFOIA guarantees that records maintained in computer databases are as accessible as paper records. Among other things, the law requires that agencies make regulations, opinions, policy statements and similar information available on-line, on CD-ROM or on computer disc. It also requires agencies to provide information in the format requested whenever possible.[52] And it allows reporters expedited access if they can demonstrate a "compelling need" for the federal records they request under FOIA.[53]

Agencies are required to respond faster in two situations: (1) when failure to obtain records can pose an imminent threat to an individual's life or physical safety and (2) when a request is made by a person "primarily engaged in disseminating information ... to inform the public concerning actual or alleged federal government activity."[54] According to the law, expedited access requests must be processed within ten days. In addition, the law changes the time limit for other requests from ten to twenty days.

Under the EFOIA, agencies must make reasonable efforts to search for requested records in electronic form, except when a search would significantly interfere with agency information. Programming created to facilitate a database search does not amount to the creation of records.[55]

Commentators believe that the legislative history surrounding the law may ultimately provide broader access to governmental information and limit the Supreme Court's problematic ruling in *Department of Justice v. Reporters Committee.*[56] In *Reporters Committee*, the Supreme Court limited access to governmental records that revealed information relevant to the agency's "core purpose." Access advocates, including those in Congress, disagreed with the Court's decision. Congressional leaders indicated they crafted this FOIA amendment to address this restrictive view of access to public records.

"The purpose of the FOIA is to require agencies of the federal government to make records available to the public through public inspection and upon the request of any person for any public or private use," according to the findings of the Senate.[57] With this finding, Congress challenges the Supreme Court's narrow interpretation of the purpose of FOIA in *Reporters Committee*.

In language intended to clarify the FOIA's purpose, one of the bill's sponsors, Senator Patrick Leahy of Vermont, said:

> The purpose of the FOIA is not limited to making agency records and information available to the public only in cases where such material would shed light on the activities and operations of government. Efforts by the courts to articulate a "core purpose" for which information should be released imposes a limitation on the FOIA that Congress did not intend and that cannot be found in its language, and distorts the broader import of the Act in effectuating government openness.[58]

## DO FOIA AND EFOIA WORK?

Many access advocates have been disappointed with the government's response to the FOIA and its amendments. It is not unusual to wait for months or even years for a response. A recent study revealed that the oldest request has been pending for seventeen years.[59]

---

[50] U.S. Dept. of Justice FOIA Post, *available at* http://www.usdoj.gov/oip/foiapost/2004foiapost12.htm.

[51] 5 U.S.C. § 552 (1996).

[52] This provision was intended to overrule a 1983 federal district court decision, *Dismukes v. Dep't of the Interior*, 603 F. Supp. 760 (D.D.C. 1984), which held that agencies had no obligation to accommodate a requester's preference for computer access as long as the information was available in a reasonably accessible form.

[53] 5 U.S.C. § 552 (a)(6)(vi) (1996).

[54] 5 U.S.C. § 552 (a)(6)(E)(v)(II) (1996).

[55] 5 U.S.C. § 552(a)(3)(C) (1996).

[56] 489 U.S. 749 (1989).

[57] 5 U.S.C. § 522 (a)(2)(a) (1996).

[58] S. Rep. No. 104-272 (additional views of Sen. Patrick Leahy, at 23).

[59] *See* The National Security Archive, *Secrecy Report Card 2006, available at* http://www.gwu.edu/~nsarchiv/NSAEBB/NSAEBB182/index.htm.

Agencies say they do the best they can with their resources. The government spent more than $334 million in 2005 responding to almost twenty million requests, according to one report.[60] Contrary to a popular belief, journalists use the FOIA relatively infrequently. According to federal reports, most FOI requests come from individuals, not from the news media.[61] These requests are from people seeking personal information from the Department of Veterans Affairs, the Department of Health and Human Services and the Social Security Administration.[62] A new study found that FOIA is a critical tool for businesses seeking government information. According to the study, 60 percent of requests from other agencies come from commercial interests.[63]

Many agencies meet the time limits to respond to requests. Some do not. For example, three agencies that handle complex and security-related issues — the State Department, the CIA and the National Science Foundation — responded fully less than 20 percent of the time.[64]

While the EFOIA has triggered major reforms in electronic information processing, including the development of numerous government-agency Web pages filled with useful information, the courts and executive branch have ignored the amendment's findings intended to broaden FOIA's use to serve "any public or private purpose." As a result, legislation that would create a government ombudsman, tighten FOIA compliance deadlines and set up penalties for failing to adhere to the law has been introduced in Congress.

While using the FOIA and EFOIA takes patience and many of its promises have yet to be fulfilled, many of the nation's most important stories, including numerous Pulitzer Prize winners, have come from government documents accessed through the FOIA. Such stories have focused on human rights violations, corruption by public officials, workplace and aircraft accidents, bridge safety, cocaine trafficking, unsafe consumer products, serious health hazards and questionable research programs on humans.[65]

## FEDERAL OPEN MEETINGS LAWS

To supplement the Freedom of Information Act, Congress enacted the Sunshine Act in 1976.[66] The law requires the meetings of high-level decision-makers in about fifty executive-branch agencies to be open. Information available under the FOIA often represents only what was done, sometimes in a general or cursory way. The Sunshine Act lets the public observe how and why an agency makes the decisions it does.

The act has limited impact. Only agencies that are subject to the FOIA are affected. Thus, groups as important as the President's Council of Economic Advisors and the Board of Governors of the Federal Reserve aren't covered. Moreover, for the law to apply, the agency must be headed by a body of two or more members. Others are exempt on the premise that where an agency is headed by an individual, the need to observe give-and-take discussion among equals is absent.

The law is evaded regularly. Staff members, who aren't subject to the act, represent the views of their bosses to staffers of other agency heads, who then pass the information on to their bosses. In agencies where a quorum for a meeting is larger than two, agency heads can meet two at a time and discuss public matters. Some acknowledge that this isn't an efficient way to work and may not lead to good decision-making, but many agency heads argue that complying is just as inefficient. In April 1995, fifteen current and former agency heads asked Congress to amend the Sunshine Act to allow "broad outlines of policy" to be discussed in closed meetings.[67]

As it stands, the law requires that meetings be announced at least one week in advance and that the announcement include the time, place and subject of the meeting. It prohibits informal discussions and decision-making. The meetings opened by the Sunshine Act "are not intended to be merely reruns staged for the public after agency members have discussed the issue in private and predetermined their views," one Senate report concluded. "The whole decision-making process, not merely the results, must be exposed to public scrutiny."[68]

The act does not give the public a right to participate in the meetings.

The act allows, but does not require, portions of meetings to be closed when the subject matter falls into one or more of ten exemptions. If an exemption applies, the agency must balance the public interest in openness against the particular interest the exemption is designed to protect before closing a meeting.

Seven of the Sunshine Act's ten exemptions parallel those of the FOIA. The act has nothing like FOIA Exemption 5 (inter- and intra-agency memoranda) or Exemption 9 (geological or geophysical data). Instead, the act's Exemption 5 protects agency discussions that "involve accusing any person of a crime, or formally censuring any person." A general discussion doesn't qualify. It must focus on a specific person and, if it concerns a crime, a specific charge.

[60] See OpenTheGovernment.org, *Secrecy Report Card 2006, available at* http://www.openthegovernment.org/otg/SRC2006.pdf.

[61] See Coalition of Journalists for Open Government, *A Review of the Federal Government's FOI Act Performance, 2006, available at* http://www.cjog.net/documents/Combined_reports.pdf.

[62] *Id.*

[63] See Coalition of Journalists for Open Government, *Frequent Filers: Businesses Make FOIA Their Business, available at* http://www.sunshineweek.org/files/cjogfoiarpt06.pdf.

[64] See Rebecca Carr, *Open Government Advocates Push for FOIA Reform*, Cox News Service, May 11, 2005.

[65] See *FOI-Based Journalism*, Quill, Sept. 1997, at 34-36.

[66] 5 U.S.C. § 522(b) (1996).

[67] Cindy Skrycki, *Getting a Little Burned Up About the Sunshine Act*, Wash. Post, Apr. 28, 1995, at F1.

[68] Allan Robert Adler, Litigation under the Federal Open Government Laws 316-17 (1993) (quoting Senate Report No. 354, 94th Congress, 1st Session).

Exemption 9 shields two kinds of discussions: those that might jeopardize the stability of a financial institution or might trigger significant speculation in financial instruments, and those that might "significantly frustrate implementation of a proposed agency action." One court has limited the exemption to matters whose disclosure would allow someone to profit at government expense or allow an agency regulation to be evaded.[69] Exemption 10 of the Sunshine Act permits closure when discussions concern a subpoena or participation in a civil action or proceeding, such as arbitration or adjudication.

The Sunshine Act governs the conduct of government agencies; the Federal Advisory Committee Act, enacted in 1972, governs the advisory committee process and opens "to public scrutiny the manner in which government agencies obtain [information] from private individuals."[70] Whether called a "council," "task force," "commission" or something else, an advisory committee is a private group that is either established or utilized by the executive branch to obtain advice. One can also be created by statute.

FACA was passed to expose any waste of government funds on committee meetings that serve no useful function and to allow the public to observe any undue influence of lobbyists and special interest groups on federal decision-makers. In addition to opening deliberations, the act provides for public access to all committee records, reports, transcripts, appendices, working papers, drafts, studies, agenda or other documents that were prepared by or made available to the advisory committee. FACA is complex and riddled with qualifications, but it can be useful at times.

## ACCESS IN AN AGE OF TERRORISM

The terrorists' attacks on September 11, 2001, in New York City and Washington, D.C., had an immediate impact on federal freedom of information laws and access to information. Following the attacks, the federal government adopted numerous measures that increased government secrecy and restricted the public's right to know. It is now more difficult to get information from federal agencies under FOIA, access information from governmental web sites and review presidential records.

A month after the attacks, Attorney General John Ashcroft issued an official memorandum directing agencies to withhold information from FOI requesters if there were any "sound legal basis."[71] This action reversed a policy adopted during the Clinton administration that created a presumption of "maximum responsible disclosure of information."[72] Then Attorney General Janet

Reno had instructed federal agencies not to use discretionary exemptions to FOIA unless they could point to a "foreseeable harm" that would occur from disclosure.[73] As a result, the presumption of openness to federal records was reversed and agencies were encouraged to withhold many types of information formerly available to the public.[74]

In 2002, Congress passed and President Bush signed the Homeland Security Act.[75] Senator Patrick Leahy, a Democrat, called it "the most severe weakening of the Freedom of Information Act in its 36-year history."[76] The act provides mandatory confidentiality for information submitted to the government by business. The section is designed to protect information about the vulnerabilities of the country's critical infrastructure. The new act criminalizes agency disclosure of critical infrastructure information without the consent of the business. Companies that voluntarily share information with the government are guaranteed that the government will keep the information secret. In addition, they become immune from civil liability if the information reveals wrongdoing and immunity from antitrust suits for sharing the information with the government and each other.[77]

Citizen activists, public interest groups and environmental groups insisted that FOIA already protected against any legitimate risk of harmful disclosure. The groups argued, unsuccessfully, that knowing about vulnerabilities is the first step to correcting them.[78]

A number of public interest groups filed suit to force the government to disclose information about potential terrorists and their supporters, including the names of potential detainees arrested after September 11.[79] The federal appellate court reversed a lower court's decision, ruling the government did not have to release the information. "Both the Supreme Court and this Court have expressly recognized the propriety of deference to the executive in the context of FOIA claims which implicate national security," the court ruled.[80]

---

[69] See Common Cause v. NRC, 674 F.2d 921 (D.C. Cir. 1982).

[70] Nat'l Anti-Hunger Coalition v. Executive Comm. of the President's Privacy Sector Survey on Cost Control, 711 F.2d 1071, 1072 (D.C. Cir. 1983).

[71] U.S. Dept. of Justice, *Memorandum for Heads of All Federal Department and Agencies*, available at http://www.usdoj.oip/foiapost/2001foiapost19.htm. *See also* Don Wycliff, *Top Secret: Just Whose Government Is It?*, CHICAGO TRIB., Jan. 17, 2002, at 23.

[72] Eric Sinrod, *Defanging the Freedom of Information Act*, N.Y. L.J., Jan. 22,

2002, at 5.

[73] Office of the Attorney General, *Memorandum for Heads of Departments and Agencies*, available at http:///www.fas.org/sgp/clinton/reno.html. *See also* Tamara Lytle, *White House Clamps Down on Information*, ORLANDO SENT., Mar. 10, 2002, at A22.

[74] See Jane Kirtley, *Hiding Behind National Security*, AM. JOURN. REV., Jan.-Feb. 2002, at 62.

[75] P.L. 107-296 § 214 (2002).

[76] Dan Morgan, *Disclosure Curbs in Homeland Bill Decried; Information From Companies at Issue*, WASH. POST, Nov. 16. 2002, at A13.

[77] Homeland Security Act of 2002, Pub. L. No. 107-296; 116 Stat. 2135 (2002) (codifying various new surveillance and security measures and creating the Department of Homeland Security).

[78] HOMEFRONT CONFIDENTIAL: HOW THE WAR ON TERRORISM AFFECTS ACCESS TO INFORMATION AND THE PUBLIC'S RIGHT TO KNOW 55 (3d ed. 2003), available at http://www.rcfp.org.

[79] Ctr. for Nat'l Sec. Studies v. United States Dep't of Justice, 215 F. Supp. 2d 94 (D.D.C. 2002).

[80] Ctr. for Nat'l Sec. Studies v. United States Dep't of Justice, 331 F.3d 918, 927 (D.C. Cir. 2003).

Information available on the Internet was also severely limited following the terrorists' attacks. A number of federal agencies removed information from their Web sites, posting notices on the site that the information had been removed because of its possible usefulness to terrorists.[81] OMB Watch, a Washington, D.C., group that encourages citizen participation and open government, reported that twenty-one online sources have been partially or completely shut down since September 11.[82]

"The atmosphere of terror induced public officials to abandon this country's culture of openness and opt for secrecy as a way of ensuring safety and security," wrote Lucy Dalglish, executive director of the Reporters Committee for Freedom of the Press. "No one has demonstrated however, that an ignorant society is a safe society."[83]

In late 2001, President Bush also issued an executive order restricting access to presidential papers.[84] This order reverses the policy of increased openness in presidential records following the Watergate scandal of the early 1970s. It modified the Presidential Records Act of 1978,[85] signed into law by President Jimmy Carter, which made presidential records public property and created a mechanism for the records to be released over a specific period of time. Under the act, papers from Ronald Reagan's presidency should have been released in January 2001. Bush's order gives the president the authority to order the National Archives to withhold records. It also allows a former president to control the release of his records, keeping them secret if he wishes.

Open government advocates are also concerned about the dramatic increase in government secrets created by the way the government now classifies documents. According to one recent report, the government spent $7.7 billion to classify 14 million new documents in 2005.[86]

In 2005, President Bush signed Executive Order 13,392, "Improving Agency Disclosure of Information," which focuses on a "citizen centered" and "results-oriented" approach to FOIA.[87] Access advocates say the president's order is a good first step, but legislation is still needed to prod public officials to release information.[88]

While federal officials rushed to restrict access to information af-

ter September 11, most state legislatures moved more slowly. A number of legislatures are struggling with how to balance law enforcement's need to collect and protect sensitive data without infringing on individual liberties and exempting important information from their state's public records law.[89]

## STATE RIGHT-TO-KNOW LAWS

All states have laws requiring government records and meetings to be open to the public. In addition to these broad laws, states have specific statutes applicable to particular kinds of records. For example, Florida's public records law played a critical role in the 2000 post-presidential election process. Florida is the only state that provides for immediate access to ballots.[90] Newspapers and other groups used the law to review the state's ballots in an effort to determine who really received most of the votes for president in Florida. Other state statutes provide access to land deeds or voter registration records or to particular kinds of meetings.

Citizens are more likely to use these state laws than the federal laws; there are more state and local records, and there are more state and local issues. It's important, therefore, to have some knowledge of both the general and the specific laws where one works and lives.

For reporters, this is never more true than with meetings. If access to a record is denied, a requester will almost always have plenty of time to find help and consider the next step. No law requires that a record be handed over immediately; officials are given time to find and deliver it.

Meetings, however, are timely, and decisions have to be made on the spot. When the city council orders the public to leave the room so that "financial matters" can be discussed, for example, an observer must quickly answer several questions. Does the open meetings law allow secrecy when "financial matters" are discussed? Has the city council taken the required procedural steps, like taking a vote to close them meeting? If there are violations of the law, should the observer object immediately or file some kind of complaint? Or do nothing?

Answers to these questions require a working knowledge of the law, a feel for the workings of the particular governmental body and, sometimes, an understanding of what the observer's boss will authorize — like paying a lawyer to file an action.

Each state right-to-know law is unique. Each differs, not only in its language, but in its political setting and judicial arena. There is no substitute for becoming acquainted with state law. In most states, there are several sources of help, and some suggestions for finding help will be offered later in this chapter. Still, some general observations can be made.

As with any law, a good starting point is the policy behind the

---

[81] *See* Kevin Galvin, *Wary Agencies Stem Flow of Information,* SEATTLE TIMES, Dec. 11, 2001, at A1.

[82] *See* Dale Dempsy, *Databases Shut Down for Security; Federal Agencies Strive to Thwart Terror Attacks,* Nov. 11, 2001, DAYTON DAILY NEWS (LEXIS).

[83] *White House Embarked on Path of Secrecy After Sept. 11, Report Says, available at* http://www.rcfp.org/2002/0315report.html (Mar. 15, 2002).

[84] Exec. Order No. 13,233, 66 Fed. Reg. 56,025 (Nov. 1, 2001), *available at* http://www.whitehouse.gov/news/releases/2001/11/20011101.12.html.

[85] 44 U.S.C. § 2201 (1978).

[86] *See* OpenTheGovernment.org, *Secrecy Report Card 2006, available at* http://www.openthegovernment.org/otg/SRC2006.pdf.

[87] Exec. Order No. 13,392,70 Fed. Reg. 75,373, *available at* http://www.whitehouse.gov/news/releases/2005/12/20051214-4.html.

[88] *See* Rebecca Carr, *FOIA Overhaul Stalled,* Cox News Service, Aug. 3, 2006.

[89] *See* Greg McDonald, *No Stampede for New Terrorism Laws* (Apr. 5, 2002), *at* www.stateline.org.

[90] FLA. STAT. ch. 119.07(1)(c)(2000).

law. Precisely what did a legislature attempt to accomplish when it enacted the statute? Many state freedom of information statutes begin with a statement of policy. Some may not be particularly helpful. Kentucky, for example, says only that: "It is declared to be the public policy of this state that public records shall be open for inspection by any person...."[91] Others have a richer texture. Michigan, for example, declares:

> It is the public policy of this state that all persons are entitled to full and complete information regarding the affairs of government and the official acts of those who represent them as public officials and public employees.... The people shall be informed so that they may fully participate in the democratic process.[92]

When a custodian or court must decide whether to release information or open a meeting whose subject matter falls into a gray area, a statute like Michigan's is immensely more helpful to the analysis and may prove persuasive.

The nuts and bolts of the state right-to-know laws share similarities. They generally declare that all records and meetings are open to the public unless exemptions apply. Some states follow the federal lead and exempt only a few broad categories. This broad approach makes for a tidy-looking statute but probably causes more litigation because of the case-by-case balancing that inevitably goes with it.

Other states opt for specific, narrow exemptions, and, over the years, many have built a rather lengthy list. Virginia, for example, exempts nearly 100 types of records. Because of its length and apparent complexity, this narrow, specific approach results in an ugly looking law, but one that often works surprisingly well day-to-day because of its precision in describing what is accessible and what is not.

Many policy and legal issues are common to the federal FOIA and state right-to-know statutes. The decisions of federal courts in interpreting the FOIA, of course, are in no way binding on state courts interpreting their own laws. But the experience of federal courts in freedom of information issues may provide persuasive reasoning for states. So a careful review of the federal FOIA is not a bad place to acquire a background to understand local law.

Electronic records raise special issues that courts and legislatures are only beginning to address. Right-to-know laws were passed in an era of paper, folders and filing cabinets. Today many records are kept in electronic databases, accessible only through computers. Many states have amended their laws to accommodate this fundamental change, broadening the definition of "record" to include information on computer disks and tapes. For example, in Florida, "public records" mean "all documents, papers, letters, maps, books, tapes, photographs, films, sound recordings,

data processing software, or other material, regardless of the physical form, characteristics, or means of transmission...."[93]

Florida was one of the first states to amend its public records statute to reflect changing technology. Florida law, in its statement of policy, says:

> The legislature finds that given advancement in technology, providing access to public records by remote electronic means is an additional method of access that agencies should strive to provide to the extent feasible. If an agency provides access to public records by remote electronic means, then such access should be provided in the most cost-effective and efficient manner available to the agency providing the information.[94]

The revisions also include a statement regarding accessibility of electronic records. It reads:

> The legislature finds that providing access to public records is a duty of each agency and that automation of public records must not erode the right of access to those records. As each agency increases its use of and dependence on electronic recordkeeping, each agency must ensure reasonable access to records electronically maintained.[95]

However, keeping pace with technology remains the biggest challenge for most states.

First, there are physical complications. In earlier days, a request for a record required a custodian to locate and retrieve a specific piece of paper from a filing cabinet. The law, not unreasonably because of the labor needed, did not require a custodian to create a record that did not already exist or to abstract or manipulate data from those that did.

Today, however, a custodian can use this reasoning in ways never intended when the laws were passed. In one sense, an electronic record does not exist until someone does something to create it. Thus, every request, in a narrow, literal sense, requires the creation of a record. And the law, based on an era of paper records, never requires the creation of a record.

Custodians rarely, if ever, go to that extreme with routine requests. Requesters tend to get the same information they received when records were on paper. But there is a serious problem with the borderline requests — those that require more than minimal personnel intervention with the computer. At what point does programming, because of the quantity or quality of the data manipulation required or because of the novelty of the finished product, cross the line between the routine (which is required) and the extraordinary (which isn't)? No legislative body has developed a satisfactory answer. Finding and describing that point, at

91 KENTUCKY REV. STAT § 61.870 (1994).
92 MICHIGAN COM. LAWS ANN. § 15.231 (1993).
93 FLA. STAT. ch. 119.01(1) (1995).
94 FLA. STAT. ch. 119.01(2) (1995).
95 FLA. STAT. ch. 119.01(3) (1995).

the federal and state levels, is a pressing legal challenge.

Closely related are paper-era prohibitions against abstracting or manipulating data. A right-to-know request to manually abstract data from a particular paper document and then manually correlate it with that taken from other paper records was at one time a practical impossibility. But the development of modern relational databases, accurate scanners and the promise of further advances can make filling these requests no more trouble than a trip to the filing cabinet. Indeed, developments in software and expanded opportunities for direct public access through on-line gateways or public-use terminals promise to eliminate, fairly soon, the physical issues with record access and manipulation. If they are being resolved, other computer-related issues are being worsened.

As a matter of public policy, many state and local governments sell computer-generated data to pay for computer systems and to provide a regular stream of additional revenue. Commercial interests, direct-mail firms and utilities, for example, are willing to pay well for this data. But if state law requires an agency to provide information virtually free to all comers, it can hardly expect to profit from the data. So many states have either amended or are trying to amend their right-to-know laws to allow them to enter the business of selling government information. The inevitable result is that less data in less powerful forms is available to the public.

E-mail communication regarding government business is considered a public record by many states. Most states do not explicitly address e-mail in their open records statutes – only four do.[96] One of the four, Montana, specifies that "public records, kept in this state, of private writings, including electronic mail" are open for inspection.[97]

Though e-mail is not directly addressed in the open record statutes of thirty-seven states, their statutory definitions of records could include e-mail.[98] Oklahoma, for example, includes in its definition of a public record "data files created by or used with computer software, computer tape, disk ... or other material regardless of physical form or characteristic."[99] In Florida, whose public record statute does not directly address e-mail, its supreme court in 2003 held that though e-mail can be a public record, private e-mails of public employees are not subject to the public record law.[100] The remaining states do not specifically mention e-mail or computer records in their open record statutes.[101]

However, confusion still reigns over how to handle e-mail in many states. The lack of a specific statute in Michigan allowed two agencies to develop radically different e-mail practices: The University of Michigan made e-mail private to the "fullest extent permitted by law;" Washtenaw County, where the university's Ann Arbor campus is located, adopted a policy that makes the county's e-mail open to the public.[102]

The same power that makes electronic information so attractive to many private and commercial interests raises grave privacy concerns to others. One recalls that the Supreme Court found a computer database to be much more than the sum of its parts. It was not the release of the individual rap sheet that the Court found to be an invasion of privacy — it was the vast power of the computer to acquire and manipulate the data. Privacy advocates are successfully raising these issues in many states and at the federal level.

In 1994, Congress, concerned about protecting privacy, passed legislation that controls access to state government records. The Drivers Protection Privacy Act is a complex federal statute that prevents public access to personal information in state drivers' records.[103] The act is filled with irony. Congress passed it following the 1989 death of Rebecca Schaeffer, who was killed by an obsessed fan. The fan hired a private investigator to obtain the actress' address by accessing her California motor vehicle record. The irony is that private investigators continue to have access to this information under the relatively new federal law.

The Supreme Court upheld the Drivers Protection Privacy Act in early 2000, ruling in *Reno v. Condon*[104] that Congress has the authority to tell state governments not to release certain records otherwise available under state law. The attorney general of South Carolina had challenged the federal statute. He argued that it violated the Tenth Amendment to the Constitution. That amendment prohibits the federal government from intruding on the states' right to govern themselves. The Supreme Court ruled that the DPPA was a valid exercise of congressional power. As a result, federal law trumps state law, and even states that want to keep the records open must obey the federal mandate.

Finally, access to public records and meetings may rest on the statutory enforcement provisions. Despite the statutory directive to open their processes to public scrutiny, government agencies often try to hide behind exemptions for records and meetings. Government attorneys, funded with taxpayer money, often litigate with the hope of establishing a precedent of closure.

Some states vest enforcement power with the local prosecutor, who has the power to investigate and file charges against public officials for violating open government laws. Florida law, for example,

---

[96] The four are California, Colorado, Montana and Tennessee.

[97] MONT. CODE ANN. § 2-6-101 (2004).

[98] Statutory definitions of public records could be interpreted to include e-mail in Alaska, Arkansas, Connecticut, Delaware, District of Columbia, Florida, Georgia, Hawaii, Idaho, Indiana, Illinois, Iowa, Kansas, Kentucky, Louisiana, Maine, Maryland, Michigan, Minnesota, Mississippi, Missouri, Nebraska, New Mexico, New York, North Carolina, North Dakota, Ohio, Oklahoma, Oregon, Rhode Island, South Carolina, Texas, Vermont, Virginia, Washington, West Virginia, Wisconsin and Wyoming.

[99] OKLA. STAT. tit. 51, § 24A.3 (2004).

[100] State v. City of Clearwater, 863 So. 2d 149 (Fla. 2003).

[101] Computer records are not specifically mentioned in the open record laws of Arizona, Colorado, Delaware, Idaho, Nevada, North Dakota, Ohio,

Pennsylvania and South Dakota.

[102] REPORTERS COMMITTEE FOR FREEDOM OF THE PRESS, ACCESS TO ELECTRONIC RECORDS: A GUIDE TO REPORTING IN THE COMPUTER AGE (1998), *at* http://www.rcfp.org/elecaccess.

[103] 18 U.S.C. § 2721-2725 (1994 & Supp. IV. 1998).

[104] 528 U.S. 141 (2000).

# Tips on Getting Access to State Public Records and Meetings

1. **Be prepared.**
   Do your homework. Know the law. Understand how the process works. Be aware of possible exemptions.
2. **Understand the agency you are investigating.**
   Identify the official responsible for the records or meetings you want and be as specific as possible with your requests.
3. **Be firm.**
   Remind public officials of their obligations under the law. Explain the law when necessary, but be polite.
4. **Put your request in writing.**
   Even if a written request is not required by your state, this serves as an official record of the request. In many states, it triggers the law requiring an official response.
5. **Don't give up when you hear "no."**
   Many records custodians use the initial denial as a test and count on your giving up. Also, most states require an agency to document denials, citing appropriate exemptions and explaining the appellate process.
6. **Report the story.**
   When you get shut out of a meeting or denied a record, that's news; report it.
7. **Don't explain why you want the information.**
   Keep your request formal and your description of why you want the information broad. Explaining the purpose of your request can sometimes alert the records custodian, making it more difficult to get your information.
8. **Be prepared for some delays.**
   This is especially true when you ask for a lot of information or access to sensitive documents. Remember tip number 5.
9. **Understand computers.**
   Computers are being used more and more to store the information you want and how you can get electronic access. This is often the cheapest and the most efficient way to get records.
10. **Consider calling your lawyer.**
    When records custodians deny your request and clearly violate the law, you need to consider your legal alternatives. Individuals need to consider whether they're willing to pay a lawyer for advice. Journalists typically make these decisions in consultation with editors and station managers.

---

authorizes state prosecutors to file civil or criminal complaints against public officials who knowingly violate the public records law. Those officials can be removed from office and face criminal penalties of up to a year in jail and $1,000 fines.[105]

For the first time in Florida's history, a public official who was convicted of a criminal violation of the state's public records law was actually sent to jail in 1999. Vanette Webb, a school board member, spent seven days in jail before being released, pending an appeal. A jury convicted Webb of knowingly violating the law. The judge sentenced her to eleven months and fifteen days in jail. She was also suspended from office by the governor.[106] In 2003, a former Florida Speaker of the House, W.D. Childers, was sentenced to sixty days in jail for violating the state's open meetings part of its Sunshine Law.[107]

In most cases, however, officials who violate the law face no penalties. Research shows that almost 70 percent of prosecutors across the nation charged with enforcing their states' open meetings laws never initiated an investigation into an alleged violation.[108] Even where state statutes allow private citizens to file civil suits to enforce the law, the high costs of litigation discourages many people. Citizens, who make far more complaints about open government than the news media, know that fighting City Hall can be an expensive, time-consuming process. As a result, major media organizations bear the burden of filing lawsuits to enforce the law.

## SUMMARY

Access to government records and meetings is essential to meaningful participation in government. As vital and as obvious as that axiom is, only recently has there been a widespread and sustained

---

[105] Fla. Stat. ch. 119.02 (1909).

[106] Associated Press, *School Board Member Free*, Palm Beach Post, May 22, 1999, at A24.

[107] *See* Ginny Graybiel, *Childers Gets 60 Days; Bass Avoids Jail Time*, Pensacola News J., May 13, 2003, at 1A.

[108] *See* Charles Davis, Sandra Chance & Bill Chamberlin, *Constant Fight for State Records*, Quill, Oct. 1996, at 50.

effort to guarantee citizen access to governmental information.

The federal constitution and some state constitutions provide limited access, particularly in the criminal justice system. Viewed optimistically, the decisions hint at a broader, emerging right of access, but only after a workable rule can be crafted that will draw a sharp, easily applied line between those things that need to be public and those that don't. This can take years.

The common law can supplement other access tools, mainly statutes. The elastic qualities of the common law, one of its historic weaknesses, is an asset to exploit when a tool must be found to reach information inaccessible by other means.

Federal and state statutes — freedom of information or right-to-know laws — are the front-line means of access. There is a federal records law (the Freedom of Information Act) and a federal meetings law (the Sunshine Act). Access to federal electronic records is covered in the Electronic Freedom of Information Act. Each state has its own counterpart to the federal laws, and many states are including access to electronic records, as well. As a group, these laws give each citizen the right to inspect and copy government documents or attend government meetings.

Some agencies and, in fact, entire branches of government, typically the judicial branch, are exempt. Each statute also identifies kinds of records or subjects of meetings that are exempt from required disclosure. In most, but not all of these exempt categories, secrecy is not required. The government may open the record or meeting if the public interest in access outweighs the competing interest of the exception.

## FOR ADDITIONAL READING

There are many sources of practical help for gaining access to meetings and records, but a few stand out:

**Federal Access Law.** The Reporters Committee for Freedom of the Press publishes "How to Use the Federal FOI Act," a detailed guide to using the Freedom of Information Act. The publication is available on the RCFP Web site at: http://www.rcfp.org/foiact/index.html.

**State Access Law.** The Reporters Committee also publishes "Tapping Official's Secrets," a guide to open government in the fifty states. It's available on the RCFP Web site at: http://www.rcfp.org. Written for and by lawyers, these publications are important resources for information about specific state laws. In addition, most state press associations are willing, even eager, to help with understanding local, right-to-know laws.

**Sunshine Week:** The American Society of Newspaper Editors and the Coalition of Journalists for Open Government are promoting Sunshine Week, which typically occurs around James Madison's birthday, March 16. Sunshine Week is a national effort to focus on the importance of open government. The Web site features stories, studies, research, editorials and editorial cartoons focused on access to information. The resource material can be found at: http://www.sunshineweek.org.

In addition, the Brechner Center for Freedom of Information's Citizen Access Project charts and ranks different aspects of access in the fifty states. Information about the various state rankings is available at http://www.citizenaccess.org.

# 18

# Newsgathering

*By Charles N. Davis*

---

☞ **Headnote Questions**

- *To what extent does the First Amendment protect the right to gather news?*
- *What restrictions can constitutionally be placed on journalists covering newsworthy events in public places?*
- *Where has the battle to gather news in public places been most successfully fought?*
- *Do reporters have a First Amendment right to interview prisoners, view executions and gather news at schools or private businesses?*
- *Do reporters have a First Amendment right to enter private property to gather news?*
- *Does the First Amendment protect journalists who violate the law?*

---

Information is the lifeblood of communications. Journalists report on what happens in city halls and in the halls of Congress, in local courthouses and in the Supreme Court, in statehouses and in the White House. These reports help broaden the understanding of the public and help citizens make decisions vital to maintaining a democracy. To get the information they need from all those venues, however, reporters must have access to people, to places and to government documents.

The U.S. Supreme Court has steadfastly ruled that the First Amendment protects the right to disseminate information, news and opinions. In *Branzburg v. Hayes*, for example, it recognized the press' First Amendment right to gather information because, "without some protection for seeking out the news, freedom of the press could be eviscerated."[1] But the level of First Amendment protection for newsgathering activities is not clear. In that same *Branzburg* decision, the Court held that "the First Amendment does not guarantee the press a constitutional right of special access to information not available to the public generally."[2]

While the Court has acknowledged that the First Amendment protects newsgathering activities, the extent of that protection remains uncertain at best. The September 11, 2001, terrorist attacks have renewed the age-old debate over the news media's ability to gather news of military conflict abroad and at home.

## NEWSGATHERING IN PUBLIC PLACES

Newsworthy events occur in public, and journalists are free to gather news from any places where activities "could be observed by passers-by."[3] As one court held, once an individual is exposed to public observation, the individual "is not entitled to the same degree of privacy that she would enjoy within the confines of her own home."[4]

Streets, sidewalks, parks and similar places are known as "traditional public forums," and the public and the press enjoy a general right of access to them and activities that occur there. In addition, the government often makes other property available for public use. Those places are known as "dedicated public forums." In most circumstances, the government may not limit or deny access to public forums, but it may impose reasonable time, place and manner restrictions on activities that go on there.

Reporters do not have free rein to go wherever they want, whenever they want. Access to people and places – even public places – is often restricted. There are restrictions, for example, on how and when reporters can gather news in prisons, at disaster scenes, on military installations and other public places.

---

[1] 408 U.S. 665, 681 (1972). *See also* California First Amendment Coal. v. Calderon, 150 F.3d 976 (9th Cir. 1998).
[2] *Id*. at 684.

[3] Forster v. Manchester, 189 A.2d 147, 150 (Pa. 1963).
[4] *Id*.

## Judicial Proceedings

The battle over the First Amendment right to gather news in public places has been most successfully fought in the area of access to judicial proceedings. In 1980, the Supreme Court acknowledged a First Amendment right of public access to judicial proceedings. In *Richmond Newspapers v. Virginia*,[5] it held that the First Amendment provided the public and the press with a right to attend trials. That "watershed decision"[6] laid the groundwork for the evolving First Amendment right of access to other judicial proceedings,[7] as well as to other governmental activities. Access to courts is covered in depth in Chapter 16.

## Disaster, Accident and Crime Scenes

When a train crashes or there is a school bus accident, cameras and news crews are not far behind. And, while reporters have an "undoubted right to gather news from any source by means within the law,"[8] officials have the authority to restrict access to public property when there is such a disaster in the interest of safety or administrative efficiency. Indeed, the Supreme Court noted in *Branzburg* that "newsmen have no constitutional right of access to the scenes of crime or disaster when the general public is excluded."[9] So, if a crime or disaster occurs on private property or a police or fire department restricts admittance to the scene, generally there is no First Amendment right of access, and journalists have been arrested for refusing to obey orders from officials to leave disaster scenes.

Some courts, however, have acknowledged a First Amendment right for journalists to cover news at accident scenes, so long as there is no interference with emergency activities.[10] In addition, at least three states – California, Ohio and Virginia – have statutes that specifically recognize a right of press access to emergency and disaster scenes.[11] "Members of the news media must be afforded special access to disaster sites in order that they may properly perform their function of informing the public," a California appeals court held.[12] But even in California, authorities may curtail access where law enforcement officials are investigating a crime.[13]

In addition to state laws allowing access to disaster scenes, access might be granted through the doctrines of implied consent and custom and usage. In *Florida Publishing Co. v. Fletcher*,[14]

reporters entered a fire-ravaged house and photographed a silhouette left on the floor after a victim's body was removed. The victim's mother, who was out of town at the time of the fire and learned of her daughter's death through the news report, was outraged and sued the newspaper.

The Florida Supreme Court ruled that there was a "long-standing custom and practice throughout the country," which protected the media in such situations.[15] It ruled that because it was customary for journalists to accompany officials onto private property and the photographer was asked to take photographs for the fire officials, the journalists were protected. That reasoning, however, has not been widely adopted.

## NEWSGATHERING ON PUBLIC PROPERTY

While journalists are generally free to gather and report on news that occurs in public forums, newsgathering activities can be restricted on government property not open for general public use, that is, in nonpublic forums.

## Prisons

The Supreme Court outlined some of the limitations of the First Amendment right of access to prisons and prisoners in three cases in the 1970s. In *Pell v. Procunier*,[16] *Saxbe v. Washington Post*[17] and *Houchins v. KQED*,[18] it declared that the First Amendment does not guarantee the press access to correctional facilities or specifically identified prisoners.

In *Pell*, the Court upheld California's correctional rules that restricted the ability of media representatives to interview specific prisoners. While the First Amendment prohibits the government from interfering with a free press, the Court held, the Constitution doesn't guarantee the press more access to correctional facilities than the average citizen. In *Saxbe*, decided the same year, the Court upheld the constitutionality of a federal prison regulation that, like the California rule, prohibited interviews with specific prisoners. Finally, in *Houchins*, four years later, it held that, because the First Amendment does not require the release of information within the control of government, it does not require a sheriff to grant journalists access to a county jail.

In this triad of cases, the Court balanced the responsibility of prison officials to maintain order and provide a secure environment against the right of journalists to gather news in volatile environments, and ruled in favor of the government. The decisions gave prison officials considerable latitude in restricting access to prisons and prisoners. According to a study sponsored by the Society of Professional Journalists, many state correctional systems have seized upon the Court's rulings to restrict inmates' access to the outside world. Some regulations include outright bans on face-to-face interviews; others discriminate between so-

---

[5] 488 U.S. 555 (1980).

[6] *Id.* at 582-83 (Stevens, J., concurring).

[7] *See, e.g.*, Press-Enter. Co. v. Riverside County Superior Court, 478 U.S. 1 (1986); Press-Enter. Co. v. Riverside County Superior Court, 464 U.S. 501 (1984); Globe Newspaper Co. v. Superior Court, 457 U.S. 596 (1982).

[8] City of Oak Creek v. King, 436 N.W.2d 285, 292 (Wis. 1989).

[9] 408 U.S. 665, 684-85 (1972).

[10] *See, e.g.*, Connell v. Town of Hudson, 733 F. Supp. 465 (D.N.H. 1990).

[11] CAL. PENAL CODE § 409.5(a), (d) (2006); OHIO REV. CODE ANN. § 2917.13(B) (2006); VA. CODE §§ 15.2-17.14 and 27-15.5 (1950).

[12] Leiserson v. City of San Diego, 184 Cal. App. 3d 41, 51-52 (Cal. 1986).

[13] *Id.* at 51.

[14] 340 So. 2d 914 (Fla. 1976).

[15] *Id.* at 918.

[16] 417 U.S. 817 (1974).

[17] 417 U.S. 843 (1974).

[18] 438 U.S. 1 (1978).

called "legitimate" and "entertainment media"; still others ban the use of electronic equipment within the prison.[19]

California, responding to complaints from officials of an overwhelming number of requests from reporters to interview so-called "celebrity" prisoners, such as Charles Manson and the Menendez brothers, was the first state to embrace new, more restrictive policies designed to prevent high-profile criminals from becoming celebrities. The restrictions, which prohibit face-to-face interviews, make it almost impossible for reporters to cover other important prison-related stories, such as allegations of beatings, rapes and administrative abuses. Prisoners have even been punished in California for contacting the news media to report possible abuses.[20]

In Connecticut, journalists are required to prepare written requests for interviews, including statements of any "perceived benefit to law enforcement agencies." The regulations require requests for access to be based on "whether a print or electronic report results in a significant benefit to law enforcement agencies."[21]

## Executions

Executions usually occur in prisons. So access to these events, particularly by broadcasters and photographers, is also subject to government fiat.

In 1994, talk show host Phil Donahue tried unsuccessfully to get permission to televise the execution of a convicted murderer in North Carolina. The prison warden refused, and the North Carolina Supreme Court ruled that the First Amendment did not require officials to allow taping of executions.[22]

In 2001, two Internet companies lost a lawsuit in which they sought the right to broadcast the execution of Oklahoma City bomber Timothy McVeigh over the Internet. A federal judge in Terre Haute, Ind., said there is no First Amendment right to broadcast an execution from within a prison.[23]

In addition, a federal appeals court ruled that California officials can bar the public and press during the preparation of inmates for execution.[24] The court acknowledged that executions are "unquestionably matters of great public importance" and that "more information leads to a better informed public,"[25] but it ruled that officials were justified in barring public access out of concern for the anonymity of execution team members. The ruling overturned a federal judge's decision that the public and press have a First Amendment right to attend executions.[26]

## Military Bases, Operations and War Zones

Neither military bases nor battlefields are public forums.[27] During the 1960s and 1970s, the press enjoyed broad rights of access to battlefields. In fact, media reports on the Vietnam War are often credited with changing Americans' feelings about the war. During the 1983 invasion of Grenada, however, the press was much more controlled by the military. Reporters whom military escorts accompanied on battlefields complained of attempts to censor their reports. As a result, an inquiry by a special panel of the Joint Chiefs of Staff concluded that "it is essential that the U.S. news media cover U.S. military operations to the maximum degree possible consistent with mission security and the safety of U.S. forces."[28]

Despite the military's position on providing access to the media following Grenada, eight years later journalists again complained bitterly about restrictions during Operation Desert Storm. A group of journalists maintained in a special report to the Department of Defense that the military restrictions "made it impossible for reporters and photographers to tell the public the full story of the war in a timely fashion."[29] In a report to the Defense Department, executives representing seventeen of the country's major news organizations – including ABC, CBS, NBC, CNN, the *Washington Post* and the *New York Times* – formally protested about the pool system that limited the number of journalists who were allowed to cover certain stories and the long delays in getting copy to newsrooms in the United States.[30] They also charged that reporters' copy was altered during military security reviews.[31] Ultimately the Defense Department, key press associations and representatives from twenty news organizations agreed that "open and independent reporting" will be the "principle means" by which U.S. wars are covered.[32]

The conflict in Afghanistan that the terrorist attacks of September 11, 2001, precipitated also has been marked by access debates and tight controls on battlefield journalists. The escalation of U.S. forces before the Oct. 7, 2001, attacks on Al-Qaeda and the Taliban generally occurred without a media presence, and press restrictions early in the conflict constrained press coverage so severely that American reporters learned second-hand about the fall of Mazar-e-Sharif, a strategic gateway to U.S. troops based in nearby Uzbekistan.[33]

Defense officials have described the war in Afghanistan as a

---

[19] *See* Charles N. Davis, *Access to Prisons,* QUILL, May 1998, at 19-28.

[20] *Id.* at 22.

[21] Conn. Dept. of Corrections, Directive No. 15, at 3 (1995). *See also* Davis, *supra* note 19, at 24.

[22] Lawson v. Dixon, 446 S.E.2d 799 (N.C. 1994).

[23] Entm't Network v. Lappin, 134 F. Supp. 2d 1002 (S.D. Ind. 2001).

[24] California First Amendment Coal. v. Calderon, 150 F.3d 976 (9th Cir. 1998).

[25] *Id.* at 982.

[26] California First Amendment Coal. v. Calderon, 956 F. Supp. 883 (N.D. Cal. 1997).

[27] *See* United States v. Albertini, 472 U.S. 675 (1985).

[28] CHAIRMAN OF THE JOINT CHIEFS OF STAFF MEDIA-MILITARY RELATIONS PANEL 3 (1984).

[29] REPORT OF 17 NEWS EXECUTIVES TO SECRETARY RICHARD CHENEY, COVERING THE PERSIAN GULF WAR 2 (June 14, 1991).

[30] *See* Jane DeParles, *17 News Executives Criticize U.S. for "Censorship" of Gulf Coverage,* N.Y. TIMES, July 3, 1991, at A4.

[31] *See* Paul McMasters, *Free Press Falls Victim to War,* QUILL, Oct. 1991, at 7.

[32] Howard Kurtz & Barton Gellman, *Guidelines Set for News Coverage of Wars,* WASH. POST, May 22, 1992, at A23.

[33] REPORTERS COMMITTEE FOR FREEDOM OF THE PRESS, HOMEFRONT CONFIDENTIAL: HOW THE WAR ON TERRORISM AFFECTS ACCESS TO INFORMATION AND THE PUBLIC'S RIGHT TO KNOW 1 (2002), *available at* http://www.rcfp.org/homefrontconfidential/covering.html, at 1.

different kind of war, one that required restrictions on journalists so that military operations and soldiers' lives would not be endangered. The compromises reached after the Gulf War did not hold, and journalists struggled to provide full coverage.

Relations between American military officials and reporters were strained. *Washington Post* reporter Doug Struck claimed that a U.S. soldier, whom he did not identify, threatened to shoot him if he went near the scene of a U.S. Hellfire missile strike in 2002. The administration denied that a troop leader would knowingly threaten an American citizen, a response that Struck asserted was "an amazing lie."[34] At the end of February 2002 – when the war was more than four months old – the Pentagon began allowing journalists to accompany U.S. ground troops in combat, but only after the reporters agreed to withhold filing their reports until military officials gave them permission.[35]

Journalists can do little more than negotiate with the Defense Department and complain when access to military operations limits the amount of independent reporting that the press can do. Legal challenges to restrictions on press access to military operations have been unsuccessful.

The beginning of hostilities in Iraq in the spring of 2003 ushered in a new form of reporting, and with it a new word in the lexicon: embedding. Responding to the criticism of the first Gulf War conflict, the Pentagon launched an embedding policy that placed journalists within military units in the field. Reporters traveled, ate and slept alongside soldiers, in a carefully planned system that resulted in compelling images of live firefights and U.S. bombing runs as well as its share of criticism for tight controls on the movements of reporters.

### Polling Places

Newsgathering near polling places has become controversial in recent years, a situation to which anyone who witnessed the 2000 presidential election can attest. Critics of exit polls claim that such polls interfere with the election process, influencing undecided voters and discouraging potential voters from casting their ballots. Pollsters, however, assert that political speech about the electoral process is core First Amendment speech and must be protected.

The Supreme Court has not ruled on the issue of exit polling,[36] but at least one federal appellate court has. In 1988, the Ninth U.S. Circuit Court of Appeals struck down as unconstitutional a Washington law prohibiting exit polling within 300 feet of polling places. It said the law was a content-based restriction on voters' First Amendment rights to discuss their political views and the press' right to gather news. It acknowledged the state's compelling interest in preserving peace, order and decorum at polling places, but as one judge wrote, the law "restricts the me-

dia's right of access to information crucial to the political process, and for that reason, violates the principles embodied in the First Amendment."[37]

Though not ruling on exit polling, the Supreme Court has upheld a law restricting campaign activities near polling places. In *Burson v. Freeman*, it upheld a Tennessee law prohibiting solicitation of votes and regulating the display and distribution of campaign material within one hundred feet of a polling place.[38] The Court acknowledged that the law regulated core political speech but that it satisfied the strict scrutiny test, because the "restricted zone is necessary in order to serve the states' compelling interest in preventing voter intimidation and election fraud."[39]

### Schools

Governments own public schools. When school business is being conducted, however, schools are usually not open to the public. Journalists who want to gather news on school property, therefore, generally need permission from school officials. In addition, reporters and photographers need to be aware that minors cannot legally waive their rights, meaning they cannot legally consent to interviews or be photographed. Many schools are sending standard photograph releases home, asking parents to give permission for their children to be photographed while at school.

The First Amendment, however, protects the right of reporters and photographers to cover events on school property from adjacent public property, such as sidewalks and streets.

### NEWSGATHERING ON PRIVATE PROPERTY

When owners of private property and journalists clash over journalists' efforts to gather news on that property, courts frequently focus on whether the journalists had consent to enter the property. Reporters and photographers often don't have permission – sometimes they enter over the objections of property owners; other times, a property owner is not present to grant permission.

Some states recognize a common law right of journalists to enter private property to gather news. In other states, however, entry without an owner's permission is trespassing, and both criminal and civil penalties could attach. In any event, remaining on private property after being ordered to leave by a property owner or a custodian of the property is almost always considered trespassing.

### Ride-Alongs

Some of the most popular TV shows involve journalists accompanying and recording the activities of law enforcement officers

---

[34] *Id.* at 2.

[35] *Id.*

[36] *But see* Mills v. Alabama, 384 U.S. 214, 218 (1966), in which the Court indicated that a state may have power to regulate conduct in and around polls to maintain peace, order and decorum.

[37] Daily Herald Co. v. Munro, 838 F. 2d 380, 389 (9th Cir. 1988) (Reinhardt, J., concurring).

[38] 504 U.S. 191 (1992).

[39] *Id.* at 206.

and emergency personnel. Police agencies sometimes encourage these so-called "ride-alongs" because they tend to put officers in a human, and sometimes heroic, light. And journalists argue that the practice serves a significant public interest by enabling public oversight of law enforcement, deterring crime and danger to police, and curbing potential police misconduct. All that may be true, but the practice still has come under increased scrutiny.

It has also been threatened by legal action. In 1999, the Supreme Court, in two unanimous opinions, struck a blow against ride-alongs. In both cases, the targets of searches sued law enforcement officials, claiming that by inviting the press to accompany them on raids, the officials violated Fourth Amendment rights against unreasonable searches. The Court agreed, ruling in *Hanlon v. Berger*[40] and *Wilson v. Layne*[41] that police can be sued for allowing journalists to accompany them onto private property.

In *Layne*, U.S. marshals and county sheriff's deputies allowed a reporter and photographer from the *Washington Post* to join their early-morning raid of a home where they expected to find a fugitive. The fugitive was not there, but his parents were rousted from bed in full view of the journalists. The photographs, one showing Wilson in his underwear with a police officer's gun to his head, were never published; but the couple, claiming an invasion of privacy, sued the officials.

In *Berger*, CNN crews accompanied fish and wildlife agents onto a Montana ranch in search of eagles that may have been poisoned by pesticides. The ranch owners sued the U.S. Fish and Wildlife agents who invited the journalists along on the search.

Writing for the Court, Chief Justice William Rehnquist held that the public interest benefit of ride-alongs did not justify the Fourth Amendment violation. "Surely the possibility of good public relations for the police is simply not enough, standing alone, to justify the ride-along intrusion into a private home," he wrote. "And even the need for accurate reporting on police issues in general bears no direct relation to the constitutional justification for the police intrusion into a home in order to execute a ... warrant."[42]

The legal liability for the news media who accompany police on ride-alongs remains unclear.

### Private Businesses Open to the Public

Reporters and photographers often face access problems when they cover events in places that are privately owned but open to the public, like restaurants and shopping malls. In 1968, the Supreme Court held that a shopping mall was the modern equivalent of a downtown business district.[43] It retreated from that position in 1972, however, when it ruled that property does not "lose its private character merely because the public is generally

invited to use it for designated purposes."[44]

So, the First Amendment does not require owners of private businesses, including malls, to permit reporters to gather news on their property. But some states have laws that protect free speech rights on such property. California's constitution, for example, protects the rights to speak, write and publish, and the state supreme court has interpreted these rights to apply to activities at shopping malls. The Supreme Court affirmed that interpretation.[45]

### Restricting Paparazzi

In 1997, Princess Diana of England was killed in an automobile accident. Reports of the accident indicate that it might have been caused, in part, because Diana's driver was attempting to elude cars driven by celebrity photographers – called "paparazzi." As a result of the accident, an outcry arose for laws restricting the activities of paparazzi. Lawmakers responded to the outcry.

Legislation was adopted in California, for example, that severely limits the use of telephoto lenses and other electronic equipment to gather news.[46] The law creates a civil cause of action against photographers who trespass on private property in order to obtain photographs, or who "technologically trespass" by employing enhancement devices, including telephoto lenses or high-powered microphones. The law establishes liability when a person

knowingly committed an act of trespass in order to physically invade the privacy of the plaintiff with the intent to capture any type of visual image, recording or other physical impression of the plaintiff engaging in a personal or familial activity and the physical invasion occurs in a manner that is offensive to a reasonable person.

In the wake of Princess Diana's death, Congress considered three separate bills – the so-called "paparazzi bills" – that would provide punishment for harassment by photojournalists.[47] After several hearings, at which some celebrities testified about their lack of privacy, the bills died.

The controversy was rekindled in 2005 when a photographer rammed his minivan into Disney star Lindsay Lohan's Mercedes Benz. Spurred by Justin Timberlake, Cameron Diaz and others, Los Angeles police and prosecutors opened a criminal investigation into what they describe as a hyperaggressive new breed of paparazzi willing to go to almost any lengths to get photographs. The emphasis on criminal law indicates the lack of success by celebrities in seeking civil damages, which time and again run into

---

[40] 526 U.S. 808 (1999).
[41] 526 U.S. 603 (1999).
[42] *Id.* at 620.
[43] Amalgamated Food Employees Union Local 590 v. Logan Valley Plaza, Inc., 391 U.S. 308 (1968).
[44] Lloyd Corp. Ltd. v. Tanner, 407 U.S. 551, 569 (1972).
[45] *See* Robins v. Pruneyard Shopping Ctr., 592 P.2d 341 (Cal. 1979), *aff'd* Pruneyard Shopping Ctr. v. Robins, 447 U.S. 74 (1980).
[46] CAL. CIV. CODE § 1708.8 (1998).
[47] Personal Privacy Protection Act, S. 2103, 105th Cong. (1998); Privacy Protection Act of 1998, H.R. 3224, 105th Cong. (1998); Protection from Personal Intrusion Act, H.R. 2448, 105th Cong. (1997).

First Amendment problems.[48]

## LEGAL AND ILLEGAL NEWSGATHERING TECHNIQUES

How far can a journalist go to gather news? What behavior constitutes a newsgathering tort? Does the First Amendment protect a journalist from misleading a source? Can he use stolen documents? Can she conduct ambush interviews? Can a journalist secretly tape conversations?

The answers to these questions, and others like them, have, in recent years, driven the discussion about newsgathering, about how much journalists can push beyond traditional boundaries and about the use of new technologies. The Supreme Court has never ruled on a reporter's liability for publishing information from illegally obtained documents. In general, if a reporter lawfully acquires information about matters of public concern, states may not punish publication of the information absent a compelling interest.[49] But a reporter, of course, may be punished for illegal activities.

In 1998, a reporter for the *Cincinnati Enquirer* learned this lesson the hard way. Michael Gallagher admitted to illegally gaining access to Chiquita Brands International corporate voice-mail system.[50] The newspaper then fired him, and the state prosecuted him on multiple counts of violating Ohio's electronic communication privacy law and for unauthorized access to a computer. He pleaded guilty to two counts and was sentenced to five years of probation and 200 hours of community service work.[51] Chiquita also sued him for defamation and for breaking into its voice mail system. Gallagher settled that lawsuit in 1999, and the terms have not been released.[52]

The *Cincinnati Enquirer* also suffered from the experience. It renounced the stories about Chiquita's business practices, apologized and paid more than $10 million to the company to avoid a lawsuit.[53] The newspaper *was* sued, however, by a former lawyer for Chiquita who was the reporter's source for the story. He accused the newspaper of breach of contract, fraud and negligence for breaking a promise by identifying him.[54] Indeed, the Supreme Court has held that liability can be found when journalists break promises to sources.[55] The *Cincinnati Enquirer* has called the entire episode "one of the most unfortunate, and em-

barrassing, failures of modern investigative journalism."[56]

Another hotbed of controversy in newsgathering involves tape-recorded conversations. In a highly anticipated 2001 decision, the Supreme Court held that the First Amendment protects the release of illegally tape-recorded conversations when neither the source nor the reporter plays a role in the unlawful interception. In a 6-3 decision, it held in *Bartnicki v. Vopper*[57] that the First Amendment rights of the media outweigh a federal wiretapping statute designed to prevent interception of private conversations.

The case involved the dissemination of an illegal tape recording of a cell phone conversation between Gloria Bartnicki, the chief negotiator for a teacher's union in Wyoming Valley West School District in Pennsylvania, and Anthony Kane, the union's president. The tape included Bartnicki's complaints about the school board's reluctance to approve a proposal for a three-percent pay raise, and a discussion about blowing up the front porches of uncooperative school board members. An unknown person gave a copy of the tape to Jack Yocum, the leader of the group opposed to the union's wage proposals. Yocum passed a copy of the tape to Frederick Vopper, a radio talk show host, who played it repeatedly on his show.

Justice John Paul Stevens, writing for the majority, held that although the privacy of communications and the minimization of harm to those whose communications were illegally intercepted represented strong government interests, these interests did not outweigh the First Amendment right to publish matters of public concern.

Although they signed on to the majority's opinion, Justices Stephen Breyer and Sandra Day O'Connor concurred in a narrower opinion, written by Justice Breyer, stating that the publication was protected because the recording was of public interest and the speakers were public figures.[58] Breyer and O'Connor were swayed by the fact that the federal statutes were broader than necessary to deter the relevant bad conduct and that the publication concerned a potential threat to public safety, decreasing the speaker's legitimate interest in maintaining the privacy of the communication.

Chief Justice William Rehnquist, joined by Justices Antonin Scalia and Clarence Thomas dissented, citing concern for privacy in electronic communications.[59]

Journalists have also been successfully sued for breaching a duty of loyalty. In 1997, Food Lion sued Capital Cities/ABC, Inc., for an undercover report on the grocery store's food-handling policies.[60] Reporters assumed false identities to get the jobs at Food Lion stores and used hidden cameras to expose practices

---

[48] *See* David M. Halbfinger & Allison Hope Weiner, *As Paparazzi Push Ever Harder, Stars Seek a Way to Push Back,* N.Y. Times, June 9, 2005, at A1.

[49] *See* Florida Star v. B.J.F., 491 U.S. 524 (1989); Smith v. Daily Mail Publishing Co., 443 U.S. 97 (1979); Landmark Communications, Inc. v. Virginia, 435 U.S. 829 (1978).

[50] *See* Ben Kaufman, *Former Chiquita Layer Sues Paper,* CINCINNATI ENQUIRER, Sept. 28, 1999, at B2.

[51] *See* Dan Horn, *Former Reporter Given Probation,* CINCINNATI ENQUIRER, July 17, 1999, at B1.

[52] *See Reporter Gets Probation in Chiquita Case,* July 20, 2000, *available at* http:www.freedomfreedom.org/professional/1999/7/16chiquita.ap.

[53] *See* James C. Goodale, *Why Did the "Enquirer" Pay $10 Million?,* N.Y. L.J., Aug. 7, 1998, at 3.

[54] *See* Dan Horn, *Enquirer Denies It Divulged a Source,* CINCINNATI ENQUIRER, Nov. 30, 1999, at B2.

[55] *See* Cohen v. Cowles Media Co., 501 U.S. 663 (1991).

[56] *See* Dan Horn, *Gannett: Suit Dodges Blame,* CINCINNATI ENQUIRER, June 21, 2000, at B2. (Former editor Lawrence Beaupre sued Gannett for fraud, breach of contract, attorney malpractice and conspiracy to injure his reputation. Gannett has denied the allegations.)

[57] 532 U.S. 514 (2001).

[58] *Id.* at 535 (Breyer, J., concurring).

[59] *Id.* at 541 (Rehnquist, C.J., dissenting).

[60] Food Lion, Inc. v. Capital Cities/ABC, Inc., 887 F. Supp. 811 (M.D.N.C. 1995).

in the grocer's delicatessens. Food Lion claimed intentional misrepresentation, deceit, fraud, negligent supervision, trespass, breach of fiduciary duty, civil conspiracy, violation of federal wiretap statutes, unfair and deceptive trace practices and violations of the Racketeer Influenced and Corrupt Organizations Act (RICO). A jury awarded Food Lion almost $1,500 in compensatory damages and $5.5 million in punitive damages, which the trial court reduced to $315,000.[61] ABC appealed the decision, and the Fourth U.S. Circuit Court of Appeals cut the verdict to $2, $1 for trespass and $1 for breach of loyalty.[62]

While some lower courts have allowed lawsuits against the media for engaging in fraud to obtain stories or footage, courts typically dismiss fraud claims where the claim is an alternative to a libel claim.[63]

## SUMMARY

The U.S. Supreme Court has noted that the First Amendment protects newsgathering. Specifically, both the First Amendment and the common law provide for the right of journalists to gather news from traditional public forums. In addition, the Court has interpreted the First Amendment to ensure a right of access to criminal judicial proceedings.

But the Court has also said that the First Amendment does not guarantee an unrestricted right to gather news on all public property and in all public places. Not all government-owned properties are public forums. Military bases and public schools are two examples. In addition, activity around polling places – including newsgathering – may be restricted. Legislative bodies also have passed laws restricting some newsgathering activities of paparazzi.

In 1999, the Supreme Court ruled on two cases involving journalists accompanying police on raids, known as "ride-alongs." It unanimously held that law enforcement officials violate the Fourth Amendment protections against unreasonable searches by allowing television crews and other journalists to accompany them.

The First Amendment does not require private businesses, including shopping malls and restaurants, to allow reporters unfettered access to their property. As a result, reporters do not have a right to remain on private property after being told to leave, and in some jurisdictions it may be illegal to enter the property at all without first gaining the permission of the property owner. Shopping malls and restaurants are considered private property.

While successful journalists have to be cunning and persistent, sometimes gaining access to information and people in unconventional ways, they must remember that the First Amendment will not protect them when they commit a crime, such as trespassing. The media have also been held liable for fraud, breach of promise of confidentiality and breach of duty of loyalty to employers when reporters pose as employees to gain access to nonpublic areas.

## FOR ADDITIONAL READING

Alexander, Marc C. "Attention, Shoppers: The First Amendment in the Modern Shopping Mall," 41 *Arizona Law Review* 927 (1992).

Davis, Charles N. "Access to Prisons," *Quill*, May 1988, p. 14.

Dienes, Thomas C., Lee Levine, Robert C. Lind. *Newsgathering and the Law*, Dayton, Ohio: Lesis, 1997.

Dyk, Timothy B. "Newsgathering, Press Access, and the First Amendment," 44 *Stanford Law Review* 927 (1992).

Goodale, James C., ed. *Communications Law*. New York: Practicing Law Institute, 1998.

LeBel, Paul A. "Symposium: Undercover Newsgathering Techniques: Issues and Concerns: The Constitutional Interest in Getting the News: Toward a First Amendment Protection from Tort Liability for Surreptitious Newsgathering," 4 *William & Mary Bill of Rights Law Journal* 1145 (1996).

Reporters Committee for Freedom of the Press, *Homefront Confidential: How the War on Terrorism Affects Access to Information and the Public's Right to Know*, Arlington, Va.: Reporters Committee for Freedom of the Press, 2002.

Sager, Kelli L. and Karen N. Frederiksen. "People v. Simpson: Perspectives on the Implications for the Criminal Justice System: Televising the Judicial Branch: In Furtherance of the Public's First Amendment Rights," 69 *Southern California Law Review* 1519 (1996).

Sharkey, Jacqueline E. "The Television War," *American Journalism Review*, May 2003, p. 18.

Smolla, Rodney A. *Suing the Press*. New York: Oxford University Press, 1986.

---

[61] Food Lion, Inc. v. Capital Cities/ABC, Inc., 984 F. Supp. 923 (M.D.N.C. 1997).

[62] Food Lion, Inc. v. Capital Cities/ABC, Inc., 194 F.3d 505 (4th Cir. 1999).

[63] *See, e.g.*, La Luna Enter, Inc. v. DBS Corp., 74 F. Supp. 2d 384 (S.D.N.Y. 1999).

# The Constitution
# of the United States of America*

We the People of the United States, in Order to form a more perfect Union, establish Justice, insure domestic Tranquility, provide for the common defence, promote the general Welfare, and secure the Blessings of Liberty to ourselves and our Posterity, do ordain and establish this Constitution for the United States of America.

## Article I

### Section 1

All legislative Powers herein granted shall be vested in a Congress of the United States, which shall consist of a Senate and House of Representatives.

### Section 2

The House of Representatives shall be composed of Members chosen every second Year by the People of the several States, and the Electors in each State shall have the Qualifications requisite for Electors of the most numerous Branch of the State Legislature.

No Person shall be a Representative who shall not have attained to the Age of twenty five Years, and been seven Years a Citizen of the United States, and who shall not, when elected, be an Inhabitant of that State in which he shall be chosen.

[Representatives and direct Taxes shall be apportioned among the several States which may be included within this Union, according to their respective Numbers, which shall be determined by adding to the whole Number of free Persons, including those bound to Service for a Term of Years, and excluding Indians not taxed, three fifths of all other Persons.][1] The actual Enumeration shall be made within three Years after the first Meeting of the Congress of the United States, and within every subsequent Term of ten Years, in such Manner as they shall by Law direct. The Number of Representatives shall not exceed one for every thirty Thousand, but each State shall have at Least one Representative; and until such enumeration shall be made, the State of New Hampshire shall be entitled to chuse three, Massachusetts eight, Rhode-Island and Providence Plantations one, Connecticut five, New-York six, New Jersey four, Pennsylvania eight, Delaware one, Maryland six, Virginia ten, North Carolina five, South Carolina five, and Georgia three.

When vacancies happen in the Representation from any State, the Executive Authority thereof shall issue Writs of Election to fill such Vacancies.

The House of Representatives shall chuse their Speaker and other Officers; and shall have the sole Power of Impeachment.

### Section 3

The Senate of the United States shall be composed of two Senators from each State, [chosen by the Legislature thereof,][2] for six Years; and each Senator shall have one Vote.

Immediately after they shall be assembled in Consequence of the first Election, they shall be divided as equally as may be into three Classes. The Seats of the Senators of the first Class shall be vacated at the Expiration of the second Year, of the second Class at the Expiration of the fourth Year, and of the third Class at the Expiration of the sixth Year, so that one third may be chosen every second Year; [and if Vacancies happen by Resignation, or otherwise, during the Recess of the Legislature of any State, the Executive thereof may make temporary Appointments until the next Meeting of the Legislature, which shall then fill such Vacancies.][3]

No Person shall be a Senator who shall not have attained to the Age of thirty Years, and been nine Years a Citizen of the United States, and who shall not, when elected, be an Inhabitant of that State for which he shall be chosen.

The Vice President of the United States shall be President of the Senate, but shall have no Vote, unless they be equally divided.

The Senate shall chuse their other Officers, and also a President pro tempore, in the Absence of the Vice President, or when he shall exercise the Office of President of the United States.

The Senate shall have the sole Power to try all Impeachments. When sitting for that Purpose, they shall be on Oath or Affirmation. When the President of the United States is tried, the Chief

---

* The Constitution was adopted in 1788.
[1] Changed by section 2 of the Fourteenth Amendment.

374

Justice shall preside: And no Person shall be convicted without the Concurrence of two thirds of the Members present.

Judgment in Cases of Impeachment shall not extend further than to removal from Office, and disqualification to hold and enjoy any Office of honor, Trust or Profit under the United States: but the Party convicted shall nevertheless be liable and subject to Indictment, Trial, Judgment and Punishment, according to Law.

### Section 4

The Times, Places and Manner of holding Elections for Senators and Representatives, shall be prescribed in each State by the Legislature thereof; but the Congress may at any time by Law make or alter such Regulations, except as to the Places of chusing Senators.

The Congress shall assemble at least once in every Year, and such Meeting shall be on [the first Monday in December,][4] unless they shall by Law appoint a different Day.

### Section 5

Each House shall be the Judge of the Elections, Returns and Qualifications of its own Members, and a Majority of each shall constitute a Quorum to do Business; but a smaller Number may adjourn from day to day, and may be authorized to compel the Attendance of absent Members, in such Manner, and under such Penalties as each House may provide.

Each House may determine the Rules of its Proceedings, punish its Members for disorderly Behaviour, and, with the Concurrence of two thirds, expel a Member.

Each House shall keep a Journal of its Proceedings, and from time to time publish the same, excepting such Parts as may in their Judgment require Secrecy; and the Yeas and Nays of the Members of either House on any question shall, at the Desire of one fifth of those Present, be entered on the Journal.

Neither House, during the Session of Congress, shall, without the Consent of the other, adjourn for more than three days, nor to any other Place than that in which the two Houses shall be sitting.

### Section 6

The Senators and Representatives shall receive a Compensation for their Services, to be ascertained by Law, and paid out of the Treasury of the United States. They shall in all Cases, except Treason, Felony and Breach of the Peace, be privileged from Arrest during their Attendance at the Session of their respective Houses, and in going to and returning from the same; and for any Speech or Debate in either House, they shall not be questioned in any other Place.

No Senator or Representative shall, during the Time for which he was elected, be appointed to any civil Office under the Authority of the United States, which shall have been created, or the Emoluments whereof shall have been encreased during such time; and no Person holding any Office under the United States, shall be a Member of either House during his Continuance in Office.

### Section 7

All Bills for raising Revenue shall originate in the House of Representatives; but the Senate may propose or concur with Amendments as on other Bills.

Every Bill which shall have passed the House of Representatives and the Senate, shall, before it become a Law, be presented to the President of the United States; If he approve he shall sign it, but if not he shall return it, with his Objections to that House in which it shall have originated, who shall enter the Objections at large on their Journal, and proceed to reconsider it. If after such Reconsideration two thirds of that House shall agree to pass the Bill, it shall be sent, together with the Objections, to the other House, by which it shall likewise be reconsidered, and if approved by two thirds of that House, it shall become a Law. But in all such Cases the Votes of both Houses shall be determined by yeas and Nays, and the Names of the Persons voting for and against the Bill shall be entered on the Journal of each House respectively. If any Bill shall not be returned by the President within ten Days (Sundays excepted) after it shall have been presented to him, the Same shall be a Law, in like Manner as if he had signed it, unless the Congress by their Adjournment prevent its Return, in which Case it shall not be a Law.

Every Order, Resolution, or Vote to which the Concurrence of the Senate and House of Representatives may be necessary (except on a question of Adjournment) shall be presented to the President of the United States; and before the Same shall take Effect, shall be approved by him, or being disapproved by him, shall be repassed by two thirds of the Senate and House of Representatives, according to the Rules and Limitations prescribed in the Case of a Bill.

### Section 8

The Congress shall have Power To lay and collect Taxes, Duties, Imposts and Excises, to pay the Debts and provide for the common Defence and general Welfare of the United States; but all Duties, Imposts and Excises shall be uniform throughout the United States;

To borrow Money on the credit of the United States;

To regulate Commerce with foreign Nations, and among the several States, and with the Indian Tribes;

To establish an uniform Rule of Naturalization, and uniform Laws on the subject of Bankruptcies throughout the United States;

To coin Money, regulate the Value thereof, and of foreign Coin, and fix the Standard of Weights and Measures;

To provide for the Punishment of counterfeiting the Securities and current Coin of the United States;

---

[4] Changed by section 2 of the Twentieth Amendment to January 3.

To establish Post Offices and post Roads;

To promote the Progress of Science and useful Arts, by securing for limited Times to Authors and Inventors the exclusive Right to their respective Writings and Discoveries;

To constitute Tribunals inferior to the supreme Court;

To define and punish Piracies and Felonies committed on the high Seas, and Offences against the Law of Nations;

To declare War, grant Letters of Marque and Reprisal, and make Rules concerning Captures on Land and Water;

To raise and support Armies, but no Appropriation of Money to that Use shall be for a longer Term than two Years;

To provide and maintain a Navy;

To make Rules for the Government and Regulation of the land and naval Forces;

To provide for calling forth the Militia to execute the Laws of the Union, suppress Insurrections and repel Invasions;

To provide for organizing, arming, and disciplining, the Militia, and for governing such Part of them as may be employed in the Service of the United States, reserving to the States respectively, the Appointment of the Officers, and the Authority of training the Militia according to the discipline prescribed by Congress;

To exercise exclusive Legislation in all Cases whatsoever, over such District (not exceeding ten Miles square) as may, by Cession of particular States, and the Acceptance of Congress, become the Seat of the Government of the United States, and to exercise like Authority over all Places purchased by the Consent of the Legislature of the State in which the Same shall be, for the Erection of Forts, Magazines, Arsenals, dock-Yards, and other needful Buildings; —And

To make all Laws which shall be necessary and proper for carrying into Execution the foregoing Powers, and all other Powers vested by this Constitution in the Government of the United States, or in any Department or Officer thereof.

## Section 9

The Migration or Importation of such Persons as any of the States now existing shall think proper to admit, shall not be prohibited by the Congress prior to the Year one thousand eight hundred and eight, but a Tax or duty may be imposed on such Importation, not exceeding ten dollars for each Person.

The Privilege of the Writ of Habeas Corpus shall not be suspended, unless when in Cases of Rebellion or Invasion the public Safety may require it.

No Bill of Attainder or ex post facto Law shall be passed.

No Capitation, or other direct, Tax shall be laid, unless in Proportion to the Census or Enumeration herein before directed to be taken.[5]

No Tax or Duty shall be laid on Articles exported from any State.

No Preference shall be given by any Regulation of Commerce or Revenue to the Ports of one State over those of another: nor shall Vessels bound to, or from, one State, be obliged to enter, clear, or pay Duties in another.

No Money shall be drawn from the Treasury, but in Consequence of Appropriations made by Law; and a regular Statement and Account of the Receipts and Expenditures of all public Money shall be published from time to time.

No Title of Nobility shall be granted by the United States: And no Person holding any Office of Profit or Trust under them, shall, without the Consent of the Congress, accept of any present, Emolument, Office, or Title, of any kind whatever, from any King, Prince, or foreign State.

## Section 10

No State shall enter into any Treaty, Alliance, or Confederation; grant Letters of Marque and Reprisal; coin Money; emit Bills of Credit; make any Thing but gold and silver Coin a Tender in Payment of Debts; pass any Bill of Attainder, ex post facto Law, or Law impairing the Obligation of Contracts, or grant any Title of Nobility.

No State shall, without the Consent of the Congress, lay any Imposts or Duties on Imports or Exports, except what may be absolutely necessary for executing its inspection Laws: and the net Produce of all Duties and Imposts, laid by any State on Imports or Exports, shall be for the Use of the Treasury of the United States; and all such Laws shall be subject to the Revision and Controul of the Congress.

No State shall, without the Consent of Congress, lay any Duty of Tonnage, keep Troops, or Ships of War in time of Peace, enter into any Agreement or Compact with another State, or with a foreign Power, or engage in War, unless actually invaded, or in such imminent Danger as will not admit of delay.

# Article II

## Section 1

The executive Power shall be vested in a President of the United States of America. He shall hold his Office during the Term of four Years, and, together with the Vice President, chosen for the same Term, be elected, as follows

Each State shall appoint, in such Manner as the Legislature thereof may direct, a Number of Electors, equal to the whole Number of Senators and Representatives to which the State may be entitled in the Congress: but no Senator or Representative, or Person holding an Office of Trust or Profit under the United States, shall be appointed an Elector.

[The Electors shall meet in their respective States, and vote by Ballot for two Persons, of whom one at least shall not be an Inhabitant of the same State with themselves. And they shall make a List of all the Persons voted for, and of the Number of Votes for each;

---

[5] But the Sixteenth Amendment allowed for the collection of income taxes.

which List they shall sign and certify, and transmit sealed to the Seat of the Government of the United States, directed to the President of the Senate. The President of the Senate shall, in the Presence of the Senate and House of Representatives, open all the Certificates, and the Votes shall then be counted. The Person having the greatest Number of Votes shall be the President, if such Number be a Majority of the whole Number of Electors appointed; and if there be more than one who have such Majority, and have an equal Number of Votes, then the House of Representatives shall immediately chuse by Ballot one of them for President; and if no Person have a Majority, then from the five highest on the List the said House shall in like Manner chuse the President. But in chusing the President, the Votes shall be taken by States, the Representation from each State having one Vote; A quorum for this Purpose shall consist of a Member or Members from two thirds of the States, and a Majority of all the States shall be necessary to a Choice. In every Case, after the Choice of the President, the Person having the greatest Number of Votes of the Electors shall be the Vice President. But if there should remain two or more who have equal Votes, the Senate shall chuse from them by Ballot the Vice President.][6]

The Congress may determine the Time of chusing the Electors, and the Day on which they shall give their Votes; which Day shall be the same throughout the United States.

No Person except a natural born Citizen, or a Citizen of the United States, at the time of the Adoption of this Constitution, shall be eligible to the Office of President; neither shall any Person be eligible to that Office who shall not have attained to the Age of thirty five Years, and been fourteen Years a Resident within the United States.

[In Case of the Removal of the President from Office, or of his Death, Resignation, or Inability to discharge the Powers and Duties of the said Office, the Same shall devolve on the VicePresident, and the Congress may by Law provide for the Case of Removal, Death, Resignation or Inability, both of the President and Vice President, declaring what Officer shall then act as President, and such Officer shall act accordingly, until the Disability be removed, or a President shall be elected.][7]

The President shall, at stated Times, receive for his Services, a Compensation, which shall neither be encreased nor diminished during the Period for which he shall have been elected, and he shall not receive within that Period any other Emolument from the United States, or any of them.

Before he enter on the Execution of his Office, he shall take the following Oath or Affirmation:— "I do solemnly swear (or affirm) that I will faithfully execute the Office of President of the United States, and will to the best of my Ability, preserve, protect and defend the Constitution of the United States."

## Section 2

The President shall be Commander in Chief of the Army and Navy of the United States, and of the Militia of the several States, when called into the actual Service of the United States; he may require the Opinion, in writing, of the principal Officer in each of the executive Departments, upon any Subject relating to the Duties of their respective Offices, and he shall have Power to grant Reprieves and Pardons for Offences against the United States, except in Cases of Impeachment.

He shall have Power, by and with the Advice and Consent of the Senate, to make Treaties, provided two thirds of the Senators present concur; and he shall nominate, and by and with the Advice and Consent of the Senate, shall appoint Ambassadors, other public Ministers and Consuls, Judges of the supreme Court, and all other Officers of the United States, whose Appointments are not herein otherwise provided for, and which shall be established by Law: but the Congress may by Law vest the Appointment of such inferior Officers, as they think proper, in the President alone, in the Courts of Law, or in the Heads of Departments.

The President shall have Power to fill up all Vacancies that may happen during the Recess of the Senate, by granting Commissions which shall expire at the End of their next Session.

## Section 3

He shall from time to time give to the Congress Information of the State of the Union, and recommend to their Consideration such Measures as he shall judge necessary and expedient; he may, on extraordinary Occasions, convene both Houses, or either of them, and in Case of Disagreement between them, with Respect to the Time of Adjournment, he may adjourn them to such Time as he shall think proper; he shall receive Ambassadors and other public Ministers; he shall take Care that the Laws be faithfully executed, and shall Commission all the Officers of the United States.

## Section 4

The President, Vice President and all civil Officers of the United States, shall be removed from Office on Impeachment for, and Conviction of, Treason, Bribery, or other high Crimes and Misdemeanors.

## Article III

### Section 1

The judicial Power of the United States, shall be vested in one supreme Court, and in such inferior Courts as the Congress may from time to time ordain and establish. The Judges, both of the supreme and inferior Courts, shall hold their Offices during good Behaviour, and shall, at stated Times, receive for their Services, a Compensation, which shall not be diminished during their Continuance in Office.

---

[6] Changed by the Twelfth Amendment.
[7] Changed by the Twenty-Fifth Amendment.

## Section 2

The judicial Power shall extend to all Cases, in Law and Equity, arising under this Constitution, the Laws of the United States, and Treaties made, or which shall be made, under their Authority;—to all Cases affecting Ambassadors, other public Ministers and Consuls;—to all Cases of admiralty and maritime Jurisdiction;—to Controversies to which the United States shall be a Party;—to Controversies between two or more States; [—between a State and Citizens of another State;][8]—between Citizens of different States, —between Citizens of the same State claiming Lands under Grants of different States, [and between a State, or the Citizens thereof, and foreign States, Citizens or Subjects.][9]

In all Cases affecting Ambassadors, other public Ministers and Consuls, and those in which a State shall be Party, the supreme Court shall have original Jurisdiction. In all the other Cases before mentioned, the supreme Court shall have appellate Jurisdiction, both as to Law and Fact, with such Exceptions, and under such Regulations as the Congress shall make.

The Trial of all Crimes, except in Cases of Impeachment, shall be by Jury; and such Trial shall be held in the State where the said Crimes shall have been committed; but when not committed within any State, the Trial shall be at such Place or Places as the Congress may by Law have directed.

## Section 3

Treason against the United States, shall consist only in levying War against them, or in adhering to their Enemies, giving them Aid and Comfort. No Person shall be convicted of Treason unless on the Testimony of two Witnesses to the same overt Act, or on Confession in open Court.

The Congress shall have Power to declare the Punishment of Treason, but no Attainder of Treason shall work Corruption of Blood, or Forfeiture except during the Life of the Person attainted.

## Article IV

### Section 1

Full Faith and Credit shall be given in each State to the public Acts, Records, and judicial Proceedings of every other State. And the Congress may by general Laws prescribe the Manner in which such Acts, Records and Proceedings shall be proved, and the Effect thereof.

### Section 2

The Citizens of each State shall be entitled to all Privileges and Immunities of Citizens in the several States.

A Person charged in any State with Treason, Felony, or other Crime, who shall flee from Justice, and be found in another State,

shall on Demand of the executive Authority of the State from which he fled, be delivered up, to be removed to the State having Jurisdiction of the Crime.

[No Person held to Service or Labour in one State, under the Laws thereof, escaping into another, shall, in Consequence of any Law or Regulation therein, be discharged from such Service or Labour, but shall be delivered up on Claim of the Party to whom such Service or Labour may be due.][10]

### Section 3

New States may be admitted by the Congress into this Union; but no new State shall be formed or erected within the Jurisdiction of any other State; nor any State be formed by the Junction of two or more States, or Parts of States, without the Consent of the Legislatures of the States concerned as well as of the Congress.

The Congress shall have Power to dispose of and make all needful Rules and Regulations respecting the Territory or other Property belonging to the United States; and nothing in this Constitution shall be so construed as to Prejudice any Claims of the United States, or of any particular State.

### Section 4

The United States shall guarantee to every State in this Union a Republican Form of Government, and shall protect each of them against Invasion; and on Application of the Legislature, or of the Executive (when the Legislature cannot be convened) against domestic Violence.

## Article V

The Congress, whenever two thirds of both Houses shall deem it necessary, shall propose Amendments to this Constitution, or, on the Application of the Legislatures of two thirds of the several States, shall call a Convention for proposing Amendments, which, in either Case, shall be valid to all Intents and Purposes, as Part of this Constitution, when ratified by the Legislatures of three fourths of the several States, or by Conventions in three fourths thereof, as the one or the other Mode of Ratification may be proposed by the Congress; Provided that no Amendment which may be made prior to the Year One thousand eight hundred and eight shall in any Manner affect the first and fourth Clauses in the Ninth Section of the first Article; and that no State, without its Consent, shall be deprived of its equal Suffrage in the Senate.

## Article VI

All Debts contracted and Engagements entered into, before the Adoption of this Constitution, shall be as valid against the United States under this Constitution, as under the Confederation.

This Constitution, and the Laws of the United States which shall be made in Pursuance thereof; and all Treaties made, or

---

[8] Changed by the Eleventh Amendment.
[9] Changed by the Eleventh Amendment.

---

[10] Changed by the Thirteenth Amendment.

which shall be made, under the Authority of the United States, shall be the supreme Law of the Land; and the Judges in every State shall be bound thereby, any Thing in the Constitution or Laws of any State to the Contrary notwithstanding.

The Senators and Representatives before mentioned, and the Members of the several State Legislatures, and all executive and judicial Officers, both of the United States and of the several States, shall be bound by Oath or Affirmation, to support this Constitution; but no religious Test shall ever be required as a Qualification to any Office or public Trust under the United States.

### Article VII

The Ratification of the Conventions of nine States, shall be sufficient for the Establishment of this Constitution between the States so ratifying the Same. Done in Convention by the Unanimous Consent of the States present the Seventeenth Day of September in the Year of our Lord one thousand seven hundred and Eighty seven and of the Independence of the United States of America the Twelfth In witness whereof We have hereunto subscribed our Names.... [The names of signers follow.]

# The Bill of Rights*

### Amendment I

Congress shall make no law respecting an establishment of religion, or prohibiting the free exercise thereof; or abridging the freedom of speech, or of the press; or the right of the people peaceably to assemble, and to petition the government for a redress of grievances.

### Amendment II

A well regulated militia, being necessary to the security of a free state, the right of the people to keep and bear arms, shall not be infringed.

### Amendment III

No soldier shall, in time of peace be quartered in any house, without the consent of the owner, nor in time of war, but in a manner to be prescribed by law.

### Amendment IV

The right of the people to be secure in their persons, houses, papers, and effects, against unreasonable searches and seizures, shall not be violated, and no warrants shall issue, but upon probable cause, supported by oath or affirmation, and particularly describing the place to be searched, and the persons or things to be seized.

### Amendment V

No person shall be held to answer for a capital, or otherwise infamous crime, unless on a presentment or indictment of a grand jury, except in cases arising in the land or naval forces, or in the militia, when in actual service in time of war or public danger; nor shall any person be subject for the same offense to be twice put in jeopardy of life or limb; nor shall be compelled in any criminal case to be a witness against himself, nor be deprived of life, liberty, or property, without due process of law; nor shall private property be taken for public use, without just compensation.

### Amendment VI

In all criminal prosecutions, the accused shall enjoy the right to a speedy and public trial, by an impartial jury of the state and district wherein the crime shall have been committed, which district shall have been previously ascertained by law, and to be informed of the nature and cause of the accusation; to be confronted with the witnesses against him; to have compulsory process for obtaining witnesses in his favor, and to have the assistance of counsel for his defense.

### Amendment VII

In suits at common law, where the value in controversy shall exceed twenty dollars, the right of trial by jury shall be preserved, and no fact tried by a jury, shall be otherwise reexamined in any court of the United States, than according to the rules of the common law.

### Amendment VIII

Excessive bail shall not be required, nor excessive fines imposed, nor cruel and unusual punishments inflicted.

### Amendment IX

The enumeration in the Constitution, of certain rights, shall not be construed to deny or disparage others retained by the people.

### Amendment X

The powers not delegated to the United States by the Constitution, nor prohibited by it to the states, are reserved to the states respectively, or to the people.

---

* The first ten amendments to the Constitution were ratified effective December 15, 1791.

# A Short Glossary of Legal Terms

## A

**absolute privilege** – an immunity from **defamation** suits that attaches to government officials protecting those officials from actions based on speech or writings made within their official capacities.

**absolutism** – the belief that the First Amendment pronouncement that no law should be made restricting free speech or a free press is absolute and, therefore, that there may be no restrictions on expression.

**acquit** – in criminal law, to find a defendant not guilty; in contract law, to release from an obligation.

**act** – **statutory law;** used interchangeably with "law."

**actionable** – giving rise to a **cause of action**.

**actual damages** – a monetary award in a lawsuit for actual injury or loss, such as harm to reputation, emotional distress or mental suffering; also called **compensatory damages**.

**actual malice** – knowledge of falsity or reckless disregard for whether material is true or false; this standard, sometimes called *"New York Times* actual malice," which all public officials and public figures must prove in order to prevail in libel actions, was first enunciated by the U.S. Supreme Court in *New York Times Co. v. Sullivan*.

**adjudication** – giving or pronouncing a judgment or decree; also, the judgment itself.

**advance sheet** – a pamphlet form of a decision issued at the time the decision is delivered.

**allegation** – a charge or declaration made in a lawsuit which the plaintiff is required to prove.

**all-purpose public figure** – in a libel or privacy action, a person of widespread fame or notoriety; a person of special prominence within society or of pervasive power and influence; a "household name."

***amicus curiae*** – literally, "friend of the court"; a person, organization, company or government that provides information to a court — in the form of a **brief** or argument — who is not a party in the case being litigated.

**appeal** – a plea to a higher court to alter or overturn a judgment of a lower court because of errors of law.

**appellant** – the party who appeals a court's decision, requesting that a higher court review the ruling or rulings of the lower court.

**appellate court** – a court that has jurisdiction to hear cases on appeal.

**appellee** – the party against whom an appeal is taken; that is, the party who won the case in the lower court.

**appropriation** – in privacy law, the use of a person's name, image or likeness without permission for trade purposes.

**arraignment** – a judicial proceeding at which a criminal defendant is formally informed of the charges against him or her and to which the defendant enters a plea.

**Articles of Confederation** – the first constitution of the United States; it was replaced by the constitution of 1787, which is still in force.

## B

**bad tendency test** – a judicial test that allows restrictions on expression when a court finds that the speech might have even the slightest tendency to cause harm.

**bail** – money or property that will be forfeited if a criminal defendant does not appear at a judicial proceeding.

**bail bond (or bond)** – a signed obligation with collateral attached to assure the appearance in court of an individual.

**bait-and-switch** – a sales technique whereby an item is advertised at a very low price, but shoppers are pressured to buy a more expensive item; in some cases, the low-priced item is not available or is available only on a very limited basis.

**balancing** – a court's weighing of competing interests guaranteed by law to determine which rights must give way.

**Bill of Rights** – the first ten amendments to the U.S. Constitution.

**black letter law** – an informal term indicating the basic principles of law generally accepted by the courts and/or embodied in the **statutes** of a particular jurisdiction.

**Bluebook** – the popular name of *A Uniform System of Citation*, the standard reference work for legal writing; the *Bluebook* was originally developed by the *Harvard Law Review*, but, now in its 17th edition, is produced by the law reviews at Harvard, Columbia, Yale and the University of Pennsylvania.

**bootstrapping** – an attempt by a media libel defendant to elevate a plaintiff to **public figure** status as a result of the attention brought to the plaintiff by the defendant's coverage of the lawsuit.

**brief** – a written argument prepared by attorneys involved in an appeal, supporting the attorneys' positions. It contains a summary of the facts, the pertinent law and an argument of how the law applies to the facts. Briefs are prepared by counsel for both sides, but often *amicus curiae* briefs will also be filed. A **brief** should not be confused with a **case brief**, which is a synopsis of an opinion.

**burden of proof** – the elements a plaintiff must prove in order to prevail in a **civil action**, or that a prosecutor must prove in order to successfully convict a criminal **defendant**.

## C

**case brief** – a synopsis of an opinion, generally only one or two pages long, highlighting the facts, question, holding and rationale of the opinion.

**CATV** – community antenna television; the early name for cable television, reflecting the perception that cable was a regional service designed to expand the reach of broadcast television.

**cause of action** – those facts which give rise to a right to sue.

**censorship** – the halting of expression at its source by the government; also called **prior restraint**.

*certiorari* – the name of a **writ** issued by the U.S. Supreme Court when it agrees to review a case; it is an order to the lower court to send up the records. Some state supreme courts also use the term.

**change of venire** – the transfer of a jury pool from a distant jurisdiction to a location in which a crime was committed in order to seat jurors who have not been biased by publicity about the case.

**change of venue** – the moving of a trial to a location other than that in which the crime was committed in order to seat jurors who have not been biased by publicity about the case.

**child pornography** – material containing depictions of children in sexually explicit situations; it is not protected by the First Amendment; also called "kiddie porn."

**citation** – a notation indicating the location of legal authority. Also called a "cite."

**civil action** – a lawsuit alleging a private wrong, as opposed to a criminal wrong.

**clear and present danger test** – a test first enunciated by Justice Oliver Wendell Holmes in 1919 allowing restrictions on speech and press when the expression would cause substantive, immediate harm.

**code** – a classified arrangement of public laws in effect. Also called "compiled statutes" or "revised statutes."

**collateral bar rule** – the rule that a person who disobeys a court order may not challenge the constitutionality of the order as a defense to a **contempt of court** charge.

**colloquium** – a libel plaintiff's proof of special circumstances in establishing that a defamatory statement is about or understood to be about the plaintiff.

**commercial speech** – communication intended to promote a business or service or sell a product.

**common carrier** – the regulatory category traditionally applied to service providers – like telephone services – that must provide universal, nondiscriminatory service to all on a first-come-first-served basis and may not control the messages they carry.

**common law** – court-created law; in modern usage, case law as opposed to statutory law; in theory, the common law was "discovered" rather than created by historical Anglo-Saxon courts. The discovery was based on the common customs of the times, thus the term "common." "Common" law was also distinguished from "ecclesiastical" or church law.

**common law malice** – ill will, hatred or spite.

**compelling government interest** – an overriding interest advocated by the government that must be proved in order for a regulation aimed at suppressing expression to be found constitutional. In such cases – which require **strict scrutiny** – the government must also prove that the regulation is narrowly tailored.

**compensatory damages** – a monetary award in a lawsuit for actual injury or loss, such as harm to reputation, emotional distress or mental suffering; also called **actual damages**.

**complainant** – the person bringing a legal complaint; the **plaintiff**.

**complaint** – the first legal argument filed by a plaintiff.

**constitution** – a document outlining the organization of a government, specifying the rights, responsibilities and limits of that government.

**contempt of court** – willful disobedience of a lawful order of a court or any act calculated to embarrass, hinder or obstruct a court in the administration of justice.

**content neutral restrictions** – restrictions that are not related to the content of expression, but on circumstances related to the **time**, **place or manner** of the expression.

**continuance** – a judicial order that a criminal or civil action be delayed.

**copyright** – protection for the ownership of an original work that has been fixed in a tangible medium of expression.

**copyright infringement** – copying the form or expression of an idea without permission; punishable by a civil or criminal action or both.

**criminal libel** – a malicious publication that exposes or tends to expose a living person or the memory of a deceased person to hatred, contempt ridicule or obloquy in violation of a statute; a prosecutor brings the criminal charges against the publisher of the publication.

**cross-ownership** – an array of FCC rules and statutory provisions aimed to protect diversity of ownership and content by preventing consolidation of media ownership.

## D

**damages** – compensation recovered by a **plaintiff** from a **defendant**.

**DBS** – direct broadcast satellites; they operate in **geosynchronous orbits** to create a stable broadcast imprint or coverage area for transmission of messages and programming to receiving dishes eighteen to twenty-four inches in diameter.

*de novo* – a second time; totally new.

**defamation** – communication that injures another's reputation, that is, that holds one up to scorn, ridicule or spite; **slander** is oral defamation; **libel** is written defamation.

**defendant** – the party against whom a lawsuit is brought.

**demurrer** – an allegation by a defendant that even if the facts alleged by a plaintiff are true, they do not state a sufficient **cause of action**.

**deposition** – a formal interview by an attorney of a witness who answers questions under oath, but not in open court; also, the transcript of the interview.

**deregulation** – a policy of eliminating laws and regulations in favor of market pressures.

*dictum* – technically *obiter dictum,* this is an incidental comment in an opinion; a comment not necessary to the determination of the issue at hand; it is not binding precedent. The plural is *"dicta."*

**digital sampling** – converting sounds from existing songs to digital bits and then manipulating and combining notes to create a new song.

**discovery** – a proceeding through which parties in a case are informed of facts known by the adversarial parties.

**diversity of citizenship action** – a civil action in which the parties are residents of different states; the U.S. Constitution allows federal district courts to hear such cases, even if the subject matter of the suit is one of state law, as long as the amount in the controversy exceeds $75,000.

**docket number** – the numerical designation assigned to each case by a court; it is used to identify the case as it progresses through the judicial system.

**DTH** – direct-to-home; the services send video signals to home dishes or receivers in the United States, including the relatively high-power **DBS** systems and lower-power **HSD** systems.

**DTV** – see **HDTV**.

**due process** – a term used to describe the proper operation of legal proceedings according to the rules and principles that have been established to protect the rights of individuals.

## E

**effective competition** – the standard that allows cable systems to operate without rate regulation; it exists when substantial overlap of services offered by cable and other providers exists.

*en banc* – a session in which the entire court — rather than a panel — hears and participates in the determination of a case.

**enjoin** – to require, by a judicial action, an individual to perform or refrain from performing some act.

**equity** – justice administered according to fairness as contrasted with the strict, formulated rules of **common law;** it renders the administration of justice more complete, by affording relief where

courts of law are incompetent to give it or enforce it.

**erotica** – sexually explicit material; generally "erotica" is a neutral term that refers to material that can be distinguished from **pornography** or **obscenity;** erotica is protected by the First Amendment.

**exemplary damages** – a monetary award designed to punish a defendant in a lawsuit for some action; the same as **punitive damages**.

*ex parte* – by, for or on behalf of one party.

## F

**fair comment and criticism** – a **common law** defense against a defamation claim in which the defendant avows a right to express an opinion, based on well-known or truthfully stated facts, without **common law malice** against a person who has entered the public sphere.

**fair use** – a provision in copyright law that allows copying of protected material for use in certain specific circumstances.

**false light** – the privacy tort which protects individuals from the publication of material that is not necessarily defamatory but is false and offensive.

**fault** – culpability; it must be proved in order for an individual to prevail in a libel action; the most common types of fault are **negligence** and **actual malice**.

**felony** – a serious crime punishable by imprisonment in a penitentiary, or more serious punishment.

**fighting words** – language that is likely to cause an immediate, violent response; it lies outside First Amendment protection.

**first sale** – the doctrine that permits a copyright owner to collect royalties the first time each copy of a work is sold. The purchaser may then rent or resell that copy without permission, but may not make derivative works, reproduce or publicly perform the work.

**franchise agreement** – the contract between local authorities and cable operators that imposes conditions on cable systems in exchange for permission for them to string their cables along public rights-of-way.

## G

**gag order** – an order by a court not to speak or write about matters before the court.

**geosynchronous orbit** – an orbit that enables a satellite to maintain its position relative to the earth.

**grand jury** – an investigatory panel; a panel whose duty is to hear the state's evidence in a criminal case and determine whether there is probable cause to believe a crime has been committed and whether the accused should stand trial; the grand jury does not determine guilt or innocence.

**group libel** – a **defamation** aimed at a group rather than an individual; if the group is large, members of the group are precluded from bringing libel actions because they are not sufficiently identified.

# H

*habeas corpus* – literally, "you have the body"; a **writ** through which a person can be brought before a court to determine whether the person has been denied liberty without **due process** of law.

**headnote** – a summary of legal principles in a case, printed immediately before the text of the opinion in a **reporter**; a case may be preceded by a number of headnotes, depending upon the findings of the court.

**HDTV** – high definition television or digital television (DTV); it uses digital technology and a new transmission standard to improve picture and sound quality and to provide an image area shaped more like a movie theater screen than a traditional television screen.

**headend** – the control center of a cable system, where the cable operator brings together programming from diverse sources before distributing it to subscribers.

**holding** – the declaration in an **opinion** of the conclusion of law reached by a court.

**HSD** – home satellite dish services; they are more properly called "fixed satellite services" and require a receiving dish approximately four to eight feet in diameter to receive their low-power signals.

# I

**implied consent** – consent that is not explicit, but may be available based on the facts of the case.

**in camera** – in private; in a judge's chambers.

**incorporation** – in constitutional law, the process by which portions of the **Bill of Rights**, including the First Amendment, have been applied to the states *via* the Fourteenth Amendment's due process clause.

**indict/indictment** – a written accusation by a **grand jury** charging a person with a crime.

**inducement** – a libel plaintiff's allegation that extrinsic facts make a statement defamatory although it is not defamatory on its face.

*infra* – a signal indicating that further information appears later in the text or footnotes.

**injunction** – a court order halting some activity or commanding someone to undo a wrong.

*inter alia* – literally "among other things."

**interconnection rules** – the rules that govern the ability of communication service providers to link up with and use the network facilities of a competitor.

**Internet** – an international network created by high-speed, broadband connections and satellite links.

**interrogatory** – a list of written questions posed by a party in a lawsuit to the opposing party.

# J

**judgment** – the **holding** of a court in a case.

**judgment n.o.v.** – a judgment rendered in favor of one party in a case, notwithstanding a verdict in favor of the opposing party; that is, the overruling of a jury verdict by a judge.

**jurisdiction** – the area over which a court has authority; the power and authority of a court to hear and determine a judicial proceeding; the area may be geographic or based on the subject matter of the case. If a court does not have jurisdiction, it may not render a legal decision in the matter.

# K

**Key Number** – a permanent number assigned to a specific point of law in a case, as developed by the West Publishing Company, to aid in the discovery of material on the same topic of law in other cases.

# L

**leased-access channels** – channels provided by cable systems for commercial lease, which, when not leased, cable operators may use to carry cable programming.

**liable** – responsible or answerable for some action.

**libel** – written communication that damages a person's reputation, that is, that holds a person up to hatred, ridicule or scorn; a type of **defamation**.

**libertarianism** – a governmental theory allowing absolute and unrestricted liberty, especially of thought and speech.

**licensing** – a governmental policy under which express permission must be granted before material may be published.

**likelihood of confusion** – grounds for legal action to protect a **trademark** from being confused with another trademark; courts compare the two marks on a variety of factors to determine whether consumers are likely to be confused as to the source, sponsorship or approval of a product.

**limited-purpose public figure** – in libel law, a person who voluntarily injects himself or herself into a public controversy in order to influence the outcome; also known as a "vortex public figure."

**lock boxes** – television set-top devices that can be programmed to eliminate certain channels or content.

# M

**malice** – see **common law malice**, **actual malice**.

**mandamus** – an order by a court directing a lower court or government official to do something.

**marketplace of ideas theory** – the theory that the government should exercise minimal control on speech, based on the notion that when all ideas are allowed to be expressed – that is, are allowed in the "marketplace of ideas" – truth will prevail.

**misdemeanor** – a criminal offense that is not serious enough to warrant a prison sentence; penalties are usually fines and community service or a sentence to a local jail.

**moot** – the absence of a genuine controversy or contention of law. Courts will rarely decide "moot" points of law unless there is an indication that the point of law is likely to recur in another case.

**MSO** – multiple system operator; a person who runs cable systems in several geographically dispersed locations.

**multiplexing** – a technology that enables the transmission of up to four television signals on one channel.

**must-carry rules** – a series of FCC rules requiring cable systems to carry all local broadcast signals.

## N

**negligence** – a standard of **fault** in **tort** law; an act or omission that a reasonably careful person would not take; in libel law, it is acting other than in a manner in which a reasonably careful or ordinarily prudent person would act or failure to follow accepted professional practices or standards.

**network nonduplication rules** – rules that allow television stations affiliated with a broadcast network to demand that a cable system black out network programming being carried on an imported station.

**nonsuit** – termination of an action without adjudicating the issues on the merits.

## O

**obscenity** – pornographic material that has been determined by a court to meet the Supreme Court's test for obscene material articulated in *Miller v. California* and, therefore, lies outside First Amendment protection.

**opinion** – an explanation of the rationale for a judicial decision, that is, the holding of a court and the rationale for that holding; in libel law, a communication that cannot be proved to be true or false and, therefore, cannot be the subject of a successful libel action.

**overbroad/overbreadth** – a term used to refer to a law that prohibits or punishes legal as well as illegal conduct or speech.

## P

**parallel citation** – a citation reference to the same case printed in a different reporter. (See definition of "reporter.")

**PEG channels** – cable television channels reserved by law for public, educational and government access.

*per curiam* – an opinion "by the court"; that is, an unsigned opinion.

**peremptory challenges** – rights by which an attorney may dismiss potential jurors without providing a reason; the number is generally limited based on the nature of the trial.

**petit jury** – a panel whose function it is to decide the facts of a case, that is, to determine guilt or innocence in a criminal suit and the party that prevails in a civil suit.

**petitioner** – the party who starts an **equity** proceeding or the party who appeals a judgment to a higher court.

**plaintiff** – the party who brings a lawsuit.

**pleading** – a legal argument, filed in writing, outlining the contentions of a party in a lawsuit.

**pocket supplement** – also called a "pocket part," a supplement found in the back of a legal source book, updating the information contained within the book.

**pornography** – sexually explicit material that is in some way demeaning; it is protected by the First Amendment.

**precedent** – legal authority that must be followed, absent a sound legal basis for variance; previous cases on the same point of law.

**preliminary injunction** – a temporary order, generally to stop a person from doing something.

**preponderance of evidence** – the standard of proof in a civil action, determined by balancing the evidence and determining which allegations or contentions are more likely to be true.

*prima facie* **case** – a case that unless contradicted would likely prevail before a reasonable jury.

**primary authority** – mandatory legal authority; that is, judicial precedent or legislative enactment; authority that must be followed or contended with.

**prior restraint** – the prohibition of expression at its source by the government; also called **censorship**.

*promissory estoppel* – a legal doctrine similar to contract law that holds that when a clear promise is intended to and does induce a specific action, that promise is binding if injustice can be avoided only by enforcing it.

**publication** – in libel law, the exposure of material to a third party.

**public domain** – material no longer protected by **copyright** falls into the public domain, meaning that it is available for anyone to use without authorization.

**public figure** – see **all-purpose public figure** and **limited-purpose public figure**.

**public official** – a government employee who has or appears to have substantial responsibility for or control over the conduct of government affairs.

**punitive damages** – a monetary award designed to punish a defendant in a lawsuit for some action; the same as **exemplary damages**. The U.S. Supreme Court has said that libel plaintiffs must prove **actual malice** in order to recover punitive damages.

## Q

**qualified privilege** – a privilege to report information that appears in absolutely privileged *fora,* if certain conditions or qualifications are met, that is, if the report is accurate, fair and made without **common law malice**.

**quash** – to vacate, abate or annul.

# R

***ratio decidendi*** – the rationale of a decision; that is, the legal point in the case which leads to the result.

**reckless disregard** – extreme indifference as to the truth or falsity of a defamatory statement; indifference that is tantamount to conscious, deliberate or intentional ignoring of the truth or falsity of a statement.

**remand** – to send back to a lower court for further proceedings, usually based upon the findings of a higher court.

**report** – to publish a decision of a court.

**reporter** – one in a series of books in which legal decisions are published; to publish the decisions.

**reporter's privilege** – the right of a journalist to keep the identities of sources or other information confidential.

**respondent** – in an **equity** case, the party who answers the **petitioner's** bill of particulars; in appellate practice, the party who contests or opposes an **appeal**.

**retraction** – a published statement acknowledging that a publication was in error; "taking back" an incorrect statement.

# S

**scienter** – guilty knowledge; prior knowledge.

**scope note** – a short note identifying and limiting the content of a topic; it appears immediately after the topic's heading in a legal reference work.

**search warrant** – an order issued by a magistrate or other officer of the court authorizing law enforcement officials to search for and seize evidence of a crime.

**secondary authority** – persuasive but not mandatory (**primary**) authority; supporting material; it may include legal encyclopedias, treatises, law journal articles or text books.

**sedition** – attacks on the government punishable by law because they could cause unrest.

**seditious libel** – harsh criticism of the government.

**sequestration** – the isolation of members of a jury during the taking of evidence and/or the deliberations on the facts of a case.

**service mark** – any word, name, symbol or device, or any combination thereof, adopted and used by a manufacturer or merchant to identify its services and distinguish them from services provided by others.

**session laws** – published laws of a state, as enacted by each assembly in each session; laws listed in chronological, rather than topical, order.

***Shepardizing*** – to use a *Shepard's* citator index to locate all subsequent references to or uses of a case or other legal authority.

**shield law** – a statute providing journalists a testimonial privilege.

**slamming** – the illegal practice of switching a person's long-distance service provider without permission.

**slander** – oral communication that damages someone's reputation, that is, that would tend to hold a person up to scorn, ridicule or hatred; a type of **defamation**.

**SMATV** – also known as "private cable," a cable system within a single apartment building or bloc of buildings that does not use public rights-of-way; the system collects local television signals through antennas and satellite signals through receiving dishes and transmits them through the buildings.

**special damages** – a monetary award for financial or pecuniary loss.

**standing** – the right to bring a legal action.

**star paging** – a pagination scheme in reprint editions of court reporters, showing on its pages where the pages of the official text begin and end.

***stare decisis*** – literally, "let the decision stand"; the legal doctrine of precedent; the tendency to follow, rather than overrule, precedent, i.e., the doctrine that a court will follow the principle established by a previous court when the facts of the cases are substantially the same.

**statute of limitations** – the time period in which a civil or criminal action must be brought.

**statute/statutory law** – law adopted by legislative bodies.

**stay** – a court order stopping some judicial action or order.

**strict liability** – the doctrine that a person is **liable** for an act even if that action was unintentional and without **fault**.

**strict scrutiny** – a test to determine whether a regulation is constitutional; the test is used when the regulation is directed at the suppression of expression; under the test, the regulation is constitutional if it meets a **compelling government interest** and is narrowly tailored.

**subpoena** – a command to appear in court at a certain time to testify about a certain matter; a **subpoena duces tecum** requires that the subpoenaed party bring certain documents or other materials to the hearing.

**summary judgment** – a ruling by a judge that there is no dispute of material fact between the two parties in a case, and that one party should win the case as a matter of law.

***supra*** – a signal indicating that further information on a point or case is provided earlier in the text or footnotes.

**syllabus** – a summary of the case and the court's holding, prepared by the publisher of a **reporter**.

**syndicated exclusivity** – an FCC rule that prohibits cable companies from importing syndicated programs to which television stations possess exclusive contracts.

# T

**temporary restraining order** – a court order to temporarily prevent an action.

**time, place and manner restrictions** – restrictions on expression based on the circumstances surrounding the expression rather than the content of the expression.

**tort** – a civil wrong by one person against another.

**trade name** – any name used by a person to identify his or her business or vocation.

**trademark** – a word, name, symbol or device or any combination thereof used to identify goods and distinguish them from those manufactured or sold by others.

**trademark dilution** – using a famous trademark in ways that blur its distinctiveness or tarnish or disparage it.

**transformative** – among the factors used to determine whether a use of copyrighted material is a **fair use** or a **copyright infringement;** courts examine whether the secondary use added value to the original copyrighted work.

## V

**vagueness** – a rationale for finding a law unconstitutional because the law is not specific enough to give fair warning as to the parameters of the law.

**venire** – the potential jurors in a trial.

**venue** – the place in which a trial occurs.

**voir dire** – literally "to see, to say"; the process through which attorneys and a judge question potential jurors to determine whether they are qualified to serve.

## W

**wireless cable** – a system licensed and regulated by the FCC that includes multi-point distribution services and multi-channel distribution services. It sends up to thirty-three channels by microwave signals to small antennas on subscribers' homes but does not cross public rights-of-way, so it does not require a local franchise.

**work made for hire** – intellectual property created as part of one's employment so that the employer, rather than the creator of the work, owns the **copyright;** there are two types: (1) work done by an employee for an employer within the scope of employment; (2) a work specially commissioned or ordered for inclusion in a collective work if a work-for-hire agreement is signed.

**writ** – an order by a court requiring some action or giving authority and commission to that act.

# The Authors

**Dorothy Bowles,** a professor at the University of Tennessee, has taught communications law at the graduate and undergraduate levels for more than twenty-five years. She is the author of *Kansas Media Law Guide* and *Media Law in Tennessee,* as well as numerous journal articles. She is an emeritus member of the board of directors of the Student Press Law Center and has held several offices in the Association for Education in Journalism and Mass Communications. She has worked as a newspaper reporter and editor and is co-author of one of the leading editing textbooks. In 2005, she received The Jefferson Prize, a top faculty award at the University of Tennessee. Her bachelor's degree is from Texas Tech University, her master's from the University of Kansas and her Ph.D. from the University of Wisconsin. Her e-mail address is bowles@utk.edu.

**Sandra F. Chance** is an associate professor and director of the Brechner Center for Freedom of Information at the University of Florida. She teaches law of mass communication at the undergraduate and graduate levels. She practiced media law with one of the country's largest law firms before joining the faculty at Florida. She has published articles in *Communication Law and Policy, Journal of Broadcasting & Electronic Media, Journalism & Mass Communication Quarterly, Journal of Law and Public Policy, UALR Law Review, Quill, Editor & Publisher* and other journals. She is on the board of directors of the First Amendment Foundation and is Sunshine Chair for the Society of Professional Journalists. She is a past head of the Association for Education in Journalism and Mass Communication Law Division and an active member of the Florida Bar's media and communications law committee. She was invited by the U.S. State Department to present FOI seminars in Brazil and Jamaica in 1999. She was named the College's Outstanding Teacher in 1997 and was named one of the university's Outstanding Teachers in 1998. She holds B.A., M.A. and J.D. degrees from the University of Florida. Her e-mail address is schance@jou.ufl.edu.

**Charles N. Davis** is an associate professor and director of the National Freedom of Information Coalition at the University of Missouri School of Journalism. He worked as a journalist in Georgia, Florida and Ireland for nearly ten years after graduating from North Georgia College. He received a master's degree from the University of Georgia and a Ph.D. degree from the University of Florida, where he assisted reporters and others with freedom of information questions for the Brechner Center for Freedom of Information. He taught at Georgia Southern University and was department chair at Southern Methodist University before joining the faculty at Missouri. He edited *Access Denied: Freedom of Information in the Information Age,* his first book, for Iowa University Press. His e-mail address is DavisCN@missouri.edu.

**Thomas Eveslage** is a professor of journalism in Temple University's School of Communications and Theater. He has directed the Master of Journalism program and chaired the Department of Journalism, Public Relations and Advertising. He holds an M.A. degree in journalism from the University of Minnesota and a Ph.D. in journalism from Southern Illinois University at Carbondale. He has served on the board of directors of the Student Press Law Center, the Pennsylvania School Press Association and Quill and Scroll Society. He has written a column on student press law issues for more than ten years and has received the Lawrence Campbell Research Award three times from the Scholastic Journalism Division of the Association for Education in Journalism and Mass Communication. A member of Temple University's Teaching Academy, he was named Journalism Teacher of the Year in 2003 by AEJMC's Scholastic Journalism Division. He is a former copy editor and university news director. His e-mail address is eveslage @temple.edu.

**Karla K. Gower** is an associate professor in the Advertising and Public Relations Department of the College of Communication and Information Sciences at the University of Alabama, where she teaches public relations courses. She has published two books on communication law topics and has published articles in *Journalism and Mass Communication Quarterly, Journalism History,*

*Communication Law and Policy* and other journals. She has also served as editor of *American Journalism*, a history journal. Her research focuses on legal issues affecting corporate communication and the history of public relations. She received her bachelor's and law degrees from the University of Western Ontario, Canada, her master's degree from Arizona State University and her doctorate from the University of North Carolina at Chapel Hill. Her e-mail address is gower@apr.ua.edu.

**F. Dennis Hale** is an emeritus professor and former director of the School of Mass Communication at Bowling Green State University. He lives in Edwardsville, Illinois. He has published more than eighty book chapters, convention papers and journal articles, many about mass media law. He is a former head of the Law Division of the Association for Education in Journalism in Mass Communication and has received research grants from the U.S. Justice Department and the Newspaper Research Council. His Ph.D. degree is from Southern Illinois University. His e-mail address is dhale@bgnet.bgsu.edu.

**Steven Helle** is a professor and former head of the Department of Journalism at the University of Illinois in Urbana-Champaign. He is co-author of *Last Rights: Revisiting Four Theories of the Press* and has published numerous articles on communication law in, among others, *Duke Law Journal, Journalism and Mass Communication Quarterly, Villanova Law Review, University of Illinois Law Review, Iowa Law Review, Illinois Bar Journal, Journalism and Mass Communication Educator* and *DePaul Law Review*. A former head of the Law Division of the Association for Education in Journalism and Mass Communication, Dr. Helle has been named to the editorial boards of the *Illinois Bar Journal, Journalism Monographs* and *Communication Law and Policy*. He is past chair of the Media Law Committee of the Illinois State Bar Association. Twice he has been named one of the outstanding undergraduate teachers at the University of Illinois, most recently in 1996, when he received the Luckman Undergraduate Distinguished Teaching Award. He was also selected Freedom Forum Journalism Teacher of the Year in 1998. His J.D. and M.A. degrees are from the University of Iowa. His e-mail address is s-helle@uiuc.edu.

**W. Wat Hopkins** is a professor of communication at Virginia Tech University, where he teaches journalism and communication law courses. He has published three books and a number of articles on First Amendment topics and is editor of *Communication Law and Policy,* the research journal of the Law Division of the Association for Education in Journalism and Mass Communication. He is a past head of the Law Division and is on the editorial board of *Journalism & Mass Communication Quarterly*. He is also vice president of the Virginia Coalition for Open Government and is a member of Virginia's first Freedom of Information

Advisory Council, an advisory and educational group established by the Virginia General Assembly. He received his bachelor's degree from Western Carolina University and his master's and Ph.D. degrees from the University of North Carolina at Chapel Hill. His e-mail address is whopkins@vt.edu.

**Matt Jackson** is an associate professor and head of the telecommunications department in the College of Communications at Pennsylvania State University. He teaches telecommunications regulation and policy, programming, management and communication law. He has published articles in *Journal of Broadcasting & Electronic Media, Federal Communications Law Journal, Communications Law and Policy, Hastings Communication and Entertainment Law Journal* and other journals. His research focuses on the evolution of intellectual property law and its impact on communication networks and free speech. He received his bachelor's and master's degrees from the University of Florida and his doctorate from Indiana University at Bloomington. His e-mail address is mattj@psu.edu.

**Paul E. Kostyu** is the Ohio statehouse bureau chief for Copley Newspapers, a San Diego-based chain. He is also an adjunct associate professor of journalism at Ohio Wesleyan University where he has taught courses in reporting, editing, journalism history and communication law. His bachelor's degree is from Heidelberg College, and his master's and Ph.D. degrees are from Bowling Green State University. He is an award-winning journalist who was a 2004 Pulitzer Prize nominee. He is a frequent panelist on *Capitol Square*, a news show broadcast by the Ohio News Network, and for six years he has been editor of *The Working Press,* the student-produced national convention newspaper of the Society of Professional Journalists. In 2005, he was a Kiplinger Fellow in Public Affairs Journalism at Ohio State University. He also has published research in *Communications and the Law, American Journalism* and the *Journal of Mass Media Ethics*. His e-mail address is paul.kostyu@cantonrep.com.

**Jeremy Harris Lipschultz** is the Robert T. Reilly Professor and director of the School of Communication at the University of Nebraska at Omaha, where he won the university's Distinguished Research or Creativity Award in 2004 and Alumni Teaching Award in 2001. He co-authored *Mass Media, An Aging Population and the Baby Boomers* in 2005 and *Crime and Local Television News* in 2002, and is co-editor of *Studies in Media & Information Literacy Education*. He is also author of *Broadcast Indecency: F.C.C. Regulation and the First Amendment*. He received his bachelor's degree from the University of Illinois, his master's degree from Sangamon State University (now the University of Illinois-Springfield) and his doctorate from Southern Illinois University. His e-mail address is jlipschultz@mail.unomaha.edu.

**Greg Lisby** is a professor of communication at Georgia State University, where he teaches mass communication law and policy, and communication ethics. In addition to serving as a member of the editorial board of *Communication Law and Policy*, he has had articles published in *Journalism Monographs, Communication Law and Policy, Communications and the Law, Journalism Quarterly, Journal of Communication Inquiry, Newspaper Research Journal* and *Georgia Historical Quarterly*. The fourth edition of his book *Mass Communication Law in Georgia* was published in 2005. He was executive producer of a PBS documentary on film censorship in 2000. He is past head of the Law Division of the Association for Education in Journalism and Mass Communication and a past member of the editorial board of *American Journalism*. He was the 2003 recipient of the American Journalism Historians Association's book of the year award, the 2000 recipient of the *Georgia Historical Quarterly's* article of the year award, and the 1990 recipient of the Henry W. Grady Prize for Research in Journalism History. He received his bachelor's degree from Auburn University, his master's degree from the University of Mississippi, his doctorate from the University of Tennessee and his law degree from Georgia State University College of Law. He is a member of the State Bar of Georgia. His e-mail address is glisby@gsu.edu.

**Mike McGregor** is an associate professor of telecommunications at Indiana University, where he teaches electronic media law and policy courses and introductory telecommunications courses. His research, which focuses on telecommunications policy making, the effects of policy decisions and e-government, has been published in *Journalism and Communication Monographs, Federal Communications Law Journal, COMM/ENT, Journalism Quarterly, Journal of Broadcasting and Electronic Media* and *Telecommunications Policy*. He has been a staff attorney at the Cable Television Information Center of the Urban Institute and has been an attorney/advisor in the Mass Media Bureau of the Federal Communications Commission. He received his bachelor's degree in history from Purdue University and his J.D. from Georgetown University Law Center. His e-mail address is mcgregom@indiana.edu.

**Cathy Packer** is an associate professor in the School of Journalism and Mass Communication at the University of North Carolina at Chapel Hill. She teaches media law and reporting and is the author of *Freedom of Expression in the American Military: A Communication Modeling Analysis* and is co-editor of *The North Carolina Media Law Handbook*. She received her master's and doctoral degrees from the University of Minnesota and her bachelor's degree from UNC. Her e-mail address is clpacker@email.unc.edu.

**Thomas A. Schwartz** is an associate professor in the School of Journalism and Communication at Ohio State University where he teaches reporting, mass communication law and legal research. He is a former newspaper and magazine editor, reporter and photographer. His recent research emphasizes the U.S. Supreme Court and the First Amendment and South African freedom of expression. He is past editor of the journal *Communication Law and Policy*. His e-mail address is tschwart@magnus.acs.ohio-state.edu.

**Sigman L. Splichal** is an associate professor in the School of Communication at the University of Miami, where he teaches media law and ethics, and is director of undergraduate and graduate journalism and photography programs. He began his journalism career in 1971 and was a newspaper writer and editor in Georgia, Florida and Virginia. He received his bachelor's, master's and Ph.D. degrees from the University of Florida. He is co-editor of *Access Denied: Freedom of Information in the Information Age* and is author of numerous law and academic journal articles on legal and ethical topics. His e-mail address is sig@miami.edu.

**Samuel A. Terilli** is an assistant professor in the School of Communication at the University of Miami, where he teaches media law, ethics, reporting and related courses. He is also a practicing attorney and has represented and advised a variety of media organizations for twenty-two years. He received his bachelor's degree from the State University of New York at Albany and his juris doctorate from the University of Michigan. His e-mail address is sterilli@Miami.edu.

**Ruth Walden** is the James Howard and Hallie McLean Parker Distinguished Professor and associate dean for graduate studies in the School of Journalism and Mass Communication at the University of North Carolina at Chapel Hill. She has held academic positions in Utah and Wisconsin-Madison and was a newspaper reporter in Wisconsin and Illinois. She was also assistant director of judicial education for the Wisconsin Supreme Court. She is the author of *Insult Laws: An Insult to Press Freedom* and *Mass Communication Law in North Carolina* and has published a number of articles on media law and First Amendment theory. A former head of the Law Division of the Association for Education in Journalism and Mass Communication, Dr. Walden serves on the editorial boards of *Journalism & Mass Communication Quarterly* and *Communication Law and Policy*. She holds B.A., M.A. and Ph.D. degrees from the University of Wisconsin-Madison. Her e-mail address is walden@email.unc.edu.

**Kyu Ho Youm** is a professor and Jonathan Marshall First Amendment Chair in the School of Journalism and Communication at the University of Oregon. He has published scholarly articles on communication law subjects in major U.S. and foreign academic journals, including *Journalism & Mass Communication*

*Quarterly, Hastings Communication/Entertainment (COMM/ENT) Law Journal* and the *International and Comparative Law Quarterly* of London. His articles have been cited by American and English courts, including the House of the Lords (the United Kingdom equivalent of the Supreme Court) and the High Court of Australia. A former head of the AEJMC Law Division and a former chair of the Communication Law and Policy Group of the International Communication Association, he serves on editorial boards of thirteen communication law journals in the United States and England. He received his bachelor's degree in South Korea and his master's and doctoral degrees from Southern Illinois University. He holds master of law degrees from the Yale Law School and Oxford University. His e-mail address is youm@uoregon.edu.

## AUTHORS EMERETI

**Louise Williams Hermanson** was a professor in the Department of Communication at the University of South Alabama, until her death in 2001. She taught law, ethics, print journalism and media history. Her research interests focused on alternative dispute resolution in conflicts between media and the public. She had published articles in *Journalism & Mass Communication Monographs, Journalism & Mass Communication Quarterly, Journalism & Mass Communication Educator* and *Oral History Review* and chapters in several books. Her bachelor's and master's degrees were from the University of South Carolina, and her Ph.D. was from the University of Minnesota. She had worked as a professional journalist in South Carolina. She wrote Chapter 1, The Law and Modern Society, for the first three editions of *Communication and the Law*.

**Robert L. Hughes** is an attorney in Richmond. He taught law for nineteen years at the Virginia Commonwealth University School of Mass Communications. Before that, he was a reporter and editorial writer for newspapers in Charlotte and West Palm Beach. He has a B.A. degree from Davidson College, an M.J. degree from the University of Missouri and a J.D. degree from the University of Florida. He wrote Chapter 16, Access to Documents and Meetings, for the 1998 edition of *Communication and the Law*.

**Arati R. Korwar** has taught courses in media law, visual communication and online journalism, most recently in the Manship School of Mass Communication at Louisiana State University. Her research in communication law and First Amendment issues has been published in *Communication Law and Policy, Journalism and Mass Communication Monographs* and other journals, and by the Freedom Forum First Amendment Center. As an American Society for Newspaper Editors fellow, she worked at *The New York Times on the Web*. She also worked at *The Times of India* as a reporter and copy editor. She received a bachelor's degree from

the University of Massachusetts at Amherst and master's and doctorate degrees from the University of North Carolina at Chapel Hill. She wrote Chapter 9, Regulating Advertising, for the 2001-04 editions of *Communication and the Law*.

**Michael Perkins** was chair of the Department of Communication at Brigham Young University until early fall 2003 when he was killed in a kayaking accident. He taught primarily mass communications law and ethics. He had also taught at Drake University and the University of Costa Rica. His research, which focused on mass communication law internationally as well as in the United States, has been published in *Journalism and Mass Communication Quarterly, Communication Law and Policy, Journal of Mass Media Ethics, Gazette* and *Newspaper Research Journal*. He was the head of the AEJMC Law Division at the time of his death.

**Milagros (Millie) Rivera-Sanchez** teaches telecommunication courses at the National University of Singapore. She has published articles in *Journalism and Mass Communication Monographs, Journalism and Mass Communication Quarterly, Journalism History, The Federal Communications Law Journal, Communications and the Law, Hastings Communications and Entertainment Law Journal* and other journals. Her research interests include regulation of the electronic media in the United States and in Latin America. She holds a bachelor's degree from the University of Puerto Rico and master's and doctorate degrees from the University of Florida. She spent the summer of 1999 in Chile as a Fulbright Scholar. Millie wrote the chapter on broadcast regulation for the 2000-2003 editions of the textbook.

**Susan Dente Ross** is an associate professor in the Edward R. Murrow School of Communication at Washington State University. She teaches media law, First Amendment theory, access to public records and journalism skills courses. In addition to conducting research on the regulation of emerging communication technologies, she examines the application of the First Amendment to speech and studies how media coverage frames marginalized groups and affects social change. She wrote Chapter 11, Regulating New Communication Technologies, for the 1999 and 2000 editions of *Communication and the Law*, and Chapter 12, Regulating Cable Communications, for the 2001 edition.

**Joseph Russomanno** is an associate professor in the Walter Cronkite School of Journalism and Mass Communication at Arizona State University. His articles have appeared in *Communication Law and Policy, Communications and the Law, Hamline Law Review*, the *Journal of Broadcasting and Electronic Media* and the *Journal of Communication Inquiry*. He is also the author of *Speaking Our Minds: Conversations With the People Behind Landmark First Amendment Cases* and editor of *Defending the First: Commentary on First Amendment Issues and*

*Cases.* He worked as a television news journalist — primarily as a producer and executive producer — for ten years. He received his master's degree from the University of Missouri and his doctorate from the University of Colorado.

**Robert Trager** is associate dean for graduate studies in the School of Journalism and Mass Communication at the University of Colorado at Boulder. He holds a Ph.D. in journalism and mass communication from the University of Minnesota and a J.D. from the Stanford Law School. He has practiced law in Washington, D.C., and with Time Warner Cable. He is also the founding editor of *Communication Law and Policy,* the law journal of the Law Division of the Association for Education in Journalism and Mass Communication. He wrote Chapter 10, Broadcast Regulation, and Chapter 11, Regulating New Communication Technologies, for the 1998 edition of *Communication and the Law.*

# Case Index

# Subject Index

Luther, Martin, 53

**M**

Macaulay, Thomas B., 55
MacKinnon, Catherine, 73
Madison, James, 27, 36, 56, 274, 349
Mailer, Norman, 83
malice, *see* actual malice; common law malice
Malvo, Lee Boyd, 346
*Man-Woman,* 75
mandamus, writ of, 353
Manhattan, 82
Mapplethorpe, Robert, 71, 76
Marconi, Guglielmo, 181
Marconi Wireless Company, 181
*Marital Intercourse,* 75
marketplace of ideas, 25, 33, 58, 205, 254, 258
Marshall, Howard, 319
Marshall, John, 316
Marshall, Thurgood, 65-66, 75, 79, 130, 325, 327, 335
Martin, Kevin, 40
Marvel Comics, Ltd., 146
Marxist League for Industrial Democracy, 101
Maryland, 30, 31, 40, 114, 260
    Germantown, 30
    Montgomery County, 282
    Rockville, 282
Mason, Jackie, 287
Massachusetts, 27, 38, 46, 55, 100, 109, 110, 156, 164, 262, 269, 270, 276, 296, 300, 336
    Norfolk County, 336
    *See also* Boston
Mattel, Inc., 133
Mauro, Tony, 40
Mazar-e-Sharif, 369
McAuliffe, Steven, 269
McCarthy, Joseph, 241
MCI, 230, 231
McDonald's Corp., 146, 167
McDougal, James B., 344
McFee, Thomas, 267
McGraw-Hill, 66, 67, 326
McLeod USA, 230
McMahon, Ed, 286
McMasters, Paul, 23, 24, 25
McNealy, Raymond, 30
McVeigh, Timothy, 292, 322, 369
Mead Data Central, 146
Media Institute, 25
Media Law Resource Center, 89, 113
MediaOne, 211, 218, 230
Medina, Howard, 324
Meese, Edwin, 73
Meese Commission, *see* Attorney General's
    Commission on Pornography
Meiklejohn, Alexander, 32, 33-34, 35, 96, 105
Memoirs Test, 74, 75
    *See also* Roth/Memoirs Test
Memphis, 81-82, 238
*Memphis Press-Scimitar,* 92
*Men in Black,* 286
Menendez, Erik and Lyle, 326
mergers, media, 211, 230-31
Merritt, Gilbert S., 67
Metallica, 143, 244
Mexico, 5

MGM, 142
Miami, 283, 326, 345
Miami Beach, 290, 345
Miami-Dade County, 290
*Miami Herald,* 183, 278, 284-85, 291, 333
Miami University of Ohio, 261, 262
Michigan, 92, 100, 247, 264, 265, 271, 274, 340, 352, 363
    Ann Arbor, 364
    Washternaw County, 364
Michigan, University of, 260, 364
Michigan Press Association, 271
Microsoft Corp., 236, 240, 245
Midler, Bette, 286
Milford Central School, 257
Milkin, Michael, 170
Mill, John Stuart, 33, 274
Miller, Arthur, 83
Miller, Darlene, 73
Miller, Judith, 34, 295, 296
Miller, Marvin, 75
*Miller* Test, 75-77, 78, 82, 239
Milton, John, 25-26, 55, 57, 59, 63
Minneapolis, 60, 170, 217, 239
*Minneapolis Star and Tribune,* 311, 312
Minnesota, 50, 59, 60, 239, 270, 312, 343
    *See also* Minneapolis; St. Paul
Miranda warnings, 11
Mississippi, 23, 156, 328
    Jackson, 190
*Mississippi Burning,* 268
Missouri, 93, 110, 261, 262, 267, 270, 277
    *See also* Kansas City; St. Louis
Mitchell, Margaret, 133
Mitchell, Nellie, 284
Mobile Oil Co., 98
Mokhiber, Russell, 342
Monroe, James, 26-27
Montana, 296, 351, 364, 371
Mooney, Michael, 120
Morehouse College, 133
Morgan, Philip, 247
Morpheus software, 142, 144, 163
Morris, Stan, 290
Moseley, Victor, 148, 167
Motion Picture Association of America, 84, 144, 197, 245
Motorola, 119
Mount St. Clare College (Iowa), 262
movie ratings, *see* ratings, movie
MP3, 141, 244
MP3.com, 142
Muhammad, John Allen, 346
Multipoint Distribution Service, 234
Murdoch, Rupert, 189
MusicMatch, 144
MusicNet, 244
Muslims, 31
must-carry rules, *see* cable television and must
    carry rules
Myers, Michael, 343

**N**

NAACP, 288
*NAD Case Reports,* 160
Namath, Joe, 286
Napster, 142, 144, 244, 245, 256

NASA, 290
Nashville, 139
Nashville Network, The (TNN), 146
"Nastiest Place on Earth, The," 81
*Nation, The,* 128-30
National Academy of Sciences, 171
National Advertising Division, 160
National Advertising Review Board, 160, 161
National Association of Broadcasters, 198
National Basketball Association, 119, 145
National Conference of Chief Justices, 341, 342
*National Enquirer,* 98
National Film Preservation Act, 139
National Football League (NFL), 149, 220
National Geographic Society, 124
National Guard, 23
National Lawyers Guild, 101
National Parks Service, 291
National Public Radio, 81, 299
National Restaurant Association, 122
National Science Foundation, 360
National Security Administration, 23, 68, 293
National Security Agency, 246
National Society of Art Directors, 83
National Telecommunications and Information
    Administration, 203
National Television System Committee, 234-35
Navasky, Victor, 129
Nazis, 49, 114, 330
NBC, 83, 142, 198, 300, 304, 369
Near, Jay M., 59
Nebraska, 3, 63, 64, 89, 270, 324, 325, 345
    Lincoln County, 324
    North Platte, 324
    Sutherland, 324
Nebraska Press Association, 63
negligence, 95, 99-100
Neilson/Net Ratings, 225
Netherlands, The, 299
Network Network, 146
neutral reporting, *see* defamation and neutral
    reporting
Nevada, 269, 330
New Deal, 17, 349
*New England Courant,* 55
New Hampshire, 12, 38, 265, 269, 309, 351
New Jersey, 38, 40, 104, 120, 155, 262, 267, 271, 279, 328, 332, 341, 353
    Flemington, 320
    Middlesex, 83
    Newark, 341
    *See also* Princeton
New Mexico, 255
New Orleans, 156
New York, 27, 28, 30, 51, 74, 80, 82, 84, 88, 104, 107, 110, 114, 119, 124, 125, 137, 138, 152, 154, 244, 262, 271, 275, 282, 285, 286, 289, 299, 304, 309, 319, 330, 345, 351
    Bellmore, Long Island, 80
    Long Island, 271
    *See also* New York City; Manhattan
New York, State University of, 154
New York City, 83, 84, 132, 152, 195, 340, 361
    *See also* Manhattan; Times Square
New York Bar Association Special Committee on
    Radio, Television and the Administration of
    Justice, 324